RANDOM HOUSE WEBSTER'S

# *American Sign Language Dictionary*

COMPACT EDITION

ELAINE COSTELLO, PhD

RANDOM HOUSE REFERENCE

NEW YORK TORONTO LONDON SYDNEY AUCKLAND

Published in the United States by Random House Reference, an imprint of The Random House Information Group, a division of Random House, Inc., New York and simultaneously in Canada by Random House of Canada Limited, Toronto.



This is a revised and updated work based on the *Random House American Sign Language Dictionary* originally published in hardcover in 1994.

Illustration: Lois Lenderman, Paul M. Setzer, Linda C. Tom
Book design and composition: Jan Ewing, *Ewing Systems,* New York, NY



Printed in the United States of America

**Library of Congress Cataloging-in-Publication Data**
Costello, Elaine.
Random House Webster's American sign language dictionary / by Elaine Costello ; illustrated by Lois Lenderman, Paul M. Setzer, Linda C. Tom. — 1st. ed.
p. cm.
Rev. updated ed. of: Random House American sign language dictionary. © 1994.
ISBN 978-0-375-72277-6 (pbk.)
1. American Sign Language—Dictionaries. I. Costello, Elaine. Random House American sign language dictionary. II. Title.
HV2475.C66 1997 97-21538
419'.03—dc21 CIP

Visit the Random House Reference Web site at www.randomwords.com.

10 9 8 7 6 5 4 3 2 1
Proprietary ISBN: 978–0–525–61540–8

# Contents

# Preface

## Why This Dictionary?

This dictionary represents a commitment to American Sign Language, known familiarly as ASL—a commitment to its authenticity as a living, evolving, fully functional language and to its role as a cohesive force among the large numbers of its regular deaf and hearing users known as the Deaf community.

Numbering more than 16 million, people with hearing loss form the largest disability group in this country. Adding to this number are the 4,000 to 5,000 babies who are born deaf every year, countless numbers of people who suffer injuries or illnesses that cause deafness, and those whose hearing is deteriorating as a natural result of the aging process.

After a long and controversial history, American Sign Language has emerged in recent decades not only as the standard means of communication for deaf people and for their families, friends, and colleagues, but also as a symbol of cultural unity. Sign language is in fact the native language, i.e., the language learned before any other, of some 300,000 to 500,000 users in North America. At any given time there are roughly 100,000 people actively learning ASL, both in formal institutions of learning and in classes conducted by social agencies, churches, and other groups. It is estimated that 13 million people, including members of both the deaf and hearing populations, can now communicate to some extent in sign language. If we count all of them, this would make ASL the fourth most commonly used language in the United States.

American Sign Language is becoming even more important as federal law increasingly mandates acceptance and accommodation of deaf people in the workplace, the education system, and public accommodations. Most recently, the landmark Americans with Disabilities Act (ADA), which became law on July 26, 1990, has extended to deaf people what may be the world's strongest civil rights legislation for people with disabilities. Businesses and public entities of all kinds must now be prepared to communicate effectively—

through sign language if necessary—with job applicants, employees, customers, and service users who are deaf.

Clearly, the need for reference materials in sign language is great. To help meet this need, the *Random House Webster's American Sign Language Dictionary* offers a comprehensive and up-to-date treasury of signs, faithfully recording their formation and usage. In addition to the standard signs used in day-to-day communication throughout the nation, this book features signs from an expanding technical vocabulary and new signs for countries of the world reflecting the way natives of those countries refer to themselves. Thus this dictionary is a broad reference designed to be useful to a wide range of users, from novices seeking "survival signs" for rudimentary communication to sophisticated users already fluent in ASL and looking to enlarge their vocabularies. This compendium is drawn from an ever-growing collection, maintained by the author and continually augmented by contributions from members of the Deaf community.

This dictionary does not depend on simple one- or two-word translations to indicate the meanings of the signs. Since different meanings of the same English word may be represented by entirely different signs in ASL, the main entry for each sign in this book is expanded by one or more short definitions to clarify the exact meanings covered by the sign. The formation of each sign is depicted in relation to the entire upper torso, in illustrations prepared by Deaf artists using models from the Deaf community. And each illustration is accompanied by a complete verbal description of how the sign is made and, often, by a "hint" to help the reader remember the sign.

As with any other living, growing language, American Sign Language can never be fully and finitely documented: it constantly evolves and changes; it has variant forms that shift according to individual, group, or regional usage; and most saliently, as a language transmitted not by writing but by gesture, it is in many respects a language to which no printed reference book can fully do justice. What this dictionary can do, however, is provide the fundamental building blocks of this language: a comprehensive vocabulary of ASL signs. Of course, language consists of more than just vocabulary; the words or signs are put into phrases and sentences according to grammatical principles, and they are used in a cultural context. These larger aspects of ASL are discussed in the Introduction.

And so, welcome to the beautiful visual language called American Sign Language! Enjoy the physical character of each sign and the messages that its gestures convey. Through interaction with its community of users, add the nuances of the language that come so naturally to its native speakers. Above all, put aside inhibitions, physically and emotionally entering into the essential conceptual nature of the language.

# Introduction

## American Sign Language in Context

### Deafness and the Deaf Community

#### What Is the Deaf Community?

A presentation of American Sign Language (ASL) would not be complete without some perspective on *deafness,* the medical condition, and *Deaf* people, the native users of ASL. The definition of deafness—the partial or total inability of a person to hear sound unaided—focuses purely on the medical aspects of deafness. However, Deaf people tend to find this view restrictive and limiting, in that it fails to describe the sociological implications of deafness. Terminology like "hearing impaired" is considered undesirable because it refers to a presumed disability.

ASL users generally prefer to view deafness not as a handicap but as a shared experience underlying their sense of community. As a symbol of pride and identity within this community, the word *Deaf* is often capitalized when referring to this group. Thus, the Deaf community is a cultural group, sharing common experience, concerns, and language.

Since the primary binding force of this cultural group is its shared language, the deaf people who do not use American Sign Language are not considered part of the Deaf community. Conversely, some hearing people do belong to the Deaf community, particularly the hearing children of Deaf parents, who acquire the language naturally from infancy.

The Deaf community now includes perhaps as many as half a million people throughout the United States. In part because of the presence of postsecondary schools with special programs to accommodate their needs, there are significant populations of Deaf people in the large metropolitan areas of the East and West Coasts; unlike members of many subcultures, however, they are not usually concentrated in particular neighborhoods. Deaf people are found in all walks of life, but because of common interests and ease of communication, they tend to gravitate toward one another and often travel great distances to take part in activities with other Deaf people.

In recent years, technical devices have opened up many aspects of the hearing world to deaf people. Captioned television provides real-time and prerecorded access to programming. Recent legislation requires that new televisions with 13-inch or larger screens have a built-in microchip to decode printed captions that are transmitted with the image. Telecommunications devices for the deaf (TDDs), also known as TTYs and Text Telephones, have allowed deaf people to communicate by telephone for some time now, if each party has appropriate equipment. More recently, relay services have been established to give deaf and hearing people easy telephone access to one another: the hearing person is connected by regular telephone to a human link, or "relay," who in turn is connected to the deaf person through a Text Telephone. Deaf people also use flashing lights to signal doorbells, a baby crying, and other sounds of everyday life. But the natural, primary means of communication among Deaf people themselves remains American Sign Language.

## Types of Hearing Loss

The causes of hearing loss and deafness are diverse. The primary cause among children is heredity, although seldom is there a direct link from one generation to the next; in fact, about 90 percent of deaf children are born to hearing parents. Other causes of hearing loss include illness, medications, and trauma to the head. Many children have, over the years, become deaf from meningitis or, especially in the 1930s and 1940s, from drugs such as mycins used to treat meningitis. In the 1960s, a large number of infants were born deaf because their mothers had contracted rubella (German measles) during the first trimester of pregnancy. Prolonged exposure to noise in the workplace or to loud music can cause hearing loss. But among the 16,000,000 people with hearing loss, the most common cause is presbycusis, the loss of hearing through the aging process.

By and large, deafness is a permanent condition. For some whose hearing loss is a result of either a malformation or deterioration of the neural auditory structures in the cochlea of the inner ear, surgery has recently become an option. In the past decade, surgeons have been able to perform a type of microscopic surgery called a *cochlear implant* on select patients, with whom they have had a degree of success. The vast majority of deaf people, however, depend upon a selection of assistive technical devices, special education strategies, and communication options.

## Educational Impact of Hearing Loss

It is generally agreed that children pass through a critical period of time, usually before the age of four, that is optimal for language acquisition. During this period, they easily absorb the structure and vocabulary of their native language, and can even acquire several languages simultaneously. The impact of deafness on language development is felt most severely when a baby is born deaf and therefore does not have the opportunity to learn spoken language naturally by hearing and using it. Unless such prelingually deaf children are born into a household of sign language users, and so have natural access to a system of communication, they often spend their formative years with no language at all. They must then learn both sign language and English with great difficulty, much like learning a second language but without the advantages and understanding conferred by a native language. On the other hand, postlingually deaf people—those who acquired a spoken language prior to losing their hearing—have a much less difficult time in school, since they have a particular language on which to base their learning and, even more fundamentally, have a sense of the very concept of language as a means of communication. Similarly, those individuals who have only a slight hearing loss, commonly referred to as hard of hearing, also have an educational advantage over those who have a severe and profound hearing loss.

For all children with any degree of deafness, communication and educational choices must be made by others, usually by hearing parents and other caregivers who, more likely than not, have had no contact with Deaf people. Typically, a parent's desire to have the child function in a hearing society plays a large role in the choices that are made. On the surface, teaching the child to speak English and *speechread* (the older term was *lipread*) seems desirable. However, the paucity of language stimuli during the critical years of language acquisition takes its toll, and the barriers to learning spoken language are enormous. Spoken language must be learned by memorizing the physical movements of the speech organs that go together to make up a word or sound, and many of these movements are difficult or impossible to see, distinguish from one another, and replicate. Speechreading as the sole vehicle for reception is seldom successful, and a deaf child's own speech very often remains unintelligible. Therefore, language learning and usage on the part of these children is rarely up to age or grade level.

In the past, deaf children have generally attended segregated residential schools, going home only for holidays and summer vacations. Through the mandates of federal law, deaf children can now attend mainstream schools with their hearing peers and live at home with their families. Most often, however, deaf children remain in segregated classrooms in the public school, although, with the assistance of an educational interpreter, they sometimes attend integrated classes. Because deafness impacts language acquisition in such a dramatic way, deaf children usually begin special training very early.

Although the first teacher of the deaf in the United States was deaf himself, most such teachers today are hearing persons trained in special education. Because hearing parents and educators often have difficulty learning the structures of American Sign Language, and because English is the predominant language of the nation, various artificial sign systems, commonly referred to as Manually Coded English, have been invented for educational purposes. These systems, such as Seeing Exact English, Signed English, and Seeing Essential English, use the vocabulary of sign language (i.e., signs) to display English visually by putting the signs in English word order. In effect, they take the vocabulary of one language and use it with the grammar of another. Since there is not a one-to-one equivalency between ASL signs and English words, these artificial systems employ additional signs invented specifically to reflect English syntax.

Some of these systems are well-meaning and even useful, especially when they have as their goal assisting deaf children to learn English, thereby helping them to become literate in the language of the hearing world. On the other hand, some of their problematic features include real violations of the principles of sign formation in ASL. Signs are forced into configurations and combinations that obscure their conceptual references. Conventions relating to symmetry and point of contact are ignored. English (rather than ASL) word formation techniques are employed, such as the frequent use of prefixes and suffixes, commonly represented by an extra gesture added to the ASL sign. All of these violations occur because the underlying principle of all Manually Coded English is "one sign for one English word," regardless of consequent distortions of sign language structure. It should be noted that these invented systems are not natural languages, in that they do not have native users and do not have other requisites and characteristics of true languages. Over the years, however, some of the signs and structures of Manually Coded English have by a natural process been incorporated into American Sign Language.

The use of Manually Coded English systems to the virtual exclusion of ASL has been pervasive in the field of deaf education, to the dismay of concerned linguists and the Deaf community. However, as more Deaf teachers are being hired by schools, the use of American Sign Language is increasing in the classroom, becoming the preferred mode of communication through which English and all other subjects are taught.

# The Nature of American Sign Language

## Origins

As its name suggests, American Sign Language is a product of North America. Its use is heavily concentrated in the United States, but it has also spread to other parts of the world, notably Canada, Africa, and the Philippines. Note that there is no universal sign language, one single language of gesture used worldwide. Any country or other geographical region with a sizable population of deaf people is likely to have one or more sign languages of its own, and the list of such languages in current use is large indeed.

The first recorded instance of deafness in the United States occurred in the eighteenth century following the marriage of one Thomas Bolling to his first cousin, a common practice of that time. The Bollings had three deaf children and, subsequently, some deaf grandchildren. They founded a small school for the deaf, but it was short-lived. Other small schools were founded, but they, too, failed to survive.

The first permanent school for the deaf was founded in 1817 in Hartford, Connecticut, to serve the growing deaf population in the United States. Now known as the American School for the Deaf, this school was the first to receive state funding. It was established as a residential school to serve a wide geographical population. It is at this school that sign language was formally established in America through its first teacher, a deaf Frenchman named Laurent Clerc.

The fact that the Hartford school used sign language as its means of communication and instruction was somewhat a matter of happenstance. In 1815, a clergyman named Thomas Hopkins Gallaudet, challenged with teaching a neighbor's young deaf daughter, had traveled to Europe to learn techniques for educating deaf people. In order to learn the oral teaching techniques used in England, Gallaudet found that he would have been required to stay there as an apprentice for several years. Not willing to be away from home that long, and frustrated by philosophical differences he had with the teachers in England, Gallaudet went to a school in Paris where he was welcomed and initiated into the use of manual communication, or sign language, as a system for teaching deaf children. It was there that Gallaudet came to know Laurent Clerc, who agreed to return to the United States to teach sign language at the Hartford school. This accounts for the considerable component of French Sign Language in the fledgling system of gestures that has evolved into American Sign Language, and for the fact that, even today, American Sign Language has much more in common with French Sign Language than it has with British Sign Language.

## Is American Sign Language a Language?

All languages share common features. For example, they are composed of symbols that can be combined and manipulated in order to express meaning. The use of the symbols of any language is organized and governed by rules specific to that language. A *natural language* is a language with native users, who learn it from birth and for whom it fulfills the diverse communicative needs of daily life. No matter who else learns such a language as a second language, a natural language is defined by the existence of its native users.

Although American Sign Language may have originated as a consciously constructed system, adapted from the French system, the strong consensus among linguistics scholars is that ASL has long since become a natural language, exhibiting all of the defining features of language. For example, ASL has principles governing the formation of signs and their use in combination. Just like spoken languages, it has a native-speaker population for whom it provides all the needs of daily discourse. Indeed, infants who are exposed to ASL from birth go through all the sequential language-learning phases experienced by any group of babies learning their first language, including the hand-movement equivalents of the babbling engaged in by babies before they speak their first words. Moreover, American Sign Language is a growing language, one that continues to evolve as new terminology is developed and as older forms of signs are replaced with newer ones. And like living languages everywhere, ASL displays considerable regional variation, though with the growing cohesiveness of the Deaf community nationwide and increasing ease of travel, the degree of variation may be diminishing.

## The Structure of American Sign Language

### *Phonology: The Parts of a Sign*

In spoken language, *phonology* is the study of how basic units of sound combine to make up a language. Just as the words in a spoken language consist of specific combinations of individual sounds (the different vowel and consonant sounds), so each of the "words"—that is, the *signs*—in American Sign Language consists of a combination of gestures. These gestural components fall into certain clearly defined categories: the *location* in which a sign is produced in relation to the body; the *handshape(s)* used in the formation of the sign; the *movement* of the hands used in executing the sign; and finally, the *orientation* of the palms. These four units or features of signs have been used for descriptive purposes since linguists first began to describe and transcribe signs more than thirty years ago. More recently, linguists have added a fifth feature, *nonmanual* cues, which are discussed in more detail in a later section. Some linguists have also begun to describe sign formation in terms of a *movement* segment and a *hold* segment, the latter defined as a period of time during which the hands pause momentarily. Using all these phonological features of sign language, scholars have designed intricate notation systems to facilitate written transcription of American Sign Language for linguistic analysis and study.

Just as changing a single sound in a spoken word may change its meaning or render it meaningless, so changing any one of the phonological features of a sign may change the meaning of the sign or result in a meaningless gesture. The following examples show how changing one phonological feature can completely change the meaning of a sign:

### Location

*eleven*
**(in front of shoulder)**

*understand*
**(near the temple)**

### Handshape

*principal*
**("P hand")**

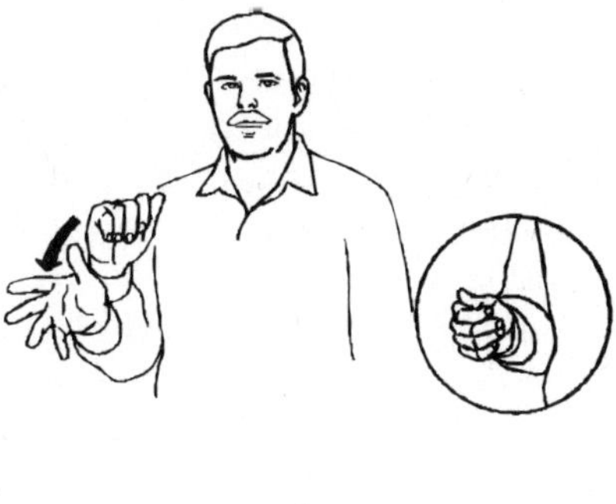

*appointment*
**("A hand")**

## Movement

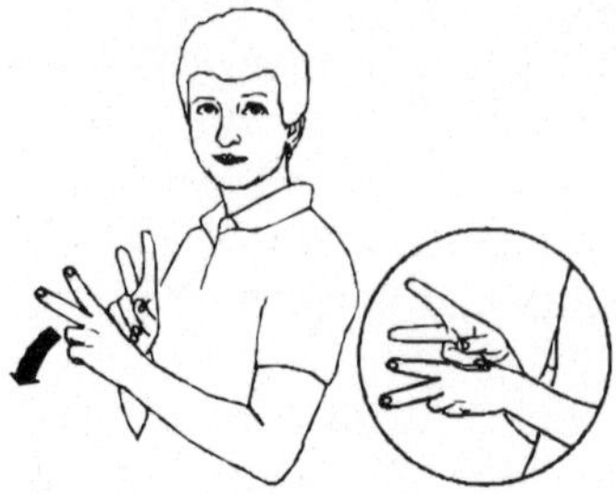

*(I) lend*

**(forward toward another)**

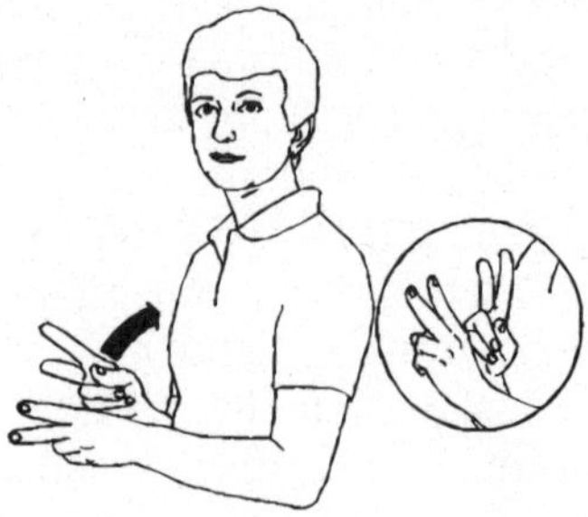

*(I) borrow*

**(back toward the body)**

## Orientation

*your*

**(palm facing forward)**

*my*

**(palm facing back)**

As these examples illustrate, careful production of each phonological feature of a sign is essential to clear communication.

The number of permissible variants of location, handshape, movement, and orientation is limited. Fewer than fifty different handshapes exist, and there are at most twenty-five different locations relative to the body where signs can be made. These various handshapes and locations can be used in connection with some twelve movements and twelve orientations. However, every language operates according to phonetic rules that restrict the way its elements are combined. For example, although English has both *k*-sounds and *b*-sounds, the combination *kb* never occurs in a single syllable. In ASL, the possible ways in which the various phonological elements (handshape, movement, etc.) can be combined in signs are likewise limited; thus learning the patterns of signing is a more manageable task than it might at first appear.

### *Morphology: The Meaningful Units of a Sign*

Morphology is the study of word formation, or how a language uses small meaningful linguistic units, called *morphemes*, to build larger ones. An example of such construction in English would be the addition of an *s*-sound (representing a morpheme for plurality) to *hat* (a morpheme representing a particular article of clothing) to form the word *hats*. The vocabulary of every language—including the signs of ASL—is built up of such units of meaning, which are classified as *free morphemes* if they can stand alone, like *hat* in English, and *bound morphemes* if, like the pluralizing morpheme in English, they exist only in combination with other morphemes. Of course, the morphemes in American Sign Language consist of signs or gestures rather than words or sounds.

One of the simplest examples of how words can be formed from smaller units is compounding, in which distinct words combine to form a single new word. This occurs very commonly both in English and in American Sign Language. Thus, just as English has compound words like *textbook* and *housewife*, so ASL often blends two or more signs together (usually with some streamlining of form) to create a new sign with its own particular meaning, as in *Jesus* + *book* (forming one of the signs for *Bible*) and *girl* + *hat* + *scarf* (forming the sign for *bonnet*).

Another close parallel between English and ASL morphology is in the formation of a particular kind of noun. Certain suffixes, such as *-er*, *-or*, and *-ist*, can be added to English words to mean "one who…"; e.g., *run* + *-er* = *runner*, "a person who runs." American Sign Language has a morpheme, referred to in this dictionary as the person marker, which serves the same purpose:

*person marker*

As in English, this marker is added to the sign that expresses what the person does, as in the following examples:

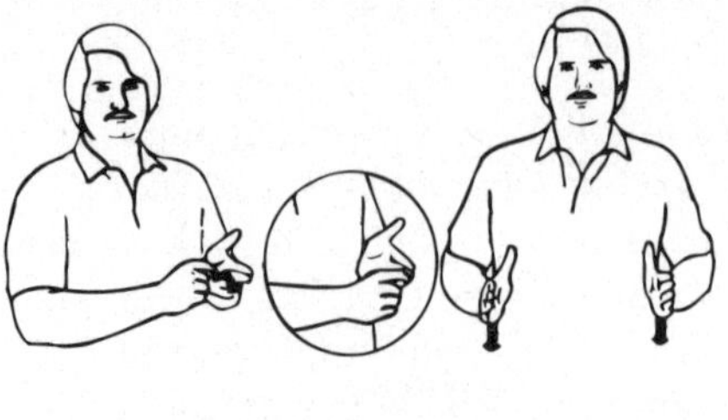

*writer*
**(write + person marker)**

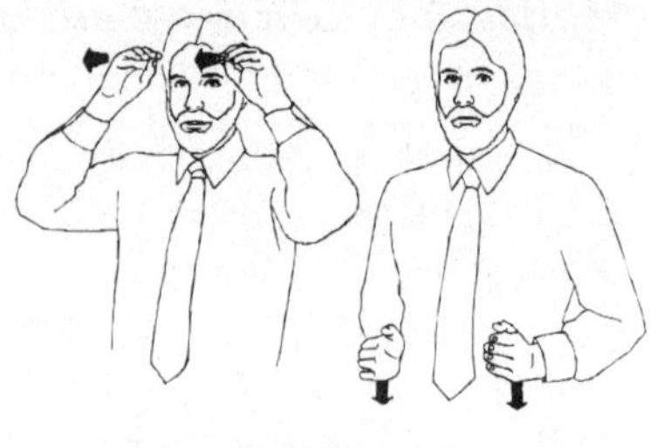

*teacher*
**(teach + person marker)**

In general, however, morphological and grammatical processes in American Sign Language are quite different from those of English. ASL shares many such structures with a wide range of spoken languages other than English; in some structures, however, ASL utilizes three-dimensional space in ingenious ways that could be closely paralleled only in other sign languages. The fact that American Sign Language has evolved its own blend of linguistic features so distinct from English is one of the major reasons that linguists have come to regard ASL as an independent member of the world's family of mature natural languages.

The frequent lack of parallelism between English and American Sign Language may be illustrated by considering how ASL performs some of the functions served in English by affixation—the addition of prefixes and suffixes, either to convey grammatical information (like the pluralizing *-s* in *hats*) or to derive new words from old (like the *-er* in *runner*). Whereas affixation is an extremely common linguistic device in English, it is quite rare in American Sign Language, which employs a wide array of different techniques to achieve the same purposes.

For example, the concept of plurality in American Sign Language may be expressed in a number of ways. One of the most common is simply to sign a number or other quantifier before signing the noun. Thus, the term *cat* can be made plural by signing *three cat* or *horde cat* (i.e., a lot of cats). Note that, as in many of the world's spoken languages, there is no change in the form of the noun itself (the sign for *cat*) to make it plural: no bound morpheme analogous to the English *-s* is added to it. Another pluralizing strategy (and again, one that is also found in many other natural languages) is reduplication of the noun. For example, since the singular *cat* is formed with a single movement, the plural *cats* can be formed by repeating the sign one or more times. Not all nouns can be reduplicated, although many can. A third method of forming plurals is to reduplicate the verb, though often the result may be to express duration or repetitive action rather than plurality. An example of verb reduplication that works to show the plural of a noun is *wash-wash-wash dish,* which indicates that one has washed (many) dishes. In yet another technique, the signer can point or gesture toward several locations to indicate a plural noun, such as *there-there-there cat.* As can be seen, a wealth of strategies is available, and signers can be guided by both context and their own personal style.

English uses a complex system of suffixes, auxiliary verbs, and form changes to express various tenses and time aspects of verbs (*-ed, -ing, -en, will, had,* etc.). In American Sign Language, the basic concept of tense may be represented in relation to an imaginary time line running from behind the speaker's body (the past) through the torso and out away from the body (stretching into the future). Within this framework, specific signs can be used to signal that the action being discussed concerns the past (indicated by a wave back over the shoulder), the present (a sign directly in front of the body), or the future (a sign moving forward from the body). (See entries *ago, new,* and *will*[2] in this dictionary.) The more expansive the gesture along this line, the more remote the time being indicated ("long ago" vs. "recently," "in the distant future" vs. "soon"). In discourse, a signer generally establishes the time frame being discussed by using a time sign; the entire discourse, including the verbs, from that point until the time is changed, remains in the established time frame. When a verb refers to actions of a continuous nature (as might be indicated in English by adding *-ing* to the verb), or actions that take place repeatedly or over an extended period of time, these time-related aspects of the sentence can often be signified by repeating the verb one or more times, sometimes with certain additional movements.

In many cases, meanings communicated by an affix in English are simply conveyed by separate, independent signs in ASL, as with the English prefix *un-*:

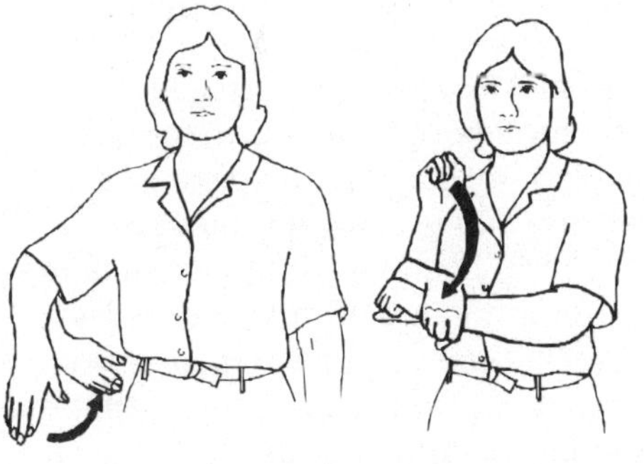

*unbeaten*
**(yet + defeat)**

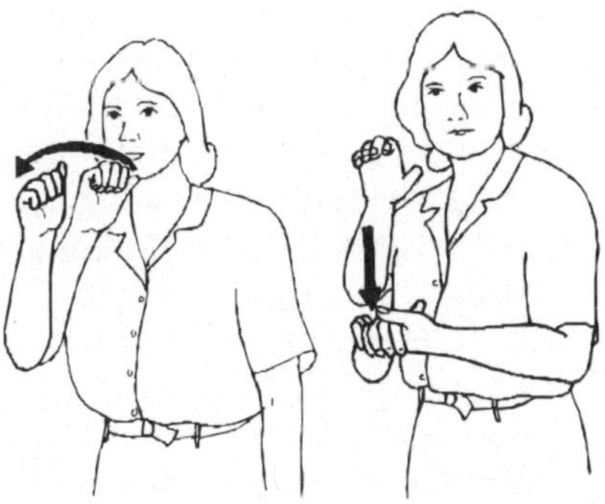

*unbelievable*
**(not + believe)**

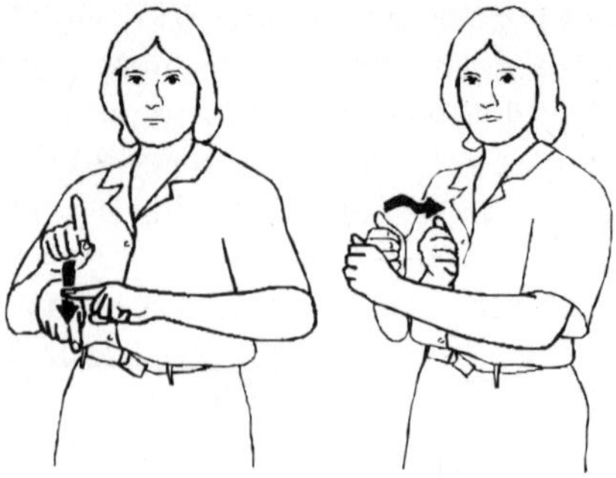

*unavoidable*
**(can't + avoid)**

Often, however, an English suffix such as *-ment, -tion,* or *-ful* simply has no corresponding structure in American Sign Language. For example, a single sign serves for both the verb *congratulate* and the noun *congratulations,* another sign for both the noun *beauty* and the adjective *beautiful.* At first glance this might seem confusing, but in fact it is no different from the use in English of a word like *spy* (which can be either a verb or a noun) or *red* (which can be either a noun or an adjective); in context, the particular grammatical function being served by the word is clear. Nevertheless, inventors of various types of Manually Coded English, in order to create a system that mimics the structure of English as closely as possible, have devised special gestures for such suffixes as these, some of which are now seen from time to time in ASL.

### *Functions of Space*

We have just seen how American Sign Language uses space to divide time into past, present, and future. But space is used in ASL to convey a number of other grammatical features as well, including pronouns, location, and directionality.

English pronouns can be expressed in ASL with specific signs. Frequently, however, the functions performed by pronouns in English are carried out by establishing a location in space for the person or thing referred to and then *indexing*—that is, pointing, gesturing, or even just glancing—toward that location in lieu of signing the name of the referent. In this way, the location of a number of people or objects can be established around the speaker and pointed to throughout the conversation. The conversational partner is able to index these same locations to refer to the persons and objects under discussion.

Location can be directly incorporated into a sign through the use of space. Papers can be indicated as lying everywhere on one's desk or stacked neatly on the corner of the desk, as distinguished through appropriate spatial gestures. People can walk side by side, cars can pass one another, and a dog and cat can have a face-to-face encounter through clear spatial manipulation.

Yet another use of space can be seen in *directional verbs,* which indicate the direction of an action. For example, as we have already noted (in the section *"Phonology"* above), the difference between the signs for *(I) borrow* and *(I) lend* is simply the direction in which the handshape moves. Similarly, the direction in which the sign for *give* is executed shows who is the giver and who is the receiver:

*(I) give*

*give-me*

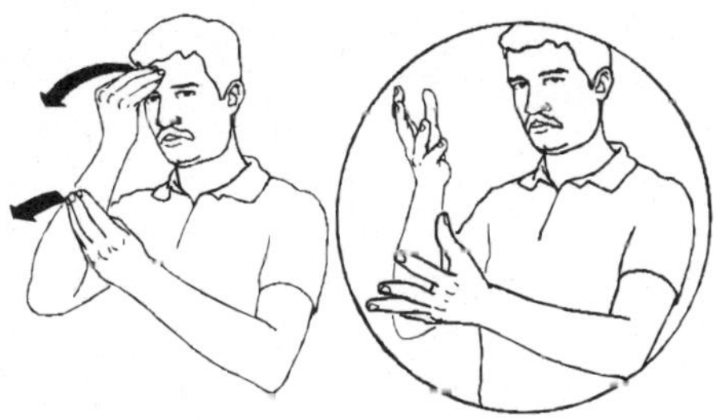

*(I) inform*

*inform-me*

### *Classifiers*

A noteworthy characteristic of American Sign Language is its use of *classifiers*—morphemes that can stand for any member of a large class of nouns and that have special grammatical functions. This is a linguistic feature common to many Asian, African, and Native American languages but largely unknown among English and European languages.

The classifiers in American Sign Language are handshapes (not complete signs) that serve to categorize the subject of a verb of motion or location. Such a handshape is a bound morpheme; that is, it is never used in isolation. Rather, it combines with the movement, location, and orientation elements of the verb as a mandatory part of any complete expression describing the movement, existence, or location of a previously specified person or thing.

Classifiers often represent some common characteristic of a class of nouns, such as size, shape, or manner of use; their existence as part of the total verb sign makes it unnecessary for signers to keep making separate signs or gestures to refer to the subject, and so gives the language great fluidity and flexibility. In discussing a car, for example, the use of the classifier for "vehicle" permits the signer to show the car starting or stopping (either abruptly or smoothly), moving around, or even—through use of an additional classifier with the other hand—trailing along after, passing, crossing, or running into another vehicle, animal, or person.

### *Related Noun-Verb Pairs*

We have already noted that in American Sign Language, as in English, it is common for nouns and verbs that are closely related in meaning to be similar or even identical in form. For example, in English, *fish* represents both the noun (a creature that swims) and the verb (to catch fish); similarly, a single sign in ASL represents both the verb *congratulate* and the noun *congratulations.* And in ASL, as in English, a noun like *teacher* is derived from the corresponding verb (*teach*) simply by the addition of a suffix: the person marker in ASL and *-er* in English.

Another important and very common derivational process in American Sign Language, however, has no parallel in English: verbs can often be turned into nouns by reduplication, that is, repeating the sign. Typically, the repeated movements of the noun are short, sharp, and quick, in contrast to the one long, smooth motion of the verb. This phonological difference—a change in the movement element of the sign, while the handshape and other elements remain unchanged—along with the reduplication, serve to distinguish the nouns from their related verbs in such pairs, as in the following examples:

*fly (v.)*

*airplane (n.)*

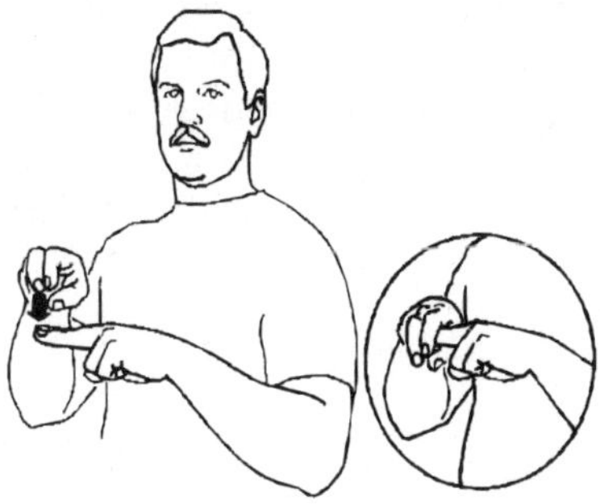

*sit (v.)*

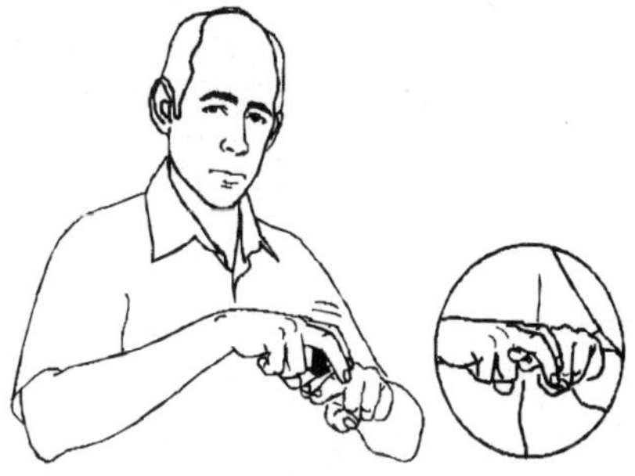

*chair (n.)*

### ***The Role of Nonmanual Cues***

Facial expression and body position play an important part in the grammar of American Sign Language. These nonmanual features are in many ways analogous to intonation in spoken language and punctuation in written language: they organize and add meaning to the words and signs. Such cues are not mere improvisations; rather, they are chosen from a repertoire of gestures that are understood among ASL users as serving specific purposes.

Perhaps the most basic role of nonmanual cues is in specifying sentence type. In English, intonation or punctuation can make the difference between a statement ("He's going.") and a question ("He's going?") or between a question ("Stop?") and a command ("Stop!"); in American Sign Language, this function is performed by nonmanual cues. Thus, a simple declarative sentence typically carries a neutral facial expression, whereas a question may be signaled by raised eyebrows and a subtle tilt forward of the head or body, and an imperative sentence by a furrowed brow and intense eye contact.

Additional functions for nonmanual cues include intensification, modification of verbs, and indexing. For example, exaggerated movement combined with a furrowed brow and pinched lips can convert *beautiful* to *very beautiful,* while signing *ago* with a constrained movement accompanied by hunched shoulders and squinted eyes makes it *just a short while ago.* Adverbs of manner are often indicated nonmanually while signing a verb or sentence; thus, a slightly open mouth, head tilt, and the tongue pressed against the lower lip indicates that the activity described in the sentence was done carelessly or lackadaisically. And as noted above in the section *"Functions of Space,"* a glance or nod toward the location previously identified with a particular person or object under discussion suffices to refer to that person or object without the need for any sign at all.

Finally, it may be noted that some facial expressions seem to accompany certain signs quite naturally, without altering the meaning. The sign for *fatten,* for example, is usually accompanied by a puffing out of the cheeks, and *thick* is seldom signed without squinting the eyes as if to contemplate the measure of thickness being discussed.

## Signs: The Vocabulary of American Sign Language

### *The Conceptual Nature of Sign Language*

It is axiomatic that there is never a one-to-one correspondence between the words or grammatical structures of one language and those of another, and that a simple word-for-word translation from one language to another is therefore never possible. For example, the French *j'ai dix ans* would be put into English as "I'm ten" or "I'm ten years old," rather than the literal "I have ten years"; and the German *Welt* might be rendered variously as "world," "society," or "humanity" depending upon the context, while *Weltanschauung* could only be adequately explained with an entire phrase, such as "a comprehensive view of the universe and humanity's relation to it."

So, too, the concept embodied in any individual sign in American Sign Language often cannot be conveyed by a single all-purpose English word; the sign representing the dimming of automobile headlights, for example, might be glossed in different circumstances as the adjective *dim,* as the verb *darken,* or as the noun and verb *tint.* And conversely, a single English word may have variations in meaning requiring different signs in ASL. This is most obvious in the case of homonyms (words that look and sound alike but have completely different meanings), as in the word *right,* which can mean "correct," "opposite of left," or "a just claim." Whereas in English these meanings can only be determined from the context in which the word appears, ASL has a distinct sign for each of these concepts:

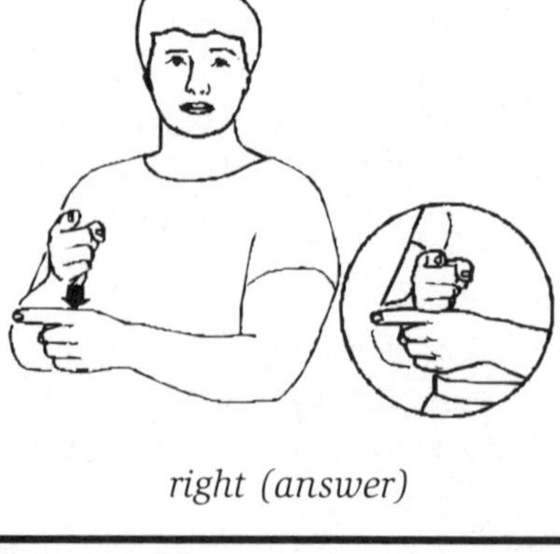

*right (answer)*

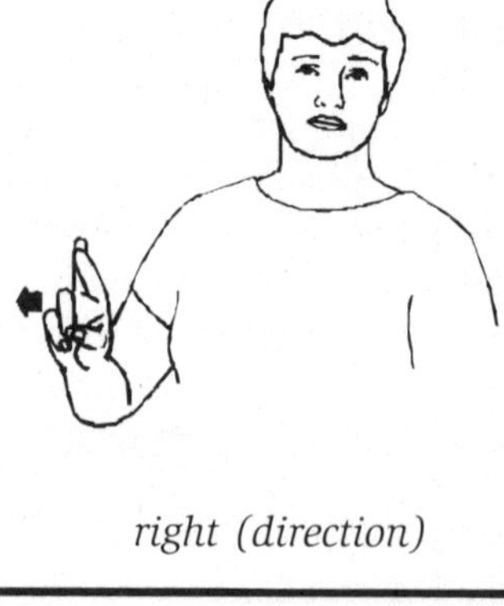

*right (direction)*

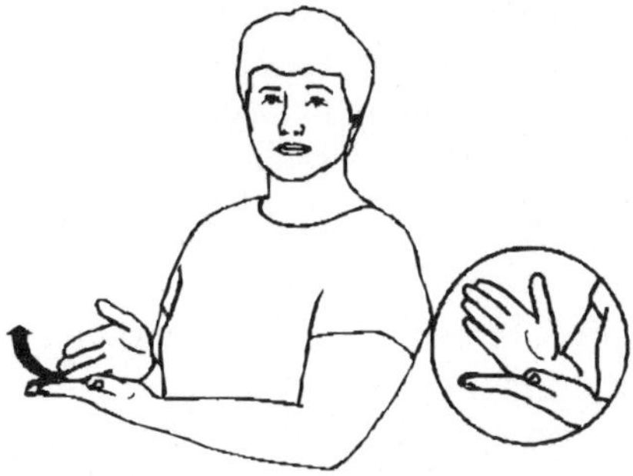

*right (legal)*

But the inevitable lack of symmetry between languages goes even further in American Sign Language. As a visual-gestural language, ASL exploits the medium of space and so is not confined to the strict linearity of spoken and written languages. In space, many things can be going on at the same time. We have seen, for example, how nonmanual cues can modify or intensify verbs and adjectives as they are being signed, how the use of classifiers with both hands can describe simultaneously how two different subjects are situated or moving in relation to each other, how several different persons and objects under discussion can be assigned locations in space and then indexed nonmanually without interrupting the flow of signs. In these ways, concepts that require a whole sentence in English—"John drove recklessly"; "The car crashed into the tree"—may be conveyed in a single gesture in American Sign Language. Indeed, ASL even has a sign meaning "I love you!"

This incongruence between the structures of sign language and those of spoken language is perhaps what most stymies students learning ASL as a second language. Unlike the various systems of Manually Coded English, the signs of American Sign Language cannot be thought of as standing for English words and structures, and statements in one language cannot be mechanically rendered into the other word by word and sign by sign. Such a literal approach is tempting for the beginner but can lead to meaningless or ludicrous results even in situations where the structures of the two languages are sufficiently parallel to make such an attempt possible. (For example, the phrase *kick the bucket,* rendered literally into ASL, would not be understood to mean "die," because *kick the bucket* is an English idiom, not an idiom of American Sign Language.) Instead, in translating from English to ASL or vice versa, the interpreter must understand the concept being expressed in the first language and then render it in the words, signs, and structures appropriate to the second language.

### *Arbitrariness and Iconicity*

All languages have both arbitrary and iconic forms. An arbitrary form of word or sign is simply an abstract symbol; an iconic word or sign is one that resembles or is somehow analogous to some aspect of the thing or activity it represents. In spoken language, iconicity takes the form of onomatopoeia, the imitative quality found in such words as *bang, boom, fizz, buzz,* and *hum.*

A widespread misconception about signing is that it is largely or entirely iconic—that it is simply the use of pantomime as a substitute for language. But in fact, just as with spoken languages, most signs in American Sign Language bear no evident relationship to the concepts they represent; either they were created as arbitrary symbols in the first place, or their original similarity to some referent has been lost through time.

It is nevertheless true that the medium in which sign language is expressed—space—invites a much broader range of iconicity than is possible in spoken languages. The wide variety of imaginative ways in which American Sign Language exploits this opportunity for iconism is one of the delights of the language, and certainly its most accessible feature for beginners. Here are a few examples:

#### What the Referent Looks Like

*airplane*
**(shape of wings)**

*tree*
**(shape of trunk)**

#### What the Referent Does

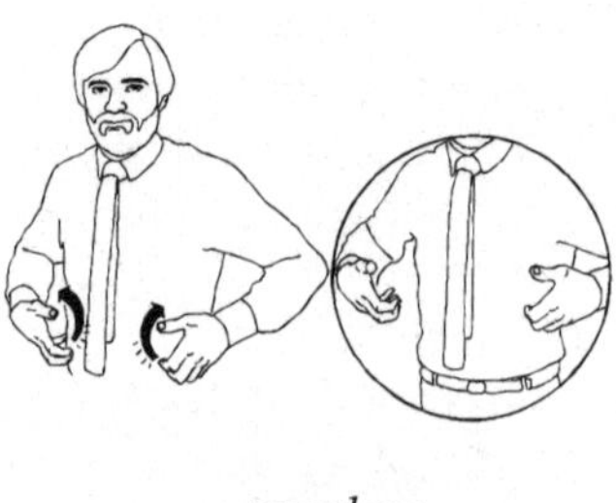

*monkey*
**(scratches itself)**

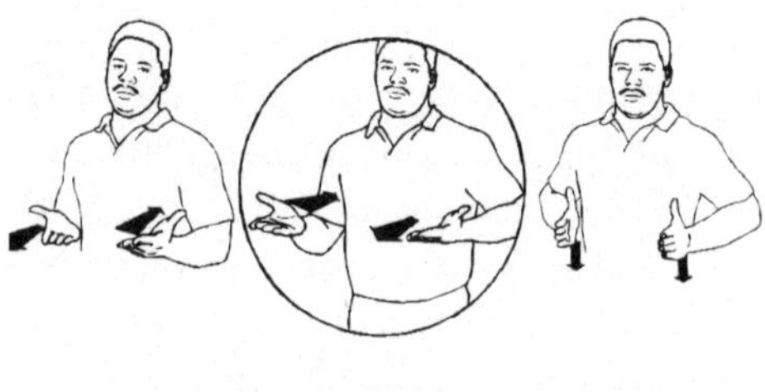

*waiter*
**(serves)**

## What You Do with the Referent

*car*
**(drive it)**

*flower*
**(smell it)**

## A Concrete Expression of an Abstract Referent

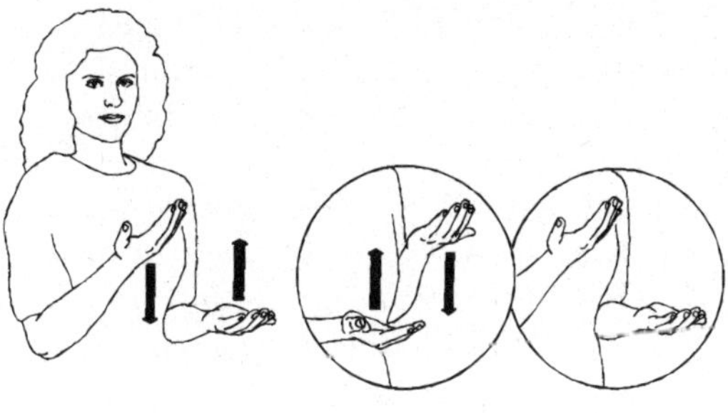

*maybe*
**(weighing possibilities)**

*affiliation*
**(connection to another)**

The actual history of many signs is not known; it is therefore often a matter of speculation whether a sign that appears to mime some aspect of its referent is truly iconic or whether the resemblance is coincidental. In either case, the similarity can be extremely helpful to the learner; accordingly, in this dictionary the apparent iconic significance of signs is pointed out in the form of "hints" as an aid in remembering the meaning of the sign and the way it is formed.

### *Fingerspelling*

Just as English words can be spelled out orally by naming each of the letters in turn, they can also be *fingerspelled* in American Sign Language, using a set of 26 handshapes called the American Manual Alphabet, reproduced in full on p. xxxviii. The sign languages of other countries have their own manual alphabets for the spoken and written languages prevailing in those countries.

Another misunderstanding about sign language is that it consists entirely of fingerspelling; and in fact some attempts have been made to educate deaf children solely through the medium of fingerspelling. But even for a hearing child who is a native English speaker, spelling is a skill that takes years to develop. And even for an adult with a complete mastery of English, spelling out every word in a speech or conversation would be extremely difficult and cumbersome, as can easily be appreciated simply by trying to carry on such a conversation for a few minutes, or by reciting out loud a familiar story or joke using letters instead of words. It is clear that fingerspelling is not a practical substitute for sign language.

Nevertheless, the manual alphabet is a useful tool in a number of situations. Fingerspelling provides an important bridge between English speakers who are just learning American Sign Language and signers competent in written English. Within the Deaf community the manual alphabet is commonly used to spell out proper names (in full or in shortened form), in borrowing English technical terms having no exact equivalent in sign, for emphasis (compare English "This means Y-O-U!"), and, often in a streamlined form, as the sign for certain concepts that can be expressed with very short English words or abbreviations such as *on, dog, TV,* or *a-p-t* for "apartment." Some words borrowed from English in full fingerspelled form have evolved into ASL signs employing only the first and last letters of the word, joined by a transitional movement. Linguists refer to words taken into one language from another as "loanwords"; these signs from English are regarded as "loan signs."

In fingerspelling, the handshapes of the manual alphabet are typically formed comfortably in front of the right shoulder (left shoulder in the case of left-handed signers). But the handshapes found in the manual alphabet are also combined with a variety of movements, locations, and orientations to make other signs, the formation of which can then be described by reference to use of the *"A hand,"* the *"P hand,"* and the like. This is a particularly prominent feature of *initialized* signs, that is, signs intentionally designed to employ the handshape of a key letter of a corresponding English word, as in signs for days of the week.

Many initialized signs began as ASL signs with different handshapes, then were adapted for use in Manually Coded English by substitution of the handshape for the initial letter of a specific English word. For example, the traditional sign for *try* employs the S hand, but the same gesture may now be seen with the T hand (for *try*), the A hand (corresponding to English *attempt*), or the E hand (for English *effort*). Some variants of this sort may be in the process of being incorporated into ASL from Manually Coded English.

### *Numbers*

Like letters, numbers are formed with one hand, held in front of the signing shoulder and moving smoothly from number to number. The chart on page 583 shows handshapes for the numbers from *zero* to *twenty-nine*; the remaining two-digit numbers are made by signing the two digits in order (30 = *three-zero,* 31 = *three-one,* etc.), with a slight shift to the signer's right (to the left for left-handed signers) between the first and second digit. The numbers *eleven* through *fifteen* are always signed with the palm facing in toward the signer, and when counting discrete objects up to five the palm likewise faces in; in all other contexts and in all higher numbers the palm should face forward. In what is probably a carryover from French sign language, the concepts of *hundred, thousand,* and *million* are represented by the signed letters *C, M,* and *MM*:

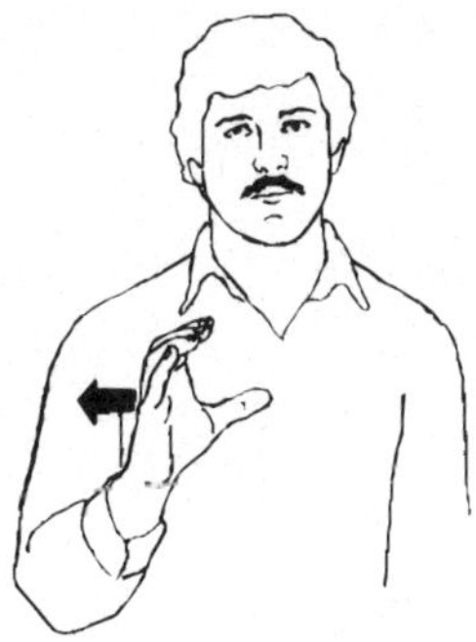

*hundred*

*thousand*

*million*

The general rule is to sign numbers just as they are spoken in English. Thus 15,671 is signed as *fifteen thousand six hundred seventy-one* (i.e., *fifteen M six C seven-one*), 3311 Russell Road as *thirty-three eleven,* the year 1994 as *nineteen ninety-four,* and the time 3:45 as *three forty-five.* The dollar amount $49.32 may be signed as *forty-nine dollars and thirty-two cents* (i.e., four-two dollar and three-two cent).

Like the letter shapes, handshapes for the numbers up to *ten* are employed in many signs, which are described as using the *"3 hand,"* the *"5 hand,"* and so on. In most such signs these handshapes have no numerical significance. But indexing with a number hand can convey such concepts as *"you two," "we three,"* or *"the four of them"*; and number handshapes can be incorporated into certain other signs, such as those for *week* and *month,* specifically to add a numerical component:

*two weeks*

*six months*

Ordinal numbers corresponding to the numerals one through nine are formed by the addition of a twisting motion, and these same signs can also be used to express dollar amounts up to nine. The chart on p. xlv shows the signs used for ordinals from *first* to *tenth.*

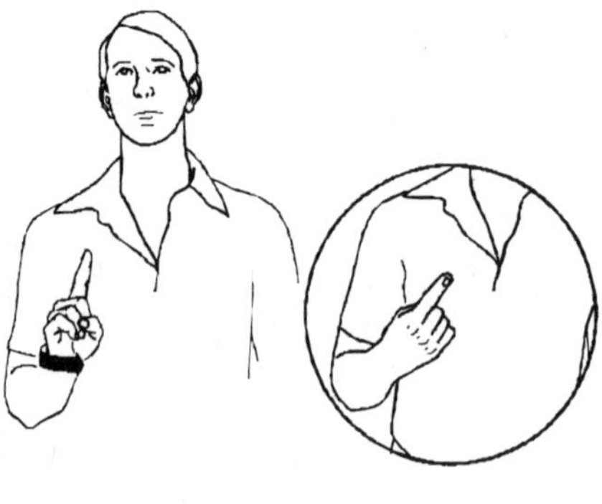

*first or one dollar*

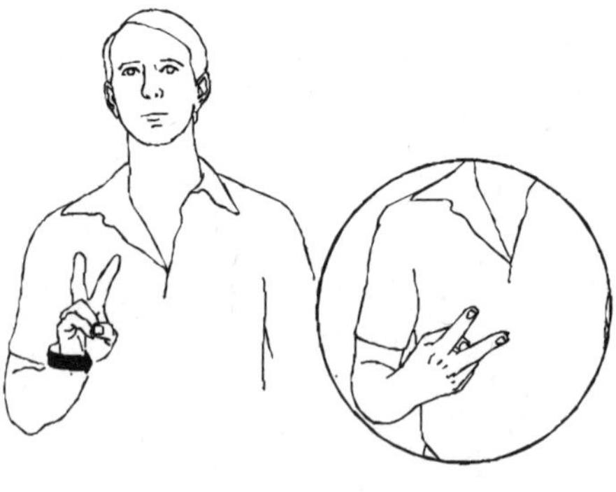

*second or two dollars*

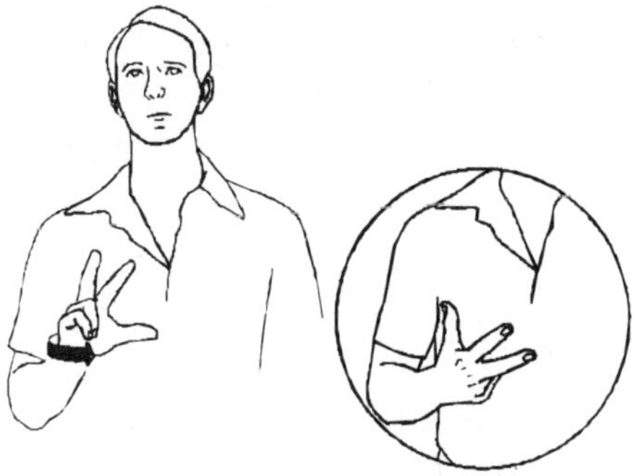

*third or three dollars*

## Historical Change in Sign Language

Like all living languages, American Sign Language grows and changes continuously. In fact, within the twentieth century alone, some 20 percent of signs recorded early in the century have undergone formational changes. The process of linguistic change is never completely uniform and predictable; in ASL, for example, some signs formerly made with two hands have become one-handed at the same time that some signs made with one hand have become two-handed. However, linguists studying the history of American Sign Language have noted some general trends in the evolution of the language, including:

*Centralization.* Older signs involving wide-ranging gestures have generally become confined to a signing space within easy view of the listener—roughly from the waist to the top of the signer's head and extending about a foot out to each side of the signer. And even within this space there has been a tendency for one-handed signs to move toward the middle, where more detailed handshapes and movements can be utilized because they are near the center of the listener's visual field. At the same time, some signs that originally involved movement of both hands with different handshapes now employ the same handshape with both hands, again reducing the amount of detail that the listener must perceive through peripheral vision.

*Assimilation.* A compound sign, that is, one originally made up of two separate signs, may have changed in various ways to make the parts more alike, to smooth out the transition between them, and generally to make the compound simpler and more unified. For example, in the sign for *agree* (*think* + *same*), certain movements of the two component signs have disappeared, and the resulting compound simply joins the final positions of both.

*Abstraction.* Perhaps the most pronounced overall trend has been for signs that originated through pantomime to lose their iconic quality. Unique handshapes and movements may evolve into more familiar, standard forms; broad gestures may become more restrained and centralized; facial expressions and other nonmanual features associated with the original mime may disappear, and dissimilar features may be smoothed out through assimilation, until the iconic origin of the sign is no longer apparent and the sign becomes purely an abstract manual symbol (see the section *"Arbitrariness and Iconicity"* above). The cumulative effect of decades of such evolutionary changes has been to regularize sign formation and make the language more systematic.

In addition to changes in formation of existing signs, the vocabulary of American Sign Language, like that of every living language, is continually augmented through the appearance of new slang and idiom, borrowing of terminology of other languages, and creation of new signs to reflect the explosive growth of knowledge in all fields.

A notable example of change through the borrowing of signs from other languages may be seen in names of countries and nationalities. The traditional—and still most commonly used—American signs for other nationalities were often iconic. Although never intended to be insulting, some of these historical signs have been considered offensive by the people of the countries referred to; and within the Deaf community there is a growing awareness that their use is not in keeping with modern sensibilities and with the internationalization of community spirit among deaf people. In a recent trend, these traditional American signs are being replaced by the signs used by deaf people in each country to refer to themselves. The section beginning on p. 567 shows the signs for selected countries and other geographic locations, including the preferred signs used by natives as well as the signs traditionally used by Americans when referring to other countries.

## In Conclusion

There is something fascinating and compelling about sign language. People from the hearing world who have occasion to take it up find themselves caught up in this new way of communicating—intrigued by the shift from a language of sound to a language of gesture, delighted by the pantomimic quality of many of the signs. But as a person becomes more fluent in ASL, it is the more subtle aspects of the language, such as the charm of classifiers, the sophisticated use of space, and the role of nonmanual cues, that keep the learner challenged and stimulated. Although this dictionary provides a foundation in the vocabulary of American Sign Language, the nuances of the language can be absorbed only from its native speakers—Deaf people themselves. In the end, it is through interaction with the Deaf community that this marvelous language can be learned and made to come alive.

# Guide

## How to Use This Dictionary

### What This Dictionary Contains

#### *Requirements of a Lexicon of Sign Language*

Like any specialized dictionary, such as a legal or medical lexicon, this one contains a specialized vocabulary. Rather than embracing the full spectrum of terms—from common to technical—that one finds in a standard dictionary of English, this book focuses on the body of signs most responsive to the needs of users and students of American Sign Language (ASL).

This means that while a broad range of concepts is covered, many English words are not included. In some cases this is simply because their signs are used infrequently. Other terms do not have a corresponding sign; their meanings are communicated quite differently in sign language—e.g., as an integrated component of some other sign, as a nonmanual cue accompanying a sign, as a pointing (or "indexing") movement, or by fingerspelling.

Conversely, there are strings of words in this book—phrases and entire clauses—that would be out of place in a standard dictionary. Here they represent concepts expressed in one unified signing gesture in ASL. Examples are **I love you** and **Now I remember.**

#### *Sources of Signs*

For the most part, the signs in this dictionary are firmly established elements of American Sign Language. New signs for nations and nationalities and some signs from systems of Manually Coded English (see *Introduction,* p. x) have also been included, to reflect recent borrowings into ASL. In addition, the dic-tionary includes a few fingerspelled forms, like **ha ha,** which are considered to be ASL signs (see *Introduction*, p. xxv), although no attempt is made to give a comprehensive listing of these terms.

Although some regional variation is represented, the signs have been collected primarily from up and down the East Coast. The general tendency is for these signs to spread westward.

### *Usage Levels: The Social Appropriateness of Signs and Their English Translations*

Like English and every other language, American Sign Language contains its share of terms that would be inappropriate in polite conversation. If a dictionary is to present an accurate picture of a language, it must include even vulgar or disparaging terms. In this dictionary, to prevent the novice from inadvertently insulting a conversational partner by unwittingly using a sign that would cause offense, cautionary notations or labels have been included for such signs. For example, a note at the end of the description of the sign might indicate that the sign is used disparagingly, or a cautionary usage label may be added to an English translation.

## How to Find a Sign

### *Complete Entries*

All entries—whether words or phrases, and whether common terms or proper nouns—are presented in large boldface type in a single alphabetical listing, following a strict letter-by-letter order that disregards spaces between words, e.g., **ever, everlasting, ever since.** An exception to this order is made for verb phrases, which are shown as a group; for example, **cast off** and **cast out** are grouped together after **cast,** and so precede **castle.**

Most signs can be found by looking them up under any of several English words or phrases, only one of which, however, will set forth a complete description of the sign. That complete entry usually includes one or more part-of-speech labels (*n.* for noun, *v.* for verb, etc.), and one or more short definitions and sample phrases or sentences, to make it clear exactly what meanings and uses of the main entry word are encompassed by the sign.

Additional words for concepts covered by that sign are often listed within the entry in small boldface type, although the list of words with equivalent or related meanings is by no means exhaustive. Typical examples may be seen at the entry for **confident,** which lists the related form **confidence** as another meaning for that sign, and the entry for **earn,** which notes that the same sign is used for **deserve, income, salary,** and **wages.** Where appropriate, these additional words are given usage labels (e.g., informal, slang, vulgar, diminutive) to emphasize that the sign portrayed in that entry may be interpreted in those various ways depending upon the context and manner in which it is used, and that it should therefore be used with some caution.

### *Cross References*

A cross-reference entry, at its own alphabetical listing, shows neither definitions nor signs. Such an entry simply sends the reader to one or more complete entries, where appropriate signs will be found. An example is the entry for **fatigue,** which states: See signs for TIRED, WEAK.

An additional type of cross reference, signaled by the instruction to "See also sign for...," is found within complete entries. This occurs when the signs for two different words are interchangeable. For example, at **achieve** there is an instruction to "See also sign for SUCCESSFUL," while at **successful** we find a matching instruction to "See also sign for ACHIEVE." This means that either sign may be used to represent either concept.

Because the range of additional meanings for a sign may differ widely from the meanings of its closest English translation, the relationship between a main entry and its cross references—all of which share the same sign—is sometimes obscure to a person who is not fluent in ASL. Although a cross reference may be virtually synonymous with the main entry (**officer** refers to entries for **captain** and **chief**), it is more likely to be linked to the main entry in some more nebulous, conceptual fashion, without being directly substitutable for it in an English sentence (at **farm** the reader is referred not only to the noun **agriculture,** but also to the adjective **sloppy**). Occasionally, the dictionary suggests a connection, as at the entry for **alert**, which reads: "See sign for INSOMNIA. Shared idea of remaining awake."

### *Multiple Entries for the Same Word*

Often there are two or more separate entries for the same word, each marked by a small identifying superscript number. These numerically sequenced groups of entries are of three sorts:

(1) Entries that have different signs because they differ in meaning (**country**$^{1}$ "foreign nation" and **country**$^{2}$ "rural land") or in part of speech (**fish**$^{1}$ a noun and **fish**$^{2}$ a verb). Each one is handled separately as a complete entry.

(2) Separate entries for a word that, though not varying in meaning or part of speech, may be expressed by two or more interchangeable signs. In these cases each numbered entry includes a sign and sign description, but only the first entry in the group is defined; those that follow are simply labeled "alternate sign." See, for example, the two interchangeable signs at the entries **nosy**[1] and **nosy**[2].

(3) Entries with at least one of the terms in the group are cross referenced to a different sign elsewhere in the alphabet—e.g., **pile**[1], a complete main entry, and **pile**[2], a cross reference to **amount** and **stack.** Cross-reference entries are always shown last in any such sequence.

## How to Make a Sign

### *Illustrations*

Formation of the sign is illustrated at every complete entry and at every entry labeled "alternate sign," sometimes by a single picture but more often by a series of full-torso line drawings that take the reader step by step through a sequence of movements. Arrows show the direction in which the hands move, and the accompanying description gives any special instructions needed on how to execute the movement.

All the illustrations demonstrate how a right-handed signer would execute each sign as seen by the listener; the model's right hand is on the reader's left. A left-handed signer should transpose the illustrated hands as well as the arrows when forming the sign—in other words, treating the picture as if it were the reader's mirror image.

In a sequence of pictures, the illustrations in a circle focus on some significant portion of the movement, often the final position of the hands. The reader should execute the signs in the order shown, from left to right.

### *Descriptions*

Each illustration is supplemented by a verbal description giving detailed instructions for making the sign. The formation of the sign is described in terms of the four component parts of a sign (see *Introduction*, the section on *Phonology*, p. xii). These four parts are: (1) handshape, (2) location in relation to the body, (3) movement of the hands, and (4) orientation of the palms. Occasionally a fifth component, a description of nonmanual cues, is added, as at the entry for **small**[2], where "while hunching the shoulders" signifies an intensification of the smallness, making the term mean "very small," "meager," or "tiny."

In cases where the rhythm of the movement is a critical component of the sign's formation, the description may state that, for example, the hands "move quickly" or the sign is "made with a deliberate movement." An indication is also given when a double movement is required or when a movement is to be "repeated"—that is, made two or more times.

Within the description, italicized terms such as *A hand* and *C hand* refer to handshapes shown in the chart of the Manual Alphabet (p. xxxviii). Terms such as *1 hand* or *10 hand* refer to handshapes for numbers (p. xli). Other special handshapes, such as *bent hand, open hand,* and *flattened C hand,* are shown on page xxxvii.

### *Hints*

Beginning most descriptions is a bracketed memory aid, or *hint.* These hints use a number of devices to help the reader understand the nature of the sign and better remember how it is made. For a *pantomimic sign,* for example, the reader may be instructed to perform an appropriate imitative action, as at **golf:** [Mime swinging a golf club]. The hint for an *iconic sign* might point out the sign's resemblance to the thing depicted or to some aspect of that thing, e.g., at **camp** [Shape of a tent] or, at **ear**: [Location of an ear].

The hint for a *compound sign,* one formed by combining two or more independent signs, tells the reader which signs are to be combined, as at **income**[1], where the hint is: [**money** + **earn**]. Superscript numbers specify which of the multiple entries for the same word the reader may use in forming the compound. For example, the hint [**gather**[1,2] + **meeting**] at **conference**[1] reveals that one may form **conference** using either of the two signs for **gather,** although both the description and the illustration refer only to **gather**[1]. The sign for a compound often involves some streamlining of the component signs, which is reflected in the description.

An *initialized sign* is formed with the handshape for the salient letter in the English term, taken from the American Manual Alphabet (see chart on p. xxxviii). The hint for **Dallas:** [Initialized sign], reminds the reader that the handshape required is the *D hand.* Similarly, the hint for **hum** is: [Initialized sign using **m** indicating the sound that is made when humming].

*Fingerspelled signs* use the Manual Alphabet to spell out a short word or abbreviation, as indicated by such hints as: [Fingerspell **n-o**] for **no** and, at **jack-o'-lantern:** [Abbreviation **j-o-l**].

Two special notations used in the hints need a word of explanation. First, an occasional reference is made to "the finger used for feelings." Signs made with the bent middle finger often refer to concepts of sensitivity, feelings, or personal contact; examples include the signs for **mercy, sick,** and **network.** Second, allusions to the "male" and "female" areas of the head relate to the fact that signs referring to men, such as **father** and **uncle**, begin at or are made near the forehead, whereas signs referring to women, such as **mother** and **aunt**, begin at or are made near the chin. A clear example of the importance of this distinction may be seen in the signs for **cousin**, made near the temple for a male cousin and near the lower cheek to refer to a female cousin.

# Abbreviations Used in This Dictionary

| | |
|---|---|
| *adj.* | adjective |
| *adv.* | adverb |
| *adv. phrase* | adverbial phrase |
| *auxiliary v.* | auxiliary verb |
| *conj.* | conjunction |
| *interj.* | interjection |
| *n.* | noun |
| *n. phrase* | noun phrase |
| *pl. n.* | plural noun |
| *prep.* | preposition |
| *prep. phrase* | prepositional phrase |
| *pron.* | pronoun |
| *v.* | verb |
| *v. phrase* | verb phrase |

# Handshapes Used in This Dictionary

*Open*

*Bent*

*Curved 5*

*Flattened C*

*Bent V*

*Modified X*

*Flattened O*

*Modified C*

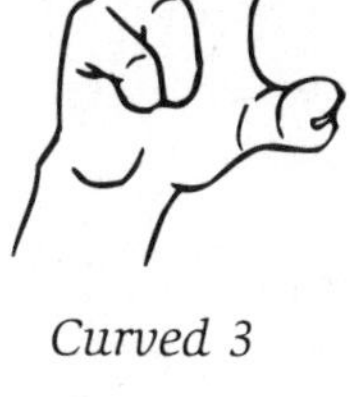

*Curved 3*

# Manual Alphabet and Fingerspelling

The American Manual Alphabet is a series of handshapes used to represent each letter of the English alphabet. Many countries have their own manual alphabets, just as they have their own sign languages. It is important to note that although English is spoken in the United States and in England, the English Manual Alphabet, which is formed by using two hands, is very different from the American Manual Alphabet.

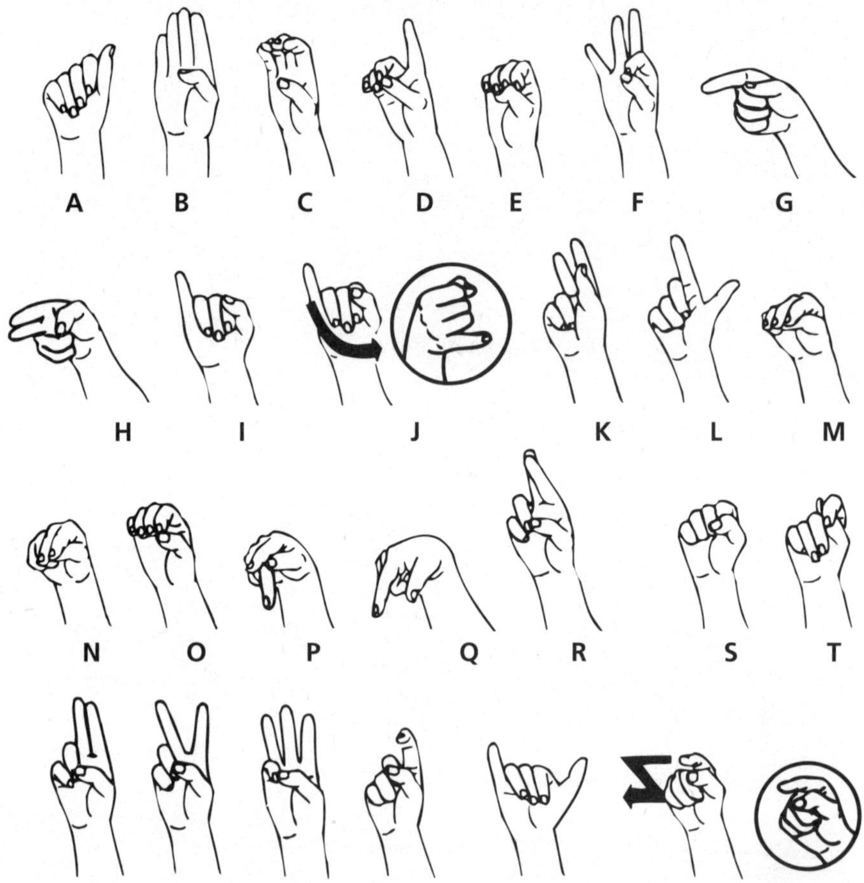

# Fingerspelling

## Expressive

"Letters" from the manual alphabet are used to fingerspell words. Fingerspelling, an important tool for communication, supplements American Sign Language when a person does not know a sign, or no sign exists for a concept. Fingerspelling is also used for proper nouns, like people's names or the names of companies. Often Deaf people use fingerspelling to be sure that an idea is exactly communicated or for emphasis. A beginning signer whose sign vocabulary may be limited can use fingerspelling to fill in for unknown signs.

Mastering the art and skill of fingerspelling is a task requiring time and practice. Some basic hints for clearer fingerspelling include the following:

1. Keep your hand stable; try not to bounce your hand or to allow it to "slip away" from its initial position.
2. Keep your hand in position, palm out, near the shoulder.
3. Avoid extraneous movements; they are distracting and cause confusion in the intended message.
4. Try to maintain a smooth and steady rhythm in your fingerspelling. Avoid choppy or irregular speed or flow.
5. Give adequate breaks between words.
6. Mouth or say the entire word, not each letter.
7. Concentrate on clearly forming the letters. Do not worry about speed; speed will occur naturally as you become more comfortable with your fingerspelling.
8. When forming double letters, while holding the letter's handshape, move your hand slightly to the side with a little bounce. In words with double letters made with a closed handshape (e.g., *o*, *s*, and *t*), open your hand slightly between the two letters.
9. Watch the person with whom you are communicating and not your hand.

## Receptive

Most people find reading and comprehending fingerspelled words to be a much more arduous task than fingerspelling itself. Practicing to understand fingerspelling during actual conversations with deaf individuals is probably the best way to improve your receptive skills.

Here are several suggestions that may be helpful in becoming skillful in reading another person's fingerspelling.

1. Do not focus on each letter individually; instead, try to see the whole word.
2. Let the content of the conversation lead you to predict the word being fingerspelled.
3. Watch the fingerspelling peripherally; do not drop your eyes from the overall signing space.

**abandon** *v.* To give up with the intent of not reclaiming: *Abandon your wild ways.* Related form: **abandonment** *n.* Same sign used for: **discard, evict, expel, forsake, throw out.**

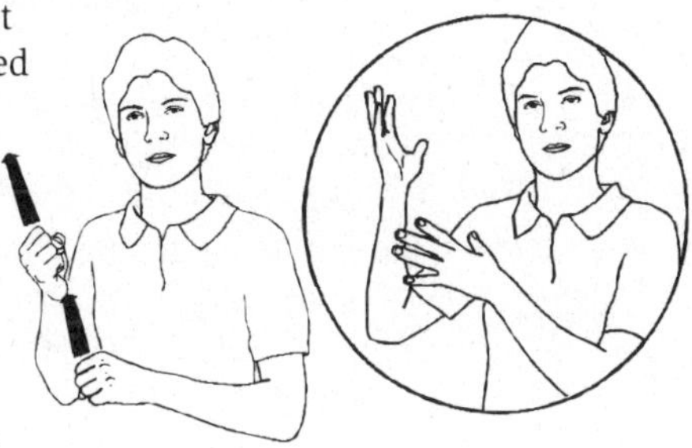

■ [Natural gesture of giving up hope] Beginning with both *S hands* in front of the chest, both palms facing in and the right hand above the left hand, quickly throw the hands upward to the right while opening into *5 hands* in front of the right shoulder, ending with the palms facing back and the fingers pointing up.

---

**abate** *v.* See sign for STOP[1].

---

**abbreviate** *v.* See sign for BRIEF.

---

**abdomen** *n.* See sign for STOMACH.

---

**ability** *n.* Same sign as for **able** but made with a double movement. See also sign for SKILL.

---

**able**[1] *adj.* Having the skill or power to do something: *able to swim.*

■ [Both hands sign **yes,** indicating ability to do something] Move both *A hands,* palms facing down, downward simultaneously in front of each side of the body.

---

**able**[2] *adj.* See sign for SKILL.

---

**abolish**[1] *v.* See sign for DAMAGE. Shared idea of destruction.

---

**abolish**[2] *v.* See signs for ELIMINATE[1], REMOVE[1].

---

**abort** *v.* See signs for ELIMINATE[1], REMOVE[1]. Related form: **abortion** *n.*

---

**abortion** *n.* The removal or expulsion of a fetus prior to natural birth before it can survive: *to have an abortion before the fourth month of pregnancy.*

■ [Represents removing the fetus and throwing it away] Beginning with the palm of the left *open hand,* palm facing down, resting on the palm side of the right *A hand,* palm facing up, turn the right hand over and move it outward to the right while opening into a *5 hand* in front of the right side of the body, palm facing down.

---

**about**[1] *prep.* Having something to do with: *a movie about tropical rain forests.* Same sign used for: **concerning, regarding.**

■ [One thing moving about another] Move the extended right index finger, palm facing in and finger pointing left, around the fingertips of the left *flattened O hand,* palm facing in and fingers pointing right.

---

**about**[2] *adv.* See signs for ALMOST[1], APPROXIMATELY.

---

**above** *prep.* **1.** At or to a higher place than: *The kite floated above the trees.* —*adv.* **2.** Higher or overhead: *the sky above.* See also sign for: OVER[2].

■ [Indicates area above] Beginning with the right *open hand* on the back of the left *open hand,* both palms facing down, bring the right hand upward in an arc, ending several inches above the left hand.

---

**abrasive** *adj.* See sign for ROUGH.

---

**abrupt** *adj.* Sudden: *The road came to an abrupt end.* Related form: **abruptly** *adv.* Same sign used for: **accelerate, quick, quickly, snap.**

■ [A sudden action] Snap the thumb of the right hand off the right middle finger, forming an *A hand* in front of the right shoulder.

---

**absent** *adj.* **1.** Not present: *absent from class.* —*v.* **2.** Keep (oneself) away: *Do not absent yourself from class without a good excuse.* Related form: **absence** *n.* Same sign used for: **drain, extinct, gone, miss, missing.**

■ [Something seems to go down the drain] Pull the right *flattened C hand,* palm facing in, downward through the left *C hand,* palm facing right, while closing the fingers and thumb of the right hand together.

---

**absent-minded** *adj.* See sign for BLANK[1].

---

**absolute** *adj.* Free from restriction or doubt: *the absolute truth.* Related form: **absolutely** *adv.* Same sign used for: **certain, truly.**

■ [**true** + a gesture that is used when one gives a promise] Beginning with the thumb side of the extended right index finger against the chin, palm facing left and finger pointing up, move the hand forward while opening into an *open hand,* palm facing forward and fingers pointing up.

**absorb**[1] *v.* To take in or suck up: *A sponge will absorb the liquid.* Related forms: **absorbent** *adj.*, **absorption** *n.* Same sign used for: **attract, magnetic.**

■ [The hands seem to be pulled together as if by a magnet] Beginning with both *5 hands* in front of each side of the body, palms facing down and fingers pointing forward, bring the hands back while forming *flattened O hands,* ending with the fingers of both hands touching in front of the chest.

**absorb**[2] *v.* See sign for RAPTURE.

**abstain**[1] *v.* To do without voluntarily: *to abstain from eating candy.* Related form: **abstinence** *n.*

■ [Initialized sign sealing the lips closed] Move the fingertips of the right *F hand,* palm facing in, from left to right across the mouth.

**abstain**[2] *v.* To voluntarily refrain from sexual relations: *to abstain from sex until after marriage.* Related form: **abstinence** *n.* Same sign used for: **celibate.**

■ [**sex**[1]; **none**[1]] Touch the index-finger side of the right *X hand* first near the right eye and then to the right side of the chin. Then move both *flattened O hands* from in front of the chest outward to each side.

**absurd**[1] *adj.* Ridiculous: *It is absurd to think that a broken mirror causes bad luck.*

■ Beginning with the index finger of the right *4 hand* touching the right side of the forehead, palm facing left, bring the hand forward in a series of small arcs.

**absurd**[2] *adj.* See sign for SILLY.

**abuse** *v.* See signs for BEAT[3], BEAT UP, TORTURE.

**accelerate** *v.* See sign for ABRUPT.

**accept** *v.* To receive with favor: *to accept the invitation.* Related form: **acceptance** *n.* Same sign used for: **adopt, adoption, approval, approve.**

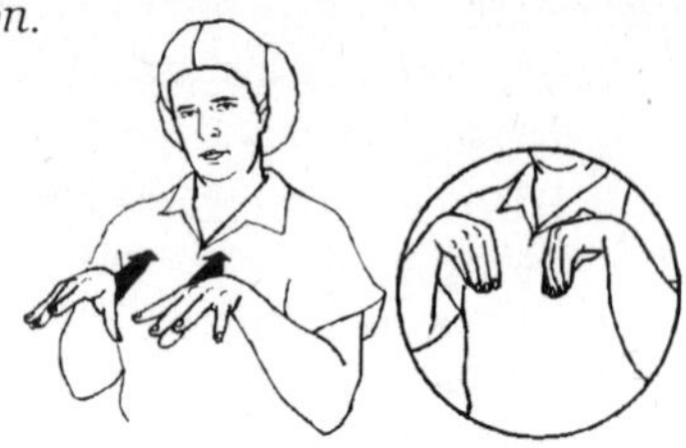

■ [Bring something that is accepted toward oneself] Beginning with both *5 hands* in front of the chest, fingers pointing forward, bring both hands back toward the chest while pulling the fingers and thumbs of each hand together.

**access** *v.* See signs for ANALYZE, ENTER[1].

**access code** *n. phrase.* See sign for PASSWORD[1].

**accident**[1] *n.* An unintended, damaging incident involving vehicles: *injured in a car accident.* Same sign used for: **collide, collision, crash.**

■ [Two things collide with each other] Move both *5 hands* from in front of each side of the chest, palms facing in and fingers pointing toward each other, while changing into *A hands,* ending with the knuckles of both *A hands* touching in front of the chest.

**accident**[2] *n.* See signs for HAPPEN, MISTAKE.

**accidentally** *adv.* By chance: *spilled the milk accidentally.* Alternate form: **by accident.** Related form: **accidental** *adj.* Same sign used for: **amiss, by mistake.**

■ [Similar to sign for **mistake** except made with a twisting movement] Twist the knuckles of the right *Y hand,* palm facing in, on the chin from right to left.

**acclaim** *v.* See sign for ANNOUNCE.

**acclamation** *n.* See sign for PRAISE.

**accompany** *v.* See sign for GO WITH.

**accomplish** *v.* See sign for SUCCESSFUL. Related form: **accomplishment** *n.*

**according to** In agreement with: *Modify your exercise routine according to your goals.* Same sign used for: **proportion, ratio.**

■ [Initialized sign similar to sign for **proportion** showing two similar things] Move both *P hands,* palms facing down, from in front of the left side of the body to the right side of the body by bringing the hands upward simultaneously in a large arc.

**accredit** *v.* To give official acceptance to: *to accredit a college.* Related forms: **accreditation** *n.*, **accredited** *adj.* Same sign used for: **adopt, certify.**

■ [Stamping something with a seal] Beginning with the right *S hand* in front of the right shoulder, palm facing down, twist the wrist to hit the little-finger side of the upturned left *open hand* with a deliberate movement.

**accrue** *v.* See signs for ADD[1,2].

**accumulate**[1] *v.* To collect or pile up in increasing quantities: *Dust accumulated on the furniture.* Related form: **accumulation** *n.* Same sign used for: **amass.**

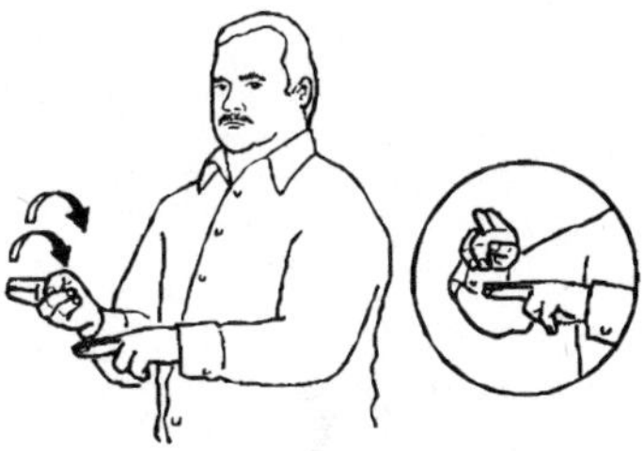

■ [More and more of something being piled up on top of other things] Beginning with the right *U hand,* palm facing left, beside the left *U hand,* palm facing down, flip the right hand over with a double movement, tapping the right fingers across the left fingers each time.

**accumulate**[2] *v.* See signs for ADD[1], COLLECT.

**accurate** *adj.* See signs for PERFECT, PRECISE, RIGHT[3].

**accusation**[1] *n.* An allegation against: *The landlord accused the tenant of not paying the rent on time.* Same sign used for: **allegation, charge.**

■ [Similar to sign for **blame** except formed with a double movement] Push the little-finger side of the right *A hand,* palm facing left, forward with a double movement across the back of the left *A hand,* palm facing down.

**accusation**[2] *n.* See sign for FAULT[2].

**accuse** *v.* See sign for BLAME[1].

**accustomed to** See sign for HABIT.

**ache** *v., n.* See signs for HURT[1], PAIN[1].

**achieve** *v.* To succeed in doing or getting by one's own efforts: *achieve one's purpose; achieve fame.* Related form: **achievement** *n.* See also sign for SUCCESSFUL. Same sign used for: **chalk up, success.**

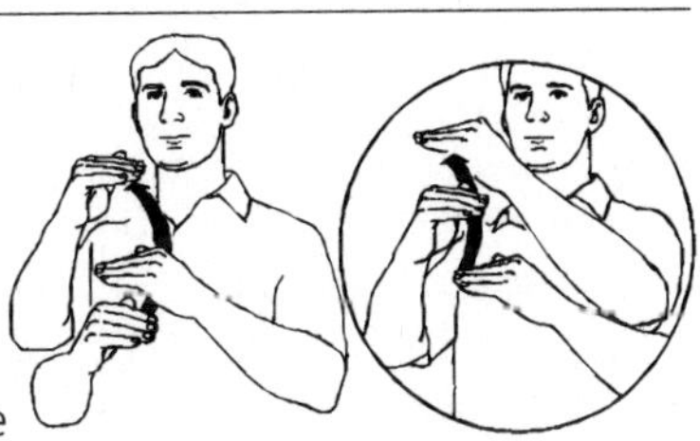

■ [An accumulation of something] Beginning with the left *bent hand* over the right *bent hand* in front of the chest, both palms facing down, move the hands with an alternating movement over each other to in front of the face.

**acid** *n.* **1.** A sour substance: *Vinegar is an acid.* **2.** A chemical substance that unites with a base to form a salt: *The acid ate holes in the marble.* Related form: **acidic** *adj.* Same sign used for: **cancer, eat up.**

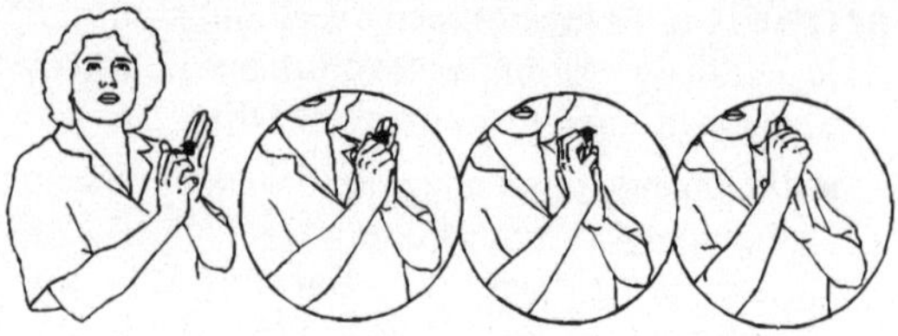

■ [Action of acid eating something] Open and tightly close the fingers of the right *curved 5 hand* as it moves with a crawling movement from the heel to the fingertips of the left *open hand,* palm facing right.

---

**acquaint** *v.* See sign for ASSOCIATE.

---

**acquire** *v.* See signs for GET, LEARN, TAKE.

---

**acquit** *v.* See sign for DISMISS[1].

---

**acquittal** *n.* See sign for EXCUSE[1].

---

**acreage** *n.* See sign for LAND[1].

---

**across** *prep.* **1.** From one side to another of: *to walk across the street.* **2.** On the other side of: *The mailbox is across the street.* —*adv.* From one side to another: *How can we get across?* Same sign used for: **after, afterward, cross, over.**

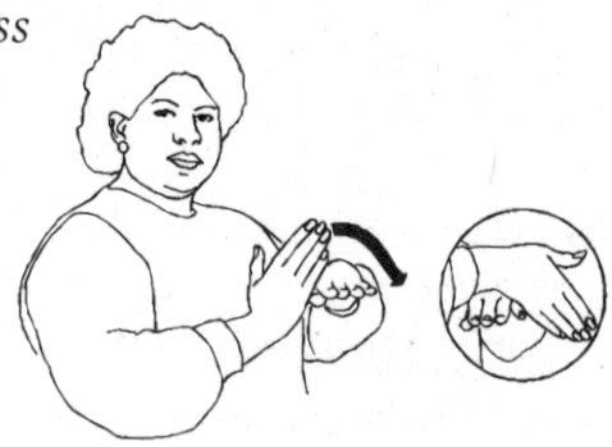

■ [Movement across another thing] Push the little-finger side of the right *open hand,* palm facing left, across the back of the left *open hand,* palm facing down.

---

**act**[1] *v.* **1.** To perform an action: *to act quickly in an emergency.* —*n.* **2.** Anything done or being done: *an act of mercy.* Related forms: **action** *n.*, **activity** *n.* Same sign used for: **deed.**

■ [The hands seem to be actively doing something] Move both *C hands,* palms facing down, simultaneously back and forth in front of the body with a swinging movement.

---

**act**[2] *v.* To play a part: *to act in the school play.* Same sign used for: **drama, perform, play, show, theater.**

■ [Initialized sign] Bring the thumbs of both *A hands,* palms facing each other, down each side of the chest with alternating circular movements.

---

**active**[1] *adj.* Doing things or moving much of the time: *She is an active child.* Related forms: **action** *n.*, **activity** *n.* Same sign used for: **deed, labor, work.**

- [The hands seem to be actively doing something] Move both *C hands,* palms facing down, back and forth in front of the body in opposite directions with a double swinging movement.

**active**[2] *adj.* See sign for AMBITIOUS[1].

**actual** *adj.* See signs for REAL, TRUE.

**actually** *adv.* See sign for TRUE.

**adapt** *v.* See sign for CHANGE[1].

**add**[1] or **add up** *v.* or *v. phrase.* To combine so as to find the sum: *to add 2 and 2; to add up the numbers.* Related forms: **addition** *n.* **additional** *adj.* Same sign used for: **accrue, accumulate, amount, plus, sum, total.**

- [Hands bring two quantities together] Beginning with the right *5 hand* from above the right shoulder, palm facing down, and the left *5 hand* near the left side of the waist, palm facing up, bring the hands toward each other while changing into *flattened O hands,* ending with the fingertips touching each other in front of the chest.

**add**[2] or **add to** *v.* Put together with something else: *to add sugar to tea.* Related forms: **addition** *n.* **additional** *adj.* Same sign used for: **accrue, amend, amount, bonus, extra, supplement.**

- [One hand brings an additional amount to the other hand] Swing the right *5 hand* upward from the right side of the body while changing into a *flattened O hand,* ending with the right index finger touching the little-finger side of the left *flattened O hand* in front of the chest, both palms facing in.

**addition** *n.* See sign for PLUS[1].

**addicted**[1] *adj.* Being a slave to a habit: *addicted to drugs.* Related form: **addiction** *n.* Same sign used for: **hooked.**

- [Gesture indicates that one is "hooked"] With the index finger of the right *X hand* hooked in the right corner of the mouth, pull the mouth outward to the right.

**addicted**[2] *adj.* (alternate sign)

■ [**become + habit**] With the palms of both *open hands* together, right hand on top of left hand, twist the wrists in opposite directions in order to reverse positions. Then with the heel of the right *C hand* across the wrist of the left *S hand,* palm facing down, move the hands down simultaneously in front of the chest.

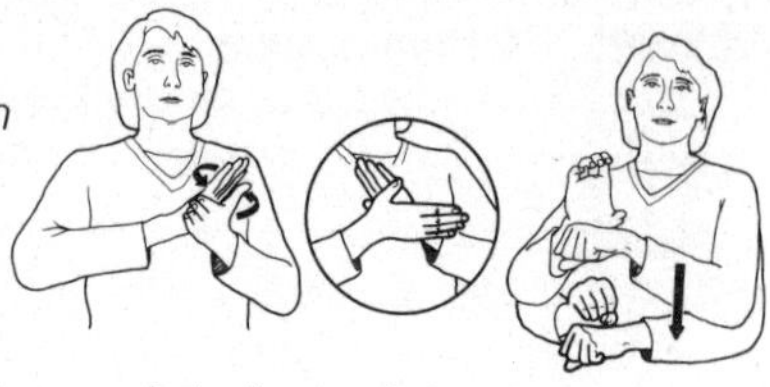

**address**[1] *n.* **1.** The designation of a place where a person or business resides or may be reached: *Write the address on the envelope.* —*v.* **2.** To affix directions for delivery on: *to address the envelope.* Same sign used for: **residence.**

■ [Initialized sign similar to sign for **live**] Move both *A hands,* palms facing in, upward on each side of the chest with a double movement.

**address**[2] *v.* See sign for SPEAK[2].

**adept** *adj.* See sign for ADROIT.

**adequate** *adj.* See sign for ENOUGH.

**adhere** *v.* See signs for APPLY[3], STICK[1].

**adhesive** *n., adj.* See sign for STICK[1].

**adhesive tape** *n.* See sign for BANDAGE.

**adjacent** *adj.* See sign for BESIDE.

**adjust** *v.* See sign for CHANGE[1].

**administer** *v.* See sign for MANAGE. Alternate form: **administrate.**

**admission** *n.* The right to enter: *The university approved the applicant's request for admission.* Alternate form: **admittance.** Same sign used for: **enter, entrance, entry.**

■ [Similar to sign for **enter** except formed with a double movement] Move the back of the right *open hand* forward in a downward arc under the palm of the left *open hand,* both palms facing down, with a double movement.

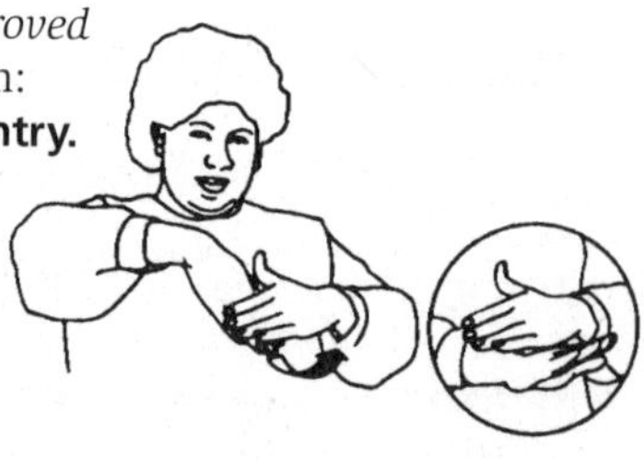

**admit**[1] *v.* To acknowledge as true: *Admit that you made a mistake.* Related form: **admission** *n.* Same sign used for: **confess, confession, submit, willing.**

■ [Hand seems to bring a confession from the chest] Move the right *open hand,* palm facing in, from the chest forward in an arc while turning the palm slightly upward.

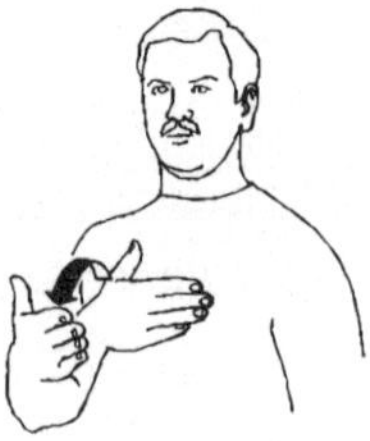

**admit**[2] *v.* See sign for ENTER.

**admonish** *v.* See sign for SCOLD, WARN.

**adopt** *v.* See signs for ACCEPT, ACCREDIT, APPROVE, TAKE. Related form: **adoption** *n.*

**adore** *v.* See sign for WORSHIP[1].

**adrift** *adj.* See sign for ROAM.

**adroit** *adj.* Skillful: *an adroit mountain climber.* Same sign used for: **adept, expert, good at, skillful, whiz** (*informal*).

■ Beginning with the fingertips of the right *F hand* touching the chin, palm facing forward, twist the hand to turn the palm inward.

**adult** *n.* **1.** A fully grown person, animal, or plant: *Children must be accompanied by an adult.* —*adj.* **2.** Mature, as befitting adults: *an adult movie.* Same sign used for: **grown-up.**

■ [Initialized sign formed in the traditional male and female positions; can be formed with an opposite movement] Move the thumb of the right *A hand,* palm facing forward, from the side of the forehead to the lower cheek.

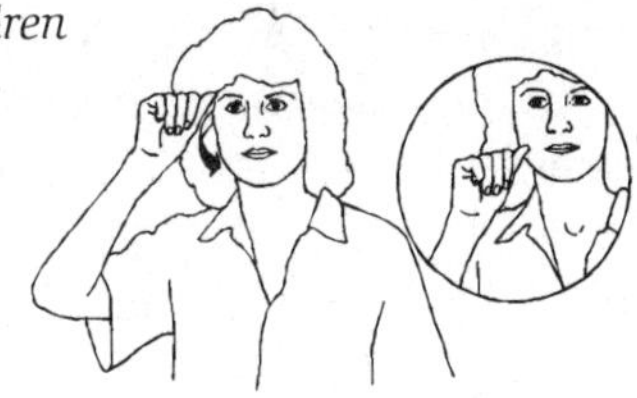

**adultery** *n.* Unfaithfulness of a husband or wife: *a wife guilty of adultery.*

■ [Initialized sign indicating moving from one partner to another] Tap the knuckles of the right *A hand,* palm facing down, first on the index fingertip and then on the middle fingertip of the left *V hand.*

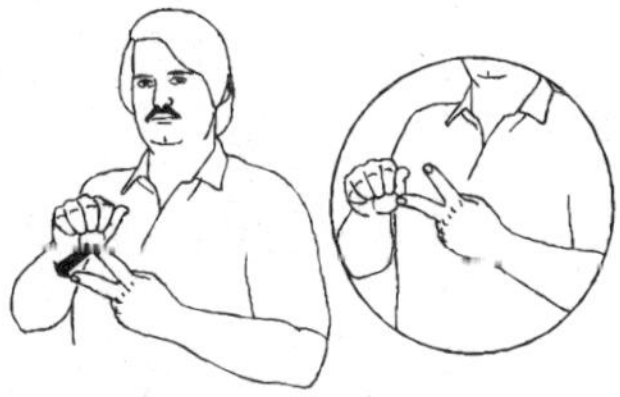

**advance** *v.* **1.** To move forward or upward: *The army advanced a short distance.* **2.** To further the development or progress of: *to advance the research regarding AIDS.* Same sign used for: **exalt.**

■ [Moving to a more advanced position] Beginning with the back of the right *bent hand* touching the palm of the left *open hand,* both palms facing in, move the right hand upward and forward of the left hand.

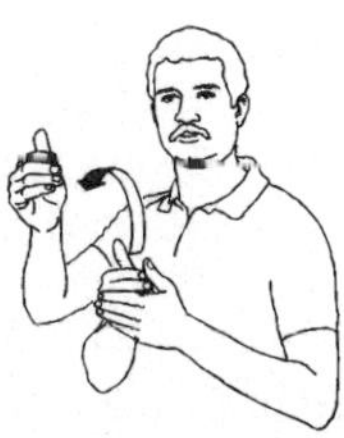

**advanced** *adj.* Beyond a beginning level: *advanced algebra.* Same sign used for: **elevate, elevated, elevation, exalt, exalted, exaltation, higher, prominent, promote, promotion, supreme.**

■ [Moving to a more advanced position] Move both *bent hands,* palms facing each other, from near each side of the head upward a short distance in a deliberate arc.

**advantage**[1] *n.* Anything in one's favor: *Her knowledge of Spanish gave her a great advantage over me.* Same sign used for: **scrounge, take advantage of.**

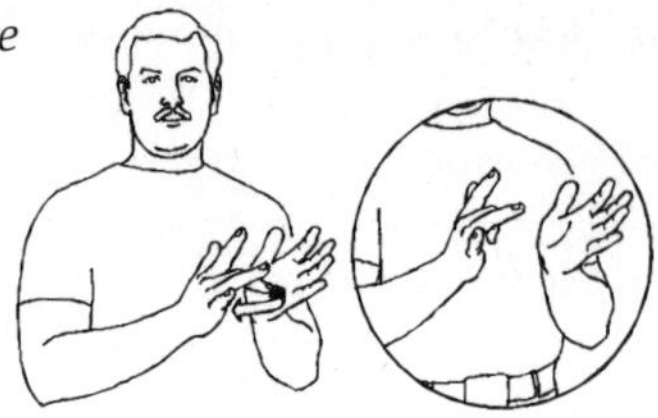

■ Flick the bent middle finger of the right *5 hand* upward off the heel of the left *open hand.*

**advantage**[2] *n.* See sign for BENEFIT.

**advertise** *v.* To announce or praise publicly in order to sell: *to advertise a new soap on television.* Related form: **advertisement** *n.* Same sign used for: **broadcast, commercial, propaganda, publicity, publicize.**

■ Beginning with the thumb side of the right *S hand,* palm facing left, against the little-finger side of the left *S hand,* palm facing right, move the right hand forward and back. The noun form of this sign is formed with a double movement.

**advice** *n.* Someone's opinion about what should be done: *He gave them good advice.* Same sign used for: **effect.**

■ [Sending information to another] Beginning with the fingertips of the right *flattened O hand* on the back of the left *open hand,* palm facing down, move the right hand forward while spreading the fingers into a *5 hand.*

**advise**[1] *v.* Same sign as for ADVICE but made with a double movement.

**advise**[2] *v.* See sign for COUNSEL.

**advisor** *n.* A person with the authority to give advice to another person: *The student met with her advisor.* Same sign used for: **consultant, counselor.**

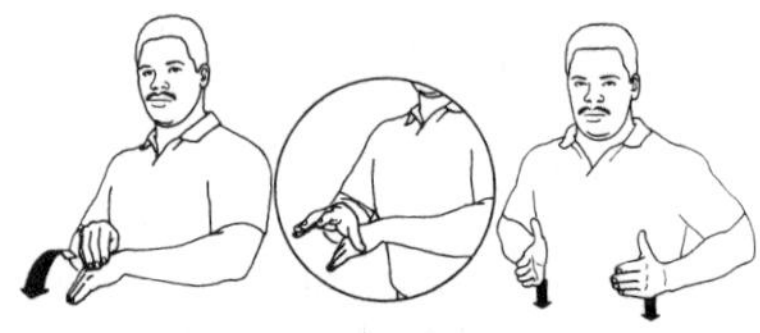

■ [**advice** + **person marker**] Beginning with the fingertips of the *flattened O hand* on the back of the left *open hand*, palm facing down, move the right hand forward while spreading the fingers into a *5 hand*. Then move both *open hands*, palms facing each other, downward along each side of the body.

**advocate** *v.* See sign for SUPPORT.

**aerial** *n.* See sign for ANTENNA.

**affect** *v.* See signs for COUNSEL, INFLUENCE.

**affection** *n.* See sign for HUG. Related form: **affectionate** *adj.*

**affiliation** *n.* See sign for COOPERATION.

**affirm** *v.* See sign for PROMISE.

**affix** *v.* See sign for APPLY[3].

**afford** *v.* To have money for: *We can't afford a new car.* Same sign used for: **debt, due, liability, owe, payable.**

■ [Indicates that money should be deposited in the palm] Tap the extended right index finger on the palm of the left *open hand* with a double movement.

**affront** *v.* See signs for INSULT.

**afraid** *adj.* Feeling fear: *afraid of heights.* Same sign used for: **fright, frightened, panic, scare, scared, terrified, terrify, timid.**

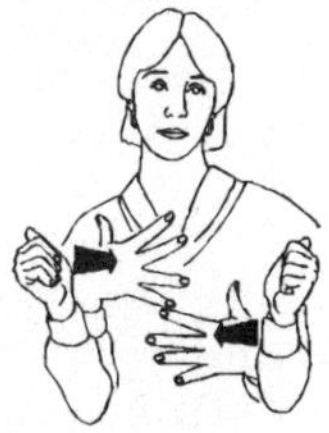

■ [Hands put up a protective barrier] Beginning with both *A hands* in front of each side of the chest, spread the fingers open with a quick movement, forming *5 hands,* palms facing in and fingers pointing toward each other.

**after**[1] *prep.* **1.** Later in time than: *after dinner.* —*conj.* **2.** Subsequent to the time that: *The speaker arrived after you left.* —*adv.* **3.** Afterward: *the day after.* Same sign used for: **afterward, beyond, from now on, rest of.**

■ [A time frame occurring after another thing] Beginning with the palm of the right *bent hand* touching the back of the fingers of the left *open hand,* both palms facing in, move the right hand forward a short distance.

**after**[2] *prep.* See sign for ACROSS.

**after a while** See sign for LATER.

**afternoon** *n.* The part of the day between noon and evening: *this afternoon.* Same sign used for: **matinee, P.M.**

■ [The sun going down in the afternoon] With the bottom of the right forearm resting on the back of the left *open hand,* palm facing down, move the right *open hand* downward with a double movement.

**afterward** *adv.* See signs for ACROSS, AFTER[1], LATER.

**again** *adv.* Once more: *do it again.* Same sign used for: **encore, over, reiterate, repeat.**

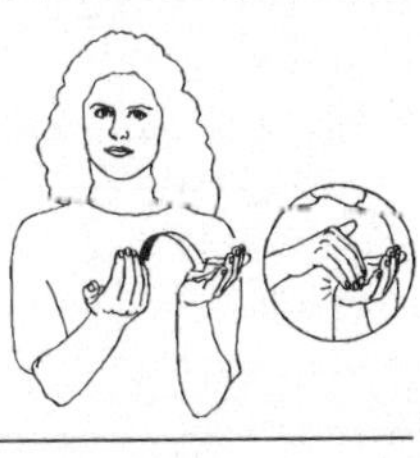

■ Beginning with the right *bent hand* beside the left *curved hand,* both palms facing up, bring the right hand up while turning it over, ending with the fingertips of the right hand touching the palm of the left hand.

**against** *prep.* In opposition to: *I was against the idea.* Same sign used for: **anti-** [prefix], **opposed to, prejudice.**

■ [Demonstrates making contact with a barrier] Hit the fingertips of the right *bent hand* into the left *open hand,* palm facing right.

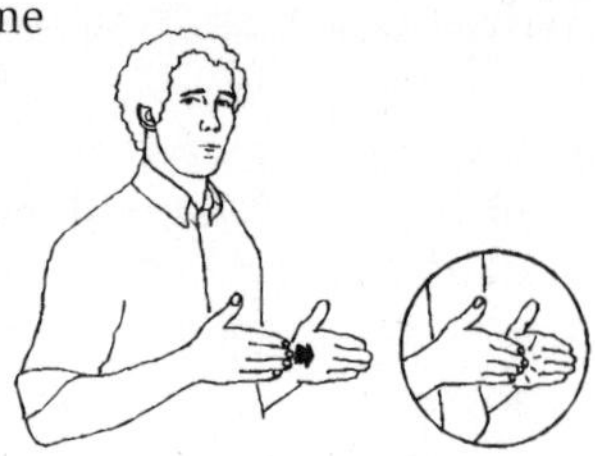

**age** *n.* Length of life or existence: *She left school at age sixteen.*

■ [An old man's beard] Move the right *O hand,* palm facing left, downward a short distance from the chin while changing into an *S hand.*

**agency** *n.* See sign for ASSOCIATION.

**agenda** *n.* A list of things to deal with: *on the agenda for the next meeting.*

■ [Initialized sign similar to sign for **list**] Move the palm side of the right *A hand* from first touching the fingers and then the heel of the left *open hand,* palm facing right.

**aggravate** *v.* **1.** To make worse or more severe: *By doing that you're aggravating an already bad situation.* **2.** To annoy: *Stop aggravating me with your silly questions.* Related forms: **aggravated** *adj.*, **aggravation** *n.*

■ [Mixing up emotions] Move both *curved 5 hands,* palms facing in, in large alternating circles on each side of the chest.

**aggravated** *v.* See sign for DISGUSTED[1].

**aggressive** *adj.* See sign for AMBITIOUS[1].

**agile** *adj.* See sign for SKILL.

**ago** *adj.* Past: *two weeks ago.* Same sign used for: **last, past, was, were.**

■ [Indicates a time in the past] Move the right *bent hand* back over the right shoulder, palm facing back.

**agree**[1] *v.* **1.** To have the same opinion: *I agree with the association rules.* **2.** To consent: *He agreed to finish the work for us.* **3.** To suit: *The climate doesn't agree with me.* Same sign used for: **all in favor, compatible, compromise, concur, deal, in accord, in agreement.**

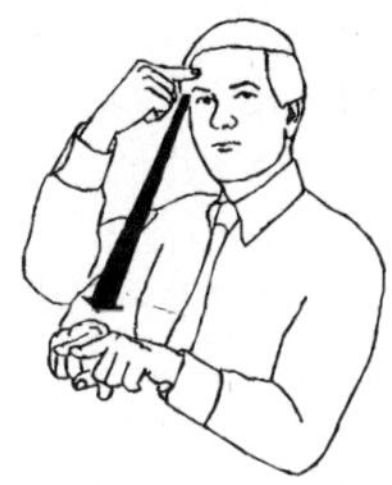

■ [**think** + lining up two things to show they agree with each other] Move the extended right index finger from touching the right side of the forehead downward to beside the extended left index finger, ending with both fingers pointing forward in front of the body, palms facing down.

**agree**[2] *v.* To have the same opinion as the person one is conversing with or within view: *I agree with you.* Same sign used for: **me, too.**

■ [Directional sign showing that two people share the same opinion] Move the right *Y hand,* palm facing left, from the right shoulder forward and back with a double movement.

**agriculture** *n.* See sign for FARM.

**ahead** *adv.* In front: *Walk ahead of me.* Same sign used for: **forward, further.**

■ [The hand moves to a position ahead] Beginning with the palm sides of both *A hands* together, move the right hand forward in a small arc.

**aid** *n.* See sign for HELP.

**aide** *n.* See sign for ASSISTANT.

**aim** *v.* See sign for GOAL.

**air conditioning** *n.* A system for cooling air within a building or vehicle: *turn up the air conditioning.* Related form: **air conditioner.**

■ [Abbreviation **a-c** + a gesture showing air blowing at one's face] Form an *A* and then a *C* in front of the right shoulder. Then with both *open hands* near each side of the face, palms facing back and fingers pointing up, bend the fingers up and down with a double movement.

**airplane** *n.* A vehicle for flying in the air: *fly in an airplane.* Same sign used for: **airport, jet, plane.**

■ [Shape and movement of an airplane] Move the right hand with the thumb, index finger, and little finger extended, palm facing down, forward with a short repeated movement in front of the right shoulder.

**airtight** *adj.* See signs for SEAL[2], SEAL ONE'S LIPS[1].

**alarm** *n.* A warning or a device to sound a warning: *a burglar alarm.* Same sign used for: **alert, drill.**

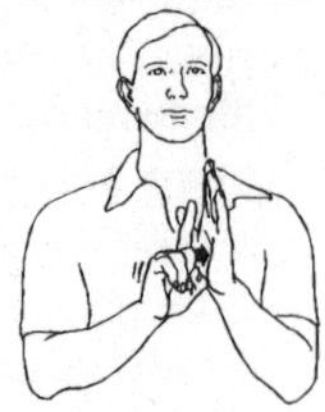

■ [Action of clapper on alarm bell] Tap the extended index finger of the right hand, palm facing forward, against the left *open hand,* palm facing right, with a repeated movement.

**alas** *interj.* Exclamation of grief or regret: *Alas, it was too late!* Same sign used for: **drat, shoot.**

■ [Natural gesture] Snap the middle finger off the thumb of the right *3 hand,* palm facing in, while swinging the right hand in toward the center of the chest.

**alcohol** *n.* See sign for WHISKEY.

**alcoholic drink** *n. phrase.* See sign for COCKTAIL.

**alert**[1] *n.* See sign for ALARM.

**alert**[2] *n.* See sign for INSOMNIA. Shared idea of remaining awake.

**algebra** *n.* A branch of mathematics that deals with relations between quantities, using letters and other symbols to represent numbers: *study algebra.*

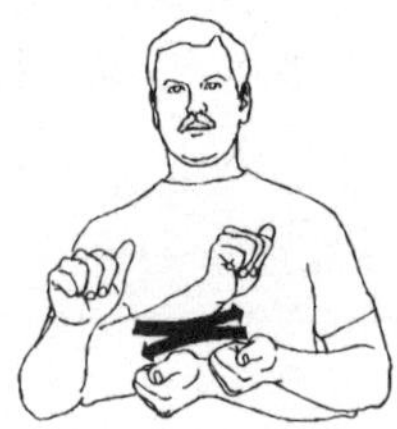

■ [Initialized sign similar to sign for **arithmetic**] With a repeated movement, brush the palm side of the right *A hand* as it moves left in front of the chest, palm facing down, against the palm side of the left *A hand,* palm facing up, as it moves right.

**align**[1] *v.* To bring into line: *align the chairs in a row.*

■ [Putting something into alignment with another thing] Move the little-finger side of the right *B hand,* palm facing left and fingers pointing forward, forward with a wavy movement along the extended left index finger, palm facing right and finger pointing forward.

**align**[2] *v.* See sign for LINE UP.

**alike**[1] *adj.* **1.** Similar (used for two people or things): *The twins are alike in many ways.* —*adv.* **2.** In the same manner (used for two people or things): *to treat them both alike.* See also sign for LIKE[3]. Same sign used for: **identical, look alike, same, similar.**

■ [Sign moves between two people or things that are similar] Move the right *Y hand,* palm facing down, from side to side with a short repeated movement in front of the body.

**alike**[2] *adj.* **1.** (Used for more than two that are similar): *They are all alike.* —*adv.* **2.** In the same manner (used for more than two people or things): *to treat them all alike.* See also signs for LIKE[3], SAME[2]. Same sign used for: **similar, uniform.**

- [Sign shows things that are similar] Move the right *Y hand,* palm facing down, in a flat circle in front of the body.

**alimony** *n.* Court-ordered periodic allowance paid following a divorce or separation: *She received alimony on the first of every month from her ex-husband.* Same sign used for: **maintenance, spousal support.**

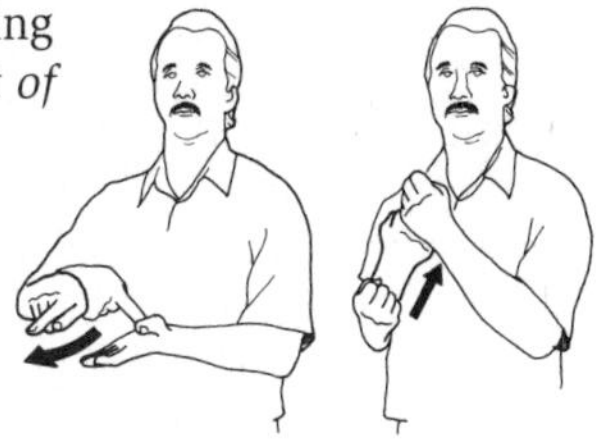

- [**pay** + **support**] Beginning with the extended right index finger touching the palm of the left *open hand,* palms facing each other, move the right finger forward with a double movement off the left fingertips. Then push the knuckles of the right *S hand* against the little finger of the left *S hand,* both palms in, pushing the left hand upward a short distance in front of the chest.

**alive** *adj.* See sign for LIVE.

**all** *pron.* Everyone or everything: *All the hot dogs were eaten.* Same sign used for: **entire, total, whole.**

- [The hand encompasses the whole thing] Move the right *open hand* from near the left shoulder in a large circle in front of the chest, ending with the back of the right hand in the left *open hand* held in front of the body, palms facing in.

**all afternoon** *adv.* Through the whole afternoon: *worked all afternoon.*

- [**afternoon** formed with a continuous movement indicating duration] With the right forearm on the back of the left *open hand,* palm facing down, move the right *B hand* smoothly downward from in front of the right shoulder.

**all along** *adv.* See signs for GO ON[1], SINCE[1].

**all day** *adv.* Through the whole day: *stayed all day.*

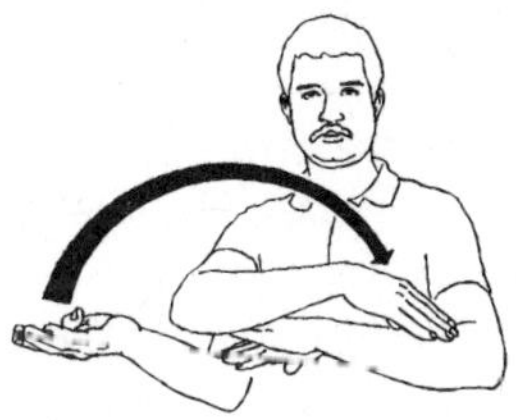

- [Shows movement of the sun through the day] With the fingers of the left *open hand* in the crook of the right arm, move the right *B hand* smoothly from the right side of the body in a large arc in front of the body, ending with the right hand, palm facing down, on the back of the left arm near the elbow.

**allegation** *n.* See sign for ACCUSATION[1].

**allegiance** *n.* See sign for SUPPORT.

**all gone** *adj.* See signs for NOTHING[5], RUN OUT OF.

**alligator** *n.* A large reptile with a broad head and powerful jaws: *the alligator's teeth.* Same sign used for: **jaws.**

- [Mimes action of alligator's jaws] Beginning with the fingertips and heels of both *curved 5 hands* touching, right hand on top of the left hand and fingers forward, bring the hands apart and together again with a double movement.

**all in favor** See sign for AGREE[1].

**all morning** *adv.* Through the whole morning: *worked all morning without a break.*

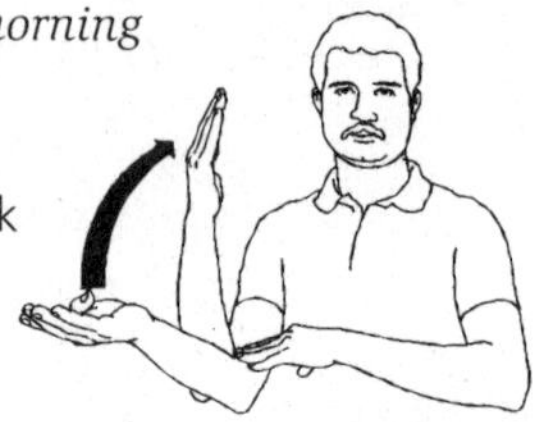

- [**morning** formed with a continuous movement indicating duration] With the fingers of the left *open hand* in the crook of the right arm, move the right *B hand* smoothly upward from in front of the right side of the body to in front of the right shoulder, palm facing back.

**all night** *adv.* Through the whole night: *to lie awake all night.* Same sign used for: **overnight.**

- [**night** formed with a continuous movement indicating duration] With the fingers of the left *open hand* in the crook of the right arm, move the right *B hand* smoothly downward from in front of the right side of the chest, ending under the left arm, palm facing back.

**all over** *adv.* Everywhere: *spread the paint all over.* Same sign used for: **overall.**

- [Surrounds entire thing] Move the right *5 hand* from in front of the right side of the body, palm facing forward, in a large arc in front of the face, ending in front of the left side of the body.

**allow** *v.* See sign for LET.

**allowance** *n.* See sign for PENSION.

**all right** *adv.* See sign for RIGHT[2].

**all the time** *adv.* Continuously: *The baby cries all the time.* Same sign used for: **ever since, total.**

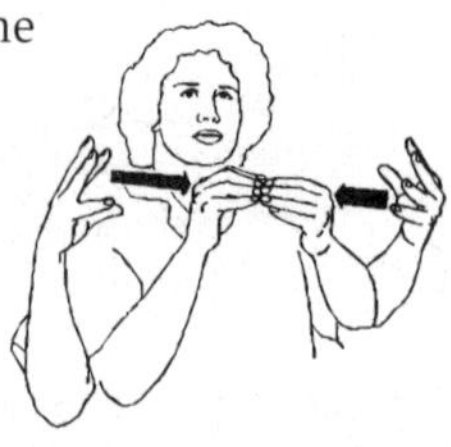

- [Hands bring together a total amount of time] Move both *curved 5 hands* from in front of each shoulder, palms facing each other, toward each other while closing the fingers, ending with the fingertips of both *flattened O hands* touching in front of the chest.

**ally** *n.* See sign for RELATIONSHIP.

**almost**[1] *adv.* A little less than; very nearly: *almost time to go.* Same sign used for: **about, barely, nearly.**

■ Brush the fingertips of the right *open hand* upward off the back of the left fingers, both palms facing up.

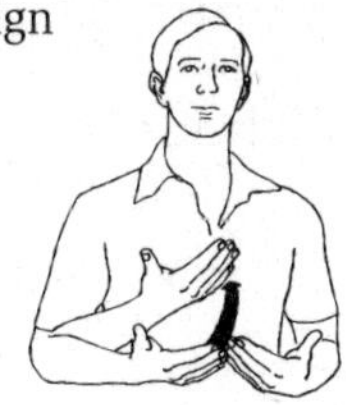

**almost**[2] *adv.* See sign for CLOSE CALL.

**alone**[1] *adv.* **1.** Without company: *He played alone.* —*adj.* **2.** Separate or without help from others: *She alone knows how to open the safe.* Same sign used for: **isolated, lone, only, orphan, solely.**

■ [Shows one thing alone] With the right index finger extended up, move the right hand, palm facing back, in a small repeated circle in front of the right shoulder.

**alone**[2] *adj.* See sign for SINGLE.

**a lot** *adv.* See signs for MANY, MUCH.

**aloud** *adv.* See sign for NOISE.

**alphabet** *n.* The letters of a language in sequential order: *26 letters in the English alphabet.*

■ [**a-b-c** + **fingerspell**] With the right hand, palm facing forward, sequentially form the first three manual alphabet letters in front of the right shoulder, moving the hand slightly to the right after each letter. Then move the right *5 hand,* palm facing down, to the right in front of the right shoulder while wiggling the fingers.

**already** *adv.* See sign for FINISH[1].

**altar** *n.* A table used for religious ceremonies: *worship at the altar.*

■ [Initialized sign showing the shape of an altar] Beginning with the thumbs of both *A hands* touching in front of the body, palms facing down, move the hands apart and then down in front of each side of the body.

**alter** *v.* See sign for CHANGE[1].

**alternate** *v.* See sign for TURN[1].

**alternative** *n.* See sign for EITHER[1].

**although** *conj.* See sign for BUT.

**altitude** *n.* See sign for HIGH.

**alumnus** *n.* A graduate of a specific school: *The alumni came together for a reunion.*

■ [Initialized sign similar to sign for **year**] Beginning with the right *A hand,* palm facing left, over the left *A hand,* palm facing right, move the right hand forward in a complete circle around the left hand, ending with the little-finger side of the right hand on the thumb side of the left hand.

**always** *adv.* Every time: *Night always follows day.* Same sign used for: **ever.**

■ [A continuous circle signifying duration] Move the extended right index finger, palm facing in and finger angled up, in a repeated circle in front of the right side of the chest.

**amass** *v.* See signs for ACCUMULATE[1], COLLECT.

**amaze** *v.* See signs for SURPRISE, WONDERFUL. Related form: **amazement** *adj.*

**amazed** *v.* See sign for INCREDIBLE[1].

**ambiguous** *adj.* See signs for VAGUE, ZEAL.

**ambitious**[1] *adj.* Having a strong desire for success: *an ambitious actress.* Related form: **ambition** *n.* Same sign used for: **active, aggressive.**

■ [Initialized sign] Move both *A hands,* palms facing in, in large alternating circles upward on each side of the chest.

**ambitious**[2] *adj.* See sign for GOAL.

**ambulance** *n.* A vehicle for carrying sick or injured people, usually to a hospital: *Call an ambulance!* Same sign used for: **siren.**

■ [Represents flashing light on an ambulance] Move the right *flattened O hand* in a circular movement near the right side of the head by repeatedly twisting the wrist and opening the fingers into a *5 hand* each time.

**amen** *interj.* Expression of solemn agreement: *forever and ever, amen.* Same sign used for: **pray, prayer.**

■ [Natural gesture for folding one's hands to pray] Bring the palms of both *open hands* together, fingers angled upward, while moving the hands down and in toward the chest.

---

**amend** *v.* See sign for ADD[2].

---

**America** *n.* The lands of the Western Hemisphere: *North America;* the United States: *50 states in the United States.* Related form: **American** *adj., n.*

■ With the fingers of both hands loosely entwined, palms facing in, move the hands in circle in front of the chest.

---

**American Sign Language** or **ASL** *n.* A visual-gestural language used by deaf people in the United States: *to communicate in American Sign Language.*

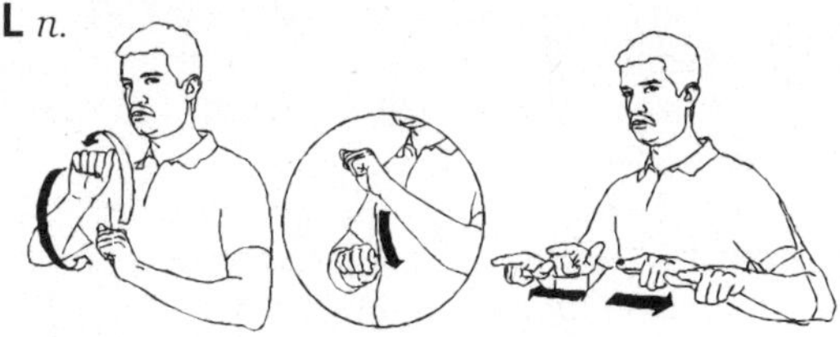

■ [Initialized sign similar to **gesture** + **language**] With both *A hands* in front of chest, palms facing forward and right hand higher than the left, move the hands in an alternating circular movement toward the chest. Then move both *L hands* from together in front of the chest, palms facing down, simultaneously apart to each side of the chest.

---

**amid** or **admidst** *prep.* See sign for AMONG.

---

**amiss** *adj.* See sign for ACCIDENTALLY.

---

**among** *prep.* **1.** In the middle of or surrounded by: *You are among friends.* **2.** With a share for each of: *divided it among ourselves.* **3.** By the joint action of: *argued among ourselves.* Same sign used for: **amid, admidst, midst.**

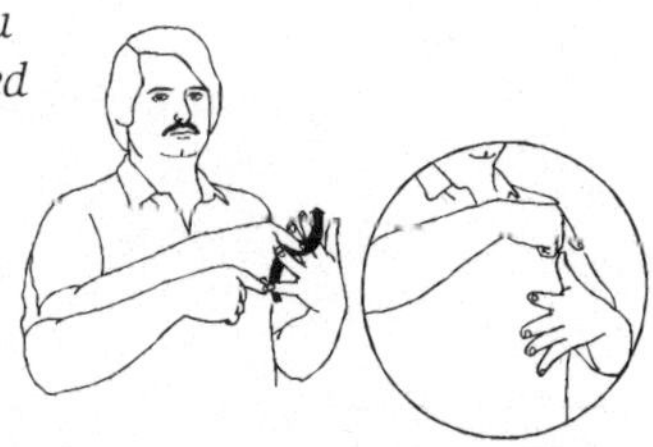

■ [Shows one moving among others] Move the extended right index finger in and out between the fingers of the left *5 hand,* both palms facing in.

---

**amount**[1] *n.* A quantity: *a small amount of money.* Same sign used for: **heap, lump, pile.**

■ [Shows a small amount in a pile] Move the extended right index finger, palm facing down, in an arc from near the heel to the fingers of the upturned left *open hand,* ending with the right palm facing in toward the chest.

**amount**[2] *n.* See sign for ADD[1].

**amusing** *adj.* See sign for FUNNY.

**analyze** *v.* To examine carefully: *analyze the situation.* Related form: **analysis** *n.* Same sign used for: **access, diagnose, diagnosis, evaluate, examine, gauge, investigate.**

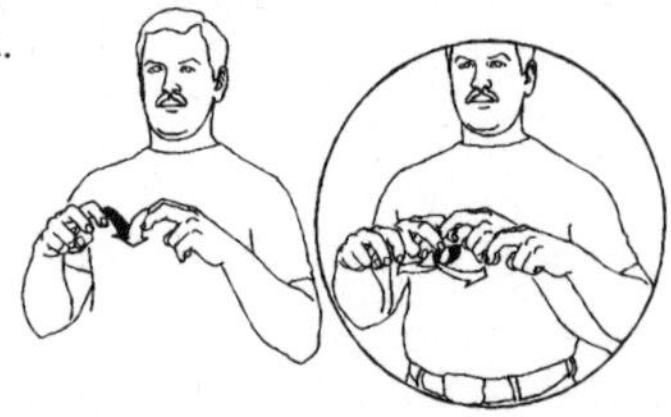

- [Taking something apart to analyze it] With both *bent V hands* near each other in front of the chest, palms facing down, move the fingers apart from each other with a downward double movement while bending the fingers.

**ancestor** *n.* A person from whom one is descended: *My ancestors came from Germany.*

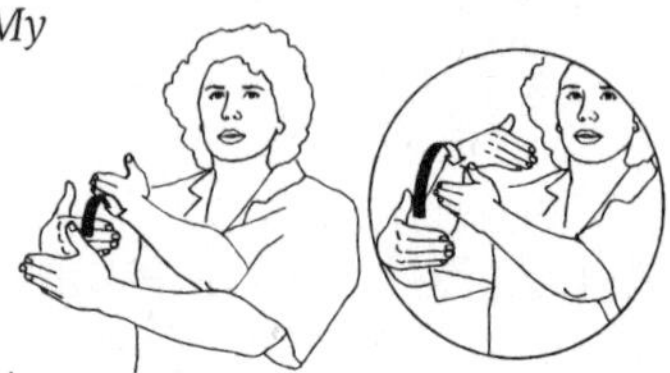

- [Shows moving back into the past] Beginning with both *open hands* in front of the right shoulder, palms facing in and right hand above the left hand, roll the hands over each other with an alternating movement while moving the hands back over the right shoulder.

**anchor** *n.* A piece of iron fastened by a chain or rope to a ship to hold it in place: *drop the anchor.*

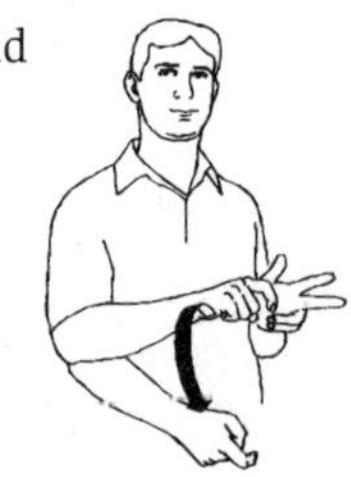

- [Represents unhooking an anchor and dropping it] Beginning with the thumb side of the right *X hand,* palm facing down, against the palm of the left *3 hand,* palm facing right and fingers pointing forward, bring the right hand downward in an arc, ending with the palm facing left.

**ancient** *adj.* See sign for LONG AGO.

**and** *conj.* As well as: *you and I.*

- Move the right *curved 5 hand,* palm facing left, to the right in front of the body while closing the fingers to the thumb, ending in a *flattened O hand.*

**and so forth** See sign for VARIETY.

**angel** *n.* A spiritual being serving God: *an angel from heaven.* Same sign used for: **wings.**

- [Shows movement of an angel's wings] Beginning with the fingertips of both *bent hands* touching each shoulder, palms facing down, twist the hands forward and outward and bend the fingers up and down with a repeated movement.

**anger**[1] *n.* A strong feeling of displeasure and hostility: *broke the vase in anger.* Related form: **angry** *adj.* See also sign for CROSS[2]. Same sign used for: **cross, enrage, fury, mad, outrage, rage.**

■ [Hands bring up feeling of anger in the body] Beginning with the fingertips of both *curved 5 hands* on the lower chest, bring the hands upward and apart, ending in front of each shoulder.

**anger**[2] *n.* (alternate sign) Related form: **angry** *adj.* Same sign used for: **cross, furious, grouchy, grumpy, mad, rage.**

■ [Hand seems to pull the face down into a scowl] With the palm of the right *5 hand* in front of the face, fingers pointing up, bring the hand slightly forward while constricting the fingers into a *curved 5 hand.*

**angle** *n.* The shape formed by two surfaces or lines meeting: *A right angle is an angle of 90°.*

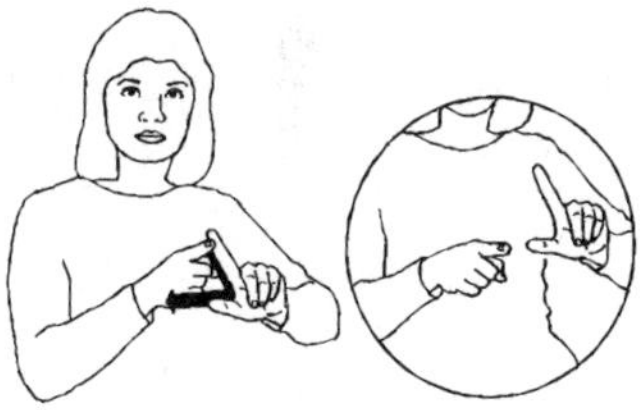

■ [Shape of an angle] With the extended right index finger, trace along the index finger and thumb of the left *L hand,* palm facing forward.

**angry** *adj.* See sign for CROSS[2].

**animal** *n.* A living thing not a plant: *Dogs are my favorite animals.* Same sign used for: **beast.**

■ Beginning with the fingertips of both *curved 5 hands* on the chest near each shoulder, roll the fingers toward each other on their knuckles with a double movement while keeping the fingers in place.

**annex** *v.* See sign for BELONG[1].

**anniversary**[1] *n.* The yearly return of a special date: *celebrate our wedding anniversary.*

■ [**annual** + **celebrate**] Beginning with the little-finger side of the right *S hand* on the thumb of the left *S hand,* flick the right index finger forward and back with a double movement. Then move both modified *X hands* in large simultaneous circles, palms facing back, near each side of the head.

**anniversary**[2] *n.* See sign for CELEBRATE.

**announce** *v.* To give public notice: *announce the score.* Related form: **announcement** *n.* Same sign used for: **acclaim, declaration, declare, proclaim, proclamation, reveal, tell.**

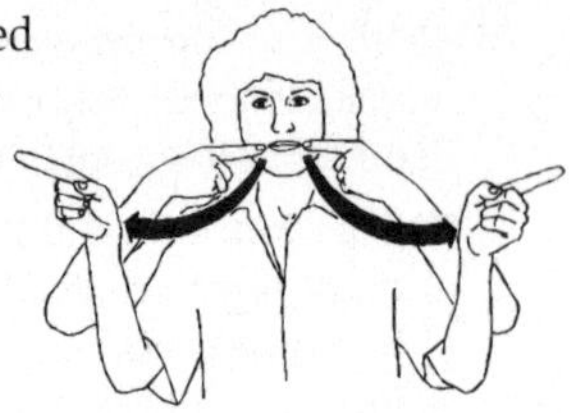

■ [**tell** with a movement that shows a general announcement] Beginning with the extended index fingers of both hands pointing to each side of the mouth, palms facing in, twist the wrists and move the fingers forward and apart from each other, ending with the palms facing forward and the index fingers pointing outward in opposite directions.

**annoy** *v.* To disturb in a way that irritates: *annoy the teacher with constant interruptions.* Same sign used for: **bother, disturb, interfere, interrupt, intervene, irritate, nuisance.**

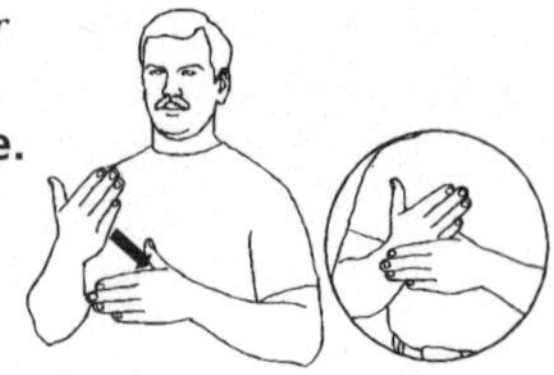

■ [A gesture showing something interfering with something else] Sharply tap the little-finger side of the right *open hand,* palm facing in at an angle, at the base of the thumb and index finger of the left *open hand* with a double movement.

**annual** *adj.* **1.** Once a year: *annual event.* **2.** Of or for one year: *annual salary.* Related form: **annually** *adv.* Same sign used for: **every year, per annum.**

■ [Formed like **year** as it moves into the future] Beginning with the little-finger side of the right *S hand* on the thumb side of the left *S hand,* palms facing in opposite directions, flick the right index finger forward and back with a double movement.

**anoint** *v.* To put oil on (a person), especially in a religious ceremony: *anoint the king.*

■ [Mime pouring oil on something] Move the extended thumb of the right *10 hand,* palm facing right, and thumb pointing down, in a flat circle over the left *S hand,* palm facing down, with a double movement.

**anonymous** *adj.* Not named or identified: *The newspaper received an anonymous letter.*

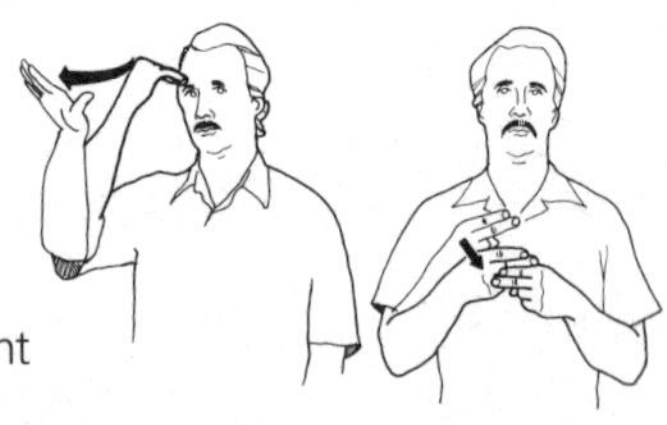

■ [**don't know** + **name**[1]] Beginning with the fingers of the right *bent hand* touching the right side of the forehead, swing the hand forward by twisting the wrist, ending with the fingers pointing forward in front of the right shoulder. Then tap the middle-finger side of the right *H hand* across the index-finger side of the left *H hand* with a double movement.

**another** *adj.* **1.** A different or additional (one): *another glass of water.* —*pron.* **2.** A different or additional one: *He went from one thing to another.* Same sign used for: **other.**

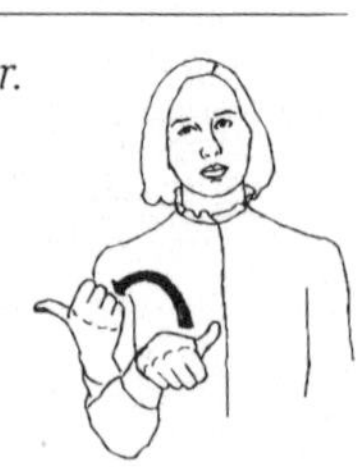

■ [Points away to another] Beginning with the right *10 hand* in front of the body, palm facing down and thumb pointing left, flip the hand over to the right, ending with the palm facing up and the thumb pointing right.

**answer** *n.* **1.** A response to a question: *the right answer.* —*v.* **2.** To respond to a question: *Please answer the question.* Same sign used for: **react, reply, respond, response.**

■ [Indicates directing words of response to another] Beginning with both extended index fingers pointing up in front of the mouth, right hand nearer the mouth than the left and both palms facing forward, bend the wrists down simultaneously, ending with fingers pointing forward and the palms facing down.

**ant** *n.* A small insect that lives in large groups: *ants crawling all over the picnic table.*

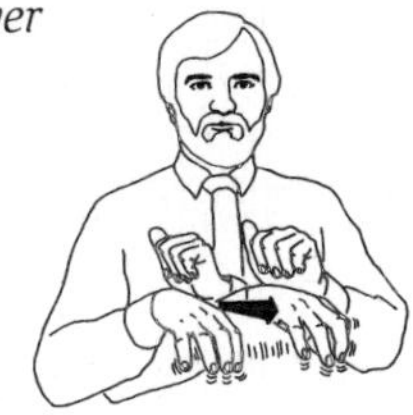

■ [Initialized sign showing the movement of an ant's legs] With the heel of the left *A hand* on the back of the right *curved 5 hand,* palm facing down, move the right hand forward while wiggling the fingers.

**antagonism** *n.* See sign for STRUGGLE.

**antagonistic** *adj.* See sign for CONTRARY[1].

**antenna** *n.* A wire or rod for conducting radio or television signals: *adjust the antenna to get a better picture.* Same sign used for: **aerial.**

■ [Shape of an antenna] Place the palm of the right *3 hand* on the extended left index finger pointing up, palm facing right.

**anti-** *prefix.* See signs for AGAINST, RESIST.

**anticipate** *v.* See sign for HOPE. Related form: **anticipation** *n.*

**antsy** *adj.* See sign for RESTLESS.

**anxiety** *n.* See signs for CONCERN[2], NERVOUS.

**anxious** *adj.* See signs for NERVOUS, TROUBLE[1], ZEAL.

**any** *adj.* **1.** One or some, no matter which: *Choose any book you like.* —*pron.* **2.** An unspecified person or thing: *I don't want any.*

■ Beginning with the right *10 hand* in front of the chest, palm facing left, twist the wrist and move the hand down and to the right, ending with the palm facing down.

**anybody** *pron.* Any person: *Anybody can make a mistake.*

- [**any** + **you**] Beginning with the right *10 hand* in front of the chest, palm facing left, twist the wrist and move the hand down and to the right, ending with the palm facing down. Then move the extended right index finger, palm facing left and finger pointing forward, in an arc from left to right in front of the body.

**anyone** *pron.* Any person: *Is anyone home?*

- [**any** + **one**] Beginning with the right *10 hand* in front of the chest, palm facing left, twist the wrist and move the hand down and to the right, ending with the palm facing down. Then hold the extended right index finger up in front of the chest, palm facing in.

**anything** *pron.* A thing of any kind: *Do you want anything from the store?*

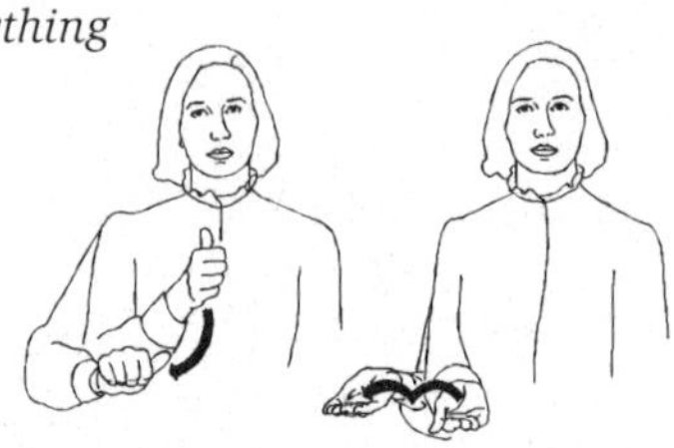

- [**any** + **thing**] Beginning with the right *10 hand* in front of the chest, palm facing left, twist the wrist and move the hand down and to the right, ending with the palm facing down. Then move the right *curved hand* from the right side of the body, palm facing up, outward to the right in a double arc.

**anyway** *adv.* In any case: *I will do it anyway, whether you want me to or not.* Same sign used for: **despite, doesn't matter, even though, hardly, however, nevertheless, regardless, whatever.**

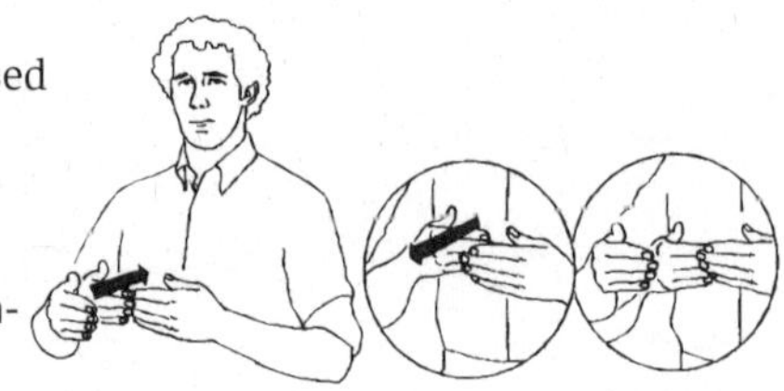

- [Flexible hands signify no firm position] Beginning with both *open hands* in front of the body, fingers pointing toward each other and palms facing in, move the hands forward and back from the body with a repeated alternating movement, striking and bending the fingers of each hand as they pass.

**anywhere** *adv.* In or to any place: *Put it anywhere.*

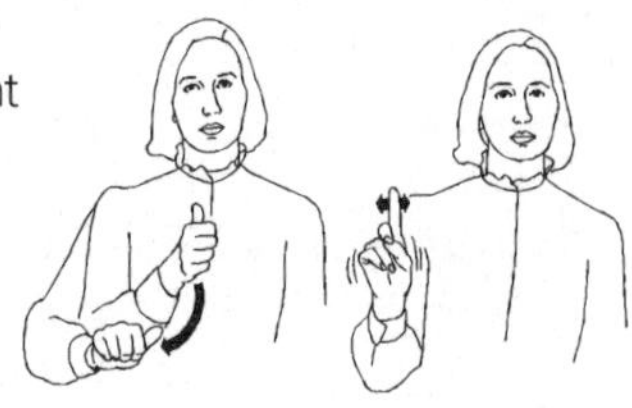

- [**any** + **where**] Beginning with the right *10 hand* in front of the chest, palm facing left, twist the wrist and move the hand down and to the right, ending with the palm facing down. Then move the extended right index finger, pointing up in front of the chest and palm facing forward, back and forth with a repeated movement.

**apart** *adv.* See signs for PART[2], SEPARATE.

**ape** *n.* See signs for GORILLA, MONKEY.

**apiece** *adv.* See sign for EACH.

**apologize** *v.* See sign for SORRY. Related form: **apology** *n.*

**apostrophe** *n.* The mark, ', used in contractions or with possessive nouns: *The word "don't" has an apostrophe.* Same sign used for: **comma.**

- [Mime drawing an apostrophe in the air] Draw an apostrophe in the air with the extended right index finger, pointing forward, by twisting the wrist in front of the right shoulder.

**apparel** *n.* See sign for CLOTHES.

**apparently** *adv.* See sign for SEEM.

**appeal** *v.* See sign for SUGGEST.

**appear** *v.* See signs for SEEM, SHOW UP.

**appearance** *n.* One's outward look: *He has a sinister appearance.*

- [Shows area of facial appearance] Move the right *5 hand,* palm facing in, in a large circle in front of the face.

**appease** *v.* See sign for SATISFY.

**appendix** *n.* A small tube attached to the intestine: *The doctor is going to remove your appendix.*

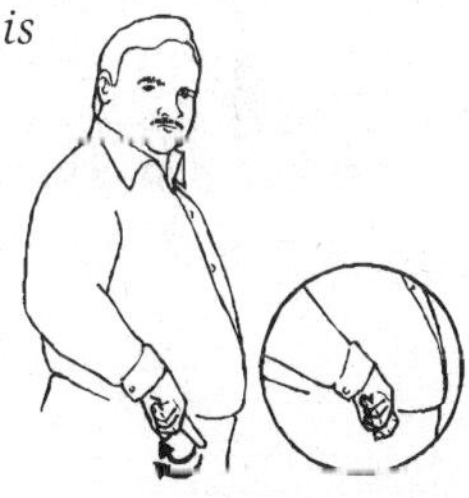

- [Shape and location of appendix] Bend the extended right index finger, palm facing back, forward and back with a double movement near the right side of the waist.

**appetite**[1] *n.* A desire for food: *Teenagers have big appetites.*

- [**hungry** + **food**] Beginning with the fingertips of the right *C hand* touching the chest, palm facing in, move the hand downward a short distance. Then bring the fingertips of the right *flattened O hand,* palm facing down, to the lips with a double movement.

**appetite**[2] *n.* See sign for HUNGRY.

**applaud** *v.* To express approval by clapping the hands: *applaud your favorite candidate.* Related form: **applause** *n.* Same sign used for: **clap, commend, praise.**

■ [Natural gesture for clapping] Pat the palm of the right *open hand* across the palm of the left *open hand* with a double movement.

**apple** *n.* A rounded firm fruit with red, green, or yellow skin: *eat an apple.*

■ With the knuckle of the right *X hand* near the right side of the mouth, twist the wrist downward with a double movement.

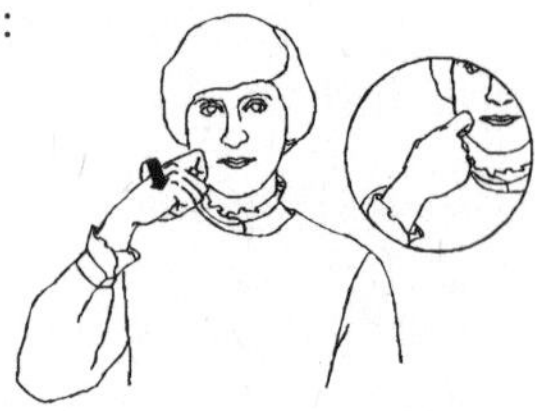

**apply**[1] *v.* To assign for a specific purpose: *apply the payment to the loan.* Related form: **applicable** *adj.* Same sign used for: **charge, file, implement, install, post, use.**

■ [Put messages on a spindle] Move the fingers of the right *V hand,* palm facing forward, downward on each side of the extended left index finger, pointing up in front of the chest.

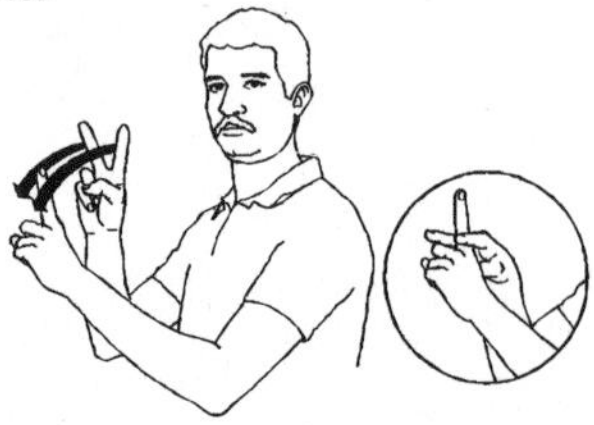

**apply**[2] *v.* To make a formal request: *to apply for a job.* Related form: **application** *n.* Same sign used for: **candidate, eligible, nominate, voluntary, volunteer.**

■ [Seems to pull oneself forward to apply for something] Pinch a small amount of clothing on the right side of the chest with the fingers of the right *F hand* and pull forward with a short double movement.

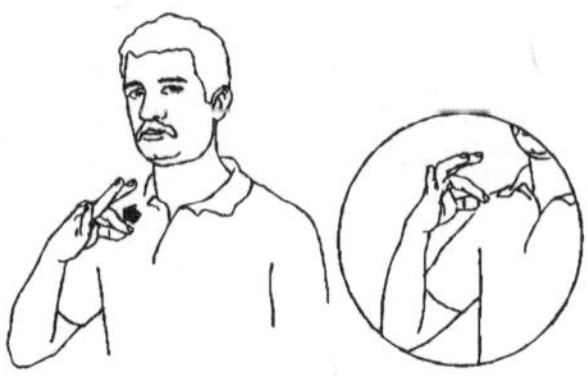

**apply**[3] *v.* To put on: *apply glue on the envelope's flap.* Same sign used for: **adhere, affix.**

■ [Mime applying tape or a label] Move the fingers of the right *H hand,* palm facing left, against the palm of the left *open hand,* palm facing right, and pull downward to the heel of the left palm.

**apply**[4] *v.* See sign for LABEL.

**appoint**[1] *v.* To choose for a position: *appoint a committee to study the issue.* Same sign used for: **choose, elect, select.**

■ [Fingers seem to pick someone] Beginning with the thumb side of the right *G hand,* palm facing down and fingers pointing forward, against the left *open hand,* palm facing right and fingers pointing up, pull the right hand in toward the chest while pinching the index finger and thumb together.

**appoint**[2] *v.* To assign officially, as to an office or position: *to be appointed chairman.* Related form: **appointment** *n.* Same sign used for: **assign.**

■ [Hand seems to grab someone and set that person aside] Beginning with the right *curved 5 hand* in front of the right side of the body, palm facing left, move the hand to the left while closing into an *S hand.* Then move the right *S hand* forward and to the left in a short arc.

**appointment** *n.* A meeting at an established time: *I have a doctor's appointment at 5:00.* Same sign used for: **assignment, book, engagement, reservation.**

■ Move the right *S hand,* palm facing down, in a small circle and then down to the back of the left *A hand,* palm facing down in front of the chest.

**appreciate**[1] *v.* To recognize and think highly of: *appreciate good music.* Related form: **appreciation** *n.*

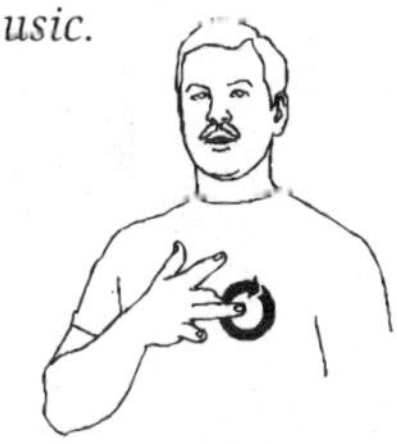

■ [Similar to sign formed for **enjoy**] Move the bent middle finger of the right *5 hand* in a small circle on the chest.

**appreciate**[2] *v.* See sign for ENJOY. Related form: **appreciation** *n.*

**appreciative** *adj.* See sign for GRATEFUL.

**apprehend** *v.* See sign for UNDERSTAND.

**approach**[1] *v.* **1.** To come near: *A storm is approaching.* —*n.* **2.** An act of coming nearer: *the approach of the train.* Same sign used for: **close to, near.**

■ [One hand moves to approach the other] Move the back of the right *bent hand* from near the chest forward with a double movement toward the palm of the left *bent hand,* both palms facing in and fingers pointing in opposite directions.

**approach**[2] *v.* See sign for CLOSE[1].

**appropriate** *adj.* Particularly suitable: *wear appropriate clothes to church.* Related form: **appropriately** *adv.* Same sign used for: **proper, suitable.**

■ [**right**[3] formed with a double movement] With the index fingers of both hands extended forward at right angles, palms angled inward and the right hand above the left, hit the little-finger side of the right hand down across the thumb side of the left hand with a double movement.

**approve** *v.* See sign for ACCEPT. Related form: **approval** *n.*

**approximate** *adj.* See sign for ROUGH.

**approximately** *adv.* Nearly: *approximately the correct amount.* Related form: **approximate** *adj.* Same sign used for: **about, around.**

■ [Natural gesture of vagueness] Move the right *5 hand,* palm facing forward, in a circle in front of the right shoulder with a double movement.

**arbitration** *n.* See sign for DEBATE[1].

**arc** *n.* See sign for ARCH.

**arch** *n.* A curved structure, usually over an opening: *Walk under the arch into the garden.* Same sign used for: **arc, curve.**

■ [Shape of an arch] Beginning with the right *B hand* in front of the chin, palm facing forward and fingers pointing to the left, move the hand in a large arc, ending in front of the right side of the body, palm facing left.

**arctic** *n.* **1.** The north polar region, the most northern part of the world: *traveled to the arctic.* —*adj.* **2.** Of the north polar region: *explored the arctic wilderness.* Same sign used for: **bitter cold, frigid.**

■ [Natural gesture used when one is very cold] Beginning with both *S hands* in front of each shoulder, palms facing down, move the hands downward toward each other in front of the chest with a sharp deliberate movement, ending with the palms facing in.

**area**[1] *n.* **1.** A geographical region: *living in the New York area.* **2.** A place with a designated function: *the playground area.* Same sign used for: **place, region, space, vicinity.**

■ [Indicates an area] Move the right *5 hand,* palm facing down and fingers pointing forward, in a flat forward arc in front of the right side of the body.

**area**[2] *n.* See sign for DISTRICT.

**argue** *v.* To express disagreement in words: *argue about the bill in Congress.* Related form: **argument** *n.* Same sign used for: **controversy, debate, dispute, fight, quarrel, squabble.**

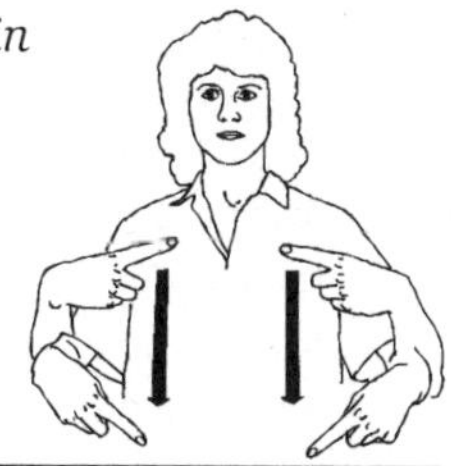

- [Represents opposing points of view] Beginning with both extended index fingers pointing toward each other in front of the chest, palms facing in, shake the hands up and down with a repeated movement by bending the wrists.

**argument** *n.* See sign for DISCUSS.

**arithmetic** *n.* The method or process of computing with numbers by addition, subtraction, multiplication, or division: *Your arithmetic is incorrect.* Same sign used for: **estimate, figure, figure out, multiplication.**

- Brush the back of the right *V hand* across the palm side of the left *V hand,* both palms facing up, as the hands cross with a double movement in front of the chest.

**army** *n.* A military organization for fighting on land: *join the army.* Same sign used for: **military.**

- [Holding a gun while marching] Tap the palm side of both *A hands* against the right side of the chest, right hand above the left hand, with a repeated movement.

**around**[1] *adv.* **1.** On all sides: *A crowd gathered around.* —*prep.* **2.** On all sides of: *build a fence around the yard.* Same sign used for: **orbit, revolve, rotary, surrounding.**

- [Demonstrates moving in a circle around something] Move the extended right index finger, pointing down, in a small circle around the extended left index finger, pointing up in front of the chest.

**around**[2] *prep.* See sign for APPROXIMATELY.

**arouse** *v.* See sign for AWAKE[1].

**arrange** *v.* See signs for PLAN[1], PREPARE. Related form: **arrangement** *n.*

**arrest** *v.* See signs for CAPTURE, CATCH[2].

**arrive** *v.* To reach a destination: *arrive home.* Related form: **arrival** *n.* Same sign used for: **reach.**

- [Hand moves to arrive in other hand] Move the right *bent hand* from in front of the right shoulder, palm facing left, downward, landing the back of the right hand in the upturned left *curved hand.*

**arrogant** *adj.* See signs for CONCEITED, PROUD.

**art** *n.* **1.** The production of drawings, paintings, or sculpture: *study art.* **2.** The class of objects subject to aesthetic criteria, as drawings, paintings, or sculpture: *an exhibit of Mexican art.* Same sign used for: **drawing, illustration, sketch.**

- [Demonstrates drawing something] Move the extended right little finger with a wiggly movement down the palm of the left *open hand* from the fingers to the heel.

**article** *n.* A part of a newspaper, magazine, or book dealing with one subject: *read the article on rock climbing.* Same sign used for: **journal.**

- [Shape of a column of newspaper type] Move the right *modified C hand* down the palm of the left *open hand* from the fingers to the heel with a double movement.

**artificial** *adj.* See sign for FAKE[2].

**ascend**[1] *v.* To go up or rise: *ascend the mountain.* Related form: **ascent** *n.*

- [Represents climbing upward] Beginning with both *H hands* in front of the chest, right palm up and left palm down, repeatedly flip the hands over to place the right *H hand* across the fingers of the left *H hand* as the hands move upward in front of the face.

**ascend**[2] *v.* See sign for CLIMB.

**ashamed** *adj.* Feeling shame or disgrace: *ashamed of myself for losing my temper.* Same sign used for: **shame, shameful, shy.**

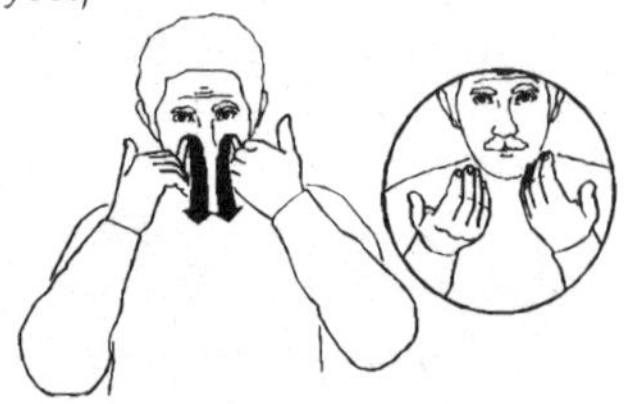

- [Blood rising in the cheeks when ashamed] Beginning with the back of the fingers of both *curved hands* against each cheek, palms facing down, twist the hands forward, ending with the palms facing back.

**aside** *adv.* Away to the side: *Put your work aside.* Same sign used for: **put aside, put away.**

- [Natural gesture for pushing something aside] Beginning with both *open hands* in front of the body, both palms facing right and fingers pointing forward, push the hands deliberately to the right.

**ask** *v.* To make a request: *to ask for help.* Same sign used for: **pray, request.**

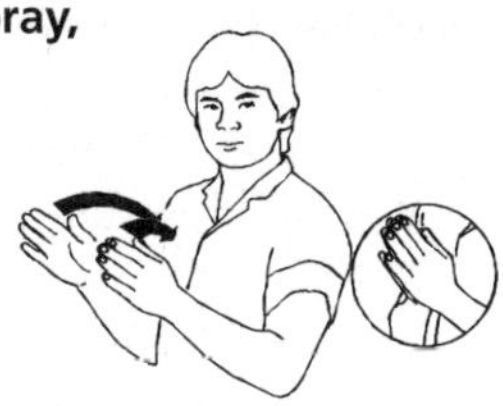

- [Natural gesture used for asking] Bring the palms of both *open hands* together, fingers angled upward, while moving the hands down and in toward the chest.

**ASL** *n.* See sign for AMERICAN SIGN LANGUAGE.

**asleep** *adv.* See sign for FALL ASLEEP.

**aspire** *v.* See sign for ZEAL. Related form: **aspiration** *n.*

**assemble**[1] *v.* To put together: *assemble the parts of a car.* Same sign used for: **put together.**

- [Mime putting parts together] Bring the fingertips of both *flattened O hands* together, palms facing down, with a double movement in front of the chest, changing the angle of the hands each time.

**assemble**[2] *v.* See signs for GATHER[1,2].

**assembly**[1] *n.* The process of putting together the parts of a machine or other products in a sequence of operations: *the assembly of an automobile's parts.*

- [Initialized sign] Tap the side of the right thumb of the *A hand* on the back of the left *open hand,* palm facing down, with a repeated movement.

**assembly**[2] *n.* See sign for MEETING.

**assembly line** *n.* An arrangement of equipment and workers for assembling a product, piece by piece, in sequence: *The engines were put together on an assembly line.* Same sign used for: **mass-produce.**

- [Pushing things along on an assembly line] With both *4 hands* near each other in front of the chest, right palm facing down and left palm facing up, push the hands off to the right with a double movement.

**assign** *v.* See signs for APPOINT[2], CHOOSE[1].

**assignment** *n.* See sign for APPOINTMENT.

**assist** *v.* See sign for HELP.

**assistant** *n.* **1.** One who helps in a job: *the teacher's assistant.* —*adj.* **2.** Assisting or subordinate: *the assistant manager of the store.* Same sign used for: **aide.**

- [Initialized hand showing giving a boost or aid to another] Use the thumb of the right *A hand* under the little-finger side of the left *A hand* to push the left hand upward in front of the chest.

**associate** *v.* **1.** Come together with others: *to associate with criminals.* —*n.* **2.** A person who shares actively in an enterprise: *a business associate.* Same sign used for: **acquaint, brotherhood, each other, fellowship, fraternity, interact, mingle, mutual, one another, socialize.**

- [Represents mingling with each other] With the thumb of the left *A hand* pointing up and the thumb of the right *A hand* pointing down, circle the thumbs around each other while moving the hands from left to right in front of the chest.

**association** *n.* An organization of people with common interests: *a professional association.* Related form: **associate** *v.* Same sign used for: **agency.**

- [Initialized sign similar to sign for **class**] Beginning with the thumbs of both *A hands* touching in front of the chest, palms facing each other, move the hands apart and forward in a circular movement by twisting the wrists until the little fingers touch and the palms face in.

**assume** *v.* See signs for GUESS, TAKE. Related form: **assumption** *n.*

**assure** *v.* See sign for VOW. Related form: **assurance** *n.*

**asterisk** *n.* See sign for STAR.

**astonish** *v.* To surprise greatly: *astonished at the huge donation.* Related form: **astonishment** *n.*

- [Represents jumping up with bent legs and falling over in astonishment] Beginning with the fingertips of the right *V hand,* palm facing in, on the palm of the left *open hand* held in front of the chest, palm facing up, bring the right hand upward in front of the chest while crooking the fingers and then down again, landing with the back of the *bent V hand* on the left palm.

**astound** *v.* See signs for FLABBERGAST, SURPRISE.

**astounded** *adj.* See sign for SHOCK[1].

**astray** *adv., adj.* Off the right path or course: *The letter went astray.* Same sign used for: **backslide, deviate, estranged, offshoot, off the point, off track, out of the way, sidetracked, stray.**

- [Shows one hand veering off the path] Beginning with both index fingers touching in front of the chest, palms facing down, slide the right index finger forward along the side of the left index finger, moving the right hand off to the right as it moves forward.

**at fault** *adj.* See sign for BLAME[1].

**athletics** *pl. n.* See sign for RACE[1].

**at last** *adv. phrase.* See sign for FINALLY.

**at odds** *adj.* See sign for STRUGGLE.

**atop** *prep.* On top of: *atop the mountain.*

- [Indicates location of something atop another thing] Place the fingertips of the right *curved hand,* palm facing down, on the back of the left *S hand* held in front of the chest, palm facing down.

**attach** *v.* See sign for BELONG[1].

**attack**[1] *v.* **1.** To set upon with violence: *attack the enemy.* —*n.* **2.** The act of attacking: *set up a defense against an attack.*

- [**hit**[1] + forcing another down] Bring the knuckles of the right *S hand,* palm facing in, forward from in front of the right shoulder to hit against the extended left index finger, palm facing forward and finger pointing up, forcing the left finger downward in front of the body.

**attack**[2] *v.* See sign for HIT[1].

**attain** *v.* See sign for GET.

**attempt** *v.* See sign for TRY[1].

**attend** *v.* To be present at: *attend church.* Same sign used for: **gather, go to.**

- [**go** formed with a directed movement] Beginning with both extended index fingers pointing up in front of the chest, right hand closer to the chest than the left and both palms facing forward, move both hands forward simultaneously while bending the wrists so the fingers point forward.

**attention** *n.* Careful concentration on something: *Pay close attention to what I'm doing.* Related form: **attend** *v.* Same sign used for: **concentrate, concentration, focus on, pay attention, watch.**

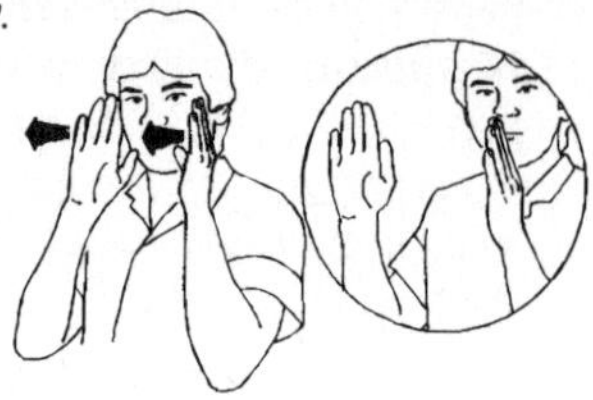

■ [Forms blinders to direct one's attention] Move both *open hands* from near each cheek, palms facing each other, straight forward simultaneously.

**attitude** *n.* A general way of feeling about something: *a bad attitude toward work.*

■ [Initialized sign similar to sign for **character**] Move the thumb of the right *A hand* in a circular movement around the heart, palm facing left, ending with the thumb against the chest.

**attract**[1] *v.* To draw by appeal: *attract a crowd of admirers.* Same sign used for: **draw.**

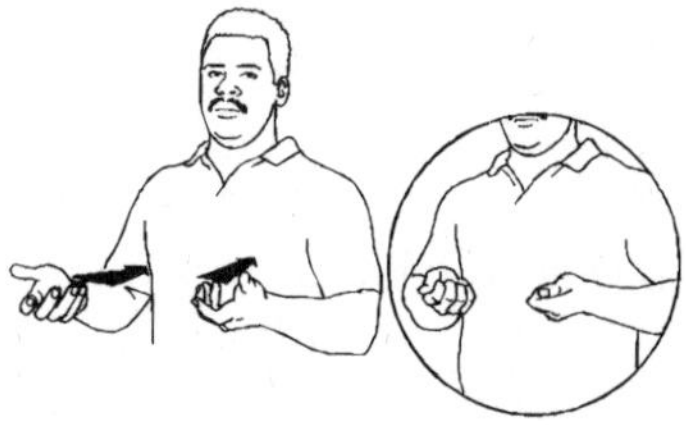

■ [Hands pull something to oneself] Beginning with both *curved hands* in front of each side of the body, palms facing up, bring the hands back toward the body while closing into *A hands.*

**attract**[2] *v.* See sign for ABSORB[1].

**attractive** *adj.* Having a pleasant appearance: *an attractive smile.* Related form: **attracted to.**

■ Beginning with the right *C hand* in front of the face, palm facing left, and the left *C hand* somewhat forward, palm facing right, move both hands forward while closing into *S hands,* ending with the little-finger side of the right hand near the thumb side of the left hand.

**auction** *n.* **1.** A public sale of goods by bidding: *to sell a painting at an auction.* —*v.* **2.** to sell at auction: *to auction off your furniture.* Same sign used for: **bid.**

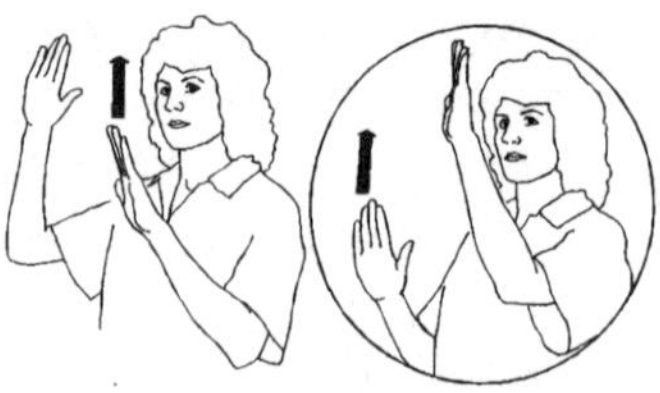

■ [Mime raising one's hand to bid at an auction] Move both *open hands,* palms facing forward, in an alternating upward movement beside each side of the head.

**audience** *n.* **1.** A group assembled at a performance: *a large audience in the theater.* **2.** A regular public with interest in (a book, a play, or the like): *The audience for this book is parents of children with disabilities.* See also sign for HORDE. Same sign used for: **congregation, crowd.**

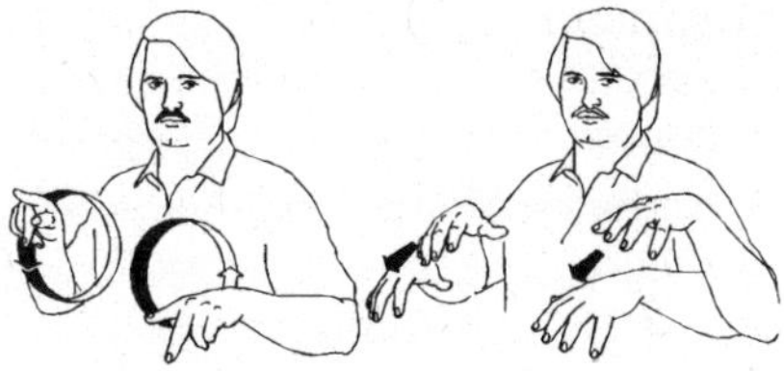

■ [**people** + **horde**] Move both *P hands,* palms facing down, in alternating forward circular movements in front of each side of the body. Then move both *curved 5 hands,* palms facing down, from in front of each side of the body forward with a simultaneous movement.

**audit** *n.* **1.** A formal examination of financial records: *The comptroller reviewed the audit of the company records.* —*v.* **2.** To make an audit of (accounts, records, etc.): *audit the company's books.*

■ [Initialized sign similar to sign for **count**] Swing the palm side of the right *A hand* with a double movement from the fingers to the heel of the left *open hand* held in front of the body, palm facing up.

**auditory** *adj.* See sign for HEAR.

**aunt** *n.* The sister of one's mother or father: *my aunt and uncle.*

■ [Initialized sign formed near the right cheek] Shake the right *A hand,* palm facing forward, near the right cheek.

**authority** *n.* A person with power or expertise: *My boss is the real authority in this office.*

■ [Shows muscle in arm symbolizing strength and authority] Beginning with the extended right thumb of *A hand,* palm facing left, near the left shoulder, move the hand down in an arc while twisting the right wrist, ending with the little-finger side of the right hand in the crook of the left arm, bent across the body.

**automatic**[1] *adj.* Having a self-acting mechanism: *automatic starter in the new car.* Same sign used for: **automatic transmission.**

■ [Indicates repetitive movement of something operating automatically] Move the extended right curved index finger, palm facing in, back and forth on the back of the left *open hand,* palm facing in, with a repeated movement.

**automatic**[2] *adj.* See sign for FAST.

**automobile** *n.* See sign for CAR.

**autopsy** *n.* A medical examination of a dead body to find the cause of death: *the autopsy revealed cancer.*

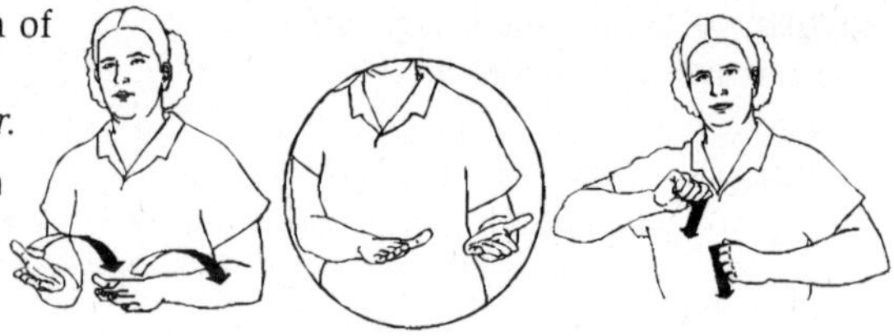

■ [**die** + **operate**[1]] Beginning with both *open hands* in front of the body, right palm facing up and left palm facing down, flip the hands to the left, turning the right palm down and the left palm up. Then move the thumbs of both *10 hands* downward on each side of the chest, in short alternating movements.

**autumn** *n.* See sign for FALL[2].

**available** *adj.* See sign for EMPTY.

**avenge** *v.* See sign for REVENGE.

**avenue** *n.* See sign for ROAD.

**average** *adj.* Approximately midway: *average score.* Same sign used for: **mean, medium.**

■ [Shows split down the middle] Beginning with the little-finger side of the right *open hand* across the index-finger side of the left *open hand,* palms angled down, twist the wrists down, bringing the hands apart a short distance with a double movement, palms facing down.

**avoid** *v.* Keep away from: *avoid the cold.* Related form: **avoidable** *adj.* Same sign used for: **back out, elude, evade, fall behind, get away, shirk.**

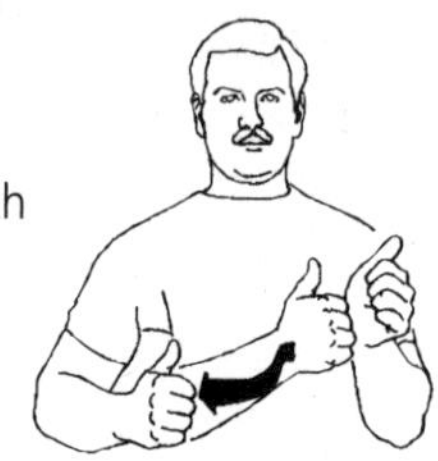

■ [One hand moves away from the other to avoid it] Beginning with the knuckles of the right *A hand,* palm facing left, near the base of the thumb of the left *A hand,* palm facing right, bring the right hand back toward the body with a wiggly movement.

**awake**[1] *v.* Cease sleeping: *awake in the morning.* Related form: **awaken** *v.* Same sign used for: **arouse, wake up.**

■ [Indicates eyes opening when becoming awake] Beginning with the *modified X hands* near each eye, palms facing each other, quickly flick the fingers apart while widening the eyes.

**awake**[2] *adj.* See sign for INSOMNIA.

**award**[1] *n.* Something given as a prize: *win the award for the best essay.*

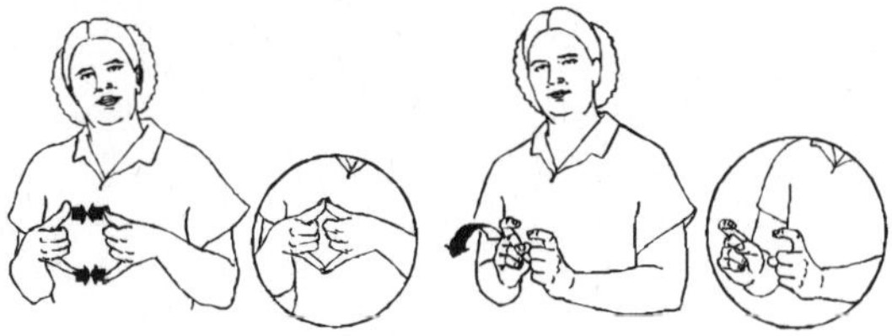

■ [**trophy** + **gift**] Tap the thumbs and little fingers of both *Y hands,* palms facing in, against each other with a double movement in front of the chest. Then, beginning with both *X hands* in front of the chest, palms facing each other, move the right hand forward in a small arc.

---

**award**[2] *n.* See signs for GIFT, TROPHY[1].

---

**aware**[1] *adj.* Having knowledge: *I was not aware of his illness.* Same sign used for: **familiar, knowledge.**

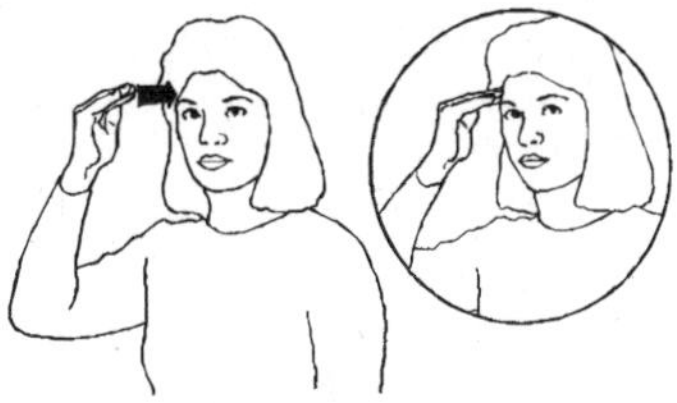

■ [Shows location of awareness] Tap the fingertips of the right *bent hand,* palm facing in, against the right side of the forehead with a double movement.

---

**aware**[2] *adj.* See sign for NOTICE[1].

---

**away** *adj., adv.* In or to another place: *She is away. Go away.* Same sign used for: **get away, go, gone.**

■ [Natural gesture as if shooing something away] Flip the fingers of the right *open hand* from pointing down near the right side of the body outward to the right by flicking the wrist upward with a quick movement.

---

**awesome** [slang] *adj.* See signs for FINEST, FLABBERGAST.

---

**awful** *adj.* Disagreeable or dreadful: *awful chance.* Same sign used for: **disastrous, dreadful, fierce, horrible, sordid, terrible.**

■ [Natural gesture used when indicating something terrible] Beginning with both *8 hands* near each side of the head, palms facing each other, flip the fingers open to *5 hands* while twisting the palms forward.

---

**awkward** *adj.* Not graceful: *awkward movements.* Same sign used for: **clumsy.**

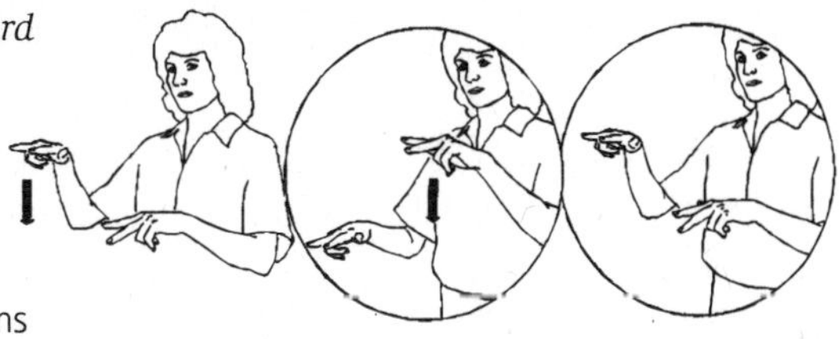

■ [Represents walking awkwardly] Beginning with both *3 hands* in front of the body, right hand higher than the left and both palms facing down, raise the left and then the right hand in alternating movements.

**babble** *v.* See sign for BLAB.

**baby** *n.* A very young child: *a six-month-old baby.* Same sign used for: **infant.**

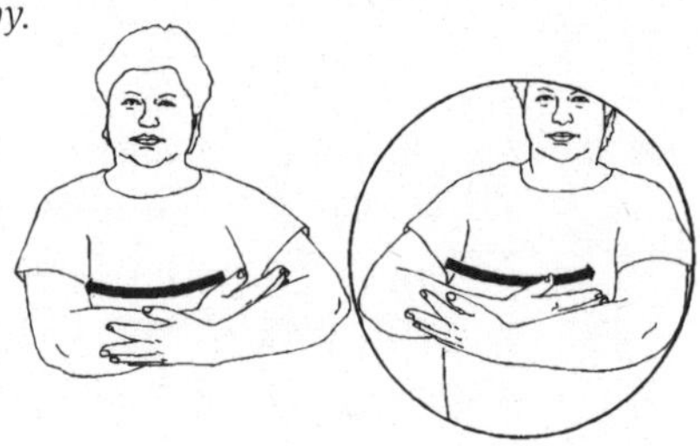

- [Action of rocking a baby in one's arms] With the bent right arm cradled on the bent left arm, both palms facing up, swing the arms to the right and the left in front of the body with a double movement.

**bachelor** *n.* A man who has never married: *He's 45 years old and still a bachelor.* Related form: **bachelorette** *n.*

- [Initialized sign] Move the index finger of the right *B hand* from touching the left side of the chin, palm facing left, in an arc to touch the right side of the chin.

**back** *n.* The rear upper portion of the body below the neck: *Scratch my back.* Same sign used for: **dorsal, lumbar, rear.**

- [Natural gesture indicating location] Pat the fingertips of the right *open hand* behind the right shoulder with a repeated movement.

**backache** *n.* A pain or ache in the back, usually in the lumbar region: *He does exercises for the pain from his backache.* Same sign used for: **lumbago.**

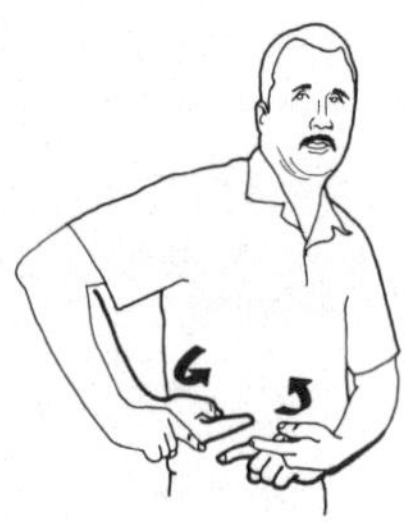

- [**pain**[1] formed near the back] Beginning with the extended index fingers of both *1 hands* pointing toward each other near the right side of the body, right palm facing down and left palm facing up, twist the wrists in opposite directions, ending with the right palm facing up and the left palm facing down.

**back and forth** *adv.* See sign for COMMUTE.

**background** *n.* **1.** Past experience, training, or family origins: *a background in journalism. She comes from a working-class background.* **2.** The part of a scene behind the main objects: *The volcano was far in the background behind the pastoral scene.* **3.** The circumstances leading up to or explaining an event or situation: *the background of the war.*

■ [Initialized sign] In quick succession tap the index-finger side of the right *B hand* and then *G hand,* palm facing forward, against the left *open hand,* palm facing right.

**back out** *v. phrase.* See signs for AVOID, RESIGN.

**backpack** *n.* **1.** A bag with straps designed to be carried on the back: *carried his books in a backpack.* —*v.* **2.** To go hiking with a bag of food and equipment on the back: *to go backpacking in the hills.*

■ [Action of putting on a backpack] Move the thumbs of both *curved 3 hands,* palms facing forward, downward toward each shoulder with a double movement.

**backslide** *v.* See signs for ASTRAY, BEHIND.

**backspace** *n.* **1.** A keyboard key: *press the backspace.* —*v.* **2.** A keyboard operation that moves the cursor one place to the left, allowing modification of what has already been typed: *backspace and correct the mistake.*

■ [Indicates a location in the past] Beginning with the right *10 hand* in front of the chest, palm down, twist the hand upward to the right, ending with the palm up and the extended thumb pointing right.

**backup**[1] *n.* **1.** A duplicate copy of computer data or a software program for use if the original fails: *Keep a backup of your file.* —*adj.* **2.** Designating such a copy: *a backup copy to be kept in a safe place.* —*v.* **back up. 3.** To make such a copy: *Back up your program.*

■ [Hand moves to provide support for the other hand] Beginning with the right *10 hand,* palm facing down, beside the left *10 hand,* palm facing right, move the right hand clockwise in an arc and then forward to the heel of the left hand, ending with the right palm facing left.

**backup**[2] *n.* See sign for SUPPORT.

**bacon** *n.* Smoked meat from a hog, usually in thin slices: *bacon and eggs for breakfast.*

■ [Hands indicate wavy shape of fried bacon] With the thumbs of both hands pointing up and fingers of both *U hands* touching in front of the chest, palms facing in, bring the hands apart while bending the fingers back into each palm with a double movement.

**bad** *adj.* **1.** Not good; harmful: *Sugar is bad for your teeth.* **2.** Inaccurate or invalid: *a bad idea.* **3.** Unpleasant or unfavorable: *to have a bad time at the party.* Related form: **badly** *adv.* Same sign used for: **evil, nasty, naughty, wicked.**

■ [Gesture tosses away something that tastes bad] Move the fingers of the right *open hand* from the mouth, palm facing in, downward while flipping the palm quickly down as the hand moves.

**badge**[1] *n.* A small sign worn for identification: *wear a name badge.* Same sign used for: **button, emblem.**

■ [Putting on a badge] Bring the index-finger side of the right *F hand,* palm facing left, against the left side of the chest with a double movement.

**badge**[2] *n.* See sign for POLICE.

**bag** *n.* A soft container that opens at the top: *a bag of potato chips.* See also sign for BASKET. Same sign used for: **sack.**

■ [Shows shape of filled bag] Beginning with the little fingers of both *curved hands* touching in front of the body, palms facing up, bring the hands apart and upward in an arc while spreading the fingers, ending with both *curved 5 hands* in front of each side of the chest, palms facing each other.

**baggage** *n.* The containers one carries when traveling, as trunks and suitcases: *The airline misplaced my baggage when I changed planes.* Same sign used for: **luggage.**

■ [Shows carrying a bag in each hand] Shake both *S hands,* palms facing in, up and down with a short movement near each side of the waist with the elbows bent.

**bake**[1] *v.* To cook by dry, indirect heat, especially in an oven: *bake a cake.*

■ [Putting something in the oven] Move the fingers of the right *open hand,* palm facing up, forward under the left *open hand* held in front of the chest, palm facing down.

**bake**[2] *v.* See sign for COOK.

**balance** *v.* **1.** To be or hold steady: *to balance on one leg.* **2.** To be or make equivalent in weight, amount, or proportion: *to balance work and pleasure.* —*n.* **3.** Equal distribution of weight, amount, etc.: *An excess of goods destroyed the trade balance.* **4.** An instrument for weighing: *to weigh gold on a balance.*

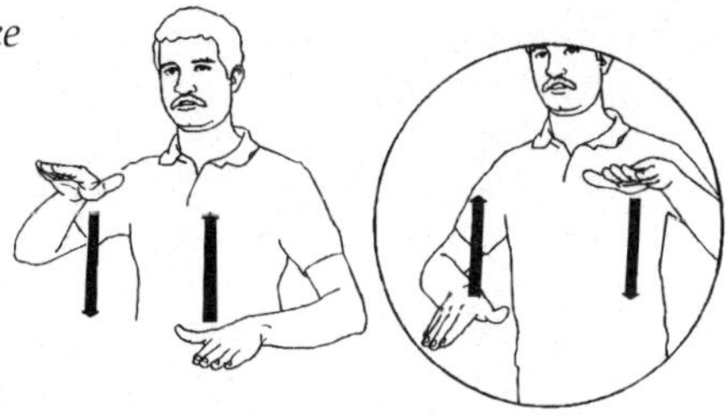

■ [Action shows trying to balance something] With a simultaneous movement bring the right *open hand* and the left *open hand,* both palms facing down, up and down in front of each side of the chest, shifting the entire torso slightly with each movement.

**bald** *adj.* Without hair: *a bald head.* Related form: **baldness** *n.* Same sign used for: **bareheaded, scalp.**

■ [Indicates bare area of head] Move the bent middle finger of the right *5 hand,* palm facing down, in a circle around the top of the head.

**ball** *n.* A round object used in games: *throw the ball.*

■ [The shape of a ball] Touch the fingertips of both *curved 5 hands* together in front of the chest, palms facing each other.

**balloon** *n.* An airtight bag that can be inflated, used as a toy or decoration: *blowing up balloons for a party.* Same sign used for: **expand.**

■ [Shows shape of balloon as it expands] Beginning with the left fingers cupped over the back of the right *S hand* held in front of the mouth, move the hands apart while opening the fingers, ending with both *curved 5 hands* near each side of the face, palms facing each other.

**ban** *v.* See signs for FORBID, PREVENT.

**banana** *n.* A long, curved, yellow tropical fruit: *peel a banana.*

■ [Mime peeling a banana] With the extended left index finger pointing up in front of the chest, palm facing forward, bring the fingertips of the right *curved 5 hand* downward, first on the back and then on the front of the index finger, while closing the right fingers to the thumb each time.

**band** *n.* A group of musicians: *plays drums in the band.* Same sign used for: **choir, orchestra.**

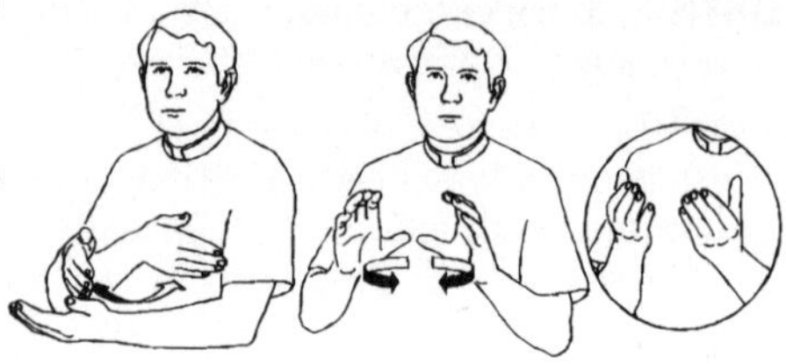

- [**music** + **class**] Swing the little-finger side of the right *open hand,* palm facing in, back and forth across the length of the bent left forearm. Then, beginning with the thumbs of both *C hands* near each other in front of the body, palms facing, bring the hands apart and outward in an arc, ending with the hands in front of the chest, palms facing in.

**bandage** *n.* A strip of material used in dressing a wound: *Put a bandage on the cut.* Same sign used for: **adhesive tape, Band-Aid** (*trademark*), **tape.**

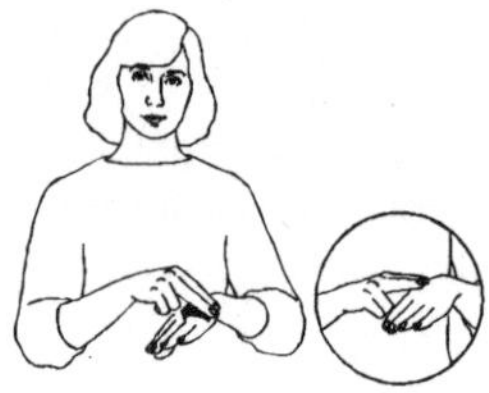

- [Mime putting on a bandage] Pull the right H fingers, palm facing down, across the back of the left *open hand,* palm facing down.

**banquet** *n.* A large meal prepared for a special occasion: *a wedding banquet.* Same sign used for: **feast, reception.**

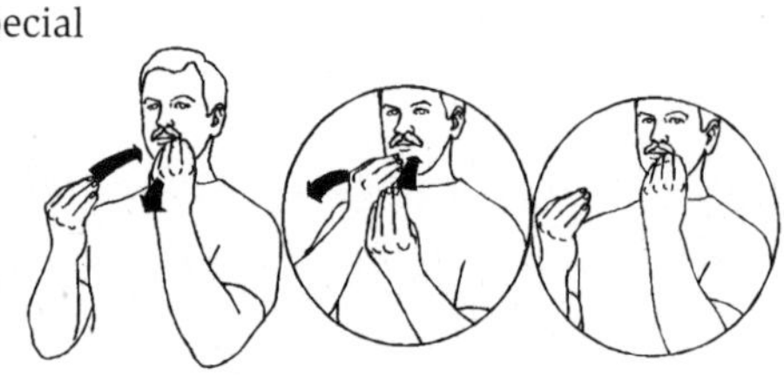

- [Indicates continuous eating] Bring the fingertips of both *flattened O hands,* palms facing down, to the mouth with repeated alternating movements.

**banter** *v., n.* See sign for STRUGGLE.

**bar** *n.* See sign for DRINK[2].

**barcode** *n.* See sign for STRIPE.

**bare**[1] *adj.* Without covering: *bare shoulders.*

- [Indicates a bare area] Move the bent middle finger of the right *5 hand,* palm facing down, in a double circle on the back of the left *open hand,* palm facing down.

**bare**[2] *adj.* See signs for EMPTY, NUDE.

**bareheaded** *adj.* See sign for BALD.

**barely** *adv.* See signs for ALMOST[1], CLOSE CALL.

**bark** *v.* To make the loud, sharp sound a dog makes: *The dog always barks at strangers.*

■ [The movement of a dog's jaws when barking] Beginning with the fingertips of both *open hands* touching, palms facing each other and heels apart, bring the fingers apart and then together again with a repeated movement.

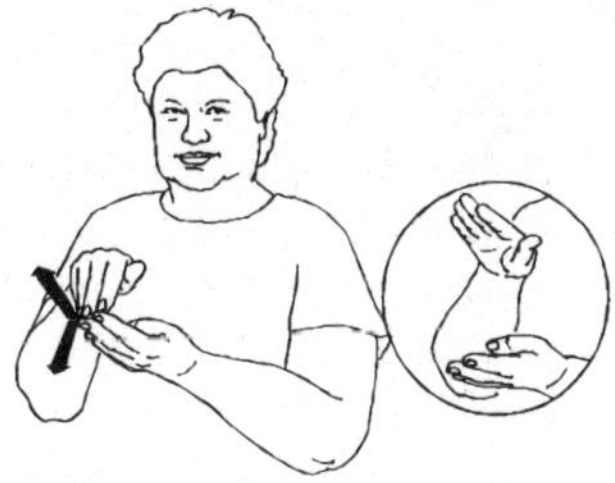

**barrier** *n.* See sign for PREVENT.

**base**[1] *n.* The bottom or supporting part: *the base of the statue.* Related forms: **basic** *adj.*, **basis** *n.*

■ [Initialized sign] Move the right *B hand,* palm facing left, in a flat circle under the left *open hand,* palm facing down.

**base**[2] *n.* See sign for BASEMENT. Related forms: **basic** *adj.*, **basis** *n.*

**baseball** *n.* **1.** A game played with a ball and bat by two teams on a field with four bases: *Baseball is the most popular American sport.* **2.** The ball used in this game: *Throw the baseball to me.* Same sign used for: **softball.**

■ [Natural gesture of swinging a baseball bat] With the little finger of the right *S hand* on the index finger of the left *S hand,* palms facing in opposite directions, move the hands from near the right shoulder downward in an arc across the front of the body with a double movement.

**based on** *v. phrase.* See sign for ESTABLISH.

**basement** *n.* The lowest story of a building, below ground: *a washing machine in the basement.* Same sign used for: **base, basic, basis, beneath, cellar, underlying.**

■ [Indicates an area beneath a house] Move the right *10 hand,* palm facing in, in a flat circle under the left *open hand* held across the chest, palm facing down.

**bashful**[1] *adj.* Shy or easily embarrassed: *a bashful child.*

■ [Shows a blush rising in the face] Move the palms of both *open hands* slowly upward from each side of the chin to each side of the forehead, palms facing in and fingers pointing up.

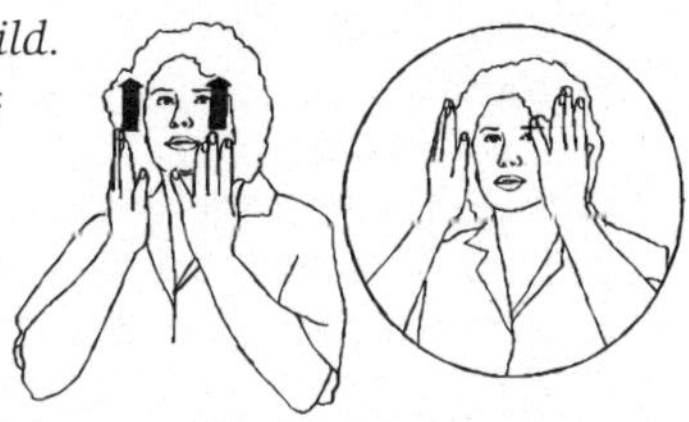

**bashful**[2] *adj.* See sign for SHY.

**basket**[1] *n.* A woven container: *a picnic basket.* See also sign for BAG. Same sign used for: **suitcase.**

■ [Initialized sign showing where a basket hangs from the arm] Move the index-finger side of the right *B hand* from the wrist to near the elbow of the bent left arm.

**basket**[2] *n.* See sign for BOWL.

**basketball** *n.* **1.** A game played by two teams that try to throw a large ball through a high hoop: *I'm too short to play basketball.* **2.** The ball used in the game of basketball: *She handles that basketball like a pro.*

■ [Mime tossing a basketball] Move the *curved 5 hands* from in front of the chest, palms facing each other, upward with a double movement by twisting the wrists upward.

**batch** *n.* See sign for PILE[1].

**bath** *n.* A washing of the whole body, especially by immersion in a tub: *take a hot bath.* Related form: **bathe** *v.*

■ [Washing oneself when bathing] Rub the knuckles of both *10 hands,* palms facing in, up and down on each side of the chest with a repeated movement.

**bathrobe** *n.* See sign for COAT.

**bathroom**[1] *n.* A room with a bathtub or shower and usually a sink and toilet: *a hotel room with a private bathroom.*

■ [**bath** + **room**] Rub the knuckles of both *10 hands,* palms facing in, up and down on each side of the chest with a repeated movement. Then, with both *open hands* in front each side of the chest, palms facing each other and fingers pointing forward, move hands in opposite directions, ending with the left hand near the chest and the right hand several inches forward, both palms facing in.

**bathroom**[2] *n.* See sign for TOILET.

**bathtub** *n.* A tub to bathe in: *The baby likes to take a bath in the little bathtub.*

■ [**bath** + a sign similar to **sit**] Rub the knuckles of both *10 hands,* palms facing in, up and down on each side of the chest with a repeated movement. Then bring the fingers of the right *H hand,* palm facing down and fingers pointing forward, down on the palm of the left *open hand,* palm facing up.

**batter** *n.* See sign for BEAT[1].

**battery** *n.* See sign for ELECTRIC.

**battle** *n.* **1.** A fight between opposing forces: *The army won the battle.* —*v.* **2.** To engage in a fight or struggle: *The opponents battled over first place.* Same sign used for: **war.**

■ [Indicates opponents in warlike maneuvers] Beginning with both *5 hands* in front of the right shoulder, palms facing down and fingers pointing toward each other, move the hands toward the left shoulder and then back toward the right shoulder.

**bawl out** *v. phrase.* To scold severely: *bawled me out for breaking the dish.* Same sign used for: **burst, burst out, chew out, tell off, yell at.**

■ [Represents a sudden burst of words] Beginning with the little finger of the right *S hand* on the top of the index-finger side of the left *S hand,* flick the hands forward with a deliberate double movement while opening the fingers into *5 hands* each time.

**beads** *pl. n.* Small ornaments with holes through them for stringing: *a string of beads.* Same sign used for: **necklace.**

■ [Location and shape of a necklace of beads] Move the index-finger side of the right *F hand,* palm facing left, from the left side of the neck smoothly around to the right side of the neck.

**bean** *n.* The long, smooth pod of a climbing plant, eaten as a vegetable: *Eat your green beans.*

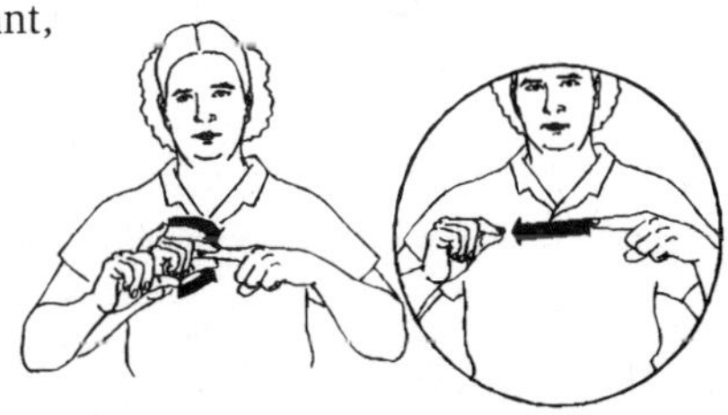

■ [Shape of a string bean] Beginning with the extended left index finger, palm facing in and finger pointing right, held between the index finger and thumb of the right *G hand,* palm facing left, pull the right hand outward to the right with a double movement.

**bear**[1] *n.* A large, heavy mammal with thick, rough fur: *a grizzly bear.*

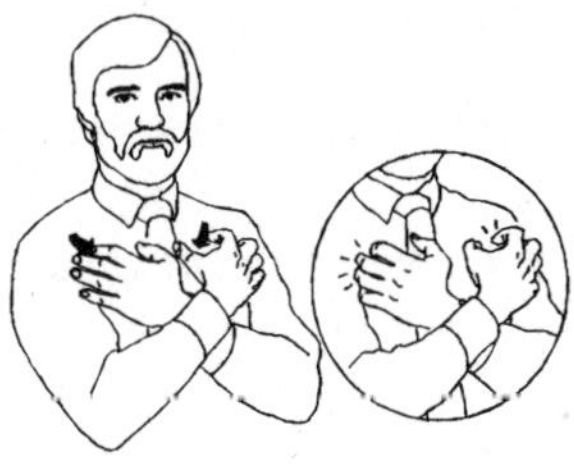

■ [Action of a bear scratching itself] With the arms crossed at the wrist on the chest, scratch the fingers of both *curved hands* up and down near each shoulder with a repeated movement.

**bear**[2] *v.* See signs for BURDEN, HURT[2], PATIENT[1].

**bear up** *v. phrase.* See sign for ENCOURAGE.

**beard** *n.* Hair covering a man's chin and cheeks: *He shaved off his beard.*

- [Location and shape of beard] Beginning with the right *C hand* around the chin, palm facing in, bring the hand downward while closing the fingers to the thumb with a double movement.

**beast** *n.* See sign for ANIMAL.

**beat**[1] *v.* To mix by stirring rapidly: *beat the eggs.* Same sign used for: **batter, mix, stir, whip.**

- [Mime beating using a spoon in a bowl] Move the right *A hand,* palm facing the chest, in a quick repeated circular movement near the palm side of the left *C hand,* palm facing right.

**beat**[2] *n.* The accent or rhythm of music: *dance to the beat.* Same sign used for: **vibrate, vibration.**

- [Feeling the rhythm of music] Move both *5 hands,* palms facing down, from side to side with a short repeated alternating movement in front of each side of the body.

**beat**[3] *v.* To strike again and again: *He beat his hand against the wall.* Same sign used for: **abuse, hit, strike.**

- [Indicates beating something] Hit the back of the right *S hand,* palm facing in, against the palm of the left *open hand,* palm facing right, with a double movement.

**beat**[4] *v.* See signs for: DEFEAT[1,2].

**beat up** *v. phrase.* To strike repeatedly so as to injure: *The man constantly beat up his wife and children.* Same sign used for: **abuse, hit, strike.**

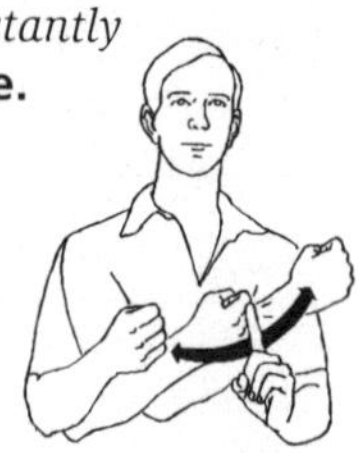

- [Indicates beating something repeatedly] Swing the right *S hand,* palm facing in, in a large arc in front of the chest, repeatedly striking the extended left index finger, palm facing right, each time it passes and returns.

**beau** *n.* See sign for SWEETHEART.

**beautiful** *adj.* Very pleasing, especially to the eye or other senses: *a beautiful view of the mountains.* Related form: **beauty** *n.* See also sign for PRETTY. Same sign used for: **lovely.**

- [Hand encircles a beautiful face] Move the right *5 hand* in a large circular movement in front of the face while closing the fingers to the thumb, forming a *flattened O hand.* Then move the hand forward while spreading the fingers quickly into a *5 hand.*

**be careful** *v. phrase.* See sign for CAREFUL.

**because** *conj.* For the reason that: *They canceled the picnic because it was raining.* Same sign used for: **since.**

- Bring the index finger of the right *L hand* with a sweeping movement across the forehead from left to right, changing to a *10 hand* near the right side of the head.

**beckon** *v.* To signal by a gesture to come: *Beckon the child to come here.* Same sign used for: **come here, recruit.**

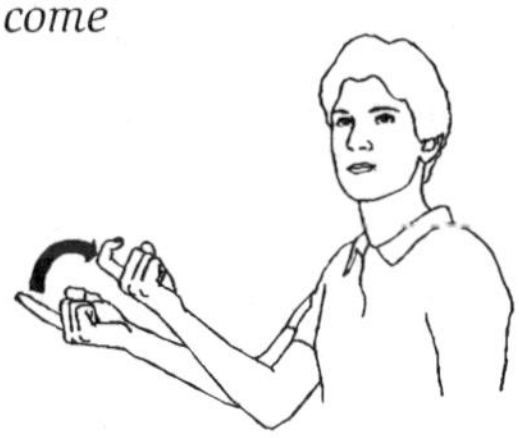

- [Natural beckoning gesture] Beginning with the extended right index finger pointing forward in front of the chest, palm facing up, bend the index finger into an *X hand* while bringing the hand back toward the chest, with a double movement.

**become** *v.* To grow to be: *to become accustomed to the cold.* Same sign used for: **turn into.**

- [Hands reverse positions as if to change one thing into another] Beginning with the palm of the right *open hand* laying across the upturned palm of the left *open hand,* rotate the hands, exchanging positions while keeping the palms together.

**become successful** See sign for SHOOT UP.

**bed** *n.* A piece of furniture used for sleeping: *lying in bed.*

- [Mime laying the head against a pillow] Rest the right cheek at an angle on the palm of the right *open hand.*

**bedroom** *n.* A room to sleep in: *fast asleep in the bedroom.*

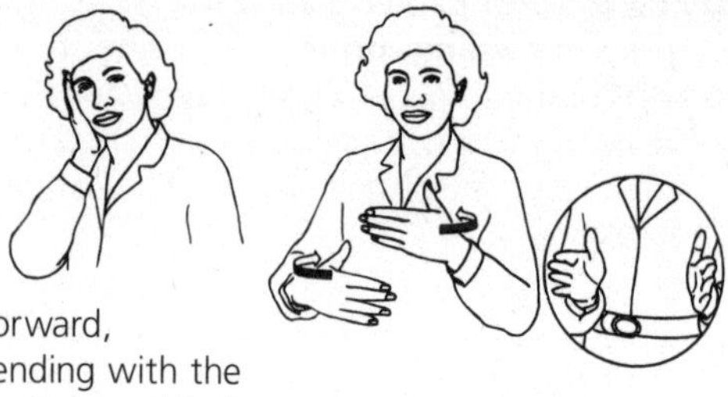

■ [**bed** + **box**] Rest the right cheek at an angle on the palm of the right *open hand.* Then, beginning with both *open hands* in front of each side of the chest, palms facing each other and fingers pointing forward, move the hands in opposite directions, ending with the left hand near the chest and the right hand several inches forward of the left hand, both palms facing in.

**bee** *n.* A stinging insect with four wings that produces wax and honey: *A bee stung me.* Same sign used for: **mosquito.**

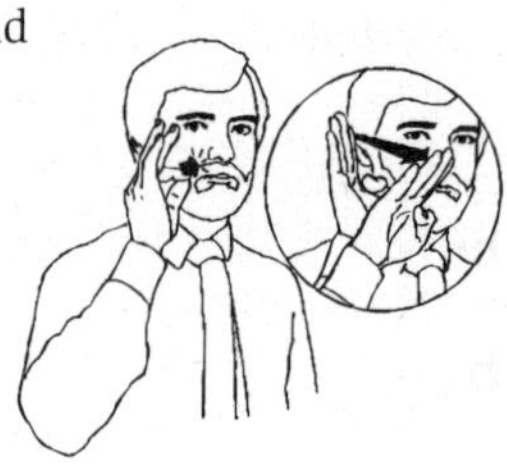

■ [The biting action of an insect and then a natural gesture of brushing it away] Press the index finger and thumb of the right *F hand* against the right cheek. Then brush the index-finger side of the right *B hand,* palm facing forward, from near the right ear forward by bending the wrist.

**beef** *n.* See sign for MEAT.

**been** *v.* See sign for SINCE.

**been (there)** (Sign indicates that one has visited or stayed at a place previously): *I've been to Hawaii.* Same sign used for: **finish.**

■ [Similar to sign for **touch** except made more quickly] Bring the bent middle finger of the right *5 hand* downward to tap quickly the back of the left *open hand* held across the chest, both palms facing down.

**beer** *n.* An alcoholic drink made from malt and hops: *drink a cold beer.*

■ [Initialized sign] Slide the index-finger side of the right *B hand,* palm facing forward, downward on the right cheek with a double movement.

**before**[1] *adv.* In the past: *I had never skied before.* Same sign used for: **last, past, previous, prior.**

■ [Indicates a time or place in the past] Move the fingertips of the right *open hand,* palm facing back, from near the right cheek back and down to touch the right shoulder.

**before**[2] *prep.* Earlier than: *a nap before dinner.* Same sign used for: **pre-, preceding, prior.**

■ [Indicates a time or place experienced in the past] Beginning with the back of the right *open hand,* palm facing in and fingers pointing left, touching the back of the left *open hand,* palm facing forward and fingers pointing up, move the right hand in toward the chest.

**beg**[1] *v.* To ask for urgently or as charity: *beg for food.* Same sign used for: **implore, plead.**

■ [Mime extending a hand while begging] While holding the wrist of the upturned right *curved 5 hand* in the left palm, constrict the right fingers with double movement.

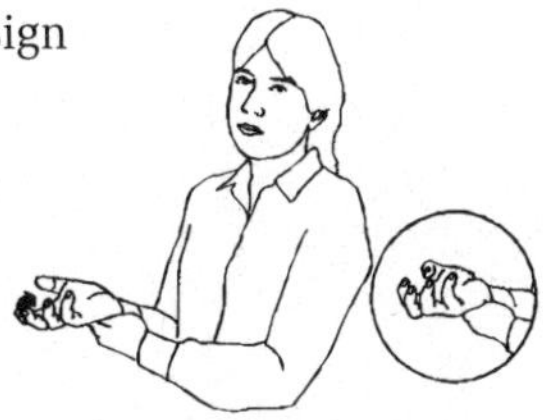

**beg**[2] *v.* See sign for WORSHIP[1].

**beginning** *n.* See sign for START[1].

**behind** *prep.* At or to the rear of: *standing behind the chair.* Same sign used for: **backslide.**

■ [Indicates a position behind another] Move the right *10 hand,* palm facing left, from in front of the left *10 hand,* palm facing right, back toward the chest in a large arc.

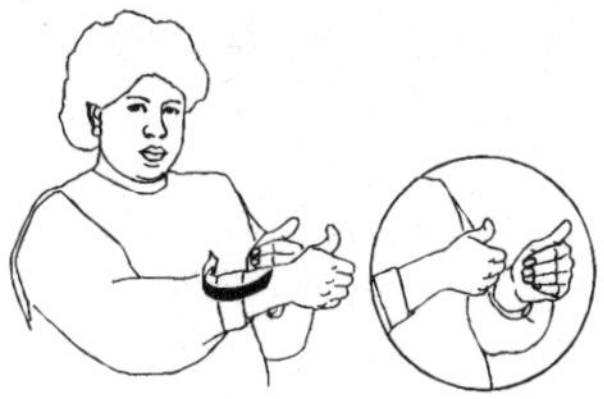

**belch** *v.* **1.** To pass gas from the stomach through the mouth: *belched after dinner.* —*n.* **2.** An act or instance of belching: *Everyone around the table heard his belch.* Same sign used for: **burp.**

■ [Indicates gas moving up from the stomach] Move the fingertips of the right *bent hand,* palm facing in, up and down on the chest with a double movement.

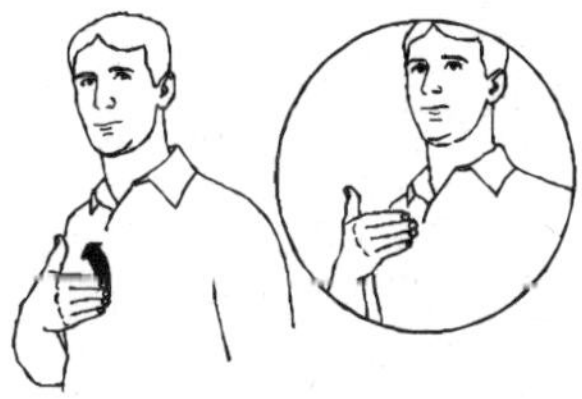

**believe** *v.* To think something is true or real: *to believe in ghosts.* Related form: **belief** *n.*

■ [**true** + clasping one's beliefs close] Move the extended right index finger from touching the right side of the forehead downward while opening the hand, ending with the right hand clasping the left *open hand,* palm facing up, in front of the body.

**bell** *n.* A hollow metal cup that rings when struck by a clapper: *ring the bell.* Same sign used for: **reverberate, reverberation, ring.**

■ [Indicates the striking of a bell's clapper and the sound reverberating] Hit the thumb side of the right *S hand,* palm facing down, against the palm of the left *open hand.* Then move the right hand to the right while opening the fingers into a *5 hand,* wiggling the fingers as the hand moves.

**belly button** *n. phrase.* See sign for NAVEL.

**belong**[1] *v.* To be a member: *to belong to a church.* Same sign used for: **annex, attach, combine, connect, fasten, hook up, join, joint, link, online, unite.**

■ [Two things coming together] Beginning with both *curved 5 hands* in front of each side of the body, palms facing each other, bring the hands together while touching the thumb and index fingertips of each hand and intersecting with each other.

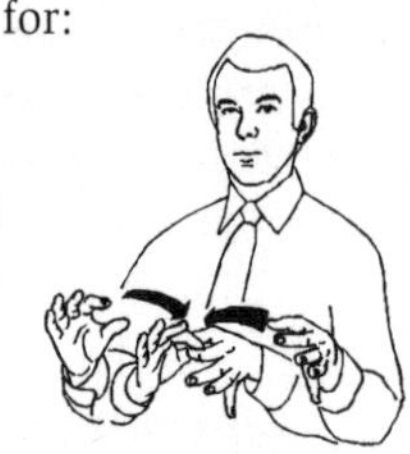

**belong**[2] *v.* To be one's property: *Does this book belong to you?* Same sign used for: **entitle, truly yours.**

■ [**true** + **your**] Move the extended right index finger, palm facing left, from in front of the mouth forward while changing into an *open hand,* palm facing forward.

**below**[1] *prep.* **1.** Lower than: *an apartment below ground level.* —*adv.* **2.** In a lower place: *a two-story house with a full basement below.* Same sign used for: **beneath, bottom.**

■ [Indicates a position below] Beginning with the left *open hand* on the back of the right *open hand,* both palms facing down, bring the right hand downward in an arc, ending several inches below the left hand.

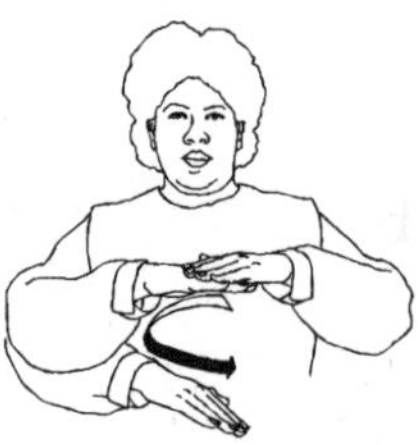

**below**[2] *prep.* See sign for MINIMUM.

**belt** *n.* A strip of leather or cloth fastened around the waist: *Wear a belt with these pants.*

■ [Location of a belt] Move both *H hands* from each side of the waist around toward each other until the fingers overlap in front of the waist.

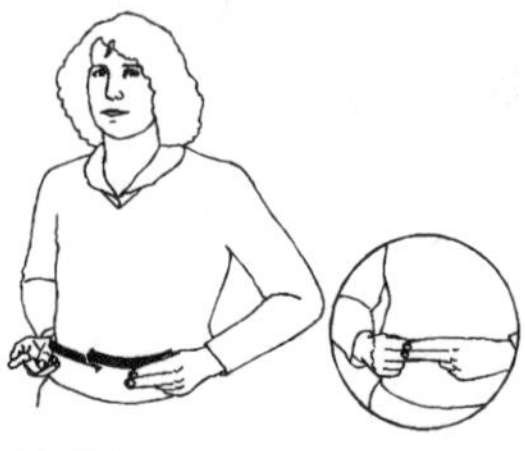

**bend**[1] *v.* To force into a curved or angular shape: *bend the pipe.* Related form: **bent** *adj.*

■ [Indicates the ability to bend] Grasp the fingers of the left *open hand,* palm facing right, with the fingers of the right *flattened O hand,* and then bend the left fingers downward until both palms are facing down and hands are bent.

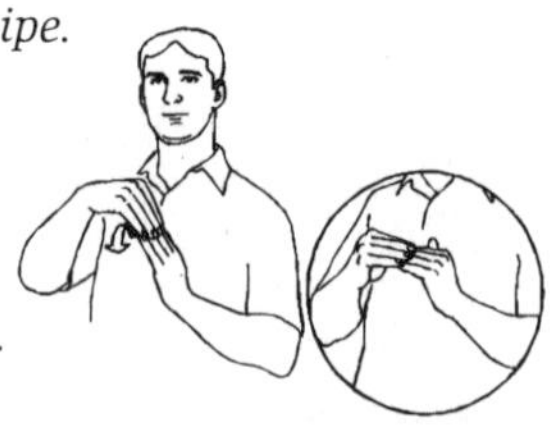

**bend**[2] *v.* See signs for BOW, DENT.

**beneath** *prep., adv.* See signs for BASEMENT, BELOW.

**benefit** *n.* Something useful or good; an advantage or aid: *for your personal benefit.* Same sign used for: **advantage.**

■ [Pocketing a beneficial item] Push the thumb side of the right *F hand* downward on the right side of the chest, palm facing down, with a short double movement.

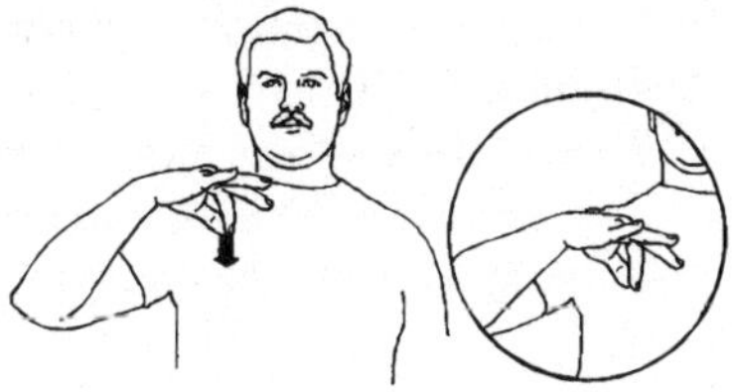

**benevolent** *adj.* See sign for GOOD.

**bent** *adj.* See sign for DENT.

**bequeath** *v.* See sign for GIVE.

**berry** *n.* A small edible fruit: *to pick just one ripe berry from the bush.*

■ [Twisting a berry to pick it from the vine] Grasp the extended little finger of the left hand, palm facing in, with the fingertips of the right *O hand* and twist the right hand outward with a double movement.

**beside** *prep.* By the side of: *beside the door.* Same sign used for: **adjacent, next to.**

■ [Indicates a location beside another] Beginning with the palm of the right *bent hand,* palm facing in and fingers pointing left, touching the back of the left *bent hand,* palm facing in and fingers pointing right, move the right hand forward in a small arc.

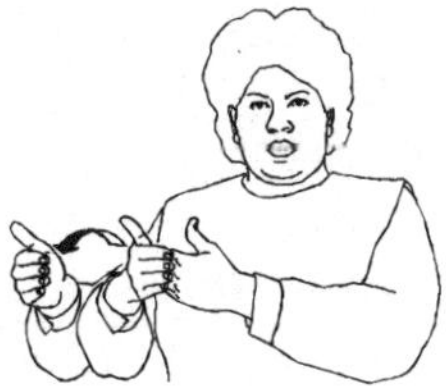

**best** *adj.* **1.** Most excellent: *the best part.* —*adv.* **2.** To the highest degree or in the most excellent way: *Who reads best?*

■ [Modification of **good,** moving the sign upward to form the superlative degree] Bring the right *open hand,* palm facing in and fingers pointing left, from in front of the mouth upward in a large arc to the right side of the head, changing to a *10 hand* as the hand moves.

**bet** *n.* **1.** A promise to forfeit something if you prove wrong in predicting the outcome of an activity; wager: *make a bet on the fifth race.* **2.** an amount of money so wagered: *place your bet.* —*v.* **3.** To make a bet: *It is illegal for a player to bet on the game.* Same sign used for: **bid, gamble, wager.**

■ [Initialized sign showing the turning of dice] Beginning with both *B hands* in front of each side of the body, palms facing each other and fingers pointing forward, turn the hands toward each other, ending with the palms facing down.

**betray**[1] *v.* To be unfaithful to: *betray a trust; betray a friend.* Same sign used for: **con, deceive, fib, fool, swindle.**

- Strike the knuckles of the right *A hand,* palm facing forward, against the extended left index finger, palm facing forward, with a double movement.

**betray**[2] *v.* See signs for CHEAT, DECEIVE[1].

**better** *adj.* **1.** Superior, as in quality or excellence: *a better deal at the other store.* —*adv.* **2.** To a greater degree or in a more excellent manner: *a child trying to read better.*

- [Modification of **good,** moving the sign upward to form the comparative degree] Bring the right *open hand,* palm facing in and fingers pointing left, from in front of the mouth upward in an arc to the right side of the head, changing to a *10 hand* as the hand moves.

**between** *prep.* In the interval separating (two things): *put the picture between the two windows.* Same sign used for: **gap, lapse.**

- [Indicates space between two things] Brush the little-finger side of the right *open hand,* palm facing left, back and forth with a short repeated movement on the index-finger side of the left *open hand,* palm angled right.

**beverage** *n.* See sign for DRINK[1].

**bewilder** *v.* See sign for SURPRISE.

**bewildered** *adj.* See sign for PUZZLED.

**beyond** *prep., adv.* See sign for AFTER[1].

**biannual** *adj.* Happening two times each year: *The biannual convention is held in May and November.* Same sign used for: **semiannual, six months.**

- [**six** handshape used to sign **month**] Move the right *6 hand,* palm facing forward and fingers pointing up, downward with a double movement on the extended left index finger held in front of the chest, palm facing right and finger pointing up.

**bias** *n.* See sign for PREJUDICE[1]. Related form: **biased** *adj.*

**bicycle** *n.* A lightweight vehicle with two wheels in tandem: *ride a bicycle.*

- [Shows action of pedaling a bicycle] Move both *S hands* in alternating forward circles, palms facing down, in front of each side of the body.

**bid** *n., v.* See signs for AUCTION, BET, SUGGEST.

**big** *adj.* See sign for LARGE.

**big-headed** *adj.* See sign for CONCEITED.

**big shot** *n. phrase.* See sign for CONCEITED.

**bill** *n.* See sign for DOLLAR.

**billiards** *n.* See sign for POOL.

**billion** *n.* **1.** One thousand millions: *The young woman is now worth several billion in her own right.* *—adj.* **2.** Having multiples of one thousand millions: *a billion dollars.*

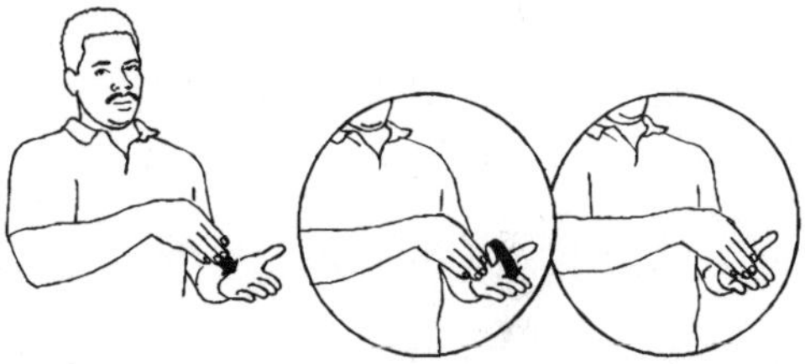

■ [Initialized sign similar to sign for **million**] Tap the fingertips of the right *bent B hand,* palm facing in, first on the heel and then on the fingers of the left *open hand,* palm facing up.

**bimonthly** *adj.* **1.** Happening once every two months: *The bimonthly newsletter is sent out six times a year.* **2.** Every two months: *The elevators are inspected bimonthly.* Same sign used for: **every two months.**

■ [**month** formed with a **two** handshape] Move the back of the right *2 hand,* palm facing in and fingers pointing left, downward on the extended left index finger held in front of the body, palm facing right and finger pointing up.

**bind** *v.* To fasten or tie in place: *bind the hostage to the chair.* Same sign used for: **bondage, bound, locked into, tie up.**

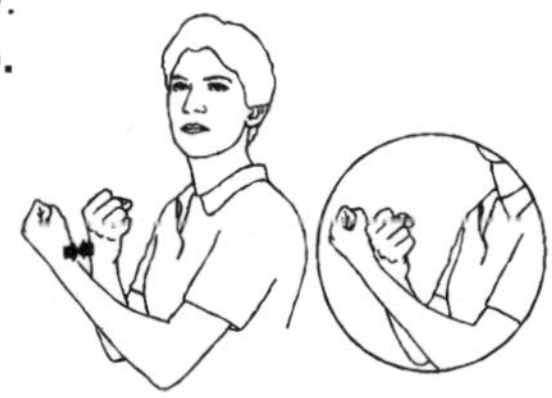

■ [Shows wrists bound together] Beginning with the wrists of both *S hands* crossed in front of the chest, but slightly apart, palms facing in, bring the wrists against each other.

**binoculars** *n.* A small, hand-held double telescope made for viewing with both eyes: *I can see the dancers' faces through the binoculars.*

■ [Mime looking through binoculars] Beginning with both *C hands* near each side of the face, palms facing each other, twist the hands upward and toward each other in a double arc.

**biology** *n.* The scientific study of living matter, including plants and animals: *a course in biology.*

- [Initialized sign similar to sign for **science**] Move both *B hands,* palms facing forward, in large alternating circles toward each other in front of the chest.

**bird** *n.* An animal that lays eggs, is covered with feathers, and has wings: *Some birds can't fly.* Same sign used for: **chicken, coward, fowl.**

- [Mime the action of a bird's beak] Close the index finger and thumb of the right *G hand,* palm facing forward, with a repeated movement in front of the mouth.

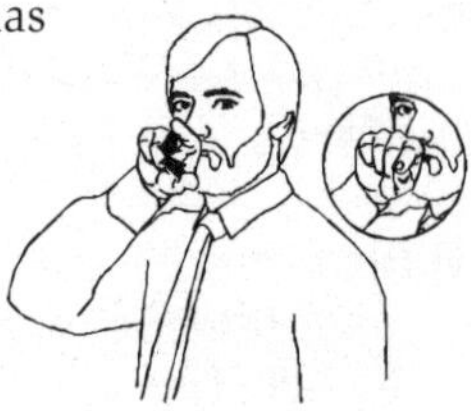

**birth** *n.* A coming into life: *the birth of a baby.* Same sign used for: **born.**

- [Indicates the birth of a baby] Bring the right *open hand,* palm facing in, from the chest forward and down, ending with the back of the right hand in the upturned palm of the left *open hand.*

**birthday** *n.* The day on which a person was born: *to celebrate my birthday.*

- [**birth** + **day**] Bring the right *open hand,* palm facing in, from the chest forward and down, ending with the back of the right hand in the upturned palm of the left *open hand.* Then, with the right elbow resting on the back of the left hand held across the body, palm down, bring the extended right index finger downward toward the left elbow in a large sweeping arc.

**biscuit** *n.* See sign for COOKIE.

**bite** *v.* To seize with the teeth: *to bite an apple.*

- [Mimes teeth biting into something] Bring the fingertips of the right *C hand,* palm facing down, down to close around the index-finger side of the left *open hand.*

**bitter** *adj.* See sign for SOUR.

**bitter cold** *adj. phrase.* See sign for ARCTIC.

**biweekly** *adj.* **1.** Happening once every two weeks: *The homeowners' association has biweekly meetings on the first and third Mondays of the month.* —*adv.* **2.** Every two weeks: *The homeowners' association meets biweekly on the first and third Mondays of the month.* Same sign used for: **every two weeks, two weeks.**

■ [**week** formed with a **two** handshape] Move the palm side of the right *2 hand* from the heel to the fingertips of the left *open hand* held in front of the body, palm facing up.

**bizarre** *adj.* See sign for STRANGE.

**blab** *v.* To talk too much or indiscreetly: *blabbed to his sister about the secret.* Same sign used for: **babble, chat, chatter, gab, gossip, talk, talkative.**

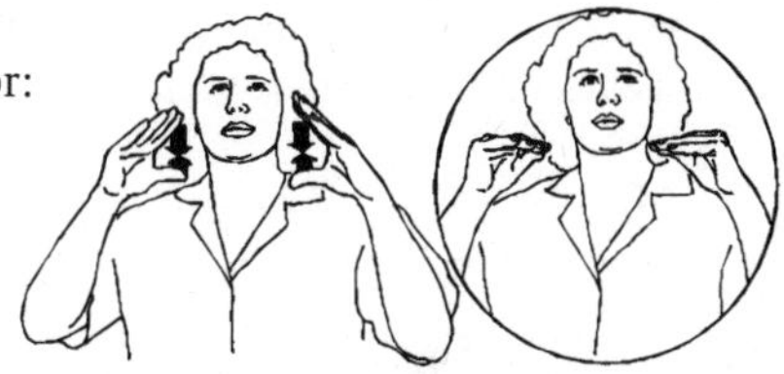

■ [Action of the mouth opening and closing] Beginning with both *flattened C hands* near each side of the face, palms facing each other, close the fingers and thumbs together simultaneously with a double movement.

**black** *adj.* **1.** Of the darkest color: *a simple black dress, appropriate anywhere.* —*n.* **2.** A dark-skinned person, especially one of African descent.

■ Pull the side of the extended right index finger, palm facing down and finger pointing left, from left to right across the forehead.

**blackboard** *n.* See sign for BOARD[1].

**blah** *n.* See sign for NEVER MIND.

**blame**[1] *v.* To hold responsible: *They blamed me for the accident.* Same sign used for: **accuse, at fault, charge.**

■ [Shoves blame at someone] Push the little-finger side of the right *A hand,* palm facing left, forward across the back of the left *A hand,* palm facing down.

**blame**[2] *v.* See sign for FAULT.

**blank**[1] *adj.* Unable to think of or remember something: *My mind is blank.* Same sign used for: **absent-minded.**

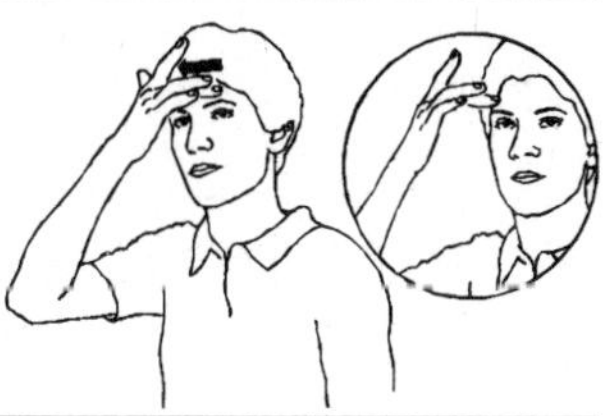

■ [Indicates a blank mind] Bring the bent middle finger of the right *5 hand,* palm facing in, from left to right across the forehead.

**blank**[2] *adj.* See sign for EMPTY.

**blanket** *n.* A large rectangular piece of soft fabric, used as a covering: *Cover the baby with a blanket.*

■ [Initialized sign miming pulling up a blanket to the chest] Move both *B hands* from in front of the body, palms facing down and fingers pointing toward each other, upward, ending with both index fingers against the upper chest.

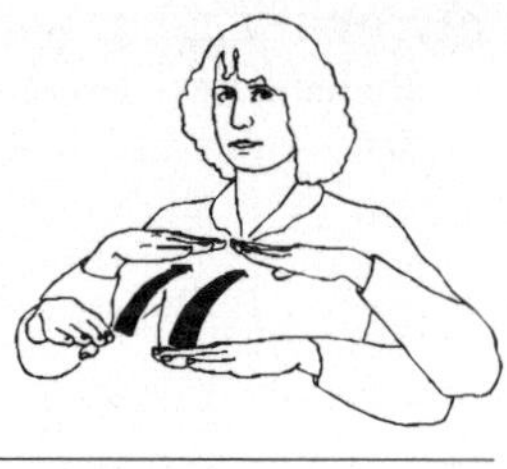

**blaze** *n.* See sign for FIRE[1].

**blend** *v.* See signs for CIRCULATE, COMBINE[1], MAINSTREAM, MESH, MIX[1].

**bless** *v.* To make or pronounce holy: *to bless the sacramental wine.* Related form: **blessed** *adj.*

■ [Taking a blessing from the lips and distributing it] Beginning with the thumbs of both *A hands* touching the lips, palms facing each other, move the hands down and forward while opening into *5 hands* in front of each side of the chest.

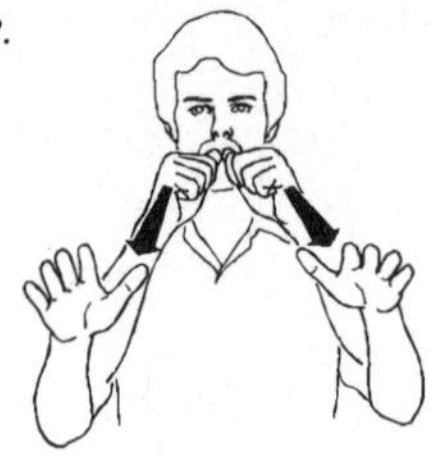

**blind** *adj.* Not able to see: *a blind person listening to books on tape.*

■ [Poking out the eyes] Jab the fingertips of the right *bent V hand* back toward the eyes with a short, deliberate movement.

**blinds** *pl. n.* Something that keeps out light, especially a window covering: *Close the blinds before you leave the house.* Same sign used for: **venetian blinds.**

■ [Represents opening the slats of venetian blinds] Beginning with the little fingers of both *B hands* touching in front of the chest, palms facing in and fingers pointing in opposite directions, move the left hand down to bring the hands slightly apart while spreading the fingers into *5 hands.*

**blizzard** *n.* A fierce snowstorm with very high winds: *The blizzard left high snowdrifts along the street.*

■ [**snow** + **wind**] Beginning with both *5 hands* in front of the face, palms facing out and fingers pointing upward, wiggle the fingers while moving the hands downward with a wavy movement. Then, beginning with both *5 hands* over the right shoulder, palms facing forward and fingers angled up, bring the hands downward to the left with a double movement.

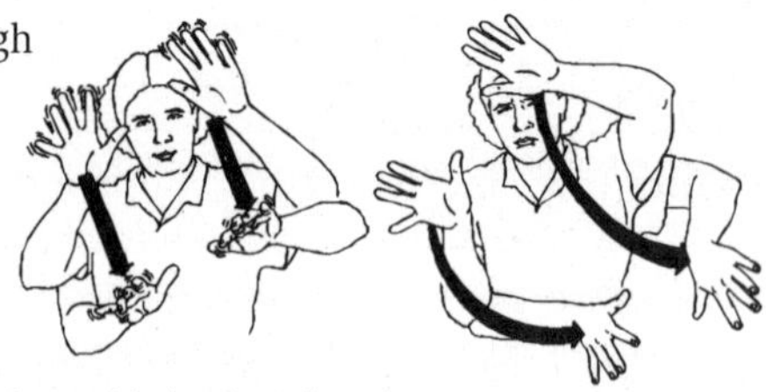

**block**[1] *n.* A solid object, as of wood, with flat sides: *children playing with blocks.* Same sign used for: **cube.**

■ [Shape of a cube or block] Beginning with both *B hands* in front of each side of the chest, palms facing each other and fingers pointing up, bend the hands sharply, ending with the left hand above the right hand, both palms facing down.

**block**[2] *v.* See sign for PREVENT. Related form: **blockage** *n.*

**blond** or **blonde** *adj.* Light in color: *blond hair.*

■ [**yellow** + **hair**] Wiggle the right *Y hand,* palm facing left, near the right side of the head. Then grasp a small strand of hair with the thumb and index finger of the right *F hand,* palm facing left.

**blood** *n.* The red fluid flowing through veins and arteries: *donating blood for the accident victims.* Related forms: **bleed** *v.*, **bloody** *adj.* Same sign used for: **shed.**

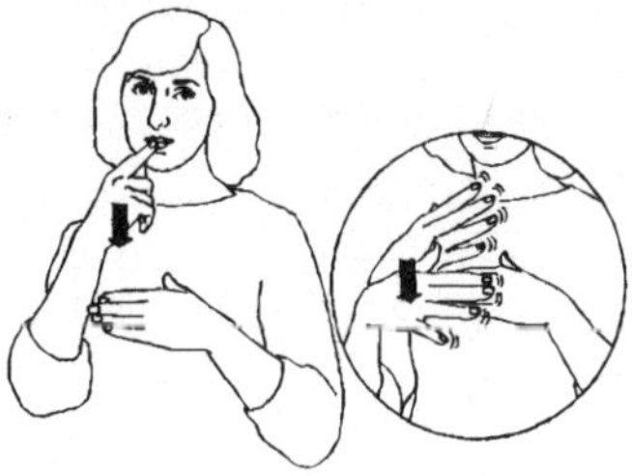

■ [**red** + a gesture representing the flow of blood from a wound] Brush the extended right index finger, palm facing in, downward on the lips. Then open the right hand into a *5 hand* and bring it downward while wiggling the fingers, palm facing in, past the open left hand held across the chest, palm facing in and fingers pointing right.

**bloom** *v.* **1.** To produce blossoms: *The daffodils bloom in spring.* —*n.* **2.** The flower of a plant: *Cut the blooms and put them in a vase.* Same sign used for: **blossom.**

■ [Shows a bloom opening up] Beginning with the fingertips and heels of both *curved 5 hands* touching in front of the chest, palms facing each other, while keeping the heels together, move the fingers away from each other while opening slightly.

**blossom** *n.* See sign for BLOOM.

**blouse** *n.* A garment worn on the upper body: *wearing a silk blouse with a wool skirt.*

■ [Location and shape of woman's blouse] Touch the bent middle fingers of both *5 hands* on each side of the upper chest, and then bring the hands down in an arc, ending with the little fingers of both hands touching the waist, palms facing up and fingers pointing toward each other.

**blow**[1] *v.* To force air through the nose, as to clear it: *Blow your nose.* Same sign used for: **fool.**

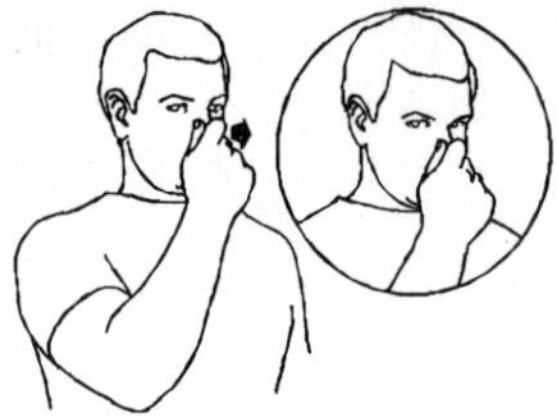

- [Mimes blowing one's nose] Squeeze the nose with the thumb and index finger of the right *A hand* while pulling the hand slightly forward.

**blow**[2] *v.* To force a current of air onto or into: *blowing out the candles; blowing up an air mattress.*

- [Indicates the flow of air through the mouth] Beginning with the back of the *flattened O hand* at the mouth, palm facing forward and fingers pointing forward, move the hand forward a short distance while opening the fingers into a *5 hand.*

**blowup** *n.* **1.** An outburst of temper or a violent quarrel: *They had a terrible blowup just before the wedding.* —*v. phrase.* **2. blow up** To become violently angry: *blew up at his mother for no reason.* Same sign used for: **blow one's top, burst, bust, erupt, temper.**

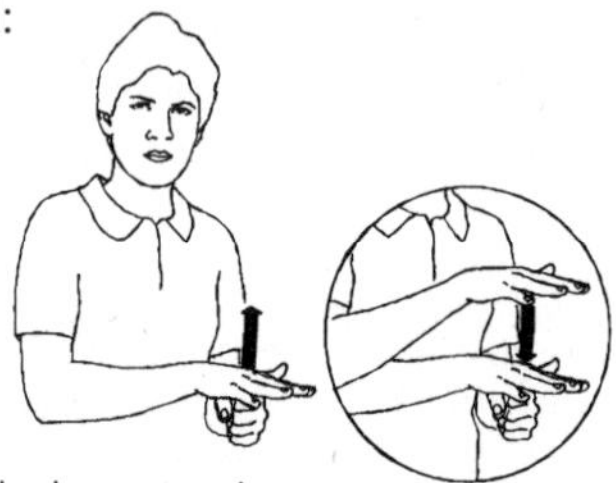

- [Demonstrates the top blowing off of something] Beginning with the palm of the right *5 hand,* palm facing down, on the thumb side of the left *S hand,* palm facing right, bring the right hand upward and back down again.

**blue** *adj.* Having the color of the sky: *a blue flower.*

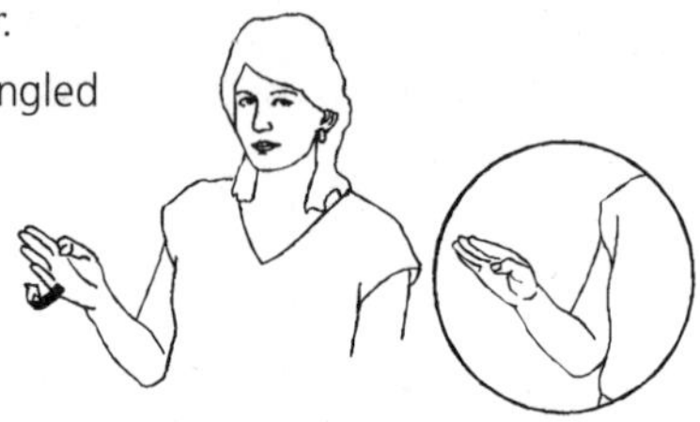

- [Initialized sign] Move the right *B hand,* fingers angled up, back and forth by twisting the wrist in front of the right side of the chest.

**bluff** *v.* See sign for FLATTER. Shared idea of insincerity.

**blur** *v.* To make indistinct or cloudy: *Tears blurred my vision.*

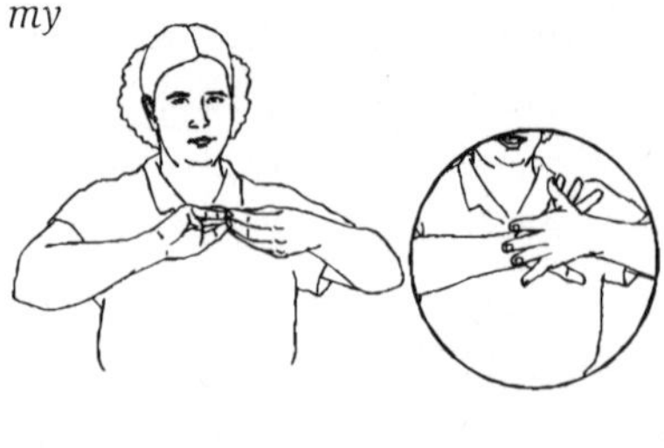

- [Obstructing the view] Beginning with the fingertips of both *flattened O hands* touching in front of the upper chest, left palm facing in and right palm facing out, move the hands in opposite directions across each other while opening into *5 hands,* palms facing each other.

**blurry** *adj.* See sign for VAGUE.

**blush** *v.* To redden, especially in the face: *She blushed at the compliment.* Same sign used for: **flush.**

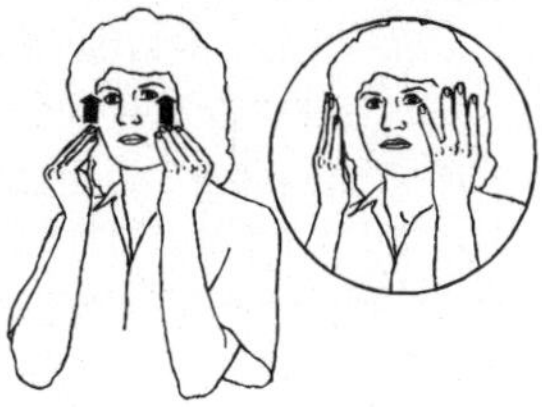

- [Blood rising in the face when blushing] Beginning with both *flattened O hands* near each cheek, palms facing in and fingers pointing up, spread the fingers slowly upward, forming *5 hands.*

**board**[1] *n.* A hard smooth surface used for writing on with chalk: *write on the board.* Same sign used for: **blackboard, chalkboard, wall.**

- [Initialized sign showing the flatness of a chalkboard or a wall] Beginning with the index-finger sides of both *B hands* together in front of the chest, palms facing forward and fingers pointing up, move the hands apart to in front of each shoulder.

**board**[2] *n.* A group of people who supervise the management of an institution: *a school board.*

- [Initialized sign formed in a similar manner to **member**] Touch the index-finger side of the right *B hand,* palm facing left, first to the left side of the chest and then to the right side of the chest.

**board**[3] *n.* A thin rectangular card containing or imprinted with various electronic components and microchips that can be inserted into a computer to provide additional capabilities, such as increased memory or graphics capabilities: *insert a new graphics board.* Same sign used for: **circuit board, expansion board, expansion card.**

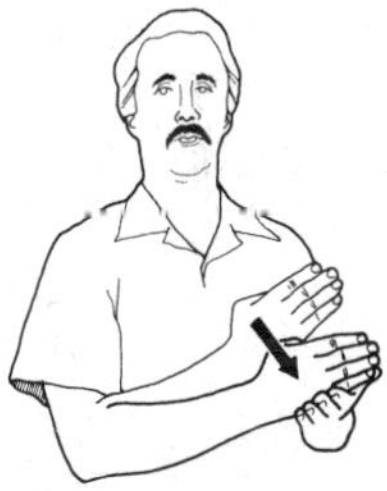

- [Insertion of board in slot] Bring the little-finger side of the right *B hand,* palm left, sharply against the palm of the left *C hand* held in front of the chest, palm up.

**board of directors** *n. phrase.* An elected or appointed group who govern the affairs of a business or corporation: *The board of directors had an emergency meeting to replace the president of the company.*

- [Abbreviation **b-d** similar to sign for **member**] Touch the index-finger side of the right *B hand* to the left side of the chest, and then move the hand in an arc while changing to a *D hand* to touch again on the right side of the chest.

**boast** *v.* See sign for BRAG.

**boat** *n.* An open vessel for traveling on the water: *go fishing in a small boat.* Related form: **boating** *n.* Same sign used for: **cruise, sail, sailing, ship.**

- [Shows the shape of a boat's hull] With the little-finger sides of both *curved hands* together, palms facing up, move the hands forward in a bouncing double arc.

**body** *n.* The trunk or torso of a person or animal, excluding the head and limbs: *to wrap a blanket around my body.*

- [Location of the body] Touch the fingers of both *open hands,* palms facing in and fingers pointing toward each other, first on each side of the chest and then on each side of the waist.

**boiling mad** *adj. phrase.* Extremely angry and upset; stirred up: *I was boiling mad when I saw the repair bill.* Same sign used for: **burning mad, flare up, fume, furious, resent, seethe, smolder.**

- [**fire**[1] formed close to the body as if boiling inside] Wiggle the fingers of the right *5 hand,* palm facing the chest, in a flat circle under the left *open hand,* held close to the chest, palm facing down.

**bold** *adj.* See signs for BRAVE, CONFIDENT, STRICT, WELL[1].

**bologna** or **baloney** *Informal n.* A large cooked and smoked sausage: *slices of bologna on the sandwich.*

- [The shape of sausage links] Beginning with the thumbs and index fingers of both *C hands* touching in front of the chest, palms facing down, move the hands apart while closing the fingers, ending with both *S hands* in front of each side of the chest.

**bolt** *n.* See sign for LIGHTNING.

**bomb** *n.* See sign for EXPLODE.

**bond** *n.* See sign for RELATIONSHIP.

**bondage** *n.* See sign for BIND.

**bone**[1] *n.* One of the structures forming the skeleton of a vertebrate animal: *I broke a bone in my arm.*

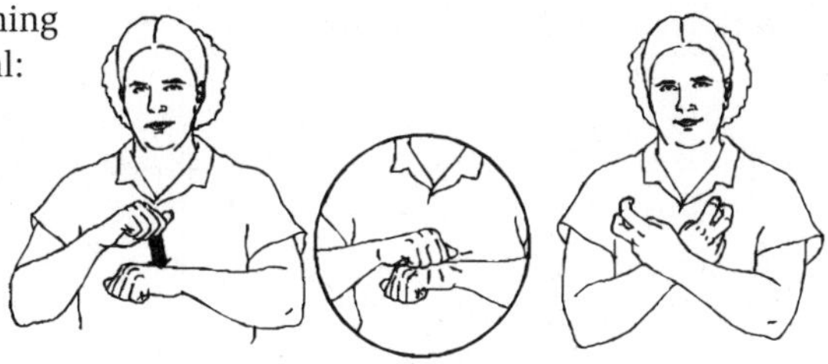

■ [**rock**[1] + **skeleton**] Tap the palm side of the right *A hand,* palm facing down, against the back of the wrist of the left *A hand.* Then, with the hands crossed at the wrists, tap the fingers of both *bent V hands* on the opposite side of the chest, palms facing in.

**bone**[2] *n.* See sign for SKELETON.

**bonus** *n.* See sign for ADD[2].

**book**[1] *n.* A long printed work on consecutive sheets of paper bound together between covers: *to read a book on the plane.*

■ [Represents opening a book] Beginning with the palms of both *open hands* together in front of the chest, fingers angled forward, bring the hands apart at the top while keeping the little fingers together.

**book**[2] *v.* See sign for APPOINTMENT.

**boom** *v.* See sign for EXPLODE.

**boost** *n.* See sign for SUPPORT.

**boots** *n.* A pair of coverings for the foot and lower part of the leg, made of rubber, leather, etc.: *to wear boots in cold weather.* Same sign used for: **galoshes.**

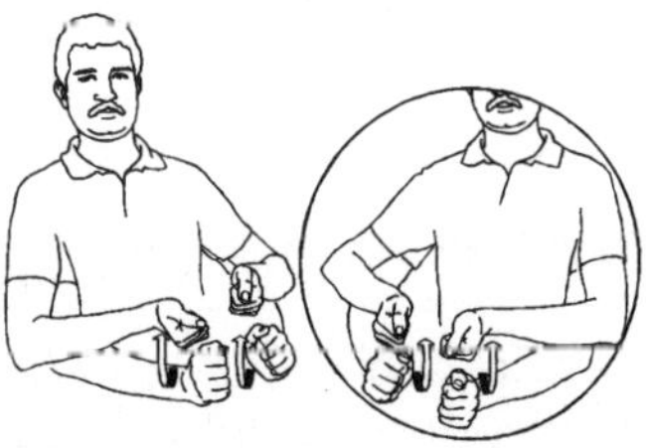

■ [Mime pulling on boots] Beginning with both *A hands* in front of the left side of the waist, palms facing each other, bring the hands sharply back and upward toward the body by twisting the wrists. Repeat in front of the right side of the waist.

**boring**[1] *adj.* Uninteresting; tedious; tiresome: *a boring lecture.* Related forms: **bore** *v.,* **bored** *adj.* Same sign used for: **dull, monotonous, tedious.**

■ [Boring a hole on the side of the nose] With the tip of the extended right index finger touching the side of the nose, palm facing down, twist the hand forward.

**boring**[2] *adj.* See sign for DRY.

**born** *adj.* See sign for BIRTH.

**borrow** *v.* Get something from another with the understanding that it will be returned: *I'd like to borrow your sweater till tomorrow.* Same sign used for: **lend me.**

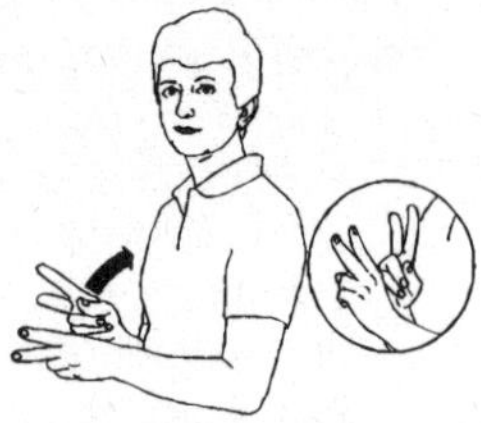

- [Bring borrowed thing toward oneself; opposite of movement for **lend**] With the little-finger side of the right *V hand* across the index-finger side of the left *V hand,* bring the hands back, ending with the right index finger against the chest.

**bosom** *n.* See sign for BREAST.

**boss** *n.* See signs for CAPTAIN, CHIEF.

**both** *adj.* **1.** Being the two: *Both houses are mine.* —*pron.* **2.** The two together: *I like both, but I live in the smaller one.* Same sign used for: **pair.**

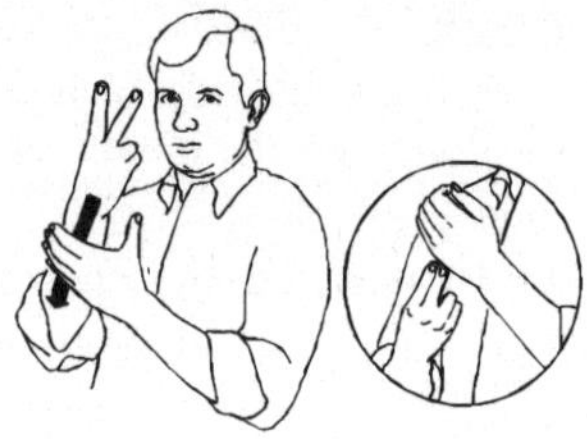

- [Two things pulled together to form a pair] Bring the right *2 hand,* palm facing in, downward in front of the chest through the left *C hand,* palm facing in and fingers pointing right, closing the left hand around the right fingers as they pass through and pulling the right fingers together.

**bother** *v.* See sign for ANNOY.

**bottle** *n.* A glass or plastic container with a narrow neck: *a medicine bottle.* Same sign used for: **glass.**

- [Shape of a bottle] Beginning with the little-finger side of the right *C hand,* palm facing left, on the upturned left *open hand,* raise the right hand.

**bottom** *n.* See sign for BELOW[1].

**boulevard** *n.* See sign for ROAD.

**bounce** *v.* To cause to spring into the air after striking a surface: *bounce a ball.* Same sign used for: **dribble.**

- [Mime bouncing a ball] Move the right *open hand,* palm facing down, up and down in front of the right side of the body with a repeated movement.

**bound** *v.* See sign for BIND.

**boundary** *n.* The limiting line of an area or between two areas: *to put a fence on the boundary between their yard and ours.*

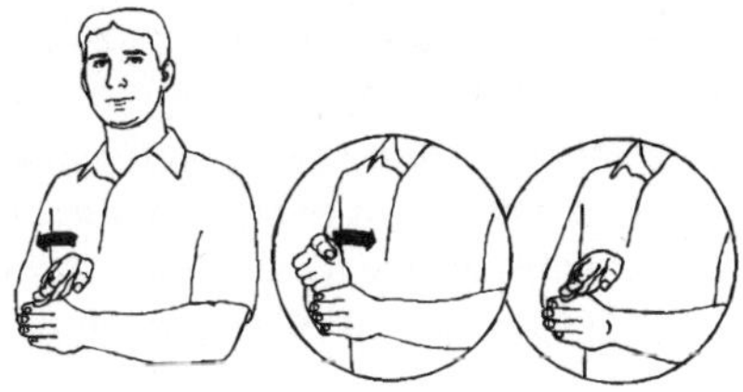

■ [Demonstrates the boundary of something] Beginning with the little-finger side of the right *B hand,* palm facing left and fingers pointing forward, on the index-finger side of the left *B hand,* palm facing right and fingers pointing forward, tip the right hand from side to side with a double movement.

**bow**[1] *v.* To bend the head or body: *to bow before the king.* Same sign used for: **bend, nod.**

■ [Represents bowing one's head] Beginning with the forearm of the right *S hand,* palm facing forward, against the thumb side of the left *B hand,* palm facing down and fingers pointing right, bend the right arm downward while bending the body forward.

**bow**[2] *n.* A knotted ribbon with two large loops: *She likes to wear a bow in her hair.* Same sign used for: **ribbon.**

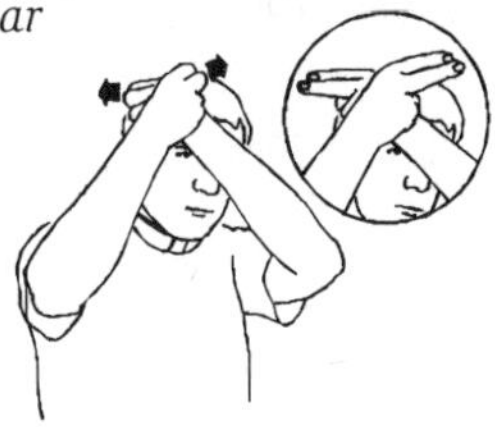

■ [The shape of a hair bow] With both *S hands* crossed on the right side of the head, palms facing in, flip the *H fingers* of both hands outward with a deliberate movement.

**bow**[3] *v.* See sign for HAIL[2].

**bowl** *n.* **1.** A somewhat deep, rounded dish or basin: *using a large bowl for soup.* **2.** The contents of a bowl; bowlful: *a bowl of cereal.* Same sign used for: **basket, pot.**

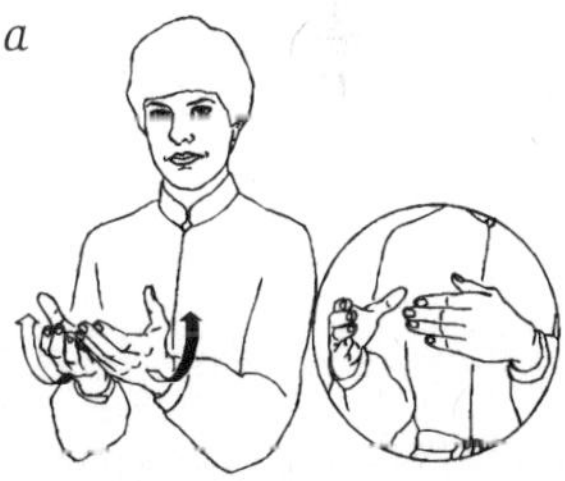

■ [The shape of a bowl] Beginning with the little fingers of both *C hands* touching, palms facing up, bring the hands apart and upward, ending with the palms facing each other.

**bowling** *n.* An indoor game in which players take turns rolling a large, heavy ball at a group of pins: *to go bowling.* Related form: **bowl** *v.*

■ [Mime throwing a bowling ball] Swing the right *bent 3 hand,* palm facing forward and fingers pointing down, from near the right hip forward and upward in an arc.

**box** *n.* A container with four sides: *a box of toys.* Same sign used for: **package, present, room.**

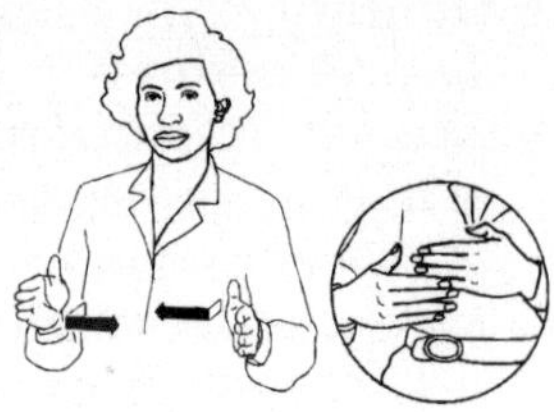

■ [Shape of a box] Beginning with both *open hands* in front of each side of the chest, palms facing each other and fingers pointing forward, move the hands deliberately in opposite directions, ending with the left hand near the chest and the right hand several inches forward of the left hand, both palms facing in. (This sign may also be formed with the hands beginning in the final position and then changing to the first position.)

**boy** *n.* A male child: *a little boy.* Same sign used for: **male.**

■ [Grasping the visor of a boy's cap] Beginning with the index-finger side of the right *flattened C hand* near the right side of the forehead, palm facing left, close the fingers to the thumb with a repeated movement.

**boycott** *v.* See sign for COMPLAIN.

**bracelet** *n.* An ornamental band for the wrist: *a gold bracelet.*

■ [The location of a bracelet] With the right thumb and middle finger encircling the left wrist, twist the right hand forward with a double movement.

**braces** *pl. n.* An oral appliance consisting of wires and bands used to correct misalignment of the teeth and jaws: *The teenager's teeth hurt from her braces.* Same sign used for: **retainer.**

■ [Shows location of braces] Bring the fingertips of the right *bent V hand* from left to right in front of the teeth.

**bracket** *n.* See sign for CLASS.

**brag** *v.* To praise oneself; speak with excess pride about one's appearance, accomplishments, possessions, etc.: *Please stop bragging about your new car.* Same sign used for: **boast, show off.**

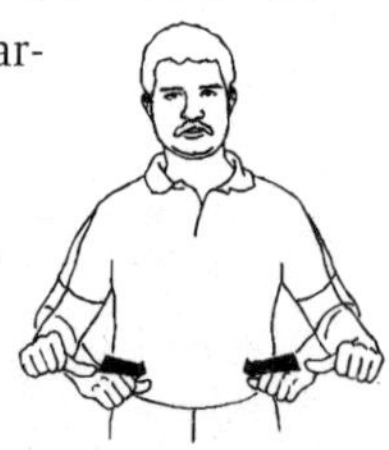

■ [Natural gesture while bragging] Tap the thumbs of both *10 hands,* palms facing down, against each side of the waist with a double movement.

**braid** *n.* **1.** Strands of hair woven together: *to wear a braid.* —*v.* **2.** To weave strands of hair together: *braiding her hair.*

■ [Represents hair being braided] Beginning with both *X hands* near the left side of the head, palms facing each other, twist the wrists with a repeated alternating movement while moving the hands downward.

**brain** *n.* See sign for MIND.

**brake** *n.* **1.** A device for stopping or slowing the movement of a vehicle or other mechanism: *Step on the brake.* —*v.* **2.** To slow or stop by using a brake: *I brake for animals.*

- [Shows action of stepping on the brake] Push the right *A hand* downward in front of the right side of the body, palm facing forward, with a double movement.

**brand** *n.* See signs for LABEL, STAMP[2].

**brandy** *n.* See sign for WHISKEY.

**brat** *n.* See sign for CONCEITED.

**brave** *adj.* Having the inner strength to confront danger: *a brave soldier.* Same sign used for: **bold, courage.**

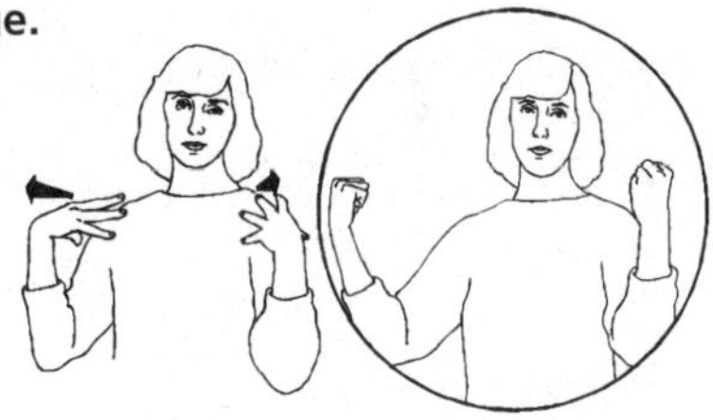

- [Hands seem to take strength from the body] Beginning with the fingertips of both *5 hands* on each shoulder, palms facing in and fingers pointing back, bring the hands deliberately forward while closing into *S hands*.

**bread** *n.* A baked food made with flour and raised with yeast: *eating bread and butter.*

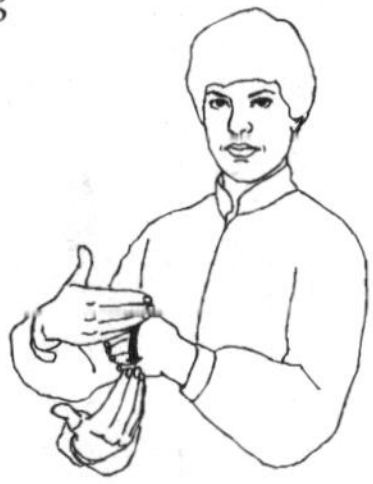

- [Slicing a loaf of bread] Move the fingertips of the right *bent hand* downward on the back of the left *open hand* with a repeated movement, both palms facing in.

**break**[1] *v.* To force to come apart violently: *break a dish.* Same sign used for: **tear apart.**

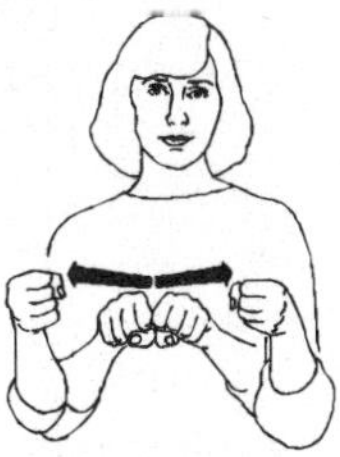

- [Mime breaking something] Beginning with both *S hands* in front of the body, index fingers touching and palms facing down, move the hands away from each other while twisting the wrists with a deliberate movement, ending with the palms facing each other.

**break**[2] *n.* See signs for HALFTIME, INTERMISSION.

**break**[3] *n., v.* See sign for FRACTURE. Related form: **broken** *adj.*

**break down** *v. phrase.* To cease to function; become inoperative: *The engine broke down.* Same sign used for: **cave in, collapse, crash, destruction, fall through, tear down.**

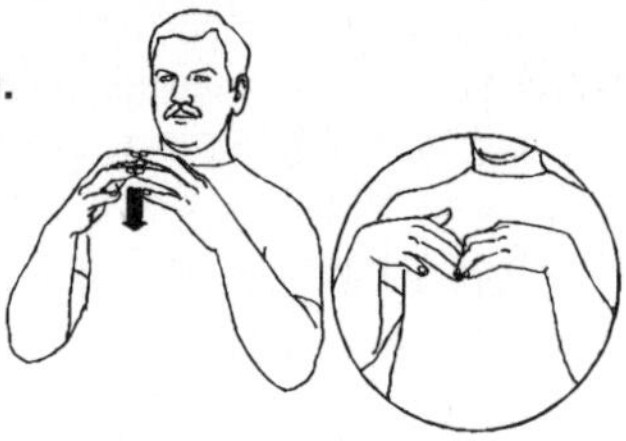

■ [Indicates things crumbling down] Beginning with the fingertips of both *curved 5 hands* touching in front of the chest, palms facing each other, allow the fingers to loosely drop, ending with the palms facing down.

---

**breakfast** *n.* The first meal of the day: *It's wise to eat breakfast.*

■ [**eat** + **morning**] Bring the fingertips of the right *flattened O hand* to the lips. Then, with the left *open hand* in the crook of the bent right arm, bring the right *open hand* upward, palm facing in.

---

**breast** *n.* **1.** Either of the two mammary organs on the upper front part of the female body: *the baby fed from the mother's breast.* **2.** The female chest: *clutched the child to her breast.* Same sign used for: **bosom, bust.**

■ [Location of breasts] Touch the fingertips of the right *bent hand* first on the right side of the chest and then on the left side of the chest.

---

**breath** *n.* **1.** The air inhaled and exhaled from the lungs: *I am all out of breath from running.* **2.** a single such inhalation: *Take a big breath.* Related form: **breathe** *v.* Same sign used for: **exhale, expel, inhale, pant, respiration.**

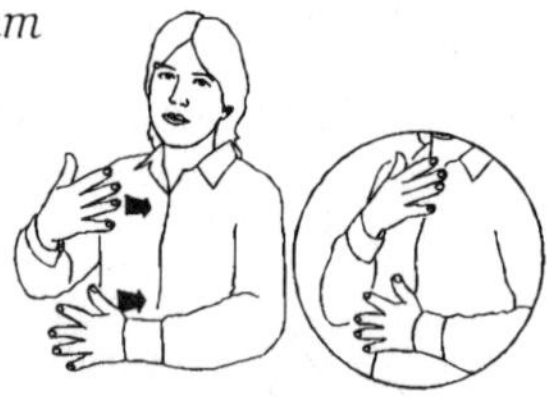

■ [Indicates the movement of the lungs when breathing] With the right *5 hand* in front of the chest above the left *5 hand,* fingers pointing in opposite directions and palms in, move both hands forward and back toward the chest with a double movement.

---

**breed** *v.* See signs for CONFLICT[1], PREGNANT[1].

---

**breeze** *n.* A light, gentle wind: *A breeze blew through the window.*

■ [Shows movement of the wind] Beginning with both *4 hands* in front of the body, palms in and fingers pointing toward each other, swing the hands forward then back with a double movement by bending the wrists.

---

**bride** *n.* A newly married woman or one about to be married: *the bride and groom.* Same sign used for: **bridesmaid.**

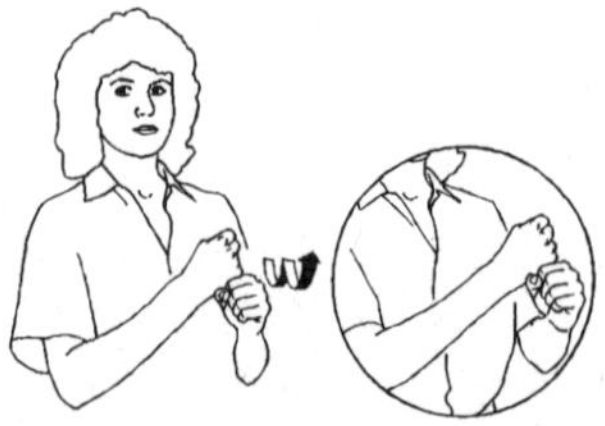

■ [Mime walking with a bride's bouquet] With the little-finger side of the right *S hand* on the thumb-side of the left *S hand,* move the hands forward a short distance and then forward again.

**bridesmaid** *n.* See sign for BRIDE.

**bridge** *n.* A structure built to provide a passage over a river or road: *to walk over the bridge.*

■ [Shows the structure of supports for a bridge] Touch the fingertips of the right *V hand,* palm facing left, first to the bottom of the wrist and then near the elbow of the left arm held in front of the chest, palm facing down.

**brief** *adj.* Lasting for a short time or using few words: *a brief announcement.* See sign for SHORT. Same sign used for: **abbreviate, condense, reduce, squeeze, summarize.**

■ [Squeeze information together as if to condense] Beginning with both *5 hands* in front of the chest, right hand above the left hand and fingers pointing in opposite directions, bring the hands toward each other while squeezing the fingers together, ending with the little-finger side of the right *S hand* on top of the thumb side of the left *S hand*.

**bright** *adj.* Very light or clear: *a room full of bright sunlight.* Same sign used for: **clarify, clear, light, radiant.**

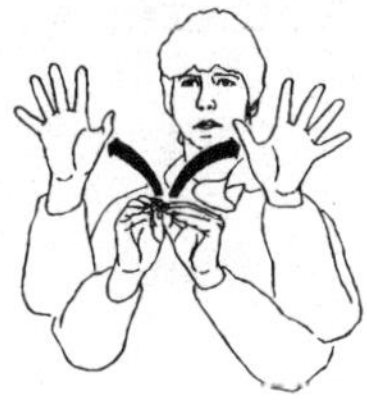

■ [Hands spread to reveal brightness] Beginning with the fingertips of both *flattened O hands* touching in front of the chest, palms facing each other, move the hands quickly upward in arcs to above each shoulder while opening to *5 hands*.

**brilliant** *adj.* See sign for SMART.

**bring** *v.* To carry something along: *You'd better bring your jacket to the picnic.* Same sign used for: **deliver, return, transport.**

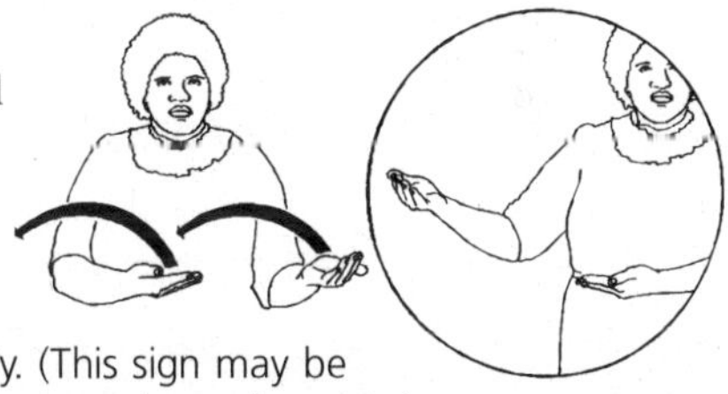

■ [Moving an object from one location to another] Move both *open hands,* palms facing up, from in front of the left side of the body in large arcs to the right side of the body. (This sign may be formed in the direction of the referent or its proposed new location.)

**broad** *adj.* See signs for GENERAL[1], WIDE.

**broadcast** *v., n.* See sign for ADVERTISE.

**broad-minded** *adj.* Free of prejudice: *The jury should remain broad-minded throughout the trial.* Same sign used for: **liberal, open-minded, tolerant.**

■ Beginning with both *open hands* near each other in front of the forehead, palms angled toward each other, move the hands forward and outward away from each other.

**brochure** *n.* See sign for MAGAZINE.

**broke** *adj. Informal.* See sign for PENNILESS.

**broom** *n.* A brush with a long handle for sweeping: *to sweep the floor with a broom.* Same sign used for: **sweep.**

- [Mime sweeping] Beginning with both *S hands* in front of the right side of the body, right hand above the left hand and palms facing in, move the hands to the right with a double swinging movement.

**brother** *n.* A son of the same parents: *presents from my uncle for my brother and me.*

- Beginning with the thumb of the right *L hand* touching the right side of the forehead, palm facing left, move the right hand downward, landing across the thumb side of the left *L hand,* palm facing right.

**brotherhood** *n.* See sign for ASSOCIATE.

**brother-in-law** *n.* The brother of one's husband or wife or the husband of one's sister: *to visit my brother-in-law.*

- [**brother** + **law**] Beginning with the thumb of the right *L hand* touching the right side of the forehead, palm facing left, move the right hand downward, placing the palm side of the right *L hand* first on the fingers and then on the heel of the palm of the left *open hand,* palm facing up and fingers pointing forward.

**brown** *adj.* Having the color of coffee: *a brown bear.*

- [Initialized sign] Slide the index-finger side of the right *B hand,* palm facing left, down the right cheek.

**browse** *v.* See sign for LOOK OVER.

**brush**[1] *n.* **1.** A tool with bristles used for grooming the hair: *a brush and comb.* —*v.* **2.** To use a brush to groom the hair: *brush my hair.* Same sign used for: **hairbrush.**

- [Mime brushing one's hair] Move the palm of the right *A hand* down the right side of the head with a repeated movement.

**brush**[2] *n.* See sign for PAINT.

**bubble** *n.* A thin spherical film of liquid, usually forming an envelope filled with air: *covered with soap bubbles.*

■ [Shows action of bubbles] Wiggle the fingers of both *curved 5 hands,* palms facing down, while moving them upward a short distance.

**bucket** *n.* A pail made of wood, plastic, or metal: *a bucket of coal.* Same sign used for: **pail, pot.**

■ [Shape of a bucket + mime holding a bucket's handle] Beginning with both *C hands* in front of each side of the chest, palms facing each other, move them upward a short distance. Then move the right *S hand* upward a short distance in front of the right side of the body with a double movement.

**buckle** *n.* **1.** A clasp used to fasten two loose ends, as on a belt: *a gold buckle.* —*v.* **2.** To fasten with a buckle: *Buckle your seat belt.* Same sign used for: **seat belt.**

■ [Mime fastening a seat belt] Bring both *bent V hands* from in front of each side of the waist, palms facing each other, around to mesh the fingers together in front of the waist.

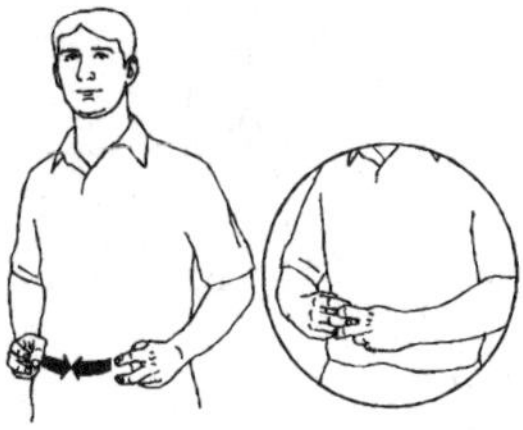

**budget**[1] *n.* **1.** A plan for spending money based on an estimate of expected income for a given period: *to make a monthly budget.* —*v.* **2.** To make a such a plan: *They carefully budgeted to save for a car.* Same sign used for: **exchange.**

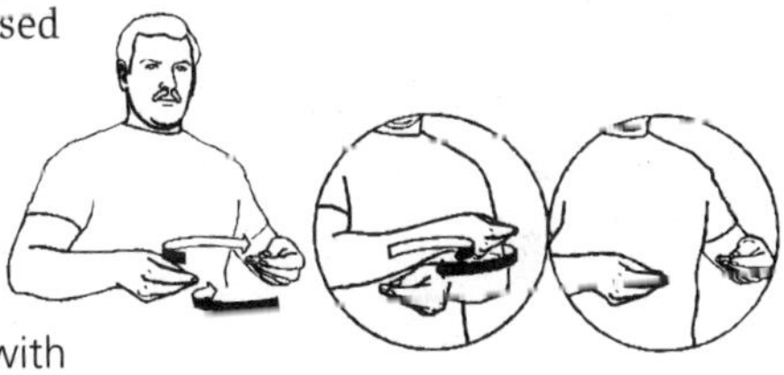

■ [Shows moving money around] Beginning with both *flattened O hands* in front of each side of the body, palms facing each other, move the right hand in a circle back toward the body, over the left hand, and forward to return to its original position.

**budget**[2] *n.* See sign for TRADE.

**bug** *n.* **1.** An insect, especially one that crawls: *a bug under a rock.* **2.** A mistake in a computer program or system or a malfunction in computer hardware: *The system has a bug that makes it shut down without warning.* Same sign used for: **insect.**

■ With the extended thumb of the right *3 hand* on the nose, palm facing left, bend the extended index and middle fingers with a repeated movement.

**build** *v.* To construct by putting materials or parts together: *to build a boat.* Related form: **building** *n.* Same sign used for: **construct, construction.**

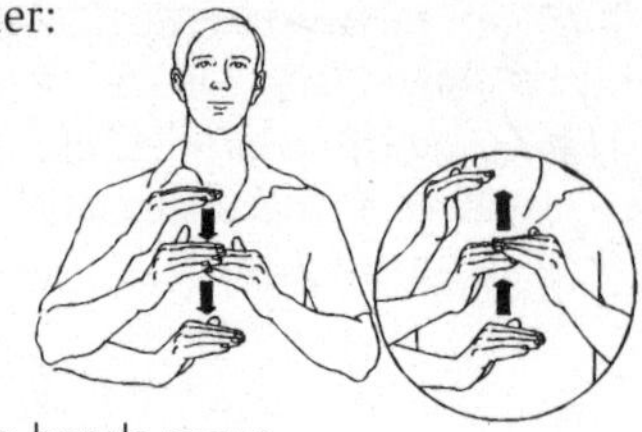

■ [Shows putting one thing upon another to build something] Beginning with the fingers of the right *bent hand* overlapping the fingers of the left *bent hand* in front of the chest, palms facing down, reverse the position of the hands with a repeated movement as the hands move upward.

**bulk** *n.* See sign for PILE[1].

**bulletin board** *n. phrase.* A board on which notices are posted: *Put the rest of the announcements on the bulletin board.* Same sign used for: **post, post a notice, poster.**

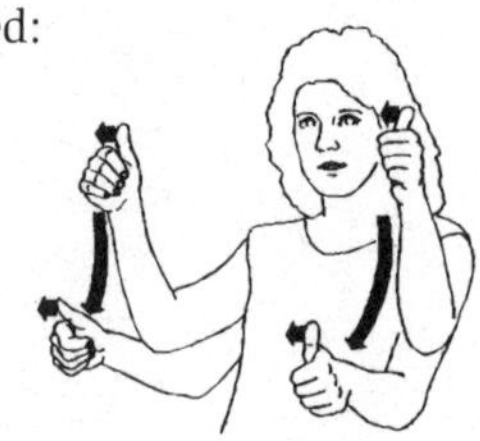

■ [Mime posting something on a wall] Push the thumbs of both *10 hands,* palms facing each other, forward with a short movement, first in front of each shoulder and then in front of each side of the body.

**bullheaded** *adj.* See sign for CONTRARY[1].

**bully** *n.* See sign for CONCEITED.

**bum** *n. Informal.* See sign for FARM. Shared idea of a country bumpkin.

**bump**[1] *n.* A swelling, as one caused by a blow: *a large bump on his head.* Same sign used for: **lump, node.**

■ [Shape of a bump on the head] Beginning with the fingertips of the right *curved 5 hand* on the right side of the head, palm facing in, move the hand upward a short distance.

**bump**[2] *n.* (alternate sign) Same sign used for: **lump, node.**

■ [Shape of small swelling] Beginning with the side of the extended right index finger, palm facing left, on the back of the left *open hand,* palm facing down, bring the right finger upward in a small arc, ending near the left fingers.

**bumper-to-bumper** *adj.* Characterized by long lines of slow-moving cars: *bumper-to-bumper traffic.*

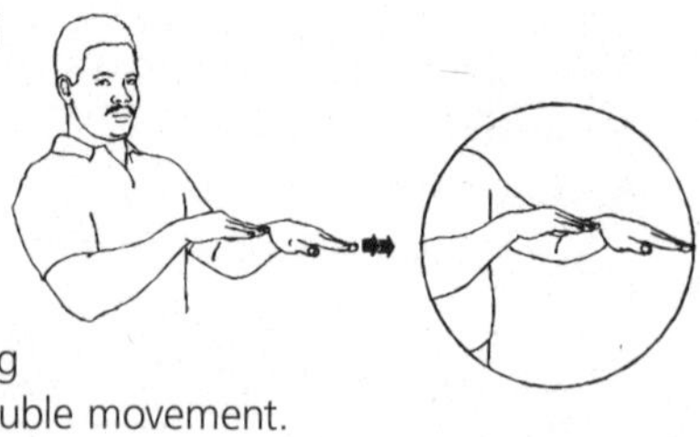

■ [Demonstrates a vehicle very close behind another vehicle] Beginning with the right *open hand* near the base of the thumb of the left *open hand,* both palms facing down and fingers pointing forward, move the hands forward with a short double movement.

**bunch** *n.* See sign for CLASS.

**bunk beds** *n. phrase.* Narrow beds stacked one above another: *to sleep in bunk beds.*

■ [**bed** + the location of one bunk bed above another] Rest the right cheek at an angle on the palm of the right *open hand.* Then place the left *H hand* above the right *H hand,* both palms facing down and fingers pointing forward.

**burden** *n.* A load, especially one that is carried with difficulty: *to carry the burden of supporting the family.* Same sign used for: **bear, fault, liability, obligation, responsible, responsibility.**

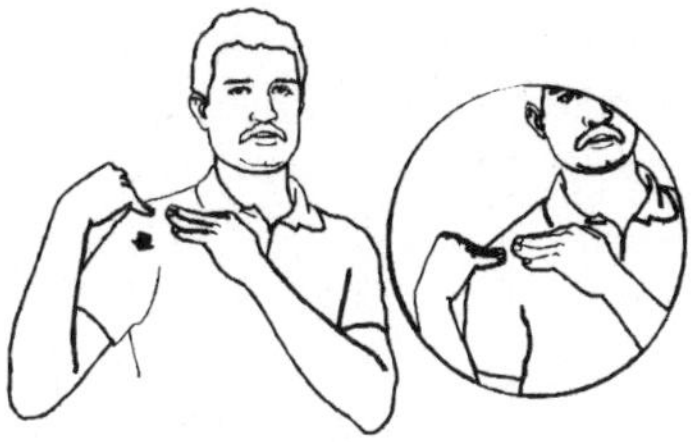

■ [The weight of responsibility on the shoulder] With the fingertips of both *bent hands* on the right shoulder, push the shoulder down slightly.

**burglary** *n.* See signs for ROB, SHOPLIFT, STEAL.

**burn**[1] *v.* **1.** To be on fire: *The house is burning.* **2.** To damage or destroy by fire: *The furniture was badly burned.* **3.** To produce by fire: *burned a hole in the rug.*

■ [Flames leaping up from a fire] Wiggle the fingers of both *curved 5 hands* with a repeated movement in front of each side of the body, palms facing up.

**burn**[2] *v.* See sign for LASER.

**burning mad** *adj. phrase.* See sign for BOILING MAD.

**burp** *n., v.* See sign for BELCH.

**burst** *v.* See signs for BAWL OUT, BLOWUP.

**burst out** *v. phrase.* See sign for BAWL OUT.

**bury** *v.* To put a dead body in the earth: *to bury the dead bird.* Same sign used for: **grave.**

■ [Shape of a mound of dirt on a grave] Move both *curved hands,* palms facing down and fingers pointing down, back toward the body in double arcs.

**bus** *n.* A large motor vehicle with seats to carry many passengers: *I took a bus to Chicago.*

- [Initialized sign] Beginning with the little-finger side of the right *B hand* touching the index-finger side of the left *B hand,* palms facing in opposite directions, move the right hand back toward the right shoulder.

**bust**[1] *v.* See sign for BLOWUP.

**bust**[2] *n.* See sign for BREAST.

**bust**[3] *v.* See sign for MEAN[1].

**busy**[1] *adj.* **1.** Actively engaged in doing something; thoroughly involved: *I'm too busy with work to relax.* **2.** Filled with activity: *a busy day.*

- [Initialized sign] Brush the base of the right *B hand,* palm facing forward, with a repeated rocking movement on the back of the left *open hand,* palm facing down.

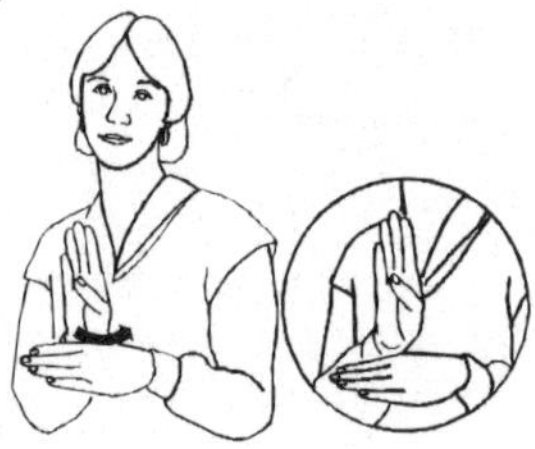

**busy**[2] *adj.* (alternate sign) Same sign used for: **lots to do.**

- [Fingerspell **d-o** in a continuous pattern] With both *D hands* in front of the chest, palms facing up, pinch the index fingers and thumbs together repeatedly while moving the hands in repeated circles. [Note: the number of repetitions increases to reflect an increase in things to be done.]

**but** *conj.* On the other hand: *You may go, but come home early.* Same sign used for: **although, different, however, unlike.**

- [Indicates opinions moving in opposite directions] Beginning with both extended index fingers crossed in front of the chest, palms facing forward, bring the hands apart with a deliberate movement.

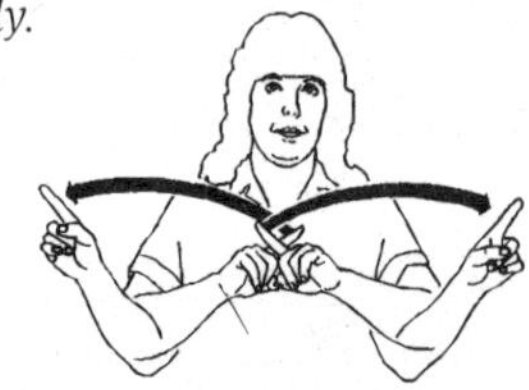

**butter** *n.* A yellowish fatty solid that separates from milk or cream when it is churned, used as a spread: *put butter on my bread.* Same sign used for: **margarine.**

- [Mime spreading butter] Wipe the extended fingers of the right *U hand,* palm facing down and thumb extended, across the palm of the left *open hand* with a repeated movement, drawing the right fingers back into the palm each time.

**butterfly** *n.* An insect with a slender body and large, colored wings: *a butterfly poised on the flower.*

■ [Symbolizes shape of butterfly's wings] With the thumb of the right *open hand* hooked around the thumb of the left *open hand,* both palms facing the chest, bend the fingers of both hands in and out with a repeated movement.

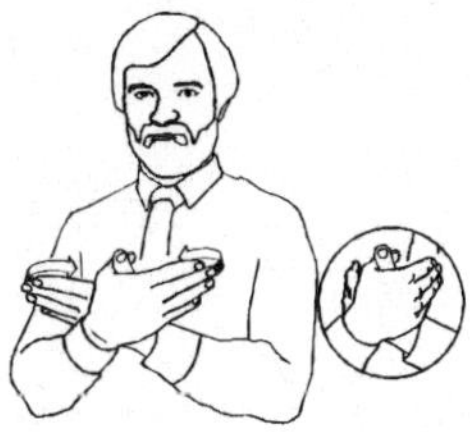

**butt in** *v. phrase.* See sign for NOSY[2].

**button**[1] *n.* A small disk or knob that fastens one piece of cloth to another when passed through a buttonhole or loop: *a row of buttons on the sweater.*

■ [Shape and location of buttons] Touch the index-finger side of the right *F hand,* palm facing left, first in the center of the chest, and then lower on the chest.

**button**[2] *n.* See sign for BADGE.

**buy** *v.* To acquire by paying a price: *buy a toy.* Same sign used for: **purchase.**

■ [Shows taking money from the hand to buy something] Beginning with the back of the right *flattened O hand,* palm facing up, in the upturned palm of left *open hand,* move the right hand forward in an arc.

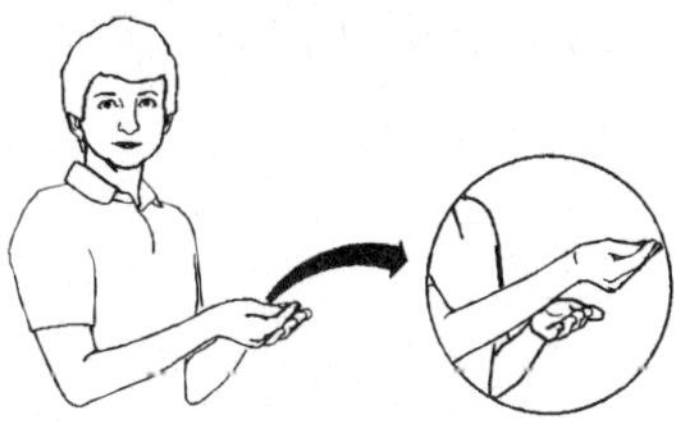

**buyer** *n.* See sign for CUSTOMER[1].

**by** *prep.* See sign for PASS.

**by accident** *prep. phrase.* See sign for ACCIDENTALLY.

**bye** *interj.* See sign for GOOD-BYE.

**by mistake** *prep. phrase.* See sign for ACCIDENTALLY.

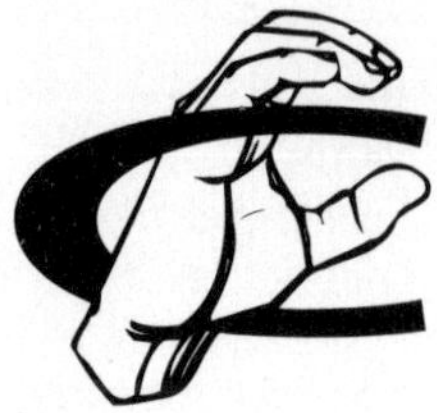

**cab** *n.* A public passenger automobile that can be hired with its driver for individual trips: *to take a cab to the airport.* Same sign used for: **taxi.**

- [Represents the lighted dome on top of a taxi] Tap the fingertips of the right *C hand,* palm facing down, on the top of the head with a double movement.

---

**cabbage** *n.* A vegetable with thick leaves forming a round, compact head: *eat corned beef and cabbage.* Same sign used for: **lettuce.**

- [The head represents a head of cabbage] Tap the heel of the right *curved hand* against the right side of the head with a repeated movement.

---

**cabinet** *n.* A piece of furniture with shelves and drawers or doors: *Put the dishes in the cabinet.*

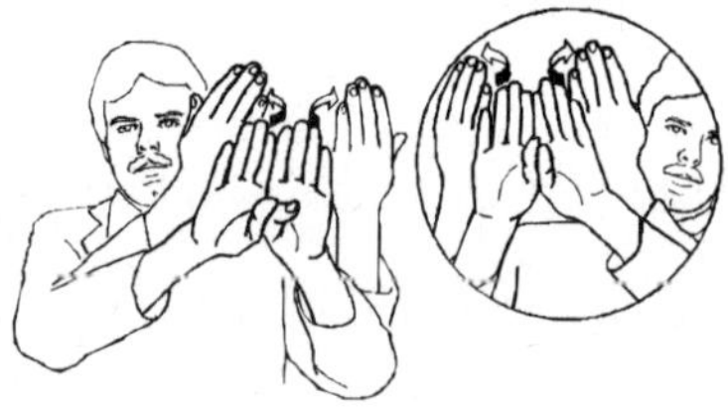

- [Demonstrates opening and closing of multiple cabinet doors] Beginning with the index-finger sides of both *B hands* together in front of the left side of the head, palms facing forward, bring the hands apart by twisting the wrists in opposite directions, ending with the palms facing back. Repeat in front of the right side of the head.

---

**cable** *n.* See sign for WIRE.

---

**cable television** or **CATV** (*Originally: Community Antenna Television*) *n. phrase.* A system for providing televison signals to consumers through optical fibers or coaxial cables as contrasted with satellite signals: *I subscribe to cable TV.*

- [Shows shape of cable + **T-V**] Beginning with both *S hands* held in front of the chest, left hand nearer the chest than the right hand and both palms facing down, bring the right hand back toward the chest to hit on the little-finger side of the left hand. Then form a T and a V in front of the chest.

---

**cafeteria** *n.* A restaurant where people carry their own food to the tables: *to eat in the school cafeteria.* Alternate form: **café.**

■ [Initialized sign similar to sign for **restaurant**] Touch the index-finger side of the right *C hand,* palm facing left, first on the right side of the chin and then on the left side.

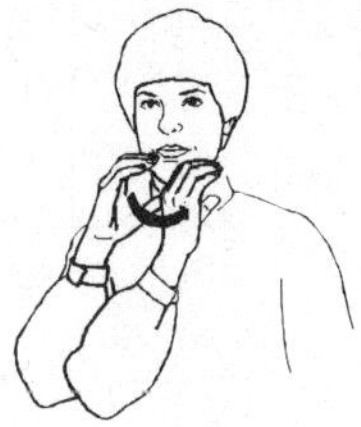

**cage** *n.* A place enclosed with wire or bars: *a bird cage.*

■ [Shape of a wire cage] Beginning with the fingertips of both *4 hands* touching in front of the chest, palms facing in, bring the hands away from each other in a circular movement back toward the chest, ending with the palms facing forward.

**cake** *n.* A sweet baked food made of a batter containing flour, eggs, sugar, and other ingredients: *a chocolate cake.*

■ [Represents a cake rising] Beginning with the fingertips of the right *curved 5 hand* on the palm of the left *open hand,* raise the right hand upward in front of the chest.

**calculator** *n.* An electronic device used for mathematical calculations: *Add up the total on the calculator.*

■ [Mime using a calculator] Alternately tap each fingertip of the right *5 hand* while moving up and down the upturned left *open hand* held in front of the body.

**calculus** *n.* A system of calculation in advanced mathematics: *studying calculus in college.* Related form: **calculate** *v.*

■ [Initialized sign similar to sign for **arithmetic**] Beginning with both *C hands* in front of each side of the chest, palms facing each other, move the hands past each other with a repeated movement.

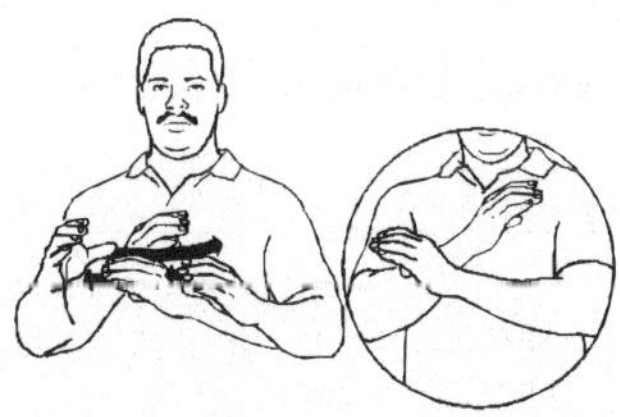

**calendar** *n.* A table showing the days, weeks, and months of the year: *According to the calendar, next Friday is the 10th.*

■ [Initialized sign indicating turning pages on a calendar] Move the little-finger side of the right *C hand,* palm facing left, from the heel upward in an arc over the fingertips of the left *open hand,* palm facing in and fingers pointing up.

**call**[1] *v.* To ask to come: *The boss called me into her office.* Same sign used for: **summon.**

■ [Tap on the hand to get one's attention] Slap the fingers of the right *open hand* on the back of the left *open hand,* palm facing down, dragging the right fingers upward and closing them into an *A hand* in front of the right shoulder.

**call**[2] or **call out** *v.* or *v. phrase.* To shout loudly: *Call out the names during the ceremony.* Same sign used for: **cry, holler, yell.**

■ [Natural gesture of cupping the mouth when yelling] Place the index-finger side of the right *C hand* against the right side of the chin.

**call**[3] *v.* To give a name to: *called the baby "John."* Same sign used for: **name.**

■ [Similar to sign for **name**] With the middle-finger side of the right *H hand* across the index-finger side of the left *H hand,* move the hands forward in an arc in front of the body.

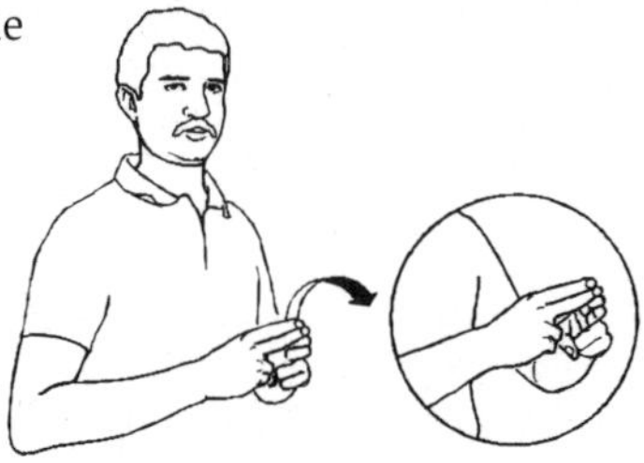

**call**[4] *v.* See sign for TELEPHONE.

**call out** *v. phrase.* See signs for CALL[2], SCREAM.

**calm** *adj., v.* See signs for QUIET[1, 2], SETTLE.

**calm down** *v. phrase.* See signs for QUIET, SETTLE, SILENT.

**camcorder** *n.* See signs for VIDEOTAPE[1, 2].

**camera**[1] *n.* An apparatus for taking photographs: *Take my picture with the new camera.*

■ [Mime taking a picture with a camera] Beginning with the *modified C hands* near the outside of each eye, palms facing each other, bend the right index finger up and down with a repeated movement.

**camera**[2] *n.* See sign for MOVIE CAMERA.

**camp** *n.* A place where people live for a short time in tents or similar temporary shelters: *sending the children to summer camp.* Same sign used for: **tent.**

■ [Shape of a tent] Beginning with the extended index fingers and little fingers of both hands touching at an angle in front of the chest, bring the hands downward and apart with a repeated movement. The same sign is used for the verb, as in *to camp on the beach for the weekend,* but the sign is made with a single movement.

**camper** *n.* A vehicle outfitted for camping: *We can sleep in the camper during the whole trip.*

■ [Represents a camper on top of a truck] Tap the fingertips of the right *flattened C hand* on the back of the left *open hand,* palm facing down, with a double movement.

**can**[1] *auxiliary v.* To be able to do something: *She can run fast.* Same sign used for **may.**

■ [Similar to sign for **able**] Move both *S hands*, palms facing down, downward simultaneously with a short double movement in front of each side of the body.

**can**[2] *n.* See sign for CUP.

**cancel** *v.* **1.** To decide or announce that something planned will not take place: *cancel an appointment.* **2.** To put a stop to or revoke: *to cancel an order.* Same sign used for: **condemn, correct, criticize, null, revoke, void.**

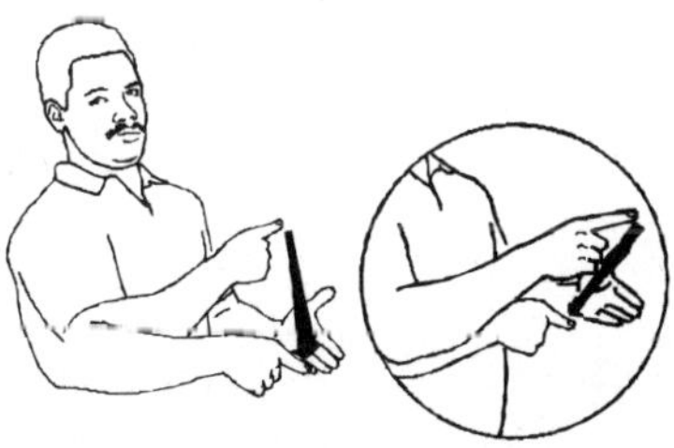

■ [Finger crosses out something to cancel it] With the right index finger extended, draw a large X across the upturned left *open hand.*

**cancer** *n.* See sign for ACID.

**candle** *n.* A stick of wax with a wick for burning: *light a candle.* Same sign used for: **flame, glow.**

■ [Represents the flame on a candle] With the extended right index finger touching the heel of the left *5 hand,* palm facing right, wiggle the left fingers.

**candy**[1] *n.* A confection made with sugar and flavoring: *a box of chocolate candy.* Same sign used for: **sugar.**

■ [Similar to sign for **sweet**] Bring the fingers of the right *U hand* downward on the chin with a repeated movement, bending the fingers each time.

**candy**[2] *n.* (alternate sign)

■ Twist the extended right index fingertip in the right cheek with a repeated movement.

**cannabis** *n.* See sign for MARIJUANA.

**can't** *contraction.* To be unable to do something: *I can't see through the fog.* Alternate form: **cannot.**

■ Bring the extended right index finger downward in front of the chest, striking the extended left index finger as it moves, both palms facing down.

**cantankerous** *adj.* See sign for CONTRARY[1].

**cap** *n.* A close-fitting covering for the head, often with a visor: *wearing a baseball cap.*

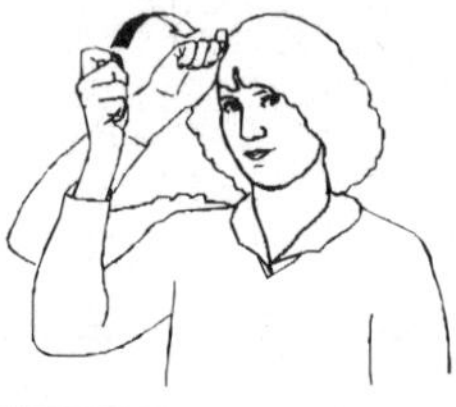

■ [Mime tipping a cap with a visor] Bring the right modified *X hand* from in front of the head, palm facing left, back to the top of the head.

**capable** *adj.* See sign for SKILL.

**capital**[1] *adj.* **1.** Designating a letter belonging to the series A, B, C, . . . , Z, rather than a, b, c, . . . , z: *a capital letter to start each sentence.* —*n.* **2.** A capital letter: *Start each sentence with a capital.*

■ [Shows size of capital letter] Hold the right *modified C hand,* palm facing forward, in front of the right side of the body.

**capital**[2] *n.* The city where the government of a country or state is located: *Harrisburg is the capital of Pennsylvania.*

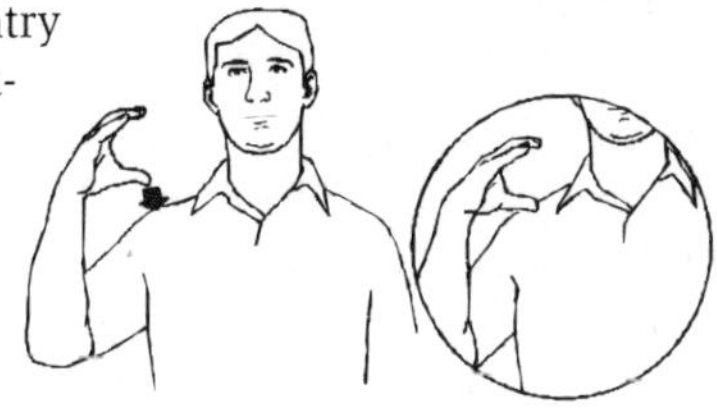

- [Initialized sign] Tap the thumb of the right *C hand*, palm facing left, on the right shoulder with a double movement.

**capsule** *n.* See sign for PILL.

**captain** *n.* **1.** A high-ranking military officer: *He is a captain in the army.* **2.** The head of a group: *captain of the basketball team.* Same sign used for: **boss, chair, chairperson, chief, general, officer.**

- [Location of epaulets on captain's uniform] Tap the fingertips of the right *curved 5 hand* on the right shoulder with a repeated movement.

**capture** *v.* To take prisoner: *to capture a rabbit in a trap.* Same sign used for: **arrest, catch, claim, conquer, nab, occupy, possess, repossess, seize, takeover.**

- [Mime grabbing at something to capture it] Beginning with both *curved 5 hands* in front of each shoulder, palms facing forward, move the hands downward while closing into *S hands.*

**car** *n.* A passenger vehicle for driving on an ordinary road or street: *The cars were bumper-to-bumper on the freeway.* Same sign used for: **automobile.**

- [Mime driving] Beginning with both *S hands* in front of the chest, palms facing in and the left hand higher than the right hand, move the hands in an up-and-down motion with a repeated alternating movement.

**card**[1] *n.* A stiff rectangular piece of paper: *to keep notes on index cards.* Same sign used for: **check, envelope.**

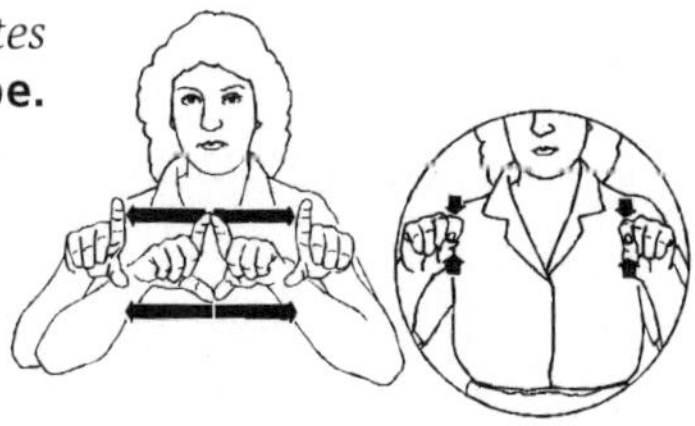

- [Shows shape of a rectangular card] Beginning with the fingertips of both *L hands* touching in front of the chest, palms facing forward, bring the hands apart to in front of each shoulder, and then pinch each thumb and index finger together.

**card**[2] *n.* A credit card: *You can charge the dinner to my card.* Same sign used for: **credit card.**

- [Initialized sign showing shape of credit card] With the fingers of the right *C hand* curved around the left *open hand,* palm facing in and fingers pointing right, pull the right hand from the base of the left thumb to the fingertips with a double movement.

**cards** *n.* Any of several games played with one or more sets of cards (playing cards) that typically are marked with numbers and symbols or pictures: *The two couples play cards once a week.* Same sign used for: **play cards.**

- [Mime dealing cards] Beginning with both *A hands* in front of the body, palms facing each other, flick the right hand to the right with a repeated movement off the left thumb.

**care**[1] *n.* Serious attention: *to work on the project with care.* Same sign used for: **monitor, patrol, supervise, take care of.**

- [Represents eyes watching out in different directions] With the little-finger side of the right *K hand* across the index-finger side of the left *K hand,* palms facing in opposite directions, move the hands in a repeated flat circle in front of the body.

**care**[2] *v.* See sign for TROUBLE.

**careful** *adj.* Taking care: *Be careful moving the painting.* Same sign used for: **be careful, cautious, take care, watch out.**

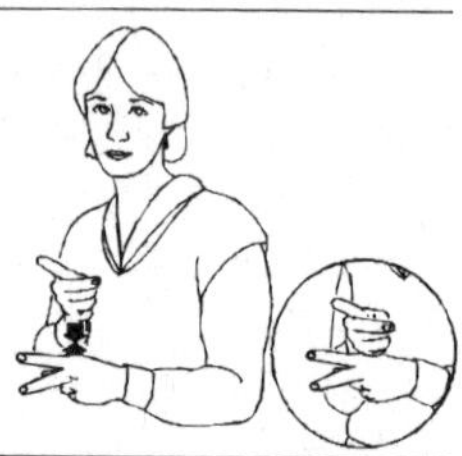

- Tap the little-finger side of the right *K hand* with a double movement across the index-finger side of the left *K hand,* palms facing in opposite directions.

**carefully** *adv.* In a careful manner: *Walk carefully on the rough sidewalk.* Same sign used for: **cautiously.**

- With the little-finger side of the right *K hand* across the index-finger side of the left *K hand,* palms facing in opposite directions, move the hands upward and forward in large double circles.

**caregiver** *n.* See sign for GUARDIAN.

**careless** *adj.* Showing lack of due care: *a careless mistake.* Related form: **carelessly** *adv.* Same sign used for: **reckless.**

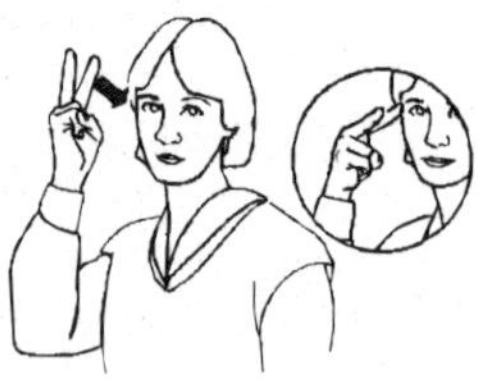

- [Misdirected eyes] Move the right *V hand* from near the right side of the head, palm facing left and fingers pointing up, down to the left in front of the eyes with a double movement.

**carry** *v.* To take from one place to another: *Carry the boxes inside.* Alternate forms: **carry on** or **onto.**

- [Having something in one's hands to transfer to another place] Beginning with both *curved hands* in front of the right side of the body, move the hands in a series of simultaneous arcs to the left, ending in front of the left side of the body.

**cart** *n.* A small vehicle on wheels, moved by hand: *push the grocery cart down the aisle.*

■ [Mime pushing a cart] Beginning with both *S hands* in front of the body, palms facing down, push the hands forward.

**carton** *n.* A box made of cardboard: *a carton of cigarettes.*

■ [Initialized sign showing shape of carton] Beginning with the fingertips of the index fingers and thumbs of both *C hands* touching in front of the chest, palms facing forward, bring the hands apart to in front of each side of the body.

**cartoon** *n.* A drawing or filmed sequence of drawings designed to entertain: *watch cartoons on television.*

■ [Initialized sign similar to sign for **funny**] Move the right *C hand,* palm facing left, downward with a double movement from in front of the nose.

**carve** *v.* **1.** To cut into pieces or slices: *carve the turkey.* **2.** To form by cutting: *to carve a statue out of marble.* Same sign used for: **engrave, sculpt.**

■ [Mime action of carving] Flick the right thumb of the right *10 hand* upward off the heel of the upturned left *open hand.*

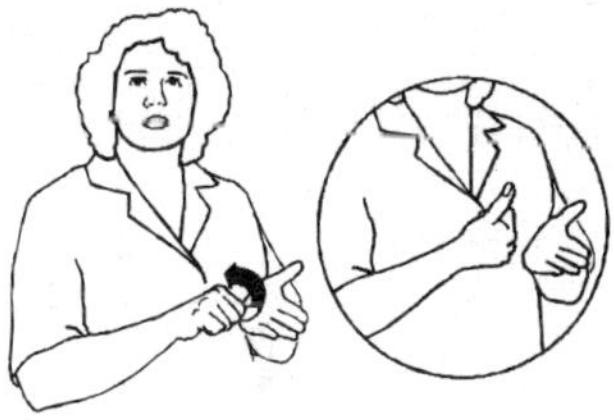

**cash register** *n.* A business machine that records sales, totals receipts, and has a drawer for holding money: *Ring this sale up on the cash register.*

■ [Mime action of using a cash register] Move the right *open hand,* palm facing down, from in front of the right shoulder downward with a repeated movement while wiggling the fingers.

**cast** *v.* See sign for THROW.

**casual** *adj.* See signs for DAILY, FARM.

**cat** *n.* A small, furry mammal with whiskers and sharp claws, bred in a number of varieties and often kept as a pet: *my pet cat.*

■ [Cat's whiskers] Move the fingertips of both *F hands,* palms facing each other, from each side of the mouth outward with a repeated movement.

**catalog** *n.* See sign for MAGAZINE.

**catch**[1] *v.* To take and hold, especially a moving object: *to catch a ball.*

■ [Mime catching ball] Beginning with both *5 hands* in front of the body, palms facing each other, bring the hands back toward the body while constricting the hands into *curved 5 hands.*

**catch**[2] *v.* (alternate sign) Same sign used for **arrest, convict, nab.**

■ [Hand moves to "catch" the finger on the other hand] Move the right *C hand* from in front of the right shoulder, palm facing left, forward to meet the extended left index finger, palm facing right and finger pointing up, while changing into an *A hand.*

**catch**[3] *v.* To incur a disease: *catch a cold.* Same sign used for: **prone.**

■ [One's fingers receive something and bring it to oneself] With an alternating movement, move first the right *curved 5 hand* and then the left *curved 5 hand* from in front of the chest, palms facing down and fingers pointing forward, back to the chest while changing into *flattened O hands.*

**catch**[4] *v.* See sign for CAPTURE.

**catch up** *v. phrase.* To come from behind and be even: *to catch up with my work.*

■ [One hand catches up with the other hand] Bring the right *A hand* from near the right side of the chest, palm facing left, forward to the heel of the left *A hand,* palm facing right, held in front of the body.

**category** *n.* See sign for CLASS.

**catsup** *n.* See sign for KETCHUP.

**cattle** *n.* See sign for COW.

**caught in the act** *v. phrase.* See sign for NAB.

**cause** *v.* To make happen: *caused a fire in the house by playing with matches.*

■ Beginning with both *S hands* near the body, palms facing up and left hand nearer the body than the right hand, move both hands forward in an arc while opening into *5 hands.*

**caution** *v.* See sign for WARN.

**cautious** *adj.* See sign for CAREFUL.

**cautiously** *adv.* See sign for CAREFULLY.

**cave in** *v. phrase.* See sign for BREAK DOWN.

**cease** *v.* See sign for STOP[1].

**celebrate** *v.* To observe a special time or event with planned activities: *to celebrate your birthday with a party.* Related form: **celebration** *n.* Same sign used for: **anniversary, festival, gala, rejoice.**

■ With *modified X hands* in front of each shoulder, move both hands in large repeated outward movements, palms angled up.

**celery** *n.* A pale green vegetable with crisp stalks: *Eating a stalk of celery.*

■ [**green** + action of eating celery stalk] Beginning with the right *G hand* in front of the right shoulder, palm facing in, twist the hand back and forth with a double movement. Then move the right *G hand* from near the right side of the mouth, palm facing up, in toward the mouth while moving the mouth as if eating.

**celibate** *adj.* See sign for ABSTAIN[2].

**cellar** *n.* See sign for BASEMENT.

**cell phone** or **cellular phone** *n. phrase.* Mobile telephone using a system of radio transmitters, each covering separate areas: *call home on a cell phone.*

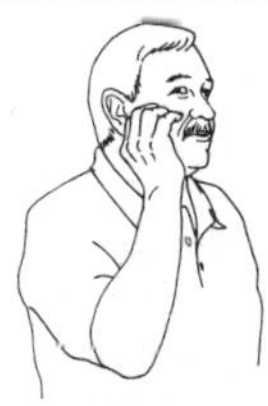

■ [Holding a cell phone] Hold the right *curved hand* near the right ear.

**cemetery** *n.* A place for burying the dead: *She placed flowers on the grave at the cemetery.* Same sign used for: **graveyard.**

■ [Shape of mounds of dirt on graves] Move both *curved hands,* palms facing down and fingers pointing forward, with a double movement back toward the body in double arcs.

**cent** *n.* A monetary unit or coin worth 1/100 of a dollar: *This newspaper still costs 30 cents.* Same sign used for: **penny.**

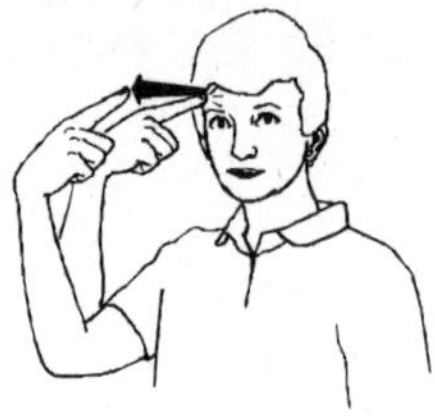

- With a double movement, move the extended right index finger forward at an outward angle from touching the right side of the forehead, palm facing down.

**center** *n.* The middle point of anything: *standing in the center of the room.* Related form: **central** *adj.* See also sign for MIDDLE.

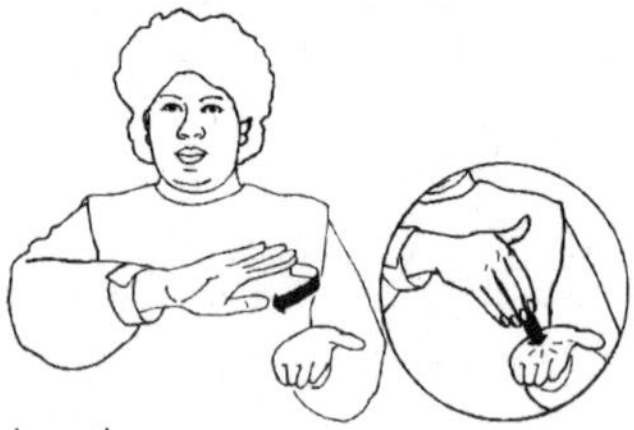

- [Indicates location in center of something] Move the right *open hand,* palm facing down, in a circular movement over the upturned left *open hand,* bending the right fingers as the hand moves and ending with the fingertips of the right *bent hand* touching the middle of the left palm.

**cereal** *n.* Food made from grain: *eat cereal for breakfast.*

- [Action of scooping cereal from bowl to mouth] Move the right curved hand, palm facing up, from the palm of the left *open hand,* palm facing up, upward to the mouth with a double movement.

**certain** *adj.* See signs for ABSOLUTE, SURE, TRUE.

**certainly** *adv.* See sign for TRUE.

**certificate** *n.* An official document attesting to a fact: *a birth certificate.* Related forms: **certification** *n.*, **certify** *v.*

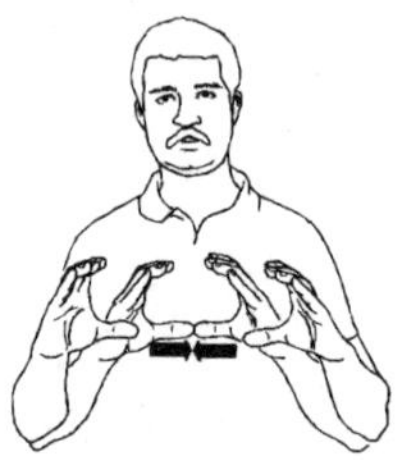

- [Initialized sign showing shape of certificate] Tap the thumbs of both *C hands* together in front of the chest with a repeated movement, palms facing each other.

**certify** *v.* See sign for ACCREDIT.

**chain** *n.* A series of connected metal links: *tied to the roof of the car with a chain.* Same sign used for: **Olympics.**

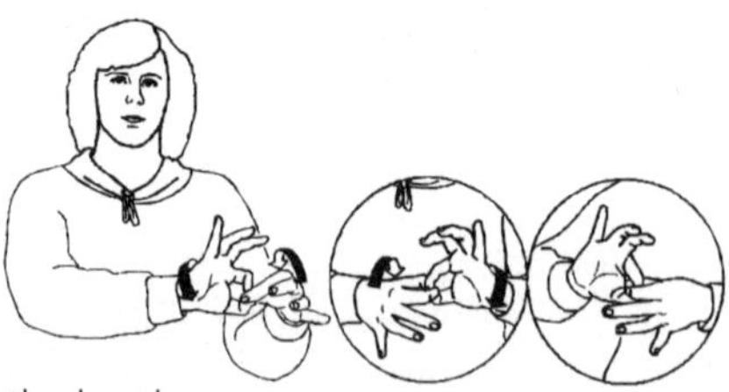

- [Shape of chain] Beginning with the index fingers and thumbs of both *F hands* intersecting in front of the left side of the chest, palms facing each other and the right hand above the left hand, release the fingers, flip the hands in reverse positions, and connect the fingers again with a repeated alternating movement as the hands move across the front of the body from left to right.

**chair** *n.* A seat with a back intended for one person: *sit in a chair.* Same sign used for: **seat.**

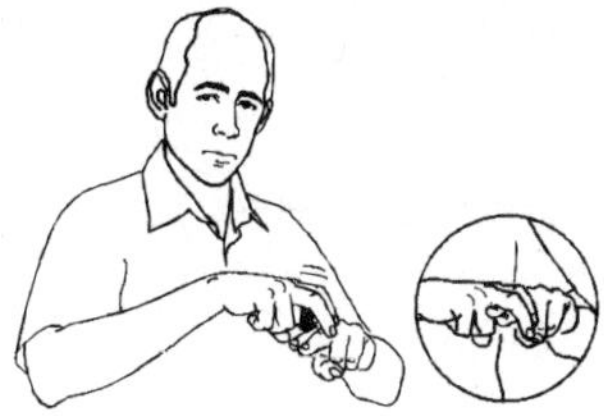

- [Fingers represent legs hanging down when sitting] With a double movement, tap the fingers of the right *curved U hand* across the fingers of the left *U hand,* both palms facing down.

**chairperson** or **chair** *n.* See signs for CAPTAIN, CHIEF.

**chalkboard** *n.* See sign for BOARD[1].

**chalk up** *v. phrase.* See sign for ACHIEVE.

**challenge** *v.* **1.** To call or summon to a contest: *challenged me to a game of tennis.* —*n.* **2.** A call or summons to engage in a contest: *accepted our challenge to see which office would raise more money for charity.* Same sign used for: **dare, play against, versus.**

- [Hands seem to confront each other] Swing both *10 hands,* palms facing in, from in front of each side of the chest toward each other, ending with the knuckles touching in front of the chest, thumbs pointing up.

**champagne** *n.* See sign for COCKTAIL.

**champion** *n.* The winner in a contest: *the swimming champion in the ten-meter race.* Same sign used for: **trophy.**

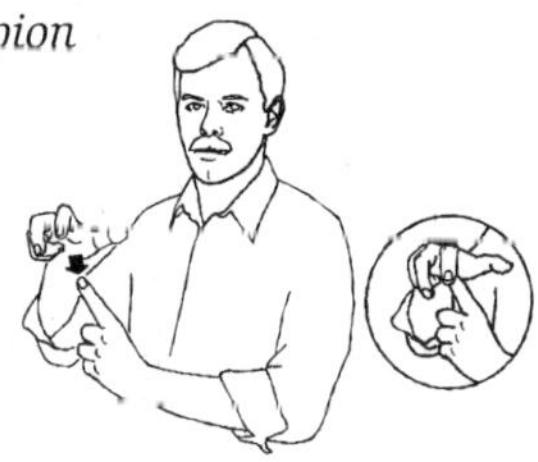

- [Symbolizes placing crown on head of winner] With the fingers of the right *curved 3 hand,* tap the right palm on the extended left index finger pointing up in front of the chest.

**chance** *n.* An opportunity: *a chance to earn some extra money.*

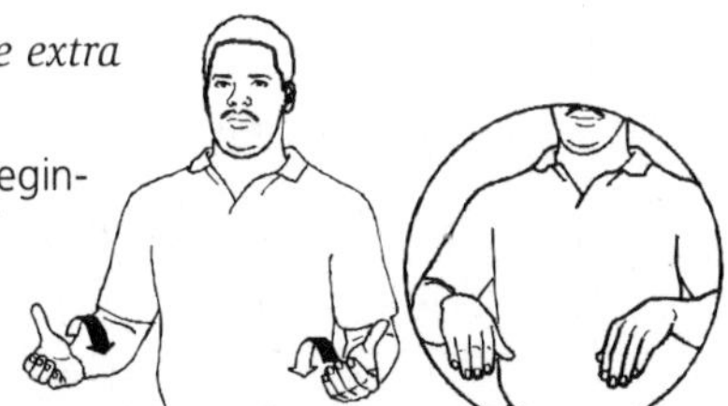

- [Initialized sign formed like turning over dice] Beginning with both *C hands* in front of each side of the body, palms facing up, flip the hands over, ending with the palms facing down.

**change**[1] *v.* To make or become different: *to change the color of the bedroom walls; plans that suddenly changed.* Same sign used for: **adapt, adjust, alter, justify, modify, shift, switch, turn.**

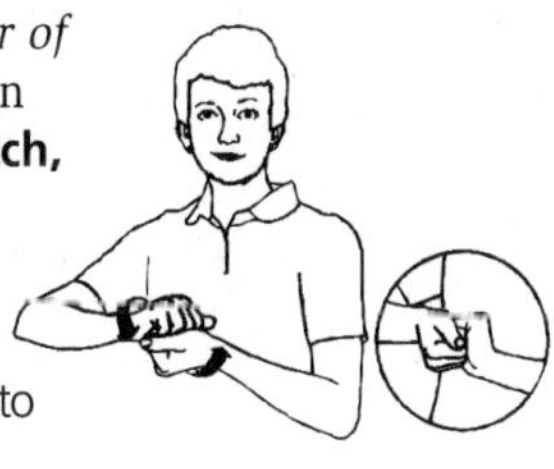

- [Hands seem to twist something as if to change it] With the palm sides of both *A hands* together, right hand above left, twist the wrists in opposite directions in order to reverse positions.

**change**[2] *n.* See sign for SHARE. Shared idea of dividing an amount of money to be shared.

**change places** See sign for TRADE PLACES.

**change the subject** *v. phrase.* To shift from the topic under discussion to another topic: *He changed the subject whenever someone mentioned his past.* Same sign used for: **change the topic.**

- [One hand moves away to another topic] Beginning with both *bent V hands* near each other in front of the chest, palms facing down, swing the right hand off to the right.

**change the topic** *v. phrase.* See sign for CHANGE THE SUBJECT.

**chant** *n.* See sign for MUSIC.

**chaos** *n.* See sign for MESSY.

**chap** *n.* See sign for CRACK.

**chapel** *n.* See sign for CHURCH.

**chapter**[1] *n.* A main division of a book, usually having a number or a title: *to read a chapter before going to bed.*

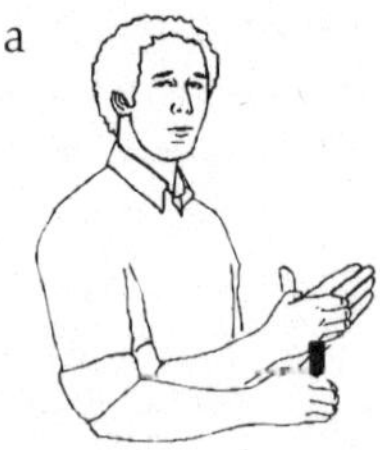

- [Initialized sign showing a column of text] Move the fingertips of the right *C hand* down the upturned left *open hand* with a repeated movement.

**chapter**[2] *n.* See sign for COURSE.

**character**[1] *n.* **1.** The quality and nature of someone or something: *a fine leader of sterling character.* **2.** A person in a story, play, or film: *The court jester is my favorite character in the play.* Related form: **characteristic** *n.*

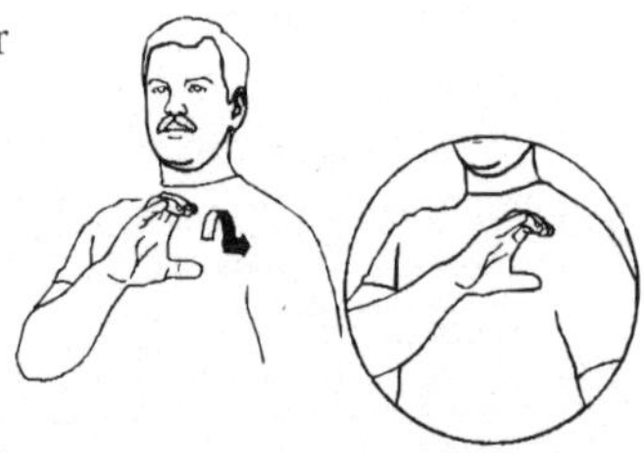

- [Initialized sign similar to sign for **personality**] Move the right *C hand,* palm facing left, in a small circle and then back against the left side of the chest.

**character**[2] *n.* (alternate sign for the character in a story, play, or film)

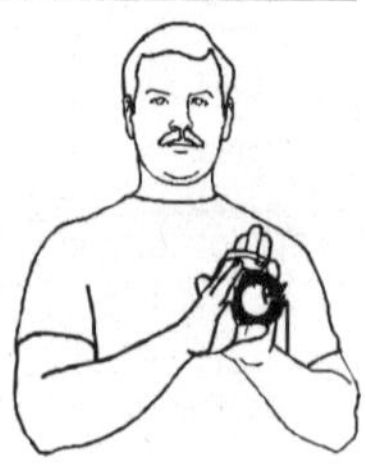

- [Initialized sign similar to sign for **role**] Move the right *C hand,* palm facing left, in a small circle against the left *open hand,* palm facing forward.

**charge**[1] *v.* To put down as a debt to be paid: *to charge the purchase to the corporate account.* Same sign used for: **credit card.**

■ [Represents getting impression of credit card charge] Rub the little-finger side of the right *S hand,* palm facing in, back and forth on the upturned left *open hand.*

**charge**[2] *v.* See signs for ACCUSE[1], APPLY[1], BLAME[1], COST[1].

**charity**[1] *n.* **1.** Donating one's money or time to the poor or to organizations set up to help them: *a philanthropist noted for his charity.* **2.** An institution or fund set up to help those in need: *raising money for charity.* Same sign used for: **contribute, contribution, donate, donation.**

■ [**gift** formed repeatedly to indicate frequent contributions] With the right *X hand* closer to the chest than the left *X hand,* move each hand, palms facing each other, forward from the chest with a double alternating movement.

**charity**[2] *n.* See sign for GIFT.

**charley horse** *n. phrase.* See sign for CRAMP.

**chart** *n.* See sign for SCHEDULE[1].

**chase** *v.* To run after to catch: *to chase a bus for a whole block.* Same sign used for: **pursue.**

■ [One hand seems to pursue the other hand] Move the right *A hand,* palm facing left, in a spiraling movement from in front of the chest forward, to behind the left *A hand* held somewhat forward of the body.

**chat**[1] *v.* To talk in an easy, informal manner: *to chat about the weather.* Same sign used for: **talk.**

■ Move both *5 hands,* palms angled up, from in front of each shoulder downward at an angle toward each other with a repeated movement.

**chat**[2] *v.* See sign for BLAB.

**chatter** *v.* See signs for BLAB, JABBER.

**cheap** *adj.* Costing relatively little; inexpensive: *It doesn't pay to buy cheap shoes.* Same sign used for: **inexpensive.**

■ Brush the index-finger side of the right *B hand* downward on the palm of the left *open hand,* bending the right wrist as it moves down.

**cheat** *v.* To behave in a manner that is not honest: *to cheat on the test.* Same sign used for: **betray, deceive, fraud.**

■ Slide the right *3 hand* between the index and middle fingers, palm facing in, onto the index-finger side of the left *B hand,* palm facing down, with a double movement.

**check**[1] *v.* To inspect for accuracy: *Check your work before you hand it in.* Same sign used for: **examine, inspect.**

■ [Bringing one's attention to something to inspect it] Move the extended right index finger from the nose down to strike sharply off the upturned palm of the left *open hand,* and then upward again.

**check**[2] *n.* See sign for CARD[1].

**checkers** *n.* A board game played by two people, using red and black disks as playing pieces: *I haven't played a game of checkers since I was a child.*

■ [Action of moving a checker on a checkerboard] Move the fingers of the right *curved 3 hand,* palm facing down, in a small arc to the right and then to the left, in front of the right side of the body.

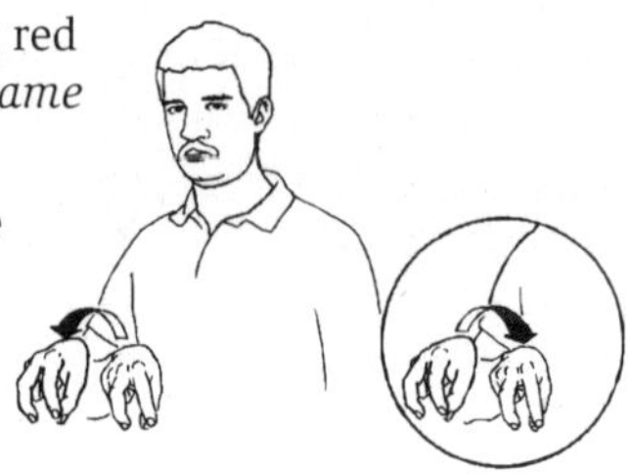

**check for** *v. phrase.* See sign for LOOK FOR.

**cheek** *n.* The side of the face below the eye: *a child with beautiful rosy cheeks.*

■ [Location of cheek] Touch the fingertips of the right *flattened C hand* against the right cheek.

**cheer** *n.* See sign for HAPPY.

**cheerful** *adj.* See signs for FRIENDLY, HAPPY.

**cheese** *n.* A solid food made from the curds of milk: *some cheese in the sandwich.*

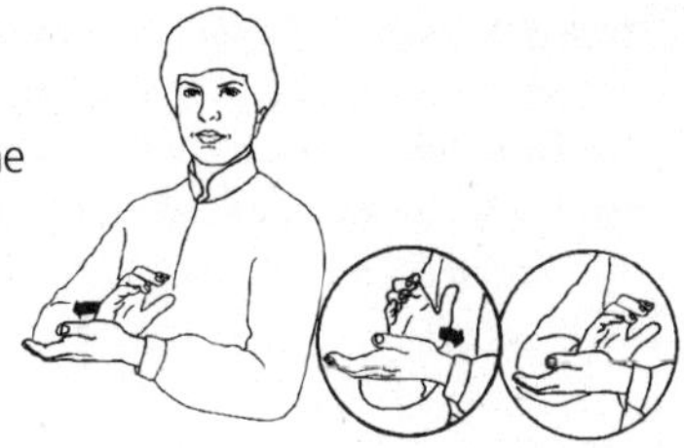

■ With the heel of the right *open hand* pressed on the heel of the upturned left *open hand,* palms facing each other and perpendicular to each other, twist the right hand forward and back slightly with a repeated movement.

**chemistry** *n.* See sign for SCIENCE. Related form: **chemical** *adj.*

**cherish** *v.* See sign for PRECIOUS.

**cherry** *n.* A small, round, usually red fruit with a pit: *a bowl of beautiful ripe cherries.*

■ [The stem of a cherry] Move the fingertips of the right *F hand,* palm facing left, from near the mouth forward and downward with a wavy movement.

**chest** *n.* The top, front part of the body: *a pain in my chest.*

■ [Location of chest] Rub the fingertips of both *open hands,* palms facing in and fingers pointing toward each other, up and down on the chest with a repeated movement.

**chew** *v.* To crush or grind with the teeth: *Chew your food well before swallowing it.* Same sign used for: **grind.**

■ [Represents grinding motion of teeth when chewing] With the palm sides of both *A hands* together, right hand on top of the left hand, move the hands in small repeated circles in opposite directions, causing the knuckles of the two hands to rub together.

**chewing gum** *n. phrase.* A sweetened and flavored substance made of chicle for chewing: *a pack of chewing gum.* Same sign used for: **gum.**

■ [Action of jaw when chewing gum] With the fingertips of the right *V hand* against the right side of the chin, palm facing down, move the hand toward the face with a double movement by bending the fingers.

**chewing tobacco** *n. phrase.* See sign for TOBACCO.

**chew out** *v. phrase.* See sign for BAWL OUT.

**chicken**[1] *n.* **1.** A domestic fowl raised for its eggs or for food: *to raise chickens.* **2.** The flesh of this fowl used for food: *having roast chicken for dinner.* Same sign used for: **hen.**

- Tap the thumb of the right *3 hand,* palm facing left and fingers pointing up, against the chin with a repeated movement.

**chicken**[2] *n.* See sign for BIRD.

**chief**[1] *n.* The person of highest authority in an organized group: *the chief of police.* —*adj.* **2.** Highest in rank or authority: *the chief copyeditor in the publishing house.* Same sign used for: **boss, chairperson, officer, prominent, superior, VIP.**

- [Shows higher location] Move the right *10 hand* upward from in front of the right side of the chest, palm facing in and thumb pointing up.

**chief**[2] *n.* See sign for CAPTAIN.

**child** *n.* A young boy or girl: *The child is lost.*

- [Patting child on the head] Pat the right *bent hand* downward with a short repeated movement in front of the right side of the body, palm facing down.

**children** *pl. n.* Young boys and/or girls: *games for children.*

- [Patting a number of children on their heads] Pat the right *open hand,* palm facing down, in front of the right side of the body and then to the right with a double arc.

**chilly** *adj.* See sign for COLD[2].

**chimpanzee** *n.* See sign for MONKEY.

**chip in** *v. phrase.* To join others in giving money for a common cause: *We all chipped in to buy her a gift.* Same sign used for: **pool.**

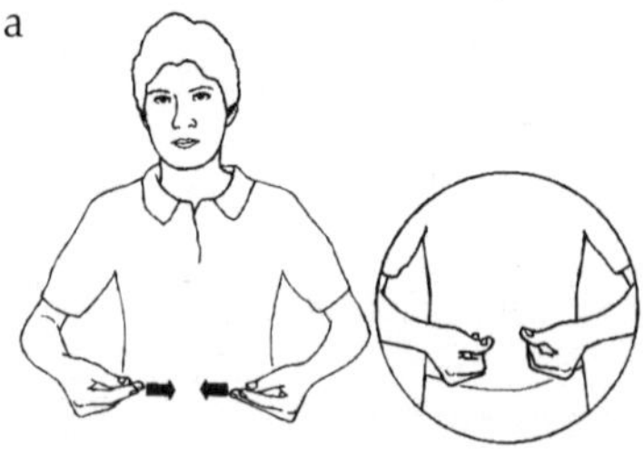

- Beginning with both *flattened O hands* in front of each side of the body, palms facing up and fingers pointing toward each other, bring the hands toward each other while sliding the fingers closed into *A hands.*

**chocolate** *n.* **1.** A brown food substance made from grinding cacao seeds, often sweetened and flavored: *I like chocolate better than vanilla.* —*adj.* **2.** Made with chocolate: *chocolate cake.*

- [Initialized sign] Move the thumb side of the right *C hand,* palm facing forward, in a repeated circle on the back of the left *open hand* held in front of the chest, palm facing down.

**choice** *n.* See sign for EITHER[1].

**choir** *n.* See sign for BAND.

**choose**[1] *v.* To select from a number of possibilities: *to choose a partner for the dance.* Related form: **choice** *n.* Same sign used for: **assign, draw, option, pick, select.**

- [Hand picks from alternatives] Beginning with the bent thumb and index finger of the right *5 hand* touching the index finger of the left *5 hand,* palms facing each other, pull the right hand back toward the right shoulder while pinching the thumb and index finger together.

**choose**[2] *v.* See sign for APPOINT[1].

**chop**[1] *v.* To cut (food) into small pieces by hitting with something sharp: *to chop onions.*

- [Mime chopping food] Sharply hit the little-finger side of the right *open hand,* palm facing left, on the upturned left *open hand* with a triple movement.

**chop**[2] *v.* See sign for HARVEST.

**Christmas** *n.* The annual Christian holiday celebrated on December 25, commemorating the birth of Jesus: *plans to go home for Christmas.*

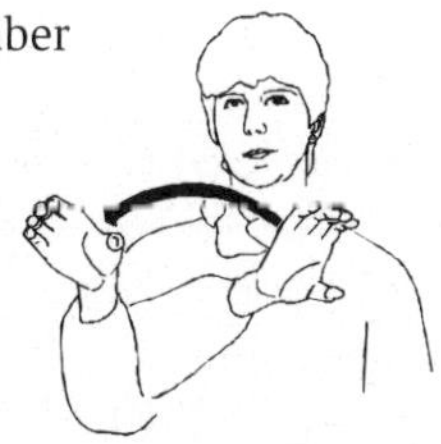

- [Initialized sign showing the shape of a wreath] Move the right *C hand,* palm facing forward, in a large arc from in front of the left shoulder to in front of the right shoulder.

**chronic** *adj.* Of or pertaining to long-term, continuing illnesses that are usually not curable, although symptoms can be controlled.

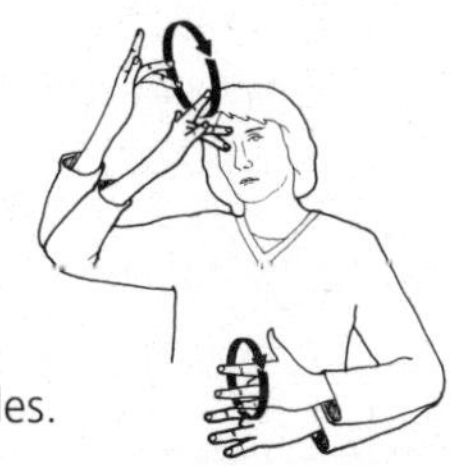

- [**sick** formed with both hands in a continuing movement] With the bent middle finger of the right *5 hand* pointing toward the forehead and the bent middle finger of the left *5 hand* pointing toward the abdomen, move both hands in repeated inward circles.

**chubby** *adj.* See sign for FAT.

**church** *n.* **1.** A building for public Christian worship: *raised funds to build a new church.* **2.** A religious service held in a church: *go to church every Sunday.* Same sign used for: **chapel.**

- [Initialized sign similar to sign for **rock**[1]] Tap the thumb of the right *C hand,* palm facing forward, on the back of the left *S hand,* palm facing down.

**cigarette** *n.* A small roll of finely cut tobacco for smoking, usually wrapped in thin paper: *You're allowed to smoke a cigarette at the tables along the wall.*

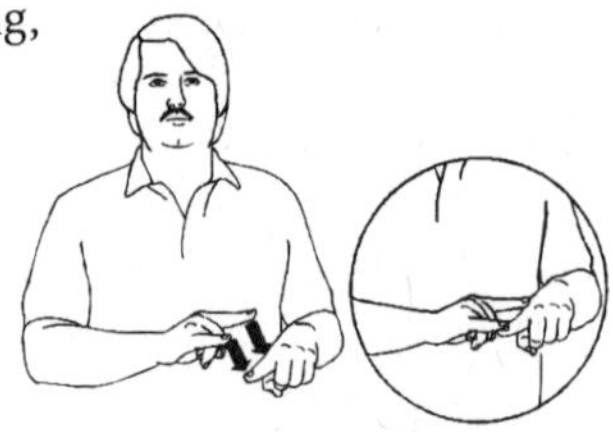

- [Tapping a cigarette to settle the tobacco] Tap the extended index finger and little finger of the right hand with a double movement on the extended left index finger, both palms facing down.

**cinema** *n.* See sign for FILM[1].

**circle**[1] *n.* A round line: *draw a circle.* Same sign used for: **cycle, round.**

- [Shape of circle] Draw a circle in the air in front of the right side of the chest with the extended right index finger, palm facing down and finger pointing forward.

**circle**[2] *n.* A circular or ringlike pattern: *Let's sit in a circle for the group discussion.*

- [Represents a number of people sitting in a circular pattern] Beginning with both *4 hands* in front of the chest, palms facing forward, bring the hands away from each other in outward arcs while turning the palms in, ending with the little fingers together.

**circuit board** *n. phrase.* See sign for BOARD[3].

**circulate** *v.* To go around or pass around: *blood circulating through the body; to circulate the paper.* Related form: **circulation** *n.* Same sign used for: **blend, merge, mix, random.**

- [Movement of circulating similar to sign for **mix**] Beginning with the right *5 hand* hanging down in front of the chest, palm facing in and fingers pointing down, and the left *5 hand* below the right hand, palm facing up and fingers pointing up, move the hands in circles around each other.

**circumcise** *v.* To cut off the foreskin of: *the baby was circumcised.* Related form: **circumcision** *n.*

■ [**operate** around a thumb representing a penis] Move the thumb of the right *10 hand* in a circle around the thumb of the left *10 hand,* both palms facing down.

**circumstance** *n.* See sign for CONDITION.

**circus** *n.* See sign for CLOWN.

**city** *n.* A large or important town: *I'm going to meet friends in the city for lunch and some shopping.* Same sign used for: **community.**

■ [Multiple housetops] With the palms of both *bent hands* facing in opposite directions and the fingertips touching, separate the fingertips, twist the wrists, and touch the fingertips again with a double movement.

**claim**[1] *v.* To assert ownership of: *I claim that book.*

■ [**my** + pointing to possession] Pat the palm of the right *open hand* on the chest with a double movement while pointing the extended index finger of the left hand downward.

**claim**[2] *v.* See sign for CAPTURE.

**clap** *v.* See sign for APPLAUD.

**clarify** *v.* See sign for BRIGHT.

**class** *n.* **1.** A group of people considered as belonging together by reason of common characteristics: *catering to the interests of writers as a class.* **2.** A group of students taught together: *Join our art class.* Same sign used for: **bracket, bunch, category, group, mass, section, series.**

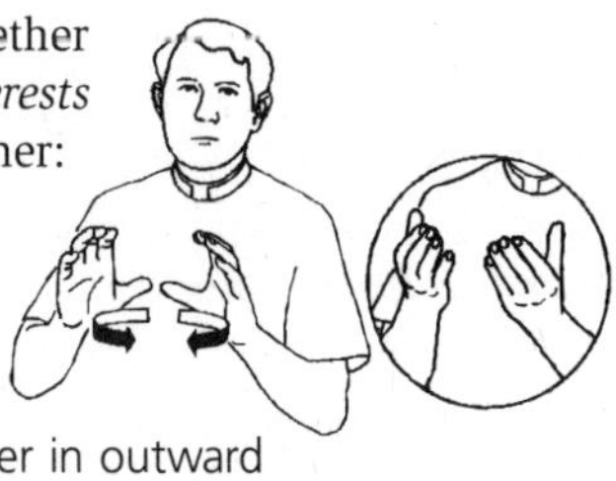

■ [Initialized sign showing an identifiable group] Beginning with both *C hands* in front of the chest, palms facing each other, bring the hands away from each other in outward arcs while turning the palms in, ending with the little fingers near each other.

**classical** *adj.* See sign for FANCY.

**classified** *adj.* See sign for SECRET.

**clean** *v.* To remove dirt: *to clean the windows with a special cleaner.* Same sign used for: **neat, pure.**

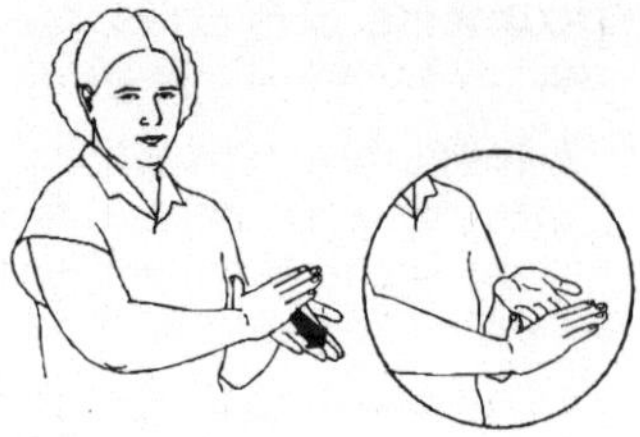

- [Wiping dirt off something to clean it] Slide the palm of the right *open hand* from the heel to the fingers of the upturned palm of the left *open hand.* For the adjective, the same sign is used, but made with a double movement.

**cleaners** *n.* A place for dry-cleaning clothing: *Take the soiled coat to the cleaners.* Same sign used for: **dry cleaners.**

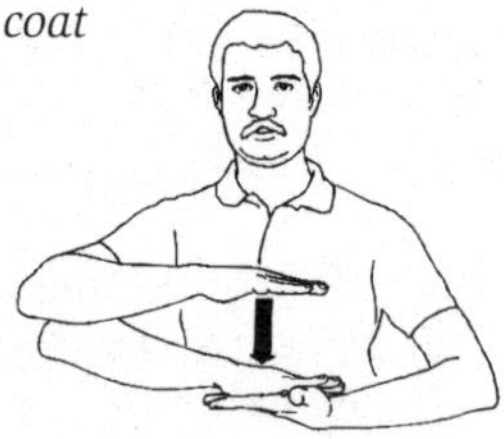

- [Action of a presser] Bring the palm of the right *open hand,* palm facing down and fingers pointing left, with a double movement down on the palm of the left *open hand,* palm facing up and fingers pointing right.

**clean up** *v. phrase.* Same sign as CLEAN but formed with a repeated movement.

**clear** *adj.* See sign for BRIGHT.

**clever** *adj.* See sign for SMART.

**click** *v.* To quickly press and release the button on a computer mouse to place the cursor at a particular position on a document or to make a selection: *right click on the mouse.*

- [Action of pressing button on mouse] Beginning with the right index finger pointing forward in front of the chest, bend the finger deliberately downward.

**client** *n.* A person seen in a clinical setting by a therapist: *a counseling session with the client.* Same sign used for: **customer.**

- [Initialized sign similar to sign for **person**] Move both *C hands,* palms facing each other, downward on each side of the chest.

**climate** *n.* See sign for WEATHER.

**climb** *v.* To go up with the help of the hands: *to climb the ladder.* Same sign used for: **ascend, ladder.**

- [Mime climbing a ladder] Beginning with both *curved 5 hands* in front of the chest, palms facing forward and right hand higher than the left, move the hands upward one at a time with an alternating movement.

**cling to** *v. phrase.* See sign for DEPEND.

**clippers** *pl. n.* See sign for SCISSORS.

**clock** *n.* An instrument for measuring and showing time: *The clock says that it's ten past three.*

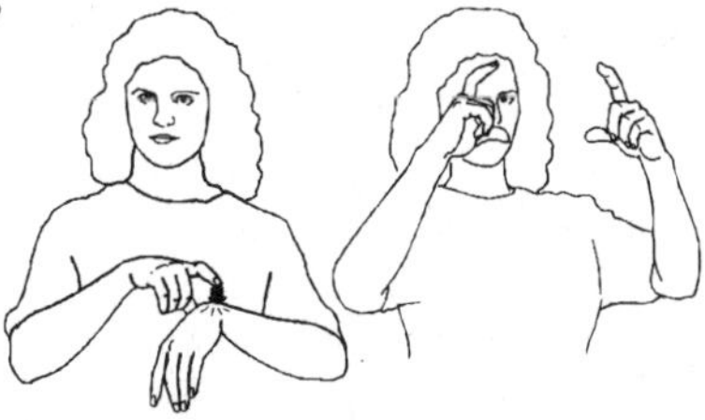

■ [**time**[2] + round shape of a clock's face] Tap the curved right index finger on the back of the left wrist. Then hold both *modified C hands* in front of each side of the face, palms facing each other.

**close**[1] *adv.* Separated by very little; near: *Sit close together.* Same sign used for: **approach, near.**

■ [Moves one hand close to the other] Beginning with the right *bent hand* somewhat forward of the chest and the left *bent hand* near the chest, palms facing in and fingers pointing in opposite directions, move the right palm to the back of the left hand, pushing the left hand toward the chest.

**close**[2] *adv.* (alternate sign) Same sign used for: **approach, near.**

■ [Moves one hand close to the other] Bring the back of the right *bent hand* from the chest forward toward the left *bent hand,* both palms facing in and fingers pointing in opposite directions.

**close call** *n. phrase.* A narrow escape, as from something dangerous: *Whew! That was a close call.* Alternate form: **close shave.** Same sign used for: **almost, barely.**

■ Beginning with the fingertips of the right *F hand* against the right side of the forehead, palm facing left, bring the hand forward a short distance.

**closet**[1] *n.* A small room for storing clothes: *Hang your coat up on the long bar in the closet.*

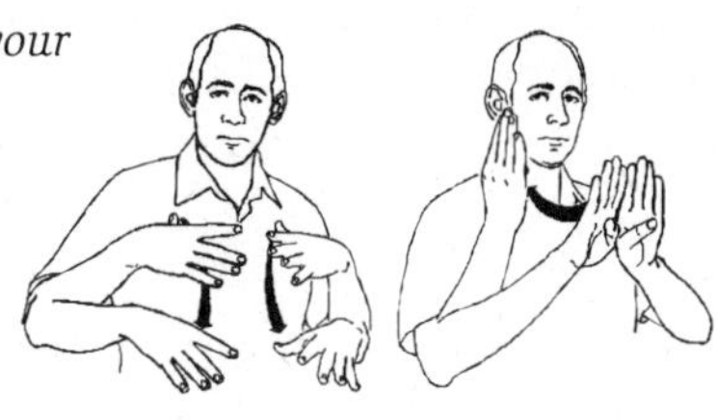

■ [**clothes** + **door**] Brush the thumbs of both *5 hands* downward on each side of the chest with a double movement. Then, beginning with the index-finger side of both *B hands* touching in front of the chest, palms facing forward and fingers pointing up, swing the right hand back toward the right shoulder with a double movement by twisting the wrist.

**closet**[2] *n.* (alternate sign) Same sign used for **locker.**

■ [Represents hangers] Beginning with the fingers of both *H hands* crossed in front of the left shoulder, twist the wrists to alternate positions.

**close to** *adj.* See sign for APPROACH[1].

**close up** *adv.* At a near distance: *I saw it happen close up.*

■ [Location of something close up to the face] Move the right *open hand,* palm facing in and fingers pointing up, back toward the face.

**cloth** *n.* See sign for MATERIAL.

**clothes** *pl. n.* Wearing apparel: *It's time to put on my clothes and go to work.* Same sign used for: **apparel, costume, dress, fashion, garment, suit.**

■ [Location of clothes on body] Brush the thumbs of both *5 hands* downward on each side of the chest with a double movement.

**cloud** *n.* A visible mass of water particles suspended in the air above the earth's surface: *dark clouds covering the sun.*

■ [Shape and location of clouds] Beginning with both *C hands* near the left side of the head, palms facing each other, bring the hands away from each other in outward arcs while turning the palms in, ending with the little fingers close together. Repeat the movement near the right side of the head.

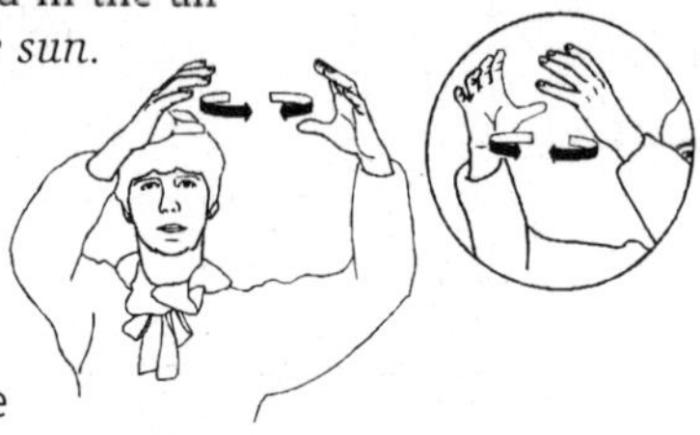

**clown** *n.* A costumed comedy performer, as in a circus: *act like a clown.* Same sign used for: **circus.**

■ [Shape of clown's big nose] Put the fingertips of the right *curved 5 hand* on the nose.

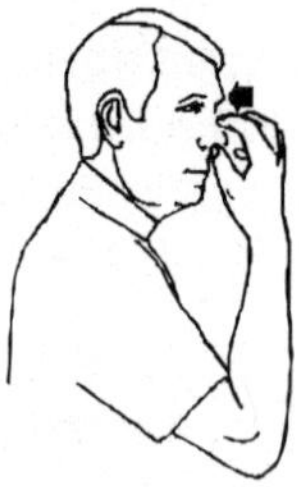

**clumsy**[1] *adj.* Awkward in movement; lacking grace: *The clumsy girl bumped into the furniture.* Same sign used for: **inexperienced.**

■ While holding the thumb of the right *5 hand* tightly in the left *S hand,* twist the right hand forward and down.

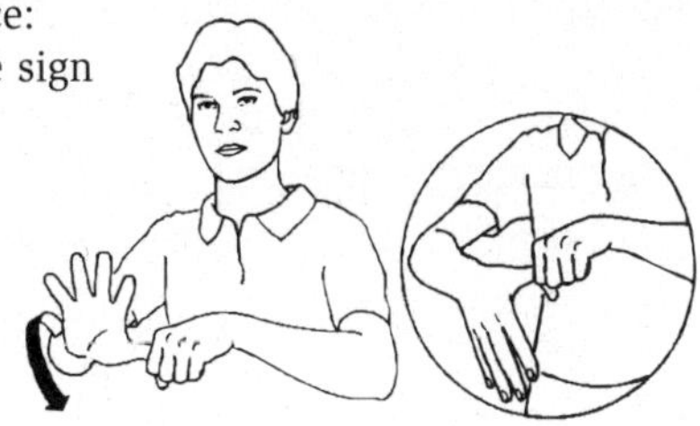

**clumsy**[2] *adj.* See signs for AWKWARD, UNSKILLED.

**coach** *n.* A person who trains athletic teams: *a football coach.*

■ [Initialized sign similar to sign for **captain**] Tap the thumb of the right *C hand,* palm facing left, against the right shoulder with a double movement.

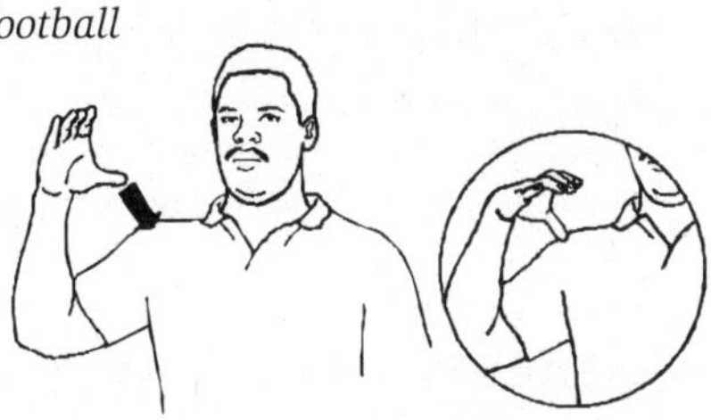

**coarse** *adj.* See sign for ROUGH.

**coat** *n.* An outer garment with sleeves: *wearing a warm coat.* Same sign used for: **bathrobe, jacket, overcoat.**

■ [A coat's lapels] Bring the thumbs of both *A hands* from near each shoulder, palms facing in, downward and toward each other, ending near the waist.

**cocaine** or **coke** *n.* A bitter addictive narcotic used as an illicit drug and also used as a local anesthetic to deaden pain: *The addict used cocaine.* Same sign used for **crack, crack cocaine.**

■ [Shows method of ingesting cocaine] Wipe the extended thumb of the right *10 hand,* palm facing left, first on the right nostril and then on the left nostril.

**cochlear implant** *n. phrase.* A surgically implanted hearing device that converts sound reaching the cochlea into electrical impulses that are transmitted by wire to the auditory nerve.

■ Touch the fingertips of the right *bent V hand,* palm facing left, to behind the right ear.

**cocktail** *n.* A mixed alcoholic drink: *Would you like a cocktail while we're waiting for dinner?* Same sign used for: **alcoholic drink, champagne, drink, liquor.**

■ [Mime drinking from a small glass] Beginning with the thumb of the right *modified C hand* near the mouth, palm facing left, tip the index finger back toward the face.

**coffee** *n.* **1.** A drink made from the ground roasted seeds (coffee beans) of a tropical tree, as by pouring boiling water through the ground coffee beans: *I drink three cups of hot coffee every morning.* **2.** The whole or ground seeds themselves: *buy a can of coffee.*

■ [Grind coffee beans] Move the little-finger side of the right *S hand* with a circular movement on the index-finger side of the left *S hand,* palms facing in opposite directions.

**cogitate** *v.* See sign for MULL.

**coin** *n.* A flat piece of metal with a designated value, issued by a government for use as money: *a pocketful of coins.*

■ [Shape of coin held in the hand] Move the extended right index finger, palm facing in and finger pointing down, in a double circular movement on the left *open hand,* palm facing up.

**coincidence** *n.* See sign for HAPPEN.

**Coke** *n. Trademark.* A carbonated soft drink containing an extract made from kola nuts, together with sweetener and other flavorings: *to order a Coke and a hamburger.* Alternate form: **Coca-Cola** (*trademark*).

■ [Mime injecting a drug] With the index finger of the right *L hand,* palm facing in, touching the upper left arm, move the right thumb up and down with a double movement.

**cold**[1] *n.* A common respiratory illness characterized by a runny nose and often a cough and sore throat: *to catch a cold when the weather changes.*

■ [Mime blowing one's nose] Grasp the nose with the thumb and index finger of the right *A hand,* palm facing in, and pull the hand forward off the nose with a double movement.

**cold**[2] *adj.* Lacking warmth: *cold hands.* Same sign used for: **chilly, frigid, shiver, winter.**

■ [Natural gesture when shivering from cold] Shake both *S hands* with a slight movement in front of each side of the chest, palms facing each other.

**collapse** *n.* See sign for BREAK DOWN.

**collar** *n.* The band around the neck of a garment, often folded down, rolled over, or standing up: *a pointed collar.*

■ [Shape and location of a collar] Move the fingertips of the right *G hand,* palm facing in, from the right side of the neck around to the front.

**collate** *v.* To arrange (pages) in proper order: *collate the copies of the annual report.*

■ [Shows filing things in order] Beginning with the palms of both *open hands* together in front of the chest, fingers pointing forward, move the right hand in a series of double arcs to the right.

**collect** *v.* To receive payment of: *to collect dues from the membership.* Related form: **collection** *n.* Same sign used for: **accumulate, amass, deserve, gather, reap.**

■ [Pulling money to oneself] With a double movement, bring the little-finger side of the right *curved hand,* palm facing left, across the palm of the left *open hand,* palm facing up, from its fingertips to the heel while changing into an *S hand.*

**college** *n.* A school beyond high school that provides a general education and grants degrees: *go away to college.*

■ [Similar to sign for **school** but moves upward to a higher level] Beginning with the palm of the right *open hand* across the palm of the left *open hand* in front of the chest, move the right hand upward in an arc, ending in front of the upper chest, palm angled forward and fingers angled upward toward the left.

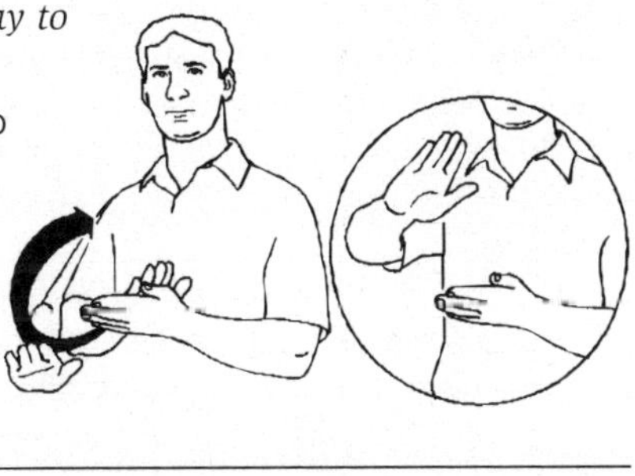

**collide** *v.* See sign for ACCIDENT[1]. Related form: **collision** *n.*

**color**[1] *n.* Any of the hues of the rainbow and their variations, as produced by the quality of the light reflected from an object: *My favorite color is purple.*

■ Wiggle the fingers of the right *5 hand* in front of the mouth, fingers pointing up and palm facing in.

**color**[2] *v.* **1.** To put color on: *to color the picture with crayons.* —*n.* **2.** Something used for coloring: *Choose a color from the box of crayons.* Same sign used for: **crayon.**

■ [Action of coloring with a crayon] Rub the extended right little finger, palm facing down, back and forth on the upturned left *open hand* with a repeated movement.

**color**[3] *n.* See sign for RACE[2].

**column**[1] *n.* **1.** A slender, upright structure: *Greek temples supported by columns.* **2.** One of the sections of an arrangement into vertical divisions on a page: *a page divided into two columns.* **3.** A vertical arrangement of items: *a column of numbers.*

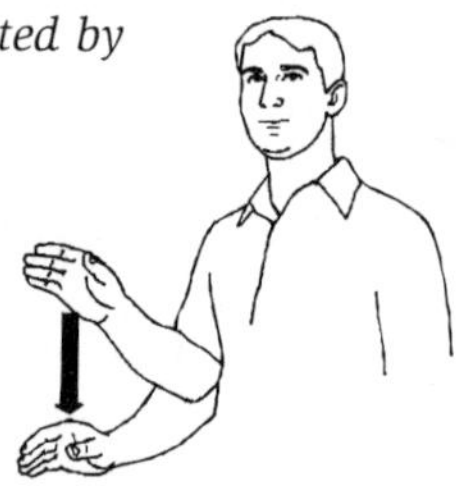

■ [Shape of a column] Move the right *C hand* from in front of the right side of the chest, palm facing forward, downward a short distance, ending with the palm facing left.

**column**[2] *n.* See sign for PILLAR.

**coma** *n.* See sign for FAINT.

**comb** *n.* A small device with a row of teeth used to arrange hair: *lost my comb.*

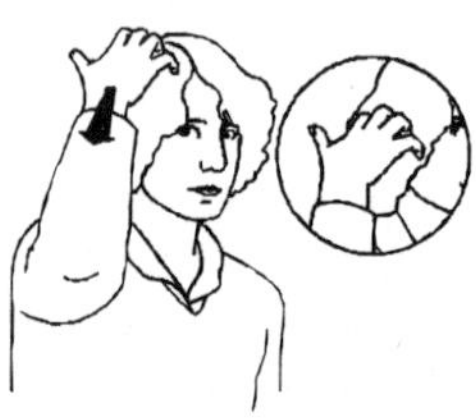

■ [Mime combing hair] Drag the fingertips of the right *curved 5 hand* through the hair on the right side of the head with a short double movement. The verb is the same sign as the noun, but made with a longer double movement.

**combat** *n.* **1.** A fight or struggle, as between ideas or people: *to participate in a combat over leadership of the organization.* **2.** Battle, as in war: *soldiers engaged in combat.* Same sign used for: **fight.**

■ [Represents two people hitting each other] Beginning with both *S hands* in front of each shoulder, palms facing each other, move the hands toward each other with a double movement by bending the wrists.

**combination** *n.* A sequence of numbers used to set the locking mechanism of a combination lock: *figure out the combination to the padlock on my locker.*

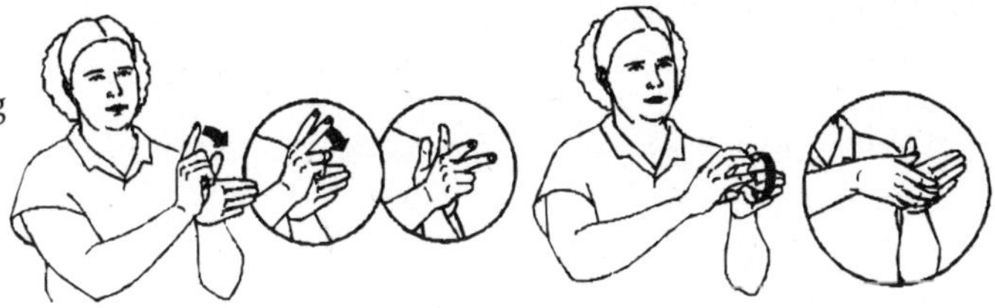

■ [**1-2-3** + mime twisting a combination on a lock] With the heel of the right hand on the left *open hand,* palm facing right, form a 1-2-3 with the right hand. Then move the right *curved 5 hand,* palm facing left, with a double movement by twisting the wrist forward near the palm of the left *open hand,* palm facing right and fingers pointing forward.

---

**combine**[1] *v.* To join or mix two or more things together to form a whole: *First we'll combine the dry ingredients in the mixing bowl.* Same sign used for: **blend.**

■ [**match**[1] + **mix**] Beginning with both *curved 5 hands* in front of each side of the chest, palms facing in, bring the hands together, ending with the fingers meshed together in front of the chest. Then, with the right *curved 5 hand* over the left *curved 5 hand,* palms facing each other, move the hands simultaneously in repeated circles around each other.

---

**combine**[2] *v.* See signs for BELONG[1], MATCH[1], MESH.

---

**come** *v.* To move toward or reach the speaker or a particular place: *come home.*

■ [Indicates direction for another to come toward oneself] Beginning with both extended index fingers pointing up in front of the body, palms facing in, bring the fingers back to each side of the chest.

---

**come back** *v. phrase.* See sign for REFUND.

---

**come here** *v. phrase.* See sign for BECKON.

---

**come on** or **come in** *v. phrase.* To approach: *Come on—the door's open.*

■ [Natural gesture beckoning someone] Move the right *open hand,* palm angled up, back toward the right shoulder.

---

**come up** *v. phrase.* See sign for SHOW UP.

**comfortable** *adj.* Having or providing physical ease: *not comfortable standing outside in the cold; a comfortable chair.* Same sign used for: **convenient, cozy.**

■ [Stroking as a gesture of comfort] Wipe the palm of the right *curved hand* down the back of the left *curved hand,* and then repeat with the palm of the left *curved hand* on the back of the right *curved hand,* both palms facing down.

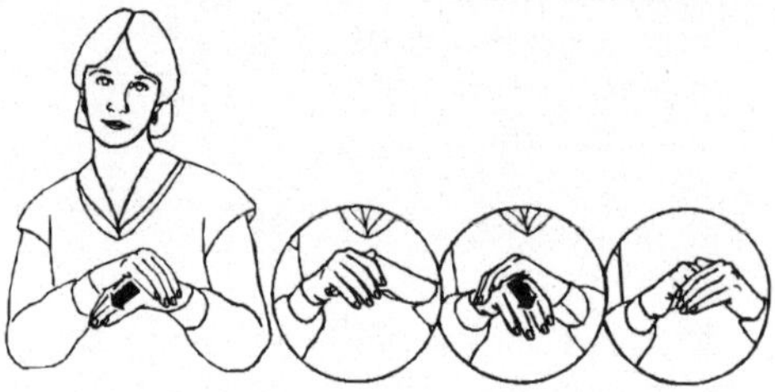

**comical** *adj.* See sign for HUMOROUS.

**comma** *n.* See sign for APOSTROPHE.

**command** *n., v.* See sign for ORDER.

**commence** *v.* See sign for START[1].

**commend** *v.* See sign for APPLAUD.

**comment** *v.* See sign for SAY.

**commercial** *n.* See sign for ADVERTISE.

**commit**[1] *v.* To do something wrong: *The shoplifter committed a felony.* Related form: **commission** *n.*

■ [**do** + **wrong**] Move both *C hands,* palms facing down, simultaneously back and forth in front of the body with a swinging movement. Then bring the middle fingers of the right *Y hand,* palm in, back against the chin with a deliberate movement.

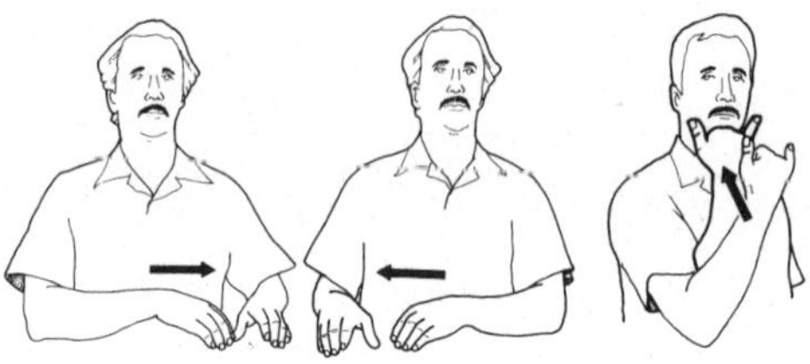

**commit**[2] *v.* See signs for DO, PROMISE, VOW.

**committee** *n.* A group of people selected to perform a special function: *appoint a committee of teachers to study the problem of cheating.*

■ [Initialized sign similar to sign for **member**] Touch the fingertips of the right *curved 5 hand* first to the left side of the chest and then to the right side of the chest, palm facing in.

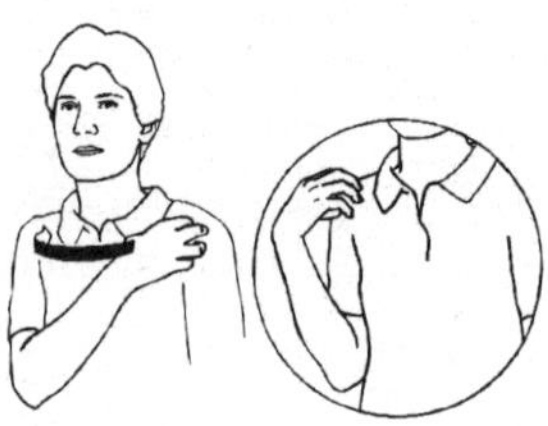

**common sense** *n.* Practical intelligence and sound judgment: *He never went to college, but he shows common sense in handling problems.*

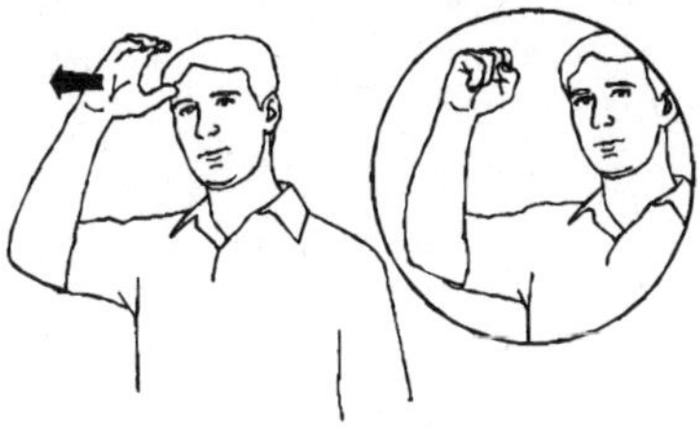

■ [Initials **c-s** formed near the brain for "common sense"] Beginning with the right *C hand* in front of the right side of the forehead, palm facing left, move the right hand forward while changing into an *S hand.*

**common** *n., adj.* See sign for STANDARD.

**communication** *n.* The exchange of information, thoughts, or opinions: *important for friends to have good communication.* Related form: **communicate** *v.* Same sign used for: **conversation, converse.**

■ [Initialized sign indicating words moving both to and from a person] Move both *C hands,* palms facing each other, forward and back from the chin with an alternating movement.

**community** *n.* See signs for CITY, TOWN.

**commute** *v.* To travel back and forth regularly: *commute to work.* Same sign used for: **back and forth.**

■ [Demonstrates movement to and from] Move the right *10 hand,* palm facing left, from in front of the right side of the body to in front of the left side of the body with a double movement.

**companion** *n.* See sign for STEADY.

**compare** *v.* To examine to identify likenesses or differences: *compare ideas.* Related form: **comparison** *n.*

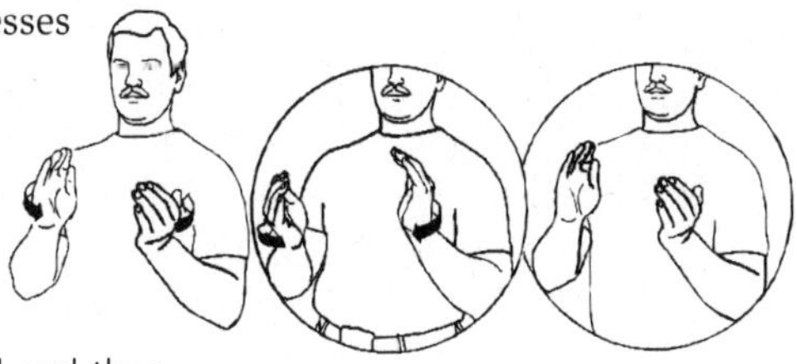

■ [Holding something in one hand and comparing it with something in the other hand] With both *curved hands* in front of each side of the chest, palms facing, alternately turn one hand and then the other toward the face while turning the other hand in the opposite direction, keeping the palms facing each other and the fingers pointing up.

**compatible**[1] *adj.* Able to exist together or with another in harmony: *a compatible couple; a compatible friend.* Related form: **compatibility** *n.*

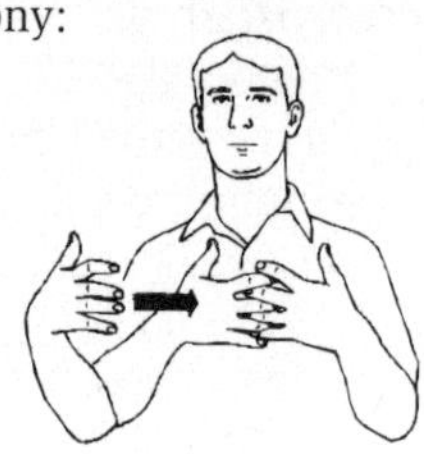

■ [Bringing something to combine with something else] Beginning with both *curved 5 hands* in front of each side of the chest, palms facing in, move the right hand to the left to mesh the fingers with the bent fingers of the left hand.

---

**compatible**[2] *adj.* See sign for AGREE[1].

---

**competent** *adj.* Possessing sufficient skill, knowledge, or experience for a specified purpose: *The prisoner was competent enough to stand trial.*

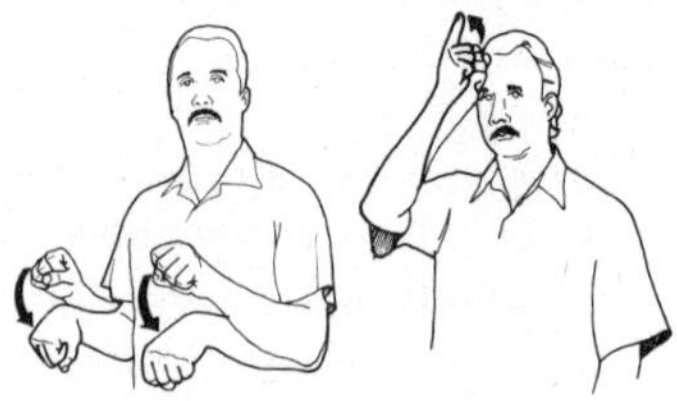

■ [**can + understand**] Move both *S hands,* palms facing down, downward simultaneously in front of each side of the body. Then beginning with the right *modified X hand*, palm in, near the right side of the forehead, flick the index finger upward with a deliberate movement.

---

**complain** *v.* To express dissatisfaction or pain: *The employee complained about the long hours with no overtime pay.* Same sign used for: **boycott, grievance, gripe, grumble, object, protest, riot, strike.**

■ Tap the fingertips of the right *curved 5 hand* against the center of the chest.

---

**complaint** *n.* See sign for PROTEST[1].

---

**complete** *v., adj.* See signs for END[1], FINISH[1], FULL[2].

---

**complex**[1] *adj.* Having many elements that are difficult to analyze: *a complex situation.* Same sign used for: **complicated.**

■ Beginning with both extended index fingers pointed toward each other in front of each side of the face, both palms facing down, continuously bend the fingers up and down as the hands move past each other in front of the face.

---

**complex**[2] *adj.* See sign for MIX[1].

---

**compliment** *v., n.* See sign for PRAISE.

---

**comprehend** *v.* See sign for UNDERSTAND.

**compromise**[1] *n.* The settlement of a disagreement by yielding on both sides: *They came to a compromise over wages and hours.*

■ [Initialized sign indicating two minds coming into agreement] Beginning with both *C hands* near each side of the head, palms facing each other, turn the hands downward, ending with the palms facing down and fingers pointing forward.

**compromise**[2] *n.* See sign for AGREE[1].

**computer** *n.* A programmable electronic machine for processing data at high speeds, including performing calculations, word processing, and database management: *using a computer to keep track of inventory and customers.*

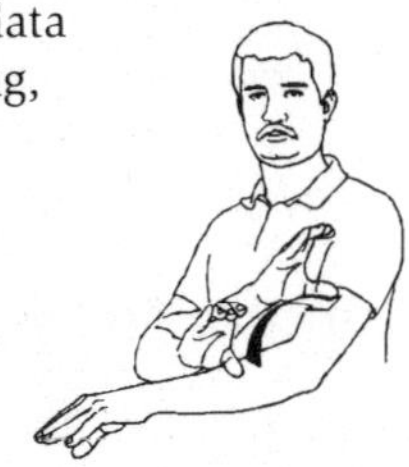

■ [Initialized sign] Move the thumb side of the right *C hand,* palm facing left, from touching the lower part of extended left arm upward to touch the upper arm.

**comrade** *n.* See sign for FRIEND.

**con** *v., n.* See signs for BETRAY, TRICK.

**conceal** *v.* See sign for HIDE.

**conceited** *adj.* Having excessive pride in oneself: *You can tell from his arrogant behavior how conceited he is.* Same sign used for: **arrogant, big-headed, big shot, brat, bully.**

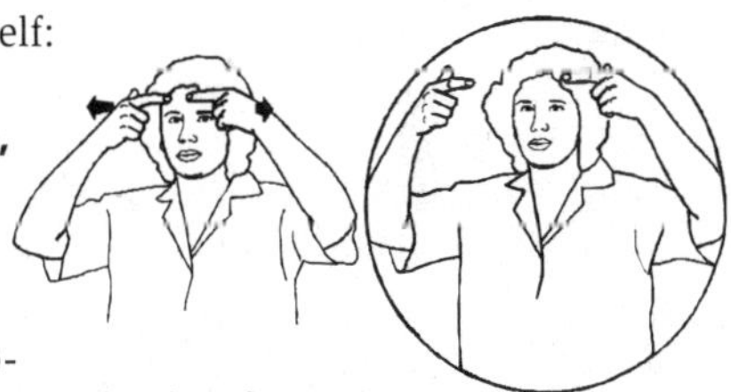

■ [**big** formed near the head, signifying a person with a "big head"] Beginning with both *L hands* in front of each side of the forehead, index fingers pointing toward each other and palms facing in, bring the hands outward away from each other a short distance.

**conceive** *v.* See sign for PREGNANT.

**concentrate** *v.* See sign for ATTENTION. Related form: **concentration** *n.*

**concept** *n.* A general idea: *The concept for the TV show is good, but the actors are terrible.* Same sign used for: **creative.**

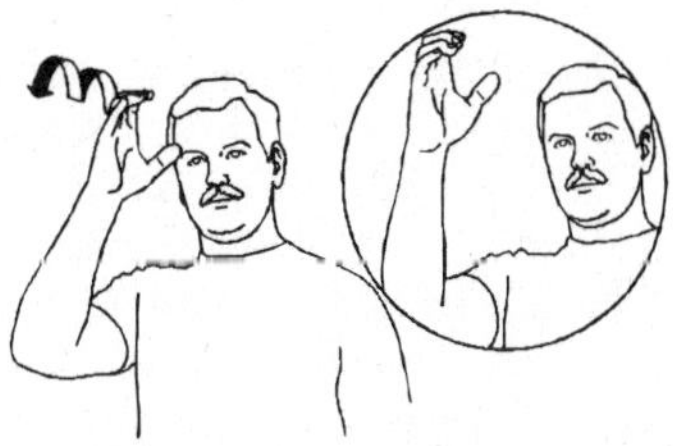

■ [Initialized sign similar to sign for **invent**] Move the right *C hand,* palm facing left, from the right side of the forehead forward and slightly upward in a double arc.

**concern**[1] *v.* To trouble, worry, or disturb: *concerned about my grades.* Same sign used for: **consider, think.**

- [Thoughts moving through the brain] Beginning with both extended index fingers in front of each side of the forehead, palms facing in and fingers angled up, move the fingers in repeated alternating circular movements toward each other in front of the face.

**concern**[2] *v.* To be of interest to: *The environment is an issue that concerns me.* Same sign used for: **anxiety.**

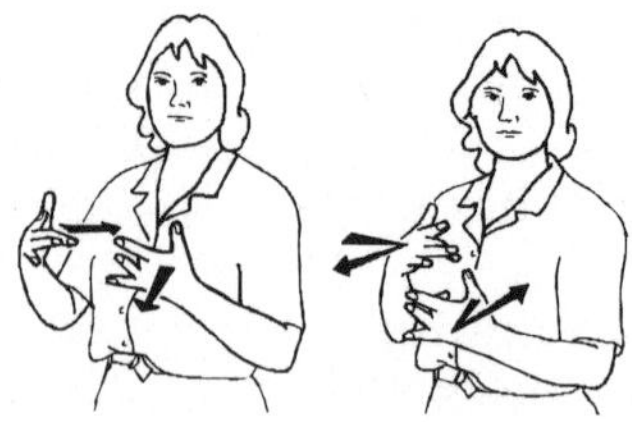

- Beginning with the bent middle fingers of both *5 hands* pointing to each side of the chest, left hand closer to the chest than the right hand and palms facing in, bring the hands forward and back to the chest with a repeated alternating movement.

**concern**[3] *n.* See sign for TROUBLE[1].

**concerning** *prep.* See sign for ABOUT.

**concise** *adj.* See sign for PRECISE.

**conclude** *v.* See sign for END[1].

**concur** *v.* See sign for AGREE[1].

**condemn** *v.* See signs for CANCEL, CURSE.

**condense** *v.* See sign for BRIEF.

**condition** *n.* The existing state or situation of a person or thing: *a used car in good condition.* Same sign used for: **circumstance, culture.**

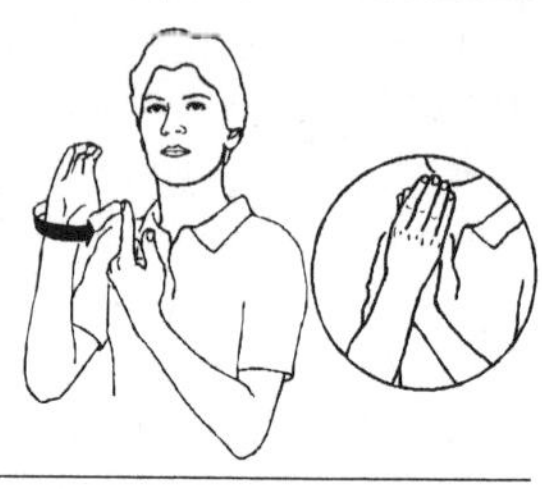

- [Initialized sign showing area around a thing] Beginning with the right *C hand,* palm facing left, near the extended left index finger, palm facing right, move the right hand in a circle forward and around the left finger.

**conduct** *v.* See signs for DO, LEAD.

**conference**[1] *n.* A meeting of interested persons to discuss a topic: *attend a conference on crime prevention.*

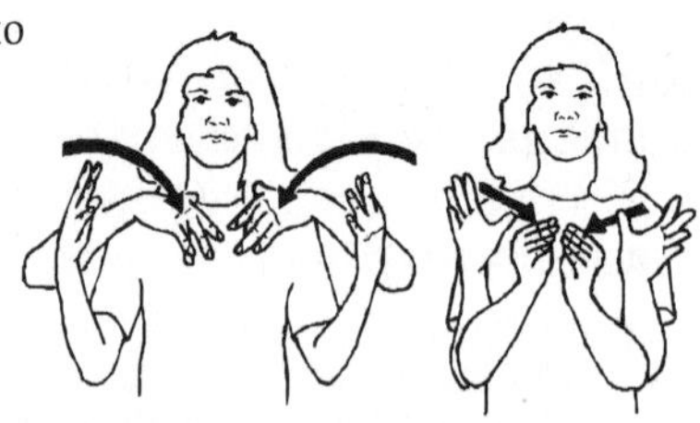

- [**gather**[1,2] + **meeting**] Beginning with both *5 hands* in front of each side of the chest, palms facing each other, bring the hands together in front of the chest, fingers pointing down. Then, beginning with both *5 hands* in front of each shoulder, palms facing each other and fingers pointing up, close the fingers into *flattened O hands* while moving the hands together with a double movement.

**conference**[2] *n.* See sign for MEETING.

**confess** *v.* See sign for ADMIT. Related form: **confession** *n.*

**confident** *adj.* Being certain; sure of oneself, one's abilities, and one's future prospects: *I am confident that we will win the election.* Related form: **confidence** *n.* Same sign used for: **bold, trust.**

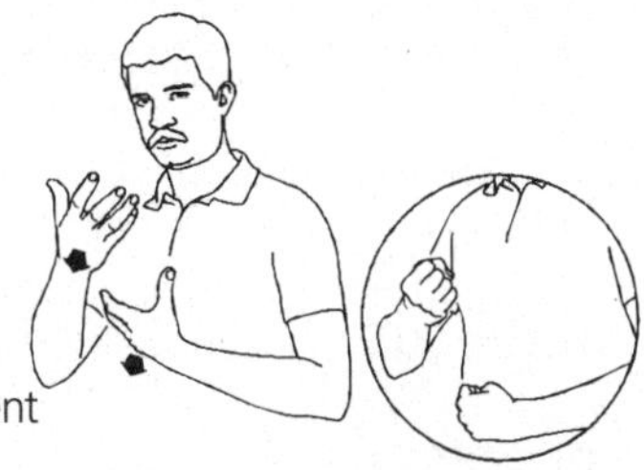

- [Holding firmly to one's beliefs] Beginning with both *curved 5 hands* in front of the chest, right hand above the left and palms facing in, bring both hands downward a short distance with a deliberate movement while closing into *S hands.*

**confidential** *adj.* See sign for SECRET.

**confined** *adj.* See sign for STUCK.

**conflict**[1] *n.* **1.** Active opposition: *The discussion ended in conflict.* —*v.* **2.** To clash or disagree: *Their stories conflicted as to what happened.* **3.** To differ: *Although their methods conflict, they are able to work together.* Same sign used for: **breed, contradict, cross-purposes, fertilize.**

- [Represents a crossing of opinions] Beginning with both extended index fingers in front of each side of the body, palms facing in and fingers angled toward each other, move the hands toward each other, ending with the fingers crossed.

**conflict**[2] *v., n.* See sign for STRUGGLE.

**confront** *v.* To encounter someone or something in order to be dealt with: *The lawyer confronted the defendant with the evidence.* Related form: **confrontation** *n.*

- [Bringing two things to a face-to-face encounter] Beginning with both *open hands* in front of the lower chest, palms facing each other and fingers pointing up, move both hands upward toward the left in an arc with a deliberate movement.

**confuse**[1] *v.* **1.** To mix up: *confuse the two packages.* **2.** To bewilder: *I was confused by your explanation.* Related form: **confusion** *n.* Same sign used for: **mixed up.**

- [**think** + **mix**] Bring the extended right index finger from touching the right side of the forehead, palm facing in, down to in front of the chest, changing into a *curved 5 hand.* Then, with the right *curved 5 hand* over the left *curved 5 hand,* palms facing each other, move the hands simultaneously in repeated circles going in opposite directions.

**confuse**[2] *v.* See sign for MIX[1].

**congratulate** *v.* To express pleasure at the good fortune of (another person): *congratulate the groom.* Related form: **congratulations** *pl. n., interj.*

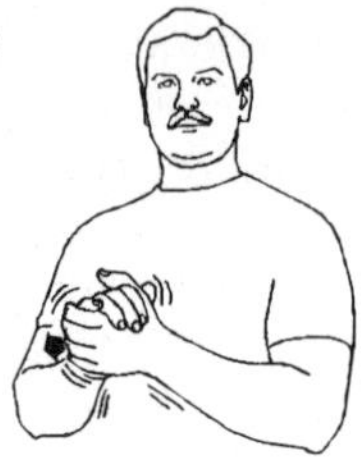

- [Mime clasping hands to congratulate another] Clasp both *curved hands* together in front of the body and shake them with a repeated movement.

**congregation** *n.* See sign for AUDIENCE.

**Congress** *n.* **1.** The national law-making body of the United States, consisting of the Senate and the House of Representatives: *Congress passed the law.* **2. congress** An association of similar organizations: *a meeting of a congress of teachers.*

- [Initialized sign similar to sign for **committee**] Touch the thumb of the right *C hand,* palm facing left, first on the left side of the chest and then on the right side.

**connect** *v.* See sign for BELONG[1].

**connection** *n.* See sign for RELATIONSHIP.

**conquer** *v.* See signs for CAPTURE, DEFEAT.

**consequence** *n.* See sign for RESULT.

**consider** *v.* See signs for CONCERN[1], WONDER.

**consistent**[1] *adj.* Staying constant in activity, principle, or course: *consistent in her philosophy throughout her life.* Related form: **consistently** *adv.* Same sign used for: **faithful, regular.**

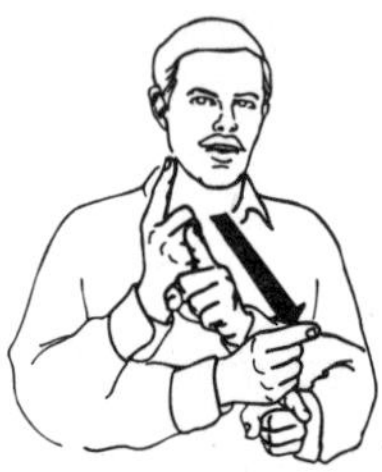

- [Similar to sign for **right**[2] formed with a continuous movement] With the little-finger side of the right *1 hand* across the index-finger side of the left *1 hand*, palms facing in opposite directions, move the hands downward in front of the chest.

**consistent**[2] *adj.* See sign for CONSTANT[2, 3].

**constant**[1] *adj.* Continuing without stopping: *The rain was constant.* Same sign used for: **continuous, momentum.**

- [Similar to sign for **alike**[2] but formed with two hands] Beginning with both *Y hands* in front of each side of the chest, palms facing down, move the hands in simultaneous circles, moving inward in opposite directions.

**constant**[2] *adj.* **1.** Always the same; unchanging; steady: *Keep a constant temperature in the room.* **2.** Steadfast and loyal: *a constant friend.* Same sign used for: **consistent, even, steady.**

■ [Indicates a steady movement] Beginning with the right *open hand* in front of the right shoulder, palm facing down and fingers pointing forward, move the hand straight forward in a slow movement.

**constant**[3] *adj.* **1.** Recurring regularly: *the constant ringing of the telephone.* **2.** Not changing: *to keep the room at a constant temperature.* **3.** Loyal; faithful; steadfast: *The dog was his constant companion.* Same sign used for: **consistent, continual, persistent, steadfast, steady.**

■ [Indicates continuing movement] Beginning with the thumb of the right *10 hand* on the thumbnail of the left *10 hand*, both palms facing down in front of the chest, move the hands downward and forward in a series of small arcs.

**construct** *v.* See sign for BUILD. Related form: **construction** *n.*

**consult** *v.* See sign for COUNSEL. Related form: **consultation** *n.*

**consultant** *n.* See sign for ADVISOR.

**consume** *v.* To use up: *consumes too much time.* Related form: **consumption** *n.* Same sign used for: **devour, eat up, gullible.**

■ [Represents food entering the mouth to be consumed] Move the right *bent hand,* palm facing in, past the right cheek with a deliberate movement.

**consumer**[1] *n.* A person who purchases goods or services: *The merchandise was displayed so a consumer could see it easily.*

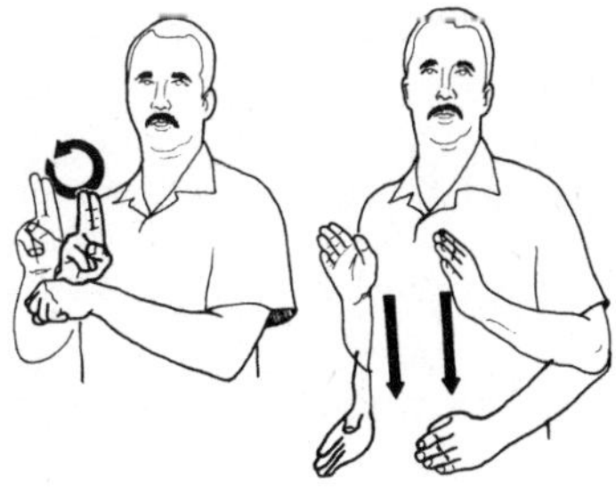

■ [**use** + **person marker**] With the heel of the right *U hand* on the back of the left *S hand,* move the right hand in a small circle. Then move both *open hands*, palms facing each other, downward along the sides of the body.

**consumer**[2] *n.* See sign for CUSTOMER[1].

**contact** *n.* **1.** The state of touching or being in communication: *Stay in contact with me.* —*v.* **2.** To get in touch with: *Contact me later.* Same sign used for: **in touch with.**

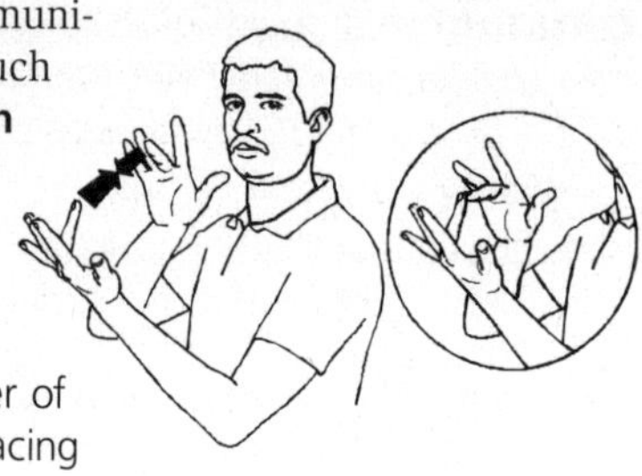

- [Indicates two things coming into contact with each other] With the right hand above the left hand in front of the chest, touch the bent middle finger of the right *5 hand* to the bent middle finger of the left *5 hand* with a double movement, palms facing each other.

**contact lens** *n. phrase.* A thin plastic disk designed to fit on the cornea to improve vision: *wear contact lenses instead of glasses.*

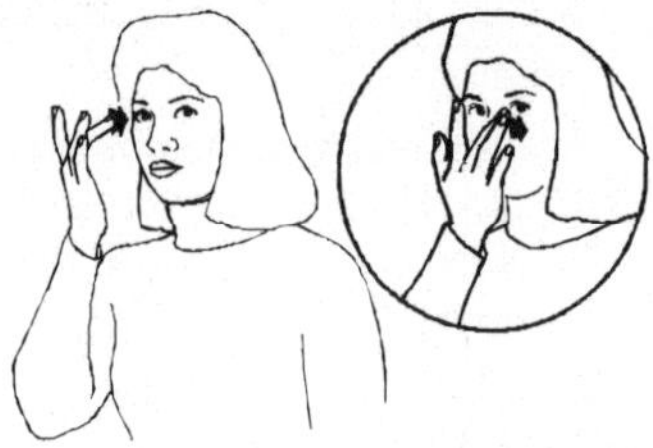

- [Action of putting in contact lenses] Bring the bent middle finger of the right *5 hand,* palm facing in, first toward the right eye, and then toward the left eye.

**contained in** *adj. phrase.* See sign for INCLUDE.

**contemplate** *v.* See sign for WONDER.

**contempt** *n.* A feeling or expression of disdain for something or someone mean, vile, and low: *looked at him with contempt.* Same sign used for: **look down at** or **on, scorn.**

- [Represents eyes looking down on another] Beginning with both *V hands* in front of each side of the chest, palms facing forward and fingers pointing up, twist the wrists downward to point the fingers forward with a slow movement.

**content**[1] *n.* See sign for MEAT.

**content**[2] *adj.* See signs for RELIEF, SATISFY[1]. Related form: **contentment** *n.*

**contingent** *v.* See sign for DEPEND.

**continuance** *n.* See sign for POSTPONE.

**continue**[1] *v.* To go on or keep on: *to continue going to work.* Same sign used for: **last, lasting, remain.**

■ [Indicates continuous movement] Beginning with the thumb of the right *10 hand* on the thumbnail of the left *10 hand,* both palms facing down in front of the chest, move the hands downward and forward in an arc.

**continue**[2] *v.* See sign for GO ON.

**continuous** *adj.* See sign for CONSTANT[1].

**contradiction** *n.* See sign for CRAMP.

**contradict** *v.* See sign for CONFLICT[1].

**contrary**[1] *adj.* Opposite in nature, character, or opinion: *contrary to popular opinion.* Same sign used for: **antagonistic, bullheaded, cantankerous.**

■ [Two opposing things meeting head-on] Bump the heels of both *Y hands* sharply against each other and then apart in front of the chest.

**contrary**[2] *adj.* See sign for OPPOSITE.

**contrast** *v.* See signs for DISAGREE, OPPOSITE.

**contribute** *v.* See signs for CHARITY, GIVE. Related form: **contribution** *n.*

**control**[1] *v.* To restrain (one's feelings): *Control your temper.* Same sign used for: **restrain, suppress, tolerate.**

■ [The hands seem to suppress one's feelings] Beginning with the fingertips of both *curved 5 hands* against the chest, palms facing in, bring the hands downward while forming *S hands,* palms facing up.

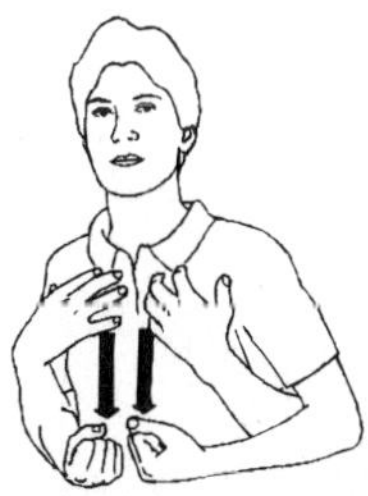

**control**[2] *v.* See sign for MANAGE.

**controlled substance** *n. phrase.* See sign for DRUG[1].

**controversy** *n.* See signs for ARGUE, STRUGGLE.

**convenient** *adj.* See signs for COMFORTABLE, EASY.

**convention** *n.* See sign for MEETING.

**converse** *v.* See sign for COMMUNICATION. Related form: **conversation** *n.*

**conversion** *n.* See sign for UPDATE.

**convertible** *n.* An automobile with a folding top: *to ride in a convertible with the top down.*

■ [Represents lowering and raising a convertible top] Beginning with both *X hands* in front of each shoulder, palms facing each other, bring the hands upward and backward, and then forward again, in a simultaneous double arc.

**convey** *v.* See sign for NARROW DOWN.

**convict** *v.* See sign for CATCH².

**convince**[1] *v.* To persuade by argument or evidence: *I remain convinced of his innocence.* Same sign used for: **persuade.**

■ Beginning with both *open hands* in front of each shoulder, palms angled upward, bring the hands down sharply at an angle toward each other.

**convince**[2] *v.* (alternate sign, used especially when referring to convincing one other person)

■ [One hand hits the other hand to influence it] Move the little-finger side of the right *open hand*, palm facing up, sharply against the extended left index finger held up in front of the chest.

**convince**[3] *v.* (alternate sign, used especially when referring to being convinced by the influence of another or others)

■ [Strike the sides of the neck to convince someone] Hit the little-finger sides of both *open hands*, palms facing down and fingers pointing back, against each side of the neck with a sharp movement.

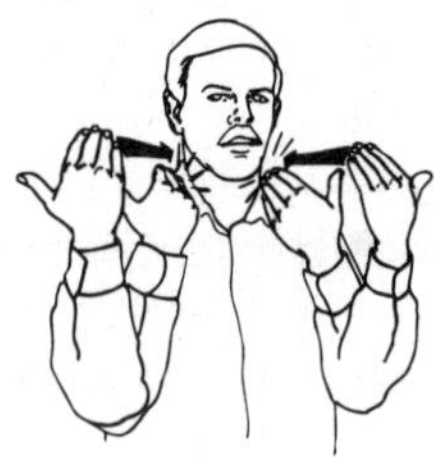

**convocation** *n.* See sign for MEETING.

**cook** *v.* To prepare food by using heat: *to cook dinner.* Same sign used for: **bake, flip, fry, turn over.**

- [As if turning food in a frying pan] Beginning with the fingers of the right *open hand,* palm facing down, across the palm of the left *open hand,* flip the right hand over, ending with the back of the right hand on the left palm.

**cookie** *n.* A small, flat cake: *chocolate chip cookies.* Same sign used for: **biscuit.**

- [Mime using a cookie cutter] Touch the fingertips of the right *C hand,* palm facing down, on the upturned palm of the left *open hand.* Then twist the right hand and touch the left palm again.

**cool** *adj.* Lacking in warmth: *a cool day.* Same sign used for: **pleasant, refresh.**

- [As if fanning oneself] With both *open hands* above each shoulder, palms facing back and fingers pointing up, bend the fingers up and down with a repeated movement.

**cooperate** *v.* United effort: *If everyone cooperates we can finish on time.* Related form: **cooperation** *n.* Same sign used for: **affiliation, union, unity, universal.**

- With the thumbs and index fingers of both *F hands* intersecting, move the hands in a flat circle in front of the chest.

**coordinate** *v.* To arrange or combine so as to function harmoniously: *Coordinate your plans with the rest of the committee.* Same sign used for: **relate.**

- With the thumbs and index fingers of both *F hands* intersecting, move the hands forward and back with a double movement.

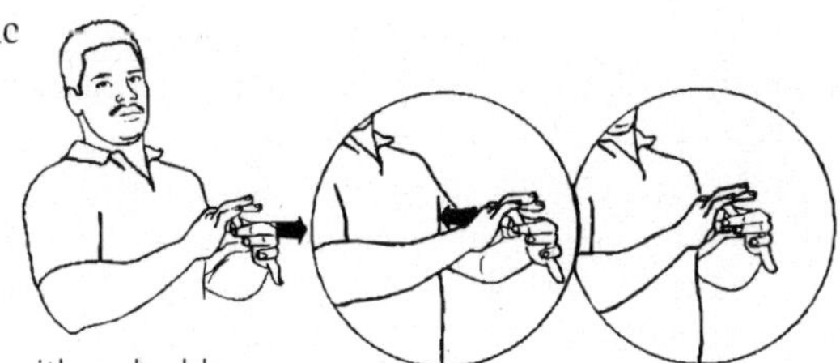

**cop** *n.* See sign for POLICE.

**copy**[1] *v.* To reproduce from another source: *Copy the homework assignment from the board.* Same sign used for: **duplicate, imitate, impose, parrot.**

■ [Represents taking information and recording it on paper] Move the right *curved hand* in front of the chest, palm facing forward, down to touch the palm of the left *open hand* while closing the right fingers and thumb into a *flattened O hand.* The noun is formed in the same way except with a double movement.

**copy**[2] *v.* **1.** To reproduce by photocopying: *Copy this report for everyone.* —*n.* **2.** A photocopy: *Make a copy for each person.* Same sign used for: **duplicate, imitate, impose, photocopy.**

■ [Represents the action of a photocopy machine] Move the fingers of the right *curved hand,* palm facing up, downward from touching the palm of the left *open hand* while closing the right fingers and thumb into a *flattened O hand.*

**copy**[3] *n.* See sign for EXCERPT.

**cord** *n.* A small flexible cable or thin rope: *Tie the package with cord.* Same sign used for: **thread, wire.**

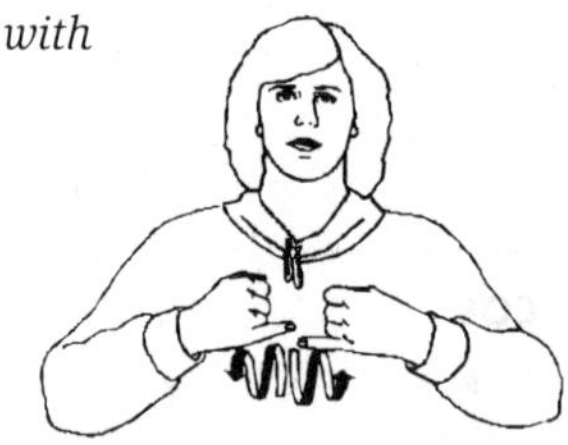

■ [Shape of a coiled cord] Beginning with both extended little fingers pointing toward each other in front of the chest, palms facing in, move the fingers in circular movements while moving the hands away from each other.

**corn** *n.* A cereal plant that bears small, usually yellow, kernels on large ears: *eating corn for dinner.*

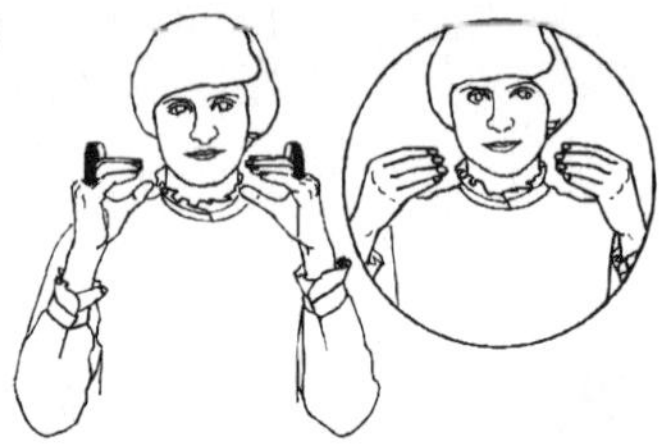

■ [Mime eating corn on the cob] With both *flattened C hands* held near each side of the face, palms facing each other, twist both hands forward simultaneously with a repeated movement.

**corner**[1] *n.* A place where two lines or surfaces meet: *standing in the corner of the room.*

■ [Hands form the shape of a corner] Move the fingertips of both *open hands,* palms angled toward each other, to touch each other at an angle with a repeated movement.

**corner**[2] *v.* See sign for NAB.

**coronary** *n.* See sign for HEART ATTACK.

**correct** *v.* See signs for CANCEL, EDIT[1], RIGHT[3].

**correspond** *v.* To communicate by letter: *close friends who correspond every week.* Related form: **correspondence** *n.*

■ [Represents the sending and receiving of letters] Beginning with *modified X hands,* palms facing each other and the right hand closer to the chest than the left, flick the index fingers toward each other with a repeated alternating movement.

**corridor** *n.* See sign for HALL.

**cosmetics** *pl. n.* See sign for MAKE-UP.

**cost**[1] *n.* **1.** The price paid or charged for something: *The cost is $5.00 for each ticket.* —*v.* **2.** To have a price of: *The candy costs 50 cents.* Same sign used for: **charge, fare, fee, fine, price, tax.**

■ Strike the knuckle of the right *X hand,* palm facing in, down the palm of the left *open hand,* palm facing right and fingers pointing forward.

**cost**[2] *n.* (alternate sign) Same sign used for: **price, value, worth.**

■ Tap the fingertips of both *F hands* together, palms facing each other, with a repeated movement.

**costly** *adj.* See sign for EXPENSIVE.

**costume** *n.* See sign for CLOTHES.

**couch** *n.* A long upholstered piece of furniture for seating two to four people: *Sit over there, on the couch.* Same sign used for: **pew, sofa.**

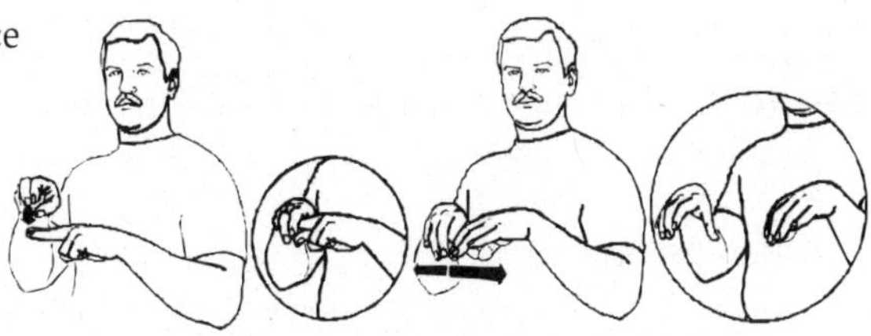

■ [**sit** + **loaf** to indicate the elongated shape of a couch] Place the fingers of the right *curved U hand* across the fingers of the left *U hand,* both palms facing down. Then, beginning with the index-finger sides of both *C hands* touching, palms facing down, bring the hands apart to each side of the body.

**cough** *v.* **1.** To force air from the lungs with a sharp noise: *I coughed all night.* —*n.* **2.** The act or sound of coughing: *The baby's cough woke me up.*

■ [Location of the origin of a cough in the chest] With the fingertips of the right *curved 5 hand* on the chest, palm facing in, lower the wrist with a repeated movement while keeping the fingertips in place.

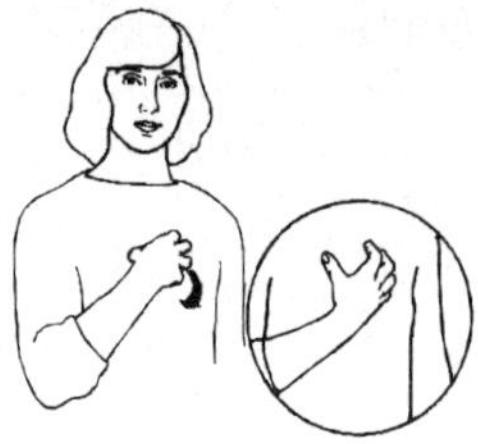

**council** *n.* See sign for MEETING.

**counsel** *v.* To give advice to: *to counsel the students.* Same sign used for: **advise, affect, consult, consultation.**

■ [Represents the spreading of one's counsel to others] Beginning with the fingertips of the right *flattened O hand* on the back of the left *flattened O hand,* palm facing down, move the right hand forward with a double movement while spreading the fingers into a *5 hand* each time.

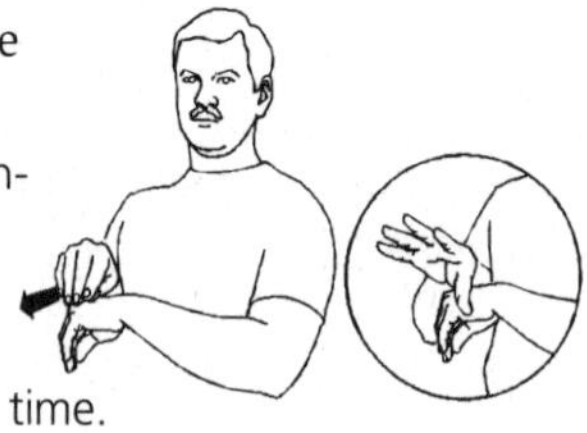

**counselor** *n.* See sign for ADVISOR.

**count** *v.* **1.** To name consecutive numbers: *See if the child can count to ten.* **2.** To find or determine the total number of: *count the chairs.*

■ Move the fingertips of the right *F hand,* palm facing down, across the upturned palm of the left *open hand* from the heel to the fingers.

**counter** *adj.* See sign for OPPOSITE.

**counterfeit** *n.* See sign for FAKE[2].

**country**[1] *n.* A state or nation or its territory: *to live in a foreign country.* Same sign used for: **land.**

■ Rub the bent fingers of the right *Y hand,* palm facing in, in a circle near the elbow of the bent left arm with a repeated movement.

**country**[2] *n.* **1.** (alternate sign) **2.** Rural areas, as opposed to cities and towns: *to spend a day in the country, away from the noise and the crowds.*

■ Rub the palm of the right *open hand* in a circle near the elbow of the bent left arm with a repeated movement.

**couple** *n.* **1.** Two people paired together: *a newly married couple.* **2.** Two things thought of or used together: *a couple of diaper pins.* Same sign used for: **pair, partners.**

- [Pointing to two people making up a couple] Move the right *V fingers,* palm facing up and fingers pointing forward, from side to side in front of the right side of the body with a repeated movement.

**courage** *n.* See sign for BRAVE.

**course** *n.* A series of classes on a subject: *register for the course in word processing.* Same sign used for: **chapter, lesson.**

- [Initialized sign similar to sign for **list**] Move the little-finger side of the right *C hand,* palm facing in, in an arc, touching first on the fingers and then near the heel of the upturned left hand.

**court** *n.* See sign for JUDGE.

**courteous** *adj.* See sign for POLITE. Related form: **courtesy** *n.*

**cousin** *n.* A child of one's uncle or aunt: *my cousins, John and Mary.*

- [Male cousin: Initialized sign formed near the male area of the head] Move the right *C hand,* palm facing left, with a shaking movement near the right side of the forehead.
- [Female cousin: Initialized sign near the female area of the head] Move the right *C hand,* palm facing left, with a shaking movement near the right side of the chin.

male

female

**cover**[1] *n.* **1.** Something placed over or upon, as to protect or conceal: *the cover of the book.* —*v.* **2.** To put something over or upon to protect or conceal it: *to cover your face with your hands.*

- [Demonstrates pulling a cover over something] Move the right *open hand,* palm facing down, from in front of the right side of the body in a large circular movement over the bent left arm held across the body.

**cover**[2] *n.* See sign for LID.

**cover-up** *n.* **1.** An action calculated to hide the truth or impede an investigation: *a high-level cover-up designed to avert scandal.* —*v. phrase.* **cover up** **2.** To conceal and prevent exposure of (a crime, scandal, etc.): *Everyone tried to cover up the judge's part in the crime.* Same sign used for: **fraud, hide.**

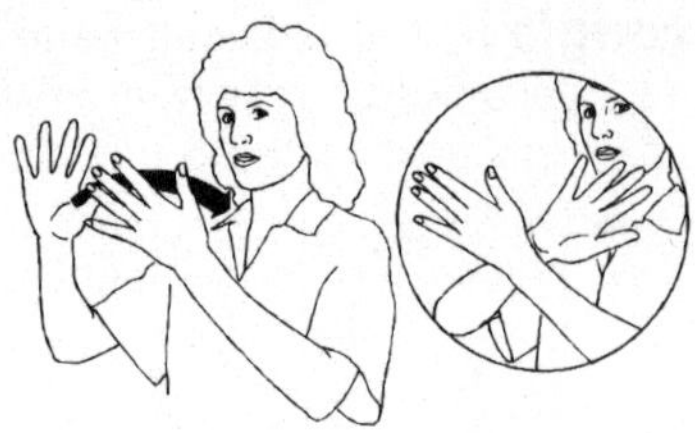

- [Hands seem to try to blur the truth] Beginning with the left *5 hand* in front of the chest, palm facing in, and the right *5 hand* by the right side of the body, palm facing forward, bring the right hand in an arc past the left hand, ending with the wrists crossed.

**cow** *n.* A full-grown female bovine animal: *Milk comes from a cow.* Same sign used for: **cattle.**

- [A cow's horns] With the thumbs of both *Y hands* on both sides of the forehead, palms facing forward, twist the hands forward.

**coward** *n.* See signs for BIRD, FEAR.

**cozy** *adj.* See sign for COMFORTABLE.

**crack**[1] *n.* A narrow break: *a crack in the sidewalk.* Same sign used for: **chap, split.**

- [Shape of a crack] Move the little-finger side of the right *open hand,* palm facing left, down the palm of the left *open hand,* palm facing up, with a jagged movement.

**crack**[2] *n.* See sign for RAGGED. Related form: **cracked** *adj.*

**crack**[3] or **crack cocaine** *n., n. phrase.* See sign for COCAINE.

**cracker** *n.* A dry, thin biscuit: *to eat crackers with the soup.* Same sign used for: **Passover.**

- Strike the palm side of the right *A hand* near the elbow of the bent left arm with a repeated movement.

**cramp** *n.* An involuntary muscle contraction or spasm: *I got a cramp in my leg.* —*v.* To have an involuntary muscle contraction, usually painful: *My muscles cramped up in the cold water.* Related form: **cramps** *pl. n.* Same sign used for: **charley horse, contraction, spasm.**

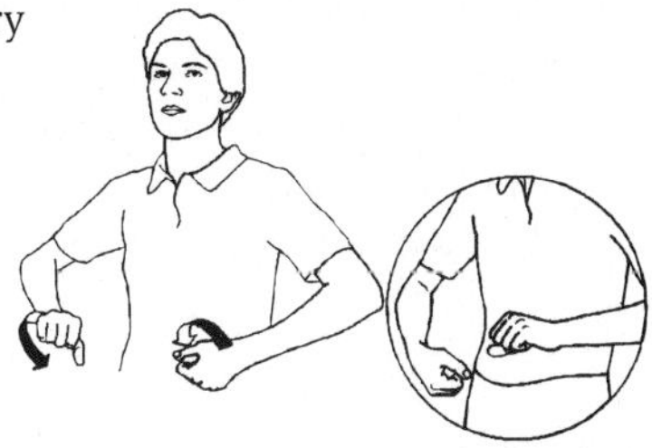

■ [A gesture indicating a cramp] Beginning with both *A hands* in front of each side of the body, right palm facing down and left palm facing up, twist the hands in opposite directions.

**cramped** *adj.* See sign for CROWDED[1].

**crash**[1] *n.* **1.** The violent and noisy striking of one solid thing against another: *There was a terrible crash when two cars ran into each other head-on.* —*v.* **2.** To strike against another thing or collide violently and noisily: *The car crashed into a tree.*

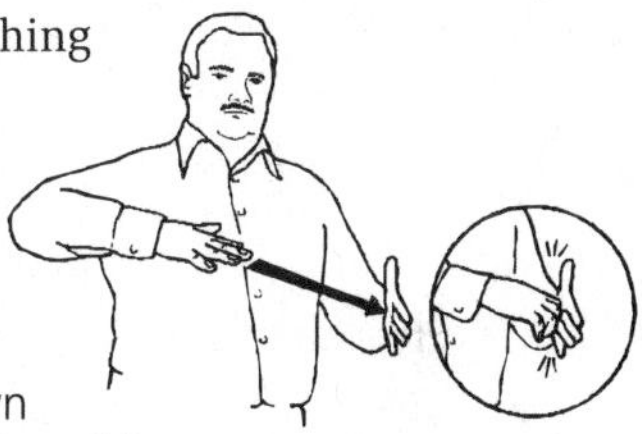

■ [Shows impact of a crash] Beginning with the right *5 hand* near the right side of the chest, palm facing down and fingers angled forward, move the hand deliberately to hit against the palm of the left *open hand,* bending the right fingers as it hits.

**crash**[2] *n.* See sign for ACCIDENT[1].

**crash**[3] *n.* See sign for BREAK DOWN.

**crave** *v.* See sign for DROOL, HUNGRY.

**crawl** *v.* **1.** To move with the body near the ground, as on one's hands and knees: *The baby has learned to crawl across the floor.* **2.** To move slowly: *The traffic is crawling today.*

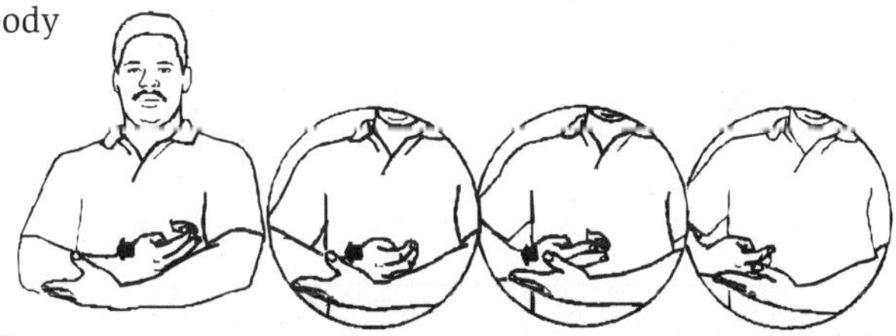

■ [Represents movement of crawling] Beginning with the back of the right *bent V hand,* palm facing up, on the inside of the bent left forearm, move the right hand down the forearm toward the left hand while crooking the finger of the *bent V hand* with a repeated movement.

**crayon** *n.* See sign for COLOR[2].

**crazy** *adj.* **1.** Mentally disordered: *behaving like a crazy person.* **2.** Wildly impractical: *crazy ideas.* **3.** Unusual; bizarre: *a crazy day.* Same sign used for: **wacky** (*slang*), **wild.**

■ [Indicates that things are confused in one's head] Twist the *curved 5 hand,* palm facing in, forward with a repeated movement near the right side of the head.

**cream** *n.* The yellowish part of whole milk containing butterfat, tending to rise to the surface in milk that is not homogenized: *a pint of cream.*

■ [Initialized sign representing skimming cream from the top of milk] Bring the little-finger side of the right *C hand,* palm facing left, back toward the chest in a circular movement across the palm of the left *open hand.*

**create** *v.* See signs for INVENT, MAKE.

**creative** *adj.* See sign for CONCEPT.

**credit card** *n. phrase.* See signs for CARD[2], CHARGE[1].

**creek** *n.* See sign for RIVER.

**crime**[1] *n.* An act that is contrary to laws established for the welfare of the public at large: *to commit the crime of robbery.* Same sign used for: **felony, illegal, infraction, misdemeanor, offense, unlawful, violation.**

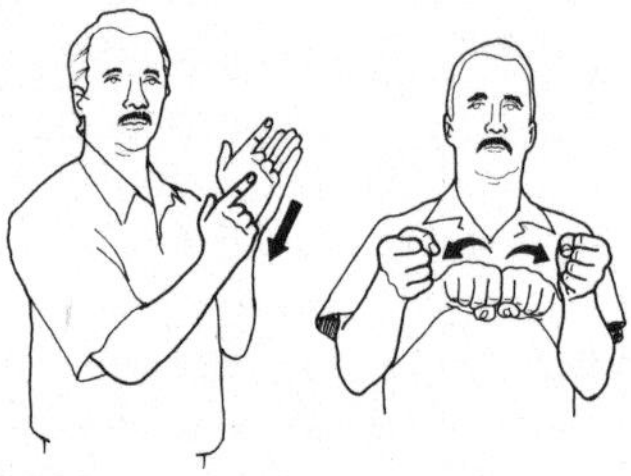

■ [**law** + **break**] Place the palm side of the right *L hand,* palm facing left, first on the fingers and then on the heel of the left *open hand,* palm facing right and fingers pointing up. Then beginning with both *S hands* in front of the body, index fingers touching and palms down, move the hands away from each other while twisting the wrists with a deliberate movement, ending with the palms facing each other.

**crime**[2] *n.* (alternate sign) Same sign used for: **felony, illegal, infraction, misdemeanor, offense, unlawful, violation.**

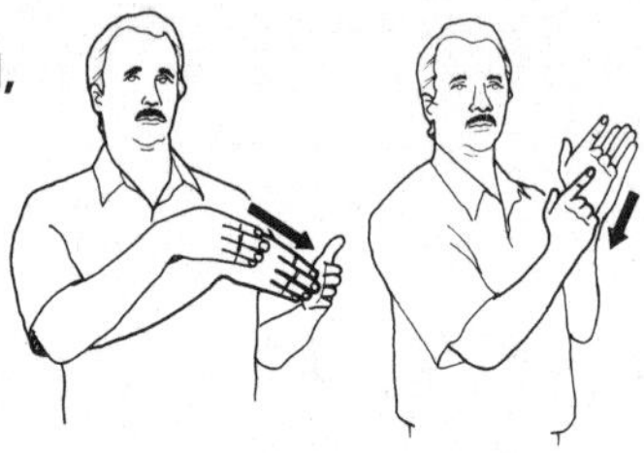

■ [**against** + **law**] Hit the fingertips of the right *bent hand* into the left *open hand,* palm right and fingers pointing forward. Then place the palm side of the right *L hand,* palm facing left, first on the fingers and then on the heel of the left *open hand,* palm facing right and fingers pointing up.

**crisis** *n.* **1.** A time of intense difficulty or danger: *Strain in the couple's marriage had reached a crisis.* **2.** The turning point of a disease, when it becomes clear whether the patient will recover or not: *The patient's condition reached a crisis during the night.* Same sign used for: **critical point, turning point.**

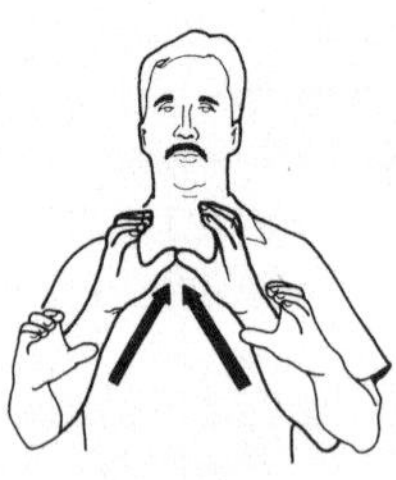

■ [Initialized sign moving up to a critical point] Bring both *C hands,* palms facing each other, upward from each side of the chest to meet in front of the neck.

**critical point** *n. phrase.* See sign for CRISIS.

**cross**[1] *n.* **1.** A structure made of an upright beam with a horizontal bar across it: *a cross on the top of the church.* **2.** A representation of a cross used as a symbol of the Christian faith: *to wear a cross on a chain around the neck.* Same sign used for: **crucifix.**

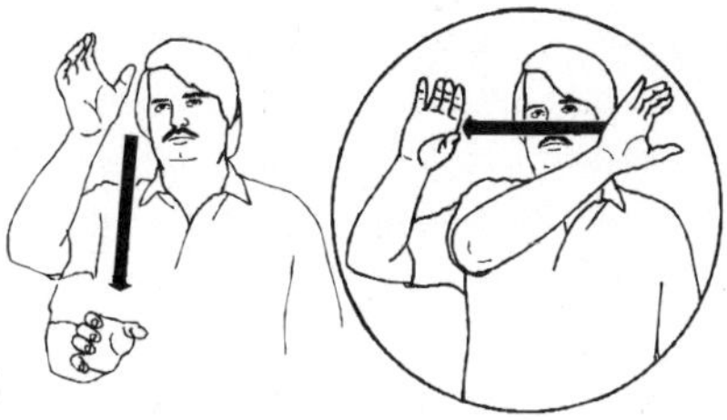

■ [Shape of a cross] Bring the right *C hand,* palm facing forward, first downward in front of the right side of the body and then from left to right.

**cross**[2] *adj.* See sign for ANGER[1,2].

**cross**[3] *prep., adv.* See sign for ACROSS.

**crossing** *n.* See sign for INTERSECTION.

**cross-purposes** *n.* See sign for CONFLICT.

**crowd** *n.* See signs for AUDIENCE, HORDE.

**crowded**[1] *adj.* Having many people or things packed into a small space: *a crowded room.* Same sign used for: **cramped, crushed.**

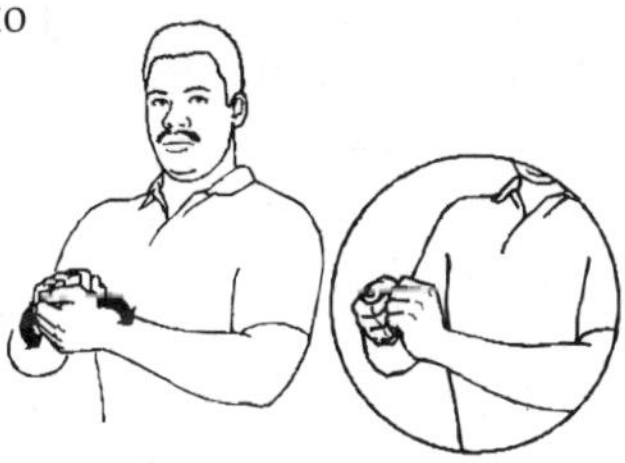

■ Beginning with the palms of both *A hands* together in front of the chest, twist the hands in opposite directions.

**crowded**[2] *adj.* See sign for JAM[1].

**crucifix** *n.* See sign for CROSS[1].

**crude** *adj.* See sign for ROUGH.

**cruel** *adj.* See signs for MEAN[1], MEANNESS, ROUGH.

**cruise** *n.* See signs for BOAT, SHIP.

**crushed** *adj.* See sign for CROWDED.

**cry**[1] *v.* To shed tears, as from grief or pain: *I cried for a long time when my grandmother died.* Same sign used for: **weep.**

■ [Tears flowing down the cheeks] Bring both extended index fingers, palms facing in and fingers pointing up, downward from each eye with an alternating movement.

**cry**[2] *v.* See signs for CALL[2], SCREAM.

**cube** *n.* See sign for BLOCK[1].

**culture** *n.* See sign for CONDITION.

**cup** *n.* An open drinking vessel: *drinking a cup of tea.* Same sign used for: **can, glass, jar.**

- [Shape of a cup] Bring the little-finger side of the right *C hand,* palm facing left, down to the upturned left *open hand* with a double movement.

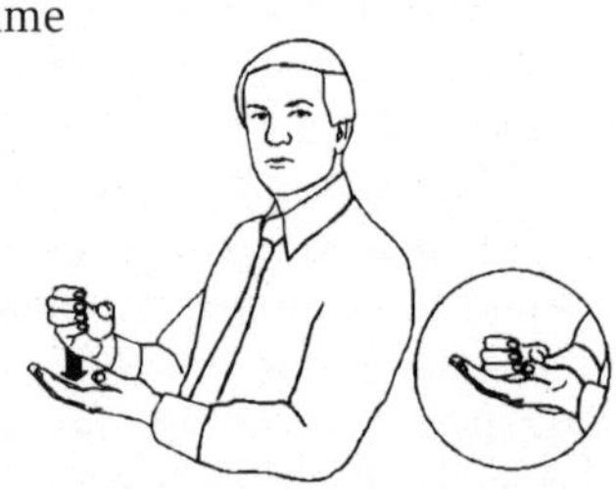

**cure** *n., v.* See signs for DISSOLVE, WELL.

**curious** *adj.* Eager to know: *curious about their Christmas presents.* Related form: **curiosity** *n.*

- With the fingertips of the right *F hand* against the neck, palm facing left, twist the hand downward with a double movement.

**curly** *adj.* Forming coils or ringlets: *curly hair.*

- [Shape of curly hair] Move both *curved 5 hands,* palms facing in, in alternating circles near each ear.

**current** *adj.* See sign for NOW.

**curse** *n.* **1.** A word or phrase calling for evil and misfortune to fall upon someone or something: *yelled a curse at the driver of the car as it sped past, barely missing us.* —*v.* **2.** To ask that evil and misfortune be brought on: *cursed those who had stolen his inheritance.* **3.** To swear at, as from annoyance: *cursed the dog for tripping him on the stairs.* Same sign used for: **condemn, cuss, swear.**

- Beginning with the right *curved 5 hand* near the mouth, palm facing in, bring the hand upward with a deliberate movement while closing into an *S hand.*

**curtain** *n.* A piece of cloth hung at a window: *to open the curtains.*

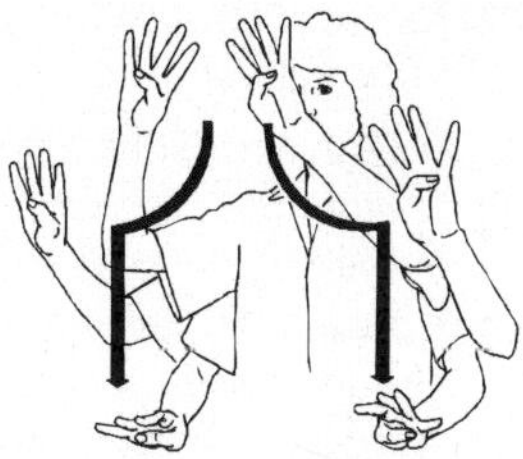

■ [Shape of curtains hanging on a window] Beginning with both *4 hands* in front of the face, palms facing forward, bring the hands downward in an arc to about shoulder width and then straight down, ending with the palms facing down.

**curve**[1] *n.* A line that has no straight part: *a curve in the road.*

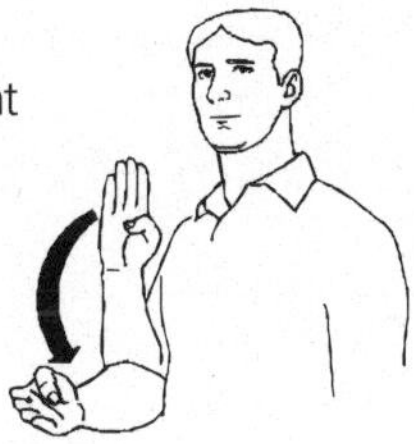

■ [Shape of a curve] Move the right *B hand* from in front of the right shoulder, palm facing left, downward in an arc, ending with the palm facing up and the fingers pointing forward.

**curve**[2] *n.* See sign for ARCH.

**cuss** *Informal* See sign for CURSE.

**custom** *n.* See sign for HABIT.

**customer**[1] *n.* A person who buys: *The store was filled with customers.* Same sign used for: **buyer, consumer, shopper.**

■ [**buy** + **person marker**] Beginning with the back of the right *flattened O hand*, palm facing up, in the upturned palm of the left *open hand*, move the right hand forward in an arc. Then move both *open hands*, palms facing each other, downward along each side of the body.

**customer**[2] *n.* See sign for CLIENT.

**cut**[1] *v.* To shorten (hair): *I just cut my hair before the trip.* Same sign used for: **haircut.**

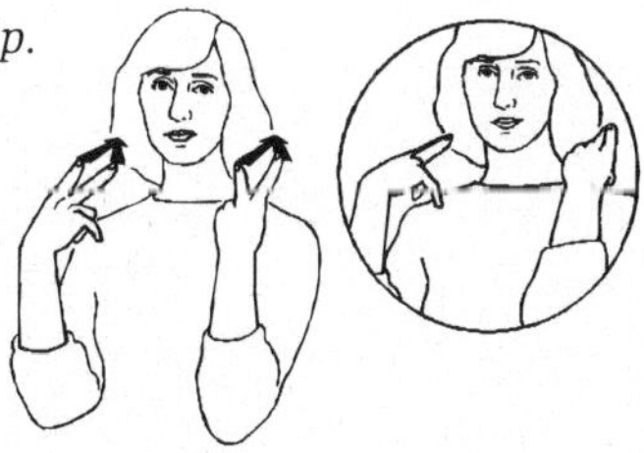

■ [Mime cutting hair] Move both *V hands,* palms facing down, back over each shoulder while opening and closing the fingers of the *V hands* repeatedly as the hands move.

**cut**[2] *v.* To separate or remove with scissors: *to cut the wrapping paper the right size.*

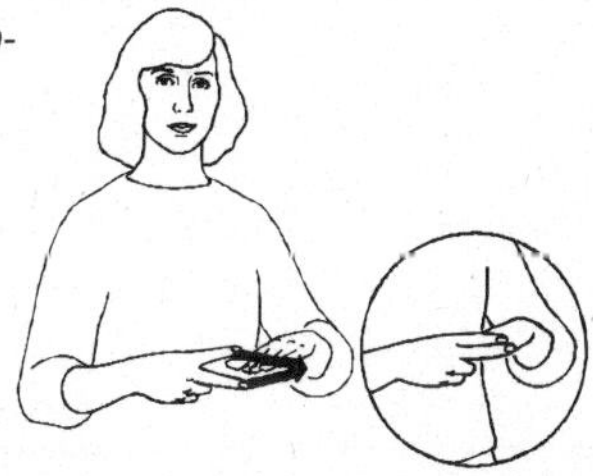

■ [Represents cutting across a piece of paper] Move the right *V hand,* fingers pointing left, across the fingertips of the left *open hand,* palm facing down, with a deliberate movement while closing the *V fingers* together.

**cut**[3] *v.* or **cut out** *v. phrase* (alternate sign)

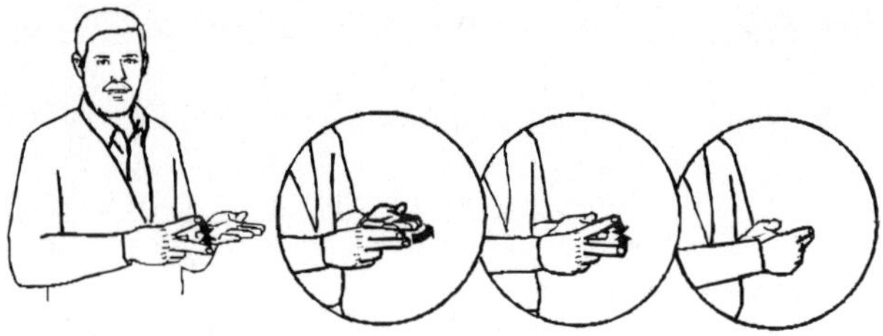

- [Represents cutting around a clipping] Move the right *V hand,* palm facing left, around the fingertips of the left *open hand,* palm facing up, while opening and closing the right index and middle fingers with a repeated movement as the hand moves.

**cut**[4] *v.* See sign for INCISION.

**cut back** *v. phrase.* See sign for LESS[1].

**cut down** *v. phrase.* See sign for HARVEST.

**cut off** *v. phrase.* See sign for INTERCEPT.

**cute** *adj.* Pleasingly pretty or endearing: *a cute doll.*

- With the right thumb extended, brush the fingers of the right *U hand,* palm facing down, downward on the chin while changing into a *10 hand.*

**cutthroat** *adj.* See sign for RISK.

**cycle** *n.* See signs for CIRCLE, YEAR-ROUND.

**dad** *n.* See sign for FATHER. Related form: **daddy** *n.*

**daily** *adj.* **1.** Of, done, or occurring every day: *Daily attendance at school is required.* **2.** Pertaining to the home, family, and other everyday matters: *to do one's daily chores.* —*adv.* **3.** Every day: *to exercise daily.* Same sign used for: **casual, domestic, everyday, every day, ordinary, routine, usual.**

■ [Similar to sign for tomorrow, only repeated to indicated recurrence] Move the palm side of the right *A hand* forward on the right side of the chin with a repeated movement.

**damage** *n.* **1.** Harm or injury that reduces something's value or usefulness: *The crash caused severe damage to the car.* —*v.* **2.** To cause such harm or injury: *Wet cups will damage the finish on the table.* Same sign used for: **abolish, demolish, destroy, ruin.**

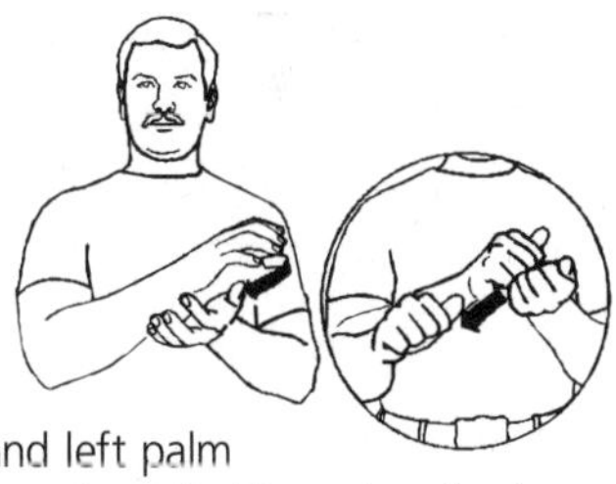

■ [Hands seem to take something and pull it apart] Beginning with both *curved 5 hands* in front of the chest, right hand over the left, right palm facing down and left palm facing up, bring the right hand in a circular movement over the left. Then close both hands into *A hands* and bring the knuckles of the right hand forward past the left knuckles with a deliberate movement.

**damp** *adj.* See sign for WET.

**dance** *v.* **1.** To move one's body in rhythm to music: *Dance with me.* —*n.* **2.** A series of rhythmic bodily movements performed to music: *an exciting new dance with a Latin beat.* **3.** A social gathering where dancing occurs: *go to a dance.* Same sign used for: **disco, gala.**

■ [Represents legs moving in rhythm to dance music] Swing the fingers of the right *V hand,* palm facing in and fingers pointing down, back and forth over the upturned left *open hand* with a double movement.

**danger** *n.* Risk of injury or harm: *These days, there is danger in the city.* Related form: **dangerous** *adj.* Same sign used for: **endanger, harassment, harm, hazard, peril, risk, threat, unsafe.**

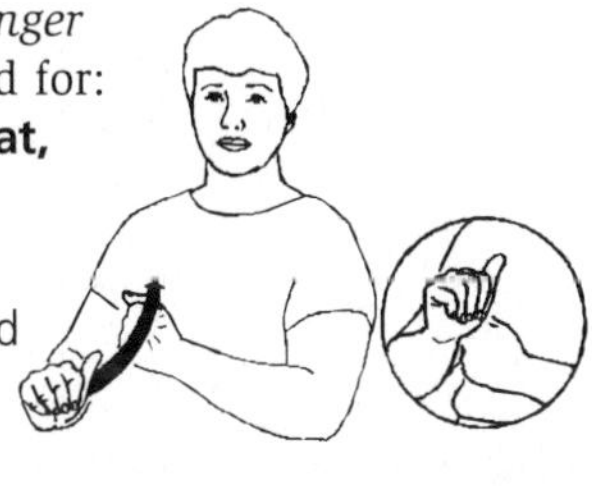

■ [Movement of hidden danger coming at a person] Move the thumb of the right *10 hand,* palm facing left, upward on the back of the left *A hand,* palm facing in, with a repeated movement.

**dare** *v.* See signs for CHALLENGE, GANG.

**dark** *adj.* Being without light: *a dark room with the shutters drawn.* Related form: **darkness** *n.* Same sign used for: **dim, dusk, shadow.**

- [Hands shade the eyes from light] Beginning with both *open hands* in front of each shoulder, palms facing back and fingers pointing up, bring the hands past each other in front of the face, ending with the wrists crossed and the fingers pointing in opposite directions at an angle.

**darken** *v.* See sign for DIM.

**darn** *adj., adv., interj.* Damned: *That darn cat keeps eating the plants.* Same sign used for: **drat.**

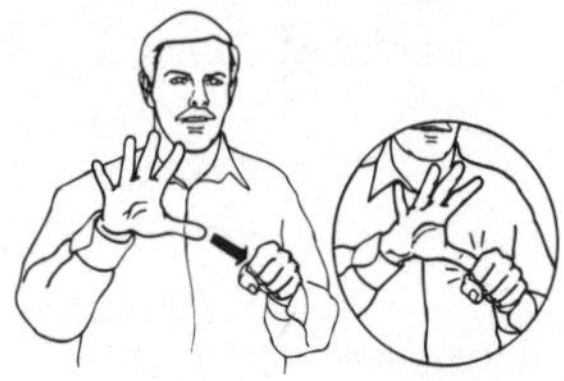

- Forcibly insert the thumb of the right *5 hand*, palm facing forward, into the opening of the left *S hand* held in front of the chest.

**daughter** *n.* A female child in relation to her parents: *my oldest daughter.*

- [Begins at the female area of the head + **baby**] Beginning with the index-finger side of the right *B hand,* palm facing left, touching the right side of the chin, swing the right hand downward, with the bent right arm cradled in the bent left arm held across the body.

**day** *n.* **1.** The period between sunrise and sunset: *a nice sunny day.* **2.** A period of 24 hours: *to complete the project in one day.*

- [Symbolizes the movement of the sun across the sky] Beginning with the bent right elbow resting on the back of the left hand held across the body, palm facing down, bring the extended right index finger from pointing up in front of the right shoulder, palm facing left, downward toward the left elbow.

**daydream** *v., n.* See sign for DREAM.

**dead** *adj.* See sign for DIE.

**deadline** *n.* The time by which something should be finished, accomplished, etc.: *He missed the deadline for applying to college.*

- [**die** + **line**] Beginning with both *open hands* in front of the body, right palm facing down and left palm facing up, flip the hands to the right, turning the right palm up and the left palm down. Then, beginning with both extended little fingers pointing toward each other in front of the chest, palms facing in, move the hands away from each other.

**deaf** *adj.* Being partially or wholly unable to hear: *a deaf person.*

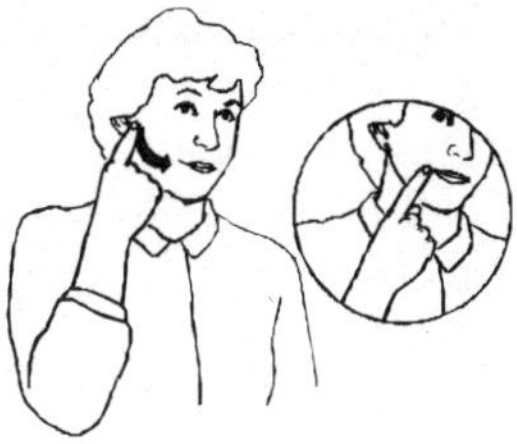

■ [Points to the ear and mouth to indicate that a person cannot hear or talk] Touch the extended right index finger first to near the right ear and then to near the right side of the mouth.

**deal** *v.* See signs for AGREE[1], PASS AROUND, PASS OUT[1].

**death** *n.* See sign for DIE.

**debate**[1] *v.* **1.** To discuss opposing viewpoints: *to debate the issues during a campaign.* —*n.* **2.** A discussion involving opposing viewpoints: *Neither candidate won the debate.* Same sign used for: **arbitration.**

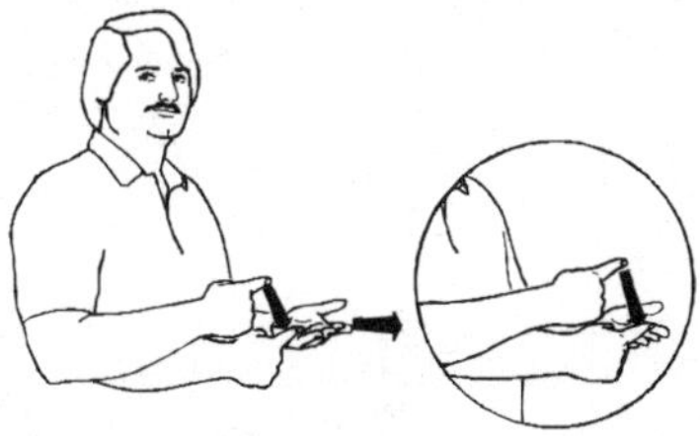

■ [**discuss** formed while moving toward another person] Tap the side of the right extended index finger, palm facing in and finger pointing left, across the upturned left *open hand,* first on the palm and then again on the fingers as the left hand moves forward slightly.

**debate**[2] *n.* See sign for ARGUE.

**debt** *n.* See sign for AFFORD.

**decal** *n.* See sign for LABEL.

**decay** *v.* See sign for WEAR OUT.

**deceive**[1] *n.* The act or practice of deceiving: *to be guilty of deceit.* Related forms: **deceit** *v.*, **deceitful** *adj.* Same sign used for: **betray, defraud, fraud.**

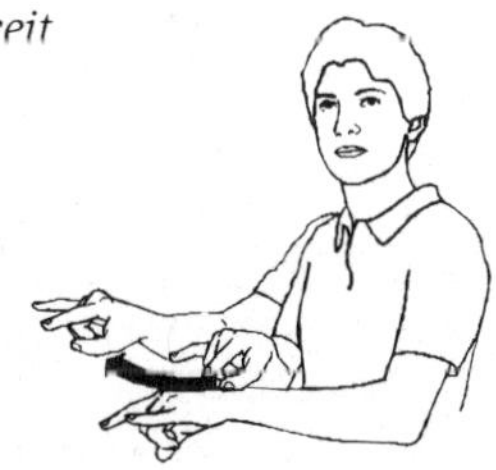

■ Slide the palm side of the right *Y hand,* palm facing down, from the wrist forward on the back of the left *Y hand,* palm facing down.

**deceive**[2] *v.* See signs for BETRAY[1], CHEAT.

**decide** *v.* To make up one's mind; come to a conclusion: *decide where to go.* Related form: **decision** *n.* Same sign used for: **determine, make up your mind, officially.**

■ [**think** + laying one's thoughts down decisively] Move the extended right index finger from the right side of the forehead, palm facing left, down in front of the chest while changing into an *F hand,* ending with both *F hands* in front of the body, palms facing each other.

**decimal point** *n. phrase.* See sign for PERIOD[1].

**declare** *v.* See sign for ANNOUNCE. Related form: **declaration** *n.*

**decline**[1] *v.* **1.** To lose or fail in power, strength, or value: *His health declined with age.* —*n.* **2.** A change to a lower or worse level: *a decline in prices.* Same sign used for: **deteriorate, diminish.**

- [Hands move downward in location] Beginning with both *10 hands* in front of each shoulder, palms facing in and thumbs pointing up, move both hands down in front of each side of the chest.

**decline**[2] *v., n.* (alternate sign) Same sign used for: **deteriorate.**

- [Shows a movement downward] Touch the little-finger side of the right *open hand,* palm facing in, first near the shoulder, then near the elbow, and finally near the wrist of the extended left arm.

**decline**[3] *v.* To refuse politely: *to decline to attend the reception.* Same sign used for: **drop, refuse, turn down.**

- [**true** + **excuse**] Move the extended right index finger from pointing up in front of the mouth, palm facing left, downward while opening the hand, ending with the fingers of the right *open hand* wiping forward across the length of the upturned left *open hand.*

**decorate** *v.* To add something to in order to make more attractive; adorn; embellish: *to decorate the cake.* Related form: **decoration** *n.* Same sign used for: **elaborate.**

- [Hands seem to arrange ornamental items] Beginning with both *flattened O hands* in front of each side of the chest, palms facing forward, move them in alternating circles with a repeated movement.

**decrease**[1] *n.* **1.** A lessening: *a decrease in spending.* —*v.* **2.** To make or become less: *I plan to decrease my use of salt.* Same sign used for: **lessen, lose, reduce, reduction.**

- [Taking some off to decrease it] Beginning with the fingers of the right *U hand* across the fingers of the left *U hand,* both palms facing down, take the right fingers off by flipping the right hand over with a double movement.

**decrease**[2] *n., v.* (alternate sign, used especially to indicate a total reduction or depletion) Same sign used for: **deflate, reduce, shrink.**

■ [Shows amount decreasing in size] Beginning with the thumb of the right *C hand,* palm angled forward, on the back of the left *curved hand,* palm facing down, close the right fingers to the thumb, forming a *flattened O hand.*

**decrease**[3] *n., v.* (alternate sign) Same sign used for: **lessen, reduce.**

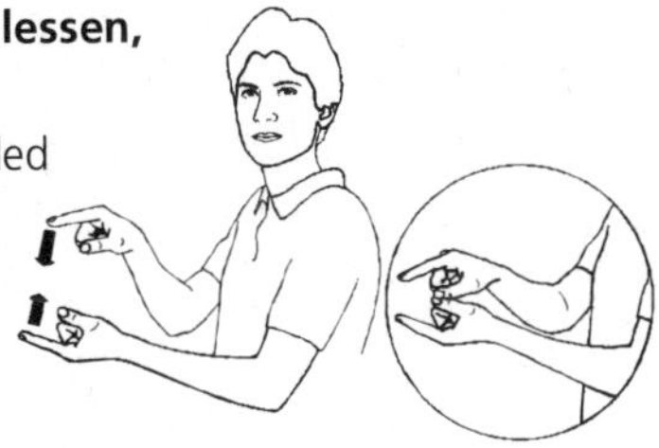

■ [Shows decreasing size] Beginning with both extended index fingers pointing forward in front of the chest, right hand over the left hand and palms facing each other, bring the hands toward each other.

**deduct** *v.* See signs for REMOVE[1], SUBTRACT. Related form: **deduction** *n.*

**deed** *n.* See signs for ACT[1], ACTIVE, DO.

**deep** *adj.* **1.** Having a great distance from top to bottom: *deep water at one end of the pool.* **2.** Not superficial; profound: *a deep discussion of all aspects of the problem.* Same sign used for: **depth, detail.**

■ [Indicates direction of bottom of something deep] Move the extended right index finger, palm facing down, downward near the fingertips of the left *5 hand,* palm facing down.

**deer** *n.* A cud chewing mammal that has hooves and, in the male, antlers; known for its grace: *The deer bounded off into the woods.* Same sign used for: **reindeer.**

■ [A deer's antlers] Tap the thumbs of both *5 hands,* palms facing forward, against each side of the forehead with a repeated movement.

**defeat**[1] *v.* To overcome, as in a war or game: *to defeat the enemy in hand-to-hand combat.* Same sign used for: **conquer, overcome, subdue, vanquish.**

■ [Represents forcing another down in defeat] Move the right *S hand* from in front of the right shoulder, palm facing forward, downward and forward, ending with the right wrist across the wrist of the left *S hand,* both palms facing down.

**defeat**[2] *v.* (alternate sign) Same sign used for: **beat.**

- [Directing a single blow] Beginning with the right *S hand* in front of the right shoulder, palm facing left, move the hand quickly forward while opening the fingers to form an *H hand*.

**defend** *v.* To guard from harm or attack: *She swore to defend him from slander.* Related forms: **defense** *n.*, **defensive** *adj.* Same sign used for: **protect, security, shield.**

- [Blocking oneself from harm] With the wrists of both *S hands* crossed in front of the chest, palms facing in opposite directions, move the hands forward with a short double movement.

**defensive** *adj.* See sign for RESIST.

**defer**[1] *v.* To put off until a later time: *The committee deferred a decision until there was a quorum present.* Same sign used for: **delay, procrastinate, put off.**

- [Represents taking something and putting it off several times] Beginning with both *F hands* in front of the body, palms facing each other and the left hand nearer to the body than the right hand, move both hands forward in a series of small arcs.

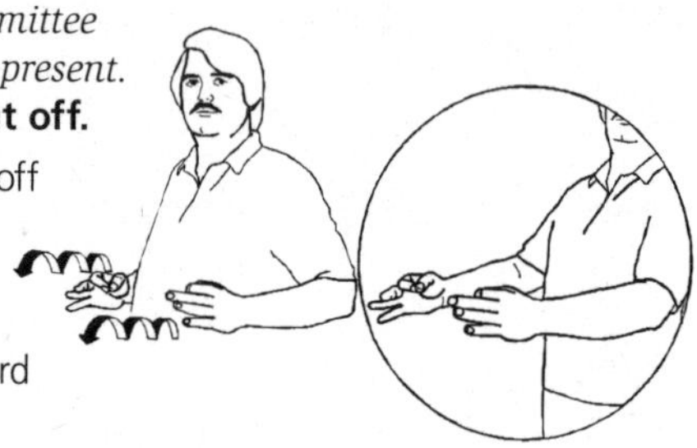

**defer**[2] *v.* See sign for POSTPONE.

**define** *v.* See sign for DESCRIBE. Related form: **definition** *n.*

**deflate** *v.* See sign for DECREASE[2].

**defraud** *v.* See sign for DECEIVE[1].

**degree** *n.* See sign for DIPLOMA.

**dejected** *adj.* See sign for DEPRESSED.

**delay** *n.*, *v.* See signs for DEFER, LATE, POSTPONE.

**delegate** *n.* **1.** A person given authority to act for others: *a delegate to the political convention.* —*v.* **2.** To give (powers or functions) to another as one's agent: *He seems unable to delegate tasks to his subordinates.*

- [Initialized sign] Brush the fingers of the right *D hand,* palm facing in and index finger pointing up, downward on the right side of the chest with a double movement.

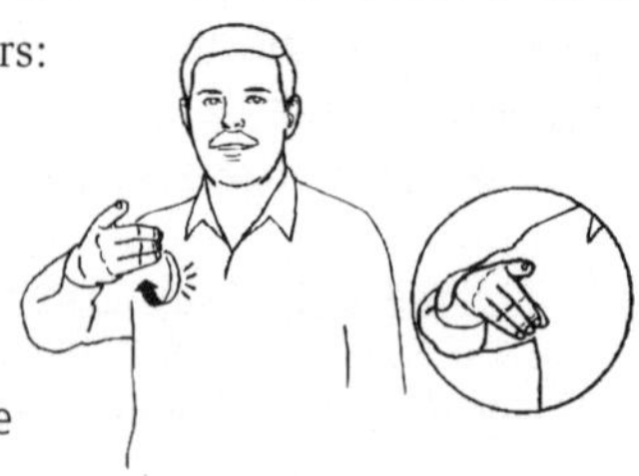

**delete** *v.* See sign for ELIMINATE.

**deliberate** *v.* See sign for MULL.

**delicious** *adj.* Highly pleasing to the taste: *This sandwich is absolutely delicious.* Same sign used for: **tasty.**

- Touch the bent middle finger of the right *5 hand* to the lips, palm facing in, and then twist the right hand quickly forward.

**delighted** *adj.* See sign for HAPPY.

**deliver** *v.* See sign for BRING.

**deluxe** *adj.* See sign for FANCY.

**demand** *v.* To ask or ask for with authority; claim as a right: *I demand to see the supervisor.* Same sign used for: **insist, require.**

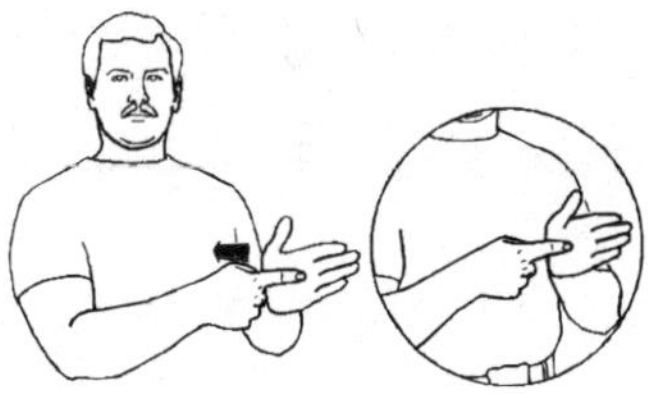

- With the extended right index finger, palm facing in, touching the palm of the left *open hand,* bring both hands back toward the chest.

**demise** *n.* See sign for DIE.

**Democrat** *n.* A member of the Democratic party: *The polls predict that a Democrat will win the election.*

- [Initialized sign] Shake the right *D hand,* palm facing forward, from side to side in front of the right shoulder.

**demolish** *v.* See sign for DAMAGE.

**demon** *n.* See sign for DEVIL.

**demonstrate** *v.* See sign for SHOW. Related form: **demonstration** *n.*

**demote** *v.* See sign for LOW.

**dent** *v.* **1.** To form a depression in, as from a blow or pressure: *He dented the bumper on the new car.* —*n.* **2.** A depression caused by a blow or pressure: *a small dent in the fender.* Same sign used for: **bend, bent.**

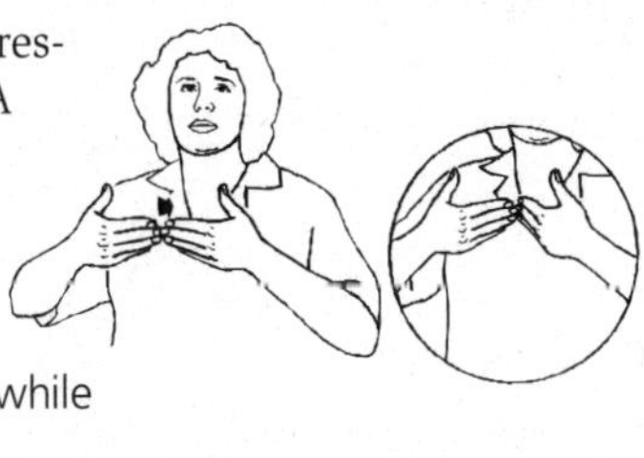

- [Bending of a surface] Beginning with the fingertips of both *open hands* touching in front of the chest, palms facing in, bend the fingers in toward the chest while keeping fingertips together.

**dentist** *n.* A doctor who treats diseases of and damage to the teeth and gums: *The dentist had to fill three cavities in my teeth.*

■ [Initialized sign formed similar to **tooth**] Tap the fingers of the right *D hand,* palm facing in and index finger pointing up, against the right side of the teeth with a repeated movement.

**dentures** *pl. n.* See sign for FALSE TEETH.

**deny**[1] *v.* To declare not to be true: *to deny the rumor.*

■ [**not**[1] with a repeated movement] Beginning with the thumb of the right *A hand* under the chin, palm facing left, and the left *A hand* held somewhat forward, palm facing right, move the right hand forward while moving the left hand back. Repeat the movement with the left hand.

**deny**[2] *v.* (alternate sign)

■ [Hand seems to hold oneself back or suppress oneself] Beginning with the fingertips of the right *C hand* on the upper chest, palm facing in, bring the hand straight down while quickly closing into an *S hand.*

**deodorant** *n.* A liquid preparation for inhibiting or masking unpleasant odors, esp. one applied by spraying: *to use an underarm deodorant.*

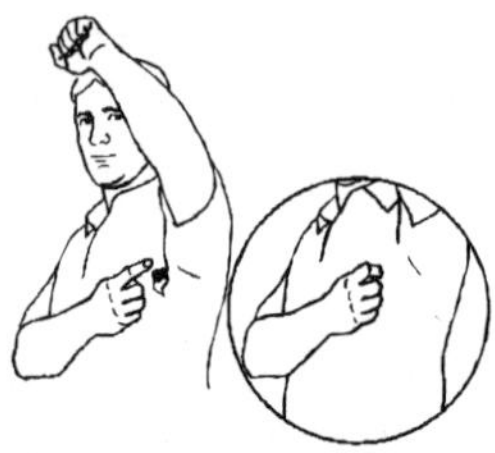

■ [Mime spraying on deodorant] With the left arm raised above the head, bend the extended right index finger up and down with a double movement near the left armpit.

**depart** *v.* See signs for FORSAKE, GO, LEAVE[1], PARTING. Related form: **departure** *n.*

**department** *n.* One of the official parts or branches of an organization, as a government or business: *the payroll department.* Same sign used for: **division.**

■ [Initialized sign similar to sign for **class**] Beginning with the fingertips of both *D hands* touching in front of the chest, palms facing each other, bring the hands away from each other in outward arcs while turning the palms in, ending with the little fingers together.

**depend** *v.* or **depend on** *v. phrase.* To rely for help: *I can always depend on my mother.* Related forms: **dependency** *n.*, **dependent** *adj.* Same sign used for: **cling to, contingent, rely.**

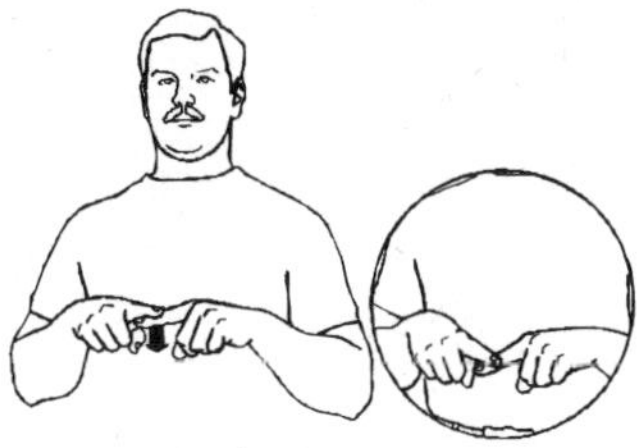

■ [Represents resting on another] With the extended right index finger across the extended left index finger, palms facing down, move both fingers down slightly with a double movement.

**deplete** *v.* See sign for RUN OUT OF.

**deposit**[1] *v.* **1.** To put (money) in the bank: *I'd better deposit my check before the bank closes.* —*n.* **2.** Money put in the bank for safekeeping: *My bank deposit was small this week.*

■ [Sealing a deposit envelope with the thumbs] Beginning with the thumbs of both *10 hands* touching in front of the chest, both palms facing down, bring the hands downward and apart by twisting the wrists.

**deposit**[2] *n., v.* See sign for INVEST.

**depreciation** *n.* The gradual decrease in the value of tangible property that occurs because of wear and tear: *take a depreciation of the rental property on your taxes.* Related form: **depreciate** *v.*

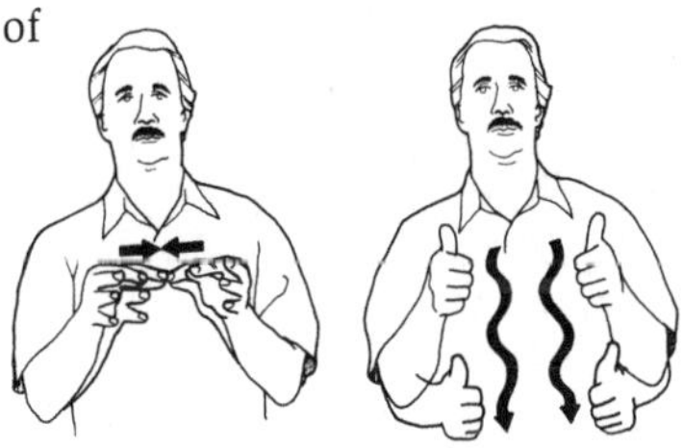

■ [**cost**[2] + **decline**[1]] lap the fingertips of both *F hands* together, palms facing each other, with a repeated movement. Then beginning with the thumbs of both *10 hands* pointing up in front of the chest, palms facing each other, move both hands down in wavy movements in front of the body.

**depressed** *adj.* Being low-spirited: *She feels depressed about losing her job.* Related forms: **depressing** *adj.*, **depression** *n.* Same sign used for: **dejected, despair, discouraged.**

■ [Feelings moving downward in the body] Beginning with the bent middle fingers of both *5 hands* on each side of the chest, palms facing in and fingers pointing toward each other, move the hands downward with a simultaneous movement.

**depth** *n.* See sign for DEEP.

**descend** *v.* To move from a higher to a lower place; go down: *descend the stairs.*

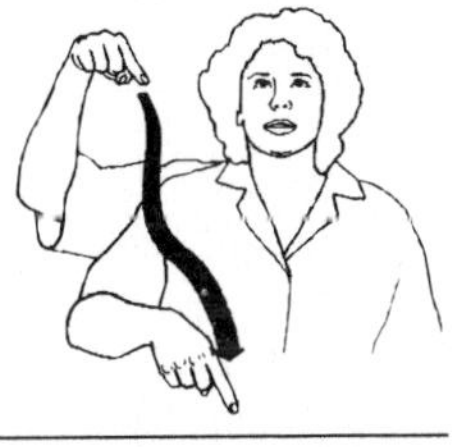

■ [Movement of someone or something to a lower place] Move the extended right index finger, palm facing down, downward with a wavy movement from near the right side of the head to in front of the body.

**describe** *v.* To tell about in words: *to describe the event in detail.* Related form: **description** *n.* Same sign used for: **define, definition, direct, direction, explain, explanation, instruct, instruction.**

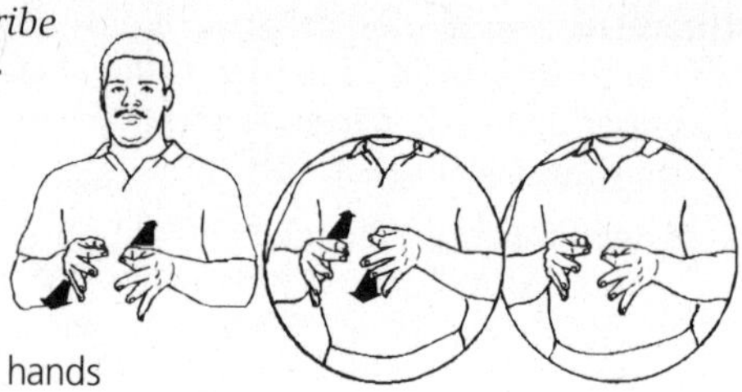

- Beginning with both *F hands* in front of the chest, palms facing each other and index fingers pointing forward, move the hands forward and back with an alternating movement.

**desert** *v.* See sign for LEAVE[1].

**deserve** *v.* See sign for COLLECT.

**design** *v.* To conceive and make preliminary drawings or plans for: *to design a new apartment building.* Same sign used for: **draw, drawing, draft.**

- [Initialized sign similar to sign for **art**] Move the fingertips of the right *D hand,* palm facing left, down the palm of the left *open hand* with a wavy movement.

**desire**[1] *n.* See sign for PASSIONATE.

**desire**[2] *v.* See signs for WANT, WISH.

**desist** *v.* To stop: *ordered to desist from smuggling across the border.* Same sign used for: **stop.**

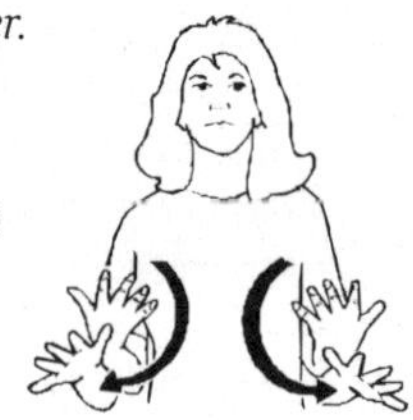

- [Natural gesture used when asking another to stop doing something] Beginning with the fingers of both *5 hands* in front of each side of the chest, palms facing in, twist the wrists to flip the hands in a quick movement, ending with the palms facing down.

**desk** *n.* See signs for TABLE[1,2].

**despair** *n., v.* See sign for DEPRESSED.

**desperate** *adj.* Nearly hopeless and driven to take any risk: *The day after he quit smoking, he became desperate for a cigarette.*

- [**must** + **have**] Move the bent index finger of the right *X hand,* palm facing forward, downward with a deliberate movement in front of the right side of the body while bending the wrist down. Then bring the fingertips of both *bent hands,* palms facing in, back to touch each side of the chest.

**despise** *v.* See signs for DETEST, HATE.

**despite** *prep.* See sign for ANYWAY.

**dessert** *n.* A course of sweet food served at the end of a meal: *Let's have ice cream for dessert.*

■ [Initialized sign] Tap the fingertips of both *D hands,* palms facing each other, together with a repeated movement in front of the chest.

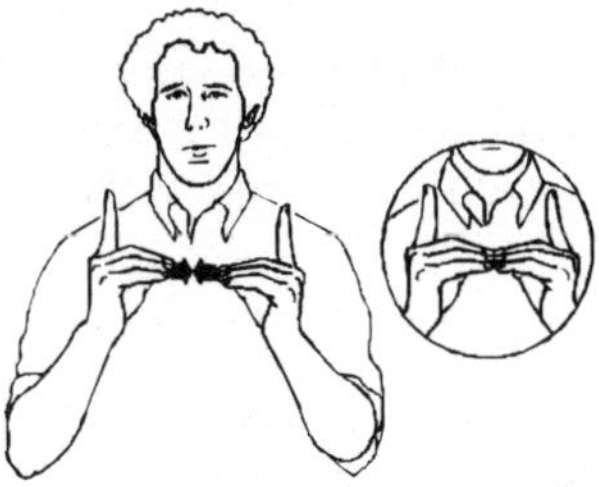

**destitute** *adj.* See sign for POOR.

**destroy** *v.* See sign for DAMAGE.

**destruction** *n.* See sign for BREAK DOWN.

**detach** *v.* See sign for DISCONNECT.

**detail** *n.* See sign for DEEP. Shared idea of careful attention to important matters.

**detective** *n.* A person whose business is to obtain information and evidence, as of criminal activity: *They plan to hire a detective to find the missing jewels.* Same sign used for: **private eye** (*informal*).

■ [Initialized sign similar to sign for **police**] Move the right *D hand,* palm facing left, in a circular movement on the left side of the chest.

**deteriorate** *v.* See signs for DECLINE[1,2].

**determine** *v.* See sign for DECIDE.

**determined** *adj.* See sign for STUBBORN.

**detest**[1] *v.* To dislike intensely; hate: *Why do so many children detest spinach?* Same sign used for: **despise, loathe.**

■ [Similar to sign for **vomit**] Beginning with the right *5 hand* near the chin, palm facing left, and the left *5 hand* somewhat forward, palm facing right, move both hands forward with a deliberate movement.

**detest**[2] *v.* See sign for HATE.

**detour** *n.* **1.** A path that is used when the direct path cannot be traveled: *to take a detour around the construction.* —*v.* **2.** To go another way because of an obstruction: *to detour through back streets.*

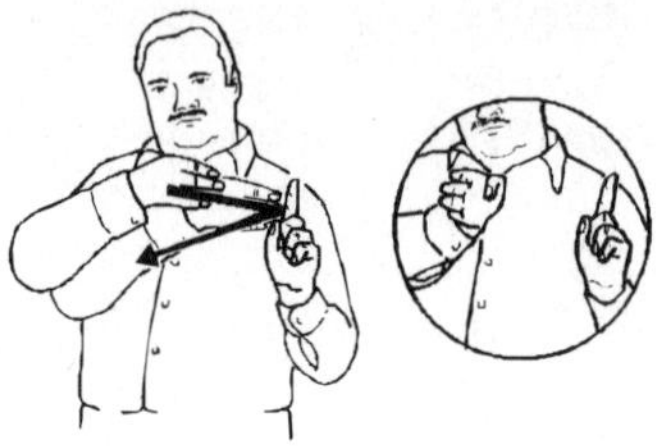

■ [Shows changing the course of movement] Beginning with the right *B hand* in front of the right shoulder, palm facing in and fingers pointing left, move the fingers toward the extended left index finger, palm facing right, and then twist the wrist to bring the right hand back outward to the right, ending with the palm facing forward.

**develop** *v.* To make or become bigger, more advanced, or more useful: *develop a new interest.*

■ [Initialized sign moving upward to represent growth or development] Move the fingertips of the right *D hand,* palm facing left, upward from the heel to the fingers of the left *open hand,* fingers pointing up and palm facing right.

**deviate** *v.* See sign for ASTRAY.

**device** *n.* See sign for EQUIPMENT.

**devil** *n.* **1.** (*cap.*) The supreme evil being: *Such crimes are the work of the Devil.* **2.** An evil, cruel, or mischievous person: *The little devil broke the television set on purpose.* Related form: **devilish** *adj.* Same sign used for: **demon, evil, mischief, mischievous, naughty, rascal, Satan, wicked.**

■ [Represents a devil's horns] With thumbs of both *3 hands* on each side of the forehead, palms facing forward, bend the index and middle fingers of both hands downward with a double movement.

**devour** *v.* See sign for CONSUME.

**dew** *n.* See sign for WET.

**diagnose** *v.* See sign for ANALYZE. Related form: **diagnosis** *n.*

**dialect** *n.* See sign for LANGUAGE.

**diamond** *n.* A very hard transparent precious stone: *a diamond ring.*

■ [Initialized sign showing location of a diamond ring] Tap the right *D hand,* palm facing down, with a double movement on the base of the ring finger of the left *5 hand,* palm facing down.

**dice** *n.* See sign for GAMBLE[1].

**dictionary**[1] *n.* A reference book listing words and their definitions, often including pronunciations, inflections, and other information, and usually arranged in alphabetical order: *to look up difficult words in the dictionary.* Same sign used for: **directory, folder.**

■ [Initialized sign formed similar to **page**] Move the fingertips of the right *D hand,* palm facing down, upward with a double movement on the heel of the upturned left *open hand.*

**dictionary**[2] *n.* See sign for PAGE.

**didn't mean that** *v. phrase.* See sign for SHUT UP[2].

**didn't say that** *v. phrase.* See sign for SHUT UP[2].

**die** *v.* To stop living: *The flowers died.* Same sign used for: **dead, death, demise, perish.**

■ [Represents a body turning over in death] Beginning with both *open hands* in front of the body, right palm facing down and left palm facing up, flip the hands to the right, turning the right palm up and the left palm down.

**diet** *n.* A special selection of foods eaten, as to lose weight: *on a diet to control his weight.* Same sign used for: **lean, shrink, slim, thin.**

■ [Shows slimmer body] Beginning with both *L hands* in front of each side of the chest, palms facing in, swing the hands downward by twisting the wrists, ending with the hands in front of each side of the waist, both palms facing down.

**different** *adj.* See sign for BUT.

**difficult** *adj.* Hard to do, understand, solve, or deal with: *faced with a difficult problem.* Related form: **difficulty** *n.* Same sign used for: **hard, problem, trouble.**

■ Beginning with both *bent V hands* in front of the chest, right hand higher than the left hand, palms facing in, move the right hand down and the left hand upward with an alternating movement, brushing the knuckles of each hand as the hands move in the opposite direction.

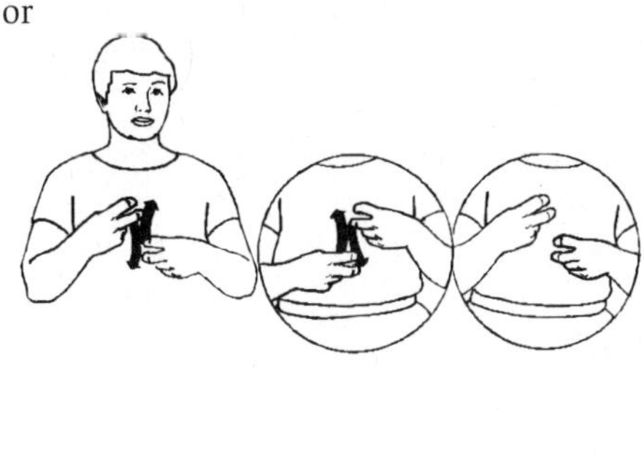

**dig**[1] *v.* To use a shovel or other tool to make a hole or turn over ground: *to dig a hole in the back yard.* Same sign used for: **shovel.**

- [Mime using a shovel to dig] Beginning with both modified *X hands* in front of each side of the waist, left hand lower than the right, palms facing each other, move the hands downward with a deliberate movement and then upward in a large arc over the right shoulder.

**dig**[2] *v.* See sign for SPATULA.

**digit** *n.* See sign for NUMBER.

**dignity** *n.* Conduct or manner showing self-respect and seriousness: *She maintained her dignity in the face of hostile questions.*

- [Holding one's head up with dignity] Place the extended right index finger, palm facing left, against the bottom of the chin.

**digress** *v.* To depart or wander from the main topic one is discussing: *The speaker digressed for a moment to tell a joke.* Same sign used for: **distracted, off the point, off the subject, off track.**

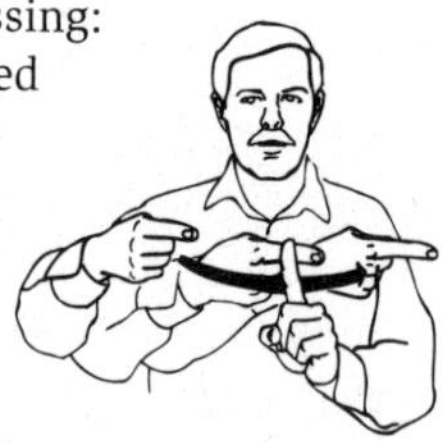

- [Begins similarly to sign for **goal** and then veers off to the side] Move the extended right index finger from in front of the right shoulder, palm facing left, forward toward the extended left index finger held up in front of the chest, turning sharply to the left near the left index finger.

**dim**[1] *adj.* **1.** Less bright; lacking intense light: *a dim light seen across the road.* —*v.* **2.** To make less bright: *Dim your headlights on the city streets.* Same sign used for: **darken, tint.**

- [Represents headlight beams going down to dim] Beginning with both *5 hands* in front of each shoulder, palms facing forward, bring the hands downward while constricting the fingers into *curved 5 hands.*

**dim**[2] *adj.* See sign for DARK.

**dime** *n.* A coin of the U.S. and Canada worth 10 cents: *Do you have two dimes and a nickel as change for my quarter?* Same sign used for: **ten cents.**

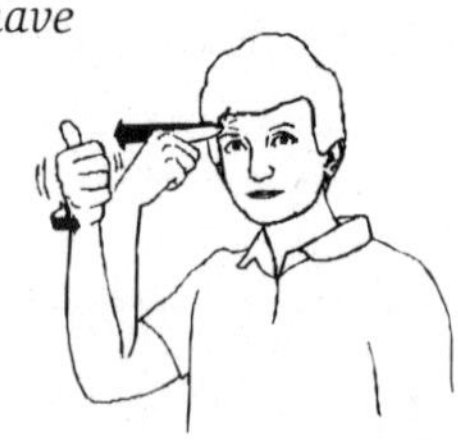

- [**cent** + **ten**] Beginning with the extended right index finger touching the right side of the forehead, palm facing down, bring the right hand forward while changing into a *10 hand.* Then slightly twist the right *10 hand* with a repeated movement, palm facing in and thumb pointing up.

**diminish** *v.* See sign for DECLINE[1].

**dimple** *n.* A small indentation usually in the cheek or chin: *He has dimples when he smiles.*

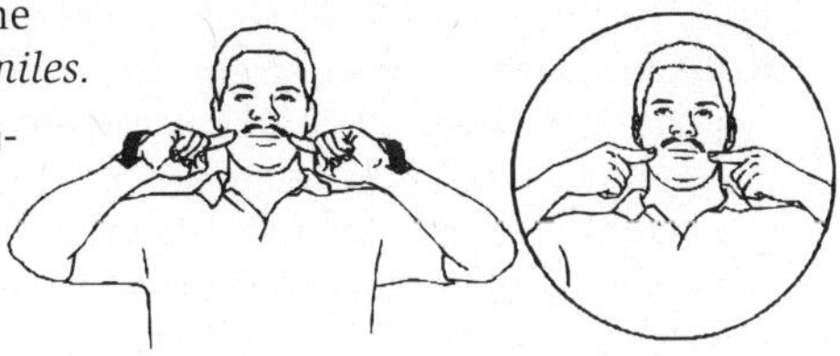

■ [Location of dimples in the cheeks] Beginning with both extended index fingers touching the cheeks on each side of the mouth, twist the hands forward with a double movement.

**dining room** *n.* A room in which meals are eaten: *Dinner is served in the dining room.*

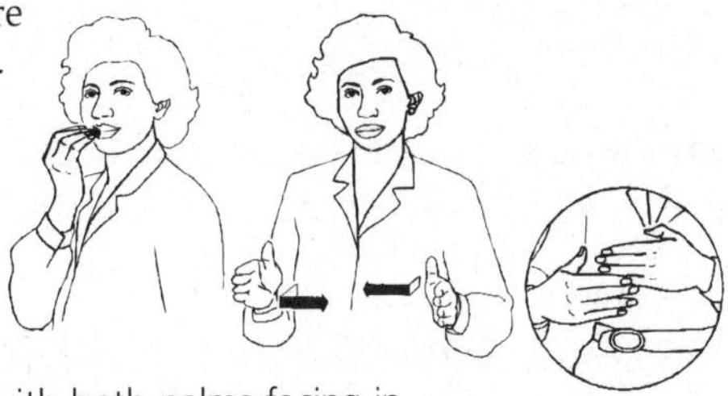

■ [**eat** + **room**] Tap the fingertips of the right *flattened O hand* to the lips with a double movement. Then, beginning with both *open hands* in front of each side of the body, palms facing each other, turn the hands sharply in opposite directions by bending the wrists, ending with both palms facing in.

**dinner** *n.* The main meal of the day: *We're having roast chicken for dinner.*

■ [**eat** + **night**] Tap the fingertips of the right *flattened O hand* to the lips with a double movement. Then tap the heel of the right *bent hand,* palm facing down, with a double movement against the index-finger side of the left *B hand* held in front of the chest, palm facing down.

**dinosaur** *n.* An extinct reptile: *to see the skeleton of a large dinosaur in the museum.*

■ [Initialized sign showing the long neck typical of some dinosaurs] Move the right *D hand* up and back in an arc from the forehead, ending with the hand above the head, palm facing left.

**dip** *v.* See sign for DYE.

**diploma** *n.* A document given by a school certifying that a student has successfully completed a designated course of study: *received a high-school diploma.* Same sign used for: **degree.**

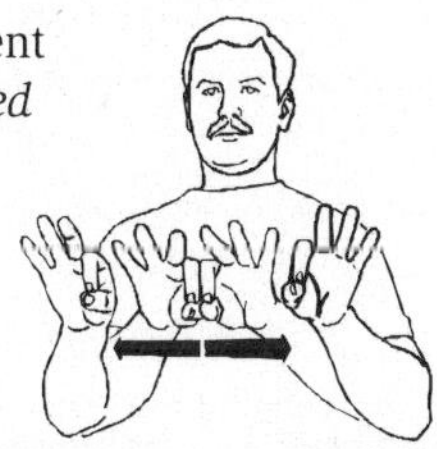

■ [Shape of rolled diploma] Beginning with the index-finger sides of both *F hands* in front of the chest, palms facing forward, move the hands apart to in front of each side of the chest.

**direct**[1] *adj.* Proceeding without interruption in a straight course or line; not deviating or swerving: *The child followed a direct path home.* Related form: **directly** *adv.*

■ [Shows direct direction] Beginning with the right *B hand* in front of the right side of the chest, palm facing in and fingers pointing left, and the left index finger pointing up somewhat forward in front of the left side of the chest, move the right hand to touch the fingers against the left index finger.

**direct**[2] *v., adj.* See signs for DESCRIBE, MANAGE, ORDER, STRAIGHT[1]. Related form: **direction** *n.*

**directory** *n.* See sign for DICTIONARY[1].

**dirt** *n.* **1.** A filthy substance: *to scrub the dirt off the kitchen floor.* **2.** Loose earth or soil: *We need some dirt to repot the plants.* Same sign used for: **ground, land, soil.**

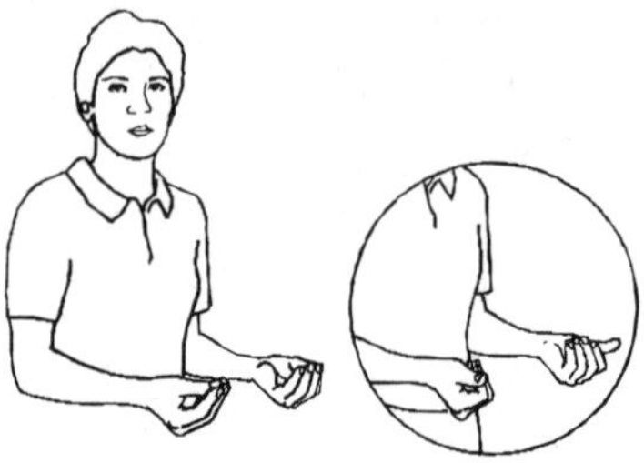

■ [Feeling the texture of dirt] Beginning with both *flattened O hands* in front of each side of the body, palms facing up, move the thumb of each hand smoothly across each fingertip, starting with the little fingers and ending as *A hands.*

**dirty** *adj.* Not clean: *Please wash the dirty dishes.* Same sign used for: **filthy, nasty, pollution, soiled.**

■ [Represents a pig's snout groveling in a trough] With the back of the right *curved 5 hand* under the chin, palm facing down, wiggle the fingers.

**disability** *n.* **1.** A disease or injury that renders a person unable to do one's usual occupation. **2.** A physical or mental condition making it impossible to hold gainful employment: *the disability of spinal injury.* Same sign used for **handicap.**

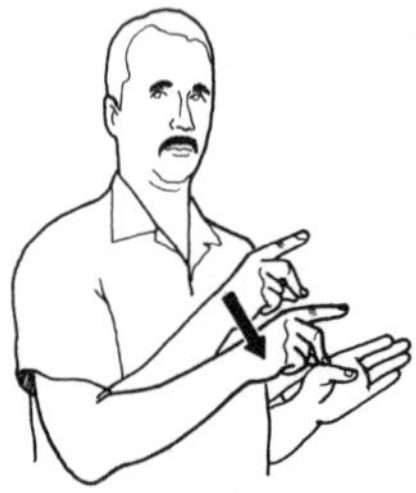

■ [Initialized sign] Tap the fingertips of the right *D hand,* palm down, on the base of the thumb of the left *B hand,* palm down.

**disagree** *v.* To differ in opinion: *I disagree with you about that movie.* Same sign used for: **contrast, dissent, object.**

■ [**think** + **opposite**] Move the extended right index finger from touching the right side of the forehead downward to meet the extended left index finger held in front of the chest. Then, beginning with both index fingers pointing toward each other, palms facing in, bring the hands apart to each side of the chest.

**disappear**[1] *v.* **1.** To cease to be visible: *The sun disappeared behind a cloud.* **2.** To go or be removed to another place: *When I turned my back, my purse disappeared.* Related form: **disappearance** *n.* Same sign used for: **vanish.**

- [Moving out of sight] Beginning with the extended right index finger, palm facing left, pointing up between the index and middle fingers of the left *5 hand,* palm facing down, pull the right hand straight down a short distance.

**disappear**[2] *v.* See sign for DISSOLVE.

**disappointed** *adj.* Feeling that expectations were not satisfied: *to feel disappointed about not getting a promotion.* Related form: **disappointment** *n.* Same sign used for: **miss.**

- Touch the extended right index finger to the chin, palm facing down.

**disastrous** *adj.* See sign for AWFUL.

**discard** *v.* See sign for ABANDON.

**discharge** *v.* See sign for DISMISS.

**disco** *n.* See sign for DANCE.

**disconnect** *v.* To break or interrupt the connection of or between: *to disconnect the phone.* Same sign used for: **detach, let go, loose, part from, withdraw.**

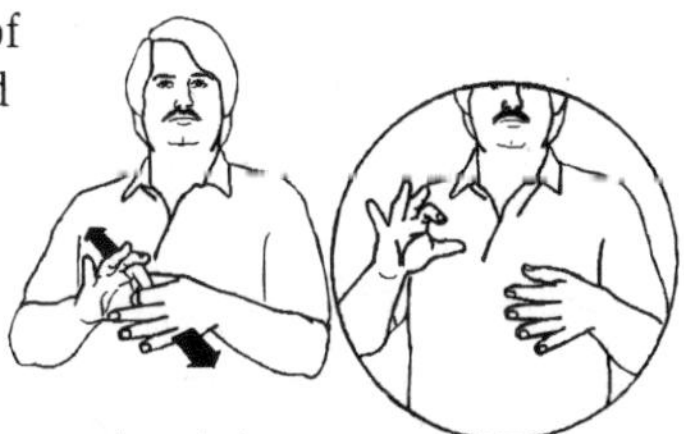

- [Demonstrates releasing of a connection] Beginning with the thumb and index fingertips of each hand intersecting with each other, palms facing each other and right hand nearer the chest than the left hand, release the fingers and pull the left hand forward and the right hand back toward the right shoulder.

**discount**[1] *n.* An amount taken off a price: *The coupon entitles you to a 15% discount.*

- [Initialized sign showing reduction] Beginning with both *D hands* in front of the chest, right hand above the left hand, palms facing each other, and index fingers pointing forward, bring the hands toward each other.

**discount**[2] *v.* See sign for SUBTRACT.

**discouraged** *adj.* See sign for DEPRESSED[1].

**discover** *v.* See sign for FIND.

**discriminate** *v.* To show a difference in treatment, esp. based on membership in a group or class: *to discriminate against women.* Related form: **discrimination** *n.*

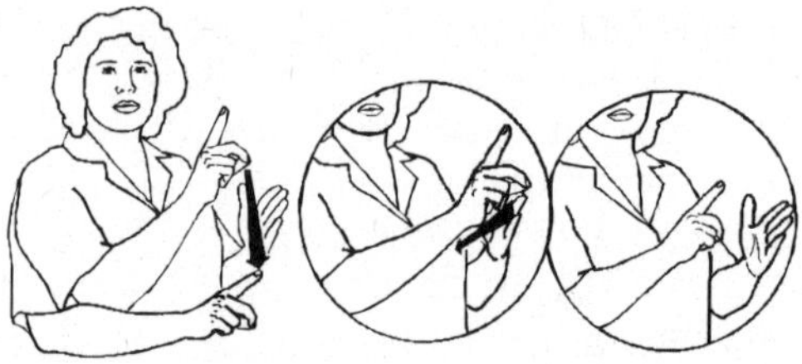

- [Initialized sign similar to sign for **cancel**] With the fingertips of the right *D hand,* palm facing left and index finger pointing up, draw a large X across the palm of the left *open hand.*

**discuss** *v.* To talk about at length: *It is time to discuss the topic thoroughly.* Related form: **discussion** *n.* Same sign used for: **argument, dispute.**

- Tap the side of the extended right index finger, palm facing in, on the upturned left *open hand* with a double movement.

**disgusted**[1] *adj.* Having a strong dislike or repugnance; sickened: *I am disgusted by your rude behavior.* Related form: **disgust** *n., v.* Same sign used for: **aggravated, nausea, stomachache, revulsion, upset.**

- [Represents one's stomach churning in disgust] Move the fingertips of the right *curved 5 hand* in a repeated circle on the stomach.

**disgusted**[2] *adj.* (alternate sign, used especially when referring to one's own actions or mistakes) Same sign used for: **I should have thought of it before** and **Now I remember.**

- [Represents internal grumbling because of an oversight] Move the fingertips of the right *curved 5 hand,* palm facing in, in a double circle on the chest.

**dish** *n.* A shallow container for serving food: *a dish of spaghetti.*

- [Shape of a dish] Beginning with the fingertips of both *curved hands* touching in front of the chest, palms facing in, move the hands away from each other in a circle, ending with the heels together close to the chest.

**disk** or **diskette** *n.* A round, flat, plate-like object used for storing electronic computer programs or data: *Oddly enough, you can store more data on the smaller disk.*

■ [Initialized sign representing recording on a disk] Move the fingertips of the right *D hand,* palm facing down and index finger pointing forward, in a double circle on the upturned left *open hand.*

---

**dislike** *v.* See sign for DON'T LIKE.

---

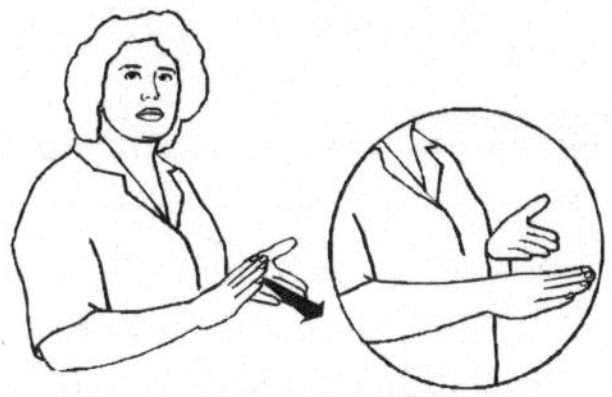

**dismiss**[1] *v.* To send away: *to dismiss the class from school early.* Related form: **dismissal** *n.* Same sign used for: **acquit, discharge, exempt, lay off, pardon, parole, waive.**

■ [Movement seems to wipe person away] Wipe the right *open hand,* palm down, deliberately across the upturned left *open hand* from the heel off the fingertips.

---

**dismiss**[2] *v.* See sign for FIRE[2].

---

**disobey** *v.* To fail or refuse to obey: *a defiant child who always disobeys the rules.* Related form: **disobedience** *n.*

■ [Hands move as in protest] Beginning with the thumbs of both *A hands* touching each side of the forehead, palms facing down, swing the hands outward to each side of the head by twisting the wrists, ending with both palms facing forward.

---

**disorder** *n.* See signs for MESSY, MIX[1].

---

**dispute** *v.* See signs for ARGUE, DISCUSS.

---

**disseminate** *v.* See sign for SPREAD.

---

**dissent** *n., v.* See sign for DISAGREE.

---

**dissolve** *v.* To make or become liquid: *The sugar dissolved in the hot coffee.* Same sign used for: **cure, disappear, evaporate, fade away, melt, perish, resolve, solve, solution.**

■ [Something in the hands seems to melt away to nothing] Beginning with both *flattened O hands* in front of the body, palms facing up, move the thumb of each hand smoothly across each fingertip, starting with the little fingers and ending as *10 hands* while moving the hands outward to each side.

---

**distance** *n.* See sign for FAR. Related form: **distant** *adj.*

**distracted** *adj.* See sign for DIGRESS.

**distribute** *v.* See signs for SELL, SPREAD.

**district** *n.* A designated region established for administrative purposes: *the fifth Congressional district.* Same sign used for: **area.**

■ [Indicates an area] Beginning with the left *open hand* held in front of the body, palm facing down, bring the right *open hand* in a large arc from the right side of the body forward and back over the left hand, ending with the right fingertips on the left wrist.

**disturb** *v.* See sign for ANNOY.

**dive** *v.* **1.** To plunge into water, esp. headfirst with arms extended above the head: *to dive into the pool.* —*n.* **2.** An act or instance of diving: *a beautiful dive that won her a gold medal.*

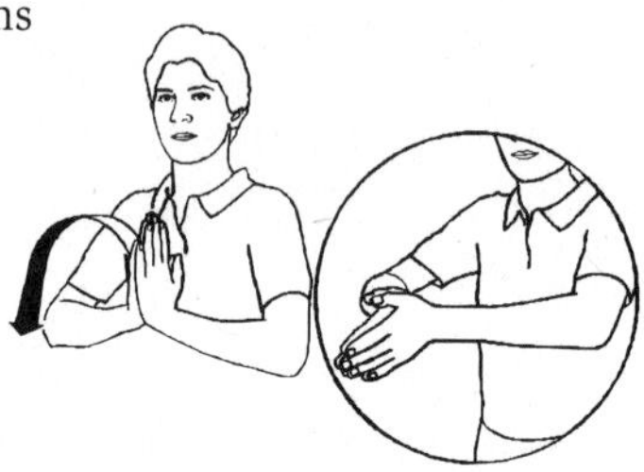

■ [Mime hand position when diving] Beginning with the palms of both *open hands* together in front of the chest, fingers pointing up, move the hands forward and downward in a large arc.

**divide** *v.* To separate into two or more parts: *to divide the money among the survivors.* Same sign used for: **split, split up.**

■ [Split something as if to divide it] Beginning with the little-finger side of the right *B hand* at an angle across the index-finger side of the left *B hand,* palms angled in opposite directions, move the hands downward and apart, ending with the hands in front of each side of the body, palms facing down.

**division** *n.* See sign for DEPARTMENT.

**divorce**[1] *v.* **1.** To terminate a marriage legally: *She had to divorce her husband.* **2.** To break one's marriage contract legally: *a couple planning to divorce.* —*n.* **3.** A legal dissolution of a marriage: *In spite of problems, they want to avoid a divorce.*

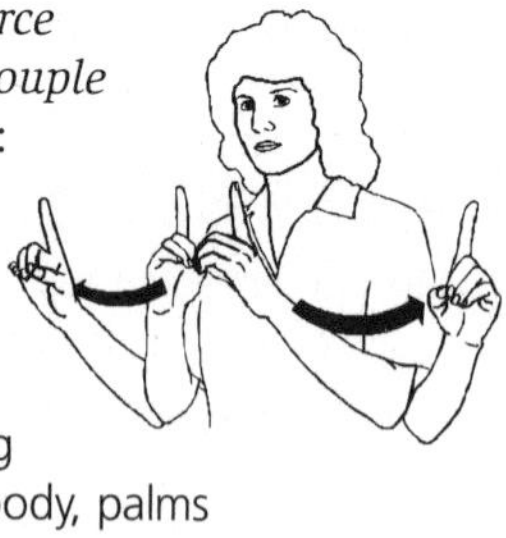

■ [Initialized sign representing two people moving apart] Beginning with the fingertips of both the *D hands* touching in front of chest, palms facing each other and index fingers pointing up, swing the hands away from each other by twisting the wrists, ending with the hands in front of each side of the body, palms facing forward.

**divorce**[2] *v., n.* (alternate sign)

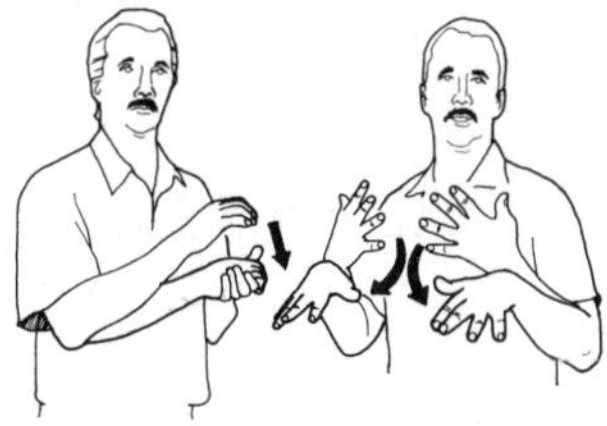

- [**marry** + **finish**[1]] Beginning with the right *curved hand*, palm facing down, moving down to clasp the left *curved hand,* palm facing up. Then beginning with both *5 hands* in front of the chest, palms facing in and fingers pointing up, flip the hands quickly downward, ending with the palms facing down.

**dizzy** *adj.* Feeling unsteady or giddy: *The merry-go-round made me feel dizzy.*

- [Indicates confusion or a spinning sensation in the head] Beginning with the right *curved 5 hand* near the right side of the head, palm facing left, move the hand in a double circular movement.

**do** *v.* To engage in or carry out: *Do your homework now, please.* Related form: **done** *adj.* Same sign used for: **commit, conduct, deed, perform, performance.**

- [Hands seem to be actively doing something] Move both *C hands,* palms facing down, from side to side in front of the body with a repeated movement.

**do better** *v. phrase.* See sign for IMPROVE[1].

**doctor** *n.* A person trained and licensed to treat diseases and injuries: *You'd better see the doctor about your cough.* Same sign used for: **medical, physician.**

- [Formed at the location where one's pulse is taken] Tap the fingertips of the right *M hand,* palm facing left, on the wrist of the upturned left *open hand* with a double movement.

**document** *v.* See sign for PUT DOWN[1].

**doesn't** *v.* or **does not** *v. phrase.* See sign for DON'T.

**doesn't matter** See sign for ANYWAY.

**dog** *n.* A domestic, four-legged, flesh-eating mammal, bred in many varieties: *my pet dog.*

- [Natural gesture for signaling or calling a dog] With a double movement, snap the right thumb gently off the right middle finger, palm facing up, in front of the right side of the chest.

**doll** *n.* A child's toy formed like a human figure: *children playing with their dolls.*

■ Bring the index finger of the right *X hand,* palm facing left, downward on the nose with a repeated movement.

**dollar** *n.* The basic unit of money in the U.S. and Canada: *One dollar doesn't buy much these days.* Same sign used for: **bill.**

■ Beginning with the fingertips of the right *flattened C hand* holding the fingertips of the left *open hand,* both palms facing in, pull the right hand to the right with a double movement.

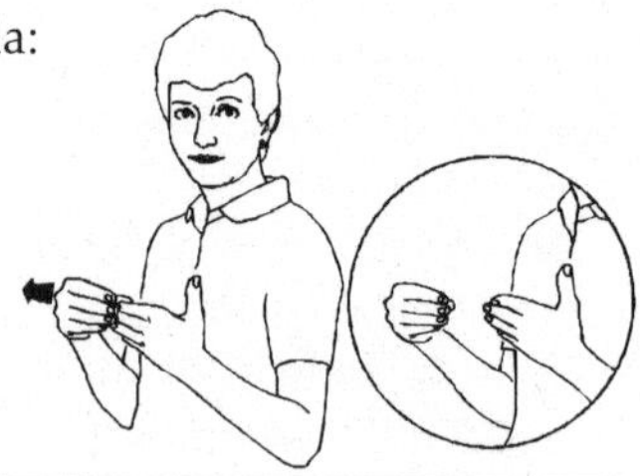

**dolphin** *n.* See sign for PORPOISE.

**domestic** *adj.* See sign for DAILY.

**dominoes** *n.* A game played with oblong playing pieces marked with dots: *to play a game of dominoes.*

■ [Represents moving two dominoes end to end with each other] Bring the fingertips of both *H hands,* palms facing in, together in front of the body with a double movement.

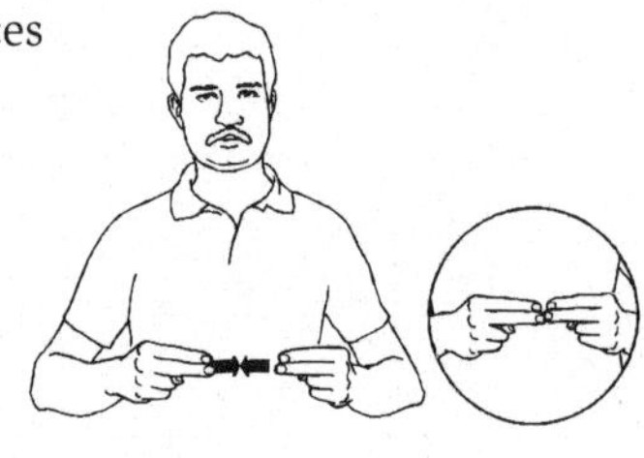

**donate** *v.* See signs for CHARITY, GIVE. Related form: **donation** *n.*

**done** *adj.* See sign for FINISH[1].

**donkey** *n.* A long-eared mammal that looks something like a small horse: *ride a donkey.* Same sign used for: **mule, stubborn.**

■ [Represents a donkey's ears] With the thumb side of the right *B hand* against the right side of the forehead, palm facing forward, bend the fingers up and down with a repeated movement.

**don't**[1] Contraction of *do not. Don't do it.* Same sign used for: **doesn't, does not.**

■ [Natural gesture of denial] Beginning with both *open hands* crossed in front of the chest, palms angled in opposite directions, swing the hands downward away from each other, ending at each side of the body, palms facing down.

**don't**[2] See signs for NOT.

**don't believe** See sign for DOUBT[1].

**don't care** Have no concern or any other feeling for: *I don't care what they think.* Same sign used for: **don't mind, indifferent, nonchalant.**

■ [Outward movement indicates the negative] Beginning with the extended right index finger touching the nose, palm facing down, swing the hand forward by twisting the wrist, ending with the index finger pointing forward in front of the right shoulder.

**don't know** Have no knowledge or information (of): *I can't give you the answer because I just don't know it.* Same sign used for: **unaware, unconscious, unknown.**

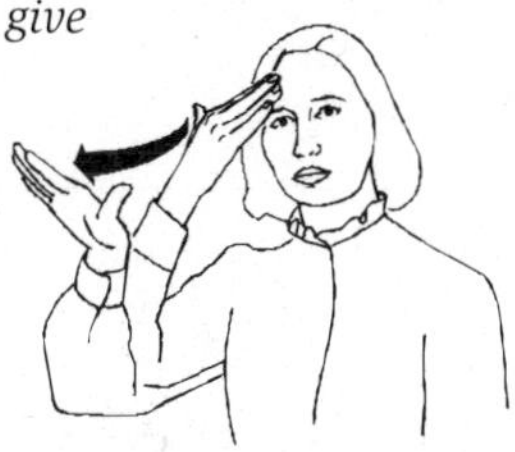

■ [**know** + an outward gesture indicating the negative] Beginning with the fingers of the right *open hand* touching the right side of the forehead, palm facing in, swing the hand forward by twisting the wrist, ending with the fingers pointing forward in front of the right shoulder.

**don't like** Regard with distaste: *I don't like horror movies.* Same sign used for: **dislike.**

■ [**like**[1] formed with an outward gesture indicating the negative] Beginning with the fingertips of the right *8 hand* touching the chest, palm facing in, swing the hand forward by twisting the wrist, and then release the fingers into a *5 hand,* palm facing down.

**don't mind** See sign for DON'T CARE.

**don't want** Have no desire for: *We don't want any dessert.* Same sign used for: **unwanted.**

■ [**want** formed with an outward gesture indicating the negative] Beginning with both *curved 5 hands* in front of the body, palms facing up, swing the hands downward by twisting the wrists, ending with the palms facing down.

**door** *n.* A solid barrier that moves to open and close an entrance: *Please close the door when you leave the room.*

■ [Shows movement of a door being opened] Beginning with the index-finger sides of both *B hands* touching in front of the chest, palms facing forward, swing the right hand back toward the right shoulder with a double movement by twisting the wrist.

**dorsal** *n.* See sign for BACK.

**dot** *n.* See sign for PERIOD.

---

**doubt**[1] *v.* **1.** To be uncertain about; fail to believe or trust: *You may say so, but I doubt it.* —*n.* **2.** An uncertain state of mind: *I should trust her, but I am filled with doubt.* Same sign used for: **don't believe.**

■ [As if one is blind to what is doubted] Beginning with the fingers of the right *bent V hand* in front of the eyes, palm facing in, pull the hand downward a short distance while constricting the fingers with a single movement.

---

**doubt**[2] *n.* See sign for INDECISION.

---

**doubtful** *adj.* See signs for INDECISION, SKEPTICAL.

---

**down** *adv.* **1.** From a higher place or level to a lower one: *The temperature went down overnight.* —*prep.* **2.** To a lower place on or along: *rolling down the hill.*

■ [Shows direction] Move the extended right index finger downward in front of the right side of the body.

---

**download** *v.* To copy a file from a main source to a peripheral device: *download the file to a flash drive.* Same sign used for: **import.**

■ [Action of information flowing down] Beginning with both *V hands,* palms facing each other and fingers pointing up, near the right shoulder, bring the hands down to the left while bending the extended fingers.

---

**downstairs** *adv.* Same sign as for DOWN but made with a double movement. Same sign used for: **downward.**

---

**doze** *v.* See signs for FALL ASLEEP, SLEEP.

---

**draft**[1] *v.* See signs for DESIGN, DRAW.

---

**draft**[2] *n.* See signs for ROUGH, SKETCH.

---

**drafting** *v.* See sign for ENGINEERING.

---

**drag** *v.* To pull along with effort: *to drag the heavy suitcase into the airline terminal.* Same sign used for: **draw, haul, pull, tow.**

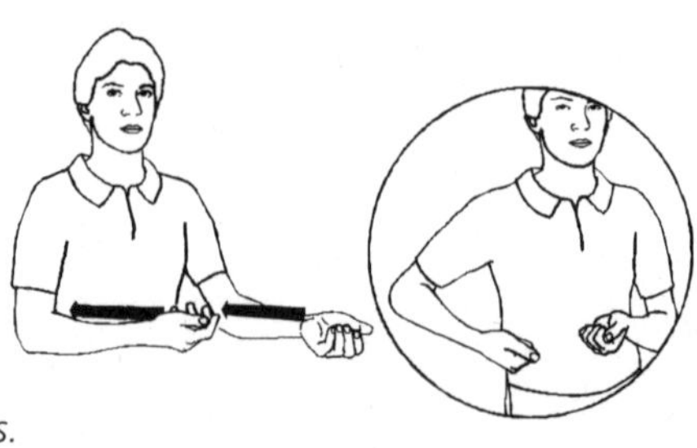

■ [Mime pulling something] Beginning with the right *curved hand* in front of the body and the left *curved hand* somewhat forward, both palms facing up, bring the hands back toward the right side of the body while closing them into *A hands.*

---

**drain** *adj.* See signs for ABSENT, LEAK.

**drama** *n.* See sign for ACT[2].

**drapes** *pl. n.* Long curtains, usually of a heavy decorative fabric, hung at a window: *closing the drapes to keep the chill out.*

- [Shape of drapes] Beginning with both *4 hands* in front of each shoulder, palms facing forward, drop the hands downward while turning the palms down.

**drat** *interj.* See signs for ALAS, DARN.

**draw**[1] *v.* To make (a picture or a picture of) using a pen, pencil, or the like: *to draw a picture; to draw a house.* Same sign used for: **draft, illustrate, sketch.**

- [Initialized sign similar to sign for **art**] Move the extended right little finger, palm facing left, down the palm of the left *open hand.*

**draw**[2] *v.* See signs for ATTRACT[1], CHOOSE, DESIGN, DRAG, FIND.

**draw back** *v. phrase.* See sign for RESIGN.

**draw blood** *v. phrase.* To take blood for medical purposes: *The nurse drew blood from my arm to send to the lab.* Same sign used for: **give blood.**

- [Hand seems to extract blood from the arm] Beginning with the fingers of the right *curved 5 hand,* palm facing up, near the crook of the left arm held extended in front of the left side of the body, pull the right hand to the right while closing the fingers to the thumb, forming a *flattened O hand.*

**drawer** *n.* A sliding open boxlike compartment in a piece of furniture: *I keep my socks in the top drawer of my bureau.* Same sign used for: **dresser.**

- [Mime opening a drawer] With the fingers of both *A hands* tightly curled in front of each side of the body, palms facing up, pull the hands back toward the body with a repeated movement.

**drawing**[1] *n.* Same sign as for DRAW but made with a double movement.

**drawing**[2] *n.* See sign for ART, DESIGN, SKETCH.

**dreadful** *adj.* See sign for AWFUL.

**dream** *v.* **1.** To have a series of images pass through the mind during sleep: *I dreamed about you last night.* —*n.* **2.** A series of such images that pass through the mind: *I had a bad dream last week.* Same sign used for: **daydream, fantasize.**

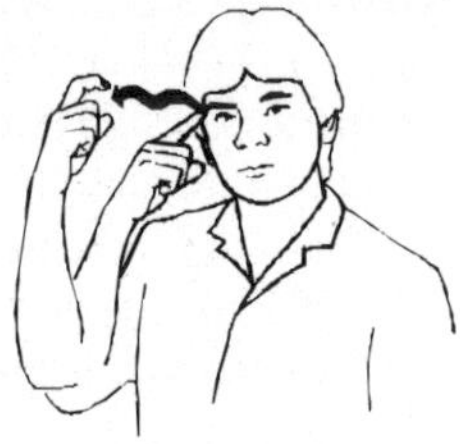

- [Represents an image coming from the mind] Move the extended right index finger from touching the right side of the forehead, palm facing down, outward to the right while bending the finger up and down.

**dress**[1] *v.* To put clothes on: *to dress yourself.*

- [Location of dress] Brush the thumbs of both *5 hands* downward on each side of the chest.

**dress**[2] *n.* See sign for CLOTHES.

**dresser** *n.* See sign for DRAWER.

**dribble** *v.* See signs for BOUNCE, DRIP.

**drill** *n.* See signs for ALARM, PRACTICE.

**drink**[1] *n.* **1.** A liquid suitable for drinking: *Cranberry juice is a refreshing drink.* **2.** A portion of such a liquid: *a drink of milk.* —*v.* To swallow something liquid: *Drink some milk.* Same sign used for: **beverage.**

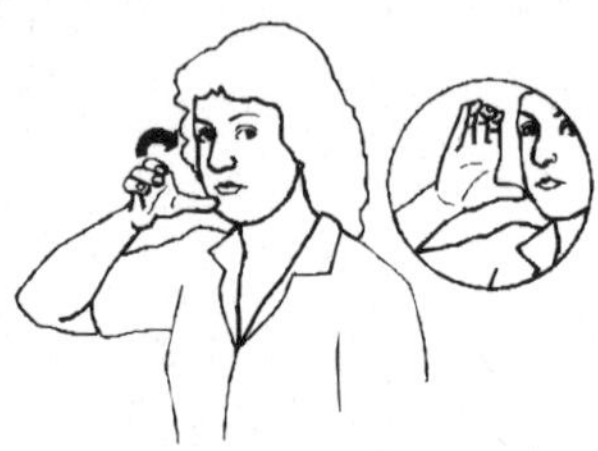

- [Mime drinking from a glass] Beginning with the thumb of the right *C hand* near the chin, palm facing left, tip the hand up toward the face, with a single movement for the noun and a double movement for the verb.

**drink**[2] *n.* Alcoholic liquor or a portion of this: *to have a mixed drink before dinner.* Same sign used for: **bar, drinking.**

- [Initialized sign made with **a** to represent an alcoholic drink] Move the thumb of the right *A hand,* palm facing left, back toward the mouth with a double circular movement.

**drink**[3] *n.* See sign for COCKTAIL.

**drip** *n.* **1.** The act or sound of liquid falling in drops: *I can hear the drip of rain on the roof.* **2.** The liquid so falling: *Catch the drip in this pan.* —*v.* **3.** To fall or allow liquid to fall in drops: *the faucet drips.* Same sign used for: **dribble, drop, leak.**

- [Represents action of water dripping] Beginning with the right *S hand,* palm facing down, near the fingertips of the left *open hand,* palm facing down and fingers pointing right, flick the right index finger downward with a repeated movement.

**drive** *v.* To guide the movement of a vehicle: *to drive carefully through the traffic.*

- [Similar to the sign for **car** except made with a larger movement] Beginning with both *S hands* in front of the chest, palms facing in and one hand higher than the other hand, move the hands in an up-and-down repeated alternating movement.

**drive to** *v. phrase.* To go in a vehicle to (a particular destination): *to drive to church.*

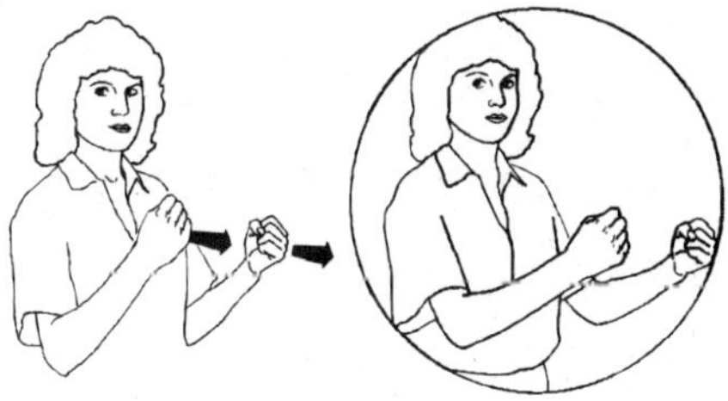

- [Represents continuous driving] Beginning with both *S hands* in front of the chest, palms facing in, move the hands forward with a deliberate movement.

**drool** *v.* To let saliva run from the mouth: *to drool just looking at the delicious food.* Same sign used for: **crave.**

- [Indicates saliva running from corner of mouth] Beginning with the index finger of the right *4 hand* near the right side of the mouth, palm facing in and fingers pointing left, bring the hand downward in front of the chest.

**drop**[1] *v.* To let fall: *Try not to drop the dish.*

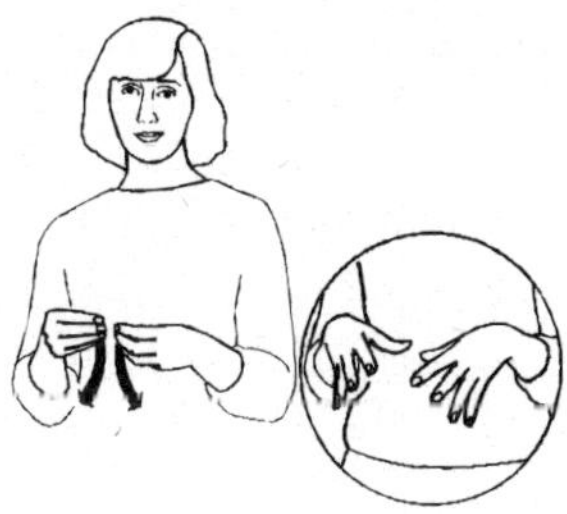

- [Represents dropping something held in the hands] Beginning with both *flattened O hands* in front of the body, palms facing in and fingers pointing toward each other, drop the fingers of both hands downward while opening into *5 hands,* ending with both palms facing in and fingers pointing down

**drop**[2] *v.* See sign for DECLINE[3].

**drop**[3] *n.* See sign for DRIP.

**drop out** *v. phrase.* See sign for RESIGN.

**drown** *v.* To die or cause to die of suffocation under water: *drown in the pool.*

■ [Symbolizes a person's head going under the water] Beginning with the thumb of the right *10 hand,* palm facing in, extended up between the index finger and middle finger of the left *open hand,* palm facing down and fingers pointing right, pull the right hand straight down.

**drug**[1] *n.* A medicinal substance taken by injection (used especially for illicit substances): *a new drug administered intravenously.* Same sign used for: **controlled substance.**

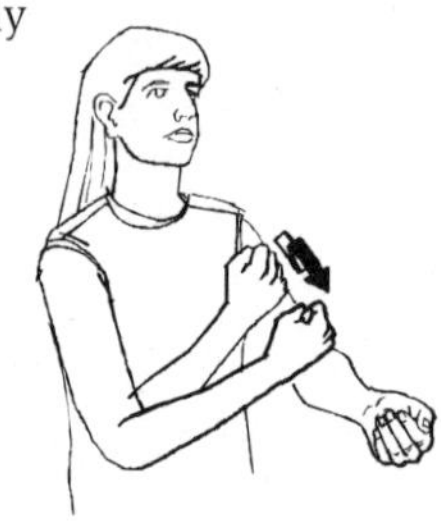

■ [Represents injecting a drug] Pound the little-finger side of the right *S hand,* palm facing up, with a double movement near the crook of the extended left arm.

**drug**[2] *n.* See sign for MEDICINE.

**drum** *n.* A musical percussion instrument struck with the hands or a pair of sticks: *beat the drum.*

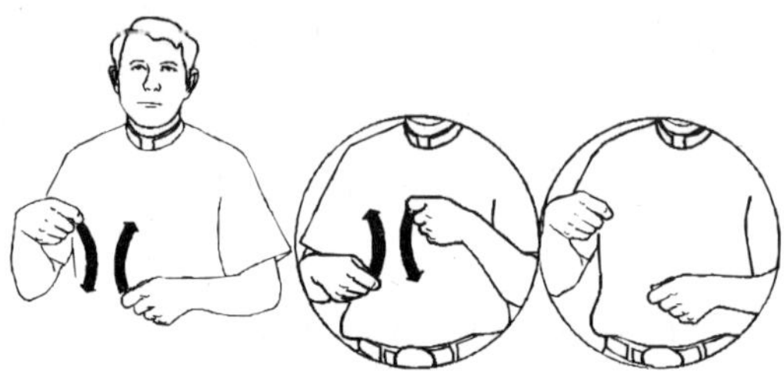

■ [Mime playing a snare drum] Move both modified *X hands,* palms facing in and knuckles pointing toward each other, up and down in front of the chest with a repeated alternating movement.

**drunk** *adj.* Being in a state in which one's faculties are impaired by alcoholic liquor: *He is so drunk that he can't talk coherently.* Same sign used for: **intoxicated.**

■ Move the thumb of the right *10 hand,* palm facing left, in an arc from right to left past the chin.

**dry** *adj.* **1.** Not wet or moist: *suffering from dry, flaky skin.* **2.** Having or characterized by insufficient rain: *a spell of dry weather.* **3.** Dull and uninteresting: *a dry lecture that we could hardly sit through.* Related form: **dried** *adj.* Same sign used for: **boring.**

- [Wiping the chin dry] Drag the index-finger side of the right *X hand,* palm facing down, from left to right across the chin.

**dry cleaners** *n.* See sign for CLEANERS.

**duck** *n.* A swimming bird with a short neck, flat bill, and webbed feet: *a wild duck.*

- [A duck's bill] Close the extended index and middle fingers of the right hand, palm facing forward, to the right thumb with a repeated movement in front of the mouth.

**due** *adj.* See sign for AFFORD.

**dull** *adj.* See sign for BORING[1].

**dumb** *adj.* **1.** Slow in understanding: *He's good with words but dumb in math.* **2.** Revealing lack of intelligence: *That's a dumb idea.* Same sign used for: **stupid.**

- [Natural gesture] Hit the palm side of the right *A hand* against the forehead.

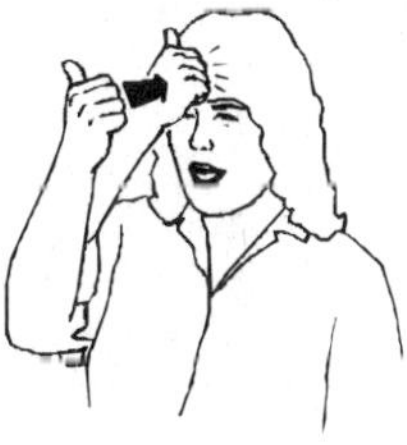

**dumbfounded** *adj.* See sign for SHOCK.

**dump** *v.* See sign for THROW.

**duplicate** *v., n.* See signs for COPY[1,2].

**during** *prep.* **1.** Throughout the entire length or existence of: *They're both at the office during the day.* **2.** At some time during the course of: *She sings once during the first act of the opera.* Same sign used for: **meanwhile, while.**

- [Shows two events occurring simultaneously] Beginning with both extended index fingers in front of each side of the body, palms facing down, move them forward in parallel arcs, ending with the index fingers angled upward.

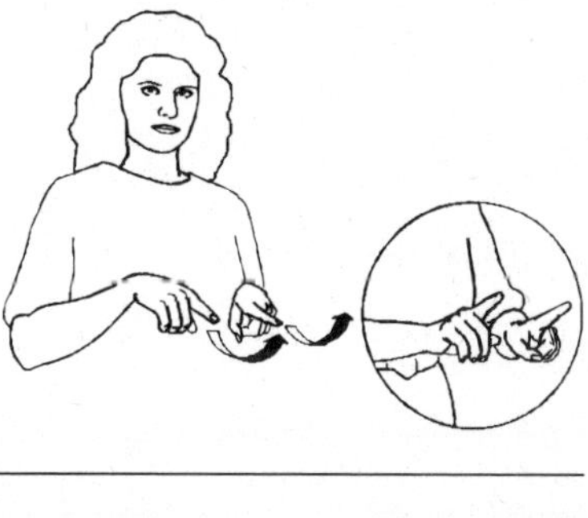

**dusk** *n.* See sign for DARK.

**duty** *n.* See sign for COST[1].

**dwell** *v.* See sign for LIVE.

**dye** *n.* **1.** A coloring matter: *Dip the t-shirt in the dye.* —*v.* **2.** To color or stain with a dye, esp. by dipping: *We can dye the cloth blue.* Same sign used for: **dip, rinse.**

- [Dipping cloth in dye] Move both *F hands,* palms facing down, with a slight up and down repeated movement in front of each side of the body.

**each** *adj.* **1.** Being every one out of two or more considered individually: *Each person gets a door prize.* —*pron.* **2.** Each one: *each of us.* —*adv.* **3.** Apiece: *The candies cost 10 cents each.* Same sign used for: **apiece, every, per.**

■ Bring the knuckle side of the right *10 hand* down the knuckles of the left *10 hand,* palms facing each other and thumbs pointing up.

**each other** *pron.* See sign for ASSOCIATE.

**eager** *adj.* See sign for ZEAL.

**eagle** *n.* A large predatory bird with a hooked beak, noted for its acute vision: *the keen eyesight of a young eagle.*

■ [Represents an eagle's beak] Tap the back of the index finger of the right *X hand,* palm facing forward, against the nose with a double movement.

**ear** *n.* **1.** The organ of hearing and balance in a mammal: *The noise hurt my ears.* **2.** The external, or outer, ear: *Cover your ears with earmuffs if they're cold.*

■ [Location of an ear] Wiggle the right earlobe with the thumb and index finger of the closed right hand.

**earache** *n.* A pain in the ear: *I have an earache.*

■ [**hurt**[1] formed near the ear] Jab both extended index fingers toward each other with a repeated movement near the right ear or near the ear with an earache.

**earbuds** *pl. n.* A tiny pair of loudspeakers connected to a signal source that fit within the ear canals: *wear earbuds to listen to music while jogging.*

■ [Placing earbuds in ears] Beginning with both *G hands* in front of the body, fingers pointing toward each other, bring the hands upward to each ear.

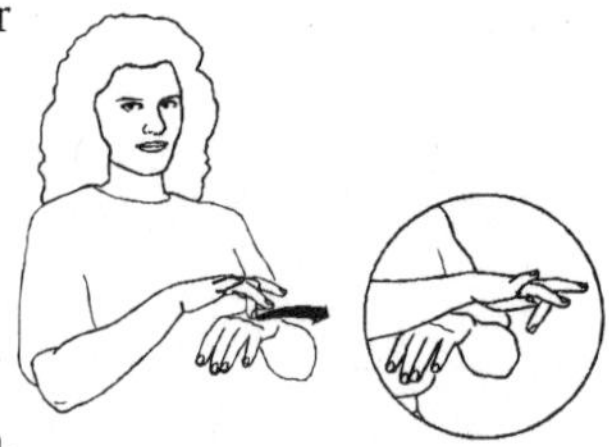

**early** *adv.* **1.** Before the usual time: *to arrive early.* **2.** Near the beginning of a period of time, series of events, or the like: *To wake up early in the morning.* —*adj.* **3.** Occurring before the usual time: *an early winter.* **4.** Of or occurring near the beginning, as of a period of time: *born sometime in the early 1950s.*

■ Push the bent middle finger of the right *5 hand* across the back of the left *open hand,* both palms facing down.

**earmuffs** *pl. n.* See sign for EARPHONES.

**earnest** *adj.* See sign for ZEAL.

**earnings** *pl. n.* Money acquired in return for one's work: *the teenager's earnings were meager.* Same sign used for: **income, salary, wages.**

■ [Bringing earned money toward oneself] Bring the little-finger side of the right *curved hand,* palm facing left, across the upturned left *open hand* from fingertips to heel while changing into an *S hand* with a double movement.

**earphones** *pl. n.* A set of receivers worn over or in the ears to transmit sound from a sound source: *to wear earphones to listen to the portable tape player.* Same sign used for: **earmuffs.**

■ [Putting on earphones] Tap the fingertips of both *curved 5 hands,* palms facing in, on each side of the head around each ear with a repeated movement.

**earring** *n.* An ornament for the lobe of the ear: *He now wears an earring in one ear.*

■ [Location of earring] Shake the right earlobe with the index finger and thumb of the right *F hand* with a repeated movement. For the plural, use the same sign but made with both hands, one at each ear.

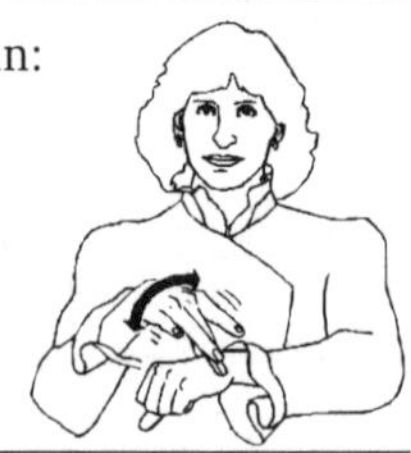

**Earth** *n.* The planet on which we live; the third planet from the sun: *Dinosaurs once lived on Earth.* Same sign used for: **geography.**

■ Grasp each side of the left *S hand,* palm facing down, with the bent thumb and middle finger of the right *5 hand,* palm facing down. Then rock the right hand from side to side with a double movement.

**east** *n.* **1.** The general direction 90 degrees to the right of north: *The sun rises in the east. —adj.* **2.** Lying toward or located in the east: *a house on the east side of the street. —adv.* **3.** To, toward, or in the east: *going east to attend college.*

■ [Initialized sign showing an easterly direction on a map] Move the right *E hand,* palm facing forward, a short distance to the right in front of the right shoulder.

**easy** *adj.* Not difficult: *an easy lesson.* Same sign used for: **convenient, simple.**

■ Brush the fingertips of the right *curved hand* upward on the back of the fingertips of the left *curved hand* with a double movement, both palms facing up.

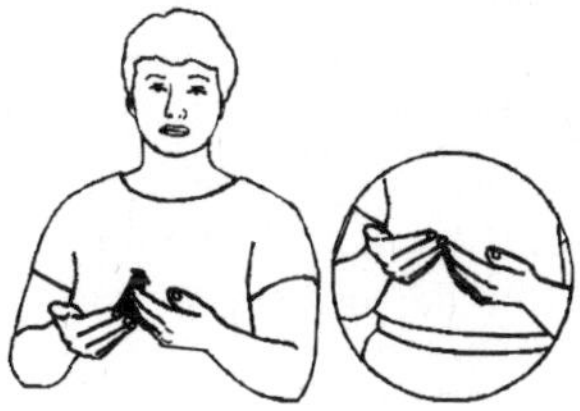

**eat** *v.* To take food into the mouth and swallow it for nourishment: *to eat only when you're hungry; to eat dinner.*

■ [Putting food in the mouth] Bring the fingertips of the right *flattened O hand,* palm facing in, to the lips with a repeated movement.

**eat up** *v. phrase.* See signs for ACID, CONSUME.

**eavesdrop** *v.* See sign for LISTEN.

**edge** *n.* A line or border where an object or surface begins or ends: *trace the edge of the circle.*

■ [Shows edge of fingers] Slide the palm of the right *open hand,* palm facing left and fingers pointing forward, back and forth with a double movement on the fingertips of the left *B hand,* palm facing down and fingers pointing right.

**edit**[1] *v.* To correct and prepare for publication: *to edit the document.* Same sign used for: **correct.**

■ [Crossing out text in order to correct it] With the extended right index finger, palm facing forward, make small repeated crosses on the palm of the left *open hand,* palm facing in, in front of the chest.

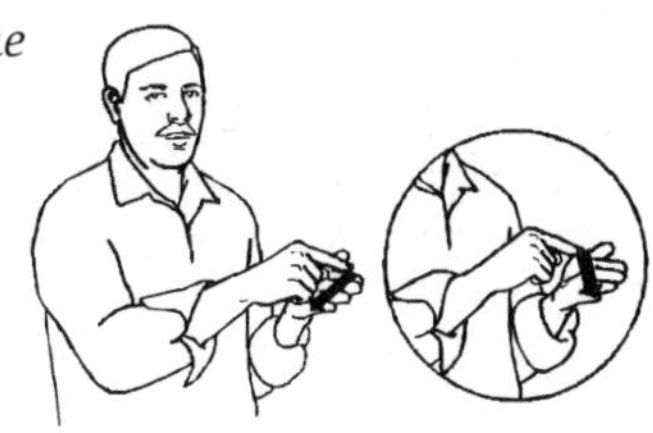

**edit**[2] *v.* See sign for WRITE.

**educate** *v.* See signs for LEARN, TEACH. Related form: **education** *n.*

**education** *n.* The process of conveying or acquiring knowledge and judgment, as through teaching or reading: *Children are entitled to a good education.* Related form: **educate** *v.*

■ [Initialized sign **e-d** similar to sign for **teach**] Beginning with both *E hands* near each side of the head, palms facing each other, move the hands forward a short distance while changing into *D hands.*

---

**effect** *n.* See signs for ADVICE, INFLUENCE.

---

**efficient** *adj.* See sign for SKILL.

---

**effort** *n.* The use of physical or mental energy or strength to do something: *The students made a real effort to pass the test with high scores.*

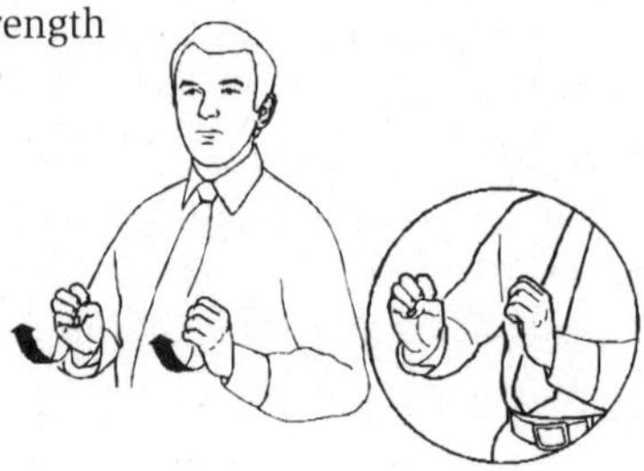

■ [Initialized sign similar to sign for **try**] Move both *E hands* from in front of each side of the body, palms facing each other, downward and forward simultaneously in an arc.

---

**egg** *n.* **1.** A roundish or oval reproductive body produced by the female of some animals: *a bird's nest with three eggs ready to hatch.* **2.** Such a body, oval and with a brittle shell, produced by a domestic bird, especially the hen; used as food for human beings: *eat scrambled eggs.*

■ [Represents cracking eggs] Beginning with the middle-finger side of the right *H hand* across the index-finger side of the left *H hand,* palms angled toward each other, bring the hands downward and away from each other with a double movement by twisting the wrists each time.

---

**egotistic** or **egotistical** *adj.* Having or displaying an exaggerated sense of self-importance; vain and selfish: *an egotistic disregard for the feelings of others.* Related forms: **ego** *n.*, **egotism** *n.*

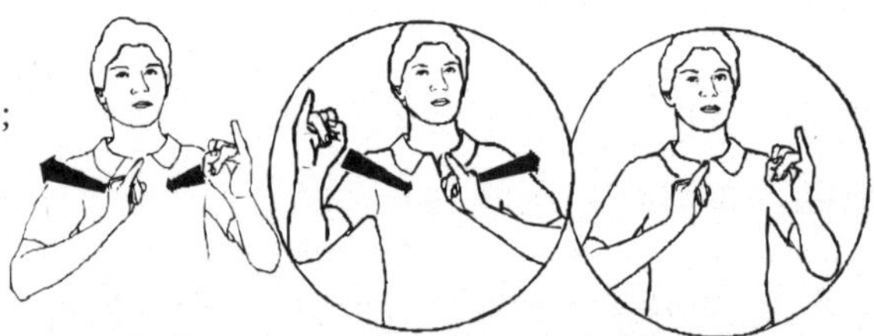

■ [The repeated **I** sign represents concentrating on oneself] Beginning with the right *I hand* in front of the right side of the chest and the left *I hand* somewhat forward of the left side of the chest, palms facing in opposite directions, bring the right hand forward and the left hand back to the chest with an alternating movement.

**either**[1] *adj.* **1.** One or the other of two: *We can go either way to get there.* *—pron.* **2.** One or the other: *I'll take either.* *—conj.* **3.** (Used before the first of two words or groups of words that represent alternatives and are separated by **or**): *It will either rain or snow; either it will rain or it won't.* See also sign for OR. Same sign used for: **alternative, choice.**

- [Shows alternative choices] Tap the fingertips of the right *V hand* with a repeated alternating movement on the fingertips of the left *V hand,* palms facing each other.

**either**[2] *adj., pron., conj.* See sign for WHICH.

**ejaculate** *v.* to eject or discharge, especially semen from the penis. Related form: **ejaculation.** Same sign used for **emission.**

- [Shows movement of semen] While touching the wrist of the right *S hand* with the left extended index finger, palms facing in opposite directions, move the right hand forward while opening into a *4 hand,* ending with the right palm facing left and fingers pointing forward.

**elaborate**[1] *v.* To give additional details: *Would you please elaborate on the story?* Same sign used for: **extend.**

- [Stretching out the facts] Beginning with the thumb side of the right *S hand* against the little-finger side of the left *S hand,* move the right hand forward with a wavy movement.

**elaborate**[2] *adj.* See sign for DECORATE.

**elaborate**[3] *v.* See sign for EXAGGERATE.

**elastic** *adj.* See sign for STRETCH.

**elect** *v.* See signs for APPOINT[1], VOTE. Related form: **election** *n.*

**electric** or **electrical** *adj.* Of or run by electricity: *an electric fan.* Related form: **electricity** *n.* Same sign used for: **battery.**

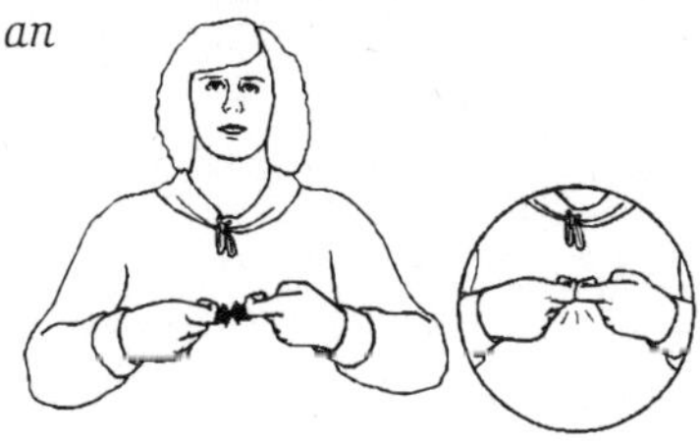

- [An electrical connection] Tap the knuckles of the index fingers of both *X hands* together, palms facing in, with a double movement.

**elegant** *adj.* See sign for FANCY.

**elementary** *adj.* Dealing with simple, basic, or introductory information: *elementary school.*

■ [Initialized sign similar to sign for **base**] Move the right *E hand,* palm facing forward, from side to side with a repeated movement below the left *open hand,* palm facing down and fingers pointing right, in front of the chest.

**elephant** *n.* A huge mammal with large ivory tusks and a long, flexible prehensile trunk: *ride an elephant in the circus parade.*

■ [Shape of elephant's trunk] Beginning with the back of the right *bent B hand* against the nose, palm facing down, move the hand downward and forward with a large wavy movement.

**elevate** *v.* See sign for ADVANCED. Related forms: **elevated** *adj.*, **elevation** *n.*

**elevator** *n.* A moving platform or compartment used to carry people or things to different levels in a building or other structure: *Take the elevator to the top floor.*

■ [Initialized sign showing movement of elevator] Move the index-finger side of the right *E hand,* palm facing forward, up and down with a repeated movement against the left *open hand,* palm facing right and fingers pointing up.

**eligible** *adj.* See sign for APPLY[2].

**eliminate**[1] *v.* To get rid of: *Try to eliminate sugar and fats from your diet.* Same sign used for: **abolish, abort, delete, omit, remove, repel, rid, terminate.**

■ [Natural gesture] Beginning with the back of the right *modified X hand,* palm facing in, touching the extended left index finger, palm facing in and finger pointing right, bring the right hand upward and outward to the right while flicking the thumb upward, forming a *10 hand.*

**eliminate**[2] *v.* See sign for SUBTRACT.

**else** *adj., adv.* See sign for OTHER.

**elude** *v.* See sign for AVOID.

**e-mail**[1] *n., v.* Short for *electronic mail.* Correspondence or data transmitted over computer telephone lines: *read your e-mail.* Same sign used for: **mail.**

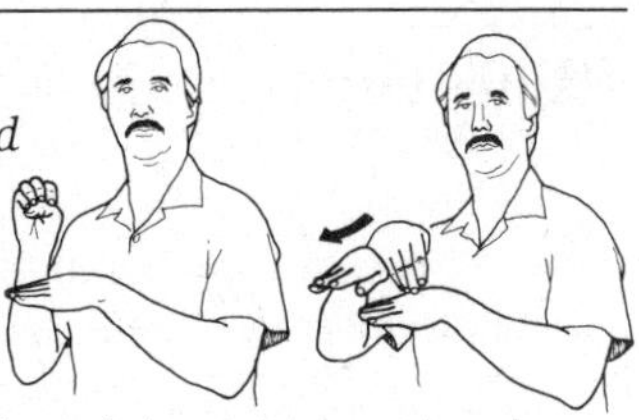

■ [Initialized sign + **mail**[1]] Hold the index-finger side of the left *B hand,* palm down and fingers pointing right, against the wrist of the right *E hand* held in front of the right shoulder, palm forward. Then flick the fingertips of the right *bent hand* forward across the back of the left *open hand,* both palms facing down, with a quick movement, straightening the right fingers as the right hand moves forward.

**e-mail**[2] *n., v.* (alternate sign) Same sign used for: **mail.**

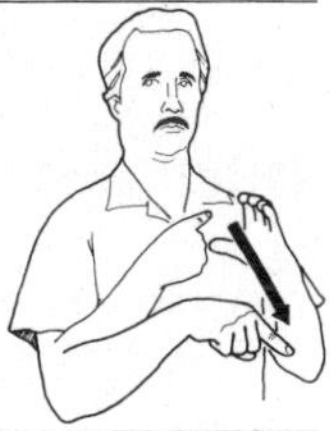

■ [e-mail being sent] Move the extended right index finger from pointing left in front of the chest past the palm side of the left *C hand,* palm right, ending with the right index finger pointing forward.

**embarrass** *v.* To cause to feel uneasy and self-conscious: *You embarrassed me by mentioning my grades.* Related form: **embarrassed** *adj.*

■ [Indicates blood rising in the face when embarrassed] Move both *5 hands,* palms facing each other, in repeated alternating circles near each cheek.

**emblem** *n.* See sign for BADGE.

**embrace** *v.* See sign for HUG.

**emerge** *v.* See sign for MAINSTREAM.

**emergency** *n.* A sudden occurrence requiring immediate action: *Dial 911 in an emergency.*

■ [Initialized sign] Move the right *E hand,* palm facing forward, back and forth with a double movement in front of the right shoulder.

**emery board** *n.* See sign for PUMICE.

**emission** *n.* See sign for EJACULATE.

**emit** *v.* To give off: *emitted a strange light.*

■ [Represents a beam of light] Beginning with the left *S hand* on the back of the right *S hand,* both palms facing down, move the right hand forward with a double movement, opening into a *5 hand* each time.

**emotional** *adj.* Involving, experiencing, or likely to have a strong feeling, as joy, love, hate, or sorrow: *an emotional homecoming; a person who is rarely emotional.* Related form: **emotion** *n.*

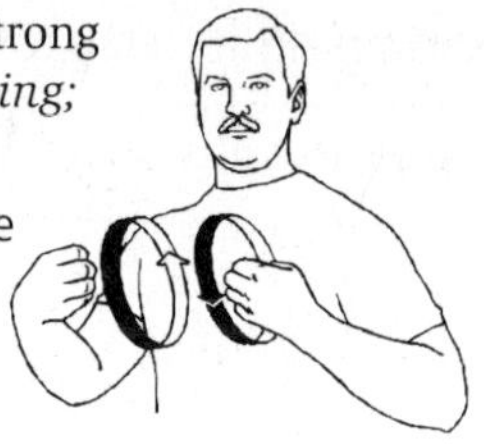

- [Initialized sign showing feeling welling up in the body] Move both *E hands,* palms facing in and knuckles pointing toward each other, in repeated alternating circles on each side of the chest.

**emphasis** *n.* See sign for IMPRESSION.

**employ** *v.* See sign for INVITE.

**employment** *n.* See sign for WORK.

**empty** *adj.* Containing nothing; lacking contents: *an empty can.* Same sign used for: **available, bare, blank, naked, vacancy, vacant, void.**

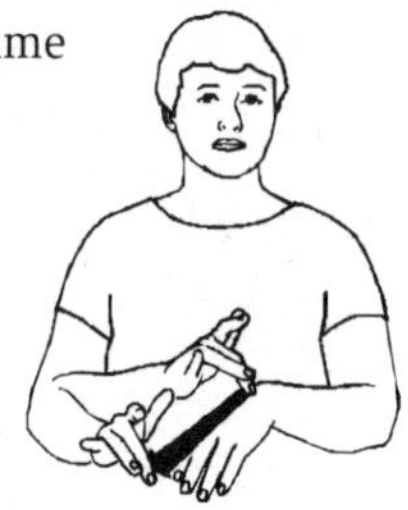

- [Indicates a vacant space] Move the bent middle fingertip of the right *5 hand* across the back of the left *open hand* from the wrist to off the fingertips, both palms facing down.

**enable** *v.* See sign for SKILL.

**encore** *n.* See sign for AGAIN.

**encourage** *v.* To give support and confidence to: *encouraged her to go to college.* Related form: **encouragement** *n.* Same sign used for: **bear up, coax, persuade.**

- [Hands seem to give someone a push of encouragement] Beginning with both *open hands* outside each side of the body, palms and fingers angled forward, move the hands toward each other and forward with a double pushing movement.

**end**[1] *v.* To come to or bring to a conclusion: *The story ended suddenly.* Same sign used for: **complete, conclude, finish, over, wind up.**

- [Demonstrates going off the end] Beginning with the little-finger side of the right *open hand,* palm facing left, across the index-finger side of the left *open hand,* palm facing in, bring the right hand deliberately down off the left fingertips.

**end**[2] *n.* See sign for LAST[1].

**endanger** *v.* See sign for DANGER.

**endorse** *v.* See signs for SIGN[2], SUPPORT.

**enemy** *n.* Someone who hates, opposes, or wishes to harm another: *difficult to face the enemy.* Same sign used for: **foe, opponent, rival.**

■ [**opposite** + **person marker**] Beginning with both extended index fingers touching in front of the chest, palms facing down, pull the hands apart to in front of each side of the chest. Then move both *open hands,* palms facing each other, downward along each side of the body.

**engaged** *adj.* Being pledged to marry: *She's engaged to him. They are engaged.* Related form: **engagement** *n.*

■ [Initialized sign showing the location of an engagement ring] Beginning with the right *E hand* over the left *open hand,* both palms facing down, move the right hand in a small circle and then straight down to land on the ring finger of the left hand.

**engagement** *n.* See sign for APPOINTMENT.

**engineering** *n.* The design and construction of machines, roads, bridges, electrical systems, computer hardware and software systems, etc.: *engineering for the field of electronics.* Same sign used for: **drafting, measuring.**

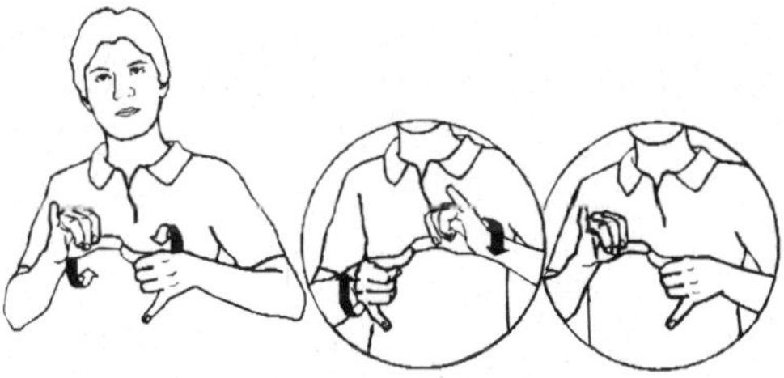

■ [Similar to sign for **measure**] With the thumbs of both *Y hands* touching in front of the chest, right palm facing forward and left palm facing in, twist the hands in opposite directions with a double movement.

**engrave** *v.* See sign for CARVE.

**enjoin** *v.* See signs for FORBID, STOP[1].

**enjoy** *v.* To be happy with; take pleasure in: *We always enjoy the performance at the opera.* Related form: **enjoyment** *n.* Same sign used for: **appreciate, leisure, like, please, pleasure.**

■ [Hands rub the body with pleasure] Rub the palms of both *open hands* on the chest, right hand above the left hand and fingers pointing in opposite directions, in repeated circles moving in opposite directions.

**enlarge** *v.* See sign for EXPAND.

**enormous** *adj.* See sign for LARGE.

**enough** *adj.* **1.** Adequate to answer a purpose or satisfy a need; sufficient: *enough water for the crops.* —*pron.* **2.** An adequate amount: *Be sure you eat enough for breakfast.* —*adv.* **3.** In or to an adequate quantity or degree: *The room is warm enough.* Same sign used for: **adequate, plenty, sufficient.**

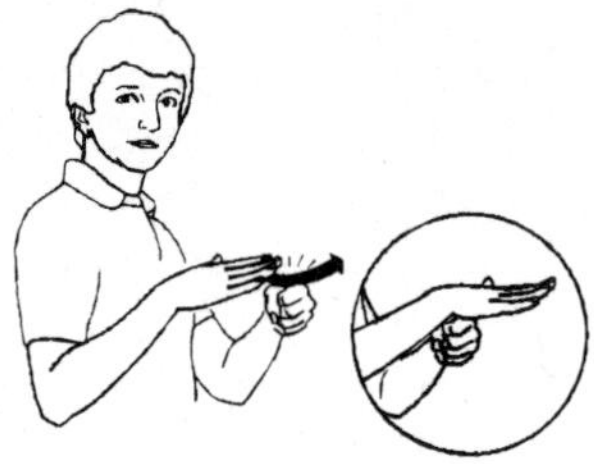

- [Represents leveling off a container filled to the top] Push the palm side of the right *open hand,* palm facing down, forward across the thumb side of the left *S hand,* palm facing in.

**enrage** *v.* See sign for ANGER.

**enter**[1] *v.* To go into: *enter the house.* Related forms: **entrance** *n.*, **entry** *n.* Same sign used for: **access, enroll, immigrate, into.**

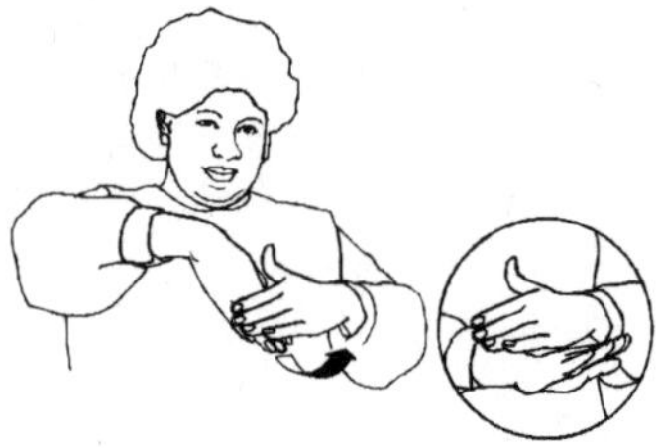

- [Represents movement of entering] Move the back of the right *open hand* forward in a downward arc under the palm of the left *open hand,* both palms facing down.

**Enter**[2] (key) or **Return** (key) *n.* The keyboard key that is pressed to execute a command or to move the cursor down to the next line: *Press Enter at the end of the paragraph.*

- [Initialize sign showing a change in direction] Beginning with the right *R hand*, palm facing down and fingers pointing forward, in front of the right side of the chest, twist the hand over, ending with the palm facing up.

**enthusiastic** *adj.* See sign for ZEAL.

**entice** *v.* See sign for TEMPT.

**entire** *adj.* See sign for ALL.

**entitle** *v.* See signs for BELONG[2], TITLE.

**entrance** *n.* See sign for ADMISSION. Related form: **entry** *n.*

**envelope** *n.* See sign for CARD[1].

**envious** *adj.* See sign for JEALOUS.

**envy** *n.* **1.** A feeling of discontent, resentment, and unreasoning desire for another's attributes, possessions, accomplishments, or status: *filled with envy over her promotion.* —*v.* **2.** To regard with envy; be envious of: *How I envy her slim figure.* Related form: **envious** *adj.*

■ [Natural gesture used when a person envies another's possessions] Touch the teeth on the right side of the mouth with the right bent index fingertip.

**epilepsy** *n.* See sign for SEIZURE. Related form: **epileptic** *adj.* Shared idea that a seizure is one possible symptom of epilepsy.

**equal** *adj.* **1.** Having the same amount, size, value, etc.: *equal portions.* —*v.* **2.** To be the same as: *two nickels equal 10 cents.* Same sign used for: **even, fair, get even, just, tie.**

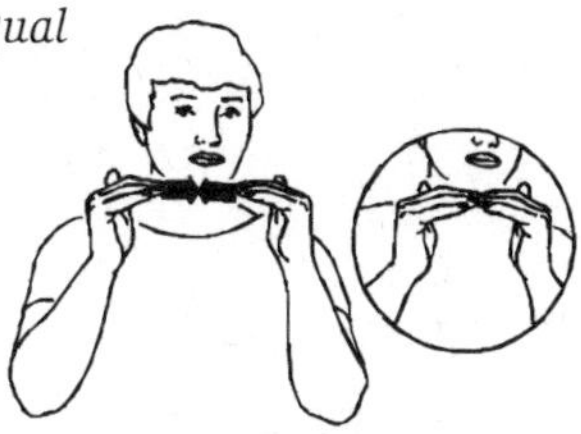

■ [Demonstrates equal level] Tap the fingertips of both bent hands, palms facing down, together in front of the chest with a double movement.

**equipment** *n.* Articles used or needed for a specific purpose: *camping equipment.* Same sign used for: **device, hardware.**

■ [Initialized sign similar to sign for **thing**] Move the right *E hand,* palm facing up, from lying on the upturned palm of the left *open hand* to the right in a double arc.

**era** *n.* See sign for TIME[1].

**erect** *v.* See sign for SET UP.

**erupt** *v.* See sign for BLOWUP.

**escape** *v.* To get safely away (from): *to escape from prison; to escape the mugger.* See also sign for RUN AWAY. Same sign used for: **estranged, get away.**

■ [Represents one person going off alone] Beginning with the extended right index finger, palm facing down and finger pointing forward, under the palm of the left *open hand,* palm facing down and fingers pointing forward, move the right hand straight forward.

**escrow** *n.* Money deposited with a third party for delivery upon the fulfillment of some condition: *pay the homeowner's insurance out of escrow.*

■ [**money** + a gesture showing holding something] Tap the back of the right *flattened O hand,* with a double movement against the palm of the left *open hand,* both palms facing up. Then move the right *S hand,* palm facing up, in a circular movement in front of the right side of the body.

**especially** *adv.* See sign for SPECIAL.

**essential** *adj.* See sign for IMPORTANT.

**establish** *v.* To set up or bring into being on a firm basis: *establish a schedule to which we can all adhere.* Same sign used for: **based on, founded, set up.**

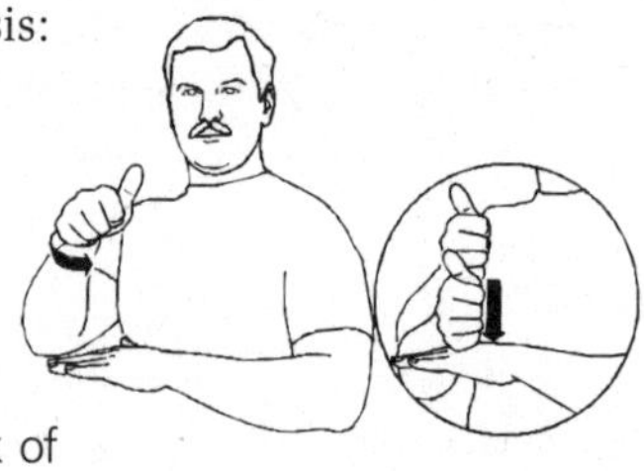

- [Represents setting something up firmly] Beginning with the right *10 hand* in front of the right shoulder, palm facing down, twist the wrist upward with a circular movement and then move the right hand straight down to land the little-finger side on the back of the left *open hand,* palm facing down.

**estimate** *n., v.* See signs for ARITHMETIC, GUESS, MULTIPLY, ROUGH.

**estranged** *adj.* See signs for ASTRAY, ESCAPE.

**et cetera** *adv.* See sign for VARIETY.

**eternal** *adj.* See sign for FOREVER.

**evade** *v.* See sign for AVOID.

**evaluate**[1] *v.* To appraise the value or quality of: *a committee to evaluate the effectiveness of the program.* Related form: **evaluation** *n.*

- [Initialized sign with a movement that signifies weighing choices] Move both *E hands,* palms facing forward, up and down with a repeated alternating movement in front of each side of the chest.

**evaluate**[2] *v.* See sign for ANALYZE.

**evaporate** *v.* See signs for DISSOLVE, RAPTURE.

**even**[1] *adj.* Being at the same level: *The piles of books on the floor were even.* Same sign used for: **fair, level.**

- [Shows things of equal level] Beginning with the fingertips of both bent hands touching in front of the chest, both palms facing down, bring the hands straight apart from each other to in front of each shoulder.

**even**[2] *adj., v.* See sign for CONSTANT[2], EQUAL.

**evening** *n.* The latter part of the day and early part of the night: *this evening, just before supper.*

■ [Represents the sun low on the horizon] Tap the heel of the right *bent hand,* palm facing forward, with a double movement against the thumb side of the left *open hand* held across the chest, palm facing down.

**event**[1] *n.* A happening or experience: *The reunion was a well-attended event.*

■ Beginning with the bent middle fingers of both *5 hands* touching the chest, palms facing in, bring the hands upward and to the sides with a quick double movement.

**event**[2] *n.* See sign for HAPPEN.

**even though** *conj.* See sign for ANYWAY.

**ever** *adv.* See sign for ALWAYS.

**everlasting** *adj.* See sign for FOREVER.

**ever since** *adv. phrase.* See signs for ALL THE TIME, SINCE.

**every** *adj.* See sign for EACH.

**everyday** *adj.* See sign for DAILY.

**everything**[1] *pron.* Every single thing in a group or total: *I think you should keep everything you bought today.*

■ Beginning with both *A hands* held in front of each side of the body, palms facing up, bring the knuckles of the right hand to the left, brushing across the top of the left hand and back again to the right while opening into a *5 hand.*

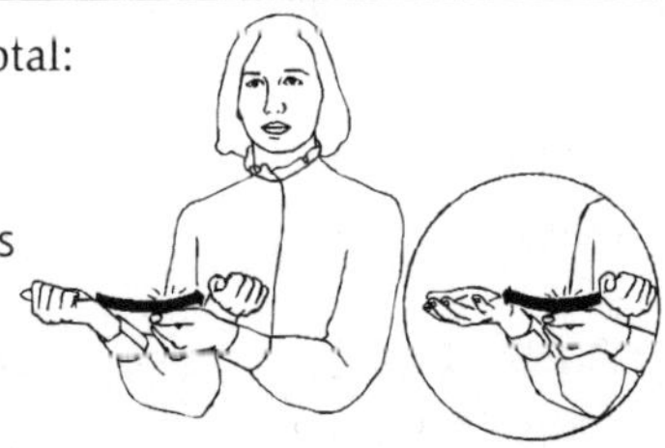

**everything**[2] *pron.* (alternate form)

■ [**every + thing**] Bring the knuckle side of the right *10 hand* down the thumb side of the left *10 hand.* Then beginning with the fingers of both *5 hands* together in front of the chest, throw the hands out to each side, palms up.

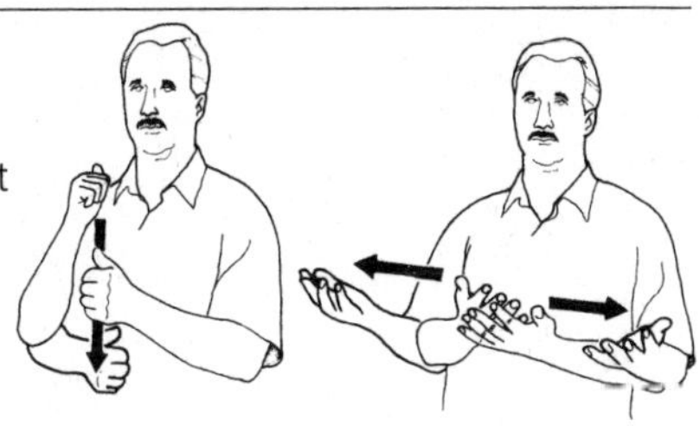

**everything**[3] *pron.* See sign for INCLUDE.

**every three months** See sign for QUARTERLY.

**every two months** See sign for BIMONTHLY.

**every two weeks** See sign for BIWEEKLY.

**every year** See sign for ANNUAL.

**evict** *v.* See sign for ABANDON.

**evidence**[1] *n.* Anything that tends to prove or disprove something: *required to show the evidence of the accused swindler's guilt in court.*

■ [Initialized sign similar to sign for **proof**] Move the right *E hand* from near the right eye, palm facing left, downward to land the back of the right *E hand* in the left *open hand,* both palms facing up.

**evidence**[2] *n.* See sign for PROOF.

**evil** *adj.* See signs for BAD, DEVIL.

**exact** *adj.* See sign for PRECISE.

**exaggerate** *v.* To make claims beyond the limits of truth: *tends to exaggerate the extent of the difficulties.* Related form: **exaggeration.** Same sign used for: **elaborate, prolong, stretch.**

■ [Hands seem to stretch the truth] Beginning with the thumb side of the right *S hand,* palm facing left, against the little-finger side of the left *S hand,* palm facing right, move the right hand forward with a large wavy movement.

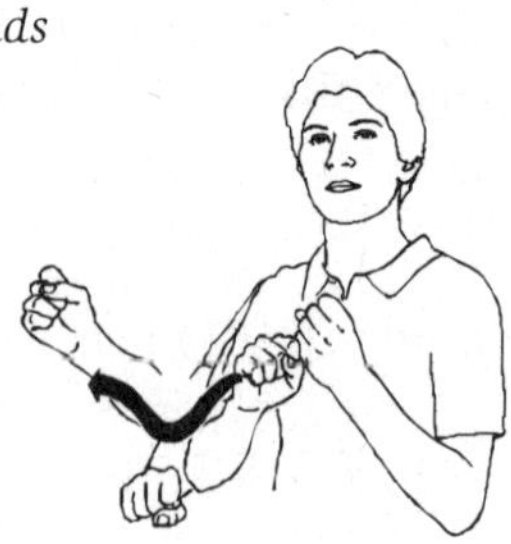

**exalt** *v.* See signs for ADVANCE, ADVANCED. Related forms: **exalted** *adj.*, **exaltation** *n.*

**examination** *n.* See signs for INVESTIGATE, TEST.

**examine** *v.* See signs for ANALYZE, CHECK[1], INVESTIGATE, LOOK FOR, TEST. Related form: **examination** *n.*

**example**[1] *n.* One thing used to show what others are like or should be like: *This essay is a fine example of what a good student can do.* Same sign used for: **exhibit.**

■ [Initialized sign similar to sign for **show**] With the index-finger side of the right *E hand,* palm facing forward, against the left *open hand,* palm facing right and fingers pointing up, move the hands forward together a short distance.

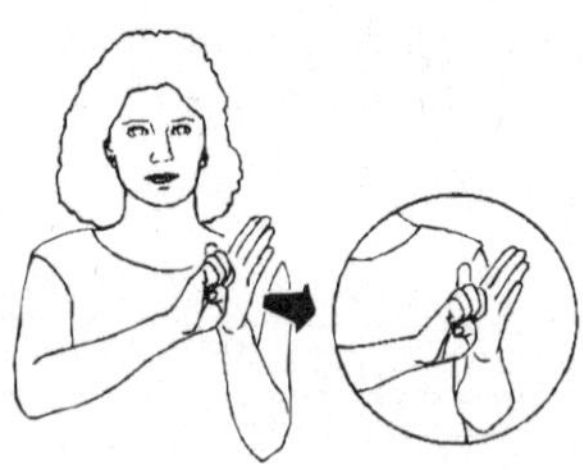

**example**[2] *n.* See sign for SHOW[1].

**exceed** *v.* See signs for EXCESS, OVER.

**excellent** *adj.* See signs for FINEST, SUPERB, WONDERFUL.

**excerpt** *n.* **1.** A passage taken from a book, document, or the like: *permission to quote an excerpt from the book in a forthcoming article.* —*v.* **2.** To take (a passage) from a book, document, or the like: *Scenes from the movie were excerpted for use on television.* Same sign used for: **copy, quotation.**

■ [Similar to sign for **quotation**] Beginning with both *bent V hands* in front each side of the body, palms facing each other, bring the hands back toward the chest while constricting the fingers.

**excess** *n.* **1.** An amount or degree beyond what is necessary or usual: *If your shopping cart is full, I'll carry the excess.* —*adj.* **2.** Being more than what is necessary or usual: *The airline charges for excess baggage.* Related form: **excessive** *adj.* Same sign used for: **exceed, massive, more than, too much.**

■ [Demonstrates an amount that is more than the base] Beginning with the right *bent hand* on the back of the left *bent hand,* both palms facing down, bring the right hand upward in an arc to the right.

**exchange** *n., v.* See signs for BUDGET, TRADE.

**excite**[1] *v.* To stir up feelings in: *The trip excited me.* Related forms: **excited** *adj.*, **exciting** *adj.*

■ Move the bent middle fingers of both *5 hands,* palms facing in and fingers pointing toward each other, in repeated alternating circles on each side of the chest.

**excite**[2] *v.* See sign for WHAT'S HAPPENING? Related forms: **excitement** *n.*, **exciting** *adj.*

**exclude** *v.* To keep out: *excluded from the meeting.* See also sign for REJECT.

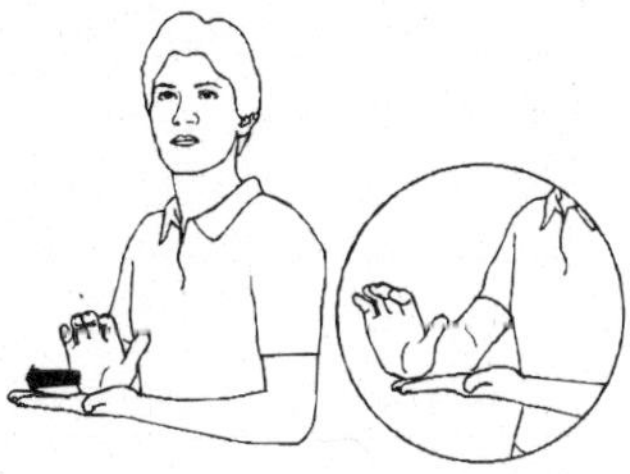

■ [Shoving something away to exclude it] Beginning with the heel of the right *curved hand,* palm facing forward, against the heel of the left *open hand,* palm facing up, move the right hand across the left hand and off the fingertips.

**excuse**[1] *n.* An explanation offered as justification for an action, apology for a fault, or plea for release from an obligation: *He didn't have a very good excuse for staying home from work.* Same sign used for: **acquittal, forgiveness, pardon, parole.**

- [The hand seems to wipe away a mistake] Wipe the fingertips of the right *open hand* across the upturned left *open hand* from the heel off the fingertips.

**excuse**[2] *v.* See sign for FORGIVE.

**excuse me** *v. phrase.* Same sign as **excuse** except made with a shorter double movement.

**execute** *v.* To process and put into effect (a computer program or command): *Clicking the mouse on this icon will execute the spreadsheet program.* Same sign used for: **run.**

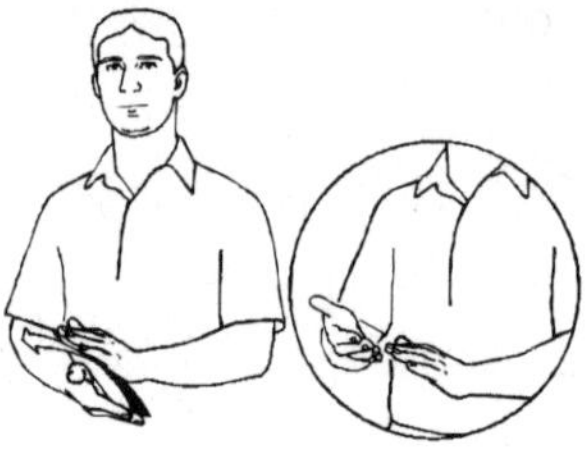

- Slide the palm of the right *open hand,* palm facing up, at an angle across the palm of the left *open hand,* palm facing down, with a double movement.

**exempt** *v.* See signs for DISMISS[1], SUBTRACT.

**exercise**[1] *n.* **1.** Activity or an activity designed to make the body healthier, stronger, and more flexible: *lifting weights for exercise; do my exercises every morning.* —*v.* **2.** To perform such activity, as to promote physical fitness: *I exercise by jogging.* Same sign used for: **work out.**

- [Mime exercising] Beginning with both *S hands* near each shoulder, palms facing each other, bring both arms up and down with a double movement.

**exercise**[2] *n., v.* See sign for PRACTICE.

**exhale** *v.* See sign for BREATH.

**exhausted** *adj.* See sign for TIRED.

**exhibit**[1] *v.* To show publicly: *to exhibit his paintings at the new gallery.* Related form: **exhibition** *n.*

- [Initialized sign similar to sign for **show**[2]] Beginning with the index-finger side of the right *E hand,* palm facing forward, against the palm of the left *open hand,* palm facing right and fingers pointing up, move both hands in a flat circle in front of the chest.

**exhibit**[2] *n., v.* See signs for EXAMPLE, SHOW[2].

**expand**[1] *v.* To make or become larger: *expanding the business by opening another store.* Related form: **expanse** *n.* Same sign used for: **enlarge, explosion.**

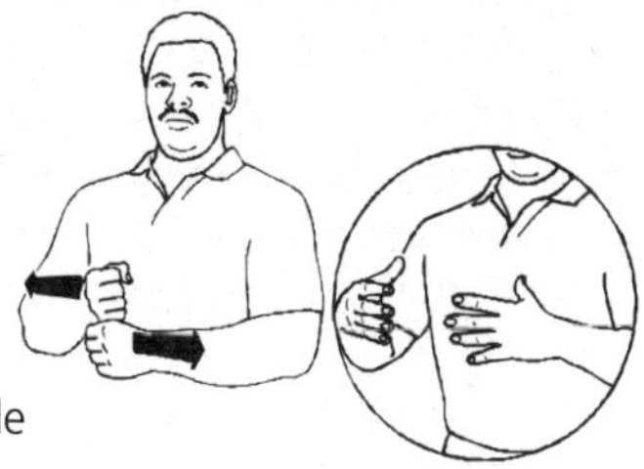

- [Demonstrates something expanding] Beginning with the little-finger side of the right *S hand* on top of the index-finger side of the left *S hand,* palms facing in opposite directions, bring the hands apart while opening into *curved 5 hands* in front of each side of the chest, palms facing each other.

**expand**[2] *v.* See sign for BALLOON.

**expansion board** *n. phrase.* See sign for BOARD[3].

**expansion card** *n. phrase.* See sign for BOARD[3].

**expect** *v.* See sign for HOPE. Related form: **expectation** *n.*

**expel**[1] *v.* To cut off from membership; drive out: *to expel from class.*

- [Initialized sign similar to sign for **fire**[2]] Swing the knuckles of the right *E hand,* palm facing up, across the index-finger side of the left *B hand*, palm facing in and fingers pointing right.

**expel**[2] *v.* See signs for ABANDON, BREATH.

**expensive** *adj.* High-priced: *an expensive coat.* Same sign used for: **costly.**

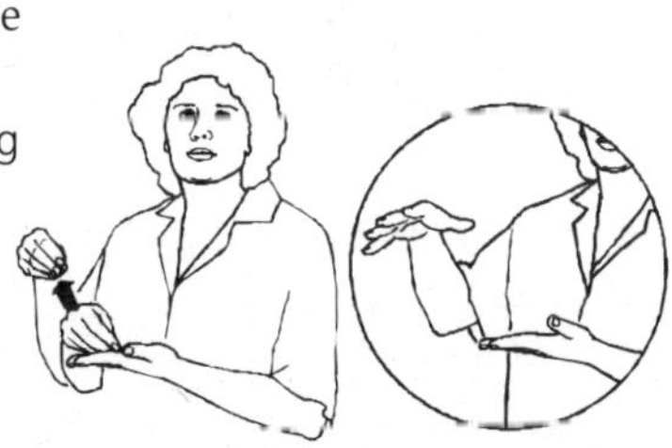

- [**money** + a gesture of throwing it away] Beginning with the back of the right *flattened O hand* on the upturned left *open hand,* bring the right hand upward to the right while opening into a *5 hand* in front of the right shoulder, palm facing down.

**experience** *n.* **1.** Something lived through or encountered: *a terrifying experience.* **2.** The undergoing of events in the course of time: *My life experiences would make a good novel.* **3.** Knowledge and wisdom gained from these events: *His experience qualifies him for the job.* —*v.* **4.** To have happen to one: *Experience it for yourself.* Same sign used for: **ordeal.**

- Beginning with the fingertips of the right *5 hand* on the right cheek, palm facing in, bring the hand outward to the right while closing the fingers into a *flattened O hand.*

**experiment** *n.* **1.** A test or trial to discover something: *a scientific experiment.* —*v.* **2.** To conduct such a test or trial: *experiment with combining the chemicals.*

■ [Initialized sign similar to sign for **science**] Beginning with both *E hands* in front of the chest, palms facing forward and the right hand higher than the left hand, move the hands in repeated alternating circles.

**expert** *adj.* See signs for ADROIT, GOOD AT, SKILL.

**explain** *v.* See sign for DESCRIBE. Related form: **explanation** *n.*

**explode** *v.* To burst or erupt violently; blow up: *The bomb exploded.* Related form: **explosion** *n.* Same sign used for: **bomb, boom.**

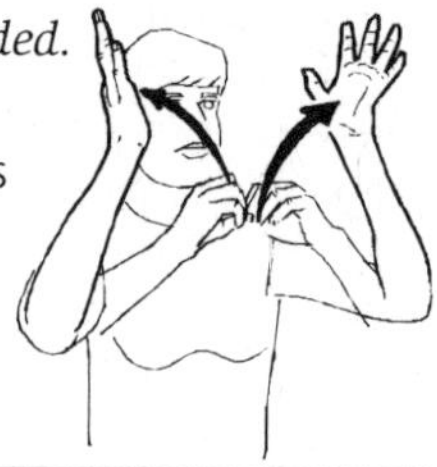

■ [Demonstrates something blowing up] Beginning with the fingers of both *flattened O hands* together in front of the chest, palms facing each other, move the hands suddenly upward and outward while opening into *5 hands,* ending with the palms angled upward near each side of the head.

**explosion** *n.* See sign for EXPAND.

**export** *v.* See sign for UPLOAD.

**expose** *v.* See signs for SHOW[1], STICK.

**exposure** *n.* **1.** The act of presenting a photosensitive surface, as film, to light: *The exposure didn't work in the afternoon light.* **2.** The amount of time taken or the amount of light received during such an exposure: *The new camera automatically sets the exposure.* **3.** The photographic image thus produced: *This looks like a double exposure.*

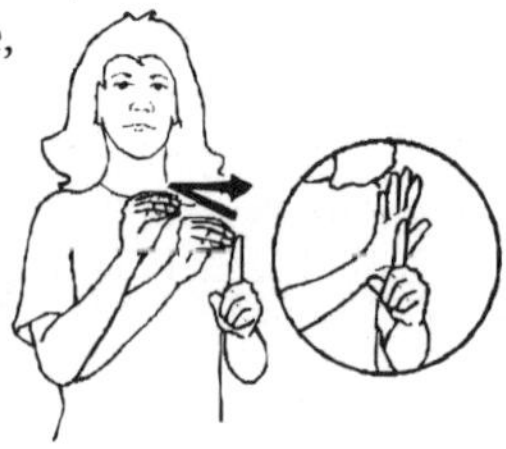

■ [Represents the shutter of a camera opening and closing while taking a picture] Beginning with the fingertips of the right *flattened O hand,* palm facing left, against the extended left index finger, palm facing right, bring the right hand back and then forward again to the index finger while changing into a *5 hand.*

**expression** *n.* An outward indication on the face that reveals one's feelings: *a sad expression in her eyes.*

■ [Indicates the face's movement when changing expression] Move both *modified X hands,* palms facing forward, up and down with a repeated alternating movement in front of each side of the face.

**extend** *v.* See sign for ELABORATE.

**external** *n., adj.* See sign for OUTSIDE.

**extinct** *adj.* See sign for ABSENT.

**extra** *n.* See sign for ADD$^2$.

**eye** *n.* One of a pair of organs of the body through which one sees: *I have something in my eye.*

- [Location of the eye] Point the extended right index finger, palm facing in, toward the right eye with a double movement. For the plural, point to each eye.

**eyeglasses** *pl. n.* See sign for GLASSES.

**eyesight** *n.* See sign for SEE.

**eyewitness** *n.* See sign for WITNESS.

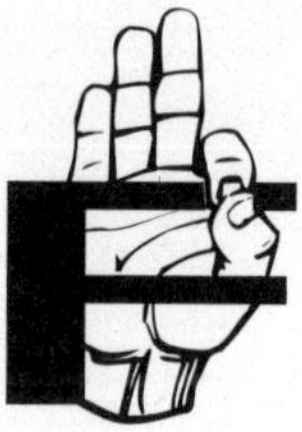

**fable** *n.* See sign for STORY.

**face** *n.* The front part of the head, from the forehead to the chin: *You shouldn't let your hair hide your face.*

- [Location and shape of face] Draw a large circle around the face with the extended right index finger, palm facing in.

**face-to-face** *adj. phrase., adv. phrase.* See sign for IN FRONT OF.

**facing** *adj., v.* (*pres. participle of* FACE) See sign for IN FRONT OF.

**fact** *n.* See sign for TRUTH.

**factory** *n.* See sign for MACHINE.

**fade** *v.* See sign for VAGUE.

**fade away** *v. phrase.* See sign for DISSOLVE.

**fail**[1] *v.* To not succeed: *failed his final exam.* Related form: **failure** *n.*

- Beginning with the back of the right *V hand* on the heel of the left *open hand,* palm facing up, move the right hand across the left palm and off the fingers.

**fail**[2] *v.* See sign for FLUNK.

**faint** *v.* To lose consciousness temporarily: *He fainted from hunger.* Same sign used for: **coma, unconscious.**

- Touch both extended index fingers, palms facing down, to each side of the forehead. Then drop the hands down while opening into *5 hands,* ending with both palms facing in and fingers pointing down in front of each side of the chest.

**fair**[1] *adj.* Not favoring one over others: *a fair test.* Related form: **fairly** *adv.*

- [Initialized sign] Tap the middle finger of the right *F hand,* palm facing left, against the chin with a repeated movement.

**fair**[2] *adj.* Neither good nor bad: *I feel just fair, but I'm getting better.* Same sign used for: **sort of, so-so.**

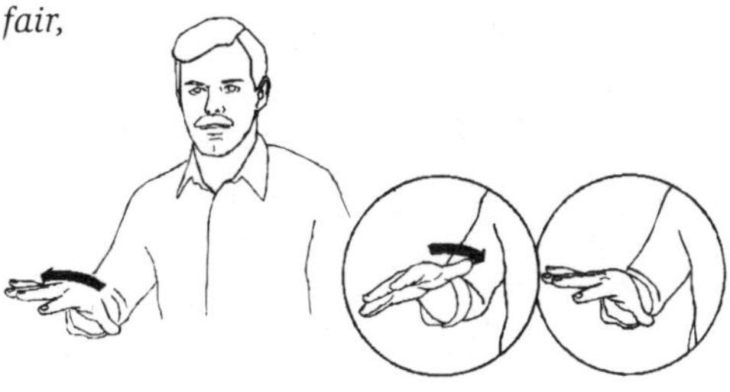

- [Natural gesture showing ambivalence] Rock the right *5 hand,* palm facing down, from side to side with a repeated movement in front of the right side of the body.

**fair**[3] *adj.* See signs for EVEN, EQUAL.

**faith** *n.* Belief without proof: *faith in God.*

- [**think** + initialized sign similar to sign for **confident**] Move the extended right index finger from touching the right side of the forehead downward while changing into an *F hand,* ending with the index finger of the right *F hand* on top of the index finger of the left *F hand* in front of the body, palms facing each other.

**faithful** *adj.* See sign for CONSISTENT.

**fake**[1] *n.* **1.** A product of the imagination: *The story is a well-constructed fake.* —*adj.* **2.** Of, pertaining to, or created by the imagination: *a fake tale of woe.* Same sign used for: **fiction.**

- [Indicates a source in the imagination rather than reality] Beginning with the index-finger side of the right *4 hand* touching the right side of the forehead, palm facing left, move the hand forward in a double arc.

**fake**[2] *adj.* Designed to deceive or trick: *a fake mustache; fake money.* Same sign used for: **artificial, counterfeit, imposter, pseudo, sham.**

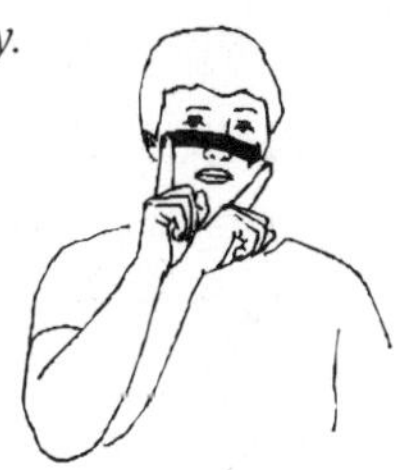

- [Formed similar to sign for **false,** indicating pushing the truth aside] Brush the extended right index finger, palm facing left, with a double movement across the tip of the nose from right to left by bending the wrist.

**fake**[3] *adj.* See sign for HYPOCRITE.

**fall**[1] *v.* **1.** To come down or drop down quickly from a standing position: *to fall on the ice.* —*n.* **2.** An act or instance of falling down: *had a bad fall.*

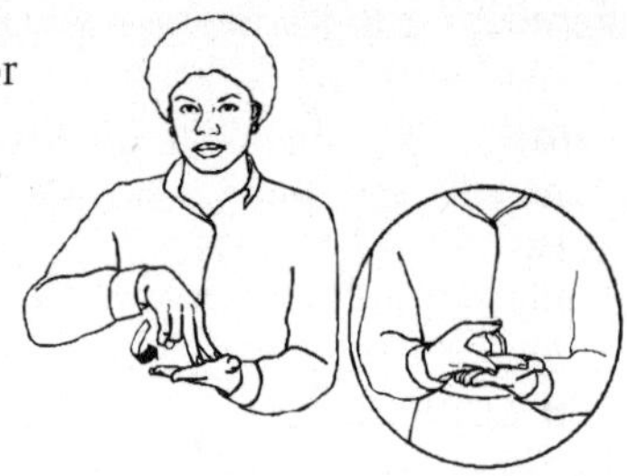

■ [Represents legs slipping out from under a person] Beginning with the fingertips of the right *V hand* pointing down, palm facing in, touching the upturned palm of the left *open hand,* flip the right hand over, ending with the back of the right *V hand* lying across the left palm.

**fall**[2] *n.* The season between summer and winter: *expecting cool weather in the fall.* Same sign used for: **autumn.**

■ Brush the index-finger side of the right *B hand,* palm facing down, downward toward the elbow of the left forearm, held bent across the chest.

**fall asleep** *v. phrase.* To go to sleep: *The baby fell asleep at last.* Same sign used for: **asleep, doze.**

■ [Represents the head falling forward when dozing off] Beginning with the right *5 hand* in front of the face, palm facing in and fingers pointing up, bring the hand down while changing into an *A hand,* ending with the right hand, palm down, on top of the left *A hand,* palm up, in front of the body.

**fall behind** *v. phrase.* See sign for AVOID.

**fall through** *v. phrase.* See sign for BREAK DOWN.

**false** *adj.* Not true or correct: *a false statement.*

■ [Similar to sign for **fake**[2], indicating pushing the truth aside] Brush the extended right index finger, palm facing left, across the tip of the nose from right to left by bending the wrist.

**falsehood** *n.* See sign for LIE[1].

**false teeth** *pl. n. phrase.* Artificial teeth: *to wear false teeth.* Same sign used for: **dentures.**

■ [Mime putting in false teeth] Push upward on the front top teeth with the fingers of the right *flattened O hand,* palm facing in.

**familiar** *adj.* See sign for AWARE[1].

**family** *n.* **1.** A group of closely related people, especially parents and their children: *I live with my family.* **2.** An extended group of related people, including grandparents, uncles, aunts, and cousins: *We're having the family over for Thanksgiving dinner.*

■ [Initialized sign similar to sign for **class**] Beginning with the fingertips of both *F hands* touching in front of the chest, palms facing each other, bring the hands away from each other in outward arcs while turning the palms in, ending with the little fingers touching.

**famished** *adj.* See sign for HUNGRY.

**famous** *adj.* Very well known: *a famous American.* Related form: **fame** *n.* Same sign used for: **notorious.**

■ [Similar to sign for **tell,** except spreading the words far and wide] Beginning with both extended index fingers pointing to each side of the mouth, palms facing in, move the hands forward and outward in double arcs, ending with the index fingers pointing upward in front of each shoulder.

**fancy** *adj.* Not plain; ornamental; decorative: *a fancy blouse to wear for a special occasion.* Same sign used for: **classical, deluxe, elegant, formal, grand, luxury, prim, proper.**

■ Move the thumb of the right *5 hand,* palm facing left, upward and forward in a double circular movement in the center of the chest.

**fantasize** *v.* See sign for DREAM.

**fantastic** *adj.* See signs for SUPERB, WONDERFUL.

**far** *adv.* **1.** At or to a great distance; a long way off: *They live far from here.* —*adj.* **2.** Being at or extending to a great distance: *explored the far frontiers.* Related form: **farther** *adv., adj.* Same sign used for: **distance, distant, remote.**

■ [Moves to a location at a far distance] Beginning with the palm sides of both *A hands* together in front of the chest, move the right hand upward and forward in a large arc.

**fare** *n.* See sign for COST[1].

**farewell** *interj., n.* See sign for GOOD-BYE.

**farm** *n.* A tract of land, plus a house, barn, etc., used for raising crops or animals for a livelihood: *lived on a small dairy farm in Vermont.* Same sign used for: **agriculture, bum, casual, ranch, sloppy.**

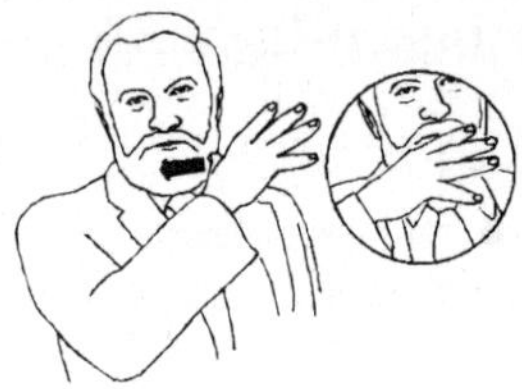

- Drag the thumb of the right *5 hand,* fingers pointing left, from left to right across the chin.

**far-out** *adj. Slang.* Exceedingly strange; unconventional and offbeat: *a far-out idea.*

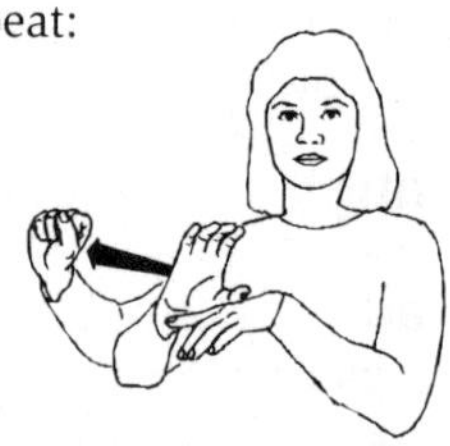

- [Represents something getting smaller as it moves farther away] Beginning with the thumb of the right *C hand*, palm facing left, on the back of the left *open hand*, palm facing down, bring the right hand across the left fingers and outward to the right while changing into an *S hand*.

**fascinating** *adj.* See sign for INTEREST[1].

**fashion** *n.* See sign for CLOTHES.

**fast** *adj.* **1.** Moving or able to move quickly: *a fast runner.* —*adv.* **2.** Quickly: *ran fast.* Same sign used for: **automatic, quick, sudden.**

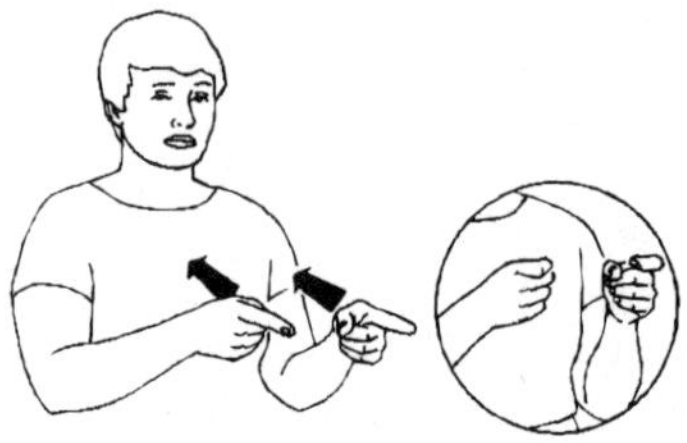

- [Demonstrates quickness] Beginning with both extended index fingers pointing forward in front of the body, palms facing each other, pull the hands quickly back toward the chest while constricting the index fingers into *X hands*.

**fasten** *v.* See signs for BELONG, STICK.

**fat** *adj.* **1.** Having more flesh than is usual; obese: *dieting to avoid getting fat.* **2.** Well-fed; plump; chubby: *a fat baby.* Same sign used for: **chubby, gain weight, obese, overweight, plump.**

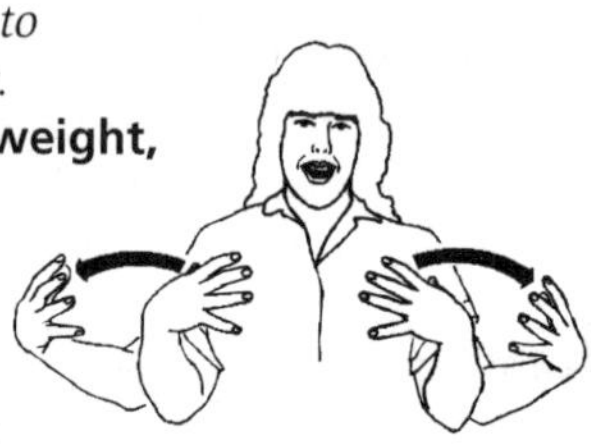

- [Shows shape of fat body] Move both *curved 5 hands* from in front of each side of the chest, palms facing in and fingers pointing toward each other, outward in large arcs to each side of the body.

**father** *n.* A male parent: *a picture of my father and mother on their wedding day.* Same sign used for: **dad, daddy, papa.**

- Tap the thumb of the right *5 hand,* palm facing left and fingers pointing up, against the middle of the forehead with a double movement.

**father-in-law** *n.* The father of one's husband or wife: *My father-in-law is coming to visit us.*

■ [**father** + **law**] Tap the thumb of the right *5 hand* against the forehead, palm facing left, with a repeated movement. Then place the palm side of the right *L hand* first on the fingers and then on the wrist of the left *open hand* held in front of the body, palm facing up.

**fatigue** *n.* See signs for TIRED, WEAK.

**faucet** *n.* A device for turning the flow of water on and off: *Turn on the cold water faucet.*

■ [Mime turning on faucets] Beginning with both *curved 3 hands* in front of each side of the body, palms facing down, turn the fingers outward and away from each other with a double movement.

**fault**[1] *n.* Personal responsibility for doing something wrong, failing to act, or the like: *It was my fault that we were late.*

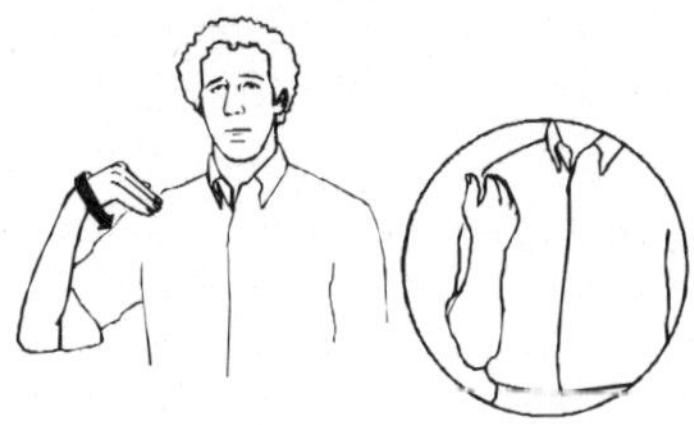

■ [Weight of faults on one's shoulders] Beginning with the fingers of the right *bent hand* on the right shoulder, palm facing down, pivot the hand downward while keeping the fingers in place.

**fault**[2] *n.* Another's responsibility for doing something wrong, failing to act, or the like: *This argument is all your fault.* Same sign used for: **accusation, blame.**

■ [Pushes blame toward another] Push the little-finger side of the right *10 hand,* palm facing left, forward and upward in an arc across the back of the left *S hand,* palm facing down.

**fault**[3] *n.* See sign for BURDEN.

**favor** *v.* See sign for PET.

**favorite**[1] *adj.* **1.** Being liked or preferred above others: *Eggdrop soup is my favorite soup.* —*n.* **2.** A contestant with the best chance to win: *Joe is the favorite in the broad-jump.* **3.** A person or thing that is preferred: *I was always daddy's favorite.* Related form: **favor** *v.* Same sign used for: **flavor, prefer, preference, rather, type, typical.**

■ [Taste something on the finger] Touch the bent middle finger of the right *5 hand,* palm facing in, to the chin with a double movement.

**favorite**[2] *adj.* See sign for PARTIAL TO.

**fear** *n.* **1.** A distressing feeling of anxiety and worry, as over impending danger: *shaking with fear during the battle.* —*v.* **2.** To regard with fear; be in dread of: *What they fear most is losing their jobs.* Related form: **fearful** *adj.* Same sign used for: **coward, frightened, scared.**

- [Natural gesture of protecting the body from the unknown] Beginning with both *5 hands* in front of each side of the chest, palms facing in and fingers pointing toward each other, move the hands toward each other with a short double movement.

**feast** *n.* See sign for BANQUET.

**federal** *adj.* See sign for GOVERNMENT.

**fed up** *adj. phrase.* See sign for FULL.

**fee** *n.* See sign for COST[1].

**feeble** *adj.* See sign for WEAK.

**feed** *v.* To supply for use: *feed the paper into the copier.* Same sign used for: **supply.**

- [Offering something to another] Beginning with both *flattened O hands* in front of each side of the body, palms facing up and right hand somewhat forward of the left hand, push the hands forward a short distance with a double movement.

**feedback** *n.* Reaction and response directed to an original source of information: *Good feedback from his first class allowed him to improve his teaching.* Same sign used for: **impeach.**

- [Initialized sign indicating information going both ways] Beginning with both *F hands* in front of each side of the chest, right palm facing forward and left palm facing in, move the hands with a double movement in opposite directions to and from the chest.

**feel** *v.* To sense by touch or awareness: *The wool blanket feels rough. I feel happy.* Related form: **feeling** *n.* Same sign used for: **motive, sensation, sense.**

- [Bent middle finger indicates feeling in sign language] Move the bent middle finger of the right *5 hand,* palm facing in, upward on the chest. Sometimes formed with a repeated movement.

**fellowship** *n.* See sign for ASSOCIATE.

**felony** *n.* See signs for CRIME[1,2].

**female** *n.* See signs for GIRL, LADY, WOMAN.

**fence** *n.* A barrier, as of wooden posts or wire, used to enclose a field, yard, etc.: *A fence around the yard will keep the stray dogs out.*

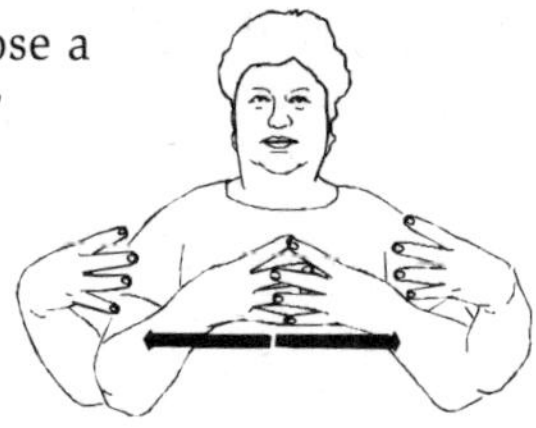

■ [Shape of interlocking fence rails] Beginning with both *4 hands* in front of the chest, fingers pointing in opposite directions and overlapping, both palms facing in, move the hands outward to in front of each shoulder.

**fertilize** *v.* See sign for CONFLICT.

**festival** *n.* See sign for CELEBRATE.

**fever** *n.* See sign for TEMPERATURE.

**few** *adj.* Not many but more than one: *costs a few dollars more than I would like.* Same sign used for: **several.**

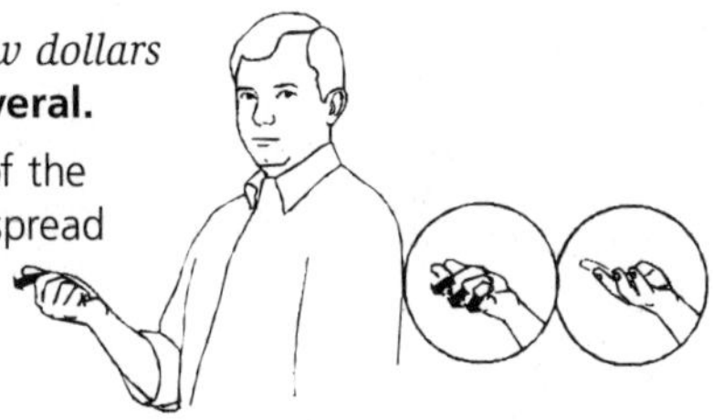

■ Beginning with the right *A hand* held in front of the right side of the chest, palm facing up, slowly spread out each finger from the index finger to the little finger, ending with an upturned *4 hand.*

**few days ago, a** *n. phrase.* At a recent time in the past, less than a week previous but more than one or two days: *She arrived from Canada a few days ago.*

■ [The fingers move into the past] Beginning with the thumb of the right *A hand* on the right cheek, palm facing down, twist the hand up while changing into a *3 hand* and keeping the thumb in place on the cheek.

**few minutes ago, a** *n. phrase.* See sign for RECENTLY[1].

**fib** *v.* See signs for BETRAY, LIE.

**fiction** *n.* See sign for FAKE[1].

**fiddle** *n.* See sign for VIOLIN.

**field**[1] *n.* A range or sphere of interest or of professional activity: *studying the field of biology.*

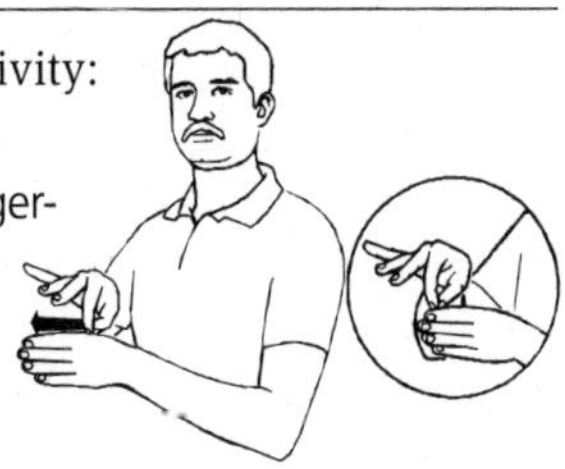

■ [Initialized sign similar to sign for **specialize**] Move the fingertips of the right *F hand,* palm facing down, forward along the length of the index finger of the right *B hand*, palm facing right, from the base to the tip.

**field**[2] *n.* See signs for LAND, SPECIALIZE.

**fierce** *adj.* See sign for AWFUL.

**fight**[1] *n.* **1.** An angry dispute or a violent struggle: *having a fight over money.* —*v.* **2.** To engage in such a dispute or struggle: *to fight with their fists.* Related form: **fighting.**

- [Mime two people striking at each other] Beginning with both *S hands* in front of each shoulder, palms facing each other, move the hands deliberately toward each other, ending with the wrists crossed in front of the chest.

**fight**[2] *v.* See sign for ARGUE.

**fight**[3] *n.* See sign for COMBAT.

**figure** *n., v.* See signs for ARITHMETIC, COUNT, MULTIPLY, SHAPE[1].

**figure out** *v. phrase.* See signs for ARITHMETIC, MULTIPLY.

**file**[1] *v.* To put away in convenient order for storage and reference: *File the forms in the drawer.* Same sign used for: **sort.**

- [Insert something in order to file it] Slide the little-finger side of the right *B hand,* palm angled up, between the middle finger and ring finger of the left *B hand* held in front of the chest, palm facing in.

**file**[2] *v.* See sign for APPLY[1].

**fill in** or **fill out** *v. phrase.* To complete, as by supplying information: *fill in the blanks.*

- [Represents documenting something on paper] Touch the fingertips of the right *flattened O hand,* palm facing down, on the upturned left *open hand* in several places.

**fill up**[1] *v. phrase.* To fill completely: *fill up the tank with gas.*

- [Shows rising level of something in a container] Bring the right *B hand,* palm facing down and fingers angled left, upward until level with the index-finger side of the left *C hand,* palm facing right.

**fill up**[2] *v. phrase.* See sign for REFILL.

**film**[1] *n.* A series of consecutive pictures projected onto a screen so rapidly that they appear to move, often telling a story: motion picture: *watching a rented film on the VCR.* Same sign used for: **cinema, movie, show.**

- [Flicker of film on a screen] With the heel of the right *5 hand,* palm facing forward, on the heel of the left *open hand,* palm facing in, twist the right hand from side to side with a repeated movement.

**film**[2] *n.* See MOVIE CAMERA.

**filthy** *adj.* See sign for DIRTY.

**final** *adj.* See sign for LAST[1]. Related form: **finally** *adv.*

**finally** *adv.* At last; at the final moment: *They finally decided to move out of town.* Same sign used for: **at last, pah!, succeed.**

- Beginning with both extended index fingers pointing up near each cheek, palms facing in, twist the wrists forward, ending with the index fingers pointing up in front of each shoulder, palms facing forward.

**find** *v.* To locate or come upon, on purpose or by chance: *found a quarter in my pocket.* Same sign used for: **discover, draw.**

- Beginning with the right *curved 5 hand* inserted in the palm side of the left *curved 5 hand,* palm facing right in front of the body, bring the right hand upward while closing the thumb and index finger, forming an *F hand.*

**fine**[1] *adj.* **1.** Of superior quality; very good: *served a fine wine.* **2.** In good health: *I feel fine, thank you.* Same sign used for: **okay, well.**

- Beginning with the thumb of the right *5 hand* touching the chest, palm facing left, move the hand forward a short distance.

**fine**[2] *adj.* Consisting of minute particles: *Grind the coffee beans to a fine powder.*

- [The fingers feel a fine texture] Beginning with the right *F hand* in front of the right shoulder, palm facing forward, rub the tip of the index finger and thumb together with a quick small movement.

**fine**[3] *n.* See sign for COST[1].

**finest** *adj.* Of the best or most desirable quality: *the finest day we've had this week.* Same sign used for: **awesome, excellent, terrific, whew.**

■ With the thumb of the right *5 hand* touching the chest, palm facing left and fingers pointing up, wiggle the fingers with a repeated movement.

**finger** *n.* Any of the jointed appendages of the hand (sometimes excluding the thumb): *broke my finger.*

■ [Location of finger] Rub the fingertip of the extended right index finger back and forth along the length of the index finger of the left *5 hand* with a repeated movement.

**fingerspell** *v.* To spell out words with the hands using the Manual Alphabet: *to fingerspell your name.* Related form: **fingerspelling** *n.* Same sign used for: **spell.**

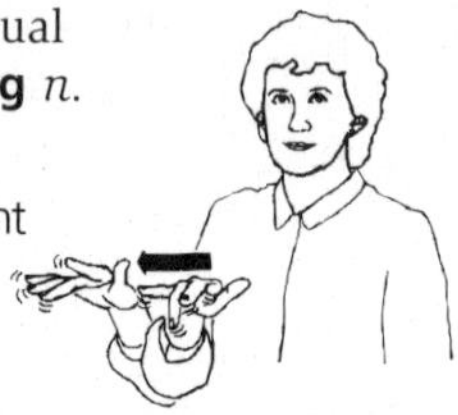

■ [Represents action of fingers when fingerspelling] Move the right *5 hand,* palm facing down, from in front of the chest to the right while wiggling the fingers.

**finish**[1] *v.* To bring or come to an end; complete: *to finish the project on time; waiting for the movie to finish.* Same sign used for: **already, complete, done, over, then, through.**

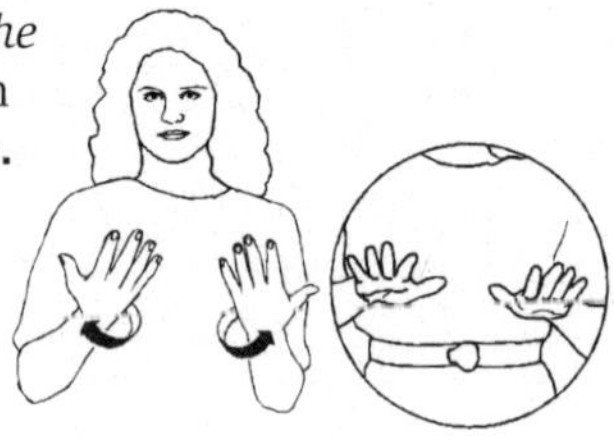

■ Beginning with both *5 hands* in front of the chest, palms facing in and fingers pointing up, flip the hands over with a sudden movement, ending with both palms facing down and fingers pointing forward.

**finish**[2] *v.* See signs for BEEN THERE, END[1].

**fire**[1] *n.* Flames, heat, and light produced by something burning: *start a fire with a match.* Same sign used for: **blaze, flames.**

■ [Represents flames] Move both *5 hands,* palms facing up, from in front of the waist upward in front of the chest while wiggling the fingers.

**fire**[2] *v.* To dismiss from a job: *They fired the three employees for theft.* Same sign used for: **dismiss, let go, terminate.**

■ [Indicates cutting a job short] Swing the back of the right *open hand,* palm facing up, across the index-finger side of the left *B hand,* palm facing in.

**firefighter** *n.* A person trained to put out destructive fires: *The firefighters arrived too late to save the house.*

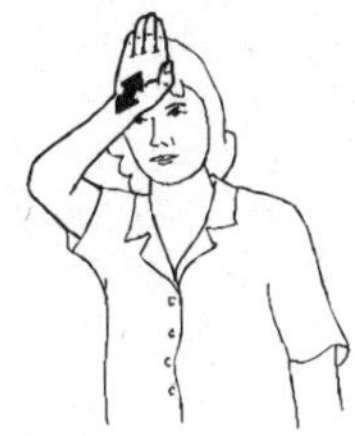

■ [Represents the raised front of a firefighter's helmet] Bring the back of the right *B hand,* fingers pointing up and palm facing forward, against the center of the forehead.

**fireworks** *n.* A display of patterns of color and light produced by explosive devices that burst loudly into the air: *watching the fireworks on the Fourth of July.*

■ [Represents the bursting of fireworks] Beginning with both *S hands* in front of each side of the body, palms facing forward, bring the hands upward and together in front of the chest and then upward and outward to each side near the head while opening into *5 hands.*

**firm** *adj.* See sign for STRICT.

**first** *adj.* **1.** Coming before others, as in time or order: *the first book I ever read.* —*n.* **2.** The one before all others, as in rank or order, in any series: *the first to finish.* —*adv.* **2.** In the first place; before others: *You can eat first.* Same sign used for: **one dollar.**

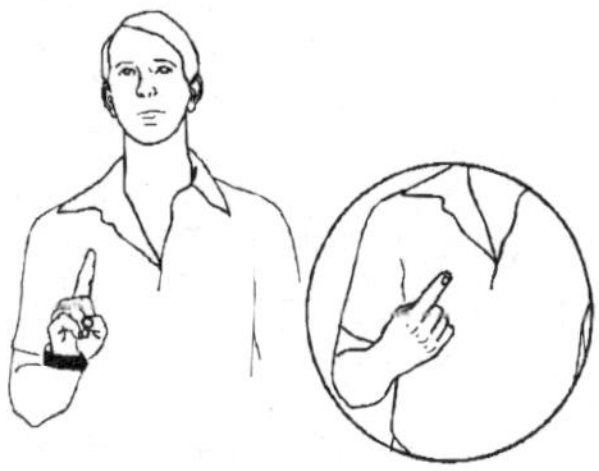

■ [**one** formed with a twisting movement used for ordinal numbers] Beginning with the extended right index finger pointing up in front of the right side of the chest, palm facing forward, twist the hand, ending with the palm facing in.

**fish**[1] *n.* Any of various cold-blooded animals with gills and fins that live in water: *a beautiful fish swimming in the stream.*

■ [The movement of a fish in water] While touching the wrist of the right *open hand,* palm facing left, with the extended left index finger, swing the right hand back and forth with a double movement.

**fish**[2] *v.* To use a hook, line, and fishing pole to try to catch fish: *fish all day for trout.* Related form: **fishing** *n.*

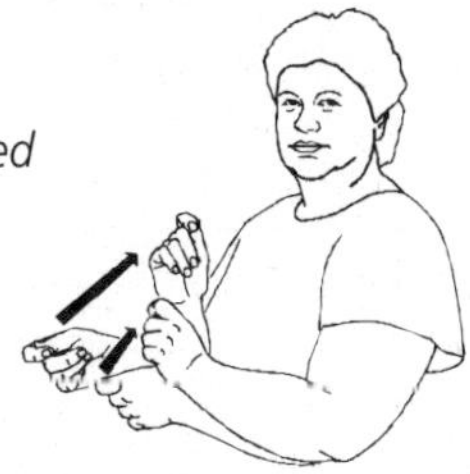

■ [Mime fishing with a fishing pole] Beginning with both *modified X hands* in front of the body, right hand forward of the left hand and palms facing in opposite directions, move the hands upward by bending the wrists with a double movement.

**fit**[1] *v.* **1.** To be of the right size (for): *Does the dress fit? Will it fit me, if I shorten it?* **2.** To be adapted to or suitable for: *a speech that fits the occasion.* Same sign used for: **suit.** —*n.* **3.** The way in which something fits: *The fit of the jacket is perfect.*

■ [Initialized sign showing that two things fit together] Beginning with the right *F hand* in front of the right shoulder, palm angled down, and the left *F hand* in front of the left side of the body, palm angled up, bring the fingertips together in front of the chest.

**fit**[2] *v., n.* See sign for MATCH.

**five cents** *pl. n.* See sign for NICKEL.

**fix** *v.* To mend or repair: *fix the flat tire.* Same sign used for: **maintain, mend, repair.**

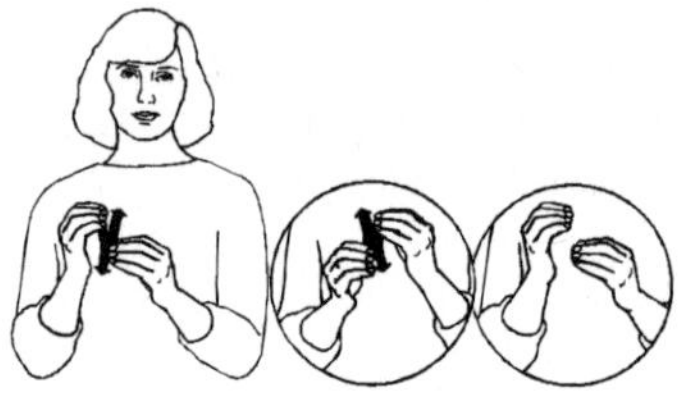

■ [The fingers seem to put things together] Brush the fingertips of both *flattened O hands* across each other repeatedly as the hands move up and down in opposite directions in a double movement.

**flabbergast** *v.* To overcome with shock and surprise; astound: *The news flabbergasted her.* Same sign used for: **astound, awesome, startle.**

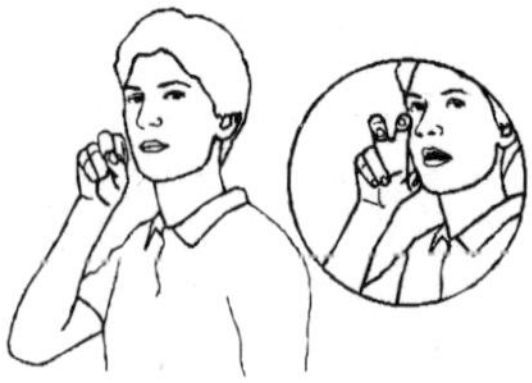

■ [Represents a person's mouth opening in amazement] Beginning with the right *S hand* near the right side of the chin, palm facing forward, open the fingers into a *bent 3 hand* while opening the mouth.

**flabby** *adj.* See sign for LOOSE[1].

**flag** *n.* A piece of cloth, typically rectangular, marked with distinctive colors or designs and used often as a symbol, as of a country: *watching the parade and waving the American flag.*

■ [Represents a waving flag] While holding the elbow of the raised right arm in the left palm, wave the right *open hand* back and forth with a repeated movement in front of the right shoulder.

**flame** *n.* See sign for CANDLE.

**flames** *pl. n.* See sign for FIRE[1].

**flare up** *v. phrase.* See sign for BOILING MAD.

**flash** *n.* **1.** A sudden, brief, bright light from a camera attachment: *The flash hurt my eyes.* **2.** The attachment producing this light: *Use a flash to take a picture in dim indoor light.*

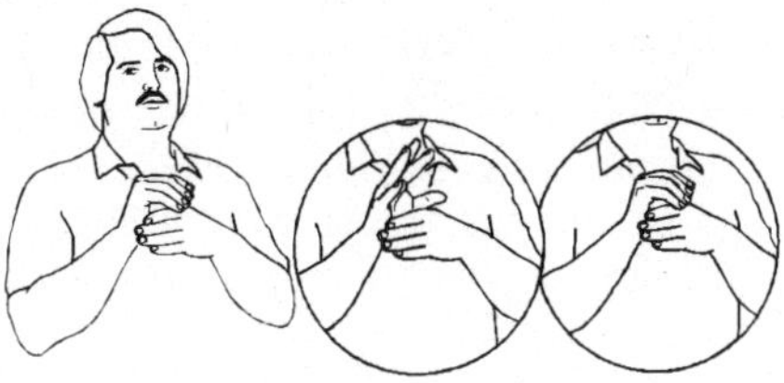

■ [Shows a flash of light] Beginning with the heel of the right *flattened O hand,* palm facing down, on the index-finger side of the left *B hand,* palm facing in, flick the right fingers quickly to form a *curved 5 hand* and back again to form a *flattened O hand.*

**flashlight** *n.* A small portable electric light, often shaped like a cylinder and usually powered by batteries: *Keep a flashlight handy in case the electricity goes out.*

■ [Light from a flashlight] While holding the wrist of the right *flattened O hand* with the left hand, flick the right fingers open into a *5 hand,* palm facing down.

**flat** *adj.* Smooth and level: *a flat surface to write on.*

■ [Shows flat surface] Beginning with the index-finger side of the right *bent hand* against the little-finger side of the left *bent hand,* both palms facing down, move the right hand forward a short distance.

**flatter** *v.* To praise or compliment excessively and insincerely: *Don't try to flatter me just because you want a job.* Related form: **flattery** *n.* Same sign used for: **bluff.**

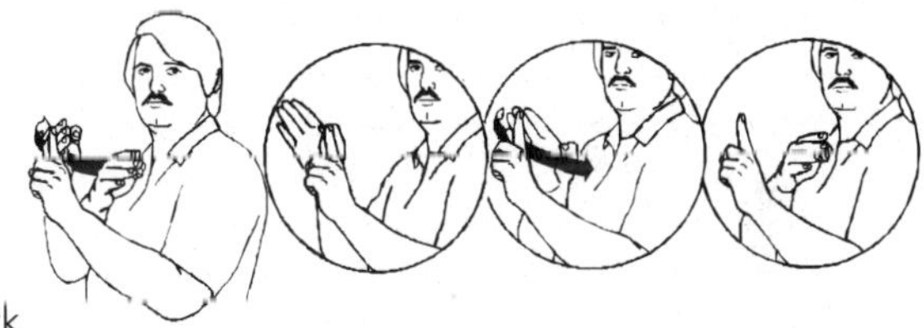

■ Swing the right *open hand* back and forth with a repeated movement, brushing the fingers against the extended left index finger held in front of the chest, palm facing right, each time it passes.

**flat tire** *n. phrase.* A tire with too little air for proper support: *My car has a flat tire.*

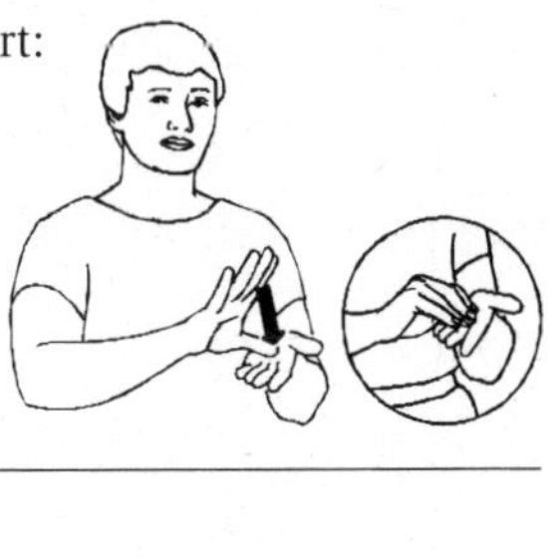

■ [Represents air going out of a tire] Beginning with the thumb of the right *open hand,* palm facing down, on the palm of the upturned left *open hand,* close the right fingers to the thumb, forming a *flattened O hand.*

**flavor** *n.* See sign for FAVORITE.

**flesh** *n.* See signs for MEAT, SKIN.

**flexible**[1] *adj.* Being easily bent: *a flexible plastic straw.* Same sign used for: **floppy.**

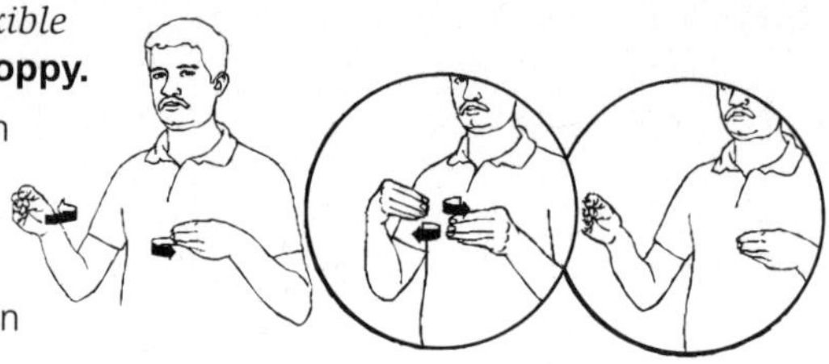

■ [Shows something easily bent] With both *flattened O hands* in front of each side of the chest, palms facing in, bend the wrists to move the hands forward and back with an alternating repeated movement.

**flexible**[2] *adj.* See sign for PLIABLE.

**flip** *v.* See sign for COOK.

**flip-flop** *n.* See sign for SANDAL.

**flirt** *v.* To behave amorously without having serious intentions: *He flirted with every girl at the party.* Same sign used for: **philander.**

■ [Represents batting one's eyelashes] Beginning with the thumbs of both *5 hands* touching in front of the chest, palms facing down and fingers pointing forward, wiggle the fingers up and down with an alternating movement.

**flood** *n.* **1.** A great flow or overflow of water, especially covering land not usually submerged: *The basement was damaged in the flood.* —*v.* **2.** To cover with a flood: *Water flooded the kitchen floor.* **3.** To overflow: *The river flooded during the heavy rain.*

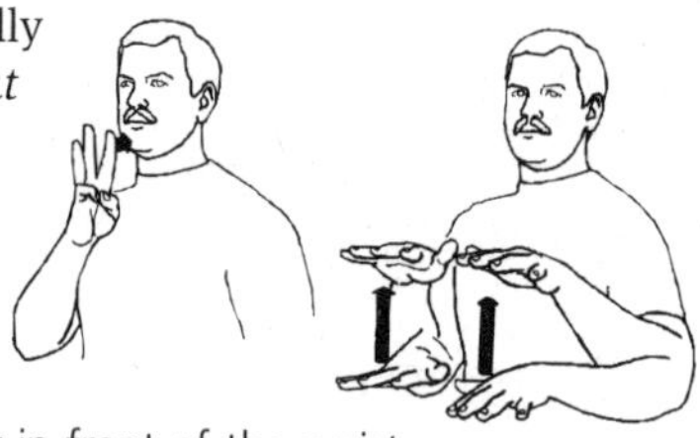

■ [**water** + showing level of water rising] Tap the index finger of the right *W hand,* palm facing left, against the chin. Then, beginning with both *5 hands* in front of the waist, palms facing down and fingers pointing forward, raise the hands to in front of the chest.

**floor** *n.* The horizontal surface that is walked upon at the bottom of a room: *mop the floor.*

■ [Shows flatness of a floor's surface] Beginning with the index-finger side of both *B hands* touching in front of the waist, palms facing down and fingers pointing forward, move the hands apart to each side.

**floppy** *adj.* See sign for FLEXIBLE[1].

**flow** *v.* See sign for STREAM.

**flower** *n.* The blossom part of a plant, often having a pleasing color and fragrance: *Smell the flowers.*

■ [Holding a flower to the nose to smell it] Touch the fingertips of the right *flattened O hand,* palm facing in, first to the right side of the nose and then to the left side.

**fluent** *adj.* See signs for SMOOTH[2], SMOOTHLY. Related form: **fluently** *adv.*

**flunk** *v. Informal.* **1.** To fail in a course or exam: *The teacher says I just flunked.* **2.** To get a failing grade in: *to flunk math.* **3.** To give a failing grade to: *I was shocked when the teacher flunked me.* Same sign used for: **fail.**

■ [Initialized sign] Strike the index-finger side of the right *F hand,* palm facing forward, against the palm of the left *open hand,* palm facing right and fingers pointing up.

**flush** *v.* See sign for BLUSH.

**flute** *n.* A slender pipelike musical instrument with a high range played by holding it to the side and blowing: *plays a flute in the school orchestra.*

■ [Mime playing a flute] Move both *curved 4 hands,* palms facing in, with a repeated movement from side to side in front of the mouth while wiggling the fingers.

**fly** *v.* To move through the air with wings: *watching the birds fly south.* Same sign used for: **wings.**

■ [Mime flapping wings to fly] Beginning with both *open hands* near each shoulder, and fingers angled outward in opposite directions, bend the wrists repeatedly, causing the hands to wave.

**focus**[1] *v.* To adjust the lens of so as to make an image clear: *focusing the camera on a cloudy day.*

■ [Mime adjusting the focus on a lens] Beginning with both *C hands* near each other in front of the chest, palms facing each other and left hand nearer the chest than the right hand, twist the right hand downward to the left.

**focus**[2] *v.* **1.** To concentrate on a single thing: *Focus on your work.* —*n.* **2.** The central point of attention: *the focus of the conversation.*

■ [Directing one's attention] Beginning with both *B hand*s near each side of the face, palms facing each other and fingers pointing up, bring the hands down while tipping the fingers downward and toward each other.

**focus on** *v. phrase.* See signs for ATTENTION, NARROW DOWN.

**foe** *n.* See sign for ENEMY.

**fold** *v.* To bend over on itself: *Fold the letter before putting it in the envelope.*

■ [Mime folding paper in half] Beginning with both *open hands* near each other in front of the chest, palms facing up, flip the right hand over in an arc, ending with the right palm on the left palm.

**folder**[1] *n.* A folded piece of cardboard used for holding papers: *Put the new information in the sales folder.*

■ [Represents inserting papers into a folder] Slide the little-finger side of the right *open hand,* palm facing up, with a double movement into the opening formed by the left *flattened C hand,* palm facing up.

**folder**[2] *n.* See sign for DICTIONARY[1].

**folk** *n.* See sign for PEOPLE.

**follow** *v.* To come after, as in sequence or time: *Look at the children following the parade. The late night movie follows the news.* Same sign used for: **go after, track down, trail.**

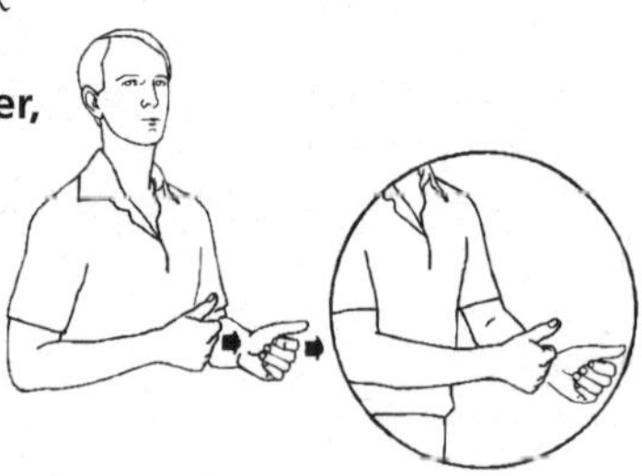

■ [One hand follows the other hand] With the knuckles of the right *10 hand,* palm facing left, near the wrist of the left *10 hand,* palm facing right, move both hands forward a short distance.

**food** *n.* Anything eaten that sustains life: *to shop for food for dinner.* Same sign used for: **groceries, meal.**

■ [Putting food in one's mouth] Bring the fingertips of the right *flattened O hand,* palm facing in, to the lips with a double movement.

**food store** *n. phrase.* See sign for GROCERY STORE.

**fool** *v.* See signs for BETRAY, BLOW[1], TRICK.

**fool around** *v. phrase.* See sign for RUN AROUND.

**foolish** *adj.* See sign for SILLY.

**foot** *n.* The end part of the leg, below the ankle joint, that is stood upon or is moved for walking: *These shoes hurt my feet.*

■ Move the bent middle finger of the right *5 hand,* palm facing down, up and down the length of the left *open hand,* palm facing down, with a repeated movement.

**football** *n.* A game, played by two teams defending goals at opposite ends of a large field, in which an oval leather ball is kicked, carried, or thrown so as to get it across the opposing team's goal line: *played football in high school.*

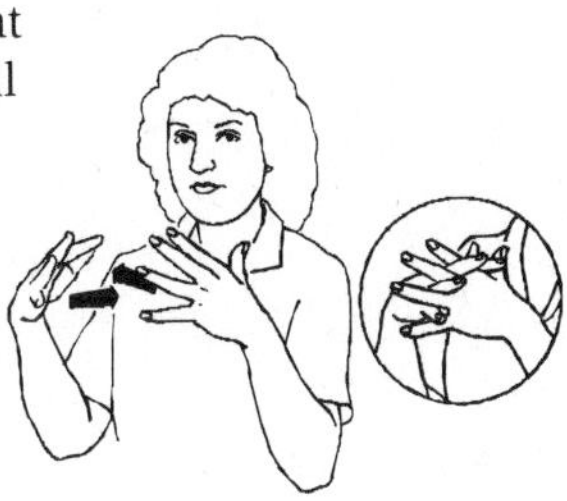

■ [Represents scrimmage between two teams] Beginning with both *5 hands* in front of each side of the chest, palms facing in and fingers pointing toward each other, bring the hands together with a short double movement, interlocking the fingers of both hands each time.

**for** *prep.* **1.** With the purpose of: *reads for pleasure.* **2.** Intended to be used by: *art supplies for the students.* **3.** So as to obtain: *sells them for profit.* **4.** With regard to: *bad for your health.* **5.** During or to the extent of: *worked there for several years.* **6.** Instead of: *a replacement for the retiring secretary.* **7.** Because of: *shouting for joy.*

■ Beginning with the extended right index finger touching the right side of the forehead, palm facing down, twist the hand forward, ending with the index finger pointing forward.

**forbid** *v.* To not allow: *to forbid visitors.* Same sign used for: **ban, enjoin, illegal, prohibit.**

■ Bring the palm side of the right *L hand,* palm facing left, sharply against the palm of the left *open hand,* palm facing right and fingers pointing up.

**fore** *adj., n.* See sign for FRONT.

**forecast** *v.* See sign for PREDICT.

**foreign** *adj.* Of or having to do with another country: *a foreign language.*

■ [Initialized sign similar to sign for **country**] Move the thumb side of the right *F hand,* palm facing left, in a double circular movement near the bent left elbow.

**foresee** *v.* See sign for PREDICT.

**forest** *n.* A tract of land covered with trees: *to walk through the forest.* Same sign used for: **jungle, orchard, woods.**

■ [**tree** is repeated] Beginning with the bent right elbow resting on the back of the left hand held across the body, palm facing down, twist the right *5 hand* forward with a double movement, moving the arms to the right each time.

**foretell** *v.* See sign for PREDICT.

**forever** *adv.* Without coming to an end: *music whose beauty will last forever.* Same sign used for: **eternal, everlasting.**

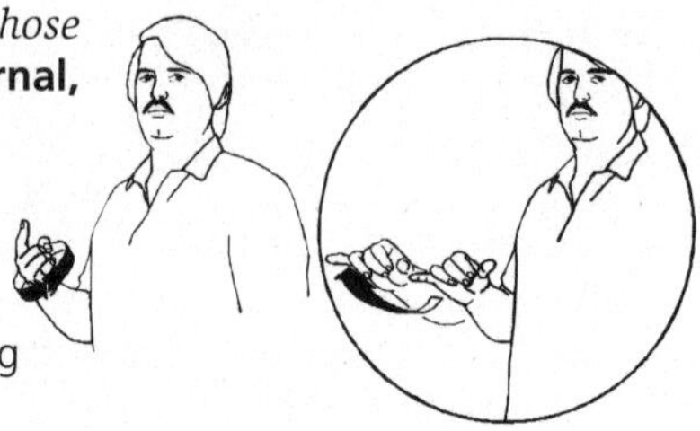

■ [**always** + **still**] Move the right *1 hand,* palm facing up, in a circle in front of the right side of the body. Then move the right *Y hand* from in front of the right side of the body, palm facing down, forward and upward in an arc.

**forgery** *n.* The crime of making a writing, recording, coin, or other document and passing it off as genuine when it is not: *The signature was a forgery.* Alternate form: **forge** *v.*

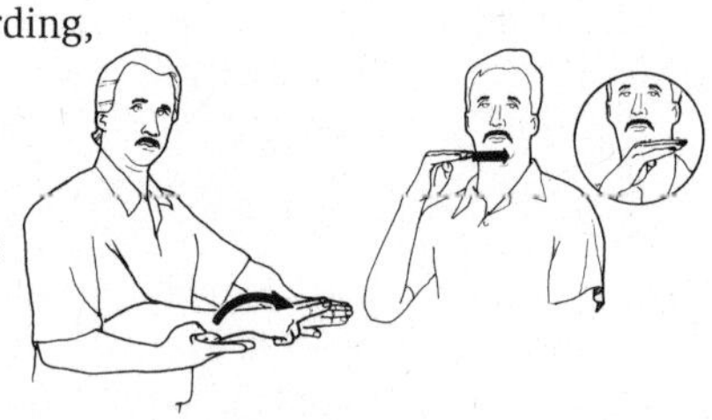

■ [**sign**[2] + **lie**[1]] Place the extended fingers of the right *H hand,* palm down, with a double movement on the back of the left *open hand* held in front of the chest. Then move the index-finger side of the right *bent hand,* palm down and fingers pointing left, across the chin from right to left.

**forget** *v.* To cease to remember: *I'm sorry, but I forgot your name.*

■ [Wipes thoughts from one's memory] Wipe the fingers of the right *open hand,* fingers pointing left, across the forehead from left to right while closing into a *10 hand* near the right side of the forehead.

**forgive** *v.* **1.** To cease to have hard feelings toward: *Forgive me for not writing to you sooner.* **2.** To grant pardon for; absolve: *forgive my sins.* Same sign used for: **excuse, pardon.**

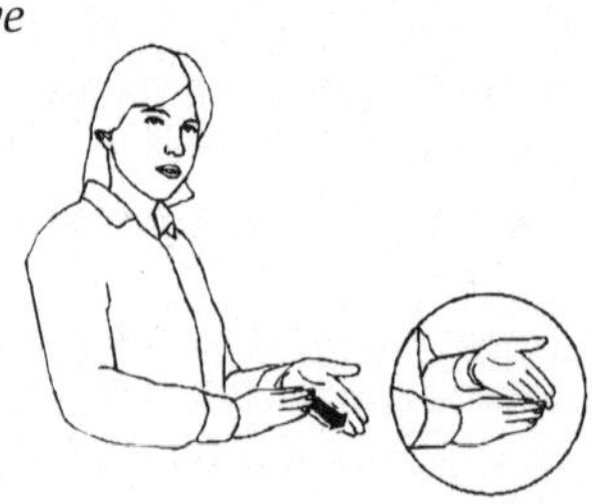

■ [Wipes away mistake] Brush the fingertips of the right *open hand,* palm facing down, across the palm of the upturned left *open hand* from the heel off the fingertips with a double movement.

**fork** *n.* An instrument with a handle and two or more projecting prongs used for piercing food: *a toddler learning to eat with a fork.*

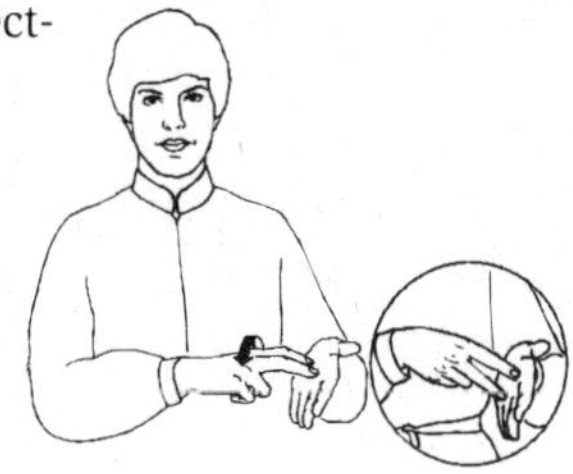

■ [Tines of a fork] Touch the fingertips of the right *V hand,* palm facing down, on the palm of the upturned left *open hand.* Then quickly turn the right hand so the palm faces the body and touch the left palm again.

**form**[1] *n.* A printed document with blank spaces, usually labeled, to be filled in with information: *Fill out the application form and hand it to the clerk.* Same sign used for: **format.**

■ [Initialized sign showing the shape of a form] Beginning with the fingertips of both *F hands* touching in front of the chest, palms facing each other, bring the hands away from each other to about shoulder width and then straight down a short distance, ending with the palms facing forward.

**form**[2] *n., v.* See sign for SHAPE.

**formal** *adj.* See sign for FANCY.

**former** *adj.* Of, pertaining to, or having existed in the past: *a former roommate.* Same sign used for: **previous.**

■ [Hand moves back into the past] Move the right *5 hand,* palm facing left and fingers pointing up, back toward the right shoulder in a double circular movement.

**formerly** *adv.* See sign for LONG AGO.

**forsake**[1] *v.* To leave completely; desert: *to forsake your home and friends.* Same sign used for: **abandon, depart, withdraw.**

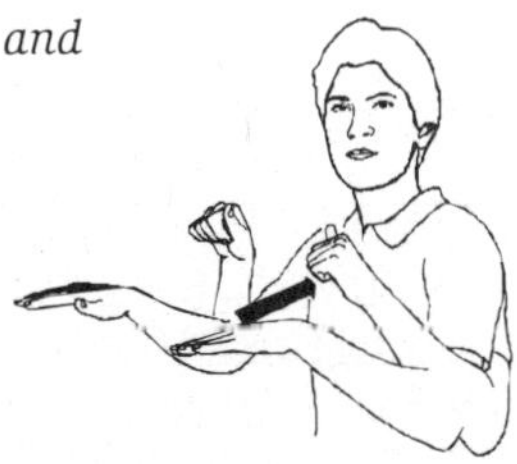

■ [Represents picking things up to leave] Beginning with both *open hands* in front of the body, palms facing down and fingers pointing forward, bring the hands back toward each side of the chest with a quick movement while closing into *A hands.*

**forsake**[2] *v.* See sign for IGNORE.

**foretell** *v.* See sign for PREDICT.

**fortunate** *adj.* See sign for LUCK.

**forward** *adv.* See signs for AHEAD, GO ON.

**forward slash** *n. phrase.* See sign for SLASH.

**founded** *adj.* See signs for ESTABLISH, RECOVER, SET UP.

**fountain** *n.* A structure producing a spray of water rising in the air: *There are colored lights in the fountain.*

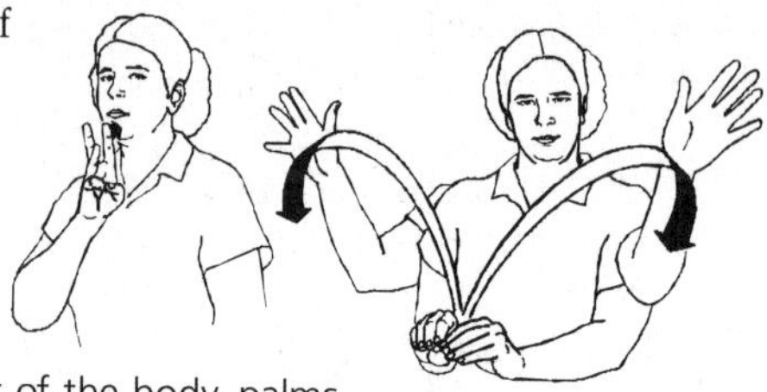

■ [**water** + spray of water coming up in a fountain] Tap the index-finger side of the right *W hand,* palm facing left, against the chin. Then, beginning with the fingers of both *flattened O hands* touching in front of the body, palms facing down, bring the hands upward and forward in large arcs while opening into *5 hands* in front of each shoulder, palms facing forward.

**fowl** *n.* See sign for BIRD.

**fox** *n.* A wild animal of the dog family having a bushy tail and pointed face: *hunting for foxes in England.*

■ [Initialized sign showing the shape of a fox's nose] With the index finger and thumb of the right *F hand* encircling the nose, palm facing left, twist the hand with a repeated movement, ending with the palm facing down.

**fraction** *n.* A number showing one or more equal parts of a whole: *to write one-third as the fraction 1/3.*

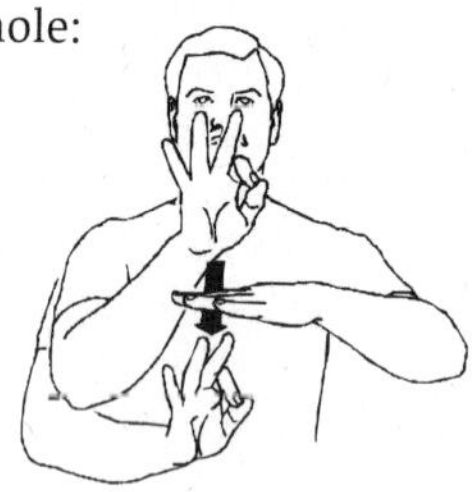

■ [Initialized sign showing that a fraction is expressed above and below a dividing line] Move the right *F hand,* palm facing forward, downward in front of the chest, past the index-finger side of the left *open hand* held in front of the chest, palm facing down.

**fracture** *n.* **1.** The injury caused by a broken bone. —*v.* **2.** The breaking of a bone: *She fractured her shoulder in the fall.* Same sign used for: **break, broken.**

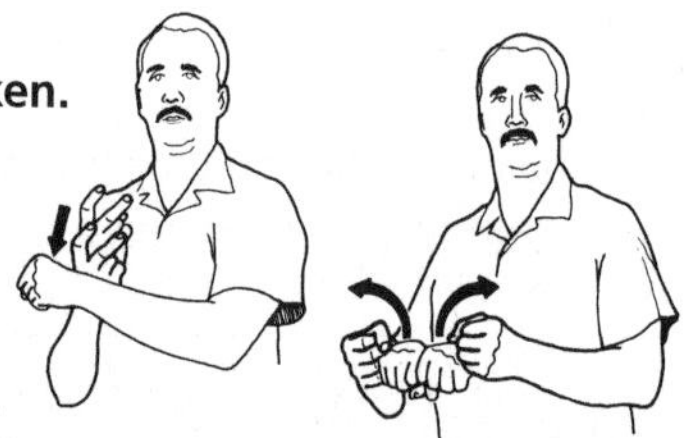

■ [**bone** + **break**] With a double movement, tap the back of the right *bent V hand,* palm facing up, on the back of the left *S hand,* palm facing down. Then beginning with both *S hands* in front of the body, index fingers touching and palms facing down, move the hands away from each other while twisting the wrists with a deliberate movement, ending with the palms facing each other.

**fragrance** *n.* See sign for SMELL.

**frail** *adj.* See sign for WEAK.

**frame** *n.* **1.** A decorative border or supporting structure in which a picture, mirror, or the like can be set or enclosed: *an ornately carved picture frame.* —*v.* **2.** To provide with or place into a frame: *three photographs that I want to frame.*

■ [Shape of a frame] Beginning with the extended fingers of both *G hands* touching in front of the chest, palms facing each other, move the hands apart to in front of each shoulder, then straight down, and finally back together in front of the lower chest.

**frank** *adj.* See sign for HONEST. Related form: **frankly** *adv.*

**fraternity** *n.* See sign for ASSOCIATE.

**fraud** *n.* See signs for CHEAT, COVER-UP, DECEIVE.

**freak** *n., adj.* See sign for STRANGE.

**free**[1] *adj.* **1.** Not under another's control; having personal, political, or civil liberties: *a free nation.* **2.** Provided without charge: *The neighborhood newspaper is free.* Related form: **freedom** *n.* Same sign used for: **liberty.**

■ [Initialized sign similar to sign for **save**[1]] Beginning with both *F hands* crossed at the wrists in front of the chest, palms facing in opposite directions, twist the wrists to move the hands apart to in front of each shoulder, ending with the palms facing forward.

**free**[2] *adj.* See sign for SAVE[1]. Related form: **freedom** *n.*

**freeway** *n.* See sign for HIGHWAY.

**freeze** *v.* To become hard because of loss of heat, especially to turn into ice: *so cold out that the lake froze over.* Same sign used for: **frost, frozen, ice, rigid, solidify.**

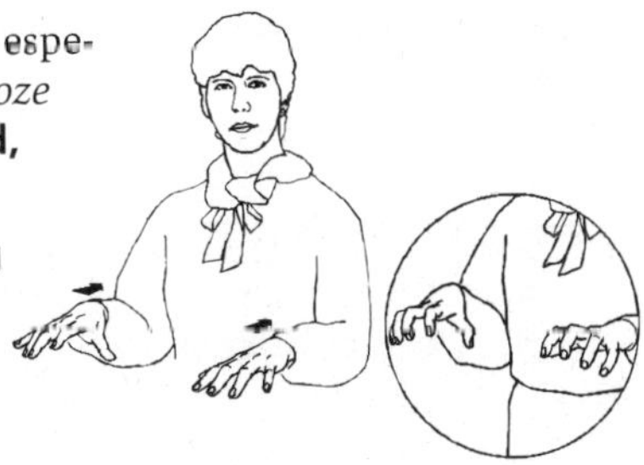

■ [Shows things hardening when frozen] Beginning with both *5 hands* in front of each side of the body, palms facing down and fingers pointing forward, pull the hands back toward the body while constricting the fingers.

**french fries** *pl. n. phrase.* Strips of potato cooked by deep-frying in hot oil: *I always put catsup on french fries.*

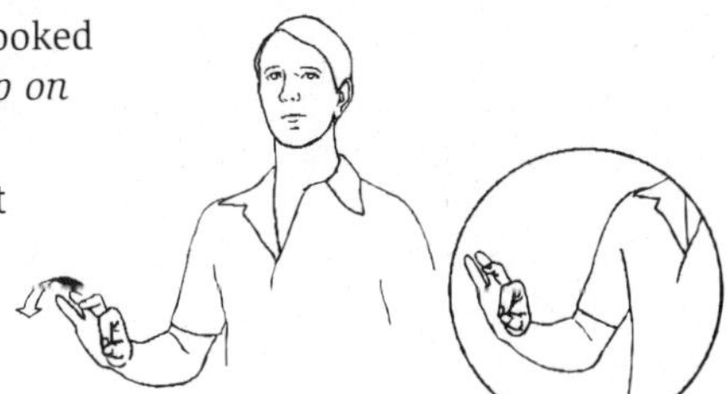

■ [Initialized sign **f-f**] Form an *F* with the right hand, palm facing forward, in front of the right side of the body and then again slightly to the right.

**frequently** *adv.* See sign for OFTEN.

**Friday** *n.* The sixth day of the week, following Thursday: *to get out of work early on Friday.*

■ [Initialized sign] Move the right *F hand,* palm facing in, in a repeated circle in front of the right shoulder.

**friend** *n.* A person whom one knows and likes well: *She's been my best friend for many years.* Same sign used for: **comrade, pal.**

■ [Indicates the entwined lives of friends who have a close relationship] Hook the bent right index finger, palm facing down, over the bent left index finger, palm facing up. Then repeat, reversing the position of the hands.

**friendly** *adj.* Characteristic of or like a friend, as in attitude and behavior: *a friendly smile.* Same sign used for: **cheerful, pleasant.**

■ With both *5 hands* near the cheeks, palms facing back, wiggle the fingers.

**fright** *n.* See sign for AFRAID. Related form: **frightened** *adj.*

**frightened** *adj.* See sign for FEAR.

**frigid** *adj.* See signs for ARCTIC, COLD[2].

**frog** *n.* A small, leaping animal with hairless skin and webbed feet, living in water or on land: *a green frog near the pond.*

■ Beginning with the index-finger side of the right *S hand* against the chin, palm facing left, flick the index and middle fingers outward to the left with a double movement.

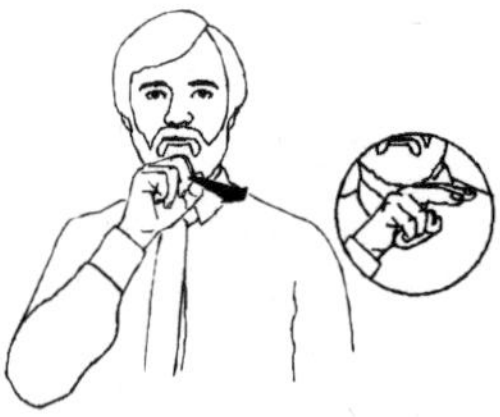

**from** *prep.* Out of or starting at: *took a bus from New York to Boston.*

■ [Moving from another location] Beginning with the knuckle of the right *X hand,* palm facing in, touching the extended left index finger, palm facing right and finger pointing up, pull the right hand back toward the chest.

**from now on** See sign for AFTER[1].

**front** *n.* **1.** The first part: *The preface is in the front of the book.* **2.** The part that faces forward: *a large door on the front of the house.* —*adj.* **3.** Situated in or at the front: *the front door.* Same sign used for: **fore.**

■ [Location in front of the person] Move the right *open hand,* palm facing in and fingers pointing left, straight down from in front of the face to in front of the chest.

**frost** *v.* See sign for FREEZE.

**frown** *v.* **1.** To wrinkle the forehead by contracting the brow, as to show disapproval: *He frowned at the naughty boy.* —*n.* **2.** a frowning look: *The teacher's face always had a frown.*

■ [Eyebrows turning down when frowning] Beginning with both extended index fingers near each side of the forehead, palms facing each other and fingers pointing up, bend the fingers downward to form *X hands* near the side of each eye.

**frozen** *adj.* See sign for FREEZE.

**fruit** *n.* A juicy or fleshy, often sweet product of a plant: *to eat a piece of fruit.*

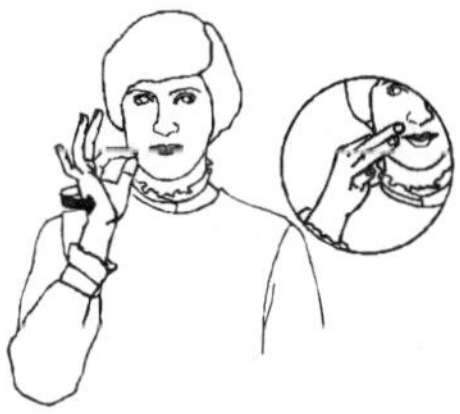

■ [Initialized sign] Beginning with the fingertips of the right *F hand* on the right side of the chin, palm facing left, twist the hand forward with a double movement, ending with the palm facing in.

**frustrate** *v.* To thwart, get in the way of, or disappoint: *frustrated in trying to get a perfect score.* Related form: **frustration** *n.*

■ Bring the back of the right *B hand,* palm facing forward, back against the mouth with a double movement or, sometimes, a single movement.

**fry** *v.* See sign for COOK.

**fuel** *n.* See sign for GAS.

**full**[1] *adj.* Filled to capacity; unable to eat more without becoming uncomfortable: *too full for dessert.* Same sign used for: **fed up, sated, satisfied, stuffed.**

■ [Represents feeling full] Move the right *B hand,* palm facing down, from the center of the chest upward with a deliberate movement, ending with the back of the right fingers under the chin.

**full**[2] *adj.* Unable to hold more: *a full cup.* Related form: **filled** *adj.* Same sign used for: **complete.**

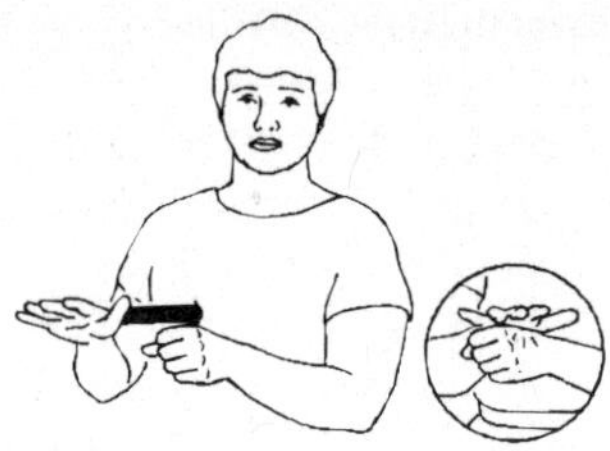

- [Leveling off something that is full] Slide the palm of the right *open hand,* palm facing down, from right to left across the index-finger side of the left *S hand,* palm facing right.

**fume** *n., v.* See signs for BOILING MAD, SMELL.

**fun** *n.* **1.** Something that provides enjoyment, pleasure, or amusement: *Playing tennis is fun.* **2.** The pleasurable feelings so provided: *We had fun at the party.* Same sign used for: **leisure, recreation.**

- Bring the fingers of the right *H hand* from near the nose downward, ending with the fingers of the right *H hand* across the fingers of the left *H hand* in front of the chest, both palms facing down.

**function** *n.* **1.** The normal action, activity, or work of a person or thing: *The chief function of the manager is to see that the work gets done.* —*v.* **2.** To perform a particular action or activity: *I don't understand the way the old pendulum clock functions.*

- [Initialized sign similar to sign for **practice**] Move the fingertips of the right *F hand,* palm facing forward, back and forth across the length of the left *open hand,* palm facing down, with a double movement.

**fund** *n.* See signs for MONEY, SUPPORT.

**funeral** *n.* A ceremony performed before the burial or cremation of someone who has died: *left town to attend his grandfather's funeral.*

- [Represents a procession following a casket] Beginning with both *V hands* in front of the chest, right hand closer to the chest than the left hand and both palms facing forward, move the hands forward simultaneously in a double arc.

**funny** *adj.* **1.** Causing laughter; providing fun: *a funny joke.* **2.** Able to amuse: *a genuinely funny comedian.* Same sign used for: **amusing, humorous.**

- With a double movement, brush the nose with the fingertips of the right *U hand,* palm facing in and thumb extended, bending the fingers of the *U hand* back toward the palm each time.

**furious** *adj.* See signs for ANGER[2], BOILING MAD.

**furniture** *n.* Movable articles, as tables, chairs, and storage units, used in a house or office: *to polish the furniture.*

■ [Initialized sign] Move the right *F hand,* palm facing forward, from side to side in front of the right side of the chest with a repeated movement.

**further** *adv.* See sign for AHEAD.

**fury** *adj.* See sign for ANGER.

**future** *n.* Time that is to come: *I don't know what the future will bring.* Same sign used for: **some day.**

■ [Hand moves forward into the future] Move the right *open hand,* palm facing left and fingers pointing up, from near the right cheek forward in a double arc.

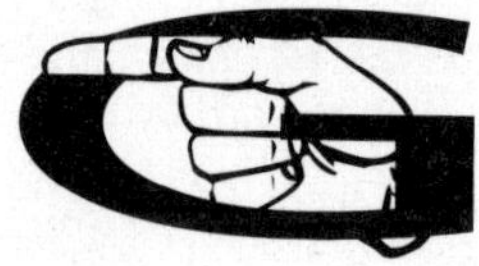

**gab** *v., n. Informal.* See sign for BLAB.

**gain** *v., n.* See signs for INCREASE, PROFIT.

**gain weight** *v. phrase.* See sign for FAT.

**gala** *adj., n.* See signs for CELEBRATE, DANCE.

**galoshes** *pl. n.* See sign for BOOTS.

**gamble**[1] *v.* **1.** To play a game of chance, especially for money: *They go to Las Vegas to gamble.* **2.** To bet or take a risk on an uncertain outcome: *to gamble on the results of the election.* —*n.* **3.** A risky undertaking: *to leave the organization and take a gamble on getting a better job.* Same sign used for: **dice.**

■ [Mime tossing dice] Beginning with the right *A hand* in front of the right side of the body, palm facing up, thrust the hand forward to the left while opening into a *5 hand.*

**gamble**[2] *n., v.* See sign for BET.

**game** *n.* A contest played according to a set of rules, often between two opposing teams of players: *Now that everyone is here, we can play the game.*

■ [Represents opposing teams sparring] Bring the knuckles of both *10 hands,* palms facing in, against each other with a double movement in front of the chest.

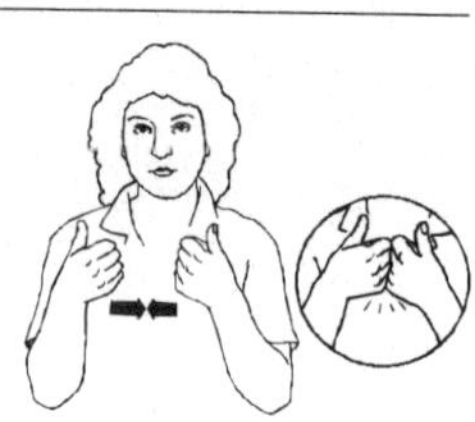

**gang** *n.* A group of persons associated for criminal or antisocial purposes: *Since he joined a gang, he just hangs out on the street.* Related form: **gangster** *n.* Same sign used for: **dare, tough.**

■ Move the right *S hand,* palm facing in, downward on the right side of the chest with a double movement.

**gap** *n.* See sign for BETWEEN.

**garage** *n.* A building or other shelter for vehicles: *Park in the garage.*

[Represents a car moving into a garage] Move the right *3 hand,* palm facing left, forward with a short repeated movement under the palm of the left *open hand,* palm facing down and fingers pointing right.

**garbage** *n.* Scraps of waste, as animal and vegetable matter from a kitchen, to be thrown away: *to take out the garbage.* Same sign used for: **gross, junk, trash.**

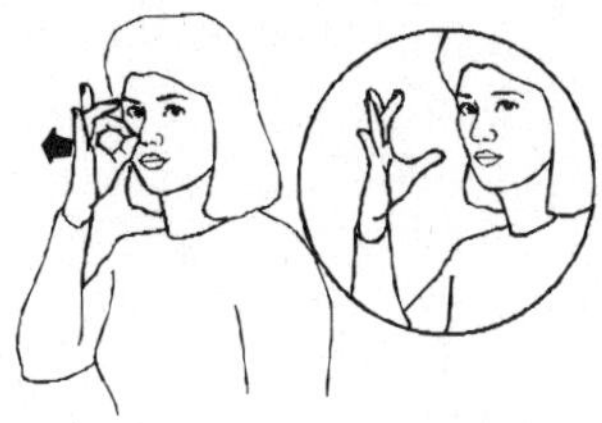

- [Natural gesture of holding one's nose when something smells bad] Beginning with the fingertips of the right *F hand* touching the nose, palm facing in, bring the right hand forward a short distance while opening the index finger and thumb in front of the face.

**garbled** *adj.* See signs for MESSY, MIX[1].

**garden** *n.* A plot of ground, usually near a house, for growing flowers, shrubs, vegetables, and other plants: *gathered a bouquet from my own garden.*

- [Initialized sign encircling an area of land] Move the right *G hand,* palm facing left, in a large circular movement over the bent left arm, beginning near the elbow and ending near the left fingers.

**garment** *n.* See sign for CLOTHES.

**gas** *n.* A liquid used as fuel to propel a vehicle: *We have to fill the tank with gas before the trip.* Alternate form: **gasoline.** Same sign used for: **fuel.**

- [Mime pouring gas into the gas tank of a vehicle] Tap the extended thumb of the right *10 hand,* palm facing forward, downward with a repeated small movement into the thumb-side opening of the left *S hand.*

**gasp** *v.* See sign for GULP.

**gate** *n.* A movable section of a fence, usually on hinges, that can be swung back and forth for opening or closing: *Unlock the gate for the letter carrier.*

- [Shows a gate swinging open] Beginning with both *open hands* in front of the body, palms facing in and the fingers touching, swing the fingers of the right hand forward and back with a double movement.

**gather**[1] *v.* To bring or come together into one group: *to gather the eggs. We will all gather in front of the restaurant.* Same sign used for: **assemble, get together.**

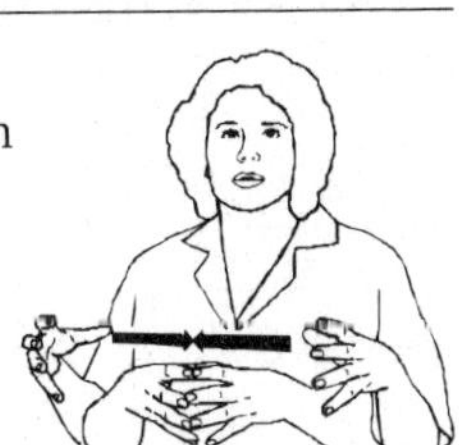

- [Represents people coming together] Beginning with both *curved 5 hands* in front of each side of the body, palms facing each other, bring the fingers together in front of the body.

**gather**[2] *v.* (alternate sign) Same sign used for: **assemble, attend, get together, go to.**

- [Represents people coming together] Beginning with both *5 hands* in front of each shoulder, palms angled forward, bring the hands forward toward each other, ending with the palms facing down.

**gather**[3] *v.* See signs for COLLECT.

**gauge** *v.* See sign for ANALYZE.

**gay**[1] *adj.* **1.** Pertaining to or being a homosexual person: *a gay employee.* **2.** Pertaining to homosexuality: *gay rights.* —*n.* **3.** A homosexual person: *gays demonstrating on behalf of AIDS research.* Same sign used for: **homosexual, queer** (*Slang, disparaging and offensive*).

- [Initialized sign] Bring the fingertips of the right *G hand,* palm facing in, back to touch the chin with a double movement.

**gay**[2] *adj.* See sign for HAPPY.

**gelatin** *n.* A food product made of a nearly transparent, glutinous, jellylike substance: *A strawberry gelatin was served for dessert.* Same sign used for: **Jell-O** (*Trademark*).

- [Shows the shaking movement of gelatin] Shake the right *curved 5 hand,* palm facing down, with a repeated back and forth movement over the left *open hand,* palm facing up.

**gender** *n.* See sign for SEX[1].

**general**[1] *adj.* **1.** Not specific or detailed; approximate: *traveling in the general direction of New York.* **2.** Concerned or dealing with extensive or important aspects rather than details: *The college catalog provides a general description of the biology course.* Same sign used for: **broad.**

- [Hands open up broadly] Beginning with both *open hands* in front of the chest, fingers angled toward each other, swing the fingers away from each other, ending with the fingers angled outward in front of each side of the body.

**general**[2] *adj.* See sign for WIDE.

**general**[3] *n.* See sign for CAPTAIN.

**generous** *adj.* See sign for KIND.

**genius** *n.* See sign for SCHOLARLY[1].

**gentle** *adj.* See signs for KIND, POLITE, SOFT, SWEET.

**gentleman** *n.* See sign for MAN.

**genuine** *adj.* See sign for REAL.

**geography** *n.* See sign for EARTH.

**gesture** *n.* A movement of the hands, arms, and body used in sign language: *The gestures used in signing are very expressive.*

■ [Mime gesturing with the hands; similar to sign for **sign**[1]] Beginning with both *curved 5 hands* in front of the chest, left hand higher than the right hand and palms facing in opposite directions, move both hands in alternating forward circles.

**get** *v.* To gain possession of: *They want to get a new car.* Same sign used for: **acquire, attain, obtain, receive, retrieve.**

■ [Reaching for something and bringing it to oneself] Beginning with both *curved 5 hands* in front of the chest, right hand above the left and palms facing in opposite directions, bring the hands back toward the chest while closing into *S hands,* ending with the little-finger side of the right hand on the index-finger side of the left hand.

**get along** *v. phrase.* See sign for GO ON.

**get away** *v. phrase.* See signs for AVOID, AWAY, ESCAPE, RUN AWAY.

**get even** *v. phrase.* See signs for EQUAL, REVENGE.

**get together** *v. phrase.* See signs for GATHER[1,2].

**get up** *v. phrase.* See sign for RAISE.

**ghost** *n.* See sign for SPIRIT.

**gift** *n.* **1.** A present, as for a special occasion: *Bring a gift to the birthday party.* **2.** Something given to provide aid to another: *a gift to your favorite charity.* **3.** A presentation to honor a person or an occasion: *presented with a $1,000 gift at the awards banquet.* Same sign used for: **award, charity, contribution, donation, grant, present, reward, tribute.**

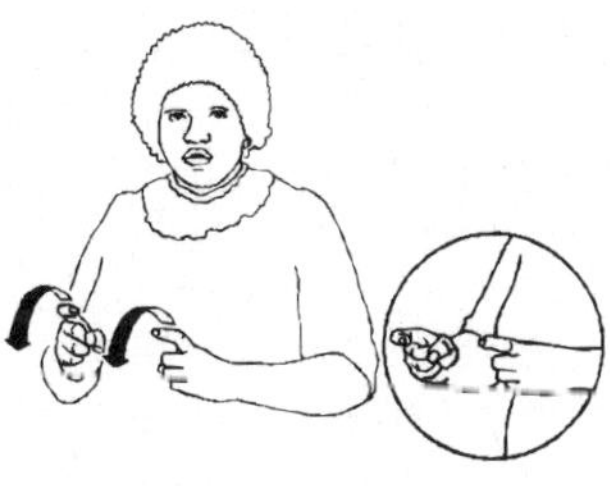

■ [Presenting something to another] Move both *X hands* from in front of the body, palms facing each other, forward in simultaneous arcs.

**giggle** *n.* **1.** A silly laugh: *the child was full of delightful giggles.* —*v.* **2.** To laugh in a silly way: *The audience giggled when the speaker forgot what he was saying.*

■ [Represents the stomach of a jolly person heaving when laughing] Beginning with the right *bent hand* in front of the chest under the left *bent hand,* both palms facing down, curve the right hand toward the chest with a double movement by bending the wrist.

**gingivitis** *n.* See sign for GUMS. Related form: **gingiva.**

**giraffe** *n.* A tall spotted African mammal with long, slender legs and a long neck: *We saw a giraffe at the zoo nibbling leaves from a tree.*

■ [Shows shape of giraffe's neck] Beginning with the little-finger side of the right *C hand* on the index-finger side of the left *C hand,* both palms facing in at the neck, move the right hand upward in front of the face.

**girl** *n.* A female child: *boys and girls in the school playground.* Same sign used for: **female.**

■ [Formed in the female area of the head] Move the thumb of the right *A hand,* palm facing left, downward on the right cheek to the right side of the chin.

**give** *v.* To present or donate: *to give a donation to the fund.* Same sign used for: **bequeath, contribute, donate, grant, present, provide.**

■ [Presenting something to another] Move the right *X hand* from in front of the right side of the chest, palm facing left, forward in a large arc.

**give blood** *v. phrase.* See sign for DRAW BLOOD.

**give up** *v. phrase.* To surrender: *I give up—you've convinced me.* Same sign used for: **relinquish, surrender, waive, yield.**

■ [Natural gesture used when surrendering] Beginning with both *curved hands* in front of the body, palms facing down, flip the hands upward in large arcs while opening into *5 hands,* ending in front of each shoulder, palms facing forward.

**glad** *adj.* See sign for HAPPY.

**glance** *v.* **1.** To look quickly or briefly: *She glanced at the map and drove off.* —*n.* **2.** A quick or brief look: *You could tell at a glance that the paintings were wonderful.*

■ [Represents the eyes moving quickly around] Beginning with the right *V hand* in front of the right side of the face, palm facing down and fingers pointing to the right eye, move the hand forward and outward to the right by twisting the wrist outward with a quick movement, following the fingers with the eyes.

**glare** *n.* **1.** A strong, harsh, dazzling light: *She turned her head away from the glare.* —*v.* **2.** To shine with a harsh, dazzling light: *The sun glared off the windshield.*

■ [Represents light shining down and reflecting off the face] Move the right *flattened O hand,* palm facing left, downward from near the right side of the head toward the face with a double movement, opening into a *curved 5 hand* each time.

**glass**[1] *n.* A hard, brittle, transparent substance: *large windows made of glass.*

■ [Shows porcelain on teeth] Tap the fingertip of the right bent index finger against the front teeth with a repeated movement.

**glass**[2] *n.* See signs for BOTTLE, CUP.

**glasses** *pl. n.* Corrective eyewear consisting of two glass or plastic lenses set in a frame, usually with earpieces: *had to wear glasses for nearsightedness.* Same sign used for: **eyeglasses, spectacles.**

■ [Shape and location of eyeglasses] Tap the thumbs of both *modified C hands,* palms facing each other, near the outside corner of each eye with a repeated movement.

**glitter** *v., n.* See sign for SHINY.

**glory** *n.* Worshipful praise: *Glory to God.*

■ [Shows light and splendor rising from something glorified] Beginning with the palm of the right *open hand* on the upturned left *open hand,* bring the right hand upward in front of the chest while opening the fingers and wiggling them.

**glossy** *adj.* See sign for SHINY.

**glove** *n.* A covering for the hand with a close-fitting cover for each finger and the thumb: *He lost a glove on the bus.*

- [Represents pulling on a glove] Pull the right *5 hand,* palm facing down, from the fingers up the length of the back of the left *5 hand,* palm facing down. To indicate the plural, repeat with the other hand.

**glow** *v., n.* See signs for CANDLE, SHINY.

**glue** *n.* **1.** An adhesive substance that causes two surfaces to stick together: *Use glue to mount the pictures.* —*v.* **2.** To cause to adhere with or as if with glue: *Glue the address label to the envelope.*

- [Initialized sign seeming to squeeze glue on paper] Move the fingertips of the right *G hand,* palm and fingers facing down, in a circular movement over the upturned left *open hand.*

**go**[1] *v.* To leave or depart, especially to a place distant from the starting location: *to go on vacation.* Same sign used for: **depart, go away, go out, leave.**

- [Represents something getting smaller as it disappears into the distance] Beginning with the *flattened C hand* in front of the right shoulder, fingers pointing left, move the hand quickly to the right while closing the fingers into a *flattened O hand.*

**go**[2] *v.* See sign for AWAY.

**go after** *v. phrase.* See sign for FOLLOW.

**go ahead** *v. phrase.* See sign for GO ON.

**go away** *v. phrase.* See sign for GO[1].

**go by train** *v. phrase.* See sign for TRAIN.

**go on** *v. phrase.* **1.** To move forward: *too tired from walking to go on.* **2.** To continue: *Let's go on with the meeting.* Same sign used for: **all along, continue, forward, get along, go ahead, move on, onward, proceed.**

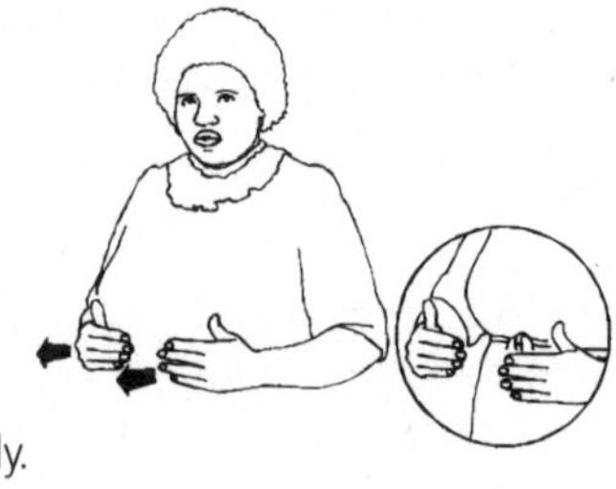

- [Shows shoving something along ahead of oneself] Beginning with both *open hands* in front of the body, palms facing in and fingers pointing toward each other, move the hands forward a short distance simultaneously.

**go out** *v. phrase.* See sign for GO[1].

**go smoothly** *v. phrase.* See signs for SMOOTH[2], SMOOTHLY.

**go steady** *v. phrase.* See sign for STEADY.

**go to** *v. phrase.* See signs for ATTEND, GATHER[2].

**go to bed** *v. phrase.*

■ [Indicates a person's legs getting under a blanket] Insert the fingers of the right *U hand,* palm facing down, into the hole formed by the left *O hand,* palm facing down.

**go with** *v. phrase.* To accompany: *He may go with his sister to the movies.* Same sign used for: **accompany.**

■ [Similar to sign for **with** but moving toward a destination] With the palm sides of both *A hands* together in front of the chest, move the hands forward and downward with a deliberate movement.

**goal** *n.* The end or result to which effort is directed: *The store manager will exceed her goal this week by $10,000.* Same sign used for: **aim, ambitious, objective, target.**

[Indicates directing something toward something else] Move the extended right index finger from touching the right side of the forehead, palm facing down, forward to point toward the extended left index finger held in front of the face, palm facing forward and finger angled up.

**goat** *n.* A cud-chewing, horned mammal closely related to sheep and found in mountainous regions: *a goat with a small, pointed beard.*

■ [Represents a goat's beard and horns] Move the right *S hand* from the chin, palm facing in and the heel of the hand pointing down, forward a short distance while flicking up the index and middle fingers. Then repeat the same movement from the forehead.

**God** *n.* The Supreme Being; the Creator: *to believe in God.*

[Indicates the spirit of God moving down from above] Move the right *B hand,* palm facing left and fingers angled upward, from above the head downward in front of the face in an inward arc.

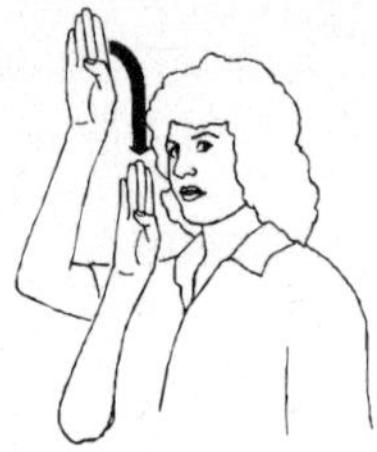

**gold** *n.* **1.** A valuable yellow metallic element, used in jewelry: *a bracelet made of gold.* —*adj.* **2.** Made of gold: *gold coins.* Same sign used for: **golden.**

■ [Shows a gold earring + **yellow**] With the thumb, index finger, and little finger of the right hand extended, palm facing in, touch the index finger near the right ear. Then bring the right hand downward and forward with a shaking movement while turning the wrist forward and changing into a *Y hand.*

**golden** *adj.* See sign for GOLD. Shared idea of yellow color.

**golf** *n.* An outdoor game played by hitting a small ball into a series of holes with as few strokes as possible, using a set of long-handled clubs: *plays nine holes of golf every Saturday.*

■ [Mime swinging a golf club] Beginning with the right *modified X hand* near the right hip, palm facing left, and the left *modified X hand* in front of the right side of the body, palm facing in, swing the right hand upward and to the left.

**gone**[1] *v., adj.* See signs for ABSENT, AWAY.

**gone**[2] *v., adj.* See sign for NOTHING[3].

**good** *adj.* **1.** Of a favorable character; virtuous: *good people, who care about others.* **2.** Satisfactory in quality or degree: *a good doctor; in good health.* **3.** Palatable or tasty: *This is a good hamburger.* Same sign used for: **benevolent, well.**

■ [Presents something good for inspection] Beginning with the fingertips of the right *open hand* near the mouth, palm facing in and fingers pointing up, bring the hand downward, ending with the back of the right hand across the palm of the left *open hand,* both palms facing up.

**good at**[1] *adj. phrase.* Skilled in doing, performing, or playing: *good at volleyball.* Same sign used for: **expert, proficient.**

■ Bring the fingertips of the right *F hand,* palm facing in, back against the chin.

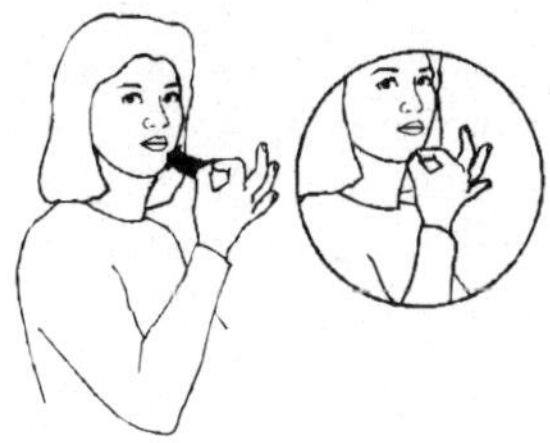

**good at**[2] *adj. phrase.* See signs for ADROIT, SKILL.

**good-bye** *interj.* **1.** (A conventional expression used as a parting remark): *Good-bye, everyone, we're leaving.* —*n.* **2.** An act of saying good-bye: *Say your good-byes and go.* Same sign used for: **bye, farewell.**

■ [Natural gesture for waving good-bye] Beginning with the right *open hand* in front of the right shoulder, palm facing forward and fingers pointing up, bend the fingers up and down with a repeated movement.

**good enough** *adj. phrase.* See sign for MAKESHIFT.

**good-looking** *adj.* See sign for LOOKS.

**good luck** *interj.* (A conventional expression used to wish someone favorable circumstances and good fortune): *Good luck to you in the competition.*

■ [**good** + a natural "thumbs up" gesture for wishing luck] Beginning with the fingertips of the right *open hand* near the mouth, palm facing in and fingers pointing up, bring the hand downward and forward while changing into a *10 hand,* ending with the thumb pointing up, palm facing left, in front of the right shoulder.

**Google** *(Trademark)* or **google** *n.* **1.** A computer search engine used to obtain information on the World Wide Web: *use Google to find the weather in Greece for tomorrow.* —*v.* **2.** To search for information on the World Wide Web by using any search engine: *He googled the name of the author to find out the title of the book.*

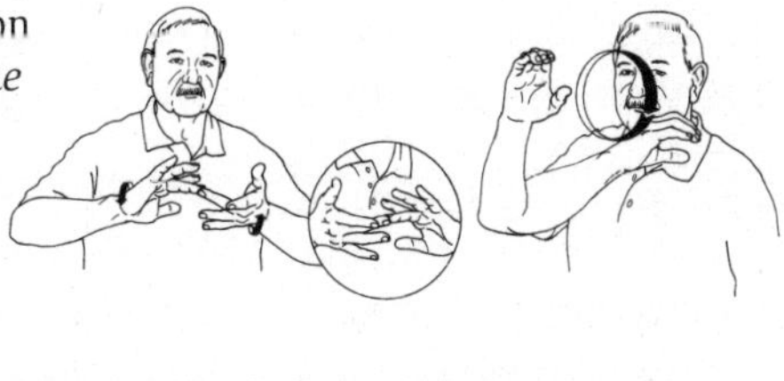

■ [**network** + **look for**] Beginning with the bent middle fingers of both *5 hands* pointing toward each other in front of the chest, twist both wrists to change positions. Then move the right *C hand,* palm facing left, with a double movement in a circle in front of the face.

**goose** *n.* **1.** A long-necked, web-footed, swimming bird, resembling but larger than a duck: *watching ducks and geese swimming in the pond.* **2.** The flesh of this fowl used as food: *serving a Christmas goose.*

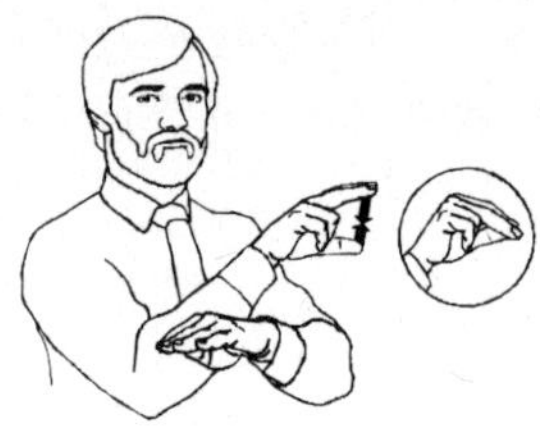

■ [Shows long neck of a goose and the movement of a goose's bill] With the left *open hand* held across the chest, palm facing down, rest the right forearm on the back of the left wrist while closing the extended right index and middle fingers to the right thumb, palm facing forward, with a repeated movement.

**gorilla** *n.* A large and powerful ape: *Gorillas live in the jungles of Africa.* Same sign used for: **ape.**

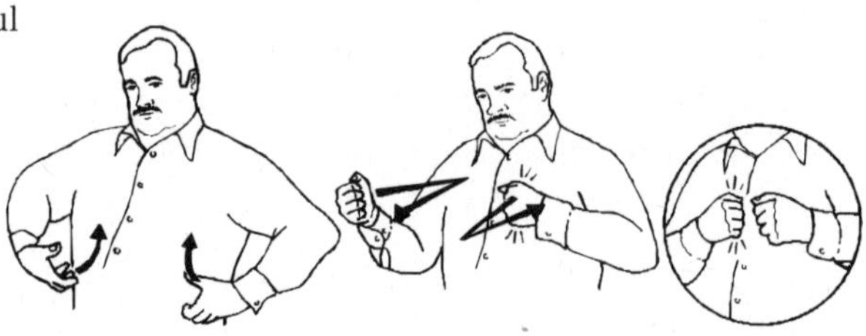

■ [**monkey** + miming a gorilla beating its chest] Beginning with the fingertips of both *curved 5 hands* against each side of the body near the waist, palms facing in, brush the fingertips upward with a double movement. Then pound the palm side of both *S hands* against the chest with an alternating double movement.

**gossip**[1] *n.* **1.** Idle talk filled with rumors about the private lives of others: *There has been malicious gossip about her since she started working here.* **2.** Chatty, light, convivial talk: *to enjoy a bit of harmless gossip over coffee.* —*v.* **3.** To engage in gossip: *They never gossip about their friends.* Same sign used for: **rumor.**

■ [Represents mouths opening and closing repeatedly] Move both *G hands,* palms facing each other, in a flat circular movement in front of the chest while pinching the index finger and thumb of each hand together with a repeated movement.

**gossip**[2] *n., v.* See sign for BLAB.

**got you!** or **gotcha!** *interj.* See sign for ZAP.

**govern** *v.* See sign for MANAGE.

**government** *n.* A political unit that directs and restrains the actions of its citizens: *the federal government; the state government.* Same sign for: **federal.**

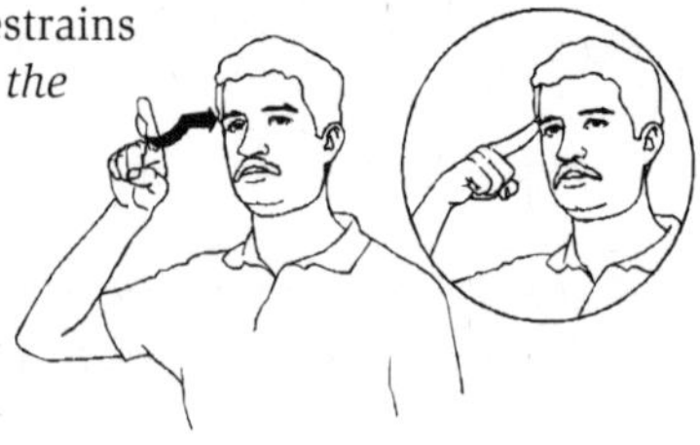

■ Beginning with the extended right index finger pointing upward near the right side of the head, palm facing forward, twist the wrist to touch the finger to the right temple.

**grab** *v.* To snatch suddenly: *Grab your hat and let's get out of here.* Same sign used for: **take a chance.**

- [Hand seems to snatch something from the other hand] Bring the right *curved 5 hand* from in front of the right side of the body, palm facing left and fingers pointing forward, in toward the body in a downward arc while changing into an *S hand,* brushing the little-finger side of the right *S hand* across the palm of the left *open hand,* palm facing up in front of the chest.

**gracious** *adj.* See sign for KIND.

**grade** *n.* A slope in the terrain: *The road has a steep grade.* Same sign used for: **incline, slope.**

- [Demonstrates the shape of an incline] Beginning with the right *open hand* on top of the left *open hand* in front of the chest, both palms facing down and fingers pointing forward, move the right hand upward and forward at an angle.

**graduate** *v.* To receive an academic degree upon completion of a course of study: *graduate from high school.* Related form: **graduation** *n.*

- [Initialized sign similar to sign for **college**] Beginning with the right *G hand* in front of the right side of the chest, palm facing left and fingers angled forward, move the hand in a small circular movement and then straight down, ending with the little-finger side of the right hand on the left upturned open palm.

**grammar** *n.* **1.** The ways in which the words and sentences of a language are structured: *spent several years studying the grammar of French.* **2.** A set of rules derived from such structure: *to produce a grammar of English.* **3.** Language constructed according to these rules: *They always use good grammar.* Same sign used for: **syntax.**

- [Initialized sign similar to sign for **sentence**] Beginning with both *G hands* in front of the chest, fingers pointing toward each other, bring the hands apart with a wavy movement to in front of each side of the body.

**grand** *adj.* See signs for FANCY, LARGE.

**grandfather** *n.* The father of one's father or mother: *One of my grandfathers was born in Vermont.* Alternate form: **grandpa** (*informal*).

- [**man** + moving forward one generation] Beginning with the thumb of the right *A hand* touching the forehead, palm facing left, bring the hand downward while opening into a *curved 5 hand* in front of the face, palm angled up.

**grandma** *n. Informal.* See sign for GRANDMOTHER.

**grandmother** *n.* The mother of one's father or mother: *My grandmother owns a store.* Alternate form: **grandma** (*informal*).

■ [**girl** + moving forward one generation] Beginning with the thumb of the right *A hand* touching the chin, palm facing left, bring the hand downward while opening into a *curved 5 hand* in front of the chest, palm facing up.

**grandpa** *n. Informal.* See sign for GRANDFATHER.

**grant** *n., v.* See signs for GIFT, GIVE, LET.

**grapes** *pl. n.* Smooth-skinned, edible berries that grow in clusters on vines: *to buy a bunch of grapes.*

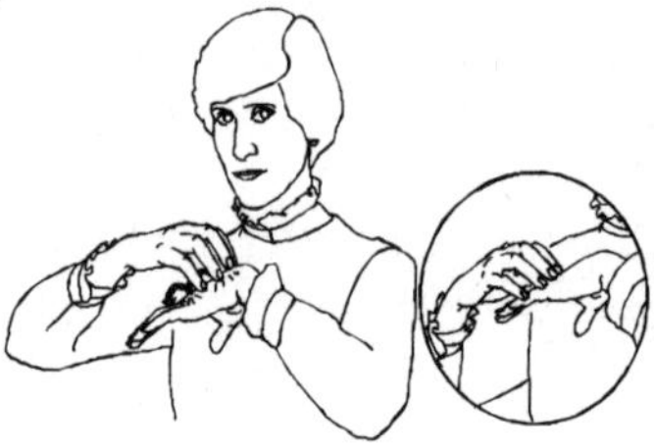

■ [Shows bumpy shape of a bunch of grapes] Tap the fingertips of the right *curved 5 hand,* palm facing down, down the back of the left *open hand,* palm facing down, from the wrist to the fingers with a bouncing movement.

**graph** *n.* See sign for SCHEDULE.

**grass** *n.* A plant with bladelike leaves used as ground cover: *time to cut the grass.*

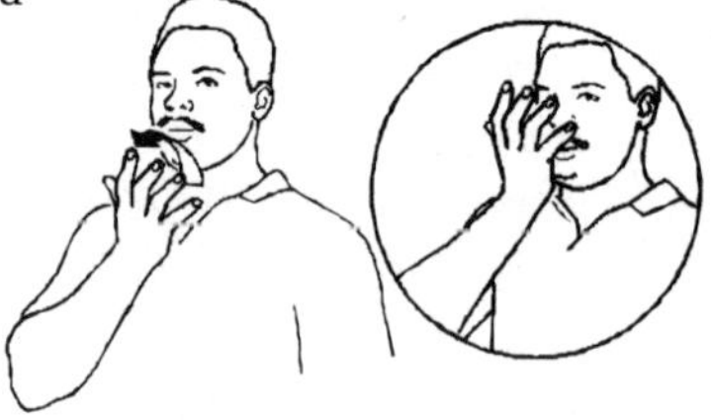

■ Push the heel of the right *curved 5 hand,* palm facing up, upward a short distance on the chin.

**grateful** *adj.* Warmly appreciative of kindness or a favor received: *I am grateful for your help.* Same sign used for: **appreciative, thankful.**

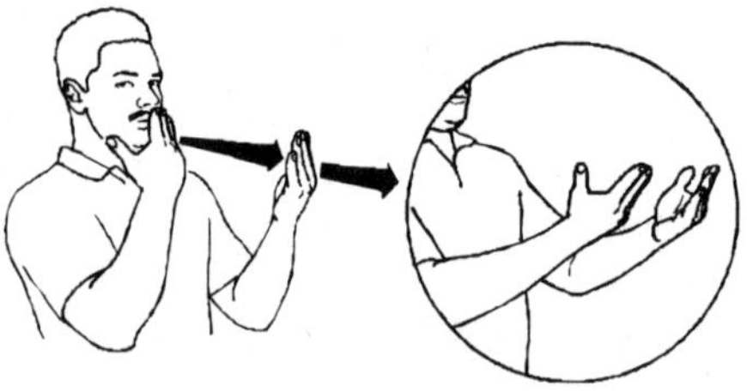

■ [**thank** moving forward toward another] Beginning with the right *open hand* near the mouth and the left *open hand* somewhat forward, palms facing in and fingers pointing up, move both hands forward.

**grave** *n., adj.* See signs for BURY, SAD.

**graveyard** *n.* See sign for CEMETERY.

**gravity** *n.* The natural force that pulls objects toward Earth: *Using the pull of gravity to roll the boulder downhill.*

■ [**Earth** + a movement showing being pulled downward] Grasping the top of the left hand, palm facing down, with the bent thumb and middle finger of the right *5 hand,* palm facing down, rock the right hand from side to side with a double movement. Then bring the back of the right *S hand,* palm facing in near the neck, downward, ending with the back of the right wrist on the thumb side of the left *open hand,* palm facing down, angled across the chest.

**gravy** *n.* Sauce for meat, potatoes, and other food made from the juices of cooked meat: *Put beef gravy on the potatoes.* Same sign used for: **grease, syrup.**

■ [Represents dripping gravy] Beginning with the extended thumb and index finger of the right *G hand* grasping the little-finger side of the left *open hand,* both palms facing in, bring the right hand downward with a double movement while closing the index finger to the thumb each time.

**gray** *adj.* Having a neutral color between black and white: *a gray, cloudy sky.*

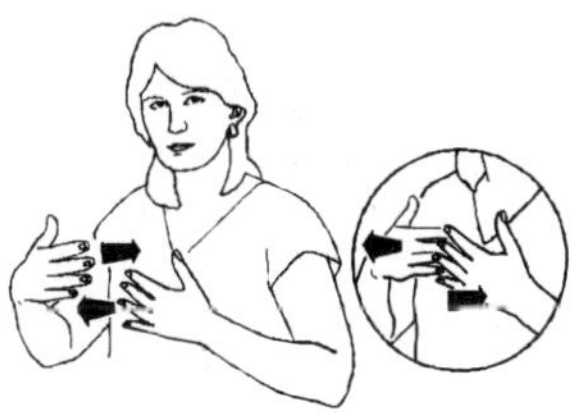

■ Beginning with both *5 hands* in front of the chest, fingers pointing toward each other and palms facing in, move the hands forward and back in opposite directions, lightly brushing fingertips as the hands pass each other.

**grease** *n.* See signs for GRAVY, OIL. Related form: **greasy** *adj.*

**great** *adj.* See signs for LARGE, WONDERFUL.

**greedy**[1] *adj.* Having an excessive, selfish desire: *greedy for wealth.* Same sign used for: **covetous, miser, niggardly, possessive, selfish, thrifty, tight, tightwad.**

■ Beginning with the right *curved 5 hand* in front of the chin, palm facing in, bring the hand downward with either a single or double movement while closing the hand into an *S hand.*

**greedy**[2] *adj.* See sign for STINGY[2].

**green** *adj.* Of a color between blue and yellow: *the rich green shades of summer foliage.*

■ [Initialized sign] Twist the right *G hand,* palm facing left, back and forward with a small repeated movement in front of the right shoulder.

**greet** *v.* See signs for INVITE, MEET.

**greeting** *n.* See sign for HELLO.

**grievance** *n.* See signs for COMPLAIN, PROTEST.

**grimace** *n.* **1.** A twisted or contorted facial expression: *With a grimace of pain, he lifted the heavy box.* —*v.* **2.** To contort the face in a grimace: *grimaced at the site of the mess all over the floor.*

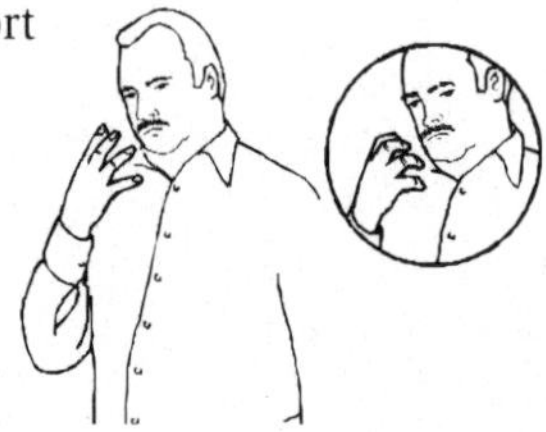

■ [Shows shape of face when grimacing] Place the right *5 hand,* palm facing in, near the right side of the face. Then constrict the fingers into a *curved 5 hand.*

**grin** *v., n.* See sign for SMILE.

**grind**[1] *v.* **1.** To reduce to fine particles by crushing or pounding: *to grind the kernels of corn into cornmeal.* **2.** To rub harshly; grate together: *to grind one's teeth.*

■ [Represents teeth grinding together] Beginning with the palm sides of both *A hands* together in front of the chest, right hand over the left hand, move the hands in opposite directions in double circles while rubbing on each other.

**grind**[2] *v.* See sign for CHEW.

**grind out** *v. phrase.* To produce in a mechanical way: *The students ground out their homework assignments day after day.* Same sign used for: **monotonous.**

■ Beginning with the extended right index finger touching the nose, palm facing in, move the hand forward while changing into an *S hand.* Then rub the index-finger side of the right *S hand,* palm facing forward, on the palm of the left *open hand,* palm facing right and fingers pointing up, with a double movement.

**grip** *n., v.* See sign for HOLD[1].

**gripe** *v.* See sign for COMPLAIN.

**groceries** *pl. n.* See sign for FOOD.

**grocery store** *n.* A store displaying and selling food: *Our local grocery store has the brand of frozen food you want.* Same sign used for: **food store, market.**

■ [**food** + **store**[1]] Bring the fingertips of the right *flattened O hand,* palm facing in, to the lips with a repeated movement. Then, beginning with both *flattened O hands* in front of the body, fingers pointing down, swing the fingertips upward and downward from the wrists with a repeated movement.

**gross** *adj.* See signs for GARBAGE, PROFIT.

**grouchy** *adj.* See sign for ANGER[2].

**ground** *n.* See sign for DIRT.

**group**[1] *n.* A number of people or things considered as a unit: *a group of children.*

■ [Initialized sign similar to sign for **class**] Beginning with both *G hands* in front of the chest, palms facing each other, bring the hands away from each other in outward arcs while turning the palms in, ending with the little fingers near each other.

**group**[2] *n.* See sign for CLASS.

**grow** *v.* **1.** To develop to maturity, as a plant: *The rose bush has grown another six inches.* **2.** To cause to grow: *They grow tulips in the Netherlands.* Same sign used for: **sprout.**

■ [Represents a plant coming up through the soil] Bring the right *flattened O hand,* palm facing in, up through the left *C hand,* palm facing in and fingers pointing right, while spreading the right fingers into a *5 hand.*

**grow up** *v. phrase.* To develop to maturity: *grow up on a farm.* Same sign used for: **raise, rear.**

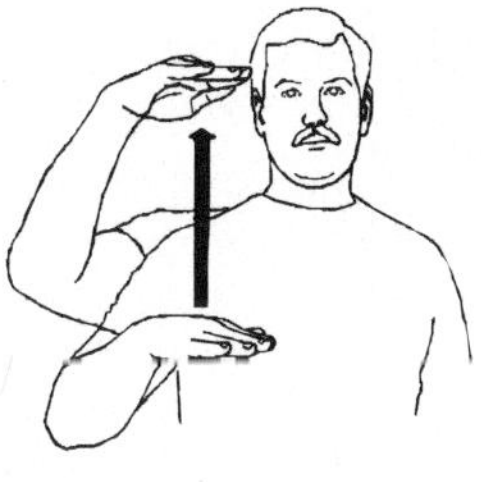

■ [Shows height as one grows] Bring the right *open hand,* palm facing down and fingers pointing left, from in front of the chest upward.

**grown-up** *n.* See sign for ADULT.

**grumble** *v.* See sign for COMPLAIN.

**grumpy** *adj.* See sign for ANGER².

**guage** *v.* See sign for ANALYZE.

**guarantee** *n., v.* See signs for PROMISE, STAMP².

**guardian** *n.* A person with responsibility for the care of a child or an incompetent adult, having control over their affairs: *The girl lived with a guardian when her mother went to jail.* Same sign used for: **caregiver.**

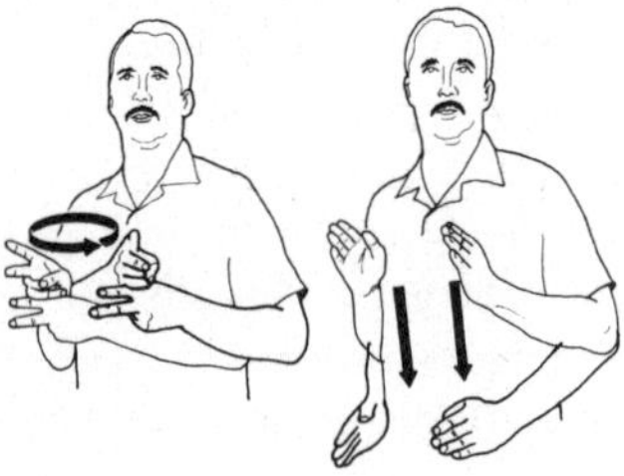

■ [**care**[1] + **person marker**] With the little-finger side of the right *K hand* on the thumb side of the left *K hand,* palms facing in opposite directions, move the hands in a flat circle in front of the body. Then move both *open hands,* palms facing each other, downward along the sides of the body.

**guess** *v.* **1.** To make assumptions based on limited facts; estimate; conjecture: *I can't begin to guess your age.* —*n.* **2.** An opinion based on limited facts: *Without looking the information up, I can only give you an educated guess.* Same sign used for: **assume, estimate.**

■ [Hand seems to snatch at an idea as it passes the face] Move the right *C hand,* palm facing left, from near the right side of the forehead in a quick downward arc in front of the face while closing into an *S hand,* ending with the palm facing down by the left side of the head.

**guide** *v.* See sign for LEAD.

**guilt** *n.* **1.** A feeling of remorse for committing an offense: *A feeling of guilt for lying stayed with her all day.* **2.** The fact that one has committed an offense: *The accomplice denied his guilt.* Related form: **guilty** *adj.*

■ [Initialized sign formed near the heart] Bring the thumb side of the right *G hand,* palm facing left, back against the left side of the chest.

**guitar** *n.* A stringed instrument with a flat, violinlike body, played with the fingers or a pick: *He learned to play the guitar when he was 12 and joined a rock band at 16.*

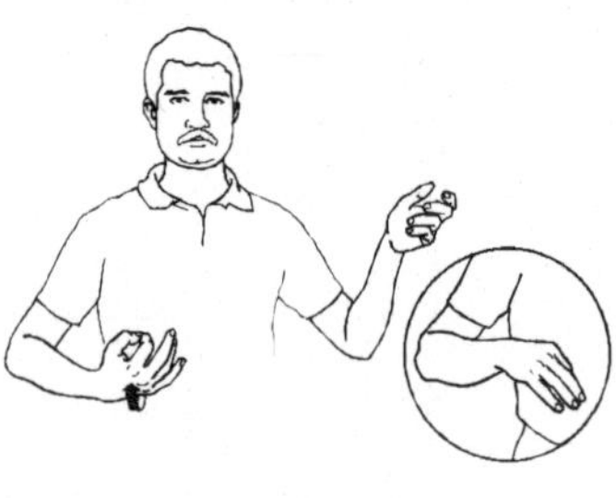

■ [Mime playing a guitar with a pick] With the left *curved 5 hand* in front of the left shoulder, palm facing right, and the right *F hand* in front of the right side of the body, palm facing in, twist the right hand downward with a double movement.

**gullible** *adj.* See sign for CONSUME.

**gulp**[1] *v.* To suppress or choke back, as in nervousness: *He gulped when caught in a lie.* Same sign used for: **gasp.**

■ [Represents the throat constricting as one swallows] Beginning with the right *C hand* near the throat, palm facing in, close the fingers to change into an *S hand.*

**gulp**[2] *v.* See sign for SWALLOW.

**gum** *n.* See sign for CHEWING GUM.

**gums** *pl. n.* The firm, fleshy tissue along the jaws that surrounds the necks of the teeth: *The gums were inflamed from an infection.* Same sign used for: **gingivitis.**

■ [Point to location] Touch the upper gums with the extended right index finger.

**gun** *n.* A portable firearm: *According to the movies, you had to carry a gun in the Old West.* Same sign used for: **pistol.**

■ [Demonstrates pulling back the hammer on a pointed gun] With the index finger of the right *L hand* pointing forward in front of the right side of the body, palm facing left, wiggle the thumb up and down with a repeated movement.

**guy** *n.* See sign for MAN.

**gym** *n.* **1.** A class for training in sports and exercises: *time to go to gym.* **2.** A building or room designed for sports or exercise: *The basketball game is in the gym.* Related form: **gymnasium** *n.*

■ Beginning with the *modified X hands* in front of each shoulder, palms facing each other, move the hands forward in small double circles by moving the arms and the wrists.

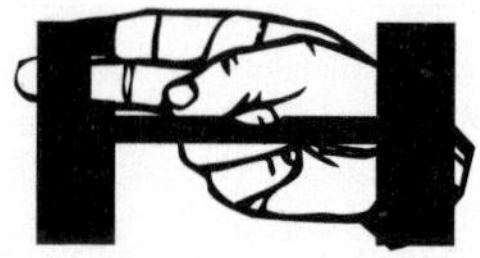

**habit** *n.* A pattern of behavior acquired through repeated experience or exposure: *an irritating habit of turning her head away and mumbling.* Same sign used for: **accustomed to, custom.**

- [Symbolizes being bound by tradition] With the heel of the right *S hand* across the wrist of the left *S hand,* both palms facing down, move the hands down simultaneously in front of the chest.

**hack** *v.* To cut, chop, or sever with repeated blows (often followed by *off, up,* or *down*): *to hack off the tree branch.* Same sign used for: **karate.**

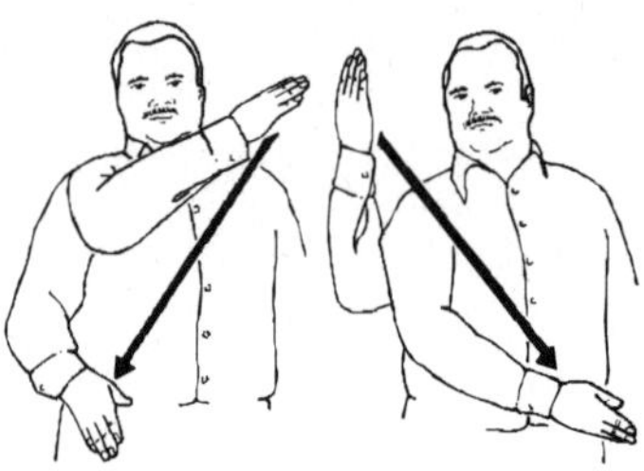

- [Mime hacking something down] Beginning with the right *B hand* in front of the left shoulder, palm facing down, bring the hand deliberately down across the body to in front of the right side of the body. Then, beginning with the right *B hand* near the right shoulder, palm facing left, bring the hand down across the body, ending in front of the left side of the body.

**had** *v.* See sign for HAVE.

**ha ha** *interj.* (A conventionalized exclamation of joy representing the sound of laughter or, sometimes, sarcastic laughter): *"Ha ha," the man laughed at the joke.*

- [Spell **h-a, h-a**] Beginning with the right *H hand* in front of the right shoulder, palm facing in and the thumb extended up, close the fingers with a double movement, forming an *A hand* each time.

**hail**[1] *n.* **1.** Precipitation in the form of small lumps of ice that form in and fall from cumulonimbus clouds: *Hail hit the roof.* **2.** A shower of hail: *The hail started at noon.* —*v.* **3.** To pour down hail: *It hailed all morning.*

- [Shapes and movement of hail] Beginning with the right *F hand* above the right shoulder and the left *F hand* in front of the left side of the body, both palms facing down, lower the right hand and raise the left hand in a repeated alternating movement.

**hail**[2] *v.* To greet with respect, as by bowing: *The crowd hailed the king.* Same sign used for: **bow, worship.**

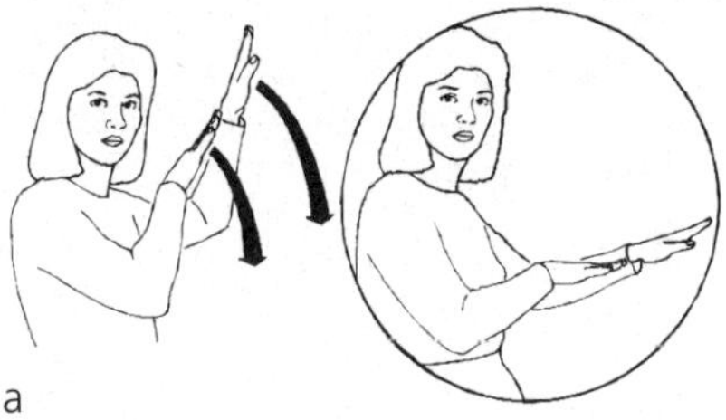

■ [Mime bowing before someone] Beginning with both *open hands* in front of the face, left hand somewhat higher than the right hand, both palms facing forward and fingers pointing up, move the hands downward with a double movement, ending with the palms facing down and the fingers pointing forward.

**hair** *n.* **1.** A threadlike filament growing from the skin: *I found another gray hair this morning.* **2.** A collection of such filaments on the human head: *He has brown hair.*

■ [Location of hair] Hold a strand of hair with the thumb and forefinger of the right *F hand,* palm facing left, and shake it with a repeated movement.

**hairbrush** *n.* See sign for BRUSH.

**haircut**[1] *n.* **1.** An act of shaping the hair by cutting it: *to get a haircut every six weeks.* **2.** The style in which the hair is cut: *an attractive haircut.*

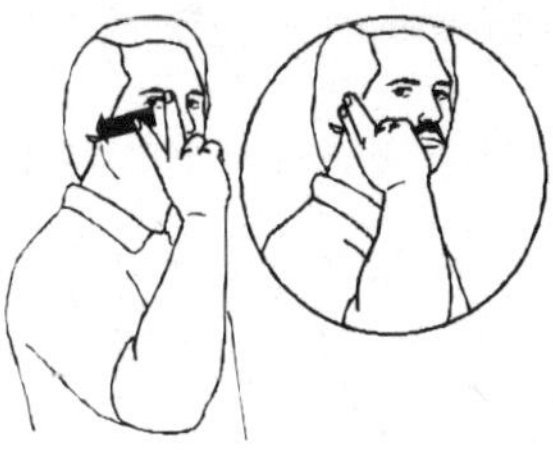

■ [Mime cutting one's hair] Move the right *V hand,* palm facing left and fingers pointing up, from near the right cheek back to near the right ear while opening and closing the index and middle fingers with a double movement.

**haircut**[2] *n.* See sign for CUT[1].

**hair spray** *n.* A fixative used on hair after styling: *The beautician sprayed hair spray on the woman's hair.*

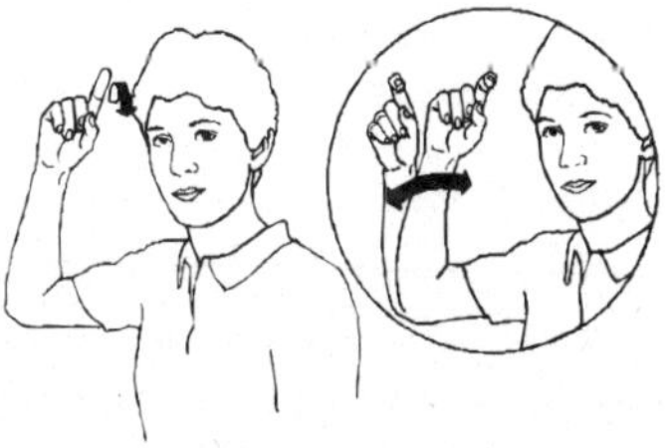

■ [**spray** formed near one's hair] Repeatedly bend the extended right index finger while moving the hand back and forth near the right side of the head.

**half** *adj.* See sign for ONE-HALF.

**half hour** *n.* Thirty minutes: *I waited a half hour.*

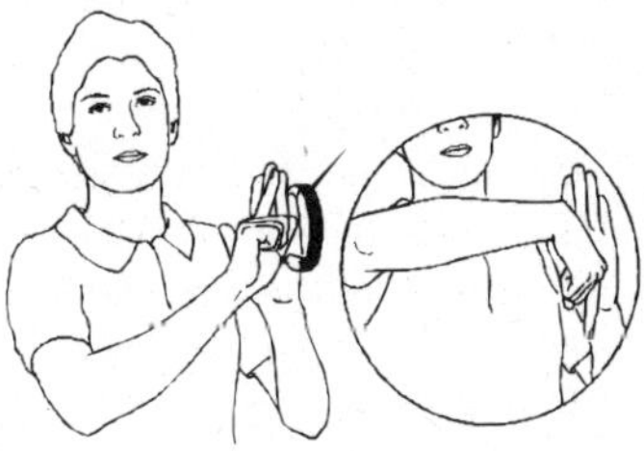

■ [Shows thirty-minute movement of minute hand on a clock] With the right index finger extended, palm facing forward, move the thumb side of the right hand in a half circle on the palm of the left *open hand,* palm facing right and fingers pointing upward, ending with the right index finger pointing straight down and palm facing in.

**halftime** *n.* A break in the middle of a football, basketball, or other game: *There was entertainment during halftime.* Same sign used for: **break, intermission.**

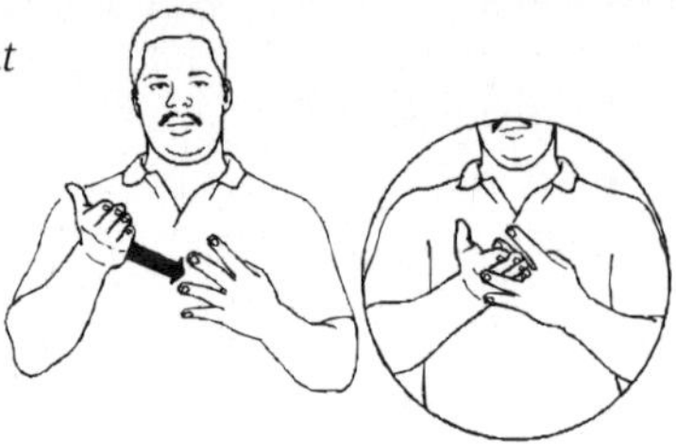

■ [Indicates a time in the middle] Insert the little-finger side of the right *open hand,* palm angled up and fingers pointing forward, between the middle finger and ring finger of the left *4 hand,* palm facing in.

**hall** *n.* A corridor in a building: *Her office is down the hall.* Alternate form: **hallway.** Same sign used for: **corridor.**

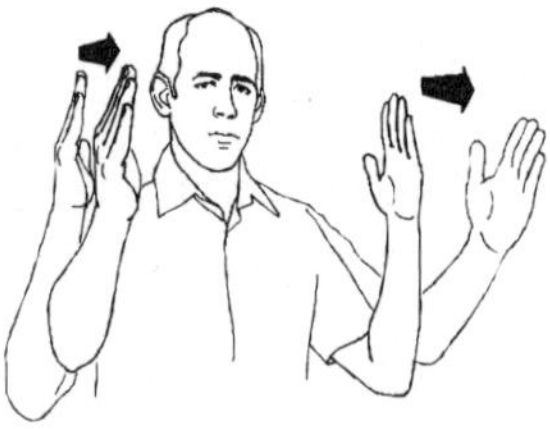

■ [Shape of a hallway] Move both *open hands,* palms facing each other and fingers pointing up, from in front of each shoulder straight forward.

**hallowed** *adj.* See sign for HOLY.

**Halloween** *n.* A holiday celebrated, especially by children, on the evening of October 31, the eve of All Saints' Day: *It's customary for children to wear costumes and play trick or treat on Halloween.* Same sign used for: **mask, masquerade.**

■ [Represents a Halloween mask] Move both *curved hands* from in front of each eye, palms facing in and fingers pointing up, around to each side of the head, ending with the palms angled forward.

**halt** *v.* See signs for HOLD[2], STOP[1].

**hamburger** *n.* **1.** A patty of ground beef: *to broil a hamburger.* **2.** A sandwich made with such a patty, usually served on a round bun: *to eat a hamburger with tomato and raw onion.*

■ [Mime making a hamburger patty] Clasp the right *curved hand,* palm facing down, across the upturned left *curved hand.* Then flip the hands over and repeat with the left hand on top.

**hammer** *n.* **1.** A hand tool with a solid head at one end of a handle, used especially for driving nails: *Hit the nail with a hammer.* —*v.* **2.** To drive (nails) with a hammer: *hammering nails into the roof.* **3.** To fasten or assemble using a hammer and nails: *hammered the roof into place.*

■ [Mime hitting something with a hammer] Move the right *A hand,* palm facing left, up and down with a repeated movement in front of the right side of the body.

**handicap** *n.* See sign for DISABILITY.

**handkerchief** *n.* See sign for TISSUE.

**handle** *v.* See signs for MANAGE, PIPE[2].

**hands** *pl. n.* The two end parts of the arms of humans and other primates: *to put gloves on my hands.*

■ [Location of one's hands] Beginning with the little-finger side of the right *B hand* at an angle on the thumb side of the left *B hand,* palms facing in opposite directions, bring the right hand down and under the left hand in order to exchange positions. Repeat the movement with the left hand.

**handshake** *n.* The act of grasping hands with another in friendship or greeting: *She has a firm handshake.* Same sign used for: **shake hands.**

■ [Mime shaking one's own hand] Grasp the left *open hand* with the right *curved hand,* both palms facing in, and shake the hands up and down with a double movement.

**hands-off** *adj. phrase.* See sign for NOT RESPONSIBLE.

**handsome**[1] *adj.* Having an attractive and imposing appearance; good looking: *He is a handsome man.*

■ [**face** + **clean**] Move the right extended index finger in a circle in front of the face, palm facing in. Then slide the palm of the right *open hand* from the heel to the fingers of the upturned left *open hand.*

**handsome**[2] *adj.* See sign for LOOKS.

**handy** *adj.* See sign for SKILL.

**hang** *v.* To suspend without support from below: *Hang your coat in the closet.*

■ [Represents placing hangers on a rod] With the index finger of the right *X hand,* palm facing left, over the left extended index finger, palm facing down, move both hands downward a short distance.

**Hanukkah** or **Chanukah** *n.* An eight-day Jewish festival, usually in December, commemorating the rededication of the Temple in Jerusalem in 165 B.C.: *to celebrate Hanukkah by lighting the candles in the menorah.*

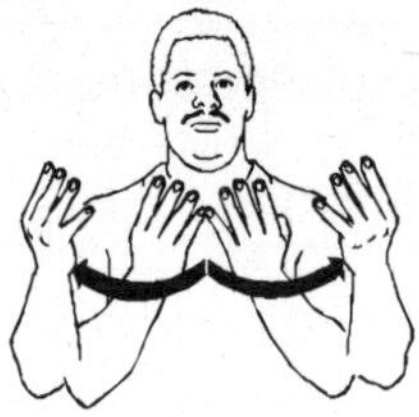

■ [Represents the shape of a Hanukkah menorah] Beginning with the little fingers of both *4 hands* touching in front of the chest, palms facing in and fingers pointing up, move the hands apart in an arc, ending with the hands in front of each shoulder.

**happen** *v.* To take place: *Let's find out what happened at the meeting.* Same sign used for: **accident, coincidence, event, incident, occur, occurrence.**

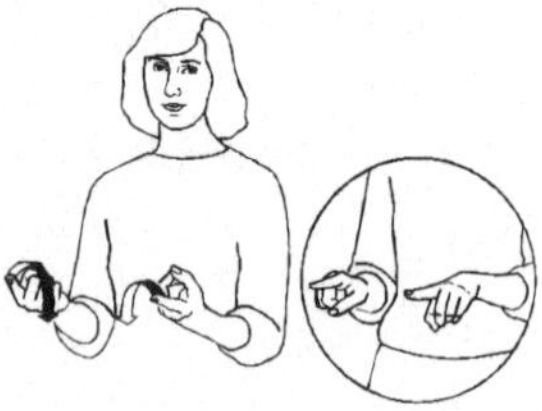

■ Beginning with both extended index fingers in front of the body, palms facing up and fingers pointing forward, flip the hands over toward each other, ending with the palms facing down.

**happy** *adj.* **1.** Enjoying a sense of well-being; delighted; pleased: *He always seems to be a happy person.* **2.** Characterized by pleasure or joy: *led a happy life.* Same sign used for: **cheer, cheerful, delighted, gay, glad, jolly, joy, merry.**

■ [Represents joy rising in the body] Brush the fingers of the right *open hand,* palm facing in and fingers pointing left, upward in a repeated circular movement on the chest.

**harassment** *n.* See sign for DANGER.

**hard**[1] *adj.* Not easily penetrated: *a hard rock.* Same sign used for: **solid.**

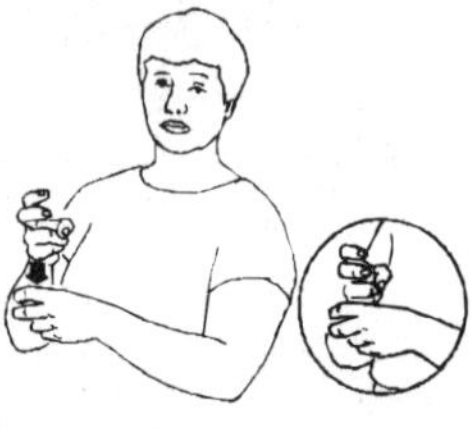

■ [Indicates a hard surface] Strike the little-finger side of the right *bent V hand* sharply against the index-finger side of the left *bent V hand,* palms facing in opposite directions.

**hard**[2] *adj.* See sign for DIFFICULT.

**hardly** *adv.* See sign for ANYWAY.

**hardware** *n.* See sign for EQUIPMENT.

**hare** *n.* See sign for RABBIT.

**harm** *v.* See signs for DANGER, HURT[1].

**harsh** *adj.* See sign for MEAN[1].

**harvest** *n.* **1.** The reaping of grain or other food crops: *a fall harvest.* —*v.* **2.** To gather grain or other food crops: *to harvest the wheat.* Same sign used for: **chop, cut down.**

■ [Represents cutting down a plant close to the ground] Move the fingers of the right *open hand,* palm facing up and fingers pointing forward, with a double movement under the elbow of the bent left arm, hand pointing up.

**has** *v.* See sign for HAVE.

**hassle** *v.* See sign for HURRY.

**haste** *n.* See sign for HURRY.

**hat** *n.* A shaped head covering, as one with a crown and brim: *to wear a hat in the winter.*

■ [Location of a hat on one's head] Pat the top of the head with the fingers of the right *open hand,* palm facing down, with a double movement.

**hate** *v.* To feel extreme dislike or aversion for: *I've always hated peas.* Same sign used for: **despise, detest.**

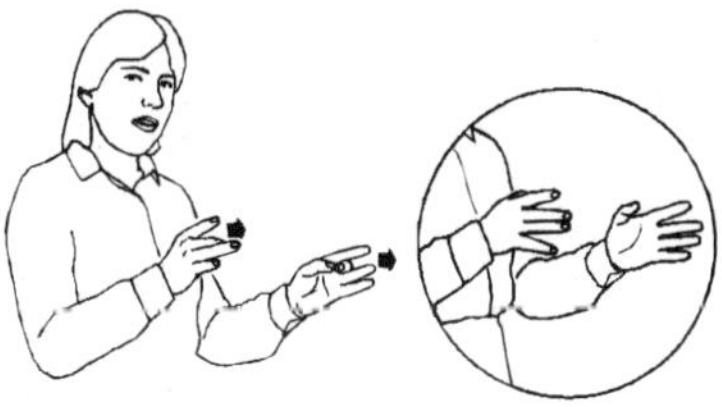

■ [The fingers flick away something distasteful] Beginning with both *8 hands* in front of the chest, palms facing each other, flick the middle fingers forward, changing into *5 hands.*

**haul**[1] *v.* **1.** To pull or drag (something heavy): *Haul that firewood over here.* **2.** To transport; carry: *The trucks haul coal across several states.* Same sign used for: **pull, tow.**

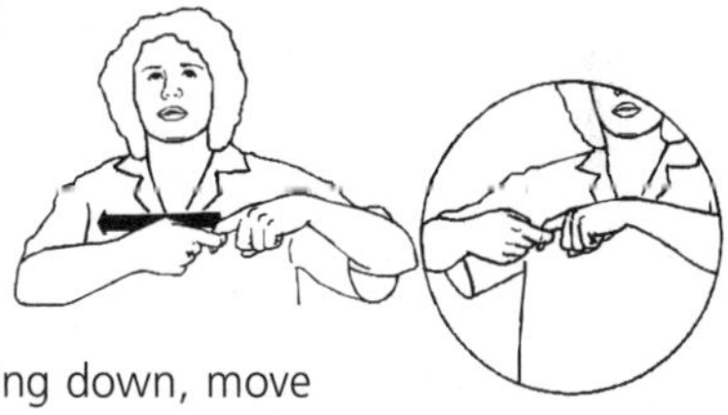

■ [Shows action of pulling another with a hitch] With the index fingers of both *X hands* around each other, right palm facing in and left palm facing down, move both hands from left to right in front of the chest.

**haul**[2] *v.* See sign for DRAG.

**haunt** *v.* See sign for MONSTER. Related form: **haunted** *adj.*

**have** *v.* To possess; own: *always wanted to have a dog.* Same sign used for: **had, has, possess.**

■ [Brings something toward oneself] Bring the fingertips of both *bent hands,* palms facing in, back to touch each side of the chest.

**have to** *auxiliary.* See sign for MUST.

**hawk** *n.* A small- to medium-size bird of prey with a short, hooked beak and curved talons: *a hawk hovering over the frightened squirrel.*

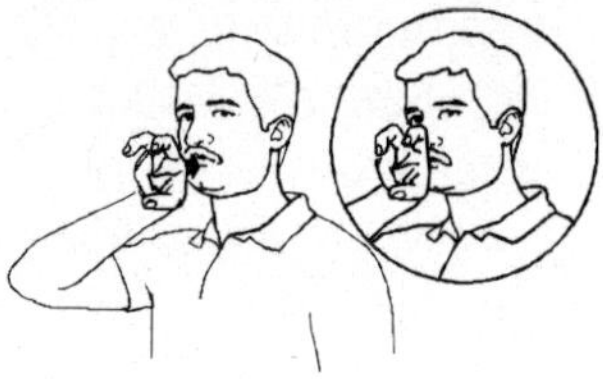

■ [Shows a hawk's claws] Beginning with the back of the right *bent V hand* in front of the mouth, palm facing forward and fingers bent, bring the hand back against the mouth with a double movement while constricting the fingers each time.

**hazard** *n.* See sign for DANGER.

**haze** *v.* See sign for TORTURE.

**hazy** *adj.* See sign for VAGUE.

**he** *pron.* The male person or animal specified, under discussion, or last mentioned: *He is the man who approached me.* Same sign used for: **her, him, it, she.**

■ [Directional sign toward another] Point the extended right index finger, palm facing down, outward to the right or in the direction of the referent.

**head**[1] *n.* The upper part of the body, containing the skull, the brain, and the face: *I hit my head on a low branch of the tree.*

■ [Location of the head] Touch the fingertips of the right *bent hand,* palm facing down, first to the right side of the forehead and then to the right side of the chin.

**head**[2] *v.* See sign for LEAD.

**headache**[1] *n.* A pain located in the head, as at the temples: *I have a headache from all that noise.*

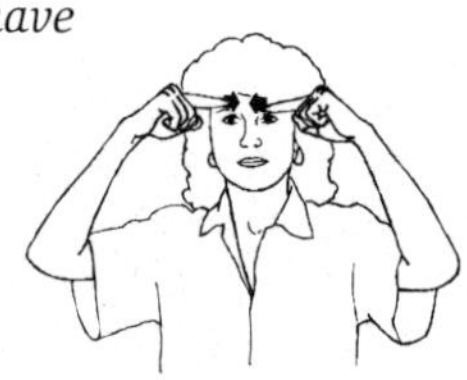

■ [**hurt**[1] formed near the forehead] With both extended index fingers pointing toward each other in front of the forehead, palms facing down, jab them toward each other with a short double movement.

**headache**[2] *n.* (alternate sign) Same sign used for: **migraine.**

■ [Location of a headache] Beginning with the thumb side of the right *modified C hand* against the forehead, bring the hand forward a short distance.

**headlight** *n.* A light on the front of a vehicle: *The approaching car's headlights were far too bright.*

- [Shows headlight beams] Beginning with both *flattened O hands* in front of the chest, palms facing down and fingers pointing forward, open the hands into *5 hands.*

**heal** *v.* See sign for WELL.

**healthy** *adj.* See sign for WELL.

**heap** *n.* See sign for AMOUNT.

**hear** *v.* To perceive through the ear: *hear a sound.* Related form: **hearing** *n.* Same sign used for: **auditory, sound.**

- [Location of the organ of hearing] Bring the extended right index finger to the right ear.

**hearing** *adj.* Having the ability to hear: *She is a hearing person who knows sign language.* Same sign used for: **public.**

- [Indicates a person who talks] Move the extended right index finger, pointing left, in a small double circular movement upward and forward in front of the lips.

**hearing aid** *n. phrase.* An electronic device used to amplify sound: *Wearing a hearing aid is helpful with some kinds of hearing loss.*

- [Shape of a hearing aid showing the location behind the ear where it is worn] Tap the index-finger side of the *modified C hand,* palm facing forward, against the head near the right ear.

**heart** *n.* The muscular organ of the body that acts as a pump to circulate the blood: *Luckily, the premature baby was born with a strong heart.*

- [Location and action of a heartbeat] Tap the bent middle finger of the right *5 hand,* palm facing in, with a repeated movement on the left side of the chest.

**heart attack** *n. phrase.* An acute episode of heart disease, in which heart function is severely disrupted: *We called an ambulance for the man who was having a heart attack.* Same sign used for: **coronary.**

- [**heart** + **beat**[3]] Beginning with the bent middle finger of the right *5 hand* on the left side of the chest, palm facing in, bring the back of the right hand forward to touch the palm of the left *open hand,* palm facing in and fingers pointing right.

**heat**[1] *n.* **1.** The condition or quality of being hot: *There is too much heat in the house.* —*v.* **2.** To make or become warm or hot (sometimes followed by *up*): *Heat some water until it boils. The oven won't heat up.*

■ [Movement of a flame heating something on the stove] Move the right *curved 5 hand,* palm facing up, in a double circular movement under the upturned left *open hand.*

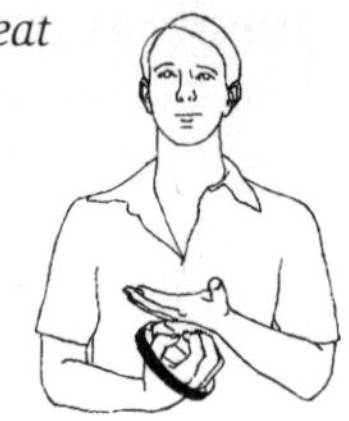

**heat**[2] *adj.* See sign for HOT.

**heaven** *n.* The dwelling place of God and the angels, conventionally thought to be in the sky: *Grandpa is in heaven now.*

■ [Location of heaven] Beginning with both *open hands* in front of each shoulder, palms facing each other and fingers angled up, bring the hands upward toward each other, passing the right hand forward under the left *open hand,* both palms facing down, as the hands meet above the head.

**heavy** *adj.* Having great weight: *a box of books too heavy for me to lift.*

■ [The hands seem to be weighted down with something heavy] Beginning with both *curved 5 hands* in front of each side of the chest, palms facing up, move the hands downward a short distance.

**hectic** *adj.* Characterized by excitement, confusion, and frantic activity: *another hectic day at work.*

■ [Natural gesture used when someone describes rushing around] Beginning with both *5 hands* in front of each side of the chest, palms facing in and fingers pointing toward each other, twist the wrists forward with a repeated movement.

**height**[1] *n.* The distance between the lowest and highest points of an upright person: *The child has grown to a height of four feet.*

■ [Indicates the top of oneself] Tap the extended right index finger, palm facing up, on the top of the head with a double movement.

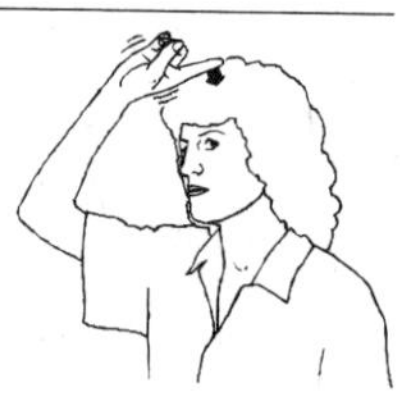

**height**[2] *n.* See sign for TALL[2].

**helicopter** *n.* An aircraft supported in the air by propellers revolving on a vertical axis: *to hover in the air in a helicopter.*

■ [Represents a helicopter's propeller] With extended thumb of the left *10 hand,* palm facing right, pointing up into the palm of the right *5 hand,* palm facing down, wiggle the right fingers while moving both hands forward a short distance.

**hell** *n.* The abode of evil and condemned souls after death: *The wicked are doomed to go to hell.*

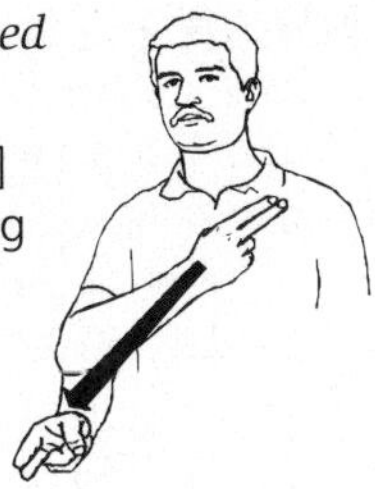

■ [Initialized sign moving downward to the traditional location of hell] Move the right *H hand* from in front of the left shoulder, palm facing in and fingers angled up, downward with a deliberate movement to the right, ending with the hand in front of the right side of the body, fingers pointing forward and palm facing left.

**hello** *interj.* **1.** (Used to express a greeting): *Hello, there. How are you?* —*n.* **2.** An act or instance of saying "hello": *Say your "hellos" to your friends and then let's go.* Same sign used for: **greeting, hi.**

■ [Natural gesture for a salute to greet someone] Beginning with the fingertips of the right *B hand* near the right side of the forehead, palm angled forward, bring the hand forward with a deliberate movement.

**helmet** *n.* A rigid covering to protect the head: *Football players now wear helmets made of a hard plastic.*

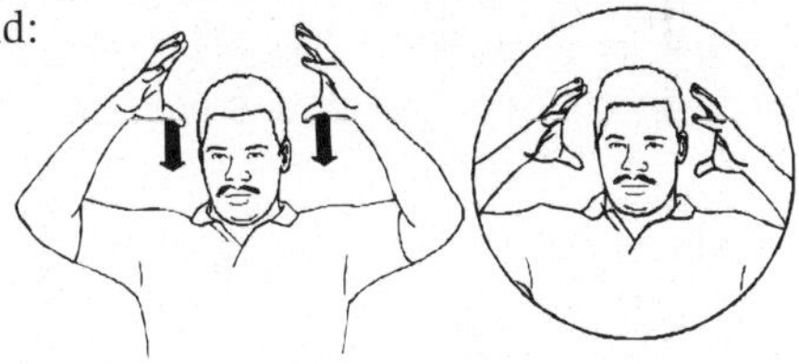

■ [Shape and location of a helmet on the head] Beginning with both *curved 5 hands* near each other at the top of the head, palms facing each other and fingers angled up, move the hands downward along the shape of the head, stopping abruptly near each side of the head.

**help** *v.* **1.** To provide needed effort, materials, etc.; give assistance: *Will you help us wash the dishes?* —*n.* **2.** The act of giving assistance: *We appreciate your help in organizing the class trip.* Same sign used for: **aid, assist.**

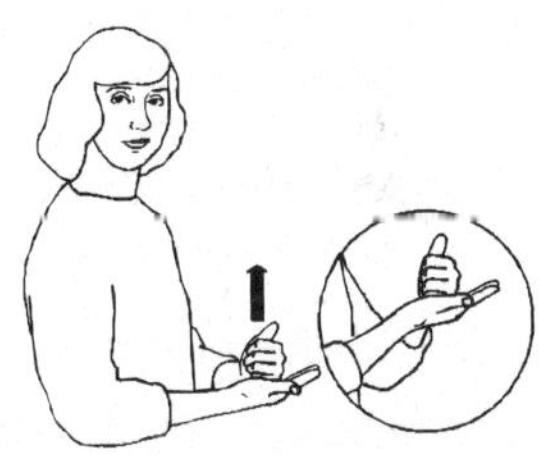

■ [The lower hand seems to give assistance to the other hand] With the little-finger side of the left *A hand* in the upturned right *open hand,* move both hands upward in front of the chest.

**hen** *n.* See sign for CHICKEN.

**henpeck** *v.* See sign for PICK ON.

**her** or **hers** *pron.* See signs for HE, HIS.

**here** *adv.* **1.** In or at this place: *The meeting will take place here.* **2.** To or toward this place: *Come here.* —*n.* **3.** This place: *From here, you go left one mile.* Same sign used for: **present.**

■ [Indicates a location near oneself] Beginning with both *curved hands* in front of each side of the body, palms facing up, move the hands toward each other in repeated flat circles.

**hermit** *n.* A person who lives alone in seclusion, especially in a solitary, isolated place: *She lives like a hermit, never seeing anyone or going out.* Same sign used for: **isolated.**

■ Beginning with both *I hands* in front of the face, palms facing in, bring the little fingers together with a double movement.

**herself** *pron.* See signs for HIMSELF, ITSELF.

**hesitate** *v.* To wait before acting, as from fear or indecision: *He hesitated to answer the question.*

■ [Natural gesture used to balk at something] With both *open hands* in front of each side of the chest, palms facing forward and fingers pointing up, pull the head and body backward with a short repeated movement.

**hi**[1] *interj.* (Used as an informal greeting): *Hi, everyone!*

■ [Natural gesture for waving in greeting] Move the right *open hand,* palm facing forward and fingers pointing up, from in front of the chest to the right in a smooth arc.

**hi**[2] *interj.* See sign for HELLO.

**hiccup** *n.* **1.** An involuntary, spasmodic inhalation, producing a short, sharp sound: *Gulping a drink gives me the hiccups.* —*v.* **2.** To have the hiccups: *Don't make me laugh or I'll hiccup.*

■ [Shows action of hiccupping] Beginning with the bent index finger of the right hand tucked under the right thumb, palm facing in, flick the index finger upward with a double movement in front of the chest.

**hide**[1] *v.* To put or get out of view: *Hide the money in the desk. You'd better hide from them.* Same sign used for: **conceal, mystery.**

■ [**secret** + a gesture putting something under the other hand as if to hide it] Move the thumb of the right *A hand,* palm facing left, from near the mouth downward in an arc to under the left *curved hand* held in front of the chest, palm facing down.

**hide**[2] *v.* See sign for COVER-UP.

**high** *adj., adv.* **1.** Having a great height; tall: *a high hill.* **2.** Having a specified height: *The table is three feet high.* **3.** Raised to an elevated position: *The shelf is too high for me to reach.* —*adv.* **4.** To or at an elevated place: *Hang the hook high enough to be out of the way.* Same sign used for: **altitude.**

■ [Initialized sign showing a location at a higher elevation] Move the right *H hand,* palm facing left and fingers pointing forward, from in front of the right side of the chest upward to near the right side of the head.

**higher** *adj.* See sign for ADVANCED.

**high school** *n. phrase.* A secondary school, usually consisting of grades 9 or 10 through 12: *attends high school in another neighborhood.*

■ [Abbreviation **h-s**] Form the fingerspelled letters H and S in front of the right side of the chest, palm facing in.

**highway** *n.* A main public road, especially one between towns or cities: *Follow the highway to the next turnoff.* Same sign used for: **freeway.**

■ [Initialized sign representing two streams of traffic going in opposite directions] Beginning with both *H hands* held in front of each side of the chest, palms facing down and fingers pointing toward each other, move the hands past each other toward the opposite sides of the chest with a repeated movement.

**hill** *n.* A rounded elevation of earth, smaller than a mountain: *to climb the hill on foot.*

■ [Shows shape of a hillside] Beginning with both *open hands* in front of each side of the waist, palms angled forward and fingers angled up, move the hands forward and upward with a large wavy movement.

**him** *pron.* See sign for HE.

**himself** *pron.* A reflexive form of HIM, used to refer back to the male last mentioned: *He will be able to do it himself.* See also sign for ITSELF. Same sign used for: **herself, itself.**

■ [Directional sign toward the person you are referring to] Push the extended thumb of the right *10 hand,* palm facing left, forward with a short double movement in front of the right side of the body.

**hinder** *v.* See sign for PREVENT.

**hindsight** *n.* The perception of the significance of an event only after it has occurred: *Their insincerity became clear in hindsight.* Same sign used for: **look back, recollect, recollection, retrospect.**

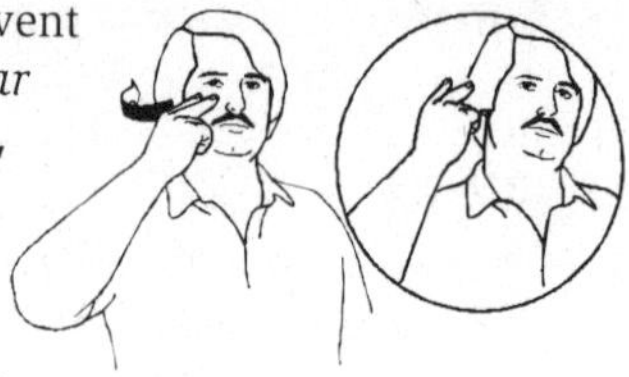

- [Represents the eyes looking back into the past] Beginning with the fingertips of the right *V hand* pointing toward the right eye, palm facing down, move the hand around to the right side of the head, ending with the fingers pointing back.

**hinge** *n.* The joint on which a door or gate moves back and forth: *The gate swung open on its hinges.*

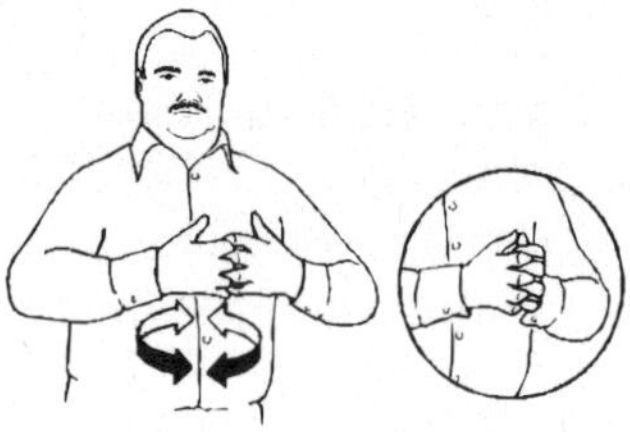

- [Shows action of a door opening on hinges] Beginning with the fingers of both *curved 5 hands* meshed together in front of the chest, palms facing in, bend the fingers forward and back with a double movement by twisting the wrists.

**hire** *v.* See sign for INVITE.

**his** *pron.* The possessive adjective form of HE: *His name is Bob.* Same sign used for: **her, hers, its.**

- [Directional sign toward the person referred to] Push the right *open hand,* palm facing forward, at an angle forward in front of the right side of the body.

**historic** *adj.* See sign for LONG AGO.

**history** *n.* **1.** The branch of knowledge dealing with significant past events: *to study history in college.* **2.** An account or record of these events regarding a particular people, period, etc.: *I am reading a history of England.* Related form: **historical** *adj.*

- [Initialized sign] Move the right *H hand,* palm facing left, downward with a double movement in front of the right side of the body.

**hit**[1] *v.* To strike with force: *He hit the wall with his fist.* Same sign used for: **attack, impact, strike.**

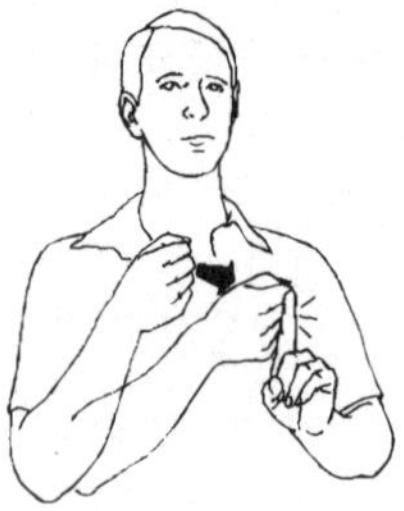

- [Demonstrates action of hitting] Strike the knuckles of the right *A hand,* palm facing in, against the extended left index finger held up in front of the chest, palm facing right.

**hit**[2] *v.* See signs for BEAT[3], BEAT UP, PUNCH.

**hitchhike** *v.* To travel by getting rides from passing vehicles, especially by standing at the side of a road and gesturing with the thumb: *He hitchhiked across the nation.* Related form: **hitch** *v.*

■ [Natural gesture for hitchhiking] Move the thumb of the right *10 hand,* palm facing in, from the front of the right shoulder to the right with a double movement.

**hockey** *n.* A game played on a field or on ice by two teams attempting to score goals at opposite ends of the playing area: *plays ice hockey on the school team.*

■ Brush the index finger of the right *X hand* against the upturned palm of the left *open hand* as the right hand moves in a double circular movement.

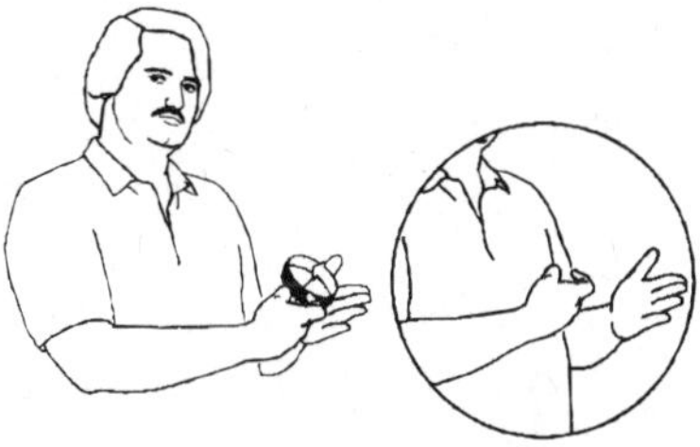

**hoe** *n.* See sign for RAKE.

**hold**[1] *v.* **1.** To have or keep in one's hand: *Please hold the package while I tie my shoe.* **2.** To have possession or use of: *to hold a job.* Same sign used for: **grip.**

■ [The hands seem to hold something securely] Beginning with the little-finger side of the right *C hand* on the index-finger side of the left *C hand,* both palms facing in, move the hands in toward the chest while closing the fingers of both hands into *S hands.*

**hold**[2] *v.* or **hold on** *v. phrase.* To restrain or delay (oneself): *Hold on until later.* Same sign used for: **halt, pause, stall, suspend.**

■ [One hand seems to suspend the other] With the index fingers of both *X hands* hooked together, palms facing down, pull both hands upward.

**hold up** *v. phrase.* See sign for ROB.

**hole** *n.* An opening in or through something: *There is a hole in the road. I have a hole in my sock.*

■ [Shape of a hole] Move the extended right index finger, palm facing back and fingers pointing down, in a large circle around the index-finger side of the left *C hand,* palm facing down.

**holiday**[1] *n.* **1.** A day officially honoring a well-known person or commemorating an important event: *to celebrate the holiday with fireworks.* **2.** A day or sequence of days of exemption from work: *I spent the holiday shopping.*

■ [Gesture often used when one is carefree] Tap the thumbs of both *5 hands* near each armpit, palms facing each other and fingers pointing forward, with a double movement.

**holiday**[2] *n.* See sign for CELEBRATE.

**holler** *v.* See sign for CALL[2].

**holy** *adj.* **1.** Declared by religious authority to be sacred: *a holy place.* **2.** Spiritually pure: *a holy love of God.* Related form: **holiness** *n.* Same sign used for: **hallowed.**

■ [Initialized sign similar to sign for **clean**] Move the right *H hand* in a circular movement over the upturned left *open hand.* Then slide the little-finger side of the right *H hand* from the base to the fingertips of the left hand.

**home** *n.* **1.** The house, apartment, or other shelter that is the principal residence of a person, family, or household: *Their home is in Montana.* —*adv.* **2.** To, toward, or at home: *It's past time for you to go home.*

■ [A modification of the signs **eat** and **sleep** indicating that a home is a place where you eat and sleep] Touch the fingertips of the right *flattened O hand* first to the right side of the chin, palm facing down, and then to the right cheek.

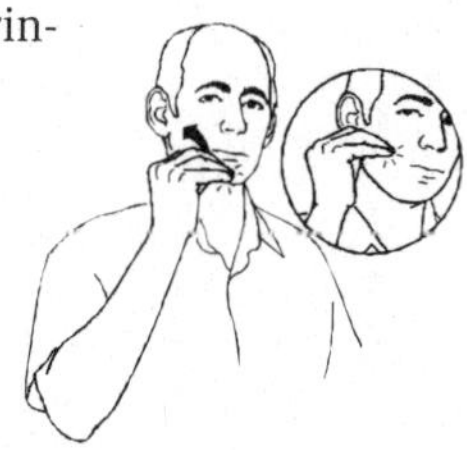

**homework** *n.* Work, especially school lessons, to be done at home: *I have a lot of math homework due tomorrow.*

■ [**home** + **work**] Touch the fingertips of the right *flattened O hand* to the right cheek, palm facing down. Then move the right hand down while changing into an *S hand* and tap the base of the right *S hand* on the back of the left *S hand* held in front of the chest, palm facing down.

**homosexual** *adj., n.* See sign for GAY.

**honest** *adj.* Tending not to lie or cheat; truthful: *an honest appraisal of their work.* Related forms: **honestly** *adv.*, **honesty** *n.* Same sign used for: **frank, frankly, sure, truth, truthful.**

■ [Initialized sign similar to sign for **clean**] Slide the extended fingers of the right *H hand,* palm facing left, forward from the heel to the fingers of the upturned left *open hand.*

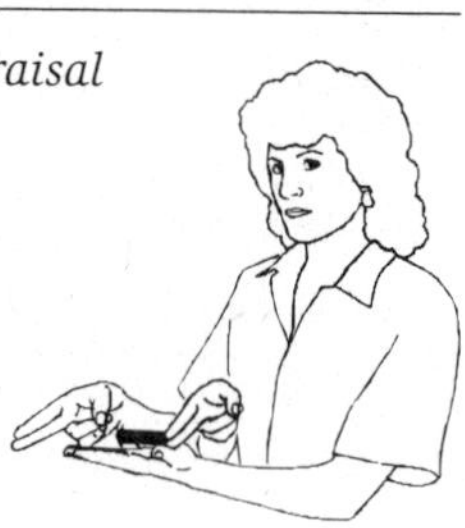

**honey** *n.* A thick, sweet liquid prepared by bees from floral nectar: *I like to put honey in my tea.*

■ [Initialized sign similar to sign for **sweet**] Beginning with the fingers of the right *H hand* near the right side of the mouth, palm facing back and fingers pointing left, move the fingers to the right with a double movement, bending the fingers back into the palm to change into an *A hand* each time.

**honeymoon** *n.* A holiday spent by a newly married couple: *They plan to go to Bermuda on their honeymoon.*

■ Touch the bent middle finger of the right *5 hand,* palm facing in, first to the left side of the chin and then to the right side of the chin.

**honor** *n.* **1.** A source of credit or distinction: *It is an honor to know you.* **2.** Credit, respect, or recognition given, as for special worth or merit: *gave him the honor of speaking at the dinner.* —*v.* **3.** To show respect: *Honor your parents.* Related form: **honorary** *adj.*

■ [Initialized sign similar to sign for **respect**] Beginning with both *H hands* in front of the face, right hand higher than the left hand and palms facing in opposite directions, bring both hands downward and forward in a slight arc.

**hood** *n.* See sign for PONCHO.

**hooked** *adj.* See sign for ADDICTED.

**hook up** *v. phrase.* See sign for BELONG[1].

**hop** *v.* To spring on one foot: *hop around the room.*

■ [Shows action of hopping] Beginning with the knuckles of the right *bent V hand,* palm facing back, on the heel of the left *open hand* held in front of the chest, palm facing up, raise the right hand while straightening the fingers into a *V hand,* and then bend the fingers again to touch down on the left palm. Repeat, touching farther toward the left fingers each time.

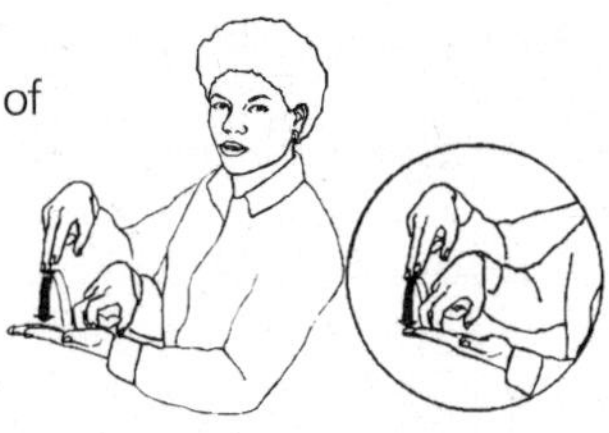

**hope** *v.* **1.** To wish or wish for and expect: *We hope for rain after the dry summer.* —*n.* **2.** A feeling that what one desires might happen: *My hope is to go to college.* Same sign used for: **anticipate, anticipation, expect, expectation.**

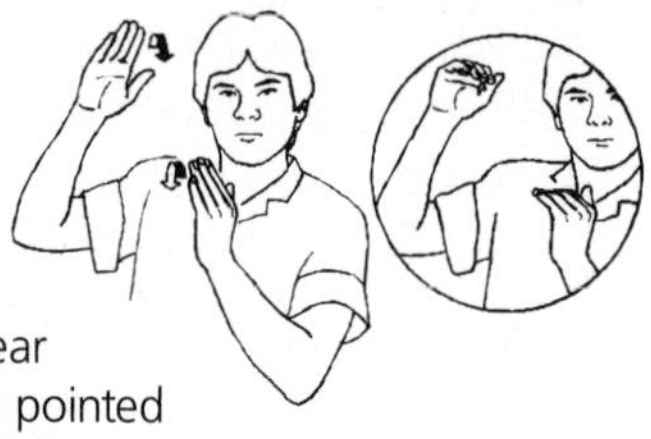

■ [The hands seem to compare a thought with the anticipated future] Beginning with the right *open hand* near the right side of the head, palm angled left and fingers pointed up, and the left *open hand* in front of the chest, palm facing right and fingers pointing up, bend the fingers toward each other with a double movement.

**horde** *n.* A multitude; crowd: *A horde of people attended the concert.* See also sign for AUDIENCE. Same sign used for: **crowd, mass.**

■ [Indicates large crowds of people] Move both *curved 5 hands,* palms facing down, from in front of each side of the upper chest forward with a simultaneous movement.

**horn** *n.* A musical instrument sounded by blowing into the smaller end; wind instrument: *Sound the horn before the hunt.*

■ [Mime holding a horn and blowing into it] Hold the left *S hand* in front of the mouth, palm facing right, and the right *C hand* in front of the face, palm facing left.

**horns**[1] *pl. n.* A pair of hard bony growths on the head of many hoofed animals: *The steer's horns got caught in the bushes.*

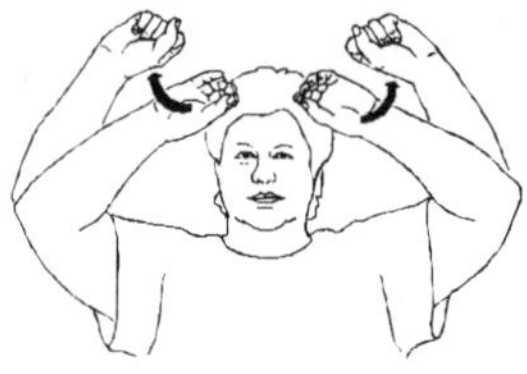

■ [Shape and location of horns on the head] Beginning with the thumb side of both *O hands* on each side of the head, palms facing forward, bring the hands upward and outward in small arcs while closing into *S hands.*

**horns**[2] *pl. n.* See sign for PRESIDENT.

**horrible** *adj.* See sign for AWFUL.

**horse** *n.* A large, four-legged mammal with solid hooves, bred for riding, pulling loads, etc.: *learned to ride a horse as a child.*

■ [Represents a horse's ears] With the extended thumb of the right *U hand* against the right side of the forehead, palm facing forward, bend the fingers of the *U hand* up and down with a double movement.

**hose**[1] *n.* A narrow tube for conveying water from a faucet to some desired point: *watering the lawn with the large garden hose.*

■ [**water** + mime holding a hose to water something] Tap the index-finger side of the right *W hand,* palm facing left, against the chin with a double movement. Then, with the little-finger side of the right *modified X hand* touching the index-finger side of the left *S hand,* palms facing in opposite directions, swing the hands from side to side with a double movement in front of the body.

**hose**[2] *n.* See signs for PANTYHOSE, STOCKING.

**hospital** *n.* An institution, staffed with doctors and nurses, in which sick and injured people are treated and cared for: *had to go to the hospital for major surgery.* Same sign used for: **infirmary.**

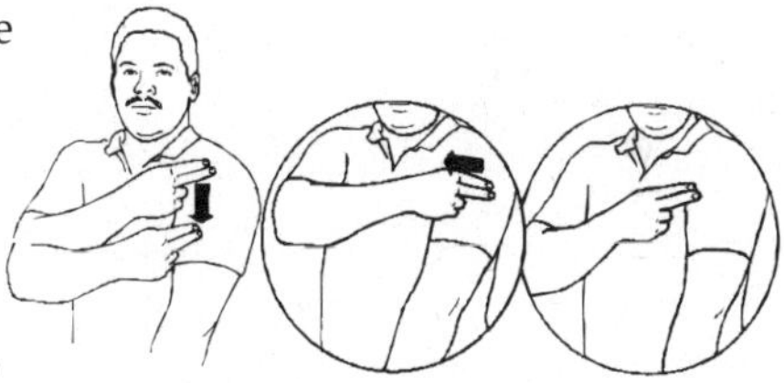

■ [Initialized sign following the shape of a cross, symbolic of the American Red Cross, a health-care organization] Bring the fingertips of the right *H hand,* palm facing right, first downward a short distance on the upper left arm and then across from back to front.

**host** *v.* See signs for LEAD, SERVE.

**hostage** *n.* A person held captive, as by an enemy, until certain conditions are met: *held as a hostage by terrorists demanding ransom.*

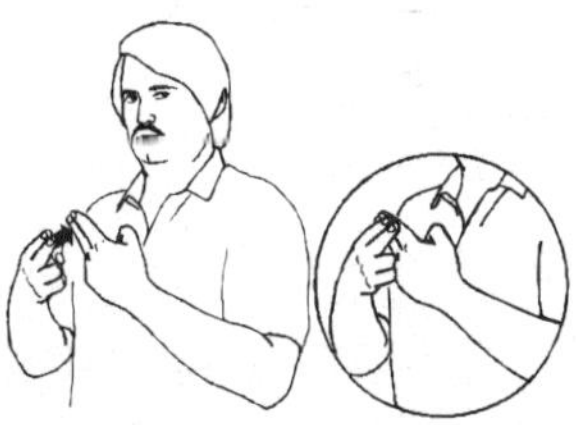

■ [Initialized sign similar to sign for **jail**] Beginning with both *H hands* in front of the chest, palms facing in and fingers pointing upward at angles in opposite directions, bring the right *H* fingers in against the left fingers.

**hot** *adj.* Having or giving off heat; having a high temperature: *a hot fire.* Same sign used for: **heat.**

■ [Hand seems to take something hot from the mouth and throw it away] Beginning with the right *curved 5 hand* in front of the mouth, palm facing in, twist the wrist forward with a deliberate movement while moving the hand downward a short distance.

**hot dog** *n.* **1.** A cooked and smoked sausage; frankfurter; wiener: *to grill hot dogs.* **2.** A sandwich made with a hot dog, usually on a long bun: *to eat a hot dog with mustard and relish.*

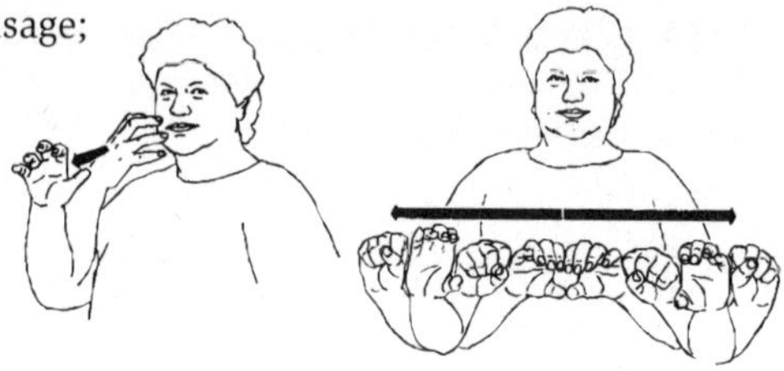

■ [**hot** + **sausage**] Beginning with the right *curved 5 hand* in front of the mouth, palm facing in, twist the wrist forward with a deliberate movement while moving the hand downward a short distance. Then, beginning with the index-finger sides of both *C hands* touching in front of the body, palms facing forward, bring the hands outward to each side while squeezing them open and closed from *C* to *S hands* repeatedly as the hands move.

**hotel** *n.* A large commercial building with rooms or suites for travelers, frequently with restaurants, stores, and other service facilities: *We plan to stay for a week in a hotel in the city.*

■ [Initialized sign] Place the fingers of the right *H hand,* palm facing in and fingers pointing left, on the back of the extended left index finger, palm facing in and index finger pointing up in front of the chest.

**hour** *n.* A period of time consisting of 60 minutes: *It will take me one hour to finish.* Same sign used for: **one hour.**

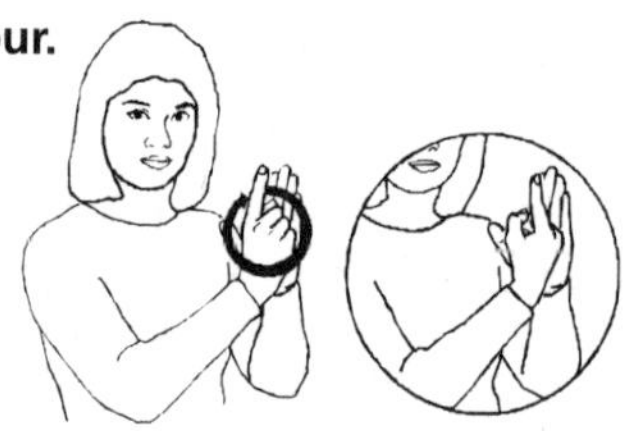

■ [Shows minute hand moving 60 minutes around a clock] With the right index finger extended, palm facing left, move the palm side of the right hand in a circle on the palm of the left *open hand,* palm facing right, while twisting the wrist, ending with the right palm facing in.

**hourly** *adj.* Same sign as for HOUR but made with a double movement.

**house** *n.* A building, typically for one or two families, in which people live: *They want to own a house in the suburbs.*

■ [Shape of house's roof and walls] Beginning with the fingertips of both *open hands* touching in front of the neck, palms angled toward each other, bring the hands at an downward angle outward to in front of each shoulder and then straight down, ending with the fingers pointing up and the palms facing each other.

**how** *adv.* **1.** By what means: *How did this happen?* **2.** To what degree or extent: *How tired are you?* **3.** In what condition: *How are you?* **4.** For what reason: *How can you say that?* —*conj.* **5.** The way in which: *I can't figure out how to do it.* **6.** About the way or condition in which: *Think how the project started!*

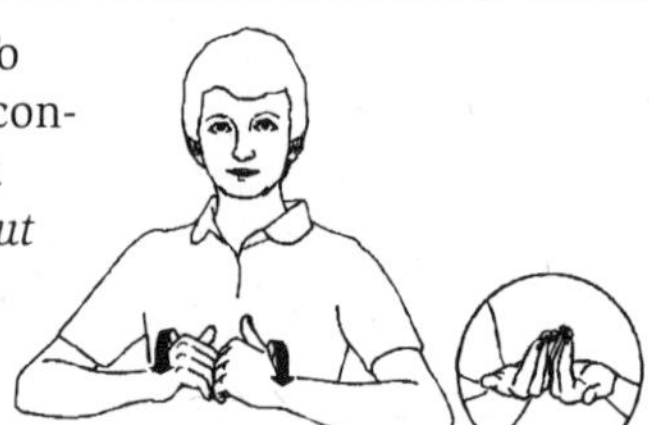

■ [Similar to gesture used with a shrug to indicate not knowing something] Beginning with the knuckles of both *curved hands* touching in front of the chest, palms facing down, twist the hands upward and forward, ending with the fingers together pointing up and the palms facing up.

**however** *adv.* See signs for ANYWAY, BUT.

**how many** See sign for HOW MUCH.

**how much** (Used to request information about the extent of something): *How much time will it take to finish?* Same sign used for: **how many.**

■ [An abbreviated form] Beginning with the right *S hand* in front of the right side of the chest, palm facing up, flick the fingers open quickly into a *5 hand.*

**hug** *v.* To put the arms around and hold close, especially as an expression of affection: *hugging the baby.* Same sign used for: **affection, affectionate, embrace.**

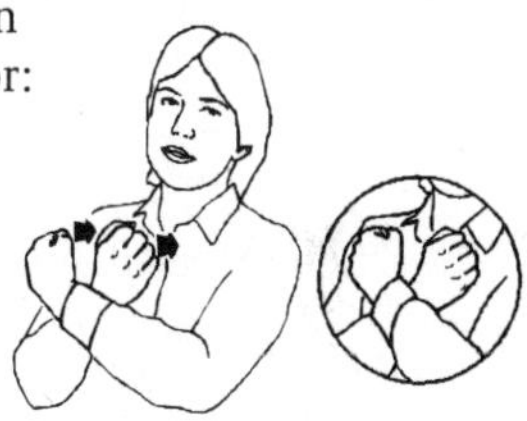

■ [Mime hugging someone] With the arms of both *S hands* crossed at the wrists, palms facing in, pull the arms back against the chest with a double movement.

**huge** *adj.* See sign for LARGE.

**hulk** *n.* A large, muscular person: *The boxer is a real hulk.* Same sign used for: **husky.**

■ [Shows shape of a hulk's shoulders] Beginning with both *modified C hands* near each side of the neck, move the hands forward from each shoulder, ending with the palms facing in.

**hum** *v.* **1.** To make a continuous droning sound: *The fan in my computer keeps humming.* **2.** To sing without words through closed lips: *The boy hummed a song.* —*n.* **3.** The sound of humming: *I heard the hum of the bees.*

■ [Initialized sign using **m** indicating the sound that is made when humming] Beginning with the index-finger side of the right *M hand* near the right side of the face, palm facing left, bring the hand forward with a wavy movement.

**humble** *adj.* Not proud; modest: *a humble man without any pretensions.* Related form: **humility** *n.* Same sign used for: **meek, modest, modesty.**

■ [Shows moving oneself under another when humbled] Bring the right *B hand,* palm facing left and fingers pointing up, from in front of the mouth downward and forward under the left *open hand* held in front of the chest, palm facing down.

**humid**[1] *adj.* Filled with moisture; containing damp air: *a humid climate.*

■ [**hot + the hands seem to be feeling something wet**] Beginning with the right *curved 5 hand* in front of the mouth, palm facing in, twist the wrist forward with a deliberate movement. Then, beginning with the fingers of both *5 hands* near the chin, palms facing in, move the hands downward and forward slightly, changing into *flattened O hands* in front of each shoulder and rubbing the thumbs and fingers together.

**humid**[2] *adj.* See sign for WET.

**humorous**[1] *adj.* Characterized by humor; funny: *a humorous story.* Same sign used for: **comical.**

■ [Similar to sign for **silly** except more exaggerated and formed with both hands] With the thumb of the right *Y hand* near the nose and the left *Y hand* somewhat lower and forward, palms facing each other, move both hands downward with repeated circular movements.

**humorous**[2] *n.* See sign for FUNNY.

**hundred** *n.* A cardinal number equal to ten times ten: *I have a hundred pages of the manuscript finished.*

■ [Abbreviation **c** representing the Roman numeral for **hundred**] Move the right *C hand,* palm facing left, from in front of the chest a short distance to the right.

**hungry** *adj.* Having a strong desire for food: *hungry for a steak.* Related form: **hunger** *n.* Same sign used for: **appetite, crave, famished, starved, yearn.**

■ [Shows passage to an empty stomach] Beginning with the fingertips of the right *C hand* touching the center of the chest, palm facing in, move the hand downward a short distance.

**hunt** *v.* To go after or search for (wild animals) to catch or kill: *to hunt for deer.* Related form: **hunting** *n., adj.*

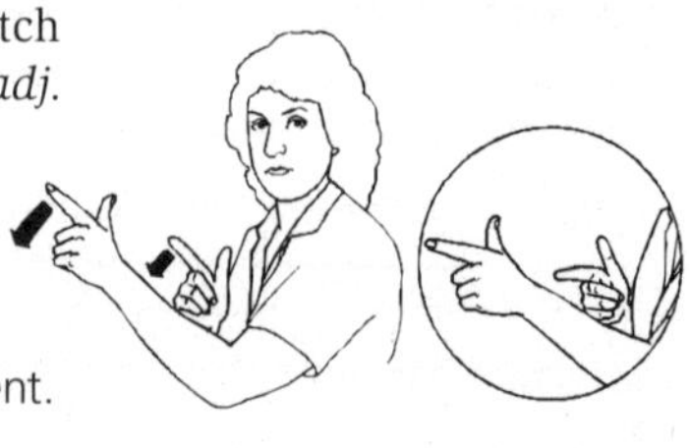

■ [Mime aiming a rifle or shotgun] With both *L hands* in front of the chest, right hand closer to the chest than the left, palms facing in opposite directions, and index fingers angled up, move the hands downward with a double movement.

**hunt for** *v. phrase.* See sign for LOOK FOR.

**hurrah** *n.* See sign for RALLY.

**hurry** *v.* **1.** To move or cause to move quickly: *Hurry home. Don't hurry me.* —*n.* **2.** An eagerness to act quickly: *always in a hurry.* Same sign used for: **hassle, haste, hustle, rush, urgent.**

■ [Initialized sign showing hurried movement] Beginning with both *H hands* in front of each side of the body, palms facing each other, move the hands up and down with a quick short repeated movement, moving the hands slightly forward each time.

**hurt**[1] *v.* **1.** To cause pain or injury: *I hurt my wrist when I twisted it.* **2.** To feel pain: *Does your head hurt?* —*n.* **3.** An injury, wound, pain, etc.: *How is the hurt on your finger?* See also signs for PAIN[1,2]. Same sign used for: **ache, harm, wound.**

■ [Fingers indicate a stabbing pain] Beginning with both extended index fingers pointing toward each other in front of the chest, palms facing in, jab the fingers toward each other with a short repeated movement.

**hurt**[2] *adj.* Physically or emotionally wounded: *a hurt pride.* See also signs for PAIN[1,2]. Same sign used for: **bear, sore, wound.**

■ [Symbolizes patience when having pain] Beginning with the thumb of the right *A hand* touching the chin, palm facing left, twist the wrist back, ending with the palm facing in.

**husband** *n.* A married man, especially in relation to his wife: *My husband will be home in an hour.*

■ [Hand moves from the male area of the head + **marry**] Move the right *C hand* from the right side of the forehead, palm facing left, down to clasp the left *curved hand* held in front of the chest, palm facing up.

**husky** *adj.* See sign for HULK.

**hustle** *v.* See sign for HURRY[1].

**hyena** *n.* A wild carnivorous animal of Africa and Asia, much like a large dog, one kind of which is noted for its noisy, laughlike call: *a laughing hyena.*

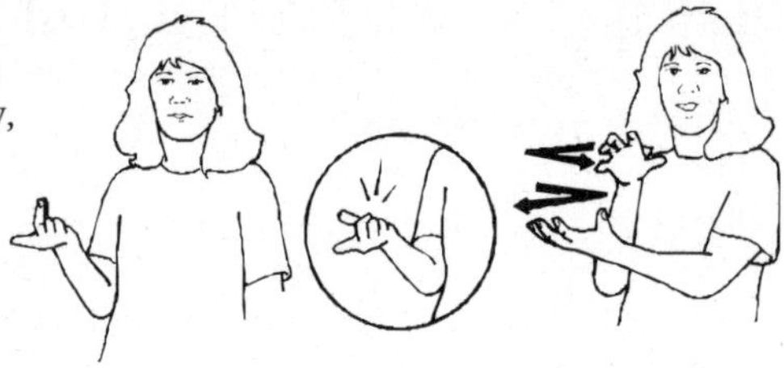

■ [**dog** + **hysterical**] Snap the right thumb gently off the right middle finger, palm facing up, in front of the right side of the chest. Then, with the right *curved 5 hand* over the left *curved 5 hand* in front of the chest, move the hands forward and back with a repeated alternating movement.

**hymn** *n.* See sign for MUSIC.

**hypnotize** *v.* **1.** To put into a trance or trancelike state; make vulnerable to control: *When hypnotized, she was able to remember the terrible experience she had blocked.* **2.** To hold spellbound; transfix; fascinate: *to hypnotize the audience.* Related form: **hypnosis** *n.*

■ [The fingers seem to put a spell on someone] Beginning with both *5 hands* in front of each side of the chest, palms facing down and fingers pointing forward, wiggle the fingers slowly.

**hypocrite** *n.* A person who espouses or pretends to exhibit virtues but is not sincere: *He is a hypocrite, who spoke against crime but embezzled funds.* Same sign used for: **fake, impostor.**

■ [Hands indicate someone covering the truth] With the palm of the right *open hand* on the back of the left *open hand,* the fingers of both hands pointing forward and palms facing down, push the fingers of the left hand down with the right fingers.

**hypodermic**[1] *adj.* **1.** Of or characterized by the injection of drugs under the skin: *a hypodermic needle.* —*n.* **2.** A hypodermic syringe: *Hand the doctor the hypodermic.* **3.** A dose of medicine administered by syringe: *prescribed a hypodermic of morphine every four hours for the pain.*

■ [Mime giving a shot in the arm with a hypodermic] Move the index finger of the right *3 hand* from in front of the right shoulder, palm facing right, back against the right upper arm while closing the middle finger to the thumb.

**hypodermic**[2] *n.* See sign for SHOT.

**hysterical** *adj.* Showing or characterized by uncontrollable outbursts: *hysterical laughter.* Same sign used for: **laugh, laughter.**

■ Beginning with both *curved 5 hands* in front of the chest, palms facing each other and the right hand above the left hand, move the hands forward and back to the chest with a repeated movement and in opposite directions.

**I**[1] *pron.* The first person singular pronoun; the person speaking: *I am happy to see you.*

■ [Initialized sign formed toward oneself] Bring the thumb side of the right *I hand,* palm facing left, back against the chest.

---

**I**[2] *pron.* See sign for ME.

---

**ice** *n.* See sign for FREEZE.

---

**ice cream** *n.* A smooth frozen dessert made with cream or milk, sugar, and flavorings: *vanilla ice cream.*

■ [Mime eating from an ice cream cone] Bring the index-finger side of the right *S hand,* palm facing left, back in an arc toward the mouth with a double movement.

---

**ice skate** *n. phrase., v. phrase.* See sign for SKATE[2].

---

**idea** *n.* A thought, conception, or notion occurring in the mind: *Having this party was a good idea.*

■ [Initialized sign representing an idea coming from the head] Move the extended right little finger from near the right temple, palm facing down, upward in an arc.

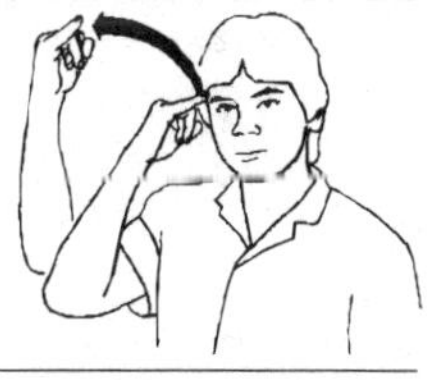

---

**ideal** *n., adj.* See sign for PERFECT.

---

**identical** *adj.* See sign for ALIKE[1].

---

**identification** *n.* Same as sign for IDENTIFY but made with a double movement. Related form: **identify** *v.*

---

**identify** *v.* To recognize as being a particular person or thing: *to identify the picture.*

■ [Initialized sign similar to sign for **show**[1]] Tap the thumb side of the right *I hand,* palm facing left, with a double movement against the left open palm held in front of the chest, palm facing forward and fingers pointing up.

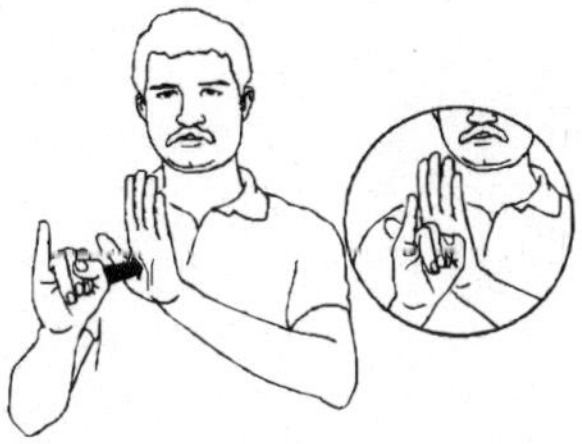

---

**idiom** *n.* A phrase or expression with a meaning different from the sum of the individual words within it: *Since "bite the bullet" is an English idiom, you should not take it literally.*

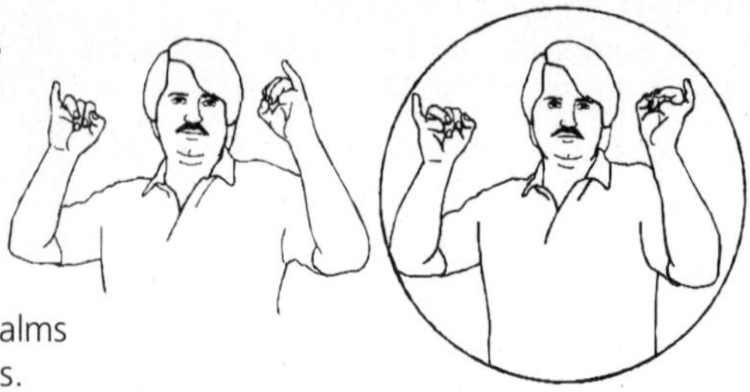

■ [Initialized sign similar to sign for **quotation**] While holding both *I hands* near each side of the head, palms angled forward, bend the little fingers.

**idiot** *n.* A very stupid or foolish person: *always acts like an idiot in public.*

■ [Initialized sign similar to sign for **ignorant**] Bring the thumb side of the right *I hand,* palm facing left, against the forehead.

**idle** *adj.* See sign for REST.

**if** *conj.* See sign for SUPPOSE.

**ignorant** *adj.* **1.** Knowing little or nothing: *an ignorant person whose insults you should ignore.* **2.** Revealing lack of knowledge, poor training, or insensitivity: *an ignorant remark.* Related form: **ignorance** *n.*

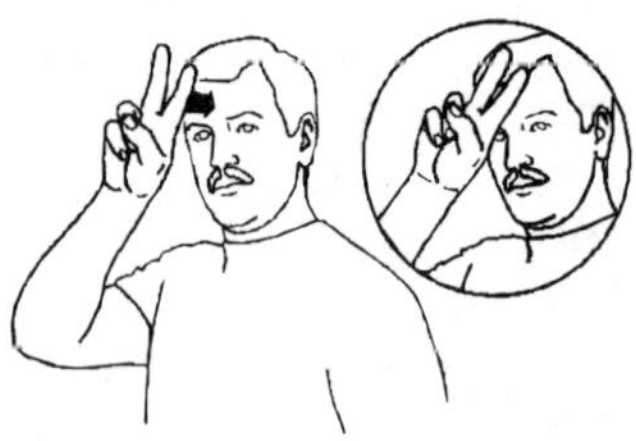

■ Bring the back of the right *V hand,* palm facing forward, against the forehead with a deliberate movement.

**ignore** *v.* To refrain from paying attention to; disregard: *Don't let the townspeople ignore the storm warning.* Same sign used for: **forsake, neglect.**

■ [Indicates attention moving away from object or person in view] While looking forward, place the index finger of the right *4 hand,* palm facing forward and fingers pointing up, near the right side of the face. Then move the hand outward to the right with a quick deliberate movement.

**ill** *adj.* See sign for SICK. Related form: **illness** *n.*

**illegal** *adj.* See signs for CRIME[1,2], FORBID.

**illegible** *adj.* See sign for VAGUE.

**illustrate** *v.* See sign for DRAW[1].

**illustration** *n.* See signs for ART, SKETCH.

**I love you** (A special handshape in American Sign Language).

■ [Abbreviation **i-l-y** formed simultaneously in a single handshape] Hold up the right hand with the thumb, index finger, and little finger extended, palm facing forward, in front of the right shoulder.

**image**[1] *n.* **1.** A physical likeness, as a photograph, painting, or statue, representing a particular person, animal, or thing: *an image of George Washington.* **2.** Something or someone strongly resembling another; counterpart; copy: *She is the image of her mother.* Same sign used for: **indicate, indicator.**

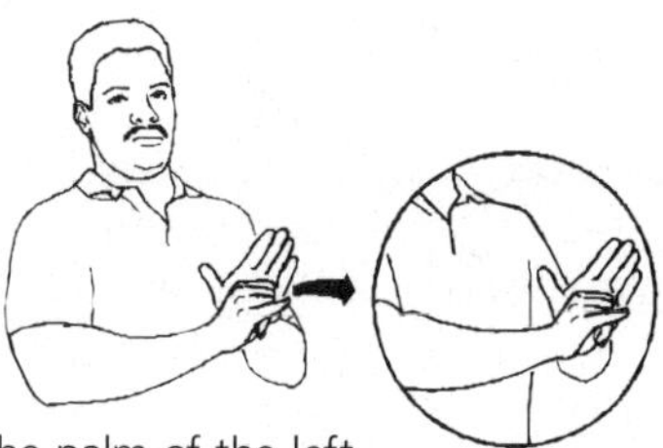

■ [Initialized sign similar to sign for **show**[1]] Beginning with the index-finger side of the right *I hand* against the palm of the left *open hand,* palm facing right and fingers pointing up, move both hands forward simultaneously.

**image**[2] *n.* See signs for PICTURE, SHAPE[1].

**imagination** *n.* The ability to form mental images of things not actually present: *a vivid imagination.* Same sign used for: **superstition, superstitious.**

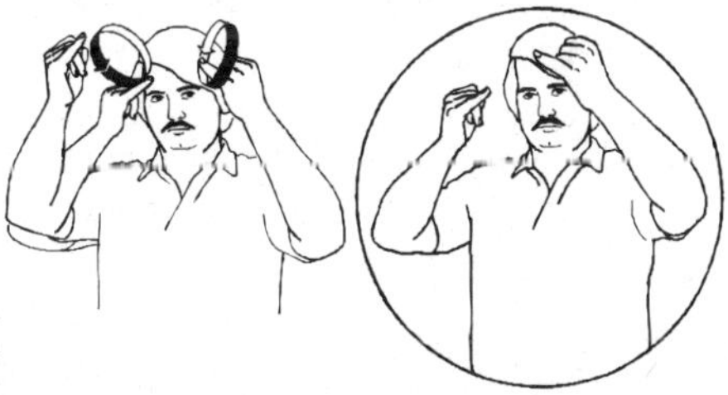

■ [Initialized sign showing ideas coming from the head] Move the extended little fingers of both *I hands,* palms facing back, in double alternating circles near each side of the head.

**imagine** *v.* To form a picture or concept in one's mind: *Imagine what it must be like to fly a plane.* Same sign used for: **make believe.**

■ [Initialized sign similar to sign for **dream**] Move the extended right little finger from near the right temple, palm facing down, upward in a double circular movement.

**imitate** *v.* See signs for COPY[1,2].

**immaterial** *adj.* Not important: *The story was immaterial to the conversation.*

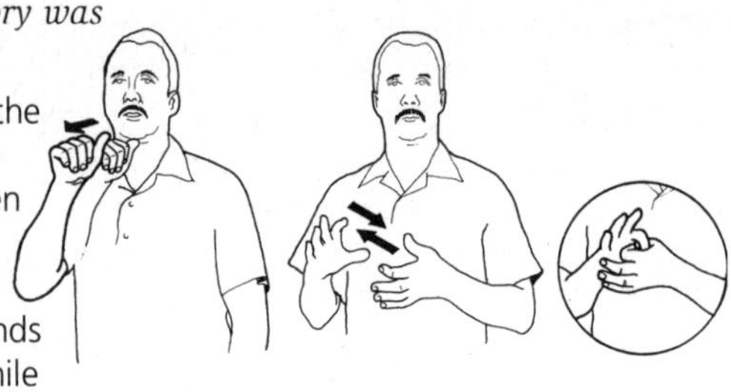

■ [**not + connect**] Bring the thumb of the right *10 hand* forward from under the chin with a deliberate movement. Then beginning with both *curved 5 hands* in front of each side of the body, palms facing each other, bring the hands together with a double movement while touching the thumb and index fingertips of each hand and intersecting with each other each time.

**immigrate** *v.* See sign for ENTER.

**immune** *adj.* See sign for RESIST.

**impact** *n.* See sign for HIT[1].

**impair** *v.* See sign for PREVENT.

**impeach** *v.* See sign for FEEDBACK.

**implement** *v.* See sign for APPLY[1].

**implore** *v.* See sign for BEG.

**import** *v.* See sign for DOWNLOAD.

**important** *adj.* Having value or significance: *an important document.* Same sign used for: **essential, main, significance, significant, value, worth.**

■ Beginning with the little-finger sides of both *F hands* touching, palms facing up, bring the hands upward in a circular movement while turning the hands over, ending with the index-finger sides of the *F hands* touching in front of the chest.

**impose** *v.* See signs for COPY[1,2].

**impossible** *adj.* Not possible: *impossible to lift the desk.*

■ Strike the palm side of the right *Y hand* against the upturned open left palm with a double movement.

**imposter** *n.* See signs for FAKE[2], HYPOCRITE.

**impoverished** *adj.* See sign for POOR.

**impression** *n.* The effect produced on one: *a good impression.* Same sign used for: **emphasis, stress.**

■ [Movement seems to press something in order to make an impression] With the extended thumb of the right *10 hand,* palm facing down, pressed into the palm of the left *open hand,* palm facing right, twist the right hand downward while keeping the thumb in place.

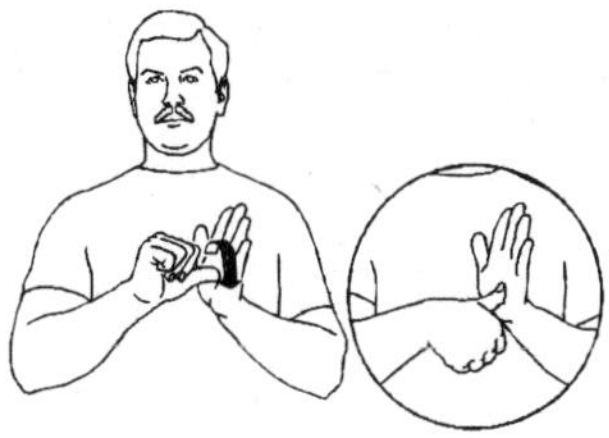

**imprisoned** *adj.* See sign for JAIL.

**improve**[1] *v.* To make or become better: *Try to improve your handwriting. The students' reading has improved.* Related form: **improvement** *n.* Same sign used for: **do better.**

■ [Hands seems to measure out an amount of improvement] Touch the little-finger side of the right *open hand,* palm facing back, first to the wrist and then near the crook of the extended left arm.

**improve**[2] *v.* To increase the value of: *We improved our house by adding an extra room.* Related form: **improvement** *n.* Same sign used for: **remodel, upgrade.**

■ [**improve**[1] formed with a movement that indicates continued improvements] Brush the little-finger side of the right *open hand,* palm facing in and fingers pointing left, upward with a circular movement on the forearm of the bent left arm.

**impulse** *n.* A sudden, involuntary driving force or inclination: *bought a new hat on impulse.*

■ [Shows spontaneity] Beginning with both *A hands* near the chest, palms facing in, move the hands suddenly forward while extending the index fingers, palms facing down and index fingers pointing forward.

**in** *prep.* (Used to indicate inclusion within something, as a place or time): *keeps the jewelry in a box.* Related form: **inner** *adj.*

■ [Shows location in something] Insert the fingertips of the right *flattened O hand,* palm facing down, into the center of the thumb side of the left *O hand,* palm facing right in front of the chest.

**in accord** See sign for AGREE[1].

**in agreement** See sign for AGREE[1].

**inauguration** *n.* See sign for OATH. Related form: **inaugural** *n.*

**in case of** See sign for SUPPOSE.

**inch** *n.* A unit of measure equivalent to one-twelfth of a foot: *He let his hair grow about six inches long.*

- Place the fingertips of the right *modified C hand,* palm facing left, against the extended thumb of the left *10 hand* held up in front of the chest, palm facing right.

**in charge of** See sign for MANAGE.

**incident** *n.* See signs for HAPPEN, SHOW UP.

**incision** *n.* A surgical cut into a tissue or an organ: *The surgeon made an incision across the stomach.* Same sign used for: **cut.**

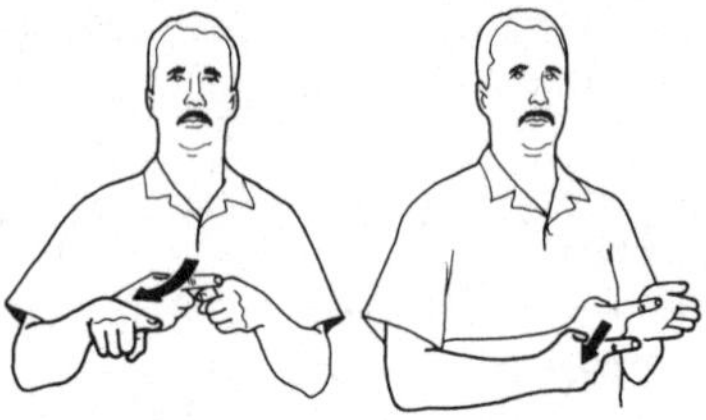

- [**cut** + **knife**] Slide the side of the extended right index finger, palm in, across the palm of the left *open hand*. Then slide the side of the extended right index finger, palm facing in, with a double movement at an angle down the length of the extended left index finger, palm facing right, turning the right palm down each time as it moves off the end of the left index finger.

**incline** *n.* See sign for GRADE.

**include** *v.* To contain as part of a whole: *The price of the hotel room includes tax.* Same sign used for: **contained in, everything, involve, within.**

- [The hand seems to encompass everything to gather it into one space] Swing the right *5 hand,* palm facing down, in a circular movement over the left *S hand,* palm facing in, while changing into a *flattened O hand,* ending with the fingertips of the right hand inserted in the center of the thumb side of the left hand.

**income**[1] *n.* Earnings that come from work, the sale of goods, investments, or other sources: *to have an annual income of $30,000.* Same sign used for: **revenue, salary, wages.**

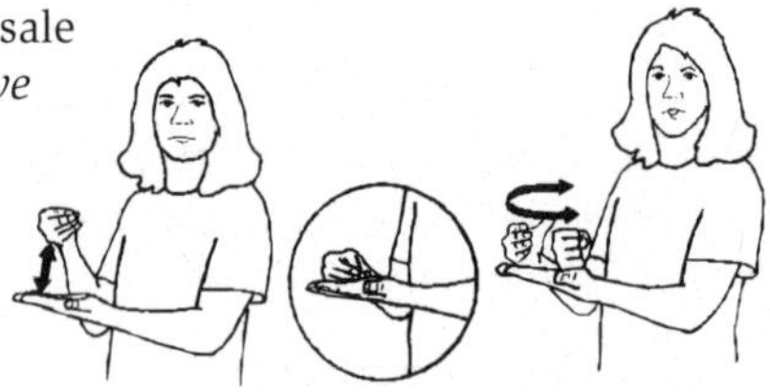

- [**money** + **earn**] Tap the back of the right *flattened O hand,* palm facing up, with a double movement against the left *open hand,* palm facing up. Then bring the little-finger side of the right *C hand,* palm facing left, with a double movement across the palm of the left *open hand,* closing the right hand into an *S hand* each time.

**income**[2] *n.* See sign for EARN.

**incorrect** *adj.* See sign for WRONG.

**increase** *n.* **1.** An act or instance of growing greater: *an increase in spending.* —*v.* **2.** To make or become greater: *increase the amount of salt.* Same sign used for: **gain, increment, raise.**

■ [Shows more and more things adding to a pile to increase it] Beginning with the right *U hand,* palm facing up, slightly lower than the left *U hand,* palm facing down, flip the right hand over, ending with the right fingers across the left fingers.

**incredible**[1] *adj.* Extraordinary; unbelievable: *This is an incredible performance.* Same sign used for: **amazed, stunned.**

■ [Represents one's mouth dropping open when amazed] Beginning with the back of the right *S hand* against the open mouth, palm facing forward, deliberately open the hand into a *bent 3 hand.*

**incredible**[2] *adj.* See sign for WONDERFUL.

**increment** *n.* See sign for INCREASE.

**indecision** *n.* Inability to decide; an act or instance of being unable to make up one's mind: *The coach has no time for indecision on the playing field.* Same sign used for: **doubt, doubtful, juggle, uncertain, undecided.**

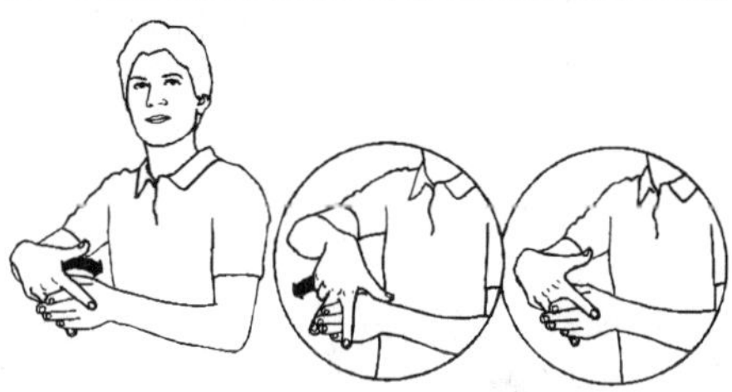

■ [Represents "sitting on the fence" when one is undecided] Beginning with the fingers of the right *V hand,* palm facing back and fingers pointing down, straddling the index finger side of the left *B hand,* palm facing right and fingers pointing forward, rock the right hand back and forth with a double movement.

**indent** *v.* To begin or add text a specific space from the left or right edge of a page: *indent one inch from the edge of the paper.* Related form: **indentation** *n.*

■ [Shows the space left by an indentation] Move the right *B hand,* palm left, from in front of the left side of the chest to the right with a deliberate movement.

**independent** *adj.* Thinking or acting for oneself: *an independent person who doesn't rely on others.* Related form: **independence.**

■ [Initialized sign similar to sign for **free**] Beginning with the wrists of both *I hands* crossed in front of the chest, palms facing in, swing the arms apart, ending with the *I hands* in front of each shoulder, palms facing forward.

**indicate** *v.* See signs for IMAGE, SHOW[1]. Related forms: **indicator** *n.*, **indication** *n.*

**indifferent** *adj.* See sign for DON'T CARE.

**individual** *n.* **1.** A single person, as distinguished from a group: *Each individual in the class is responsible for doing all the assignments.* *—adj.* **2.** Intended for a single person: *individual attention.*

■ [Initialized sign similar to sign for **person**] Bring both *I hands,* palms facing each other, from the chest down along the sides of the body.

**indoctrinate** *v.* See sign for TEACH. Related form: **indoctrination** *n.*

**indoors** *n.* See sign for INSIDE.

**induce** *v.* To influence; move to action by persuasion: *induced me to come along to the party.*

■ [Similar to sign for **hypnotize** moving toward oneself] Beginning with both *curved 5 hands* in front of the face, palms facing each other, wiggle the fingers while moving the hands in toward the eyes, closing into *S hands.*

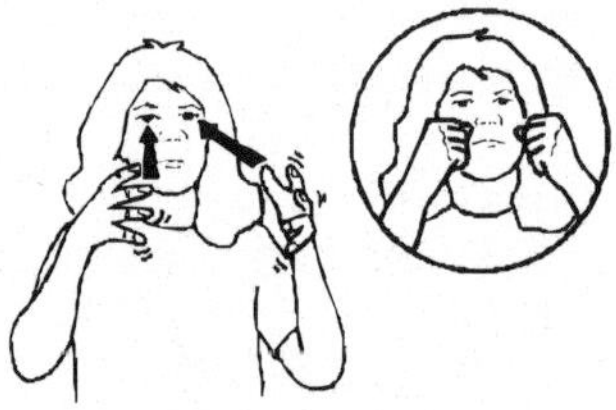

**industry** *n.* See sign for MACHINE.

**inexpensive** *adj.* See sign for CHEAP.

**inexperienced** *adj.* See signs for CLUMSY, UNSKILLED.

**infant** *n.* See sign for BABY.

**in favor of** See sign for SUPPORT.

**infection** *n.* See sign for INSURANCE.

**inferior** *adj.* Below average, as in quality or grade: *a cheap car of inferior quality.*

■ [Initialized sign similar to sign for **base**] Move the extended finger of the right *I hand,* palm angled forward, in a double circular movement under the left *open hand,* palm facing down.

**infirmary**[1] *n.* A hospital in a school or other institution: *sent by the Dean to rest in the infirmary.*

■ [Initialized sign similar to sign for **hospital**] Move the extended fingertip of the right *I hand,* palm facing in, first down and then across on the upper left arm from back to front.

**infirmary**[2] *n.* See sign for HOSPITAL.

**influence** *v.* **1.** To have an effect on: *Nothing you say will influence my thinking.* —*n.* **2.** The power to effect others without force: *Their teacher has a lot of influence on the rest of the faculty.* **3.** Someone or something that exerts influence: *Her new friend is a good influence.* Same sign used for: **affect, effect.**

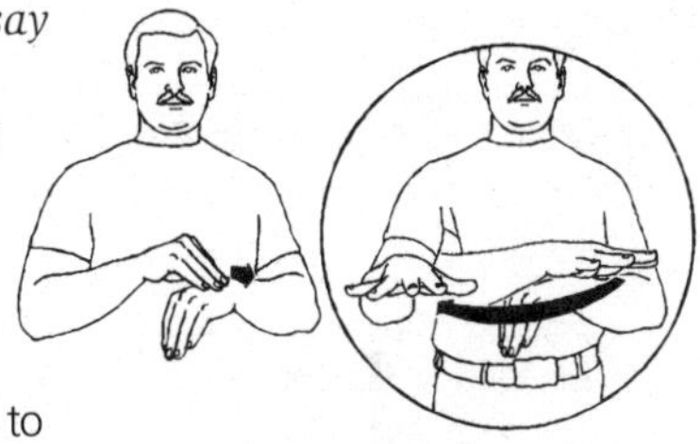

■ [Similar to sign for **advice** except spread outward to others] Beginning with the fingertips of the right *flattened O hand* on the back of the left *open hand,* palm facing down, move the right hand forward while opening into a *5 hand* and bringing the hand in a sweeping arc to in front of the right side of the body.

**inform** *v.* To give knowledge or information to: *I had to inform you of the news myself.* Same sign used for: **issue, let know, notice, notify.**

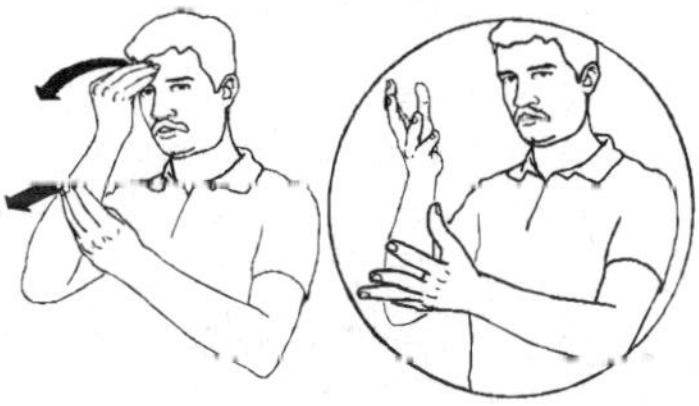

■ [Indicates taking information from one's head and giving it to others] Beginning with the fingertips of the right *flattened O hand* near the forehead and the left *flattened O hand* in front of the chest, move both hands forward while opening into *5 hands,* palms facing up.

**information** *n.* Similar to sign for **inform** except formed with a double movement.

**infraction** *n.* See signs for CRIME[1,2].

**in front of** Outside or facing the front part of; before: *in front of the house.* Same sign used for: **face-to-face, facing.**

■ [Shows two things facing each other] Beginning with both *open hands* in front of the chest, palms facing each other and fingers pointing up, move both hands forward simultaneously.

**infuse** *v.* See signs for INTERFACE, MESH.

**inhale**[1] *v.* To breathe in: *inhale the fresh air.*

■ [Shows air brought in the nose] Move the back of the right *5 hand,* palm facing down and fingers pointing forward, back toward the nose while closing into a *flattened O hand.*

**inhale**[2] *v.* See sign for BREATH.

**injection** *n.* See sign for SHOT.

**injury** *n.* See sign for PAIN[1].

**innocent** *adj.* Being free from moral or legal wrong: *an innocent baby; proved innocent in a court of law.* Same sign used for: **naive.**

■ Beginning with the fingers of both *U hands* touching the mouth, palms facing in, move the hands forward and outward to in front of each shoulder.

**inoculation** *n.* See sign for SHOT.

**inoperable** *adj.* Not suitable for surgery: *an inoperable tumor.*

■ [**can't** + **operate**] Bring the extended index finger of the right *one hand* downward hitting the extended index finger of the left *one hand* as it moves. Then move the thumb of the right *A hand,* palm facing down, across the upturned palm of the left *open hand* held in front of the chest.

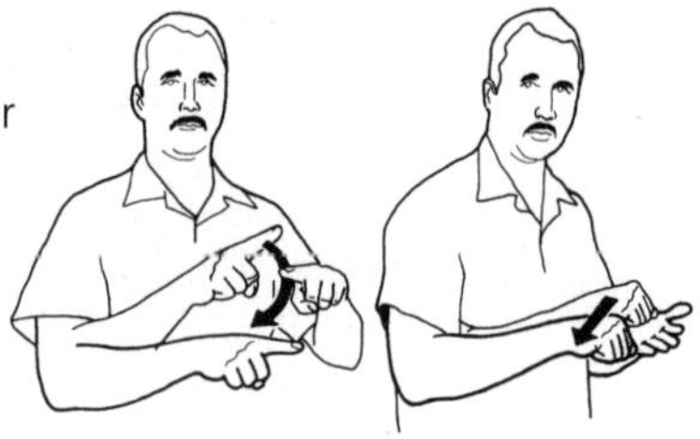

**in order** See signs for PLAN[2], PREPARE.

**inquire** *v.* See sign for TEST.

**insect** *n.* See sign for BUG.

**insert** *v.* **1.** To put in: *Insert a notice with the statement.* —*n.* **2.** Something put in: *The magazine had many advertising inserts.*

■ [Action of inserting] Slide the little-finger side of the right *open hand*, palm facing up, between the index and middle fingers of the left *4 hand,* palm facing right.

**inside** *prep.* **1.** On the inner side of; in or within: *inside the box.* —*adv.* **2.** In or into the inner part: *Come inside.* —*n.* **3.** The inner surface; the interior: *the inside of the room.* —*adj.* **4.** Being on the inside: *an inside seat.* Same sign used for: **indoors, internal, stuffing.**

■ [Shows location inside] Insert the fingertips of the right *flattened O hand,* palm facing down, into the center of the thumb side of the left *O hand,* palm facing right in front of the chest, with a repeated movement.

**insist** *v.* See sign for DEMAND.

**insomnia**[1] *n.* Inability to fall or stay asleep: *Too much coffee gives me insomnia.* Same sign used for: **alert, awake.**

■ [Represents the eyes being wide open when one can't sleep] Place both *C hands* around the wide-open eyes with the thumbs near each side of the nose, palms facing forward.

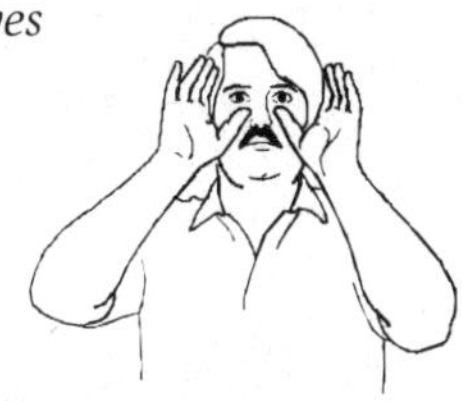

**insomnia**[2] *n.* (alternate sign)

■ [**can't** + a gesture showing the eyes closing to sleep] Bring the extended index finger of the right *one hand* downward hitting the extended index finger of the left *one hand* as it moves. Then bring the right *5 hand* downward in front of the face while closing into a *flattened O hand.*

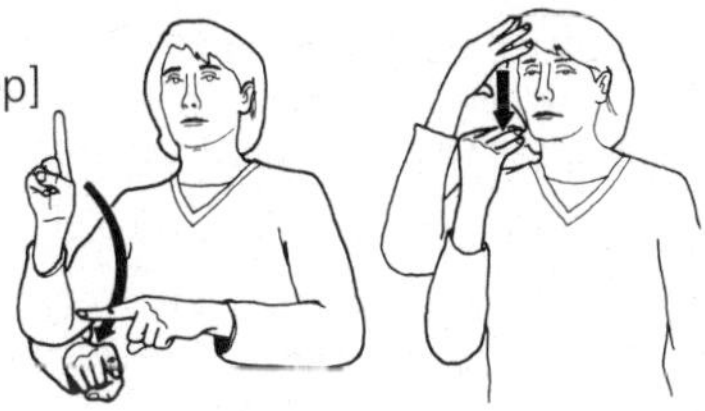

**inspect** *v.* See signs for CHECK[1], INVESTIGATE. Related form: **inspection** *n.*

**inspire** *v.* To fill with feeling: *inspired with hope.* Related form: **inspiration** *n.* Same sign used for: **pep, revive.**

■ [Represents inspiration moving up in one's body] Beginning with both *flattened O hands* in front of each side of the chest, palms facing in and fingers pointing up, move the hands upward while opening into *5 hands* in front of each shoulder.

**install** *v.* See signs for APPLY[1], PUT.

**installment plan** *n.* A system for paying for an item by making fixed partial payments over time at specified intervals: *The young couple paid for their carpeting on the installment plan.* Same sign used for: **layaway.**

■ [Pushing money away for payments] Slide the little-finger side of the right *bent hand,* palm facing in and fingers pointing left, with a short double movement from the wrist to off the fingertips of the left *open hand* held in front of the chest, palm facing up and fingers angled forward.

**instead** *adv.* As a substitute: *tea instead of coffee.*

■ [Represents substituting one thing for another] Move the fingertips of the right *F hand* forward in a circle around the fingertips of the left *F hand,* ending with the fingertips touching, palms facing each other.

**institute** *n.* An organization established for a specific purpose: *decided to go to an art institute after college.*

■ [Initialized sign showing setting something up] Beginning with the right *I hand* in front of the right side of the body, palm facing in, and the left *open hand* held across the chest, palm facing down and fingers pointing right, bring the right hand back toward the chest in a large upward arc and then down, ending with the little-finger side of the right *I hand* on the back of the left hand.

**instruct**[1] *v.* To give knowledge to, especially in a systematic way; teach; train: *to instruct the class in grammar.* Related form: **instruction** *n.*

■ [Initialized sign similar to sign for **teach**] Move both *I hands* forward a short distance with a double movement from in front of each side of the chest, palms facing each other.

**instruct**[2] *v.* See signs for DESCRIBE, TEACH. Related form: **instruction** *n.*

**insult** *v.* **1.** To say something harsh, rude, or insolent to: *She insulted me.* —*n.* **2.** A harsh, rude, or insolent statement or deed: *Not inviting me is an insult.* Related form: **insulting** *adj.* Same sign used for: **affront, put down.**

■ [Finger seems to direct an insult at another] Move the extended right index finger from in front of the right side of the body, palm facing left and finger pointing forward, forward and upward sharply in an arc.

**insurance** *n.* **1.** Coverage by contract with a business offering monetary reimbursement as protection from loss in return for payment of a premium: *It is considered important to have life insurance.* **2.** The premium paid for this coverage: *The insurance is $20 a month.* Related form: **insure** *v.* Same sign used for: **infection.**

■ [Initialized sign] Move the right *I hand,* palm facing forward, from side to side with a repeated movement near the right shoulder.

**integrate** *v.* See sign for MESH.

**intelligent** *adj.* See sign for SMART[2]. Related form: **intelligence** *n.*

**intend** *v.* See sign for MEAN[2]. Related form: **intention** *n.*

**interact** *v.* See sign for ASSOCIATE.

**intercept** *v.* To seize en route: *tried to intercept the package before it got mailed.* Same sign used for: **cut off.**

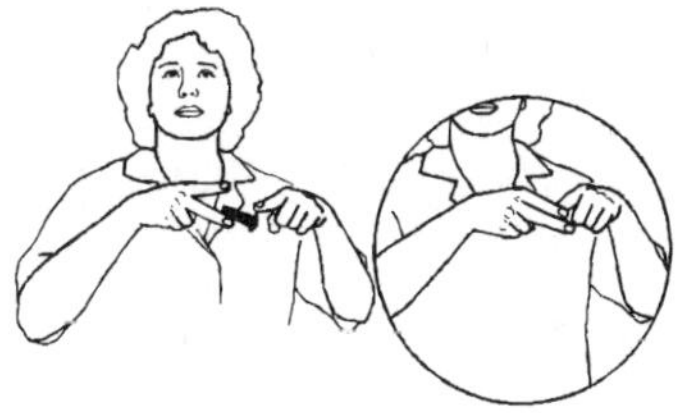

- [The hand moves forward to stop or intercept the other hand] Move the right *V hand,* palm facing left, forward while closing the index and middle fingers together near the end of the extended left index finger held in front of the chest, palm facing down and finger pointing right.

**intercourse** *n.* Sexual relations: *The man had intercourse with his wife.* Same sign used for: **sex.**

- Bring the right *V hand* downward in front of the chest to tap against the heel of the left *V hand* with a double movement, palms facing each other.

**interest**[1] *n.* A feeling of concern, involvement, and curiosity: *to have an interest in stamp collecting.* Related form: **interested** *adj.* Same sign used for: **fascinating.**

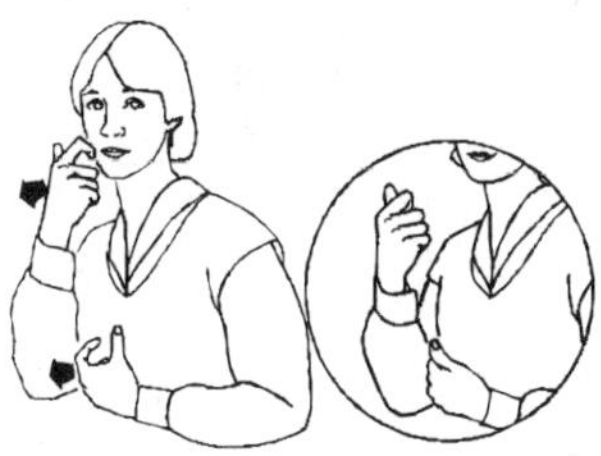

- Beginning with the right *modified C hand* in front of the face and the left *modified C hand* in front of the chest, both palms facing in, move the hands forward simultaneously while closing into *A hands.*

**interest**[2] *n.* Money paid or charged for the use of money or for borrowing money: *The bank will earn interest on the loan.*

- [Initialized sign] Rub the little-finger side of the right *I hand,* palm facing the chest, in a repeated circle on the back of the left *open hand,* palm facing down.

**interface** *n.* **1.** The connection between a computer and another entity: *an interface between the printer and the computer.* **2.** Software and hardware designed to allow communication between a computer and a user: *an easy, intuitive user interface.* Same sign used for: **infuse, merge.**

- [The hands represent things interfacing with each other] Beginning with both *5 hands* in front of each side of the chest, palms facing in and fingers angled toward each other, push the hands toward each other, causing the fingers to mesh together.

**interfere** *v.* See signs for ANNOY, MEDDLE.

**intermediate** *adj.* Occurring or situated between two points, things, persons, etc.: *the intermediate level in school.*

- [Shows a location in the middle] Slide the little-finger side of the right *open hand,* palm facing up, with a double movement between the middle and ring fingers of the left *5 hand,* palm facing right.

**intermission** *n.* **1.** A short interval between acts of a play or other performance: *saw friends in the lobby during the intermission.* **2.** A pause between periods of activity: *took a short intermission between tasks around the house.* Same sign used for: **break, halftime.**

- [Shows something being inserted halfway through something] Slide the index-finger side of the right *open hand,* palm facing down, between the index and middle fingers of the left *5 hand,* palm facing in.

**internal**[1] *adj.* Within the body: *your internal organs.*

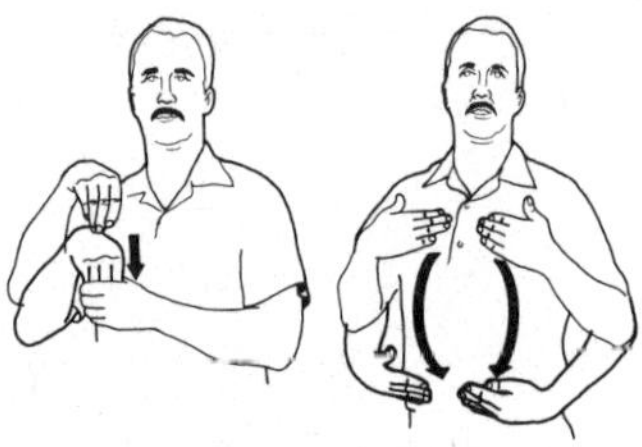

- [**inside** + **body**] Move the fingers of the right *flattened O hand* downward with a short double movement in the thumb side of the left *O hand* held in front of the chest. Then pat the palm side of both *open hands* first on each side of the chest and then on each side of the abdomen.

**internal**[2] *adj.* See sign for INSIDE.

**international** *adj.* Among nations; involving two or more nations: *Trade talks are an international affair.*

- [Initialized sign similar to sign for **world**] Move both *I hands* in circles around each other, palms facing each other, ending with the little-finger side of the right hand on the index-finger side of the left hand in front of the chest.

**Internet** *n.* See sign for NETWORK.

**internship** *n.* A period of supervised experience, especially for a recent graduate of medical school: *an internship at the local hospital.* Related form: **intern** *n.*

- [Initialized sign similar to sign for **practice**] Slide the little-finger side of the right *I hand,* palm facing left, back and forth with a double movement on the back of the left *open hand,* palm facing down and fingers pointing right.

**interpret** *v.* **1.** To explain or provide the meaning of: *to interpret the story for the class.* **2.** To translate, as from one language into another: *She interprets from Russian to French and English at the United Nations.*

■ [Uses the same movement as **change**[1]] With the fingertips of both *F hands* touching in front of the chest, palms facing each other, twist the hands in opposite directions to reverse positions.

**interrupt** *v.* See signs for ANNOY, MEDDLE.

**intersection** *n.* A place where one thing, especially a road, crosses another: *the famous intersection of Broadway and Forty-second Street.* Same sign used for: **crossing.**

■ [Represents two roads crossing each other] Bring the side of the extended right index finger, palm facing left, with a double movement across the extended left index finger, palm facing down.

**intervene** *v.* See sign for ANNOY.

**interview** *v.* **1.** To meet and talk with, as to obtain information: *to interview a movie star for a magazine article.* —*n.* **2.** A formal meeting to evaluate someone's qualifications: *to have a job interview.*

■ [Initialized sign similar to sign for **communication**] Move both *I hands,* palms facing each other, forward and back toward the mouth with an alternating movement.

**into** *prep.* See sign for ENTER.

**in touch with** See sign for CONTACT.

**intoxicated** *adj.* See sign for DRUNK.

**introduce** *v.* To present (one or more persons) to another or to each other so as to make acquainted: *Introduce yourself to the committee.* Related form: **introduction** *n.*

■ [The hands seem to bring two people together] Bring both *bent hands* from in front of each side of the body, palms facing up and fingers pointing toward each other, toward each other in front of the waist.

**invent** *v.* **1.** To create (something new) as a result of one's own planning and ingenuity: *to invent a gadget that will peel apples.* **2.** To make up out of one's imagination: *to invent a song.* **3.** To devise for one's own purposes: *to invent an excuse.* Same sign used for: **create, make up, originate.**

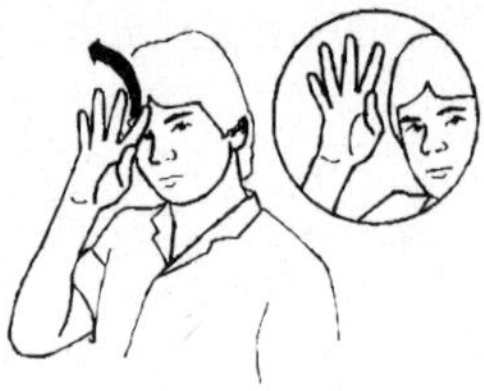

■ [The hand seems to take ideas from the head] Move the index-finger side of the right *4 hand,* palm facing left, from the forehead upward in a forward arc.

**invest** *v.* To use money to buy something that is expected to return a profit: *invest in stocks.* Related form: **investment** *n.* Same sign used for: **deposit, stocks.**

■ [Represents depositing money in a bank] Insert the fingertips of the right *flattened O hand,* palm facing left, into the center of the thumb side of the left *O hand,* palm angled forward.

**investigate**[1] *v.* To examine the details (of), especially to find a cause or motive: *We'll investigate to find out what went wrong with your travel plans. The police investigated the murder.* Related form: **investigation** *n.* Same sign used for: **examination, examine, inspect, inspection.**

■ [The finger seems to be paging through pages of documents] Brush the extended right index finger with a repeated movement from the heel to the fingertips of the upturned palm of the left *open hand.*

**investigate**[2] *v.* See sign for ANALYZE.

**invite** *v.* To ask politely for the presence or participation of, as at a gathering of friends or a meeting: *I am inviting you to my party.* Related form: **invitation** *n.* Same sign used for: **employ, greet, hire, welcome.**

■ [The hand brings another to oneself] Bring the upturned right *curved hand* from in front of the right side of the body in toward the center of the waist.

**involve** *v.* See sign for INCLUDE.

**iron**[1] *n.* **1.** A silver-colored metal valued for its strength and commonly used for making tools, machinery, etc.: *The hammer was made of iron.* —*adj.* **2.** Made of iron: *an iron fence.*

■ [Initialized sign] Slide the base of the extended little finger of the right *I hand,* palm facing left, with a double movement across the extended left index finger, palm facing down and finger pointing right in front of the chest.

**iron**[2] *n.* **1.** An appliance with a flat, smooth surface that can be heated for pressing and smoothing cloth: *The steam iron will get the wrinkles out of this jacket.* —*v.* **2.** To smooth or press cloth with an iron: *to iron the cotton shirts.*

■ [Mime using an iron] Rub the knuckle side of the right *S hand,* palm facing in, back and forth along the length of the upturned left *open hand* with a repeated movement.

**irony** *n.* **1.** The sarcastic use of words to communicate a meaning that is the opposite of what is actually said: *The irony of his words is apparent from his sarcastic tone.* **2.** A situation in which an otherwise favorable outcome cannot be enjoyed or appreciated: *The irony is that she won an award after her show was canceled.* Related form: **ironic** *adj.* Same sign used for: **sarcastic.**

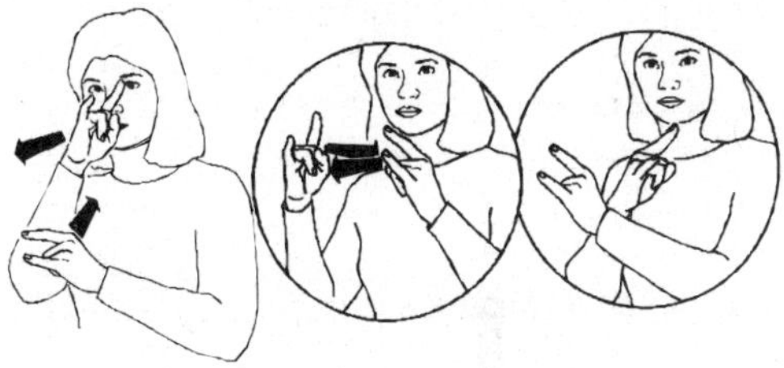

■ With the little finger and index finger of the right hand extended, palm facing left near the nose, and the little finger and index finger of the left hand extended in front of the chest, palm facing down, move the right hand forward and the left hand back until the hands are facing each other in front of the chest. Then push the hands past each other, ending with the wrists crossed in front of the chest.

**irritate** *v.* See signs for ANNOY, ITCH.

**I should have thought of it before** See sign for DISGUSTED[2].

**island** *n.* A relatively small body of land surrounded by water: *We plan to take a trip to an island in the Bahamas.*

■ [Initialized sign] Rub the side of the extended little finger of the right *I hand,* palm facing left, with a double movement in a circle on the back of the left *S hand,* palm facing down.

**isolated** *adj.* See signs for ALONE, HERMIT.

**issue** *v.* See signs for INFORM, NEWSPAPER.

**it** or **its** *pron.* See signs for HE, HIS.

**itch** *n.* **1.** A prickly, irritated feeling making one want to scratch the affected part: *If you have an itch, you can use this ointment.* —*v.* **2.** To manifest such a feeling: *My mosquito bites itch terribly.* Related form: **itchy** *adj.* Same sign used for: **irritate.**

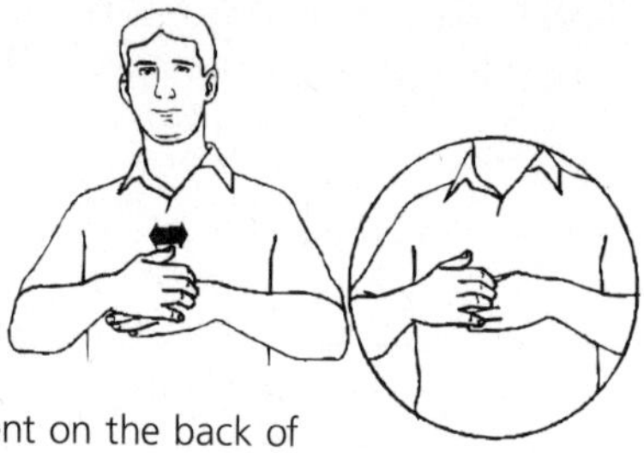

■ [Mime scratching an itchy place] Move the fingertips of the right *curved 5 hand,* palm facing in, back and forth with a double movement on the back of the left *open hand,* palm facing in and fingers pointing right.

**itself**[1] *pron.* A reflexive form of IT, used to refer back to the object last mentioned: *The door closed by itself.* See also sign for HIMSELF. Same sign used for: **herself.**

■ Bring the knuckles of the right *10 hand,* palm facing left, firmly against the side of the extended left index finger, palm facing right and finger pointing up in front of the chest.

**itself**[2] *pron.* See sign for HIMSELF.

**jab** *v.* **1.** To poke: *jabbed him with her elbow.* —*n.* **2.** A thrust with something pointed: *feel a jab in my side.*

■ [Mime jabbing someone in the ribs] Poke the extended right index finger, palm facing back, against the right side with a double movement.

**jabber** *v.* To talk very fast in a senseless way: *They jabbered away about nothing for hours.* Same sign used for: **chatter.**

■ [**talk**[1] formed with a fast repeated movement] Beginning with the right *5 hand* in front of the mouth, palm facing left and fingers pointing up, and the left *5 hand* near the little finger of the right hand, palm facing right and fingers pointing up, wiggle the fingers repeatedly.

**jacket** *n.* See sign for COAT.

**jagged** *adj.* See sign for RAGGED.

**jail** *n.* A place for holding accused persons awaiting trial or sentenced prisoners; prison: *sentenced to jail for a minor crime.* Same sign used for: **imprisoned, prison.**

■ [Represents jail bars] Bring the back of the right *4 hand* from near the chest forward with a double movement while bringing the left *4 hand* in to meet the right hand, ending with the fingers crossed at an angle, both palms facing in.

**jam**[1] *v.* **1.** To squeeze into a small space: *jammed many people into the bus.* —*n.* **2.** A mass of objects, especially vehicles, crowded together in a way that hinders movement: *caught in a traffic jam.* Same sign used for: **crowded.**

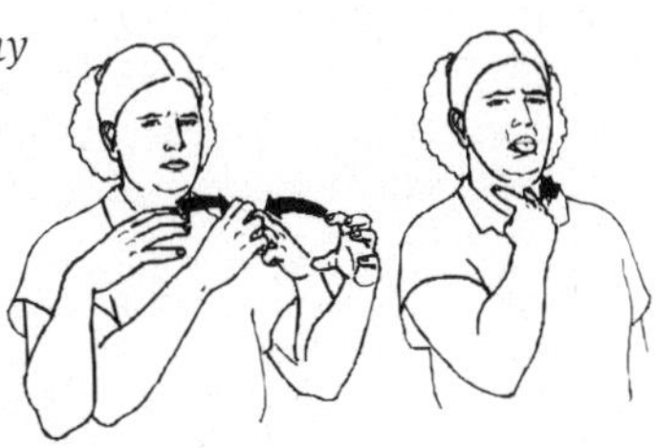

■ [**crowded** + **stuck**] Beginning with both *curved 5 hands* in front of each shoulder, palms facing each other, bring the hands together while bending the fingers and meshing them with each other in front of the chest. Then push the fingers of the right *V hand* against the neck, palm facing down.

**jam**[2] *n.* See sign for JELLY.

**jar** *n.* See sign for CUP.

**jaws** *pl. n.* See sign for ALLIGATOR.

**jealous** *adj.* **1.** Being suspicious that a rival can attract the love and attention of someone you care for: *a jealous lover.* **2.** Envious and covetous of another's accomplishments, possessions, etc.: *I'm jealous of his good luck.* Same sign used for: **envious.**

- [Initialized sign] Beginning with the extended little finger of the right *J hand* touching the right corner of the mouth, palm facing forward, twist the hand down and forward, ending with the palm facing back.

**jeans** *pl. n.* See sign for PANTS.

**jeer** *v.* See sign for MOCK.

**Jell-O** *Trademark.* See sign for GELATIN.

**jelly** *n.* A sweet, sticky spread, often translucent, made from fruit or fruit juice: *The coffee shop serves jelly with the toast.* Same sign used for: **jam.**

- [Initialized sign miming spreading jelly on bread] Strike the extended little finger of the right *J hand* on the upturned left *open hand* as it moves upward in an arc with a double movement.

**jest** *v.* See sign for TEASE.

**jet** *n.* See sign for AIRPLANE.

**jewelry** *n.* Necklaces, bracelets, rings, etc., made of precious metals and gemstones or imitations of these: *We bought some handcrafted jewelry on our trip.*

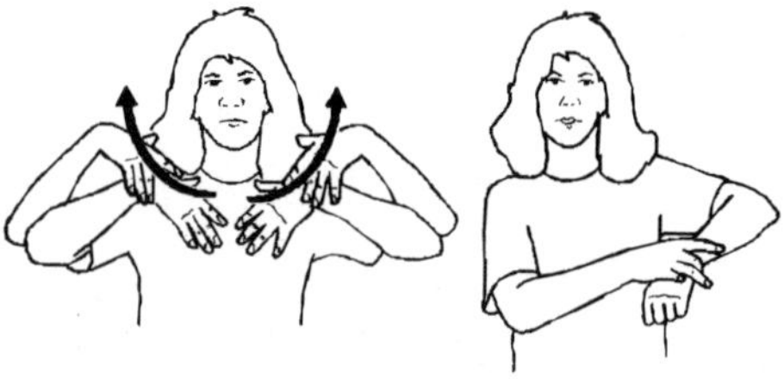

- [Location of necklace and bracelet] Beginning with the fingers of both *5 hands* in front of the chest, palms facing in, bring the hands upward to on top of each shoulder. Then grasp the left wrist with the bent middle finger and thumb of the right hand.

**jigsaw puzzle** *n. phrase.* See sign for PUZZLE.

**job** *n.* See sign for WORK.

**jog**[1] *v.* To run slowly and steadily, especially as part of an exercise program: *jog every day.* Related form: **jogging** *n.*

■ [Mime how the hands are thought to move when jogging] Move both *S hands,* palms facing each other, in repeated alternating outward circles in front of each side of the chest.

**jog**[2] *v.* See sign for RUN[1]. Related form: **jogging** *n.*

**join**[1] *v.* To become a member of: *to join the club.* Same sign used for: **participate.**

■ [Represents a person's legs entering a place where there are other people with whom one can have social exchanges] Beginning with the right *H hand* in front of the chest, palm facing left and fingers pointing forward, and the left *C hand* in front of the lower left side of the chest, palm facing right, bring the right hand down in an arc into the palm side of the left hand while closing the left fingers around the fingers of the right *H hand.*

**join**[2] *v.* See sign for BELONG[1].

**joint**[1] *n.* Structure made up of ligaments and cartilage that holds bones together and enables them to move easily in relation to each other: *My knee joint hurts.* Same sign used for: **socket.**

■ [A bone in its socket] Cover the left *S hand,* palm facing in, with the palm side of the right *curved hand.*

**joint**[2] *n.* See sign for BELONG[1].

**jolly** *adj.* See sign for HAPPY.

**journal** *n.* See signs for ARTICLE, MAGAZINE.

**journey** *n.* See sign for TRIP.

**joy** *n.* See sign for HAPPY.

**joystick** *n.* A device that can be attached to the computer to control the action of a game on the display screen.

■ [Action of using a joystick] With the little-finger side of the right *S hand,* palm left, in the palm of the left *open hand,* palm up, rock the right hand in different directions with a repeated movement.

**judge** *v.* To form an opinion or make a decision: *to judge the case on its merits.* Same sign used for: **court, justice, trial.**

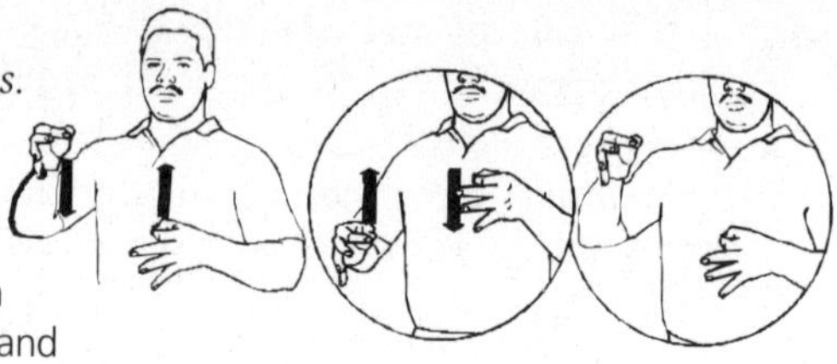

■ [The hands move up and down indicating weighing a decision] Move both *F hands,* palms facing each other, up and down in front of each side of the chest with a repeated alternating movement.

**juggle** *v.* See sign for INDECISION.

**juice** *n.* Liquid extracted from fruits: *to drink orange juice for breakfast.*

■ [**drink**[1] + initialized sign] Beginning with the thumb of the right *C hand* near the chin, palm facing left, tip the hand up toward the face. Then form a *J* near the right side of the face with the right hand.

**jump** *v.* **1.** To spring up from the ground: *Jump over the puddle.* —*n.* **2.** An act or instance of jumping: *It's a long jump from here to there.*

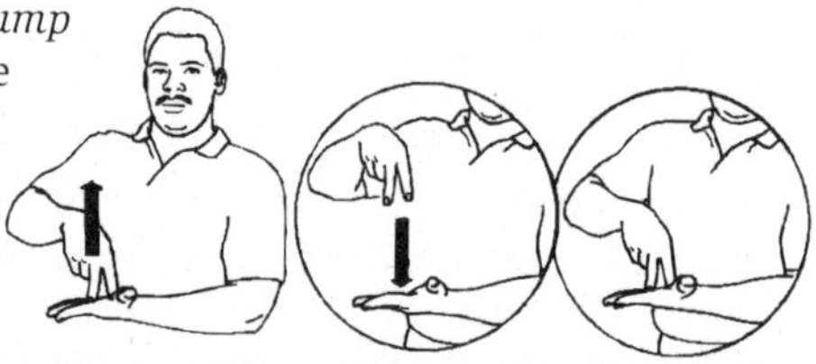

■ [Demonstrates the action of jumping] Beginning with the extended fingers of the right *V hand,* palm facing in, pointing down and touching the open left palm, move the right hand up and down in front of the chest with a double movement.

**jump rope** *n. phrase.* **1.** A children's game in which a rope is swung over the head and around under the feet of the player, who leaps over it every time it comes around again: *learned to play jump rope as a child.* **2.** The rope used in this game: *Hand me the jump rope so I can see how many times I can jump.*

■ [Mime using a jump rope oneself, with one end of the rope in each hand] Move both *A hands,* palms facing up, in simultaneous outward circles in front of each side of the body.

**jungle** *n.* See sign for FOREST.

**junk** *n.* See sign for GARBAGE.

**jury** *n.* A group of citizens called upon to hear the evidence at a trial, decide the facts, and render a verdict: *The jury listened to the defendant's case.* Same sign used for **petit jury.**

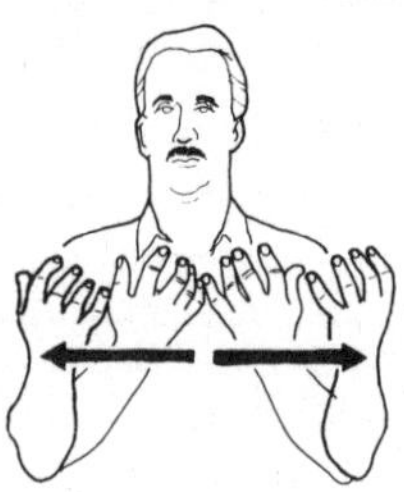

■ [Represents people in a jury box] Beginning with the little-finger sides of both *bent 4 hands,* palms in, together in front of the chest, move the hands apart to each side.

**just**[1] *adv.* A short while ago: *just arrived.* Same sign used for: **recently** and **while ago, a.**

■ [Indicates something in the recent past] Wiggle the index finger of the right *X hand,* palm facing back, up and down with a repeated movement on the lower right cheek.

**just**[2] *adv.* See signs for EQUAL, PRECISE.

**justice** *n.* See sign for JUDGE.

**justify** *v.* See sign for CHANGE.

**juvenile** *n.* **1.** A young person: *Juveniles pay half price.* —*adj.* **2.** Young: *a juvenile crowd at the movie.* **3.** Of, characteristic of, or suitable for young people: *a shelf of juvenile books.*

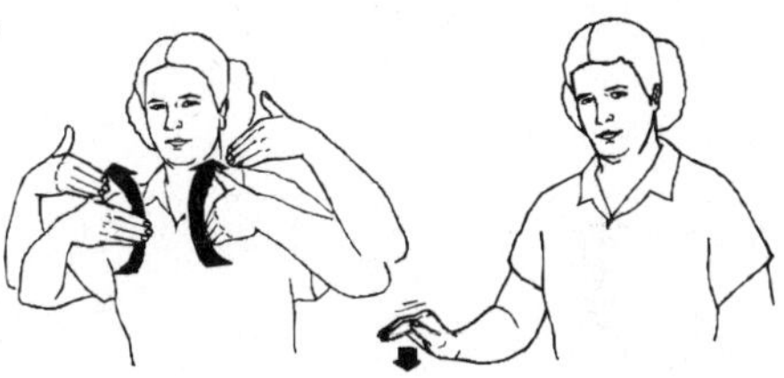

■ [**young** + **little**[2]] Beginning with the fingertips of both *bent hands* on each side of the chest, palms facing in and fingers pointing toward each other, brush the fingers upward in a double arc. Then move the right *bent hand* downward with a double movement in front of the right side of the body, palm facing down.

**kangaroo** *n.* A mammal having short forelegs and strong hind legs for leaping, with young that continue their development after birth in a pouch on the mother's abdomen: *We saw kangaroos on our trip to Australia.*

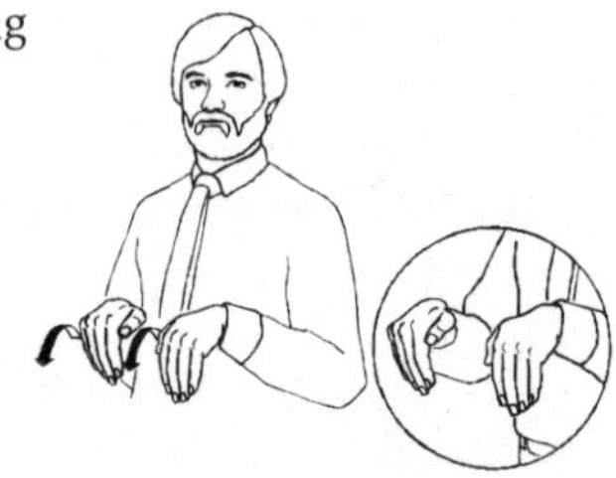

■ [Shows posture of a kangaroo] Move both *bent hands* from in front of each side of the body, palms facing in, forward in small upward arcs.

---

**karate** *n.* See sign for HACK.

---

**keen** *adj.* See sign for SHARP.

---

**keep** *v.* **1.** To hold in one's possession: *to keep the idea in mind.* **2.** To put or store: *to keep the flour in a canister.* Same sign used for: **maintain.**

■ Tap the little-finger side of the right *K hand* across the index-finger side of the left *K hand,* palms facing in opposite directions.

---

**keep quiet** *v. phrase.* See signs for SEAL ONE'S LIPS, SHUT UP[1] (*informal*).

---

**keep secret** *v. phrase.* See sign for SEAL ONE'S LIPS.

---

**ketchup** or **catsup** *n.* A sauce made of tomatoes, vinegar, sugar, spices, and other flavorings: *Please put ketchup on my hot dog.* Same sign used for **catsup.**

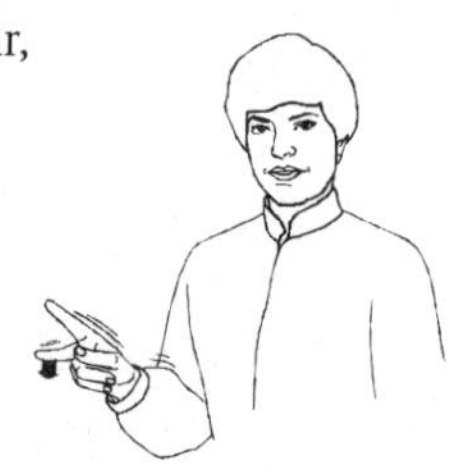

■ [Initialized sign] Shake the right *K hand,* palm facing left, up and down with a short repeated movement in front of the right side of the body.

---

**key**[1] *n.* A small instrument used to move the bolt in a lock, especially for opening and closing: *a brass key for the antique door.*

■ [Mime turning a key in a lock] Twist the knuckle of the right *X hand,* palm facing down, in the palm of the left *open hand,* palm facing right and fingers pointing forward, with a repeated movement.

---

**key**[2] *n.* A button on a keyboard: *press on a key.* Same sign used for: **keystroke.**

- [Action of pressing on a key] Push the extended thumb of the right *10 hand* downward a short distance in front of the right side of the body.

**keystroke** *n.* See sign for KEY[2].

**kick** *v.* To strike with the foot: *to kick the football through the goalposts.* Same sign used for: **kick off.**

- [Demonstrates the action of kicking something] Bring the right *B hand* in front of the right side of the body, palm facing left and fingers angled down, upward to strike the index-finger side of the right hand against the little-finger side of the left *B hand* held in front of the body, palm facing in and fingers pointing right.

**kick off** *n.* See sign for KICK.

**kid**[1] *n. Informal.* A child: *a family with two kids and a dog.*

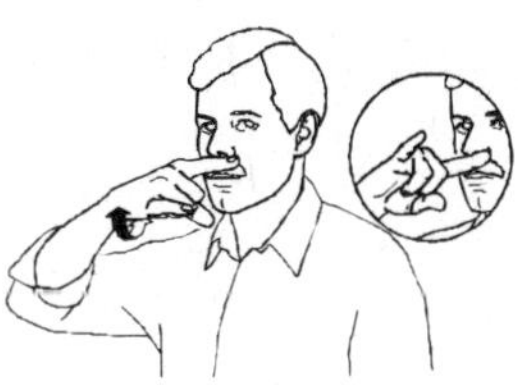

- With the right index finger and little finger extended, palm facing down, put the extended index finger under the nose, and twist the hand up and down with a small repeated movement.

**kid**[2] *v.* See sign for TEASE. Related form: **kidding** *n.*

**kill** *v.* To cause to die: *A stroke of lightning killed the old tree.* Same sign used for: **murder, slaughter, slay.**

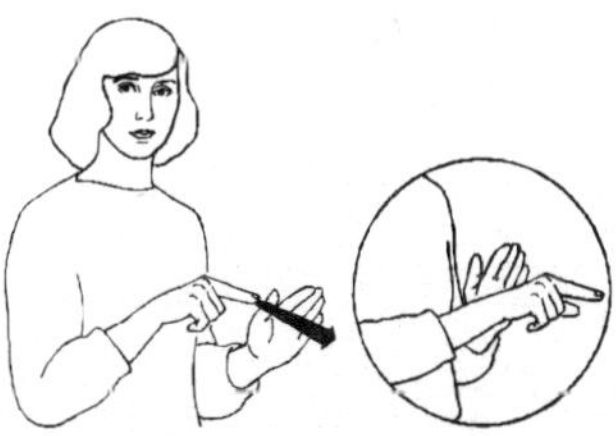

- [Represents a knife being inserted] Push the side of the extended right index finger, palm facing down, across the palm of the left *open hand,* palm facing right, with a deliberate movement.

**kind**[1] *adj.* Having a nature that prompts one to be helpful, generous, charitable, etc.: *a kind person, always generous with his time.* Same sign used for: **generous, gentle, gracious.**

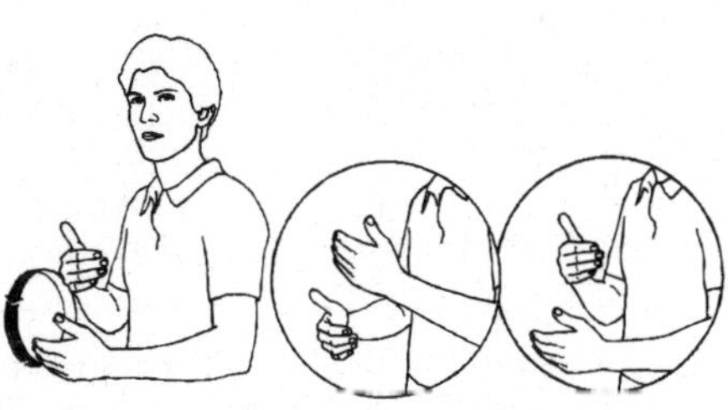

- [A comforting movement] Bring the right *open hand,* palm facing in near the middle of the chest, in a forward circle around the back of the left *open hand,* palm facing in, as it moves in a circle around the right hand.

**kind**[2] *n.* A group having characteristics in common: *can use computers of the same kind we have in the office.* Same sign used for: **sort, type.**

■ Move the right *K hand,* palm facing left, in a forward circle around the left *K hand,* palm facing right, as it moves in a circle around the right hand, ending with the little-finger side of the right hand landing on the index-finger side of the left hand.

**kind**[3] *adj.* See sign for SOFT-HEARTED.

**kindergarten** *n.* A school class for five-year-old children prior to first grade: *attending kindergarten was a real help to the child's social development.*

■ [Initialized sign similar to sign for **base**] Move the right *K hand,* palm facing left, with a repeated back-and-forth movement under the left *open hand,* palm facing down.

**king** *n.* The male ruler of a country: *the king of Spain.*

■ [Initialized sign following the location of a royal sash] Move the right *K hand,* palm facing in, from touching the left side of the chest near the shoulder downward to touch again near the right side of the waist.

**kink** *n.* See sign for KNOT.

**kiss** *v.* **1.** To touch with the lips, as to show affection or veneration: *kissed her hand.* —*n.* **2.** An act or instance of kissing: *Give me a big kiss on the cheek.*

■ [The hand takes a kiss from the mouth and puts it on the cheek] Touch the fingertips of the right *flattened O hand,* palm facing in, to the right side of the mouth, and then open the right hand and lay the palm of the right *open hand* against the right side of the face.

**kitchen** *n.* A room equipped for preparing and cooking food: *Everyone came into the kitchen while I made dinner.*

■ [Initialized sign similar to sign for **cook**] Beginning with the palm side of the right *K hand* on the upturned left *open hand,* flip the right hand over, ending with the back of the right hand in the left palm.

**Kleenex** *Trademark.* See sign for TISSUE.

**kneel** *v.* To go down on one's knees: *kneel at the altar.*

- [Represents a person's bent knees] Bring the knuckles of the right *bent V fingers,* palm facing in, down on the upturned left *open hand.*

**knife** *n.* A thin, flat metal blade fastened in a handle and used for cutting and spreading: *to cut meat with a knife.*

- [Represents the slicing movement done with a knife] Slide the bottom side of the extended right index finger, palm facing in, with a double movement at an angle down the length of the extended left index finger, palm facing right, turning the right palm down each time as it moves off the end of the left index finger.

**knob** *n.* A rounded projection forming a handle on a door or drawer, or a controlling device on an appliance: *Turn the volume up on the television with the knob on the left.*

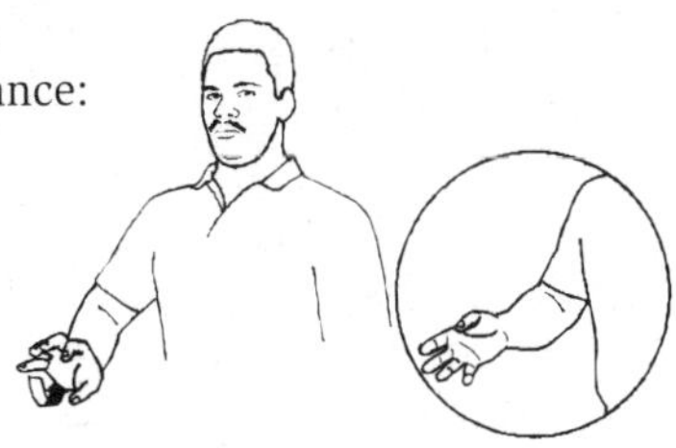

- [Mime turning a knob] Beginning with the right *curved 5 hand* in front of the right side of the body, palm facing forward, twist the hand, ending with the palm facing left.

**knock** *v.* To strike a blow with the knuckles: *knock on the door.*

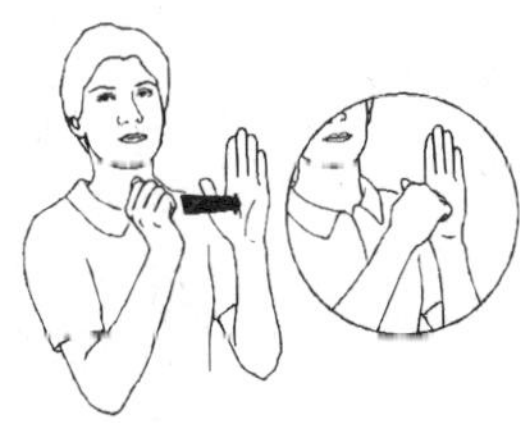

- [Mime knocking on something] Hit the palm side of the right *A hand,* palm facing left, with a double movement on the palm of the left *open hand,* palm facing right and fingers pointing up.

**knot** *n.* **1.** A fastening made by tying pieces or ends of rope, string, etc., together by looping or interlacing them: *Tie a tight knot in the shoelace.* **2.** A tangled mass: *terrible knots in my hair.* —*v.* **3.** To tie in a knot: *Knot the rope on each end.* Same sign used for: **kink.**

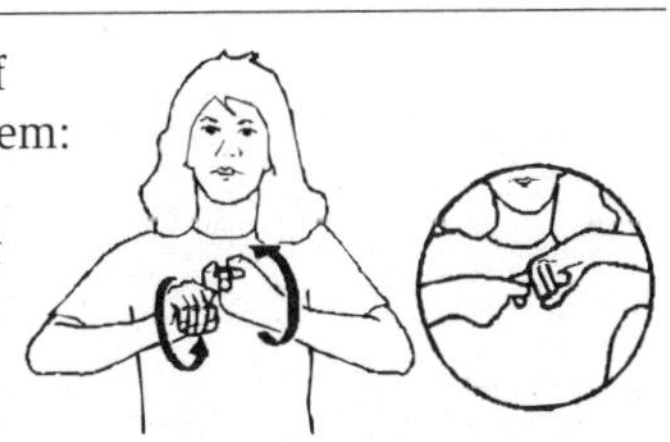

- [Represents a knotted rope] Beginning with the index finger of the right *X hand,* palm facing down, hooked over the bent left index finger, palm facing up, twist the hands in opposite directions, reversing positions.

**know** *v.* To have the facts; perceive; understand: *to know about the accident.*

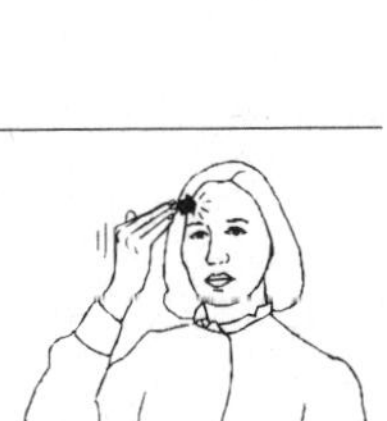

- [Location of knowledge in the brain] Tap the fingertips of the right *bent hand,* palm facing down, on the right side of the forehead.

**knowledge** *n.* See sign for AWARE.

**know nothing** *v. phrase.* Not to have the facts; be unaware: *know nothing about it.*

■ [**know** + showing zero amount] Bring the fingers of the right *bent hand,* palm facing down, from the forehead downward while changing into an *O hand,* touching the little-finger side of the right *O hand,* palm facing left, against the upturned palm of the left *open hand.*

**label**[1] *n.* **1.** A strip of paper attached to an object to specify its contents, purpose, destination, or other information: *Put a label on each file folder.* —*v.* **2.** To mark with a label; attach a label to: *to label the jelly jars.* Same sign used for: **apply, brand, decal, tag.**

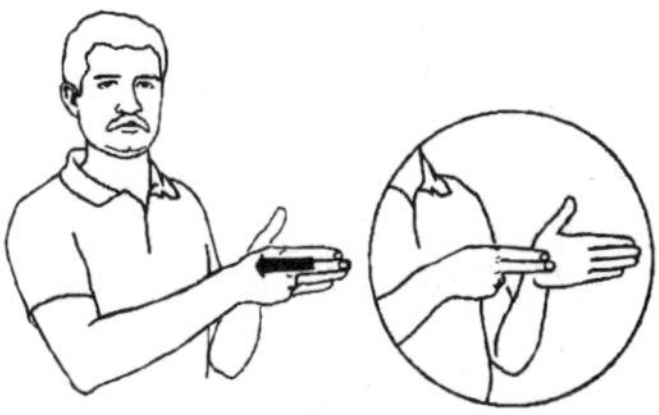

■ [Demonstrates applying a label] Wipe the extended fingers of the right *H hand,* palm facing left, from the fingers to the heel of the left *open hand,* palm facing right and fingers pointing forward.

**label**[2] *n.* See sign for NAME[1].

**labor** *v.* See signs for ACTIVE, WORK.

**lack** *n.* See sign for SKIP[1].

**ladder** *n.* See sign for CLIMB.

**lady** *n.* A well-bred woman: *She is quiet and refined and always acts like a lady.* Same sign used for: **female.**

■ [**girl** + **polite**] Bring the thumb of the right *A hand,* palm facing left, downward from the right side of the chin while opening, ending by tapping side of the thumb of the right *open hand* in the center of the chest.

**laid up** *adj. phrase.* Temporarily incapacitated or disabled, especially when confined to bed: *He was laid up with the flu.*

■ Bring both *bent V hands,* palms facing each other, from in front of each side of the body back toward each side of the chest.

**lake** *n.* A body of water surrounded by land: *to fish for trout in the lake.*

■ [**water** + shape of a lake] Tap the index finger of the right *W hand,* palm facing left, against the chin with a double movement. Then with the *modified C hands,* palms facing each other, in front of each side of the body, move the hands downward a short distance.

**lamp** *n.* Any of several devices that give out artificial light: *Turn on the lamp in the hallway.*

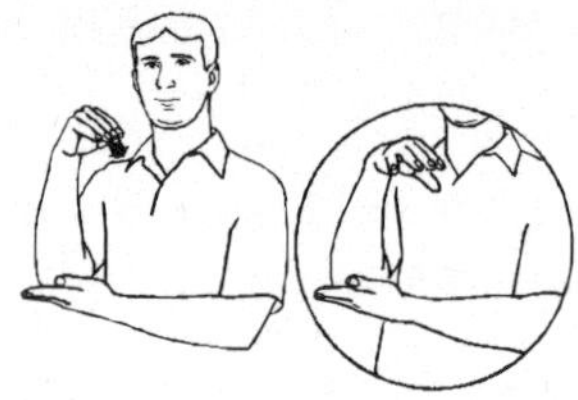

■ [Represents light coming out of a table lamp] With the elbow of the raised right arm resting on the palm of the left *open hand* in front of the right side of the chest, open the right *flattened O hand,* forming a *curved 5 hand,* palm facing down and fingers pointing forward.

---

**land**[1] *n.* **1.** Any part of the Earth not covered by water: *The lost ship finally approached land.* **2.** Soil on an area of ground with reference to its composition and potential use: *good land for planting.* Same sign used for: **acreage, field, property.**

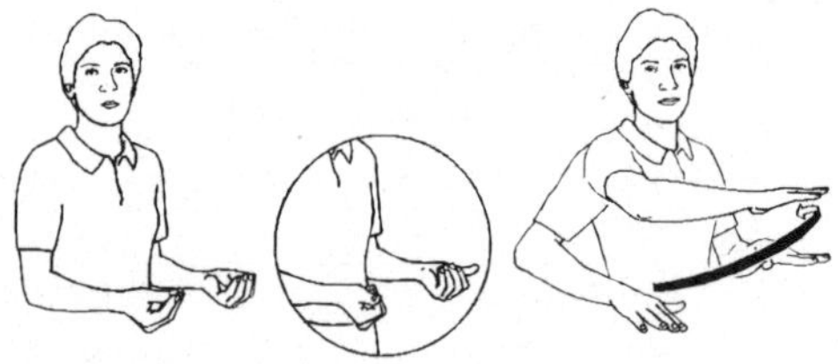

■ [**dirt** + **district**] Beginning with both *flattened O hands* in front of each side of the body, palms facing up, move the thumb of both hands smoothly with a double movement across each fingertip, starting with the little fingers and ending as *A hands* each time. Then move the right *open hand,* palm facing down and fingers pointing forward, from in front of the right side of the body in a large arc forward and in front of the chest over the back of the left *open hand,* held in front of the left side of the body, palm facing down and fingers pointing forward.

---

**land**[2] *n.* See signs for COUNTRY, DIRT.

---

**lane** *n.* See sign for ROAD.

---

**language** *n.* Structured communication using a system of arbitrary symbols, sounds, gestures, etc., to express thought: *knows the French language well.* Same sign used for: **dialect, tongue.**

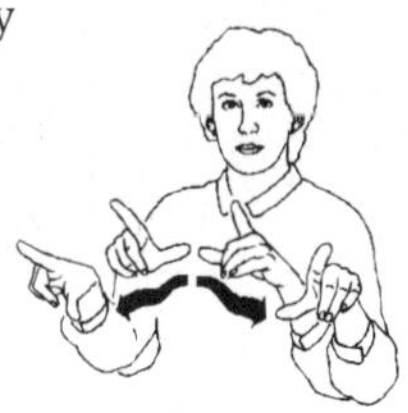

■ [Initialized sign] Beginning with the thumbs of both *L hands* near each other in front of the chest, palms angled down, bring the hands outward with a wavy movement to in front of each side of the chest.

---

**lapse** *n.* See sign for BETWEEN.

---

**laptop computer** *n. phrase.* A portable computer complete with an integrated screen and keyboard usually weighing less than 10 pounds: *take the laptop computer on the trip.* Same sign used for: **notebook computer.**

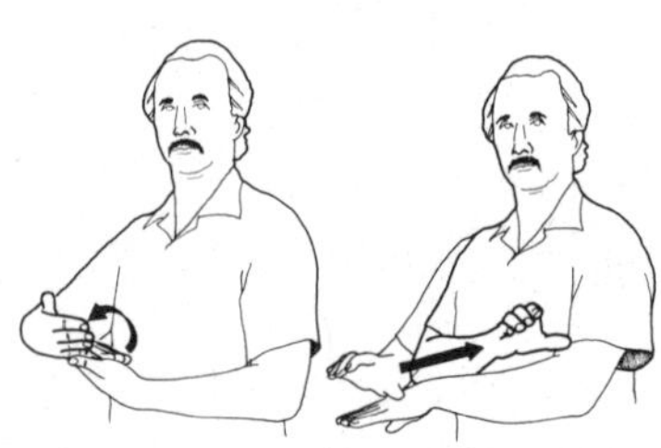

■ [Opening of a laptop + **computer**] Beginning with the palms of both *open hands* together, right hand on top of left hand and fingers pointing in opposite directions, flip the thumb side of the right hand up while keeping the little finger on the left palm. Then move the thumb side of the right *C hand,* palm left, from touching the lower part of the extended left arm upward to touch the upper arm.

**large** *adj.* Of more than the usual size, quantity, degree, etc.: *a large amount of money.* Same sign used for: **big, enormous, grand, great, huge, massive.**

■ [Initialized sign showing a large size] Move both *L hands* from in front of each side of the chest, palms facing each other, in large arcs beyond each side of the body.

**laser** *n.* A device that emits intense light of a precise wavelength: *burn a design in the wood with a laser.* Same sign used for: **burn.**

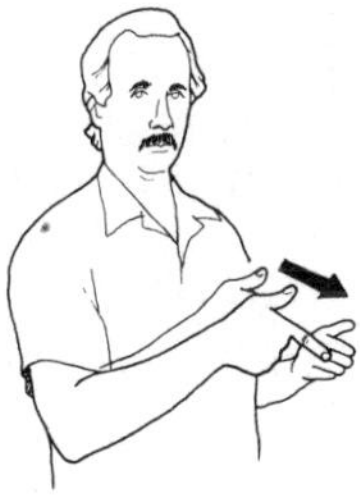

■ [Action of a laser beam] With the index finger of the right *L hand* pointing at the palm of the left *open hand,* move the right hand back and forth with a double movement.

**last**[1] *adj.* **1.** Coming after all others: *the last cookie in the box.* —*adv.* **2.** After all others: *He finished last.* —*n.* **3.** Something or someone that is last: *the last to arrive.* Same sign used for: **end, final, finally.**

■ [Indicates the last thing] Move the extended little finger of the right *I hand,* palm facing left, downward in front of the chest, striking the extended little finger of the left *I hand,* palm facing in, as it passes.

**last**[2] *adj., adv.* See signs for AGO, BEFORE[1], CONTINUE[1]. Related form: **lasting.**

**last week** *n. phrase.* During the week before this one: *went to the opera last week.*

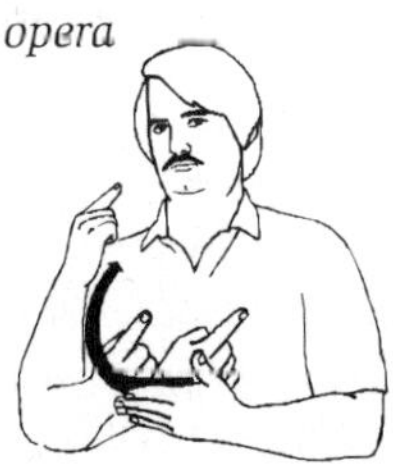

■ [**week** formed with a movement into the past] Beginning with the back of the right *one hand,* palm facing in, in the palm of the left *open hand,* palm facing in, bring the right hand across the palm and then back with a sweeping movement over the right shoulder.

**last year** *n. phrase.* During the year before this one: *attended college last year.*

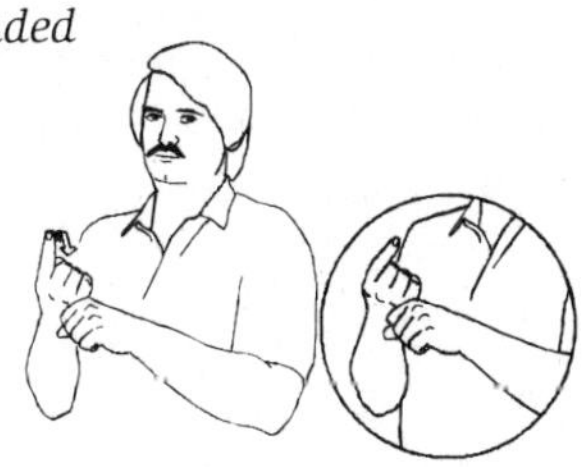

■ [An abbreviated form of **year** moving into the past] With the back of the right *one hand,* palm facing up, on the index-finger side of the left *S hand,* palm facing down, bend the right extended index finger down toward the chest with a double movement.

**late** *adj.* **1.** Occurring after the usual time: *a very late summer.* **2.** Continued past the usual time: *I just rushed over from a late meeting.* —*adv.* **3.** After the usual time: *you got here late.* **4.** Until past the usual time: *had to work late again.* Same sign used for: **delay, tardy.**

■ [Hand moves into the past] Bend the wrist of the right *open hand,* palm facing back and fingers pointing down, back near the right side of the waist with a double movement.

**lately** *adv.* See sign for SINCE.

**later** *adv.* After the present time: *talk about it later.* Alternate form: **later on.** Same sign used for: **after a while, afterward.**

■ [Initialized sign representing the minute hand on a clock moving to indicate the passing of time] With the thumb of the right *L hand,* palm facing forward, on the palm of the left *open hand,* palm facing right and fingers pointing forward, twist the right hand forward, keeping the thumb in place and ending with the right palm facing down.

**laugh**[1] *v.* To make sounds, as chuckles, giggles, or loud guffaws, expressing amusement or happiness: *The children are laughing hysterically at the clown.*

■ [Initialized sign showing the shape of the mouth when one laughs] Beginning with the extended index fingers of both *L hands* at each corner of the mouth, palms facing back, pull the hands outward to each side of the head with a double movement while closing the hands into *10 hands* each time.

**laugh**[2] *v.* See sign for HYSTERICAL. Related form: **laughter** *n.*

**laugh at** *v. phrase.* See sign for MOCK.

**lavatory** *n.* See sign for TOILET.

**law** *n.* **1.** The combination of regulations made by a government: *sworn to obey the law of the land.* **2.** An individual rule, prescribed by a city, state, or national authority, governing the behavior of its citizens: *broke the law against jaywalking.* Same sign used for: **legal.**

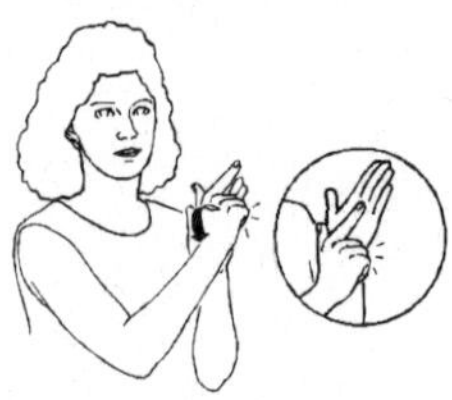

■ [Initialized sign representing recording laws on the books] Place the palm side of the right *L hand,* palm facing left, first on the fingers and then the heel of the left *open hand,* palm facing right and fingers pointing up.

**layaway** *n.* See sign for INSTALLMENT PLAN.

**layer** *n.* One thickness spread on a surface or forming a level below or beneath other thicknesses: *a layer of dust.* Same sign used for: **plush.**

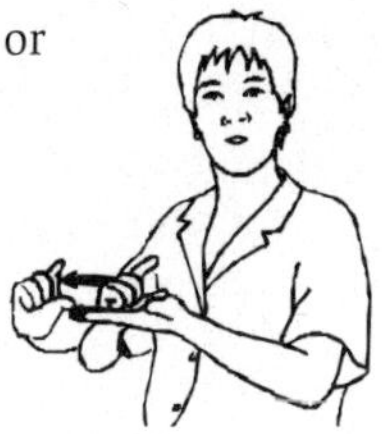

■ [Shows the shape of a layer on top of something] Slide the thumb of the right *modified C hand,* palm facing left, from the heel to off the fingers of the upturned palm of the left *open hand* held in front of the chest.

**lay off** *v. phrase. Informal.* See sign for DISMISS.

**lazy** *adj.* Not inclined to work or be active: *a lazy person, who hangs around the house all day doing nothing.* Same sign used for: **slothful.**

■ [Initialized sign] Tap the palm side of the right *L hand* against the left side of the chest with a double movement.

**lead** *v.* To show the way (to): *to lead the way; to lead the group on a hike.* Same sign used for: **conduct, guide, head, host, steer.**

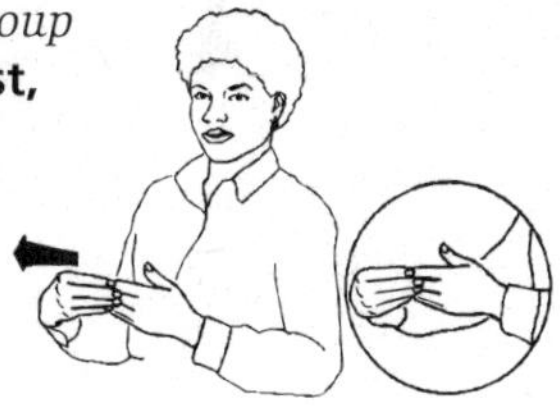

■ [One hand leads the other by pulling it] With the fingers of the left *open hand,* palm facing right, being held by the fingers and thumb of the right hand, palm facing in, pull the left hand forward a short distance.

**leaf** *n.* A thin, flat green part that grows on the stem of a plant and absorbs energy from the sun: *Rake the dried leaves that have fallen from the tree.*

■ [Represents a leaf blowing in the wind on a branch] With the extended left index finger on the wrist of the right *5 hand,* angled down and bent at the wrist, swing the right hand forward and back with a double movement.

**leak**[1] *v.* **1.** (of liquid) To escape from a hole or crack: *The water leaked onto the floor through a small hole in the pipe.* —*n.* **2.** A hole or crack that lets liquid out: *a leak in the bucket.* **3.** An act or instance of leaking: *furniture damaged by the leak in the ceiling.* Same sign used for: **drain, run.**

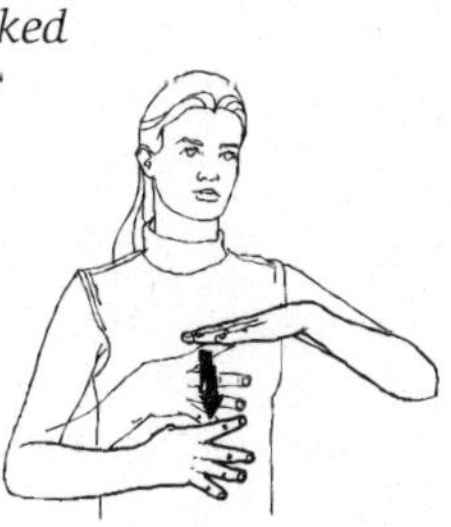

■ [Represents the flow of a leaking liquid] Beginning with the index-finger side of the right *4 hand,* palm facing in and fingers pointing left, touching the palm of the left *open hand,* palm facing down and fingers pointing right, move the right hand down with a double movement.

**leak**[2] *n., v.* See sign for DRIP.

**lean** *adj.* See signs for DIET, THIN.

**learn** *v.* To gain knowledge of or skill in: *learn a trade.* Same sign used for: **acquire, educate, education.**

■ [Represents taking information from paper and putting it in one's head] Beginning with the fingertips of the right *curved 5 hand,* palm facing down, on the palm of the upturned left *open hand,* bring the right hand up while closing the fingers and thumb into a *flattened O hand* near the forehead.

**least** *adj.* Smallest in size, amount, degree, etc.: *the least amount.*

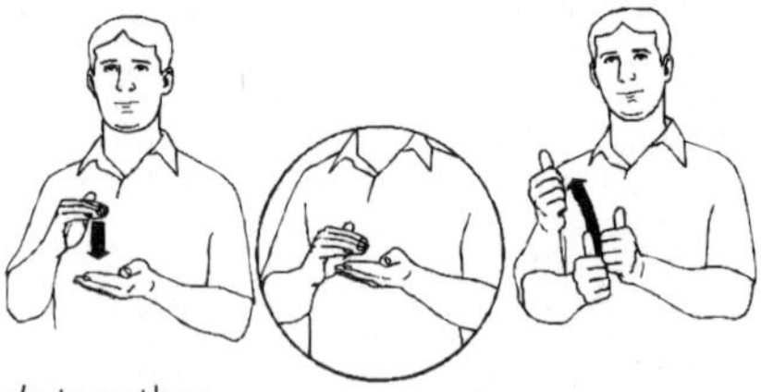

■ [**less** + **most**] Move the right *bent hand,* palm facing down and fingers pointing left, from in front of the chest downward a few inches above the left *open hand,* palm facing up and fingers pointing right. Then, beginning with the palm sides of both *10 hands* together in front of the chest, bring the right hand upward, ending with the right hand in front of the right shoulder, palm facing left.

**leave**[1] *v.* To go away (from): *to leave without saying good-bye; to leave home.* Same sign used for: **depart, desert, withdraw.**

■ Beginning with both *curved 5 hands* in front of each side of the chest, palms facing down, pull the hands back toward the right shoulder while closing the fingers and thumbs into *flattened O hands.*

**leave**[2] *v.* To let stay or be: *Leave your shoes outside.* Same sign used for: **leftover, rest.**

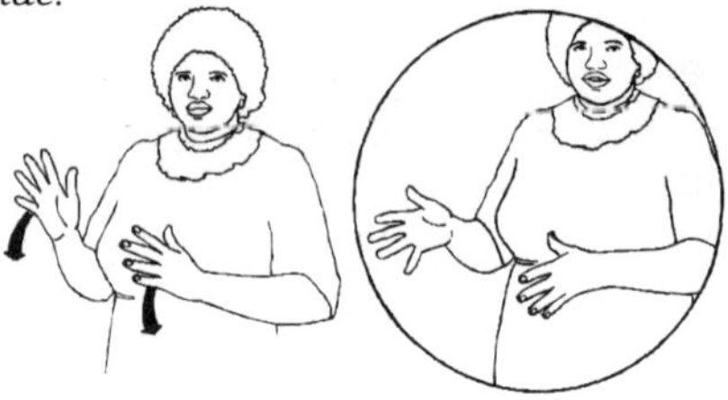

■ [The hands seem to leave something by thrusting it down] Beginning with both *5 hands* in front of each side of the body, palms facing each other and fingers angled up, thrust the fingers downward with a deliberate movement.

**leave**[3] *v.* See sign for GO[1].

**lecture** *v., n.* See sign for SPEAK[2].

**leech** *n.* A person who habitually tries to get something from others without giving anything in return: *He is a leech when it comes to cigarettes—borrowing them from everyone.* Same sign used for: **mooch** *(slang)*, **take advantage of.**

■ [One hand seems to "put the bite on" the other hand] Tap the fingers of the right *U hand* and extended thumb of the right hand, palm facing left, with a double movement on the fingertips of the left *U hand,* palm facing down and fingers pointing right.

**left** *adj.* **1.** Belonging to the left side: *his left arm.* —*adv.* **2.** On or toward the left side: *Turn left at the next light.* —*n.* **3.** The left side: *leaning toward the left.*

■ [Initialized sign indicating a direction to the left] Beginning with the right *L hand* in front of the right side of the chest, palm facing forward and index finger pointing up, move the hand deliberately to the left.

**leftover** *n., adj.* See sign for LEAVE[2].

**left turn** *n. phrase.* A turn to the left to proceed along a street, hallway, etc.: *made a left turn on Main Street.*

■ [Initialized sign demonstrating a left direction] Move the left *L hand,* palm facing in and index finger pointing right, to the left while twisting the wrist, ending with the palm facing forward and the index finger pointing left.

**leg** *n.* Either of the two lower limbs used for standing, walking, etc.: *I hurt my leg on the corner of the coffee table.*

■ [Location of the leg] Pat the palm of the right *open hand,* palm facing left, against the side of the right thigh with a double movement.

**legal** *adj.* See sign for LAW.

**leisure** *n.* See signs for ENJOY, FUN.

**lemon** *n.* A sour, juicy, citrus fruit, yellow in color: *to put lemon in the tea.*

■ [Initialized sign similar to sign for **sour**] Tap the thumb of the right *L hand,* palm facing left, against the chin with a double movement.

**lend** *v.* To let someone have temporary use of: *I will lend you my umbrella.* Same sign used for: **loan.**

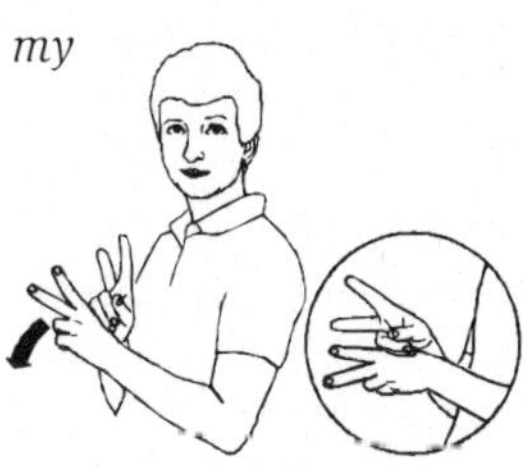

■ [Directional sign toward the person to whom something is lent] With the little-finger side of the right *V hand* across the index-finger side of the left *V hand,* move the hands from near the chest forward and down a short distance.

**lend me** *v. phrase.* See sign for BORROW.

**length** *n.* The extent of something as measured from end to end: *What is the length of that table?* See also sign for LONG.

■ [The finger measures off a designated distance] Beginning with the extended right index finger, palm facing in and finger pointing down, touching the extended left index finger, palm facing in and finger pointing right, move the right finger outward to the right.

---

**lesbian** *n.* **1.** A woman who is sexually attracted to other women; female homosexual: *She realized in her twenties that she was a lesbian.* —*adj.* **2.** Of or pertaining to lesbians or lesbianism. Related form: **lesbianism** *n.*

■ [Initialized sign] Bring the palm side of the right *L hand,* palm facing in and index finger pointing left, back against the chin with a double movement, ending with the chin within the crook between the right index finger and thumb.

---

**less**[1] *adj.* **1.** Being smaller in amount, quantity, or size: *less rain this year.* —*adv.* **2.** To a smaller extent or degree: *charity for those less fortunate.* Related form: **lessen** *v.* Same sign used for: **cutback, low, reduce.**

■ [The hands demonstrate a decreasing amount] Move the right *open hand,* palm facing down and fingers pointing left, from in front of the chest downward a few inches above the left *open hand,* palm facing up and fingers pointing right.

---

**less**[2] *adj.* See sign for MINIMUM.

---

**lessen** *v.* See signs for DECREASE[1,3].

---

**lesson**[1] *n.* **1.** A section of a course of study: *Did you study your French lesson for tomorrow?* **2.** Something to be learned or taught, especially of a moral nature: *learning from the lessons of history.*

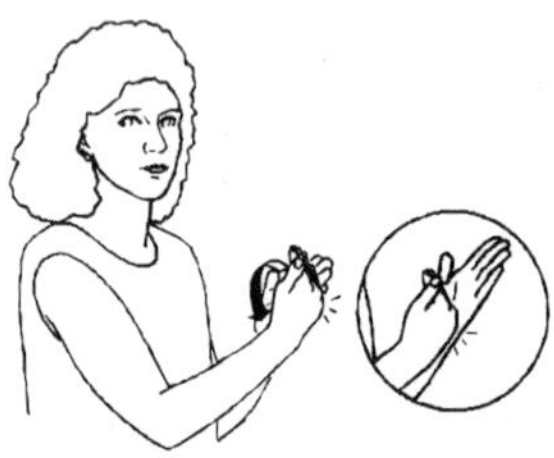

■ [The movement represents breaking up information on a page into lessons] Move the little-finger side of the right *bent hand,* palm facing in, from the fingers to the heel of the left *open hand,* palm facing up.

---

**lesson**[2] *n.* See sign for COURSE.

---

**let** *v.* To allow to: *Let me do it.* Same sign used for: **allow, grant, permit.**

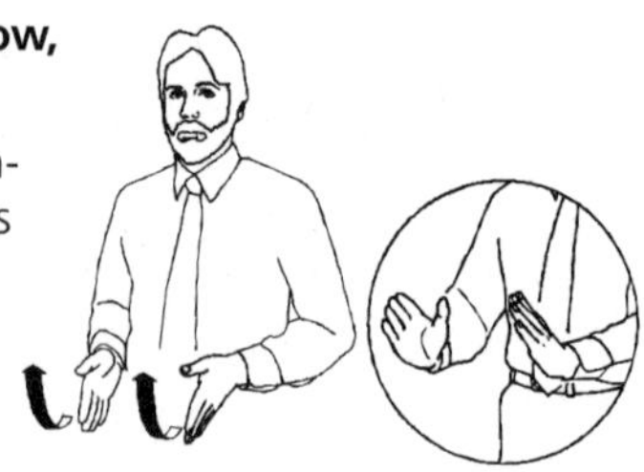

■ [The hands outline a path for a person to pass] Beginning with both *open hands* in front of the waist, palms facing each other and fingers pointing down, bring the fingers forward and upward by bending the wrists.

**let go** *v. phrase.* See signs for DISCONNECT, FIRE[1].

**let know** *v. phrase.* See sign for INFORM.

**let's see 1.** *v. phrase.* (Used to recommend the postponement of action or judgment until something specified occurs): *Let's see what happens before you make up your mind.* **2.** (Used to indicate an impending investigation): *Let's see how our patient is doing.* Same sign used for: **speculate, speculation.**

- [The fingers represent one's eyes] Tap the fingertips of the right *V hand,* palm facing left and fingers pointing up, with a double movement near the right eye.

**letter**[1] *n.* One of the 26 symbols forming the English alphabet, used in printing and writing to represent the sounds of the spoken language: *the letters A to Z.* Same sign used for: **literal.**

- [Initialized sign similar to sign for **word**] Tap the thumb of the right *L hand,* palm facing forward, with a double movement against the extended left index finger, palm facing right.

**letter**[2] *n.* A written communication sent through the postal service: *to write a letter of complaint to the utility company.* Same sign used for: **mail.**

- [Shows licking a stamp and placing it on an envelope] Touch the extended thumb of the right *10 hand* to the lips, palm facing in, and then move the thumb downward to touch the fingertips of the left *open hand* held in front of the body, palm facing up.

**lettuce** *n.* See sign for CABBAGE.

**level** *adj.* See sign for EVEN[1].

**lever** *n.* See sign for PIPE[2].

**liability** *n.* See signs for AFFORD, BURDEN.

**liberal** *adj.* See signs for BROAD-MINDED, LIBERTY.

**liberate** *v.* See sign for SAVE[1].

**liberty**[1] *n.* Freedom from governmental or other external control: *We are proud of the liberty of our citizens.* Same sign used for: **liberal.**

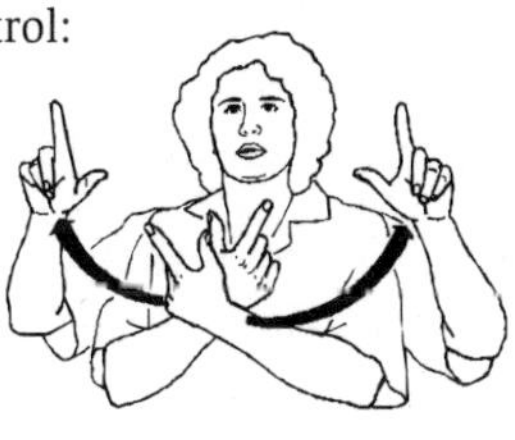

- [Initialized sign similar to sign for **save**[1]] Beginning with the wrists of both *L hands* crossed in front of the chest, palms facing in, twist the wrists to move the hands outward, ending with the hands in front of each shoulder, palms facing forward.

**liberty**[2] *n.* See signs for FREE[1], SAVE[1].

**library** *n.* **1.** A collection of books or other materials useful for reference, especially one that is organized and cataloged: *The university has a fine library.* **2.** The building in which such a collection is housed: *We can go to the library to study.*

■ [Initialized sign] Move the right *L hand,* palm facing forward, in a circle in front of the right shoulder.

**license** *n.* A permit to do something: *a driver's license.* Same sign used for: **permit.**

■ [Initialized sign similar to sign for **certificate**] Tap the thumbs of both *L hands* with a double movement in front of the chest, palms facing forward.

**lick** *v.* To stroke with the tongue: *The dog licked my hand.*

■ [The fingers represent the tongue licking something] Brush the fingertips of the right *U hand,* palm facing back and fingers pointing down, forward with a double movement along the length of the palm of the upturned left *open hand,* held in front of the chest.

**lid** *n.* A removable cover, as for a jar: *Put the lid back on the peanut butter, please.* Same sign used for: **cover, top.**

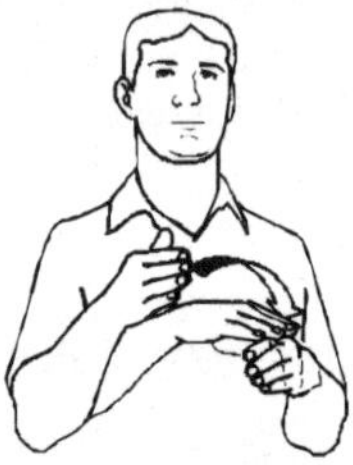

■ [Mime putting a lid on a jar] Bring the fingers of the right *open hand* from in front of the right shoulder, palm facing left and fingers pointing forward, in an arc down on top of the index-finger side of the left *C hand,* palm facing right in front of the left side of the chest.

**lie**[1] *v.* **1.** To speak or write falsely with the intention of deceiving: *lied to his lawyer about the accident.* —*n.* **2.** Something said or written that is intended to deceive: *Don't tell your mother a lie.* Same sign used for: **falsehood, fib, perjury.**

■ [The hand movement indicates that a person is speaking out of the side of the mouth when telling a lie] Slide the index-finger side of the right *bent hand,* palm facing down, with a double movement across the chin from right to left.

**lie**[2] or **lie down** *v.* or *v. phrase.* To recline the body in a horizontal position: *to lie down on the couch.* Same sign used for: **recline.**

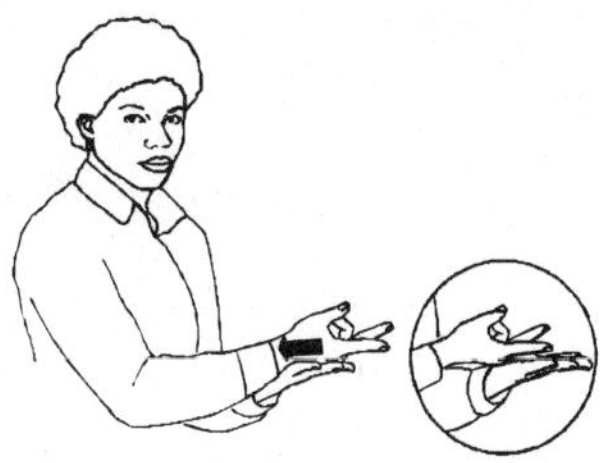

■ [The fingers represent a person's legs in a reclining position] Beginning with the back of the right *V hand,* palm facing up, on the palm of the left *open hand,* palm facing up, pull the right hand in toward the body.

**lift** *v.* See sign for RAISE.

**light**[1] *adj.* Bright; well-lighted; not dark: *a light room with plenty of sunshine.* Same sign used for: **lightbulb.**

■ Beginning with the fingertips of the right *8 hand* near the chin, palm facing in, flick the middle finger upward and forward with a double movement while opening into a *5 hand* each time.

**light**[2] *n.* Something that gives off light, as a lamp: *Turn on the light in the hallway.* Same sign used for: **shine.**

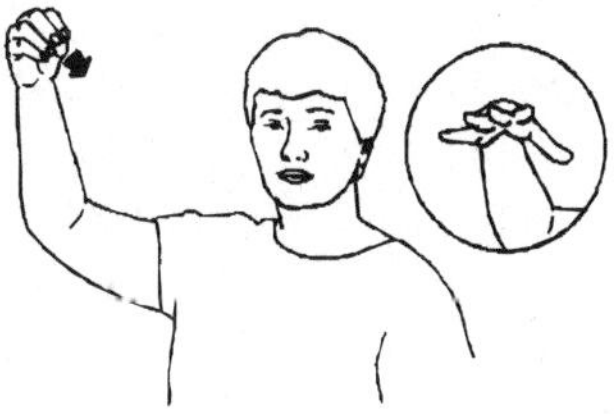

■ [The hand shows the rays of light beaming from a lamp] Beginning with the right *flattened O hand* held above the right shoulder, palm facing down, open the fingers into a *5 hand.*

**light**[3] *adj.* Not heavy: *a light load.*

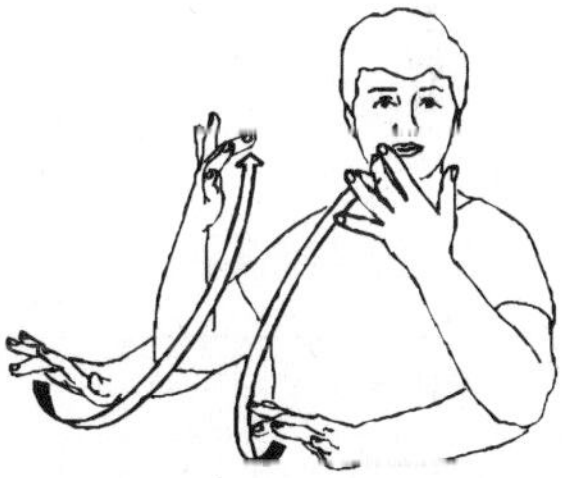

■ [The gesture represents something light floating upward] Beginning with both *5 hands* with bent middle fingers in front of the waist, palms facing down, twist the wrists to raise the hands quickly toward each other and upward, ending with the hands in front of each side of the chest, bent middle fingers pointing in.

**light**[4] *adj.* See sign for BRIGHT.

**lightbulb** *n.* See sign for LIGHT[1].

**lighter** *n.* A device with a spark used to ignite a cigarette: *He'd rather use a lighter than a match.*

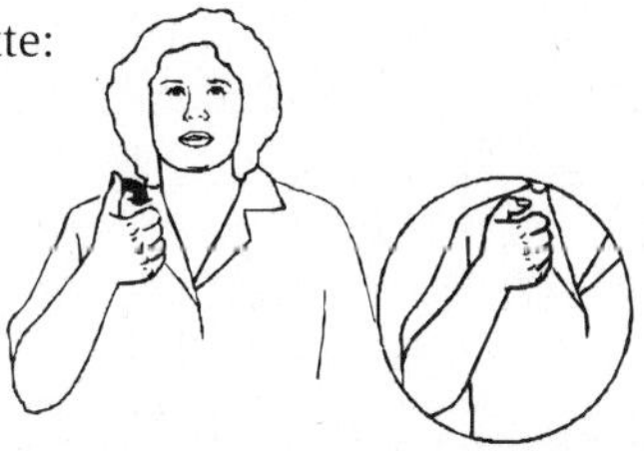

■ [Mime starting a lighter] Bend the extended thumb of the right *10 hand,* palm facing in, up and down with a double movement in front of the right side of the chest.

**lightning** *n.* A flash of electric sparks discharged in the atmosphere: *The lightning hit the tree.* Same sign used for: **bolt, thunderbolt.**

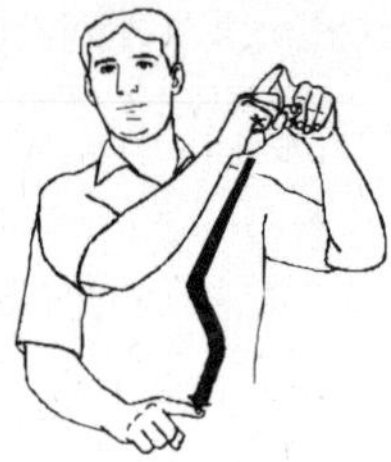

- [Shows shape of lightning bolt] Beginning with the extended index fingers of both hands touching above the left shoulder, move the right hand downward with a jagged movement in front of the chest, ending in front of the waist, finger pointing forward and palm facing down.

**like**[1] *v.* To be pleased with; find agreeable; enjoy: *like to watch TV.*

- Beginning with the bent thumb and middle finger of the right *5 hand* touching the chest, palm facing in, bring the hand forward while closing the fingers to form an *8 hand.*

**like**[2] *v.* (alternate sign)

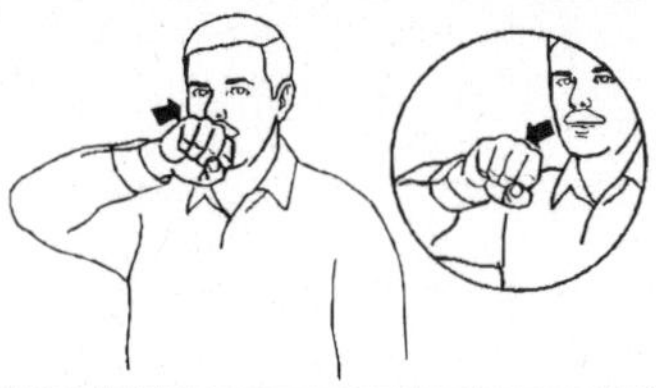

- [Mime kissing the back of one's hand to show fondness] Bring the back of the right *S hand,* palm facing forward, back to the lips and then forward again.

**like**[3] *prep.* Resembling; similar to: *looks like his father.* See also signs for ALIKE[1,2]. Same sign used for SAME.

- [A directional sign in which the hand moves back and forth between the two objects being compared] Move the right *Y hand,* palm facing forward, from side to side with a double movement in front of the right side of the body.

**like**[4] *v.* See sign for ENJOY.

**lime** *n.* A sour, juicy, citrus fruit, green in color: *I like to put lime in my soda.*

- [Initialized sign showing slicing a lime] Slide the thumb of the right *L hand,* palm facing left and index finger pointing up, down the back of the left *S hand,* palm facing in, in front of the chest.

**limit** *v.* See sign for RESTRICT.

**line** *n.* A long, thin fiber, as a cord, wire, or rope: *Unwind the line and tie the boat to the dock.* Same sign used for: **string, thread.**

- [Shows shape of a line] Beginning with the extended little fingers of both *I hands* touching in front of the chest, palms facing in, move both hands outward.

**line up** *v. phrase.* To stand or cause to stand one behind the other in a row; form or cause to form a line: *Let's have the first graders line up on the playground.* Same sign used for: **align, queue, row.**

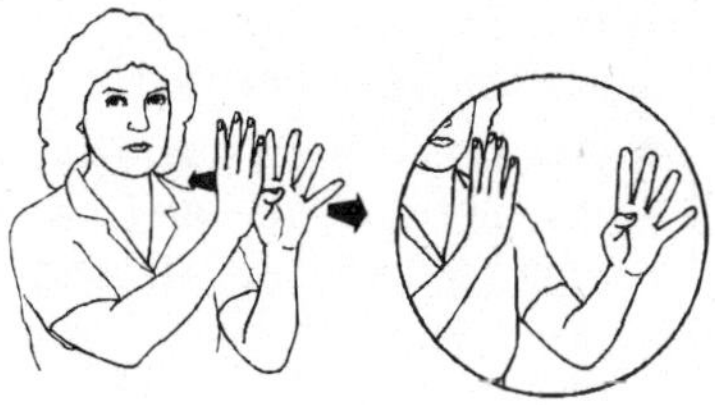

■ [Represents people lined up in a row] Beginning with the little finger of the right *4 hand,* palm facing left, touching the index finger of the right *4 hand,* palm facing right, move the right hand back toward the chest and the left hand forward.

**link**[1] *v.* See sign for BELONG[1].

**link**[2] *n.* See sign for RELATIONSHIP.

**lion** *n.* A large, tawny-colored, flesh-eating member of the cat family, the male of which has a large mane on the back of the neck: *Lions are found in Africa and Asia.*

■ [Shows shape and location of lion's mane] Beginning with the fingers of the right *curved 5 hand* pointing down over the forehead, palm facing down, move the hand back over the top of the head.

**lip** *n.* Either of the two movable fleshy folds forming the edges of the mouth: *Watch my lips move when I speak.*

■ [Location of one's lips] Draw a rectangle around the edge of the mouth with the extended right index finger, palm facing in.

**lipstick** *n.* A cosmetic used for coloring the lips: *to put on lipstick before going out.*

■ [Mime putting on lipstick] Move the fingers of the right *modified X hand* back and forth in front of the mouth with a double movement.

**liquor** *n.* See signs for COCKTAIL, WHISKEY.

**list** *n.* **1.** A series of items written or printed in a sequence: *A shopping list for Christmas.* —*v.* **2.** To record in such a sequence: *She listed all her reasons for changing schools.* Same sign used for: **record, score.**

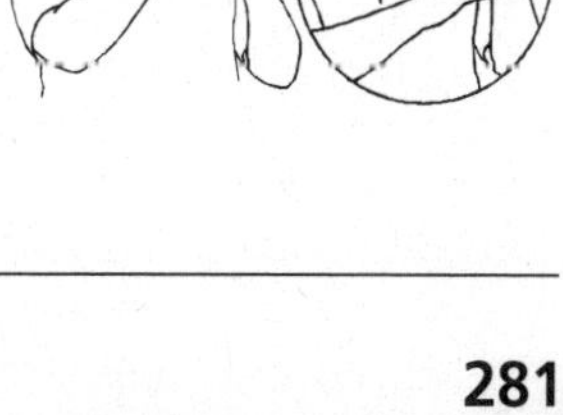

■ [The finger points out items on a list] Touch the bent middle finger of the right *5 hand,* palm facing left, several times on the palm of the left *open hand,* palm facing right and fingers pointing up, as it moves from the fingers downward to the heel.

**listen** *v.* To attend with the ears: *listen to the music.* Same sign used for: **eavesdrop.**

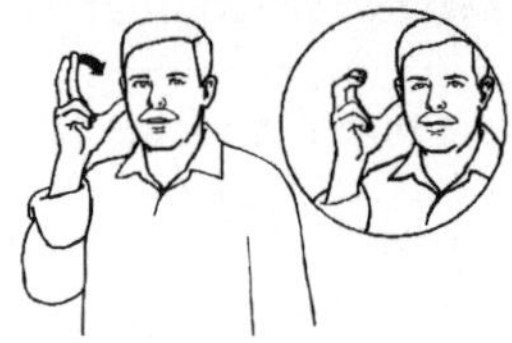

- [The fingers bring sound to the ear] With the thumb of the right *curved 3 hand,* palm facing left, touching the right ear, bend the extended index and middle fingers down with a short double movement.

**literal** *adj.* See sign for LETTER[1].

**little**[1] *adj.* Not large: *a little box that fits in a purse or pocket.* Same sign used for: **small.**

- [Shows a small size] Move both *open hands,* palms facing each other, toward each other with a short double movement in front of the body.

**little**[2] *adj.* Not tall: *a little girl.* Same sign used for: **short, small.**

- [Shows someone or something short in size] Move the right *bent hand,* palm facing down, with a short double movement in front of the right side of the body.

**little bit** *n. phrase.* See sign for TINY.

**live** *v.* To exist or dwell: *to live in Ohio.* Same sign used for: **alive, dwell, survival, survive.**

- Move both *A hands,* palms facing in, upward on each side of the chest.

**living room** *n. phrase.* A room for use by the family for leisure activities and for entertaining guests: *to sit in the living room reading.*

- [**fancy** + **room**] Brush the thumb of the right *5 hand,* palm facing left, upward on the chest with a double movement. Then, beginning with both *open hands* in front of each side of the body, palms facing each other, turn the hands sharply in opposite directions, ending with both palms facing in.

**load** *n.* See sign for PILE[1].

**loaf** *n.* Anything, especially baked food, shaped in an oblong mass with a slightly rounded top: *a loaf of bread.*

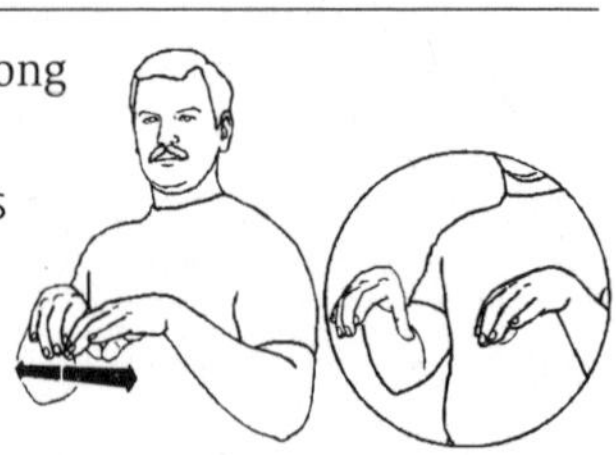

- [Shows shape of a loaf] Beginning with the index fingers of both *C hands* touching in front of the body, palms facing down, bring the hands outward to in front of each side of the body.

**loan** *v.* See sign for LEND.

**loathe** *v.* See sign for DETEST.

**lobster** *n.* **1.** A large shellfish with prominent asymmetrical pincers: *setting traps for lobsters in the bay.* **2.** The edible meat of this shellfish: *a fancy seafood restaurant where we ate lobster.*

- [Represents a lobster's claws] Beginning with both *V hands* in front of each shoulder, palms facing forward, close the index and middle fingers with a double movement.

**local** *adj.* See sign for LOCATION.

**location** *n.* **1.** A position occupied by something: *looking for the location of the document.* **2.** An area where people have settled or reside or where a particular activity can take place: *a good location to camp.* Same sign used for: **local.**

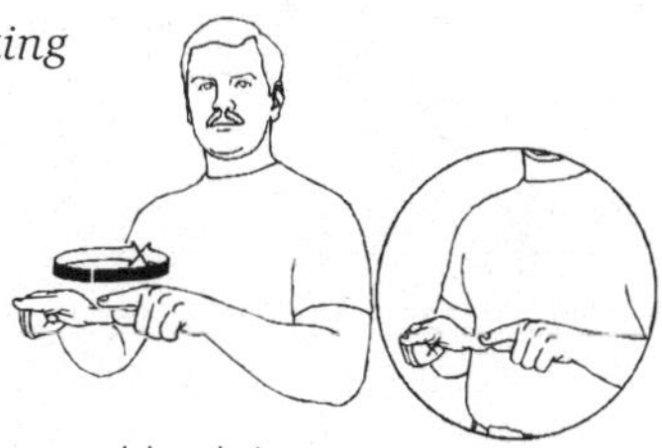

- [Initialized sign similar to sign for **area**[1]] Beginning with the thumbs of both *L hands* touching in front of the body, palms facing down, move the hands apart and back in a circular movement until they touch again near the chest.

**lock** *n.* **1.** A device for securing something when it is closed, as a door, drawer, etc.: *a house protected with a new electronic lock.* —*v.* **2.** To secure an object, as a door or drawer, with a lock: *Lock the front door when you leave.*

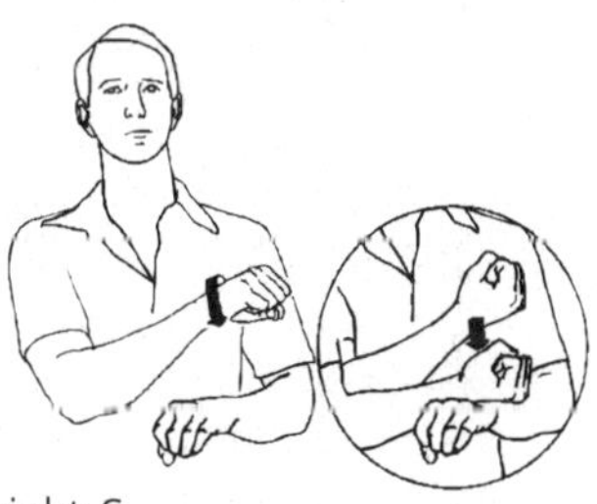

- [Represents the wrists locked together] Beginning with both *S hands* in front of the body, right hand above left and both palms facing down, turn the right hand over by twisting the wrist, ending with the back of the right *S hand,* palm facing up, on the back of the left *S hand,* palm facing down.

**locked into** *adj. phrase.* See sign for BIND.

**locker** *n.* See sign for CLOSET.

**loiter** *v.* To spend time idly lingering in or around a place: *not allowed to loiter at the bus station.*

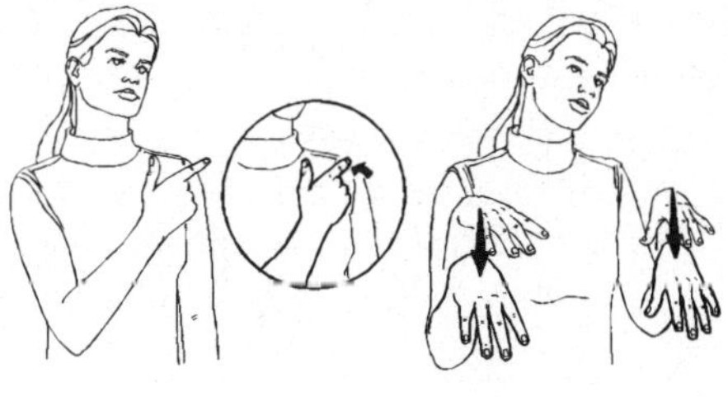

- [**lazy** + dangling the hands lazily] Tap the palm side of the right *L hand* against the left side of the chest. Then drop both *5 hands,* palms facing down, downward in front of each side of the chest.

**lollipop** *n.* A piece of hard candy on a stick: *Some people suck on a lollipop instead of smoking.* Same sign used for: **Popsicle** (*trademark*).

■ [Mime holding and licking a lollipop] Bring the thumb side of the right *X hand,* palm facing left, in a double circular movement back toward the mouth.

**lone** *adj.* See sign for ALONE. Related form: **lonely** *adj.*

**lonely** *adj.* Affected with a depressed sensation resulting from feeling alone: *a lonely person who finds it difficult to make friends.* Alternate form: **lonesome.**

■ Bring the side of the extended right index finger, palm facing left, from near the nose slowly downward in front of the mouth.

**long** *adj.* Having a greater than usual extent in space or time: *to walk a long way; to wait a long time.* See also sign for LENGTH.

■ [The finger measures out a long length] Move the extended right index finger from the wrist up the length of the extended left arm to near the shoulder.

**long ago** *n. phrase.* In the distant past: *fossils of creatures that existed a long time ago.* Repeat sign to indicate a time farther in the past. Same sign used for: **ancient, formerly, historic, primitive, used to.**

■ [The hand indicates a time far in the past] Beginning with the right *5 hand* in front of the right shoulder, palm facing left, bring the hand back to behind the right shoulder with a repeated movement.

**look alike** *v. phrase.* See sign for ALIKE[1].

**look at** *v. phrase.* Direct the eyes toward in order to see (a specific thing): *look at the picture.*

■ [**look** directed toward something] Move the right *V hand,* palm facing down and extended fingers pointing forward, forward a short distance in the direction of the referent.

**look back**[1] *v. phrase.* To recall the past: *to look back on the major events in American history.* Same sign used for: **memorial, memory.**

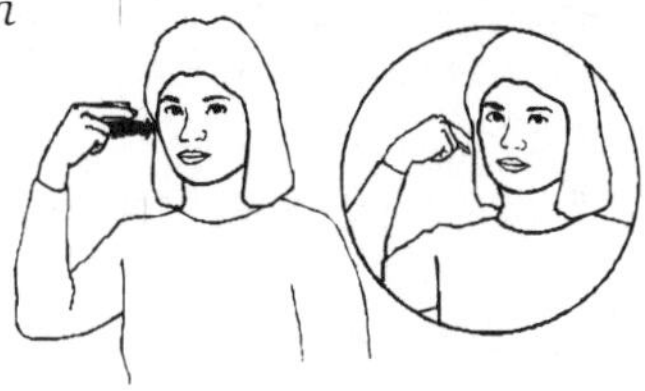

- [**look at** directed toward the past] Move the fingers of the right *V hand,* palm facing down and fingers pointing back, back beside the right side of head.

**look back**[2] *v. phrase.* See sign for HINDSIGHT.

**look down at** or **on** *v. phrase.* See sign for CONTEMPT.

**look for** *v. phrase.* To search for: *Wait while I look for my keys.* Same sign used for: **check for, examine, hunt for, search for.**

- [Shows repeated searching for something] Move the right *C hand,* palm facing left, with a double movement in a circle in front of the face.

**look like** *v. phrase.* See sign for SEEM.

**look out** *v. phrase.* To watch carefully for danger: *Look out for cars crossing the street.* Same sign used for: **watch out, yield.**

- [Represents the eyes moving quickly to observe something] Beginning with the right *V hand* near the right side of the nose, palm facing left and fingers pointing up, bring the hand forward and outward to the right and then downward in front of the chest, ending with the palm facing down and the fingers angled to the left.

**look over** *v. phrase.* To inspect or examine (something): *to look over the work he did.* Same sign used for: **browse, observe, view.**

- [Represents the eyes surveying something] Beginning with both *V hands* in front of each side of the chest, right hand higher than the left hand, both palms facing down, and fingers pointing forward, move the hands in double alternating circles.

**look up** *v. phrase.* To search for, as in a reference book or online database: *to look up a phone number.*

- [The fingers seem to page through a book to look up something] Brush the extended thumb of the right *10 hand,* palm facing down, with a double movement in an arc across the palm of the left *open hand,* palm facing up.

**loop** *n.* A sequence of computer instructions that is repeatedly executed until some specified condition is met: *caught in an endless loop because of bad programming.*

■ [Shape of a loop] Move the extended right index finger, palm facing down and finger pointing left, in a large circle with a double movement around the extended left index finger, palm facing in and finger pointing right.

**loose**[1] *adj.* Not firmly fastened: *a loose button.* Same sign used for: **flabby.**

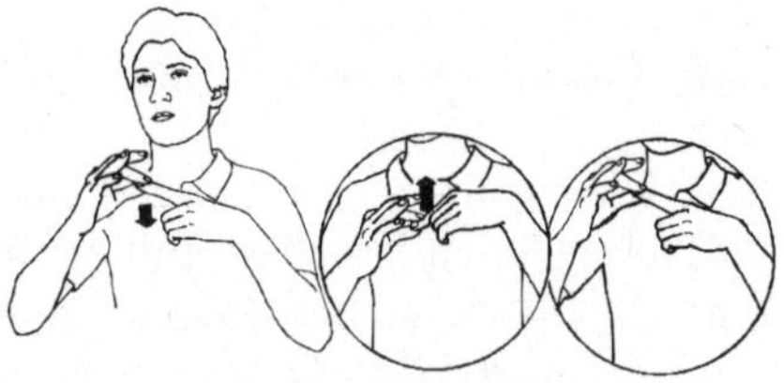

■ [Demonstrates something that is loose and moves easily] With the extended left index finger, palm facing down and finger pointing right, grasped between the thumb and bent middle finger of the right *5 hand,* palm facing left, move the right hand up and down with a double movement.

**loose**[2] *adj.* See sign for DISCONNECT.

**lopsided** *adj.* **1.** Not level; leaning to one side: *a lopsided shelf.* **2.** Larger or heavier on one side; not balanced: *trying to carry a bulky, lopsided package.*

■ Beginning with both *open hands* in front of each side of the chest, palms facing down and fingers pointing forward, and hands angled downward to the right, drop the right hand while tipping the right side of the body downward at the same time.

**lose**[1] *v.* To come to be without: *I lost my wallet at the supermarket.*

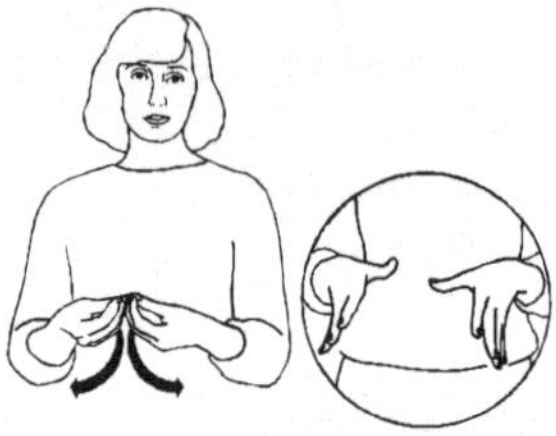

■ [The hands seem to drop something as if to lose it] Beginning with the fingertips of both *flattened O hands* touching in front of the body, palms facing up, drop the fingers quickly downward and away from each other while opening into *5 hands,* ending with both palms and fingers angled downward.

**lose**[2] *v.* To be defeated in: *to lose the game.*

■ Bring the palm side of the right *V hand* from in front of the right shoulder, palm facing forward, downward to land on the upturned palm of the left *open hand* in front of the body.

**lose**[3] *v.* See sign for DECREASE[1].

**lotion** *n.* A liquid preparation for cleansing, soothing, disinfecting, or smoothing the skin: *She put lotion on her rough hands.*

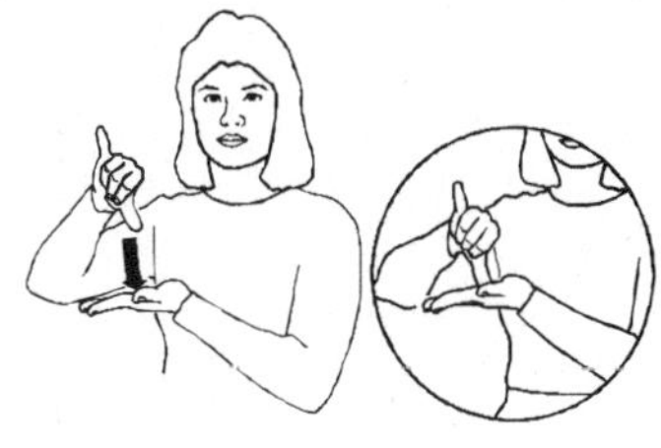

- [Shows pouring lotion from a bottle into one's hand] Bring the thumb of the right *Y hand* from in front of the right shoulder, palm facing right, downward to touch the left *open hand* held in front of the chest, palm facing up and fingers pointing right.

**lots** *pl. n. Informal.* See signs for MANY, MUCH.

**lots to do** *n. phrase. Informal.* See sign for BUSY.

**loud**[1] *adj.* (Of sound) Having marked intensity or great volume: *The horn made a loud blast.*

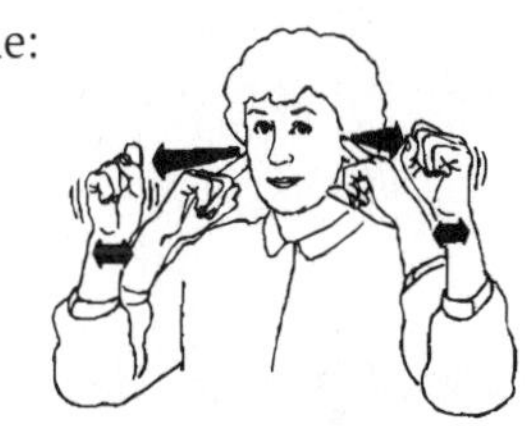

- [**hear** formed with both hands + **noise**] Move both extended index fingers from pointing to each ear forward while changing into *S hands,* and shake them with a repeated movement.

**loud**[2] *adj.* See sign for NOISE.

**lousy** *adj. Slang.* Of low quality; extremely poor: *did a lousy job painting the living room.* Related form: **louse** *n.*

- Beginning with the thumb of the right *3 hand* touching the nose, palm facing left, bring the hand downward in front of the chest.

**love** *v.* **1.** To have a deep affectionate feeling for: *I really love my dog.* —*n.* **2.** A warm regard or affectionate feeling: *to have a great love of books.*

- [The hands bring something that is loved close to oneself] With the wrists of both *S hands* crossed in front of the chest, palms facing in, bring the arms back against the chest.

**lovely** *adj.* See signs for BEAUTIFUL, PRETTY.

**lover** *n.* See sign for SWEETHEART.

**low**[1] *adj.* Existing close to the floor or ground; not high: *a low shelf.* Related form: **lower** *adj.* Same sign used for: **demote.**

- [Indicates a location lower than another location] Beginning with both *bent hands* in front of each shoulder, palms facing each other, move them downward in front of each side of the chest.

**low**[2] (amount) *adj.* See sign for LESS.

**loyal** *adj.* Faithful and devoted, as to one's country or friends: *to be a loyal follower of the cause.*

- [Initialized sign formed similarly to the sign for **respect**] Beginning with the thumb of the right *L hand,* palm facing left, touching the forehead, move the right hand forward in an arc.

**luck** *n.* **1.** Something that seems to cause things, whether good or bad, to happen by chance: *We wish you good luck.* **2.** Success; good fortune: *She's had a lot of luck in her job.* Related form: **lucky** *adj.* Same sign used for: **fortunate.**

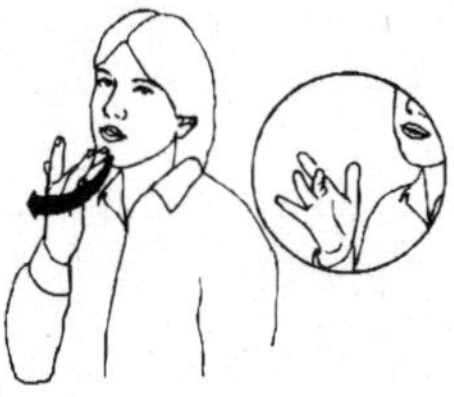

- Beginning with the bent middle finger of the right *5 hand,* palm facing in, touching the chin, twist the wrist to swing the hand forward with a quick movement, ending with the palm angled forward.

**luggage** *n.* See sign for BAGGAGE.

**lumbago** *n.* See sign for BACKACHE.

**lumbar** *adj.* See sign for BACK.

**lump** *n.* See signs for AMOUNT, BUMP[1,2].

**lunch** *n.* A light meal eaten at midday: *time for lunch.*

- [**eat** + **noon**] Bring the fingers of the right *flattened O hand* to the lips, palm facing in. Then place the elbow of the bent right arm, arm extended up and open right palm facing forward, on the back of the left *open hand* held in front of the body, palm facing down.

**lung** *n.* Either of the two respiratory organs in humans and other vertebrates used for the exchange of air so as to bring oxygen to the blood: *to take fresh air into the lungs by breathing deeply.*

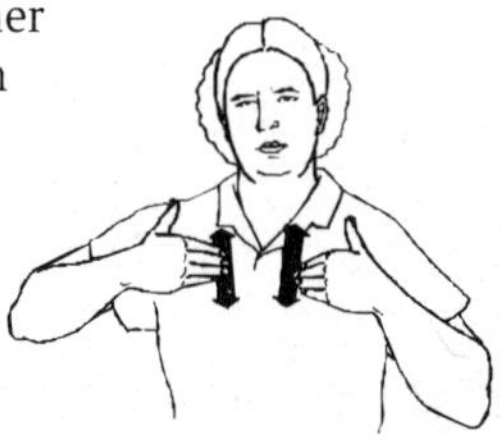

- [Shows location of one's lungs] Rub the fingertips of both *bent hands,* palms facing in, up and down near the center of the chest with a repeated movement.

**luxury** *adj.* See sign for FANCY.

**machine** *n.* An apparatus consisting of fixed and moving parts functioning together to do specific work: *a washing machine.* Same sign used for: **factory, industry, manufacture, mechanism, motor, plant, run.**

■ [Represents movement of gears meshing together] With the fingers of both *curved 5 hands* loosely meshed together, palms facing in, move the hands up and down in front of the chest with a repeated movement.

---

**mad** *adj.* See signs for ANGER[1,2], CROSS[2].

---

**magazine** *n.* A periodical publication containing stories, articles, photographs, etc.: *to read a magazine during the plane trip.* Same sign used for: **brochure, catalog, journal, pamphlet.**

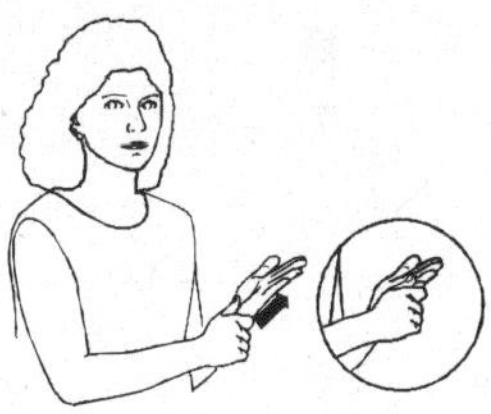

■ [Shows the spine of a magazine] Grasp the little-finger side of the left *open hand,* palm angled up, with the index finger and thumb of the right *A hand,* and slide the right hand from heel to fingertips of the left hand with a double movement.

---

**magic** *n.* **1.** The art of commanding supernatural powers to influence events or produce effects normally considered impossible: *a fictional world in which people appear and disappear by magic.* **2.** The art of creating the illusion of magical acts: *By magic, he pulled a dove out of the hat.* —*adj.* **3.** Accomplished as if by magic: *learning to do magic tricks.*

■ [The hands seem to cast a spell] Beginning with both *S hands* in front of each side of the body, palms facing forward, drop the hands downward and forward with a quick movement while opening into *5 hands.*

---

**magnet** *n.* A piece of metal that has the property of attracting smaller pieces of metal: *cars drawn upward by the giant magnet in the junkyard.* Related form: **magnetic** *adj.*

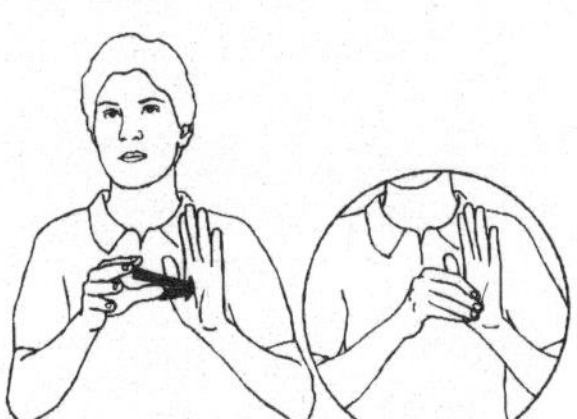

■ [Demonstrates action of a magnet pulling something to itself] Beginning with the right *flattened C hand,* palm angled forward, near the palm of the left *open hand,* palm facing right and fingers pointing up, bring the index-finger side of the right hand against the left palm while closing the right fingers into a *flattened O hand.*

---

**magnetic** *adj.* See sign for ABSORB.

---

**mail**[1] *n.* **1.** Letters, packages, etc., sent by means of the postal service or an alternate agency: *The mail doesn't get delivered on holidays.* —*v.* **2.** Alternate form: **mail out.** To send by mail: *to mail a letter; to mail out form letters to prospective clients.* Same sign used for: **send, send out.**

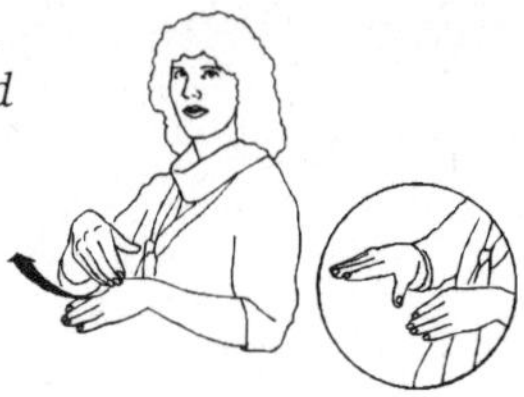

■ [Shows sending something forward] Flick the fingertips of the right *bent hand* forward across the back of the left *open hand,* both palms facing down, with a quick movement, straightening the right fingers as the right hand moves forward.

**mail**[2] *v., n.* See signs for E-MAIL[1,2], LETTER.

**main** *adj.* See signs for IMPORTANT, SPECIALIZE.

**mainstream** *n.* **1.** The principal course, trend, or direction: *This artist's work has always been in the mainstream.* —*adj.* **2.** Belonging to the most widely accepted group: *a radio station that plays mainstream music.* **3.** Being integrated into regular, especially public school programs: *to attend mainstream classes rather than special ones.* —*v.* **4.** To place in mainstream classes: *These children are ready to be mainstreamed.* Same sign used for: **blend, emerge, merge.**

■ [Represents things coming together to merge] Beginning with both *5 hands* in front of each side of the chest, palms facing down and fingers pointing toward each other, move the hands downward and forward toward each other, ending with the right hand on the back of the left hand in front of the chest.

**maintain** *v.* See signs for FIX, KEEP.

**maintenance** *n.* See signs for ALIMONY, WRENCH.

**major** *v.* See sign for SPECIALIZE.

**majority** *n.* The larger number, especially a number larger than half the total: *The majority of the first-grade class has learned to read.*

■ [**specialize** + **class**] Slide the little-finger side of the right *B hand,* palm facing left and fingers pointing forward, along the length of the index finger of the left *B hand,* palm facing right and fingers pointing forward. Then, beginning with both *C hands* in front of each side of the chest, palms facing each other, bring the hands away from each other in outward arcs while turning the palms in.

**make** *v.* To put together or bring into being: *to make a cake.* Same sign used for: **create, manufacture, produce.**

■ [The hands seem to be molding something] Beginning with the little-finger side of the right *S hand* on the index-finger side of the left *S hand,* twist the wrists in opposite directions with a small, quick, grinding movement.

**make believe** *v. phrase.* See sign for IMAGINE.

**make love** *v. phrase.* See sign for PET[2].

**make up** *v. phrase.* See sign for INVENT.

**make up your mind** *v. phrase.* See sign for DECIDE.

**makeshift** *adj.* Serving as a temporary replacement or substitute: *a makeshift handle for the pot.* Same sign used for: **good enough.**

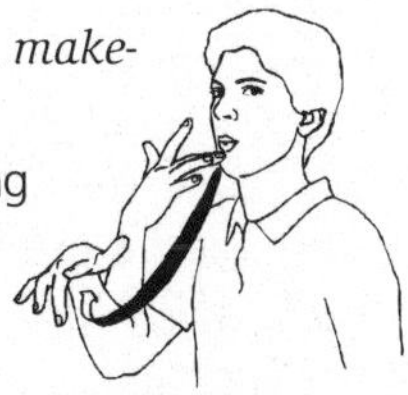

■ Beginning with the bent middle finger of the right *5 hand* touching the chin, palm facing in, move the hand forward while twisting the wrist, ending with the palm facing down.

**make-up** or **makeup** *n.* Cosmetics for the face: *to put on your make-up before the party.* Same sign used for: **cosmetics.**

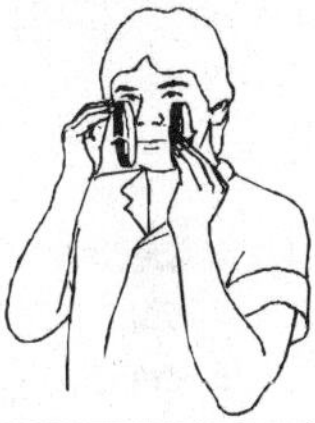

■ [Mime dabbing make-up on one's face] Move the fingertips of both *flattened O hands,* palms facing each other, in double alternating circles near each cheek.

**malady** *n.* See sign for SICK.

**male** *n.* See signs for BOY, MAN.

**maltreatment** *n.* See sign for TORTURE.

**mama** *n.* See sign for MOTHER.

**mammillary** *adj.* See sign for NIPPLE.

**man** *n.* An adult male person: *a man who owns his own business.* Same sign used for: **gentleman, guy, male.**

■ [A combination of **boy** and a gesture indicating the height of a man] Beginning with the thumb side of the right *flattened C hand* in front of the right side of the forehead, palm facing left, bring the hand straight forward while closing the fingers to the thumb.

**manage** *v.* To take charge of: *to manage a business.* Same sign used for: **administer, control, direct, govern, handle, in charge of, manipulate, operate, preside over, regulate, reign, rule, run (a meeting).**

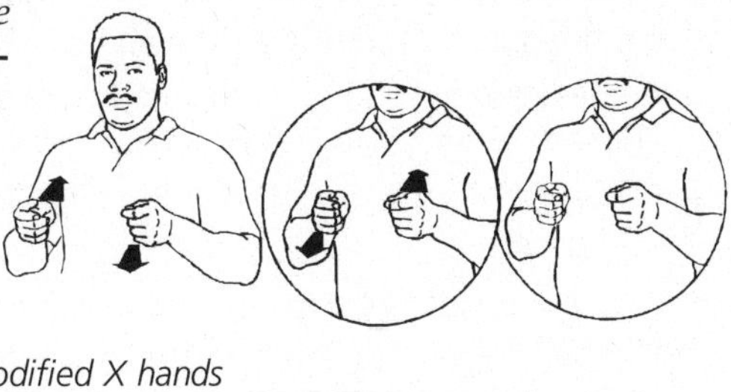

■ [Mime holding a horse's reigns indicating being in a position of management] Beginning with both *modified X hands* in front of each side of the body, right hand forward of the left hand and palms facing each other, move the hands forward and back with a repeated alternating movement.

**manipulate** *v.* See sign for MANAGE.

**manners** *pl. n.* See sign for POLITE.

**mantel** *n.* See sign for SHELF.

**manufacture** *v.* See signs for MACHINE, MAKE.

**many** *adj.* **1.** Consisting of a great number: *They own many cats.* —*pron.* **2.** A large number of persons or things: *Many couldn't come to the annual dinner this year.* Same sign used for: **a lot, lots, multiple, numerous.**

■ [Natural gesture for indicating many things] Beginning with both *S hands* in front of each side of the chest, palms facing up, flick the fingers open quickly with a double movement into *5 hands.*

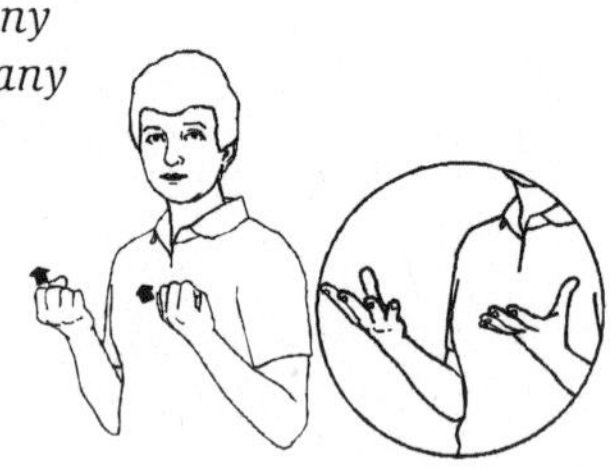

**marbles** *n.* A children's game played with small glass balls: *played marbles in the front yard.*

■ [Mime shooting a marble] Beginning with right the *modified X hand* in front of the right shoulder, palm facing left, flick the thumb upward with a double movement.

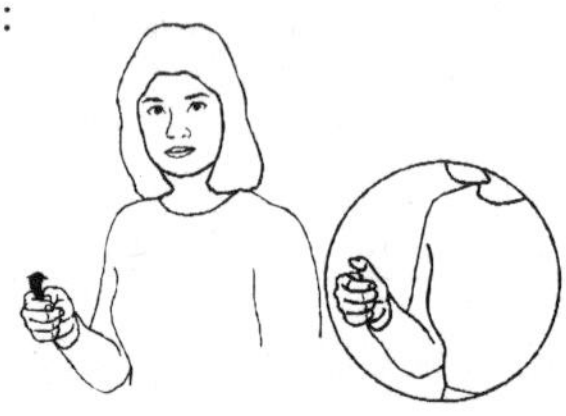

**march** *v.* **1.** To advance steadily: *Time marches on.* **2.** To move forward in time to music or in step with others: *marched in the parade.* Same sign used for: **parade, procession.**

■ [The hands represent people moving forward in a procession] Beginning with both *4 hands* in front of the body, the right hand somewhat forward of the left hand, both palms facing in, and fingers pointing down, flip the fingers forward and back with a double movement by bending the wrist.

**margarine** *n.* See sign for BUTTER.

**marijuana** *n.* The dried leaves and flowers of the hemp plant, used especially as an intoxicant: *to smoke a marijuana cigarette.* Same sign used for: **cannabis, pot** (*slang*).

■ [Mime holding and smoking a marijuana cigarette] Move the right *F hand,* palm facing left, from near the pursed mouth forward with a short double movement.

**marionette** *n.* See sign for PUPPET.

**market** *n.* See signs for GROCERY STORE, STORE.

**marry** *v.* **1.** To join one another officially as husband and wife: *They will marry in the spring.* **2.** To take in marriage as husband or wife: *Will you marry me?* **3.** To officiate at the marriage ceremony of: *They were married by a justice of the peace.*

■ [Symbolizes joining hands in marriage] Bring the right *curved hand,* palm facing down, downward in front of the chest to clasp the left *curved hand,* palm facing up.

**marshall** *n.* See sign for POLICE.

**mart** *n.* See sign for STORE.

**marvel** *n.* See sign for WONDERFUL. Related form: **marvelous** *adj.*

**mash** *v.* To crush or beat into a soft, uniform, pulpy mass: *to mash the potatoes.* Same sign used for: **smash.**

■ [Mime mashing something with the heel of the hand] Bring the heel of the right *open hand* downward on the heel of the left *open hand,* palms facing each other, while twisting the right wrist and grinding the heel on the left palm.

**mask**[1] *n.* A covering to hide all or part of the face: *The burglar wore a mask.*

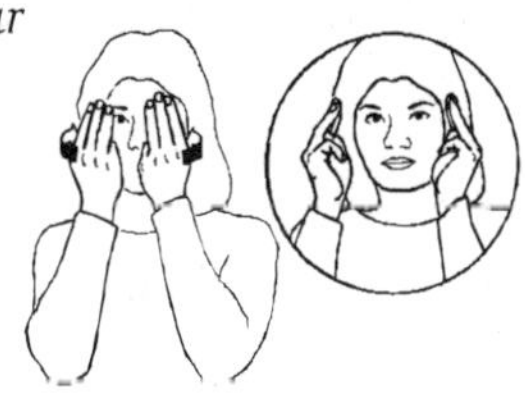

■ [Initialized sign showing the location of a mask] Beginning with both *M hands* in front of the face, palms facing in and fingers pointing up, move the hands to each side of the face while turning the palms toward each other.

**mask**[2] *n.* See sign for HALLOWEEN.

**masquerade** *n.* See sign for HALLOWEEN.

**mass** *n.* See signs for CLASS, HORDE.

**massive** *adj.* See signs for EXCESS, LARGE.

**mass-produce** *v.* See sign for ASSEMBLY LINE.

**match**[1] *v.* **1.** To correspond in essential aspects, as material, style, or color: *The chair matches the sofa.* **2.** To go well together: *These colors match quite well.* —*n.* **3.** A person or thing that matches: *This jacket is a match to that skirt.* Same sign used for: **combine, fit, mate, merge, suit.**

■ [The fingers move together to match with each other] Beginning with both *5 hands* in front of each side of the chest, palms facing in, bring the hands together, ending with the bent fingers of both hands meshed together in front of the chest.

**match**[2] *n.* A short, slender stick or piece of cardboard with a tip that ignites when struck: *to light the candles with a match.*

■ [Mime striking a match] Flick the index-finger knuckle of the *modified X hand,* palm facing left, upward with a double movement on the palm of the left *open hand,* palm facing right and fingers pointing forward.

**mate** *n.* See sign for MATCH[1].

**material** *n.* **1.** What a thing is made of: *The material of this appliance is plastic.* **2.** Fabric; cloth: *a loosely woven material.* Same sign used for: **cloth, texture.**

■ [The hands seem to feel material with the fingers] Rub the thumbs of both *flattened O hands* against the fingers of each hand in front of each side of the chest, palms facing up.

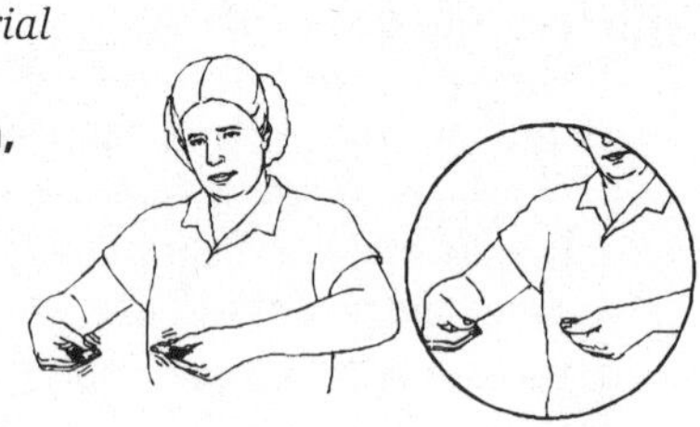

**materialize** *v.* See sign for SHOW UP.

**materials** *pl. n.* Supplies for doing or making something: *You'll have to use your own materials to make the collage.* Same sign used for: **media.**

■ [Initialized sign similar to sign for **thing**] Beginning with the right *M hand* in front of the body, palm facing up, move the hand in a double arc to the right.

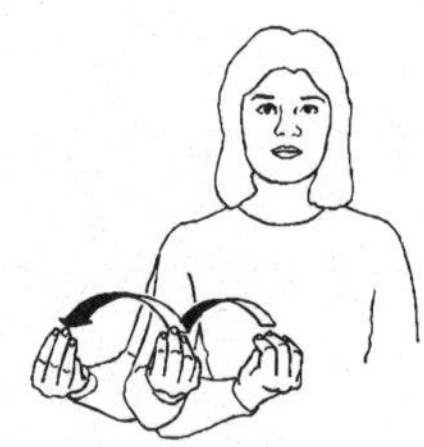

**mathematics** *n.* The science dealing with measurements, quantities, and other quantitative properties as expressed with numbers: *solved an equation using higher mathematics; to study math for an engineering degree.* Alternate form: **math.** Same sign used for: **multiplication.**

■ [Initialized sign similar to sign for **arithmetic**] Brush the back of the right *M hand* across the index-finger side of the left *M hand,* both palms facing in, as the hands cross with a double movement in front of the chest.

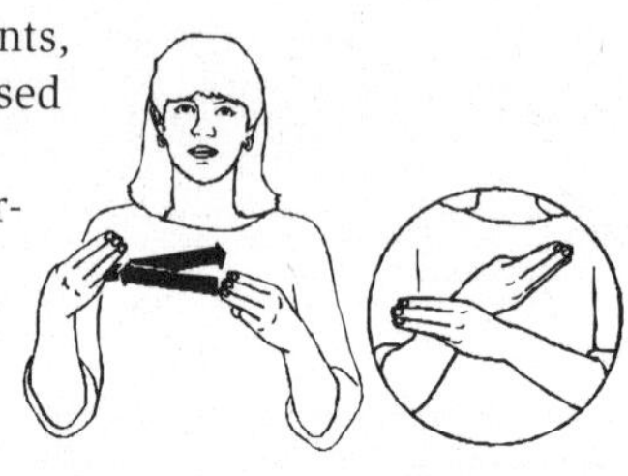

**matinee** *n.* See sign for AFTERNOON.

**maximum** *n.* **1.** The greatest possible amount: *The class score was the maximum.* —*adj.* **2.** Being the maximum: *achieved maximum production levels.* Same sign used for: **up to.**

■ [Shows reaching the top] Beginning with the right *B hand,* palm facing down and fingers pointing left, a few inches under the left *open hand,* palm facing down and fingers pointing right, bring the back of the right hand up against the left palm.

**may** *auxiliary v.* See signs for CAN[1], MAYBE.

**maybe** *adv.* Possibly: *Maybe it will snow.* Same sign used for: **may, might, perhaps, probability, probable, probably.**

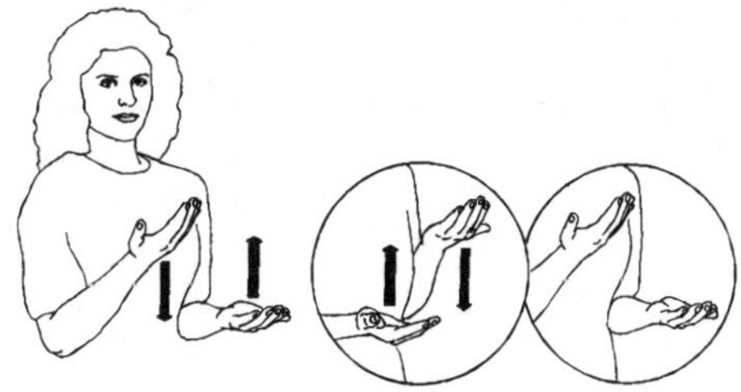

■ [Indicates weighing possibilities] Beginning with both *open hands* in front of each side of the chest, palms facing up and fingers pointing forward, alternately move the hands up and down with a double movement.

**mayonnaise** *n.* A dressing made chiefly of egg yolk, vegetable oil, and lemon juice: *I always put mayonnaise on my hamburger.*

■ [Initialized sign miming spreading mayonnaise on bread] Move the fingers of the right *M hand,* palm facing down, in a double circular movement on the palm of the left *open hand,* palm facing up.

**me** *pron.* The objective case of I, used as a direct or indirect object: *He gave it to me.* Same sign used for: **I.**

■ Point the extended right index finger to the center of the chest.

**meager** *adj.* See sign for SMALL[2].

**meal** *n.* See sign for FOOD.

**mean**[1] *adj.* Unkind; nasty; bad-tempered: *A mean person who never loses an opportunity to insult others.* Related form: **meanness** *n.* Same sign used for: **bust, cruel, harsh, rude, unkind.**

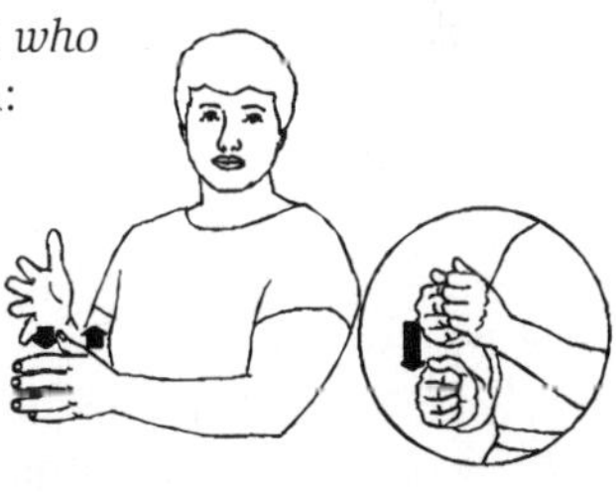

■ Beginning with both *5 hands* in front of the body, palms facing in opposite directions and the right hand above the left hand, close the hands into *A hands* while quickly moving the right hand down brushing the knuckles against the left knuckles as it passes.

**mean**[2] *v.* **1.** To indicate; signify: *What does this word mean?* **2.** To intend to express; have in mind to communicate: *What did you mean in this paragraph?* Related form: **meaning** *n.* Same sign used for: **intend, intention, purpose, stand for.**

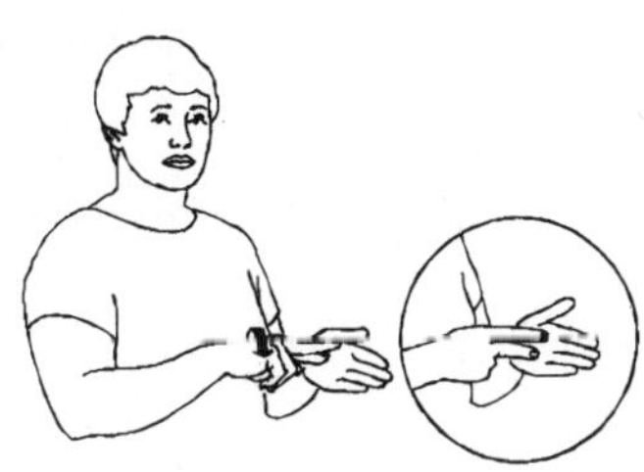

■ Touch the fingertips of the right *V hand,* palm facing down, in the palm of the left *open hand,* palm facing up and fingers pointing forward, and then twist the right wrist and touch the fingertips down again.

**mean**[3] *n.* See sign for AVERAGE.

**meanness** *n.* **1.** One or more instances of being mean and cruel: *We were shocked by their meanness to the child.* **2.** The state or quality of being mean or cruel: *notorious for their meanness.* Same sign used for: **cruel, rude.**

■ Bring the knuckles of the right *bent V hand,* palm facing in, downward, brushing the knuckles of the left *bent V hand,* palm facing in, as the right hand passes.

**meanwhile** *adv.* See sign for DURING.

**measles** *pl. n.* Any of several contagious diseases caused by viruses and characterized by symptoms resembling those of a cold and by red spots or a red rash on the skin: *Pregnant women should not be exposed to German measles.*

■ [Shows location of measles spots] Beginning with the fingers of both *curved 5 hands,* palms facing each other, on each side of the chin, move the hands upward, touching the fingertips to the cheeks in several places and then to each side of the forehead.

**measure** *v.* To find out the size or amount of: *to measure the room.* Related form: **measurement** *n.* Same sign used for: **size.**

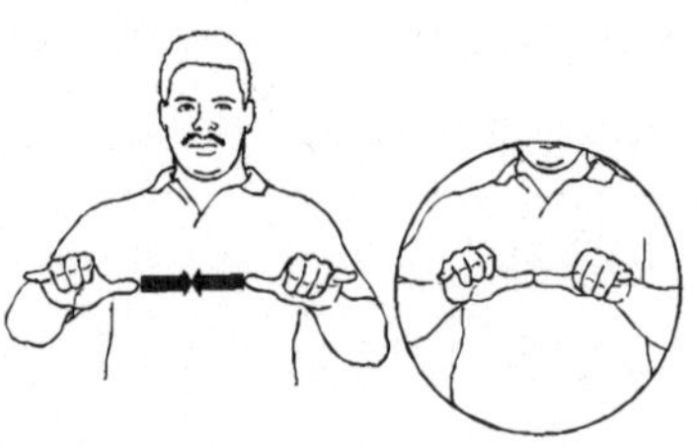

■ [The fingers seem to measure something] Tap the thumbs of both *Y hands,* palms facing down, together in front of the chest with a double movement.

**measure up** *v. phrase.* See sign for MEET.

**measuring** *n., adj.* See sign for ENGINEERING.

**meat** *n.* Animal flesh used for food: *prefers to eat meat for dinner.* Same sign used for: **beef, content, flesh, steak, substance.**

■ [Indicates the meaty part of the hand] With the bent index finger and thumb of the right *5 hand,* palm facing down, grasp the fleshy part of left *open hand* near the thumb, palm facing right and fingers pointing forward, and shake the hands forward and back with a double movement.

**mechanism** *n.* See sign for MACHINE.

**medal** *n.* An award, typically in the form of a metal disk, usually bearing an inscription: *won the gold medal in figure skating at the Olympics.* Same sign used for: **prize, ribbon.**

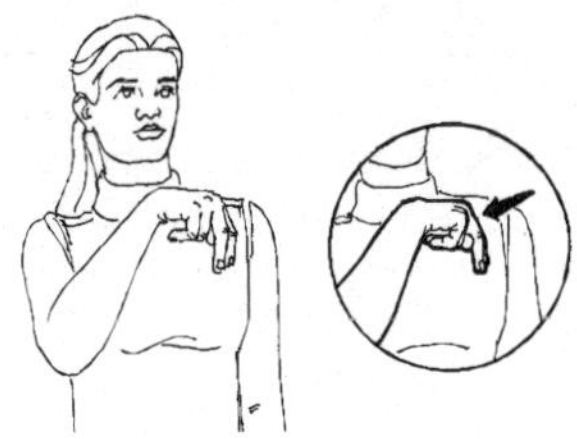

■ [Symbolizes pinning on a medal] Bring the index-finger side of the right *H hand,* palm facing down and fingers pointing down, back against the left side of the chest with a deliberate movement.

**meddle**[1] *v.* To interfere in others' affairs without their consent: *not wise to meddle in their business.* Same sign used for: **interfere, interrupt.**

■ [Hand seems to interrupt in the middle of something] Bring the little-finger side of the right *open hand,* palm facing left, downward sharply between the middle finger and ring finger of the left *5 hand* held in front of the chest, palm facing in and fingers pointing up.

**meddle**[2] *v.* See sign for NOSY[2].

**media** *pl. n.* See sign for MATERIALS.

**media card**[1] *n. phrase.* A small card having a built-in computer chip on which digital photographic images are stored: *use a 2GB media card in the digital camera.* Same sign used for **memory card.**

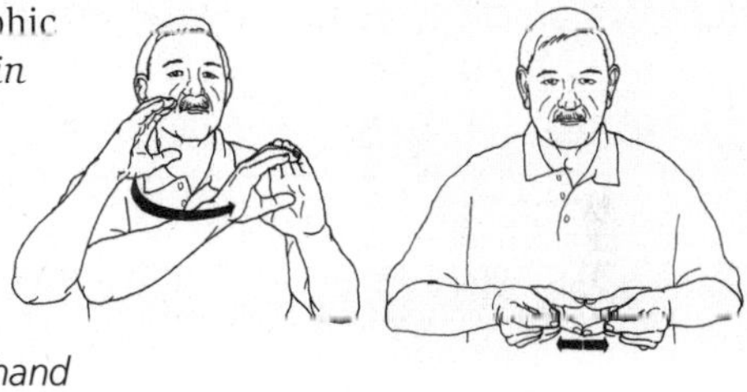

■ [**picture** + **card**] Move the right *C hand,* palm facing forward, from near the right side of the face downward, ending with the index-finger side of the right *C hand* against the palm of the left *open hand,* palm facing right. With the finger tips of both *G hands* touching in front of the chest, palms facing each other, bring the hands apart and then pinch each thumb and index finger together.

**media card**[2] *n. phrase.* (alternate sign) Same sign used for **memory card.**

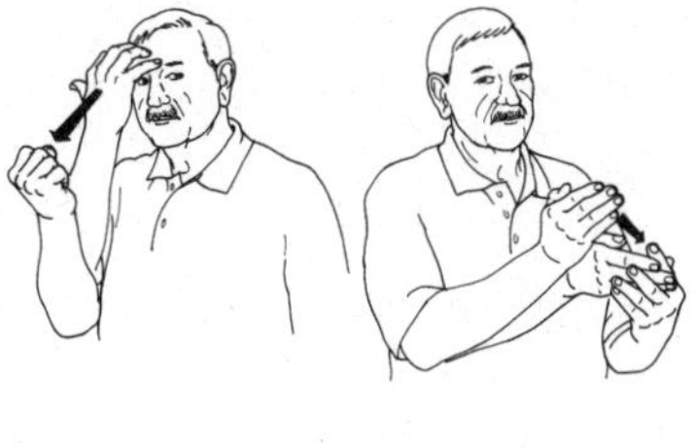

■ [**memorize** + **insert**] Beginning with the fingertips of the right *curved hand* touching the right side of the forehead, palm facing down, bring the hand forward and down while closing the fingers into an *S hand,* palm facing in. Then slide the little-finger side of the right *open hand,* palm facing up, between the index and middle fingers of the left *4 hand,* palm facing right.

**medical** *adj.* See sign for DOCTOR[1].

**medicine** *n.* A drug or other substance used to treat or prevent disease: *It's time to take your medicine.* Related forms: **medical** *adj.*, **medication** *n.* Same sign used for: **drug, poison.**

■ [Represents mixing a prescription with a mortar and pestle] With the bent middle finger of the right *5 hand,* palm facing down, in the palm of the left *open hand,* rock the right hand from side to side with a double movement while keeping the middle finger in place.

**meditate** *v.* See sign for WONDER. Related form: **meditation** *n.*

**medium** *adj., n.* See sign for AVERAGE.

**meek** *adj.* See sign for HUMBLE.

**meet** *v.* **1.** To come face to face with; encounter: *to meet a friend for lunch.* **2.** To become acquainted with; be introduced to: *It's good to meet you at last.* **3.** To be in accordance with; deal with appropriately: *Your report meets our expectations.* Same sign used for: **greet, measure up.**

■ [Represents two people approaching each other when meeting] Beginning with the extended index fingers of both hands pointing up in front of each shoulder, palms facing each other, bring the hands together in front of the chest.

**meeting** *n.* **1.** The act of coming together: *Our meeting was a lucky event.* **2.** A gathering or assembly of people for some purpose: *to attend the meeting.* Related form: **meet** *v.* Same sign used for: **assembly, conference, convention, convocation, council, session.**

■ [Represents many people coming together for a meeting] Beginning with both open hands in front of the chest, palms facing each other and fingers pointing up, close the fingers with a double movement into *flattened O hands* while moving the hands together.

**mellow** *adj.* See sign for SOFT.

**melody** *n.* See sign for MUSIC.

**melon** *n.* See sign for PUMPKIN.

**melt** *v.* See sign for DISSOLVE.

**member** *n.* A person or thing belonging to a group: *a member of the committee.*

- [Similar to sign for **committee**] Touch the fingertips of the right *bent hand,* first to the left side of the chest and then to the right side of the chest.

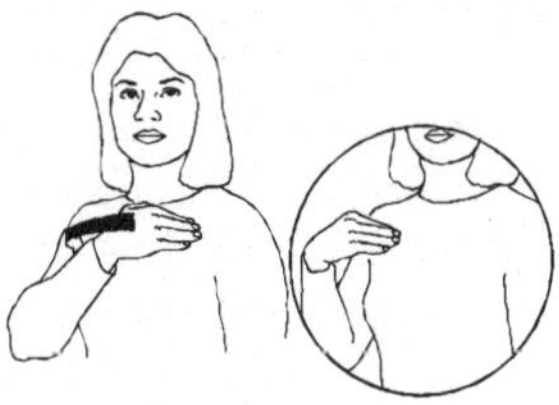

**memorial** *n.* See sign for LOOK BACK[1]. Shared idea of preserving the memory of a person or event.

**memorize** *v.* To commit to memory: *to memorize the telephone number.* Related form: **memory** *n.*

- [The hand seems to take information from the brain and then hold on to it tightly, as if to keep it in the memory] Beginning with the fingertips of the right *curved hand* touching the right side of the forehead, palm facing in, bring the hand forward and down while closing the fingers into an *S hand,* palm facing in.

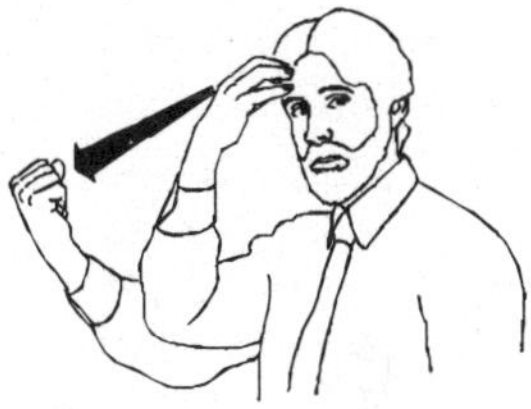

**memory** *n.* See sign for LOOK BACK.

**memory card** *n. phrase.* See signs for MEDIA CARD[1,2].

**mend** *v.* See sign for FIX.

**Mennonite** *n.* See sign for SCARF.

**menstruation** *n.* A discharging of blood and tissue from the uterus at monthly intervals, between puberty and menopause, by a nonpregnant female: *If she's almost 13, it is time to talk to her about menstruation.* Same sign used for: **period.**

- Tap the palm side of the right *A hand* against the right side of the chin with a double movement.

**mention** *v.* To speak about briefly or in passing: *Did you mention something about a rehearsal?*

- [**say** + **call**[3]] Beginning with the extended right index finger near the mouth, palm facing in and finger pointing up, bring the right hand downward while changing into an *H hand,* ending with the middle-finger side of the right *H hand* across the index-finger side of the left *H hand* in front of the chest.

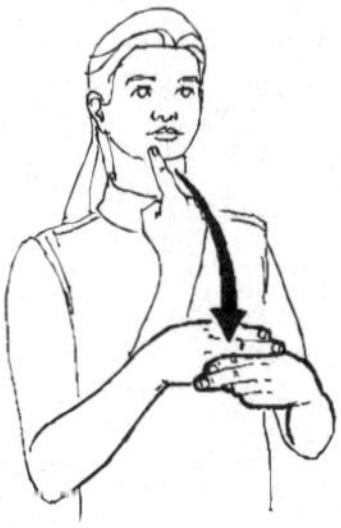

**menu** *n.* A list of foods or prepared dishes available to be served at a restaurant: *I need to look at a menu before I order.*

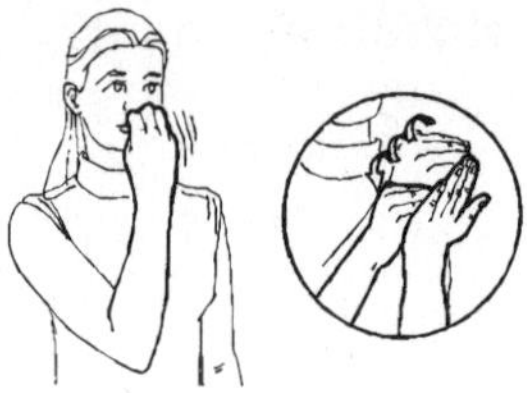

- [**food** + **list**] Bring the fingertips of the right *flattened O hand,* palm facing down, to the lips with a repeated movement. Then touch the little-finger side of the right *bent hand,* palm facing left, several times on the palm of the left *open hand,* palm facing in and fingers angled upward, as it moves from the fingertips downward to the heel of the left palm.

**merchandise** *n.* See sign for SELL.

**mercy** *n.* Kindness or compassion, especially as shown to an offender or enemy: *The judge showed mercy to the young offender.* Related form: **merciful** *adj.* Same sign used for: **poor thing**.

- [The finger used to show feeling is directed toward another] Beginning with the bent middle finger of the right *5 hand* pointing forward in front of the right shoulder, move the hand forward in a repeated circular movement.

**merge** *v.* See signs for CIRCULATE, INTERFACE, MAINSTREAM, MATCH[1], MESH.

**merry** *adj.* See sign for HAPPY.

**mesh** *v.* To fit together and engage, as gear teeth: *The gears are grinding because they don't mesh.* Same sign used for: **blend, combine, infuse, integrate, merge.**

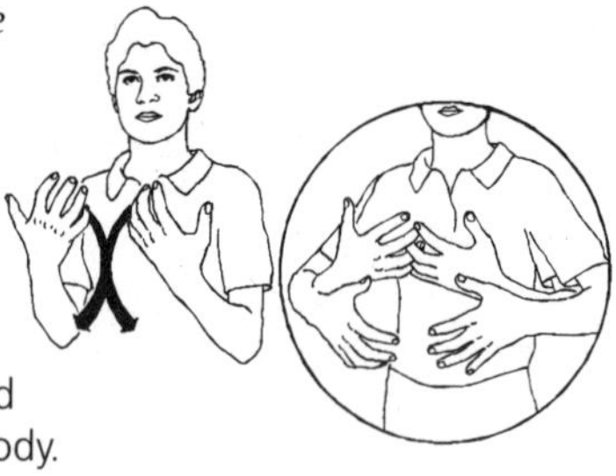

- [Shows the fingers coming together to merge] Beginning with both *curved 5 hands* in front of each side of the chest, palms facing in, drop the hands down while meshing the fingers together, and then drop them apart in front of each side of the body.

**messy** *adj.* Untidy: *a messy desk.* Same sign used for: **chaos, disorder, garbled, riot, stir, storm.**

- [Represents something turned upside down, causing a mess] Beginning with both *curved 5 hands* in front of the body, right hand over the left hand, twist the hands with a deliberate movement, reversing the positions.

**metal** *n.* **1.** Any of a group of elementary substances, as gold, silver, or iron, particularly the stronger metals and alloys used for construction: *The file cabinet is made of metal.* —*adj.* **2.** Made of metal: *a metal container.* Same sign used for: **rock, steel.**

- Bring the top of the bent index finger of the right *X hand,* palm facing left, forward from under the chin with a double movement.

**method** *n.* A procedure or technique for doing something: *developed a method for manufacturing the parts more cheaply.*

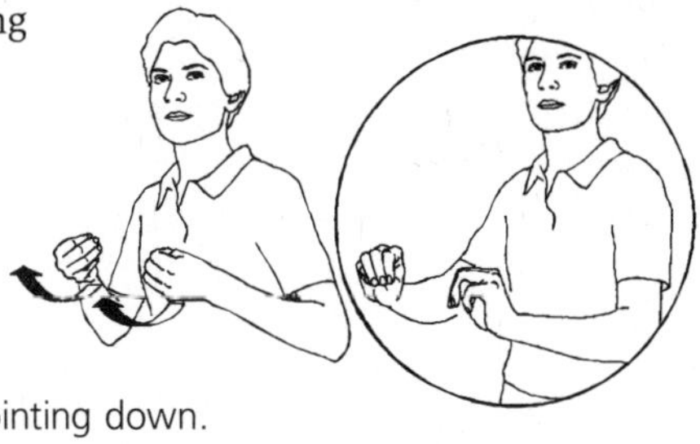

■ [Initialized sign similar to sign for **road**] Move both *M hands* from in front of each side of the body, palms facing in and fingers angled up, downward and forward simultaneously in an arc, ending with the palms facing forward and the fingers pointing down.

**me, too** See sign for AGREE[2].

**microwave** *n.* **1.** Alternate form: **microwave oven.** An oven in which food is cooked by the penetration of microwaves: *It saves time to cook dinner in the microwave.* —*v.* **2.** To cook food in a microwave oven: *I microwave my vegetables because they stay crunchy.*

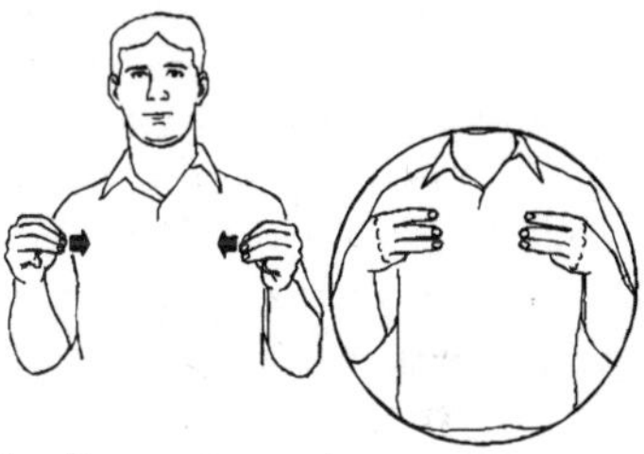

■ [Abbreviation **m-w**] Beginning with both *M hands* in front of each side of the chest, palms facing in, move the hands toward each other while extending the fingers toward each other with a double movement, changing into *W hands* each time.

**midday** *n.* See sign for NOON.

**middle** *adj.* **1.** Located in the center: *the middle chair.* —*n.* **2.** The point that is the same distance from each end or side: *to sit in the middle of the aisle.* See also sign for CENTER.

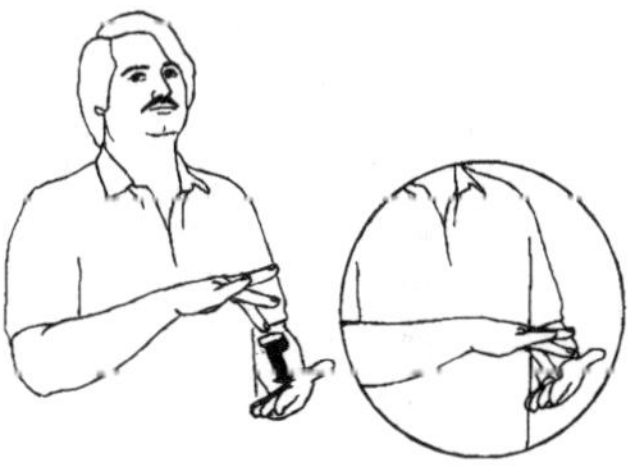

■ [Indicates the middle of something] Move the bent middle finger of the right *5 hand,* palm facing down, in a circular movement and then down into the palm of the left *open hand* held in front of the chest, palm facing up.

**middle of the night** *n. phrase.* See sign for MIDNIGHT.

**midnight** *n.* Twelve o'clock at night: *They were told to be home by midnight.* Same sign used for: **middle of the night.**

■ [Represents the sun being on the other side of the world at midnight] With the fingertips of the left *open hand,* palm facing in, touching the crook of the extended right arm, fingers pointing down and palm facing left, move the right *open hand* to the left with a short double movement.

**midst** *n., prep.* See sign for AMONG.

**might** *v.* See sign for MAYBE.

**mighty** *adj.* See signs for POWER, STRONG[1]. Alternate form: **might** *n.*

**migraine** *n.* See sign for HEADACHE[2].

**military** *n.* See sign for ARMY.

**milk** *n.* **1.** The white liquid secreted by female mammals to feed their young: *The mother cat had enough milk for her six kittens.* **2.** This liquid, secreted by certain animals, especially cows and goats, used by humans as food: *Drink your milk.*

■ [Mime squeezing a cow's udder to get milk] Beginning with the right *C hand,* palm facing left, in front of the right side of the body, squeeze the fingers together with a double movement, forming an *S hand* each time.

**million** *n.* One thousand times one thousand: *millions and millions of stars.*

■ [Initialized sign similar to sign for **thousand** except repeated] Touch the fingertips of the right *M hand,* palm facing down, first on the heel, then in the middle, and then on the fingers of the upturned left *open hand.*

**mimic** *v.* To imitate or copy: *The comedian mimicked the President.*

■ [Represents copying another repeatedly] Move the right *5 hand* from in front of the chest, palm angled forward, down with a repeated movement to touch the upturned palm of the left *open hand* while closing the right fingers and thumb into a *flattened O hand* each time.

**mind** *n.* The part of a person with the capacity to think, reason, perceive, etc.: *a good mind for mathematics.* Same sign used for: **brain, sense.**

■ [Location of the mind] Tap the bent extended right index finger, palm facing in, against the right side of the forehead with a double movement.

**mine** *pron.* See sign for MY.

**mingle** *v.* See sign for ASSOCIATE.

**mini** *adj.* See signs for SMALL[1,2].

**minimum** *n.* **1.** The least possible or allowable amount: *had to take the minimum for their house.* —*adj.* **2.** Least possible: *Use the minimum amount of salt.* Same sign used for: **below, less.**

■ [Indicates that something exceeds the base or minimum] Beginning with the back of the right *B hand,* palm facing down and fingers pointing left, touching the palm of the left *open hand,* palm facing down and fingers pointing right, bring the right hand downward a few inches.

**minister** *v.* See sign for SERVE.

**minor** *adj.* Less, as in size, amount, or importance: *a few minor problems.*

■ [Shows something taking a lesser position under another] Slide the index-finger side of the right *B hand,* palm facing left and fingers pointing forward, forward under the little-finger side of the left *B hand,* palm facing right and fingers pointing forward.

**minority** *n.* The smaller part, forming less than half of the whole: *The minority of the group voted to stay home.*

■ [**minor** + **class**] Slide the index-finger side of the right *B hand,* palm facing left and fingers pointing forward, forward under the little-finger side of the left *B hand,* palm facing right and fingers pointing forward. Then, beginning with both *C hands* in front of the chest, palms facing each other, bring the hands away from each other in outward arcs while turning the palms in toward each other.

**minus** *prep.* Less by the subtraction of: *Ten minus five equals five.*

■ [Shape of a minus sign] Touch the thumb side of the extended right index finger, palm facing down and finger pointing forward, against the palm of the left *open hand,* palm facing right.

**minute** *n.* **1.** One of the 60 equal periods of time that make up an hour: *The dinner will come out of the microwave in two minutes.* **2.** A very short period of time; moment: *Wait a minute.* Same sign used for: **moment, momentarily, one minute.**

■ [The finger represents the movement of the minute hand on a clock] Move the extended right index finger, palm facing left, forward a short distance, pivoting the closed fingers of the right hand on the palm of the left *open hand,* palm facing right and fingers pointing up.

**mirror** *n.* A smooth, shiny surface, usually a piece of glass with a silver or amalgam backing, that reflects images: *to look in a mirror to check your hair.*

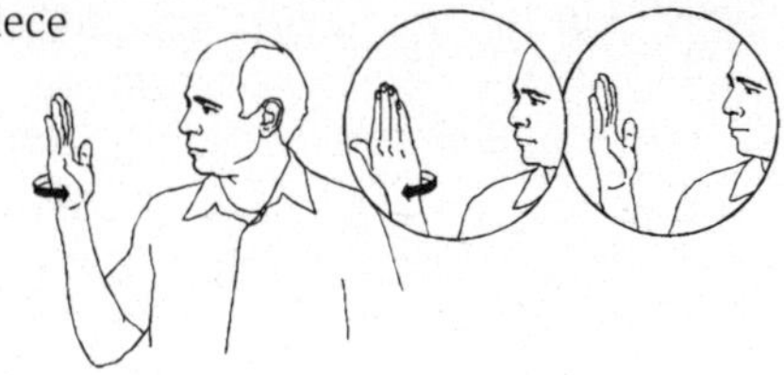

■ [The hand represents a mirror] Beginning with the right *open hand* held up near the right shoulder, palm facing left, twist the wrist to turn the palm in and back with a double movement.

**mischief** *n.* See sign for DEVIL. Related form: **mischievous** *adj.*

**misconception** *n.* See sign for MISUNDERSTAND.

**misdemeanor** *n.* See signs for CRIME[1,2].

**miser** *n.* See sign for GREEDY[1].

**miserable** *adj.* Very uncomfortable or unhappy; wretched: *I was miserable waiting for two hours in the hot sun.*

■ With a repeated alternating movement, touch the chin with the extended right index finger and then the left, palms facing in.

**miss**[1] *v.* **1.** To fail to hit or strike: *The batter swung at the ball and missed.* **2.** To fail to catch or come into the presence of: *to miss the bus.* **2.** To overlook or let go by, as an opportunity: *to miss a chance.*

■ [The hand seems to snatch at something as it passes] Move the right *C hand,* palm facing left, from near the right side of the forehead in a quick downward arc in front of the face while closing into an *S hand,* ending with the palm facing down in front of the left shoulder.

**miss**[2] *v.* To fail to pay attention when something is said, with the result that the speaker is unwilling to repeat: *The coach told the late player that he would have to sit out because he had missed the game plan.* Same sign used for: **You're too late.**

■ [**train** + **zoom**] Rub the extended fingers of the right *H hand* across the back of the extended fingers of the left *H hand,* both palms facing down. Then beginning with the thumb of the right *L hand,* palm facing forward, on the base of the extended left index finger, palm facing down, move the right hand quickly to the right while closing the index finger to the thumb.

**miss**[3] *v.* See signs for ABSENT, DISAPPOINTED, SKIP. Related form: **missing** *adj.*

**missile** *n.* A weapon propelled by a rocket: *launched the missile at the enemy target.*

■ [Shows movement of a missile ejecting] Beginning with the heel of the right *one hand,* palm facing forward, on the back of the left *open hand,* palm facing down, raise the right hand upward in front of the face.

**mistake** *n.* A blunder or error, as in action or judgment: *It was a mistake to leave without resolving the argument.* Related form: **mistaken** *adj.* Same sign used for: **accident.**

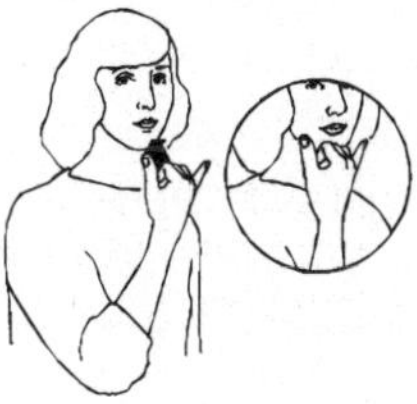

■ [Similar to sign for **wrong** but made with a double movement] Tap the middle fingers of the right *Y hand,* palm facing in, against the chin with a double movement.

**misty** *adj.* See sign for WET.

**misunderstand** *v.* To understand incorrectly: *I misunderstood the directions.* Related form: **misunderstanding** *n.* Same sign used for: **misconception.**

■ [The fingers indicate something turned around in the mind] Touch the index finger of the right *V hand* to the right side of the forehead, palm facing forward, and then twist the wrist and touch the middle finger to the forehead, ending with the palm facing back.

**mitten** *n.* A long, sometimes padded glove with a single enclosure for the four fingers and a separate one for the thumb: *wearing mittens in cold weather; an oven mitt.* Alternate form: **mitt** *n.*

■ [Shape of a mitten] With the extended right index finger, palm facing down and finger pointing forward, trace the shape of the left *open hand,* palm facing in and fingers pointing up, beginning at the base of the thumb and ending at the base of the little finger.

**mix**[1] *v.* To put together; combine: *to mix the ingredients for the cake.* Same sign used for: **blend, complex, confuse, disorder, garbled, scramble, stir.**

■ [Mime mixing things up] Beginning with the right *curved 5 hand* over the left *curved 5 hand,* palms facing each other, move the hands in repeated circles in opposite directions in front of the chest.

**mix**[2] *v.* See signs for BEAT[1], CIRCULATE.

**mix up** *v. phrase.* See sign for CONFUSE[1].

**mobile** *adj.* Easy to move: *a mobile hospital.* Same sign used for: **movable.**

- [Sign similar to sign for **move** except indicates moving in different directions] Beginning with both *flattened O hands* in front of the right side of the body, palms facing down, move the hands forward with a wavy movement.

**mobilize** *v.* See sign for TRIP.

**mock** *v.* To ridicule; make fun of: *It is insensitive of them to mock her accent.* Same sign used for: **jeer, laugh at.**

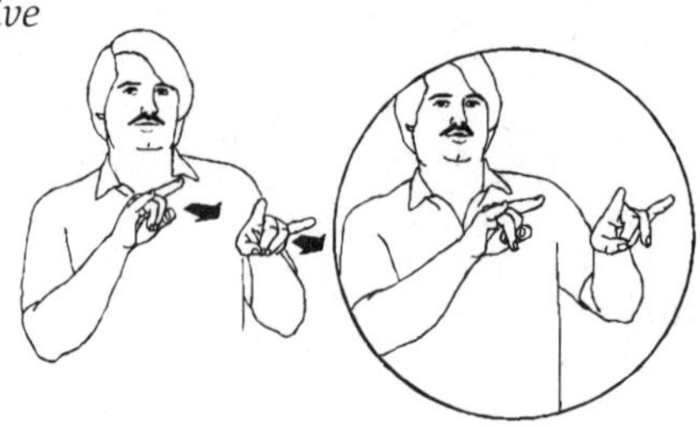

- [The fingers seem to jeer at another] Move both *Y hands,* palms facing down, forward a short distance with a double movement from in front of each side of the chest.

**modem** *n.* Acronym for *modulator-demodulator.* A device used by a computer to communicate to remote computers through telephone lines.

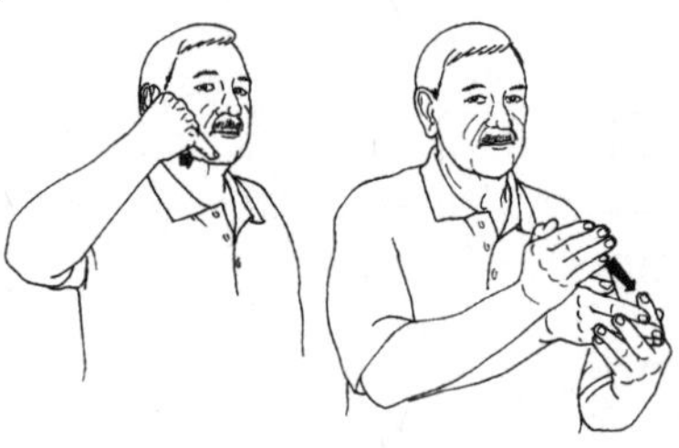

- [**telephone** + **insert**] Bring the knuckles of the right *Y hand* in to touch the lower right cheek, holding the right thumb near the right ear and the little finger in front of the mouth. Then slide the little-finger side of the right *open hand*, palm facing up, between the index and middle fingers of the left *4 hand,* palm facing right.

**modest** *adj.* See sign for HUMBLE. Related form: **modesty** *n.*

**modify**[1] *v.* To change somewhat; alter partially: *You'd better modify the tone of your letter.* Related form: **modification** *n.*

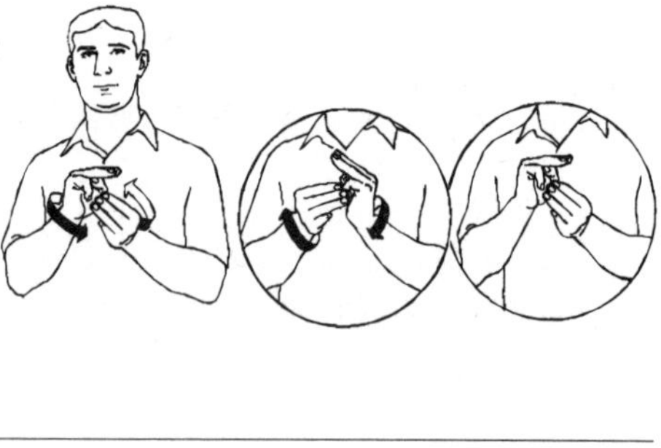

- [Initialized sign similar to sign for **change**[1]] Beginning with the palm sides of both *M hands* facing each other in front of the chest, twist the hands in opposite directions with a double movement.

**modify**[2] *v.* See sign for CHANGE[1].

**moist** *adj.* See sign for WET. Related forms: **moisten** *v.*, **moisture** *n.*

**mole**[1] *n.* A small furry mammal with rudimentary eyes that lives primarily underground: *The mole burrowed under the lawn.*

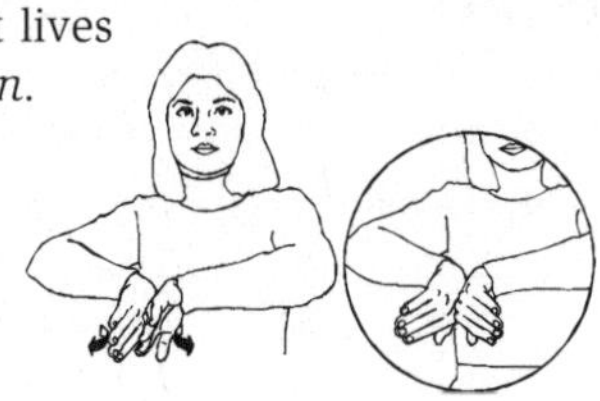

■ [Represents the action of mole burrowing through dirt] Beginning with the back of both *open hands* together in front of the chest, palms facing in opposite directions, bend the fingers of each hand downward toward each palm with a double movement.

**mole**[2] *n.* A small, often dark, raised spot on the skin: *She has a mole on her cheek.*

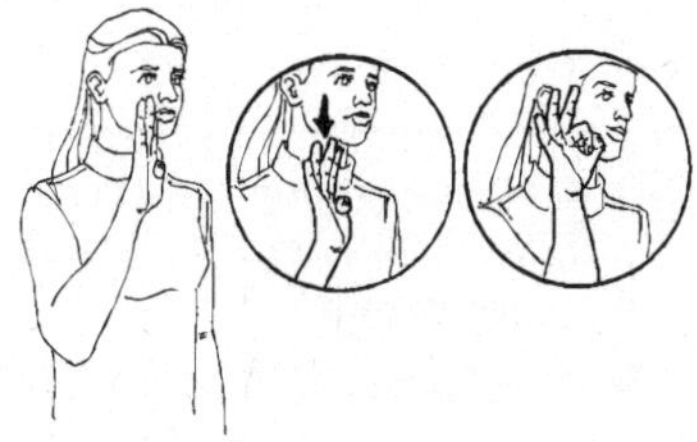

■ [**brown** + shape and location of a mole on the face] Slide the index-finger side of the right *B hand,* palm facing left, down the right cheek with a repeated movement. Then bring the thumb side of the right *F hand,* palm facing forward, against the right side of the chin.

**molest** *v.* To disturb or annoy, especially in a way that may cause harm: *Don't molest the animals in the cages.*

■ With the index finger of the left hand extended in front of the chest, palm facing right, rub the knuckles of the extended right index-finger hand, palm facing forward, back and forth with a double movement against the thumb side of the left hand.

**mom** *n.* See sign for MOTHER. Alternate form: **mommy** *n.*

**moment** *n.* See sign for MINUTE. Related form: **momentarily** *adv.*

**momentum** *n.* See sign for CONSTANT[1].

**Monday** *n.* The second day of the week, after Sunday: *The work week begins on Monday.*

■ [Initialized sign] Move the right *M hand,* palm facing in, in a double circle in front of the right shoulder.

**money** *n.* Coins and paper notes issued by a government for use in buying and selling: *Don't spend all your money at once.* Same sign used for: **fund.**

■ [Represents putting money in one's hand] Tap the back of the right *flattened O hand,* palm facing up, with a double movement against the palm of the left *open hand,* palm facing up.

**monitor**[1] *n.* See sign for TERMINAL[1].

**monitor**[2] *v.* See sign for CARE.

**monkey** *n.* A small primate, usually having a long tail: *Watch the monkey swing from the bars by its tail.* Same sign used for: **ape, chimpanzee.**

- [Mime the scratching motion done by monkeys] Beginning at the waist, scratch the fingertips of both *curved 5 hands,* palms facing in, upward on each side of the body with a double movement.

**monotone** *adj.* See sign for MONOTONOUS.

**monotonous**[1] *adj.* Lacking variety: *Working on an assembly line can be monotonous.* Related form: **monotony** *n.* Same sign used for: **monotone.**

- [Shows repetitive activity] Rub the index-finger side of the right *S hand,* palm facing down, in a repeated circular movement on the palm of the left *open hand* held in front of the chest, palm facing right.

**monotonous**[2] *adj.* See signs for BORING[1], GRIND OUT.

**monster** *n.* A creature, imaginary or not, with exaggerated features unlike those found in nature: *They claim they saw a monster rising up from the ocean.* Same sign used for: **haunt, haunted, spooky.**

- [Mime the action and facial expression of a monster] Beginning with both *curved 5 hands* held near each side of the head, palms facing down, move the hands up and down with a double movement accompanied by a menacing facial expression.

**month** *n.* **1.** One of the 12 parts into which a year is divided: *April is my favorite month.* **2.** A period of time of approximately 30 days: *I'll see you in one month.* Same sign used for: **one month.**

- [The finger moves down the weeks on a calendar] Move the extended right index finger, palm facing in and finger pointing left, from the tip to the base of the extended left index finger, palm facing right and finger pointing up in front of the chest.

**monument** *n.* A structure constructed in memory of a person or event: *the Washington Monument.*

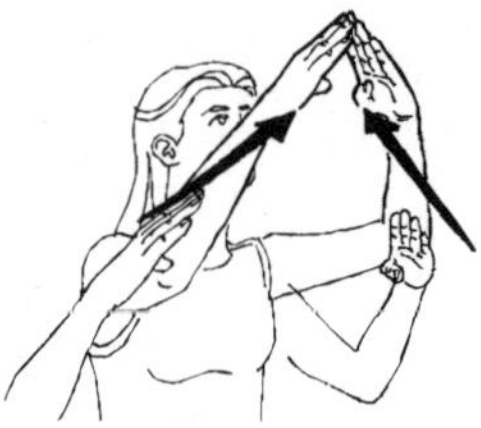

- [Shows the shape of the top of a monument] Beginning with both *B hands* in front of each shoulder, palms angled down, bring the hands upward toward each other, ending with the fingertips touching in front of the head.

**mooch** *v. Slang.* See sign for LEECH.

**moon** *n.* **1.** The natural heavenly body that revolves around the earth: *Look at the full moon shining through those trees.* **2.** Any similar body orbiting another planet: *Io is one of the moons of Jupiter.*

■ [The shape of the crescent moon] Tap the thumb of the right *modified C hand,* palm facing left, against the right side of the forehead with a double movement.

**mop** *n.* **1.** A cleaning tool with an absorbent head and long handle: *Let's use a mop to clean the kitchen floor.* —*v.* **2.** To clean with a mop: *to mop the floor.*

■ [Mime using a mop] Beginning with both *modified X hands* in front of the body, the left hand lower than the right hand, right palm angled left and left palm angled up, move the hands forward and downward with a double movement.

**moped** *n.* See sign for MOTORCYCLE.

**more** *adj.* **1.** Greater in amount, quantity, degree, etc.: *more food.* —*adv.* **2.** In or to a greater degree: *It's a more interesting excuse than most.* **3.** In addition or additionally; again: *We need to exercise more.*

■ [The hands seem to add more and more things together] Tap the fingertips of both *flattened O hands,* palms facing each other, together in front of the chest with a double movement.

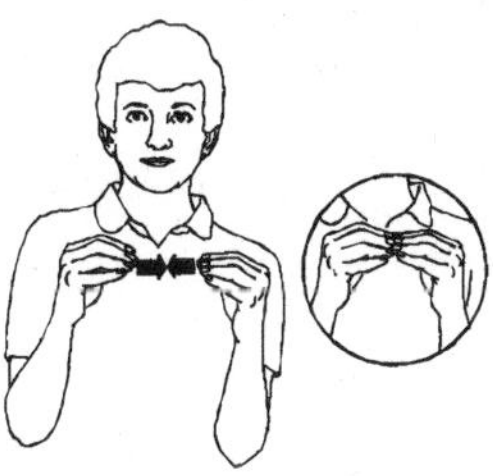

**more than** *adj.* + *prep.* See sign for EXCESS.

**morning** *n.* The early part of the day, before noon: *to eat breakfast in the morning.*

■ [Represents the sun coming up over the horizon] With the left *open hand* in the crook of the bent right arm, bring the right *open hand* upward, palm facing in.

**mortgage** *n.* An agreement conveying interest in property in return for financial obligations to pay for it: *The mortgage payment is due the first of each month.*

■ [Initialized sign similar to sign for **lend**] With the little finger of the right *M hand* on the index finger of the left *M hand*, fingers pointing in opposite directions and palms facing in, tip the hands forward.

**mosquito**[1] *n.* A small slender insect, the female of which sucks the blood of humans and animals: *bitten by a mosquito.*

■ [Represents a mosquito biting one's cheek, causing one to hit it in order to kill it] Touch the fingertips of the right *F hand,* palm facing left, on the right cheek. Then place the palm of the right *open hand* against the same place on the right cheek.

**mosquito**[2] *n.* See sign for BEE.

**most** *adj., adv.* **1.** To or in the highest degree, amount, etc.: *the most money; the most cooperative.* —*n.* **2.** The greatest amount: *Of all those at the dinner, he ate the most.*

■ Beginning with the palm sides of both *10 hands* together in front of the chest, bring the right hand upward, ending with the right hand in front of the right shoulder, palm facing left.

**mother** *n.* A female parent: *Her hair is the same color as her mother's.* Same sign used for: **mama, mom, mommy.**

■ [Formed in the female area of the head] Tap the thumb of the right *5 hand,* palm facing left, against the chin with a double movement.

**mother-in-law** *n.* The mother of one's husband or wife: *cleaning house before a visit from my mother-in-law.*

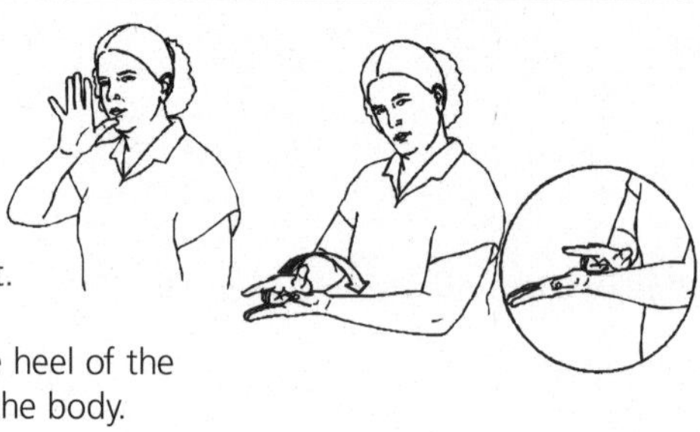

■ [**mother** + **law**] Tap the thumb of the right *5 hand*, palm facing left against the chin with a double movement. Then place the palm side of the right *L hand* first on the fingers and then on the heel of the upturned left *open hand* held in front of the body.

**motion** *v.* See sign for SUGGEST.

**motive** *n.* See signs for FEEL, ZEAL. Related form: **motivation** *n.*

**motor** *n.* See sign for MACHINE.

**motorcycle** *n.* A two-wheeled motorized vehicle: *ride a motorcycle.* Same sign used for: **moped, snowmobile.**

■ [Mime the action of one's hands on a motorcycle's handlebars] Beginning with both *S hands* held near each side of the waist, palms facing back, twist the wrists to move the hands up and down with a repeated movement.

**mount** *v.* See sign for PUT.

**mountain** *n.* A very high elevation of land, higher than a hill: *the beautiful craggy mountains of Montana.*

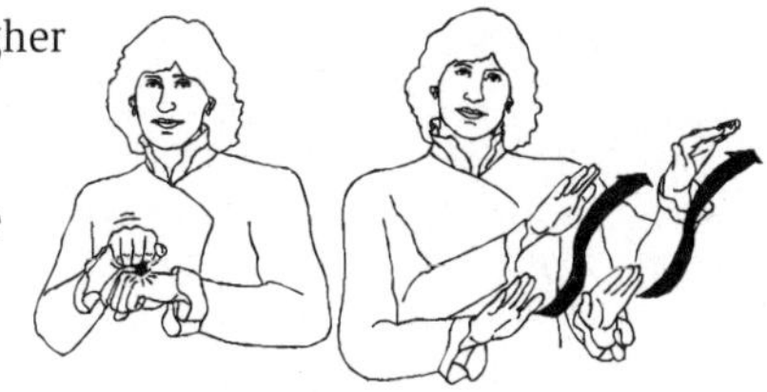

■ [**rock**[1] + the shape of a mountainside] Tap the palm side of the right *S hand* on the back of the left *S hand,* both palms facing down in front of the body. Then, beginning with both *open hands* in front of each side of the waist, palms facing down and fingers angled up, move the hands upward and forward at an angle with a large wavy movement.

**mournful** *adj.* See sign for SAD.

**mouse**[1] *n.* **1.** A small gnawing rodent with pointed ears and a long, thin tail: *Don't be surprised if you see a mouse in the pantry.* **2.** A small device for controlling the pointer on a computer's display screen: *To open the file, click twice on the file name with the left button on your mouse.*

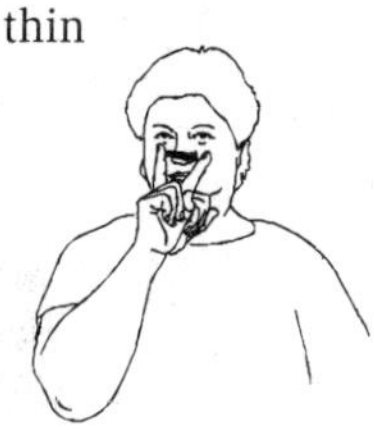

■ [Represents the twitching of a mouse's nose] Flick the extended right index finger, palm facing left, across the tip of the nose with a double movement.

**mouse**[2] *n.* A device for moving a cursor or other object around on the display screen: *Use the mouse to click on the e-mail you want to read.*

■ [Action of moving a computer mouse] Move the right *modified C hand*, palm down, around in front of the right side of the body.

**mouth** *n.* The opening through which one takes in food: *You'll have to open your mouth wide for that sandwich.*

■ [Location of the mouth] Draw a circle around the mouth with the extended right index finger, palm facing in.

**movable** *adj.* See sign for MOBILE.

**move** *v.* **1.** To change the position of: *Move the chair to the other side of the room.* **2.** To change the location of one's business or residence: *We're moving to the third floor.* Related form: **movement** *n.* Same sign used for: **relocate.**

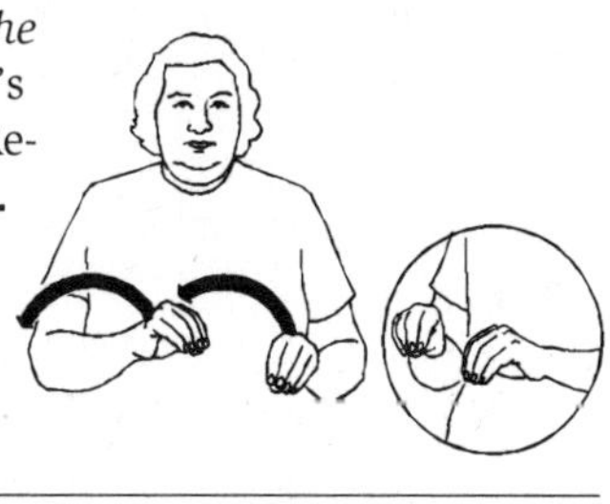

■ [The hands seem to move something from one place to another] Beginning with both *flattened O hands* in front of the body, palms facing down, move the hands in large arcs to the right.

**move on** *v. phrase.* See sign for GO ON.

**movie** *n.* See sign for FILM.

**movie camera** *n. phrase.* A camera used for making motion pictures: *Let's film the birthday party with a movie camera.* Same sign used for: **camera, film, shoot, video camera, videotape.**

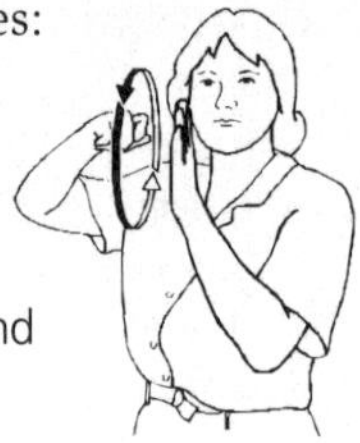

■ [Shows the action of movie film going through the camera] Move the right *modified X hand,* palm facing down, in a forward circular movement near the palm of the left *open hand,* palm facing right and fingers pointing up, in front of the upper chest.

**much** *n.* **1.** A great amount: *carried too much.* —*adj.* **2.** In a great amount: *not much time.* —*adv.* **3.** Greatly: *much pleased.* Same sign used for: **a lot, lots.**

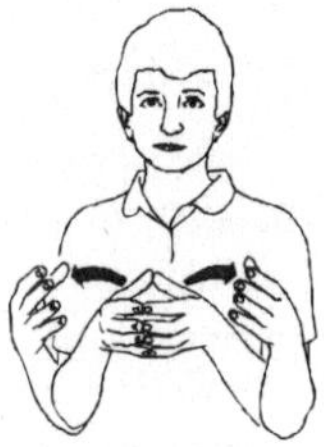

■ [The hands expand to encompass something large] Beginning with the fingertips of both *curved 5 hands* touching each other in front of the body, palms facing each other, bring the hands outward to in front of each side of the chest.

**muffle** *v.* To stop (sound) from being emitted from the mouth by covering the mouth with the hand: *The girls muffled their giggling by hiding under the covers.*

■ [Natural gesture] Place the palm side of the right *C hand* over the mouth.

**mule** *n.* See sign for DONKEY.

**mull** *v.* or **mull over** *v. phrase.* To think about carefully: *mull over whether to go or not.* Same sign used for: **cogitate, deliberate, ponder.**

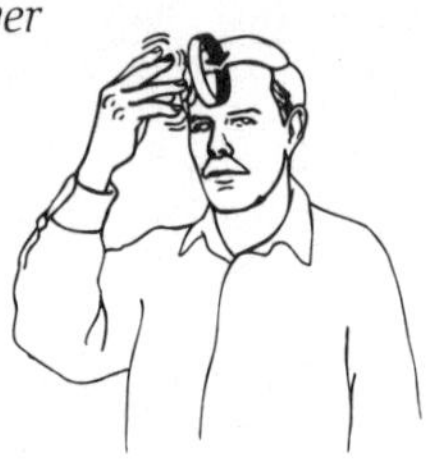

■ [Represents the brain as it cogitates] Wiggle the fingers of the right *4 hand* in a small repeated circle near the forehead, palm facing in.

**multiplication** *n.* See signs for ARITHMETIC, MATHEMATICS.

**multiply** *v.* To add a number to itself a given number of times: *If you multiply the number 12 by 7, you get 84.* Same sign used for: **estimate, figure, figure out.**

■ Brush the back of the right *V hand* across the palm side of the left *V hand,* both palms facing up, as the hands cross in front of the chest.

**mumps** *pl. n.* A contagious viral disease marked by swollen glands: *vaccinated against the mumps.*

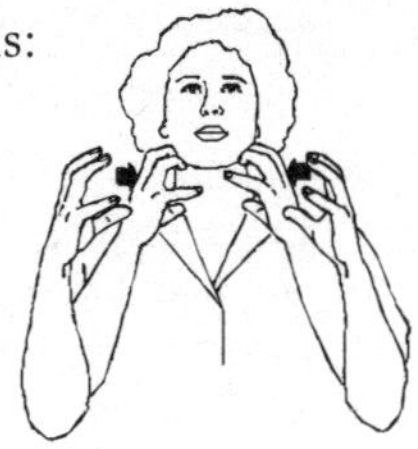

- [Shows the shape of one's swollen jaws from mumps] Beginning with both *curved 5 hands* in front of each shoulder, palms facing each other, bring the hands in to touch each side of the neck.

**murder** *v.* See sign for KILL.

**muscle** *n.* A special bundle of tissue in the body composed of long cells that contract to produce movement: *The weightlifter has enormous muscles.*

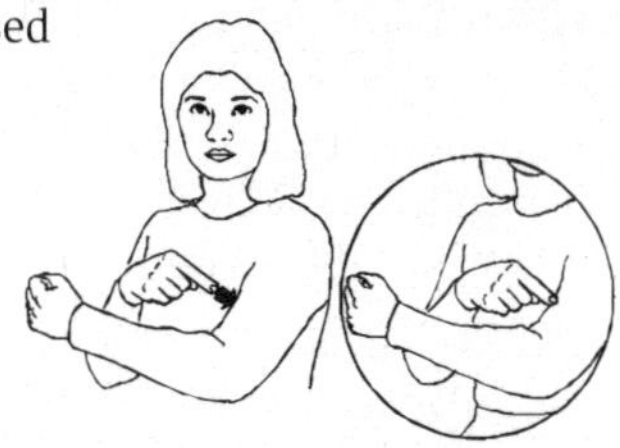

- [Location of a muscle in the arm] Tap the extended right index finger against the upper part of the bent left arm with a double movement.

**museum** *n.* A building intended for the display of objects of public interest: *The city has a wonderful art museum.*

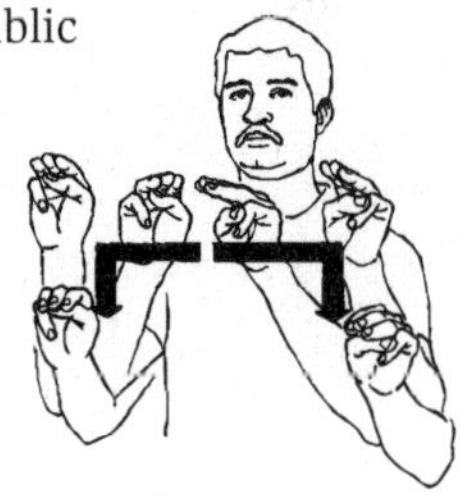

- [Initialized sign showing the shape of museum shelves] Beginning with both *M hands* in front of chest, palms facing forward, bring the hands outward to in front of each shoulder and then straight down.

**music** *n.* Pleasant or emotionally expressive arrangements of sounds, as those using rhythm, melody, and harmony: *Play some soft music.* Same sign used for: **chant, hymn, melody, sing, song.**

- [Demonstrates the rhythm of music] Swing the little-finger side of the right *open hand,* palm facing left, back and forth with a double movement across the length of the bent left forearm held in front of the chest.

**must** *auxiliary v.* (Used to express obligation, requirement, compulsion, preference, etc.): *We must attend the next concert.* Same sign used for: **have to, necessary, ought to, should.**

- Move the bent index finger of the right *X hand,* palm facing forward, downward with a deliberate movement in front of the right side of the body by bending the wrist down.

**mustache** *n.* Hair growing on the upper lip: *He wears a mustache.*

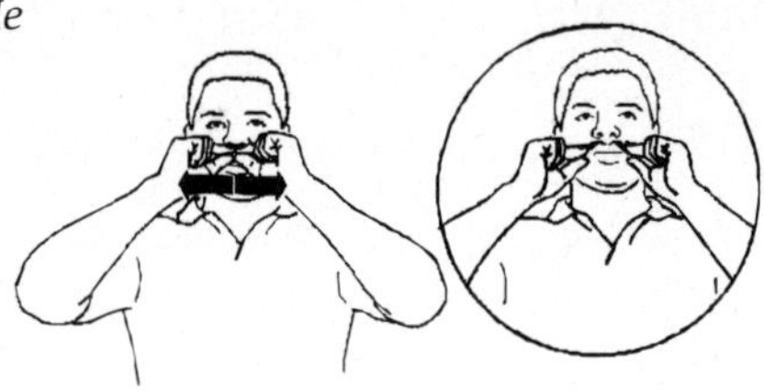

■ [Location of a mustache] Beginning with the index finger and thumb of each hand pinched together under the nose, palms facing each other, bring the hands straight apart to near each side of the mouth.

**mutilate** *v.* See sign for TORTURE.

**mutual** *adj.* See signs for ASSOCIATE, SAME[1].

**my** *pron.* A form of the possessive case of I, indicating that something specified or indicated belongs to the speaker: *my book.* Same sign used for: **mine own.**

■ [Pulling something to oneself] Place the palm of the right *open hand* on the chest, fingers pointing left.

**myself** *pron.* A reflexive form of ME: *Let me do it myself.*

■ [Sign moves toward oneself] Tap the thumb side of the right *A hand,* palm facing left, against the chest with a double movement.

**mystery** *n.* See sign for HIDE.

**nab**[1] *v.* To catch or seize: *nabbed the rabbit before it ruined the garden.* Same sign used for: **capture, catch, corner, caught in the act.**

- [The fingers seem to nab a suspect] Bring the right *bent V fingers,* palm facing down, sharply forward on each side of the extended left index finger held up in front of the chest, palm facing right.

---

**nab**[2] *v.* See signs for CATCH[2], SOLICIT.

---

**nag** *v.* See sign for PICK ON, PREACH.

---

**nail file** *n. phrase.* See sign for PUMICE.

---

**naive** *adj.* See sign for INNOCENT.

---

**naked** *adj.* See sign for NUDE.

---

**name**[1] *n.* **1.** A word that designates or identifies a person or thing: *The baby's name is John.* —*v.* **2.** To give a name to: *We named the cat Cinderella.* Same sign used for: **label.**

- Tap the middle-finger side of the right *H hand* across the index-finger side of the left *H hand.*

---

**name**[2] *v.* See sign for CALL[3].

---

**napkin** *n.* A paper or cloth towel used for wiping the mouth, protecting the clothing, etc., during meals: *Your napkin is on the table.*

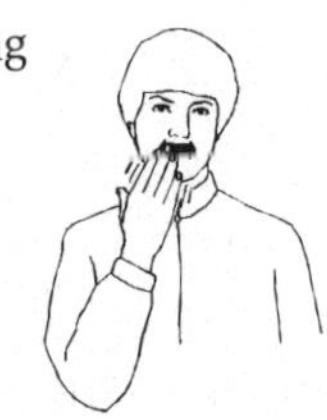

- [Mime wiping one's mouth with a napkin] Wipe fingertips of the right *open hand* from side to side over the lips with a double movement, palm facing in.

---

**narrow** *adj.* Not wide; constricted in width: *walked down a narrow hallway.*

- [The hands demonstrate something getting narrower] Bring both *open hands* from in front of each side of the body, palms facing each other, toward each other in front of the waist.

---

**narrow down** *v. phrase.* To restrict, as in amount or number, so as to eliminate what is not essential: *narrow down the number of candidates.* Same sign used for: **convey, focus on.**

■ [The hands move downward from wider to narrower] Beginning with both *open hands* in front of each shoulder, palms facing each other and fingers pointing forward, bring the hands downward toward each other in front of the body.

**nasty** *adj.* See signs for BAD, DIRTY.

**nation** *n.* A country and its people: *a great nation.* Related form: **national** *adj.* Same sign used for: **native, natural, nature, normal, of course.**

■ [Initialized sign] Beginning with the right *N hand,* palm facing down, over the left *open hand,* palm facing down, move the right hand in a small circle and then straight down to land on the back of the left *open hand.*

**native** *n.* See sign for NATION.

**natural** *adj.* See sign for NATION.

**nature** *n.* See sign for NATION.

**naughty** *adj.* See signs for BAD, DEVIL.

**nausea** *n.* See sign for DISGUSTED.

**navel** *n.* A depression in the abdomen at the point that the umbilical cord was attached: *Her navel showed above her bikini.* Same sign used for: **belly button, umbilicus.**

■ [Location of navel] Place the index-finger side of the left *F hand* on the abdomen.

**nay** *adv. Archaic.* See sign for NEVER MIND.

**near** *adv.* See signs for APPROACH[1], CLOSE[1,2].

**near future, in the** *prep. phrase.* See sign for SOON.

**nearly** *adv.* See sign for ALMOST.

**neat** *adj.* In an orderly condition: *It's easy to find things in a neat closet.*

- [Initialized sign similar to sign for **clean**] Slide the extended fingers of the right *N hand,* palm facing down, from the heel to the fingers of the upturned left *open hand,* fingers pointing forward.

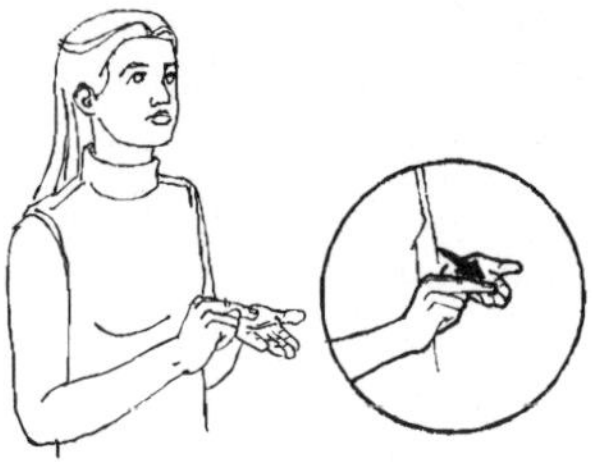

**necessary** *adj.* See sign for MUST, NEED.

**neck**[1] *n.* The part of the body that connects the head and the shoulders: *to wrap a scarf around your neck.*

- [Location of the neck] Tap the fingertips of the right *bent hand,* palm facing down, against the neck with a double movement.

**neck**[2] *v.* See sign for PET[2].

**necklace**[1] *n.* A piece of jewelry, as a chain or string of beads, worn around the neck as an ornament: *to wear a pearl necklace.*

- [Location of a necklace] Beginning with both extended index fingers touching near each side of the neck, bring the hands downward to touch near the middle of the chest.

**necklace**[2] *n.* See sign for BEADS.

**necktie** *n.* A narrow length of cloth worn around the collar and tied so that the two ends hang down the front: *The restaurant won't let a man in unless he's wearing a necktie.* Same sign used for: **tie.**

- [Initialized sign showing the location of a necktie] Touch the fingertips of the right *N hand* first to near the neck and then to the lower chest, palm facing in.

**need** *v.* **1.** To be in want of; require: *I need a pen so I can sign this.* —*n.* **2.** A requirement, as from lack or want: *to have an acute need for more sleep.* Same signs used for: **necessary, supposed to.**

- Tap the bent index finger of the right *X hand,* palm facing down, with a short, repeated downward movement in front of the right side of the body, by bending the wrist down.

**needle** *n.* A slender, pointed metal tool used in sewing: *to sew a fine stitch with a small needle.*

■ [Represents threading a needle] Move the index finger of the right *modified C hand,* palm facing left, downward with a double movement to brush the index finger of the left *L hand*, palm facing right.

**needlework** *n.* The art or process of working with a needle, as in quilting, hand sewing, or embroidery: *Mother does needlework while watching television.* Same sign used for: **sew.**

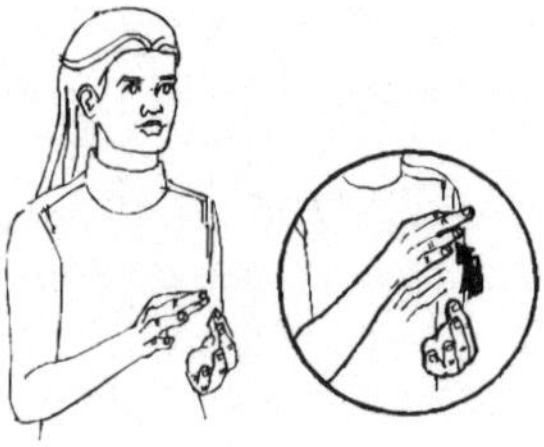

■ [Mime sewing] Beginning with the right *F hand,* palm facing down, above the left *F hand,* palm facing up, move the right hand upward with a short repeated movement.

**negative** *adj.* **1.** Expressing refusal or denial: *a negative answer.* **2.** Lacking positive qualities: *a negative attitude.*

■ [Shape of a minus sign] Tap the thumb side of the extended right index finger, palm facing down and finger pointing forward, against the palm of the left *open hand,* palm facing right and fingers pointing up, with a double movement.

**neglect** *v.* See sign for IGNORE. Related forms: **negligence** *n.*, **negligent** *adj.*

**negotiate** *v.* **1.** To discuss and arrange terms for: *to negotiate a settlement of the strike.* **2.** To deal or bargain with others so as to reach an understanding: *The management and the workers refuse to negotiate.* Related form: **negotiation** *n.*

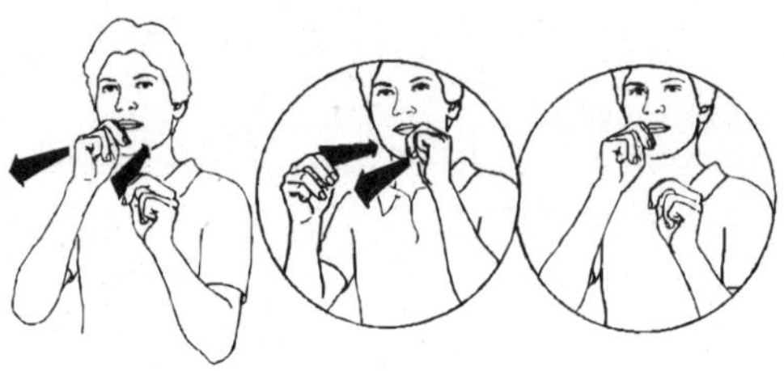

■ [Initialized sign similar to sign for **communication**] Move both *N hands,* palms facing each other, forward and back from the chin with an alternating movement.

**neighbor** *n.* A person who lives near another: *to borrow a cup of sugar from my neighbor.*

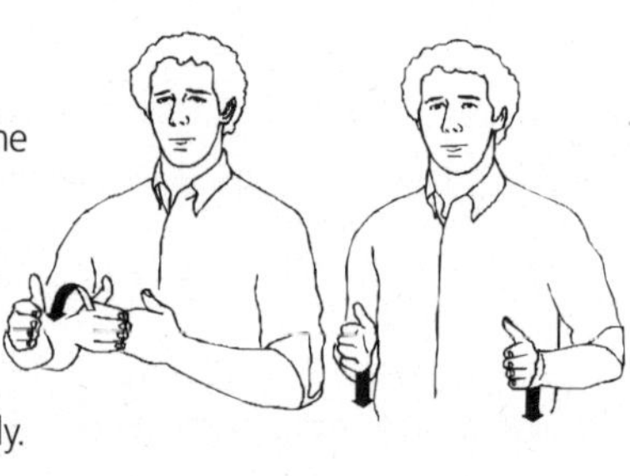

■ [**next door** + **person marker**] Beginning with the palm of the right *bent hand,* palm facing in and fingers pointing left, touching the back of the left *bent hand,* palm facing in and fingers pointing right, move the right hand forward in a small arc. Then move both *open hands,* palms facing each other, downward along each side of the body.

**neighborhood** *n.* A localized area, as in a town or city, considered a definable district by the people who live there: *a friendly neighborhood.*

■ [**next door** + **district**] Beginning with the palm of the right *bent hand,* palm facing in and fingers pointing left, touching the back of the left *bent hand,* palm facing in and fingers pointing right, move the right hand forward in a small arc.

**nephew** *n.* The son of one's brother or sister: *taking my nephew to the toy store.*

■ [Initialized sign formed near the male area of the head] Beginning with the extended fingers of the right *N hand* pointing toward the right side of the forehead, palm facing left, twist the wrist to point the fingers forward with a double movement.

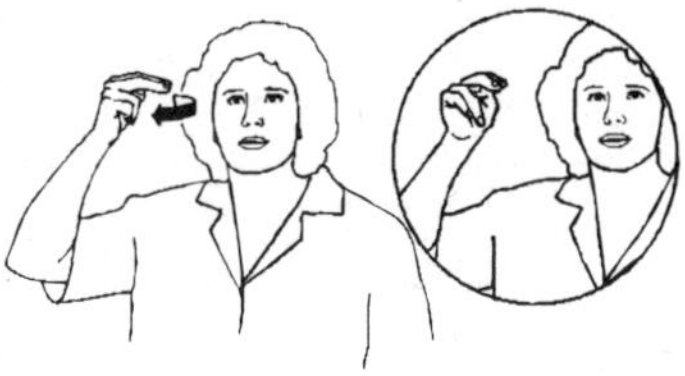

**nerve** *n.* One or more bundles of fibers that, as part of a system, convey impulses of sensation, motion, etc., between the brain or spinal cord and other parts of the body: *The needle hit a nerve in my arm.*

■ [Initialized sign] Move the fingertips of the right *N hand,* palm facing down, from the wrist to the crook of the back of the bent left arm.

**nervous** *adj.* **1.** Extremely uneasy and apprehensive; worried: *nervous about the interview.* **2.** Agitated and jittery: *Your drumming on the table is making me nervous.* Related form: **nervously** *adv.* Same sign used for: **anxiety, anxious.**

■ [Natural gesture of shaking when nervous] Shake both *5 hands* with a loose, repeated movement in front of each side of the body, palms facing each other and fingers pointing forward.

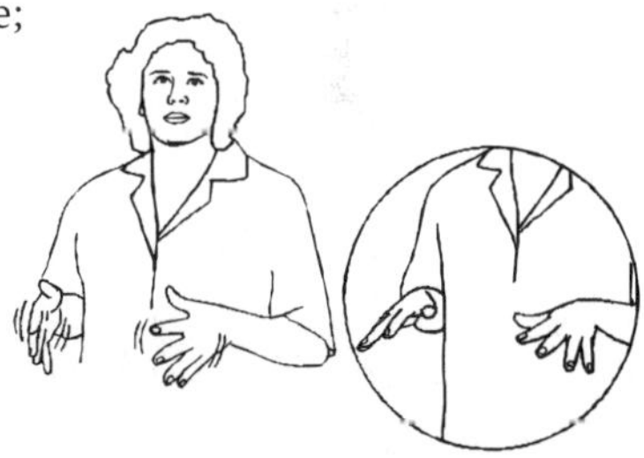

**nervy** *adj. Informal.* **1.** Rude; insolent; pushy: *a nervy reporter who won't stop bothering them.* **2.** Requiring courage: *It was nervy of me to ask for a raise so soon.* Related form: **nerve** *n.*

■ Beginning with the bent fingers of the right *V hand* against the right cheek, palm facing forward, twist the wrist, ending with the palm facing back.

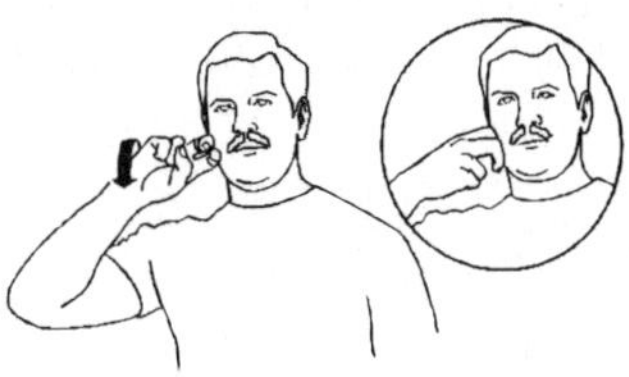

**net** *n.* A loosely woven fabric, usually made with knotted string: *to hit the volleyball over the net.* Same sign used for: **screen.**

- [Shows the mesh of a net] Beginning with the fingers of the right *4 hand* across the back of the fingers of the left *4 hand,* both palms facing forward, move the fingers of both hands slightly upward with a double movement.

**Net, the** *n.* See sign for NETWORK.

**network** *n.* **1.** A system of interconnected elements, as a group of electronically linked computers: *The data file is accessed through the network.* **2.** A group of people who share information and services, as for career advancement: *Someone in my network will know where to find a good accountant.* —*v.* **3.** To connect to a network: *to network the computer with an information system.* **4.** To get into or stay in touch with a group of people who share information and services: *learning to network early in one's career.* Same sign used for: **Internet, the Net, World Wide Web (www).**

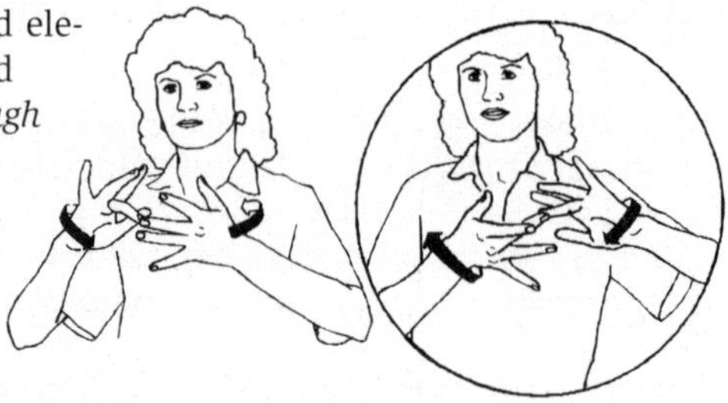

- [Similar to the sign for **contact** to indicate many contacts in a network] Beginning with the bent middle fingers of both *5 hands* touching in front of the right side of the chest, right palm angled forward and left palm facing in, twist both wrists and touch again in front of the left side of the chest, ending with the right palm facing in and left palm angled forward.

**neutral** *adj.* Being uncommitted to one side or another in a conflict: *Switzerland was a neutral country during World War II.*

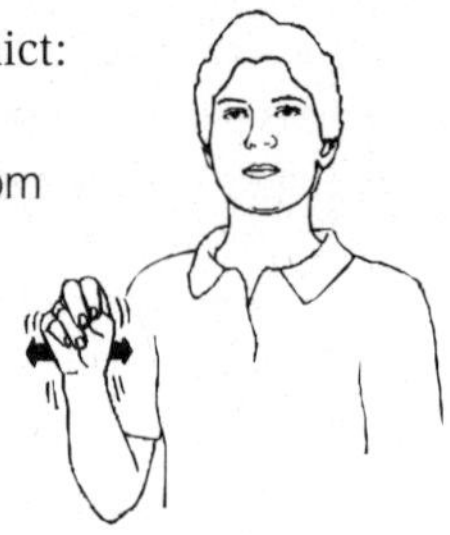

- [Initialized sign] Move the right *N hand,* palm facing forward, from side to side with a small double movement in front of the right shoulder.

**never** *adv.* Not ever: *never got married.*

- Move the right *open hand* from near the right side of the face, palm facing left, downward with a large wavy movement to in front of the right side of the body, ending with the palm facing down.

**never mind** *Slang.* (Used to tell listeners that they need not concern themselves with the matter under discussion; often said ironically): *I was going to carry that for you, but never mind.* Same sign used for: **blah** (*slang*), **nay** *(archaic)*.

- [Natural gesture] Beginning with the right *open hand* in front of the right shoulder, palm facing forward and fingers pointing up, bend the wrist to bring the hand downward to the right side of the body, ending with the fingers pointing down and the palm facing back.

**nevertheless** *adv.* See sign for ANYWAY.

**new** *adj.* **1.** Existing or known for the first time: *a new idea.* **2.** Newly produced or purchased: *bought a new coat.*

- Slide the back of the right *curved hand,* palm facing up, from the fingertips to the heel of the upturned left *open hand.*

**newspaper** *n.* A daily or weekly publication containing news, feature articles, advertising, etc.: *a newspaper with an excellent editorial page.* Same sign used for: **issue, press, print, publication.**

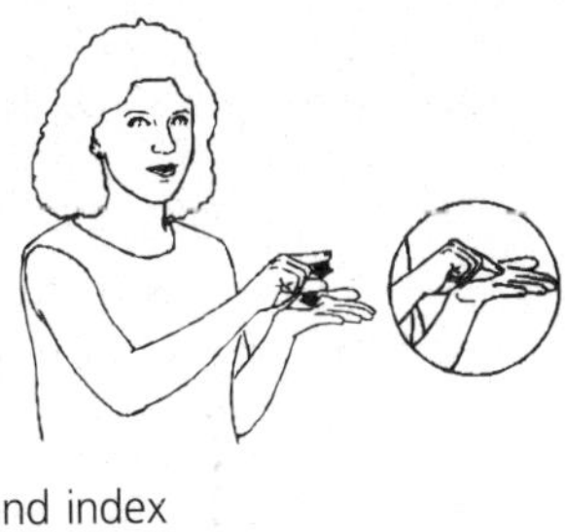

- [Represents putting movable type into place to set up a newspaper] Beginning with the right *G hand,* palm facing forward, above the left *open hand,* palm facing up, pull the right hand down toward the heel of the left hand with a double movement, closing the right thumb and index finger together each time.

**next**[1] *adj.* **1.** Immediately following: *the next train.* **2.** Nearest; closest in position: *Could you move to the next chair? —adv.* **3.** In the time or position that is nearest: *You are speaking next. She has the next highest score. —prep.* **4. next to** Nearest to: *the chair next to the window.*

- [Demonstrates one hand overcoming an obstacle to move on to the next thing] Beginning with the right *bent hand,* palm facing in and fingers pointing left, closer to the chest than the left *open hand,* palm facing in and fingers pointing right, move the right hand up and over the left hand, ending with the right palm on the back of the left hand.

**next**[2] *adj.* See sign for TURN[1].

**next door** or **next-door** *adv.* At, in, or to the next house or apartment: *he lives next door.*

■ [Shows a location next to another thing] Beginning with the palm of the right *bent hand,* palm facing in and fingers pointing left, touching the back of the left *curved hand,* palm facing in and fingers pointing right, move the right hand forward in a small arc.

**next to** *prep.* See sign for BESIDE.

**nickel** *n.* A U.S. coin valued at five cents: *Remember when candy cost a nickel?* Same sign used for: **five cents.**

■ [The sign **cents** is formed with a *5 hand*] Beginning with the bent index finger of the right *5 hand,* palm facing left, touching the right side of the forehead, bring the hand forward with a double movement.

**nickname** *n.* A name, as an affectionate shortened form, used instead of a person's given name: *Elizabeth's nickname at school was Lizard!*

■ [**short** + **name**[1]] Rub the middle-finger side of the right *H hand,* palm angled left, back and forth with a repeated movement on the index-finger side of the left *H hand,* palm angled right. Then place the middle-finger side of the right *H hand* across the index-finger side of the left *H hand.*

**niece** *n.* The daughter of one's brother or sister: *I bought a computer for my niece.*

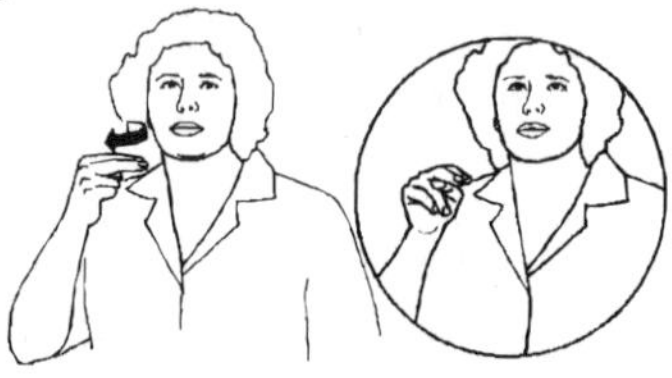

■ [Initialized sign formed near the female area of the head] Beginning with the extended fingers of the right *N hand* pointing toward the right cheek, palm facing left, twist the wrist to point the fingers forward with a double movement.

**niggardly** *adj.* See sign for GREEDY.

**night** *n.* The time between evening and morning: *The job requires him to work at night.* Same sign used for: **tonight.**

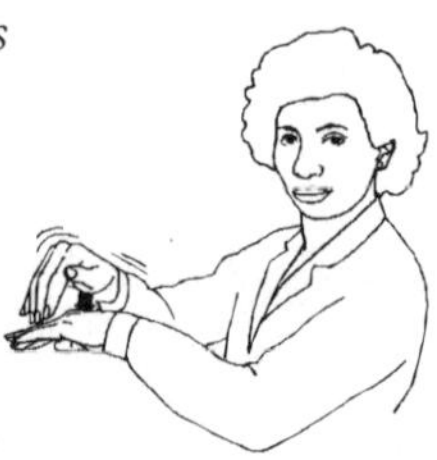

■ [Represents the sun going down over the horizon] Tap the heel of the right *bent hand,* palm facing down, with a double movement on the back of the left *open hand* held across the chest, palm facing down.

**nightgown** *n.* A loose garment worn by a woman or child for sleeping: *to wear a nightgown to bed instead of pajamas.*

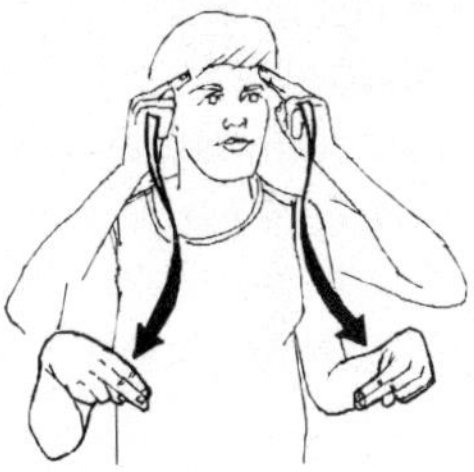

■ [Initialized sign] Beginning with the extended fingers of both *N hands* touching each side of the forehead, palms facing each other, bring the hands downward with a long wavy movement, ending with the *N hands* in front of each side of the body, fingers pointing toward each other and palms facing in.

**nipple** *n.* The small projection on a breast that, in females, contains the conduit for the milk glands: *The baby grasped the mother's nipple and began to nurse.* Same sign used for: **mammillary.**

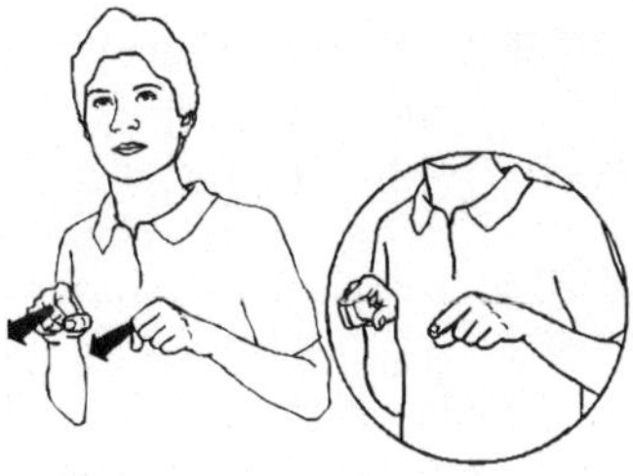

■ [Indicates position of nipples] Beginning with both *S hands* in front of the chest, palms facing down, flick each index finger forward with a double movement.

**no**[1] *adv.* (A negative expressing dissent, denial, or refusal, as in response to a question or request): *No, I won't.*

■ [Fingerspell **n-o** quickly] Snap the extended right index and middle fingers closed to the extended right thumb, palm facing down, while moving the hand down slightly.

**no**[2] *adv.* See sign for NONE[1].

**nobody** *pron.* No person; not anyone: *Nobody knows where we hid it.* Same sign used for: **no one.**

■ [Similar to sign for **none**[1] but formed with one hand] Move the right *O hand,* palm facing forward, from side to side with a double movement in front of the right shoulder.

**nod** *v.* See sign for BOW[1].

**node** *n.* See signs for BUMP[1,2].

**no good** *adj.* Not of good quality; valueless: *The term paper is no good.*

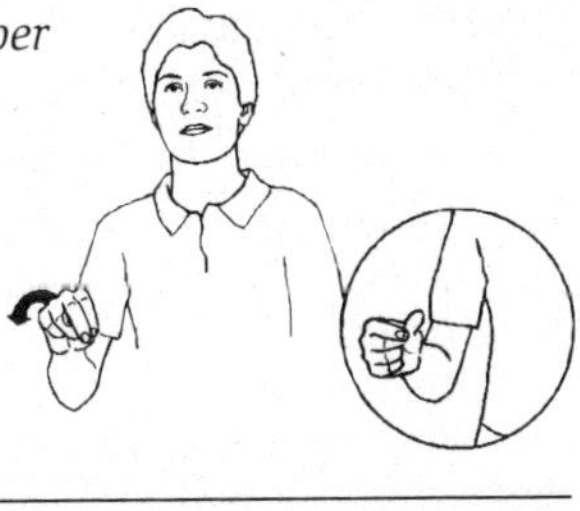

■ [Abbreviation **n-g**] Beginning with the right *N hand* in front of the right side of the chest, palm facing down, quickly twist the wrist to form a *G hand,* palm facing left.

**noise** *n.* **1.** A loud, or harsh, or grating sound: *awakened by a loud noise.* **2.** Loud sound: *I hate noise.* Same sign used for: **aloud, loud, sound.**

■ [Indicates the vibration of a loud sound coming from the ears] Beginning with the bent index fingers of both *5 hands* touching each ear, palms facing in, move the hands forward with a deliberate movement while shaking the hands.

**nominate** *v.* See signs for APPLY², SUGGEST.

**nonchalant** *adj.* See sign for DON'T CARE.

**none¹** *pron.* Not any: *I have none left.* Same sign used for: **no.**

■ [Indicates zero amount of something in the hand] Move both *flattened O hands,* palms facing forward, from side to side with a repeated movement in front of each side of the chest.

**none²** *pron.* (alternate sign) Same sign used for: **zero.**

■ [Indicates zero amount of something] Move the right *O hand,* palm facing left, from in front of the chest forward, ending with the little-finger side of the right hand on the palm of the left *open hand.*

**none³** *pron.* See sign for NOTHING².

**noodle** *n.* A typically flat, solid strip of pasta made of flour and eggs: *chicken and noodles.*

■ [The shape of a thin noodle] Beginning with the fingertips of both *I hands* touching in front of the chest, palms facing in, bring the hands apart with a double movement, bending the little fingers back toward the palms each time.

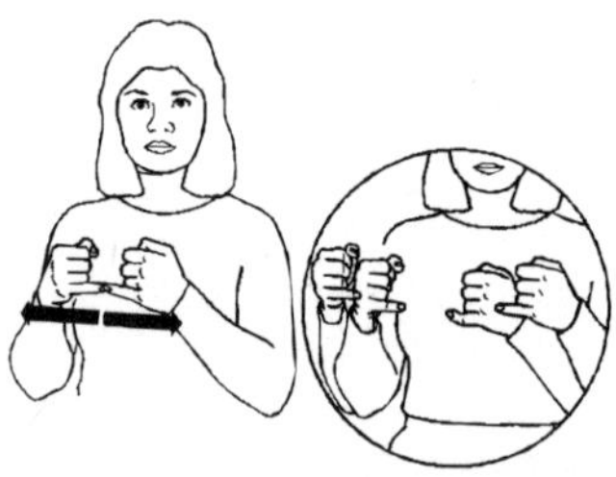

**noon** *n.* The middle of the day: *eat at 12 noon.* Alternate form: **noontime.** Same sign used for: **midday.**

■ [Represents the sun straight overhead at noon] Place the right elbow, arm extended up and right *open hand* facing forward, on the back of the left *open hand* held across the body, palm facing down.

**no one** *pron.* See sign for NOBODY.

**normal** *n., adj.* See sign for NATION.

**north** *n.* **1.** The general direction 90 degrees to the left of east and to the right of west: *moved to a suburb just north of the city.* —*adj.* **2.** Lying toward or located in the north: *the north end of town.* —*adv.* **3.** To, toward, or in the north: *Go north for three miles.*

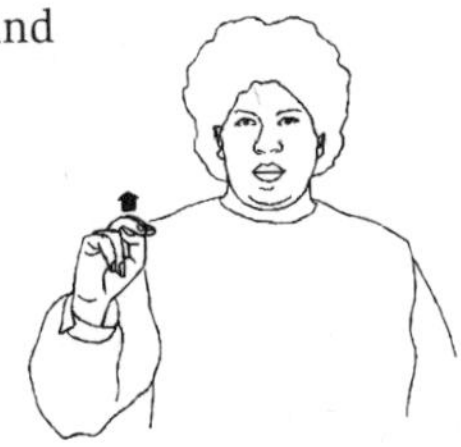

■ [Initialized sign moving in the direction of north on a map] Move the right *N hand,* palm facing forward, upward in front of the right shoulder.

**nose** *n.* The part of the face protruding above the lips and having openings for breathing and smelling: *a broken nose.*

■ [Location of the nose] Touch the extended right index finger to the right side of the nose, palm facing down.

**nosebleed** *n.* See sign for RUN[3].

**nosy**[1] *adj. Informal.* Prying: *a nosy person.*

■ [Shape of a large nose] Beginning with the extended right index finger touching the nose, palm facing down, twist the wrist to bring the finger around the end of the nose, ending with the finger under the nose, palm facing in.

**nosy**[2] *adj. Informal.* (alternate sign) Same sign used for: **butt in, meddle, peek, pry, snoop.**

■ [Represents one's nose extending to insert it into another's business] Beginning with the bent index finger of the right *X hand* beside the nose, palm facing left, bring the right hand downward and insert the bent index finger in the thumb-side opening of the left *O hand,* palm facing right.

**not**[1] *adv.* (Used to express negation, denial, refusal, etc.): *I'm not tired any more.* Same sign used for: **don't.**

■ Bring the extended thumb of the right *10 hand* from under the chin, palm facing left, forward with a deliberate movement.

**not**[2] *adv.* (alternate sign) Same sign used for: **don't.**

■ [Natural gesture forbidding something] Beginning with the right *open hand* crossed over the left *open hand* in front of the body, palms facing down, swing the hands outward to in front of each side of the body.

**notebook computer** *n. phrase.* See sign for LAPTOP COMPUTER.

**nothing**[1] *n.* **1.** Not anything: *Nothing has arrived in the mail today.* **2.** Something of no importance or value or something requiring little effort: *Don't worry about the trip—it's nothing.*

■ [The hand opens to reveal nothing in it] Beginning with the index-finger side of the right *O hand* under the chin, palm facing forward, bring the hand downward and forward while opening into a *5 hand,* palm facing down.

**nothing**[2] *n.* (alternate sign)

■ [The hand opens to reveal nothing in it] Beginning with the index-finger side of the right *S hand* under the chin, palm facing left, bring the hand downward and forward while opening into a *5 hand,* palm facing down.

**nothing**[3] *n.* (alternate sign) Same sign used for: **all gone, gone, none.**

■ [Natural gesture for showing nothing in one's hand] With the right *curved hand* in front of the upper chest, palm facing up, blow across the palm.

**notice**[1] *v.* To observe; become aware of: *I noticed a big hole in the wall.* Same sign used for: **aware, recognize.**

■ [Brings the eye down to look at something in the hand] Bring the extended curved right index finger from touching the cheek near the right eye, palm facing left, downward to touch the palm of the left *open hand,* palm facing right in front of the chest.

**notice**[2] *v.* See sign for INFORM.

**notify** *v.* See sign for INFORM.

**not my fault** See sign for NOT RESPONSIBLE.

**notorious** *adj.* See sign for FAMOUS.

**not responsible** *adj.* Without culpability: *My dog is not responsible for the holes in the yard.* Same sign used for: **hands off, not my fault.**

- [Natural gesture for flicking away responsibility] Beginning with the fingertips of both *8 hands* touching each shoulder, palms facing each other, flick the hands quickly forward while opening into *5 hands.*

**now** *adv.* At this time or moment: *Come here now!* Same sign used for: **current, present, prevailing, urgent.**

- Bring both *bent hands,* palms facing up, downward in front of each side of the body.

**Now I remember** See sign for DISGUSTED[2]. Shared idea of disgust with oneself for having forgotten.

**nude** *adj.* Wearing no clothes: *a nude model.* Same sign used for: **bare, naked.**

- [The sign **empty** formed downward on the hand representing a person's body] Move the bent middle finger of the right *5 hand,* palm facing in, downward on the back of the left *open hand,* palm facing in and fingers pointing down, from the wrist to off the fingertips.

**nuisance**[1] *n.* An annoying person, animal, thing, event, etc.: *the constant interruptions are a nuisance.* Same sign used for: **pest.**

- Move the bent middle finger of the right *5 hand* forward and back with a short, quick movement in front of the chest, palm facing forward.

**nuisance**[2] *n.* See sign for ANNOY.

**null** *adj.* See sign for CANCEL.

**number** *n.* **1.** Alternate form: **numeral.** A word, letter, or symbol representing a count of things or persons: *Write down the number of people in attendance.* **2.** A mathematical unit expressing an amount or quantity: *The number of people here is twenty-six.* Related form: **numeric** *adj.* Same sign used for: **digit.**

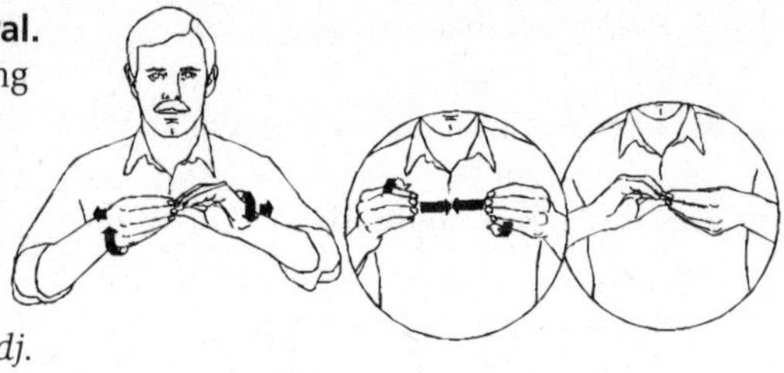

- Beginning with the fingertips of both *flattened O hands* touching, left palm angled forward and right palm facing in, bring the hands apart while twisting the wrists in opposite directions and touch the fingertips again, ending with the left palm facing in and the right palm angled forward.

**numerous** *adj.* See signs for MANY, MULTIPLE.

**nurse** *n.* A person trained to care for ill people: *The family of the sick child hired a private registered nurse.*

- [Initialized sign similar to sign for **doctor**] Tap the extended fingers of the right *N hand,* palm facing down, with a double movement on the wrist of the left *open hand* held in front of the body, palm facing up.

**nut** *n.* See sign for PEANUT.

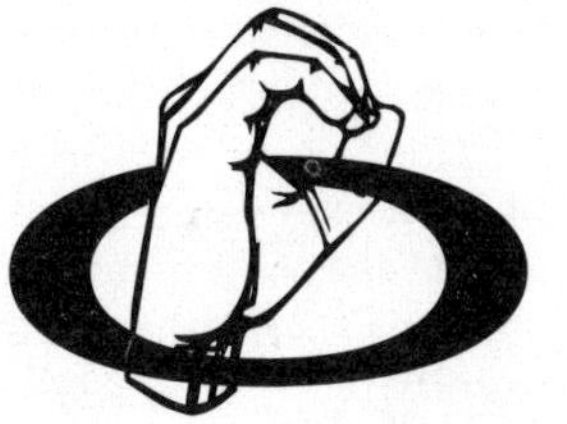

**oath** *n.* A solemn pledge to speak the truth, keep a promise, etc.: *I made an oath in the courtroom to tell the truth.* Same sign used for: **inaugural, inauguration, pledge, testify, testimony.**

■ [Natural gesture for putting one's hand on the Bible and taking an oath] Hold the left *open hand* in front of the left side of the body, palm facing down and fingers pointing forward, and the right *open hand* in front of the right shoulder, palm facing forward and fingers pointing up.

---

**obese** *adj.* See sign for FAT.

---

**obey** *v.* To comply with the orders, instructions, or wishes of: *to obey the rules.* Related forms: **obedience, obedient.**

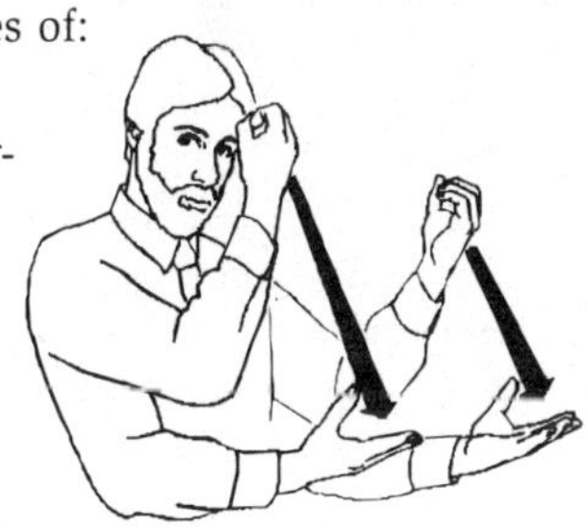

■ [Represents placing one's own ideas in a position subservient to another's] Beginning with the right *O hand* in front of the forehead and the left *O hand* in front of the left shoulder, both palms facing in, bring the hands downward simultaneously while opening the fingers, ending with both *open hands* in front of the body, palms facing up and fingers pointing forward.

---

**object**[1] *n.* See sign for THING.

---

**object**[2] *v.* See signs for COMPLAIN, DISAGREE.

---

**objection** *n.* See sign for PROTEST[1].

---

**objective**[1] *n.* A goal or purpose to be achieved: *The objective of the game is to capture all the pieces.*

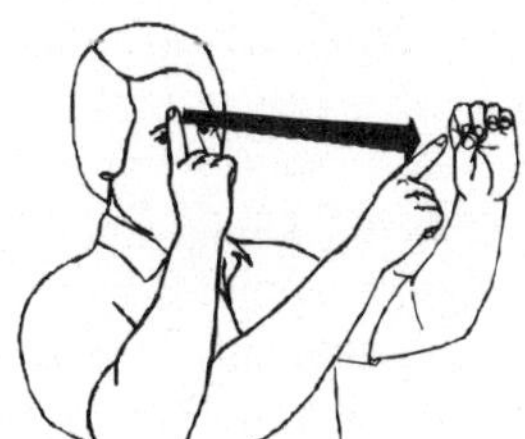

■ [Initialized sign similar to sign for **goal**] Move the extended right index finger from in front of the right side of the forehead, palm facing left and finger pointing up, forward toward the thumb-side opening of the left *O hand* held in front of the left shoulder, palm facing right.

---

**objective**[2] *n.* See sign for GOAL.

---

**obligate** *v.* See sign for VOW.

---

**obligation** *n.* See sign for BURDEN.

**obscene** *adj.* Describes any form of expression that deals with sex in a way that is regarded so offensive as to be beyond the protection of freedom of speech: *The movie was R-rated because of obscene language.* Related form: **obscenity** *n.*

■ Twist the right *Y hand* up and down with a repeated movement, striking the extended left index finger held in front of the chest each time it passes.

**observe**[1] *v.* **1.** To see and notice: *driving around and observing the scenery.* **2.** To watch carefully so as to learn from: *I observed the procedure in the operating room.* Related form: **observant** *adj.*

■ [Represents one's eyes surveying the surroundings] Beginning with both *V hands* in front of the chest, palms facing down and fingers pointing forward, swing the hands to the left, following the fingers with the eyes.

**observe**[2] *v.* See sign for LOOK OVER.

**obsession** *n.* The domination of one's thoughts by a persistent idea, desire, etc.: *an obsession with neatness.* Related forms: **obsess** *v.*, **obsessive** *n., adj.* Same sign for: **persevere, persistent.**

■ With the bent middle finger of the right *5 hand* on the back of the left *open hand,* both palms facing down, move the hands forward in a repeated circular movement in front of the body.

**obstinate** *adj.* See sign for STUBBORN.

**obstruct** *v.* See sign for PREVENT.

**obtain** *v.* See sign for GET.

**occasional**[1] *adj.* Happening irregularly or infrequently: *We have an occasional snowstorm.* Related form: **occasionally** *adv.* Same sign used for: **once in a while, periodically.**

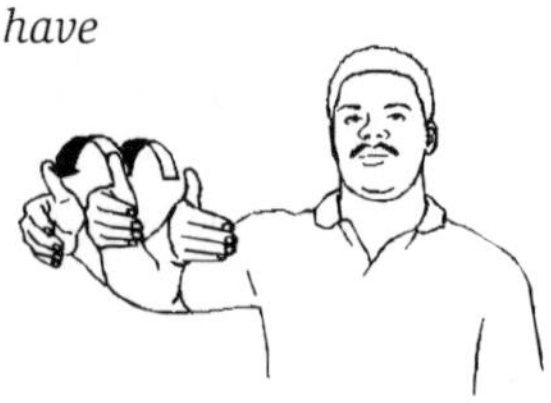

■ [**next-next-next**] Beginning with the right *bent hand* in front of the right side of the chest, palm facing left and fingers pointing left, move the hand forward in a deliberate double arc.

**occasional**[2] *adj.* See sign for SOMETIMES.

**occupation** *n.* See sign for WORK.

**occupy** *v.* See sign for CAPTURE.

**occur** *v.* See signs for HAPPEN, SHOW UP. Related form: **occurrence** *n.*

**ocean** *n.* **1.** The great body of salt water that covers most of the earth's surface: *Three quarters of the planet is covered by ocean.* **2.** Any of the divisions of this body: *the Atlantic Ocean.*

■ [**water** + the shape of an ocean wave] Tap the index-finger side of the right *W hand,* palm facing left, against the chin with a double movement. Then, beginning with both *5 hands* in front of the body, palms facing down and fingers pointing forward, move the hands upward and forward in a large wavy movement.

**odd** *adj.* See sign for STRANGE.

**odor** *n.* See sign for SMELL.

**of course** *adv. phrase.* See sign for NATION.

**off** *prep.* **1.** So as to be away from, no longer resting on, etc.: *Take your feet off the chair.* —*adv.* **2.** So as to be away from the usual position, no longer attached or supported, or the like: *Take off your coat.*

■ [Shows moving one hand off the other hand] Beginning with the palm of the right *open hand* across the back of the left *open hand* at an angle, both palms facing down in front of the body, raise the right hand upward in front of the chest.

**offense** *n.* See signs for CRIME[1,2].

**offer** *v.* See sign for SUGGEST.

**office** *n.* The place in which the work of running a business is done: *Please send copies of the annual report to the office.*

■ [Initialized sign similar to sign for **room**] Beginning with both *O hands* in front of each side of the body, palms facing each other, move the hands deliberately in opposite directions, ending with the left hand near the chest and the right hand several inches forward of the left hand, both palms facing in.

**officer** *n.* See signs for CAPTAIN, CHIEF, POLICE.

**officially** *adv.* See sign for DECIDE.

**offshoot** *n.* See sign for ASTRAY.

**off the point** *prep. phrase.* See signs for ASTRAY, DIGRESS.

**off the subject** *prep. phrase.* See sign for DIGRESS.

**off track** *prep. phrase.* See signs for ASTRAY, DIGRESS.

**often** *adv.* Many times; frequently: *We often go to the movies.* Same sign used for: **frequently.**

■ [The sign **again** formed with a repeated movement to indicate frequency of occurrence] Touch the fingertips of the right *bent hand,* palm facing left, first on the heel and then on the fingers of the left *open hand,* palm angled up.

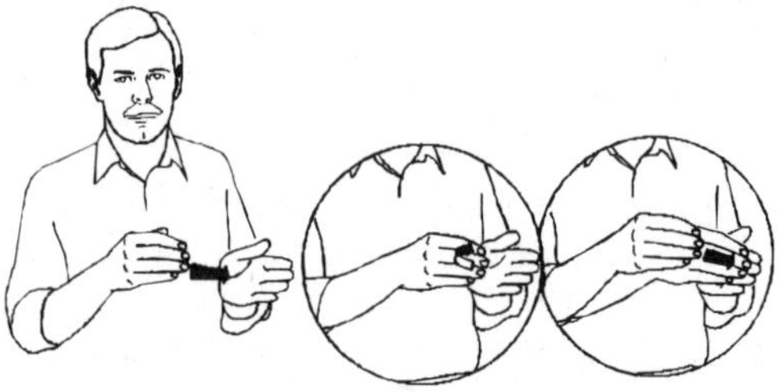

**Oh** *interj.* (Used to indicate surprise or understanding): *Oh, I see what you mean.*

■ Tap the right *Y hand,* palm angled down, downward with a small double movement in front of the right side of the body.

**oil** *n.* Any of various kinds of thick, greasy liquid used as fuel, for cooking, etc.: *I now cook in vegetable oil.* Related form: **oily** *adj.* Same sign used for: **grease, greasy.**

■ [Shows oil dripping off something] Beginning with the bent thumb and middle finger of the right *5 hand,* palm facing up, on each side of the little-finger side of the left *open hand,* palm facing right and fingers pointing forward, bring the right hand downward with a double movement, pinching the thumb and middle finger together each time.

**ointment** *n.* A substance applied to the skin, as to heal or soften: *to put ointment on a cut.*

■ [**medicine** + mime rubbing ointment on the hand] With the bent middle finger of the right *5 hand,* palm facing down, in the upturned palm of the left *open hand,* rock the right hand from side to side with a double movement while keeping the middle finger in place. Then rub the fingers of the right *open hand* with a double movement on the back of the left *open hand* held in front of the chest, both palms facing down.

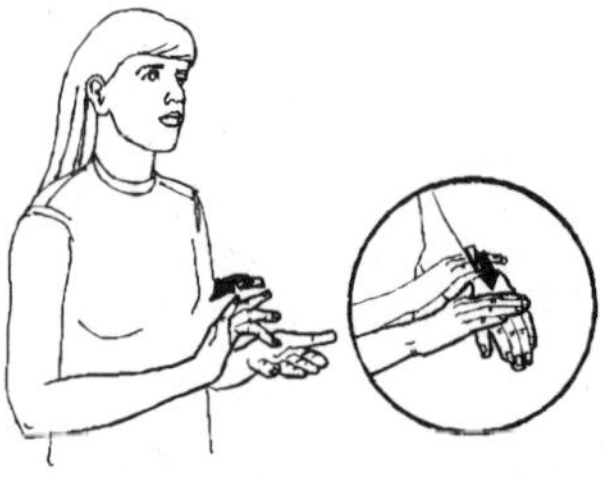

**okay**[1] or **OK** or **O.K.** *interj.* **1.** (Used to express approval or agreement): *"OK!" he yelled, "you can go ahead now."* —*adj.* **2.** All right; satisfactory: *The schedule is okay.* **3.** Feeling well: *I was sick, but now I'm O.K.* **4.** Adequate: *His work is OK, but he could do better.*

■ [Spell **o-k**] Form an *O* and a *K* quickly in front of the right side of the chest, palm facing forward.

**okay**[2] *adj.* See signs for FINE[1], RIGHT[3], SUPERB.

**old** *adj.* Having existed for a long time; not young: *an old house.*

■ [Shows the shape of a beard on an old man] Move the right *C hand* from near the chin, palm facing left, downward a short distance while closing into an *S hand.*

**old-fashioned** *adj.* Characteristic of things and ideas of an earlier era: *old-fashioned ideas.*

■ [**old** + **fashion**] Move the right *C hand* from near the chin, palm facing left, downward a short distance while closing into an *S hand.* Then move the right *F hand,* palm facing down and fingers pointing forward, from in front of the right side of the body to the right a short distance in a small arc.

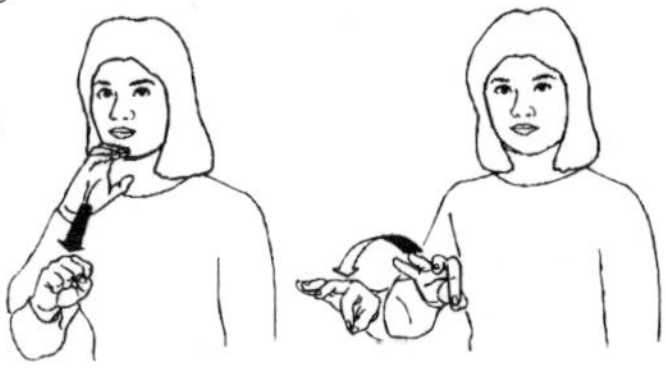

**Olympics** or **Olympic Games** *pl. n.* See sign for CHAIN.

**omit** *v.* See sign for ELIMINATE.

**on** *prep.* **1.** Above and supported by: *The purse is on the chair.* **2.** Suspended by: *a pendant on a chain.* **3.** Affixed to: *The label is on the back of the collar.*

■ [Shows moving one hand on the other] Bring the palm of the right *open hand* downward on the back of the left *open hand* held in front of the body, both palms facing down.

**on behalf of** See sign for SUPPORT.

**once** *adv.* **1.** One single time: *I'll tell you this just once.* **2.** In the past; formerly: *I once worked for a law firm.*

■ Beginning with the extended right index finger touching the left *open hand* held in front of the body, palm facing right and fingers pointing forward, bring the right finger upward with a quick movement while twisting the right wrist in, ending with the palm facing in and finger pointing up in front of the right side of the chest.

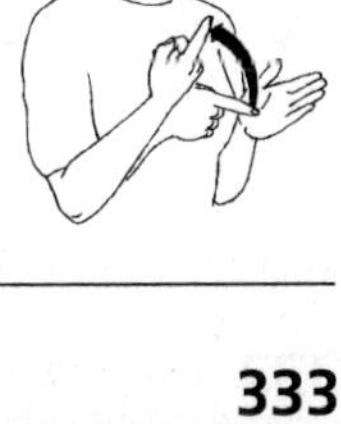

**once in a while** *adv. phrase.* See sign for OCCASIONAL[1].

**one another** *pron.* See sign for ASSOCIATE.

**one dollar** *n. phrase.* See sign for FIRST.

**one fourth** *n. phrase.* One of the four equal parts into which a whole may be divided: *one fourth of a cake.* Related form: **one-fourth** *adj.* Same sign used for: **quarter.**

■ [**one** + **four** formed over each other as in a fraction] Beginning with the extended right index finger pointing up in front of the right side of the chest, palm facing in, drop the hand while opening into a *4 hand.*

**one half** *n. phrase.* One of the two equal parts into which a whole may be divided: *one half of the pie.* Related form: **one-half** *adj.* See also sign for HALF.

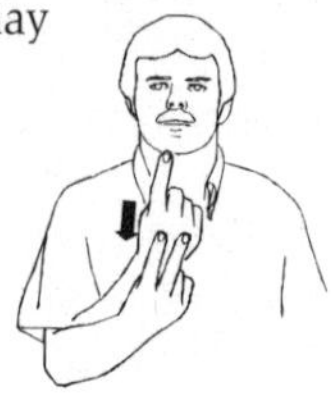

■ [**one** + **two** formed over each other as in a fraction] Beginning with the extended right index finger pointing up in front of the right side of the chest, palm facing in, drop the hand while opening into a *2 hand.*

**one minute** *n. phrase.* See sign for MINUTE.

**one month** *n. phrase.* See sign for MONTH.

**one third** *n. phrase.* One of the three equal parts into which a whole may be divided: *We gave a grade of B to one third of the class.* Related form: **one-third** *adj.* Same sign used for: **third.**

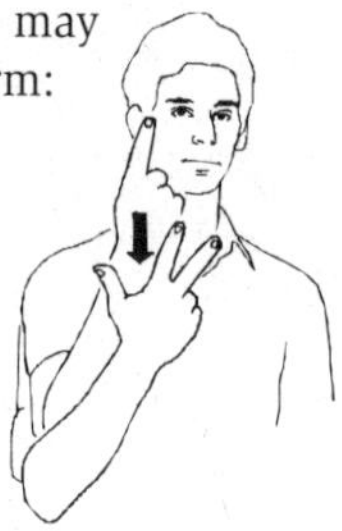

■ [**one** + **three** formed over each other as in a fraction] Beginning with the extended right index finger pointing up in front of the right side of the chest, palm facing in, drop the hand while opening into a *3 hand.*

**one week** *n. phrase.* See sign for WEEK.

**onion** *n.* An edible round bulb with a strong, pungent smell and taste, having tightly packed layers: *I like to put onions on my hamburger.*

■ [As if wiping a tear away from onion fumes] Twist the knuckle of the bent index finger of the right *X hand,* palm facing forward, with a double movement near the outside corner of the right eye.

**online** *adj.* See sign for BELONG[1]. Shared idea of connectivity.

**only**[1] *adj., adv.* See sign for ALONE.

**only**[2] *adj.* **1.** Being the single one: *only one ticket left.* —*adv.* **2.** Without others; solely: *This memo is for you only.* **3.** Merely; just: *She is only ten years old.*

■ Beginning with the extended right index finger pointing up in front of the right shoulder, palm facing forward, twist the wrist in, ending with the palm facing in near the right side of the chest.

**onward** *adv.* See sign for GO ON.

**open** *adj.* **1.** Not closed: *an open box.* —*v.* **2.** To make or become open: *The boy opened the birthday presents eagerly. Does the box open?*

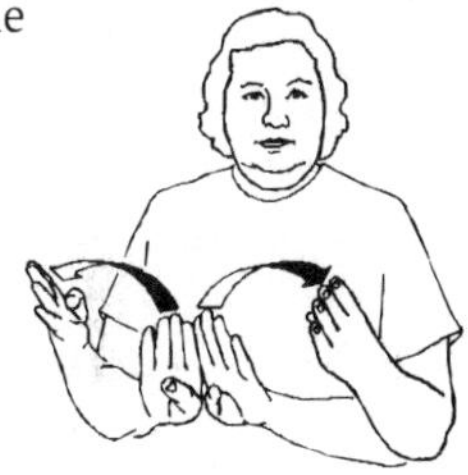

■ [Represents doors opening] Beginning with the index-finger sides of both *B hands* touching in front of the chest, palms facing forward, twist both wrists while bringing the hands apart to in front of each side of the chest, ending with the palms facing each other and the fingers pointing forward.

**open-minded** *adj.* See sign for BROAD-MINDED.

**operate**[1] *v.* To treat diseases or injuries by manipulating the body with surgical instruments: *The doctor operated on the man's arm.* Related form: **operation** *n.* Same sign used for: **surgery.**

■ [Represents the action of cutting during surgery] Move the thumb of the right *A hand,* palm facing down, from the fingers to the heel of the left *open hand,* palm facing right and fingers pointing forward.

**operate**[2] *v.* See signs for MANAGE, RUN[2].

**operating system** or **OS** *n. phrase.* A group of programs that help the computer's components function together smoothly: *The computer runs on a Windows operating system.*

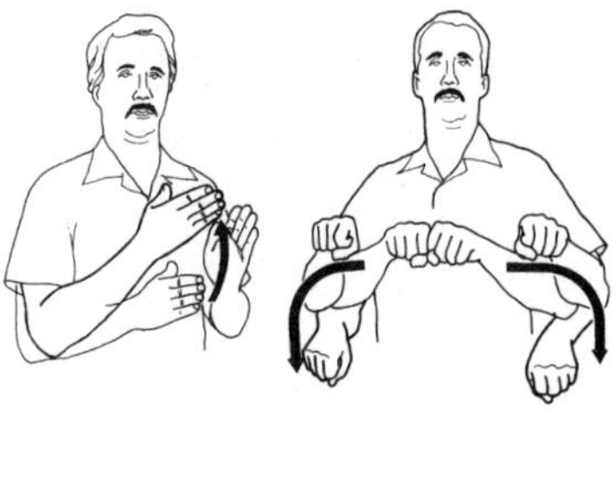

■ [**run**[3] + **system**] Brush the palm of the right *open hand* upward with a double movement on the palm of the left *open hand* held up in front of the chest. Then beginning with the index-finger sides of both *S hands* touching in front of the chest, palms down, move the hands outward to in front of each shoulder and then straight down a short distance.

**opinion** *n.* A belief or judgment, esp. one based on inadequate proof: *It's my opinion that he's innocent.*

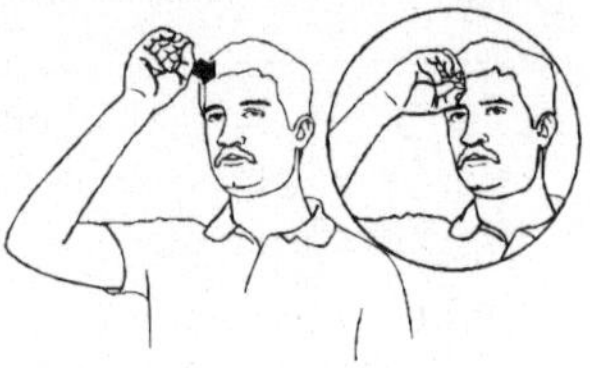

■ [Initialized sign] Move the right *O hand,* palm facing left in front of the forehead, toward the head with a double movement.

**opponent** *n.* See sign for ENEMY.

**opportunity** *n.* A favorable chance or appropriate occasion: *an opportunity to earn some money.*

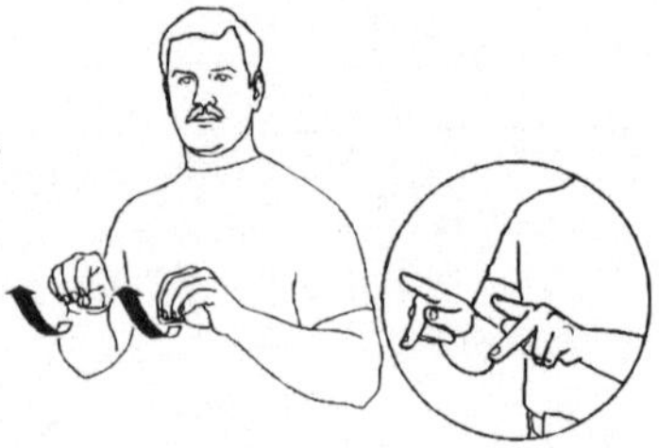

■ [Abbreviation **o-p** formed in a way that is similar to the sign for **permit**] Beginning with both *O hands* in front of the chest, palms facing down, move the hands forward and upward in an arc while changing into *P hands.*

**opposed to** *adj.* + *prep.* See sign for AGAINST.

**opposite** *adj.* Being extremely different, as in character or quality; opposed: *We have opposite opinions on that issue.* Related form: **oppose** *v.* Same sign used for: **contrary, contrast, counter.**

■ [Shows two things repelled by each other] Beginning with the fingertips of both extended index fingers touching in front of the chest, palms facing in, bring the hands straight apart to in front of each side of the chest.

**opposition** *n.* See sign for STRUGGLE.

**oppress** *v.* To weigh down: *The weather oppressed my spirits.* Related form: **oppression** *n.*

■ [Demonstrates pushing an oppressed thing down] Push the palm of the left *5 hand* downward on the extended right index finger, palm facing left and finger pointing up, forcing the right hand downward with a double movement.

**optical** *adj.* Relating to vision, light, or optics: *It was an optical illusion.*

■ [Turning an optical instrument to put it in focus] Beginning with the right *C hand*, palm facing down, near the right eye, twist the wrist to turn the palm up.

**optical zoom** *n. phrase.* The feature on a camera that allows an image to be magnified: *He used the optical zoom to get a close-up picture of the spider.*

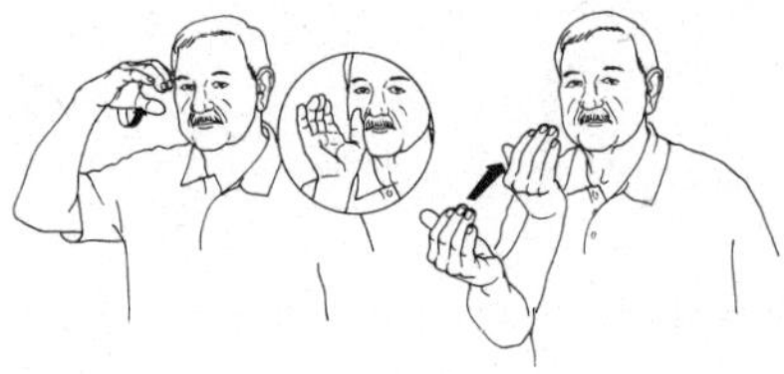

■ [**optical +** move an object into focus] Beginning with the right *C hand*, palm facing down, near the right eye, twist the wrist to turn the palm up. Then move the right *curved hand* forward and back toward the face with a double movement.

**optimistic** *adj.* Tending to expect the best: *I am optimistic about tomorrow's weather.*

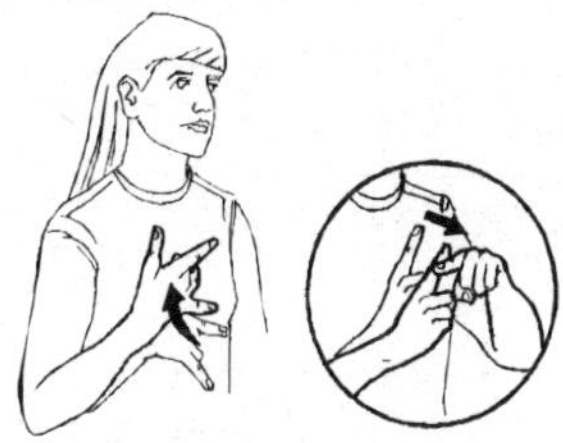

■ [**feel** + **plus**] Move the bent middle finger of the right *5 hand,* palm facing in, upward on the chest with a double movement. Then bring the side of the extended right index finger, palm facing left and finger pointing up, with a double movement against the extended left index finger, palm facing down and finger pointing right in front of the chest.

**option** *n.* See sign for CHOOSE[1].

**or** *conj.* (Used to connect alternate words, phrases, etc.): *Do you want apples or oranges?* Same sign used for: **then.**

■ [Touches two choices] Tap the extended right index finger, palm facing in, first to the thumb tip and then to the end of the index finger of the left *L hand,* palm facing right and index finger pointing forward.

**orange** *n.* **1.** A juicy, acidic, often sweet citrus fruit: *to eat an orange at breakfast.* —*adj.* **2.** Reddish-yellow in color: *an orange pumpkin.*

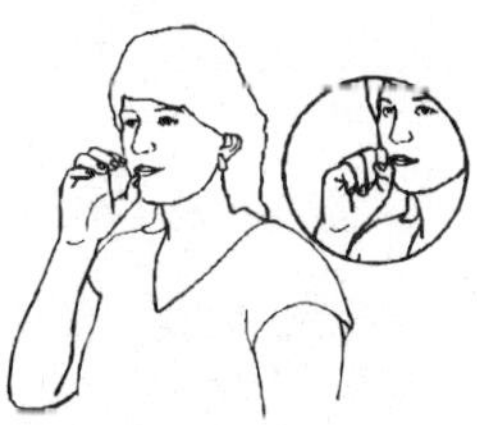

■ [The hand seems to squeeze an orange] Beginning with the right *C hand* in front of the mouth, palm facing left, squeeze the fingers open and closed with a repeated movement, forming an *S hand* each time.

**orbit**[1] *n.* **1.** The curved path of a heavenly body around another heavenly body: *studying the moon's orbit around the Earth.* —*v.* **2.** To travel in a circular movement around another object in space: *The satellite orbits the Earth every twenty-four hours.*

■ [Shows movement of one thing around another] Move the extended right index finger, palm facing down, in a circle around the fingers of the left *flattened O hand,* palm facing down in front of the chest.

**orbit**[2] *n.* See signs for AROUND[1], YEAR-ROUND.

**orchard** *n.* See sign for FOREST.

**orchestra** *n.* See sign for BAND.

**ordeal** *n.* See sign for EXPERIENCE.

**order** *n.* **1.** An instruction or command issued with authority: *When I give you an order, I expect you to obey it.* —*v.* **2.** To give an order or command to: *I order you to leave the house.* Same sign used for: **command, direct.**

■ [Represents taking words from the mouth and directing them at another] Move the extended right index finger, palm facing left and finger pointing up, from in front of the mouth straight forward while turning the palm down, ending with the finger pointing forward.

**ordinary**[1] *adj.* Usual; commonplace: *an ordinary day.*

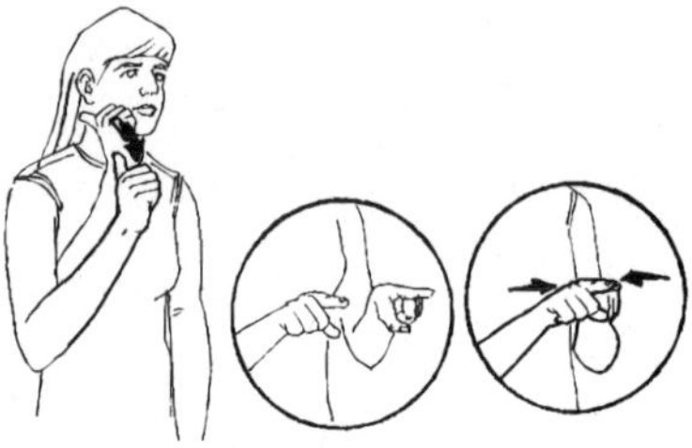

■ [**daily** + **same**] Move the palm side of the right *10 hand* forward on the right side of the chin with a double movement. Then, beginning with both index fingers pointing forward in front of the each side of the body, palms facing down, bring the hands together, ending with the index fingers side by side in front of the body.

**ordinary**[2] *adj.* See sign for DAILY, REGULAR[1]. Related form: **ordinarily** *adv.*

**organ** *n.* See sign for PIANO.

**organization** *n.* A group of people united for some purpose: *to belong to a political organization.* Related form: **organize** *v.*

■ [Initialized sign similar to sign for **class**] Beginning with the fingertips of both *O hands* touching in front of the chest, palms angled forward, bring the hands away from each other in outward arcs while turning the palms in, ending with the little fingers touching.

**organize** *v.* See signs for PLAN, PREPARE.

**orientation** *n.* An introduction or short program of training, as for a new job: *The new employees will attend an orientation.*

■ [Initialized sign similar to sign for **situation**] Move the palm side of the right *O hand* in a circle around the extended left index finger held in front of the chest, palm facing in and finger pointing up.

**origin** *n.* See sign for START[1]. Related form: **origination** *n.*

**originate** *v.* See sign for INVENT.

**orphan** *n.* See sign for ALONE[1].

**orthodox** *adj.* Conforming to generally accepted religious or other doctrinal views: *holds orthodox beliefs about behavior.*

■ [Initialized sign similar to sign for **clean**] Slide the little-finger side of the right *O hand,* palm facing in, from the heel to the fingertips of the left *open hand* held in front of the chest, palm facing up and fingers angled forward.

**other**[1] *adj.* **1.** Additional; further: *We'll be in our other house this weekend.* **2.** Different from the one under discussion: *If this pen doesn't work, try the other one.* —*n.* **3.** The other one: *I will choose the other.* Same sign used for: **else.**

■ [The thumb points over to another person, object, etc.] Beginning with the right *10 hand* in front of the chest, palm facing down, twist the hand upward to the right, ending with the palm facing up and the extended thumb pointing right.

**other**[2] *adj.* See sign for ANOTHER.

**ought to** *auxiliary v.* See sign for MUST.

**our** *adj.* Belonging to us: *This is our car.* Related form: **ours** *pron.*

■ [The hand seems to draw a possession to oneself] Beginning with the thumb side of the right *C hand* on the right side of the chest, palm facing left, bring the hand forward in an arc across the chest, ending with the little-finger side of the left hand on the left side of the chest, palm facing right.

**ourselves** *pl. pron.* A reflexive form of WE or US, used as an object or an intensifier: *We cooked for ourselves. We ourselves would never do that.*

■ [Uses the handshape used for reflexive pronouns] Beginning with the thumb of the right *A hand* touching the right side of the chest, palm facing left, bring the hand in an arc across the chest and touch again on the left side of the chest.

**out** *prep.* Movement or direction from the inside to the outside of something: *She took money out of the jar.* Same sign used for: **go out.**

- [Demonstrates a movement out of something] Beginning with the right *5 hand,* palm facing down, inserted in the thumb side opening of the left *C hand,* palm facing right, bring the right hand upward, closing the fingers and thumb together into a *flattened O hand.*

**outbreak** *n.* See sign for SPREAD.

**outcome** *n.* See sign for RESULT.

**outdoors** *adv.* See sign for OUTSIDE.

**out of the way** *prep. phrase.* See sign for ASTRAY.

**outrage** *n.* See sign for ANGER.

**outreach** *n.* **1.** An act, instance, or program of extending services and information to the larger community: *an organization engaged in outreach to the elderly.* —*adj.* **2.** Being part of an information and services network: *an outreach program providing food to the homeless.*

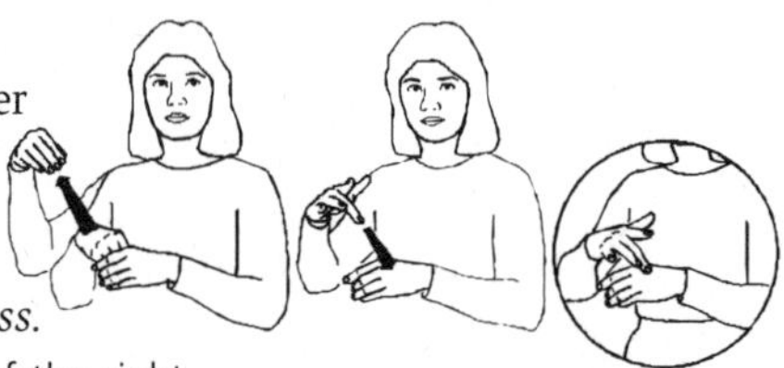

- [**out** + **touch**] Beginning with the fingertips of the right *flattened O hand,* palm facing down, inserted in the thumb side opening of the left *C hand,* palm facing right, bring the right hand upward to the right, then touch the bent middle finger of the right *5 hand,* palm facing down, to the back of the left *open hand* held across the chest, palm facing down.

**outside** *n.* **1.** The external side or surface or the area near it: *the outside of a house.* —*adj.* **2.** Located on the outside: *painting the outside walls.* —*adv.* **3.** On or to the outside: *Go outside and play.* —*prep.* **4.** Beyond the boundaries of: *outside the fence.* Same sign used for: **external, outdoors.**

- Beginning with the right *5 hand,* palm facing down, inserted in the thumb-side opening of the left *C hand,* palm facing right, bring the right hand upward and forward in an arc while closing the fingers and thumb together into a *flattened O hand* in front of the chest, fingers pointing in.

**oven** *n.* An enclosed place, as in a stove, for baking or roasting food: *Let's make the pie in the smaller oven.*

- [The hand seems to put something in the oven] Move the fingers of the right *open hand,* palm facing up and fingers pointing forward, forward with a double movement under the left *open hand* held in front of the chest, palm facing down and fingers pointing right.

**over**[1] *prep.* In excess of: *He charged over his credit limit.* Same sign used for: **exceed, too much.**

- [Shows a location higher than another] Beginning with the fingertips of the right *bent hand* on the fingertips of the left *bent hand,* palms facing each other and fingers pointing in opposite directions, bring the right hand upward a short distance in a small arc.

**over**[2] *prep., adv.* See signs for ABOVE, ACROSS, AGAIN, END, FINISH.

**overall** *adj., adv.* See sign for ALL OVER.

**overcoat** *n.* See sign for COAT.

**overcome** *v.* See sign for DEFEAT.

**overflow** *v.* **1.** To have the contents flow or spill over: *The river overflowed onto the fields.* **2.** To be plentifully supplied: *My heart overflows with love.* Same sign used for: **plenty, run over.**

- [Demonstrates a substance flowing over the sides of a container] Slide the fingers of the right *open hand,* palm facing forward, over the index-finger side of the left *open hand,* palm facing in, while opening into a *5 hand* as it goes over to the back of the left hand.

**overlook** *v.* **1.** To fail to see or notice: *He overlooked too many mistakes to be a good proofreader.* **2.** To disregard or forget: *I'm sorry I overlooked answering your letter.* Same sign used for: **oversight.**

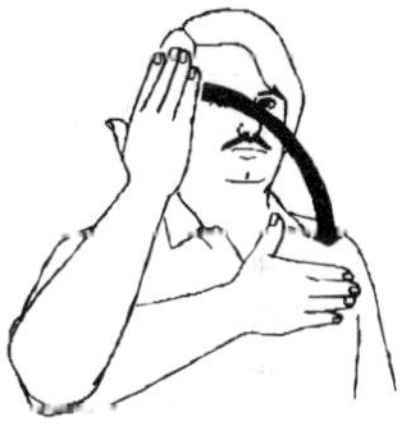

- [Represents something passing in front of the eyes without notice] Beginning with the right *open hand* near the right side of the head, palm facing left and fingers pointing up, move the hand in an arc in front of the face to the left while turning the fingers down, ending with the fingers pointing left and the palm facing in, in front of the left side of the chest.

**overnight** *adj., adv.* See sign for ALL NIGHT.

**overrule**[1] *v.* **1.** To rule against or disallow the arguments of a person. **2.** To rule unfavorably upon an objection raised in court: *The judge overruled the lawyer's objection.*

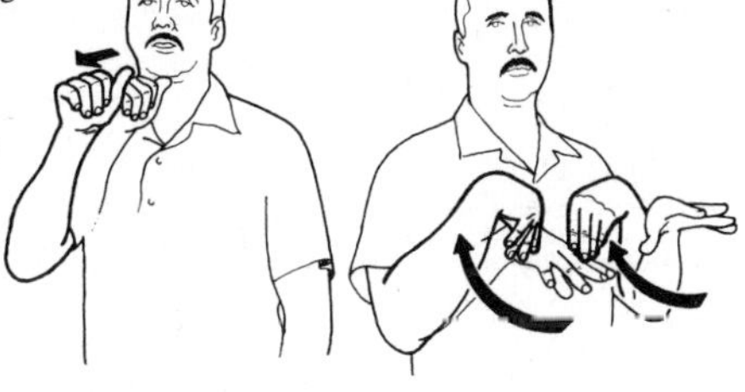

- [**not** + **accept**] Bring the thumb of the right *10 hand* forward from under the chin with a deliberate movement. Then beginning with both *5 hands* in front of the body, fingers pointing forward and palms down, pull both hands back to the chest while changing to *flattened O hands.*

**overrule**[2] *v.* (alternate sign)

■ [A shortened form of **decide** + **reject**] Move both *F hands,* palms facing each other, downward in front of each side of the body. Then beginning with the right *10 hand* in front of the right shoulder, elbow extended and palm facing down, twist the wrist downward ending with the thumb pointing down and the palm facing right.

**oversight** *n.* See sign for OVERLOOK.

**oversleep** *v.* To sleep too long: *I overslept this morning.*

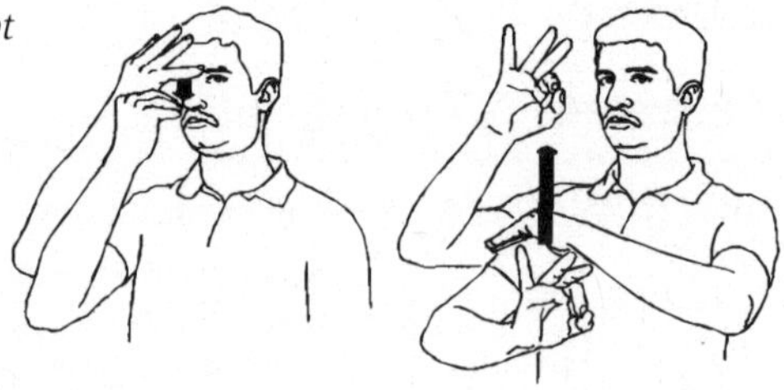

■ [**sleep** + **sunrise**] Beginning with the right *curved 5 hand* in front of the forehead, palm facing in, bring the hand downward while closing the fingers and thumb together, forming a *flattened O hand* in front of the nose. Then, beginning with the right *F hand* in front of the body, palm facing forward, bring the hands straight upward in front of the little-finger side of the left *open hand* held across the chest, palm facing down and fingers pointing right, ending with the right *F hand* in front of the face.

**overweight** *adj.* See sign for FAT.

**overwhelm** *v.* To overpower completely; burden; engulf: *overwhelmed with work.*

■ [Represents everything coming at one at once, as if to overwhelm] Beginning with both *A hands* in front of each side of the face, palms facing in, bring the hands back along each side of the head while opening into *5 hands.*

**owe** *v.* See sign for AFFORD.

**own** *adj.* **1.** Belonging to oneself: *I have my own car.* —*pron.* **2.** Something that belongs to oneself: *She has her own.* Same sign used for: **self.**

■ [The hand moves back toward oneself] Bring the knuckles of the right *10 hand,* palm facing right, back against the center of the chest.

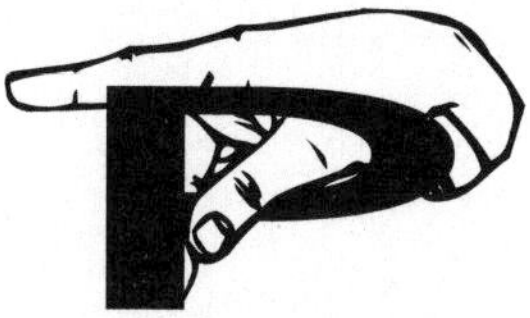

**pace** *n.* See signs for PROCEDURE, STEP. Shared idea of taking orderly steps.

**pack** *v.* To place and tightly arrange articles in: *to pack your suitcase.*

■ [Mime putting things into a suitcase] Beginning with both *flattened O hands* in front of each side of the chest, palms facing down, move the hands downward with an alternating double movement.

**package** *n.* See signs for BOX, ROOM.

**page** *n.* One side of a leaf of paper in something printed, as a book or manuscript: *to turn the page.* Same sign used for: **dictionary.**

■ [The thumb seems to flip through the pages of a book] Strike the extended thumb of the right *A hand,* palm facing down, against the left open palm with a double circular upward movement.

**pah!** *interj.* See sign for FINALLY. Used by Deaf people meaning "finally."

**pail** *n.* See sign for BUCKET.

**pain**[1] *n.* Physical suffering associated with disease or injury: *a pain in my chest.* See also signs for HURT[1,2]. Same sign used for: **ache, injury, sore.**

■ [Similar to sign for **hurt**[1] except with a twisting movement] Beginning with both extended index fingers pointing toward each other in front of the chest, right palm facing down and left palm facing up, twist the wrists in opposite directions, ending with right palm facing up and the left palm facing down.

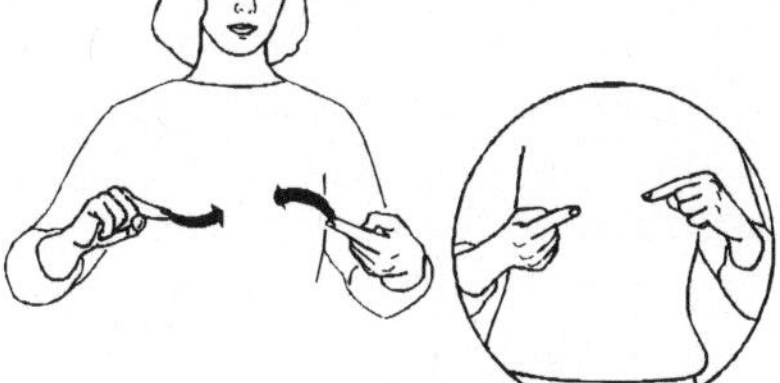

**pain**[2] *n.* See signs for HURT[1,2].

**paint** *n.* **1.** Liquid or creamy coloring matter that can be applied to a surface with a brush, as to protect or decorate: *to buy a can of paint.* —*v.* **2.** To apply paint or pigments to: *to paint the bookcase.* **3.** To produce with paint: *to paint a picture.* Same sign used for: **brush, paintbrush.**

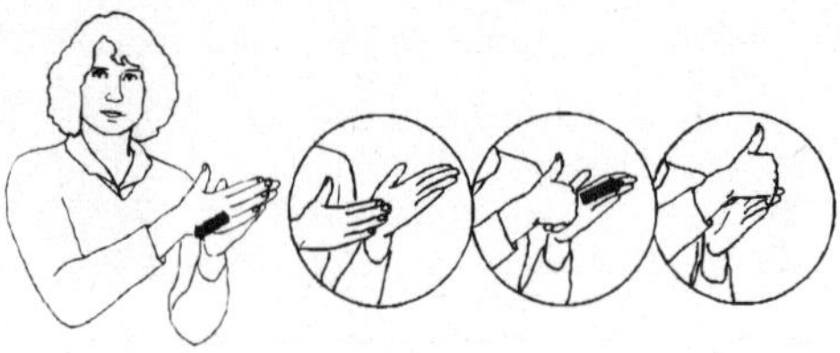

■ [Mime the action of a paintbrush's bristles moving when painting] Bring the fingertips of the right *open hand* down the length of the left palm from the fingertips to the base with a double movement, pulling the back of the right fingers up the left palm to the fingertips each time.

**paintbrush** *n.* See sign for PAINT.

**pair** *n.* See signs for BOTH, COUPLE.

**pajamas** *pl. n.* Loose clothes consisting of a jacket or shirt and trousers, designed to be worn while sleeping: *She'd rather wear pajamas than a nightgown.*

■ [Abbreviation **p-j**] Form a *P* and then a *J* with the right hand in front of the right side of the chest.

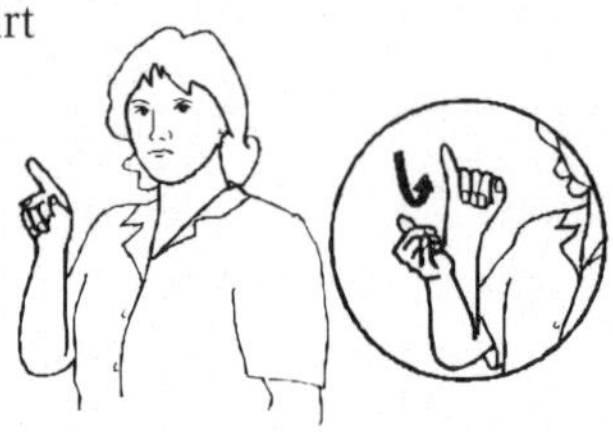

**pal** *n.* See sign for FRIEND.

**pale** *adj.* Lacking warm or intense skin color: *She looks pale after weeks indoors.* Same sign used for: **Caucasian.**

■ [**white** + a gesture indicating that a person's face is white] Beginning with the fingertips of the right *5 hand* on the chest, pull the hand forward while closing into a *flattened O hand.* Then move the hand up toward the face while changing into an *S hand.*

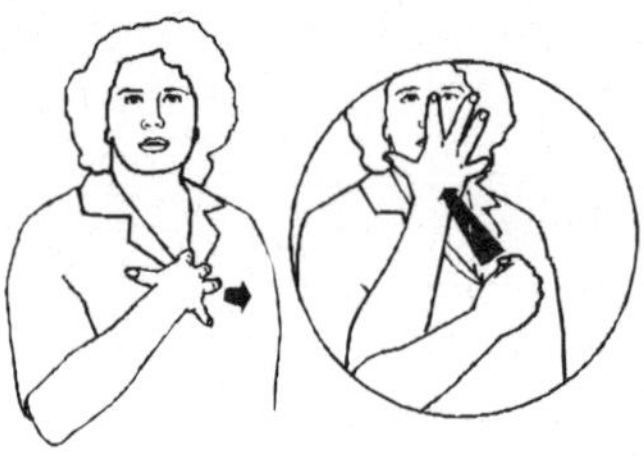

**palpitate** *v.* See sign for PULSE. Related form: **palpitation** *n.*

**pamphlet** *n.* See sign for MAGAZINE.

**pancake** *n.* A thin, flat cake made on a griddle: *ordered a stack of pancakes for breakfast.*

■ [Indicates turning a pancake over while cooking] Beginning with the back of the right *open hand* across the palm of the left *open hand,* both palms facing up, flip the right hand over, ending the right palm facing down across the left palm.

**panel** *n.* A group formed to conduct a public discussion, judge a contest, etc.: *a panel of experts.*

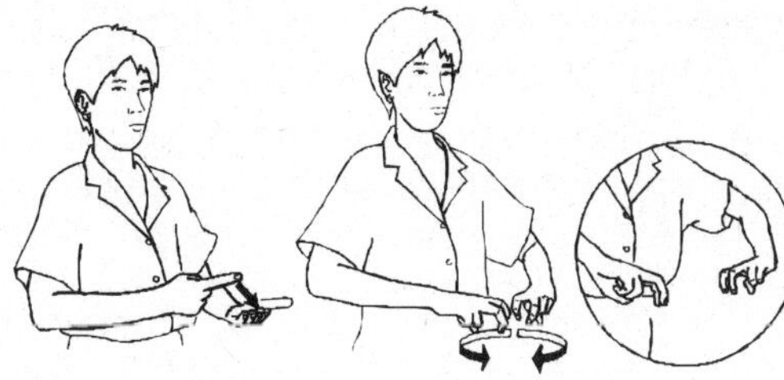

■ [**discuss** + **circle**[2]] Tap the side of the extended right index finger, palm facing in, on the upturned open left palm with a double movement. Then, beginning with the knuckles of both *bent V hands* together in front of the body, palms facing down, bring the hands away from each other in outward arcs while turning the palms out, ending in front of each side of the body.

**panic** *n., v.* See signs for AFRAID, FRIGHT.

**pant** *v.* See sign for BREATH.

**panties** *pl. n.* Short underpants for a woman or a child: *bought lace panties.*

■ [Mime pulling up panties] Beginning with the fingertips of both *F hands,* palms facing in, touching each hip, move the hands up to touch the fingertips again at the waist.

**pants** *pl. n.* A loose-fitting garment for the part of the body from the waist to the ankles; trousers: *tore his pants at the knee.* Same sign used for: **jeans, slacks, trousers.**

■ [Shows location of pants on both legs] Beginning with the fingertips of both *open hands* touching each hip, palms facing in, move the hands upward toward the waist with a double movement.

**panty hose** *pl. n.* See sign for HOSE.

**papa** *n.* See sign for FATHER.

**paper** *n.* **1.** A substance made from wood pulp and formed into thin sheets, used to write or print on, for wrapping, etc.: *We use plain white paper for the laser printer.* —*adj.* **2.** Made of paper: *a paper container.*

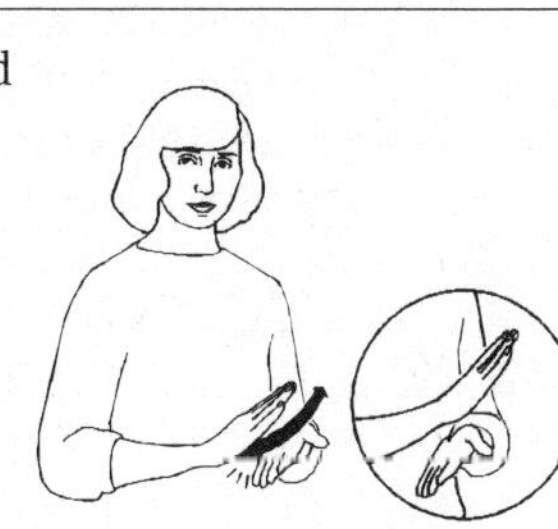

■ Brush the heel of the right *open hand,* palm facing down, on the heel of the left *open hand,* palm facing up, in front of the body with a double movement.

**paper clip** *n. phrase.* A link of bent wire used to hold papers together: *to attach the letter to the check with a paper clip.*

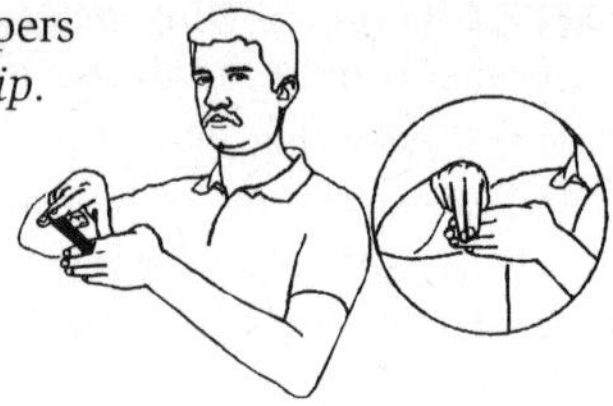

■ [Demonstrates clipping a paper clip on the edge of paper] Beginning with the extended thumb of the right *U hand* against the palm side of the left *B hand,* palm facing down, close the extended right middle and index fingers down against the back of the left hand.

**parable** *n.* See sign for STORY.

**parachute** *n.* **1.** A device, consisting of a silk or nylon expanse attached by strings to a harness, to allow something to be lowered without harm from a great height: *The parachute caught in the tree.* —*v.* **2.** To come down by parachute: *to parachute from the plane.*

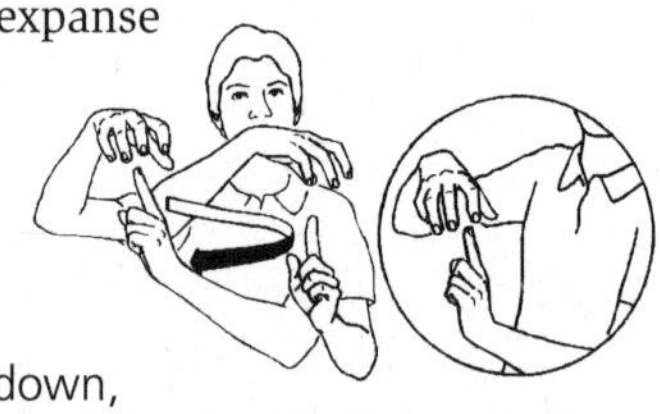

■ [Represents the shape of a parachute circling around] Beginning with the right *curved 5 hand,* palm facing down, over the extended right index finger, palm facing right and finger pointing up, in front of the right side of the body, move the hands to the left side of the chest and then outward in an arc back to the right side of the chest.

**parade** *n.* See sign for MARCH.

**paradox** *n.* See sign for PUZZLED.

**paragraph** *n.* A portion or subsection of a written document that deals with one aspect of a subject and usually starts on a new line: *a paragraph about whales and another about dolphins.* Same sign used for **section.**

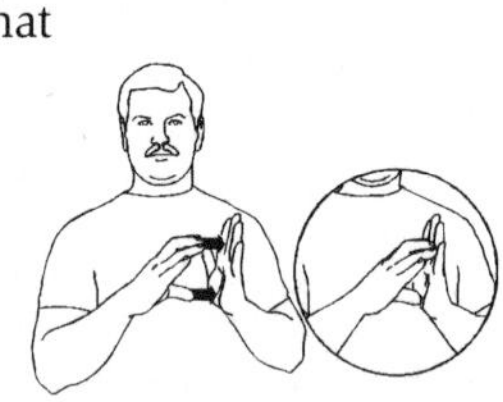

■ [Marks off the size of a **paragraph**] Tap the fingertips of the right *C hand,* palm facing left, against the palm of the left *open hand,* palm facing right and fingers pointing up, with a double movement.

**parallel** *adj.* Extending in the same direction and being always the same distance apart: *parallel lines.*

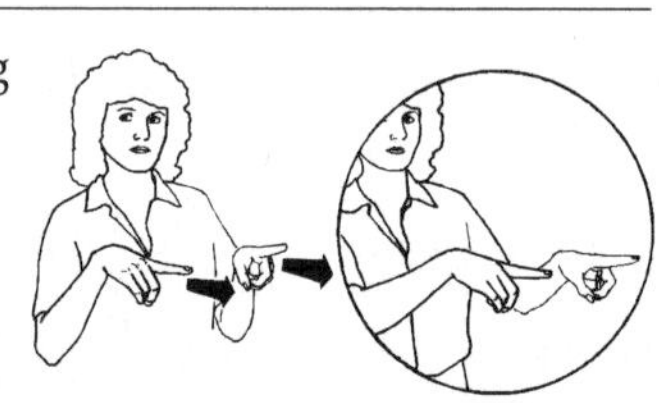

■ [Shows two things that are parallel to each other] Beginning with the index fingers of both hands in front of each side of the chest, palms facing down and index fingers pointing forward, move the hands forward simultaneously.

**paralysis** *n.* A condition in which all or part of the body has lost the ability to move or feel sensation: *He had paralysis of the left leg after his stroke.* Related form: **paralyze** *v.*

■ [Mime the rigid body of a person with paralysis] Beginning with both *5 hands* held limply in front of each side of the body, fingers pointing down and palms facing back, jerk the right hand upward in front of the right side of the chest while dropping the left hand downward, bending the hand awkwardly at the wrist near the left hip.

**paranoid** *adj.* Having exaggerated and unfounded feelings of persecution and distrust of others: *It's difficult to deal with a paranoid person.*

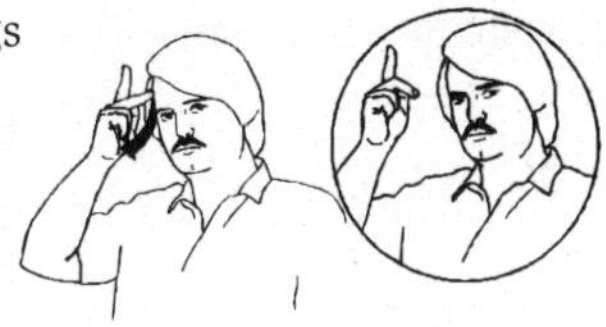

■ [Initialized sign] Beginning with the extended middle finger of the right *P hand* touching the right side of the forehead, palm facing left, move the right hand quickly forward with a double movement while bending the middle finger down.

**parched** *adj.* See sign for THIRSTY.

**pardon** *v.* See signs for DISMISS, EXCUSE[1], FORGIVE.

**pare** *v.* See sign for PEEL.

**parentheses** *pl. n.* The curved lines used as delimiters to set off something, as a group of numbers or a qualifying word or phrase: *to put parentheses around the explanatory comments.*

■ [Draw a pair of parentheses in the air] Beginning with both extended index fingers angled upward in front of each shoulder, palms facing forward, move both hands in outward and downward arcs while turning the wrists in.

**parents** *pl. n.* One's father and mother: *still lives with his parents.*

■ [**mother** + **father**] Touch the thumb of the right *5 hand,* palm facing left, first to the chin, then to the forehead.

**park** *v.* To leave a vehicle for a period of time in an appropriate place, as at curbside or in a garage: *to park downtown; to park your car.*

■ [The handshape represents a vehicle that is set on the other hand as if to park] Tap the little-finger side of the right *3 hand,* palm facing left and fingers pointing forward, on the palm of the left *open hand,* palm facing up, with a repeated movement.

**parole** *n., v.* See sign for DISMISS, EXCUSE[1].

**parrot**[1] *n.* A tropical bird of the Southern Hemisphere having a hooked bill and brightly colored feathers: *Some parrots can imitate human speech.* Same sign used for: **parakeet.**

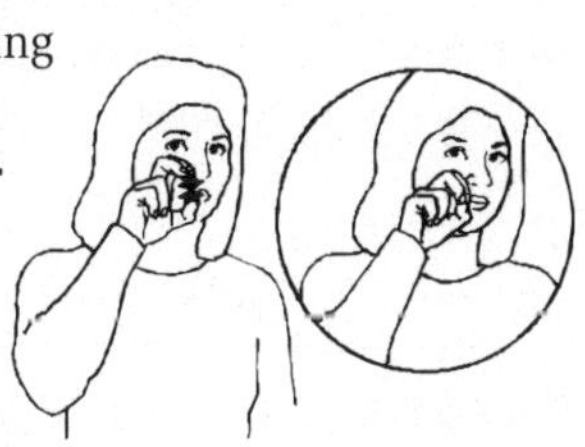

■ [Shows the action of a parrot's beak closing] Pinch the bent index and middle fingers and thumb of the right hand together near the right side of the mouth with a double movement, palm facing forward.

**parrot**[2] *v.* See sign for COPY[1].

**part**[1] *n.* A separate or distinct portion or fraction of a whole: *This is my part of the pie.* Related form: **partial** *adj.* Same sign used for: **piece, section, segment.**

■ [The hand seems to divide what is in the other hand into parts] Slide the little-finger side of the right *open hand,* palm facing left, across the palm of left *open hand,* palm facing up, with a curved movement.

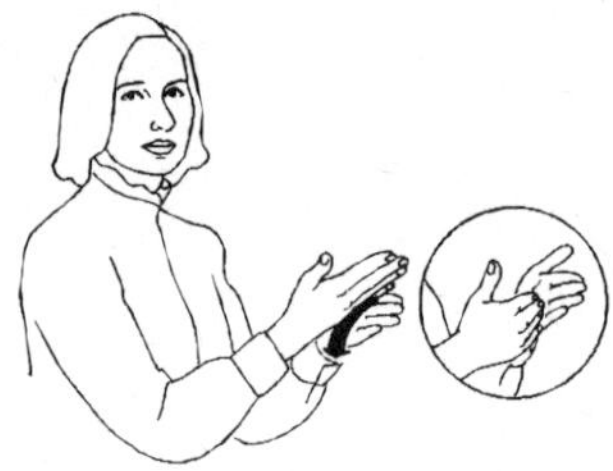

**part**[2] *v.* To separate: *We parted the two boys who were fighting.* Same sign used for: **apart, separate.**

■ [The hands separate two things] Beginning with the fingers of both *10 hands* together in front of the chest, palms facing in, bring the hands apart in front of each side of the chest.

**part**[3] *n., adj.* See sign for SOME.

**part from** *v. phrase.* See sign for DISCONNECT.

**partial to** *adj.* + *prep.* Favoring or especially fond of: *I'm partial to mint chocolate-chip ice cream.* Same sign used for: **favorite.**

■ [Pointing out a favorite] Tap the fingertips of the right *B hand,* palm facing left, with a double movement against the index finger of the left *B hand* held up in front of the chest, palm facing right.

**participate** *v.* See sign for JOIN.

**particular** *adj.* See sign for POINT[2].

**parting** *n.* An act or instance of going away: *It was a sad parting.* Same sign used for: **depart, departure.**

■ [Represents two people moving apart when parting] Beginning with both extended index fingers pointing up in front of the chest, palms facing forward, bring the hands apart to in front of each shoulder.

**partners** *pl. n.* See sign for COUPLE.

**party** *n.* A social gathering: *to have a party to celebrate her promotion.*

■ [Initialized sign] Beginning with both *P hands* in front of the right side of the body, palms facing down, swing the hands from side to side in front of the body with a large double arc.

**partying** *n.* The act of going to parties: *We went partying all night.*

■ Beginning with both *5 hands* near each side of the head, palms facing each other and fingers pointing up, flip the hands forward with a double movement, turning the palms forward each time.

**pass** *v.* To move beyond: *to pass the truck on the highway.* Same sign used for: **by, ratification, ratify.**

■ [One hand moves past the other hand] Beginning with both *A hands* in front of the body, palms facing in opposite directions and left hand somewhat forward of the right hand, move the right hand forward, striking the knuckles of the left hand as it passes.

**pass around** *v. phrase.* To distribute: *to pass the bread around.* Same sign used for: **deal, pass out.**

■ [Mime passing something around] Beginning with the fingers of both *flattened O hands* together in front of the body, palms facing up, move the right hand forward and then twist it around to the right, ending with the palm facing left.

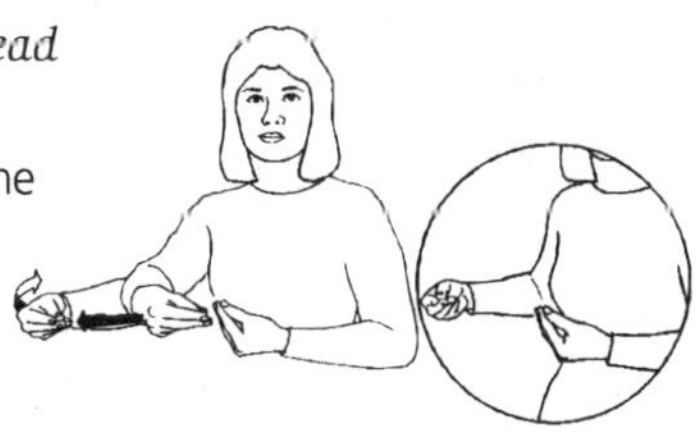

**pass out**[1] *v. phrase.* To lose consciousness: *to pass out from the heat.*

■ [Abbreviation **p-o**] Place the thumb side of the right *P hand* and, then, the right *O hand* against the forehead, palm facing left.

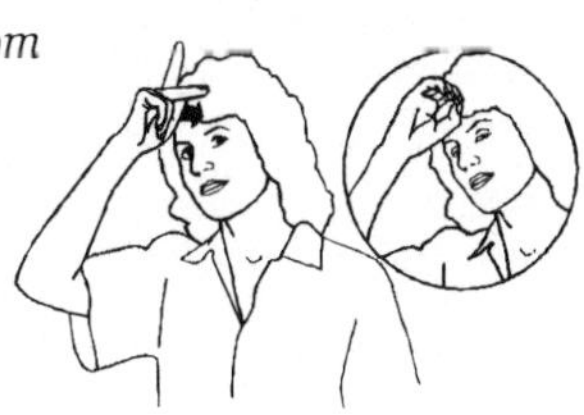

**pass out**[2] *v. phrase.* See sign for PASS AROUND.

**passion** *n.* See sign for WANT.

**passionate** *adj.* Having or expressing strong, intense feelings, as fondness or desire: *She had passionate feelings for him.* Related form: **passion** *n.* Same sign used for: **desire.**

■ [Shows the location of deep feelings] Move the fingertips of the right *C hand* down the center of the chest with a deliberate double movement.

**passive** *adj.* See sign for QUIET.

**Passover** *n.* See sign for CRACKER.

**password**[1] *n.* A secret series of characters that enables a user to access a file, computer, or program, and that is intended to prevent access by unauthorized users: *Type in a six-letter password.* Same sign used for: **access code.**

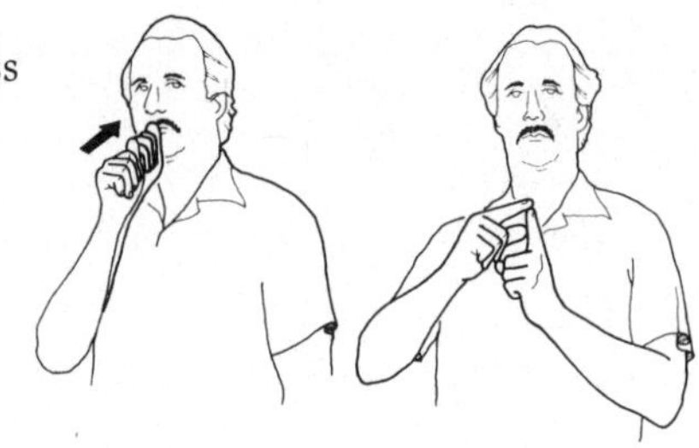

■ [**secret** + **word**] Tap the thumb side of the right *A hand*, palm left, against the mouth with a repeated movement. Then touch the extended fingers of the right *G hand,* palm left, against the extended left index finger pointing up in front of the chest, palm right.

**password**[2] *n.* See sign for SECRET.

**past** *adv.* See signs for AGO, BEFORE[1], PASS, WAS[1].

**path** *n.* See sign for ROAD. Related form: **pathway** *n.*

**patient**[1] *adj.* **1.** Bearing annoyance, suffering, etc., calmly or without complaint: *The children were remarkably patient during the long trip.* **2.** Persevering and diligent: *The teacher is patient with the slow learners in class.* Related form: **patience** *n.* Same sign used for: **bear, put up with, tolerant, tolerate.**

■ [The thumb seems to seal the lips as a person tolerates something] Move the right *A hand,* palm facing left, downward in front of the chin.

**patient**[2] *n.* A person under medical care or treatment: *The little girl is a good patient.*

■ [Initialized sign similar to sign for **hospital**] Move the extended middle finger of the right *P hand,* palm facing in, first down and then forward on the left upper arm.

**patrol** *v.* See sign for CARE[1].

**pattern** *n.* A design or guide for something to be made: *a pattern for sewing a miniskirt.*

■ [**same-same-same** indicating a repetition as in a pattern] Beginning with both *Y hands* in front of the left side of the body, palms facing down, move the hands in simultaneous repeated arcs to in front of the right side of the body.

**pauper** *n.* See sign for POOR.

**pause** *v.* See sign for HOLD[2].

**pave** *v.* To cover (a road or walk), as with concrete, so as to make smooth: *paved the road with asphalt.*

■ [Demonstrates the action of moving dirt in order to pave] Slide the little-finger side of the right *bent hand,* palm facing in, from the wrist to off the fingertips of the left *open hand,* palm facing down and fingers pointing forward.

**pawn** *v.* See sign for SELL.

**pay** *v.* To give money in return for goods or services: *to pay $5.00; to pay the cashier.*

■ [Represents directing money from the hand to pay another person] Beginning with the extended right index finger touching the palm of the left *open hand,* palms facing each other, move the right finger forward and off the left fingertips.

**pay attention** *v. phrase.* See sign for ATTENTION.

**pay for** *v. phrase.* To offer all the money required in exchange for: *Be sure you have enough money to pay for the groceries.* Same sign used for: **pay in full, pay off.**

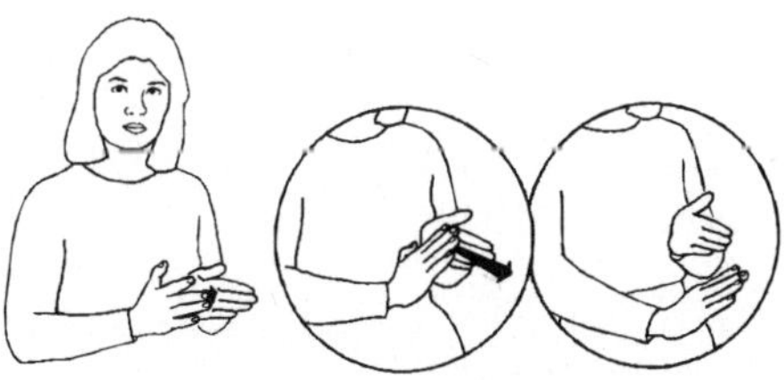

■ [Represents directing money from the hand to pay another person + **clean**] Touch the bent middle finger of the right *5 hand* to the palm of the left *open hand,* palms facing each other and fingers pointing forward. Then wipe the right *open hand* across the left *open hand* from the heel to off the fingertips with a deliberate movement.

**pay in full** *v. phrase.* See sign for PAY FOR.

**pay off** *v. phrase.* See sign for PAY FOR.

**payable** *adj.* See sign for AFFORD.

**PDA** (personal digital assistant) *n. phrase.* See sign for TEXT MESSAGE.

**peace** *n.* **1.** Freedom from war: *peace among nations.* **2.** A state of harmony in personal relations or among groups: *hoping for peace among the factions on campus.* **3.** Tranquility; calm: *All I want is a little peace and quiet.* Related form: **peaceful** *adj.*

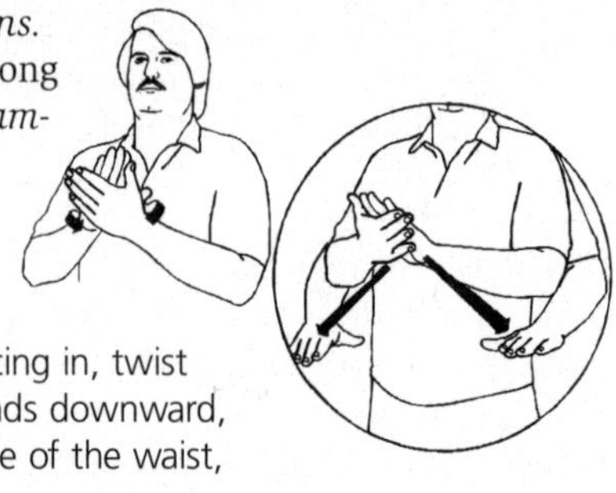

■ [**become** + **settle**] Beginning with the palms of both *open hands* together in front of the chest, right palm facing forward and left palm facing in, twist the wrist to reverse positions. Then move the hands downward, ending with both *open hands* in front of each side of the waist, palms facing down and fingers pointing forward.

**peaceful** *adj.* See sign for QUIET[1].

**peach** *n.* A sweet, juicy fruit with yellow flesh and soft, fuzzy skin: *He won't eat a peach without peeling it.*

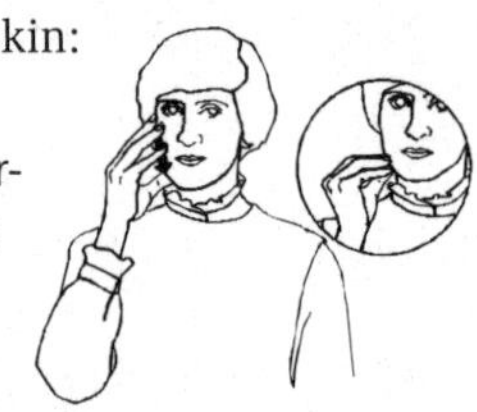

■ [The fingers seem to feel peach fuzz] Beginning with the fingertips of the right *curved 5 hand* on the right cheek, palm facing left, bring the fingers down with a double movement, forming a *flattened O hand* near the right side of the chin.

**peacock** *n.* A bird with beautiful, colorful, iridescent tail feathers that can be spread wide like a fan: *The spots on the peacock's tail look like eyes.*

■ [**bird** + a gesture indicating a peacock's tail feathers] Close the index finger and thumb of the right *G hand,* palm facing forward, with a repeated movement in front of the mouth. Then, beginning with the right *O hand,* palm facing in, near the crook of the bent left arm held across the chest, raise the right hand upward in an arc while opening into a *4 hand* as it passes in front of the face.

**peak**[1] *n.* The pointed top of a mountain or ridge: *The mountain climbers reached the peak.*

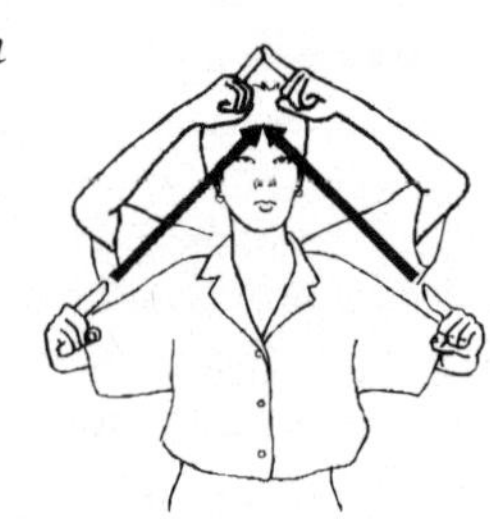

■ [The shape of a peak] Move both extended index fingers from in front of each shoulder upward toward each other until they meet in front of the head.

**peak**[2] *n.* See sign for TOP[1].

**peanut** *n.* A pod with oily, edible seeds: *Don't leave the shells around when you eat peanuts.* Same sign used for: **nut.**

- [Represents peanut butter sticking to the back of one's teeth] Flick the extended right thumb, palm facing left, forward off the edge of the top front teeth with an upward double movement.

**peanut butter** *n. phrase.* An edible paste, used as a spread, made of browned roasted peanuts: *to eat a peanut butter and jelly sandwich.*

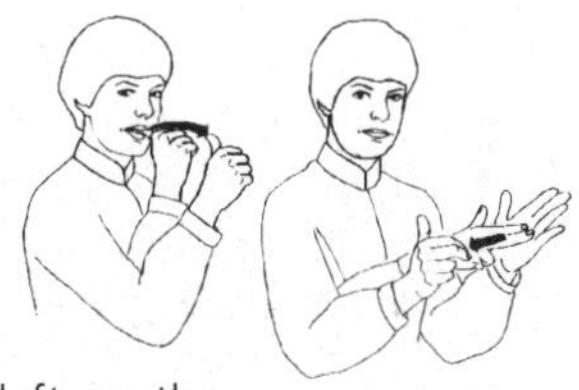

- [**peanut** + **butter**] Flick the extended right thumb, palm facing left, forward off the edge of the top front teeth with an upward double movement. Then wipe the extended middle and index fingers of the right hand, palm facing left, on the palm of the left *open hand,* palm facing right, toward the heel with a double movement, drawing the fingers back into the right palm each time.

**pear** *n.* A fleshy, juicy fruit, usually with a yellow to green skin: *I ate a pear that wasn't ripe.*

- [Shows the shape of a pear] Beginning with the fingertips of the right *curved 5 hand* cupped around the fingertips of the left *flattened O hand,* both palms facing in, bring the right hand outward to the right while closing the fingers to the thumb, forming a *flattened O hand.*

**peas** *pl. n.* The round edible seeds from the pod of a plant of the legume family: *I always put peas in the tuna casserole.*

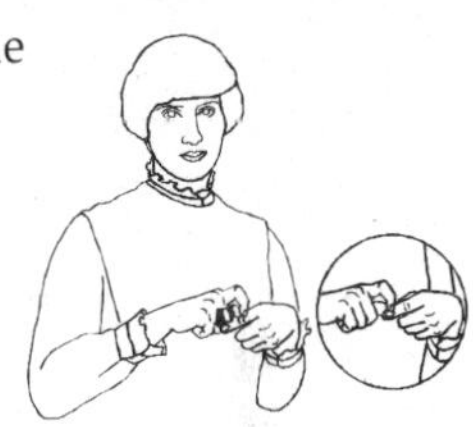

- [The finger points to peas in a pod] Touch the fingertips of the right *modified X hand,* palm facing down, on the extended left index finger, palm facing in and finger pointing right, moving from the base to the tip and touching down in several places.

**peck** *v.* See sign for PICK ON.

**peculiar** *adj.* See sign for STRANGE.

**peddle** *v.* See sign for SELL.

**pee** *n. Slang (sometimes vulgar).* See sign for PENIS.

**peek**[1] *v.* **1.** To look quickly: *to peek at the headlines.* —*n.* **2.** A quick look: *I took a peek at the headlines.*

- [Mime peeking around a partition] Beginning with the index-finger side of the right *B hand* in front of the nose, palm facing left, move the head to the right to look around the hand.

**peek**[2] *v.* See sign for NOSY[2].

**peel**[1] *v.* To strip the skin off (a fruit or vegetable): *to peel the potatoes before boiling them.* Same sign used for: **pare.**

- [Mime peeling with a small knife] Beginning with the knuckles of the right *10 hand* against the extended left index finger, both palms facing down, move the right thumb open and closed with a double movement.

**peel**[2] *v.* To strip away from something: *to peel the backing off the address label.*

- [Demonstrates the action of peeling something with the fingers] Beginning with the fingertips of the right *9 hand* touching the back of the left *S hand,* both palms facing down, move the right hand upward and forward while twisting the palm back.

**pee wee** *n.* See sign for SMALL[1].

**pen** *n.* See sign for WRITE.

**penalty** *n.* See sign for PUNISH. Related form: **penalize** *v.*

**pencil**[1] *n.* A pointed tool with a graphite core to write or draw with: *to draw a picture with a pencil.*

- [Indicates wetting the tip of a pencil and then writing with it] Touch the fingertips of the right *modified X hand,* palm facing in, near the mouth. Then move the right hand smoothly down and across the upturned left *open hand* from the heel to off the fingertips.

**pencil**[2] *n.* See sign for WRITE.

**penetrate** *v.* To get into or through: *a light that will penetrate the darkness.* Same sign used for: **pierce, pierced.**

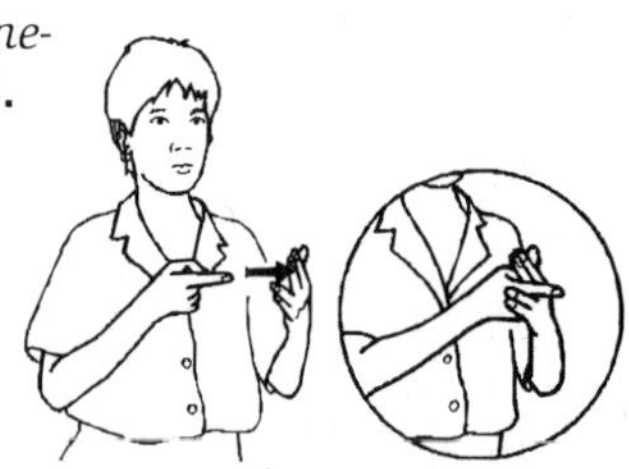

- [Demonstrates something penetrating something else] Insert the extended right index finger, palm facing left and finger pointing forward, with a deliberate movement between the middle and ring fingers of the left *open hand* held in front of the chest, palm facing in and fingers angled right.

**penis** *n.* The male organ of copulation and, in mammals, urinary excretion: *Urine leaves the man's body through the penis.* Same sign used for: **pee** (*slang, sometimes vulgar*), **urine.**

- [Initialized sign] Tap the middle finger of the right *P hand,* palm facing in, against the nose with a double movement.

**penitent** *adj.* See sign for SORRY. Related form: **pentitence** *n.*

**pennant** *n.* A long, narrow, tapering flag: *hung the team pennant on the wall of their room in the dorm.*

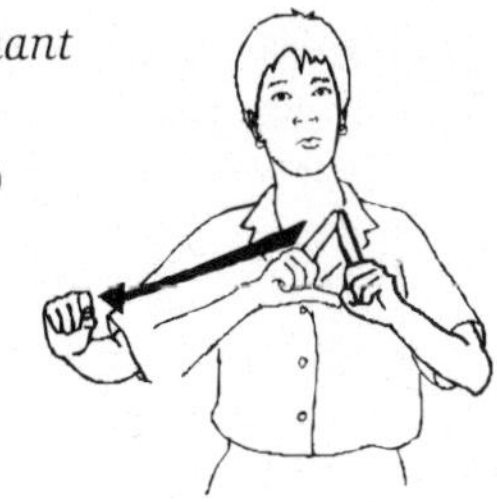

■ [The shape of a pennant] Beginning with the extended thumb and index finger of the right *L hand,* palm facing forward, touching the thumb and extended index finger of the left hand, palm facing forward, move the right hand to the right while closing the index finger to the thumb in front of the right side of the body.

**penniless** *adj.* Very poor; without any money at all: *a penniless vagrant.* Same sign used for: **broke** *(informal).*

■ [Gesture indicates a broken neck to signify being broke] Bring the little-finger side of the right *bent hand,* palm facing down and fingers pointing back, against the right side of the neck with a deliberate movement while bending the head down to the left.

**penny** *n.* See sign for CENT.

**pension** *n.* A regular payment, other than wages, made to a person, especially for past services: *to receive a pension after retirement.* Same sign used for: **allowance, royalty, subscribe, welfare.**

■ With the right *curved hand* in front of the right shoulder, palm facing back, bring the hand downward and inward toward the right side of the chest with a double movement, closing the fingers to form an *A hand* each time.

**people** *n.* **1.** Men, women, and children collectively: *Only ten people visited the museum today.* **2.** Persons in general: *People don't want their intelligence insulted by their political leaders.* Same sign used for: **folk, public.**

■ [Initialized sign] Move both *P hands,* palms facing down, in alternating forward circles in front of each side of the body.

**pep** *n.* See sign for INSPIRE.

**pepper** *n.* A seasoning with a hot, spicy taste: *to put fresh pepper on the pasta.*

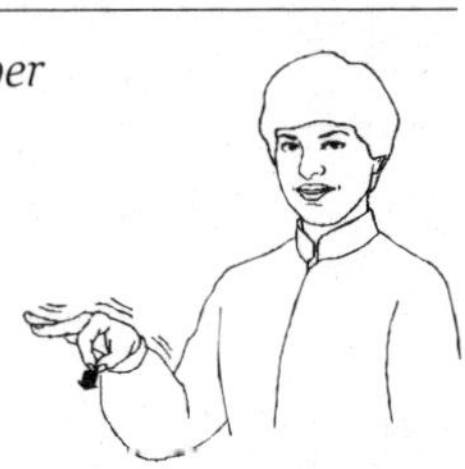

■ [The hand seems to drop pepper on food] Shake the right *F hand,* palm facing down, up and down in front of the right side of the body with a repeated movement.

**per** *prep.* See sign for EACH.

**per annum** See sign for ANNUAL.

**perceive** *v.* See signs for PREDICT, UNDERSTAND. Related form: **perception** *n.*

**percent** *n.* A proportion expressed in parts or amounts of one hundred: *Ten percent of 1,000 is 100. The agent will want ten percent of your royalties.* Related form: **percentage** *n.*

■ [Draw the shape of a percent sign in the air] Move the right *O hand* from near the right side of the face, palm facing forward, a short distance to the right, then down at an angle to in front of the right side of the chest.

**perennial** *adj.* **1.** Lasting for a long time: *a perennial leading lady.* **2.** (of plants) Having a life cycle of two or more years: *The climbing rose is a perennial flower.*

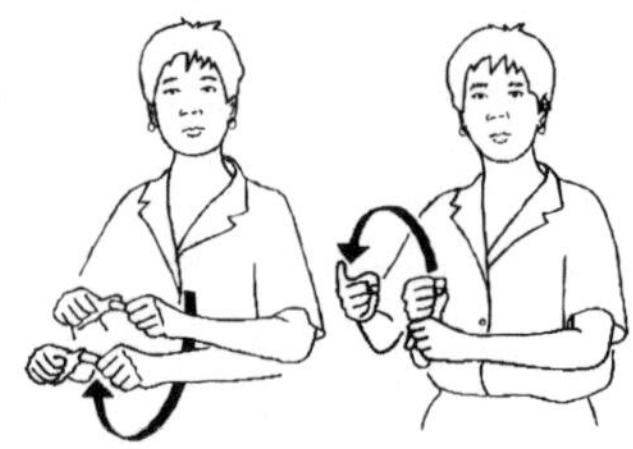

■ [**continue**[1] + **annual**] Beginning with the thumb of the right *10 hand* on the thumbnail of the left *10 hand,* both palms facing down in front of the chest, move the hands downward and forward in an arc. Then, beginning with the little-finger side of the right *S hand* on the index-finger side of the left *S hand,* palms facing in opposite directions, move the right hand upward and forward in an arc while extending the right index finger.

**perfect** *adj.* **1.** Without defect: *a beautiful, perfect face.* **2.** Conforming to or representing an ideal: *The children behaved like perfect ladies and gentlemen.* **3.** Correct and complete in every detail: *a perfect score.* Related form: **perfection** *n.* Same sign used for: **accurate, ideal.**

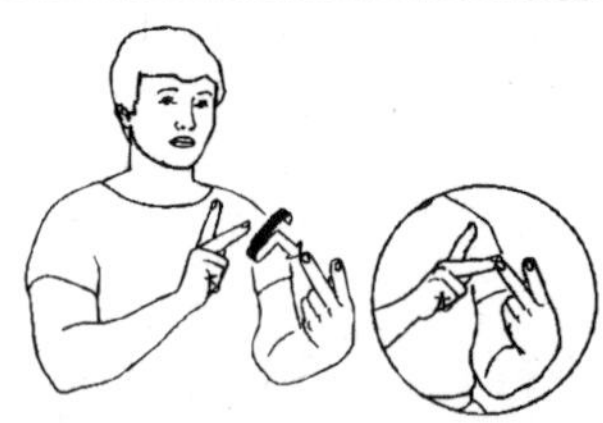

■ [Initialized sign showing things matching perfectly] Move the right *P hand,* palm facing left, in a small circle above the left *P hand,* palm facing up. Then move the right hand downward to touch both middle fingers together in front of the chest.

**perform** *n.* See signs for ACT[2], DO. Related form: **performance** *n.*

**perfume** *n.* A liquid or other substance having a fragrant, attractive smell: *puts on perfume before going out.*

■ [Represents applying perfume to the neck] Touch the thumb of the right *Y hand,* palm facing left, to the throat. Then twist the hand slightly to the left and touch the thumb to the throat again.

**perhaps** *adv.* See sign for MAYBE.

**peril** *n.* See sign for DANGER.

**period**[1] *n.* A dot used to mark the end of a sentence or an abbreviation: *to put a period at the end of the sentence.* Same sign used for: **decimal point, dot, point.**

■ [Draw a period in the air] With the right index finger and thumb pinched together, palm facing forward in front of the right side of the chest, push the right hand forward a short distance.

**period**[2] *n.* A portion of time specified for some purpose: *to play the piano for a short period every afternoon.*

■ [Initialized sign similar to sign for **time**[1]] Move the right *P hand,* palm facing left, in a small circle near the palm of the left *open hand,* palm angled forward, ending with the right palm against the left palm.

**period**[3] *n.* See signs for MENSTRUATION, TIME[1].

**periodically** *adv.* See sign for OCCASIONAL.

**perish** *v.* See signs for DIE, DISSOLVE.

**perjury** *n.* See sign for LIE[1].

**permanent wave** *n. phrase.* A wave or curl set into the hair by a special chemical process so that it will last for several months: *It's obviously time for me to get another permanent wave.* Alternate form: **permanent.**

■ [Represents the action of rollers crimping the hair] Beginning with both *C hands* near each side of the head, palms facing forward, bring the hands back toward the sides of the head while closing into *S hands.* Then move the hands downward and repeat the movement.

**permeate** *v.* To soak through or into every part of: *the water permeated my coat.* Same sign used for: **soak through.**

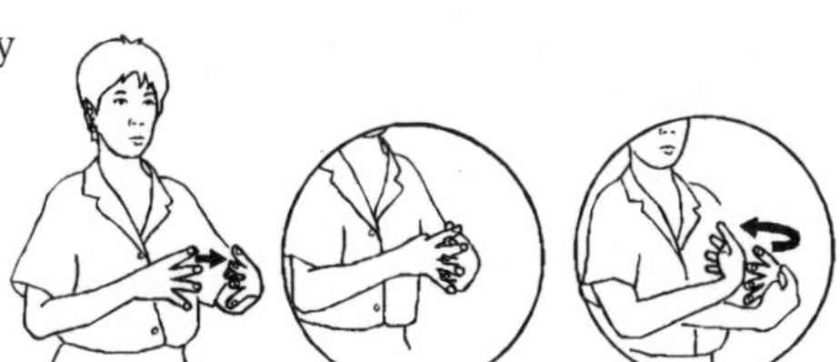

■ [Demonstrates something penetrating through something else] Beginning with both *5 hands* in front of each side of the chest, palms facing in and fingers pointing toward each other, bring the right hand forward, interlocking the left fingers. Then bring the right fingers back toward the chest, ending with the right palm facing right.

**permit**[1] *v.* To allow: *With a new baby, they don't want to permit smoking in the house.* Related form: **permission** *n.* Same sign used for: **privilege.**

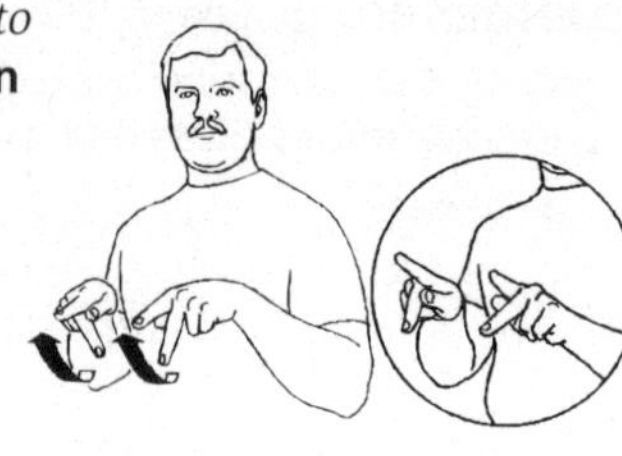

■ [Initialized sign similar to sign for **try**] Beginning with both *P hands* in front of the body, palms facing down, swing the wrists to move both hands forward and upward in small arcs.

**permit**[2] *v.* See sign for LET.

**permit**[3] *n.* See sign for LICENSE.

**perpendicular** *adj.* Straight up and down; vertical: *The shack doesn't have a single perpendicular wall.*

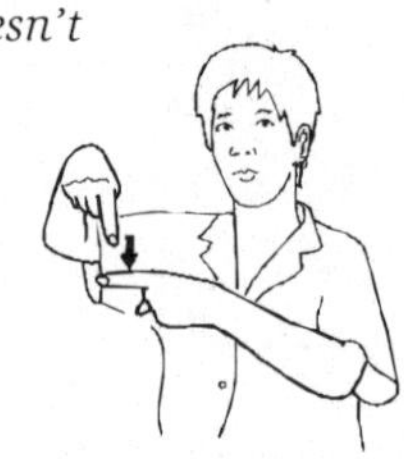

■ [Demonstrates the angle created when one thing is perpendicular to another thing] Tap the extended right index finger, palm facing in and finger pointing down, with a double movement on the extended left index finger held across the chest, palm facing in and finger pointing right.

**perpetual** *adj.* Lasting forever: *a perpetual care cemetery.*

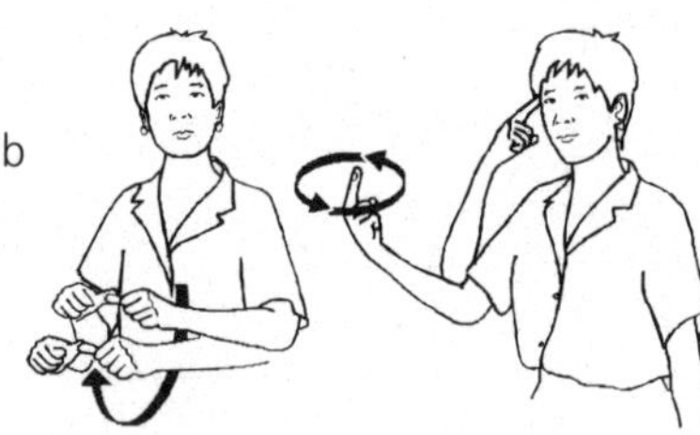

■ [**continue**[1] + **forever**] Beginning with the thumb of the right *10 hand* on the thumbnail of the left *10 hand,* both palms facing down in front of the chest, move the hands downward and forward in an arc. Then, beginning with the extended right index finger touching the right side of the forehead, palm angled in, move the hand downward and form a large circle in front of the right side of the body, palm facing in and finger pointing up.

**perplexed** *adj.* See sign for PUZZLED.

**persecute** *v.* See sign for TORTURE. Related form: **persecution** *n.*

**persevere**[1] *v.* To continue or persist in trying to do something in spite of obstacles: *We hope he will persevere in his studies.* Related form: **perseverance** *n.* Same sign used for: **persistence, persistent.**

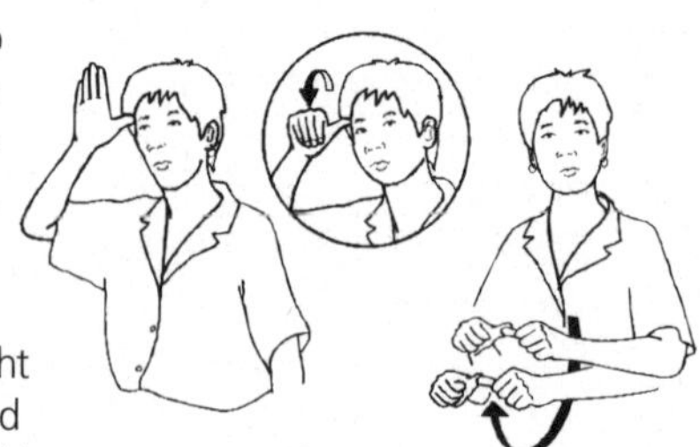

■ [**stubborn** + **continue**[1]] With the extended thumb of the right *open hand* touching the right side of the forehead, palm facing forward, bend the fingers forward and downward with a double movement. Then, beginning with the thumb of the right *10 hand* on the thumbnail of the left *10 hand,* both palms facing down in front of the chest, move the hands downward and forward in an arc.

**persevere**[2] *v.* See sign for OBSESSION.

**persistent** *adj.* See signs for CONSTANT, OBSESSION, PERSEVERE[1], STUBBORN. Related form: **persistence** *n.*

**person** *n.* A man, woman, or child: *a remarkably nice person.*

- [Initialized sign following the shape of a person] Bring both *P hands,* palms facing each other, downward along the sides of the body with a parallel movement.

**personal** *adj.* Belonging to or concerning a particular person: *personal property.* Same sign used for: **personnel.**

- [Initialized sign] Move the right *P hand,* palm facing down, in a small double circle on the left side of the chest with a double movement.

**personality** *n.* **1.** The total of individual qualities that make a person different from others: *a personality that has developed over the years.* **2.** The visible characteristics that determine a person's social appeal: *a performer with a lot of personality and energy.*

- [Initialized sign similar to sign for **character**[1]] Move the right *P hand,* palm facing down, in a small circle in front of the left side of the chest. Then bring the thumb side of the right *P hand* back against the left side of the chest.

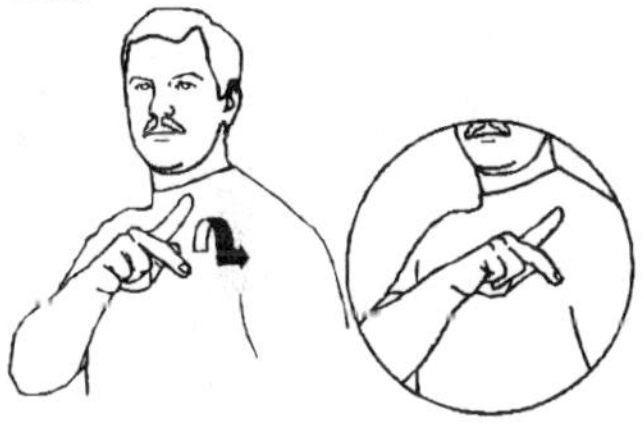

**person marker** *n. phrase.* A marker used as a suffix in sign language to denote a person.

- [The hands follow the shape of a person] Move both *open hands,* palms facing each other, downward along each side of the body.

**personnel** *pl. n.* See sign for PERSONAL.

**perspective** *n.* One's way of looking at people, facts, ideas, situations, etc., and understanding the relationships among them: *trying to see the situation in the proper perspective.* Same sign used for: **point of view, viewpoint.**

■ [Represents eyes looking at something from different directions] Beginning with the index fingers of both *V hands* near each side of the face, palms facing down and fingers pointing toward each other, bring the hands outward in an arc and then forward toward each other in front of the chest.

**perspire** *v.* See sign for SWEAT. Related form: **perspiration** *n.*

**persuade** *v.* See signs for CONVINCE, ENCOURAGE, URGE.

**pessimistic** *adj.* Having or exhibiting a tendency to expect the worst: *a pessimistic view on life.*

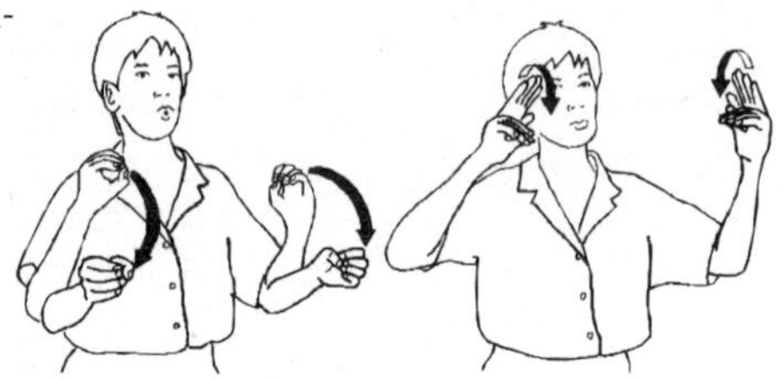

■ [**none**[2] + **hope**] Beginning with both *O hands* in front of each side of the chest, palms facing each other, move the hands forward and downward in an arc. Then, beginning with the right *open hand* near the right side of the head, palm angled forward and fingers pointing up, and the left *open hand* in front of the chest, palm facing right and fingers pointing up, bend the fingers toward each other with a double movement.

**pest** *n.* See signs for NUISANCE, PICK ON.

**pet**[1] *v.* To stroke or pat gently: *to pet the kitten.* Same sign used for: **favor, spoil, tame.**

■ [Demonstrates the action of petting something] Pull the fingertips of the right *open hand,* palm facing down, back toward the chest from the fingers to the wrist of the left *open hand,* palm facing down, with a long movement while bending the finger back into the palm.

**pet**[2] *v. Slang.* To engage in amorous physical activity: *The boy and girl petted in the back seat of the car.* Same sign used for: **make love, neck.**

■ [The fists represent two heads close together] Beginning with both *S hands* crossed at the wrists in front of the chest, palms facing in opposite directions, bend the hands downward with a short double movement.

**petition**[1] *n.* A formal request to some authority for a special privilege, a right, etc.: *a petition to the city for a new stoplight.*

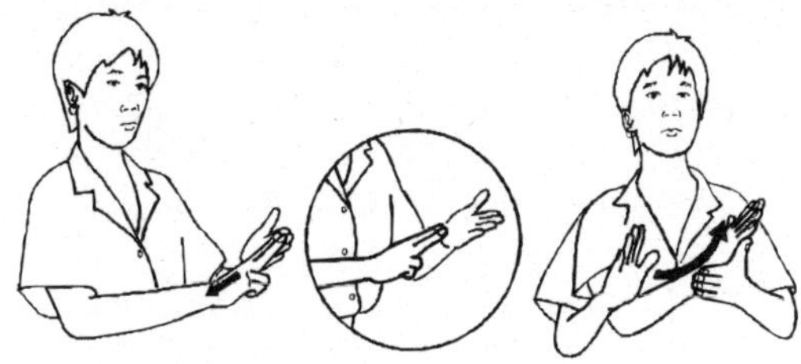

■ [**sign**[2] + **paper**] Place the extended fingers of the right *H hand,* palm facing down, on the upturned palm of the left *open hand,* fingers pointing forward. Then brush the heel of the right *open hand,* palm facing down, on the heel of the left *open hand,* palm facing up, in front of the body with a double movement.

**petition**[2] *n.* See sign for SUGGEST.

**petit jury** *n.* See sign for JURY.

**pew** *n.* See sign for COUCH.

**pharmacy** *n.* A store that sells drugs and medicines and often toiletries, stationery, and other items; drugstore: *to buy the medicine at the pharmacy.*

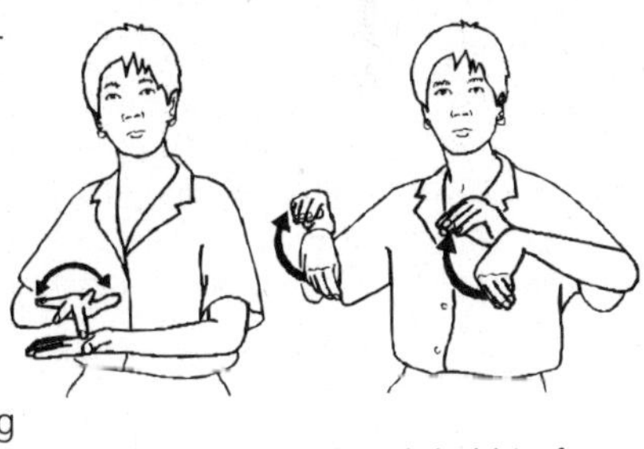

■ [**medicine** + **store**[1]] With the bent middle finger of the right *5 hand,* palm facing down, in the upturned palm of the left *open hand,* rock the right hand from side to side with a double movement while keeping the middle finger in place. Then, beginning with both *flattened O hands* held in front of each side of the chest, palms facing down and fingers pointing down, swing the fingertips upward and back by twisting the wrists.

**phew** *interj.* See sign for STINK.

**philander** *v.* See sign for FLIRT.

**philosophy** *n.* **1.** The study and investigation of the general principles of existence, knowledge, ethics, etc.: *to study the philosophy of Plato.* **2.** A system of guiding principles, values, and beliefs for everyday living: *my philosophy about learning.*

■ [Initialized sign similar to sign for **theory**] Bring the right *P hand,* palm facing left, downward with a short double movement in front of the right side of the forehead.

**phone** *n., v.* See sign for TELEPHONE.

**photo** *n.* See sign for PICTURE. Alternate form: **photograph.**

**photocopy** *v.* See sign for COPY[2].

**photograph** *v.* See sign for TAKE PICTURES.

**phrase** *n.* See sign for STORY.

**physical** *adj.* Of or pertaining to the body: *an annual physical examination.*

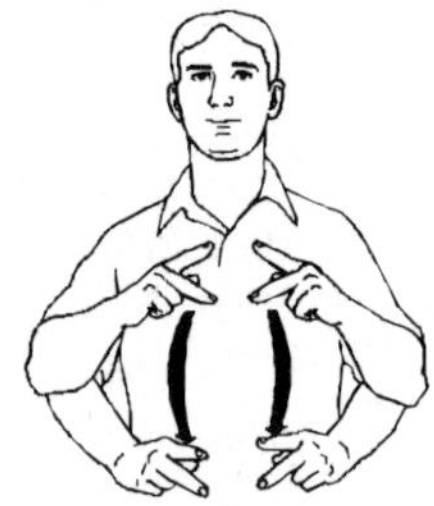

■ [Initialized sign similar to sign for **body**] Touch the palm sides of both *P hands,* palms facing in and fingers pointing toward each other, first on each side of the chest and then on each side of the waist.

**physical therapy** *n. phrase.* Treatment of diseases by physical or mechanical means of treating the skeletal, muscular, and nervous systems to help restore normal function after disease or injury: *The doctor ordered six weeks of physical therapy.*

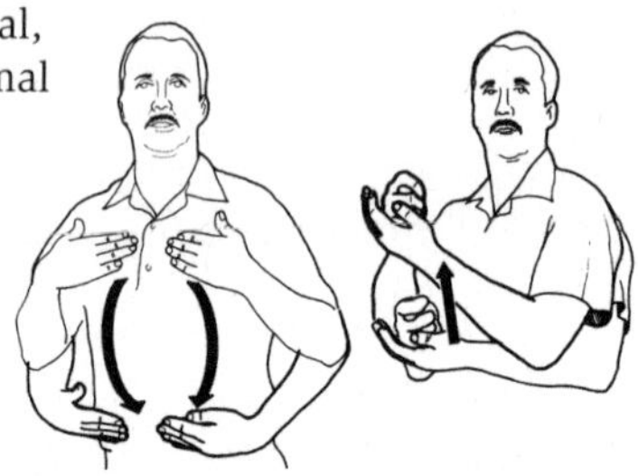

■ [**body** + **therapy**] Pat the palm side of both *open hands* first on each side of the chest and then on each side of the abdomen. Then beginning with the little-finger side of the right *T hand,* palm facing in, on the upturned palm of the left *open hand,* move both hands upward in front of the chest.

**physician** *n.* See sign for DOCTOR.

**physics** *n.* The science that deals with matter, energy, motion, and force: *to study physics in school.*

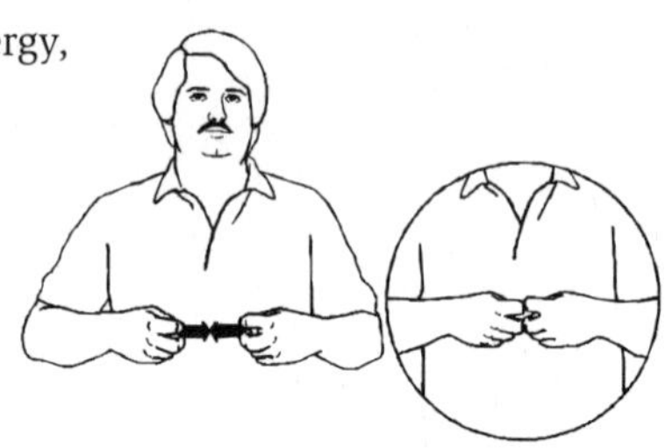

■ Tap the knuckles of both *bent V hands,* palms facing in, against each other in front of the chest with a double movement.

**physique** *n.* The general appearance, shape, development, and condition of the body: *a muscular physique.*

■ [Shows the shape of one's figure + **hulk**] Beginning with both *curved hands* near each side of the chest, palms facing each other, move the hands downward along the sides of the body with a wiggly movement, twisting the wrists up and down as the hands move. Then, beginning with both *modified C hands* in front of each shoulder, palms facing each other, move the hands outward to each side with a large movement.

**piano** *n.* A large musical instrument played by striking keys on a keyboard: *learned to play the piano as a child.* Same sign used for: **organ.**

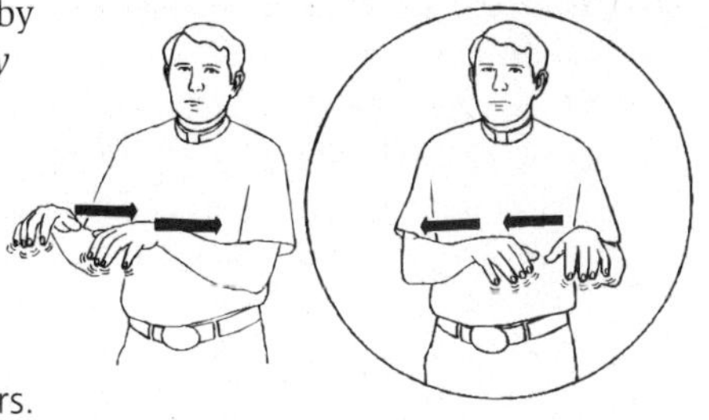

■ [Mime playing a piano] Beginning with both *curved 5 hands* in front of the right side of the body, palms facing down, move the hands to the left and then back to the right again while wiggling the fingers.

**pick**[1] *v.* To choose; select: *to pick a card from the deck.*

■ [A directional sign demonstrating picking something] Beginning with the bent thumb and index finger of the right *5 hand* pointing forward in front of the right shoulder, palm facing forward, bring the right hand back toward the right shoulder while pinching the thumb and index finger together.

**pick**[2] *v.* See signs for CHOOSE, SELECT.

**pick on** *v. phrase.* To find fault with or tease persistently: *Why do they always pick on the little guy?* Same sign used for: **henpeck, nag, peck, pest.**

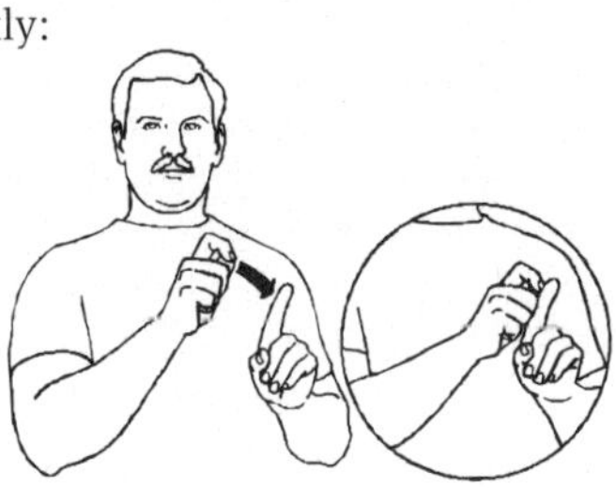

■ [Indicates picking on someone] Tap the fingertips of the right *modified X hand,* palm facing left, against the extended left index finger, palm facing right and finger pointing up, in front of the chest with a double movement.

**picket** *v.* **1.** To protest company practices during a strike, especially by demonstrating in front of the entrance to obstruct it: *to picket the factory for unfair employment practices* —*n.* **2.** A person who pickets during a strike: *The pickets marched in front of the factory carrying large placards.* Same sign used for: **protest.**

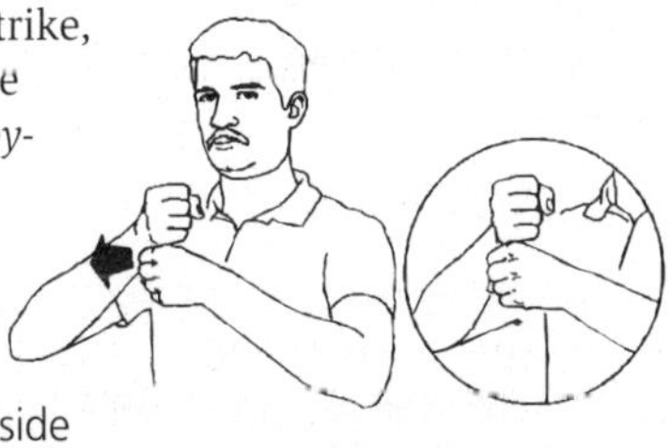

■ [Mime holding a picket sign] With the little-finger side of the right *S hand* on top of the index-finger side of the left *S hand,* both palms facing in, move the hands forward in a short double movement.

**pickle** *n.* A vegetable, especially a cucumber, preserved in brine or vinegar: *to eat a dill pickle with your hamburger.*

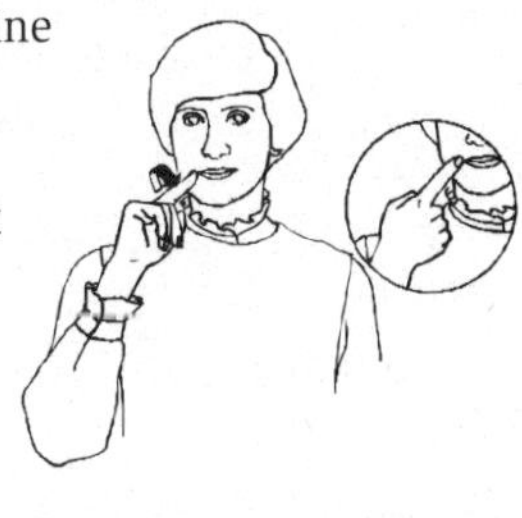

■ [Similar to sign for **sour**] Twist the tip of the extended right index finger near the right corner of the mouth with a short double movement.

**picnic** *n.* A meal in the open air, as on a trip to the country: *went on a picnic.*

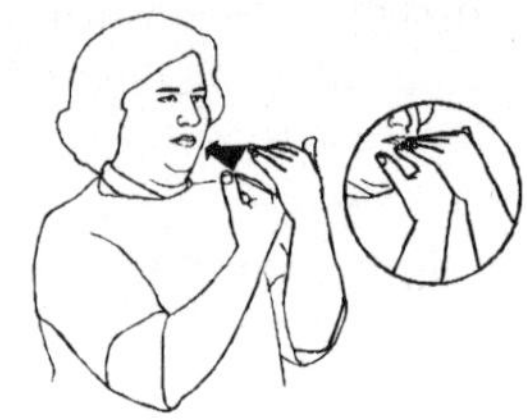

- [Represents eating a sandwich at a picnic] With the left *bent hand* over the back of the right *bent hand,* both palms facing down and fingers pointing toward the mouth, move the hands toward the mouth with a repeated movement.

---

**picture** *n.* A drawing, painting, or photograph: *a picture of my child.* Same sign used for: **image, photo, photograph.**

- [The hand seems to focus the eyes on an image and then record it on paper] Move the right *C hand,* palm facing forward, from near the right side of the face downward, ending with the index-finger side of the right *C hand* against the palm of the left *open hand,* palm facing right.

---

**pie** *n.* A baked pastry crust with fruit, custard, meat, or other filling: *a piece of apple pie.*

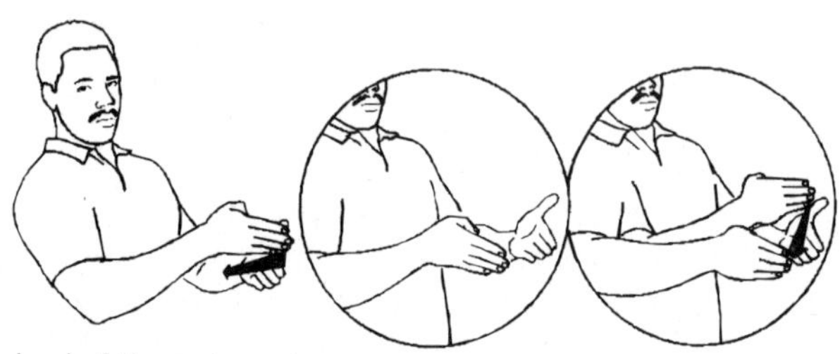

- [Demonstrates cutting a pie into slices] Slide the fingertips of the right *open hand,* palm facing left, from the fingers to the heel of the upturned left hand, fingers pointing forward, and then perpendicularly across the left palm.

---

**piece** *n.* See sign for PART[2].

---

**pierce** *v.* See sign for PENETRATE. Related form: **pierced** *adj.*

---

**pierced ears** *pl. n.* Ears with holes punctured through the lobes to allow wearing earrings: *to have pierced ears with more than one hole.*

- [Shows where holes are pierced into ears] Move the extended index fingers of both hands, palms facing down, toward each ear.

---

**pig** *n.* A four-footed stout domestic animal with a short snout and short legs, usually raised as food: *pigs wallowing in their pens.*

- [Similar to sign for **dirty**] With the back of the right *open hand* under the chin, palm facing down, bend the right fingers down and up again with a double movement.

**pigeon** *n.* A bird with a plump body and short legs: *There are many pigeons in the park.*

■ With the extended right index finger touching the right side of the neck, palm facing forward, twist the hand forward, ending with the palm facing back.

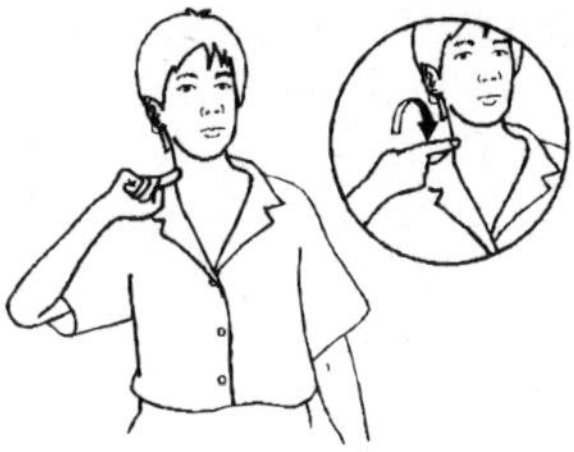

**pigment** *n.* See sign for RACE².

**pile**¹ *n.* **1.** A collection of things lying on top of one another: *a big pile of magazines on my floor.* **2.** A large number or amount: *made a pile of money in the stock market.* Same sign used for: **batch, bulk, load.**

■ [The shape and size of a pile] Move the right *5 hand* from in front of the left side of the chest, palm facing right and fingers pointing forward, upward in an arc in front of the right shoulder, ending near the right side of the body, palm facing left.

**pile**² *n.* See signs for AMOUNT, STACK.

**pill** *n.* Medicine in tablet or capsule form made to be swallowed whole: *to take a vitamin pill.* Same sign used for: **capsule, take a pill.**

■ [Represents flicking a pill into the mouth] Beginning with the index finger of the right *A hand* tucked under the thumb, palm facing in, flick the right index finger open toward the mouth with a double movement.

**pillage** *v.* See sign for STEAL¹.

**pillar** *n.* A column or similarly shaped structure used as a building support or monument: *The house had eight pillars on the front porch.* Same sign used for: **column.**

■ [The shape of a pillar] Rest the elbow of the bent right arm on the back of the left hand held across the chest, palm facing down. Then slide the left *C hand* from the elbow upward to the wrist of the bent right arm.

**pillow** *n.* A case filled with soft material used to support the head while resting: *I like to sleep on a down pillow.*

■ [The hands seem to squeeze a soft pillow] With the fingers of both *flattened C hands* pointing toward each other near the right ear, palms facing each other, close the fingers to the thumbs of each hand with a repeated movement.

**pimples** *pl. n.* A small, usually inflammatory swelling of the skin: *an excellent medication for drying up pimples.*

- [Represents a pimple popping out] Beginning with the right *S hand* against the right cheek, palm facing left, flick the right index finger upward with a double movement.

**pin** *n.* An ornament with a pointed fastener: *to wear a cameo pin on a black dress.*

- [Represents clipping on a pin] Beginning with the thumb of the right *modified C hand* against the left side of the chest, palm facing left, pinch the right index finger to the thumb.

**pinball machine** *n. phrase.* A sloping table with a mechanical device in which a ball is propelled by a plunger to score points: *to play game after game on the pinball machine.*

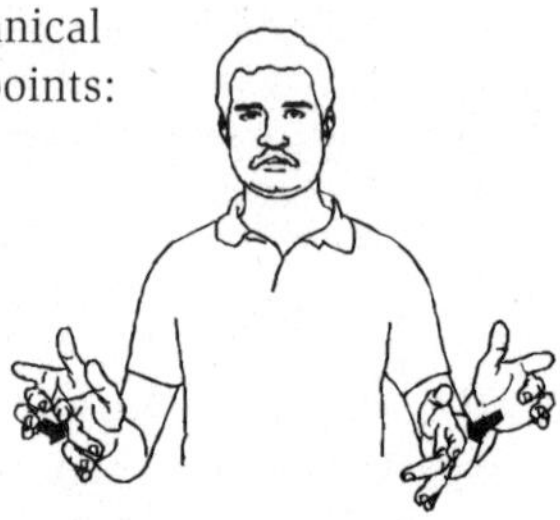

- [Mime pushing buttons to play a pinball machine] Beginning with both *curved 5 hands* in front of each side of the body, angled toward each other and fingers pointing forward, move the hands downward with a double movement toward each other while bending the middle finger of each hand.

**pinch** *v.* **1.** To squeeze between the thumb and index finger: *to pinch the baby's cheek.* **2.** To press on or constrict painfully: *My shoes are pinching my toes.*

- [Mime pinching] Move the curved index finger and thumb of the right hand downward in front of the chest, palm facing down, to pinch the back of the left *open hand,* palm facing down.

**pineapple** *n.* A juicy tropical fruit with yellow, fibrous flesh: *Fresh pineapple tastes better than canned.*

- [Initialized sign] Beginning with the middle finger of the right *P hand* touching the right cheek, palm facing left, twist the hand forward with a repeated movement, turning the palm back.

**Ping-Pong** *n. Trademark.* A table game resembling tennis, played with a paddle and a small hollow ball: *Play Ping-Pong with me.* Same sign used for: **table tennis.**

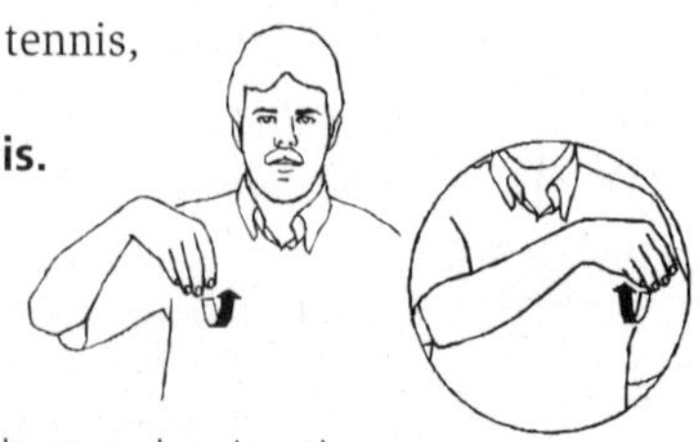

- [Mime swinging a Ping-Pong paddle] Beginning with the right *flattened O hand* in front of the right shoulder, palm facing down and fingers pointing down, swing the fingertips forward. Then move the right hand in front of the left side of the chest and swing the fingers forward again.

**pink** *adj.* Of a pale red color: *a pink rose.*

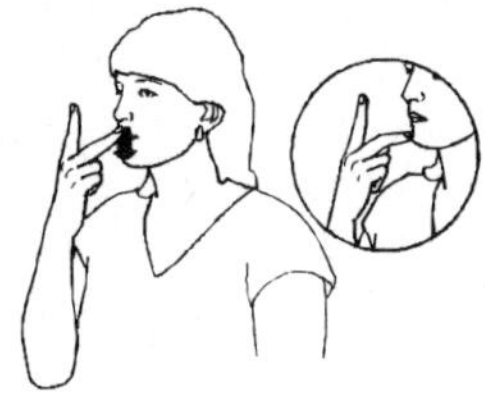

■ [Initialized sign similar to sign for **red**] Brush the middle finger of the right *P hand,* palm facing in, downward across the lips with a short repeated movement.

**pinpoint** *n.* See sign for POINT[2].

**pipe**[1] *n.* A tube with a bowl on one end used for smoking: *My professor smokes a pipe.*

■ [Represents smoking a pipe] Pat the thumb of the right *Y hand,* palm facing left, against the right side of the chin with a repeated movement.

**pipe**[2] *n.* A tube through which liquids flow: *a water pipe attached to the washing machine.* Same sign used for: **handle, lever, pole, rod, tube.**

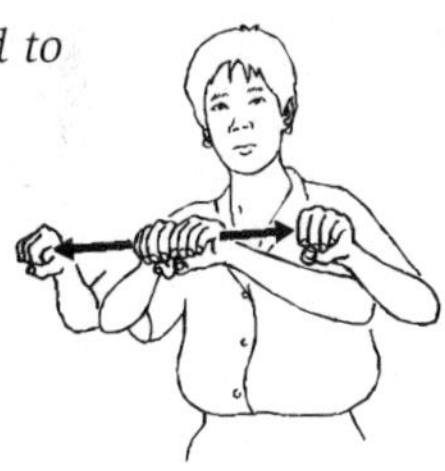

■ [The shape of a pipe] Beginning with the index-finger sides of both *O hands* touching in front of the chest, palms facing forward, move the hands apart to in front of each side of the chest.

**pipe**[3] *n.* See sign for STICK[2].

**pistol** *n.* See sign for GUN.

**pit** *n.* A cavity in the ground: *The campers dug a pit to build a fire.*

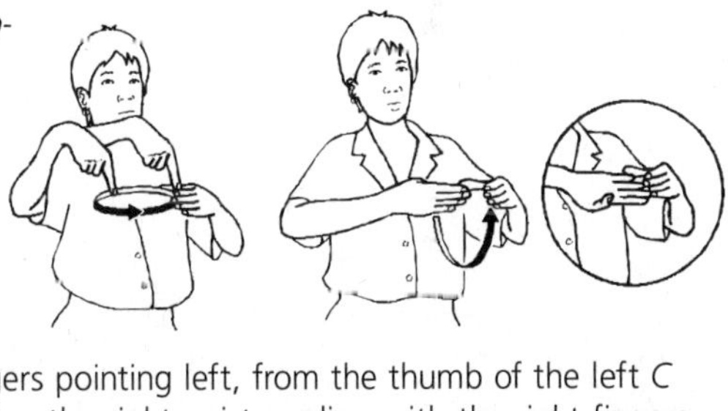

■ [**hole** + shape of a pit] Move the extended right index finger, palm facing in and finger pointing down, in a large circle near the palm side of the left *C hand,* palm facing right. Then move the right *B hand,* palm facing in and fingers pointing left, from the thumb of the left *C hand* in a downward arc while twisting the right wrist, ending with the right fingers, palm facing forward, near the little finger of the left hand.

**pitch**[1] *v.* To throw, as the ball to a batter in a baseball game: *learned to pitch the baseball in Little League.*

■ [Mime pitching a ball] Beginning with the right *curved 3 hand* near the right shoulder, palm facing left, bring the right hand downward and forward to the left with a quick double movement, ending with the palm facing up.

**pitch**[2] *v.* See sign for THROW.

**pitcher** *n.* A container with a lip on one side and a handle on the other used for pouring: *a pitcher of tea.*

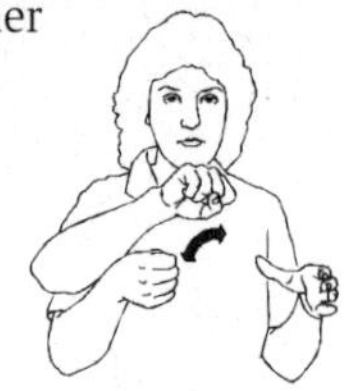

■ [Represents pouring from a pitcher into another container] Beginning with the left *C hand* in front of the left side of the body, palm facing right, and the right *S hand* in front of the right side of the body, palm facing in, bring the right hand upward in an arc while turning the palm down, and then back down again in the original position.

**pixel** *(Short for Picture Element) n.* A single point in a graphic image or the basic unit of the composition of an image on a television screen, computer monitor, or similar display. Pixels may have intensity and color: *a 7.2 pixel digital camera.*

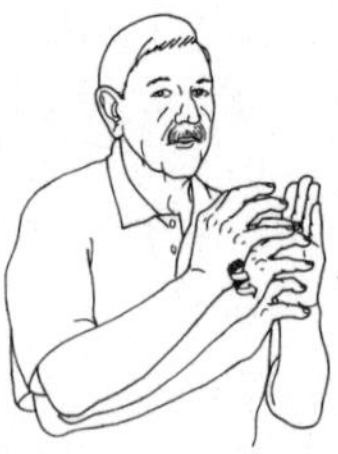

■ [The dot pattern of pixels] Tap the fingertips of the right *curved 5 hand* with a small repeated movement from the fingers to the heel of the left *open hand* held in front of the chest, palm facing right and fingers pointing up.

**pizza** *n.* An open pie made with tomato sauce, cheese, and other ingredients on a layer of dough: *to go out to an Italian restaurant for pizza.*

■ [**z** formed with *P hand*] Form a *Z* with the right *P hand,* palm facing left, in front of the right side of the chest.

**place**[1] *n.* A particular section of space, as for a designated purpose: *a place to play.* Same sign used for: **position.**

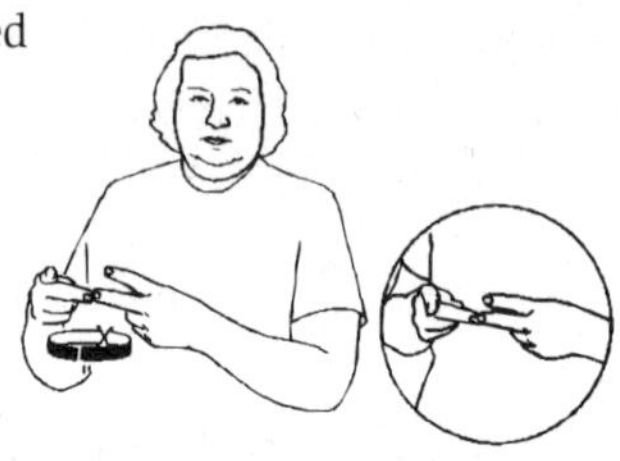

■ [Initialized sign outlining an area] Beginning with the middle fingers of both *P hands* touching in front of the body, palms facing each other, move the hands apart in a circular movement back until they touch again near the chest.

**place**[2] *v.* See sign for PUT.

**place**[3] *n.* See sign for AREA[1].

**plain** *adj.* Simple; without ornament or design: *a plain black dress.*

■ [The hand seems to clean off something to make it plain] Beginning with the index-finger side of the right *open hand* against the chin, palm facing left, move the right hand down across the palm of the left *open hand* from the heel to the fingertips, palm facing up.

**plan** *n.* **1.** A program or procedure developed in advance for accomplishing something: *Our summer plans include a trip through the Rockies.* **2.** A design, arrangement, drawing, etc.: *a seating plan for the dinner.* —*v.* **3.** To make a plan: *to plan for the future.* Same sign used for: **arrange, arrangement, schedule.**

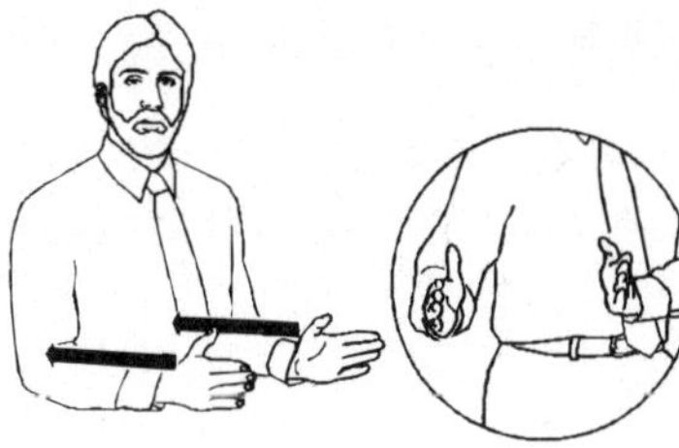

■ [The hands show a smooth and orderly flow of events] Move both *open hands* from in front of the left side of the body, palms facing each other and fingers pointing forward, in a long smooth movement to in front of the right side of the body.

**plane** *n.* See signs for AIRPLANE, SMOOTH[1].

**plant**[1] *n.* A living thing, smaller than a tree or shrub, that produces food from sunlight and inorganic substances through photosynthesis and that usually has leaves, roots, and a soft stem: *The aloe has become a popular houseplant.*

■ [Represents a seed sprouting and growing as it emerges from the ground] Bring the right *flattened O hand,* palm facing in, with a repeated movement upward through the left *C hand,* palm facing in and fingers pointing right, while spreading the right fingers into a *5 hand* each time.

**plant**[2] *v.* **1.** To put in the ground to grow: *to plant tulip bulbs; to plant roses.* **2.** To furnish with plants for growing: *to plant your garden.* Same sign used for: **sow.**

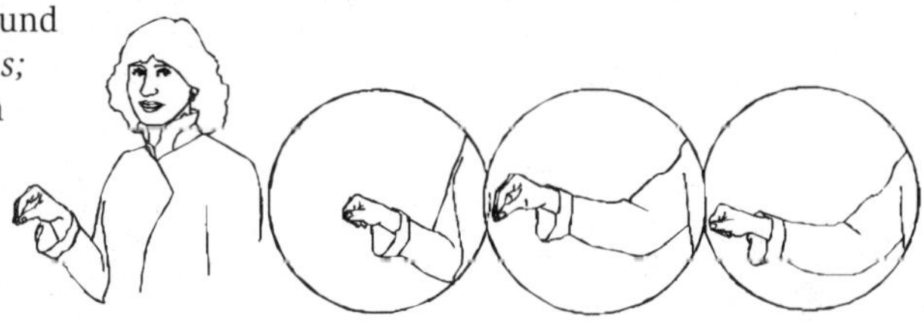

■ [Mime dropping seeds in a garden to plant them] Beginning with the right *flattened O hand* in front of the right side of the body, palm facing down, quickly close the fingers into an *A hand.* Repeat again somewhat forward from the body.

**plant**[3] *n.* See signs for MACHINE.

**plaster** *n.* **1.** A soft mixture of lime, sand, and water that hardens as it dries: *We used plaster to fill the hole in the ceiling.* —*v.* **2.** To cover, fill or spread with plaster: *We must plaster the walls before painting.*

■ [Mime spreading plaster on a wall] Beginning with the palm side of the right *S hand* on the open left palm, palms facing each other, move the right hand upward in an arc to the left.

**plate** *n.* **1.** A round, shallow dish from which food is eaten: *to serve dinner on the new china plates.* **2.** Food served on a plate: *to eat a plate of spaghetti.* Same sign used for: **saucer.**

- [The shape of a plate] Move both *modified C hands* downward with a short repeated movement in front of each side of the body, palms facing each other.

**play**[1] *v.* **1.** To engage in recreational activity, as spontaneous frolicking or participating in a game: *to play in the park; to play football.* —*n.* **2.** Spontaneous recreational activity: *children at play.* Same sign used for: **romp.**

- Swing both *Y hands* up and down by twisting the wrists in front of each side of the body with a repeated movement.

**play**[2] *n.* See sign for ACT[2].

**play against** *v. phrase.* See sign for CHALLENGE.

**play cards** *v. phrase.* See sign for CARDS.

**plead** *v.* See sign for BEG.

**pleasant** *adj.* See signs for COOL, FRIENDLY.

**please**[1] *adv.* (Used to express politeness in a request, command, etc.): *Please open the window.*

- Rub the palm of the right *open hand* in a large circle on the chest.

**please**[2] *v.* See sign for ENJOY. Related form: **pleasure** *n.*

**please**[3] *adv.* See sign for WORSHIP[1]. Used in the context of pleading only.

**pledge** *n.* See signs for OATH, PROMISE, VOW.

**plenty** *n.* See signs for ENOUGH, OVERFLOW.

**pliable** *adj.* **1.** Easily bent: *a pliable piece of plastic.* **2.** Easily influenced; adaptable: *a pliable personality.* Same sign used for: **flexible.**

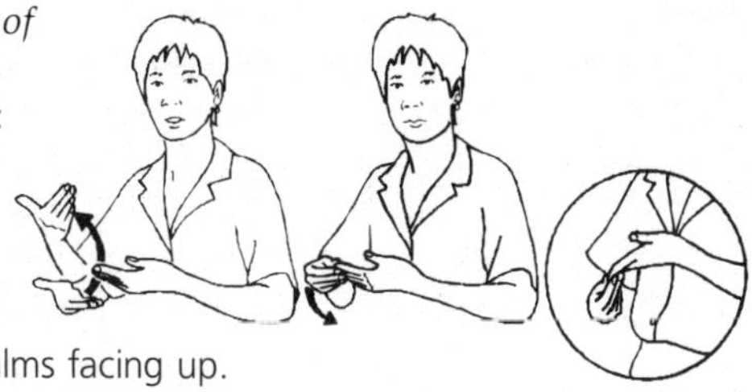

■ [**easy** + **bend**] Brush the fingertips of the right *curved hand* upward on the back of the fingertips of the left *curved hand* with a double movement, both palms facing up. Then, with the fingers of the right *flattened O hand* grasping the fingers of the left *open hand,* both palms facing in, bend the left fingers forward and back with a double movement.

**pliers** *pl. n.* A tool with long jaws for bending, cutting, or gripping objects: *Tighten the bolt with a pair of pliers.*

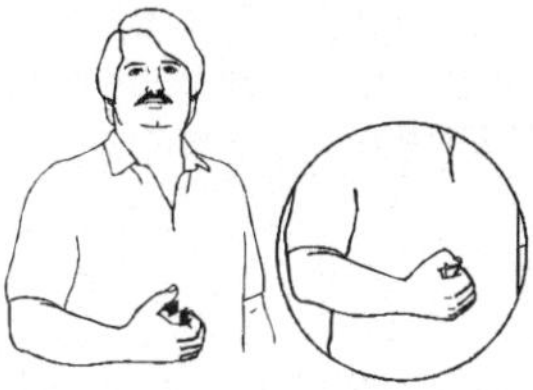

■ [Demonstrates the squeezing action used with pliers] Open and close the finger of the right *C hand* in front of the right side of the chest with a double movement, palm facing in.

**plod** *v.* To walk or move in a slow, dull way: *the horse plodded through the mud.* Same sign used for: **trudge.**

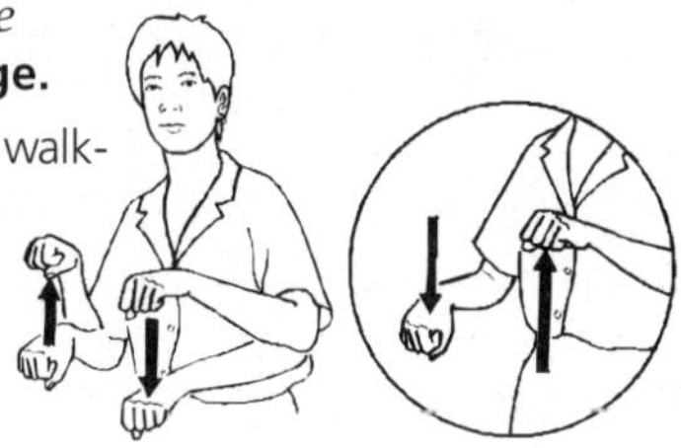

■ [Represents the movement of a horse's hooves when walking slowly] Beginning with both *S hands* in front of each side of the chest, right hand higher than the left hand, move the hands up and down with an alternating double movement by bending the wrists.

**plop** *v.* **1.** To fall dully and with full force, as onto a flat object: *The orange plopped onto the sidewalk. We plopped backwards into the pool.* —*n.* **2.** An act or sound of plopping: *The eggs fell with a loud plop.* Same sign used for: **splat.**

■ [Demonstrates something falling and spreading out as it lands] Beginning with the palm side of the right *S hand* on the index-finger side of the left *S hand,* bring the right hand forward and downward in a large arc while opening into a *5 hand* in front of the body.

**plow**[1] *n.* **1.** A large, bladed instrument, usually pulled by an animal or motorized, for turning over the soil to prepare it for planting: *Some farmers still use plows pulled by horses.* —*v.* **2.** To turn over (soil or the soil in) with a plow: *to plow the field.*

■ [Represents pushing dirt forward with a plow] Slide the little-finger side of the right *bent hand,* palm facing in and fingers pointing left, with a double movement from the wrist to off the fingertips of the left *open hand* held in front of the chest, palm facing down and fingers pointing forward.

**plow**[2] *v.* See sign for RAKE.

**plug** *n.* **1.** A small multipronged device attached to one end of an electrical cord to fit into a socket to make an electrical connection: *Pull out the plug when you're finished ironing.* —*v.* **2.** To make an electrical connection for by inserting a plug into a socket: *Plug in the TV.*

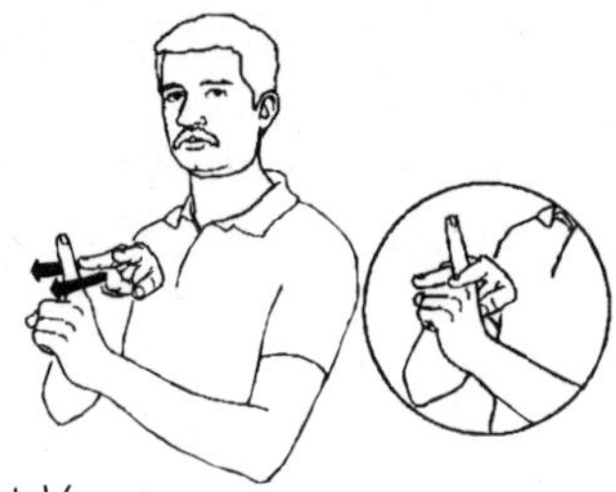

■ [Represents inserting a plug into a socket] Move the right *V hand,* palm facing down, forward from in front of the right shoulder, ending with the fingers of the right *V hand* on either side of the extended left index finger held pointing up in front of the chest, palm facing right.

**plump** *adj.* See sign for FAT.

**plus**[1] *prep.* **1.** Increased by: *Three plus two equals five.* **2.** In addition to: *She has brains plus beauty.* Same sign used for: **addition.**

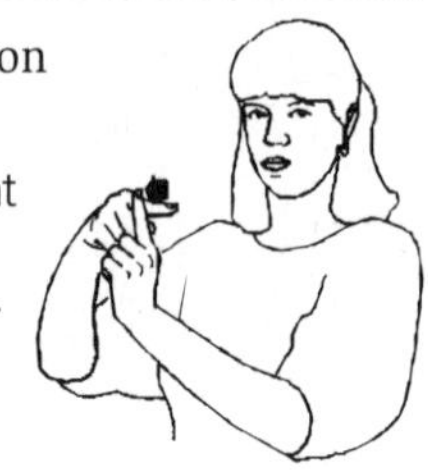

■ [Shows the shape of a plus sign] Place the side the extended right index finger, palm facing down and finger pointing left, against the extended left index finger, palm facing right and finger pointing up in front of the chest.

**plus**[2] *prep.* See sign for ADD[1].

**plush** *adj.* See sign for LAYER.

**P.M.** or **p.m.** *adj.* See sign for AFTERNOON.

**pneumonia** *n.* An infection of the lungs characterized by inflammation and congestion: *caught pneumonia during the freezing weather.*

■ [Initialized sign similar to sign for **lung**] Rub the middle fingers of both *P hands,* palms facing in and fingers pointing toward each other, up and down on each side of the chest with a double movement.

**pocket** *n.* **1.** A small opening sewn into clothing for carrying small articles: *Put the car keys in your pocket.* —*v.* **2.** To place in the pocket: *The thief pocketed the stolen wallet.*

■ [Mime putting the hand in one's pocket] Slide the fingertips of the right *open hand,* palm facing in, up and down a short distance on the right side of the body with a repeated movement.

**pocketbook** *n.* See sign for PURSE.

**pod** *n.* A long case, with side seams, in which the seeds of some plants, as peas, grow: *The seeds burst out of the pod when it ripened.*

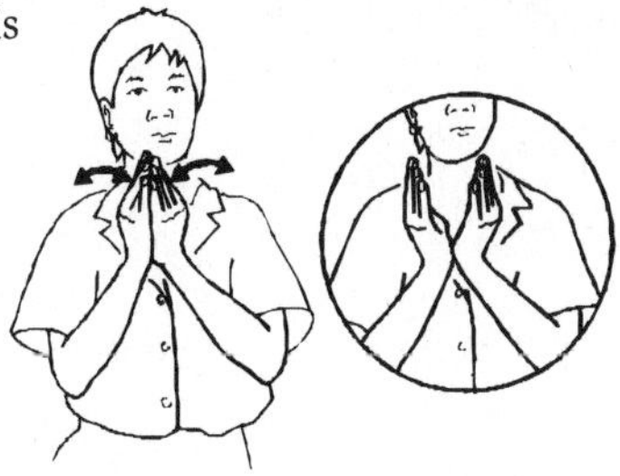

- [Shows the shape of a pod opening] Beginning with the heels and fingers of both *curved hands* together in front of the chest, open the fingers with a small double movement while keeping the heels together.

**poem** *n.* A composition in verse using imagery and rhythm: *Let's read the poem aloud.* Same sign used for: **poetry, Psalms.**

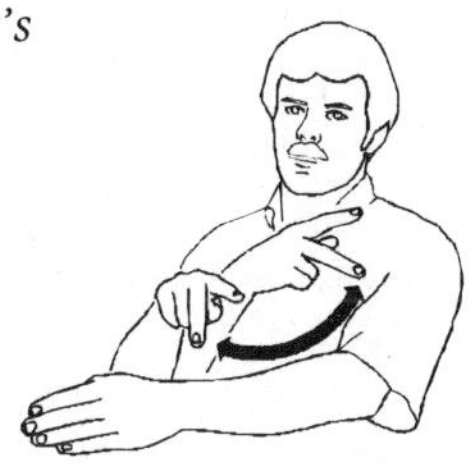

- [Initialized sign similar to sign for **music**] Swing the middle finger of the right *P hand,* palm facing in, back and forth across the length of the bent left forearm, palm facing right.

**poetry** *n.* See sign for POEM.

**point**[1] *n.* The sharp or tapering end of something: *to sharpen the pencil point.* Same sign used for: **tip.**

- [Indicates the top point of something] Tap the extended right index finger, palm facing down and finger pointing left, down on the tip of the extended left index finger, palm facing right and finger pointing up, with a double movement.

**point**[2] *n.* **1.** A specific location: *at the point where the house used to stand.* **2.** The most important element or matter: *Get to the point of your story.* Same sign used for: **particular, pinpoint, specific, target.**

- [Demonstrates pointing at a specific thing] Bring the right extended index finger from in front of the right shoulder, palm facing left and finger pointing up, downward to touch the left extended index finger held in front of the left side of the chest, palm facing right and finger pointing up.

**point**[3] *v.* See sign for THERE.

**point**[4] *n.* See sign for PERIOD.

**point of view** *n. phrase.* See sign for PERSPECTIVE.

**poison**[1] *n.* **1.** A drug or other substance that can destroy life or injure health: *searched for an antidote to the poison.* —*v.* **2.** To kill or attempt to kill with poison: *The victims were poisoned by arsenic.*

- [Represents the crossbones from the skull and crossbones symbol on labels for poison] Cross the wrists of both *bent V hands,* palms facing the body, in front of the chest.

**poison**² *n.* See sign for MEDICINE.

**pole** *n.* See signs for PIPE², POST, STICK.

**police** *n.* An organized civil force for maintaining order, preventing and detecting crime, and enforcing the law: *to report the robbery to the police.* Same sign used for: **badge, cop, marshall, officer, security, sheriff.**

- [Shows the location of a police badge] Tap the thumb side of the right *modified C hand,* palm facing left, against the left side of the chest with a double movement.

**policy** *n.* See sign for PRINCIPLE.

**polish** *v.* To make smooth and shiny, especially by rubbing: *to polish the silver.* Same sign used for: **rub, scrub.**

- [Demonstrates action of polishing something] Rub the knuckles of the right *A hand,* palm facing down, with a repeated movement on the back of the left *B hand,* palm facing down.

**polite** *adj.* Showing good manners; courteous: *a polite thank-you note.* Same sign used for: **courteous, courtesy, gentle, manners, prim.**

- Tap the thumb of the right *5 hand,* palm facing left, with a double movement against the center of the chest.

**politics** *n.* The science and art of conducting government and political affairs: *involved in politics before becoming a senator.* Related form: **political** *adj.*

- [Initialized sign similar to sign for **government**] Beginning with the right *P hand* near the right side of the head, palm facing forward, twist the wrist to turn the palm back and touch the middle finger of the right *P hand* against the right side of the forehead.

**pollution** *n.* See sign for DIRTY.

**poncho** *n.* **1.** A rectangular or circular woolen cloak, originally from South America, with a slit or hole in the middle through which the wearer inserts the head: *brought back an authentic poncho from Mexico.* **2.** A similarly styled waterproof garment with a hood: *to wear a poncho in the rain.* Same sign used for: **hood.**

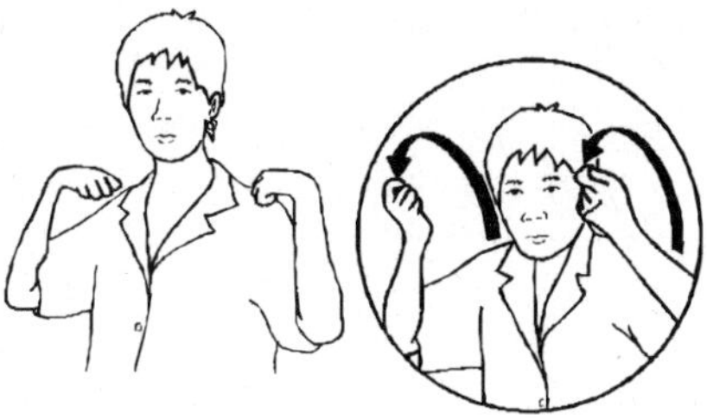

- [Mime pulling up the hood of a poncho] Beginning with both *modified X hands* near each shoulder, palms facing down, bring the hands upward and forward in an arc, ending with the palms facing up near each side of the head.

**pond** *n.* See sign for PUDDLE.

**ponder** *v.* See signs for MULL, WONDER.

**pool**[1] *n.* Any of various games played on a pool table by driving balls into pockets with a cue stick: *to play pool in the local pool hall.* Same sign used for: **billiards.**

- [Mime holding a pool cue] With the right elbow bent and extended back, move the right *A hand* forward a short distance near the right side of the body while holding the left *F hand* extended in front of the left side of the body.

**pool**[2] *v.* See sign for CHIP IN.

**poor** *adj.* Having little or no money or goods: *sending food to poor people.* Same sign used for: **destitute, impoverished, pauper, poverty.**

- [Represents the tattered sleeves on the elbows of poor people] Beginning with the fingertips of the right *curved 5 hand,* palm facing up, touching the elbow of the bent left arm, pull the right hand downward while closing the fingers to the thumb with a double movement, forming a *flattened O hand* each time.

**poor thing** *n. phrase.* See sign for MERCY.

**popcorn** *n.* Kernels of corn that burst open and puff out when heated: *to eat buttered popcorn at the movies.*

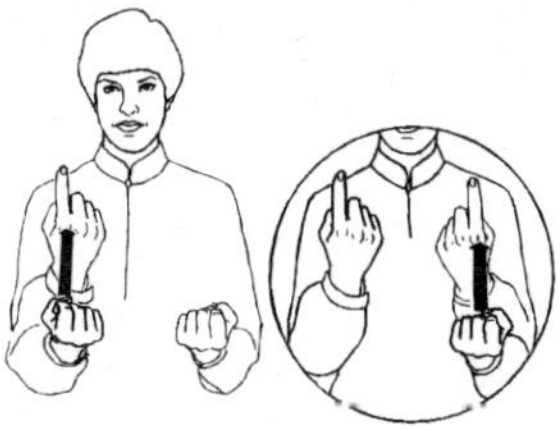

- [Shows action of popcorn popping] Beginning with both *S hands* in front of each side of the body, palms facing up, alternately move each hand upward while flicking out each index finger with a repeated movement.

**Popsicle** *n. Trademark.* See sign for LOLLIPOP.

**popular** *adj.* Liked and approved of by many people: *a popular song; a popular president.*

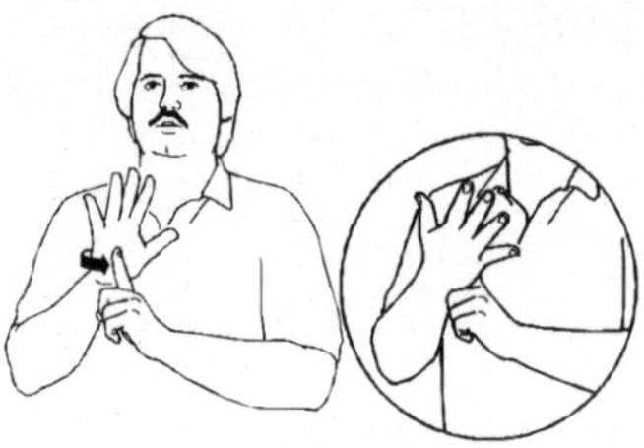

■ [Represents many people surrounding a popular person] With the extended left index finger against the palm of the right *5 hand,* palm facing forward, twist the right hand around the index finger with a double movement, ending with the palm facing in.

**population** *n.* The number of people in a city, country, district, or other defined area: *to keep track of the growing population in the suburbs.*

■ [Initialized sign similar to sign for **among**] Move the extended middle finger of the right *P hand,* palm facing in, in and out between the fingers of the left *5 hand,* palm facing in.

**pop up** *v. phrase.* See sign for SHOW UP.

**porch** *n.* An appendage to a building, including a covered entrance: *to sit on the front porch in the early evening.*

■ Strike the index-finger side of the right *S hand,* palm facing in, first near the elbow then on the forearm of the bent left arm held across the chest, palm of the left *open hand* facing down.

**porpoise** *n.* Any member of one of the varieties of small whales with blunt snouts that travel in groups: *The porpoises were swimming ahead of the ship.* Same sign used for: **dolphin.**

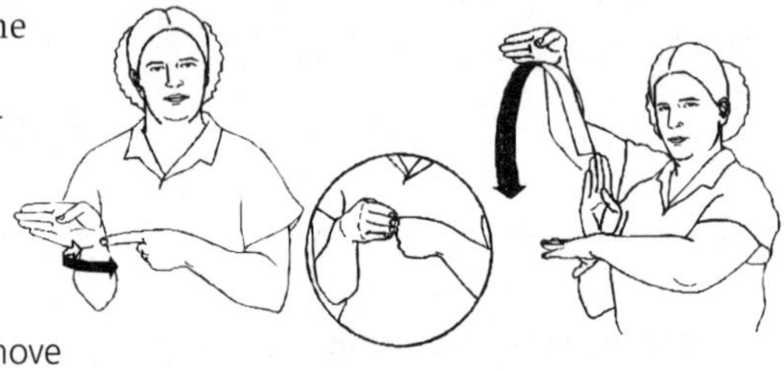

■ [**fish**[1] + diving movement] With the extended left index finger, palm facing in, touching the right wrist, move the right *B hand* from right to left with a double movement by bending the wrist. Then move the right *B hand,* palm facing left and fingers pointing up, in a large upward arc over the left arm held across the chest, ending with the right fingers pointing down in front of the left arm.

**portray** *v.* See sign for SHOW.

**position** *n.* See sign for PLACE.

**possess**[1] *v.* To have: *possess an acre of land.* Related form: **possession** *n.*

■ [**my** + **capture**] Pat the palm side of the right *open hand,* palm facing in and fingers pointing left, against the center of the chest. Then, beginning with both *curved 5 hands* in front of each side of the chest, palms facing down and fingers pointing forward, move the hands downward with a quick movement while changing into *S hands.*

**possess**[2] *v.* See signs for CAPTURE, HAVE.

**possessive** *adj.* See sign for GREEDY[1].

**possible** *adj.* **1.** Capable of existing, happening, or being achieved: *a possible candidate; possible to finish on time.* **2.** Capable of being true: *The prediction is unlikely but possible.* Related form: **possibly** *adv.* Same sign used for: **potential.**

■ [Similar to sign for **can** but made with a double movement] Move both *S hands,* palms angled forward, downward simultaneously in front of each side of the body with a double movement by bending the wrists.

**post**[1] *n.* A column set upright to support something else: *attach the clothesline to the post.* Same sign used for: **pole.**

■ [The shape of a post] Beginning with the little-finger side of the right *C hand* on the index-finger side of the left *C hand,* palms facing in opposite directions, raise the right hand upward in front of the chest.

**post**[2] *v.* See signs for APPLY[1], BULLETIN BOARD.

**postage** *n.* See sign for STAMP[1].

**postage stamp** *n. phrase.* See sign for STAMP[1].

**post a notice** *v. phrase.* See sign for BULLETIN BOARD.

**poster** *n.* See sign for BULLETIN BOARD.

**postpone** *v.* To put off until a later time; defer: *to postpone the meeting.* See also sign for PROCRASTINATE. Same sign used for: **continuance, defer, delay, put off.**

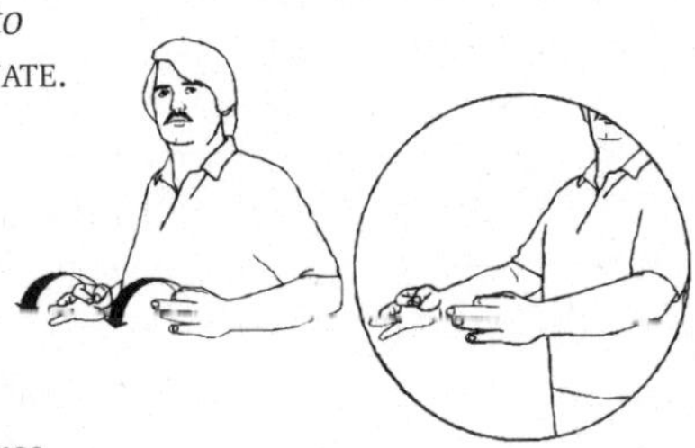

■ [Represents taking something and putting it off until the future] Beginning with both *F hands* in front of the body, palms facing each other and the left hand nearer to the body than the right hand, move both hands forward in small arcs.

**pot**[1] *n. Slang.* See sign for MARIJUANA.

**pot**[2] *n.* See signs for BOWL, BUCKET.

**potato** *n.* A hard, round edible tuber, cooked and eaten as a vegetable: *Potatoes are delicious baked, mashed, or fried.*

- [Represents putting fork tines into a baked potato to see if it is done] Tap the fingertips of the right *bent V hand,* palm facing down, with a double movement on the back of the left *open hand,* palm facing down.

**potent** *adj.* See sign for POWER.

**potential** *adj.* See sign for POSSIBLE.

**poultry** *n.* Domestic birds collectively, especially those raised for eggs or meat: *Turkeys, ducks, and chickens are kinds of poultry.*

- [**bird** + **meat**] Open and close the extended fingers of the right *G hand,* palm facing forward, with a double movement in front of the mouth. Then, with the bent index finger and thumb of the right *5 hand,* palm facing down, grasp the fleshy part of the left *open hand,* palm facing down and fingers pointing right, and shake the hands forward and back with a double movement.

**pound**[1] *v.* To hit again and again: *pound the nail.*

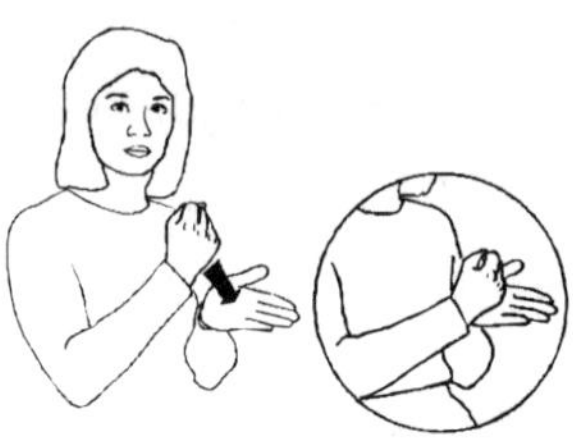

- [Mime pounding something] Strike the little-finger side of the right *S hand,* palm facing in, with a repeated movement on the upturned palm of the left *open hand* held in front of the waist, fingers pointing forward.

**pound**[2] *n.* See sign for WEIGH.

**pour** *v.* To cause to flow in a steady stream: *Pour the milk into the pitcher.*

- [Mime holding a large container and pouring from it] Beginning with both *C hands* in front of the body, palms facing each other, tip the hands so that the right hand is above the left hand, palm facing down, and the left hand is in front of the body, palm facing up.

**poverty** *n.* See sign for POOR.

**power**[1] *n.* **1.** The ability to act or do with strength: *The wrestler has great power in his arms.* **2.** Command or control; authority: *the power to sign treaties.* Related form: **powerful** *adj.* Same sign used for: **mighty, potent, strength, sturdy.**

- [Demonstrate power in one's arms] Move both *S hands,* palms facing in, forward with a short deliberate movement from in front of each shoulder.

**power**[2] *n.* See sign for STRONG[1].

**powerful** *adj.* Having great power, strength, or force: *a powerful fighter; a powerful blow.* Same sign used for: **strong**[2].

- [Shows the large muscles in the arms of a powerful person] Bring the fingertips and thumb of the right *C hand* down against the biceps of the bent left arm.

**power surge** *n. phrase.* A sudden increase in electric current delivered through a power line that may damage a computer or its memory: *The power surge shut down my computer.* Same sign used for: **spike, surge.**

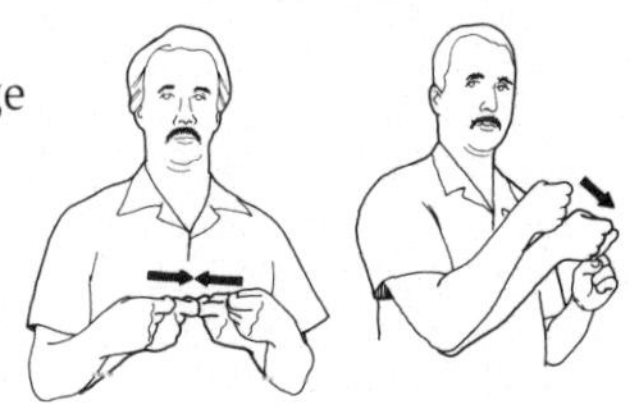

- [**electric** + **hit**[1]] Tap the knuckles of the index fingers of both *X hands* together with a double movement, palms facing in. Then strike the knuckles of the right *S hand,* palm facing in, against the extended left index finger held up in front of the chest, palm facing right.

**practice** *n.* **1.** Repetition of an activity to achieve or improve skill: *To do it well takes practice.* —*v.* **2.** To do repeatedly to improve skill: *to practice the piano every day.* Same sign used for: **drill, exercise, rehearse, training.**

- [The repetitive action symbolizes doing something again and again] Rub the knuckles of the right *A hand,* palm facing down, back and forth on the extended left index finger held in front of the chest, palm facing down and finger pointing right, with a repeated movement.

**praise**[1] *v.* **1.** To speak well of: *to praise their efforts on the job.* —*n.* **2.** An expression of approval of something: *high praise for the team.* Same sign used for: **acclamation, compliment.**

- [**real** + **applaud**] Bring the extended right index finger, palm facing left and finger pointing up, from in front of the mouth forward while changing into an *open hand.* Then clap the palms of both *open hands* together with a double movement in front of the body.

**praise**[2] *v.* See sign for APPLAUD.

**pray**[1] *v.* **1.** To petition God: *to pray for rain during a drought.* **2.** To offer praise or thanks to God: *to pray briefly before each meal.* Related form: **prayer** *n.*

- [Natural gesture for praying] With the palms of both *open hands* together in front of the chest, fingers angled upward, move the hands forward with a double circular movement.

**pray**[2] *v.* See signs for AMEN, ASK, WORSHIP[1]. Related form: **prayer** *n.*

**pre-**[1] *prefix.* Before: *prenatal.* Same sign used for: **previous.**

- [Initialized sign similar to sign for **before**] Beginning with the back of the right *P hand,* palm facing in, touching the palm of the left *open hand,* palm facing in and fingers pointing right in front of the chest, move the right hand in toward the chest a short distance.

**pre-**[2] *prefix.* See sign for BEFORE[2].

**preach** *v.* To speak on a religious subject: *preach a sermon.* Same sign used for: **nag.**

- Move the right *F hand,* palm facing forward, with a short double movement forward in front of the right shoulder.

**preceding** *adj.* See sign for BEFORE.

**precious** *adj.* **1.** Of great monetary value: *precious jewels.* **2.** Highly cherished: *My children are precious to me.* Same sign used for: **cherish, treasure.**

- [Holding something of value tightly in the hand] Beginning with the right *curved 5 hand* in front of the mouth, palm facing back, slowly close the fingers into an *S hand.*

**precise** *adj.* Accurate; clear; definite: *the precise time of day.* Same sign used for: **accurate, concise, exact, just, specific.**

■ [Demonstrates something coming together precisely] Beginning with the right *modified X hand* near the left *modified X hand,* move the right hand in a small circle and then forward to touch the hands together in front of the chest.

**predict** *v.* To forecast: *predict the future.* Same sign used for: **forecast, foresee, foretell, perceive, perception, prophecy.**

■ [Represents the eyes looking forward into the future] Beginning with the fingers of the right *V hand* pointing to each eye, move the right hand forward under the palm of the left *open hand.*

**prefer**[1] *v.* To like better: *to prefer chocolate ice cream.* Related form: **preference** *n.* Same sign used for: **rather.**

■ [**favorite** + **better**] Beginning with the bent middle finger of the right *5 hand* touching the chin, palm facing in, bring the hand forward to the right while closing into a *10 hand.*

**prefer**[2] *v.* See sign for FAVORITE. Related form: **preference** *n.*

**pregnant**[1] *adj.* Having a baby developing in the womb: *After five years of marriage, she is pregnant.* Same sign used for: **breed, conceive.**

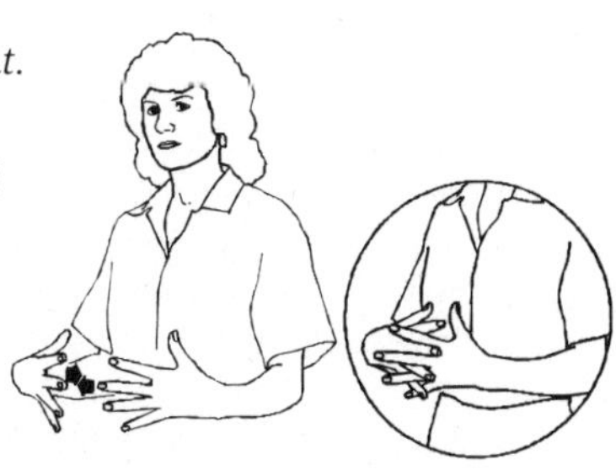

■ [The shape of a pregnant woman's stomach] Bring both *5 hands* from in front of each side of the body, palms facing in, toward each other, entwining the fingers in front of the stomach.

**pregnant**[2] *adj.* See sign for STUCK. This sign is used only when referring to an unwanted pregnancy.

**prejudice**[1] *n., v.* **1.** An unfavorable opinion or feeling formed beforehand without knowledge, thought, or reason. **2.** To pass judgment unfairly based on unreasonable feelings or opinions: *having a prejudice against fat people.* Same sign used for: **bias, biased.**

- [**mind** + **against**] Tap the extended right index finger, palm facing in, against the right side of the forehead with a double movement. Then hit the fingertips of the right *bent hand* into the left *open hand,* palm right and fingers pointing forward.

**prejudice**[2] *n.* See sign for AGAINST.

**premeditate** *v.* To plan beforehand: *The crime was premeditated.*

- [**concern**[1] + **plan**] Move both extended index fingers in large alternating circles in front of each side of the forehead. Then move both *open hands* from in front of the left side of the body, palms facing each other and fingers pointing forward, in a long smooth movement to in front of the right side of the body.

**prepare** *v.* To make or get ready: *to prepare a meal; to prepare for the picnic.* Same sign used for: **arrange, put in order, organize, sequence, sort.**

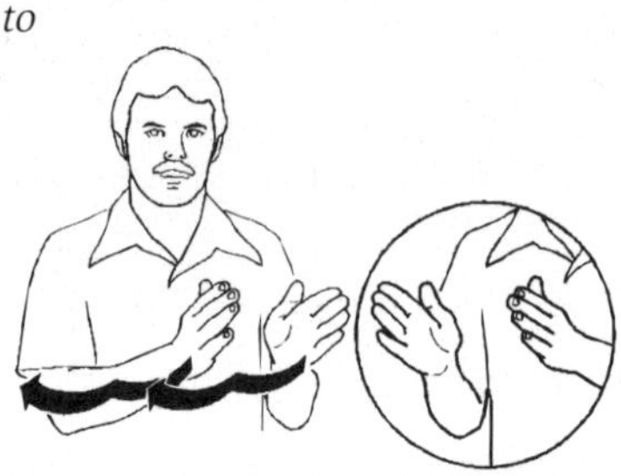

- Beginning with both *open hands* in front of the left side of the body, palms facing each other and fingers pointing forward, move the hands in double downward arcs to in front of the right side of the body.

**prepay** *v.* To pay in advance: *We prepaid the shipment.*

- [**finish** + **pay**] Beginning with both *5 hands* in front of each side of the chest, palms facing in and fingers pointing up, flip the hands over with a sudden movement, ending with both palms facing down and fingers pointing forward. Then, beginning with the extended right index finger touching the palm of the left *open hand* held in front of the body, palm facing up and fingers pointing right, move the right finger forward off the left fingertips while turning the right palm down, ending with the finger pointing forward.

**preschool** *adj.* **1.** Of or designating children of an age between infancy and five: *preschool children.* —*n.* **2.** School intended for children younger than kindergarten age: *The toddlers attend preschool.*

■ [**pre-** + **school**] Beginning with the left *open hand* in front of the chest, palm facing in and fingers pointing right, and the right *P hand* somewhat closer to the chest, palm facing in, bring the right *P hand* toward the chest. Then clap the palms of both *open hands* together with a double movement in front of the chest.

**prescribe** *v.* To order or direct a patient to use specific medicine: *The doctor prescribed aspirin three times a day.* Related form: **prescription.**

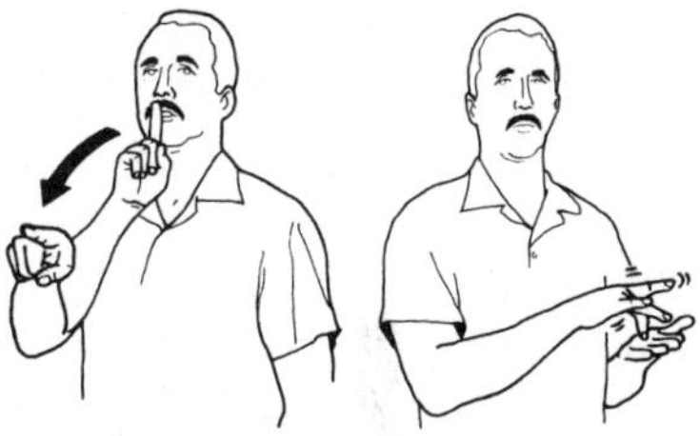

■ [**order** + **medicine**] Move the extended right index finger, palm facing forward and finger pointing up, from in front of the mouth forward and down, ending with the finger pointing forward and the palm facing down. Then with the bent middle finger of the right *5 hand* in the palm of the left *open hand,* palms facing each other, rock the right hand from side to side with a double movement while keeping the middle finger in place.

**present**[1] *n.* See signs for BOX, GIFT, ROOM[1].

**present**[2] *adv.* See signs for HERE, NOW.

**present**[3] *v.* See sign for GIVE.

**presentation** *n.* See sign for SPEAK[2].

**preserve** *v.* See sign for SAVE[2]. Related form: **preservation** *n.*

**preside over** *v. phrase.* See sign for MANAGE.

**president** *n.* **1.** The chief of state of a republic: *president of the country.* **2.** The chief executive officer of an organization: *a quarterly report from the president of the company.* Same sign used for: **horns, superintendent.**

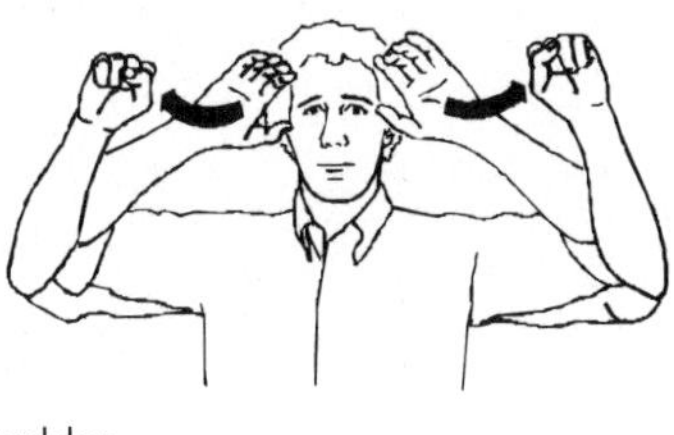

■ Beginning with the index-finger sides of both *C hands* near each side of the forehead, palms facing forward, move the hands outward to above each shoulder while closing into *S hands.*

**press** *n.* See sign for NEWSPAPER.

**pressure** *n.* **1.** Continued weight or force: *There is too much pressure on the shelf from all the books.* **2.** Stress; strain: *an executive job with a lot of pressure.* Same sign used for: **repress, repression, stress, suppress, suppression.**

■ [Demonstrates the action of applying pressure] Push the palm of the right *5 hand,* palm facing down, on the index-finger side of the left *S hand,* palm facing in, forcing the left hand downward.

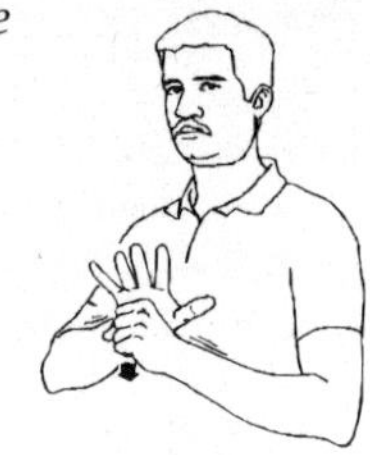

**pretty** *adj.* Pleasing to the eye or ear: *a pretty face.* See also sign for BEAUTIFUL. Same sign used for: **lovely.**

■ [The hand encircles the beauty of the face] Beginning with the right *5 hand* in front of the face, palm facing in, move it in a circular movement, closing the fingers to the thumb in front of the chin, forming a *flattened O hand.*

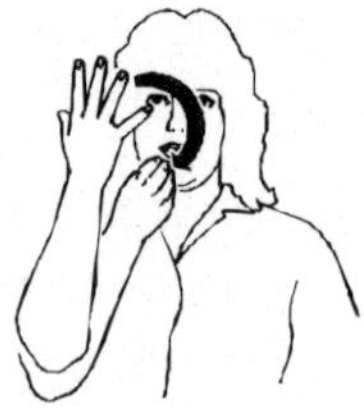

**prevailing** *adj.* See sign for NOW.

**prevent** *v.* To keep from happening: *a cream that helps to prevent sunburn.* Same sign used for: **ban, barrier, block, blockage, hinder, impair, obstruct.**

■ [The hands seem to shield the body with a barrier] With the little-finger side of the right *B hand,* palm facing down, against the index-finger side of the left *B hand,* palm facing right, move the hands forward a short distance.

**preview** *v.* **1.** To view or show beforehand: *to preview the movie.* —*n.* **2.** An advance showing, as of scenes from a movie: *went to a preview of the new film.*

■ [**see** + **before**] Bring the fingers of the right *V hand* from pointing at the eyes, palm facing in, forward a short distance. Then, beginning with the back of the right *open hand,* palm facing in and fingers pointing left, touching the palm of the left *open hand,* palm facing in and fingers pointing right, move the right hand back toward the right shoulder.

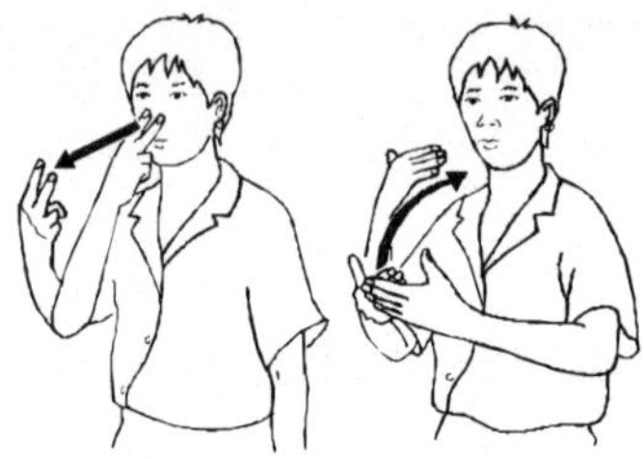

**previous**[1] *adj.* Occurring, existing, or coming before something else: *The previous owner has the key.*

■ [The hand indicates a time in the past] Tap the fingertips of the right *bent hand* on the right shoulder with a double movement.

**previous**[2] *adj.* See signs for BEFORE, FORMER, PRE-[1].

**price** *n.* See signs for COST[1,2].

**prim** *adj.* See signs for FANCY, POLITE, SOPHISTICATED.

**prime** *n.* The period of life when one has the combined advantages of vigor and experience: *She's in her 40s and in her prime.*

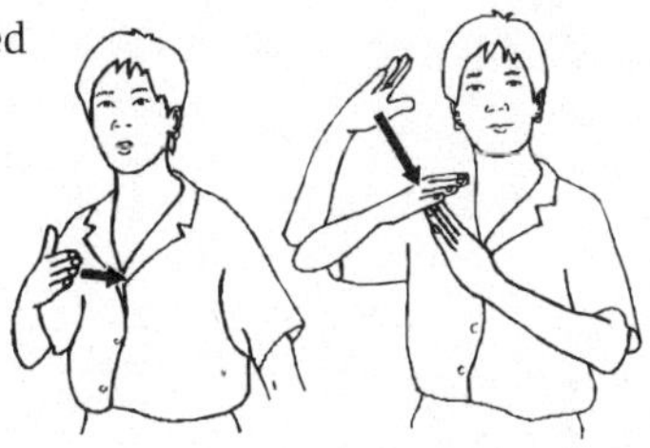

■ [**my** + **top**] Bring the palm of the right *open hand* against the chest, palm facing in and fingers pointing left. Then bring the palm of the right *open hand* from near the right side of the head downward to touch the fingertips of the left *open hand* held in front of the chest, palm facing right and fingers pointing up.

**primitive** *adj.* See sign for LONG AGO.

**principal** *n.* The head of an elementary or secondary school: *Teachers report to the school principal.*

■ [Initialized sign] Move the right *P hand,* palm facing down, in a small circle above the left *open hand,* palm facing down, ending with the middle finger of the right hand on the back of the left hand.

**principle** *n.* **1.** A fundamental truth: *Space travel is based on sound scientific principles.* **2.** A rule of conduct; standard for moral behavior: *We must live according to principles of decency.* Same sign used for: **policy.**

■ [Initialized sign similar to sign for **law**] Touch the index-finger side of the right *P hand,* palm facing down, first against the fingers and then against the heel of the left *open hand,* palm facing forward and fingers pointing up.

**print** *v., n.* See sign for NEWSPAPER.

**printer server** *n. phrase.* See sign for SERVER.

**printout** *n.* Computer output printed on paper: *He used the printout as a guide for his speech.*

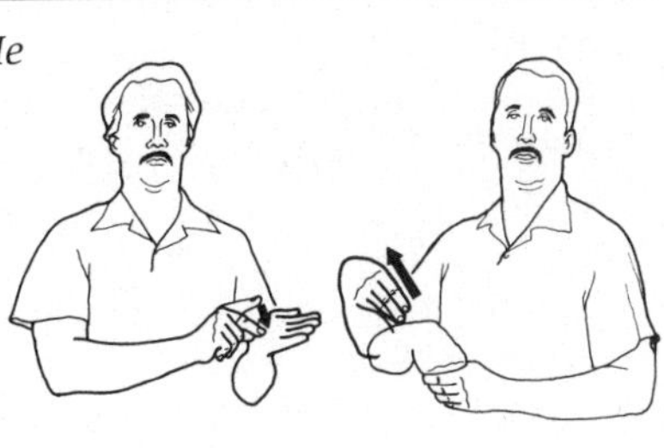

■ [**print** + **out**] Beginning with the thumb of the right *G hand* on the heel of the left *open hand,* tap the right index finger down to the thumb with a double movement. Then beginning with the right *flattened O hand* inserted in the palm side of the left *C hand,* bring the right hand upward.

**prior** *adj.* See signs for BEFORE[1,2].

**priority** *n.* Something given the right to precede other things in order of importance: *to keep your priorities in proper order.* Related form: **prioritize** *v.*

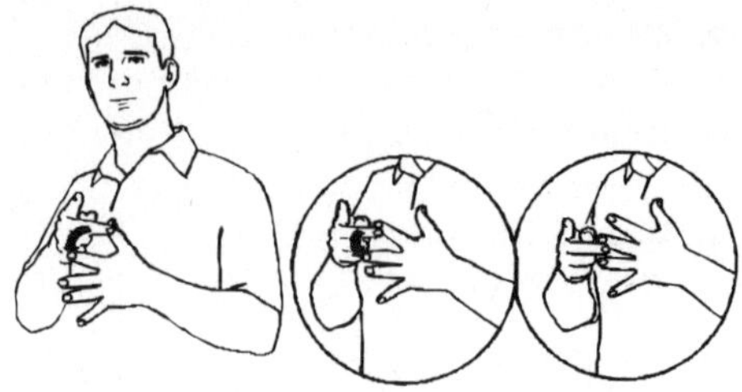

■ [Initialized sign touching each item on a list showing the order of priorities] Touch the middle finger of the right *P hand,* palm facing in, first to the thumb, then the index finger, and then the middle finger of the left *5 hand* held in front of the body, palm facing right and fingers pointing forward.

**prison** *n.* See sign for JAIL.

**private** *adj.* See sign for SECRET. Related form: **privacy** *n.*

**private eye** *n. Informal.* See sign for DETECTIVE.

**privilege** *v.* See signs for PERMIT, RIGHT[2].

**prize** *n.* See sign for MEDAL.

**probably** *adv.* See sign for MAYBE. Related forms: **probability** *n.*, **probable** *adj.*

**probation** *n.* See sign for TORTURE.

**problem**[1] *n.* Something that presents a difficulty and requires a solution: *a student having a problem with money.*

■ Beginning with the knuckles of both *bent V hands* touching in front of the chest, twist the hands in opposite directions with a deliberate movement, rubbing the knuckles against each other.

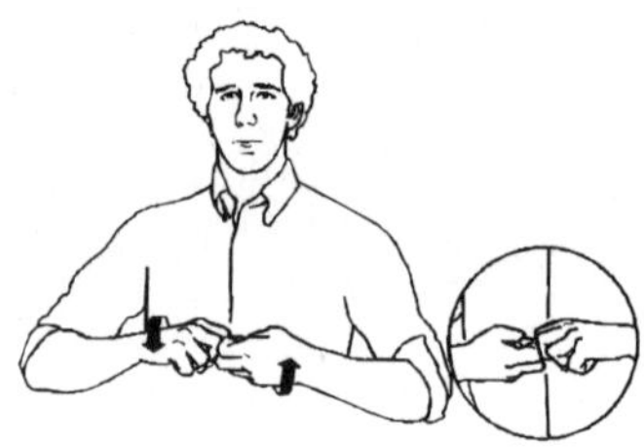

**problem**[2] *n.* See sign for DIFFICULT.

**procedure** *n.* A method or course of action: *Follow the procedure for submitting your expense report.* Related form: **procedural** *adj.* Same sign used for: **pace, process, progress, take steps.**

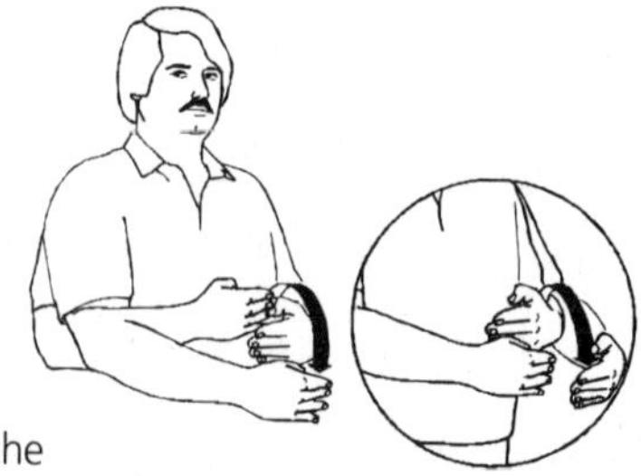

■ [Represents the progression of activities in a procedure] Beginning with both *open hands* in front of the body, palms facing in, left fingers pointing right and right fingers pointing left, and the right hand closer to the chest than the left hand, move the right hand over the left hand and then the left hand over the right hand in an alternating movement.

**proceed** *v.* See sign for GO ON.

**process** *n.* See sign for PROCEDURE.

**procession**[1] *n.* A body of persons, vehicles, etc., marching or moving forward in ceremonial order: *a wedding procession.*

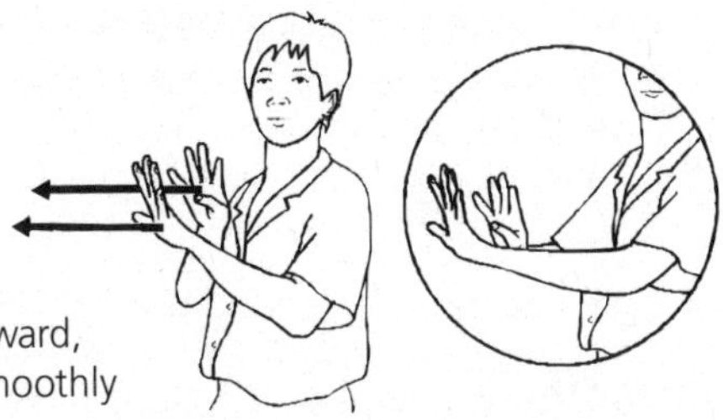

■ [Represents people marching in a procession] Beginning with both *4 hands* in front of the chest, left hand somewhat forward of the right hand, palms facing forward, and fingers pointing up, move the hands smoothly forward.

**procession**[2] *n.* See sign for MARCH.

**proclaim** *v.* See sign for ANNOUNCE. Related form: **proclamation** *n.*

**procrastinate** *v.* To put off action until a later time; delay: *If a student procrastinates, it becomes more difficult to do the homework.* See signs for DEFER, POSTPONE.

■ [The hand seems to put something off time and time again] Beginning with the fingertips of the right *F hand* touching the fingertip of the left *F hand,* palms facing each other, move the right hand forward in a series of small arcs.

**produce**[1] *v.* **1.** To bring about; cause to exist: *Study will produce better grades.* **2.** To manufacture: *The factory produces cars.*

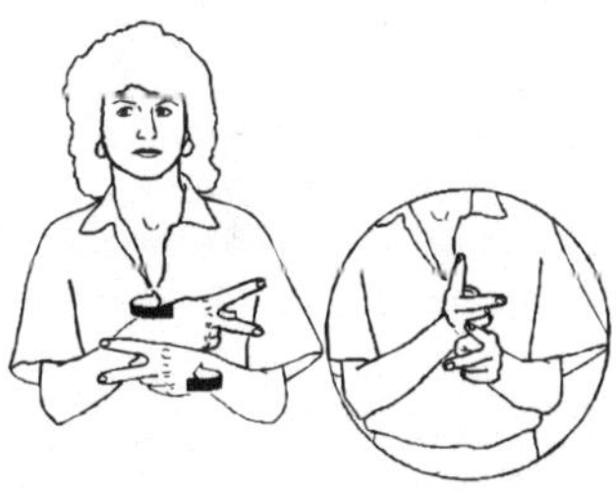

■ [Initialized sign similar to sign for **make**] Beginning with the little-finger side of the right *P hand* on the index-finger side of the left *P hand,* palms facing in, twist the hands so that the fingers point forward, ending with the palms facing in opposite directions.

**produce**[2] *v.* See sign for MAKE.

**profession** *n.* An occupation requiring special training: *to work in the legal profession.* Related form: **professional** *n., adj.*

■ [Initialized sign similar to sign for **specialize**] Move the middle finger of the right *P hand,* palm facing down, from the base of the index finger of the left *B hand,* palm facing right and fingers pointing forward, to its tip.

**proficient** *adj.* See signs for GOOD AT, SKILL.

**profit** *n.* The monetary gain made from a business or a particular transaction: *The business won't survive if it doesn't make a profit.* Same sign used for: **gain, gross.**

- [The hand seems to put a profit into one's pocket] Move the right *F hand,* palm facing down, downward with a double movement near the right side of the chest.

**program** *n.* **1.** A plan of what is to be done or accomplished: *a new school program for gifted children.* **2.** A sequence of coded instructions for a computer: *wrote a program for sorting files by date.*

- [Initialized sign] Move the middle finger of the right *P hand,* palm facing left, from the fingertips to the base of the left *open hand,* palm facing right and fingers pointing up. Repeat the movement on the back side of the left hand.

**progress** *n.* See sign for PROCEDURE.

**prohibit** *v.* See sign for FORBID.

**project** *n.* An undertaking: *plans to complete the project by March.*

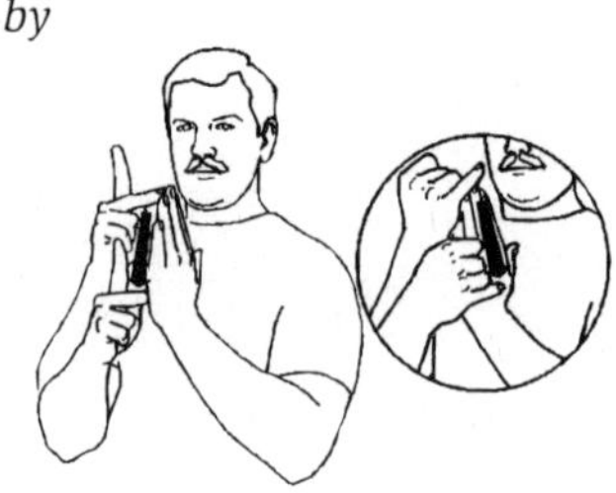

- [Abbreviation **p-j** similar to sign for **program**] Move the middle finger of the right *P hand,* palm facing left, from the fingertips to the base of the palm of the left *open hand,* palm facing right and fingers pointing up. Then move the right extended little finger from the fingertips to the base of the back of the left hand.

**prolong** *v.* See sign for EXAGGERATE.

**prominent** *adj.* See signs for ADVANCED, CHIEF.

**promiscuous** *adj.* Characterized by or having casual sexual relations with many persons: *It is becoming increasingly dangerous to be promiscuous.*

- [Represents jumping from bed to bed] Move the right *bent V hand* from in front of the right side of the body, palm facing down, in an arc to in front of the body, and then to in front of the left side of the body.

**promise** *n.* **1.** Something said or written that binds a person to do or not do something: *I hope you keep your promise to stay in touch.* —*v.* **2.** To pledge; give one's word: *Promise you'll come back.* See also sign for VOW. Same sign used for: **affirm, commit, guarantee, obligation, pledge, warranty.**

■ [**true** + a gesture seeming to seal a promise in the hand] Bring the extended right index finger, palm facing left and finger pointing up, from in front of the lips downward, changing into an *open hand* and placing the palm of the right hand on the index-finger side of the left *S hand* held in front of the body, palm facing right.

**promote**[1] *v.* To raise in importance; advance: *promoted to a new job.* Related form: **promotion** *n.* Same sign used for: **rank.**

■ [**advanced** formed with a repeated movement to indicate levels of promotion] Move both *bent hands,* palms facing each other, from near each side of the head upward in a series of deliberate arcs.

**promote**[2] *v.* See sign for ADVANCED. Related form: **promotion** *n.*

**prompt** *adj.* Quick or on time: *a prompt response.* Same sign used for: **punctual.**

■ [**fast** + **on** + **time**[2]] Beginning with the thumbs of both *A hands* tucked under the index fingers, palms facing each other in front of the body, flick the thumbs out while twisting the wrists quickly forward. Next bring the palm of the right *open hand* downward across the back of the left *open hand* held in front of the body, both palms facing down. Then tap the index finger of the right *X hand,* palm facing down, with a double movement on the wrist of the left *open hand* held across the body, palm facing down.

**promptly** *adv.* See sign for REGULAR.

**prone** *v.* See signs for CATCH[3], TEND.

**pronounce** *v.* To articulate the sounds, words, sentences, etc., of speech: *Pronounce your words carefully.*

■ [Initialized sign similar to sign for **say**] Move the middle finger of the right *P hand,* palm facing in, upward in front of the lips in an upward double arc in front of the lips.

**proof** *n.* Evidence establishing the truth or believability of something: *to show some proof that they can do the job.* Related form: **prove** *v.* Same sign used for: **evidence.**

■ [The hand seems to bring something forward to present to another as proof] Move the fingertips of the right *open hand,* palm facing in, from in front of the mouth downward, ending with the back of the right hand on the palm of the left *open hand,* both palms facing up in front of the chest.

**propaganda** *n.* See sign for ADVERTISE.

**proper** *adj.* See signs for APPROPRIATE, FANCY. Related form: **properly** *adv.*

**property** *n.* See sign for LAND[1].

**prophecy** *n.* See sign for PREDICT.

**proportion** *n.* See sign for ACCORDING TO.

**proposal**[1] *n.* A formal plan or suggestion: *She presented her proposal to the board of directors.* Related form: **propose** *v.*

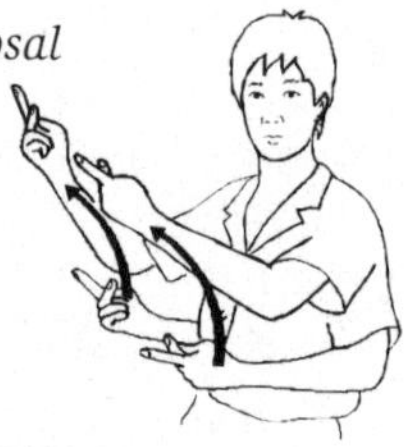

■ [Initialized sign similar to sign for **suggest**] Beginning with both *P hands* in front of each side of the body, palms facing each other, move the hands upward and forward in simultaneous arcs.

**proposal**[2] *n.* See sign for SUGGEST. Related form: **propose** *v.*

**prose** *n.* See sign for STORY.

**prosecute**[1] *v.* To pursue a civil or criminal action against someone: *prosecute the case in a court of law.* Related form: **prosecution** *n.* Same sign used for: **suit.**

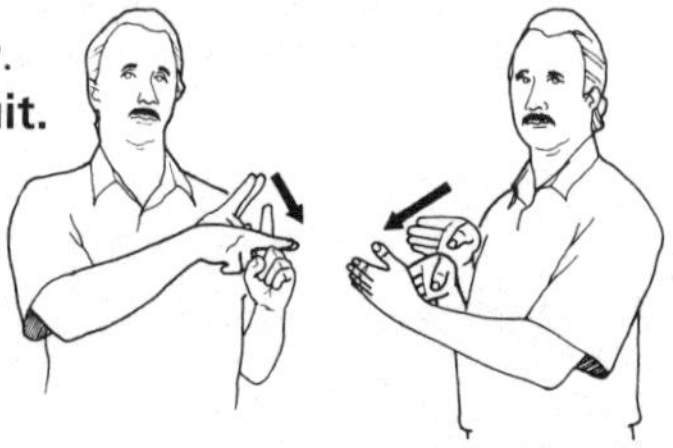

■ [**file** + **against**] Move the fingers of the right *V hand,* palm facing forward, downward on each side of the extended left index finger, pointing up in front of the chest. Then hit the fingertips of the right *bent hand* into the left *open hand,* palm right and fingers pointing forward.

**prosecute**[2] *v.* See sign for TORTURE. Related form: **prosecution** *n.*

**prosper** *v.* To be successful; thrive: *to prosper in business.* Related form: **prosperity** *n.*

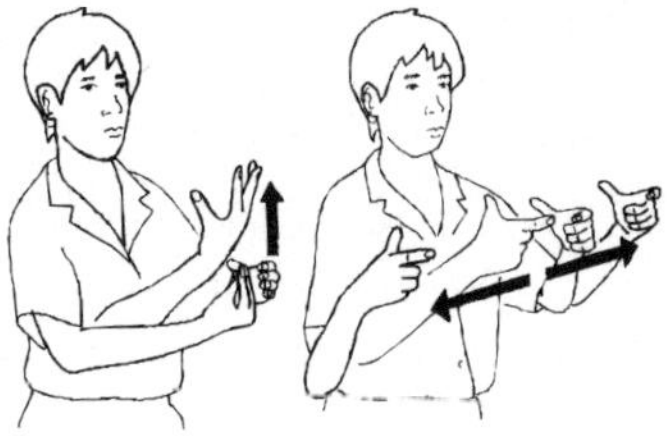

■ [**grow** + **big**] Bring the right *flattened O hand,* palm facing in and fingers pointing up, upward through the left *C hand,* palm facing right, while spreading the right fingers into a *curved 5 hand* in front of the chest. Then, beginning with both *modified C hands* together in front of the chest, palms facing each other, bring the hands apart, ending in front of each shoulder.

**prosperous** *adj.* See sign for RICH.

**prostitute** *n.* A person who has sexual relations with others for money: *prostitutes loitering on the street corner.* Same sign used for: **whore.**

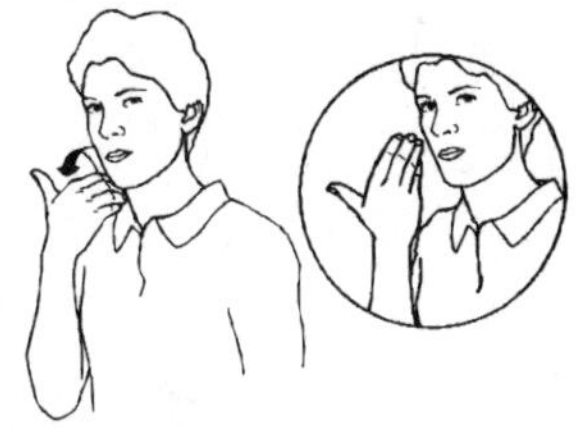

■ Twist the back of the fingers of the right *bent hand,* palm facing back, forward on the right side of the chin with a double movement, changing into an *open hand* each time.

**protect**[1] *v.* To keep safe from harm or injury: *The car seat protected the baby from sudden stops.*

■ [The hands seem to block oneself from harm] With the wrists of both *open hands* crossed in front of the chest, palms facing in opposite directions, move the hands forward a short distance.

**protect**[2] *v.* See sign for DEFEND.

**protest**[1] *n.* A strong expression of objection, dissent, etc.: *He voiced his protest.* Same sign used for: **complaint, grievance, objection.**

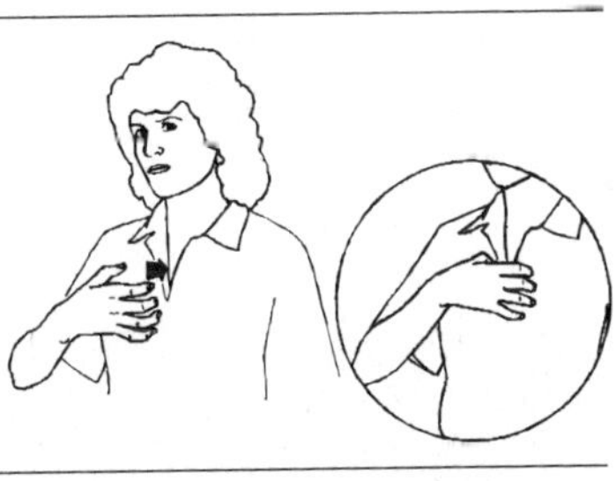

■ Strike the fingertips of the right *curved 5 hand* against the center of the chest with a double movement.

**protest**[2] *n.* **1.** An organized public demonstration against a cause or policy: *Students staged antiwar protests.* —*v.* **2.** To engage in such protests: *to protest company rules.* Same sign used for: **rebel, rebellion, revolt, revolution, strike.**

■ [Natural gesture indicating that a person is on strike] Beginning with the right *S hand* in front of the right shoulder, palm facing back, twist the hand sharply forward.

**protest**[3] *v.* See signs for COMPLAIN, PICKET.

**proud** *adj.* Feeling pleased about oneself, one's accomplishments, or the achievements of another: *I'm proud of your efforts.* Related form: **pride** *n.* Same sign used for: **arrogant.**

■ Move the thumb of the right *10 hand,* palm facing down, from the center of the lower chest upward with a smooth movement.

**provide** *v.* See signs for GIVE, SUGGEST.

**prune** *v.* To cut off excess material from: *to prune the bushes.* Same sign used for: **trim.**

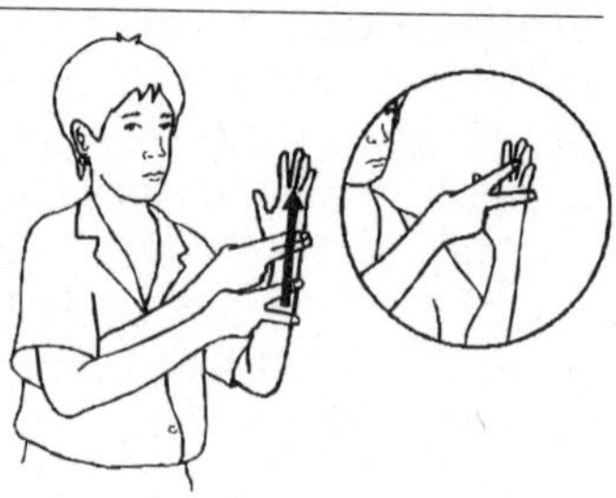

■ [The left hand represents a tree and the right hand shows trimming it] With the bent left arm held up in front of the left side of the body, palm facing right, move the fingers of the right *V hand,* palm facing left, up the left arm while closing the fingers together with a repeated movement.

**pry** *v.* See sign for NOSY[2].

**Psalms** *n.* See sign for POEM.

**pseudo** *adj.* See sign for FAKE[2].

**psychiatry** *n.* The branch of medicine dealing with mental disorders: *to study psychiatry to help people with serious mental illnesses.*

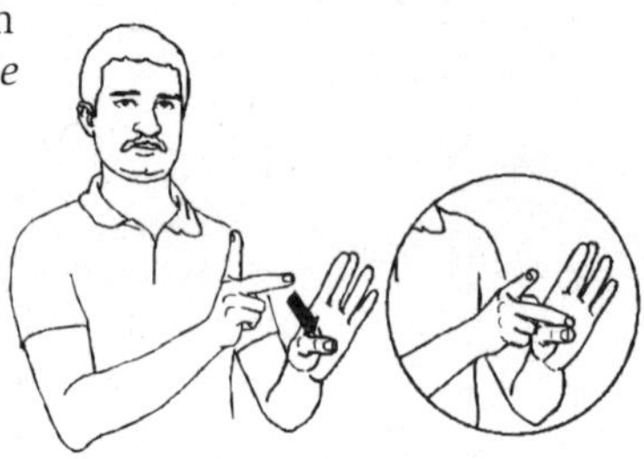

■ [Initialized sign similar to sign for **psychology**] Tap the middle finger of the right *P hand,* palm facing left, in the crook between the thumb and index finger of the left *open hand,* palm facing forward, with a double movement.

**psychology** *n.* The science dealing with the mind and human behavior: *to study psychology and become a therapist.*

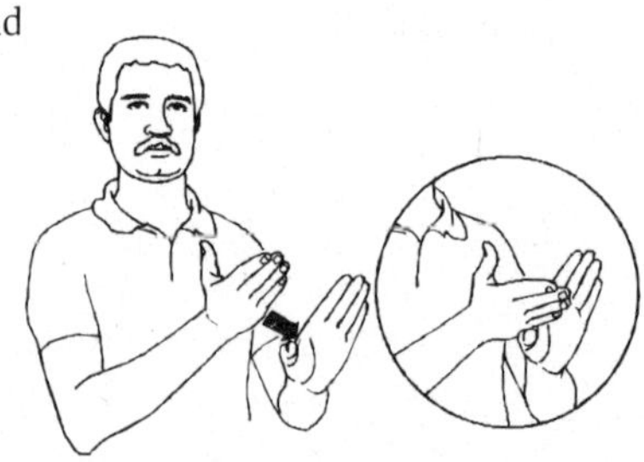

■ Tap the little-finger side of the right *open hand,* palm angled left, in the crook between the thumb and the index finger of the left *open hand,* palm facing forward, with a double movement.

**public** *n.* See signs for HEARING, PEOPLE.

**publication** *v.* See sign for NEWSPAPER.

**publicize**[1] *v.* To give publicity to; advertise: *to publicize the fall dance.* Related form: **publicity** *n.*

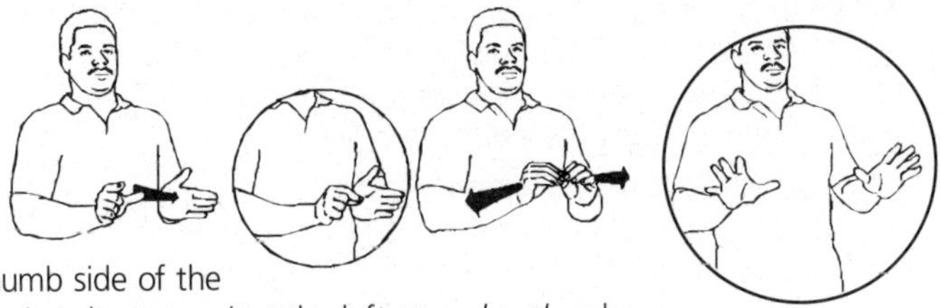

■ [**newspaper** + **spread**] Bring the thumb side of the right *G hand,* palm facing down, against the left *open hand,* palm facing up, while pinching the right index finger and thumb together with a double movement. Then, beginning with the fingers of both *flattened O hands* touching in front of the body, palms facing down, move the hands outward to each side while opening into *5 hands* in front of each side of the body.

**publicize**[2] *v.* See sign for ADVERTISE. Related form: **publicity** *n.*

**puddle** *n.* A small pool of water, especially rainwater: *Try to avoid stepping in a puddle.* Same sign used for: **pond.**

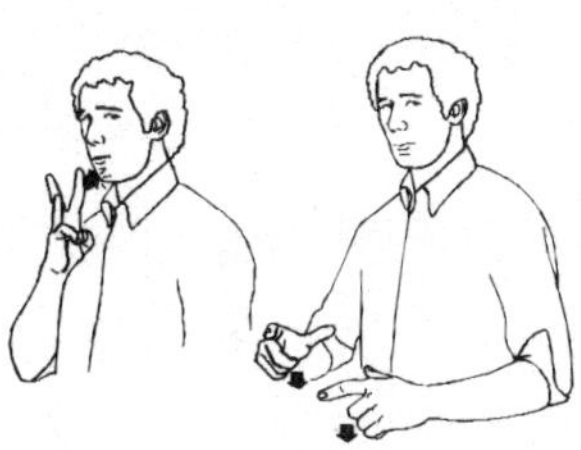

■ [**water** + indicating the size of a puddle] Tap the index-finger side of the right *W hand,* palm facing left, against the chin with a double movement. Then move both *modified C hands,* palms facing each other, downward in front of the chest a short distance.

**pull** *v.* See signs for DRAG, HAUL.

**pulse** *n.* The beating of the heart as reflected in the regular throbbing of the arteries: *a rapid pulse.* Same sign used for: **palpitate, throb.**

■ [Mime taking one's pulse] Place the fingertips of the right *flattened O hand,* palm facing down, on the upturned left wrist.

**pumice** *n.* An abrasive volcanic stone used for polishing: *Pumice is used to polish metal.* Same sign used for: **emery board, nail file.**

■ [Represents filing one's nails on pumice] Move the fingertips of the left *curved hand* downward with a repeated movement on the knuckles of the right *curved hand,* both palms facing in.

**pump** *n.* A machine used for forcing liquids or gases into or out of something: *a water pump.*

■ [Mime using a water pump] With the right elbow extended, move the right *A hand,* palm facing in, up and down in front of the right side of the body with a double movement.

**pumpkin** *n.* A large, round, edible, orange-colored fruit, the shell of which is traditionally carved into a jack-o'-lantern: *to carve a pumpkin at Halloween.* Same sign used for: **melon.**

- [Represents testing a pumpkin's ripeness by thumping it] With a double movement, flick the middle finger of the right *8 hand,* palm facing down, off the back of the left *S hand,* palm facing down, bouncing the right hand up slightly each time.

**punch** *n.* **1.** A hard, thrusting blow with the fists: *grew angry and gave the wall a resounding punch.* —*v.* **2.** To hit with the fists: *punched him in the eye.* Same sign used for: **hit.**

- [Mime giving a punch] Beginning with the right *S hand* in front of the right shoulder, palm facing forward, move the hand upward and forward in a large arc.

**punctual** *adj.* See sign for PROMPT.

**punish** *v.* **1.** To deal with harshly or strictly, especially as repayment for a crime or offense: *The justice system will punish the criminal.* **2.** To inflict a penalty for an offense or fault: *The little boy was punished for spilling his milk.* Same sign used for: **penalize, penalty.**

- Strike the extended right index finger, palm facing left, downward across the elbow of the left bent arm.

**puny** *adj.* See sign for TINY[1].

**pupil**[1] *n.* A young student, as in school or learning under a private tutor: *The shorter pupils sat in the front row.* Same sign used for: **student.**

- [**learn** + **person marker**] Beginning with the fingertips of the right *flattened C hand,* palm facing down, on the upturned palm of the left open hand, bring the right hand up while closing the fingers and thumb into a *flattened O hand* near the forehead. Then move both open hands, palms facing each other, downward along each side of the body.

**pupil**[2] *n.* The opening in the center of the iris of the eye that expands and contracts to allow light to enter: *dilated pupils.*

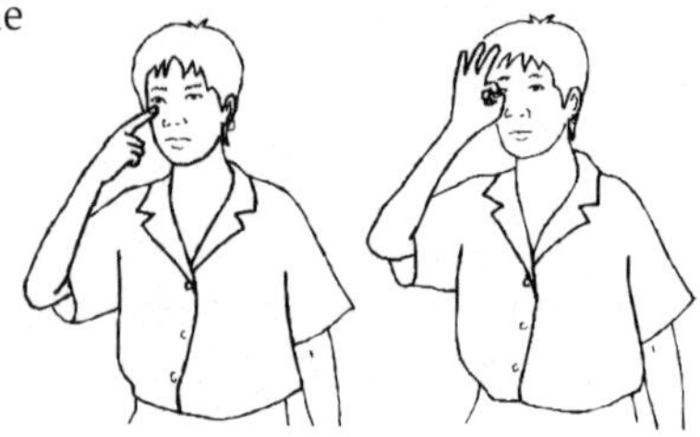

- [**eye**[1] + the shape of one's pupil in the eye] Point the extended right index finger to the right eye, palm facing in. Then place the thumb side of the right *F hand*, palm facing left, in front of the right eye.

**puppet** *n.* A small movable doll manipulated by rods, wires, the hands, etc., to emulate a living creature: *to watch the puppets in the show.* Same sign used for: **marionette.**

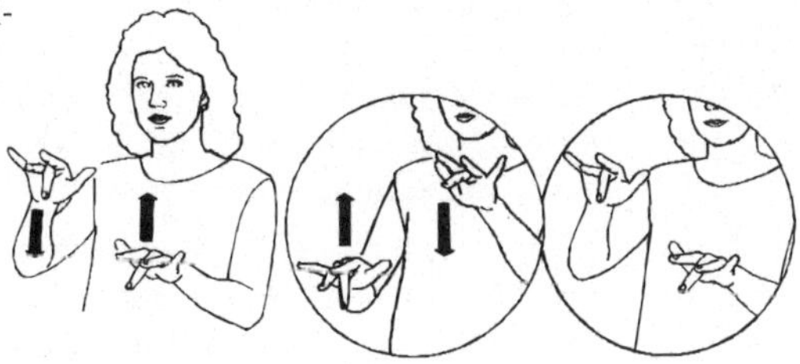

■ [Mime the action of moving a puppet's strings] With the bent middle fingers of both *5 hands* pointing down in front of each side of the chest, palms facing down, move the hands up and down with an alternating movement in front of each side of the chest.

**purchase** *v.* See sign for BUY.

**pure** *adj.* **1.** Perfectly clean; free from contaminants: *pure water.* **2.** Free from adulterating matter: *pure platinum.* **3.** Innocent; wholesome; undefiled: *a pure mind.* Related forms: **purification** *n.*, **purify** *v.*

■ [Initialized sign similar to sign for **clean**] Move the middle finger of the right *P hand* from the heel to off the fingertips of the upturned left *open hand.*

**purge** *v.* **1.** To make clean; rid of undesirable elements: to *purge the chemical mixture of all impurities.* **2.** To free of difficult or troublesome people, activities, etc.: *to purge the office of petty thieves.* Same sign used for: **remove.**

■ [Similar to sign for **remove** except mime throwing whatever is removed over the shoulder] Bring the fingertips of the right *curved 5 hand,* palm facing down, downward to the palm of the left *open hand* held in front of the body, palm facing up, while closing the right hand into an *A hand* as it lands on the left palm. Then bring the right hand upward in a large arc while twisting the palm backward and opening the fingers into a *5 hand* as it goes over the right shoulder.

**purple** *n.* **1.** A dark color made by mixing red and blue: *You can tell from my outfit that I like purple.* —*adj.* **2.** Of a purple color: *a purple dress.*

■ [Initialized sign] Shake the right *P hand,* palm facing down, back and forth in front of the right side of the body with a double movement.

**purpose** *n.* See sign for MEAN².

**purse** *n.* A bag or rigid case, often with a handle or strap, for carrying personal articles, as a wallet or cosmetics; handbag: *to carry a purse.* Same sign used for: **luggage, pocketbook, suitcase.**

■ [Mime holding a purse] Shake the right *S hand,* palm facing left, up and down near the right side of the waist with the elbow bent.

**pursue** *v.* See signs for APPROACH[1], CHASE.

**push**[1] *v.* **1.** To press against something in order to move it: *Push the stuck door harder.* **2.** To move something by pushing: *to push the cart.*

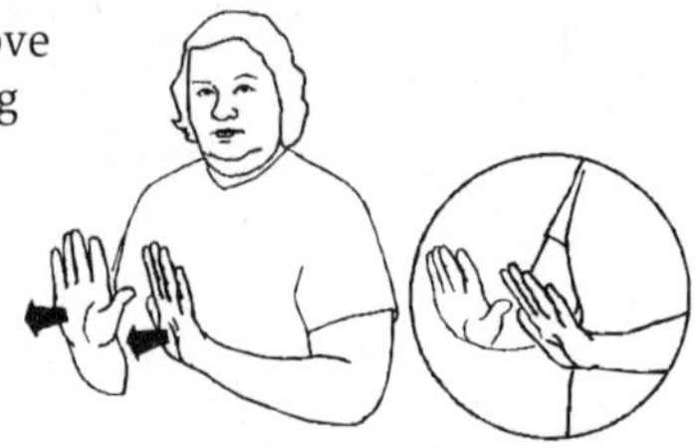

■ [Mime pushing something] Move the palms of both *open hands,* palms facing forward, with a deliberate movement forward in front of the chest.

**push**[2] *v.* See sign for SHOVE.

**pushpin** *n.* See sign for THUMBTACK.

**put** *v.* To move into a particular location; place: *Put away the toys. Put the package on the table.* Same sign used for: **install, mount, place, set.**

■ [The hands seem to take an object and put it in another location] Beginning with both *flattened O hands* in front of the body, palms facing down, move the hands upward and forward in a small arc.

**put aside** *v. phrase.* See sign for ASIDE.

**put away** *v. phrase.* See sign for ASIDE.

**put down**[1] *v. phrase.* To write down: *Put down my address.* Same sign used for: **document, record.**

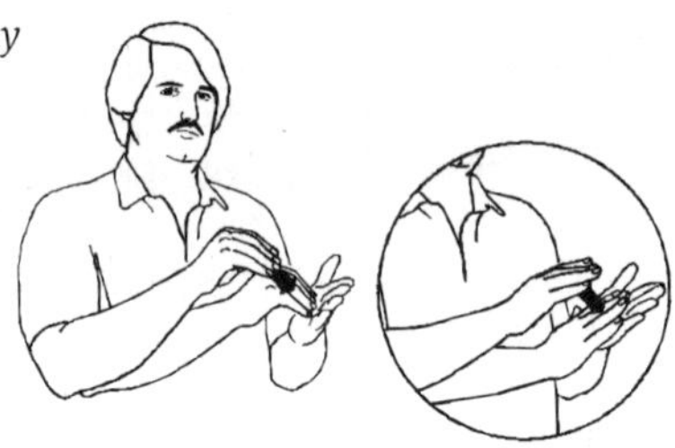

■ [The hand seems to put something on a list] Touch the fingertips of the right *flattened O hand,* palm facing down, to the palm of the left *open hand,* palm facing up. Then slap the palm of the right *open hand* against the left palm.

**put down**[2] *v. phrase.* To pay as a deposit: *to put down some money on the car.*

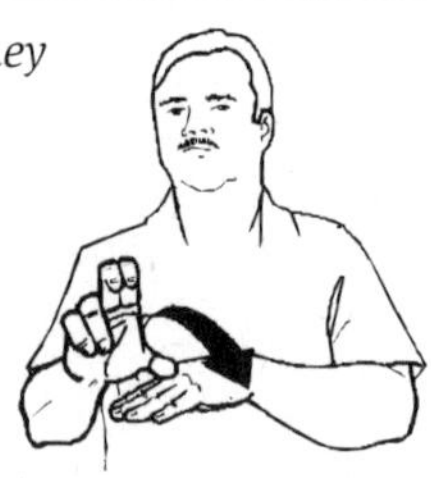

■ [Represents putting a stack of money down as a deposit] Move the right *curved 3 hand,* palm facing forward, from in front of the chest in an arc over the back of the left *open hand,* palm facing down and fingers pointing right.

**put down**[3] *v. phrase.* See sign for INSULT.

**put off** *v. phrase.* See signs for DEFER[1], POSTPONE.

**put together** *v. phrase.* See sign for ASSEMBLE[1].

**put up with** *v. phrase.* See sign for PATIENT[1].

**putrid** *adj.* See sign for STINK.

**putty** *n.* A mixture used for fastening panes of glass in a window or filling small holes in plaster or woodwork: *to seal the hole with putty.*

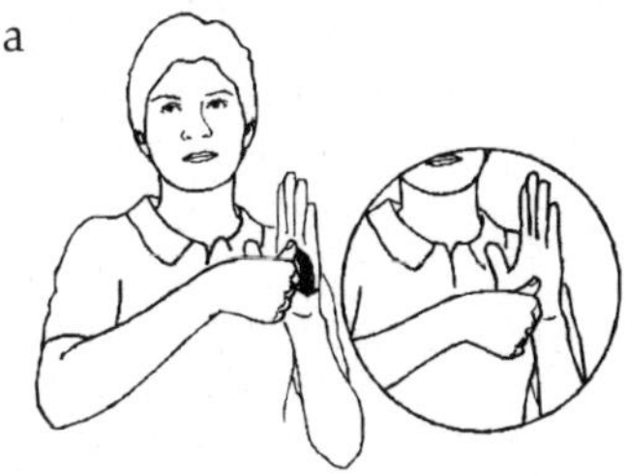

■ [Mime pushing putty into a hole in the wall] With the thumb of the right *A hand* against the palm of the left *open hand,* palm facing right and fingers pointing up, twist the right hand forward and downward with a double movement.

**puzzle** *n.* A problem or game to be solved, put together, filled in, etc.: *Put the pieces in the jigsaw puzzle. She does the Sunday crossword puzzle in ink.* Same sign used for: **jigsaw puzzle.**

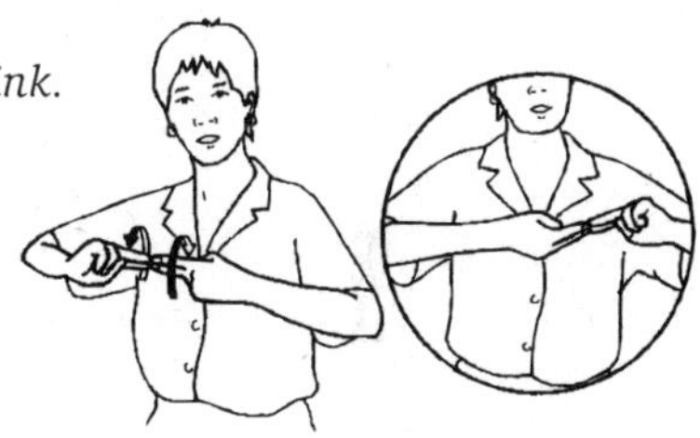

■ [Represents fitting the pieces of a puzzle together] Beginning with the extended fingertips of both *H hands* touching in front of the chest, right palm facing forward and left palm facing in, twist the hands in opposite directions to reverse positions with a double movement.

**puzzled** *adj.* A condition of being confused or perplexed: *You look puzzled about what he said.* Same sign used for: **bewildered, paradox, perplexed.**

■ [Indicates a question in the mind] Beginning with the extended right index finger in front of the forehead, palm facing forward and finger angled up, bring the back of the right hand against the forehead while bending the finger into an *X hand.*

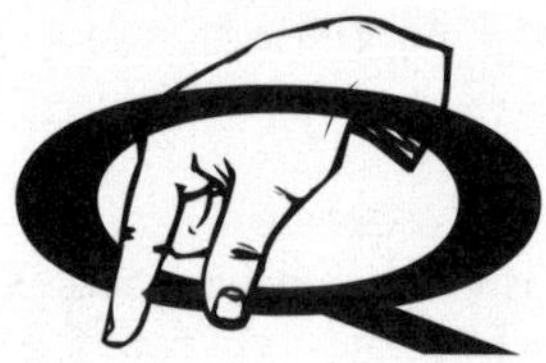

**qualification** *n.* A characteristic or accomplishment that fits someone for a job, office, award, etc.: *The interviewee has good qualifications for the job.* Related form: **qualify.**

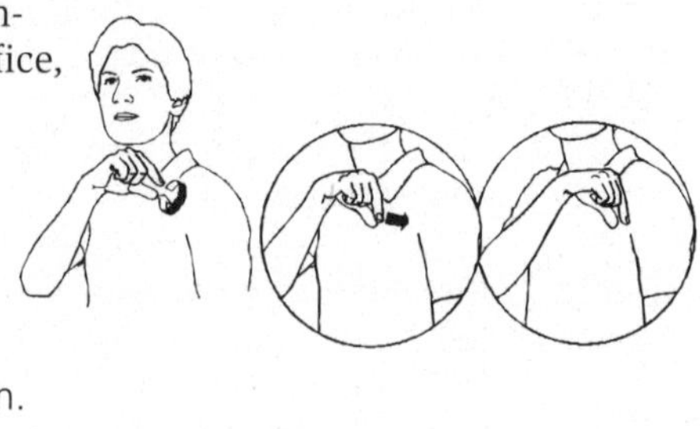

- [Initialized sign similar to sign for **character**[1]] Move the right *Q hand* in a small circle and then back against the right side of the chest, palm facing down.

---

**quarrel** *v.* See sign for ARGUE.

---

**quarter**[1] *n.* **1.** One of the four equal periods of play in certain games: *losing by 12 after the third quarter.* **2.** One of four terms of instruction in a school year: *my grades for the first quarter.*

- [Initialized sign] Move the right *Q hand,* palm facing down, in a small circle in front of the right side of the body with a double movement.

---

**quarter**[2] *n.* A coin equal to one fourth of a dollar: *change for a quarter.* Same sign used for: **twenty-five cents.**

- [**cent** + **twenty-five**] Beginning with the extended right index finger touching the right side of the forehead, palm facing left and finger pointing up, twist the hand forward while changing into a *5 hand* with a wiggling bent middle finger, palm facing forward.

---

**quarter**[3] *n.* See sign for ONE FOURTH.

---

**quarterly** *adj.* Occurring at the end of each quarter of a year: *the quarterly business report.* —*adv.* Once each quarter: *The interest is calculated quarterly.* Same sign used for: **every three months.**

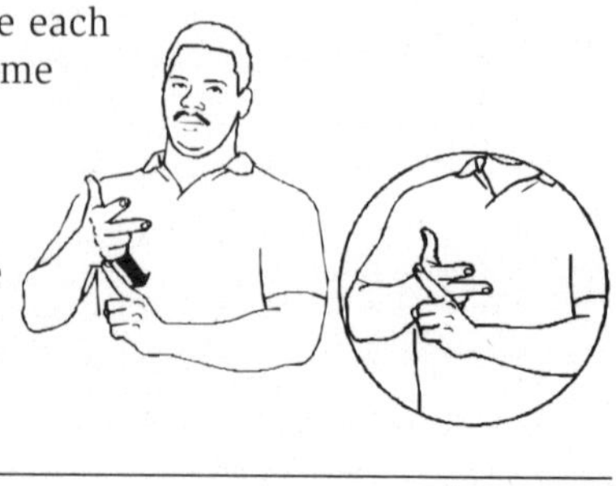

- [**three** + **month** are signed simultaneously] Move the right *3 hand,* palm facing in, with a double movement down the thumb side of the extended left index finger pointing up in front of the chest, palm facing right.

---

**queen** *n.* **1.** A woman who rules a country; female sovereign: *the Queen of England.* **2.** The wife of a king: *The king asked her to become his queen.*

- [Initialized sign similar to sign for **king**] Move the right *Q hand,* palm facing left, from touching the left side of the chest near the shoulder, downward to touch again near the right side of the waist.

**queer**[1] *adj.* See sign for STRANGE.

**queer**[2] *n.* See sign for GAY[1]. (*Slang: disparaging and offensive.*)

**query** *v.* **1.** To inquire: *to query as to whether or not the class is available.* **2.** To ask questions of: *to query the witness.* See also sign for QUESTION.

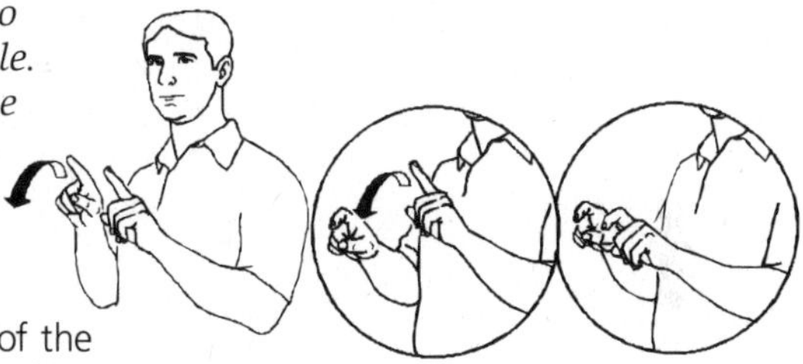

- [Form a question mark with each hand] Beginning with both extended index fingers pointing up in front of each side of the chest, palms facing forward, move the right hand down while bending into an *X hand* and then the left hand down while bending into an *X hand,* ending with both *X hands* in front of the chest.

**question** *n.* **1.** Something asked in order to get information: *Ask your question before the teacher leaves.* —*v.* **2.** To ask questions of: *The policeman questioned the driver about the accident.* See also sign for QUERY.

- [Draw a question mark in the air] Move the extended right index finger from pointing forward in front of the right shoulder, palm facing down, downward with a curving movement while retracting the index finger and then pointing it straight forward again at the bottom of the curve.

**queue** *v.* See sign for LINE UP.

**quick** *adj., adv.* See signs for ABRUPT, FAST. Related form: **quickly** *adv.*

**quick-witted** *adj.* See sign for SMART[1].

**quiet**[1] *adj.* **1.** Relatively free of sound or movement: *a quiet room.* **2.** Making very little noise: *subdued, quiet children.* See also sign for **silent.** Same sign used for: **calm, calm down, passive, peaceful, serene, silence, silent, still, tranquil.**

- [Natural gesture requesting others to be quiet] Beginning with both *B hands* crossed in front of the upper chest, palms angled outward in either direction, bring the hands downward and outward, ending with both *B hands* in front of each side of the waist, palms facing down.

**quiet**[2] *adj.* (alternate sign) Same sign used for: **silent, still.**

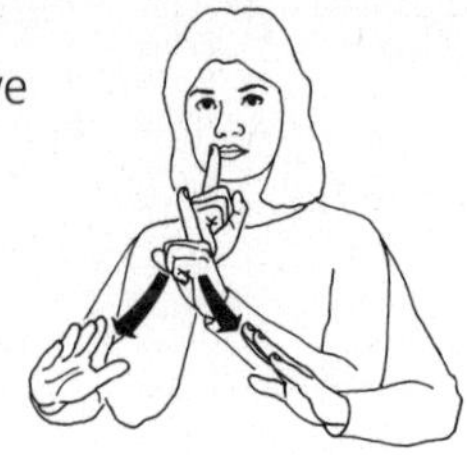

- [The fingers seem to silence the mouth, and the hands move down as if to show quiet] Beginning with both extended index fingers pointing up in front of the mouth, right hand closer to the face than the left hand and palms facing in opposite directions, bring the hands downward and outward, ending with both *open hands* in front of each side of the chest, palms angled down.

**quiet down** *v. phrase.* See sign for SETTLE.

**quit**[1] *v.* To stop: *quit working.*

- [Formed with the opposite movement as **join** and indicates withdrawing involvement with others] Beginning with the extended fingers of the right *H hand* inside the opening of the left *O hand* held in front of the body, palm facing right, bring the right hand upward, ending in front of the right shoulder, palm facing left and fingers pointing up.

**quit**[2] *v.* See signs for RESIGN, STOP[1].

**quiver** *v.* See sign for SHIVER.

**quiz** *n., v.* See sign for TEST.

**quota** *n.* See sign for RESTRICT.

**quotation**[1] *n.* Someone else's spoken or written words, as from a book or speech, repeated exactly: *"To be or not to be" is a famous quotation.* Related form: **quote** *n., v.* Same sign used for: **subject, theme, topic.**

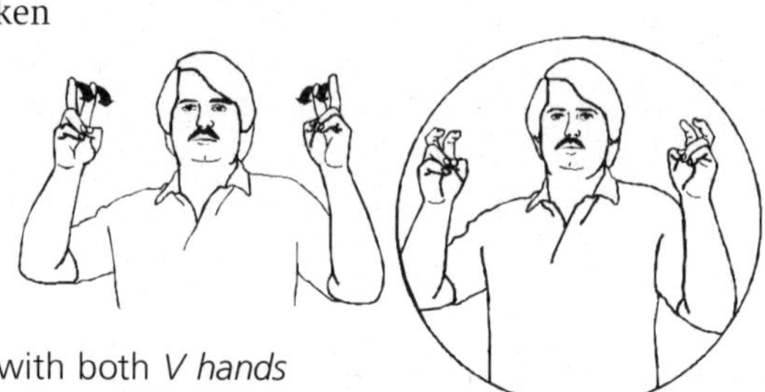

- [Natural gesture forming quotation marks in the air] Beginning with both *V hands* held near each side of the head, palms angled forward and fingers pointing up, bend the fingers downward with a double movement.

**quotation**[2] *n.* See sign for EXCERPT. Related form: **quote** *n., v.*

**quotes** *pl. n.* See sign for TITLE.

**rabbit** *n.* A small animal with soft fur and long ears: *fed their pet rabbit lettuce.* Same sign used for: **hare.**

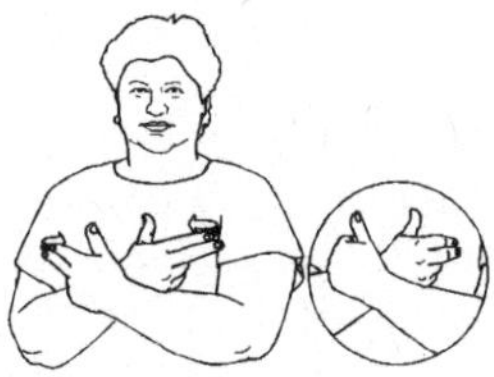

■ [Represents a rabbit's ears] With the *U hands* crossed above the wrists, palms facing in and thumbs extended, bend the fingers of both hands forward and back toward the chest with a double movement.

**raccoon** *n.* A small furry animal with a black, masklike band across the eyes and a bushy, ringed tail that lives in wooded areas and is active at night: *a raccoon in the tree.*

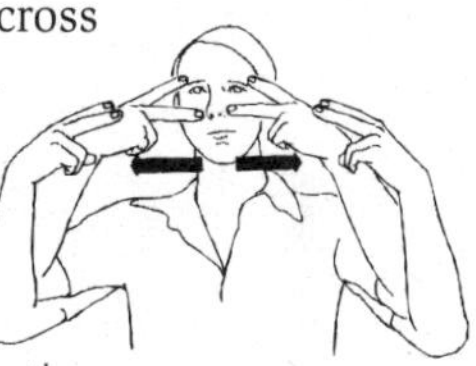

■ [Indicates the distinctive coloring around the eyes of a raccoon] Beginning with the fingers of both *V hands* pointing toward each other around each eye, palms facing back, bring the hands outward to each side of the head while closing the index and middle fingers of each hand.

**race**[1] *v.* To compete in a contest of speed: *to race against champions.* Same sign used for: **athletics, sports.**

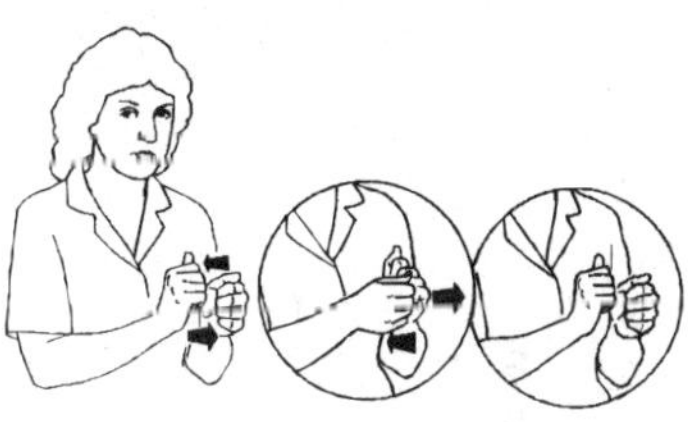

■ [The hands move back and forth as if in contention with each other in a race] With an alternating movement, move both *A hands* forward and back past each other quickly, palms facing each other in front of the body.

**race**[2] *n.* Any grouping of people based on ancestry or ethnicity: *member of the Caucasian race.* Same sign used for: **color, pigment.**

■ [**skin** + **color**] Pinch the skin of the right cheek with the index finger and thumb of the right hand, palm facing left. Then wiggle the fingers of the right *5 hand* in front of the mouth, fingers pointing up and palm facing in.

**radar** *n.* An instrument using radio waves to determine distance and direction of an object: *The ship used radar to locate the approaching plane.*

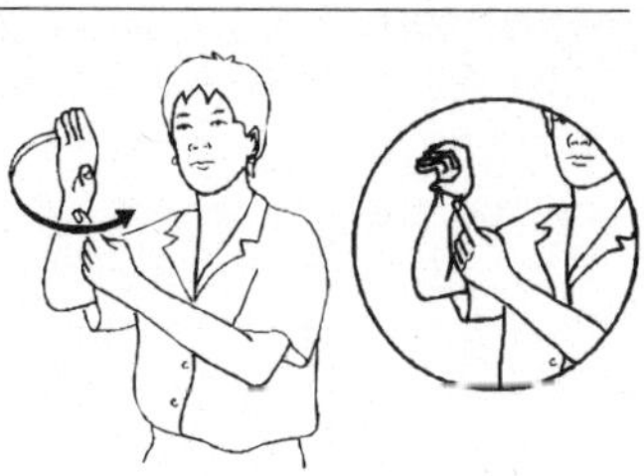

■ [Represents the screening action of a radar dish] With the extended left index finger touching the wrist of the right *C hand,* palm facing forward, twist the right wrist to move the hand outward and around.

**radiant** *adj.* See sign for BRIGHT.

**radio** *n.* **1.** A device for sending and receiving sounds by electromagnetic waves without the use of wires: *broadcast a distress signal over the ship's radio.* **2.** A similar device that receives radio broadcasts: *carries around a portable radio to listen to music.* **3.** Commercial programs broadcast for reception by a radio: *listen to the radio.*

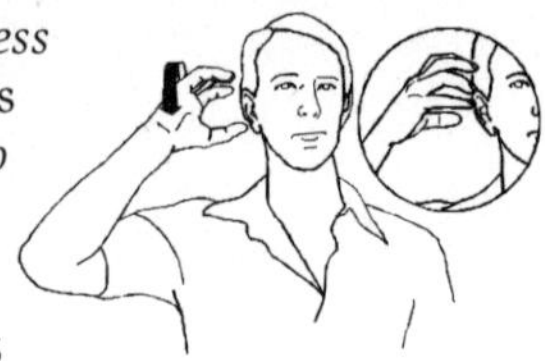

■ [Represents radio headphones on the ears] With the fingers of the right *curved 5 hand* near the right ear, twist the hand forward with a double movement.

**rage** *n.* See signs for ANGER[1,2].

**ragged** *adj.* **1.** Having loose shreds or rough projections: *a ragged edge on the paper.* **2.** (of a column of type) Set with at least one side not justified: *Set the recipes in the cookbook ragged right.* Same sign used for: **crack, cracked, jagged.**

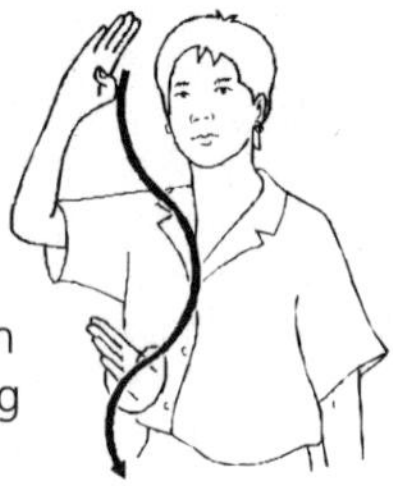

■ [Shows the shape of a ragged crack] Beginning with the right *B hand* near the right side of the head, palm facing forward and fingers pointing up, move the hand in a large jagged movement down to in front of the right side of the body, ending with the palm facing left and the fingers pointing forward.

**rah** *interj.* See sign for RALLY.

**raid** *v.* See sign for ROB.

**railroad** *n.* See sign for TRAIN.

**rain** *n.* **1.** Water falling in drops from the clouds: *walking in the rain.* —*v.* **2.** To fall in drops of water from the clouds: *It rained all day and it's still raining.*

■ [Represents raindrops falling] Bring both *curved 5 hands,* palms facing down, from near each side of the head downward to in front of each shoulder with a double movement.

**rainbow** *n.* An arch of the colors of the spectrum sometimes seen in the sky when the sun shines through mist: *to see a beautiful rainbow after the storm.*

■ [The shape of a rainbow] Beginning with the right *4 hand* in front of the left shoulder, palm facing in and fingers pointing left, bring the hand upward in front of the face, ending in front of the right shoulder, palm facing in and fingers pointing up.

**raise**[1] *v.* To move to a higher position; lift up: *to raise the flag.* Same sign used for: **get up, lift, rise.**

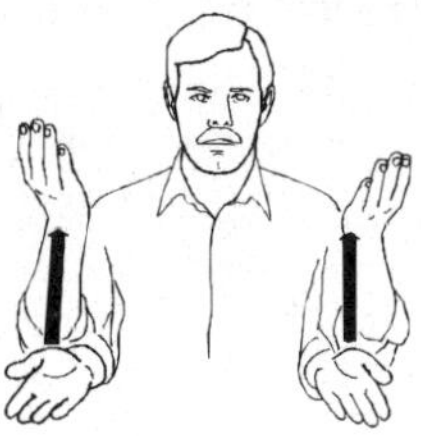

■ [Natural gesture of raising something] Beginning with both *open hands* in front of each side of the body, palms facing up, lift the hands upward to in front of each shoulder.

**raise**[2] *v.* See sign for GROW UP.

**raise**[3] *n.* See sign for INCREASE.

**rake** *n.* A long-handled agricultural tool with teeth on one end for smoothing the ground, gathering cut grass, etc.: *to rake the leaves.* Same sign used for: **hoe, plow, scratch.**

■ [Demonstrate the action of raking] Move the fingertips of the right *curved 5 hand,* palm facing down, from the fingers to the heel of the upturned left *open hand* with a double movement.

**rally** *n.* A mass meeting, usually for a common purpose: *to attend the football rally.* Same sign used for: **hurrah, rah.**

■ [Natural gesture used in leading a rally] Beginning with both *S hands* in front of each shoulder, palms facing each other, move the hands energetically forward with a double movement.

**ranch** *n.* See sign for FARM.

**random** *adj.* See signs for CIRCULATE, VARIETY.

**range** *n.* See sign for VARIETY.

**rank** *n.* See sign for PROMOTE.

**rape**[1] *n., v.* The crime of forcing a person to submit to sexual intercourse against his or her will: *She was raped by her captor.*

■ [**force** + **intercourse**] Beginning with the right *C hand* in front of the right shoulder, palm forward, and the left arm bent across the body, move the right hand downward and forward, ending with the right wrist across the left wrist, both palms down. Then bring the right *V hand* downward in front of the chest to tap against the heel of the left *V hand* with a double movement, palms facing each other.

**rape**[2] *n., v.* (alternate form)

- [Action of two bodies coming together] Beginning with both *curved 5 hands* in front of the chest, the right hand higher than the left, move the right hand down and the left hand up while changing to *S hands.*

**rape**[3] *v.* See sign for STUCK.

**rapture** *n.* Great joy; delight: *She was overcome with rapture.* Same sign used for: **absorb, evaporate, take up, vapor.**

- [Indicates something being absorbed] Beginning with both *5 hands* dangling down in front of each side of the body, palms facing in, bring the hands upward to in front of each shoulder while closing the fingers, forming *flattened O hands.*

**rascal** *n.* See sign for DEVIL.

**rat**[1] *n.* A long-tailed gnawing animal resembling a large mouse: *to see a rat scurrying around the garbage.*

- [Initialized sign similar to sign for **mouse**] Brush the index finger side of the right *R hand,* palm facing left, back and forth across the tip of the nose with a double movement.

**rat**[2] *v. Slang.* See sign for TATTLE.

**rather** *adv.* See signs for FAVORITE, PREFER[1].

**ratify** *v.* See sign for PASS. Related form: **ratification** *n.*

**ratio** *n.* See sign for ACCORDING TO.

**rational** *adj.* See sign for REASON.

**rationale** *n.* See sign for REASON.

**rattle** *v.* **1.** To make repeated short, sharp sounds: *The window rattled from the wind.* —*n.* **2.** A toy or instrument that makes a rattling noise when shaken: *a baby's rattle.*

- [**hear** + mime shaking a rattle] Point the extended right index finger to the right ear. Then shake the right *modified X hand* with a short repeated movement in front of the right side of the body, palm facing left.

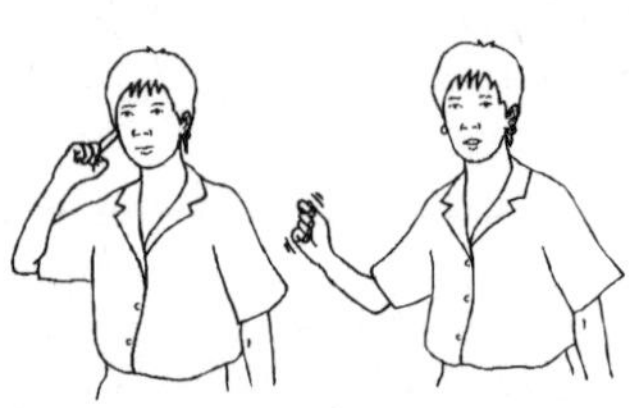

**rave** *v.* To talk excitedly and enthusiastically: *He raved on about the party.* Same sign used for: **wild.**

■ [Indicates that the head is all mixed up] Move both *5 hands* from in front of each side of the head in large repeated forward circles.

**razor** *n.* See signs for SHAVE[1,2].

**reach**[1] *v.* To touch or seize, as with an outstretched hand or other object: *to reach the books on the top shelf.*

■ [Demonstrates reaching for something] Move the right *curved 5 hand,* palm facing down, from in front of the right side of the body forward while changing into an *S hand.*

**reach**[2] *v.* See sign for ARRIVE.

**react** *v.* See sign for ANSWER, REPORT. Related form: **reaction** *n.*

**reaction** *n.* **1.** An action in response to some influence or event: *the staff's reaction to new regulations.* **2.** A physiological response, as to a disease or an irritation: *a bad reaction to smoke.* Related form: **react** *v.*

■ [Initialized sign formed similar to the sign for **opposite**] Beginning with the fingertips of both *R hands* touching in front of the chest, palms facing in, bring the hands apart to in front of each side of the chest.

**read** *v.* To get meaning from print or writing by looking: *to read a book; off in a corner reading.*

■ [Represents the movement of the eyes down a page to read it] Move the fingertips of the right *V hand,* palm facing down, from the fingertips to the heel of the left *open hand,* palm facing right.

**ready** *adj.* In a state of preparedness for action or use: *ready to go.* Related form: **readiness.**

■ [Initialized sign] Move both *R hands* from in front of the left side of the body, palms facing each other and fingers pointing forward, in a smooth movement to in front of the right side of the body.

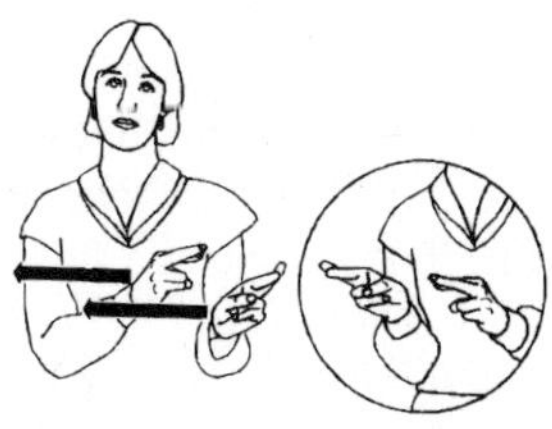

**real** *adj.* **1.** Actually existing and not imaginary: *real life.* **2.** Not artificial; authentic: *real flowers.* Same sign used for: **actual, genuine.**

■ [Movement emphasizes validity of one's statement] Move the side of the extended right index finger from in front of the mouth, palm facing left and finger pointing up, upward and forward in an arc.

**realize** *v.* See sign for REASON. Related form: **realization** *n.*

**really** *adj.* See sign for TRUTH.

**reap** *v.* See sign for COLLECT.

**rear**[1] *v.* See sign for GROW UP.

**rear**[2] *n.* See sign for BACK.

**reason** *n.* A cause or motive: *a good reason to be angry.* Related form: **reasonable** *adj.* Same sign used for: **rational, rationale, realization, realize.**

- [Initialized sign similar to sign for **think**] Move the fingertips of the right *R hand,* palm facing in, in a double circular movement in front of the right side of the forehead.

**rebel** *v.* See sign for PROTEST[2]. Related form: **rebellion.**

**recall** *v.* To call back into one's mind: *Try to recall the incident.* Same sign used for: **recollect, remember, remind.**

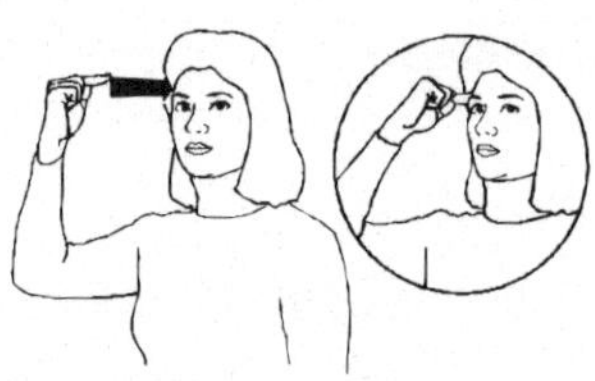

- [Represents finding something way back in one's head] Bring the extended right index finger, palm facing in, deliberately against the right side of the forehead.

**receive** *v.* See sign for GET.

**recently**[1] *adv.* At a time not long ago: *saw the movie recently.* Related form: **recent** *adj.* Same sign used for: **a few minutes ago, a while ago.**

- [Represents the minute hand on a clock moving a short distance into the past] With the little-finger side of the right *1 hand,* palm facing in and finger pointing up, against the palm of the left *open hand,* palm facing right and fingers pointing up, bend the extended right index finger back toward the chest with a double movement.

**recently**[2] *adv.* See sign for JUST. Related form: **recent.**

**reception** *n.* See sign for BANQUET.

**recess** *n.* See sign for REST.

**reckless** *adj.* See sign for CARELESS.

**recline** *v.* See sign for LIE.

**recognize** *v.* See sign for NOTICE.

**recollect** *v.* See signs for HINDSIGHT, RECALL. Related form: **recollection** *n.*

**recommend**[1] *v.* To speak in favor of: *to recommend a restaurant.* Related form: **recommendation** *n.*

■ [Initialized sign similar to sign for **suggest**] Bring both *R hands* from in front of the chest, palms facing up, forward in an upward arc.

**recommend**[2] *v.* See sign for SUGGEST.

**record**[1] *n.* A collection of related data fields treated as a unit in a computerized database: *There are ten fields in each record.*

■ [Initialized sign] With the heel of the right *R hand,* palm facing forward and fingers pointing up, on the index-finger side of the left *4 hand,* palm facing in and fingers pointing right, rock the right hand from side to side with a double movement.

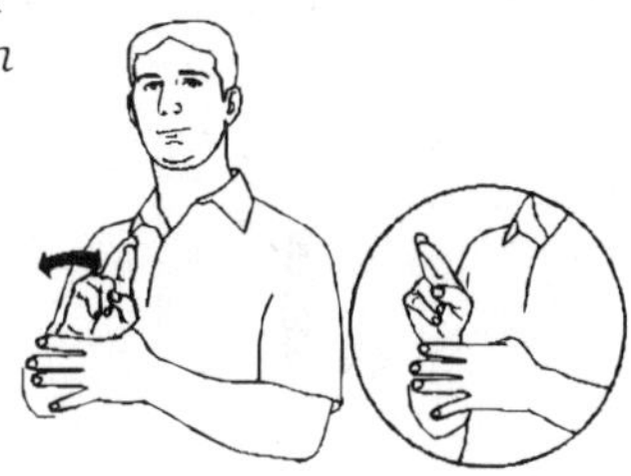

**record**[2] *n., v.* See sign for LIST.

**record**[3] *v.* See sign for PUT DOWN[1].

**recover**[1] *v.* To get well again, as after an illness: *to recover quickly from the operation.*

■ [**again** + **well**] Beginning with the bent right hand beside the left *curved hand,* both palms facing up, bring the right hand up while turning it over, ending with the fingertips of the right hand touching the palm of the left hand. Then, beginning with the fingertips of both *curved 5 hands* touching each shoulder, palms facing in, bring the hands forward with a deliberate movement while closing into *S hands.*

**recover**[2] *v.* See sign for SET UP.

**recreation** *n.* See sign for FUN.

**recruit**[1] *v.* To hire, enroll, or enlist (new members or the like): *to recruit new students.*

■ [Natural gesture for beckoning someone] Beginning with the right *X hand* in front of the right shoulder, palm facing in, swing the hand in front of the chest with a double movement, bending the index finger repeatedly as the hand moves.

**recruit**[2] *v.* See sign for BECKON.

**rectangle** *n.* A two-dimensional figure with four sides and four right angles: *A square is a rectangle with four equal sides.*

■ [Draw the shape of a rectangle in the air] Beginning with both extended index fingers side by side in front of the chest, palms angled forward and fingers pointing forward, bring the hands apart to in front of each shoulder, then straight down, and finally back together again in front of the lower chest.

**recuse** *v.* See sign for RESIGN.

**red** *adj.* Having the color of blood: *a red rose.*

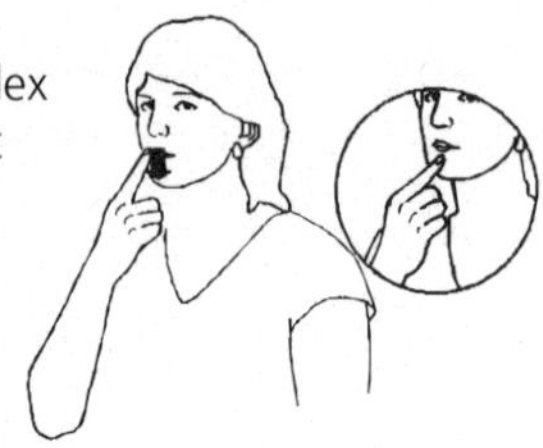

■ [Shows the redness of the lips] Bring the extended right index finger, palm facing in, from the lips downward with a short double movement.

**redeem** *v.* See sign for SAVE[1].

**reduce** *v.* See signs for BRIEF, DECREASE[1,2,3], LESS[1]. Related form: **reduction** *n.*

**refer** *v.* To send or direct to a person or place for information or help: *They'll refer you to a good doctor.*

■ [Initialized sign] Beginning with the fingers of the right *R hand,* palm facing in, on the back of the left *open hand,* palm facing in, twist the right hand forward, ending with the right palm facing down.

**referee** *n.* A person who judges the events of play according to the official rules of a game: *The referee blew the whistle to bring the action to a halt.* Same sign used for: **whistle.**

■ [Natural gesture used to whistle between one's teeth] Tap the fingertips of the right *bent V hand,* palm facing in, against the lips with a double movement.

**refill** *n.* **1.** A fresh supply of something that has been used up: *If you're out of ink, put a refill in the pen.* —*v.* **2.** To fill again: *Please refill my cup with coffee.* Same sign used for: **fill up.**

- [Shows the level of something rising to the top] Beginning with the right *open hand* in front of the waist and the left *open hand* in front of the chest, both palms facing down and fingers pointing in opposite directions, move the right hand up against the left palm.

**reflect**[1] *v.* **1.** To cast back from a surface, as light or heat: *soft light reflected from the moon.* **2.** To give back an image: *looked at his face reflected in the mirror.* Related form: **reflection** *n.*

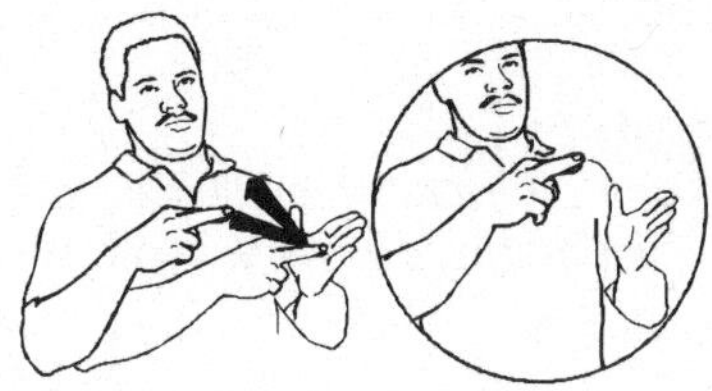

- [Initialized sign demonstrating something reflecting off another thing] With a bouncing movement, bring the extended fingertips of the right *R hand* against the open left palm and off again.

**reflect**[2] *v.* See sign for WONDER.

**refresh** *v.* See sign for COOL.

**refrigerator** *n.* An appliance run by electricity in which food is kept cool without ice: *Put the butter in the refrigerator before it melts.*

- [Initialized sign similar to sign for **door**] Beginning with the thumb side of the right *R hand,* palm facing forward and fingers pointing up, against the palm side of the left *open hand,* palm facing right and fingers pointing up, move the right hand to the right in an arc while twisting the palm back in front of the right side of the chest.

**refund** *v.* **1.** To pay back: *The store refuses to refund my money.* —*n.* **2.** Return of money paid: *You'll receive the refund in the mail.* Same sign used for: **come back, return.**

- [Shows the direction that something takes in coming back to oneself] Beginning with both extended index fingers pointing up in front of the chest, palms facing in, bring the fingers back to point at each side of the chest, palms facing down.

**refuse** *v.* See signs for DECLINE[3], WON'T.

**regarding** *prep.* See sign for ABOUT[1].

**regardless** *adv.* See sign for ANYWAY.

**region** *n.* See sign for AREA[1].

**register**[1] *v.* To enroll officially: *to register for school.* Related form: **registration** *n.*

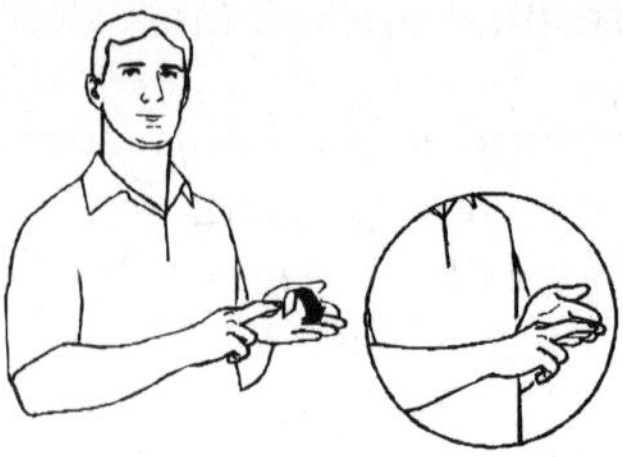

■ [Initialized sign similar to sign for **sign**[2]] Touch the fingertips of the right *R hand,* palm facing down, first to the heel and then to the fingertips of the palm of the left *open hand.*

**register**[2] *v.* See sign for SIGN[2].

**regret** *n.* See signs for REMORSE, SORRY.

**regular**[1] *adj.* Conforming to a habitual pattern, acceptable behavior, etc.: *a regular life.* Related form: **regularly** *adv.* Same sign used for: **ordinarily, ordinary, promptly, usual.**

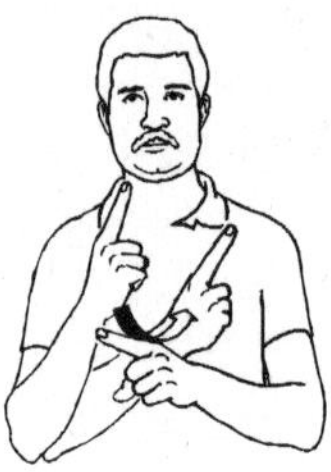

■ With the right index finger extended, brush the little-finger side of the right hand, palm facing in, across the extended left index finger, palm facing in, as the right hand moves toward the chest in a double circular movement.

**regular**[2] *adj.* See sign for CONSISTENT.

**regulate** *v.* See sign for MANAGE.

**regulation** *n.* See sign for RULE[1].

**regurgitate** *v.* See sign for VOMIT.

**rehabilitation** *n.* Restoration to good condition or appropriate functionality: *The prisoner completed his rehabilitation and was released.* Related form: **rehabilitate** *v.*

■ [Initialized sign similar to sign for **help**] With the little-finger side of the right *R hand* resting on the open left palm, raise the hands upward in front of the chest.

**rehearse**[1] *v.* To practice before performing: *rehearse the play.* Related form: **rehearsal** *n.*

■ [Initialized sign similar to sign for **practice**] Rub the heel of the right *R hand,* palm facing forward and fingers pointing up, back and forth on the back of the left *open hand* held in front of the chest, palm facing down and fingers pointing right, with a double movement.

**rehearse**[2] *v.* See sign for PRACTICE.

**reign** *v.* See sign for MANAGE.

**reindeer** *n.* See sign for DEER.

**reinforce**[1] *v.* To strengthen, as by adding support: *to reinforce the book's binding.* Same sign used for: **resource.**

■ [Initialized sign similar to sign for **help**] With the fingertips of the right *R hand,* palm facing in and fingers pointing up, touching the little-finger side of the left *S hand,* palm facing in, raise both hands upward in front of the chest.

**reinforce**[2] *v.* See sign for SUPPORT.

**reiterate** *v.* See sign for AGAIN.

**reject**[1] *v.* To refuse to accept, take, use, etc.: *rejected my help.* Same sign used for: **turn down, veto.**

■ [Natural gesture indicating turning down something] Beginning with the right *10 hand* in front of the right shoulder, elbow extended and palm facing down, twist the wrist downward, ending with the thumb pointing down and the palm facing right.

**reject**[2] *v.* To throw away: *to reject the bad copies.* See also sign for EXCLUDE.

■ [The hand brushes away something that is not desired] Brush the fingertips of the right *open hand,* palm facing in, with a forward movement from the heel to the fingertips of the left *open hand,* palm facing up.

**rejoice** *v.* See sign for CELEBRATE.

**relate** *v.* See sign for COORDINATE.

**relationship** *n.* **1.** An association or involvement: *What is your relationship to this organization?* **2.** An emotional connection between people: *involved in a relationship that may lead to marriage.* Related form: **relate** *v.* Same sign used for: **ally, connection, link, relevant, tie.**

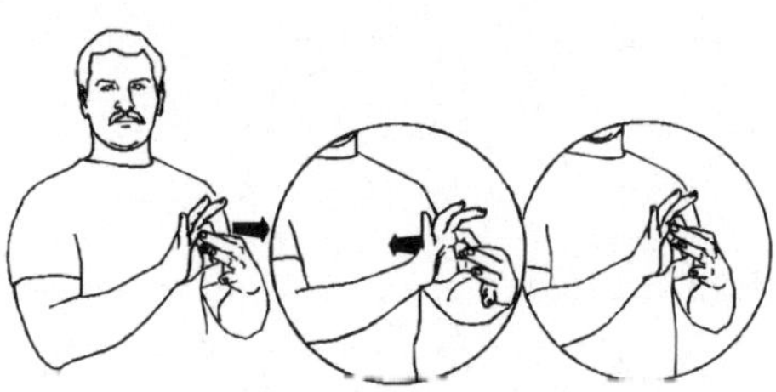

■ [Represents a link between two persons or things] With the thumbs and index fingers of both *F hands* intersecting, move the hands forward and back toward the chest with a double movement.

**relative** *n.* A person who belongs to one's family by blood, adoption, or marriage: *My relatives live nearby.*

■ [Initialized sign similar to sign for **friend**] Beginning with the extended fingers of the right *R hand,* palm facing down, across the extended fingers of the left *R hand,* palm facing up, twist the wrists in opposite directions to reverse positions.

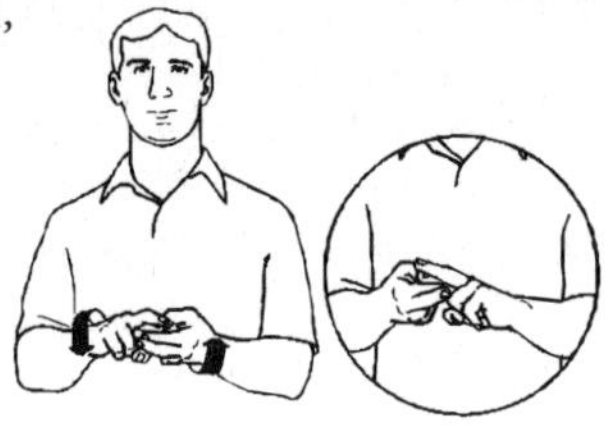

**relax** *v.* See signs for REST, SETTLE.

**relevant** *adj.* See sign for RELATIONSHIP.

**relief** *n.* An act or state of being freed from or experiencing reduction of pain or difficulty: *relief from the heat.* Related form: **relieved** *v.*

■ [Shows feeling being calmed in the body] With the index-finger sides of both *B hands* against the chest, left hand above the right hand, move the hands downward simultaneously.

**relinquish** *v.* See sign for GIVE UP.

**relocate** *v.* See sign for MOVE.

**rely** *v.* See sign for DEPEND.

**remain** *v.* See signs for CONTINUE[1], STAY.

**remark** *v.* See sign for SAY.

**remarkable** *adj.* See sign for WONDERFUL.

**remarks** *pl. n.* See signs for SAY, STORY.

**remember**[1] *v.* To call back to mind: *Remember how much we enjoyed our vacation?*

■ Move the thumb of the right *10 hand* from the right side of the forehead, palm facing left, smoothly down to touch the thumb of the left *10 hand* held in front of the body, palm facing down.

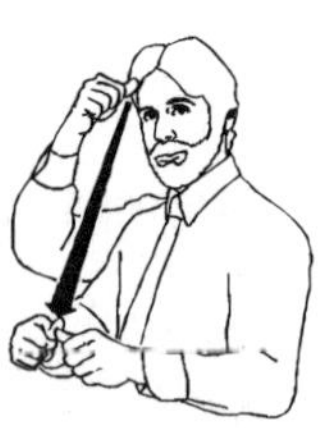

**remember**[2] *v.* See sign for RECALL.

**remind**[1] *v.* To cause (someone) to remember: *Remind me about the date of the party.*

■ [Natural gesture to tap someone to remind them of something] Tap the fingertips of the right *bent hand* with a double movement on the right shoulder, palm facing down.

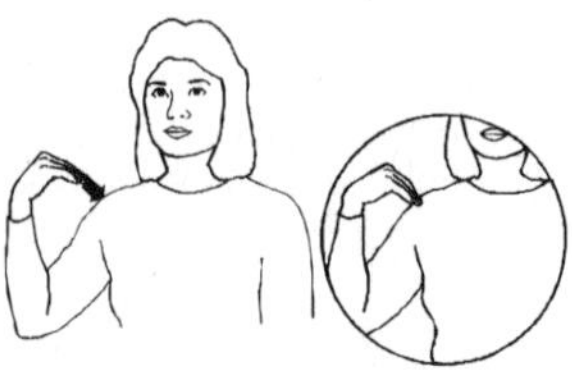

**remind**[2] *v.* (alternate sign)

■ [Tapping someone as a reminder] Tap the fingertips of the right *bent hand*, palm facing down, with a double movement against the extended left index finger held up in front of the chest.

**remind**[3] *v.* See sign for RECALL.

**remodel** *v.* See signs for IMPROVE[2], RENOVATE.

**remorse** *n.* A painful feeling of regret and guilt for having done something wrong: *The criminal showed no remorse.* Same sign used for: **regret.**

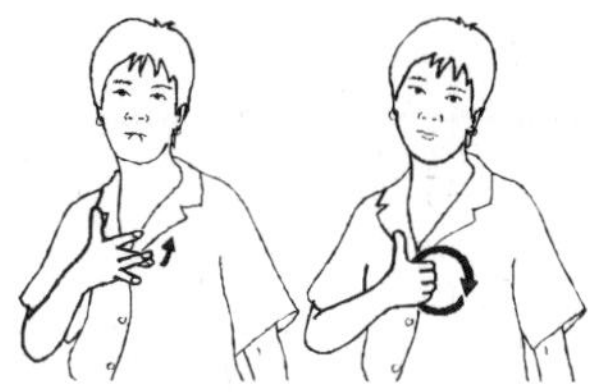

■ [**feel** + **sorry**] Move the bent middle finger of the right *5 hand,* palm facing in, upward on the chest with a repeated movement. Then rub the palm side of the right *10 hand* in a repeated circle on the left side of the chest.

**remote** *adj.* See sign for FAR.

**remote control** *n. phrase.* A device for controlling machines, appliances, etc., from a distance: *to change the channel on the TV with the remote control.*

■ [Mime operating a remote control with one's thumb] Bend the extended thumb of the right *10 hand,* palm facing in, up and down with a repeated movement in front of the right shoulder.

**remove**[1] *v.* To take away or move from a place or position: *Remove the things from the back seat of the car.* Related form: **removal** *n.* Same sign used for: **abolish, abort, abortion, deduct, deduction.**

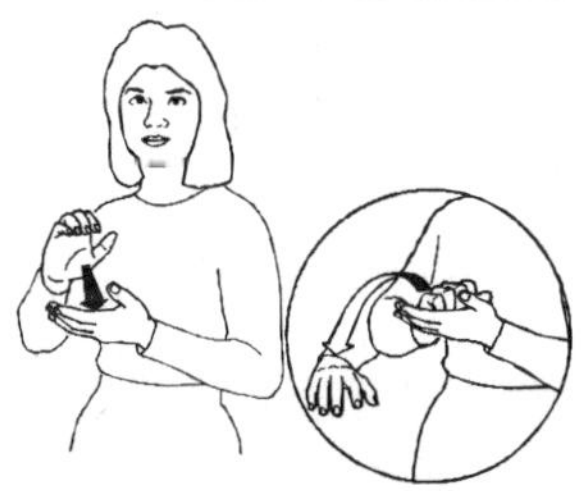

■ [Demonstrates picking something up and tossing it away to remove it] Bring the fingertips of the right *curved hand* against the palm of the left *open hand* while changing into an *A hand,* palms facing each other. Then move the right hand downward off the left fingertips while opening into a *curved 5 hand* in front of the right side of the body.

**remove**[2] *v.* See signs for ELIMINATE, PURGE, TAKE OFF.

**renovate** *v.* To restore to good condition: *to renovate the old house.* Related form: **renovation** *n.* Same sign used for: **remodel, restore.**

■ [Sign similar to **improve**[2] but made with a repeated movement] Slide the little finger side of the right *open hand,* palm facing in, in a forward circular movement on the back of the left bent arm held in front of the body with a double movement.

**rent** *v.* **1.** To make regular payments for use of (property): *to rent an apartment from the landlord.* **2.** To allow the use of in return for a payment or regular payments: *They will rent you a car at the airport.* —*n.* **3.** Payment made for use of property, a residence, etc.: *How much rent do you pay?*

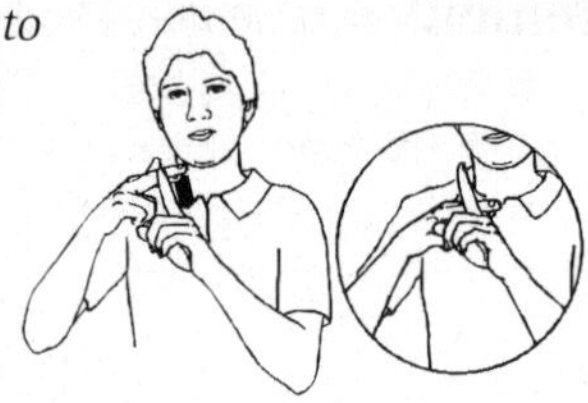

■ [Initialized sign similar to sign for **month**] Move the middle-finger side of the right *R hand,* palm facing down and fingers pointing left, downward with a double movement from the tip to the base of the extended left index finger, palm facing right and finger pointing up in front of the chest.

**repair** *v.* See sign for FIX.

**repeat** *v.* See sign for AGAIN.

**repel** *v.* See sign for ELIMINATE.

**repent** *v.* See sign for SORRY.

**replace** *v.* See sign for TRADE.

**reply** *n., v.* See signs for ANSWER, REPORT.

**report** *n.* **1.** A detailed account, as of an event: *to submit a report about the conference.* —*v.* **2.** To give a detailed account: *to report on the meeting.* Same sign used for: **react, reaction, reply, respond, response.**

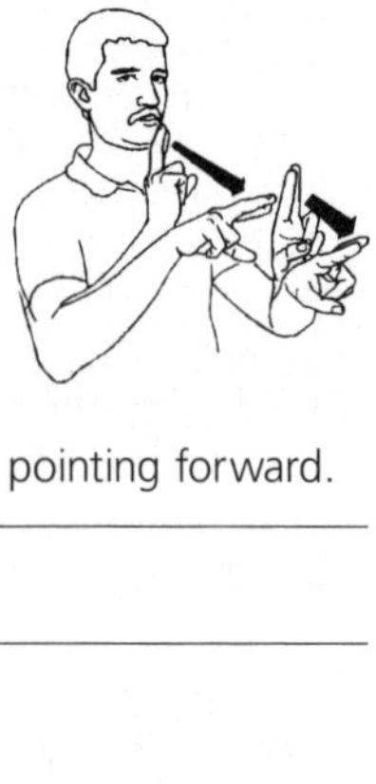

■ [Initialized sign similar to sign for **answer**] Beginning with the fingers of both *R hands* pointing up, right hand closer to the mouth than the left hand and the palms facing in opposite directions, move the hands forward and downward with a deliberate movement, ending with the palms facing down and fingers pointing forward.

**repossess** *v.* See sign for CAPTURE.

**represent** *v.* To stand for, speak for, or express: *This letter represents my opinion.*

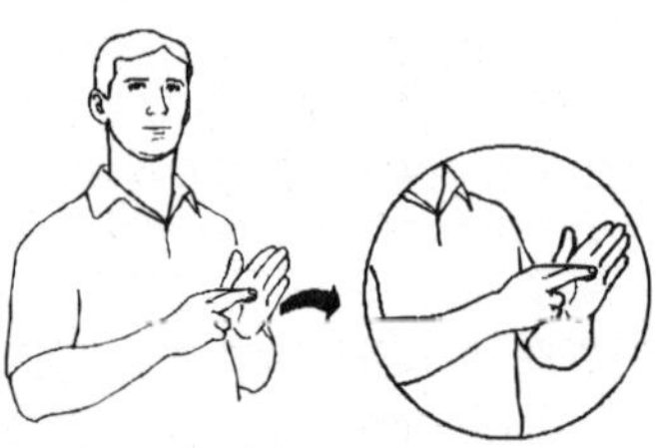

■ [Initialized sign similar to sign for **show**[1]] With the fingertips of the right *R hand,* palm facing down, against the left *open hand,* palm facing right and fingers pointing forward, move the hands forward together a short distance.

**repress** *v.* See sign for PRESSURE. Related form: **repression.**

**reprimand** *v.* See signs for SCOLD, WARN.

**reptile** *n.* See sign for SNAKE.

**republic** *n.* See sign for REPUBLICAN.

**Republican** *n.* **1.** A member of the Republican party: *The polls predict that a Republican will win the election.* Same sign used for: **republic** *n.*

- [Initialized sign] Shake the right *R hand,* palm facing forward, from side to side in front of the right shoulder with a double movement.

**reputation** *n.* **1.** The opinion of others regarding one's character, abilities, standing, etc.: *a bad reputation among his peers.* **2.** A favorable reputation; good name: *a reputation enhanced by good works.*

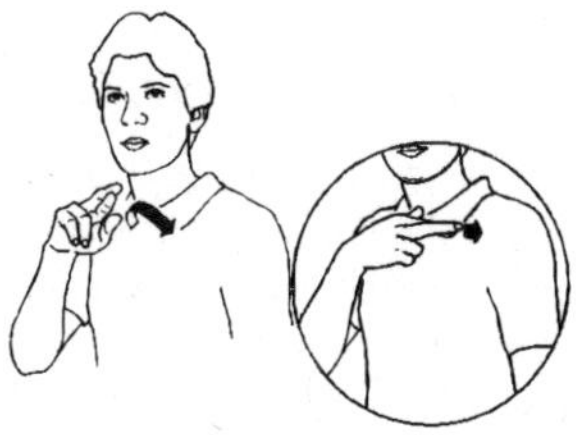

- [Initialized sign similar to sign for **character**[1]] Beginning with the right *R hand* in front of the chest, palm facing down, twist the wrist to bring the fingertips of the right *R hand* back against the left side of the chest.

**request** *v.* See sign for ASK.

**require** *v.* See sign for DEMAND.

**rescue** *v.* See sign for SAVE[1].

**research** *n.* **1.** Careful investigation to discover facts, revise theories, etc.: *engaged in medical research.* —*v.* **2.** To investigate carefully, as to discover facts: *to research the outbreak of the mysterious illness.*

- [Initialized sign similar to sign for **investigate**] Move the fingertips of the right *R hand,* palm facing down, across the open left palm from the heel to the fingertips with a double movement.

**resent** *v., n.* See sign for BOILING MAD.

**reservation** *n.* See sign for APPOINTMENT.

**residence** *n.* See sign for ADDRESS[1].

**residue**[1] *n.* Something that stays behind when the rest has been removed; remainder; remnant: *The oil spill left a residue along the shore.*

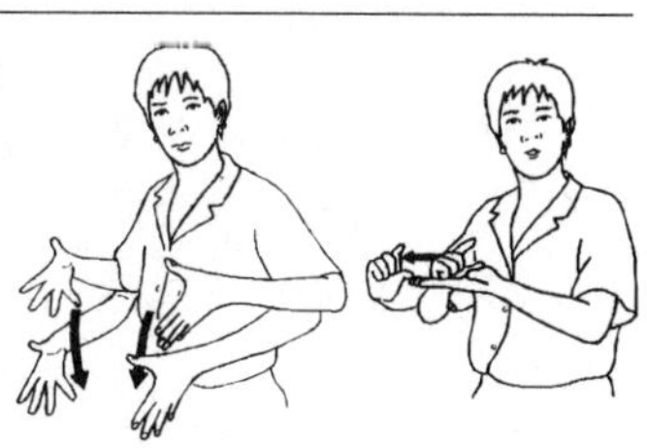

- [**leave**[2] + **layer**] Beginning with both *5 hands* in front of each side of the body, palms facing each other and fingers pointing down, thrust the fingers downward with a deliberate movement. Then slide the thumb of the right *G hand,* palm facing left, from the heel to off the fingers of the palm of the upturned left *open hand* held in front of the chest.

**residue**[2] *n.* See sign for SEDIMENT.

**resign** *v.* To give up a position, office, etc.: *to resign from his job; to resign his job.* Same sign used for: **back out, draw back, drop out, quit, recuse.**

■ [Represents pulling one's legs out of a situation] Beginning with the fingers of the right *bent U hand,* palm facing down, in the opening of the left *O hand,* palm facing right, pull the right fingers out to the right.

**resist** *v.* To oppose; fight against; combat: *to resist a bad influence.* Same sign used for: **anti-, defensive, immune, uncertain.**

■ [Natural gesture for resisting something] Move the right *S hand,* palm facing down, from in front of the right side of the body outward to the right with a deliberate movement.

**resolve** *v.* See sign for DISSOLVE.

**resource** *n.* See sign for REINFORCE.

**respect** *v.* **1.** To show honor or esteem for: *to respect your parents.* —*n.* **2.** Honor and esteem: *to show respect to older people.* Related form: **respectful** *adj.*

■ [Initialized sign similar to sign for **loyal**] Beginning with the index-finger side of the right *R hand,* palm facing left, near the right side of the forehead, bring the hand downward and forward.

**respiration** *n.* See sign for BREATH.

**respond** *v.* See signs for ANSWER, REPORT. Related form: **response** *n.*

**response** *n.* See sign for ANSWER. Related form: **respond** *v.*

**responsibility**[1] *n.* **1.** The state or fact or an instance of being accountable: *The responsibility for the mistake is mine.* **2.** A burden or obligation: *Raising children is a big responsibility.* Related form: **responsible** *adj.*

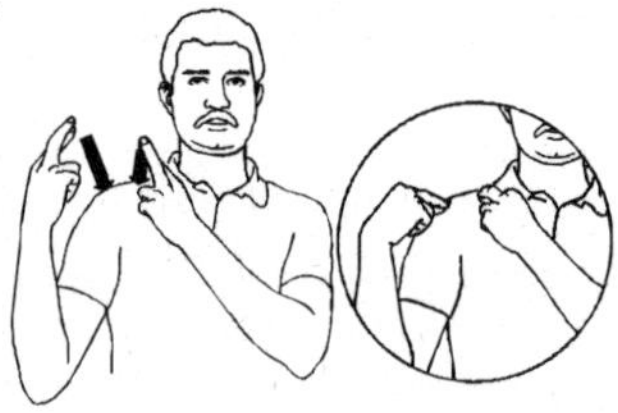

■ [Initialized sign indicating burden on one's shoulders] Tap the fingers of both *R hands,* palms facing in, on the right shoulder with a double movement.

**responsibility**[2] *n.* See sign for BURDEN. Related form: **responsible** *adj.*

**rest**[1] *v.* **1.** To be still or quiet or to sleep: *to rest after lunch.* —*n.* **2.** Repose, relaxation, or sleep: *Have a good rest.* Same sign used for: **idle, recess, relax.**

■ [Shows laying one's hands on one's chest as if in repose] With the arms crossed at the wrists, lay the palm of each *open hand* on the chest near the opposite shoulder.

**rest**[2] See sign for LEAVE[2].

**restaurant** *n.* A place to buy and eat a meal: *to eat a quiet dinner in a cozy restaurant.*

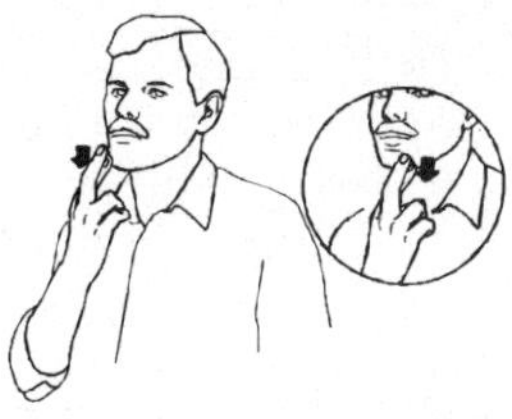

■ [Initialized sign similar to sign for **cafeteria**] Touch the fingers of the right *R hand,* palm facing in, first to the right and then to the left side of the chin.

**restless** *adj.* Characterized by an inability to rest: *to have a restless night; to be in a restless mood.* Same sign used for: **antsy.**

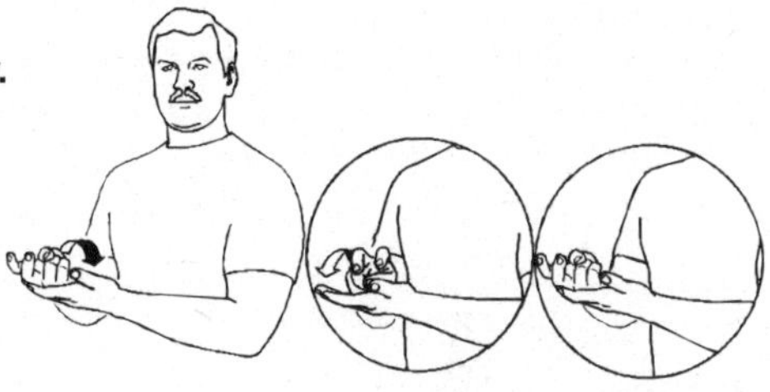

■ [Represents one's legs turning over restlessly during a sleepless night] With the back of the right *bent V hand* laying across the open left palm, both palms facing up, turn the right hand over and back with a double movement.

**rest of** *n.* + *prep.* See sign for AFTER.

**restore** *v.* See signs for RENOVATE, SAVE.

**restrain** *v.* See sign for CONTROL[1]. Related form: **restraint** *n.*

**restrict** *v.* To keep within limits; confine: *Small cages at the zoo restrict the lions' movements.* Same sign used for: **limit, quota.**

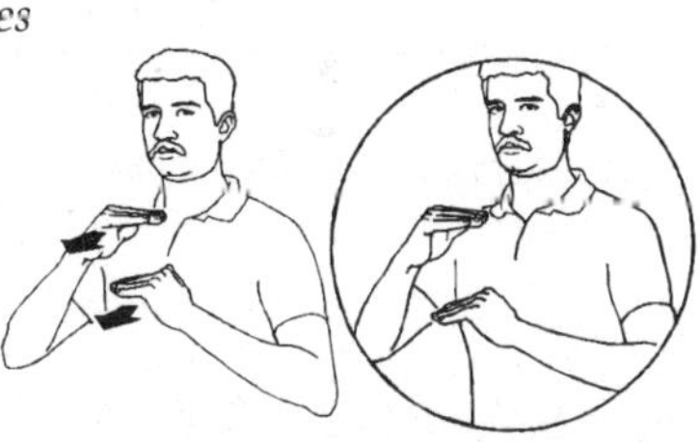

■ [Shows the level of limit] Beginning with both *bent hands* in front of the chest, right hand above the left hand and both palms facing down, move both hands forward simultaneously.

**rest room**[1] *n. phrase.* A room containing one or more sinks, toilets, counters, etc., as in a restaurant: *The rest rooms are one flight up.*

■ [Abbreviation **r-r**] Tap the right *R hand,* palm facing down and the fingers pointing forward, downward first in front of the right side of body and then again slightly to the right.

**rest room**[2] *n. phrase.* See sign for TOILET.

**result** *n.* Something that happens because of something else; outcome: *What was the result of your research?* Same sign used for: **consequence, outcome.**

- [Initialized sign similar to sign for **end**[1]] Move the fingertips of the right *R hand,* palm facing down, along the length of the index finger of the left *B hand,* palm facing in, and then down off the fingertips.

**résumé** or **resume** *n.* A short summation of one's educational and professional qualifications: *a good idea to keep your résumé up to date.*

- [Initialized sign showing the shape of a typed resume] Beginning with the fingertips of both *R hands* touching in front of the chest, palms angled forward, bring the hands apart to in front of each shoulder, then straight down, and finally back together in front of the lower chest.

**retail** *v.* See sign for SELL.

**retain** *v.* See sign for SAVE[2].

**retainer** *n.* See sign for BRACES.

**retaliate** *v.* See sign for REVENGE.

**retire** *v.* To give up an occupation or career, as when one reaches retirement age: *retired from work at age 65.*

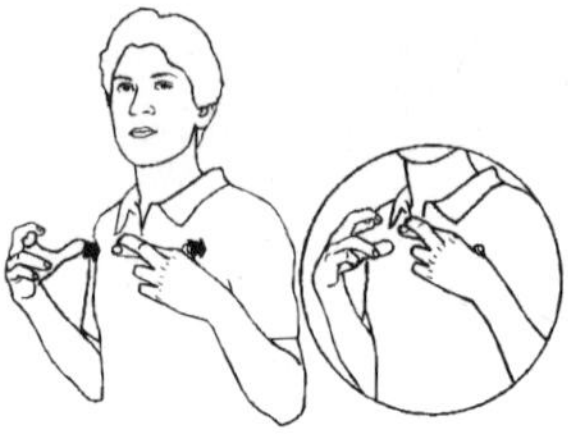

- [Initialized sign similar to sign for **holiday**] Touch the extended thumbs of both *R hands,* palms facing each other, against each side of the chest.

**retirement** *n.* Similar to sign for RETIRE but made with a double movement.

**retreat** *n.* **1.** A quiet place of rest or refuge: *The cabin in the mountains is a lovely retreat.* **2.** A short period of retirement to a quiet place for religious meditation and spiritual renewal: *to go on a retreat organized by the church.*

- [Initialized sign similar to sign for **run away**] Beginning with the extended fingers of the right *R hand,* palm facing forward, pointing up between the index finger and middle finger of the left *5 hand,* palm facing down, move the right hand outward to the right.

**retrieve** *v.* See sign for GET.

**retrospect** *n.* See sign for HINDSIGHT.

**return**[1] *v.* See signs for BRING, REFUND.

**Return**[2] (key) *n.* See sign for ENTER (key).

**reveal** *v.* See signs for ANNOUNCE, TELL[1].

**revenge** *n.* An act of retaliation for an injury or wrong: *to take revenge on the people who hurt you.* Same sign used for: **avenge, get even, retaliate, vengeance.**

- Beginning with both *modified X hands* in front of the chest, left hand above the right hand and palms facing each other, bring the right hand upward until the knuckles of both the hands touch.

**revenue** *n.* See sign for INCOME.

**reverberate** *v.* See sign for BELL. Related form: **reverberation** *n.*

**reverse** *n.* **1.** The opposite: *When you woke up, I did the reverse.* **2.** The back: *Sign the check on the reverse.* —*adj.* **3.** Opposite in position or direction: *Sign on the reverse side.* —*v.* **4.** To turn the opposite way: *Reverse direction by making a U-turn.* Same sign used for: **revert, swap, switch.**

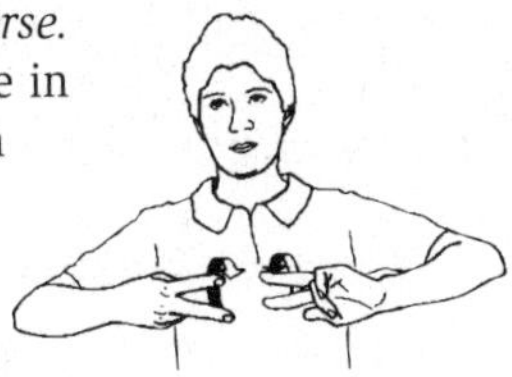

- [The fingers seem to reverse positions] Beginning with both *V hands* in front of the chest, right palm facing in and fingers pointing left, and left palm facing out and fingers pointing right, twist the hands in opposite directions to turn the palms the opposite way.

**revert** *n.* See sign for REVERSE.

**review** *v.* To look at or study again: *to review your lessons.*

- [Initialized sign] With the little-finger side of the right *R hand,* palm facing left, on the open left palm, twist the right fingers back toward the chest.

**revive** *v.* See sign for INSPIRE.

**revoke** *v.* See signs for CANCEL, TEAR.

**revolt** *v., n.* See sign for PROTEST[2]. Related form: **revolution** *n.*

**revolve** *v.* See sign for AROUND.

**revulsion** *n.* See sign for DISGUSTED[1].

**reward** *n., v.* See sign for GIFT.

**ribbon** *n.* See signs for BOW, MEDAL.

**rice** *n.* The starchy seeds from an annual grass grown in wet areas for food: *a diet of rice.*

■ [Initialized sign similar to sign for **soup**] Move the right *R hand* from touching the open left palm held in front of the body, upward to the mouth.

**rich** *adj.* Having much wealth, as money, possessions, and land: *A rich family bought the old mansion.* Same sign used for: **prosperous, wealth, wealthy.**

■ [Represents a pile of money in one's hand] Beginning with the little-finger side of the right *S hand,* palm facing left, in the open left palm held in front of the body, raise the right hand a short distance while opening into a *curved 5 hand,* palm facing down.

**rid** *v.* See sign for ELIMINATE.

**ride in a car, truck, etc.** *v. phrase.* To make a trip, as a passenger or driver, inside a car or similar vehicle: *There's room for you to ride in the car.*

■ [Represents a person sitting in a vehicle] With the fingers of the right *bent U hand,* palm facing down, hooked over the thumb of the left *C hand,* palm facing right, move the hands forward from in front of the body.

**ridicule** *v.* See sign for TORTURE.

**ridiculous** *adj.* See sign for SILLY.

**rifle** *n.* A gun with a long barrel, usually fired from the shoulder: *Rifles can be fired with great accuracy at long range.*

■ [Mime pulling a trigger on a rifle] With the index fingers of both *L hands* pointing forward in front of the body, palms facing in opposite directions and right hand nearer the chest than the left hand, wiggle the thumb of the right hand up and down with a repeated movement.

**right**[1] *n.* **1.** The side that faces east when a person or thing is facing north: *Turn to your right.* —*adj.* **2.** Of, pertaining to, or located on or toward the right side: *the right side of the road.* —*adv.* **3.** On or toward the right side: *Turn right.*

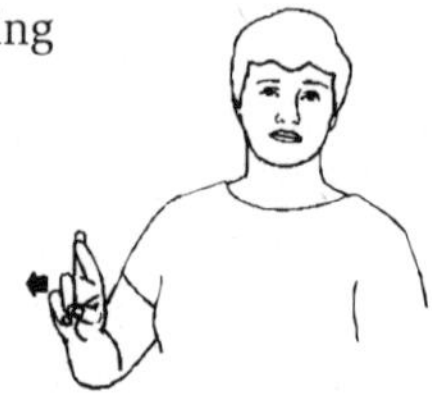

■ [Initialized sign showing a right direction] Move the right *R hand,* palm facing forward, from in front of the right side of the body to the right a short distance.

**right**[2] *n.* Something that is legally or morally due someone: *As free people, we have a right to vote.* Same sign used for: **all right, privilege.**

■ Slide the little-finger side of the right *open hand,* palm facing left, in an upward arc across the upturned left palm held in front of the body.

**right**[3] *adj.* Conforming to the truth; being correct: *the right answer.* Same sign used for: **accurate, correct, okay.**

■ With the index fingers of both hands extended forward at right angles, palms angled in and right hand above left, bring the little-finger side of the right hand sharply down across the thumb side of the left hand.

**right turn** *n. phrase.* A movement angling toward the right side: *to make a right turn.*

■ [Shows direction of a right turn] Move the right *open hand,* palm facing in and fingers pointing up, to the right by twisting the wrist, ending with the palm facing forward.

**rigid** *adj.* See sign for FREEZE.

**ring**[1] *n.* A thin circle of metal worn on the finger: *a wedding ring.*

■ [The location of a ring on the ring finger] Move the bent thumb and index finger of the right *5 hand,* palm facing down, back and forth the length of the ring finger of the left *5 hand,* palm facing down, with a repeated movement.

**ring**[2] *v.* **1.** To cause a bell to sound: *to ring the church bells.* **2.** To give forth a sound: *The doorbell rang.* —*n.* **3.** The sound of a bell: *I heard the ring of the bells.*

■ [Initialized sign similar to sign for **bell**] Quickly tap the index-finger side of the right *R hand,* palm facing forward, against the open left palm with a repeated movement.

**ring**[3] *v., n.* See sign for BELL.

**ring tone** *n. phrase.* The customized sound on a mobile phone that indicates an incoming call.

■ [sign similar to sign for **bell** + **hear**] Quickly tap the extended right index finger, palm facing left, against the open left palm with a repeated movement. Then bring the extended right index finger to the right ear.

**rinse** *n., v.* See sign for DYE.

**riot** *v., n.* See signs for COMPLAIN, MESSY.

**rip** *v.* See sign for TEAR.

**rise** *v., n.* See sign for RAISE.

**risk**[1] *n.* **1.** The possibility of loss or injury: *He took a risk in the stock market.* —*v.* **2.** To expose to hazard or danger: *risked his life.* Same sign used for: **cutthroat.**

■ [Shows the throat being cut] Move the extended right index finger from left to right across the throat, palm facing down and finger pointing left.

**risk**[2] *n.* See sign for DANGER.

**rival** *n.* See sign for ENEMY.

**river** *n.* A large, natural stream of water flowing through a channel: *sailed down the river to the ocean.* Same sign used for: **creek, stream.**

■ [**water** + a gesture showing the movement of waves] Tap the index-finger side of the right *W hand,* palm facing left, against the chin with a double movement. Then move both *5 hands,* palms facing down, forward from in front of the chest with an up-and-down wavy movement.

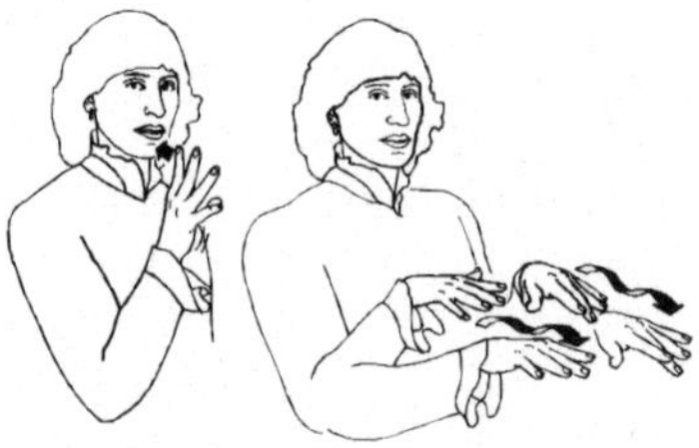

**road** *n.* A way between places for vehicles to travel on: *to take a different road.* Same sign used for: **avenue, boulevard, lane, path, route, street, trail, way.**

■ [Indicates the shape of a road] Move both *open hands* from in front of each side of the body, palms facing each other, forward with a parallel movement.

**roam** *v.* To go about without a special plan: *roam around the city.* Same sign used for: **adrift, wander.**

■ [Represents the aimless movement of a roaming person] Beginning with the extended right index finger pointing up in front of the right shoulder, palm facing forward, move the hand to in front of the chest and then outward again in a large arc.

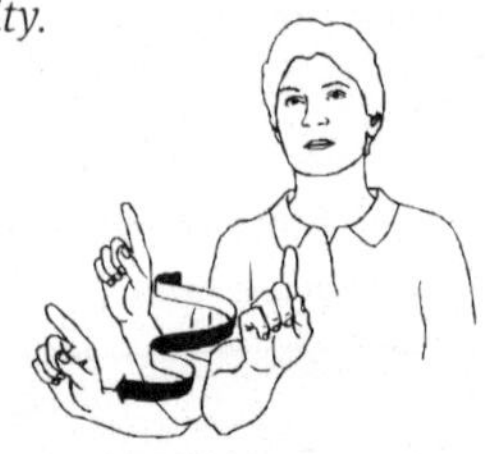

**roar** *v., n.* See sign for SCREAM.

**rob**[1] *v.* To steal or steal from: *to rob a bank.* Related form: **robbery** *n.* Same sign used for: **burglary, hold up, raid.**

■ [Represents pulling out one's guns for a robbery] Beginning with both *H hands* in front of each side of the waist, palms facing each other and fingers pointing down, twist the wrists upward, bringing the hands up in front of each side of the body, palms facing each other and fingers pointing forward.

**rob**[2] *v.* See sign for STEAL[1]. Related form: **robbery** *n.*

**robe** *n.* A long, loose garment: *to wear a robe over your pajamas.*

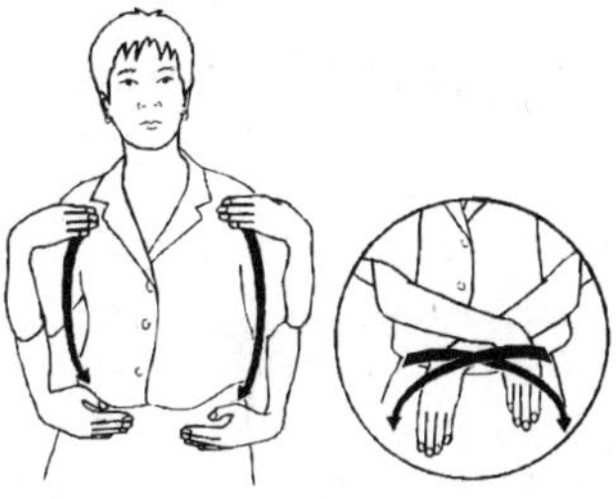

■ [Shows location of a robe on one's torso and then the way a robe overlaps] Touch the fingers of both *bent hands,* palms facing in and fingers pointing toward each other, first to the upper chest and then near the waist. Then bring both *open hands,* palms facing in and fingers pointing down, across each other in front of the waist.

**robot** *n.* A mechanical form shaped like a person, often created to do routine tasks: *The robot walked across the room.*

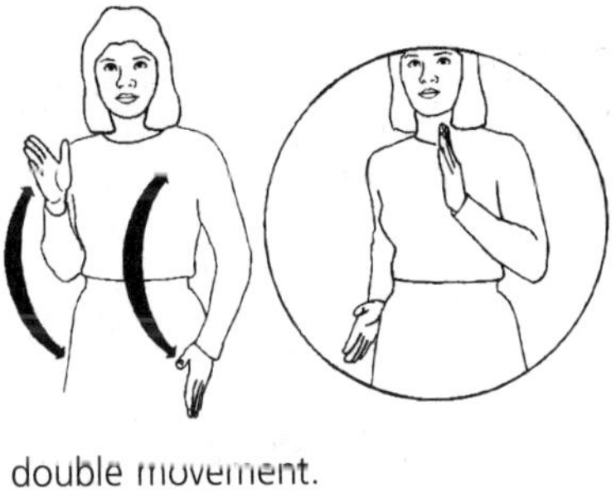

■ [Mime the traditional arm movements of a robot] Beginning with the right *open hand* in front of the right side of the body, palm facing left and fingers pointing forward, and the left *open hand* near the left hip, palm facing in and fingers pointing down, move the hands up and down with a deliberate alternating double movement.

**rock**[1] *n.* **1.** A large mass of stone, as one forming a hill: *climbed the rock.* **2.** A stone of any size: *to throw a rock.* Same sign used for: **stone.**

■ [Indicates the hardness of a rock] Tap the back of the right *S hand,* palm facing up, on the back of the left *S hand* held in front of the chest, palm facing down, with a repeated movement.

**rock**[2] *v.* To move backward and forward with rhythm and a swaying motion: *to rock in a rocking chair.* Same sign used for: **rocking chair.**

■ [Shows movement of a rocking chair] Beginning with the thumbs of both *L hands* on each side of the chest, palms facing each other and index fingers pointing up, bring the hands forward and down to in front of each side of the waist, index fingers pointing forward, and then back up again with a double movement.

**rock**[3] *n.* See sign for METAL.

**rocket** *n.* **1.** A device consisting of a tube filled with explosives that burn very quickly to force the tube rapidly upward: *sent up rockets on the Fourth of July.* **2.** A space vehicle launched or propelled by such a device: *to send a rocket to the moon.* Same sign used for: **space shuttle.**

- [Initialized sign showing the movement of a rocket being launched] Beginning with the heel of the right *R hand,* palm facing forward and fingers pointing up, on the back of the left *S hand* held in front of the chest, palm facing down, move the right hand upward in front of the face.

**rocking chair** *n. phrase.* See sign for ROCK[2].

**rod** *n.* See signs for PIPE[2], STICK[2].

**role** *n.* An actor's part in a play, movie, etc.: *an exciting role in the new TV drama.*

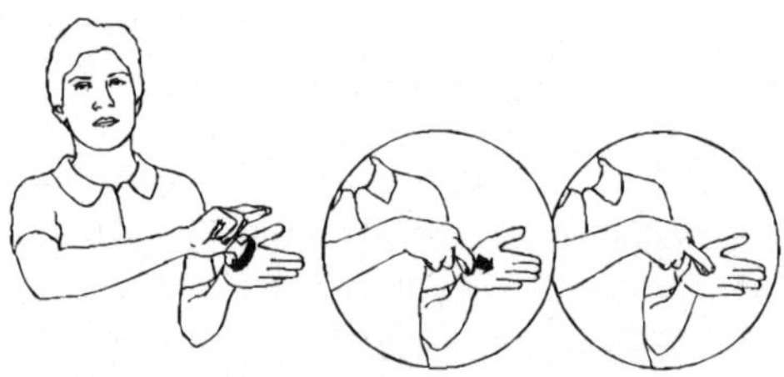

- [Initialized sign similar to sign for **character**[2]] Move the fingers of the right *R hand* in a small circle near the open left palm, ending with the right fingertips touching the left palm.

**roller skate** *n. phrase, v. phrase.* See sign for SKATE[1].

**romance** *n.* **1.** A love story: *likes to read romances.* **2.** A love affair: *the romance between a man and a woman.*

- [Initialized sign] Bring the extended fingers of the right *R hand,* palm facing back, from touching the shoulder forward in a double arc.

**romp** *v., n.* See sign for PLAY[1].

**roof** *n.* The external top covering of a building: *had to climb on the roof to fix it.*

- [Initialized sign showing the shape of a roof] Beginning with the fingertips of both *R hands* touching in front of the forehead, palms angled down, bring the hands downward and outward at an angle to about shoulder width.

**room**[1] *n.* **1.** A space within a building enclosed by walls, a floor, and a ceiling: *The apartment has 6 rooms.* **2.** Such a space designed or available for a special purpose: *the living room.* Same sign used for: **package, present.**

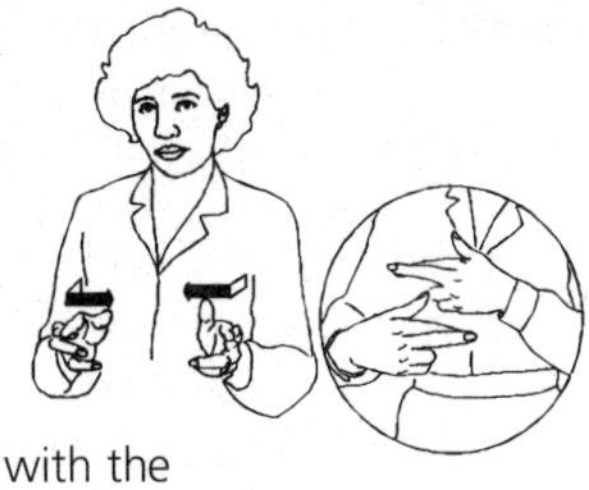

- [Shows the four walls of a room] Beginning with both *open hands* in front of each side of the chest, palms facing each other and fingers pointing forward, move the hands in opposite directions by bending the wrists, ending with the left hand near the chest and the right hand several inches forward of the left hand, both palms facing in.

---

**room**[2] *n.* See sign for BOX.

---

**root** *n.* The part of a plant that grows down into the soil and absorbs moisture and nutrients: *Water the plant so the roots are thoroughly moistened.*

- [Initialized sign representing roots growing beneath the soil] Push the fingers of the right *R hand,* palm facing in, down through the opening of the left *C hand,* palm facing right, while opening the fingers into a *5 hand* as it emerges.

---

**rope** *n.* A thick cord made by twisting smaller cords together: *tied the swing to the branch of the tree.*

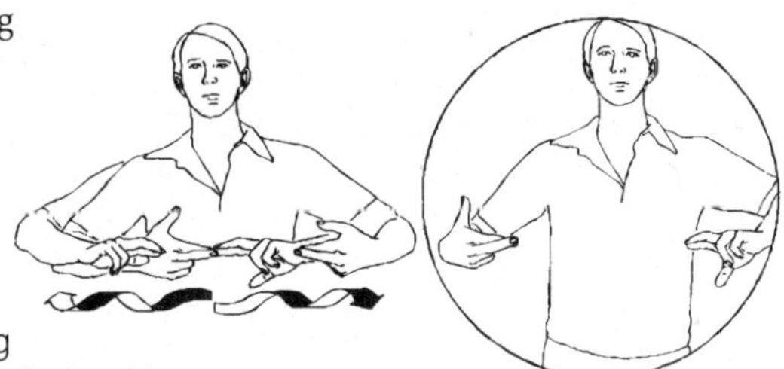

- [Initialized sign showing the shape of a rope] Beginning with the fingertips of both *R hands* pointing toward each other and touching in front of the chest, bring the hands outward to in front of each shoulder while twisting the wrists as the hands move.

---

**rose** *n.* A flower that grows on a thorny stem: *to smell the roses.*

- [Initialized sign similar to sign for **flower**] Touch the extended fingertips of the right *R hand,* palm facing in, first to the right side of the nose and then to the left side.

---

**rot** *v., n.* See sign for WEAR OUT. Related form: **rotten** *adj.*

---

**rotary** *adj.* See sign for AROUND.

---

**rotate** *v.* To turn around on an axis: *The earth rotates.* Related form: **rotation** *n.*

- [Initialized sign showing the movement of something rotating around something else] Move the extended fingers of the right *R hand,* palm facing in and fingers pointing down, in a circle around the fingertips of the left *R hand,* palm facing in and fingers pointing up.

**rough** *adj.* **1.** Not smooth: *a rough surface.* **2.** Not finished or perfected; unpolished: *a rough draft of a composition.* **3.** Lacking gentleness or refinement: *a rough crowd.* **4.** Approximate: *a rough guess.* Same sign used for: **abrasive, approximate, coarse, crude, draft, estimate.**

■ [Indicates a rough, scratchy surface] Move the fingertips of the right *curved 5 hand,* palm facing down, from the heel to the fingertips of the upturned left *open hand* held in front of the body.

**round**[1] *n.* Being shaped like a disk or a ball: *a round tire; to know that the earth is round.*

■ [Initialized sign similar to sign for **circle**[1]] Move the extended fingers of the right *R hand* from pointing down in front of the body in a large flat circle in front of the body.

**round**[2] *adj.* See sign for CIRCLE[1].

**route** *n.* See sign for ROAD.

**routine** *n.* See sign for DAILY.

**row**[1] *n.* A line of adjacent chairs facing in the same direction, as in a theater: *to sit in the front row.*

■ [Represents legs sitting in a row] Beginning with the index-finger sides of both *bent V hands* touching in front of the body, palms facing down, move the hands apart to in front of each side of the body.

**row**[2] *n.* **1.** The horizontal arrangement of data in a spreadsheet or table: *Each row of data represented one customer.* **2.** A line of text in a word-processing document or a line of text across a display screen: *Make a correction to the tenth row of the paragraph.*

■ [Shows shape of a row] Move the right *G hand,* palm forward, from in front of the chest outward to the right.

**row**[3] *n.* See sign for LINE UP.

**royalty** *n.* See sign for PENSION.

**rub**[1] *v.* To move one thing back and forth against another: *to rub the cake of soap on the dirty cloth.*

■ [Mime rubbing ointment on something] Rub the fingers of the right *open hand,* palm facing down, back and forth across the palm of the left *open hand,* palm facing up, with a double movement.

**rub**[2] *v.* See signs for POLISH, WASH.

**rubber** *n.* **1.** An elastic substance made from a certain tropical plant or a synthetic substance with similar properties: *tires made of rubber.* —*adj.* **2.** Made of this substance: *a rubber eraser.*

■ Bring the index finger side of the right *X hand,* palm facing forward, downward on the right cheek with a double movement.

**rubber band** *n. phrase.* A circular strip of rubber used to hold things together: *Put a rubber band around the index cards.*

■ [**rubber** + a sign similar to **stretch**] Bring the index-finger side of the right *X hand,* palm facing forward, downward on the right cheek with a double movement. Then, beginning with the knuckles of both *modified X hands* touching in front of the chest, palms facing in, pull the hands apart to in front of each side of the chest with a double movement.

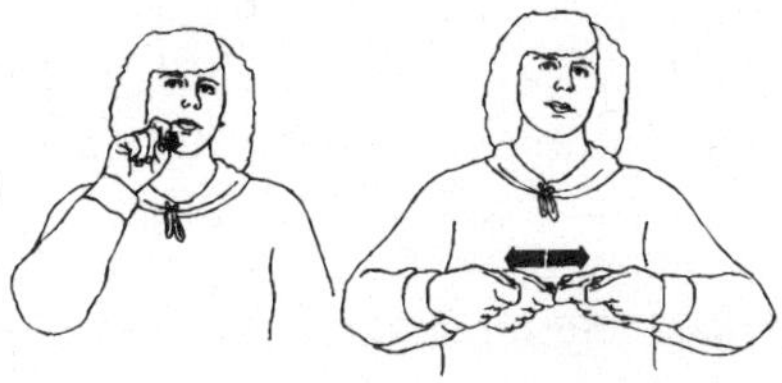

**rude** *adj.* See sign for MEAN[1].

**ruin**[1] *v.* To cause damage to: *Your muddy hands will ruin my picture.* Same sign used for: **spoil.**

■ Slide the little-finger side of the right *X hand,* palm facing left, across the index finger side of the left *X hand,* palm facing right.

**ruin**[2] *v.* See sign for DAMAGE.

**rule**[1] *n.* A statement outlining what can and cannot properly be done: *In this organization, we follow the rules.* Same sign used for: **regulation.**

■ [Initialized sign similar to sign for **law**] Touch the fingertips of the right *R hand* first on the fingers and then on the heel of the left *open hand,* palms facing each other.

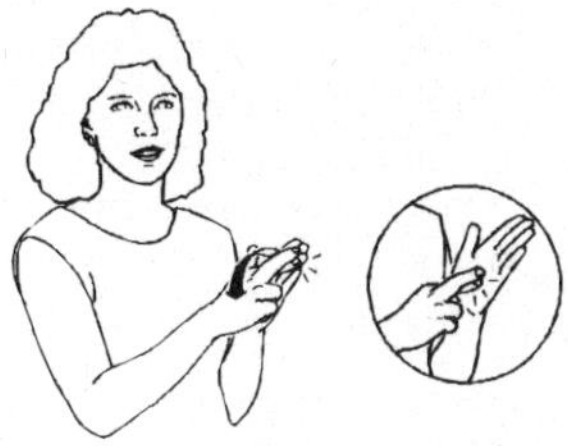

**rule**[2] *v.* See sign for MANAGE.

**ruler** *n.* A straight strip of wood, metal, or plastic marked off, as in inches, to be used for measuring: *Measure the size of the book with a ruler.*

■ [The shape of a ruler + **measure**] Beginning with the index fingers and thumbs of both *G hands* touching in front of the chest, palms angled forward, bring the hands apart to in front of each side of the chest. Then tap the thumbs of both *Y hands,* palms together angled forward in front of the chest with a double movement.

**rumor** *n.* See sign for GOSSIP[1].

**run**[1] *v.* To go by moving the legs quickly so that at some moments both legs are off the ground at the same time: *Run faster.* Related form: **running** *n.* Same sign used for: **jog, jogging.**

■ [Represents one's legs moving when running] With the index finger of the right *L hand,* palm facing left and index finger pointing forward, hooked on the thumb of the left *L hand,* palm facing right and index finger pointing forward, move both hands forward.

**run**[2] *v.* **1.** To operate or be responsible for the functioning of: *to run a business; to run the dishwasher.* **2.** To process by computer: *to run the program.* Same sign used for: **operate.**

■ Brush the palm of the right *open hand* upward with a double movement across the left *open hand,* palms facing each other and fingers pointing forward.

**run**[3] *v.* (of the nose) To discharge fluid, as during a respiratory illness: *My nose is running.* Related form: **runny** *adj.* Same sign used for: **nosebleed.**

■ [Represents fluid dripping from the nose] Beginning with the index finger of the right *4 hand* touching the nose, palm facing in and fingers pointing left, bring the hand straight down with a double movement.

**run**[4] *v.* See signs for EXECUTE, MACHINE.

**run**[5] (a meeting) *v.* See sign for MANAGE.

**run around** *v. phrase.* To go to many places: *to run around town.* Same sign used for: **fool around, tour, travel.**

- With the left extended index finger pointing up in front of the body and the right extended index finger pointing down above it, both palms facing in, move both hands in alternate circles in front of the body.

**run away** *v. phrase.* To escape: *to run away from home.* See also sign for ESCAPE. Same sign used for: **get away, split** (*slang*).

- [Represents one taking off quickly] Move the extended right index finger, palm facing left and finger pointing up, from between the index and middle fingers of the left *5 hand,* palm facing down in front of the chest, forward with a deliberate movement.

**run out of** *v. phrase.* To use up: *to run out of eggs.* Same sign used for: **all gone, deplete, used up.**

- [Indicates grabbing everything so that nothing is left] Beginning with the little-finger side of the right *5 hand,* palm facing in, on the heel of the left *open hand,* palm facing up, bring the right hand forward to the left fingertips while changing into an *S hand.*

**run over** *v. phrase.* See sign for OVERFLOW.

**rush** *v., n.* See sign for HURRY.

**sack** *n.* See sign for BAG.

**sacrifice** *n.* **1.** Someone or something surrendered, given up, or destroyed for the sake of preserving someone or something else: *sent their children to college at great financial sacrifice.* **2.** Something offered up to a deity, as in propitiation: *slew a calf upon the altar as a sacrifice.* —*v.* **3.** To make a sacrifice or offering of: *to sacrifice one's life.*

- [Initialized sign similar to sign for **suggest**] Beginning with both *S hands* in front of each side of the body, move the hands quickly upward while opening into *5 hands,* palms facing in.

**sad** *adj.* Not happy; sorrowful: *I feel sad about your misfortune.* Same sign used for: **grave, mournful, tragic, unhappy.**

- [The hands seem to pull the face down to a sad expression] Move both *5 hands* from in front of each side of the face, palms facing in and fingers pointing up, downward a short distance.

**safe**[1] *n.* A place, as a steel box, for keeping valuables: *to put jewelry in the safe.*

- [The shape of a safe + **knob**] Beginning with the index-finger sides of both *open hands* together in front of the body, palms facing down and fingers pointing forward, bring the hands apart and then straight down while turning the palms toward each other. Then turn the right *curved 5 hand,* palm facing forward, in a double movement in front of the right side of the body.

**safe**[2] *adj.* See sign for SAVE[1].

**sail** *n.* See sign for BOAT. Related form: **sailing** *n.*

**sailboat**[1] *n.* A boat that is moved by sails: *to skim over the water in a sleek sailboat.*

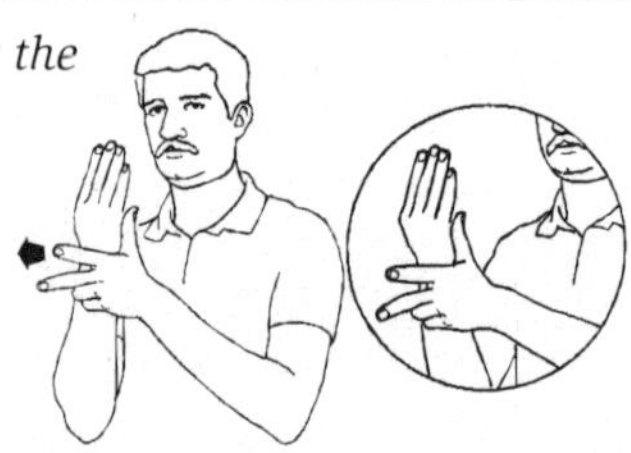

- [The right hands represents a boat's sail and the left hand represents a boat] Beginning with the little-finger side of the right *B hand,* palm facing in, against the palm side of the left *3 hand,* palm facing right, move both hands forward a short distance.

**sailboat**[2] *n.* See sign for SHIP[1].

**salad** *n.* A cold dish of raw vegetables usually tossed together and served with a dressing: *made a salad with artichokes, tomato, and avocado.*

■ [Mime tossing a salad] Move both *curved hands,* palms facing up and fingers pointing toward each other, from in front of each side of the body toward each other with a double movement.

**salad dressing** *n. phrase.* See sign for SAUCE.

**salary** *n.* See signs for EARN, INCOME.

**sale** *n.* See sign for SELL.

**salt** *n.* A white crystalline compound used as a seasoning and preservative: *to put salt on my egg.*

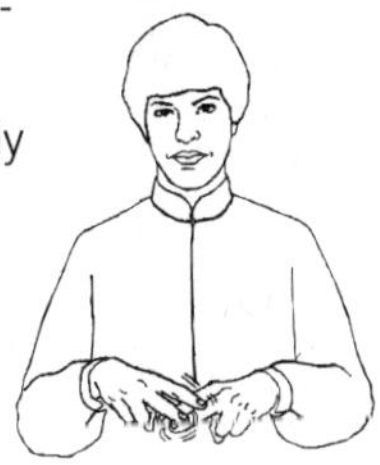

■ [Represents tapping out salt from a shaker on one's food] Alternately tap the fingers of the right *V hand* across the back of the fingers of the left *V hand,* both palms facing down.

**salute** *v.* **1.** To raise the hand to the forehead as an act of respect: *to salute the officers in the army.* —*n.* **2.** A greeting made by raising the hand to the forehead: *He answered with a salute.*

■ [Natural gesture for saluting] With a deliberate movement, bring the index-finger side of the right *B hand* against the right side of the forehead, palm angled left.

**salvation** *n.* See sign for SAVE[1].

**same**[1] *adj.* **1.** Not different; identical: *wearing the same dress I wore yesterday.* **2.** Similar or of the same kind: *I see you bought the same TV I did.* —*pron.* **3.** The same kind of thing: *She's having lasagna and I'll have the same.* —*adv.* **4. the same** In the same manner: *The twins walk and talk the same.* See also signs for ALIKE[2], LIKE[3]. Same sign used for: **mutual, similar, such as.**

■ [The fingers come together to show that they are the same] Beginning with both extended index fingers pointing forward in front of each side of the body, palms facing down, bring the hands together, ending with the index fingers together in front of the body.

**same**[2] *adj.* See signs for ALIKE[1,2].

**sample** *n.* See signs for SHOW[1], SYMBOL.

**sandal** *n.* A shoe made of a sole fastened to the foot by straps: *to wear sandals to the beach.* Same sign used for: **flip-flop.**

■ [Shows a thong coming between the toes] Beginning with the left *5 hand* in front of the body, palm facing down and fingers pointing forward, pull the extended right index finger back from between the index finger and middle finger of the left hand toward the chest with a double movement.

**sandwich** *n.* Two or more slices of bread with filling between them: *to eat a ham sandwich.*

■ [Represents a sandwich being eaten] With the palms of both *open hands* together, right hand above left, bring the fingers back toward the mouth with a short double movement.

**Santa Claus** *n. phrase.* The chubby, white-bearded man in a red suit who, according to folklore, brings gifts to children and represents Christmas giving: *Children believe in Santa Claus.*

■ [Hand follows the shape of Santa Claus's beard] Beginning with the index-finger side of the right *curved hand* held on the chin, palm facing down, bring the hand forward and downward in an arc, ending with the little-finger side against the chest, palm facing up.

**sarcastic** *adj.* See sign for IRONY.

**Satan** *n.* See sign for DEVIL.

**sated** *adj.* See sign for FULL[1].

**satisfied** *adj.* See sign for FULL[1].

**satisfy** *v.* To fulfill the desires or needs of: *A snack will satisfy my hunger.* Related form: **satisfaction** *n.* Same sign used for: **appease, content, contentment.**

■ Beginning with both *B hands* in front of the chest, right hand above the left hand and both palms facing down, bring the index-finger sides of both hands against the chest.

**Saturday** *n.* The seventh day of the week, following Friday: *She often has to work on Saturday.*

■ [Initialized sign] Move the right *S hand,* palm facing back, in a small circle in front of the right shoulder.

**sauce** *n.* A liquid served over food as seasoning: *to put a sauce on the ham.* Same sign used for: **salad dressing.**

■ [Represents pouring sauce over food] Move the extended thumb of the right *10 hand,* palm angled down, in a circle over the palm of the left *open hand,* palm facing up in front of the body.

**saucer** *n.* See sign for PLATE.

**sausage** *n.* Chopped meats stuffed into a thin tubelike casing: *likes to eat sausage with eggs.* Same sign used for: **wiener.**

■ [Shows the shape of sausage] Beginning with the index-finger sides of both *C hands* touching in front of the chest, palms facing forward, bring the hands apart while squeezing them open and closed from *C* to *S hands,* ending with *S hands* outside the sides of the body.

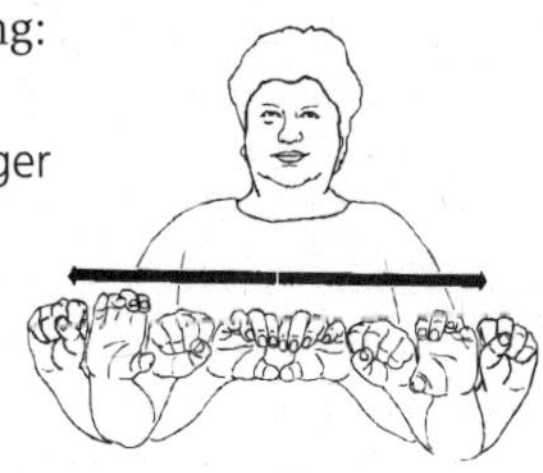

**save**[1] *v.* **1.** To rescue from harm or loss: *saved the dog's life by rushing it to the vet.* **2.** To set free from sin: *a belief that Christ saved the world.* Same sign used for: **free, freedom, liberate, liberty, redeem, rescue, safe, salvation, secure, security.**

■ [Initialized sign representing breaking the chains of captivity] Beginning with both *S hands* crossed at the wrists in front of the chest, palms facing in opposite directions, twist the wrists and move the hands apart, ending with the hands in front of each shoulder, palms facing forward.

**save**[2] *v.* To set aside for future use: *to save money in the bank.* Related form: **savings** *pl. n.* Same sign used for: **preservation, preserve, restore, retain, storage, store, stuff.**

■ Tap the fingers of the right *V hand* with a double movement on the back of the fingers of the left *V hand,* both palms facing in.

**saw** *n.* See sign for WOOD.

**say** *v.* To speak or speak about: *to say what you mean.* Same sign used for: **comment, remark, remarks, state.**

■ [Points to where words are said] Tap the extended right index finger, palm facing in, on the chin with a double movement.

**scale** *n.* See sign for WEIGH.

**scalp** *n.* See sign for BALD.

**scant** *adj.* See sign for TINY[1].

**scared** *adj.* See signs for AFRAID, FEAR. Related form: **scare** *v.*

**scarf** *n.* A piece of cloth worn on the head or around the neck: *to tie the scarf around her hair.* Same sign used for: **Mennonite.**

■ Beginning with both *modified X hands* touching each side of the head, palms facing each other, bring the hands downward around the face, ending near each other under the chin.

**scatter** *v.* To throw about in several directions: *to scatter the seeds.*

■ [Mime scattering something] Beginning with both *S hands* in front of each side of the chest, palms facing forward, move the hands alternately forward while opening into *5 hands.*

**scent** *n., v.* See sign for SMELL.

**schedule**[1] *n.* A written statement of detailed procedure: *to follow the schedule set up for the project.* Same sign used for: **chart, graph.**

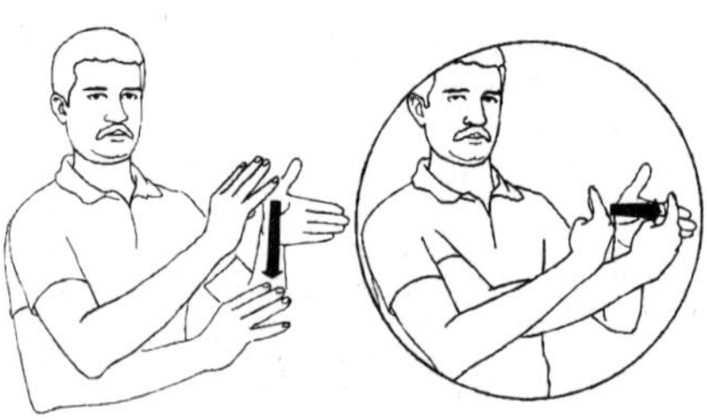

■ [Shows the rows and columns on a schedule] Beginning with the left *open hand* held in front of the left shoulder, palm facing right and fingers pointing forward, bring the fingers of the right *4 hand,* palm facing left, down the heel of the left hand, and then drag the back of the right fingers across the length of the left palm from the heel to the fingertips.

**schedule**[2] *n.* See signs for PLAN[1,2].

**scholarly** *adj.* **1.** Concerned with research and knowledge: *spent a lifetime engaged in scholarly pursuits.* **2.** Of or befitting a scholar: *to have scholarly habits.* Same sign used for: **genius.**

■ Touch the thumb of the right *C hand,* palm facing left, against the forehead.

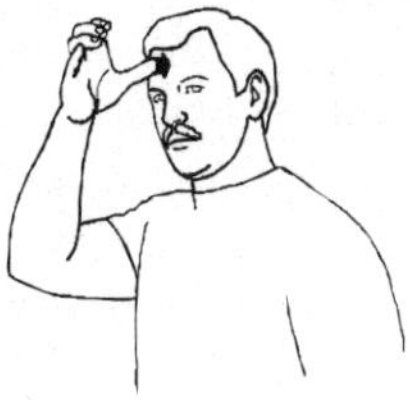

**school** *n.* An institution for teaching and learning: *old enough to go to school.*

■ Tap the fingers of right *open hand,* palm facing down, with a double movement on the upturned palm of left *open hand.*

**science** *n.* A branch of knowledge based on observed facts and tested truths: *Physics and chemistry are branches of science.* Same sign used for: **chemical, chemistry.**

■ [Represents mixing chemicals in a scientific experiment] Beginning with the right *10 hand* in front of the right shoulder and the left *10 hand* in front of the left side of the chest, both palms facing forward, move the hands in large alternating circles toward each other.

**scissors** *pl. n.* A tool, with two sharp blades held together on a pivot, used for cutting paper, cloth, etc.: *to cut the wrapping paper with the scissors.* Same sign used for: **clippers, shears.**

■ [Mime cutting with scissors] Open and close the index and middle fingers of the right *V hand,* palm facing in and fingers pointing left, with a repeated movement.

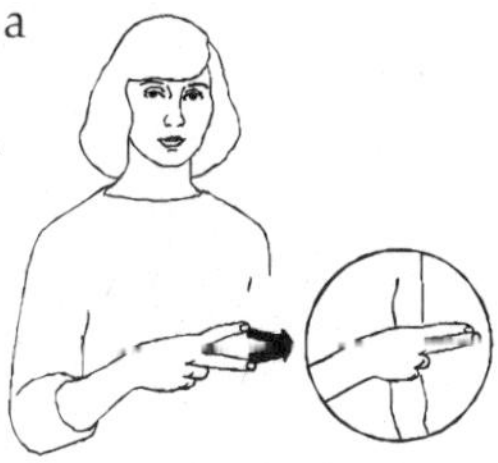

**scold** *v.* To blame and reprimand with angry words: *to scold the naughty child.* Same sign used for: **admonish, reprimand.**

■ [Natural gesture for scolding someone] Move the extended right index finger from in front of the right shoulder, palm facing left and finger pointing up, forward with a double movement.

**score** *n., v.* See sign for LIST.

**scorn** *n.* See sign for CONTEMPT.

**scramble** *v.* See sign for MIX.

**scratch**[1] *v.* **1.** To mark with a rough object: *to scratch the floor with heavy shoes.* **2.** To rub with the fingernails, as to relieve an itch: *Would you scratch my back?*

■ [Shows the action of scratching] Pull the curved extended right index finger with a short double movement downward on the palm of the left *open hand,* palm facing right and fingers pointing forward.

**scratch**[2] *v.* See sign for RAKE.

**scream** *v.* **1.** To make a loud, sharp, piercing cry: *to scream for help.* —*n.* **2.** A loud, sharp, piercing cry: *I heard a terrible scream!* Same sign used for: **call out, cry, roar, shout, yell.**

■ [The hand seems to take a loud sound from the mouth and direct it outward] Beginning with the fingers of the right *C hand* close to the mouth, palm facing in, bring the hand forward and upward in an arc.

**screen** *n.* See sign for NET.

**screw**[1] *v.* Same sign as for SCREWDRIVER but formed with a single movement.

**screw**[2] *n.* See sign for SCREWDRIVER.

**screwdriver** *n.* A tool for turning screws: *to use a screwdriver to put the bookcase together.* Same sign used for: **screw.**

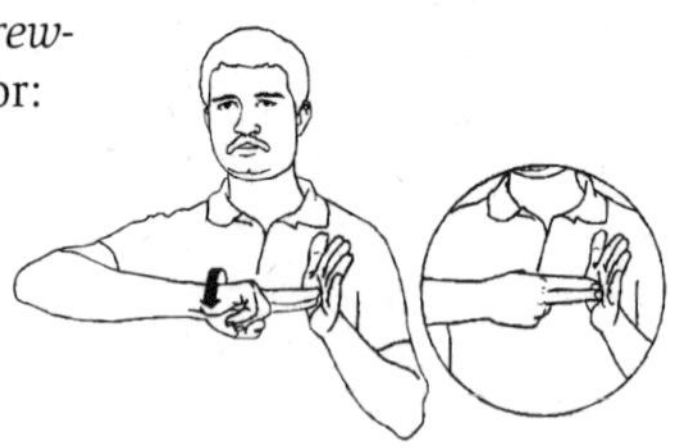

■ [Shows the action of using a screwdriver] Twist the fingertips of the right *H hand* in the palm of the left *open hand,* palm facing right, with a double forward movement.

**scribble** *v.* See sign for WRITE.

**scroll** *v.* To move through copy line by line on a computer display screen: *to scroll through the data.* Related form: **scrolling** *n.*

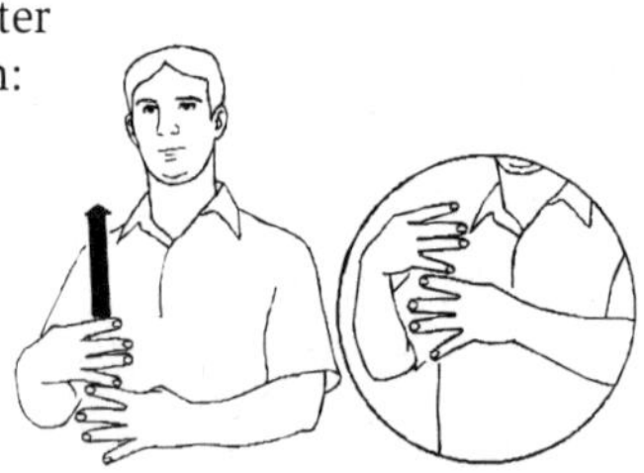

■ [Shows how information moves up a screen when scrolling] Beginning with the little finger of the right *4 hand* on the index finger of the left *4 hand,* both palms facing in and fingers pointing in opposite directions in front of the chest, move the hands upward in front of the chest with a double movement.

**scrounge** *v.* See sign for ADVANTAGE[1].

**scrub** *v.* See sign for POLISH.

**sculpt** *v.* See sign for CARVE.

**sculpture** *n.* A work of art in three dimensions made by carving, modeling, or casting: *a sculpture of an angel.* Related form: **sculpt** *v.*

■ [**carve** + showing the shape of a sculpture] Flick the thumb of the right *10 hand* upward with a double movement off the palm of the left *open hand* held in front of the chest. Then, beginning with both *5 hands* in front of each side of the chest, palms facing each other and fingers pointing forward, move the hands downward with a wavy movement, twisting the wrists up and down as the hands move.

**seal**[1] *n.* A sea animal with large flippers, living in cold regions: *The seal swims in cold water.*

■ [Shows a clapping movement often made by seals with their flippers] With the backs of both *open hands* together in front of the chest, palms facing in opposite directions and fingers pointing down, bend the fingers with a repeated movement.

**seal**[2] *v.* To close tightly: *to seal the jar.* Same sign used for: **airtight.**

■ [Represents putting a stopper on a jar] Bring the right *curved 5 hand* from in front of the chest, palm facing down, deliberately downward to land on the index-finger side of the left *S hand* held in front of the body, palm facing in.

**seal**[3] *v.* See sign for STAMP[2].

**seal one's lips**[1] *v. phrase.* To keep a secret: *My lips are sealed, and I promise not to tell.* Same sign used for: **keep quiet, keep secret.**

■ [Represents sealing one's mouth] Beginning with the index-finger side of the right *C hand* in front of the mouth, palm facing left, close the fingers together to form an *S hand.*

**seal one's lips**[2] *v. phrase.* See sign for SHUT UP[1].

**search for** *v. phrase.* See sign for LOOK FOR.

**seasoning** *n.* Something, as salt, an herb, or a spice that enhances the flavor of food: *to put some seasoning on the bland food.*

■ [Mime shaking seasoning on food] Shake the right *curved hand,* palm facing forward and fingers pointing left, downward in front of the chest with a double movement.

**seat** *n.* See sign for CHAIR.

**seat belt**[1] *n. phrase.* A belt or set of straps designed to keep an occupant secure in a vehicle: *Fasten your seat belt.*

■ [**sit** + a gesture showing pulling a seat belt across oneself and fastening] Place the fingers of the right *H hand,* palm facing down, across the extended fingers of the left *H hand* held in front of the chest, palm facing down and fingers pointing right. Then move the right *H hand* from near the right shoulder downward toward the left *H hand* held in front of the waist until the fingers overlap, both palms facing in.

**seat belt**[2] *n. phrase.* See sign for BUCKLE.

**second**[1] *n.* **1.** One of the sixty equal periods of time that make up a minute: *a watch that marks the hours, minutes, and seconds.* **2.** A moment: *Wait a second.*

■ [Shows the movement of the second hand on a clock] With the palm side of the right *1 hand* against the left open palm, fingers pointing up, twist the extended right finger forward a very short distance.

**second**[2] *adj.* **1.** Next after the first: *the second time you've done that.* —*n.* **2.** The one after the first in a series of two or more: *the second in command.* —*adv.* **3.** In the second place: *always comes in second in contests.* Same sign used for: **two dollars.**

■ [**two** + a twisting movement used to indicate ordinals] Beginning with the right *2 hand* in front of the right shoulder, palm facing forward and fingers pointing up, twist the wrist, ending with the palm facing in.

**second-hand** *adj.* Previously owned: *to buy a second-hand car.* Same sign used for: **used.**

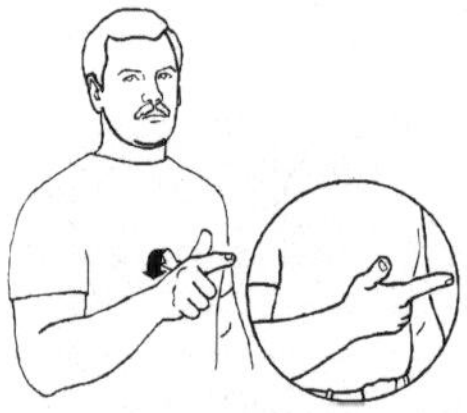

■ Beginning with the right *L hand* in front of the right side of the chest, palm facing down and index finger pointing forward, twist the wrist up and down with a double movement.

**second the motion** *v. phrase.* To offer support to a motion, as to allow further discussion or an official vote, during a parliamentary procedure: *I second that motion.*

■ Beginning with the right *L hand* in front of the right side of the head, palm facing left and index finger pointing up, move the hand deliberately forward while tipping the hand downward, ending with the index finger pointing forward.

**secret** *adj.* **1.** Hidden from the knowledge of others: *a secret hiding place.* —*n.* **2.** A piece of hidden information: *It's difficult to keep a secret.* Same sign used for: **classified, confidential, password, privacy, private.**

- [The movement seems to silence the lips to keep a secret] Tap the thumb side of the right *A hand,* palm facing left, against the mouth with a repeated movement.

**secretary** *n.* **1.** A person who keeps records, as for a company or committee meetings: *The secretary will send out the minutes of the meeting.* **2.** A person who does correspondence, typing, filing, and other support work in an office: *to work as a secretary.*

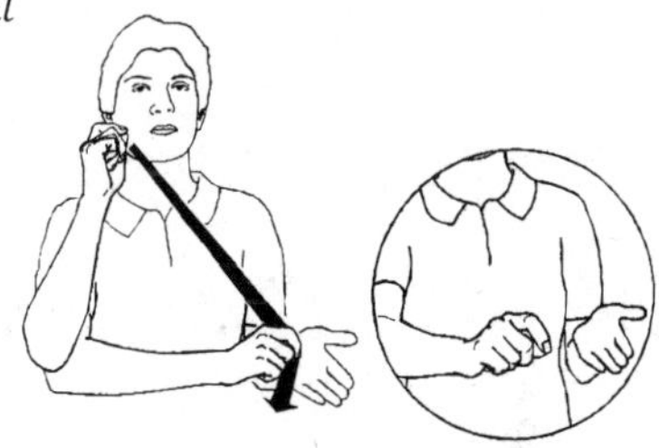

- [The hand seems to take words from the mouth and write them on paper] Bring the right *modified X hand* from near the right side of the chin downward across the palm of the left *open hand* from the heel to off the fingertips.

**secretively** *adv.* See sign for SNEAK.

**section** *n.* See signs for CLASS, PARAGRAPH, PART[1].

**secure** *v.* See sign for SAVE[1]. Related form: **security** *n.*

**security** *n.* See signs for DEFEND, POLICE, SAVE[1].

**sediment** *n.* Material left at the bottom of a liquid; dregs: *sediment left at the bottom of the bucket.* Same sign used for: **residue.**

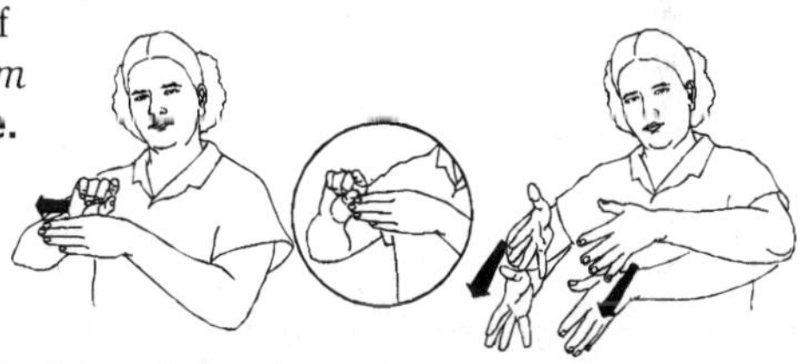

- [Showing a layer of something + **leave**[2]] Slide the thumb of the right *G hand,* palm facing forward, from the wrist to off the fingers of the index-finger side of the left *B hand* held in front of the chest, palm facing in and fingers pointing right. Then, beginning with both *5 hands* in front of each side of the body, palms facing each other and fingers angled forward, thrust the fingers downward with a deliberate movement.

**see** *v.* To perceive with the eyes: *I didn't see you come into the room.* Same sign used for: **eyesight, sight, vision, visualize.**

- [The fingers follow the direction of vision from the eyes] Bring the fingers of the right *V hand* from pointing at the eyes, palm facing in, forward a short distance.

**seem** *v.* To appear to be, do, feel, etc.: *The natives of the small town seemed to be friendly.* Same sign used for: **apparently, appear, look like.**

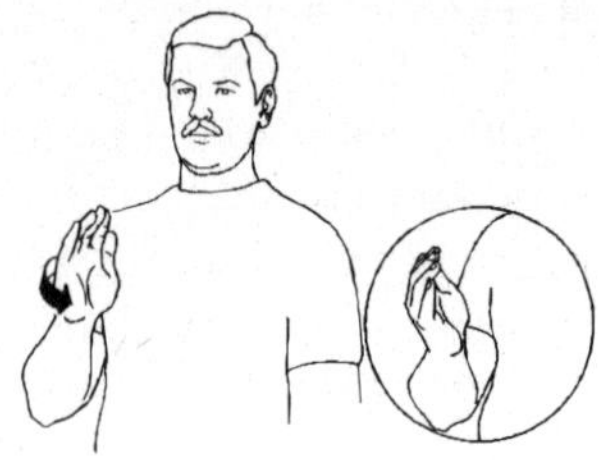

- [Looking in a mirror] Beginning with the right *open hand* near the right shoulder, palm facing forward and fingers pointing up, turn the hand so the palm faces back.

**seethe** *v., n.* See sign for BOILING MAD.

**segment** *n.* See sign for PART[1].

**seize** *v.* See signs for CAPTURE, CATCH[2].

**seizure** *n.* A sudden attack, as experienced by people with epilepsy: *His seizure caused him to fall to the ground.* Same sign used for: **epilepsy.**

- [Represents a body lying with feet up] Wiggle the right *bent V hand,* palm facing up, around on the palm of the left *open hand,* while repeatedly bending the right index and middle fingers.

**seldom** *adv.* Not often; infrequently: *He is seldom home.*

- [**once** formed with a rhythmic repeated movement] Bring the extended right index finger, palm facing in, downward against the upturned palm of the left *open hand* and then swing it upward in a slow upward arc with a double movement.

**select**[1] *v.* To choose from among others: *to select the best apples.* Related forms: **selection** *n.*, **selective** *adj.* Same sign used for: **pick.**

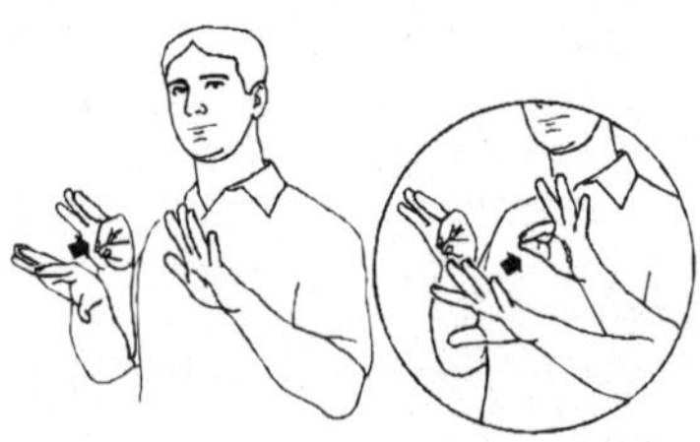

- [**pick** formed with a repeated movement] Beginning with the bent thumb and index finger of the right *5 hand* pointing forward in front of the right shoulder, palm facing forward, bring the right hand back toward the right shoulder while pinching the thumb and index finger together. Repeat with the left hand in front of the left shoulder.

**select**[2] *v.* See signs for APPOINT[1], CHOOSE.

**self** *n.* See sign for OWN.

**selfish**[1] *adj.* **1.** Caring too much for or concerned only with one's own interests: *an utterly selfish person.* **2.** Manifesting excessive concern for oneself: *selfish reasons for lending the money.* Same sign used for: **stingy.**

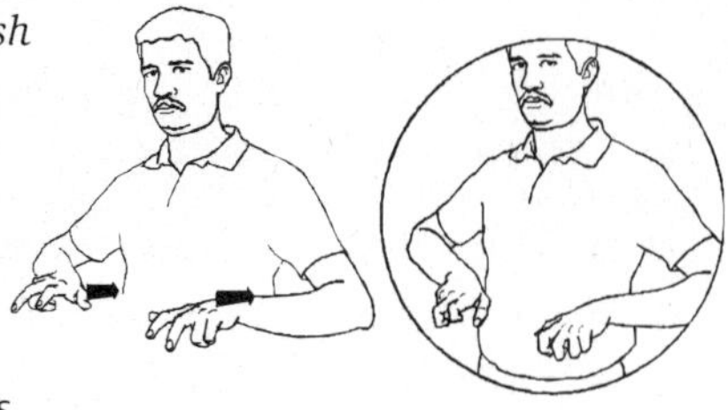

■ Beginning with both *3 hands* in front of each side of the body, palms facing down, bring the hands back toward the body while bending the fingers in toward the palms.

**selfish**[2] *n.* See sign for GREEDY.

**sell** *v.* To exchange something for payment: *to sell my house.* Same sign used for: **distribute, merchandise, pawn, peddle, retail, sale.**

■ [The hands seem to hold something out for inspection in order to sell it] Beginning with both *flattened O hands* held in front of each side of the chest, palms facing down and fingers pointing down, swing the fingertips forward and back by twisting the wrists upward with a double movement.

**semester** *n.* A portion, usually half, of a school year: *started French during the first semester.*

■ [Initialized sign] Move the right *S hand* from in front of the right shoulder, palm facing forward, a short distance to the right and then straight down in front of the chest.

**semiannual** *adj.* See signs for BIANNUAL.

**seminary** *n.* A school that prepares students for the clergy: *to study at a seminary to be a minister.*

■ [Initialized sign similar to sign for **college**] Beginning with the right *S hand,* palm facing down, on the palm of the left *open hand* held in front of the chest, palm facing up, move the right hand upward in an arc.

**senate** *n.* A powerful lawmaking assembly in a government: *a member of the senate.* Same sign used for: **staff.**

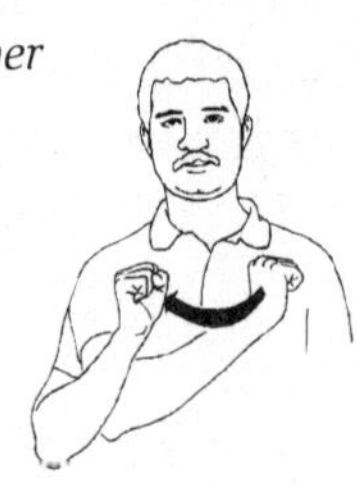

■ [Initialized sign similar to sign for **Congress**] Move the index-finger side of the right *S hand,* palm facing left, from the left side of the chest to the right side of the chest in a small arc.

**send** *v.* See sign for MAIL.

**send out** *v. phrase.* See sign for MAIL.

**senior** *n.* **1.** A student who is a member of the graduating class of a high school or college: *a scholarship to college for one of our high school seniors.* *—adj.* **2.** Of or pertaining to seniors in high school or college: *a prom for the senior class.*

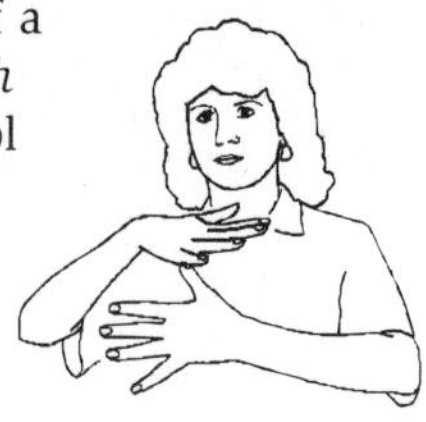

■ [Shows the top year in school] Place the palm of the right *5 hand,* palm facing down and fingers pointing left, on the thumb of the left *5 hand,* palm facing in and fingers pointing right.

**senior citizen** *n. phrase.* An older person; retiree: *The senior citizens are given bus passes.*

■ [Abbreviation **s-c** formed in the same location as the sign for **old**] With the right hand, form an *S* and then a *C* in front of the chin, palm facing left.

**sensation** *n.* See sign for FEEL.

**sense** *v., n.* See signs for FEEL, MIND.

**senseless** *adj.* Foolish: *a senseless deed.*

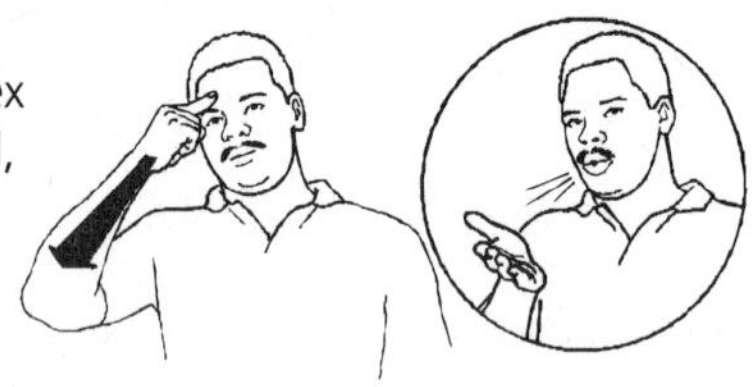

■ [**think** + **nothing**[3]] Move the extended right index finger from touching the right side of the forehead, palm facing in, forward while opening the fingers into an *open hand* in front of the right shoulder, palm facing up. Then blow across the palm of the right *open hand.*

**sensitive** *adj.* **1.** Easily affected: *sensitive feelings.* **2.** Easily offended: *Don't be so sensitive.* **3.** Responsive and sympathetic to the feelings of others: *looking for a relationship with a sensitive person.*

■ [Formed with the finger used for feelings] Beginning with the bent middle finger of the right *5 hand* touching the right side of the chest, flick the wrist forward, ending with the palm facing down.

**sentence** *n.* A group of words that express a complete thought, as a statement, question, or command, having an overt or understood subject and a predicate with a finite verb: *They never learned how to write a complete sentence.* Same sign used for: **statement.**

■ [Represents stretching out words into a sentence] Beginning with the thumbs and index fingers of both *F hands* touching in front of the chest, palms facing each other, pull the hands apart with a wiggly movement, ending in front of each side of the chest.

**separate** *v.* **1.** To bring, force, or keep apart: *The cashier separated the coins from the bills.* —*adj.* **2.** Detached; not shared: *They sat at separate tables.* Related form: **separation** *n.* Same sign used for: **apart.**

■ Beginning with the knuckles of both *A hands* touching in front of the chest, palms facing in, bring the hands apart.

**sequel** *n.* See sign for UPDATE.

**sequence** *n.* See signs for PLAN[2], PREPARE.

**serene** *adj.* See sign for QUIET[1].

**series** *n.* See sign for CLASS.

**serious** *adj.* **1.** Thoughtful; requiring thought: *a serious book.* **2.** Important; significant: *Quitting school is a serious matter.* **3.** Threatening: *a serious illness.* Same sign used for: **severe.**

■ With the extended right index finger touching the chin, palm facing left, twist the right hand, ending with the palm facing back.

**sermon** *n.* See sign for SPEAK[2].

**serpent** *n.* See sign for SNAKE.

**serve** *v.* **1.** To give service to, as by providing with food and drink: *to serve the customers at the restaurant.* **2.** To provide assistance to: *How may I serve you?* Related form: **service** *n.* Same sign used for: **host, minister, wait on.**

■ [The hands seem to carry something to serve it] Beginning with both *open hands* in front of each side of the body, palms facing up and right hand closer to the body than the left, move the hands forward and back with an alternating movement.

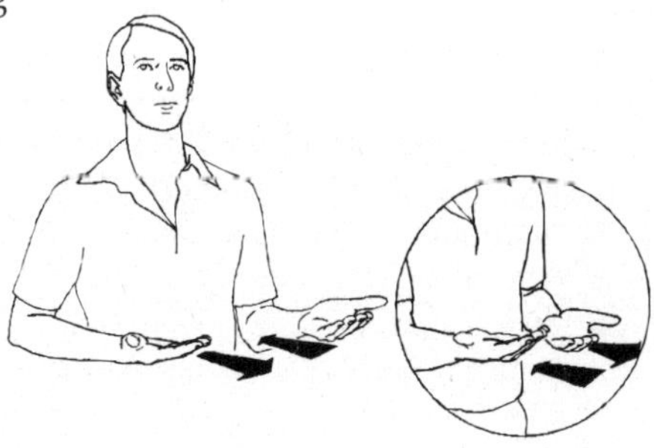

**server** *n.* A high-capacity computer with resources such as a hard disk and printer that are available to other terminals in a computer network: *The office was hooked up to a central server.* Same sign used for: **printer server, slave.**

■ [**center** + **spread**] Move the right *open hand*, palm facing down, in a circular movement over the upturned left *open hand*, bending the fingers as the hand moves and ending with the fingertips of the right *bent hand* touching the middle of the left palm. Then beginning with the fingertips of both *flattened O hands* touching in front of the chest, palms facing down, move the hands forward and away from each other while opening into *5 hands* in front of each side of the body, palms facing down.

**session** *n.* See sign for MEETING.

**set**[1] *n.* (*as in computer programming*) Shared idea of a group of instructions combined to perform certain functions. See sign for SOCIETY.

**set**[2] *v.* See sign for PUT.

**set off** *v. phrase.* See sign for ZOOM[1].

**set up**[1] *v. phrase.* **1.** To raise into place: *to set up the tent.* **2.** To get ready for something by putting things into place: *to set up for the luncheon.* Same sign used for: **erect, founded, recover.**

■ [The movement represents setting up something] Beginning with the fingertips of both *curved hands* touching in front of the chest, palms facing down, bend the fingers upward, ending with the fingers angled upward and touching each other.

**set up**[2] *v. phrase.* See signs for ESTABLISH, RECOVER.

**settle** *v.* or **settle down** *v. phrase.* **1.** To quiet down; make calm: *medicine to settle the stomach.* **2.** To come to rest: *to settle in a comfortable position.* **3.** To place in order: *to settle their business affairs.* Same sign used for: **calm, calm down, quiet down, relax.**

■ [Natural gesture for calming someone down] Beginning with both *5 hands* in front of each side of the chest, palms facing down, move the hands slowly down to in front of each side of the waist.

**several** *adj.* See sign for FEW.

**severe** *adj.* See sign for SERIOUS.

**sew**[1] *v.* **1.** To fasten with stitches by hand using a needle and thread: *to sew a button on.* **2.** To make or fix with stitches in this way: *to sew and embroider a dress.* Related form: **sewing** *n.* Same sign used for: **stitch.**

■ [Mime sewing with a needle] With the thumbs and index fingers of both *F hands* touching in front of the chest, palms facing each other, move the right hand in a double circular movement upward in front of the right shoulder, meeting the fingertip of the left hand each time it passes.

**sew**[2] *v.* To make or fix by working with needle and thread on a sewing machine: *They sew all their children's clothes.* Related form: **sewing** *n.* Same sign used for: **sewing machine, stitch.**

■ [Represents the action of a sewing machine needle moving across fabric] Move the bent index finger of the right *X hand,* palm facing down, with a double movement from the base to off the fingertip of the extended left index finger, palm facing down and finger angled to the right.

**sew**[3] *v.* See sign for NEEDLEWORK.

**sewing machine** *n. phrase.* See sign for SEW[2].

**sex**[1] *n.* **1.** Either of the two divisions, male and female, of human beings and some other species, as distinguished by their reproductive functions: *Mammals of the female sex bear the young.* **2.** Human sexual attraction and fulfillment: *a movie showing a bit of tasteful sex.* Related form: **sexual** *adj.* Same sign used for: **gender.**

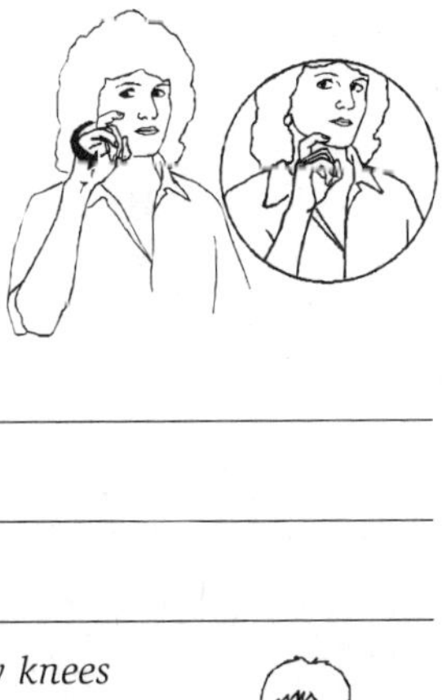

■ Touch the index finger side of the right *X hand,* first to near the right eye and then to the lower chin, palm facing forward.

**sex**[2] *n.* See sign for INTERCOURSE.

**shadow** *n.* See sign for DARK.

**shake** *v.* **1.** To move or cause to move in a jerky manner: *My knees were shaking. The baby shook the rattle.* **2.** To move violently or dislodge with violent movements: *to shake the rug; to shake the dirt out of the rug.*

■ [Mime shaking something] With both *A hands* in front of each side of the body, palms facing down, move the hands from side to side with a repeated movement.

**shake hands** *v. phrase.* See sign for HANDSHAKE.

**sham** *n.* See sign for FAKE[2].

**shame**[1] *n.* A painful feeling of having done something improper: *to blush with shame.* Related form: **shameful** *adj.*

■ Beginning with the backs of the fingers of the right *bent hand* against the right side of the chin, palm facing down, twist the hand upward and forward, ending with the right *bent hand* in front of the right side of the chest, palm facing up.

**shame**[2] *n.* See sign for ASHAMED. Related form: **shameful** *adj.*

**shampoo** *n.* **1.** A cleansing preparation for washing the hair: *My shampoo has conditioner added.* —*v.* **2.** To wash one's hair with shampoo: *to shampoo my hair every day.* Same sign used for: **wash one's hair.**

■ [Mime shampooing one's hair] Move both *curved 5 hands,* palms facing each other, in and out near each side of the head with a repeated movement.

**shape**[1] *n.* The form of the outer surface or an outline of an object: *a round shape.* Same sign used for: **figure, form, image.**

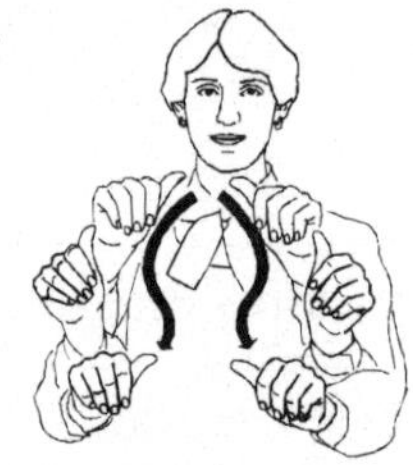

■ [The hands outline the image of a shape] Beginning with both *10 hands* in front of each side of the chest, palms facing forward, bring the hands downward with a wavy movement, ending in front of each side of the waist.

**shape**[2] *n.* See sign for STATUE.

**share** *v.* To use or participate in together: *to share the same room.* Same sign used for: **change.**

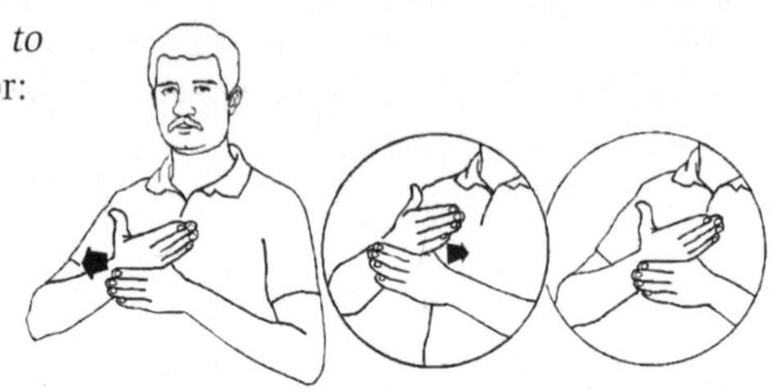

■ [The hand moves back and forth as if to share a portion of something] Move the little-finger side of the right *open hand,* palm facing in, back and forth with a double movement at the base of the index finger of the left *open hand,* palm facing in.

**sharp** *adj.* Having a thin cutting edge or fine point: *a sharp knife.* Same sign used for: **keen.**

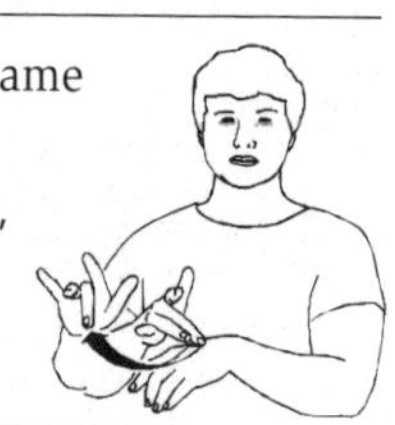

■ Flick the bent middle finger of the right *5 hand,* palm facing down, forward off the back of the left *open hand* held in front of the body.

**shave**[1] *v.* To remove a beard or excess hair growth with an electric razor: *to shave every day.* Same sign used for: **razor.**

■ [Represents holding an electric razor to shave] Move the fingertips of the right *flattened C hand* up and down on the right cheek with a repeated movement.

**shave**[2] *v.* To remove a beard or excess hair growth with a hand-held razor: *to shave every morning.* Same sign used for: **razor.**

■ [Represents holding a hand razor to shave] Move the knuckles of the right *Y hand,* palm facing left, downward on the right cheek with a repeated movement.

**she** *pron.* See sign for HE.

**shears** *pl. n.* See sign for SCISSORS.

**shed** *v.* See sign for BLOOD.

**sheep** *n.* A cud-chewing mammal, closely related to the goat, often bred for its coat of wool: *a flock of sheep.*

■ [Represents cutting the wool from sheep] Slide the back of the fingers of the right *K hand,* palm facing up, from the wrist up the inside forearm of the left bent arm with a short repeated movement.

**shelf** *n.* A flat, slablike surface fastened horizontally to the wall or in a frame to hold things: *to put books on the shelf.* Same sign used for: **mantel.**

■ [The shape of a shelf] Beginning with the index-finger sides of both *B hands* touching in front of the chest, palms facing down and fingers pointing forward, bring the hands apart to in front of each side of the chest.

**sheriff** *n.* See sign for POLICE.

**shield** *v.* See sign for DEFEND.

**shift** *v.* See sign for CHANGE.

**shine** *v.* See sign for LIGHT.

**shiny** *adj.* Reflecting light; bright; glossy: *a shiny penny.* Related form: **shine** *n., v.* Same sign used for: **glitter, glossy, glow, sparkle.**

■ [Indicates the glare reflecting off something shiny] Beginning with the bent middle finger of the right *5 hand,* palm facing down, touching the back of the left *open hand,* palm facing down, bring the right hand upward in front of the chest with a wiggly movement.

**ship**[1] *n.* A large sailing vessel: *to go to the Caribbean by ship.* Same sign used for: **cruise, sailboat.**

■ [The right hand represents a ship moving on waves] With the little-finger side of the right *3 hand,* palm facing left, resting on the palm of the left *open hand,* palm facing up, move both hands forward in a series of small arcs.

**ship**[2] *n.* See sign for BOAT.

**shirk** *v.* See sign for AVOID.

**shirt** *n.* A lightweight garment, usually with sleeves, worn on the upper part of the body: *a new shirt with a tailored collar.* Same sign used for: **top.**

■ [Indicates the location of a shirt] Pull a small portion of clothing from the upper right chest forward with the fingers of the right *F hand,* palm facing in, with a double movement.

**shiver**[1] *v.* **1.** To shake with cold or fear: *to shiver with fright.* —*n.* **2.** An act, instance, or attack of shivering: *to feel a shiver down my back.* Same sign used for: **quiver.**

■ [Represents teeth rattling together when shivering] Beginning with the heels of both *bent V hands* touching in front of the chest, twist the right hand with a double movement.

**shiver**[2] *v., n.* See sign for COLD[2].

**shock** *n.* **1.** A sudden feeling of surprise or horror: *It was a shock to learn of his illness.* —*v.* **2.** To feel a sudden sensation of surprise or horror: *shocked by what I saw.* Related form: **shocking** *adj.* Same sign used for: **astounded, dumbfounded, startled.**

■ [Represents one's eyes bulging open when shocked] Beginning with the index-finger sides of both *S hands* in front of each eye, palms facing each other, open the hands simultaneously into *C hands.*

**shoe** *n.* An outer covering for the foot, often of leather: *Time to polish your shoes.*

■ [Represents clicking the heels of shoes together] Tap the index-finger sides of both *S hands* together in front of the chest with a double movement, palms facing down.

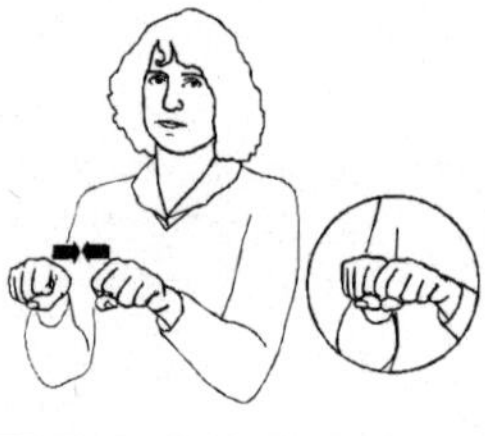

**shoot**[1] *v.* See signs for MOVIE CAMERA, TAKE PICTURES.

**shoot**[2] *interj.* See sign for ALAS.

**shoot up** *v. phrase.* To grow taller and develop rapidly: *The girl has shot up over the last six months and is now as tall as her mother.* Same sign used for: **become successful, skyrocket, zoom.**

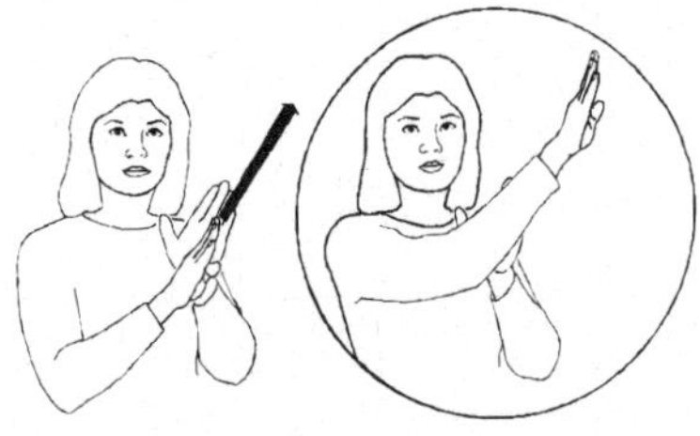

■ [An upward movement] Slide the index-finger side of the right *B hand,* palm angled forward, upward from the heel to off the fingertips of the left *open hand* held in front of the chest, palm facing right and fingers pointing up.

**shop**[1] *v.* To visit stores to look at or buy goods: *to go shopping on Saturday.* Related form: **shopping** *n.*

■ [The hand takes money and gives it in payment] Beginning with the back of the right *flattened O hand,* palm facing up, across the palm of the left *open hand,* palm facing up, move the right hand forward and slightly upward with a double movement.

**shop**[2] *n.* See sign for STORE[1].

**shoplift** *v.* To steal from a store while pretending to be a customer: *arrested for shoplifting in a department store.* See also sign for STEAL[2]. Same sign used for: **burglary, theft.**

■ [The hands spread out to grab things] Beginning with the fingers of both *5 hands* pointing toward each other in front of the body, palms facing down, bring the hands outward and away from each other in arcs, ending with the hands in front of each side of the body. Then close the fingers into *A hands.*

**shopper** *n.* See sign for CUSTOMER[1].

**short**[1] *adj.* Having little length; not long: *a short time.* Related form: **shortage** *n.* See also sign for BRIEF. Same sign used for: **soon, temporary.**

■ [The fingers measure off a short distance] Rub the middle-finger side of the right *H hand,* palm angled left, back and forth with a repeated movement on the index-finger side of the left *H hand,* palm angled right.

**short**[2] *adj.* See signs for LITTLE[2], THIN.

**shortcut** *n.* A short or quick way of doing something or getting somewhere: *to take a shortcut home.*

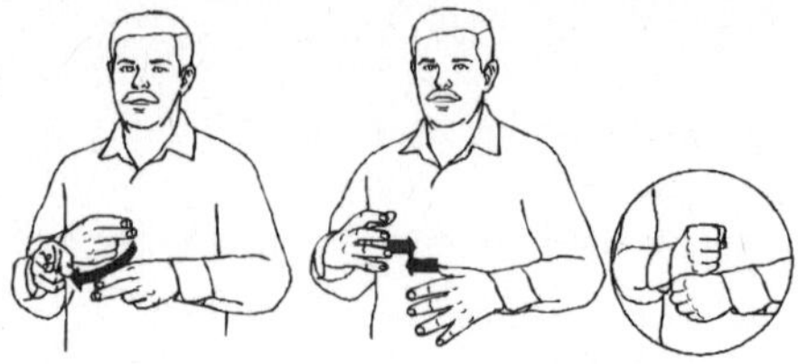

■ [**short**[1] + **brief**] Brush the middle-finger side of the right *H hand,* palm angled left, with a sweeping movement across the index-finger side of the left *H hand,* palm angled right. Then, beginning with both *curved 5 hands* in front of the chest, right hand higher than the left hand and fingers pointing in opposite directions, bring the hands toward each other while squeezing the fingers together, ending with the little-finger side of the right *S hand* on top of the thumb side of the left *S hand.*

**shortly** *adv.* See sign for SOON[1].

**shorts** *pl. n.* Loose trousers reaching to above the knees: *to wear shorts in summer.*

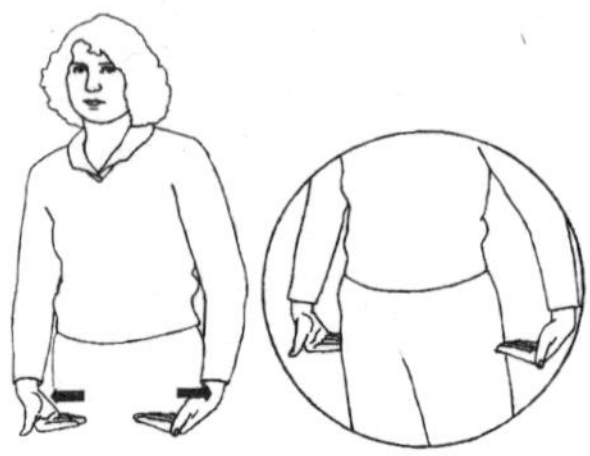

■ [Shows the length of shorts] Slide the little-finger sides of both *bent hands,* palms facing up, with a double movement from in front of each thigh around to each side, ending with the fingertips touching the sides of each thigh.

**shot** *n.* An injection, as of a vaccine, a drug, or vitamins: *a shot against polio.* Same sign used for: **hypodermic, injection, inoculation, vaccine.**

■ [Mime pushing the plunger on a hypodermic syringe] With the index finger of the right *L hand* touching the left upper arm, bend the right thumb up and down with a repeated movement.

**should** *auxiliary v.* See sign for MUST.

**shoulder** *n.* The part of the human body to which the arm is attached: *He put his hand on my shoulder.*

■ [The location of one's shoulder] Pat the palm of the right *curved hand,* palm facing down, with a single movement on the left shoulder.

**shout** *v.* See sign for SCREAM.

**shove** *v.* To push: *shove the box out of the way.* Same sign used for: **push.**

■ [Mime shoving someone or something] Move the right *5 hand,* palm facing forward, from the chest forward with a deliberate movement.

**shovel** *v.* See sign for DIG.

**show**[1] *v.* To display to or cause to be seen by another: *I want to show you this student's term paper.* Same sign used for: **demonstrate, expose, indicate, indication, portray, reveal, sample.**

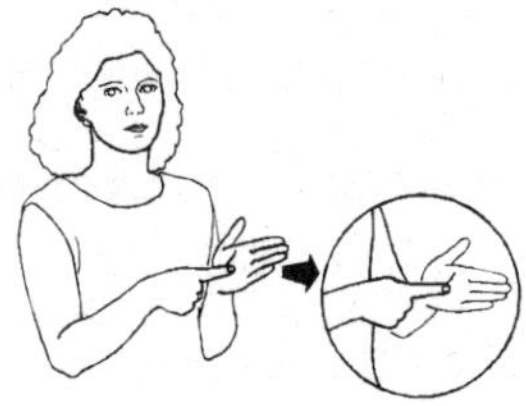

■ [The finger points to something in the hand and moves it to show it to someone else] With the extended right index finger, palm facing in, touching the open left palm, move both hands forward a short distance.

**show**[2] *v.* (alternate sign, used when something is shown to many people) Same sign used for: **exhibit.**

■ [Represents showing something around to many people] With the extended right index finger, palm facing in, touching the open left palm, move both hands in a flat circle in front of the body.

**show**[3] *v.* See sign for ACT[2].

**show**[4] *n.* See sign for FILM[1].

**show off** *v. phrase.* See sign for BRAG.

**show up** *v. phrase.* To put in an appearance; arrive: *to show up at the party.* Same sign used for: **appear, come up, incident, materialize, occur, pop up, surface, turn up.**

■ [Represents something popping up into sight] Push the extended right index finger, palm angled left, upward between the index finger and middle finger of the left *open hand,* palm facing down.

**shower** *n.* **1.** A bath in which water pours down on the body from an overhead nozzle: *to take a shower every morning.* —*v.* **2.** To take a shower: *I'd rather shower than take a bath.*

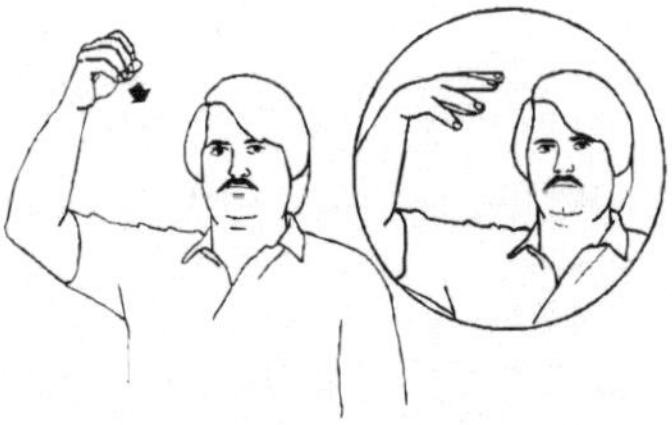

■ [Represents water coming down from a shower head] Beginning with the right *O hand* above the right side of the head, palm facing down, open the fingers into a *5 hand* with a double movement.

**shred** *v.* To tear in small pieces: *to shred the documents.* Related form: **shredder** *n.*

■ [Action of paper going through a shredder] Move the fingers of the right *4 hand* downward to intersect the fingers of the left *4 hand* held in front of the chest, both palms facing down.

**shrimp** *n.* A small, long-tailed shellfish, some species of which are used for food: *to eat shrimp at a seafood restaurant.*

■ [Represents a shrimp's tail] Beginning with the extended right index finger pointing left in front of the right side of the chest, palm facing in, bend the finger into an *X hand* with a double movement.

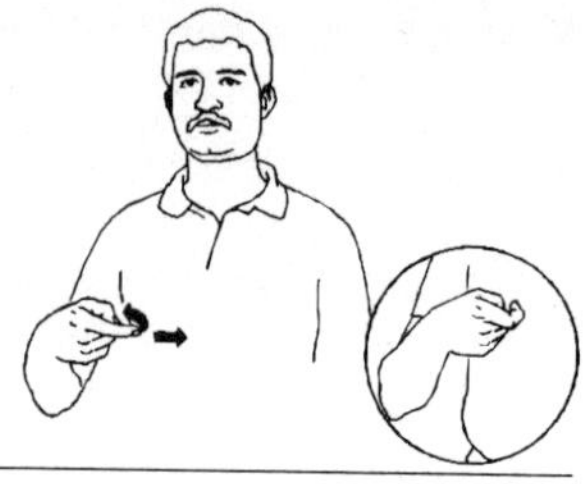

**shrink** *v.* See signs for DECREASE², DIET.

**shudder** *v.* To tremble, as in fear or horror: *We shuddered when we walked into the dark room.*

■ [Natural gesture showing a shudder] With both *5 hands* in front of each side of the chest, palms facing forward and fingers pointing up, shake the hands back and forth with a repeated movement.

**shuffle** *v.* To intermix cards to put them in random order: *to shuffle the deck before dealing the cards.*

■ [Mime mixing up a deck of cards] With the little-finger side of the right *C hand* on the index-finger side of the left *C hand* in front of the chest, palms facing in opposite directions, raise the right *C hand* upward a short distance at an angle to the right with a double movement.

**shut out** *v. phrase.* To defeat an opposing team without allowing it to score: *shut out the opponent.*

■ [Indicates a score of zero] Move the right *O hand,* palm angled forward, from near the right eye forward with a deliberate movement.

**shut up**¹ *v. phrase.* To stop talking; become silent: *Shut up and listen.* Same sign used for: **keep quiet, seal one's lips.**

■ [Represents closing one's mouth to shut it up] Beginning with the thumb of the *flattened C hand* touching the chin, palm facing in, close the fingers to the thumb, forming a *flattened O hand*.

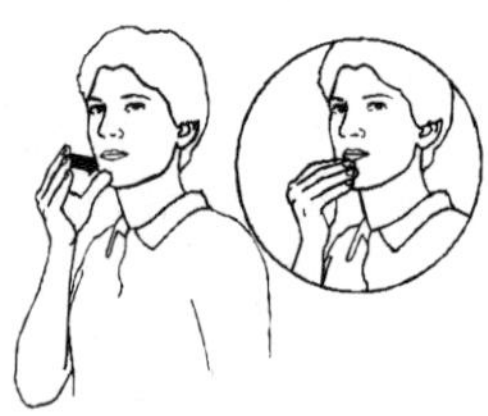

**shut up**² *v. phrase.* (alternate sign) Same sign used for: **didn't say that, didn't mean that.**

■ [The finger quiets the mouth] Bring the extended right index finger sharply against the mouth, palm facing left and finger pointing up, while shaking the head negatively.

**shy**[1] *adj.* Uncomfortable or timid in company: *a shy child.* Same sign used for: **bashful.**

■ Beginning with the palm side of the right *A hand* against the lower right cheek, twist the hand forward, ending with the palm facing back.

**shy**[2] *adj.* See sign for ASHAMED.

**sick** *adj.* In poor health or afflicted with a disease: *I feel sick from this cold.* Related form: **sickness** *n.* Same sign used for: **ill, illness, malady.**

■ [The finger used to indicate feeling touches the forehead to show that a person doesn't feel well] Touch the bent middle finger of the right *5 hand,* palm facing in, to the forehead.

**sick of** *Informal.* Weary of; exasperated with: *sick of your excuses.*

■ [**sick** formed with a deliberate twist] With the bent middle finger of the right *5 hand* touching the forehead, twist the hand to the left with a deliberate movement.

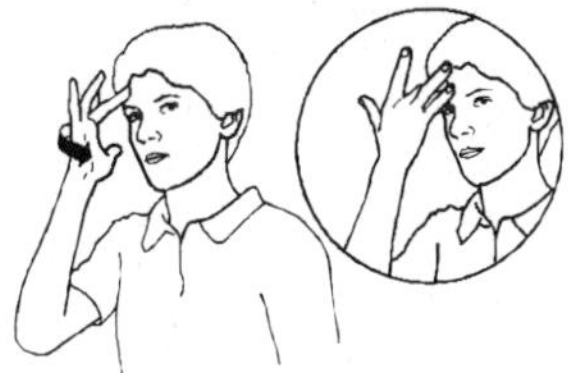

**side** *n.* **1.** One of the surfaces forming the outside of an object: *the north side of a building.* **2.** An area at the edge of something, as a room: *Everyone move to the side of the road.*

■ [Shows the shape of the side of a wall] Bring the right *open hand,* palm facing left and fingers pointing forward, downward in front of the right side of the body.

**sidestep** *v.* To avoid (an issue): *to sidestep the problem.*

■ [Represents a person's legs moving off to the side] Move the fingers of the right *bent V hand,* palm facing down, from the extended left index finger held in front of the left side of the chest, palm facing right, in a downward arc to the right.

**sidetracked** *adj.* See sign for ASTRAY.

**sight** *n.* See sign for SEE.

**sightseeing** *n.* The act of going around to see places of interest: *to go sightseeing in Washington.*

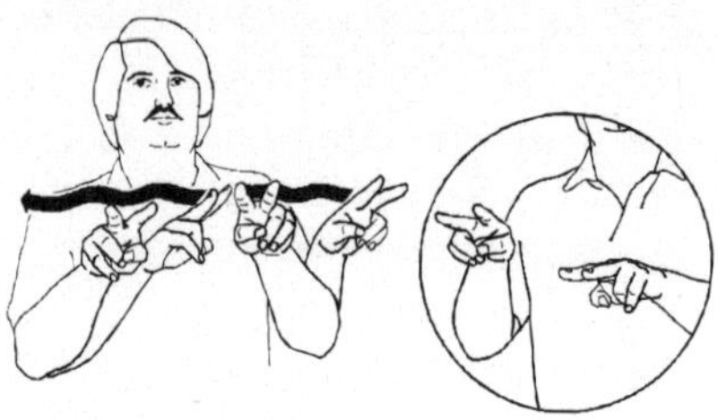

■ [The fingers represent one's vision as one goes sightseeing] Beginning with the right *V hand* in front of the chest and the left *V hand* in front of the left shoulder, move both hands to the right with a wavy movement, ending with the right *V hand* in front of the right shoulder and the left *V hand* in front of the chest, both palms facing down.

**sign**[1] *v.* **1.** To communicate in sign language: *Watch how well they sign to each other.* —*n.* **2.** A grammatical unit within sign language: *Let me show you the correct sign.*

■ [Represents one's hands moving when using sign language] Beginning with both extended index fingers pointing up in front of each side of the chest, palms facing forward and the left hand higher than the right hand, move the hands in large alternating circles toward the chest.

**sign**[2] *v.* To affix one's name in writing: *to sign the check.* Same sign used for: **endorse, register.**

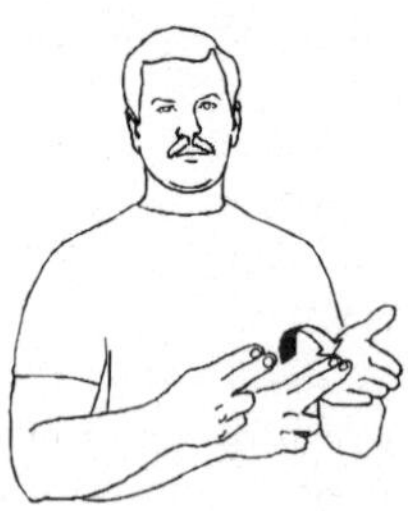

■ [Represents placing one's name on a paper] Place the extended fingers of the right *H hand*, palm facing down, firmly down on the upturned palm of the left *open hand* held in front of the chest.

**sign**[3] *n.* See signs for SQUARE, SYMBOL.

**signature** *n.* Same sign as for SIGN[2] but made with a double movement.

**significant** *adj., n.* See sign for IMPORTANT. Related form: **significance** *n.*

**sign language** *n.* The language of Deaf people in which motions, especially of the hands, stand for ideas: *learned to communicate in sign language.*

■ [**sign**[1] + **language**] Beginning with both extended index fingers pointing up in front of each side of the chest, palms facing forward and the left hand higher than the right hand, move the hands in large alternating circles toward the chest. Then move both *L hands* from in front of the center of the chest, palms angled down, away from each other to in front of each shoulder with a wavy movement.

**silence** *n.* See signs for QUIET[1,2]. Related form: **silent** *adj.*

**silky** *adj.* See sign for SMOOTH[2].

**silly** *adj.* Without sense or reason: *a silly thing to do.* Same sign used for: **absurd, foolish, ridiculous.**

- Beginning with the right *Y hand* in front of the face, palm facing in, twist the wrist outward with a double movement, brushing the right thumb across the nose with each movement.

**silver** *n.* **1.** A white precious metal used to make coins, jewelry, tableware, etc.: *a necklace made of silver.* **2.** Coins: *a pocket filled with silver.* *—adj.* **3.** Made of silver: *a silver spoon.*

- [Initialized sign similar to sign for **gold**] Bring the extended right index finger, palm facing in, from pointing to the right ear downward and forward with a shaking movement while turning the palm forward and changing into an *S hand.*

**similar** *adj.* See signs for ALIKE[1,2], SAME[1].

**simple**[1] *adj.* **1.** Easy to understand: *simple directions.* **2.** Uncomplicated: *a simple design.* **3.** Unadorned: *She chose a simple suit for her wedding dress.*

- Beginning with both *F hands* in front of the body, right hand higher than the left hand and palms facing in opposite directions, bring the right hand down, striking the fingertips of the left hand as it passes.

**simple**[2] *adj.* See sign for EASY.

**sin** *n.* **1.** An act of breaking divine laws: *Stealing is a sin.* *—v.* **2.** To commit a sin: *sinned by envying others.* Same sign used for: **trespass.**

- Beginning with both extended index fingers angled upward in front of each side of the chest, palms facing in, move the hands toward each other in double circular movement.

**since**[1] *prep.* From a past time until now: *since we moved here.* Same sign used for: **all along, been, ever since, lately, since then, so far.**

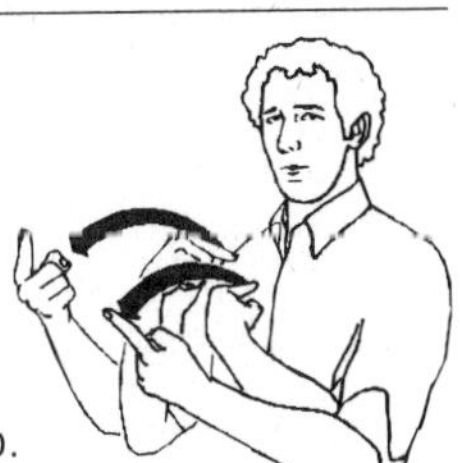

- [Shows passage of time from the past to the present] Move the extended index fingers of both hands from touching the upper right chest, palms facing in, forward in an arc, ending with the index fingers angled forward and the palms angled up.

**since**[2] *conj.* See sign for BECAUSE.

**sing** *v.* See sign for MUSIC.

**single** *adj.* Only one in number: *the single child in a room full of adults.* Same sign used for: **alone.**

- [Shows a person moving around alone] Beginning with the extended right index finger pointing up in front of the right side of chest, palm facing in, move the hand into the middle of the chest and then back to the right again.

**siren** *n.* See sign for AMBULANCE.

**sister** *n.* A female with the same parents as another person: *My sister is two years older than I am.*

- Beginning with the thumb of the right *L hand* touching the right side of the chin, palm facing left, move the right hand downward, ending with the little-finger side of the right *L hand* across the thumb side of the left *L hand* held in front of the chest, palms facing right.

**sister-in-law** *n.* The sister of one's husband or wife, or the wife of one's brother, or the wife of the brother of one's husband or wife: *going to visit my new sister-in-law.*

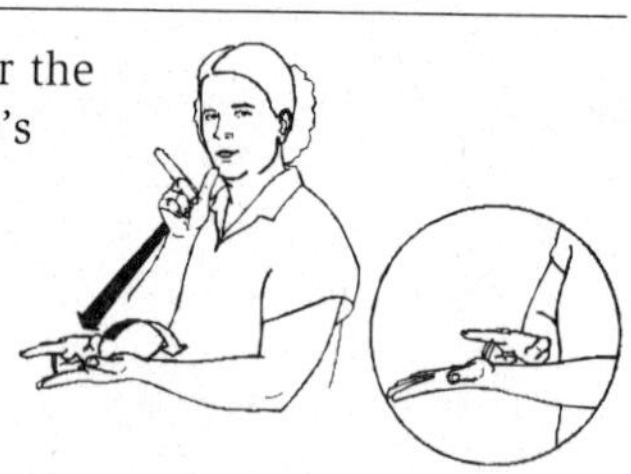

- [A combination similar to the signs for **sister** + **law**] Beginning with the thumb of the right *L hand* touching the right side of the chin, palm facing left, move the right hand downward, landing on the upturned palm of the left *open hand.* Then move the right *L hand* to touch again near the heel of the left *open hand,* palm facing up and fingers pointing forward.

**sit** *v.* To rest with the knees bent and the lower part of the body supported on the buttocks and thighs: *to sit on a comfortable chair.*

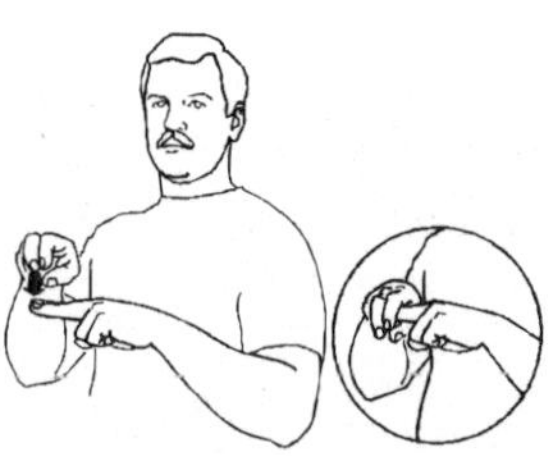

- [The bent fingers represent one's legs dangling from the edge of a seat] Hook the fingers of the right *curved U hand,* palm facing down, perpendicularly across the fingers of the left *U hand* held in front of the chest, palm facing down and fingers pointing right.

**situation** *n.* Condition; state of affairs; set of circumstances: *got himself into a bad situation with his boss.* Same sign used for: **surround.**

- Move the right *S hand* in a circle around the extended left index finger, palm facing right in front of the chest, by twisting the right wrist.

**six months** *pl. n.* See sign for BIANNUAL.

**size**[1] *n.* The proportions, dimensions, or extent of something: *What is your shoe size?*

- [The hands seem to measure out a size] Beginning with the thumbs of both *Y hands* touching in front of the chest, palms facing down, bring the hands apart to in front of each side of the chest.

**size**[2] *n.* See sign for MEASURE.

**skate**[1] *n.* **1.** A shoe fitted with rollers so that a person can glide on a surface: *to try those new in-line roller skates.* —*v.* **2.** To glide along on roller skates: *to skate down the street with my friends.* Same sign used for: **roller skate.**

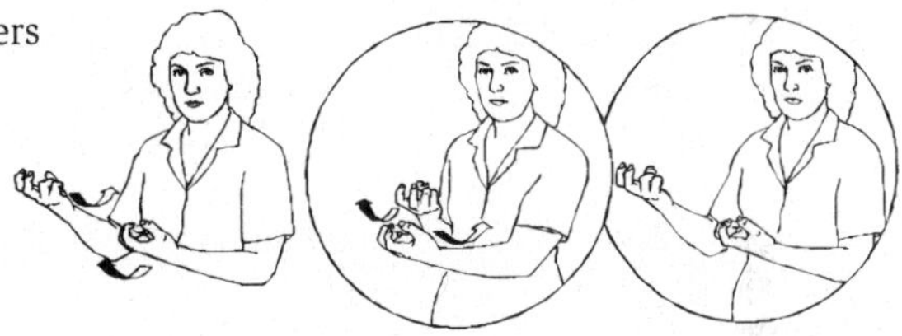

- [Shows the action of a person roller skating] With both *bent V hands* in front of each side of the chest, palms facing up, move the hands forward and back with a repeated alternating swinging movement.

**skate**[2] *n.* **1.** A shoe fitted with a blade so that a person can glide on ice: *ice skates with newly sharpened blades.* —*v.* **2.** To glide along on ice skates: *She skates so well she can do spins and triple jumps on the ice.* Same sign used for: **ice skate.**

- [Shows the action of a person who is ice skating] With both *X hands* in front of each side of the chest, palms facing up, move the hands forward and back with a repeated alternating swinging movement.

**skeleton** *n.* The framework of bones in the body: *to study the bones in the skeleton.* Same sign used for: **bone.**

- [Resembles the skull and crossbones symbol on poisons] With the arms crossed at the wrists, lay the palms of both *V hands* on the chest near the opposite shoulder and bend the fingers up and down with a repeated movement.

**skeptical** *adj.* **1.** Failing to believe or trust; uncertain: *I'm skeptical about her motivation for giving me a present.* Same sign used for: **doubtful.**

- [As if one is blind to what is doubted] Beginning with the right *bent V fingers* in front of the eyes, palm facing in, constrict the fingers with a short double movement.

**sketch**[1] *v.* **1.** To draw quickly and roughly: *sketched a map of the neighborhood showing the bus stop.* —*n.* **2.** A quickly done drawing: *did a sketch of my house.* Same sign used for: **draft, drawing, illustration.**

■ [The finger moves as if sketching something] Move the right *I hand,* palm facing in, with a repeated movement in front of the left side of the chest while holding the left *open hand* in front of the left shoulder, palm angled right and fingers pointing forward.

**sketch**[2] *n.* See sign for ART.

**sketch**[3] *v.* See sign for DRAW[1].

**ski** *n.* **1.** One of a pair of long, slender pieces of hard wood fastened to the feet to enable a person to glide on snow: *to put on a pair of skis.* —*v.* **2.** To glide over snow on skis: *to ski down the mountain.* Related form: **skiing** *n.*

■ [Represents the movement of skis on snow] Beginning with both *X hands* in front of the chest, palms facing up and right hand closer to the chest than the left hand, move the hands forward.

**skill** *n.* Ability to do something well, gained from talent, training, or practice: *skill in playing the piano.* Related form: **skilled** *adj.* Same sign used for: **ability, able, agile, capable, efficient, enable, expert, good at, handy, proficient, talent.**

■ Grasp the little-finger side of the left *open hand* with the curved right fingers. Then pull the right hand forward while closing the fingers into the palm.

**skillful** *adj.* See sign for ADROIT.

**skin** *n.* The outer layer of tissue on the body: *soft, smooth skin.* Same sign used for: **flesh.**

■ [The location of skin on one's hand] Pinch and shake the loose skin on the back of the left *open hand,* palm facing down, with the bent thumb and index finger of the right *5 hand.*

**skinny** *adj.* Very thin; emaciated: *She has skinny legs.* See also sign for THIN[2].

■ [Indicates the shape of a skinny person] Move the right *I hand,* palm facing in and finger pointing up, downward in front of the right side of the chest.

**skip**[1] *v.* To avoid attending; be absent from: *to skip class.* Same sign used for: **lack, miss.**

■ Beginning with the left *5 hand* held across the chest, middle finger bent downward, move the extended right index finger, palm facing left and finger pointing forward, from right to left in front of the chest, hitting the bent left middle finger as it passes.

**skip**[2] *n.* **1.** A light jump, especially in a series alternating from one foot to another: *moved along with a lighthearted skip.* —*v.* **2.** To move along with a series of skips: *skipped all the way home.*

■ [Shows the action of skipping] Touch the middle finger of the right *P hand,* palm facing down, on the palm of the left *open hand,* first near the base and then near the fingertips.

**skip**[3] *v.* To pass over or omit: *I skipped one of the questions on the test.*

■ [The right fingers represent a person's legs skipping on to the next item] Tap the palm side of the right *bent V hand,* palm facing forward, first on the index finger and then the middle finger of the left *5 hand* held in front of the chest, palm facing in.

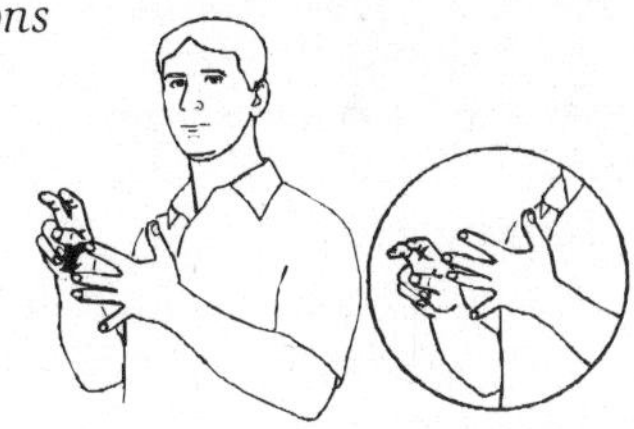

**skirt** *n.* **1.** A woman's garment, not joined between the legs, that hangs from the waist: *to wear a plaid skirt.* **2.** The lower part of a dress: *The buttons go from the collar to halfway down the skirt.*

■ [The location of a skirt] Brush the thumbs of both *5 hands,* palms facing in and fingers pointing down, from the waist downward and outward with a repeated movement.

**sky** *n.* The region of the upper air: *clouds in the sky.*

■ [The location of the sky] Bring the right *curved hand* from over the left side of the head, palm facing down, in a large arc to the right, ending above the right shoulder.

**skyrocket** *v.* See sign for SHOOT UP.

**slacks** *pl. n.* See sign for PANTS.

**slap** *v.* To strike with the open hand: *to slap someone's face.*

■ [Demonstrates the action of slapping something] Bring the fingers of the right *open hand* from in front of the right side of the chest, palm facing left and fingers pointing forward, with a deliberate movement to in front of the left side of the chest, hitting the extended left index finger held in front of the chest, palm facing forward and finger pointing up, as the right hand moves.

**slash** *n.* A mark or cut made with a sweeping stroke: *The tree made a slash across the car.* Same sign used for: **forward slash.**

■ [Shape of a slash] Bring the right *B hand*, palm left, from in front of the right shoulder downward to the left with a deliberate movement.

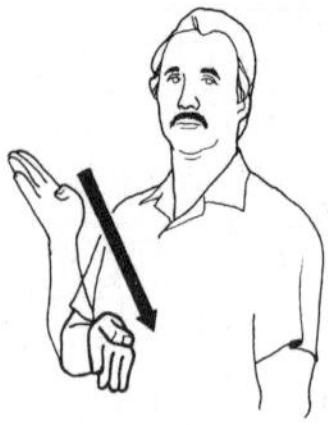

**slaughter** *v.* See sign for KILL.

**slave** *n.* See sign for SERVER.

**slavery** *n.* The condition of being the property of another and being forced to work without proper compensation: *sold people into slavery.* Related form: **slave** *n.*

■ [Represents a person's wrists being bound in slavery; formed with a continuing movement] With the wrists of both *S hands* crossed in front of the body, palms facing down, move the arms in a large, flat circle in front of the body with a double movement.

**slay** *v.* See sign for KILL.

**sled** *n.* A vehicle mounted on runners for use on ice or snow: *to pull the sled over the snow.*

■ [Represents the runners on a sled moving across the snow] Beginning with the back of the right *bent V hand,* palm facing up, across the back of the left *open hand,* palm facing down, push the right hand forward.

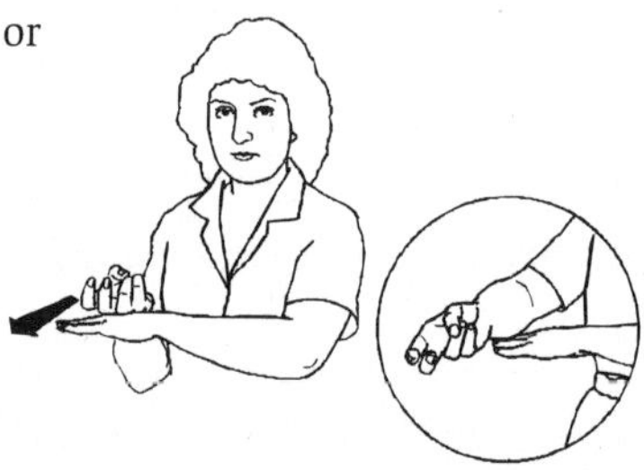

**sleep** *v.* **1.** To rest with consciousness suspended: *to sleep for eight hours a night.* —*n.* **2.** The condition or state of sleeping: *Go to sleep. Did you have a good sleep?* Same sign used for: **doze, slumber.**

■ [The hand brings the eyes and face down into a sleeping position] Bring the right *open hand,* palm facing left and fingers point up, in against the right cheek.

**slice** *v.* **1.** To cut into thin pieces: *Slice the meat for our dinner.* —*n.* **2.** A thin, broad cut of something: *a slice of bread.*

■ [Demonstrates the action of slicing off the end of something] Bring the palm side of the right *open hand,* palm facing left and fingers pointing forward, from in front of the chest straight down near the thumb side of the left *S hand* held in front of the body, palm facing down.

**slide** *v.* See signs for SLIP[1,2].

**slides** *pl. n.* Small transparent photographs, framed for use in a projector to be shown on a screen: *to look at slides.*

■ Beginning with both *H hands* in front of the chest, palms facing in, left fingers pointing right, and right fingers pointing left, move the right fingers to the left across the back of the left fingers with a double movement.

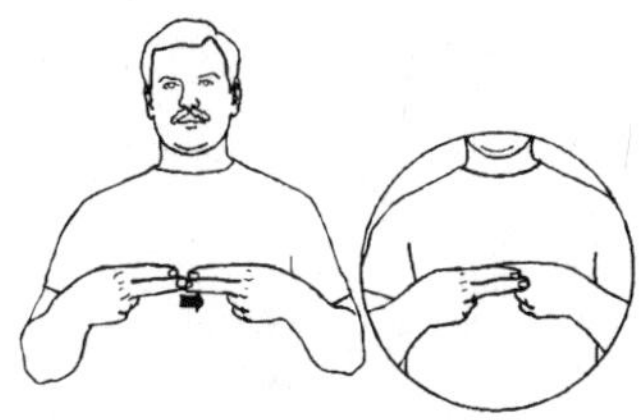

**slim** *adj.* See signs for DIET, THIN[2].

**slip**[1] *v.* To slide suddenly and accidentally: *I slipped on the ice.* Same sign used for: **slide.**

■ [Represents a person's legs slipping] Beginning with the fingertips of the right *V hand* touching the upturned palm of the left *open hand,* push the right fingers forward, ending with the right palm on the left palm.

**slip**[2] *v.* To put on or take off easily: *slip into some dry clothes.* Same sign used for: **put clothes on.**

■ [Represents pulling clothes down over one's body] Move the palm side of the right *C hand* from in front of the right shoulder, palm facing left, downward around the extended left index finger, palm facing right and finger pointing up.

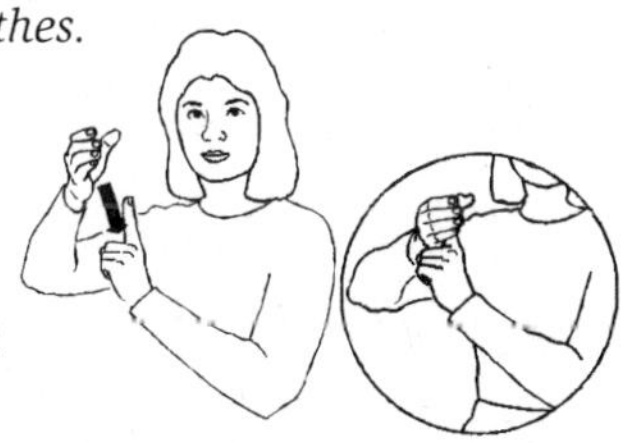

**slipper** *n.* A light shoe that is slipped on easily: *Put on your slippers and rest.*

■ [Represents sliding one's foot into a slipper] Slide the right *open hand,* palm facing down, forward across the palm of the left *curved hand,* palm facing up, while closing the left fingers around the right fingers.

**slope** *n.* See sign for GRADE.

**sloppy** *adj.* See sign for FARM.

**slothful** *adj.* See sign for LAZY.

**slow** *adj.* Proceeding with less speed than usual; not fast or quick: *slow traffic.* Related form: **slowly** *adv.*

- [Demonstrates a slow movement] Pull the fingertips of the right *5 hand,* palm facing down, from the fingers toward the wrist of the back of the left *open hand,* palm facing down.

**slumber** *n.* See sign for SLEEP.

**sly** *adj.* See sign for SNEAK.

**small**[1] *adj.* Not great in amount or extent; limited in size: *a small amount.* See also signs for LITTLE[1,2]. Same sign used for: **mini, pee wee.**

- [Shows a small size] Hold the right *G hand* beside the right side of the face, palm angled forward.

**small**[2] *adj.* (alternate sign) See also signs for LITTLE[1,2]. Same sign used for: **meager, mini, tiny.**

- [Shows a small size] Beginning with both *open hands* in front of each side of the chest, palms facing each other and fingers pointing forward, bring the palms close to each other in front of the chest.

**smart** *adj.* Showing a quick intelligence; clever: *We need a smart person to run the department.* See also sign for SCHOLARLY. Same sign used for: **brilliant, clever, intelligence, intelligent, quick-witted.**

- [Indicates brightness coming from the brain] Bring the bent middle finger of the right *5 hand* from touching the forehead, palm facing in, forward with a wavy movement.

**smash** *v.* See sign for MASH.

**smear** *v.* To spread a wet, oily, or sticky substance over something: *to smear the windows with fingerprints.*

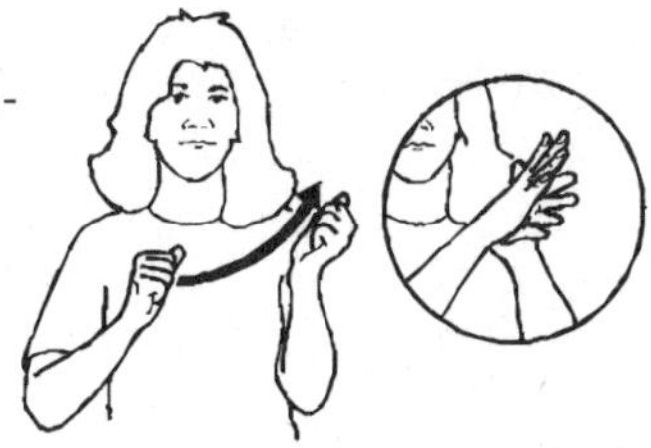

■ [Represents something spreading and smearing] Beginning with the right *A hand* in front of the right side of the chest, palm facing left, and the left *A hand* in front of the left side of the chest, palm facing right, move the right hand to the left in an arc while opening both hands into *5 hands* and rubbing the right hand across the palm of the left.

---

**smell**[1] *v.* **1.** To detect by breathing in through the nose: *to smell the food cooking.* —*n.* **2.** An odor: *the smell of roses.* Same sign used for: **fragrance, fume, odor, scent.**

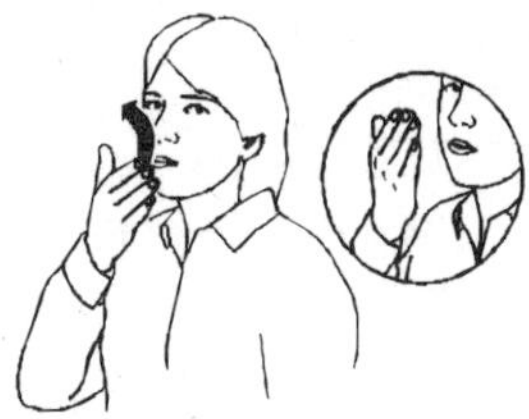

■ [Represents bringing something from in front of the nose to smell it] Brush the fingers of the right *open hand,* palm facing in, upward in front of the nose with a double movement.

---

**smell**[2] *v.* See sign for SNIFF.

---

**smile** *v.* **1.** To show pleasure, amusement, etc., on the face with an upward curve of the mouth: *He smiled when I told him how handsome he looked.* **2.** To look with favor on: *The fates smiled on the wedding.* —*n.* **3.** An act or instance of smiling: *She reacted with a big smile.* Same sign used for: **grin.**

■ [The shape of the mouth when smiling] Beginning with both *flattened C hands* near each side of the mouth, palms facing each other, pull the fingers back and upward past each cheek in the shape of a smile while pinching the fingers together, forming *flattened O hands* near each side of the head, palms facing down.

---

**smoke**[1] *v.* To draw the smoke from a pipe, cigar, or cigarette into the mouth and puff it out again: *to smoke a cigarette; to smoke after meals.* Related form: **smoking** *n.*

■ [Mime smoking a cigarette] Beginning with the fingers of the right *V hand* touching the right side of the mouth, palm facing in and fngers pointing up, bring the hand forward with a double movement.

---

**smoke**[2] *n.* A visible mixture of gases that rise from anything burning: *Smoke from the campfire told us where they were.*

■ [Shows the movement of smoke upward from a fire] Beginning with the right *curved 5 hand* above the left *curved 5 hand,* palms facing each other in front of the chest, move the hands in repeated flat circles in opposite directions.

**smolder** *v.* See sign for BOILING MAD.

**smooth**[1] *adj.* Having an even surface: *smooth boards.*

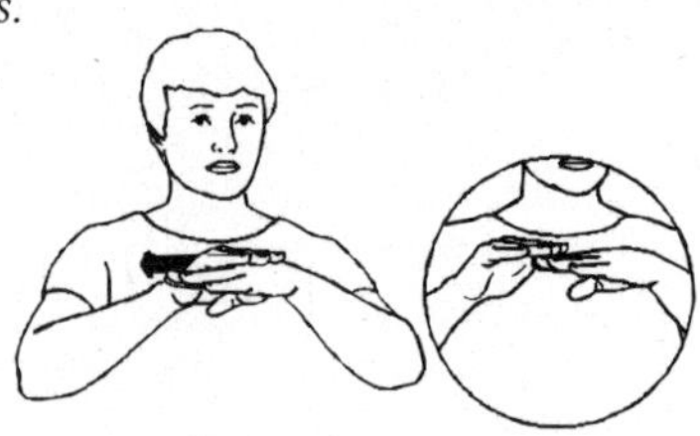

■ [Demonstrates a smooth flat surface] Move the fingers of the right *open hand,* palm facing down, from the wrist to the fingertips across the top of the left *open hand* held in front of the body, palm facing down.

**smooth**[2] *adj.* Free from unevenness; allowing an uninterrupted flow of movement: *a smooth ride.* Related form: **smoothly** *adv.* Same sign used for: **fluent, fluently, go smoothly, silky.**

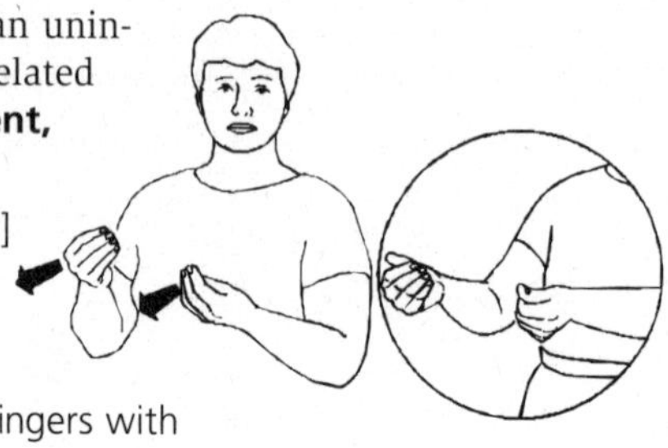

■ [The fingertips seem to feel something smooth] Beginning with both *flattened O hands* in front of each side of the chest, palms facing up, slide the thumb of each hand across the fingertips from the little fingers to the index fingers with a smooth movement, ending with *A hands.*

**smother** *v.* To suffocate or stifle: *to smother the cough.*

■ [The hand covers the mouth as if to smother a person] Bring the palm side of the right *curved hand* firmly back across the mouth.

**snack** *v.* **1.** To eat lightly, especially between regular meals: *We snacked before bedtime.* —*n.* **2.** A light meal or small portion of food or drink: *eat a snack after school.*

■ [Demonstrates picking up a snack to eat it] Move the fingertips of the right *F hand* from touching the open left palm held in front of the chest, palms facing each other, upward to the mouth with a double movement.

**snake** *n.* A long, slender, flexible, limbless reptile, some species of which are venomous: *The snake slithered across the lawn.* Same sign used for: **reptile, serpent.**

■ [Represents a snake striking with its fangs] Beginning with the back of the right *bent V hand* in front of the mouth, palm facing forward, move the hand forward in a double spiral movement.

**snap** *n., v., adj.* See sign for ABRUPT.

**sneak** *v.* To move in a stealthy, furtive way: *to sneak in by the back door.* Alternate form: **sneaky.** Same sign used for: **secretively, sly, stealthy.**

■ [Represents a person sneaking around] With the right index finger extended, move the right hand, palm facing down and finger pointing forward, in a wavy movement under the left *curved hand,* sliding the left palm up the right forearm as the right hand moves forward.

**sneakers** *pl. n.* High or low canvas shoes with rubber soles: *Please wear sneakers in the gym so you don't damage the floor.*

■ [**rubber** + **shoe**] Bring the index-finger side of the right *X hand,* palm facing forward, downward on the right cheek with a double movement. Then tap the index-finger sides of both *S hands* together in front of the chest with a double movement, palms facing down.

**sneeze** *v.* To expel air suddenly and spasmodically through the mouth and nose: *An allergy makes her sneeze.*

■ [Natural gesture used in trying to stop a sneeze] With the extended right index finger under the nose, palm facing down and finger pointing left, bend the head downward a short distance.

**sniff** *v.* To draw air through the nose in short breaths: *He sniffed the cold air.* Same sign used for: **smell.**

■ [Represents pulling air into the nostrils when sniffing] Bring the back of the *curved 5 hand,* palm facing forward and fingers pointing forward, back against the nose while closing into a *flattened O hand.*

**snob** *n.* A person who is condescending to those he or she considers inferior socially, professionally, or intellectually: *Aloof and patronizing, they were behaving like snobs.* Same sign used for: **snub.**

■ [Indicates one's nose up in the air] Push the extended right index finger, palm facing left, upward and forward in front of the nose, moving the chin upward as the finger passes the nose.

**snoop** *v.* See sign for NOSY[2].

**snow** *n.*, *v.* **1.** Ice crystals that fall to earth in the form of soft, white flakes that frequently stick together to form a layer on the ground: *A pile of snow covered the car.* —*v.* **2.** (of snow) To fall from the sky: *It snowed all day.*

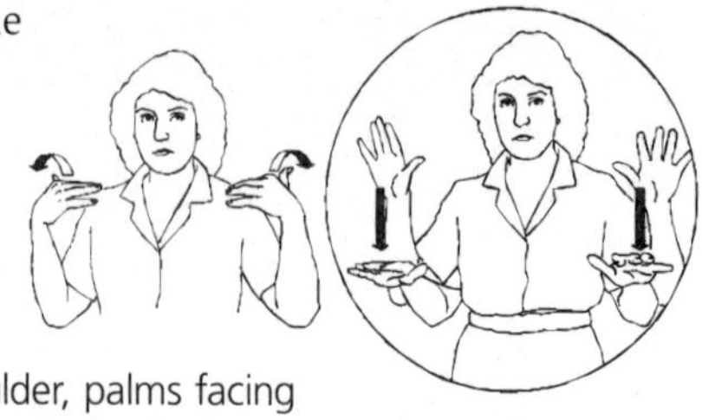

■ [Represents snow on one's shoulder + the movement of snow falling] Beginning with the fingers of both *5 hands* touching each shoulder, palms facing down, turn the hands forward and bring the hands slowly down to in front of each side of the body while wiggling the fingers as the hands move.

**snowmobile** *n.* See sign for MOTORCYCLE.

**snub** *v.* See sign for SNOB.

**soak through** *v. phrase.* See sign for PERMEATE.

**soap** *n.* A substance made from treated fat, used for washing: *Wash your hands with soap.*

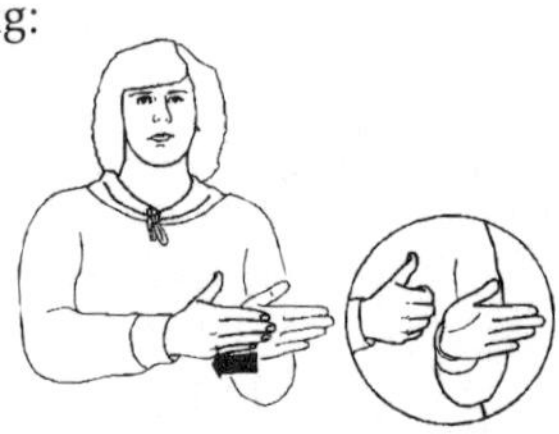

■ [Represents rubbing soap on one's hands] Wipe the fingers of the right *bent hand* on the palm of the left *open hand* from the fingers to the heel with a double movement, bending the right fingers back into the palm each time.

**so-called** *adj.* See sign for TITLE.

**soccer** *n.* A form of football played between two teams using their feet or other parts of the body except the hands and arms to propel a round ball to the opponent's goal: *to play soccer on Saturday.*

■ [Formed similar to **kick** but with a double movement] Move the right *B hand* upward in front of the body to hit the index-finger side of the right hand against the little-finger side of the left *B hand* with a double movement, both palms angled in.

**socialize** *v.* See sign for ASSOCIATE.

**society** *n.* A group of persons joined together by a common purpose: *a society of computer buffs.* Related form: **social** *n.* Same sign used for: **set** *(computer)*, **sorority.**

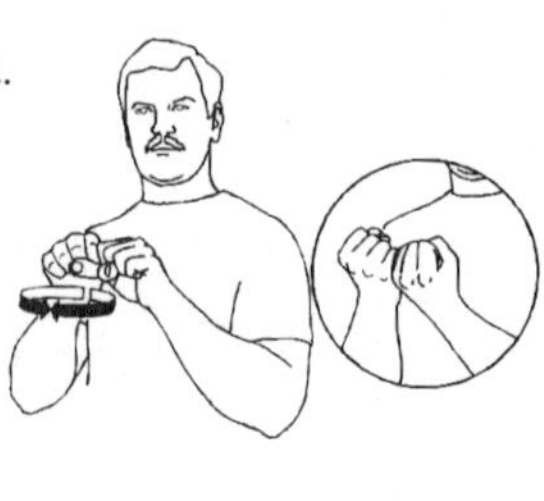

■ [Initialized sign similar to sign for **class**] Beginning with the index finger of both *S hands* touching in front of the chest, palms facing forward, move the hands away from each other and in outward arcs until the little fingers meet again in front of the chest.

**sock** *n.* Short covering for the feet and ankles, sometimes calf-length: *to wear a pair of argyle socks.*

■ Rub the sides of both extended index fingers back and forth with an alternating movement, palms facing down and fingers pointing forward in front of the body.

**socket** *n.* See sign for JOINT[1].

**soda pop** *n.* A nonalcoholic, carbonated drink: *to drink a soda pop with lunch.* Alternate forms: **soda, pop.** Same sign used for: **soft drink.**

■ [Represents recapping a soda pop bottle] Insert the bent middle finger of the right *5 hand,* palm facing down, into the hole formed by the left *O hand,* palm facing right. Then slap the right *open hand,* palm facing down, sharply on the thumb side of the left *O hand.*

**sodomy** *n.* A term referring to any type of sex act disapproved by the legislature.

■ Insert the little finger of the right *one hand* into the index-finger side of the left *S hand* held in front of the chest, palm down.

**sofa** *n.* See sign for COUCH.

**so far** *adv.* See sign for SINCE.

**soft** *adj.* Yielding or smooth to the touch; not hard or stiff: *a soft pillow; a soft silk dress.* Same sign used for: **gentle, mellow, tender.**

■ [The hands seem to feel something soft] Beginning with both *curved 5 hands* in front of each side of the chest, palms facing up, bring the hands down with a double movement while closing the fingers to the thumbs each time.

**softball** *n.* See sign for BASEBALL.

**soft drink** *n.* See sign for SODA POP.

**soft-hearted** *adj.* Sympathetic and generous of spirit; tender-hearted: *an extra bonus from our soft-hearted boss.* Alternate form: **big-hearted** *adj.* Same sign used for: **kind, tender.**

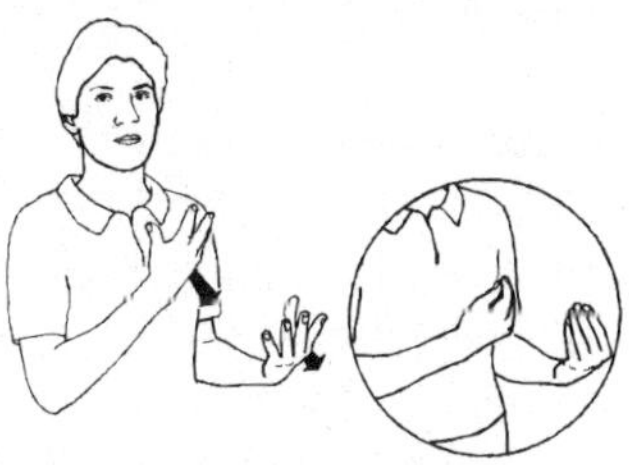

■ [**soft** formed near the heart] Beginning with the right *curved 5 hand* near the left side of the chest and the left *curved 5 hand* somewhat lower in front of the left side of the body, bring the hands downward with a double movement while closing the fingers to the thumbs each time.

**soil** *n.* See sign for DIRT.

**soiled** *adj.* See sign for DIRTY.

**solely** *adv.* See sign for ALONE.

**solicit** *v.* To try to obtain, as by petition or entreaty: *to solicit new business through the mail.* Same sign used for: **nab.**

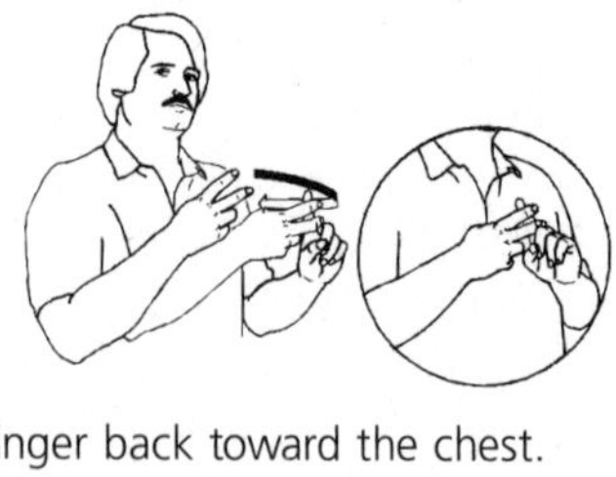

- [The fingers seem to nab one who has been solicited] Move the fingers of the right *V hand* from in front of the right side of the chest in an arc forward around to hook on the extended left index finger, palm facing forward and finger pointing up, pulling the left index finger back toward the chest.

**solid** *adj.* See signs for HARD[1], STRONG[1], STURDY[1].

**solidify** *v.* See sign for FREEZE.

**solve** *v.* See sign for DISSOLVE. Related form: **solution** *n.*

**some** *adj.* A quantity of: *Drink some milk.*

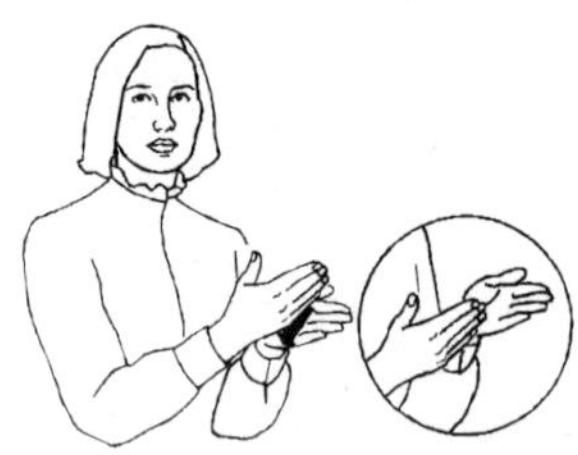

- [The hand seems to divide an object] Pull the little-finger side of the right *bent hand,* palm facing left, across the palm of the left *open hand,* palm facing up and fingers pointing forward.

**someday** *adv.* See sign for FUTURE.

**someone** *pron.* Some person: *Someone took my wallet.* Alternate form: **somebody** *adj.* Same sign used for: **something.**

- [Indicates one person] With the right extended index finger pointing up in front of the right side of the chest, palm facing in, move the right hand in a circle with a repeated movement.

**something** *n.* See sign for SOMEONE.

**sometimes** *adv.* Now and then; on some occasions: *Sometimes I forget my keys and get locked out.* Same sign used for: **occasional.**

- [Similar to sign for **once** except repeated to indicate reoccurrence] Bring the extended right index finger, palm facing in, downward against the upturned palm of the left *open hand* and up again in a rhythmic repeated circular movement.

**son** *n.* A male child in relation to his father and mother: *a younger son.*

- [A shortened form of the combination of the signs for **boy** and **baby**] Beginning with the fingertips of the right *B hand* against the forehead, palm facing left, bring the right hand downward, ending with the bent right arm cradled in the bent left arm held across the body, both palms facing up.

**song** *n.* See sign for MUSIC.

**son-in-law** *n.* The husband of one's daughter: *My son-in-law is a computer programmer.*

- [A combination similiar to the signs for **son** + **law**] Beginning with the fingertips of the right *open hand* against the forehead, palm facing left, bring the right hand downward, ending with the bent right arm cradled in the bent left arm held across the body, both palms facing up. Then move the right *L hand* from touching first on the palm of the upturned left *open hand* to touching on the left wrist.

**soon**[1] *adv.* Within a short time: *Soon it will be time to go.* Same sign used for: **near future, in the; shortly.**

- Touch the fingertips of the right *F hand,* palm facing in, to the middle of the chin.

**soon**[2] *adv.* See sign for SHORT[1].

**sophisticated** *adj.* Worldly-wise: *a sophisticated, well-traveled woman.* Same sign used for: **prim.**

- With the thumb, index finger, and little finger of the right hand extended, push the right index finger upward and forward under the chin, palm facing left.

**sordid** *adj.* See sign for AWFUL.

**sore** *adj.* See signs for HURT[2], PAIN[1].

**sorority** *n.* See sign for SOCIETY.

**sorry** *adj.* Feeling regret: *I am sorry that you have to leave so soon.* Related form: **sorrow** *n.* Same sign used for: **apologize, apology, penitence, penitent, regret, repent.**

- [Indicates rubbing the chest in sorrow] Rub the palm side of the right *A hand* in a large circle on the chest with a repeated movement.

**sort**[1] *n.* See sign for KIND[2].

**sort**[2] *v.* See signs for FILE, PLAN[2], PREPARE.

**sort of** *adv.* See sign for FAIR[2].

**so-so** *adj.* See sign for FAIR[2].

**soul** *n.* See sign for SPIRIT.

**sound**[1] *n.* What can be heard when the organs of hearing are stimulated, as noises, voices, or music: *I heard a sound coming from the next room.*

■ [Initialized sign formed near the ear] Move the right *S hand,* palm facing forward, from near the right ear outward to the right.

**sound**[2] *n.* See signs for HEAR, NOISE.

**soup** *n.* A liquid food usually made by boiling a combination of seasonings, vegetables, fish, or meat in water: *to make vegetable soup from leftovers.*

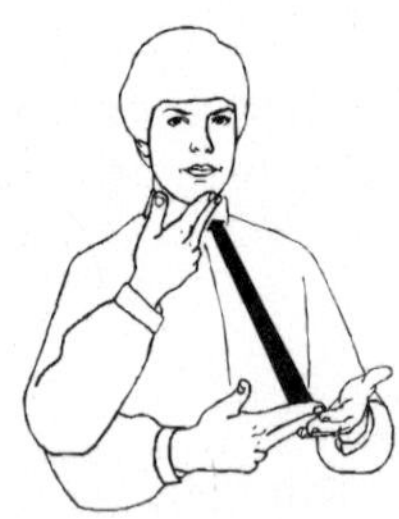

■ [Mime eating soup with a spoon] With the thumb extended, move the fingers of the right *U hand* from touching the palm of the left *open hand* upward to the mouth, both palms facing up.

**sour** *adj.* Having a sharp, acidic, biting taste, like lemon or vinegar: *The milk has turned sour.* Same sign used for: **bitter.**

■ [Points to puckered lips from eating something sour] With the tip of the extended right index finger on the chin near the mouth, palm facing left, twist the hand, ending with the palm facing back.

**source** *n.* See sign for START[1].

**south** *n.* **1.** The general direction opposite of north: *The new buildings face the south.* —*adj.* **2.** Lying toward, located in, or coming from the south: *a south wind.* —*adv.* **3.** To, toward, or in the south: *The birds travel south for the winter.* Related form: **southern** *adj.*

■ [Initialized sign indicating a southern direction on a map] Move the right *S hand,* palm facing in, downward in front of the right side of the chest.

**sow** *v.* See sign for PLANT[2].

**space** *n.* See sign for AREA.

**spacecraft** *n.* See sign for SPACESHIP.

**spaceship** *n.* A vehicle for traveling in outer space: *The astronauts were in the spaceship, getting ready for the launch.* Same sign used for: **spacecraft.**

■ [The hand shape represents a spaceship moving through space] Move the right *curved 3 hand,* palm facing in and fingers pointing left, from in front of the head to the right.

**space shuttle** *n. phrase.* See sign for ROCKET.

**spade** *n., v.* See sign for SPATULA.

**spaghetti** *n.* Long, slender strings of pasta, cooked by boiling and often served with tomato sauce: *serving the classic dish of spaghetti and meatballs.*

■ [The shape of spaghetti] Beginning with both extended little fingers touching in front of the chest, palms facing in, bring the hands apart in small arcs, ending in front of each shoulder.

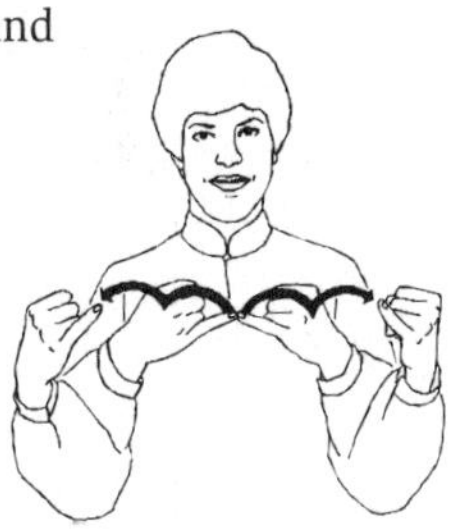

**spank** *v.* To strike as punishment with an open hand or a flat object, especially on the buttocks: *to spank the naughty child.* Related form: **spanking** *n.* Same sign used for: **whack, whip, whipping.**

■ [Demonstrates the action of spanking] Bring the palm of the right *open hand* downward from in front of the right side of the chest to strike against the palm of the left *open hand,* palm facing up, with a repeated movement.

**spark** *n.* A flash of electrical light or fire: *A spark came from the wires.*

■ Beginning with the right *modified X hand* touching the extended left index finger in front of the chest, both palms facing forward, flick the right index finger upward with a double movement.

**sparkle** *v.* See sign for SHINY.

**spasm** *n.* See sign for CRAMP.

**spatula** *n.* A tool with a flat, flexible blade, used in preparing food, spreading plaster, and the like: *Turn the pancakes with a spatula.* Same sign used for: **dig, spade.**

■ [Shows action of turning food over with a spatula] Push the fingertips of the right *open hand,* palm facing up and fingers pointing forward, with a short movement forward on the fingers of the left *open hand* held in front of the chest, palm facing up. Then flip the right hand over in an arc, ending with the palm facing down.

**speak**[1] *v.* To say words, especially to communicate: *Speak softly.* Same sign used for: **talk.**

■ [Represents words coming from the mouth] Beginning with the index-finger side of the right *4 hand* touching the chin, palm facing left, move the hand forward with a repeated movement.

**speak**[2] *v.* To express ideas in front of a group of people, as in delivering a speech: *She spoke on the broad topic of international unrest.* Same sign used for: **address, lecture, presentation, sermon, speech, talk.**

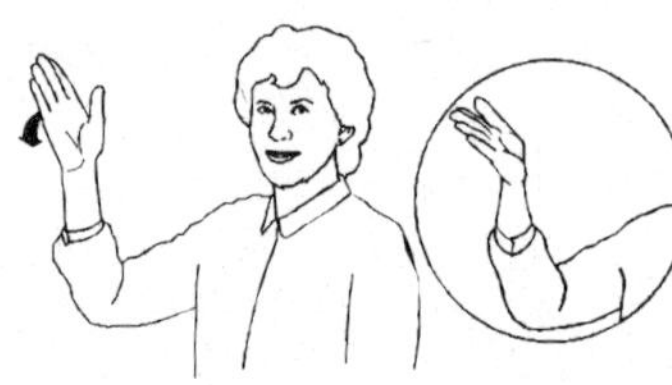

■ Beginning with the right *open hand* near the right side of the head, palm facing left and fingers pointing up, twist the wrist to move the fingers forward and back with a short repeated movement.

**special** *adj.* Distinguished from the ordinary; distinctive; unusual: *a special dessert just for you.* Same sign used for: **especially, unique.**

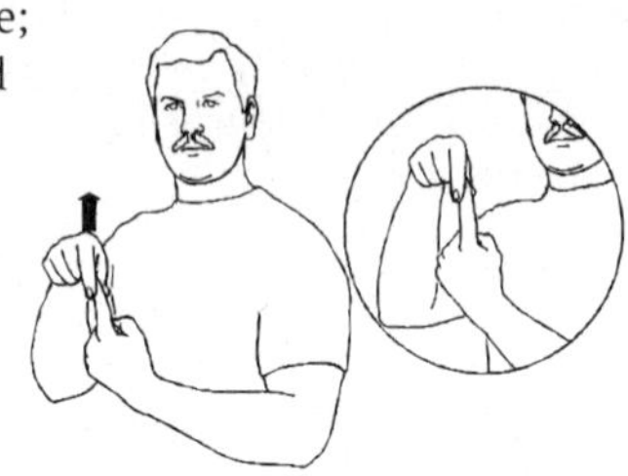

■ [Demonstrates pulling one thing out that is special] Grasp the left extended index finger, palm facing in and finger pointing up, with the fingers of the right *G hand* and pull upward in front of the chest.

**specialize** *v.* To select a field to pursue professionally or for study: *to specialize in economics.* Related form: **specialty** *n.* Same sign used for: **field, main, major, straight.**

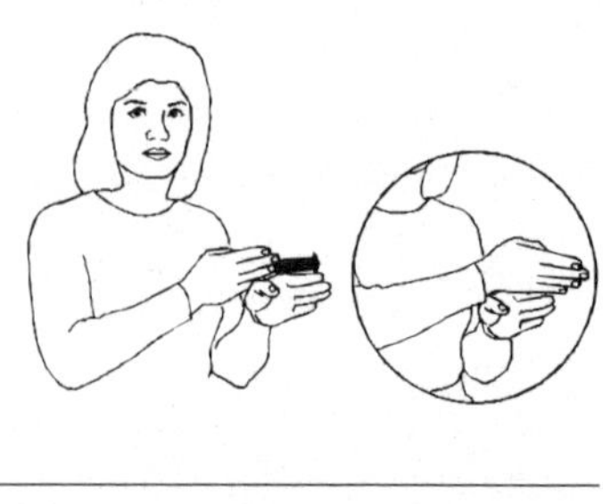

■ Slide the little-finger side of the right *B hand,* palm facing left and fingers pointing forward, along the index-finger side of the left *B hand* held in front of the chest, palm facing right and fingers pointing forward.

**specific** *adj.* See signs for POINT[2], PRECISE.

**spectacles** *pl. n.* See sign for GLASSES.

**speculate** *v.* See sign for LET'S SEE. Related form: **speculation** *n.*

**speech**[1] *n.* The ability to speak, an act of speaking, or an utterance spoken with the mouth, vocal cords, and other organs of speech: *trained to use good, understandable speech.*

■ [Shows the movement of the lips when speaking] Move the bent fingers of the right *V hand,* palm facing in, in a small repeated circle in front of the mouth.

**speech**[2] *n.* See sign for SPEAK[2].

**speed** *n.* **1.** Rapid movement, as of a vehicle: *a driver who loves speed.* **2.** Relative rate of motion or activity: *works at a fast speed.* —*v.* **3.** to go or move quickly: *The boat sped across the lake.*

■ Beginning with both extended index fingers pointing forward in front of each side of the chest, palms facing in opposite directions and right hand forward of the left hand, bend the fingers with a double movement.

**spell** *v.* See sign for FINGERSPELL.

**spend**[1] *v.* To pay out money: *to spend a fortune at the carnival.*

■ [Represents money slipping through one's hands] Beginning with both *curved hands* in front of each side of the chest, right hand nearer the chest than the left hand and both palms facing up, move the hands forward while moving the thumbs across the fingers, ending with *10 hands.*

**spend**[2] *v.* To pass time in a particular manner or place: *spend your vacation on a cruise.*

■ Beginning with the index fingers and thumbs of both hands pinched together, palms facing up in front of the body, move the hands upward while flicking the index fingers forward.

**spider** *n.* A small wingless creature with eight legs, known for spinning webs that trap insects for food: *The black widow spider is poisonous.*

■ [Represents a spider's legs] With the wrists of both *curved 4 hands* crossed in front of the body, palms facing down and right wrist over the left wrist, wiggle the fingers with a repeated movement.

**spike** *n.* See sign for POWER SURGE.

**spill** *v.* **1.** To cause or allow (liquid or other loose material) to run or fall from a container, especially accidentally: *to spill the milk.* **2.** To run out of or fall from a container, as onto a surface: *The milk spilled.*

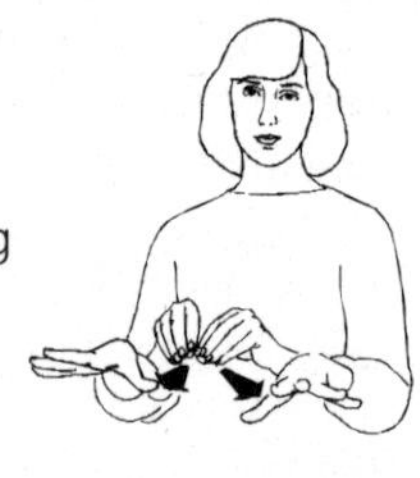

■ [Represents something spreading out when it is spilled] Beginning with both *flattened O hands* touching in front of the body, palms facing down and fingers pointing down, move the hands forward and apart while opening the fingers into *5 hands,* palms facing down.

**spiral** *n.* **1.** A winding coil: *The tornado was shaped like a spiral.* —*adj.* **2.** Having a coiled shape: *a spiral staircase.*

■ [The shape of a spiral] With the extended right index finger pointing down in front of the head, and the extended left index finger pointing up in front of the chest, both palms facing in and fingers pointing toward each other, move the hands in repeated circular movements as the hands pull away from each other.

**spirit** *n.* **1.** The intangible animating essence of human life: *Though they're gone, their spirits will live on.* **2.** One's fundamental emotional nature; temperament: *She has a bright, happy spirit.* **3.** An attitude of courage and optimism: *The soldiers in the field had amazing spirit.* **4.** A supernatural being: *God is a spirit.* Related form: **spiritual** *adj.* Same sign used for: **ghost, soul.**

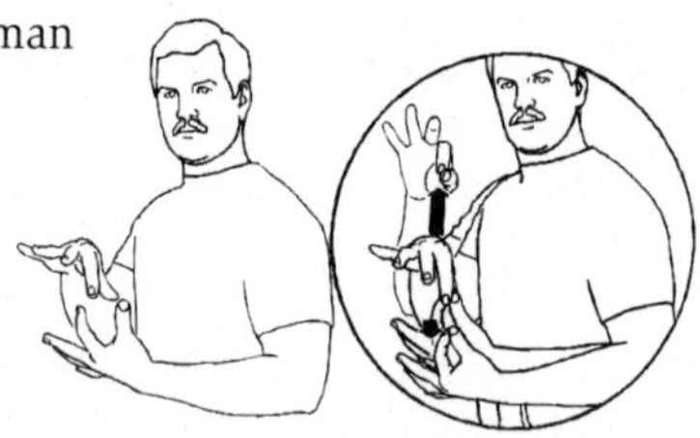

■ Beginning with the bent index finger and thumb of the right *5 hand* pointing down above the bent index finger and thumb of the left *5 hand,* palms facing each other, close the index fingers and thumbs of both hands together, touching each other. Then pull the hands apart, moving the right hand upward in front of the chest.

**spit** *v.* **1.** To eject saliva from the mouth: *The dentist said to spit into the sink.* —*n.* **2.** Saliva ejected from the mouth: *There was spit on the sidewalk.*

■ [Indicates the movement of spitting] Beginning with the thumb holding down the bent index finger of the right hand in front of the mouth, palm facing forward, move the hand forward while flicking the index finger forward.

**splash** *v.* To dash or shower, as with liquid or mud: *to splash dirty water on the sidewalk.* Same sign used for: **splatter.**

■ [Represents the movement of a liquid splashing] Beginning with both *S hands* near each other in front of the chest, palms facing forward, move the hands upward and apart while opening quickly into *5 hands,* ending in front of each shoulder, palms facing forward and fingers pointing up.

**splat** *v.* See sign for PLOP.

**splatter** *n.* See sign for SPLASH.

**splendid** *adj.* See sign for WONDERFUL.

**split**[1] *n., v.* See signs for CRACK, DIVIDE, ZOOM.

**split**[2] *v. Slang.* See sign for RUN AWAY.

**split up** *v. phrase.* See sign for DIVIDE.

**spoil** *v.* See signs for PET[1], RUIN.

**sponsor** *v.* See sign for SUPPORT.

**spooky** *adj.* See sign for MONSTER.

**spoon** *n.* A utensil with a shallow bowl at one end of a handle, used for eating, stirring, serving, etc.: *ate my soup with a large, round spoon.*

■ [The fingers represent a spoon scooping up food] Wipe the backs of the fingers of the right *U hand,* palm facing up and thumb extended, across the upturned palm of the left *open hand* from the fingers to the heel with a double movement.

**sports** *pl. n.* See sign for RACE[1].

**spot**[1] *v.* To locate, notice, or recognize: *spotted my friend in the crowd.*

■ [Indicates a person's eyes directed at whatever is spotted] Beginning with the right *S hand* near the right cheek, palm facing forward, move the hand forward while flicking the thumb and index finger open to form a *G hand.*

**spot**[2] n. **1.** A rounded mark, as a stain: *I have a spot on my blouse.* **2.** A blemish on the skin: *The sun is causing spots to come out on my hands.* Same sign used for: **stain.**

■ [Shape and location of a spot] Touch the thumb side of the right *F hand* to the left side of the chest, palm facing left.

**spousal support** *n. phrase.* See sign for ALIMONY.

**sprain** *v.* **1.** To injure the ligaments around a joint without a fracture: *sprained my wrist.* —*n.* **2.** An injury to the ligaments around a joint: *an ankle with a bad sprain.*

■ [Shows a twist causing a sprain] Beginning with both *bent V hands* in front of the chest, right palm facing out and left palm facing in, twist the hands in opposite directions, reversing the direction of the palms.

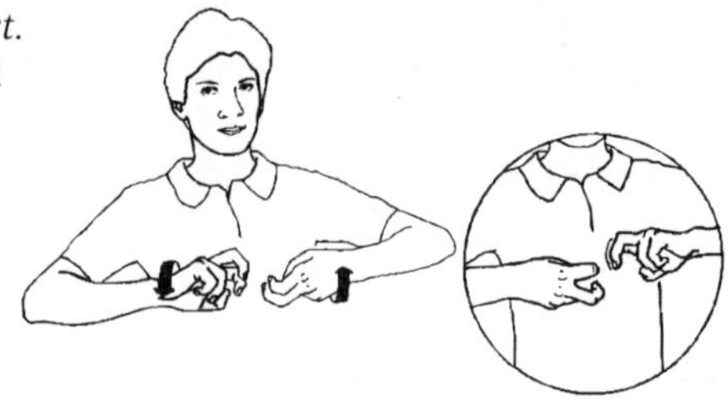

**spray** *v.* To sprinkle through the air in small drops: *to spray the bushes with insecticide.*

■ [Mime pushing down on an aerosol can] Beginning with the extended right index finger pointing up in front of the right shoulder, palm facing forward, bend the finger down to form an *X hand* with a double movement while moving the hand from side to side.

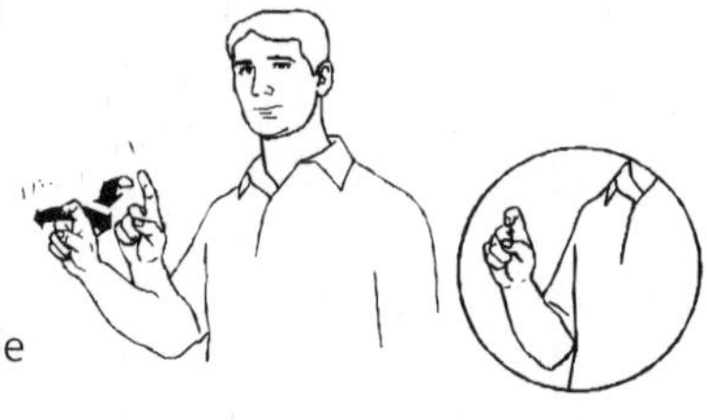

**spread** *v.* To distribute or expand over a large area: *They want to spread the news.* Same sign used for: **disseminate, distribute, outbreak.**

■ [Demonstrates something spreading outward] Beginning with the fingertips of both *flattened O hands* touching in front of the chest, palms facing down, move the hands forward and away from each other while opening into *5 hands* in front of each side of the body, palms facing down.

**spring** *n.* The season between winter and summer: *to plant a garden in the spring.*

■ [Similar to sign for **grow** except with a double movement] Beginning with the right *flattened O hand,* palm facing up, being held by the left *C hand,* palm facing in, move the right hand upward with a double movement, opening into a *5 hand* each time.

**sprinkle** *v.* To scatter drops or little pieces: *to sprinkle nuts on the cake.* Alternate form: **sprinkles** *pl. n.*

■ [Mime sprinkling something] Move the right *curved hand* forward in front of the chest while wiggling the fingers with a repeated movement.

**sprout** *v.* See sign for GROW.

**spy** *n.* **1.** A person who obtains secret information, as for a government or corporation: *The spies from the two countries traded secrets.* **2.** A person who watches others secretly: *Some spy in the office has been reading my mail!* —*v.* **3.** To watch secretly: *He spied on the neighbors.* **4.** To act as a spy for a government or corporation: *They were caught spying for a rival software company.*

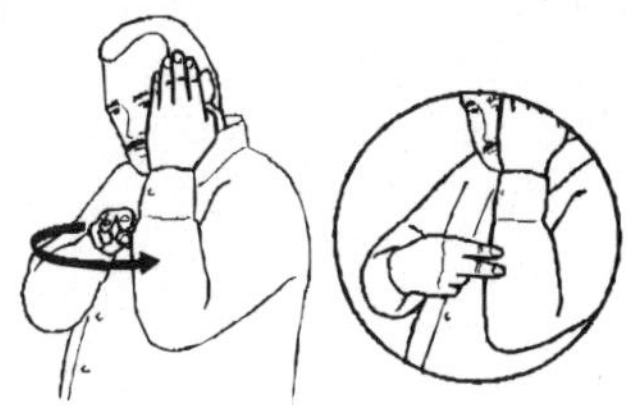

- [Represents eyes peeking around a corner to spy] Bring the right *V hand,* palm facing down, from behind the bent left arm held up in front of the left shoulder, in an arc forward and to the left around the left arm.

**squabble** *v.* See sign for ARGUE.

**squander** *v.* To spend or use wastefully: *He squandered his entire fortune.*

- [Represents throwing money away] Beginning with both *A hands* near each side of the body, palms facing in, thrust the hands upward with a double movement while changing into *5 hands* in front each shoulder, palms facing in.

**square** *n.* **1.** A two-dimensional figure with four equal sides and four equal angles: *to draw a square measuring four inches by four inches.* —*adj.* **2.** Having a square shape: *a square box.* Same sign used for: **sign.**

- [Draw a square in the air] Beginning with both extended index fingers touching in front of the upper chest, palms angled forward and fingers pointing upward, bring the hands straight out to in front of each shoulder then straight down, and finally back together in front of the waist.

**squeal** *v. Slang.* See sign for TATTLE.

**squeeze**[1] *v.* To force together by pressing from more than one direction: *Squeeze the sponge to get all the water out.*

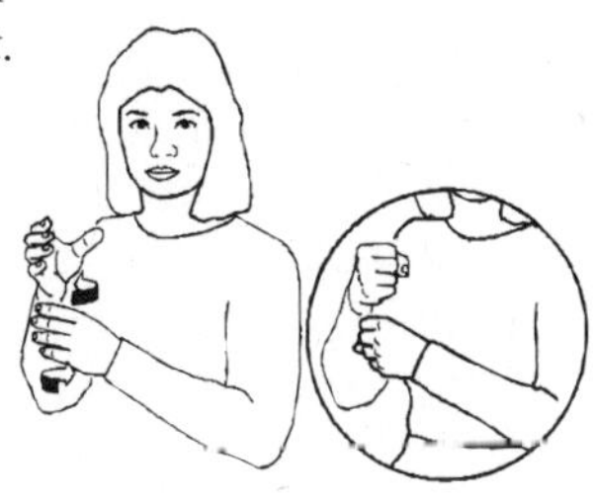

- [Mime squeezing a tube with both hands] Beginning with the little-finger side of the right *C hand,* palm facing left, above the index-finger side of the left *C hand,* palm facing right, twist the hands in opposite directions while closing into *S hands.* Repeat if desired.

**squeeze**[2] *n.* See sign for BRIEF.

**squirrel** *n.* A bushy-tailed rodent that lives in trees: *saw black squirrels in Canada.*

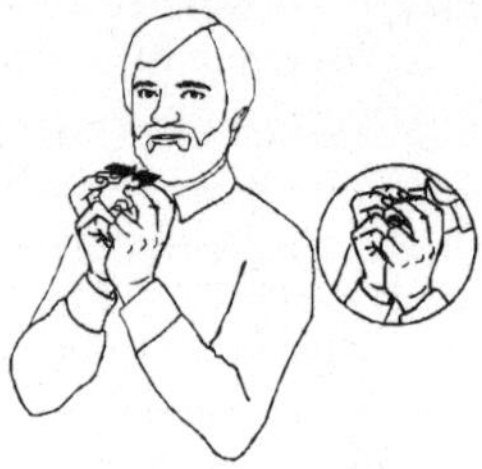

- [Represents the gnawing action of a squirrel's teeth] With the heels of both hands together in front of the chest, palms facing each other, tap the fingertips of both *bent V hands* together with a double movement.

**stab** *v.* To pierce with or as if with a pointed weapon: *to stab the meat with a knife; stabbed at me with his finger.*

- [Mime stabbing something with a knife] Bring the right *S hand* in a large arc from in front of the right shoulder forward to hit against the open left palm held in front of the chest, with a deliberate movement.

**stack** *n.* **1.** A relatively orderly pile of things, one on top of another: *a stack of books.* —*v.* **2.** To pile in a stack: *Stack the books in the corner.* Same sign used for: **pile.**

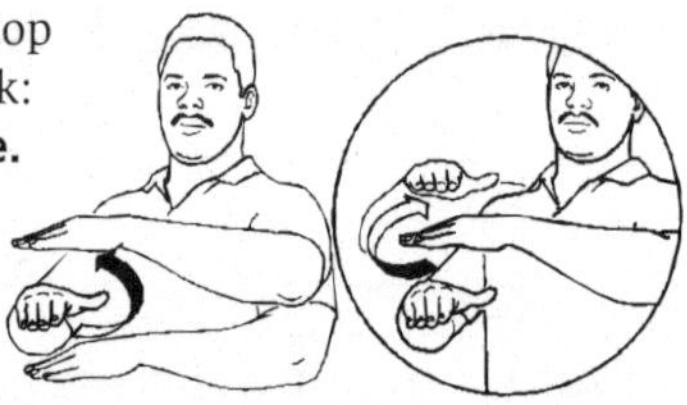

- [Shows a pile of things stacked on top of other things] With an alternating movement, bring each *open hand* upward over the other hand in a small arc as the hands rise in front of the chest, both palms facing down and fingers angled in opposite directions.

**staff** *n.* See sign for SENATE.

**stage** *n.* The platform in a theater on which the actors perform: *to walk across the stage and turn toward the audience.*

- [Initialized sign representing the stage floor] Move the right *S hand,* palm facing forward, across the back of the left *open hand,* palm facing down, from the wrist to off the fingers.

**stain**[1] *n.* **1.** A discoloration or spot, as on fabric, produced by soil, food, or other foreign matter: *a stain on my dress.* —*v.* **2.** To spot or soil: *The coffee stained the rug.*

- [**eat** + a gesture indicating food spilling on one's clothes + **spot**[2]] Bring the fingertips of the right *flattened O hand,* palm facing in, back to the mouth with a double movement. Next move the palm side of the right *5 hand* against the chest with a sudden movement. Then place the index-finger side of the right *F hand,* palm facing left, against the chest.

**stain**[2] *n.* See sign for SPOT[2].

**staircase** *n.* See sign for STAIRS.

**stairs** *pl. n.* A series of steps for going from one level or floor to another: *to climb the stairs.* Same signs used for: **staircase, stairway.**

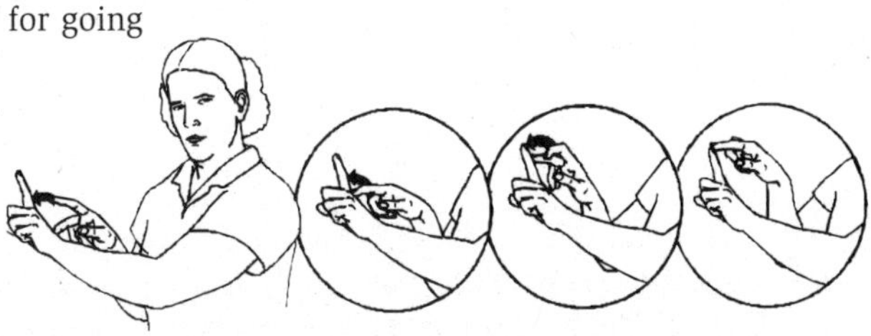

■ [Demonstrates the action of walking up stairs] Move the fingertips of the right *bent V hand,* palm facing forward, in an alternating crawling movement up the extended left index finger, palm facing forward.

**stairway** *n.* See sign for STAIRS.

**stalk** *v.* To follow a person about in such a way as to instill fear of bodily harm: *The fan stalked the movie star wherever she went.*

■ [Represents two people moving in tandem] With the palm side of the right *1 hand* on the index-finger side of the left *one hand,* both palms facing forward, move both hands forward in a random movement.

**stall** *v.* See signs for HOLD[2], SUSPEND.

**stamp**[1] *n.* **1.** A small label with a sticky back, issued by postal authorities in various denominations, to place on items for mailing as evidence that postal charges have been paid: *to lick the stamp.* —*v.* **2.** To affix a postage stamp to: *to stamp the letters.* Same sign used for: **postage, postage stamp.**

■ [The fingers seem to lick a stamp and place it on an envelope] Move the fingers of the right *H hand* from the mouth, palm facing in, down to land on the fingers of the left *open hand,* palm facing up, in front of the body.

**stamp**[2] *n.* **1.** An instrument, as a block with a raised imprinting device, to mark an item with an instruction, an official seal of approval, etc.: *Use the department stamp to mark all the bills before mailing them.* **2.** A mark made with such an instrument: *marked the invoice with the department's stamp.* —*v.* **3.** To place an official or instructional mark on an item: *Stamp the package "RUSH."* Same sign used for: **brand, guarantee, seal.**

■ [Mime stamping something with a rubber stamp] Move the right *S hand,* palm facing left, from in front of the chest downward, ending with the little-finger side of the right *S hand* on the upturned palm of the left *open hand.*

**stand** *v.* To be in or rise to an upright position on one's feet: *The teacher stood in front of the classroom.*

■ [The fingers represent erect legs] Place the fingertips of the right *V hand,* palm facing in and fingers pointing down, on the upturned palm of the left *open hand* held in front of the body.

**standard** *n.* **1.** Something considered usual and normal or accepted as a basis for comparison: *a student whose behavior provides an exemplary standard. —adj.* **2.** Generally recognized as usual or normal: *standard-size 8 1/2 by 11 paper.* Related form: **standardized** *adj.* Same sign used for: **common, uniform.**

■ [**same**[1] formed with a large circular movement to indicate everything is the same] Beginning with both *Y hands* in front of the body, palms facing down, move the hands in a large flat circle.

**stand for** *v. phrase.* See sign for MEAN[2].

**staple** *v.* Same sign as for STAPLER but formed with a single movement.

**stapler** *n.* A machine used for fastening with staples, short pieces of wire bent to hold things together: *Use a stapler, not a paper clip, to fasten the receipts to the expense report.* Related form: **staple** *n.*

■ [Mime pushing down on a stapler] Press the heel of the right *curved 5 hand,* palm facing down, on the heel of the left *open hand,* palm facing up, with a double movement.

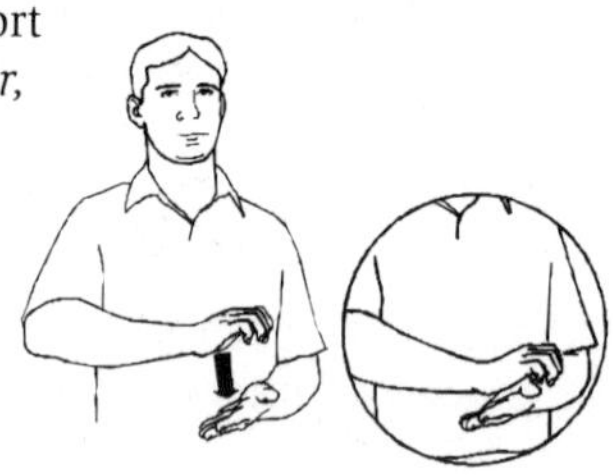

**star** *n.* A hot, gaseous heavenly body that shines by its own light: *stars in the sky.* Same sign used for: **asterisk, wildcard.**

■ Brush the sides of both extended index fingers against each other, palms facing forward, with an alternating movement as the hands move upward in front of the face.

**stare** *v.* To gaze intently and directly: *Don't stare at me like that.*

■ [Directional sign indicating that all eyes turn to look at you] Beginning with both *4 hands* in front of each side of the chest, palms facing down and fingers pointing forward, twist the wrists toward each other to point the fingers back toward the face.

**start**[1] *n.* A beginning: *a good start for the project.* Same sign used for: **beginning, commence, origin, origination, source.**

■ [Represents turning a key to start ignition] Beginning with the extended right index finger, palm facing in, inserted between the index and middle fingers of the left *open hand,* palm facing right and fingers pointing forward, twist the right hand back, ending with the palm angled forward.

**start**[2] *v.* To cause the motor of to go into action: *to start the car.*

■ [Mime turning a key to start an ignition] Beginning with the right *A hand* in front of the right side of the body, palm facing forward, twist the wrist to turn the palm to the left.

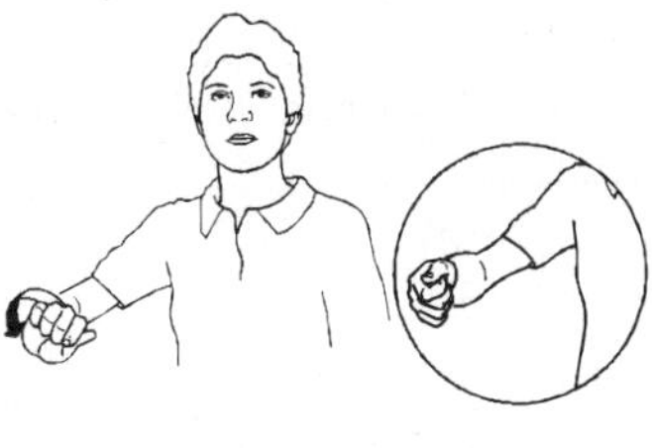

**starter** *n.* Same sign as for **start**[2] but formed with a double movement. Same sign used for: **ignition**.

**startle** *v.* See signs for FLABBERGAST, SURPRISE.

**startled** *adj.* See sign for SHOCK.

**starved** *adj.* See sign for HUNGRY.

**state**[1] *n.* A politically unified territory within a nation: *the state of Texas.*

■ [Initialized sign similar to sign for **law**] Move the index-finger side of the right *S hand,* palm facing forward, down from the fingers to the heel of the left *open hand,* palm facing right and fingers pointing up, in front of the chest.

**state**[2] *v.* See sign for SAY.

**statement** *n.* See sign for SENTENCE.

**statistics** *n.* A branch of mathematics that deals with collecting and analyzing numerical data: *used statistics to determine the probability of increased sales.*

■ [Initialized sign similar to sign for **mathematics**] Beginning with both *S hands* in front of each side of the chest, palms facing in, move the hands past each other with a double movement while rubbing the little-finger side of the right hand over the index-finger side of the left hand.

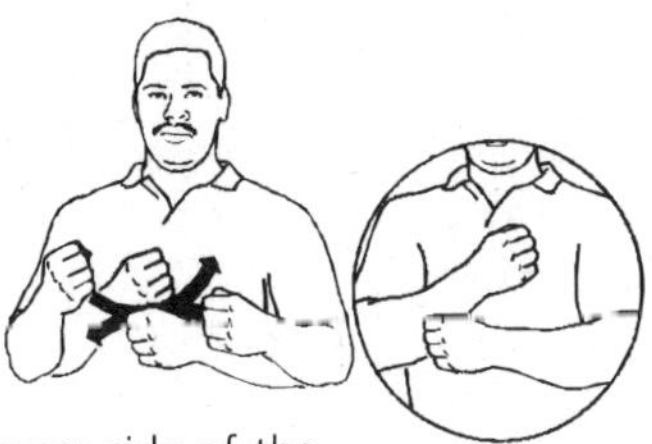

**statue** *n.* A carved or molded three-dimensional image: *a statue of a famous person.* Same sign used for: **shape.**

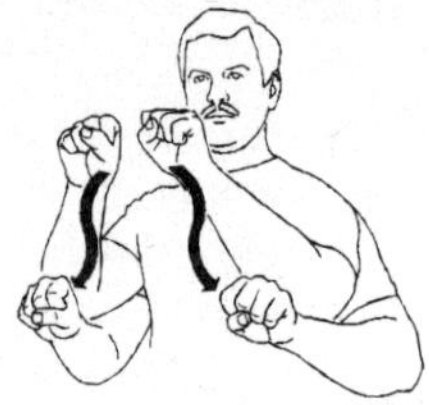

■ [Initialized sign similar to **shape**] Beginning with both *S hands* near each other in front of the face, palms facing forward, bring the hands downward and apart in a wavy movement.

**stay** *v.* To remain: *Stay here.* Same sign used for: **remain.**

■ With the thumb of the right *10 hand* on the thumbnail of the left *10 hand,* both palms facing down in front of the chest, move the hands forward and down a short distance.

**stay away** *v. phrase.* To remain far or apart from a given place, person, or thing; not come or go near: *You'd better stay away from the edge.*

■ Beginning with the thumb of the right *Y hand* touching the thumb of the left *Y hand* in front of the chest, both palms angled down, move the right hand forward and to the right in a small arc.

**steadfast** *adj.* See sign for CONSTANT[3].

**steady**[1] *Informal.* —*n.* **1.** One's exclusive sweetheart; boyfriend or girlfriend: *He is my steady.* —*adj.* **2.** Constant; regular; habitual: *my steady date.* Same sign used for: **companion, go steady.**

■ [**with** signed with a repeated movement] Beginning with the palm sides of both *A hands* together in front of the chest, move the hands forward with a repeated movement.

**steady**[2] *adj.* See signs for CONSTANT[2,3].

**steak** *n.* See sign for MEAT.

**steal**[1] *v.* To take from the rightful owner without permission: *stole the jewelry from the store.* Same sign used for: **burglary, pillage, rob, robbery, theft.**

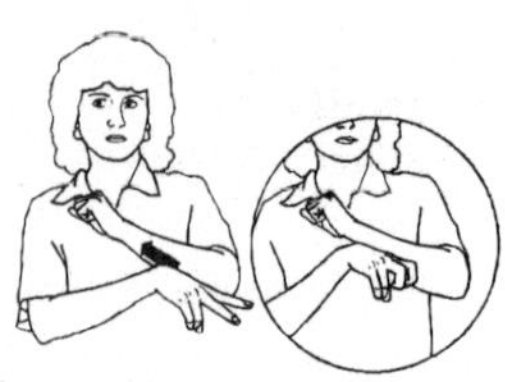

■ [The fingers seem to snatch something] Beginning with the index-finger side of the right *V hand,* palm facing down, on the elbow of the bent left arm, held at an upward angle across the chest, pull the right hand upward toward the left wrist while bending the fingers in tightly.

**steal**[2] *v.* See sign for SHOPLIFT.



482

**stealthy** *adj.* See sign for SNEAK.

**steel**[1] *n.* An alloy of iron and carbon: *beams made of steel.*

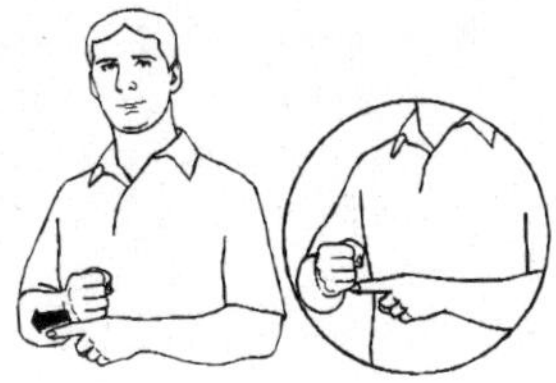

■ Move the little-finger side of the right *S hand,* palm facing in, forward from the base to the tip of the extended left index finger, palm facing in and finger pointing right, with a double movement.

**steel**[2] *n.* See sign for METAL.

**steer** *v.* See sign for LEAD.

**stem** *n.* The long, slender part of a plant that ascends above the ground: *Cut the stems of the roses with the shears.*

■ [The shape of a long stem] Beginning with the thumb and index finger of the right *G hand,* palm facing left, holding the base of the extended left index finger, palm facing right and finger pointing up, pull the right hand upward along the length of the index finger and off its tip a short distance, while pinching the thumb and index finger together.

**step** *n.* **1.** A movement made by lifting the foot and putting it down again: *Take a big step.* —*v.* **2.** To move the legs in steps, as in walking: *Step forward.* Same sign used for: **pace.**

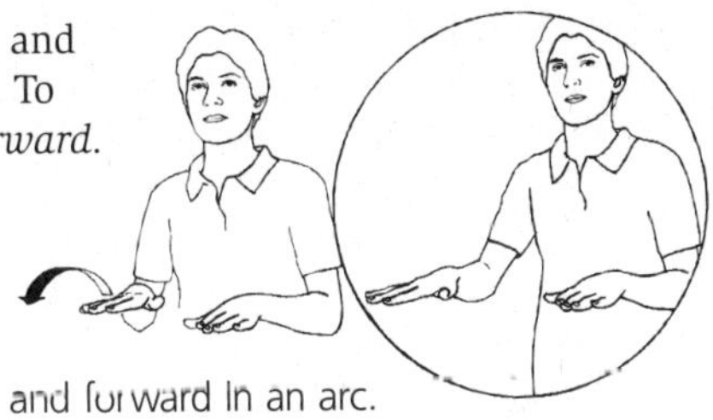

■ [Demonstrates the action of stepping forward] Beginning with both *open hands* in front of the body, palms facing down and fingers pointing forward, move the right hand upward and forward in an arc.

**stepbrother** *n.* A son of one's stepparent by a former marriage: *He is my older stepbrother.*

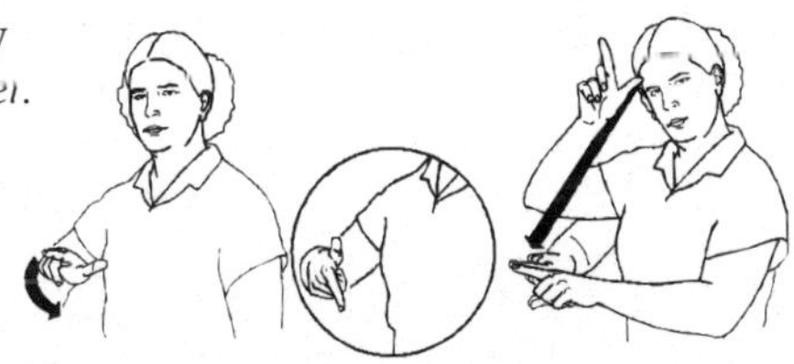

■ [**second-hand** + **brother**] Beginning with the right *L hand* in front of the right side of the chest, palm facing down, twist the wrist forward with a deliberate movement. Then bring the right *L hand,* palm facing left, from the forehead down while closing the thumb to the hand, ending with the index fingers of both *1 hands* together in front of the chest.

**stepdaughter** *n.* A daughter of one's husband or wife by a former marriage: *My stepdaughter and I are very close.*

■ [**second-hand** + **daughter**] Beginning with the right *L hand* in front of the right side of the chest, palm facing down, twist the wrist forward with a deliberate movement. Then bring the right *B hand,* palm facing left, from the chin downward while opening into an *open hand,* ending with the bent right arm cradled on the bent left arm held across the body, both palms facing up.

**stepfather** *n.* The husband of one's mother by a subsequent marriage: *We live with my stepfather.*

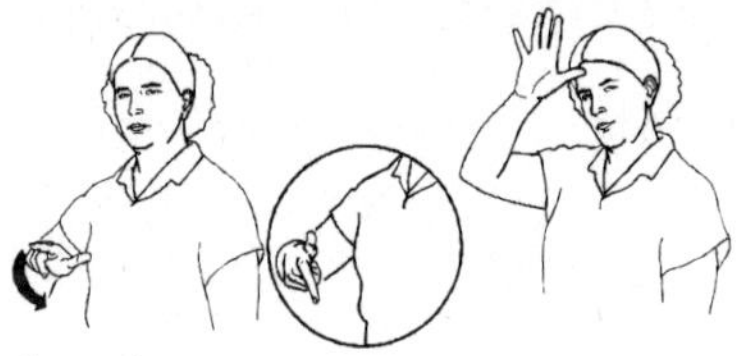

■ [**second-hand** + **father**] Beginning with the right *L hand* in front of the right side of the chest, palm facing down, twist the wrist forward with a deliberate movement. Then, tap the thumb of the right *5 hand* against the forehead, palm facing left and fingers pointing up.

**stepmother** *n.* The wife of one's father by a subsequent marriage: *the children now get along well with their stepmother.*

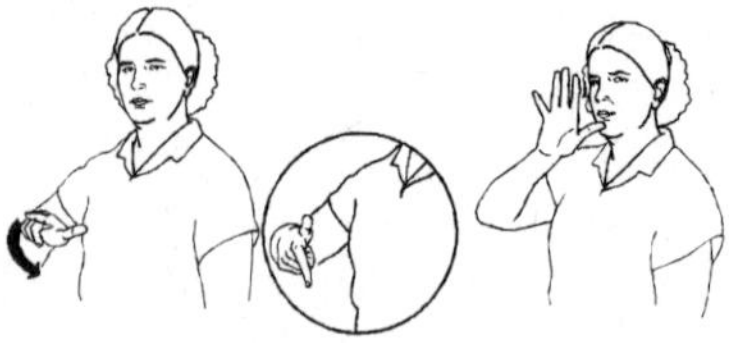

■ [**second-hand** + **mother**] Beginning with the right *L hand* in front of the right side of the chest, palm facing down, twist the wrist forward with a deliberate movement. Then, tap the thumb of the right *5 hand* against the chin, palm facing left and fingers pointing up.

**stepsister** *n.* A daughter of one's stepparent by a former marriage: *The two stepsisters look amazingly alike.*

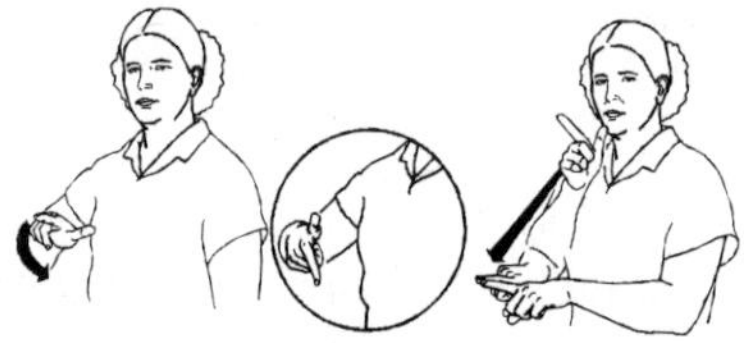

■ [**second-hand** + **sister**] Beginning with the right *L hand* in front of the right side of the chest, palm facing down, twist the wrist forward with a deliberate movement. Then bring the thumb of the right *L hand,* palm facing left, from the chin smoothly down while closing the thumb to the hand, ending with the index fingers of both *1 hands* together in front of the chest.

**stepson** *n.* A son of one's husband or wife by a former marriage: *getting to know my stepson.*

■ [**second-hand** + **son**] Beginning with the right *L hand* in front of the right side of the chest, palm facing down, twist the wrist forward with a deliberate movement. Then bring the fingers of the right *B hand* from touching the right side of the forehead downward while opening into an *open hand,* ending with the bent right arm cradled on the bent left arm held across the body, both palms facing up.

**sterilization** *n.* The tying of a woman's fallopian tubes to render her infertile: *chose sterilization to prevent further pregnancies.* Related form: **sterilize** *v.* Same sign used for: **tubal ligation, vasectomy.**

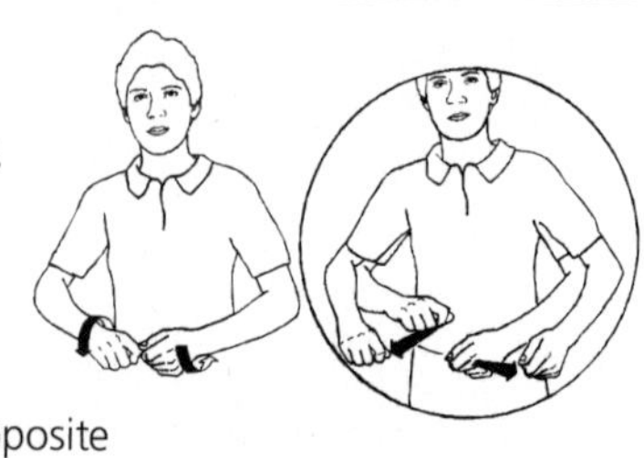

■ [Mime tying to represent tying one's tubes for sterilization] Beginning with both *modified X hands* touching in front of the waist, right palm facing down and left palm facing in, twist the wrists in opposite directions and pull the hands deliberately apart to each side of the waist.

**stern** *adj.* See sign for STRICT.

**stick**[1] *v.* To fasten or attach, as with glue: *to stick a stamp on the envelope.* Related form: **sticky** *adj.* Same sign used for: **adhere, adhesive, expose, fasten.**

■ [Demonstrates something sticky causing the finger and thumb to stick together] With the thumb of the right *5 hand,* palm facing down, touching the palm of the left *open hand,* palm facing up, close the right middle finger down to the thumb.

**stick**[2] *n.* A relatively long and slender piece of wood: *to knock down a beehive with a stick.* Same sign used for: **pipe, pole, rod.**

■ [Shape of a stick] Beginning with the thumb sides of both *F hands* touching in front of the chest, palms facing forward, move the hands apart.

**sticky** *adj.* Same sign as for STICK[1] but formed with a double movement.

**still**[1] *adv.* As previously: *still at home.* Same sign used for: **yet.**

■ [Formed with a continuing movement to show passage of time] Move the right *Y hand,* palm facing down, from in front of the right side of the body forward and upward in an arc.

**still**[2] *adj.* See signs for QUIET[1,2].

**sting** *v.* **1.** To prick and wound with a sharp, pointed organ, as on a bee or wasp: *A bee stung me!* —*n.* **2.** An act or instance of stinging: *Stings are more dangerous for the bees than for us.* **3.** A wound caused by stinging: *medicines to sooth a bee sting.*

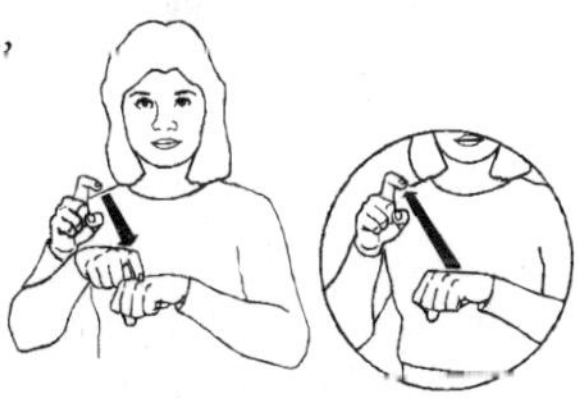

■ [Represents the stinger of an insect penetrating to wound] Beginning with the right *X hand* held in front of the right side of the chest, palm facing left, bring the bent index finger down deliberately against the back of the left *S hand,* palm facing down, and then back upward quickly.

**stingy**[1] *adj.* Unwilling or reluctant to spend money or to give in other ways: *difficult to get a donation from a stingy person.* Same sign used for: **thrifty.**

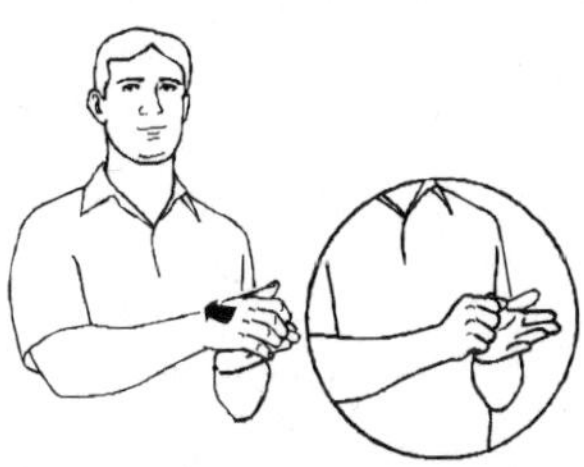

■ [Represents scraping] Beginning with the fingertips of the right *curved 5 hand* on the fingers of the left *open hand,* palm facing up, bring the right hand back toward the left heel with a double movement while closing into an *A hand* each time.

**stingy**[2] *adj.* See sign for SELFISH[1].

**stink** *v.* **1.** To give off a strong, offensive smell: *Rotting fish really stink.* —*n.* **2.** A strong, offensive smell: *a terrible stink in the room.* Related form: **stinky** *adj.* Same sign used for: **phew, putrid.**

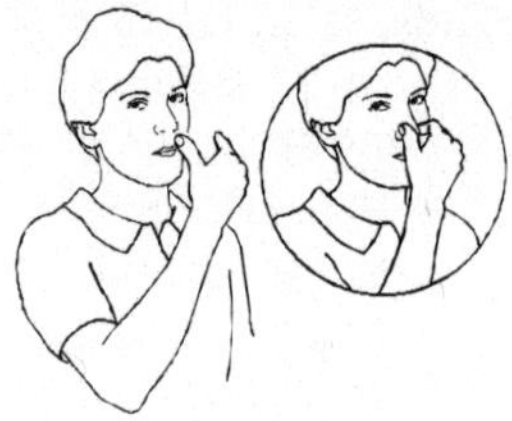

■ [Natural gesture for holding the nose when something smells bad] Bring the thumb and index finger of the right *G hand,* palm facing in, back to pinch the nose.

**stir** *v.* See signs for BEAT[1], MESSY, MIX.

**stitch** *v.* See signs for SEW[1,2].

**stocking** *n.* A knitted covering for the foot and leg: *likes to wear nylon stockings instead of panty hose.* Same sign used for: **hose.**

■ [Represents pulling on a long stocking] Bring the fingers of the right *5 hand,* palm facing in, from the wrist up the forearm of the extended left arm with a smooth movement.

**stocks** *pl. n.* See sign for INVEST.

**stomach** *n.* The mid-portion of the body, part of the alimentary canal, where food is stored and partially digested: *a pain in my stomach.* Same sign used for: **abdomen.**

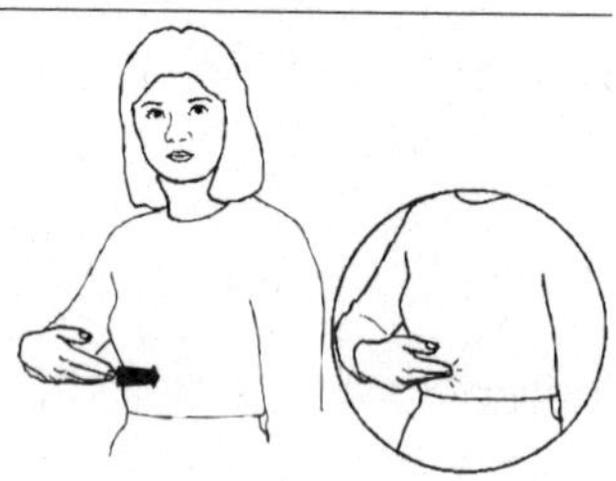

■ [Location of stomach] Tap the fingertips of the right *bent hand*, palm facing up, against the center of the body with a double movement.

**stomachache**[1] *n.* A pain in the stomach area: *I have a stomachache from eating green apples.*

■ [**hurt**[1] formed near the stomach] Beginning with both extended index fingers pointing toward each other in front of the body, palms facing up, jab the fingers toward each other with a short double movement.

**stomachache**[2] *n.* See sign for DISGUSTED[1].

**stop**[1] *v.* To cease from moving or doing: *to stop work at three o'clock.* Same sign used for: **abate, cease, enjoin, halt, quit.**

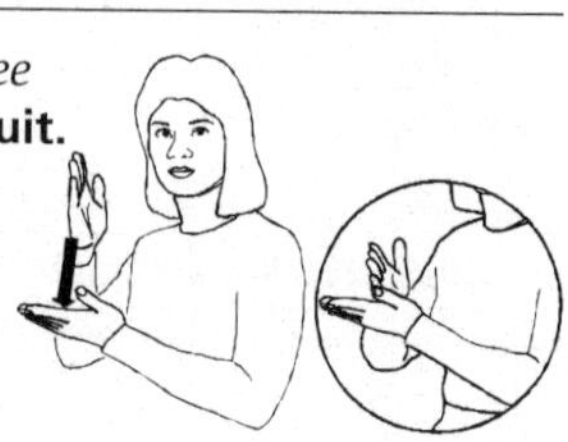

■ [Demonstrates an abrupt stopping movement] Bring the little-finger side of the right *open hand,* palm facing left and fingers pointing up, sharply down on the upturned palm of the left *open hand* held in front of the body.

**stop**[2] *v.* See sign for DESIST.

**storage** *n.* See sign for SAVE[2].

**store**[1] *n.* A place where goods are sold: *Go to the grocery store.* Same sign used for: **market, mart, shop.**

- [The hands seem to hold merchandise out for inspection and sale] Beginning with both *flattened O hands* in front of each side of the body, palms facing down and fingers pointing down, swing the fingers forward and back from the wrists with a repeated movement.

**store**[2] *v.* See sign for SAVE[2].

**storm** *n.* See signs for MESSY, WIND.

**story** *n.* An narrative account of some true or fictitious happening: *to tell a long story.* Same sign used for: **fable, parable, phrase, prose, remarks, tale.**

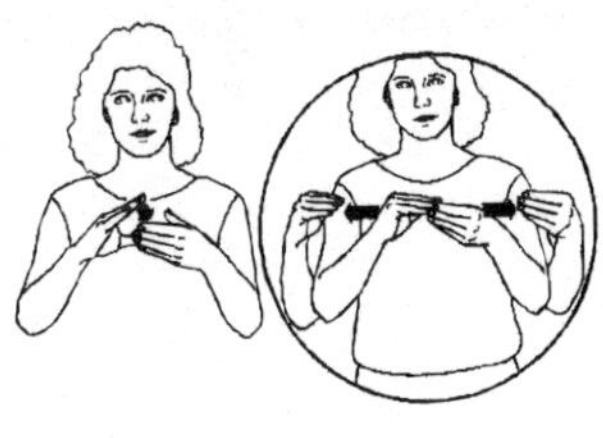

- [The hands seem to pull out sentences to form a story] Beginning with both *flattened C hands* in front of the chest, palms facing each other and the right hand slightly over the left hand, close the fingertips to the thumbs of each hand and then pull the hands straight apart in front of each shoulder with a double movement.

**straight**[1] *adj.* **1.** Without a curve: *a straight line.* —*adv.* **2.** In a straight line: *Walk straight to the corner.* Same sign used for: **direct.**

- [Indicates a straight direction] Beginning with the index-finger side of the right *B hand* against the right shoulder, palm facing left and fingers pointing up, move the hand straight forward by bending the wrist down.

**straight**[2] *adj., adv.* See sign for SPECIALIZE.

**stranded** *adj.* See sign for STUCK.

**strange** *adj.* Unusual; extraordinary: *a strange incident.* Same sign used for: **bizarre, freak, odd, peculiar, queer, unusual, weird.**

- Move the right *C hand* from near the right side of the face, palm facing left, downward in an arc in front of the face, ending near the left side of the chin, palm facing down.

**strategy** *n.* Planning for achieving a goal: *If we follow the strategy as outlined, the office will be computerized by May.*

■ [Initialized sign] Beginning with both *S hands* in front of each side of the chest, palms facing forward, move the hands downward with a wavy movement.

**straw** *n.* A slender hollow tube used for sipping: *to drink the soda with a straw.*

■ [The right hand represents a straw leading from a liquid to the mouth] Beginning with both *G hands* together in front of the body, palms facing each other and right hand closer to the lips than the left hand, move the right hand upward to touch the mouth with a short double movement.

**strawberry** *n.* A small red, fleshy fruit from a vine: *to eat strawberries and cream.*

■ Wipe the right extended index finger, palm facing in, downward on the lips. Then wipe the thumb of the right *10 hand,* palm facing in, downward on the lips.

**stray** *v.* See sign for ASTRAY.

**stream**[1] *n.* **1.** A steady flow: *a stream of light.* —*v.* **2.** To flow: *the light streamed in.* Same sign used for: **flow.**

■ [Represents liquid flowing down] Beginning with both *B hands* in front of the right side of the chest, right palm facing up and left palm facing down, move the hands downward to the left with a double movement.

**stream**[2] *n.* See sign for RIVER.

**street**[1] *n.* A usually paved public road in a city or town, often including sidewalks: *to walk down the street.*

■ [Initialized sign formed similar to **road**] Move both *S hands* from in front of the body, palms facing each other, forward with a parallel movement.

**street**[2] *n.* See sign for ROAD.

**strength** *n.* See signs for POWER[1], STRONG[1], WELL[1].

**stress** *n.* See signs for IMPRESSION, PRESSURE.

**stretch**[1] *v.* To draw out to greater size: *to stretch the elastic band.* Same sign used for: **elastic.**

■ [Mime stretching out some elastic] Beginning with the knuckles of both *S hands* touching in front of the chest, palms facing in, bring the hands apart to in front of each side of the chest with a double movement.

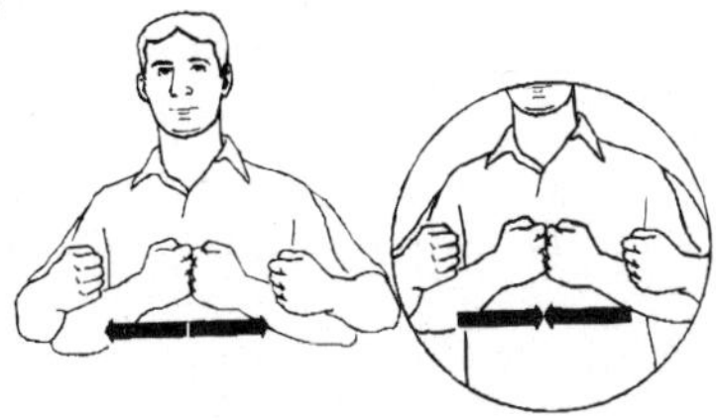

**stretch**[2] *v.* See sign for EXAGGERATE.

**strict** *adj.* Conforming to regulations, principles, and rules: *strict discipline.* Same sign used for: **bold, firm, stern.**

■ Strike the index-finger side of the right *bent V hand* against the nose with a deliberate movement, palm facing left.

**strike** *v.* See signs for BEAT[3], BEAT UP, COMPLAIN, HIT[1], PROTEST[2].

**string** *n.* See sign for LINE.

**strip**[1] *n.* A long, narrow piece of anything: *a strip of paper.*

■ [The shape of strips of something] Beginning with the thumbs and index fingers of both *G hands* touching, left palm facing down, over the right palm facing left, move the right hand straight down with a double movement in front of the chest.

**strip**[2] *v.* See sign for TEAR.

**stripe** *n.* A long, narrow band differing in color, texture, etc., from adjacent parts: *red and white stripes.* Same sign used for: **barcode, UPC.**

■ [Represents the shape of stripes] Beginning with the right *4 hand* in front of the left shoulder, palm facing in and fingers pointing left, pull the hand straight across the chest to in front of the right shoulder.

**strive** *v.* See sign for TRY.

**stroll** *v.* See sign for WALK.

**strong**[1] *adj.* Having much power or strength: *a strong personality.* Same sign used for: **might, mighty, power, solid, strength.**

■ [Initialized sign formed similar to **power**] Beginning with the index-finger side of the right *S hand* near the left shoulder, palm facing left, move the right hand down in an arc, ending with the little-finger side of the right *S hand* touching near the crook of the left arm, palm facing up.

**strong**[2] *adj.* See signs for POWERFUL, WELL[1].

**structure** *n.* **1.** Something composed of parts arranged together: *the structure of the novel.* **2.** A building: *a tall structure going up on the next street.*

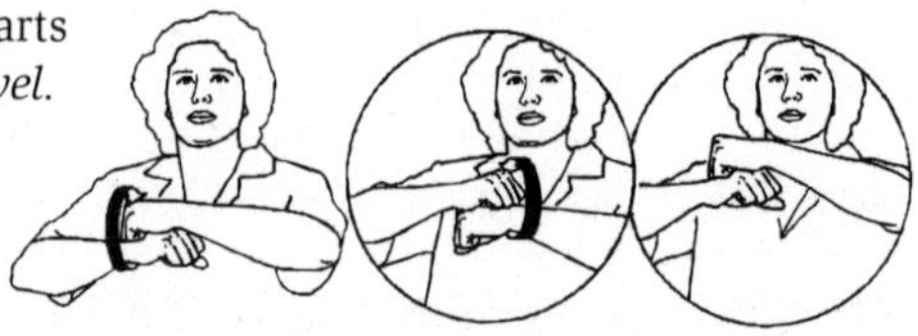

■ [Initialized sign formed similar to **build**] Beginning with the left *S hand* on the back of the right *S hand,* both palms facing down, move the right hand in a forward and upward arc to reverse positions. Repeat as the hands move upward in front of the chest.

**struggle** *v.* **1.** To contend vigorously, as with an adversary: *to struggle with the robber.* **2.** To make great efforts or perform hard work: *to struggle with a problem.* —*n.* **3.** Great effort or hard work: *a great struggle.* Same sign used for: **antagonism, at odds, banter, conflict, controversy, opposition.**

■ [Represents opposing forces struggling] Beginning with both extended index fingers pointing toward each other in front of the chest, palms facing in and right hand closer to the body than the left hand, move the hands back and forth simultaneously with a double movement.

**stubborn** *adj.* Having fixed opinions and an unyielding nature or attitude: *a stubborn person who won't listen to opposing arguments.* Same sign used for: **determined, obstinate, persistence, persistent.**

■ [Similar to sign for **donkey** signifying a donkey's stubborn nature] Beginning with the extended thumb of the right *open hand* touching the right temple, palm facing forward and fingers pointing up, bend the fingers downward with a deliberate movement.

**stuck** *adj.* Fixed in position; unable to proceed or escape: *stuck in the mud.* Same sign used for: **confined, pregnant, rape, stranded, trapped.**

■ [Indicates where food gets stuck in the throat] Move the fingertips of the right *V hand,* palm facing down, against the throat with a deliberate movement.

**student** *n.* See sign for PUPIL[1].

**study** *v.* **1.** To apply oneself to the acquisition of knowledge: *to study for an examination.* —*n.* **2.** The application of one's mind to the acquisition of knowledge: *The study of sign language is difficult but fascinating.* **3.** studies: a student's work at school or college: *He found the answer in his studies about ecology.*

■ While wiggling the fingers, move the right *5 hand,* palm facing down, with a double movement toward the left *open hand* held in front of the chest, palm facing up.

**stuff** *n.* See sign for SAVE[2].

**stuffed** *adj.* See sign for FULL[1].

**stuffing** *n.* See sign for INSIDE.

**stunned** *adj.* See sign for INCREDIBLE.

**stupid** *adj.* See sign for DUMB.

**sturdy**[1] *adj.* Strongly built: *a sturdy chair.* Same sign used for: **solid, tough.**

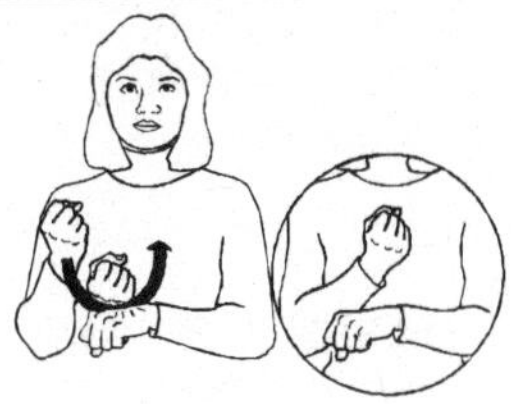

■ Move the right *S hand* from in front of the right side of the chest, palm facing in, in a downward arc across the back of the left *S hand* held in front of the chest, palm facing down, and back again.

**sturdy**[2] *adj.* See sign for POWER[1].

**style** *n.* See sign for TASTE. Shared idea that style is equivalent to good taste.

**sub-** *prefix.* Under; beneath; less than: *subway; subbasement; subnormal.*

■ [Initialized sign formed similar to sign for **base**] Move the right *S hand,* palm facing forward, in a double circular movement under the left *open hand* held across the chest, palm facing down and fingers pointing right.

**subdue** *v.* See sign for DEFEAT.

**subject** *n.* See signs for QUOTATION[1], TITLE.

**submit** *v.* See signs for ADMIT[1], SUGGEST. Related form: **submission** *n.*

**subscribe** *v.* See sign for PENSION.

**substance**[1] *n.* The physical material of which something is made: *Cement is a rough substance.*

■ [Represents feeling a substance] Grasp the left *open hand* with the fingers of the right *flattened C hand,* both palms facing down, and slide the right hand forward and back with a double movement.

**substance**[2] *n.* See sign for SAME MEAT.

**substitute** *v.* See sign for TRADE. Related form: **substitution** *n.*

**subtract** *v.* **1.** To take away, as a part from a whole: *Subtract four from seven.* **2.** To perform the mathematical operation of substraction (on): *First multiply, then subtract; to subtract the numbers.* Same sign used for: **deduct, discount, eliminate, exempt.**

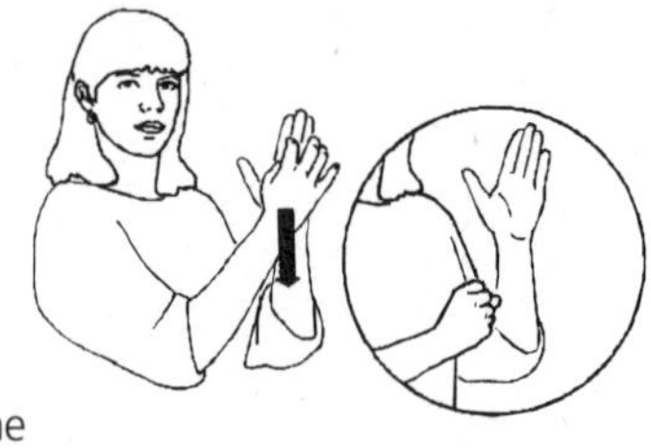

■ [Demonstrates removing something] Beginning with the fingertips of the right *curved 5 hand* touching the palm of the left *open hand* held in front of the left side of the chest, palm facing right and fingers pointing up, bring the right hand down off the base of the left hand while changing into an *S hand.*

**subway** *n.* An electric railroad running under the streets of a city: *to ride the subway.*

■ [Initialized sign formed under the left hand representing moving under street level] Move the right *S hand,* palm facing left, forward and back under the palm of the left *open hand* held across the chest, palm facing down and fingers pointing right.

**succeed** *v.* See sign for FINALLY.

**success** *n.* See sign for ACHIEVE.

**successful** *adj.* **1.** Having or manifesting a favorable result: *a successful event.* **2.** Possessing wealth, honors, professional position, etc. Related forms: **succeed** *v.*, **success** *n.* See also sign for ACHIEVE. Same sign used for: **accomplish, accomplishment, achievement, prosper, triumph.**

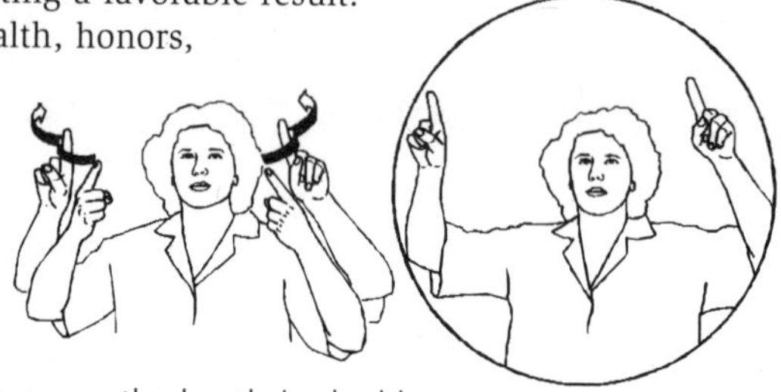

■ Beginning with both extended index fingers pointing up in front of each shoulder, palms facing back, move the hands in double arcs upward and back, ending near each side of the head.

**such as** See sign for SAME[1].

**suck** *v.* To draw something into the mouth by creating a partial vacuum: *to suck through a straw.*

■ [Represents the mouth when sucking] Open and close the fingers of the right *flattened C hand* with a double movement around the fingertips of the left *flattened O hand* held in front of the chest, left palms facing in and right palm facing forward. Then pull the right hand back toward the chest while closing the fingers into a *flattened O hand* and puckering the lips as if sucking.

**sudden** *adj., adv.* See sign for FAST.

**sue** *v.* To take legal action (against): *to sue for damages; to sue the driver after an accident.*

■ Beginning with the right *B hand* in front of the right shoulder, palm facing left and fingers angled forward, bring the hand down to sharply touch the fingertips against the palm of the left *open hand,* palm facing in and fingers angled to the right.

**suffer** *v.* To have pain or grief: *to suffer from headaches.*

■ [Similar to **hurt**[2] except formed with a double movement] Beginning with the thumb of the right *A hand* touching the chin, palm facing left, twist the hand to the left with a double movement.

**sufficient** *adj.* See sign for ENOUGH.

**sugar** *n.* See sign for CANDY.

**suggest** *v.* To mention or put forward, as an idea: *I suggest we go swimming.* Related form: **suggestion** *n.* Same sign used for: **appeal, bid, motion, offer, nominate, petition, proposal, propose, provide, recommend, submit, submission.**

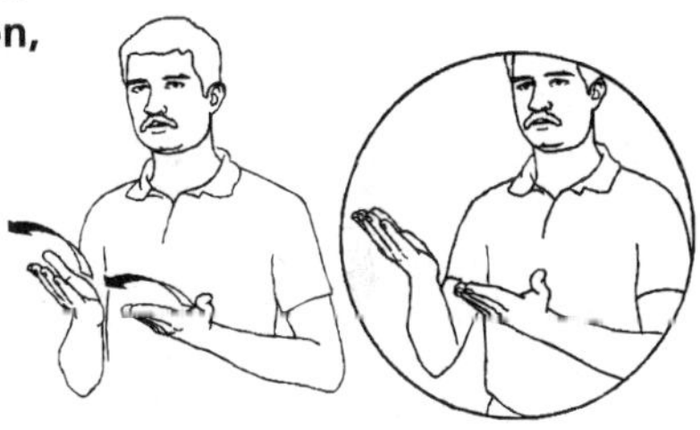

■ [The hands seem to put forward a suggestion] Beginning with both *open hands* in front of each side of the chest, palms facing up and fingers pointing forward, move the hands simultaneously upward in an arc.

**suicide** *n.* The taking of one's own life: *to commit suicide.*

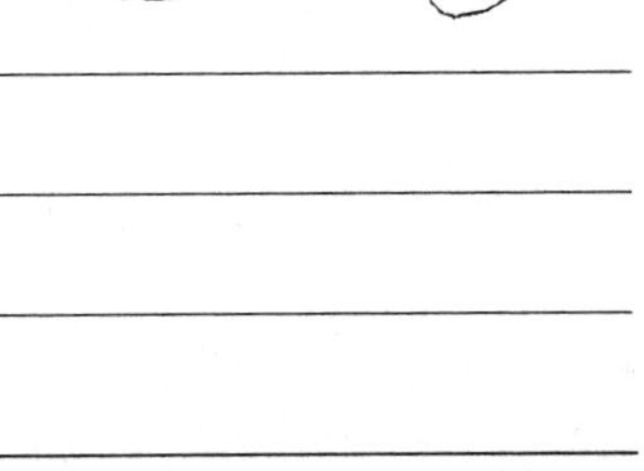

■ [**kill** + **myself**] Push the side of the extended right index finger, palm facing down, across the palm of the left *open hand,* palm facing right, with a deliberate movement. Then tap the thumb side of the right *10 hand,* palm facing left, against the chest with a double movement.

**suit**[1] *n.* See signs for AGREE[1], FIT, MATCH[1], PROSECUTE[1].

**suit**[2] *n.* See sign for CLOTHES.

**suitable** *adj.* See sign for APPROPRIATE.

**suitcase** *n.* See signs for BASKET, PURSE.

**sum** *v.* See sign for ADD[1].

**summarize** *v.* See sign for BRIEF.

**summer** *n.* The warmest season of the year, occurring between spring and autumn: *plans to go on vacation this summer.*

- [Represents wiping sweat from the brow] Bring the thumb side of the extended right index finger, palm facing down and finger pointing left, across the forehead while bending the index finger into an *X hand.*

**summon** *v.* See sign for CALL[1].

**sun** *n.* The star around which the earth and other planets of the solar system revolve and from which they receive light and heat: *the bright sun shining in the sky.*

- [Represents shielding one's eyes from the sun] Tap the thumb and index finger of the right *C hand,* palm facing forward, against the right side of the head with a double movement.

**sunburn** *n.* A skin inflammation caused by overexposure to sunlight: *The girl got a sunburn at the pool.*

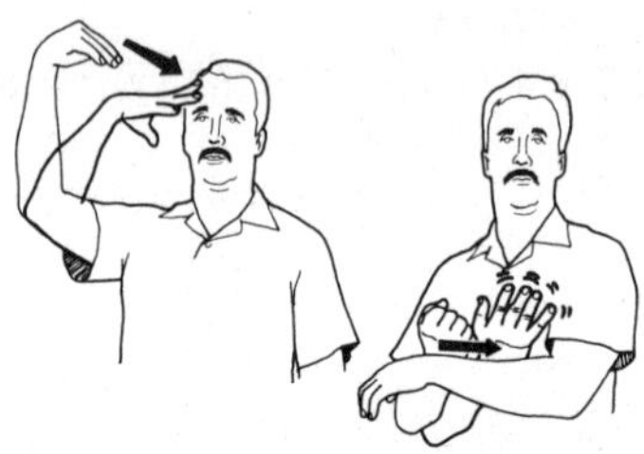

- [Gesture showing the sun's rays hitting the face + **burn**] Beginning with the right *flattened O hand* above the right shoulder, palm facing down, bring the right hand downward toward the face while opening into a *curved 5 hand.* Then begin with the right *S hand,* palm facing up, on the back of the left wrist. Then open the right hand to a *curved 5 hand* and slide the back of the right hand toward the crook of the left arm while wiggling the right fingers with a repeated movement.

**Sunday** *n.* The first day of the week, the Sabbath of most Christian denominations: *to go to church on Sunday.*

- Beginning with both *open hands* in front of each shoulder, palms facing forward and fingers pointing up, move the hands forward and back with a small double movement.

**sundown** *n.* See sign for SUNSET.

**sunrise** *n.* **1.** The first appearance of the sun above the horizon in the morning: *to wake up at sunrise.* **2.** The colorful scenic phenomena in the atmosphere accompanying this: *a beautiful sunrise.* Same sign used for **dawn.**

■ [Represents the sun coming up over the horizon] Bring the index-finger side of the right *F hand,* palm facing left, upward past the little-finger side of the left *open hand,* palm facing down and fingers pointing right, held across the chest, ending with the right *F hand* in front of the face.

**sunset** *n.* **1.** The descent of the sun below the horizon in the evening: *a walk by the river at sunset.* **2.** The colorful scenic phenomena in the atmosphere accompanying this: *to watch a beautiful sunset through multicolored clouds.* Same sign used for: **sundown.**

■ [Represents the sun going down below the horizon] Move the thumb side of the right *F hand*, palm facing left, downward past the little-finger side of the left *open* hand held across the chest, palm facing down and fingers pointing right.

**superb** *adj.* Excellent: *a superb day with the sun shining.* Same sign used for: **excellent, fantastic, okay.**

■ [Natural gesture to indicate something is superb] Move the right *F hand,* palm facing left, forward with a short double movement in front of the right shoulder.

**superintendent** *n.* See sign for PRESIDENT.

**superior** *n.* See sign for CHIEF.

**superstition** *n.* See sign for IMAGINATION. Related form: **superstitious** *adj.*

**supervise** *v.* See sign for CARE.

**supplement** *v.* See sign for ADD².

**supply** *v.* See sign for FEED.

**support** *v.* **1.** To give help, sustenance, money, or comfort to: *to support one's family.* **2.** To advocate: *to support the cause.* —*n.* **3.** An act or instance of supporting: *Your support is appreciated.* **4.** Help; backup: *He brought extra support with him when he took over the fund raising.* Same sign used for: **advocate, allegiance, backup, boost, endorse, fund, in favor of, on behalf of, reinforce, sponsor.**

■ [Initialized sign similar to sign for **help**] Push the knuckles of the right *S hand,* palm facing left, upward under the little-finger side of the left *S hand,* palm facing in, pushing the left hand upward a short distance in front of the chest.

**suppose** *v.* To consider as a possibility: *Suppose it rains this afternoon.* Same sign used for: **if, in case of.**

■ [Indicates a thought coming from the mind] Move the extended little finger of the right *I hand,* palm facing in, forward from the right side of the forehead with a short double movement.

**supposed to** *adj.* + *prep.* See sign for NEED.

**suppress** *v.* See signs for CONTROL, PRESSURE. Related form: **suppression** *n.*

**supreme** *adj.* See sign for ADVANCED.

**sure**[1] *adj.* Free from doubt: *Are you sure?* Same sign used for: **certain.**

■ [Indicates that true facts are coming straight from the mouth] Move the extended right index finger from in front of the mouth, palm facing left and finger pointing up, forward with a deliberate movement.

**sure**[2] *adj.* See sign for HONEST.

**surf** or **surf the Net** *v.* To explore the Internet, especially casually or recreationally, looking for interesting sites: *I surfed the Net for good airline prices.* Related form: **surfer** *n.*

■ [**look for** + **sneak**] Move the right *C hand,* palm facing left, with a double circular movement in front of the face. Then with the right index finger extended, move the right hand, palm facing down and finger pointing forward, in a wavy movement under the left *open hand,* sliding the left palm up the right forearm as the right hand moves forward.

**surface**[1] *n.* The outside of something: *Rub the surface of the roast with garlic.*

■ [Indicates the surface of something] Move the palm side of the right *open hand* in a circle on the back of the left *open hand,* both palms facing down in front of the chest.

**surface**[2] *v.* See sign for SHOW UP.

**surfboard** *n.* A long, narrow board used for riding the crest of waves in the surf: *to float in to shore on a surfboard.* Same sign used for: **surfing.**

■ [Represents a person standing on a surfboard] With the fingertips of the right *H hand,* palm facing down, on the back of the left *open hand,* palm facing down in front of the chest, move both hands forward.

**surge** *n.* See sign for POWER SURGE.

**surgery** *n.* See sign for OPERATE[1].

**surprise** *n.* **1.** A feeling of wonder from encountering something unexpected; astonishment: *The party was a pleasant surprise.* —*v.* **2.** To strike with surprise: *I was surprised to find out how much the bill was.* Same sign used for: **amaze, amazement, astound, bewilder, startle.**

■ [Represents the eyes widening in surprise] Beginning with the index fingers and thumbs of both hands pinched together near the outside of each eye, palms facing each other, flick the fingers apart, forming *L hands* near each side of the head.

**surrender** *v.* See sign for GIVE UP.

**surround** *v.* See sign for SITUATION.

**surrounding** *adj.* See sign for AROUND.

**surveillance** *n.* Covert monitoring of a person's movements and activities, especially by law enforcement authorities: *The cops had him under surveillance.*

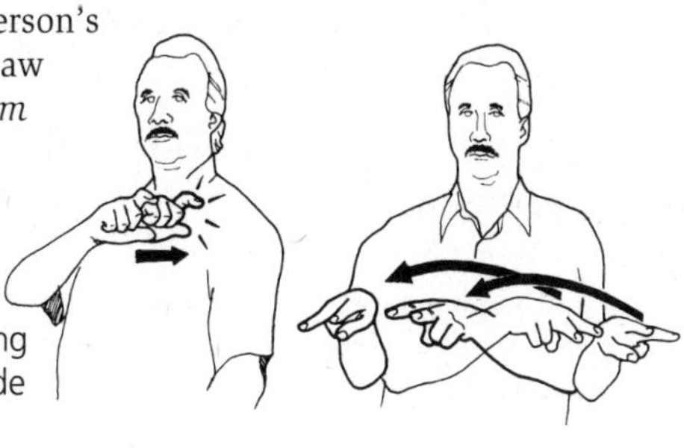

■ [**police** + **watch**] Tap the thumb side of the right *modified C hand,* palm facing left, against the left side of the chest with a double movement. Then beginning with both *V hands* in front of the left side of the body, palms down and fingers pointing forward, swing the hands in large simultaneous arcs to the right.

**survive** *v.* See sign for LIVE. Related form: **survival** *n.*

**suspect** *v.* **1.** To think something is likely: *I suspect that it will snow.* **2.** To doubt or mistrust: *Don't suspect my motives.* **3.** To believe to be guilty: *The detective suspects the butler.* Related forms: **suspicion** *n.*, **suspicious** *adj.*

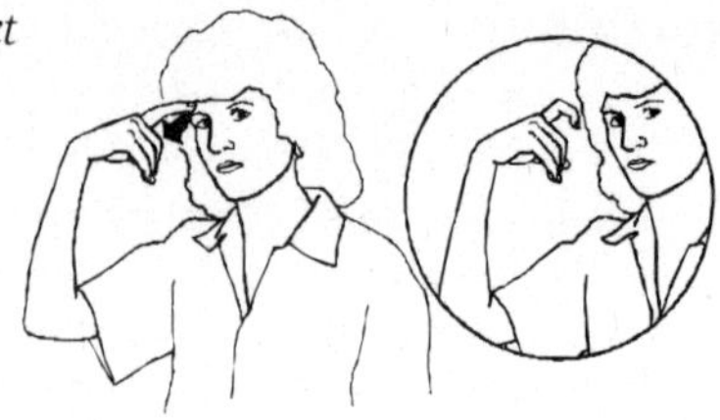

■ Beginning with the extended right index finger touching the right side of the forehead, palm facing down, bring the hand forward a short distance with a double movement, bending the index finger into an *X hand* each time.

---

**suspend** v. See sign for HOLD².

---

**swallow** *v.* To take into the stomach through the mouth and throat: *so nervous I can't swallow a bite of food.* Same sign used for: **gulp.**

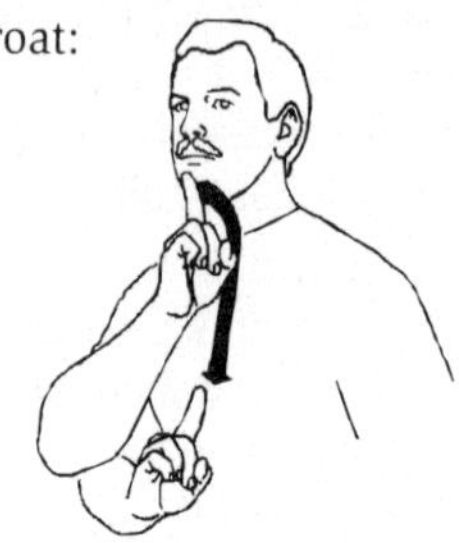

■ [Shows the path food follows when swallowed] Move the extended right index finger, palm facing left and finger angled upward, in an arc from in front of the chin down the length of the neck.

---

**swap** *v.* See signs for REVERSE, TRADE.

---

**swap places** *v. phrase.* See sign for TRADE PLACES.

---

**swear** *v.* See signs for CURSE, VOW.

---

**sweat** *v.* **1.** To emit moisture from one's pores: *tends to sweat in summer.* —*n.* **2.** The moisture so emitted: *drenched with sweat.* Same sign used for: **perspire, perspiration, toil.**

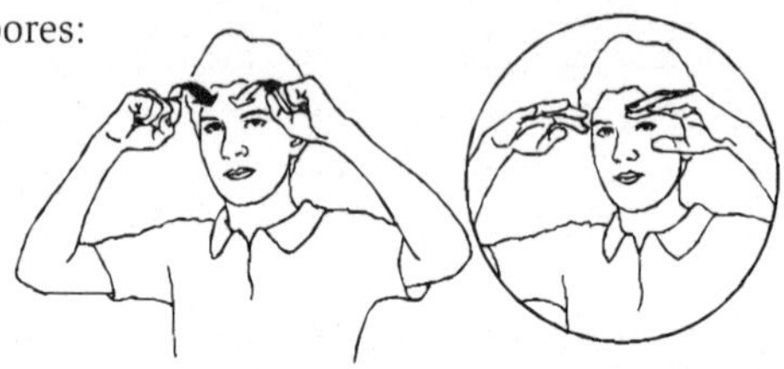

■ [Represents sweat coming from one's brow] Beginning with both *S hands* in front of each side of the forehead, move the hands forward while opening into *curved hands,* palms facing down and fingers pointing toward each other.

---

**sweater** *n.* A knitted covering, as a cardigan or pullover, for the upper torso: *to wear a sweater in the fall.*

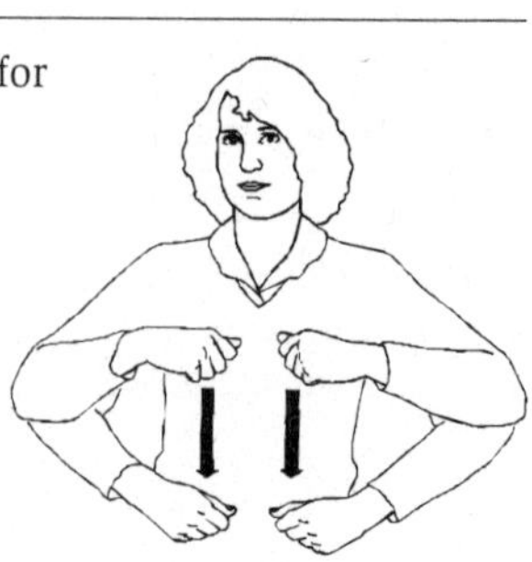

■ [Demonstrates pulling on a sweater] Beginning with the thumb sides of both *A hands* on each side of the chest, palms facing in, bring the hands straight downward.

---

**sweep** *v.* See sign for BROOM.

**sweet** *adj.* Pleasant and agreeable; amiable and kind: *a genuinely sweet person.* Same sign used for: **gentle.**

■ Wipe the fingertips of the right *open hand,* palm facing in and fingers pointing up, downward off the chin while bending the fingers.

**sweetheart** *n.* Someone with whom one shares a love relationship: *My sweetheart sent me a valentine.* Same sign used for: **beau, lover.**

■ With the knuckles of both *10 hands* together in front of the chest, palms facing in and thumbs pointing up, bend the thumbs downward toward each other with a double movement.

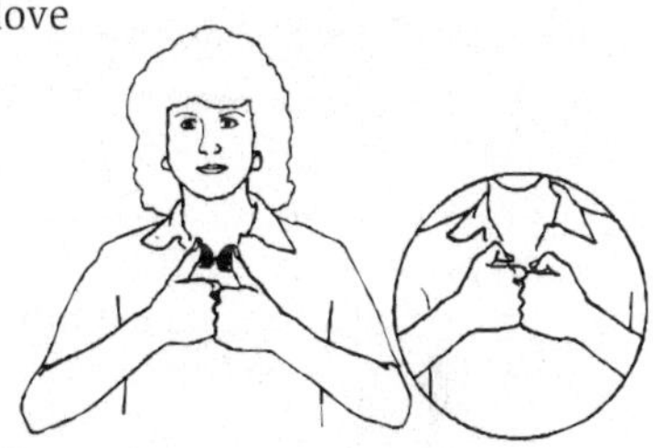

**swell** *v.* See sign for EXPAND[1].

**swim** *v.* To move through the water by moving the arms, legs, tail, or fins: *Fish swim in the ocean.* Related form: **swimming** *n.*

■ [Demonstrates the movement of the hands when swimming] Beginning with the fingers of both *open hands* crossed in front of the chest, palms facing down, move the hands apart to each side with a double movement.

**swindle** *v.* See sign for BETRAY.

**switch** *v.* See signs for CHANGE, REVERSE, TRADE.

**switch places** *v. phrase.* See sign for TRADE PLACES.

**swollen** *adj.* Enlarged abnormally, as by injury: *Her wrist is swollen from the bump on the bookcase.*

■ [Indicates the shape of a swelling on the wrist] Beginning with the right *curved 5 hand* on the back of the left *open hand* held in front of the chest, both palms facing down, raise the right hand a short distance.

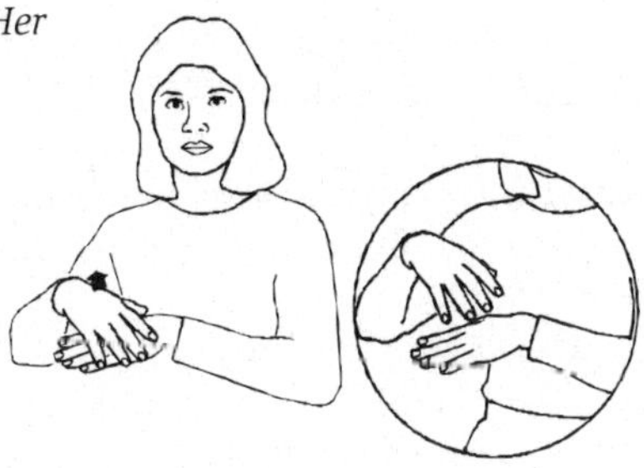

**sworn** *adj.* See sign for VOW.

**syllable** *n.* A part of a word that can be pronounced with a single uninterrupted sound: *Break the word into syllables and try to sound it out.*

■ [**word** signed in several places to show the small parts of a word] Move the right *G hand,* palm facing left, in short arcs across the length of the extended left index finger held in front of the chest, palm facing right and finger pointing forward.

**symbol** *n.* Something that represents something else: *The flag is a symbol of our country.* Same sign used for: **sample, sign, symptom.**

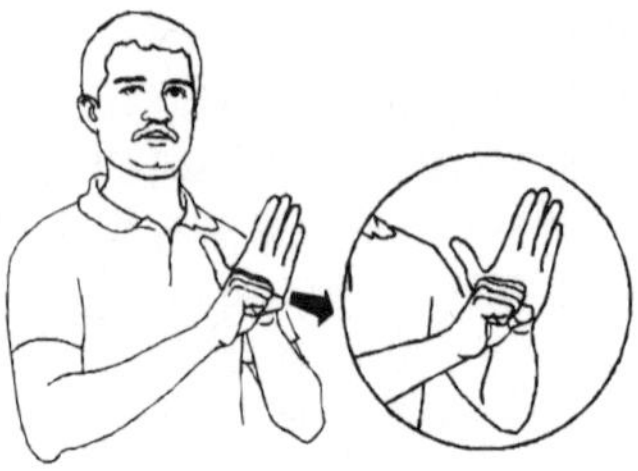

■ [Initialized sign similar to sign for **show**[1]] With the index-finger side of the right *S hand,* palm facing forward, against the palm of the left *open hand* held in front of the chest, palm facing right and fingers pointing up, move both hands forward a short distance.

**symptom** *n.* See sign for SYMBOL.

**synagogue** *n.* A Jewish house of worship, often used as well for religious instruction: *goes to the synagogue on Friday nights.*

■ [Initialized sign similar to sign for **church**] Tap the heel of the right *S hand,* palm facing forward, downward with a double movement on the back of the left *open hand* held in front of the chest.

**syntax** *n.* See sign for GRAMMAR.

**syrup**[1] *n.* A thick, sweet liquid prepared for table use: *to put syrup on pancakes.*

■ Wipe the extended right index finger, palm facing down, from under the nose across the right cheek.

**syrup**[2] *n.* See sign for GRAVY.

**system** *n.* An orderly combination of things, methods, or other parts that fit together to make a coherent whole: *an order-processing system.*

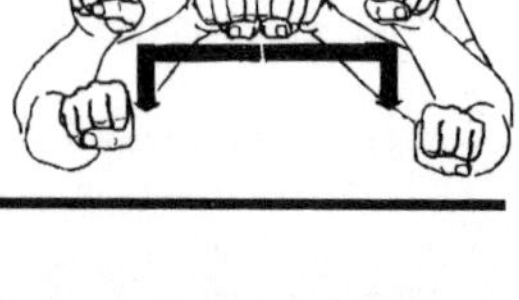

■ [Initialized sign] Beginning with the index-finger sides of both *S hands* touching in front of the chest, palms angled down, move the hands outward to in front of each shoulder and then straight down a short distance.

**tabernacle** *n.* See sign for TEMPLE.

**table**[1] *n.* A piece of furniture with a flat, horizontal top on legs, a pedestal, or other support: *to eat at the table.* Same sign used for: **desk.**

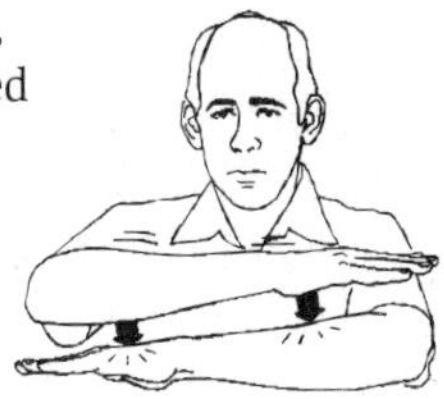

■ [Represents the flat surface of a table top] Beginning with the bent arms of both *open hands* across the chest, right arm above the left arm, move the right arm down with a short double movement.

**table**[2] *n.* (alternate sign) Same sign used for: **desk.**

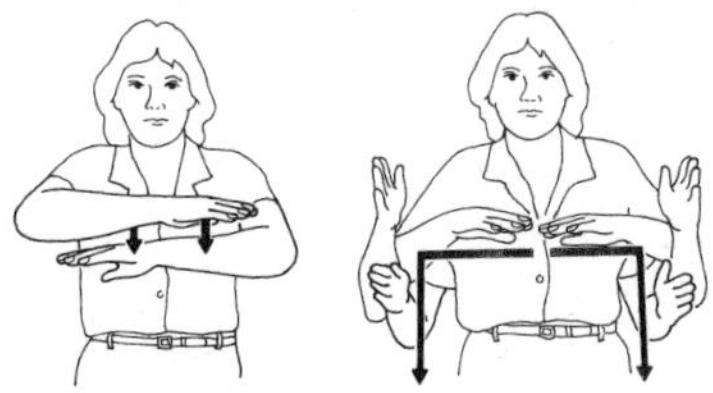

■ [**table**[1] + shape of a table] Pat the forearm of the bent right arm with a double movement on the bent left arm held across the chest. Then, beginning with the fingers of both *open hands* together in front of the chest, palms facing down, move the hands apart to in front of each shoulder and then straight down, ending with the palms facing each other.

**table tennis** *n. phrase.* See sign for PING PONG.

**tack** *n.* See sign for THUMBTACK.

**tag** *n.* See sign for LABEL.

**take** *v.* To accept or undertake, as an obligation: *to take charge of the project.* Same sign used for: **acquire, adopt, assume, assumption, takeover, take up.**

■ [The hands seem to take up something] Beginning with both *curved 5 hands* in front of each side of the body, palms facing down, move the hands upward toward the body while changing into *S hands.*

**take a chance** *v. phrase.* See sign for GRAB.

**take advantage of** *v. phrase.* See signs for ADVANTAGE[1], LEECH.

**take a pill** *v. phrase.* See sign for PILL.

**take care** *v. phrase.* See sign for CAREFUL.

**take care of** *v. phrase.* See sign for CARE.

**take off** *v. phrase.* To remove: *take off your clothes.* Same sign used for: **remove, undress.**

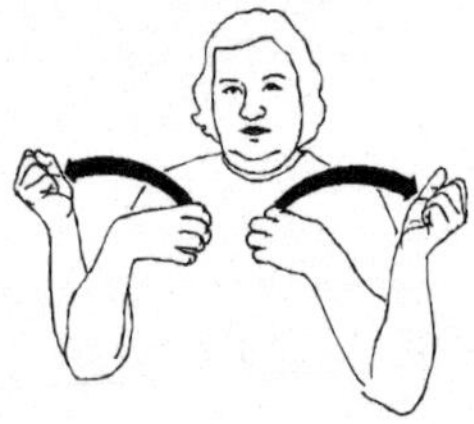

■ [Mime taking off one's clothes] Beginning with the fingers of both *curved hands* on each side of the chest, palms facing in, bring the hands outward to in front of each shoulder while closing into *S hands*, palms facing each other.

**take pictures** *v. phrase. Take pictures of the wedding.* Same sign used for: **photograph, shoot.**

■ [Represents the shutter on a camera opening and closing] Beginning with both *modified C hands* near the outside of each eye, palms facing each other, bend the right index finger downward.

**take steps** *v. phrase.* See sign for PROCEDURE.

**take up** *v. phrase.* See signs for RAPTURE, TAKE.

**takeover** *n.* See signs for CAPTURE, TAKE.

**tale** *n.* See sign for STORY.

**talent** *n.* See sign for SKILL.

**talk**[1] *v.* To exchange ideas by using words: *to talk on the phone.*

■ [Shows words coming from the mouth] Beginning with the index-finger side of the right *4 hand* in front of the mouth, palm facing left and fingers pointing up, move the hand forward with a double movement.

**talk**[2] *v.* See signs for BLAB, CHAT, SPEAK[1]. Related form: **talkative** *adj.*

**talk**[3] *v.* See sign for SPEAK[2].

**tall**[1] (for things) *adj.* Having a relatively great height: *a tall building.*

■ [Indicates the height of a tall object] Move the extended right index finger, palm facing forward and finger pointing up, from the heel upward to off the fingertips of the left *open hand,* palm facing right and fingers pointing up, ending with the right hand in front of the head.

**tall**[2] (people) *adj.* (alternate sign) Same sign used for: **height.**

■ [Shows height of a tall person] Raise the right *open hand,* palm facing down, upward from in front of the right shoulder.

**tame** *v.* See sign for PET.

**tan** *adj.* **1.** Light brown in color: *a tan sweater.* —*n.* **2.** A light brown color: *The color scheme is tan and blue.* **3.** A brown color acquired by the skin from exposure to the sun: *She has a nice tan.*

■ [Initialized sign similar to sign for **brown**] Slide the index-finger side of the right *T hand,* palm facing left, downward on the right cheek.

**tape** *n.* See sign for BANDAGE.

**tardy** *adj.* See sign for LATE.

**target** *n.* See signs for GOAL, POINT[2].

**task** *n.* See sign for WORK.

**taste** *n.* **1.** Flavor: *a spicy taste.* **2.** The sense by which flavor is perceived in the mouth: *enjoying food through the senses of taste and smell* —*v.* **3.** To sample the flavor of: *to taste the soup.* Same sign used for: **style.**

■ [The finger used for feeling points toward the sense of taste] Touch the bent middle finger of the right *5 hand,* palm facing in, to the lips.

**tasty** *adj.* See sign for DELICIOUS.

**tattle** *v.* To tell something secret about another: *The boy tattled on the girl who threw the paper airplane.* Same sign used for: **rat** *(slang),* **squeal, tattletale.**

■ Beginning with the index-finger side of the right *S hand* in front of the mouth, palm facing left, move the hand forward with a double movement, extending the right index finger each time.

**tax** *n.* See sign for COST[1].

**taxi** *n.* See sign for CAB.

**tea** *n.* A drink made by pouring hot water over specially dried and prepared tea leaves: *to drink a cup of tea.*

- [Mime dipping a tea bag in hot water] With the fingertips of the right *F hand,* palm facing down, inserted in the hole formed by the left *O hand* held in front of the chest, palm facing in, move the right hand in a small circle.

**teach** *v.* **1.** To help to pass on knowledge to: *to teach the class.* **2.** To help to pass on knowledge of: *to teach music.* Same sign used for: **educate, education, indoctrinate, indoctrination, instruct, instruction.**

- [The hands seem to take information from the head and direct it toward another person] Move both *flattened O hands,* palms facing each other, forward with a small double movement in front of each side of the head.

**team** *n.* **1.** A number of people forming one of the sides in a game: *a football team.* **2.** A number of people working together, as on a project: *a software development team of top programmers.*

- [Initialized sign similar to sign for **class**] Beginning with the index-finger sides of both *T hands* touching in front of the chest, palms angled forward, bring the hands away from each other in outward arcs while turning the palms in, ending with the little fingers touching.

**tear** *v.* To pull apart by force: *to tear the paper.* Same sign used for: **revoke, rip, strip, torn.**

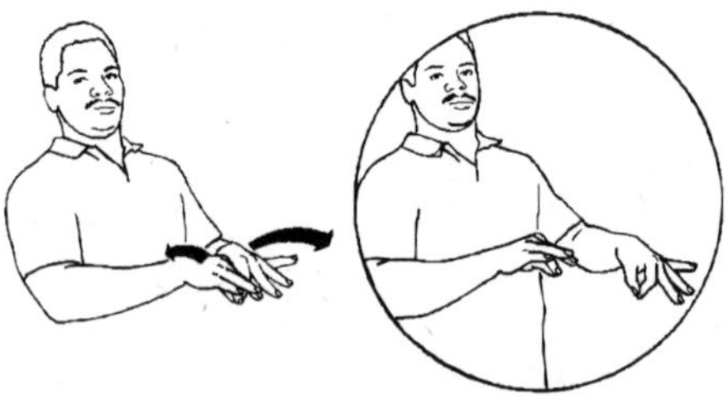

- [Mime ripping a piece of paper] Beginning with the index-finger sides of both *F hands* touching in front of the chest, palms facing down, move the right hand back toward the body with a deliberate movement while moving the left hand forward.

**tear apart** *v. phrase.* See sign for BREAK.

**tear down** *v. phrase.* See sign for BREAK DOWN.

**teardrop** *n.* See sign for TEARS.

**tears** *pl. n.* Drops of salty water coming from the eyes when crying: *His face was covered with tears.* Same sign used for: **teardrop.**

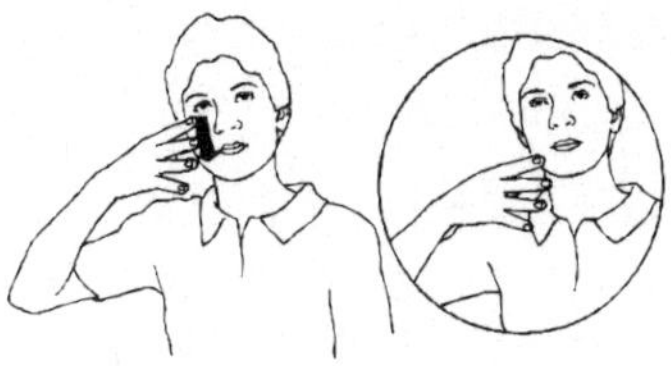

■ [Represents tears flowing from the eye] Beginning with the index finger of the right *4 hand* touching the cheek near the right eye, palm facing in and fingers pointing left, bring the hand downward a short distance.

**tease** *v.* To irritate or annoy, as with persistent taunts or playful mockery: *The grown-ups kept teasing the child about his shyness.* Related form: **teasing** *n.* Same sign used for: **jest, kid, kidding.**

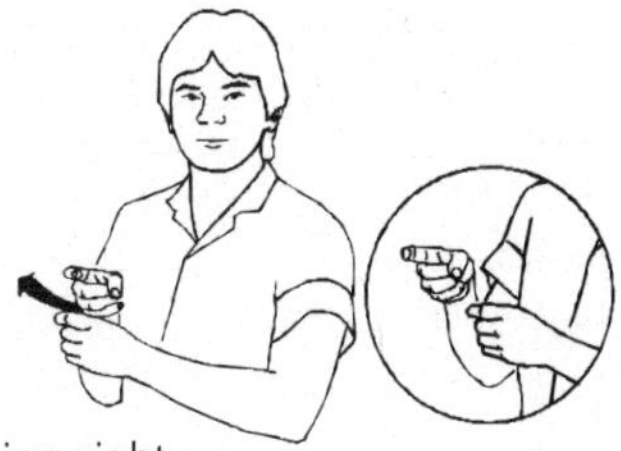

[The hand seems to direct jabbing remarks at someone] Push the little-finger side of the right *X hand,* palm facing left, forward with a repeated movement across the index-finger side of the left *X hand,* palm facing right.

**technical** *adj.* Pertaining to specialized facts and techniques of science, the arts, professions, and trades: *delivered a technical paper at the conference.* Same sign used for: **technique, technology.**

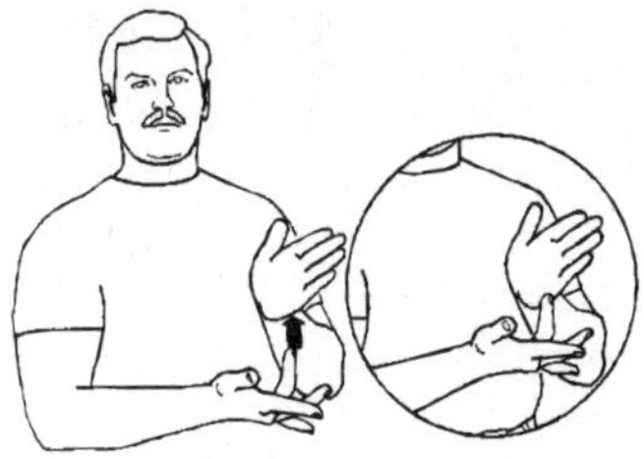

■ Tap the bent middle finger of the right *5 hand,* palm facing up, upward on the little-finger side of the left *open hand,* palm facing right and fingers pointing forward, with a double movement.

**technique** *n.* See sign for TECHNICAL.

**technology** *n.* See sign for TECHNICAL.

**tedious** *adj.* See sign for BORING[1].

**teeny** *adj.* See sign for TINY.

**teeth** *pl. n.* **1.** Plural of TOOTH: *The six-year-old lost two teeth this week.* **2.** The set of hard bodies attached in a row to each jaw, used for chewing: *Brush your teeth.*

■ [Location of the teeth] Move the curved index finger of the right *X hand* from right to left across the top front teeth, palm facing in.

**telephone**[1] *n.* An instrument or system for sending speech over distances electrically: *She used the cellular telephone to call us from her car.* —*v.* To send a message or speak by telephone: *The girl telephoned her mom to ask if she could pick her up from school.* Same sign used for: **call, phone.**

■ [Represents holding a telephone receiver to the ear] Tap the knuckles of the right *Y hand,* palm facing in, with a double movement on the lower right cheek, holding the right thumb near the right ear and the little finger in front of the mouth.

**telephone**[2] *v.* Same sign as **telephone**[1] but made with a single movement. See also signs for CALL, PHONE.

**television** or **TV** *n.* A device for transmitting transient images by an apparatus that converts light and sound into electrical waves and then reconverts them into visible light rays and audible sound: *The family watches television every night.*

- [Abbreviation of letters T and V] Form a *T* and then a *V* in front of the right shoulder with the right hand, palm facing forward.

**tell**[1] *v.* To say or make known (to): *Tell me about the party. Tell the truth.* Same sign used for: **reveal.**

- [Represents words coming from the mouth toward another person] Beginning with the extended right index finger near the chin, palm facing in and finger pointing up, move the finger forward in an arc by bending the wrist, ending with the finger angled forward.

**tell**[2] *v.* See sign for ANNOUNCE.

**tell off** *v. phrase.* See sign for BAWL OUT.

**temper** *n.* See sign for BLOWUP.

**temperature** *n.* **1.** A measure of the warmth or coldness of an object, the atmosphere, etc.: *What is the temperature today?* **2.** The degree of heat of the human body: *He has the flu, with a high temperature and a sore throat.* Same sign used for: **fever.**

- [Symbolizes the mercury in a thermometer rising and falling] Slide the back of the extended right index finger, palm facing in and finger pointing left, up and down with a repeated movement on the extended index finger of the left hand, palm facing right and finger pointing up.

**temple** *n.* A building used for worship: *The family goes to the temple for religious services.* Same sign used for: **tabernacle, tomb.**

- [Initialized sign similar to sign for **church**] Tap the heel of the right *T hand,* palm facing forward, with a double movement on the back of the left *S hand* held in front of the chest, palm facing down.

**temporary** *adj.* See sign for SHORT.

**tempt** *v.* To appeal to (someone), as to do something immoral or ill-advised: *Don't tempt me to eat that dessert.* Related form: **temptation** *n.* Same sign used for: **entice.**

■ [Shows tapping someone in order to tempt] Tap the curved right index finger, palm facing up, with a double movement on the elbow of the bent left arm.

**ten cents** *pl. n.* See sign for DIME.

**tend** *v.* To be inclined or disposed toward: *We tend to stay home on weekends.* Related form: **tendency** *n.* Same sign used for: **prone.**

■ [The fingers used for feeling move from the heart] Beginning with the bent middle fingers of both *5 hands* touching each side of the chest, palms facing in, move both hands forward in small arcs.

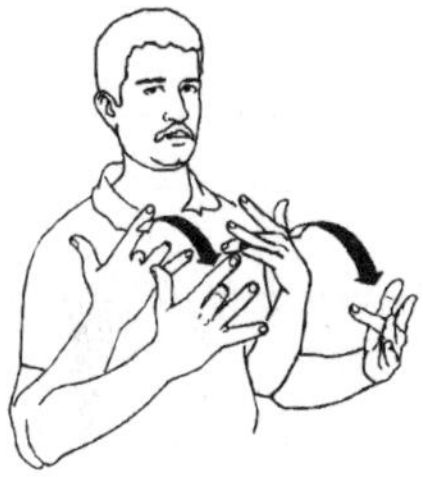

**tender** *adj.* See signs for PAIN[1], SOFT, SOFT-HEARTED.

**tent** *n.* See sign for CAMP.

**term** *n.* A specific, finite period of time during which an agreement is operative or an interest rate remains good, or at the end of which an obligation matures: *The guarantee was good for a term of one year.*

■ [**time** + **limit**] Tap the bent index finger of the right *X hand,* palm down, with a double movement on the wrist of the downturned left hand. Then beginning with both *bent hands* in front of the chest, right hand above the left hand and both palms facing down, move both hands forward simultaneously.

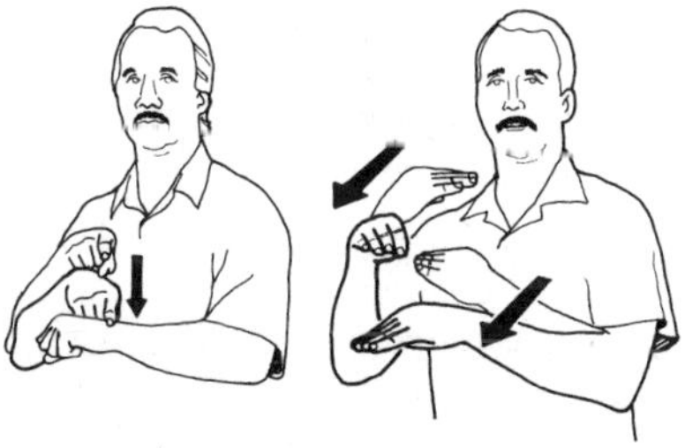

**terminal**[1] *n.* A device for entering information into a central computer: *The staff were given computer terminals instead of individual PCs.* Same sign used for: **monitor.**

■ [Initialized sign showing the shape of a terminal] Beginning with the index-finger sides of both *T hands* together in front of the chest, palms facing forward, bring the hands apart to in front of each shoulder and then straight down.

**terminal**[2] *adj.* Occurring at the end of a sequence or event: *to have terminal cancer.* Related form: **terminate** *n.*

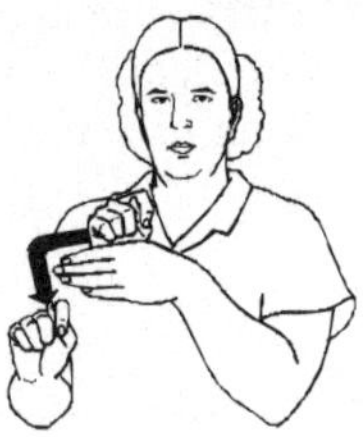

■ [Initialized sign similar to sign for **end**] Slide the heel of the right *T hand,* palm facing forward, along the index-finger side of the left *B hand* held in front of the chest, palm facing in and fingers pointing right, and then straight downward in front of the right side of the body.

**terminate** *v.* See signs for ELIMINATE, FIRE[2].

**terrible** *adj.* See sign for AWFUL.

**terrific** *adj.* See signs for FINEST, WONDERFUL.

**terrify** *v.* See sign for AFRAID. Related form: **terrified** *adj.*

**test** *n.* **1.** A means for evaluating knowledge, abilities, performance, etc.; examination: *studying to pass the test.* —*v.* **2.** To examine by subjecting to a test: *We tested the children in mathematical skills.* Same sign used for: **examine, examination, inquire, quiz.**

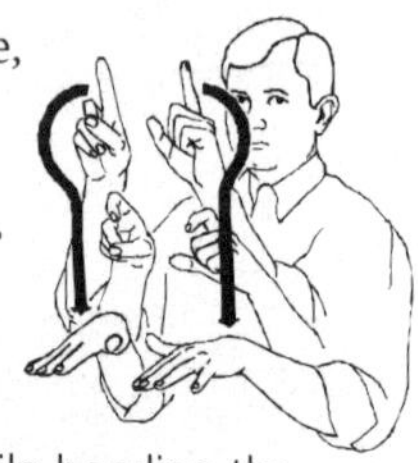

■ [Draw a question mark in the air + a gesture representing distributing the test to a group] Beginning with both extended index fingers pointing up in front of the head, palms facing forward, bring the hands in arcs to the side and then downward while bending the index fingers into *X hands* and continuing down while throwing the fingers open into *5 hands* in front of the body, palms facing down and fingers pointing forward.

**testimony**[1] *n.* A statement given under oath, used in evidence: *gave his testimony at the trial.* Related form: **testify** *v.*

■ [Sign **talk** while holding the hand up as if giving testimony in court] While holding the left *open hand* in front of the left shoulder, palm facing forward and fingers pointing up, with a double movement, move the fingers of the right *4 hand* forward a short distance in front of the mouth, palm facing left and fingers pointing up.

**testimony**[2] *n.* See sign for OATH. Related form: **testify** *v.*

**text** *n.* See sign for WORD.

**text message** *n. phrase.* A message consisting of words that are typed or entered on a keypad and sent electronically to a cell phone, especially from another cell phone: *She received a text message about the meeting.* Related form: **text** *v.* Same sign used for **PDA** (**personal digital assistant**).

■ [Mime action of thumbs when text messaging] Bend the extended thumbs of both *curved hands* with a random up and down movement.

**texture** *n.* See sign for MATERIAL.

**than** *conj.* (Used after comparatives to introduce the second item being compared): *taller than I.*

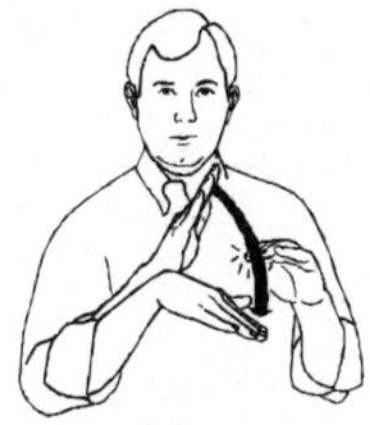

- Move the fingers of the right *open hand,* palm angled left, downward by bending the right wrist, hitting the fingers of the left *bent hand* held in front of the chest, palm and fingers angled forward, as it passes.

**thank** *v.* or **give thanks** *v. phrase.* To express gratitude to: *Thank the guests for coming.* Same sign used for: **thank you.**

- [The hand takes gratitude from the mouth and presents it to another] Move the fingertips of the right *open hand,* palm facing in and fingers pointing up, from the mouth forward and down, ending with the palm angled up in front of the chest.

**thankful** *adj.* See sign for GRATEFUL.

**Thanksgiving** *n.* A national holiday of the United States and Canada set aside for giving thanks to God: *Thanksgiving is celebrated in November in the United States.*

- [Represents the shape of a turkey's wattle] Beginning with the right *G hand* in front of the nose, palm facing left, bring the hand downward in an arc with a double movement, bringing the hand forward in front of the chest each time.

**that** *pron.* **1.** (Used to indicate a specific person, idea, or thing, as one previously mentioned: *I didn't know that.* —*adj.* **2.** Being the one spoken of: *that girl.*

- Bring the palm side of the right *Y hand* with a deliberate movement down to land on the palm of the left *open hand* held in front of the chest, palm facing up.

**theater** *n.* See sign for ACT[2].

**theft** *n.* See signs for SHOPLIFT, STEAL[1].

**their** *pron.* A form of the possessive case of THEY, used as an adjective before a noun: *It's their idea, not mine.* Related form: **theirs** *pron.*

- [Points toward the referents being discussed] Move the right *open hand,* palm facing forward and fingers pointing up, from in front of the right side of the body outward to the right.

**them** *pron.* The objective case of THEY, used as a direct or indirect object: *I like them. Give them the money.* See also signs for THOSE[1,2]. Same sign used for: **these, they.**

■ [Points toward the referents being discussed] Move the extended right index finger, palm facing down and finger pointing forward, from in front of the right side of the body outward to the right.

**theme** *n.* See signs for QUOTATION, TITLE.

**themselves** *pl. pron.* A reflexive form of THEM, used to refer back to the persons last mentioned: *They did it themselves.*

■ [This hand shape is used for reflexive pronouns and is directed toward the referents being discussed] Move the right *10 hand* from in front of the right side of the body, palm facing left, outward to the right.

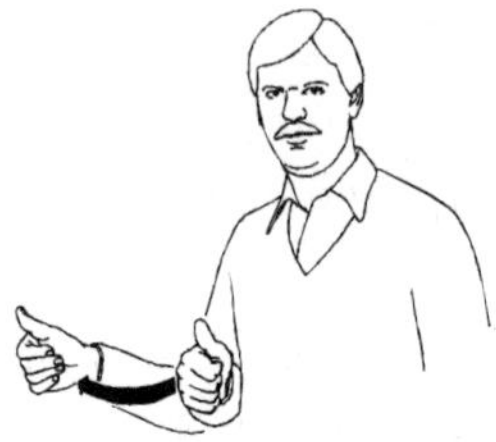

**then** *adv.* See signs for FINISH, OR.

**theory** *n.* **1.** A coherent group of principles: *Einstein's theory of relativity.* **2.** A proposed explanation: *My theory is that the key is lost.*

■ [Initialized sign similar to sign for **wonder**] Move the right *T hand,* palm facing forward, in a double circle near the right side of the forehead.

**therapy** *n.* A rehabilitation program, as for treating mental or physical disorders: *to place a student in speech therapy.*

■ [Initialized sign similar to sign for **help**] Beginning with the little-finger side of the right *T hand,* palm facing in, on the palm of the left *open hand* held in front of the body, palm facing up, move both hands upward in front of the chest.

**there** *adv.* In that place: *go over there.* Same sign used for: **point.**

■ [Points to a specific place away from the body] Push the extended right index finger from in front of the right shoulder forward a short distance, palm facing forward and finger pointing forward.

**therefore** *adv.* For that reason: *It rained; therefore we couldn't go.*

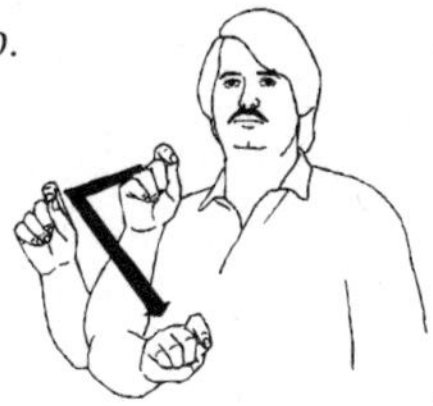

■ Move the right *modified X hand,* palm facing forward in front of the right shoulder, outward to the right and then downward in an angle to the left in front of the body.

**these** *pron.* See sign for THEM.

**they** *pron.* The plural of *he, she,* and *it,* used as the subject of a sentence. See signs for THEM[1,2].

**thick** *adj.* Fat, broad, or deep; not thin: *a thick coat of paint.*

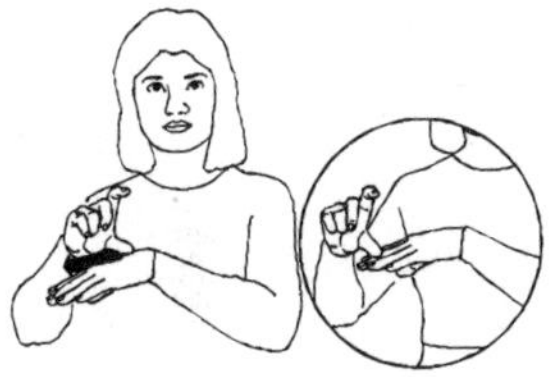

■ [Similar to the sign for **layer** except indicating a thicker layer] Slide the thumb side of the right *modified C hand,* palm facing forward, from the wrist across the back of the left *open hand* held in front of the chest, palm facing down.

**thin**[1] *adj.* Narrow; not thick: *a thin coat of paint.* Same sign used for: **short.**

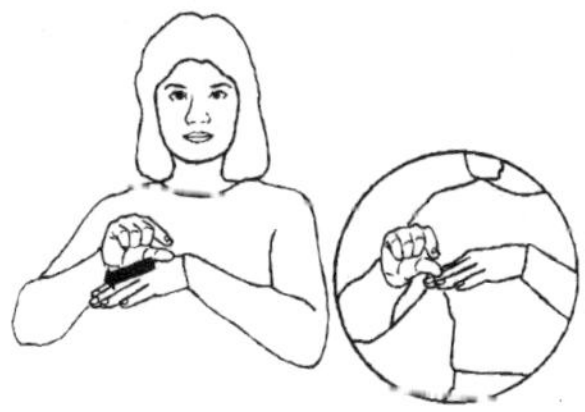

■ [Shows the thickness of a thin layer] Slide the thumb side of the right *G hand,* palm facing forward, from the wrist to the fingers of the left *open hand* held in front of the chest, palm facing down.

**thin**[2] *adj.* (alternate sign) See also sign for SKINNY. Same sign used for: **lean, slim.**

■ [Indicates something or someone that is very thin] Beginning with the extended little fingers of both *I hands* touching in front of the chest, right hand above the left hand and palms facing in, bring the right hand upward and the left hand downward.

**thin**[3] *adj.* See sign for DIET.

**thing** *n.* **1.** An inanimate object: *What is that strange-looking thing on your desk?* **2.** One of someone's personal possessions: *Pick up your things.* Same sign used for: **object.**

■ Bring the right *open hand,* palm facing up and fingers pointing forward, from in front of the body in a large arc to the right.

**think**[1] *v.* **1.** To use one's mind, as in analyzing and evaluating: *It's too noisy in here for me to think clearly.* **2.** To have as the subject of one's thoughts: *Think about what you're going to do next.* Alternate form: **thought** *n.*

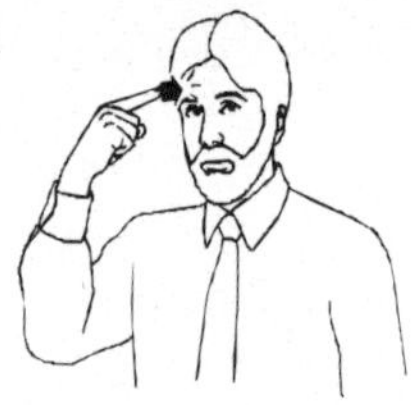

■ [Indicates the location of the mind] Tap the extended right index finger, palm facing in, to the right side of the forehead with a short double movement.

**think**[2] *v.* See signs for CONCERN[1], WONDER.

**think about** *v. phrase.* See sign for WONDER.

**thinking** *n.* See sign for WONDER.

**third** *adj.* See sign for ONE THIRD.

**thirsty** *adj.* Having a thirst; craving liquid: *After spicy food I am always thirsty.* Related form: **thirst** *n.* Same sign used for: **parched.**

■ [Indicates a dry throat] Move the extended right index finger, palm facing in and finger pointing up, downward on the length of the neck, bending the finger down as it moves.

**this** *pron.* **1.** (Used to indicate a person or thing that is nearby or a person, thing, or idea just mentioned or under discussion): *Why do you want to keep this?* —*adj.* **2.** (Used before a noun to indicate that the person or thing is close by, specified, or under discussion): *I like this idea on page twenty.*

■ [Points to a specific thing held in the hand] Move the extended right index finger, palm facing down and finger pointing down, from in front of the chest in a circular movement and then down to touch the left *open hand* held in front of the body, palm facing up.

**thoughtless** *adj.* **1.** Revealing lack of consideration for others; inconsiderate: *Going out after inviting them over was thoughtless.* **2.** Done without proper thought; careless: *Driving so quickly was thoughtless behavior.* Related form: **thoughtlessly** *adv.*

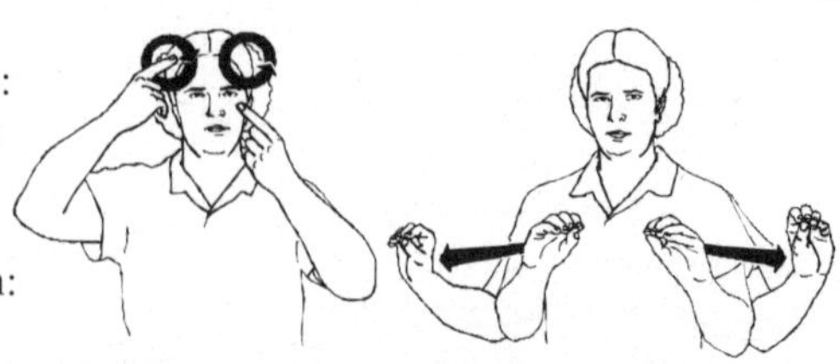

■ [**concern**[1] + a variation of the sign for **none**[1]] Beginning with both extended index fingers in front of each side of the forehead, palms facing in and fingers angled up, move the fingers in repeated alternating circular movements toward each other in front of the face. Then move both *O hands,* palms facing forward in front of the body, apart to the sides.

**thousand** *n.* **1.** A number equal to ten times one hundred: *Count to a thousand.* **2.** This number of persons or things: *If you have paper clips in stock, I'll take two thousand.* —*adj.* **3.** Amounting to one thousand in number: *A thousand people attended.*

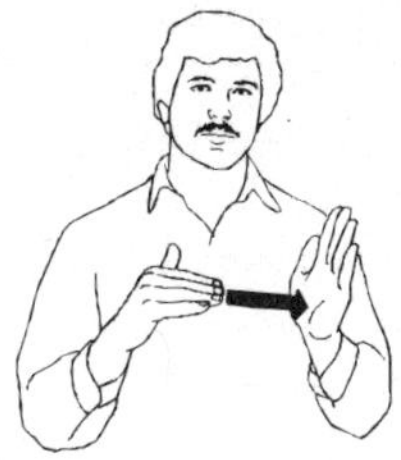

■ Bring the fingertips of the right *bent hand,* palm facing left, against the palm of the left *open hand* held in front of the body, palm facing right and fingers pointing forward.

**thread** *n.* See signs for CORD, LINE.

**threat** *n.* See sign for DANGER.

**thrifty** *adj.* See signs for GREEDY, STINGY[1].

**thrilling** *adj.* See sign for WHAT'S HAPPENING. Related form: **thrill.**

**throat** *n.* **1.** The front of the neck: *wore a pendant on a chain at her throat.* **2.** The upper part of the passageway to the lungs and stomach, extending from the back of the mouth to below the larynx: *to have a sore throat.*

■ [Location of the throat] Move the extended fingers of the right *G hand,* palm facing in, downward along the length of the neck.

**throb** *n., v.* See sign for PULSE.

**through**[1] *prep.* From one end or side of to another, between the parts of, or across the extent of: *to go through a tunnel; made their way through the crowd; drove through the countryside.* Same sign used for: **via.**

■ [Demonstrates movement through something] Slide the little-finger side of the right *open hand,* palm facing in and fingers angled to the left, between the middle finger and ring finger of the left *open hand* held in front of the chest, palm facing right and fingers pointing up.

**through**[2] *adv.* See sign for FINISH[1].

**throw** *v.* **1.** To cast away or dispose of: *to throw the trash into the trash can.* **2.** To propel with the hand by hurling or tossing: *Throw the stick to the dog.* Same sign used for: **cast, dump, pitch, throw away, toss.**

■ [Mime throwing something] Beginning with the right *S hand* in front of the right shoulder, palm facing forward, move the hand forward and downward while opening into a *5 hand,* palm facing down.

**throw out** *v. phrase.* See sign for ABANDON.

**throw up** *v. phrase.* See sign for VOMIT.

**thumbtack** *n.* A small tack with a broad, flat head: *Put the note on the bulletin board with a thumbtack.* Same sign used for: **pushpin, tack.**

■ [Mime pushing a thumbtack into a wall] Push the extended thumb of the right *10 hand,* palm angled left, first against the fingers and then the heel of the left *open hand* held in front of the left side of the chest, palm facing right and fingers pointing up.

**thunder** *n.* **1.** The loud, explosive, reverberating sound caused by the expansion of air that is heated by lightning: *I heard the thunder all during the storm.* —*v.* **2.** To emit thunder: *It thundered all evening.* **3.** To make a noise like thunder: *We heard the cannons thundering during the battle.*

■ [**hear** + a movement that represents the vibration of a loud sound] Touch the extended right index finger to the right ear, palm facing left. Then shake both *S hands* from side to side with a repeated movement in front of each shoulder, palms facing forward.

**thunderbolt** *n.* See sign for LIGHTNING.

**Thursday** *n.* The fifth day of the week, after Wednesday: *Thursday is the day before Friday.*

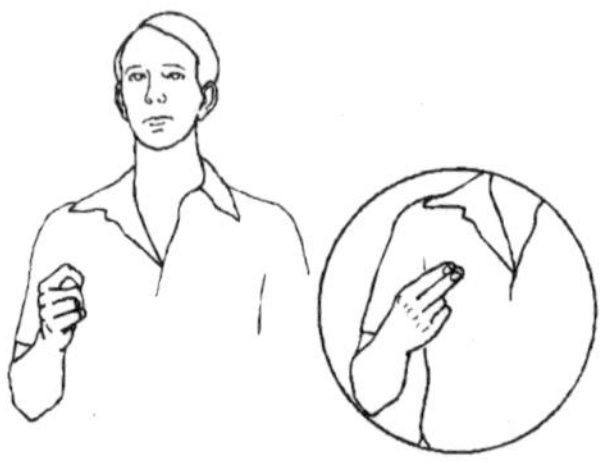

■ [Abbreviation **t-h**] Beginning with the right *T hand* in front of the right shoulder, palm facing left, flick the index and middle fingers forward, forming an *H hand.*

**tie**[1] *v.* **1.** To fasten with a cord or the like: *to tie one's shoelaces.* **2.** To form by looping and lacing together ends or pieces of cord or the like: *to tie a knot or a bow.* Same sign used for: **knot.**

■ [Mime tying a bow] Beginning with the fingers of both *F hands* together in front of the chest, move the fingers around each other and then apart, miming tying a bow.

**tie**[2] *n., v.* See sign for NECKTIE.

**tie up** *v. phrase.* See sign for BIND.

**tight**[1] *adj.* Firmly fixed into place: *a tight door.* —*adv.* In a secure manner: *The screw held tight no matter how hard he tried to turn it.*

- [Shows shaking something that is tight] With rigid, bent arms, shake both *S hands,* palms facing in, in front of each side of the chest.

**tight**[2] *adj.* See sign for GREEDY.

**tightwad** *n. Informal.* See sign for GREEDY[1].

**time**[1] *n.* A period during which something occurs or a period between given events: *at that time in history.* Same sign used for: **era, period.**

- [Initialized sign showing the movement of the minute hand around a clock face] Move the right *T hand,* palm facing left, in a circle around the left *open hand* held in front of the chest, palm facing right, ending with the right hand on the left heel.

**time**[2] *n.* A specific point in time as measured, usually in hours and minutes, in a given time zone of the earth: *What time is it?*

- [Indicates the location of a person's watch] Tap the bent index finger of the right *X hand,* palm facing down, with a double movement on the left wrist held in front of the chest, palm facing down.

**timeout** *n.* A brief suspension of activity: *The naughty child went to his room for a timeout.*

- [This is the signal used in sports to indicate a timeout] With a double movement, tap the palm of the right *open hand* held in front of the chest, palm facing down, downward on the fingertips of the left *open hand*, palm facing right.

**timepiece** *n.* See sign for WATCH[1].

**timid** *adj.* See sign for AFRAID.

**tint** *n., v.* See sign for DIM.

**tiny**[1] *adj.* Very small: *a tiny flower.* Same sign used for: **little bit, puny, scant, teeny.**

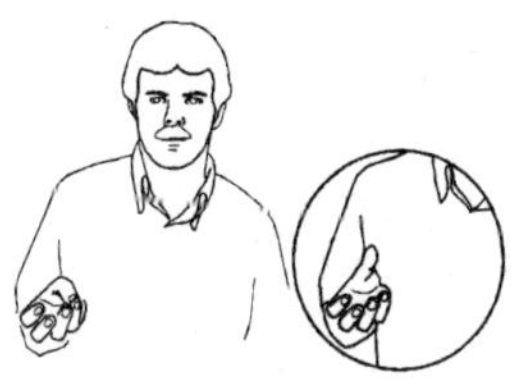

- Beginning with the right *6 hand* in front of the right side of the chest, palm facing up, flick the thumb off the little finger with a quick movement.

**tiny**[2] *adj.* See sign for SMALL[2].

**tip** *n.* See sign for POINT[1].

**tiptoe** *v.* **1.** To walk quietly on one's toes: *tiptoe through the room.* —*n.* **2.** The tips of one's toes: *walk on tiptoe.*

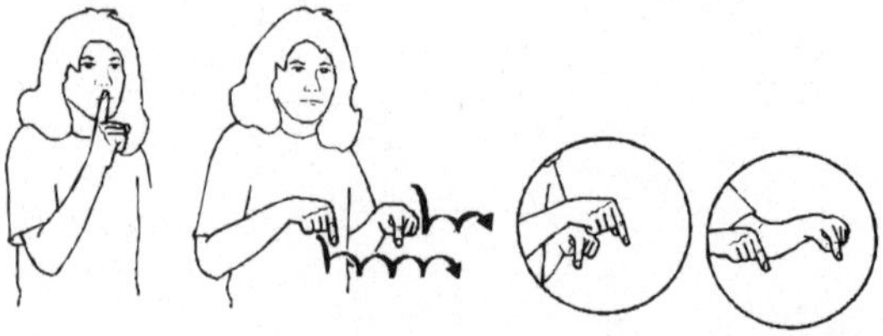

■ [Natural gesture to indicate quiet + a movement that represents a person moving on tiptoes] Bring the side of the extended right index finger, palm facing left, to the mouth. Then move both extended index fingers from in front of each side of the body, palms and fingers pointing down, forward in a series of alternating arcs.

**tired** *adj.* Weary; fatigued: *I am tired at the end of the day.* Same sign used for: **exhausted, fatigue, weary.**

■ [The hands show that energy has dropped in the body] Beginning with the fingertips of both *bent hands* on each side of the chest, palms facing in, roll the hands downward on the fingertips, ending with the little-finger sides of both hands touching the chest, palms facing outward.

**tissue** *n.* A disposable, thin sheet of paper used for wiping: *to blow one's nose in a tissue.* Same sign used for: **handkerchief, Kleenex** (*trademark*).

■ [**cold**[1] + **paper**] Bring the index finger and thumb of the right *G hand,* palm facing in, downward on each side of the nose with a double movement, pinching the fingers together each time. Then brush the heel of the right *open hand,* palm facing down and fingers pointing left, with a double movement on the heel of the left *open hand* held in front of the body, palm facing up and fingers pointing right.

**title** *n.* The distinguishing name of something, as a creative work: *the title of the book.* Same sign used for: **entitle, quotes, so-called, subject, theme, topic.**

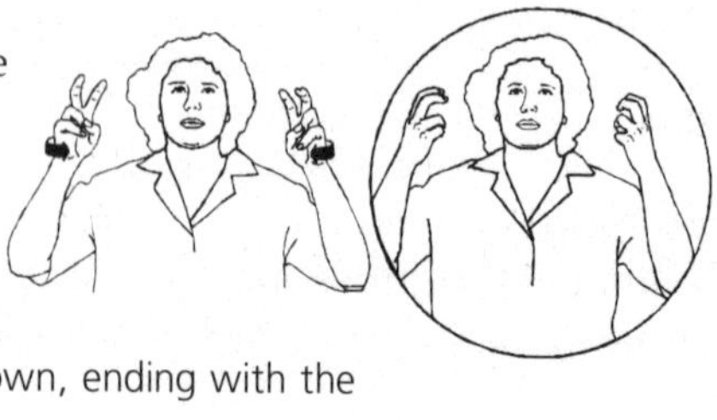

■ [Represents quotation marks around a title] Beginning with both *bent V hands* near each side of the head, palms facing forward, twist the hands while bending the fingers down, ending with the palms facing back.

**toast**[1] *n.* **1.** Sliced bread browned by exposure to dry heat: *to put jelly on the toast.* —*v.* **2.** To expose to dry heat: *toasted the rolls.*

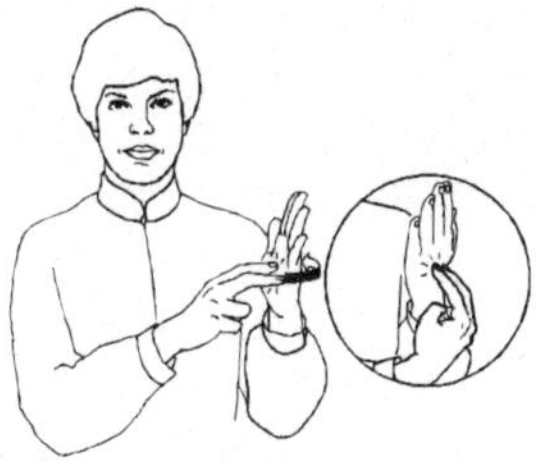

■ [Represents the prongs of a toaster holding the bread in place] Touch the fingertips of the right *bent V hand,* palm facing left, first on the palm and then on the back of the left *open hand* held in front of the chest, palm facing right and fingers pointing up.

**toast**[2] *n.* **1.** A welcome, tribute, etc., proposed in someone's honor to accompany a congratulatory drink and traditionally marked by the participants clinking their glasses together before drinking: *to propose a toast to the new director.* **2.** An act or instance of having such a congratulatory drink: *to drink a toast to the future of the project.* —*v.* **3.** To propose or drink, such as a toast in honor of: *We toast the bride and groom.*

■ [Represents clinking two glasses together in a toast] Beginning with both *C hands* in front of each side of the chest, palms facing in, bring the hands upward and toward each other in a large arc, ending with the knuckles of both hands touching in front of the face, palms facing in.

**tobacco** *n.* Leaves of certain plants of the nightshade family prepared for recreational chewing: *to chew tobacco.* Same sign used for: **chewing tobacco.**

■ [Shows tobacco in the cheek] Rotate the fingertips of the right *curved hand,* palm facing forward, against the right side of the chin while turning the palm down.

**today** *n.* **1.** This day: *Today is Monday.* **2.** This present age: *today's powerful computers.* —*adv.* **3.** During or on this day: *What are you doing today?* **4.** At the present time: *Schools today are more violent than they used to be.*

■ [Sign similar to **now** except with a double movement] Bring both *Y hands,* palms facing up, with a short double movement downward in front of each side of the body.

**together**[1] *adv.* With each other: *to go shopping together.*

■ [Sign similar to **with** except with a circular movement indicating duration] With the palm sides of both *A hands* together in front of the body, move the hands in a flat circle.

**together**[2] *adv.* See sign for WITH.

**toil** *n.* See signs for SWEAT, WORKAHOLIC.

**toilet** *n.* **1.** Same sign used for: **bathroom, lavatory, rest room, washroom.** A bathroom or washroom: *looking for the toilets at the restaurant.* **2.** A bathroom or washroom fixture with a bowl and a device for flushing with water, used for urination and defecation: *Remember to flush the toilet and close the lid.*

■ [Initialized sign] Move the right *T hand,* palm facing forward, from side to side in front of the right shoulder with a repeated shaking movement.

**tolerant** *adj.* See signs for BROAD-MINDED, PATIENT.

**tolerate** *v.* See signs for CONTROL, PATIENT. Related form: **tolerant** *adj.*

**tomato** *n.* A large juicy berry, usually red, eaten raw or cooked as a vegetable: *Put a tomato in the salad.*

■ [**red** + **slice**] Bring the extended right index finger from the lips, palm facing in, downward with a deliberate movement across the thumb side of the left *O hand* held in front of the chest, palm facing down, ending with the right palm facing down in front of the body.

**tomb** *n.* See sign for TEMPLE.

**tomorrow** *n.* **1.** The day after today: *They predict snow for tomorrow.* **2.** A future period: *Tomorrow will be the age of electronics.* —*adv.* **3.** On or during the day after today: *The new movie opens tomorrow.* **4.** At a future time: *Will there be commercial space flight tomorrow?*

■ [The sign moves forward into the future] Move the palm side of the right *10 hand,* palm facing left, from the right side of the chin forward while twisting the wrist.

**tongue** *n.* See sign for LANGUAGE.

**tonight** *n.* See sign for NIGHT.

**tonsils** *pl. n.* The mass of tissue on each side of the throat at the back of the mouth: *She had her tonsils removed when she was five.*

■ [Location of tonsils] Place the thumb sides of both *F hands,* palms facing each other and fingers pointing up, near each other on the upper neck.

**too much** *n. phrase.* See signs for EXCESS, OVER.

**tooth** *n.* One of the hard bodies attached in a row to each jaw, used for chewing: *to see the dentist about a broken tooth.*

■ [Location of a tooth] Touch a front tooth with the extended right index finger, palm facing in.

**toothache** *n.* Pain in or about a tooth: *a toothache in a molar.*

■ [**pain** formed near the location] With both extended index fingers pointing toward each other in front of the mouth, palms facing down, jab the fingers toward each other with a short double movement.

**toothbrush** *n.* A small brush with a long handle for cleaning the teeth: *The dentist recommends brushing with a softer toothbrush.*

■ [Mime the action of brushing one's teeth] Move the extended right index finger, palm facing down and finger pointing left, up and down with a repeated movement in front of the front teeth.

**top**[1] *n.* **1.** The highest point: *the top of the hill.* **2.** The upper surface: *the top of the table.* —*adj.* **3.** Located at or forming the top: *the top shelf.* Same sign used for: **peak.**

■ [The location on the top of something] Bring the palm of the right *open hand,* palm facing down and fingers pointing left, downward on the fingertips of the left *open hand* held in front of the chest, palm facing right and fingers pointing up.

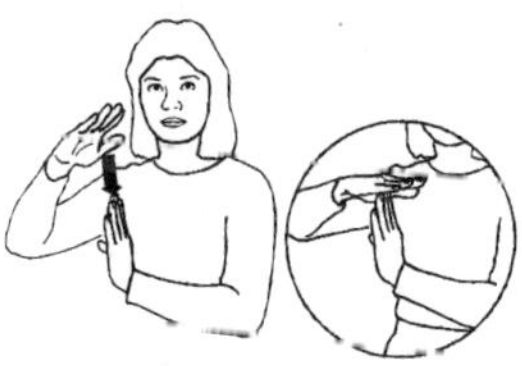

**top**[2] *n.* See signs for LID, SHIRT.

**topic** *n.* See signs for QUOTATION, TITLE.

**torment** *n.* See sign for TORTURE.

**torn** *v.* Past participle of TEAR. See sign for TEAR.

**tornado** *n.* A violent, destructive windstorm characterized by a large funnel-shaped cloud causing extreme damage as it moves along the ground: *You can tell from the utter destruction of the buildings that a tornado hit the town.*

■ [Shows the circular winds occurring during a tornado] Beginning with the extended right index finger pointing down in front of the right side of the chest, palm facing down, and the extended left index finger pointing up in front of the chest, palm facing up, move the hands in small circles around each other in opposite directions as the hands move from right to left in front of the chest.

**tortoise** *n.* See sign for TURTLE.

**torture** *n.* **1.** The act of inflicting severe pain, as to coerce someone into revealing information: *The spy suffered extreme torture before confessing.* **2.** Agony or the cause of agony: *These tight shoes are pure torture.* —*v.* **3.** To subject to torture: *tortured the prisoner.* Same sign used for: **abuse, haze, maltreatment, mutilate, persecute, persecution, probation, prosecute, prosecution, ridicule, torment.**

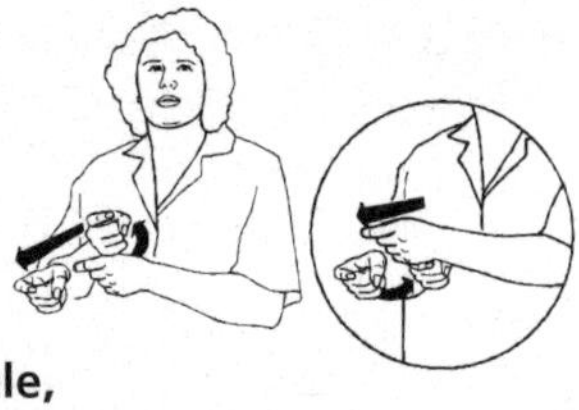

■ Shove the little-finger side of the right *X hand,* palm facing left, forward across the index-finger side of the left *X hand,* palm facing right, while moving the left hand upward to repeat the left hand movement over the right hand with a double movement.

**toss** *v.* See sign for THROW.

**total**[1] *v.* See sign for ADD[1].

**total**[2] *adj.* See signs for ALL, ALL THE TIME.

**touch** *v.* **1.** To cause a part of the body, as the hand or finger, or something held with or on a part of the body, to come in contact with: *to touch the hot pan; to touch the step with your shoe.* —*n.* **2.** The sense by which one perceives the texture, temperature, and other qualities of things around one by feeling, as with the hand: *I felt your touch on my shoulder.*

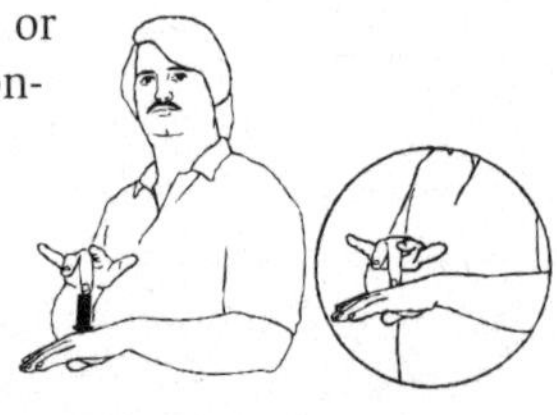

■ [Demonstrates touching something, with the middle finger used frequently to indicate feelings] Bring the bent middle finger of the right hand, palm facing down, downward to touch the back of the left *open hand* held in front of the body, palm facing down.

**tough**[1] *adj.* Difficult to do or deal with: *a tough problem.*

■ Slide the little-finger side of the right *bent V hand,* palm facing in, in an arc to the right off the back of the left *S hand* held in front of the body, palm facing down.

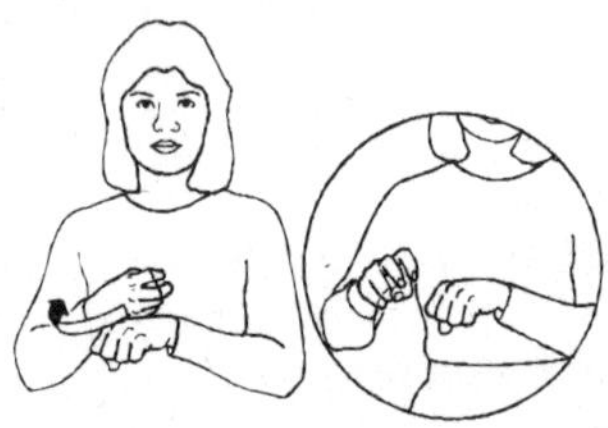

**tough**[2] *adj.* See signs for GANG, MEANNESS, STURDY.

**tour** *n.* See signs for RUN AROUND, TRIP.

**tow** *v.* See signs for DRAG, HAUL.

**toward** *prep.* In the direction of: *Drive toward town.*

■ [Demonstrates a movement toward something] Beginning with the extended right index finger in front of the right shoulder, palm facing left, move the hand in an arc to the left, ending with the right extended index finger touching the left extended index finger pointing up in front of the left side of the body, palm facing right.

**towel** *n.* **1.** A piece of absorbent cloth or paper used for drying something wet: *to dry the dishes with a towel.* —*v.* **2.** To dry with a towel: *to towel the baby after its bath.*

■ [Mime drying one's back with a towel] Beginning with the right *S hand* above the right shoulder, palm facing forward, and the left *S hand* near the left hip, palm facing back, move the hands simultaneously upward and downward at an angle with a repeated movement.

**town** *n.* A populated area, usually smaller than a city, with recognized boundaries and a local government: *always wanted to live in a small town.* Same sign used for: **community, village.**

■ [Represents the rooftops in a town] Tap the fingertips of both *open hands* together in front of the chest with a double movement, palms facing each other at an angle.

**track down** *v. phrase.* See sign for FOLLOW.

**trade** *v.* To exchange: *traded books with each other.* Same sign used for: **budget, exchange, replace, substitute, substitution, swap, switch.**

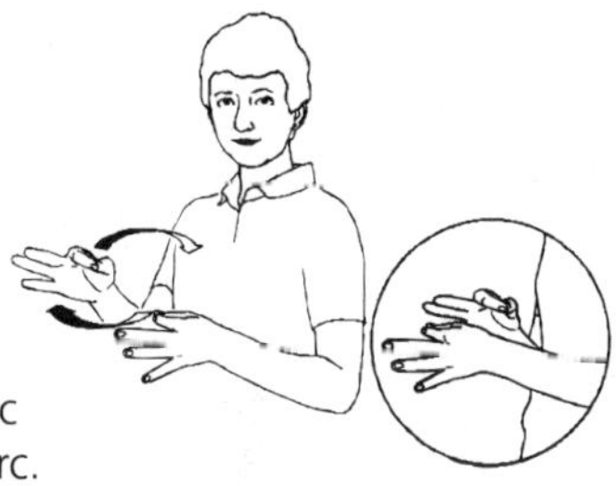

■ [Demonstrates moving something into another thing's place] Beginning with both *F hands* in front of the body, palms facing each other and right hand somewhat forward of the left hand, move the right hand back toward the body in an upward arc while moving the left hand forward in a downward arc.

**trade places** *v. phrase.* To exchange locations: *The two girls traded places in the classroom.* Same sign used for: **change places, swap places, switch places.**

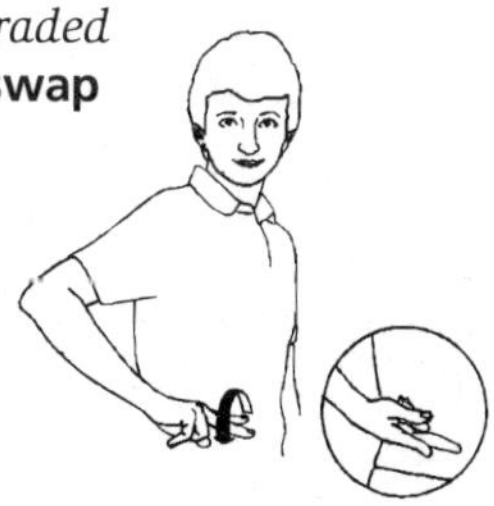

■ [Directional sign representing a person trading places with the referent toward whom the sign is formed] Beginning with the right *V hand* near the right side of the waist, palm facing down and fingers pointing forward, flip the hand over, ending with the palm facing up.

**tradition** *n.* **1.** The handing down of beliefs and customs from generation to generation, especially by word of mouth: *to preserve tradition and welcome innovation.* **2.** Something so handed down: *Birthday dinners at a restaurant are a tradition in our family.* Related form: **traditional** *adj.*

■ [Initialized sign similar to sign for **habit**] With the heel of the right *T hand,* palm facing forward, on the back of the left *S hand,* palm facing down, move both hands downward in front of the chest.

**traffic** *n.* The movement of vehicles and people coming and going along a route: *heavy traffic on Main Street during the rush hour.*

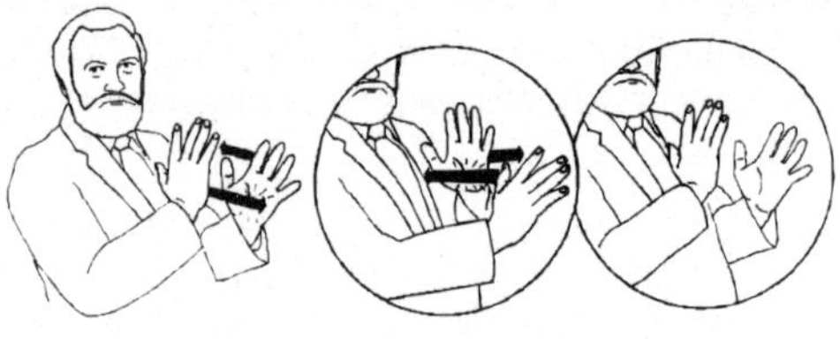

■ [Represents many vehicles moving quickly past each other in both directions] With both *5 hands* in front of the chest, palms facing each other and fingers pointing up, move the right hand forward and the left hand back with a repeated alternating movement, brushing palms as they pass each time.

**tragedy** *n.* A dreadful or catastrophic event, especially one in which one or more people die: *The accident was a tragedy.* Related form: **tragic** *adj.*

■ [Initialized sign similar to sign for **tears**] Beginning with both *T hands* near each cheek, palms facing each other, bring the hands downward simultaneously.

**tragic** *adj.* See sign for SAD.

**trail** *v.* See signs for FOLLOW, ROAD.

**trailer** *n.* See sign for TRUCK.

**train** *n.* A connected line of railroad cars: *to ride the train across the country.* Same sign used for: **go by train, railroad, travel by train.**

■ [Represents the crossties on a railroad track] Rub the fingers of the right *H hand* back and forth with a repeated movement on the fingers of the left *H hand* held in front of the body, both palms facing down.

**training** *n.* See sign for PRACTICE.

**tranquil** *adj.* See sign for QUIET.

**transfer** *v.* **1.** To remove from one place, person, or position to another: *to transfer the property to the new owner.* —*n.* **2.** A person who has transferred, as from one school to another: *She is a transfer from the junior college.*

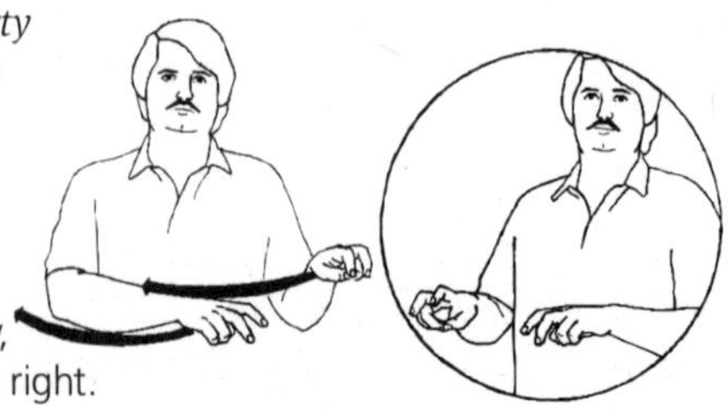

■ [Represents a person's legs moving to another place] Beginning with both *bent V hands* in front of the left side of the body, palms facing down, swing the hands to the right.

**transform** *v.* See sign for TRANSLATE.

**translate** *v.* To convert (text or speech) from one language to another: *to translate the French poems into Spanish.* Related form: **translation** *n.* Same sign used for: **transform.**

- [Initialized sign similar to sign for **change**[1]] Beginning with the palms of both *T hands* together in front of the chest, right hand over the left hand, twist the wrists to exchange positions.

**transparent** *adj.* See sign for VISIBLE.

**transport** *v.* See sign for BRING.

**trapped** *adj.* See sign for STUCK.

**trash** *n.* See sign for GARBAGE.

**travel** *v.* See signs for RUN AROUND, TRIP.

**travel by train** *v. phrase.* See sign for TRAIN.

**treasure** *v.* See sign for PRECIOUS.

**tree** *n.* A usually tall plant with a thick woody trunk and branches that emerge at some distance from the ground: *to stand in the shade of the old tree.*

- [Represents a tree trunk and branches at the top] Beginning with the elbow of the bent right arm resting on the back of the left *open hand* held across the body, twist the right *5 hand* forward and back with a small repeated movement.

**trespass** *n.* See sign for SIN.

**trial** *n.* See sign for JUDGE.

**tribute** *n.* See sign for GIFT.

**trick** *n.* **1.** Something done cleverly, maliciously, or playfully to deceive: *The class played a trick on the teacher by hiding the chalk.* —*v.* **2.** To deceive by using tricks: *We tricked the boss into closing the office early.* Same sign used for: **con, fool.**

- Tap the knuckles of the right *A hand,* palm facing forward, with a double movement against the extended left index finger held up in front of the body, palm facing right.

**trim** *v.* See sign for PRUNE.

**trip** *n.* A journey: *preparing to go on a trip.* Same sign used for: **journey, mobilize, tour, travel.**

■ [Represents legs moving as if on a trip] Move the right *bent V hand,* palm facing down, from in front of the right side of the body upward and forward in an arc, ending with the palm facing forward.

**triumph** *n.* See sign for SUCCESSFUL.

**trophy**[1] *n.* An object won as a prize and symbolizing victory or achievement: *to win an athletic trophy.* Same sign used for: **award.**

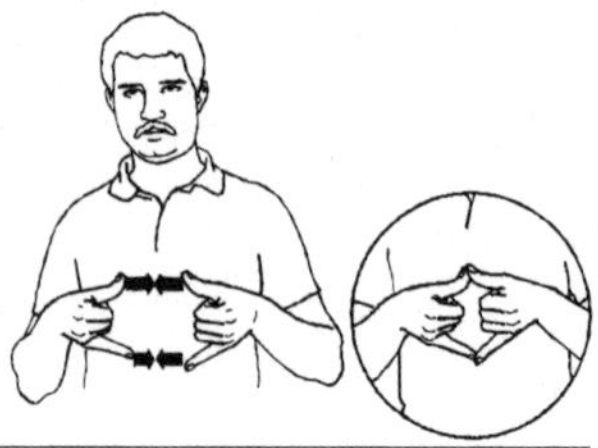

■ [The shape of a trophy] Tap the thumbs and little fingers of both *Y hands,* palms facing in, together in front of the body with a double movement.

**trophy**[2] *n.* See sign for CHAMPION.

**trouble**[1] *n.* Difficulty or annoyance: *This situation is bound to cause trouble.* Same sign used for: **anxious, care, concern, worry.**

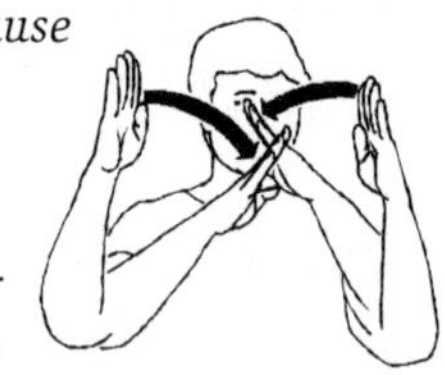

■ [Represents problems coming from all directions] Beginning with both *B hands* near each side of the head, palms facing each other, bring the hands toward each other with a repeated alternating movement, crossing the hands in front of the face each time.

**trouble**[2] *n.* See sign for DIFFICULT.

**troubleshoot** *v.* To locate an error through a process of elimination: *The technician used a program to troubleshoot the problem.*

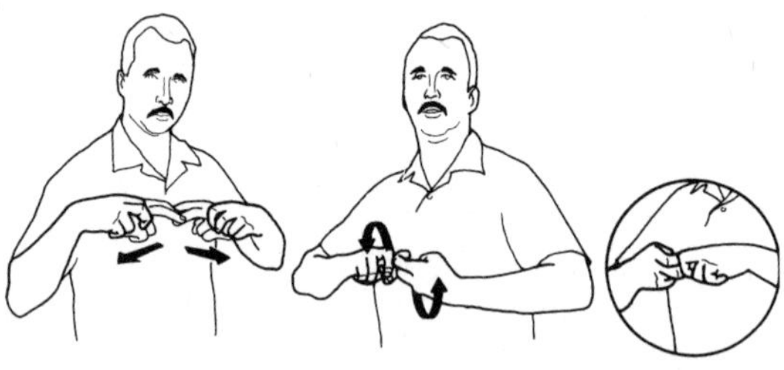

■ [**analyze** + **problem**[1]] With both *V hands* pointing toward each other in front of the chest, palms facing down, move the fingers down and apart with a double movement, bending the fingers each time. Then beginning with the knuckles of both *bent V hands* touching in front of the chest, twist the hands in opposite directions with a deliberate movement, rubbing the knuckles against each other.

**trousers** *pl. n.* See sign for PANTS.

**truck** *n.* A vehicle with an elongated back used for hauling: *The store delivered the furniture in a large truck.* Same sign used for: **trailer.**

■ [Initialized sign similar to sign for **bus**] Beginning with the little-finger side of the right *T hand,* palm facing left, touching the index-finger side of the left *T hand,* palm facing right, move the right hand back toward the chest while the left hand moves forward.

**trudge** *v.* See sign for PLOD.

**true** *adj.* In accordance with fact and reality; not false: *a true story.* Same sign used for: **actual, actually, certain, certainly, truly.**

■ [Represents words coming from the mouth] Move the side of the extended right index finger from in front of the mouth, palm facing left and finger pointing up, forward in an arc.

**truly** *v.* See sign for ABSOLUTE.

**truly yours** See sign for BELONG².

**trust** *n.* See sign for CONFIDENT.

**truth**¹ *n.* That which is true: *swore to tell the truth.* Same sign used for: **fact, really.**

■ [Represents the truth coming straight from the mouth] Move the extended right index finger from pointing up in front of the mouth, palm facing left, forward with a deliberate movement.

**truth**² *n.* See sign for HONEST. Related form: **truthful** *adj.*

**try** *v.* To make an effort to do or accomplish: *Please try to be home on time.* Same sign used for: **attempt, strive.**

■ [The hands push forward indicating effort] Move both *S hands* from in front of each side of the body, palms facing each other, downward and forward in simultaneous arcs.

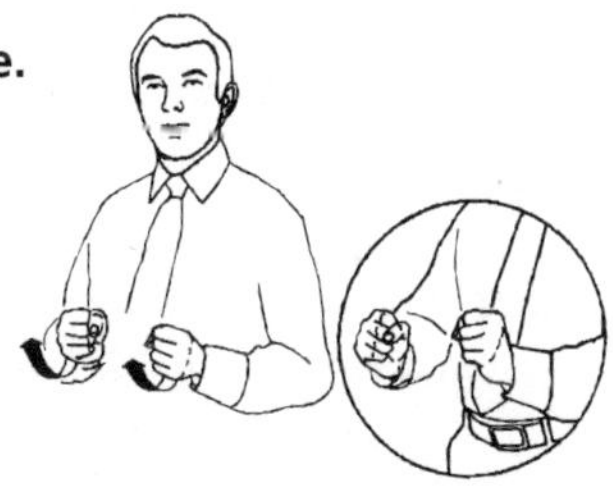

**tubal ligation** *n. phrase.* See sign for STERILIZATION.

**tube** *n.* See sign for PIPE².

**Tuesday** *n.* The third day of the week, following Monday: *If today is Tuesday, there will be a science article in the newspaper.*

■ [Initialized sign] Move the right *T hand,* palm facing in, in a circle in front of the right shoulder.

**turkey** *n.* A large, pheasantlike North American bird: *The turkey has a wattle, a fleshy lobe hanging down from the throat.*

■ [Represents the action of a turkey's wattle] With the thumb side of the right *G hand* under the chin, palm and fingers pointing down, wiggle the fingers from side to side with a repeated movement.

**turn**[1] *n.* A chance or requirement to do something in an agreed-upon order: *It's your turn to drive.* Same sign used for: **alternate, next.**

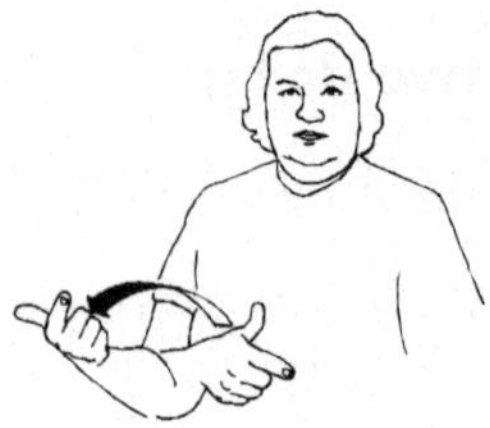

■ [Indicates alternating positions in order to take turns] Move the right *L hand* from in front of the body, palm angled left, to the right by flipping the hand over, ending with the palm facing up.

**turn**[2] *n.* See sign for CHANGE.

**turn down** *v. phrase.* See signs for DECLINE[1], REJECT[1].

**turn into** *v. phrase.* See sign for BECOME.

**turn off** *v. phrase.* Same sign as for TURN ON but the wrist twists in the opposite direction.

**turn on** *v. phrase.* **1.** To allow something to flow through: *to turn on the faucet.* **2.** To switch on or activate: *to turn on the radio.*

■ [Mime turning a knob so as to turn something on or off] While holding an imaginary switch between the thumb and bent index finger of the right *X hand* held in front of the right side of the body, palm facing up, twist the wrist, ending with the palm facing down.

**turn over** *v. phrase.* See sign for COOK.

**turn up** *v. phrase.* See sign for SHOW UP.

**turning point** *n. phrase.* See sign for CRISIS.

**turtle** *n.* A reptile with the trunk enclosed in a hard shell, inside which the animal can hide its head and appendages: *The turtle lived in the creek.* Same sign used for: **tortoise.**

■ [Represents a turtle's head coming from under the shell] Cup the left palm over the right *A hand,* palm facing left, and wiggle the right thumb with a repeated movement.

**twenty-five cents** *pl. n.* See sign for QUARTER[2].

**twin** *n.* One of two children born at the same time from the same mother: *They seem to be identical twins.*

■ [Initialized sign] Touch the index-finger side of the right *T hand,* palm facing left, first to the right side of the chin and then to the left side of the chin.

**two dollars** *pl. n.* See sign for SECOND.

**two weeks** *n. phrase.* See sign for BIWEEKLY.

**type**[1] *v.* To write with a typewriter or typewriterlike keyboard: *to type a letter on the electric typewriter; learned to type using a software tutorial.* Related form: **typing** *v.*

■ [Mime typing] Beginning with both *curved 5 hands* in front of the body, palms facing down, wiggle the fingers with a repeated movement.

**type**[2] *n.* See sign for FAVORITE. Related form: **typical** *adj.*

**type**[3] *n.* See sign for KIND[2].

**ugly** *adj.* Unpleasant in appearance; very unattractive: *an ugly color.*

■ Beginning with the extended right index finger in front of the left side of the face, palm facing left and finger pointing left, move the hand to the right side of the face while bending the index finger to form an *X hand.*

**umbilicus** *n.* See sign for NAVEL.

**umbrella** *n.* A portable circular cover of waterproof fabric on folding ribs attached to a long handle, used as protection from rain or snow: *to carry an umbrella in case it rains.*

■ [Mime raising an umbrella] Beginning with the little-finger side of the right *A hand* on the index-finger side of the left *A hand* in front of the chest, palms facing in opposite directions, raise the right hand upward in front of the head.

**unaware** *adj.* See sign for DON'T KNOW.

**uncertain** *adj.* See signs for INDECISION, RESIST.

**uncle** *n.* **1.** A brother of one's father or mother: *My uncle still teases my father.* **2.** The husband of one's aunt: *He's more friendly since becoming my uncle.*

■ [Initialized sign formed near the male area of the head] Shake the right *U hand,* palm facing forward and fingers pointing up, near the right side of the forehead.

**unclear** *adj.* See sign for VAGUE.

**unconscious** *adj.* See signs for COMA, DON'T KNOW.

**undecided** *adj.* See sign for INDECISION.

**under** *prep.* Below; beneath: *shoes under the living room couch.*

■ [Shows a location under something else] Move the right *10 hand,* palm facing left, from in front of the chest downward and forward under the left *open hand* held in front of the chest, palm facing down and fingers pointing right.

**underclothes** *pl. n.* See sign for UNDERWEAR.

**underline** *v.* In word processing, a character that produces a line under the other characters in the text: *The author underlined words that should appear in italics.* Related form: **underlined** *adj.* Same sign used for: **underscore.**

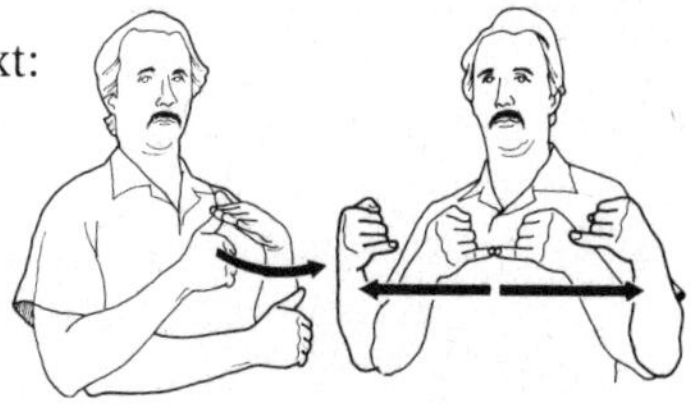

■ [**under** + **line**] Move the right *10 hand,* palm facing left, from in front of the chest downward and forward under the left *open hand* held in front of the chest, palm facing down and fingers pointing right. Then beginning with the extended little fingers of both *I hands* touching in front of the chest, palms facing in, move both hands outward.

**underlying** *adj.* See sign for BASEMENT.

**underscore** *v.* See sign for UNDERLINE.

**understand** *v.* To grasp the meaning of: *I understand your question.* Same sign used for: **apprehend, comprehend, perceive.**

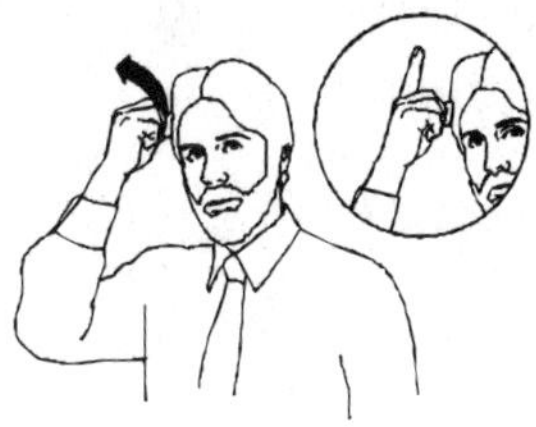

■ [Comprehension seems to pop into one's head] Beginning with the right *S hand* near the right side of the forehead, palm facing left, flick the right index finger upward with a sudden movement.

**underwear** *n.* Clothing worn next to the skin underneath one's outer clothing: *to put on fancy new underwear.* Same sign used for: **underclothes.**

■ [Location of underwear worn on the body] Beginning with the fingertips of both *bent hands* touching each side of the abdomen, palms facing in, twist the wrists upward, ending with both *open hands* in front of each side of the waist, palms facing down and fingers pointing forward.

**undress** *v.* See sign for TAKE OFF.

**unfair** *adj.* Not fair; unjust: *an unfair decision.*

■ Bring the fingertips of the right *F hand,* palm facing left, downward, striking the fingertips of the left *F hand,* palm facing right, as it passes.

**unhappy** *adj.* See sign for SAD.

**uniform** *n., adj.* See signs for ALIKE², STANDARD.

**union** *n.* See sign for COOPERATION.

**unique** *adj.* See sign for SPECIAL.

**unite** *v.* See sign for BELONG[1].

**unity** *n.* See sign for COOPERATION.

**universal** *adj.* See sign for COOPERATION.

**university** *n.* An institution of higher learning, offering undergraduate and graduate studies: *left a junior college to attend the university.*

■ [Initialized sign similar to sign for **college**] Beginning with the palm side of the right *U hand* on the left *open hand* in front of the chest, palm facing up, move the right hand in a circular movement upward and forward.

**unkind** *adj.* See sign for MEAN[1].

**unknown** *adj.* See sign for DON'T KNOW.

**unlawful** *adj.* See signs for CRIME[1,2].

**unlike** *adj.* See sign for BUT.

**unsafe** *adj.* See sign for DANGER.

**unskilled** *adj.* Lacking in required skills: *a need to provide jobs for unskilled workers.* Same sign used for: **clumsy, inexperienced.**

■ While grasping the thumb of the right *5 hand,* palm facing in and fingers pointing down, with the left *S hand,* palm facing down, twist the right wrist to move the right fingers upward, ending with the palm facing forward.

**until** *prep.* **1.** Up to the time of: *The cafeteria is open until eleven o'clock.* —*conj.* **2.** Up to the time when: *I will wait until you come.*

■ [Uses a movement indicating the passage of time] Move the extended right index finger, palm facing left, in an arc to meet the extended left index finger in front of the left side of the chest, palm facing right and finger pointing up.

**unusual** *adj.* See sign for STRANGE.

**unwanted** *adj.* See sign for DON'T WANT.

**up** *adv.* **1.** In or to a higher place: *The airplane went up.* —*prep.* **2.** To or at a higher place on or in: *to go up the mountain.* Same sign used for: **upstairs, upward.**

- [Points up] With the right extended index finger pointing up in front of the right shoulder, palm facing forward, move the right hand upward a short distance.

**UPC** (universal product code) *n. phrase.* See sign for STRIPE.

**update** *v.* **1.** To make current: *to update the files.* —*n.* **2.** New, up-to-date information: *Give me an update on the situation.* **3.** A new, updated account, version, etc.: *selling an update of the textbook.* Same sign used for: **conversion, sequel.**

- Beginning with the right *10 hand* in front of the right side of the chest, palm facing down, and the left *10 hand* in front of the left side of the chest, palm facing right, twist the right wrist to the right to turn the palm left. Then bring the knuckles of the right hand against the heel of the left hand, pushing it forward.

**upgrade** *v.* See sign for IMPROVE[2].

**upload** *v.* To transmit a file from your computer to another computer: *upload my files to the Internet.* Same sign used for: **export.**

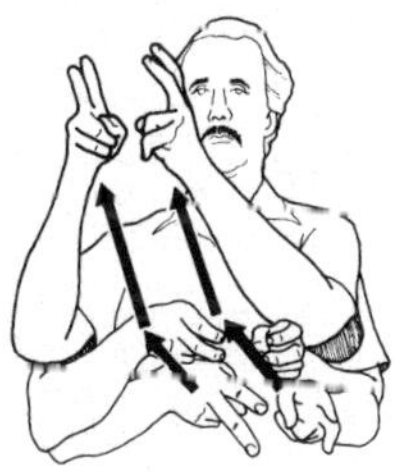

- [Action of information flowing up] Beginning with both *bent V hands,* palms facing each other and fingers pointing up, in front of the body, move the hands upward and then upward to the right while straightening the fingers forming *V hands.*

**upset**[1] *v.* **1.** To disturb or distress physically or emotionally: *His actions upset me somewhat.* —*adj.* **2.** Physically or emotionally disturbed or distressed: *an upset stomach.* —*n.* **3.** A disturbance: *a general upset over the fire downtown.*

- [The stomach seems to turn over as when upset] Beginning with the right *P hand* in front of the abdomen, palm facing down, twist the wrist forward, ending with the palm facing up.

**upset**[2] *v.* See sign for DISGUSTED[1].

**upstairs** *adv.* Same sign as for UP but made with a double movement.

**up to** *prep.* See sign for MAXIMUM.

**upward** *adv.* See sign for UP.

**urge** *v.* To encourage earnestly: *I urged him to go to college.* Same sign used for: **persuade.**

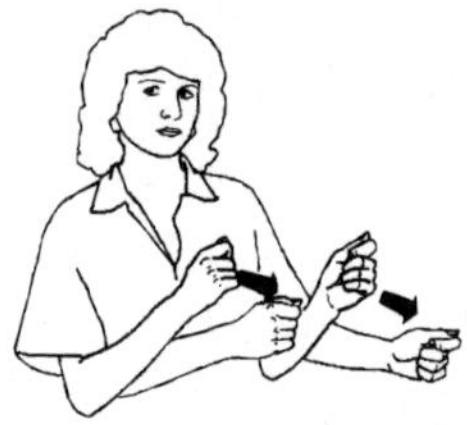

■ With both *modified X hands* in front of each side of the chest, palms facing each other and right hand closer to the chest than the left hand, move the hands forward with a short double movement.

---

**urgent** *adj.* See signs for HURRY, NOW.

---

**urine** *n.* See sign for PENIS.

---

**us** *pron.* The objective case of WE, used as a direct or indirect object; used in referring to the person speaking plus one or more others: *Take us with you. They gave us new office furniture.*

■ [Initialized sign similar to sign for **we**] Touch the index-finger side of the right *U hand,* palm facing left and fingers pointing up, to the right side of the chest. Then twist the wrist and move the hand around to touch the little-finger side of the right *U hand* to the left side of the chest, palm facing right.

---

**use**[1] *v.* To put into service; employ for some purpose: *Use a pen to write the check.* Alternate forms: **usage** *n.,* **useful** *adj.*

■ [Initialized sign] Move the right *U hand,* palm facing forward and fingers pointing up, in a repeated circle over the back of the left *S hand* held in front of the chest, palm facing down, hitting the heel of the right hand on the left hand each time as it passes.

---

**use**[2] *v.* See sign for APPLY[1].

---

**used** *adj.* See sign for SECOND-HAND.

---

**used to**[1] *adj.* + *prep.* Accustomed to: *The students got used to going home at three o'clock.* Same sign used for: **usual, usually.**

■ [Initialized sign similar to sign for **habit**] With the heel of the right *U hand,* palm facing forward and fingers pointing up, on the back of the left *S hand* held in front of the chest, palm facing down, move both hands downward.

---

**used to**[2] *adv.* See sign for LONG AGO.

---

**use up** *v. phrase.* See sign for RUN OUT OF.

---

**usual** *adv.* See signs for DAILY, REGULAR[1], USED TO. Related form: **usually** *adv.*

**vacant** *adj.* See sign for EMPTY. Related form: **vacancy** *n.*

**vacation** *n.* A free time away from one's usual duties, as for rest or travel: *to go on vacation.*

- With the thumbs of both *5 hands* near each armpit, palms facing in and fingers pointing toward each other, wiggle the fingers with a repeated movement.

**vaccinate** *v.* To inoculate with a vaccine, a preparation for producing immunity to a specific disease: *to vaccinate the city's population against smallpox.* Related form: **vaccination** *n.*

- [Shows the traditional location on the upper arm for vaccinations] With the bent index finger and thumb of the right hand pinched together, rub the fingertips downward with a double movement on the upper left arm.

**vaccine** *n.* See sign for SHOT.

**vacuum** *v.* To clean with a vacuum cleaner: *to vacuum the carpet.*

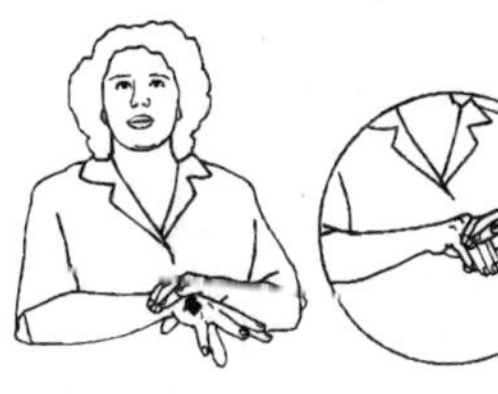

- [Demonstrates the action of a vacuum drawing in dirt] With the fingertips of the right *flattened C hand* on the fingers of the left *open hand* held in front of the chest, palm facing up and fingers pointing forward, close the right fingers with a double movement while sliding across the left palm, forming a *flattened O hand* each time.

**vague** *adj.* Not clear; indefinite; indistinct: *offered only a vague explanation that told us nothing.* Same sign used for: **ambiguous, blurry, fade, hazy, illegible, unclear.**

- [Represents a blurring of the facts] With the palms of both *5 hands* together at angles in front of the chest, move both hands in circular movements going in opposite directions rubbing the palms against each other.

**vain** *adj.* Having too much pride in or concern with one's appearance or achievements: *Vain people can be very tiresome, always thinking about themselves.* Related form: **vanity.**

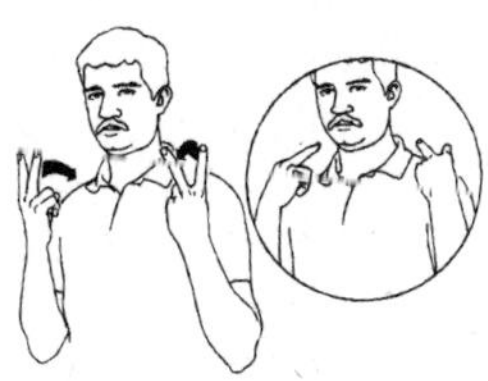

- [Initialized sign] Beginning with both *V hands* in front of each shoulder, palms facing in and fingers pointing up, move the fingers backward toward each shoulder with a double movement.

**valley** *n.* An elongated area of low land between hills or mountains: *The stream runs through the valley.*

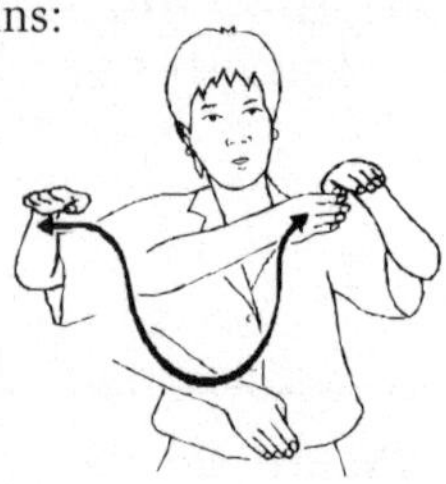

■ [Shows the shape of a valley] Beginning with the index-finger sides of both *B hands* held up in front of both shoulders, palms facing down and fingers pointing forward, bring the right hand downward and then upward again, ending with the index-finger sides of both hands touching in front of the left shoulder.

**value** *adj.* See signs for COST[2], IMPORTANT.

**vanilla** *n.* **1.** A flavoring: *to put vanilla in the cake.* —*adj.* **2.** Flavored with vanilla: *vanilla ice cream.*

■ [Initialized sign] Shake the right *V hand,* palm facing forward and fingers pointing up, from side to side with a small double movement in front of the right shoulder.

**vanish** *v.* See sign for DISAPPEAR.

**vanquish** *v.* See sign for DEFEAT.

**vapor** *n.* See sign for RAPTURE.

**variety** *n.* **1.** The state of being diverse: *Your writing lacks variety.* **2.** A collection of different forms of things in the same general category: *a variety of answers to the same question.* Same sign used for: **and so forth, et cetera, random, range.**

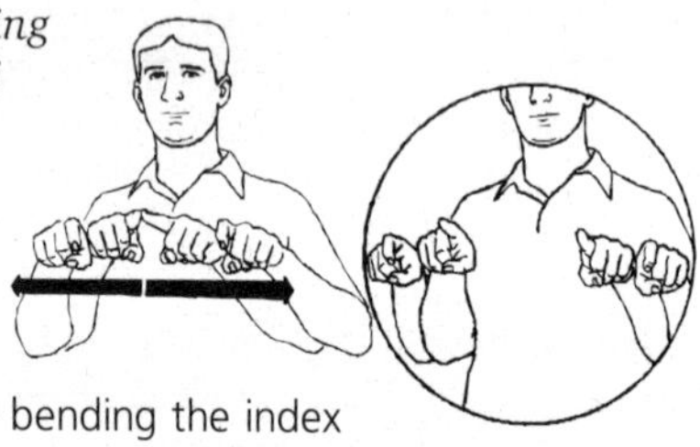

■ Beginning with the extended index fingers of both hands touching in front of the chest, palms facing down, move the hands apart while bending the index fingers downward, forming *X hands* with a repeated movement, ending with the hands in front of each side of the chest.

**vasectomy** *n.* See sign for STERILIZATION.

**vegetable** *n.* Any plant, one or more parts of which, as the leaves, flowers, stems, or roots, is eaten as food: *Vegetables are part of a balanced diet.*

■ [Initialized sign] Beginning with the index finger of the right *V hand,* palm facing forward, touching the right side of the chin, twist the wrist to turn the palm back and touch the middle finger to the right side of the chin, ending with the palm facing back.

**vending machine** *n. phrase.* A machine from which food or drink or other small items can be obtained by inserting coins: *to get a soda from the vending machine.*

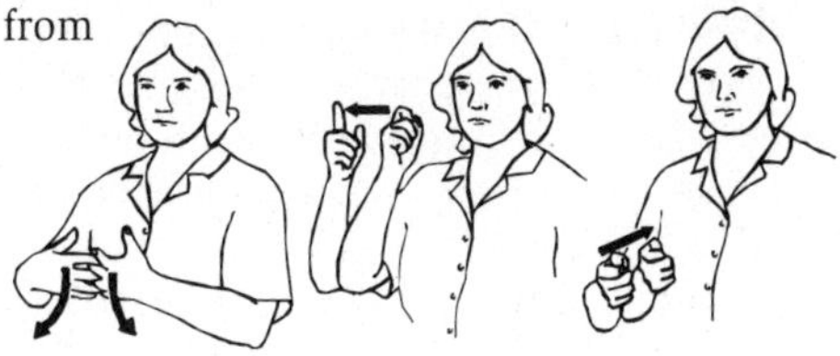

■ [**machine** + mime putting money in a vending machine and pulling a knob for one's selection] With the fingers of both *curved 5 hands* loosely meshed together, palms facing in, move the hands up and down in front of the chest with a repeated movement. Then with the right thumb holding down the bent left index finger in front of the right shoulder, palm facing left, quickly flick the index finger up. Then with the right thumb tucked under the bent right index finger, palm facing left, pull the right hand back toward the right side of the body.

**venetian blinds** *n. phrase.* See sign for BLINDS.

**vengeance** *n.* See sign for REVENGE.

**versus** *prep.* See sign for CHALLENGE.

**very** *adv.* In or to a high degree; extremely: *a very good job.*

■ [Initialized sign similar to sign for **much**] Beginning with the fingertips of both *V hands* touching in front of the chest, palms facing each other, bring the hands apart to in front of each shoulder.

**veto** *v.* See sign for REJECT[1].

**via** *prep.* See sign for THROUGH.

**vibrate** *v.* See sign for BEAT[2]. Related form: **vibration** *n.*

**vice president** *n.* The officer next in rank to the president: *The vice president called the meeting to order.*

■ [Abbreviation **v-p**] Beginning with the right *V hand* in front of the right side of the forehead, palm facing forward and fingers pointing up, move the hand downward by twisting the wrist, forming a *P hand* in front of the right shoulder.

**vicinity** *n.* See sign for AREA[1].

**victory** *n.* See sign for CELEBRATE.

**video camera** *n. phrase.* See sign for MOVIE CAMERA.

**videotape**[1] *n.* **1.** A magnetic tape on which images, often with accompanying audio, can be recorded: *to watch a videotape.* —*v.* **2.** To make a recording of, as a television program, on magnetic tape: *videotape the movie that was broadcast at midnight.* Same sign used for: **camcorder.**

- [Abbreviation **v-t**] Beginning with the index-finger side of the right *V hand,* palm facing forward and fingers pointing up, against the open left palm held up in front of the chest, move the right hand forward in a circular movement while changing into a *T hand* as the hand moves.

**videotape**[2] *v.* (alternate sign) Same sign used for **camcorder.**

- [Represents the fluttering pictures on a videotape] With the index-finger side of the right *C hand* against the palm of the left *open hand* held in front of the chest, palm facing right and fingers pointing up, bend the right fingers and thumb with a quick repeated movement.

**videotape**[3] *v.* See sign for MOVIE CAMERA.

**view** *v.* See sign for LOOK OVER.

**viewpoint** *v.* See sign for PERSPECTIVE.

**village** *n.* See sign for TOWN.

**violation** *n.* See signs for CRIME[1,2].

**violin** *n.* A musical instrument, the treble member of the modern stringed instruments, held in one arm and played with a bow drawn across the strings by the other hand: *listening to a master play the violin.* Same sign used for: **fiddle.**

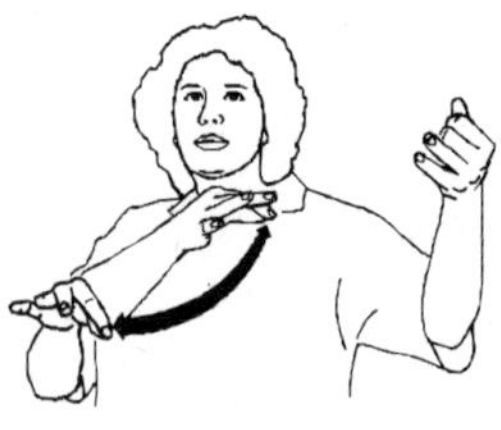

- [Mime playing a violin] While holding the left *curved hand* in front of the left shoulder, palm facing in, move the right *F hand* forward and back toward the left side of the chest with a swinging movement, palm facing down.

**VIP** (short for very important person) *n. phrase.* See sign for CHIEF[1].

**virtual** *adj.* **1.** Having the effect of, although not actually being such: *Because she had not seen him for years, he was a virtual stranger.* **2.** Simulated; functionally behaving like: *a virtual disk in RAM.*

- [Initialized sign similar to sign for **dream**] Beginning with the index-finger side of the right *V hand* touching the right side of the forehead, palm facing left, move the hand forward in a double arc.

**visible** *adj.* Able to be seen: *The trees were visible through the fog.* Same sign used for: **transparent.**

■ [**see** + **through**] Move the fingers of the right *V hand*, palm facing down and fingers pointing forward, from near the right side of the face forward between the index finger and middle finger of the left *5 hand* held in front of the face, palm facing in and fingers pointing right.

**vision** *n.* See sign for SEE.

**visit** *v.* **1.** To go and stay with or at for a short time: *to visit a friend in the hospital; to visit Vermont.* —*n.* **2.** An act or instance of visiting: *looking forward to a long visit with you.*

■ [Initialized sign] Beginning with both *V hands* in front of each side of the chest, palms facing in and fingers pointing up, move the hands in alternating repeated movements.

**visualize** *adj.* See sign for SEE.

**vocabulary**[1] *n.* **1.** The words in a language: *studying vocabulary in Russian.* **2.** The stock of words known by a person or group: *The baby has a big vocabulary for her age.*

■ [Initialized sign similar to sign for **word**] Tap the fingertips of the right *V hand*, palm facing down, with a double movement on the extended left index finger held in front of the body, palm facing in and finger pointing right.

**vocabulary**[2] *n.* See sign for WORD.

**voice** *n.* The sound made through the mouth, as by human beings in speaking or singing, especially the type of sound unique to a given individual: *a high-pitched voice.* Related forms: **vocal, vocalize.**

■ [Initialized sign showing the location of one's voice] Move the fingertips of the right *V hand*, palm facing down, upward on the throat with a double movement.

**void**[1] *v.* See sign for CANCEL.

**void**[2] *adj.* See sign for EMPTY.

**volleyball** *n.* A game played by two teams using a large ball kept in motion by the hands hitting it back and forth over a net: *to play a game of volleyball.*

■ [Mime hitting a volleyball] Beginning with both *open hands* near each side of the head, palms facing forward and fingers pointing up, push the hands upward and forward with a double movement.

**volunteer** *v.* See sign for APPLY[2]. Related form: **voluntary** *adj.*

**vomit** *v.* **1.** To eject the contents of the stomach through the mouth; throw up: *vomited because of food poisoning.* —*n.* **2.** The substance ejected from the stomach: *had to clean up the vomit.* Same sign used for: **regurgitate, throw up.**

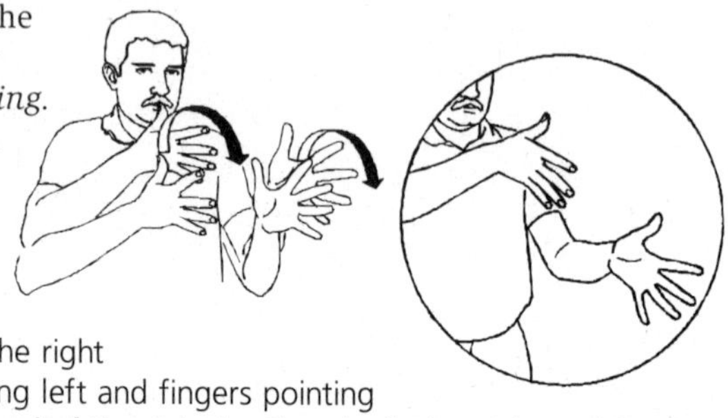

■ [Represents food being expelled from the mouth] Beginning with the right *5 hand* near the mouth, palm facing left and fingers pointing forward, and the left *5 hand* forward of the right hand, palm facing right and fingers pointing forward, move both hands upward and forward in large arcs.

**vote** *n.* **1.** A formal choice made by an individual or body of individuals: *The vote was in favor of the proposition.* **2.** A ballot or equivalent mechanism for making such a choice: *to count the votes.* —*v.* **3.** To express such a choice officially, as by casting a ballot: *to vote for your favorite candidate.* Same sign used for: **elect, election.**

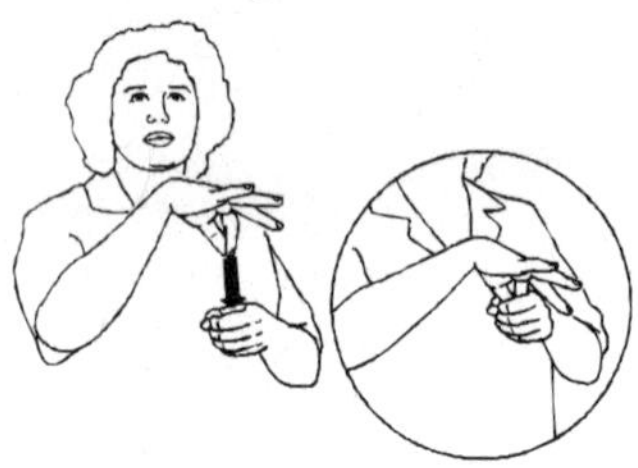

■ [Represents putting one's vote into a ballot box] Insert the fingertips of the right *F hand,* palm facing down, with a double movement in the hole formed by the left *O hand* held in front of the chest, palm facing in.

**vow** *n.* **1.** A solemn promise: *He gave his vow.* —*v.* **2.** To make a promise: *I vow not to smoke again.* See also sign for PROMISE. Same sign used for: **assurance, assure, commit, commitment, obligate, pledge, swear, sworn.**

■ [Natural gesture for making a pledge] Beginning with the extended right index finger in front of the mouth, palm facing left and finger pointing up, move the right hand forward with a deliberate movement while opening into an *open hand,* palm facing forward and fingers pointing up, and hitting the right forearm against the index-finger side of the left *open hand* held across the body, palm facing down and fingers pointing right.

**wacky** *adj.* See sign for CRAZY.

**wager** *n.* See sign for BET.

**wages** *pl. n.* See signs for EARN, INCOME.

**wait** *v.* **1.** To remain inactive or in readiness, as until something expected happens: *to wait for the bus.* —*n.* **2.** An act, instance, or state of waiting: *It was a long wait.*

■ [Seems to be twiddling the finger while waiting impatiently] Beginning with both *curved 5 hands* in front of the body, palms facing up, wiggle the fingers with a repeated motion.

**wait on** *v. phrase.* See sign for SERVE.

**waive** *v.* See signs for DISMISS, GIVE UP.

**wake up** *v. phrase.* See sign for AWAKE[1].

**walk** *v.* To go or travel on foot at a moderate speed: *to walk down the hall.* Same sign used for: **stroll, wander.**

■ [Represents a person's legs moving when walking] Beginning with both *open hands* in front of each side of the body, left palm facing in and fingers pointing down and right palm facing down and fingers pointing forward, move the fingers of both hands up and down with an alternating movement by bending the wrists.

**wall** *n.* See sign for BOARD[1].

**wander** *v.* See signs for ROAM, WALK.

**want** *v.* To wish for: *I want to eat dinner.* Same sign used for: **desire, passion.**

■ [Represents bringing a wanted thing toward oneself] Beginning with both *5 hands* in front of the body, palms facing up and fingers pointing forward, bring the hands back toward the chest while constricting the fingers toward the palms.

**war** *n.* See sign for BATTLE.

**warm** *adj.* Having or giving out a feeling of heat: *a warm room.* Related form: **warmth** *n.*

■ Beginning with the fingers of the right *E hand* near the mouth, palm facing in, move the hand forward in a small arc while opening the fingers into a *C hand.*

**warn** *v.* To give notice or advice to, as of impending danger: *They warned us about the impending snow storm.* Related form: **warning** *n.* Same sign used for: **admonish, caution, rebuke, reprimand.**

■ [Indicates tapping someone on the hand as a warning] Tap the palm of the right *open hand* with a double movement on the back of the left *open hand* held in front of the chest, both palms facing down.

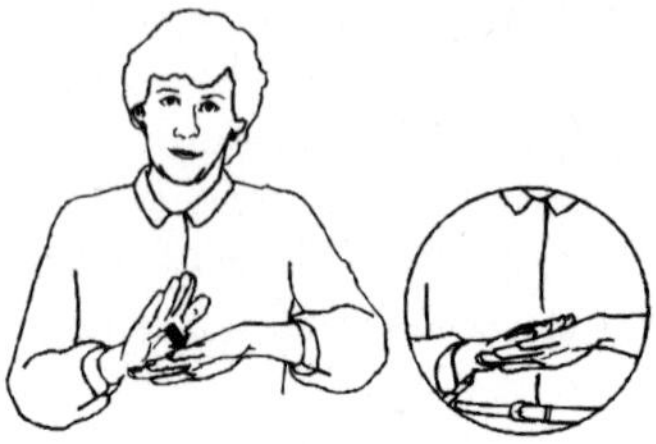

**warranty** *v., n.* See sign for PROMISE.

**was**[1] *v.* First and third person singular past tense of BE: *He was here yesterday.* Same sign used for: **past, were.**

■ [The hand gestures toward the past] Bring the fingertips of the right *bent hand,* palm facing back, down on the right shoulder.

**was**[2] *v.* See sign for AGO.

**wash**[1] *v.* To clean with water or another liquid, as by dipping and rubbing: *to wash the sweater by hand.* Same sign used for: **rub.**

■ [Demonstrates the action of rubbing something to wash it] Rub the palm side of the right *A hand* with a repeated movement across the palm side of the left *A hand,* palms facing each other.

**wash**[2] (laundry) *v., n.* See sign for WASHING MACHINE.

**wash one's hair** *v. phrase.* See sign for SHAMPOO.

**washer** *n.* See sign for WASHING MACHINE.

**washing machine** *n. phrase.* An appliance for washing clothes, linens, towels, etc.: *put the dirty laundry in the washing machine.* Same sign used for: **wash, washer.**

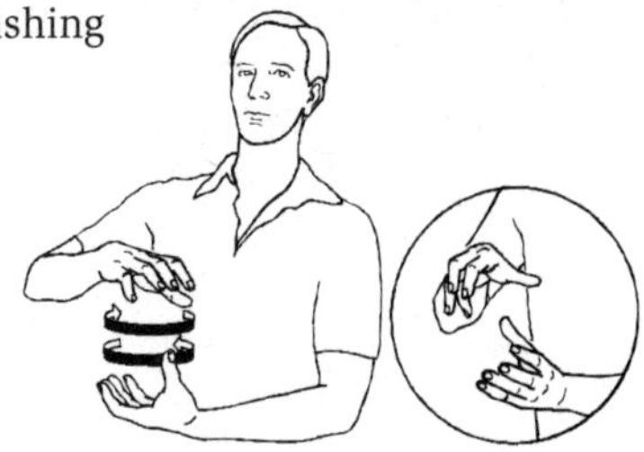

■ [Indicates the action of a washing machine's agitator] Beginning with the right *curved 5 hand* over the left *curved 5 hand* in front of the chest, palms facing each other, twist the hands with a repeated movement in opposite directions.

**washroom** *n.* See sign for TOILET.

**waste** *n.* **1.** Useless material: *The waste in the bin is to be thrown out.* **2.** Useless consumption or expenditure: *This is a total waste of my time.* —*v.* **3.** To put to poor use or to squander: *Don't waste my time with excuses.*

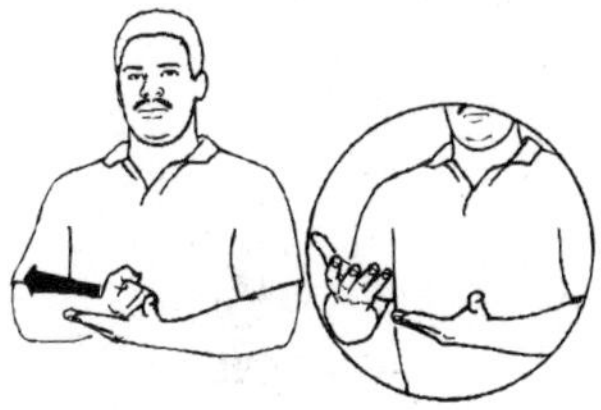

■ [The hand seems to toss waste away] Beginning with the back of the right *S hand,* palm facing up, in the palm of the left *open hand* held in front of the chest, palm facing up, move the right hand forward while opening into a *5 hand.*

**watch**[1] *n.* A small, portable device for telling time, as a wristwatch: *She refuses to wear a watch.* Same sign used for: **timepiece, wristwatch.**

■ [The shape of a watch's face] Place the palm side of the right *F hand* on the back of the left wrist.

**watch**[2] *v.* To look at carefully and attentively: *to watch the children play.*

■ [Represents the eyes looking at something] Beginning with the right *V hand* in front of the right side of the face, palm facing down and fingers pointing forward, move the hand forward.

**watch**[3] *v.* See sign for ATTENTION.

**watch out** *v. phrase.* See signs for CAREFUL, LOOK OUT.

**water** *n.* The transparent, odorless, tasteless liquid that falls from the sky as rain and is found in impure form in oceans, lakes, underground springs, etc.: *a bucket of water.*

■ [Initialized sign] Tap the index-finger side of the right *W hand,* palm facing left, against the chin with a double movement.

**watermelon** *n.* A large, oval, edible melon with a hard green rind and juicy red or pink pulp: *Watermelon is a refreshing summer dessert.*

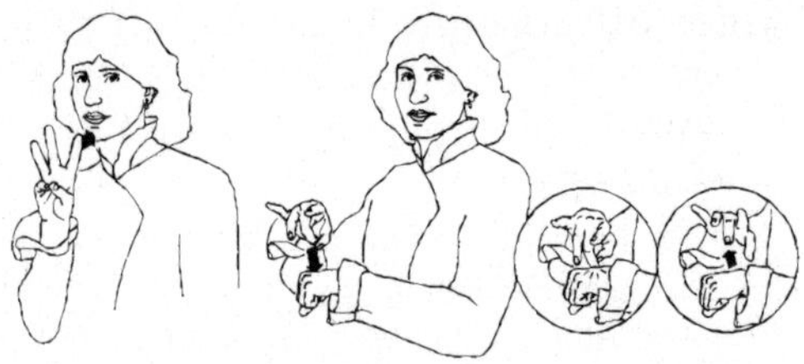

■ [**water** + **pumpkin**] Tap the index-finger side of the right *W hand,* palm facing left, against the chin with a double movement. Then with a double movement flick the middle finger of the right *8 hand,* palm facing down, off the back of the left *S hand,* palm facing down, bouncing the right hand up slightly each time.

**way**[1] *n.* Manner: *I like the way he treats the children.* **2.** A method or plan: *We came up with a way to finish sooner.* **3.** A passage on a path or course: *Can you find your way to her office?*

■ [Initialized sign similar to sign for **road**] Beginning with both *W hands* in front of each side of the body, palms facing each other, move the hands straight forward.

**way**[2] *n.* See sign for ROAD.

**we** *pron.* The nominative plural of I, used as a subject; used in referring to the person speaking plus one or more others: *We will go together.*

■ Touch the extended right index finger, palm facing down, first to the right side of the chest and then to the left side of the chest.

**weak** *adj.* Lacking in strength, vigor, or force: *feeling weak in the knees; a weak personality.* Related form: **weakness** *n.* Same sign used for: **fatigue, feeble, frail.**

■ [The fingers collapse as if weak] Beginning with the fingertips of the right *5 hand,* palm facing in, touching the palm of the left *open hand* held in front of the chest, move the right hand downward with a double movement, bending the fingers each time.

**wealth** *n.* See sign for RICH. Alternate form: **wealthy** *adj.*

**wear** *v.* To carry or have on the body as a covering or ornament: *to wear a coat; to wear jewelry.*

■ Move the right *U hand,* palm facing forward and fingers pointing up, in a circle in front of the right side of the body with a double movement.

**wear out** *v. phrase.* To use until damaged, unfit, or useless: *to wear out your shoes.* Same sign used for: **decay, rot, rotten.**

■ Beginning with both *S hands* together in front of the chest, palms facing up, move the hands forward with a sudden movement while opening into *5 hands,* palms facing up.

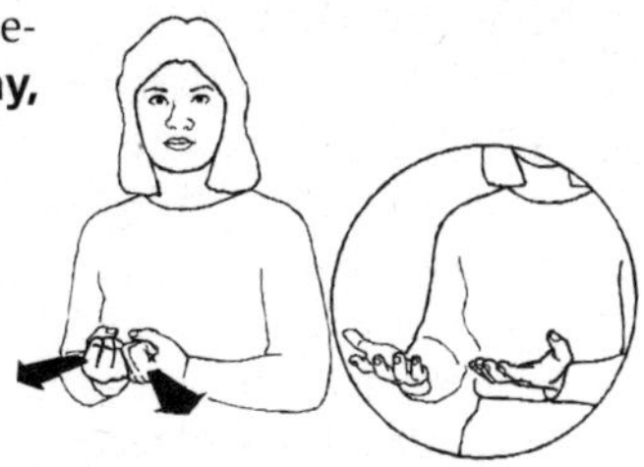

**weary** *adj.* See sign for TIRED.

**weather** *n.* The state or condition of the atmosphere regarding temperature, moisture, winds, etc.: *good weather expected this week.* Same sign used for: **climate.**

■ [Initialized sign] With the fingertips of both *6 hands* together in front of the chest, palms facing each other, twist the hands in opposite directions with a double movement.

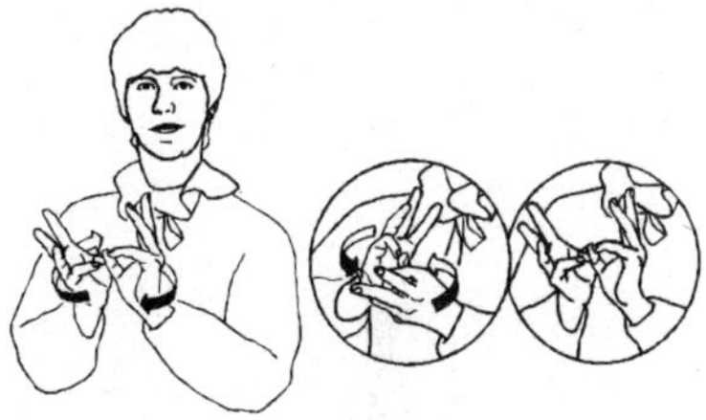

**wedding** *n.* A marriage ceremony: *a beautiful wedding.* Related form: **wed** *v.*

■ [Represents bringing the bride's and groom's hands together during a wedding] Beginning with both *open hands* hanging down in front of each side of the chest, palms facing in and fingers pointing down, bring the fingers upward toward each other, meeting in front of the chest.

**Wednesday** *n.* The fourth day of the week, after Tuesday: *a class trip planned for Wednesday.*

■ [Initialized sign] Move the right *W hand,* palm facing in and fingers pointing up, in a circle in front of the right shoulder.

**week** *n.* **1.** A period of seven successive days starting on Sunday and ending with Saturday: *the second week of the month.* **2.** A period of seven successive days starting on a specified day: *She'll be away for a week, starting Thursday.* **3.** The work week, normally thought of as a five-day period starting on Monday and going through Friday: You *can take next week off from work.* Same sign used for: **one week.**

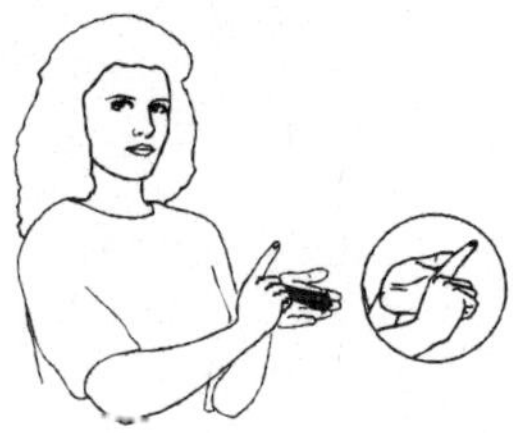

■ [The finger moves along the days of one week on an imaginary calendar] Slide the palm side of the right *1 hand* from the heel to the fingers of the left *open hand* held in front of the chest, palm facing in.

**weekend** *n.* The end of a week, usually including Friday evening, Saturday, and Sunday: *plans to go fishing this weekend.*

■ [**week** + **end**[1]] Slide the palm side of the right *1 hand* from the heel to the fingertips of the left *open hand* held in front of the chest, palm facing in. Then move the palm side of the right *open hand* downward along the fingertips of the left *open hand* held in front of the chest, palm facing right.

**weep** *v.* See sign for CRY.

**weigh** *v.* To measure how heavy something is: *to weigh the package.* Related form: **weight** *n.* Same sign used for: **pound, scale.**

■ [The fingers seem to balance something as if on a scale] With the middle-finger side of the right *H hand* across the index-finger side of the left *H hand,* palms angled toward each other, tip the right hand up and down with a repeated movement.

**weird**[1] *adj.* Strange or unearthly: *a weird sound.*

■ [Initialized sign] Move the right *W hand,* palm facing down and fingers pointing left, across the front of the face, bending the fingers as the hand moves.

**weird**[2] *adj.* See sign for STRANGE.

**welcome** *v., n., adj., interj.* See sign for INVITE.

**welfare** *n.* See sign for PENSION.

**well**[1] *adj.* **1.** In good health: *Sorry you don't feel well.* —*adv.* **2.** In a satisfactory manner: *doing well in school.* Same sign used for: **bold, cure, heal, healthy, strength, strong.**

■ [The hands seem to pull health from the body] Beginning with the fingertips of both *5 hands* on each side of the chest, palms facing in and fingers pointing up, bring the hands forward with a deliberate movement while closing into *S hands.*

**well**[2] *adj.* See signs for FINE[1], GOOD.

**were** *v.* See signs for AGO, WAS.

**west** *n.* **1.** The general direction 90 degrees to the left of north: *The coast is to the west of the mountains.* **2.** (*sometimes cap.*) The western states of the United States: *likes to read novels about cowboys in the old West.* —*adj.* **3.** Lying toward or located in the west: *the west side of the street.* —*adv.* **4.** To, toward, or in the west: *"Go west, young man."* Related form: **western** *adj.*

■ [Initialized sign showing a west direction on a map] Move the right *W hand,* palm facing forward and fingers pointing up, to the left in front of the right side of the chest.

**wet** *adj.* Covered or soaked with water or some other liquid: *a wet towel.* Same sign used for: **damp, dew, humid, misty, moist, moisten, moisture.**

■ [The hands seem to feel something wet] Beginning with the right *5 hand* near the right side of the chin, palm facing left, and the left *5 hand* in front of the left side of the chest, palm facing up, bring the hands downward while closing the fingers to the thumbs.

**whack** *v.* See sign for SPANK.

**what** *pron.* (Used interrogatively to request information): *What is your name?*

■ Bring the extended right index finger, palm facing left, downward across the left *open hand* held in front of the chest, palm facing up.

**whatever** *pron.* See sign for ANYWAY.

**what for?** Why: *What are you fixing that old thing for?*

■ [**for** formed with a repeated movement] Beginning with the extended right index finger touching the right side of the forehead, palm facing down, twist the hand forward with a double movement, pointing the index finger forward each time.

**what's happening?** (Used as a greeting) Same sign used for: **excite, excitement, exciting, thrill, thrilling, what's up?**

■ Beginning with the bent middle fingers of both *5 hands* touching the chest, palms facing in, bring the hands upward and forward with a quick double movement.

**what's the matter?** Same sign used for: **what's wrong?**

- [Similar to sign for **wrong**] Bring the knuckles of the right *Y hand,* palm facing in, against the chin with a deliberate movement while wrinkling the forehead.

**when** *adv.* At what time: *When will you go?*

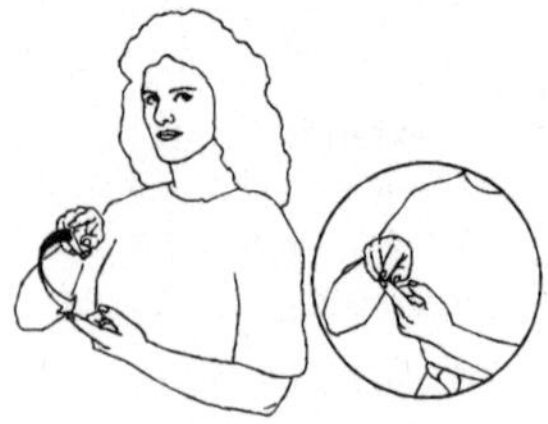

- Beginning with the extended right index finger in front of the chest, palm facing down and finger pointing forward, and the left extended index finger in front of the lower chest, palm facing in and finger pointing right, move the right index finger in a circular movement down to land on the left index finger.

**where** *adv.* At what place: *Where do you live?*

- Move the extended right index finger, palm facing forward and finger pointing up, with a short double movement from side to side in front of the right shoulder.

**whether** *pron.* See sign for WHICH.

**whew**[1] *interj.* (Used to express surprise, dismay, relief, etc.): *Whew! It's hot in here. Whew! We're finished!*

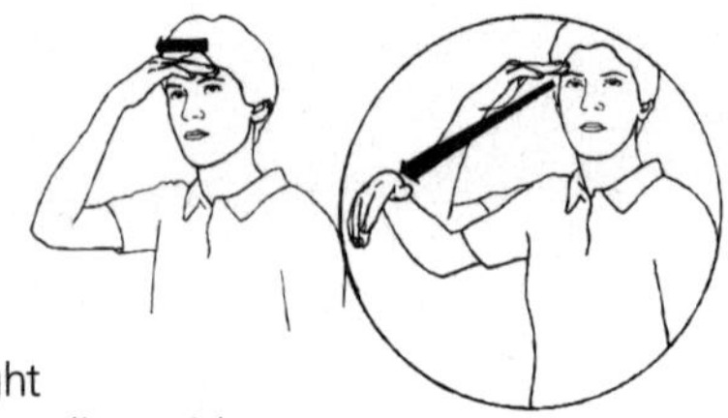

- [Natural gesture used to wipe sweat from the forehead] Wipe the index-finger side of the right *B hand,* palm facing down, from left to right across the forehead, and then throw the right hand downward to in front of the right shoulder, ending with the palm facing in and fingers pointing down.

**whew**[2] *interj.* See sign for FINEST.

**which** *pron.* **1.** What one: *Which do you want? —adj.* **2.** What one, out of a number or group mentioned or implied: *Which book is yours?* Same sign used for: **either, whether.**

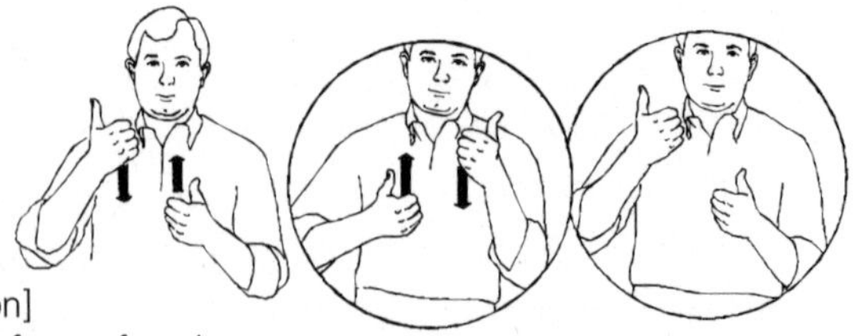

- [The movement indicates indecision] Beginning with both *10 hands* in front of each side of the chest, palms facing each other and right hand higher than the left hand, move the hands up and down with an alternating movement.

**while** *conj.* See sign for DURING.

**while ago, a** *adv. phrase.* See signs for JUST, RECENTLY[1].

**whip** *n., v.* See sign for SPANK. Related form: **whipping** *n.*

**whiskey** *n.* **1.** A strong intoxicating drink made from fermented grain: *to drink whiskey and water.* **2.** A drink of whiskey: *I'll have a whiskey and soda.* Same sign used for: **alcohol, brandy, liquor.**

■ With the index fingers and little fingers of both hands extended, tap the little finger of the right hand with a double movement on the index finger of the left hand, palms facing in opposite directions.

**whistle** *n., v.* See sign for REFEREE.

**whistleblower** *n.* An employee who reports dangerous or illegal conduct of an employer to the authorities: *The whistleblower reported the misused funds.*

■ [**tattle + person marker**] Beginning with the thumb side of the right *S hand* near the right side of the mouth, palm forward, flick the index finger upward with a deliberate movement. Then move both *open hands*, palms facing each other, downward along the sides of the body.

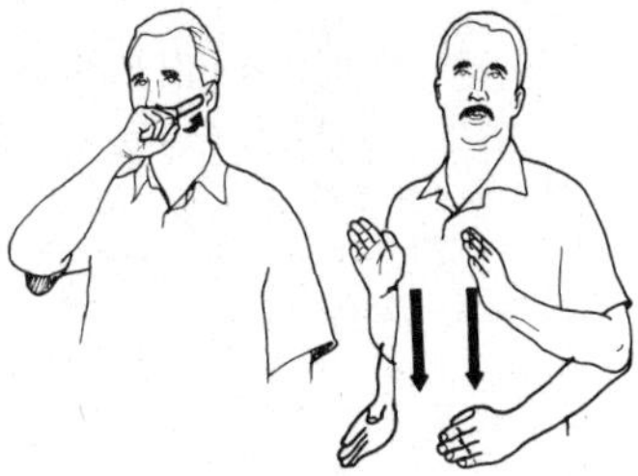

**white** *adj.* Having the color of snow: *a white flower.*

■ Beginning with the fingertips of the right *5 hand* on the chest, palm facing in, pull the hand forward while closing the fingers into a *flattened O hand.*

**whiz** *n. Informal.* See sign for ADROIT.

**who** *pron.* What person or persons: *Who is that?* Same sign used for: **whom.**

■ With the thumb of the *modified C hand* touching the chin, palm facing left, bend the index finger up and down with a double movement.

**whole** *adj., n.* See sign for ALL.

**whom** *pron.* See sign for WHO.

**whore** *n.* See sign for PROSTITUTE.

**why**[1] *adv.* For what reason: *Why did you do that?*

■ Beginning with the fingertips of the right *bent hand* touching the right side of the forehead, palm facing down, move the hand forward with a deliberate movement while changing into a *Y hand.*

**why**[2] *adv.* (alternate sign)

■ With the right index finger, little finger, and thumb extended, palm facing in, wiggle the bent middle fingers with a small repeated movement in front of the forehead.

**wicked** *adj.* See signs for BAD, DEVIL.

**wide** *adj.* Of great extent from side to side: *a wide street.* Related form: **width** *n.* Same sign used for: **broad, general.**

■ [Indicates a wide space] Beginning with both *open hands* in front of each side of the body, palms facing each other and fingers pointing forward, move the hands away from each other outward to the sides of the body.

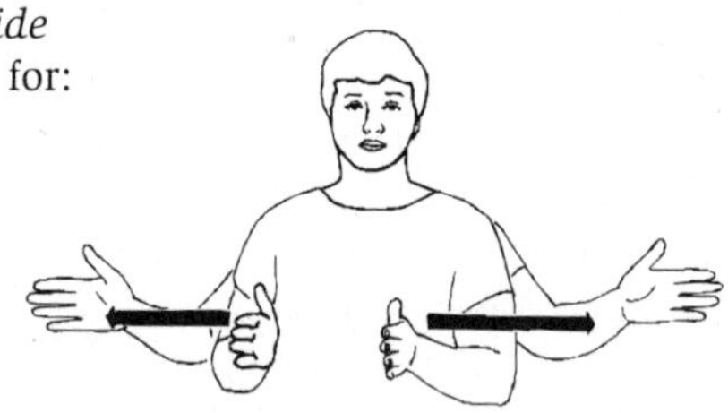

**widescreen** *adj.* Refers to a film, computer, or television image that has a wider aspect ratio than the traditional Academy frame used in older movie theaters: *She chose a widescreen video to play on their new LED widescreen television.*

■ [**wide** + **full**[2]] Beginning with both *open hands* in front of each side of the body, palms facing each other and fingers pointing forward, move the hands apart to the sides of the body. Then slide the palm of the right *open hand*, palm facing down, from right to left across the index-finger side of the left *S hand*, palm facing right.

**wiener** *n.* See sign for SAUSAGE.

**wife** *n.* A married woman: *the doctor's wife.*

■ [The hand moves from near the female area of the head + **marry**] Move the right *curved hand* from near the right side of the chin, palm facing forward, downward to clasp the left *curved hand* held in front of the body.

**wild** *adj.* See signs for CRAZY, RAVE.

**wildcard** *n.* See sign for STAR.

**will**[1] *n.* **1.** Purpose and determination, as carried out by, affecting, or required of others: *It is God's will.* **2.** The power to choose one's own actions consciously and deliberately: *I took on that job of my own free will.*

- [Initialized sign similar to sign for **against**] Hit the index-finger side of the right *W hand,* palm facing forward, against the left *open hand* held in front of the chest, palm facing right and fingers pointing up.

**will**[2] *auxiliary v.* (Used preceding another verb to express the future tense): *We will win tomorrow.*

- [The hand moves into the future] Move the right *open hand,* palm facing left and fingers pointing up, from the right side of the chin forward while turning the fingers forward.

**willing** *adj.* See sign for ADMIT.

**will not** See sign for WON'T.

**win** *v.* **1.** To be successful over others in (a game, competition, battle, etc.): *to win the contest.* —*n.* **2.** A victory: *It was a big win.*

- Beginning with the right *5 hand* in front of the right shoulder, palm facing forward and fingers pointing up, and the left *5 hand* in front of the body, palm facing right and fingers pointing forward, sweep the right hand downward in an arc across the index-finger side of the left hand while changing both hands into *S hands* and bringing the right hand upward in front of the chest.

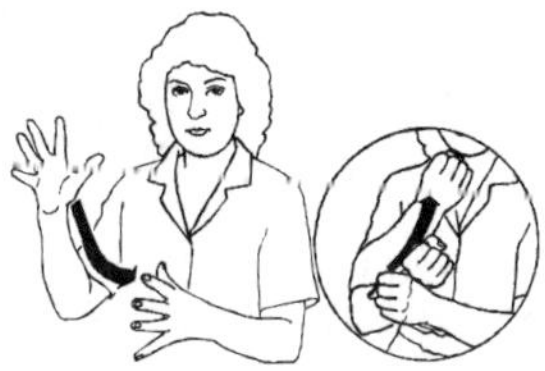

**wind** *n.* Moving air: *a strong wind.* Related form: **windy** *adj.* Same sign used for: **storm.**

- [Represents the action of wind blowing] Beginning with both *5 hands* in front of the left side of the body, palms facing each other and fingers pointing forward, move the hands back and forth in front of the chest with a repeated movement.

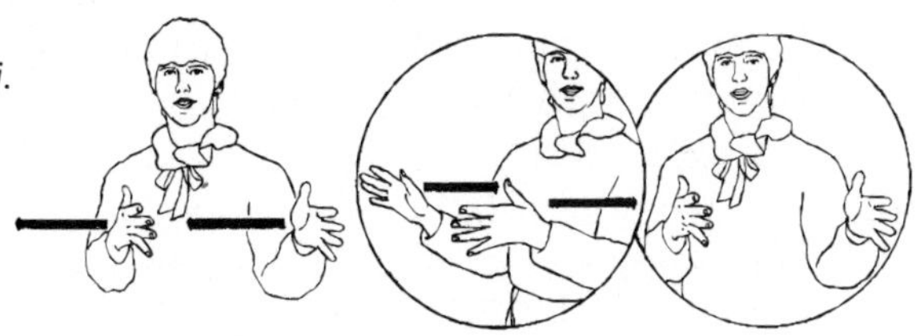

**window** *n.* **1.** An opening in a wall to let light or air in, usually fitted with one or more frames containing panes of glass: *The window is broken.* **2.** An area having data, programs, or information on a computer display screen: *The address list was open in one window and the letter was open in another window.* Same sign used for: **Windows** or **Microsoft Windows.**

- [Represents closing a window] Bring the little-finger side of the right *open hand* down sharply with a double movement on the index-finger side of the left *open hand,* both palms facing in and fingers pointing in opposite directions.

**Windows** (short for Microsoft Windows) *n. Trademark.* See sign for WINDOW.

**wind up** *v. phrase.* See sign for END[1].

**wine** *n.* An alcoholic drink made by fermenting the juice of grapes or other fruit: *a glass of wine.*

- [Initialized sign] Move the right *W hand,* palm facing left, in a small circle near the right side of the chin.

**wings** *pl. n.* See signs for ANGEL, FLY.

**winter**[1] *n.* The season between fall and spring: *It was a cold winter.*

- [Initialized sign similar to sign for **cold**[2]] Beginning with both *W hands* in front of the body, palms facing each other, move the hands toward each other with a shaking repeated movement.

**winter**[2] *n.* See sign for COLD[2].

**wipe** *v.* To rub in order to dry or clean: *It's your turn to wipe the dishes.* Same sign used for: **rub.**

- [Demonstrates the action of wiping something] Wipe the palm side of the right *A hand* with a repeated movement back and forth on the left *open hand* held in front of the body, palm facing up.

**wire**[1] *n.* A pliable metallic strand sometimes clad or electrically insulated, used chiefly for structural support or to conduct electricity: *The gardener tied up the tomato plants with a wire.* Same sign used for: **cable.**

- [Shape of a wire] Beginning with both extended little fingers pointing toward each other in front of the chest, palms facing in, move the hands apart from each other.

**wire**[2] *n.* See sign for CORD.

**wireless** *adj.* Having no wires: *use a wireless telephone.*

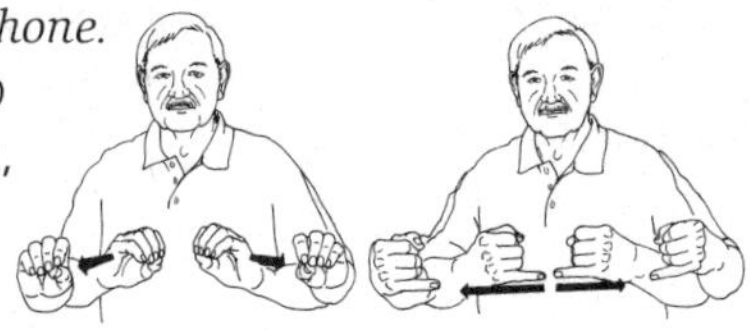

■ [**none**[2] + **wire**[1]] Beginning with both *flattened O hands,* palms facing forward, in front of the chest, move the hands apart to each side. Then beginning with both extended little fingers pointing toward each other in front of the chest, palms facing in, move the hands apart from each other.

**wise** *adj.* **1.** Having the power to judge what is true, right, beneficial, etc.: *a wise person.* **2.** Revealing or benefiting from such power: *a wise decision.* Related form: **wisdom** *n.*

■ Move the right *X hand,* palm facing left, up and down with a double movement in front of the right side of the forehead.

**wish** *v.* **1.** To desire: *to wish for a new car; to wish to leave the city.* —*n.* **2.** The expression or formation of a desire: *I made a wish.* **3.** Something one wishes for: *I hope you get your wish.* Same sign used for: **desire.**

■ Move the fingers of the right *C hand,* palm facing in, downward on the chest a short distance.

**witch** *n.* A person, especially a woman, who professes or is believed to have magic power: *The witch cast a spell.*

■ [Represents the traditional hooked nose of a witch] Move the bent index finger of the right *X hand* from near the right side of the nose, palm facing left, downward in front of the nose, ending with the palm facing down.

**with** *prep.* **1.** Accompanied by: *to serve gravy with the potatoes.* **2.** Using or showing: *to slice it with a knife; to eat with gusto.* Same sign used for: **together.**

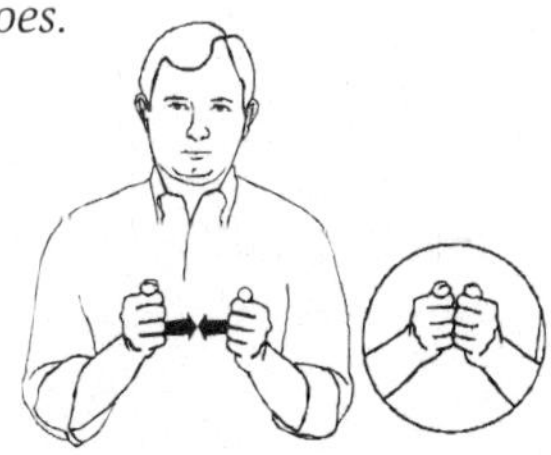

■ [Indicates two things coming together so they are with one another] Beginning with both *A hands* in front of the chest, palms facing each other, bring the hands together.

**withdraw**[1] *v.* **1.** To take or pull back: *Kindly withdraw your hand from my shoulder.* **2.** To remove oneself, as from an activity: *to withdraw from class.*

■ [Abbreviation **w-d**] Beginning with the right *W hand* in front of the right shoulder, palm facing forward, bring the hand back toward the right shoulder while changing into a *D hand.*

**withdraw**[2] *v.* See signs for DISCONNECT, FORSAKE[1], LEAVE[1].

**within** *prep.* See sign for INCLUDE.

**without** *prep.* Not having, lacking, or free from: *to go outside without a coat; a world without poverty.*

■ [**with** + releasing the hands to indicate the opposite meaning] Beginning with the palm sides of both *A hands* together in front of the chest, bring the hands apart while opening into *5 hands,* palms facing each other.

**witness** *n.* A person who has seen or heard something relevant to a case or an investigation: *The witness testified against the defendant.* Same sign used for: **eyewitness.**

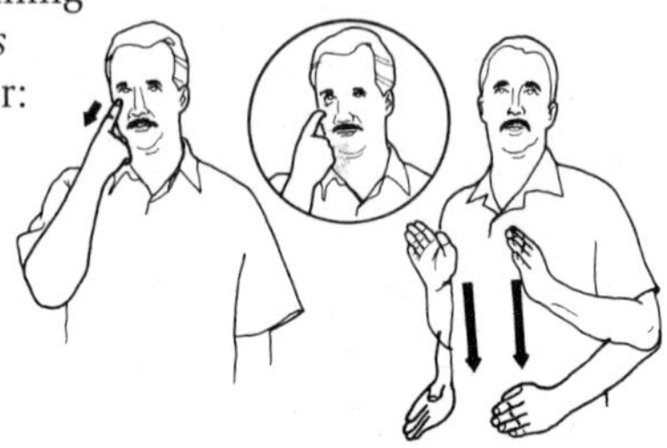

■ [A gesture indicating that one saw something + **person marker**] With the index finger of the right *X hand* pull down slightly on the cheek near the outside corner of the right eye. Then move both *open hands*, palms facing each other, downward along the sides of the body.

**woman** *n.* An adult human female: *a woman of many accomplishments.* Same sign used for: **female.**

■ [A gesture beginning near the female area of the head + **polite**] Beginning with the extended thumb of the right *open hand* touching the right side of the chin, palm facing left, bring the hand downward to touch the thumb again in the center of the chest.

**wonder** *v.* To think or speculate with curiosity: *I wonder what happened.* Same sign used for: **consider, contemplate, meditate, ponder, reflect, think, think about, thinking.**

■ [Represents thoughts going around in one's head] Move the extended right index finger, palm facing in, in a small circle near the right side of the forehead with a repeated movement.

**wonderful** *adj.* Remarkably good; excellent; marvelous: *a wonderful movie.* Same sign used for: **amaze, excellent, fantastic, great, incredible, marvel, marvelous, remarkable, splendid, terrific.**

■ Move both *5 hands,* palms facing forward and fingers pointing up, from in front of each side of the head forward with a short double movement.

**won't** *v.* Contraction of *will not*: *I won't go.* Same sign used for: **refuse, will not.**

■ [Natural gesture for refusing to do something] Beginning with the right *10 hand* in front of the right shoulder, palm facing left, move the hand deliberately back toward the shoulder while twisting the wrist up.

**wood** *n.* **1.** The hard fibrous substance composing the trunk and branches of a tree: *a piece of wood.* —*adj.* **2.** Made of wood: *a wood box.* Same sign used for: **saw.**

■ [Shows action of sawing wood] Slide the little-finger side of the right *open hand,* palm facing left and fingers pointing forward, forward and back with a double movement on the index-finger side of the left *open hand* held in front of the chest, palm facing in and fingers pointing right.

**woods** *pl. n.* See sign for FOREST.

**word** *n.* An independent unit of language that carries meaning, usually separated from other words in running text: *New words are constantly added to the vocabulary.* Same sign used for: **text, vocabulary.**

■ Tap the extended fingers of the right *G hand,* palm facing left, with a double movement against the extended left index finger pointing up in front of the left side of the chest, palm facing right.

**word processing** *n. phrase.* A type of program that transforms the computer into a tool for creating, editing, proofreading, formatting, and printing documents: *use the computer for word processing.*

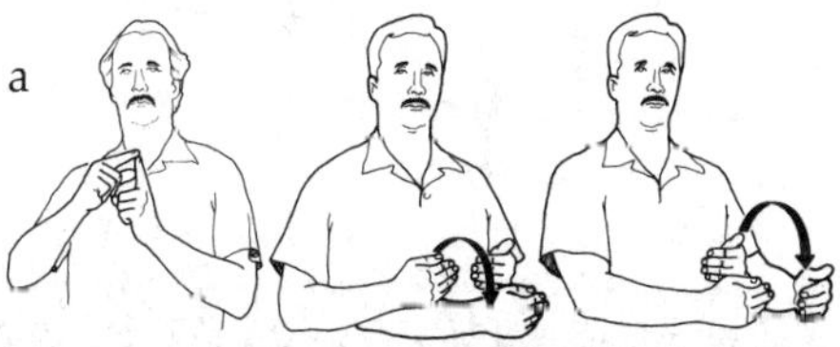

■ [**word** + **procedure**] Touch the extended fingers of the right *G hand,* palm facing out, against the extended left index finger pointing up in front of the chest, palm facing right. Then beginning with both *open hands* in front of the body, palms facing in, left fingers pointing right and right fingers pointing left and the left hand closer to the chest than the right hand, move the left hand over the right hand then the right hand over the left hand in an alternating movement.

**work**[1] *n.* **1.** Mental or physical effort: *This project takes a lot of work.* **2.** One's occupation: *to go to work.* —*v.* **3.** To labor: *to work hard all day.* **4.** To be employed: *He works in management.* **5.** To function; be in operation: *The toaster doesn't work.* Same sign used for: **employment, job, labor, occupation, task.**

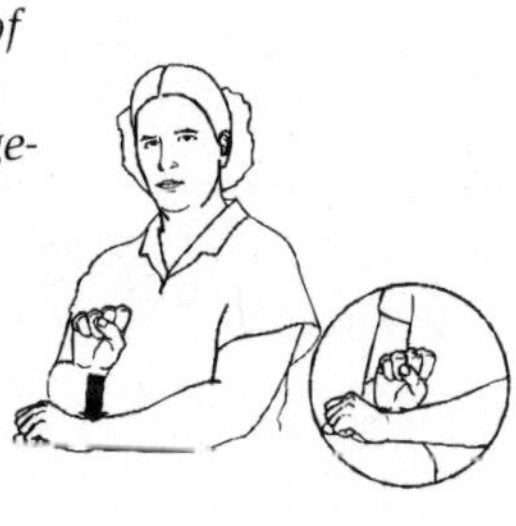

■ Tap the heel of the right *S hand,* palm facing forward, with a double movement on the back of the left *S hand* held in front of the body, palm facing down.

**work**[2] *n., v.* See sign for ACTIVE.

**work hard** *v. phrase.* See sign for WORKAHOLIC.

**work out** *v. phrase.* See sign for EXERCISE[1].

**workaholic** *n.* A person who works long hours, especially obsessively: *The boss is a workaholic—at the job till past midnight.* Same sign used for: **toil, work hard, working.**

■ [**work** formed with a repeated circular movement] Bring the heel of the right *A hand,* palm facing forward, in a double circular movement down across the back of the left *S hand* held in front of the chest.

**working** *adj.* See sign for WORKAHOLIC.

**workshop** *n.* A small group of people that meets to study, learn skills, or work together: *to attend a workshop in advanced ASL.*

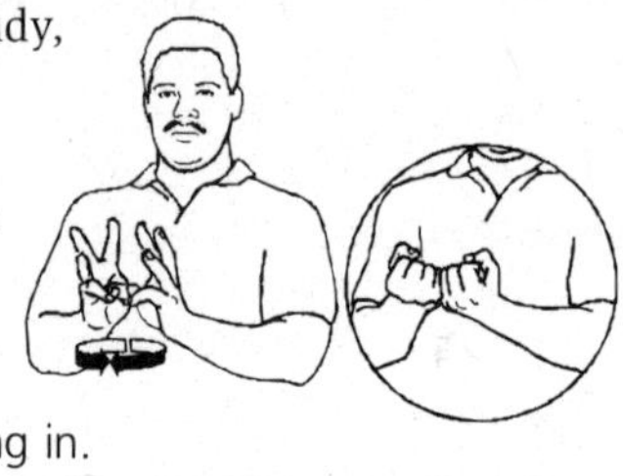

■ [Abbreviation **w-s**] Beginning with the thumbs of both *W hands* together in front of the chest, palms facing each other, move the hands outward in arcs while closing into *S hands,* ending with the little fingers of both *S hands* touching in front of the body, palms facing in.

**world** *n.* **1.** The planet Earth: *traveled around the world.* **2.** All or most of the people on the Earth; the public: *The world will hear of your accomplishments.* **3.** The universe: *The world is vast.*

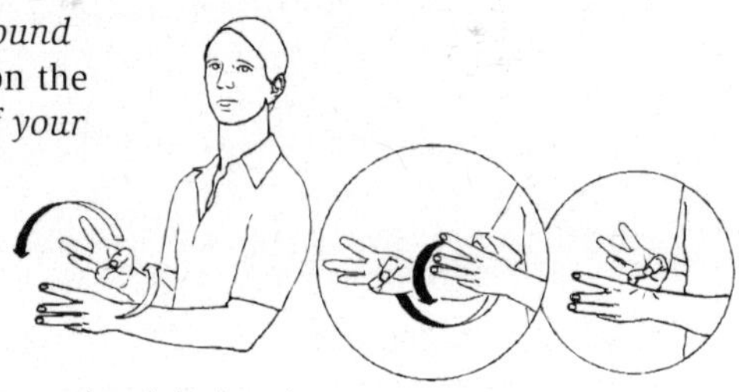

■ [Initialized sign indicating the movement of the Earth around the sun] Beginning with both *W hands* in front of the body, palms facing each other, move the right hand upward and forward in an arc as the left hand moves back and upward around the right hand, exchanging positions.

**World Wide Web** (www) *n. phrase.* See sign for NETWORK.

**worry** *v.* See signs for CONCERN[1], TROUBLE[1].

**worse** *adj.* Bad or ill to a greater degree than others: *a worse cold than ever before.* Related form: **worsen** *v.*

■ Beginning with both *V hands* in front of each shoulder, palms facing in, push the hands past each other in front of the chest, brushing the little-finger side of the right hand across the index-finger side of the left hand.

**worship**[1] *n.* **1.** A ceremony of reverent homage to God: *to attend worship every Sunday.* —*v.* **2.** To pay homage to God: *The family worshiped together regularly.* Same sign used for: **adore, beg, please, pray.**

- [Similar to sign for **amen** except formed with a double movement] With the right fingers cupped over the left *A hand,* bring the hands downward and in toward the chest with a double movement.

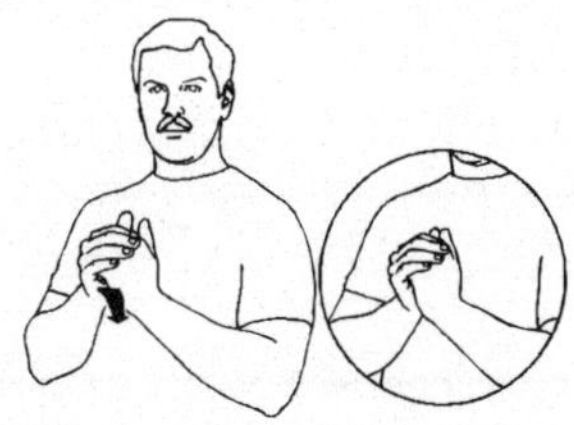

**worship**[2] *v.* See sign for HAIL[2].

**worth** *n., prep.* See signs for COST[2], IMPORTANT.

**wound** *v., n.* See signs for HURT[1,2].

**wow** *interj.* (Used to indicate surprise, wonder, amazement, etc.)

- [Natural gesture] Swing the right *5 hand,* palm facing in, limply up and down in front of the right side of the body.

**wrench** *n.* A tool used for twisting a pipe, nut, etc.: *The plumber used a pipe wrench to fix the leak.* Same sign used for: **maintenance.**

- [Shows twisting action of a wrench] With the extended left index finger inserted between the index finger and middle finger of the right *3 hand*, both palms angled in, twist the right hand up and down with a double movement.

**wristwatch** *n.* See sign for WATCH[1].

**write** *v.* **1.** To make letters, words, etc., as on paper: *to write your name.* **2.** To communicate with in writing: *wrote me a postcard from London.* **3.** To be the author of: *wrote a wonderful short story.* Related form: **written** *adj.* Same sign used for: **edit, pen, pencil, scribble.**

- [Mime writing on paper] Bring the fingers of the right *modified X hand,* palm facing left, with a wiggly movement from the heel to the fingers of the left *open hand* held in front of the body, palm facing up.

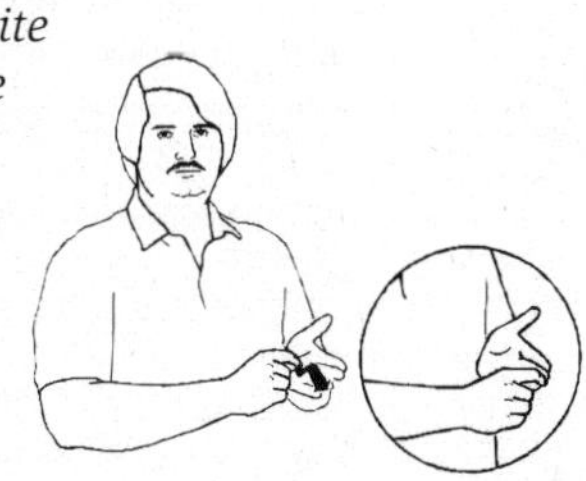

**wrong** *adj.* Not correct; in error: *the wrong answer.* Same sign used for: **incorrect.**

- Place the middle fingers of the right *Y hand,* palm facing in, against the chin with a deliberate movement.

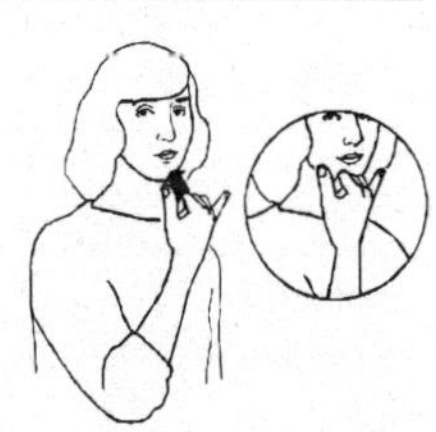

**xylophone** *n.* A musical instrument consisting of a series of wooden bars of graduated lengths played by striking with wooden hammers held in each hand: *You usually play the xylophone standing up.*

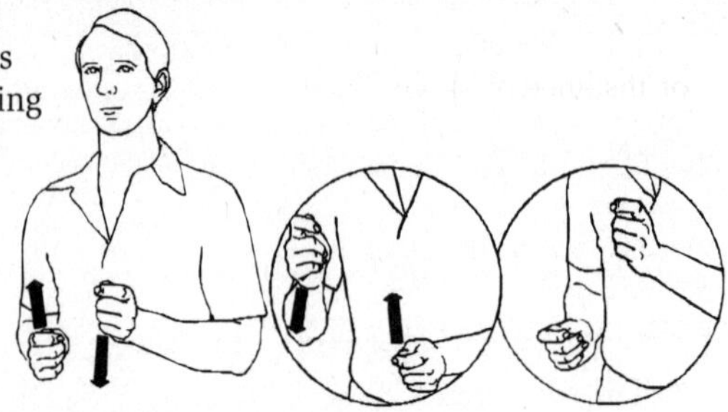

■ [Mime playing a xylophone] Beginning with the palms of both *modified X hands* facing each other in front of each side of the body, move the hands up and down with an alternating movement.

**yawn** *v.* **1.** To open the mouth wide, especially involuntarily, as because of tiredness or boredom: *He yawned during the sermon.* —*n.* **2.** An act or instance of yawning: *He stifled a yawn.*

■ [Natural gesture used to cover the mouth when yawning] Bring the fingers of the right *open hand,* palm facing in and fingers pointing up, back against the mouth with a double movement.

---

**yeah** *adv. Informal.* See sign for YES.

---

**year** *n.* **1.** A period of twelve months, especially as calculated from January through December: *I will buy a car sometime next year.* **2.** Such a twelve-month period calculated from some other point: *The next conference will be held in a year.* **3.** A period of a year or less established for some specified purpose: *the fiscal year; the academic year.*

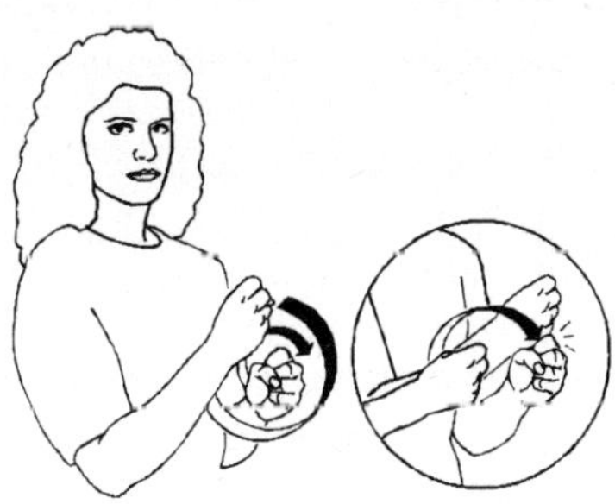

■ [Represents the movement of the Earth around the sun] Beginning with the right *S hand,* palm facing left, over the left *S hand,* palm facing right, move the right hand forward in a complete circle around the left hand while the left hand moves in a smaller circle around the right hand, ending with the little-finger side of the right hand on the thumb side of the left hand.

---

**yearlong** *adj.* See sign for YEAR-ROUND.

---

**yearn** *v.* See sign for HUNGRY.

---

**year-round** *adj.* **1.** Available for use throughout the year: *a year-round resort.* —*adv.* **2.** Throughout the year: *travels year-round.* Same sign used for: **cycle, orbit, yearlong.**

■ [Represents the movement of the Earth around the sun] Beginning with both extended index fingers pointing toward each other in front of the chest, right hand slightly higher than the left hand and both palms facing down, move the right index finger in a complete circle around the left finger.

---

**yell** *v.* See signs for CALL², SCREAM.

---

**yell at** *v. phrase.* See sign for BAWL OUT.

**yellow** *adj.* Having the color of the sun: *a yellow flower.*

■ [Initialized sign] Move the right *Y hand,* palm facing left, with a twisting double movement.

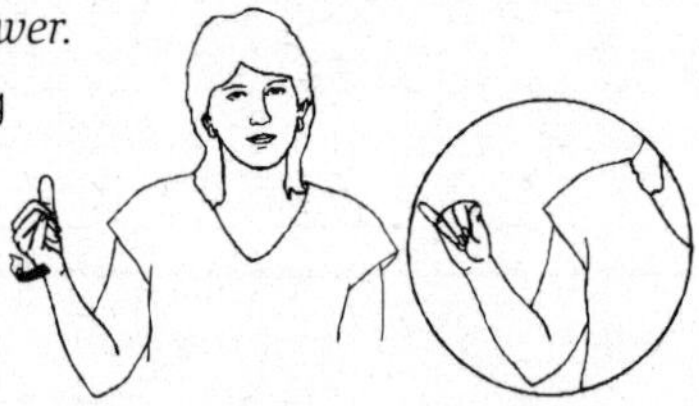

**yes** *adv.* (Used to show consent, affirmation, agreement, etc.): *Yes, I will go.* Same sign used for: **yeah** *(informal).*

■ [Represents a person's head nodding in approval] Move the right *S hand,* palm facing forward, up and down in front of the right shoulder by bending the wrist with a repeated movement.

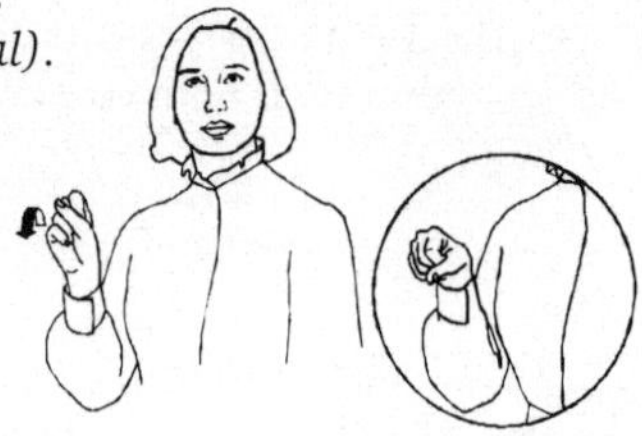

**yesterday** *n.* **1.** The day before today: *Yesterday was a cold day.* **2.** A period of time in the immediate past: *It seems like yesterday that we were young.* —*adv.* **3.** On the day before today: *I tried to call you yesterday.* **4.** In the immediate past: *Yesterday, things were less expensive.*

■ [Initialized sign moving back into the past] Move the thumb of the right *Y hand,* palm facing forward, from the right side of the chin up to the right cheek.

**yet**[1] *adv.* **1.** So far: *The package hasn't arrived yet.* **2.** At the present time; now: *Are we there yet?*

■ [The hand gestures back into the past] Bend the wrist of the right *open hand,* palm facing back and fingers pointing down, back with a double movement near the right side of the waist.

**yet**[2] *adv.* See sign for STILL[1].

**yield** *v.* See signs for GIVE UP, LOOK OUT.

**you** *pron.* (Used to designate a single person being addressed): *I want you to handle this problem alone.*

■ [Point toward the referent] Point the extended right index finger, palm facing down, toward the person being talked to.

**young** *adj.* Being in the early part of life or growth; not old: *a young boy and his older brother.* Same sign used for: **youth.**

- [Represents bringing up youthful feelings in the body] Beginning with the fingers of both *bent hands* on each side of the chest, palms facing in, brush the fingers upward with a double movement.

**your** *pron.* The possessive form of YOU used as an adjective: *your home.* Related form: **yours** *pron.*

- [The hand moves toward the referent] Push the palm of the right *open hand,* palm facing forward and fingers pointing up, toward the person being talked to.

**You're too late.** See sign for MISS[2].

**yourself** *pron.* **1.** A reflexive form of YOU, used as an object: *Ask yourself if you really want to resign.* **2.** (Used as an intensifier): *You said it yourself!* **3.** Oneself: *Do it yourself.*

- [This hand shape is used for reflexive pronouns and moves toward the referent] Push the extended thumb of the right *10 hand,* palm facing left, forward with a double movement toward the person being talked to.

**youth** *n.* See sign for YOUNG.

**zap** *v. Informal* **1.** To destroy with sudden speed: *The insect spray zapped the bugs.* —*n.* **2.** A forceful, sudden, and destructive attack: *With one zap, the older boy knocked the little one over.* Same sign used for: **got you!** or **gotcha!**

■ [The fingers mime zapping something] Beginning with the right *H hand* in front of the chest, palm facing forward and fingers pointing up, move the fingers forward and then back again with a quick movement.

**zeal** *n.* Enthusiastic fervor: *The team approached basketball practice with zeal.* Same sign used for: **ambitious, anxious, aspiration, aspire, eager, earnest, enthusiastic, motivation, motive.**

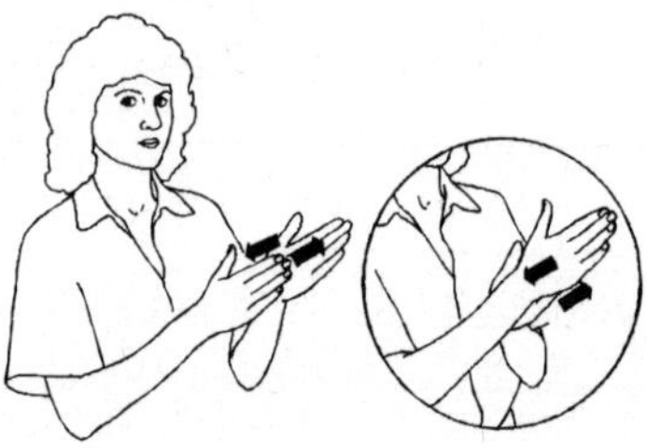

■ [Rubbing the hands together in eagerness] Rub the palms of both *open hands,* palms facing each other, back and forth against each other with a double alternating movement.

**zero** *n.* See sign for NONE².

**zip** *v.* Same sign as for ZIPPER but formed with a single movement.

**zipper** *n.* A sliding fastener for clothing, luggage, etc., consisting of two flexible tracks of teeth or coils that can be interlocked or separated by a slide: *This zipper opens easily.*

■ [Mime pulling a zipper up and down] With the right *modified X hand,* palm facing down, move the right hand up and down with a double movement in front of the chest.

**zoom**¹ *v.* To move quickly, especially away: *The airplane zoomed off beyond the clouds.* Same sign used for: **set off, split.**

■ [Represents something getting smaller as it goes off into the distance] Beginning with the thumb of the right *G hand,* palm facing forward, at the base of the extended left index finger held in front of the chest, palm facing down and finger pointing right, move the right thumb across the length of the left index finger, closing the right index finger and thumb together as the hand moves to the right.

**zoom**² *v.* See sign for SHOOT UP.

# Days of the Week

The days of the weeks are generally formed with the palm facing in, although the palm may be turned out for **Monday, Wednesday, Friday,** and **Saturday,** if desired. Except for **Sunday,** these signs are initialized signs. In the case of **Thursday,** an *H hand* is used instead of a *T hand* in order to distinguish it from **Tuesday.**

*Sunday*

*Monday*

*Tuesday*

*Wednesday*

*Thursday*

*Friday*

*Saturday*

# Colors

The following are signs used for colors in American Sign Language. Many of the signs are initialized, that is, the sign uses the handshape of the first letter of the English word for the color. Although color in American Sign Language can be signed either before or after the noun, generally it is signed after the noun. So in describing "brown hair," the signer would more likely sign *hair, brown* although signing *brown hair* would be equally correct.

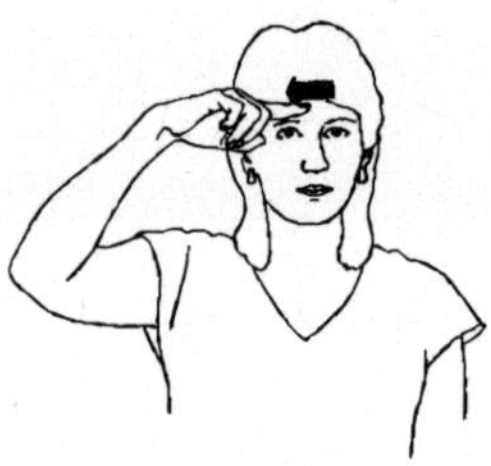

*black*

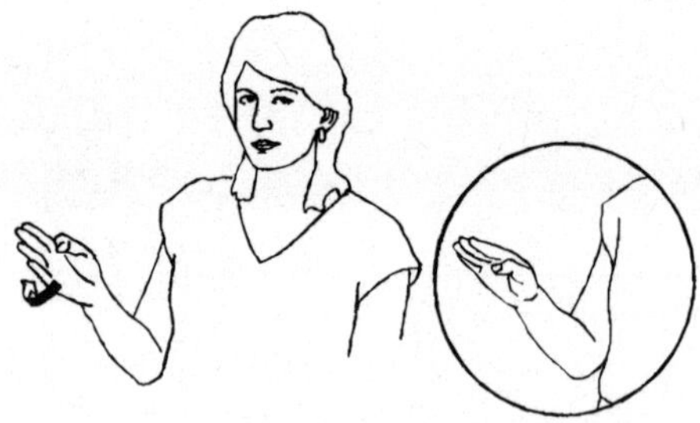

*blue*

*brown*

*gray*

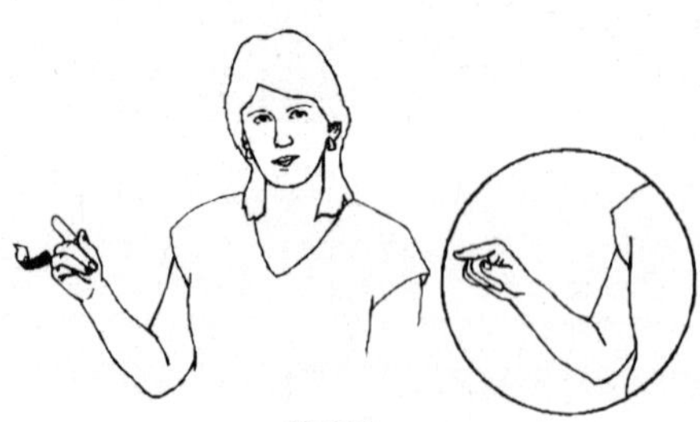

*green*

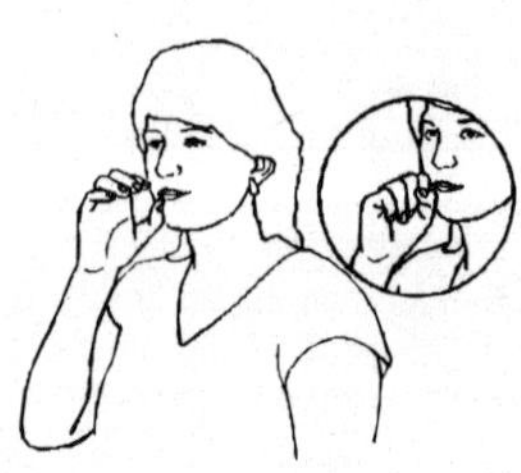

*orange*

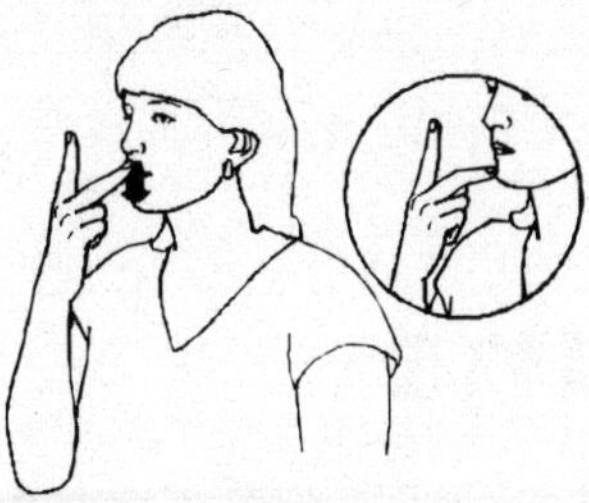

*pink*

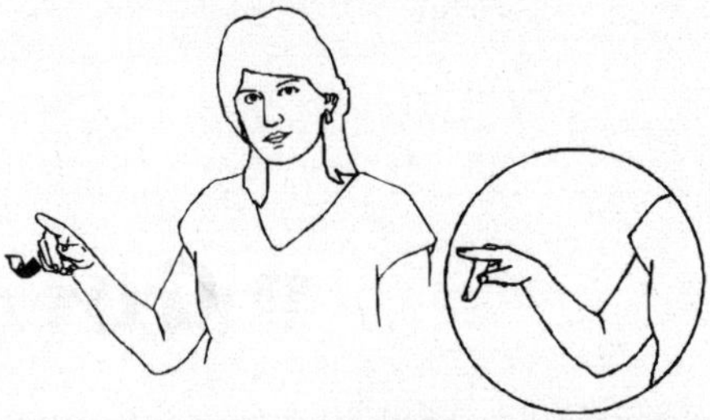

*purple*

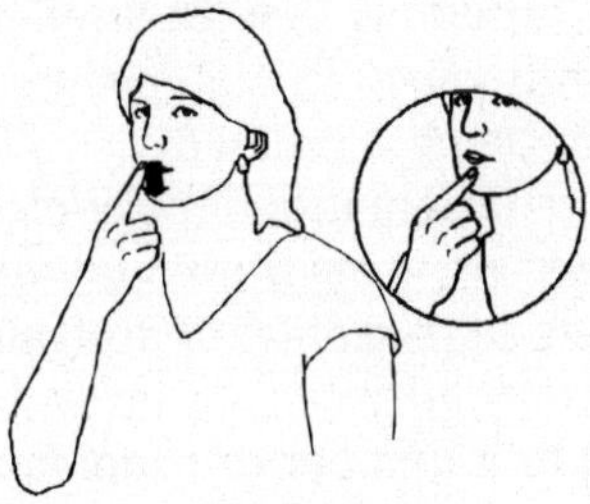

*red*

*tan*

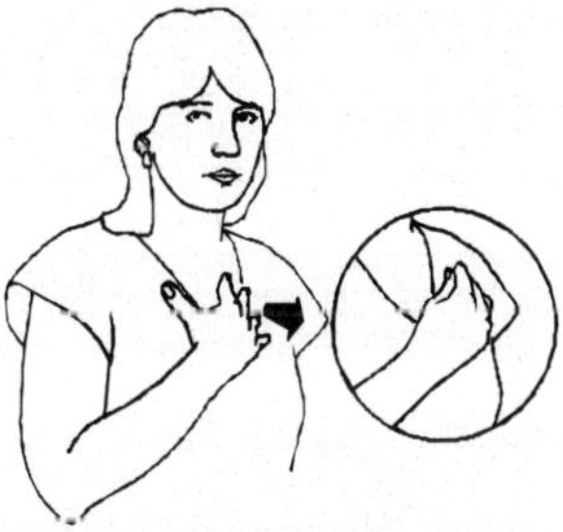

*white*

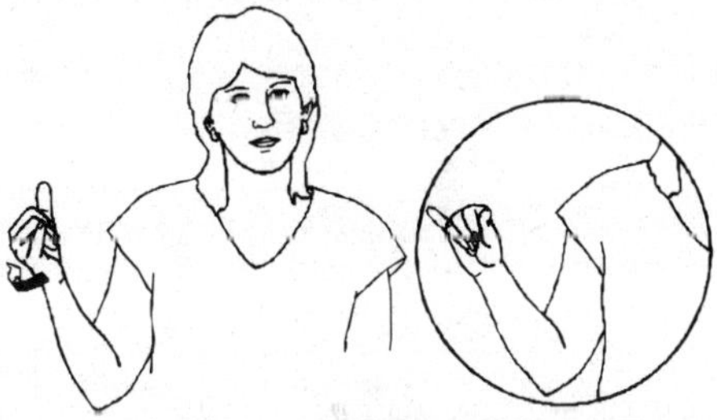

*yellow*

# Pronouns

The following are the preferred signs for pronouns that are used when referring to people or things that are within view of the conversants. The signs are directed toward the referent being discussed.

In American Sign Language, pronoun representation for people or things that are not in view is accomplished by using a pointing or *indexing* strategy. Basically, the signer sets up a marker, a designated location, to refer to a person or object. The signer can set up and identify multiple markers when referring to a number of people or objects. Then the signer can index toward the appropriate location to refer to a particular person or object. The established location for a referent should change only if the person or object referred to changes position and if all communicators are aware of the change.

## Personal Pronouns

*I, me*

*you (singular)*

*he, she, him, her, it*

*we*

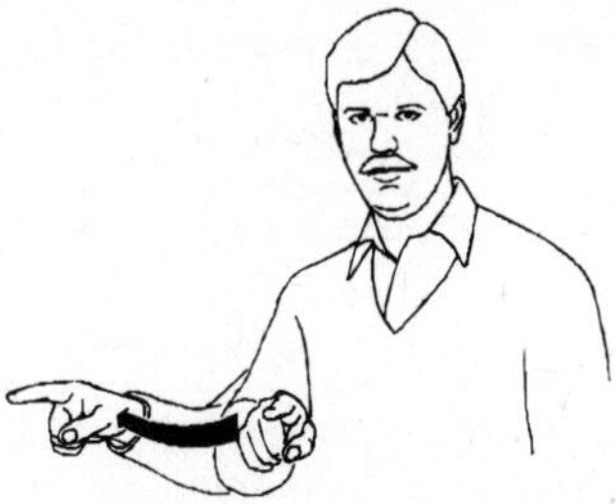

*you (plural)*

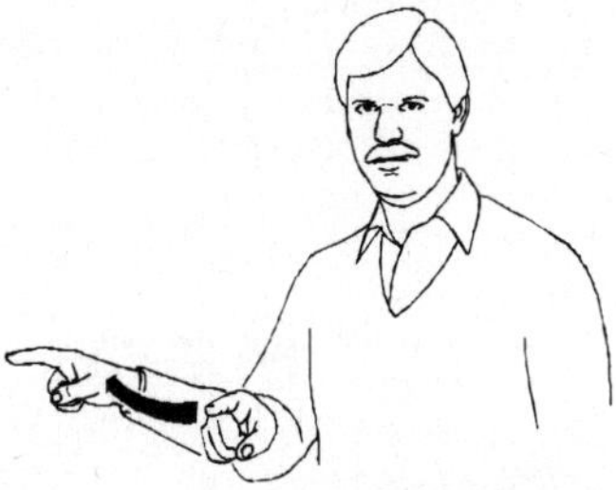

*they, them*

*us*

## Possessive Pronouns

*my, mine*

*your, yours (singular)*

*her, hers, his, its*

*our, ours*

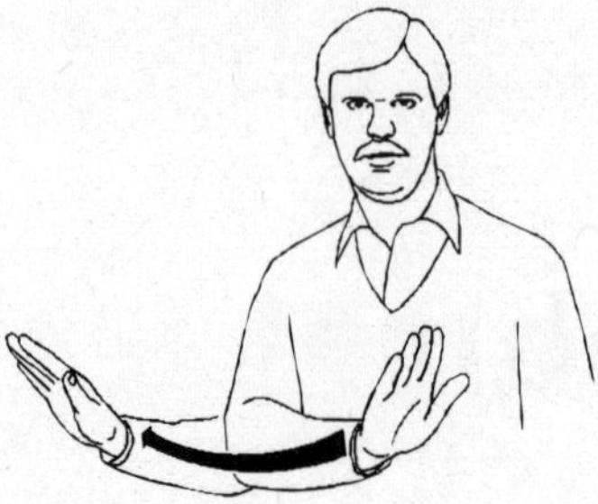

*your, yours (plural)*

*their, theirs*

## Reflexive Pronouns

*myself*

*yourself*

*herself, himself, itself*

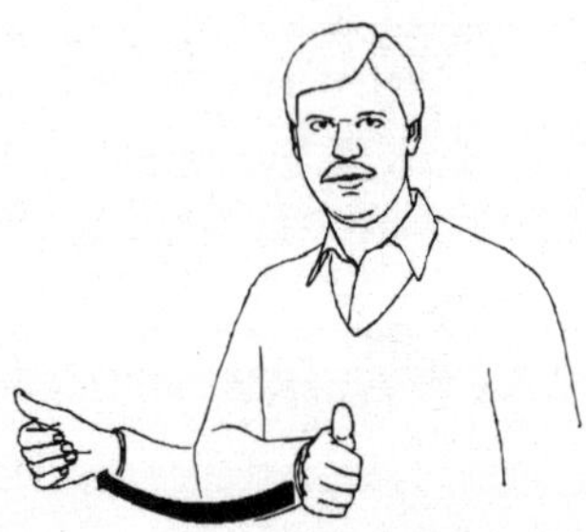

*yourselves*

*ourselves*

*themselves*

# Geographical References

Until recently, the signs Americans used for various countries have been somewhat iconic in that they hint at some characteristic of the people or activities of that country. These signs for countries were developed by Deaf Americans beginning in the 17th century, and their use spread nationwide as the country grew and Deaf people moved around and attended national meetings.

In recent years, as Deaf people have participated in international forums, they have begun to assimilate the signs that Deaf people from other countries use to refer to themselves. These signs are now becoming the preferred signs to use in America. However, these preferred country signs are not yet being used by all Deaf people, especially older Deaf Americans and those living in rural areas.

The following section of geographical locations presents both the traditional signs and the signs used by natives of the countries. In the spirit of "calling people by the name they prefer," those signs are listed first.

**Africa**[1] *n.* A continent south of Europe: *living in Zaire in west central Africa.* Related form: **African** *adj., n.*

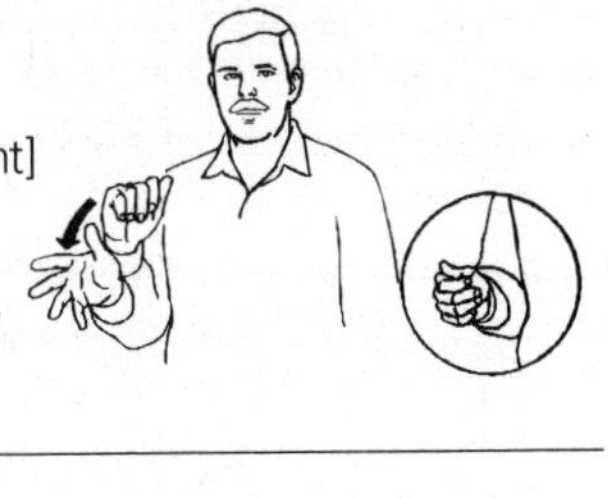

- [Initialized sign showing the shape of the African continent] Move the right *A hand,* palm facing forward, from in front of the right shoulder to the right and downward while opening into a *5 hand* and closing into an *A hand* again in front of the right side of the body.

**Africa**[2] *n.* (alternate form) Related form: **African** *adj., n.*

- [Initialized sign] Move the thumb of the right *A hand,* palm facing left, in a circle in front of the nose, ending with the thumb tip on the nose.

**Alaska**[1] *n.* A state of the United States in the northwestern part of North America: *Alaska is the biggest state.*

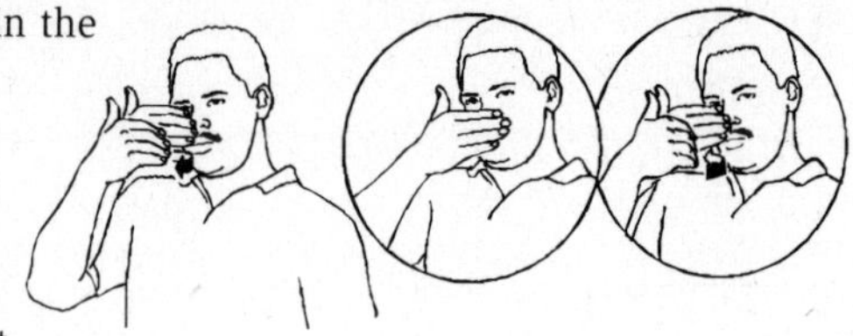

- Beginning with the fingers of the right *bent hand* in front of the nose, palm facing in, bend the right fingers from side to side with a repeated movement, brushing the nose each time.

---

**Alaska**[2] *n.* (alternate sign)

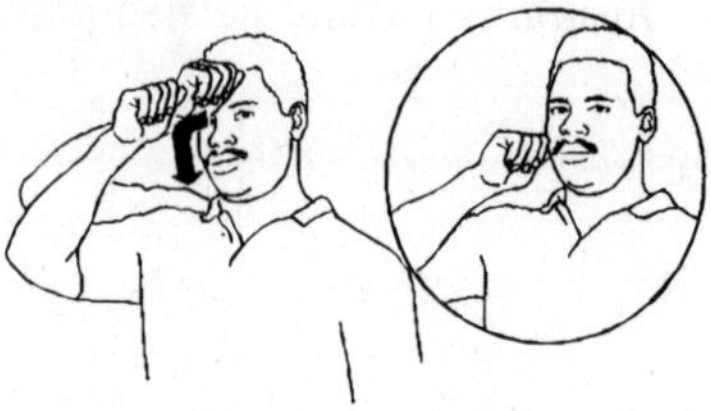

- [Initialized sign] Beginning with the thumb of the right *A hand* touching the forehead, palm facing left, move the hand forward a short distance and then down, ending with the thumb touching the right side of the chin.

---

**America** *n.* The lands of the Western Hemisphere: *North America.*; the United States: *50 states in the United States.* Related form: **American** *adj., n.*

- With the fingers of both hands loosely entwined, palms facing in, move the hands in circle in front of the chest.

---

**Arizona** *n.* A state in the southwestern United States: *The Hopi live in Arizona.*

- [Initialized sign similar to sign for **dry**] Move the thumb of the right *A hand,* palm facing left, in an arc from the right side of the chin to the left side of the chin.

---

**Asia** *n.* The largest continent, located in the Eastern Hemisphere: *India is in southern Asia.* Related form: **Asian** *adj., n.*

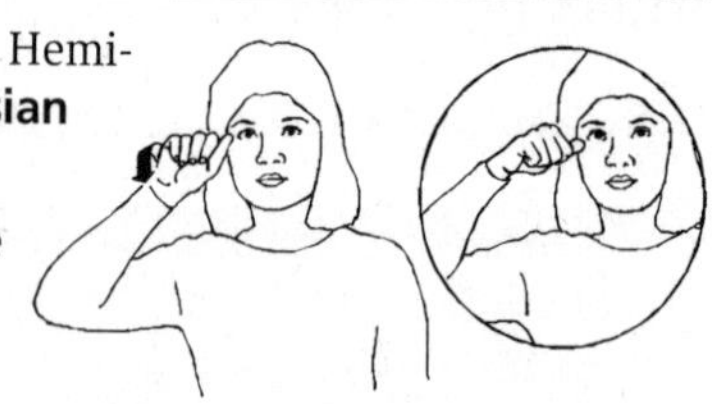

- [Initialized sign similar to sign for **China**[2]] With the thumb of the right *A hand,* palm facing out, near the outside corner of the right eye, twist the hand forward with a double movement.

---

**Australia**[1] *n.* A continent southeast of Asia, or a country consisting chiefly of this continent: *Canberra is the capital of Australia.* Related forms: **Australian** *adj., n.*; **Aussie** *n. Informal.*

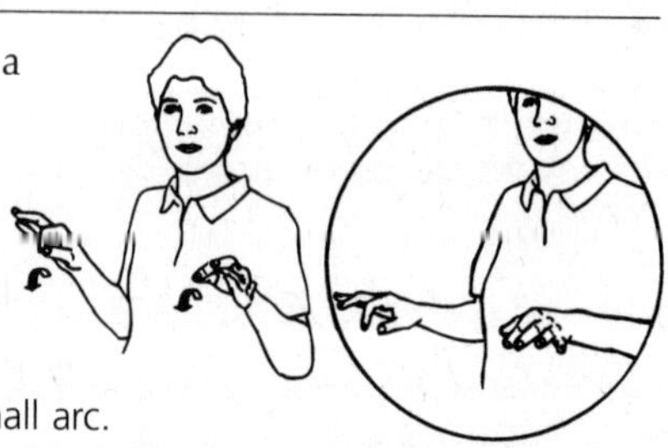

- [Mimics a kangaroo's jump] Beginning with both *F hands* in front of the body, palms facing down, move the hands forward in a small arc.

**Australia**[2] *n.* (alternate sign) Related form: **Australian** *adj., n.*; **Aussie** *n. Informal.*

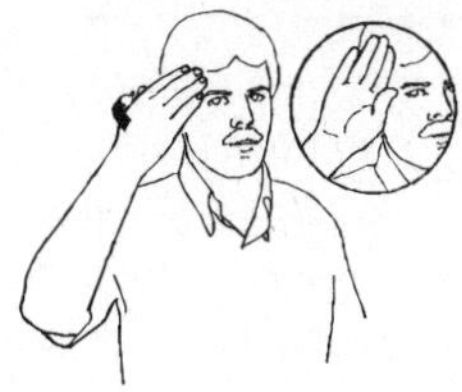

- Beginning with the fingers of the right *B hand* touching the right side of the forehead, palm facing in, flip the hand over, bringing the back of the right hand against the forehead.

**Austria** *n.* A republic in eastern Europe: *The capital of Austria is Vienna.* Related form: **Austrian** *adj., n.*

- [Design on the Austrian flag] With the wrists crossed, place the index-finger sides of both *X hands* on the chest near the opposite shoulder, palms facing in.

**Belgium**[1] *n.* A country in northwestern Europe: *The capital of Belgium is Brussels.*

- [Initialized sign] Move the index-finger side of the right *B hand,* palm facing left, from the left shoulder downward to the right hip.

**Belgium**[2] *n.* (alternate sign)

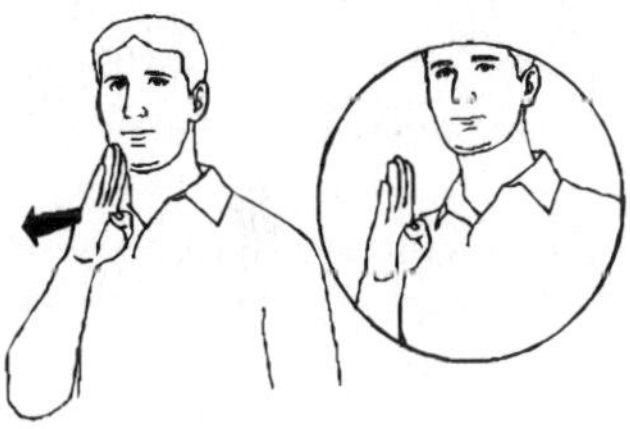

- [Initialized sign] Beginning with the index finger of the right *B hand* touching the right side of the chin, palm facing left and fingers pointing up, move the hand forward a short distance.

**Britain** *n.* See sign for ENGLAND. Related form: **British** *adj., n.*

**California** *n.* A large state on the west coast of the United States: *to visit Hollywood in California.*

- [Shows a gold earring, referring to the gold rush in California] Move the bent middle finger of the right *5 hand* from near the right ear, palm facing left, outward to the right with a wiggling movement.

**Canada** *n.* A country in the northern part of North America: *English and French are spoken in Canada.* Related form: **Canadian** *adj., n.*

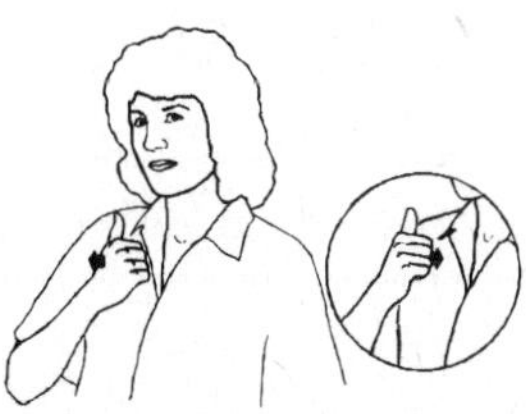

- Tap the palm side of the right *A hand,* thumb pointing up, against the right side of the chest with a double movement.

**China**[1] *n.* A large country in eastern Asia: *Taipei is the capital of the Republic of China.* Related form: **Chinese** *adj., n.*

■ [Shape of Chinese military uniforms] Move the extended right index finger, palm facing in, from the left to the right side of the chest and then straight down.

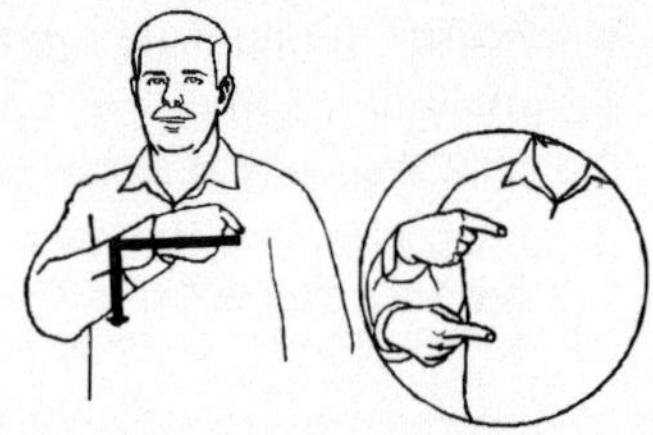

**China**[2] *n.* (alternate sign, sometimes considered offensive) Related form: **Chinese** *n., adj.*

■ [Points to characteristic shape of an Asian person's eyes] With the extended right index finger touching near the corner of the right eye, palm facing down, twist the hand forward, ending with the palm facing back.

**Czechoslovakia** *n.* A former republic in central Europe: *looked forward to a trip to Czechoslovakia.* Related form: **Czech** *adj., n.*

■ [Initialized sign] Move the right *C hand,* palm facing left, from the left shoulder diagonally down to the right side of the waist.

**Czech Republic** *n.* A republic in central Europe: *The capital of the Czech Republic is Prague.* Related form: **Czech** *adj., n.*

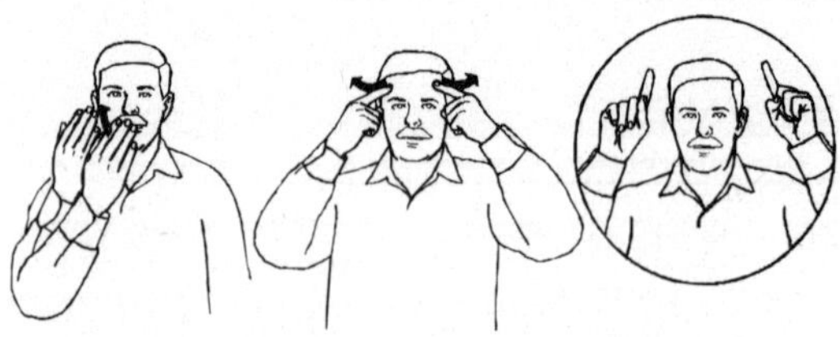

■ Move the fingers of the right *open hand,* palm facing in and fingers pointing up, from the mouth upward to in front of the right cheek. Then, beginning with both extended index fingers pointing to each side of the forehead, palms facing in, twist the hands forward and outward, ending with the palms facing forward.

**Delaware** *n.* An eastern state: *to move to Delaware when you retire.*

■ [Initialized sign showing that Delaware was the first state] Beginning with the right *D hand* in front of the right shoulder, palm facing forward and index finger pointing up, move the hand upward while twisting the wrist in to the left.

**Denmark**[1] *n.* A country in northern European: *Shakespeare's* Hamlet *takes place in Denmark.* Related form: **Danish** *adj., n.*

■ [Represents the ships for which the seafaring Danish are known] Move the right *3 hand,* palm facing in, from left to right in a wavy movement in front of the chest.

**Denmark**[2] *n.* (alternate sign) Related form: **Danish** *adj., n.*

- [Initialized sign] Move the right *D hand,* palm facing left, from in front of the right side of the forehead downward a short distance to the left in front of the face with a double movement.

**Dutch** *adj., n.* See signs for HOLLAND[1,2].

**Egypt**[1] *n.* A country in northeast Africa: *a vacation in Egypt to see the Sphinx and the pyramids.* Related form: **Egyptian** *adj., n.*

- [Represents the insignia on headdresses worn by Pharaohs] Tap the back of the right *X hand,* palm facing forward, against the center of the forehead with a double movement.

**Egypt**[2] *n.* (alternate form) Related form: **Egyptian** *adj., n.*

- [Reminiscent of Cleopatra's hairstyle] Beginning with the fingers of both *B hands* touching each side of the top of the head, bring the hands downward and outward to in front of each shoulder.

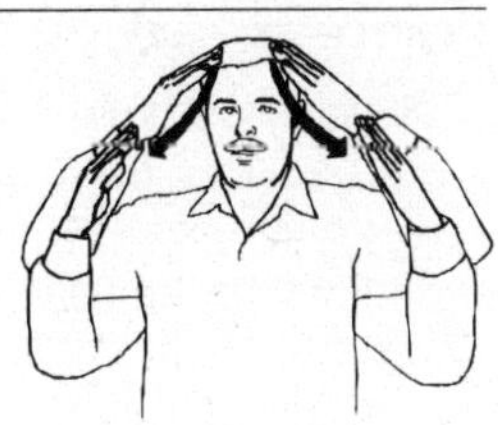

**England** *n.* The southern part of Great Britain: *reading about the royal family in England.* Related form: **English** *n., adj.* Same sign used for: **Britain, British.**

- [Suggests an English gentleman with his hands on his cane] With the right *curved hand* grasping the back of the left *curved hand,* both palms facing down, move the hands forward slightly with a shaking movement.

**Europe** *n.* A continent west of Asia: *planning to travel in Europe for three weeks.* Related form: **European** *adj., n.*

- [Initialized sign] Move the right *E hand,* palm facing back, in a repeated circular movement near the right side of the forehead.

**Finland**[1] *n.* A republic in northern Europe: *The capital of Finland is Helsinki.* Related forms: **Finnish** *adj., n.*; **Finn** *n.*

- Tap the fingertip of the right *X hand,* palm facing in, against the chin with a double movement.

**Finland**[2] *n.* (alternate sign) Related form: **Finnish** *adj., n.*; **Finn** *n.*

- [Initialized sign] Tap the thumb side of the right *F hand* against the center of the forehead with a double movement.

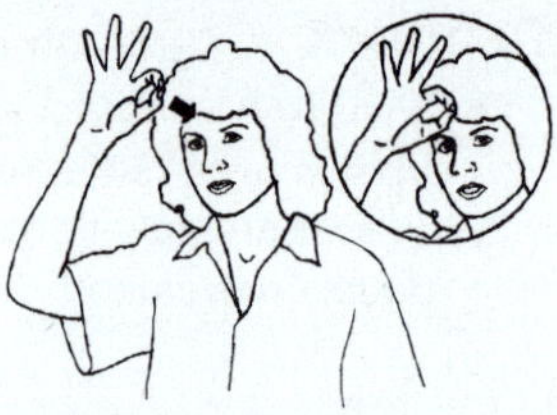

**France**[1] *n.* A country in western Europe: *France is famous for its food and wine.* Related form: **French** *adj., n.*

- [Initialized sign] Beginning with the right *F hand* near the right side of the head, palm facing back, twist the hand quickly forward.

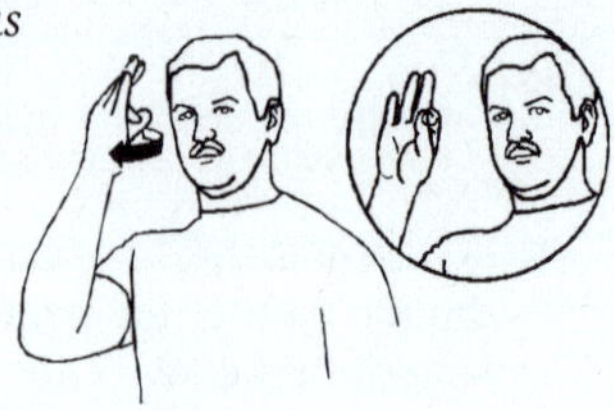

**France**[2] *n.* (alternate sign) Related form: **French** *adj., n.*

- [Initialized sign] Beginning with the index-finger side of the right *F hand,* palm facing down, touching the left side of the chest, twist the hand forward, ending with the palm facing in.

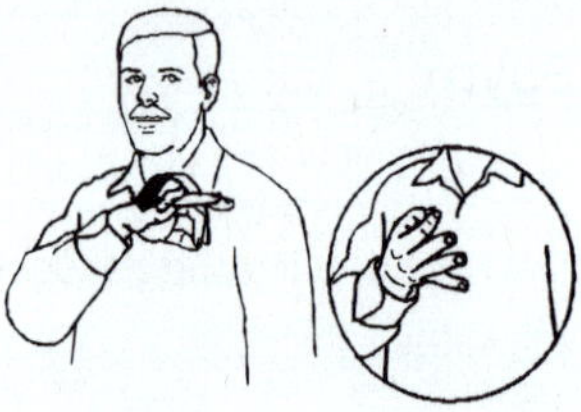

**Germany**[1] *n.* A republic in central Europe: *East and West Germany were reunited in 1990.* Related form: **German** *adj., n.*

- [Represents the raised insignia on a German helmet] Bring the back of the right *1 hand,* palm facing forward, against the center of the forehead.

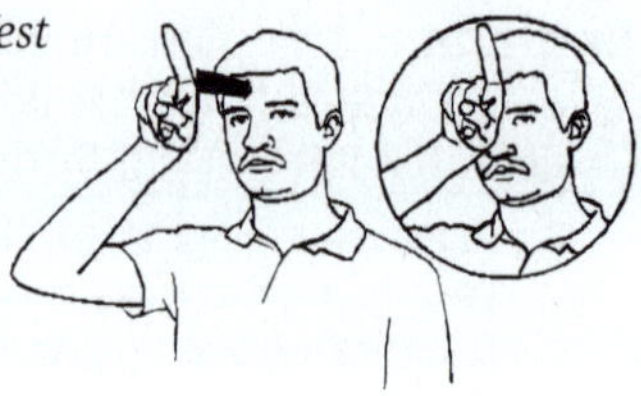

**Germany**[2] *n.* (alternate sign) Related form: **German** *adj., n.*

- [Represents the eagle on the German insignia] Beginning with right *A hand* holding the thumb of the left *A hand* in front of the chest, both palms facing in, quickly flick the fingers of both hands outward, ending with *5 hands.*

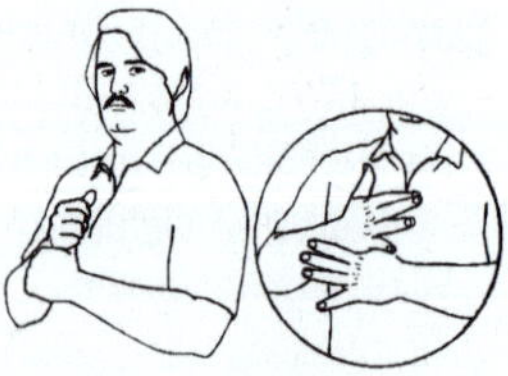

**Germany**[3] *n.* (alternate sign) Related form: **German** *adj., n.*

- [Represents the eagle on the German insignia] With the little-finger side of the right *5 hand* at the base of the thumb and index finger of the left *5 hand,* both palms angled in, wiggle the fingers of both hands with a repeated movement.

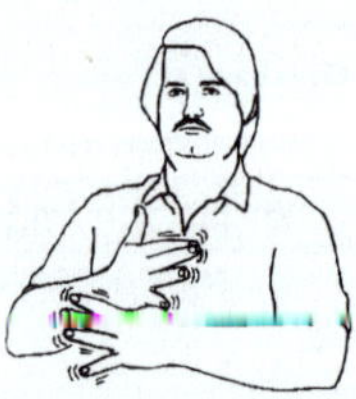

**Great Britain** *n.* See sign for UNITED KINGDOM.

**Greece**[1] *n.* A European country in the Balkan Peninsula: *Many tourists travel to see the ruins in ancient Greece.* Related forms: **Grecian, Greek** *adj., n.*

■ Cross the extended index fingers of both hands, fingers angled downward and palms facing in, in front of the lower chest.

**Greece**[2] *n.* (alternate sign) Related forms: **Grecian** *adj.* **Greek** *n., adj.*

■ [Initialized sign indicating a Grecian nose] Move the index-finger side of the right *G hand,* palm facing left and fingers pointing up, downward in front of the forehead and nose with a double movement.

**Hawaii**[1] *n.* A state of the United States located in the North Pacific: *Do they really dance the hula in Hawaii?* Related form: **Hawaiian** *adj., n.*

■ [Initialized sign] Move the fingers of the right *H hand,* palm facing in, around the face with a circular movement.

**Hawaii**[2] *n.* (alternate sign) Related form: **Hawaiian** *adj., n.*

■ [Mime doing a hula dance] Beginning with the left *open hand* somewhat to the left side of the body and the right *open hand* in front of the left side of the body, both palms facing down and fingers pointing left, move the hands upward while bending the fingers down with a swaying movement. Repeat the same movement from the right side of the body.

**Hispanic** *adj., n.* See signs for MEXICO, SPAIN[2,3].

**Holland**[1] *n.* A country in western Europe, on the North Sea: *Holland is famous for its tulips.* Same sign used for: **Dutch, the Netherlands.**

■ [Shape of a traditional Dutch hat] Beginning with the thumb of the right *Y hand* on the forehead, palm facing left, move the right hand forward in an arc.

**Holland**[2] *n.* (alternate sign) Same sign used for: **Dutch, the Netherlands.**

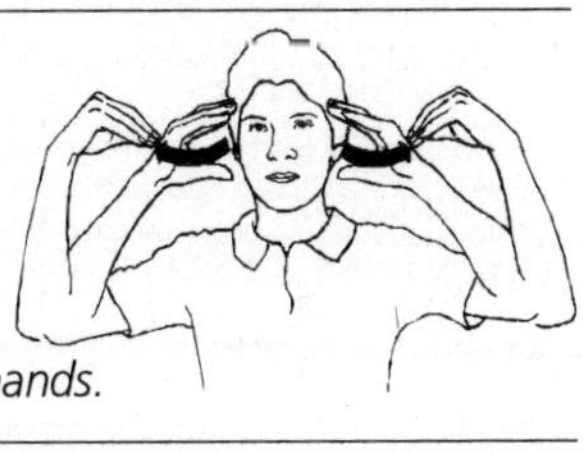

■ [Shape of a Dutch hat] Beginning with the fingertips of both *C hands* touching each side of the head, palms facing each other, bring the hands outward to each side while closing the fingers, forming *flattened O hands.*

**Hungary** *n.* A republic in central Europe: *The capital of Hungary is Budapest.* Related form: **Hungarian** *adj., n.*

■ Move the thumb side of the right *X hand,* palm angled left, from under the nose to the right and downward to the right side of the mouth.

**India**[1] *n.* A country in southern Asia: *looking at the traditional costumes of India.* Related form: **Indian** *adj., n.*

■ [Shows location of spot on Indian woman's forehead] With the extended right *10 thumb* pressed against the center of the forehead, palm facing left, twist the hand downward.

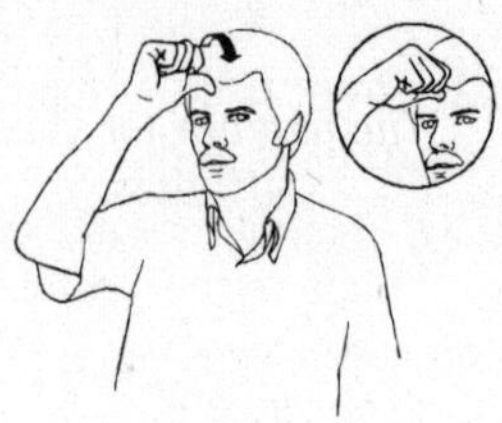

**India**[2] *n.* (alternate sign) Related form: **Indian** *adj., n.*

■ [Shows location of spot on Indian woman's forehead] Flick the extended right *10 thumb* upward and forward on the middle of the forehead with a double movement.

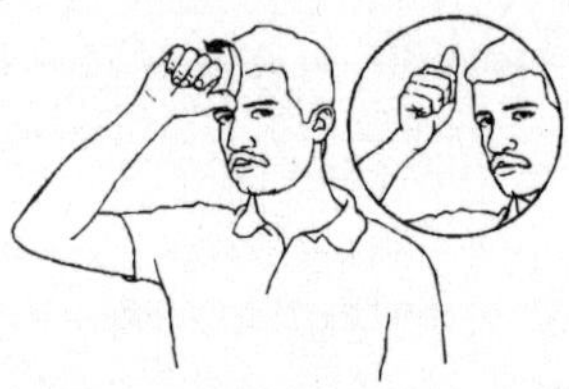

**Indiana** *n.* One of the central states in the United States: *to live in Indiana.*

■ [Initialized sign] Move the right *I hand,* palm facing forward, from in front of the right shoulder outward to the right and then downward to in front of the waist.

**Indonesia** *n.* A country in the Far East, in the Malay Archipelago: *vacationed in the islands of Indonesia.*

■ Beginning with the right *H hand* in front of the body, palm facing in and fingers pointing left, bring the hand with a wavy in-and-out movement to the right.

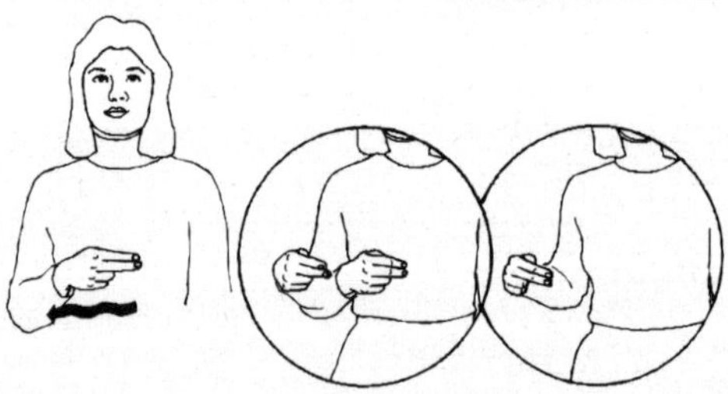

**Italy**[1] *n.* A country in southern Europe: *We ate wonderful pasta dishes in Italy.* Related form: **Italian** *adj., n.*

■ [Shows the shape of the Italian peninsula] Beginning with the right *modified C hand,* palm facing forward, in front of the right side of the body, move the hand downward while pinching the thumb and index finger together.

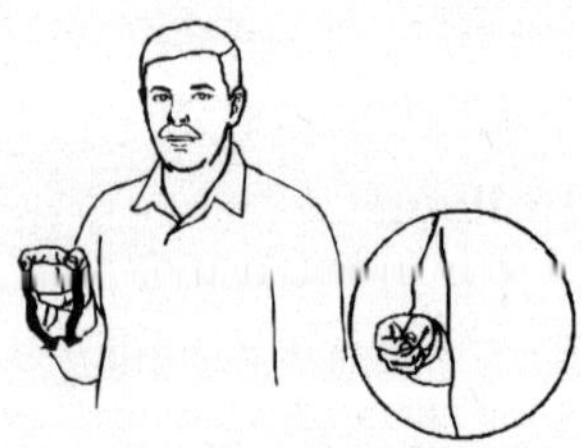

**Italy**[2] *n.* (alternate sign) Related form: **Italian** *adj., n.*

■ [Initialized sign forming a cross on the forehead refering to the center of Catholicism in Italy] Bring the extended little finger of the right *I hand,* palm facing in, first from the forehead downward in front of the face and then from left to right across the forehead.

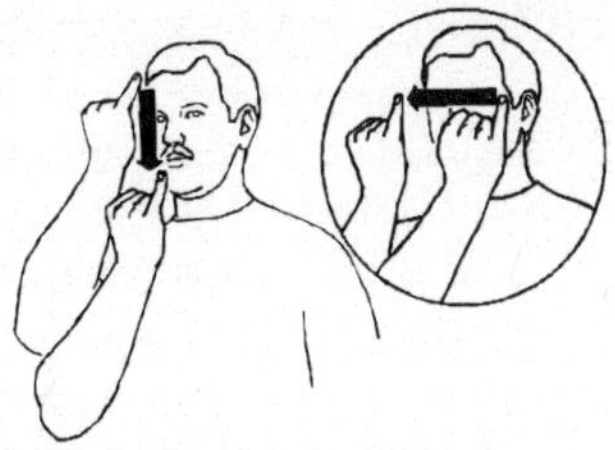

**Japan**[1] *n.* A country in the western Pacific, off the East coast of Asia: *The monitor for your computer was made in Japan.* Related form: **Japanese** *adj., n.*

■ Beginning with the extended fingers of both *G hands* pointing toward each other in front of the body, palms facing in, pull the hands apart to in front of each side of the body while pinching the fingers of the *G hand* open and closed with a repeated movement.

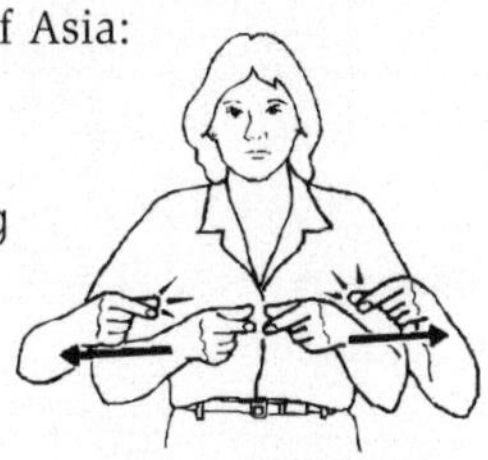

**Japan**[2] *n.* (alternate sign) Related form: **Japanese** *adj., n.*

■ Beginning with both *D hands* near each other in front of the chest, palms angled down, bring the extended index fingers toward each other.

**Japan**[3] *n.* (alternate sign) Related form: **Japanese** *adj., n.*

■ [Initialized sign showing the shape of a Japanese person's eyes] Beginning with the extended little finger of the right *J hand* touching the outside corner of the right eye, twist the hand upward with a double movement.

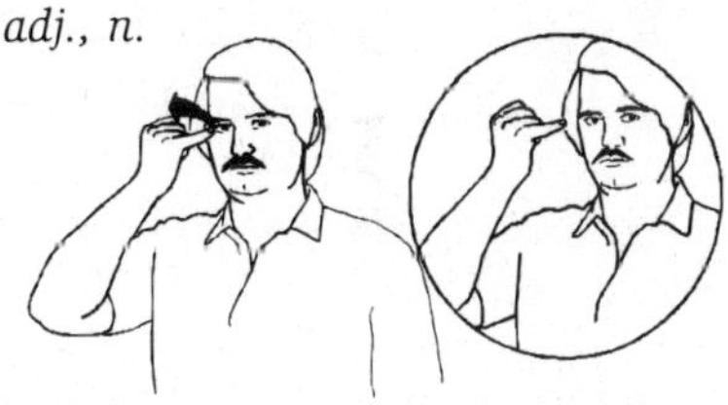

**Korea**[1] *n.* A former country in East Asia now divided into North Korea and South Korea: *diplomatic discussions about unifying Korea.* Related form: **Korean** *adj., n.*

■ [Initialized sign] With the middle finger of the right *K hand* touching near the outer corner of the right eye, palm facing in, twist the hand forward with a double movement.

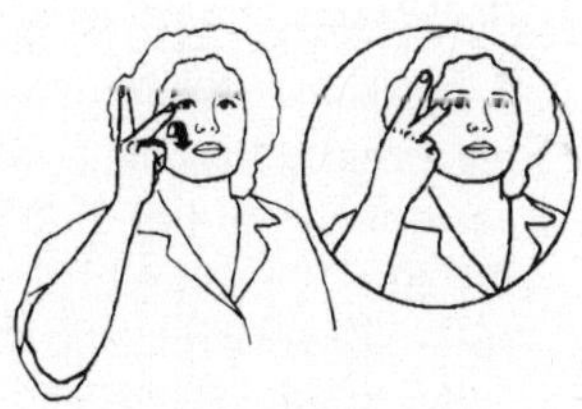

**Korea**[2] *n.* (alternate sign) Related form: **Korean** *adj., n.*

■ [Shows shape of Korean hat] Beginning with the fingertips of both *open hands* touching each side of the head, palms angled down, bring the hands downward and outward in an arc while bending the fingers.

**Latin** *adj., n.* See sign for ROME.

**Malaysia** *n.* A country in southeast Asia: *The capital of Malaysia is Kuala Lumpur.* Related form: **Malaysian** *adj., n.*

■ Beginning with both *open hands* on each side of the head, palms facing each other and fingers pointing up, move the hands up and down with an alternating movement.

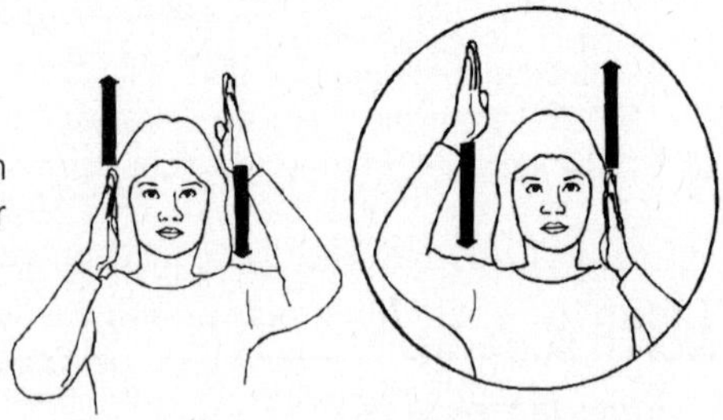

**Mexico**[1] *n.* A country in the southern part of North America, just south of the United States: *Mexico City is the capital of Mexico.* Related form: **Mexican** *n., adj.*

■ [Initialized sign showing location of mustache] Wipe the fingertips of the right *M hand,* palm facing in, downward with a double movement from the right side of the mouth.

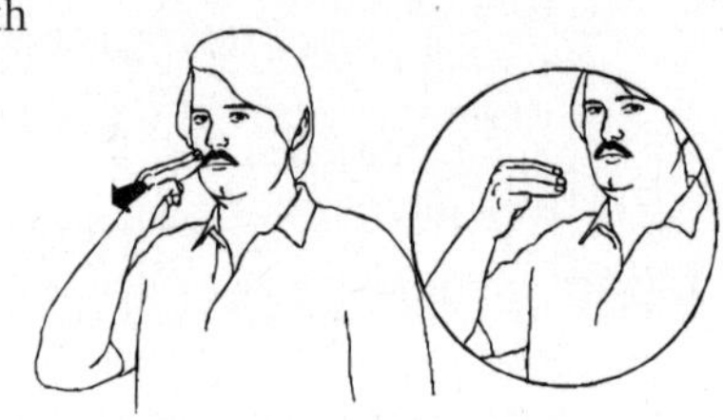

**Mexico**[2] *n.* (alternate sign) Related form: **Mexican** *adj.* Same sign used for: **Hispanic.**

■ [Shows the brim of a Mexican sombrero] Move the right *V hand,* fingers pointing down, from in front of the forehead in an arc to near the right side of the head.

**Mexico**[3] *n.* See signs for SPAIN[2,3].

**Netherlands, the** *n.* See signs for HOLLAND[1,2].

**New England** *n.* An area in the northeastern part of the United States that includes the states of Connecticut, Maine, Massachusetts, New Hampshire, Rhode Island, and Vermont: *to visit New England to see the fall foliage.*

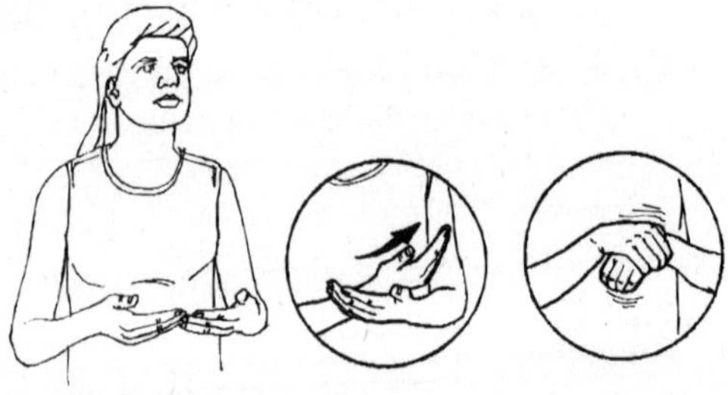

■ [**new** + **England**] Slide the back of the right *curved hand,* palm facing up, from the fingertips to the heel of the upturned left *open hand.* Then, with the right *curved hand* grasping the back of the left *curved hand,* both palms facing down, move the hands forward slightly with a shaky movement.

**New York** *n.* **1.** A state in the northeast United States: *The capital of New York is Albany.* **2.** A city in New York State at the mouth of the Hudson River: *to go to a Broadway play in New York.* Same sign used for: **Manhattan.**

■ Brush the palm side of the right *Y hand,* palm facing down, with a double movement across the palm of the upturned left *open hand.*

**North America** *n.* The northern continent in the Western Hemisphere: *The United States and Canada are in North America.*

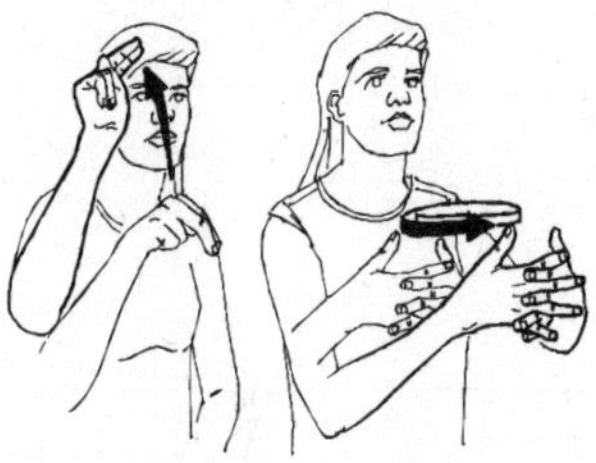

■ [**north** + **America**] Move the right *N hand,* palm facing down, upward in front of the right shoulder. Then, with the fingers of both *5 hands* loosely entwined, palms facing in, move the hands in a circle in front of the chest.

**Norway**[1] *n.* A kingdom in northern Europe; part of the Scandinavian peninsula: *Oslo is the capital of Norway.* Related form: **Norwegian** *adj., n.*

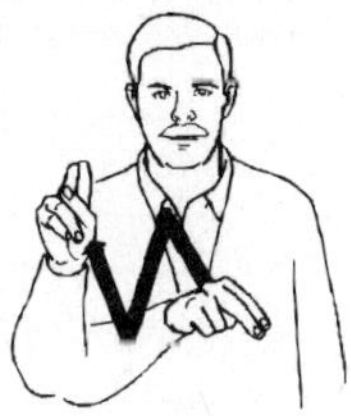

■ [Initialized sign showing the movement of waves in the sea surrounding Norway] Move the right *N hand,* palm facing down, from in front of the left side of the chest in a large up and down movement as the hand moves to the right.

**Norway**[2] *n.* (alternate sign) Related form: **Norwegian** *adj., n.*

■ [Initialized sign] Touch the extended fingers of the right *N hand,* palm facing left, to the right side of the forehead with a double movement.

**Philippines**[1] *n.* A republic in southeast Asia consisting of more than 7,000 islands: *The capital of the Philippines is Manila.* Related forms: **Filipino** or **Pilipino** *n.*; **Philippine** *adj.*

■ [Initialized sign similar to sign for **island**] Move the extended index finger of the right *P hand,* palm facing down, in a circle on the back of the left *open hand* held across the chest, palm facing down and fingers pointing right.

**Philippines**[2] *n.* (alternate sign) Related forms: **Filipino** or **Pilipino** *n.*; **Philippine** *adj.*

■ Move the thumb side of the right *9 hand,* palm facing left, in a circle in front of the face.

**Poland**[1] *n.* A country in eastern Europe: *Poland is on the Baltic Sea.* Related form: **Polish** *adj., n.*

■ Touch the fingertips of the right *curved hand,* palm facing in, first on the left side of the chest and then on the right side of the chest.

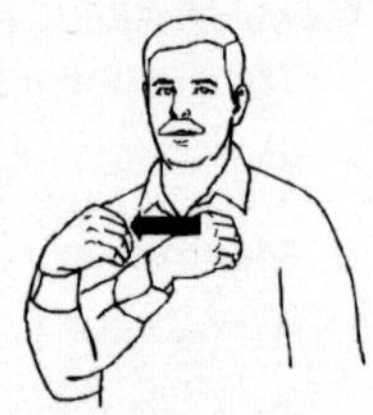

**Poland**[2] *n.* (alternate sign, considered offensive) Related form: **Polish** *adj., n.*

■ Wipe the tip of the extended thumb of the right *10 hand,* palm facing left, upward on the nose with a double movement.

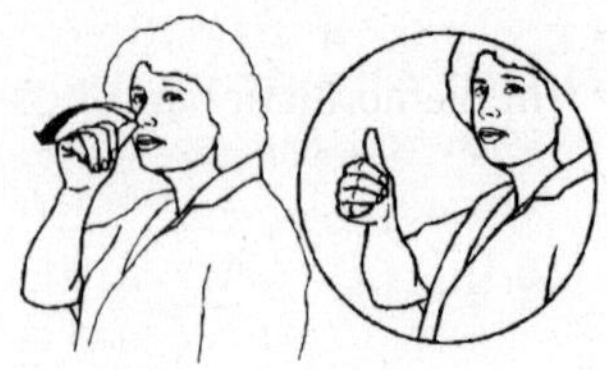

**Portugal**[1] *n.* A country on the west coast of Spain: *Portugal has mild, humid winters.* Related form: **Portuguese** *adj., n.*

■ [Initialized sign similar to sign for **Spain**[2]] Beginning with both *P hands* in front of each shoulder, palms facing in, move the hands toward each other, hooking the index fingers around each other in front of the chest.

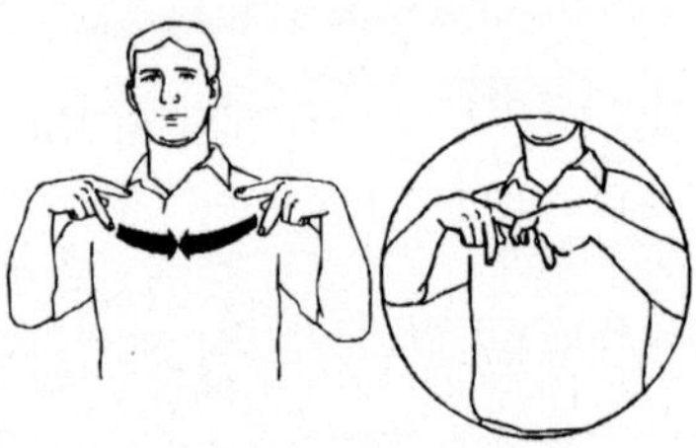

**Portugal**[2] *n.* (alternate sign) Related form: **Portuguese** *adj., n.*

■ [Shows the profile of a person from Portugal] Move the extend right index finger, palm facing in, from the forehead to the chin, following the facial profile.

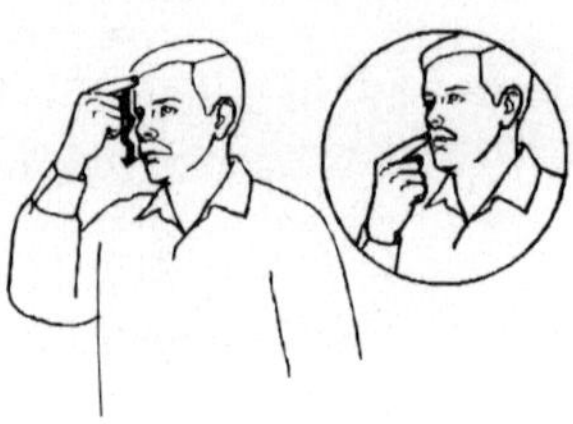

**Romania** *n.* A republic in southeast Europe: *Bucharest is the capital of Romania.* Related form: **Romanian** *adj., n.*

■ Move the fingertips of the right *modified C hand* from the left side of the chest downward at an angle to the right side of the body.

**Russia**[1] *n.* A country in eastern Europe and western and northern Asia: *The Volga River is in Russia.* Related form: **Russian** *adj., n.*

■ Move the side of the extended right index finger, palm facing down and finger pointing left, across the chin from left to right with a double movement.

**Russia**[2] *n.* (alternate sign) Related form: **Russian** *adj., n.* Same sign used for: **Soviet.**

■ [Location of the hands while doing a traditional Russian dance] Tap the index-finger sides of both *open hands,* palms facing down, against each side of the waist with a double movement.

**Scotland**[1] *n.* A division of the United Kingdom in the northern part of Great Britain: *bought a handknit wool sweater in Scotland.* Related forms: **Scotch** *adj., n.* **Scottish** *adj., n.*

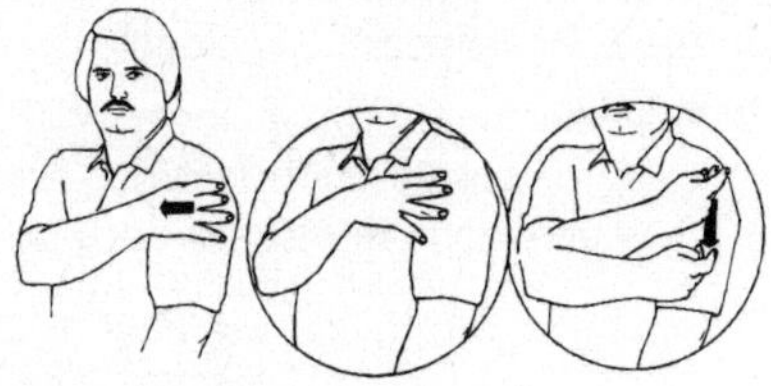

■ [Shows the plaids representative of Scottish kilts] Bring the fingertips of the right *4 hand* from back to front on the left upper arm. Then drag the back of the right fingers downward on the left upper arm.

**Scotland**[2] *n.* (alternate sign) Related forms: **Scotch** *adj., n.*; **Scottish** *adj.,* **Scots** *n.*

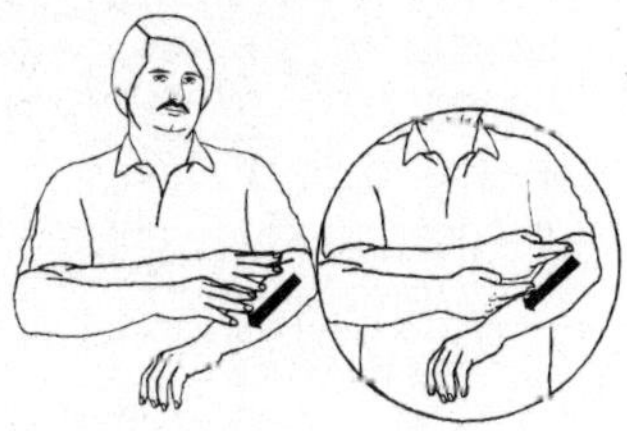

■ [Shows the plaids representative of Scottish kilts] Bring the fingertips of the right *4 hand* down the length of the extended left arm. Then drag the back of the right fingers down the length of the extended left arm.

**Singapore** *n.* A small island country in southeast Asia: *The capital of Singapore is Singapore.*

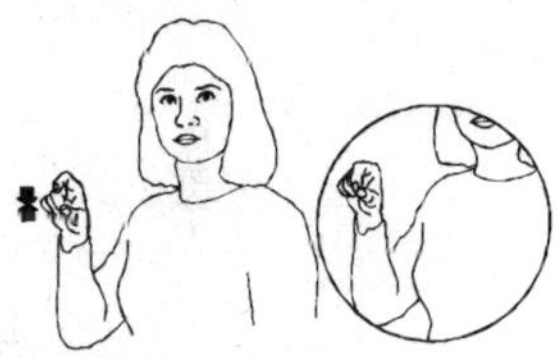

■ Pinch the curved index finger and thumb of the right hand together with a double movement in front of the right shoulder, palm facing forward.

**South America** *n.* A continent in the southern part of the western hemisphere: *Spanish and Portuguese are spoken in South America.*

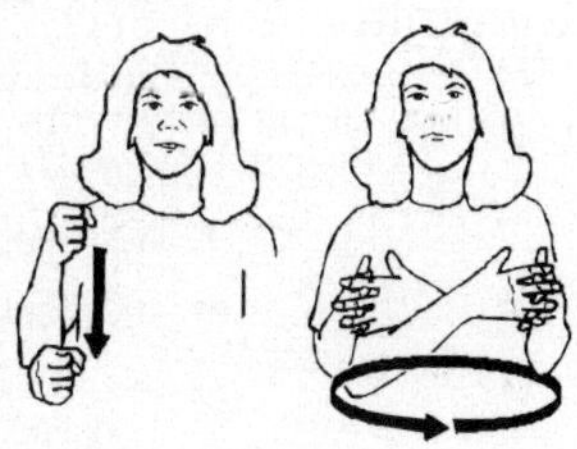

■ [**south** + **America**] Move the right *S hand,* palm facing in, downward in front of the right side of the chest. Then, with the fingers of the both hands loosely entwined, palms facing in, move the hands in a circle in front of the chest.

**Soviet** *adj., n.* See sign for RUSSIA[2].

**Spain**[1] *n.* A country in southwest Europe: *Spain is on the Iberian Peninsula, next to Portugal.* Related form: **Spanish** *adj., n.*

■ Beginning with the fingertips of the right *C hand,* palm facing in, touching the right side of the body, bring the right hand up to the left shoulder while opening into an *open hand,* palm facing forward.

**Spain**[2] *n.* (alternate sign) Related form: **Spanish** *adj., n.* Same sign used for: **Hispanic, Mexico.**

- [Represents the mantilla worn by Spanish women] Beginning with the index fingers of both *X hands* touching each side of the chest, palms facing in, twist the wrists to bring the hands downward and toward each other, ending with the index fingers hooked in front of the chest, palms facing in opposite directions.

**Spain**[3] *n.* (alternate sign) Related form: **Spanish** *adj., n.* Same sign used for: **Hispanic, Mexico.**

- Beginning with the index fingers of both *X hands* touching each side of the chest, palms facing in, bring the hands downward and forward ending in front of each side of the body.

**Switzerland**[1] *n.* A country in central Europe: *The people of Switzerland speak German, French, and Italian.* Related form: **Swiss** *adj., n.*

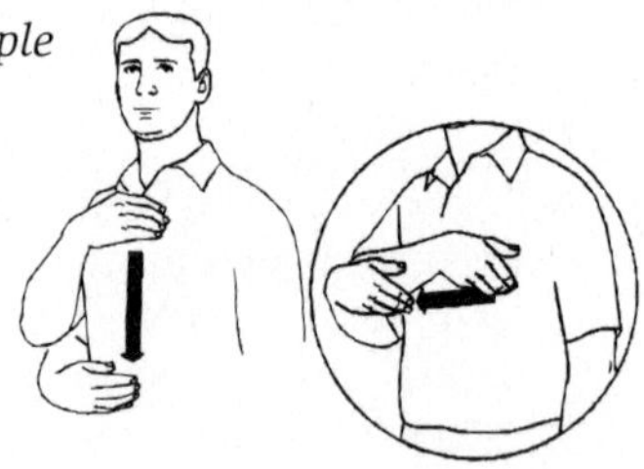

- [The shape of a cross on the Swiss flag] Move the fingertips of the right *C hand,* palm facing in, first downward and then from left to right across the chest.

**Switzerland**[2] *n.* (alternate sign) Related form: **Swiss** *adj., n.*

- [Shows the cross on a Swiss military uniform] With the extended right index finger, draw a cross on the left side of the chest by first going across from left to right and then moving downward.

**Taiwan** *n.* An island near the southeastern coast of China, the governmental seat of the Republic of China: *Taiwan was once a Japanese territory.* Related form: **Taiwanese** *adj., n.*

- Beginning with the heel of the right *S hand* touching the chin, palm facing in, twist the hand with a double movement, turning the palm forward each time.

**Texas** *n.* A southwestern state in the United States: *The capital of Texas is Austin.* Related form: **Texan** *adj., n.*

- [Initialized sign with **x** hand shape] Move the right *X hand,* palm facing forward, a short distance to the right and then straight down in front of the right side of the body.

**Thailand** *n.* A country in southeast Asia: *Thailand used to be called Siam.* Related forms: **Thai** or **Tai** *adj., n.*; **Thailander** *n.*

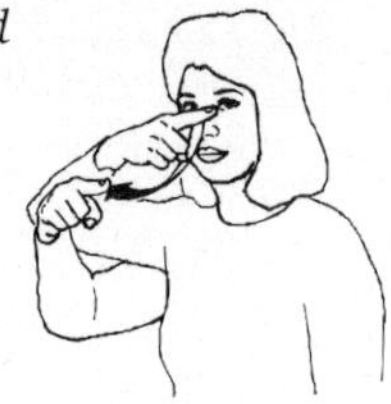

■ Beginning with the extended right index finger touching the top of the nose, palm facing down and finger pointing left, move the finger downward and forward in an arc.

**Turkey** *n.* A republic in Asia Minor and southeastern Europe: *a native of Turkey.* Related forms: **Turkish** *adj.*, **Turk** *n.*

■ Move the right *modified C hand,* palm facing left, downward with a double movement in front of the forehead.

**United Kingdom** *n.* A kingdom in northwest Europe: *London is the capital of the United Kingdom.* Same sign used for **Great Britain.**

■ Place the curved index finger and thumb of the right *modified C hand,* palm facing in, on each side of the chin.

**Washington**[1] *n.* **1.** The capital of the United States; the District of Columbia: *A new administration brings new faces to Washington.* **2.** A state in the northwest United States: *We plan to visit the outdoor market in Seattle, Washington.*

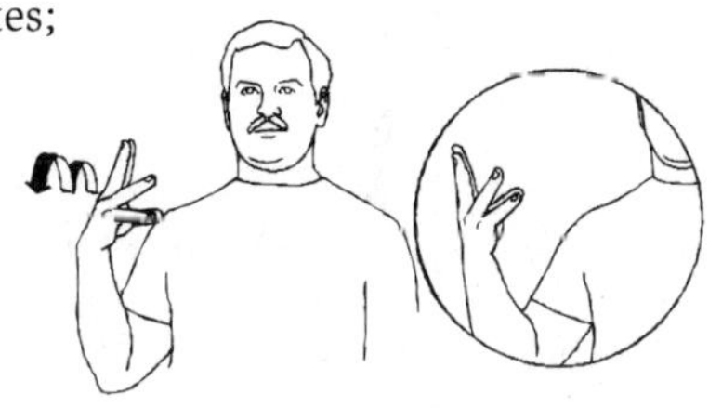

■ Beginning with the right *W hand* in front of the right shoulder, palm facing left move the hand forward in a double arc.

**Washington**[2] *n.* (alternate sign)

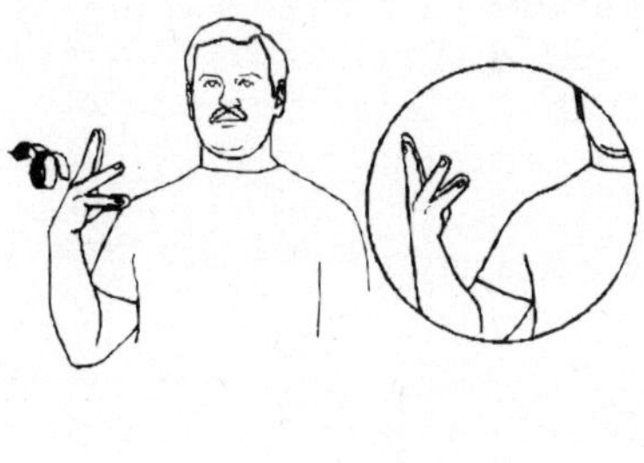

■ Beginning with the right *W hand* in front of the right shoulder, palm facing left, move the hand in a circular movement forward.

## Numbers

Zero, 0 One, 1 Two, 2 Three, 3 Four, 4 Five, 5 Six, 6 Seven, 7 Eight, 8

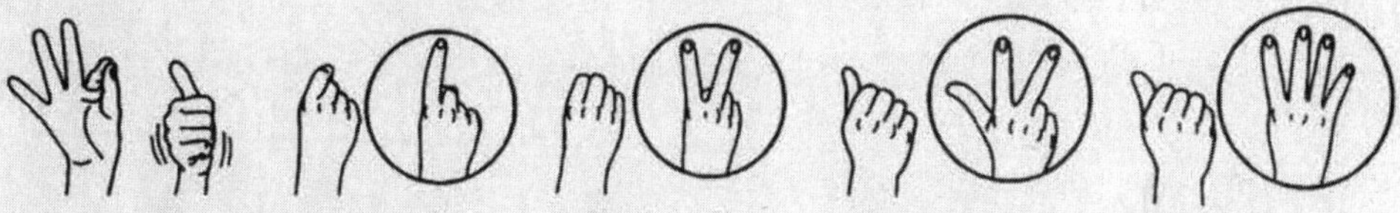

Nine, 9 Ten, 10 Eleven, 11 Twelve, 12 Thirteen, 13 Fourteen, 14

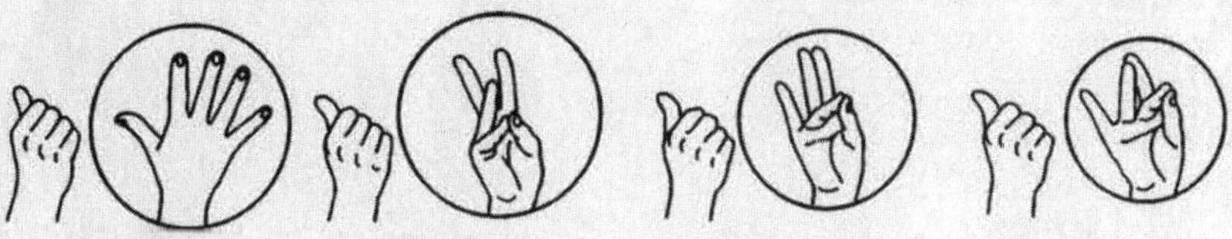

Fifteen, 15 Sixteen, 16 Seventeen, 17 Eighteen, 18

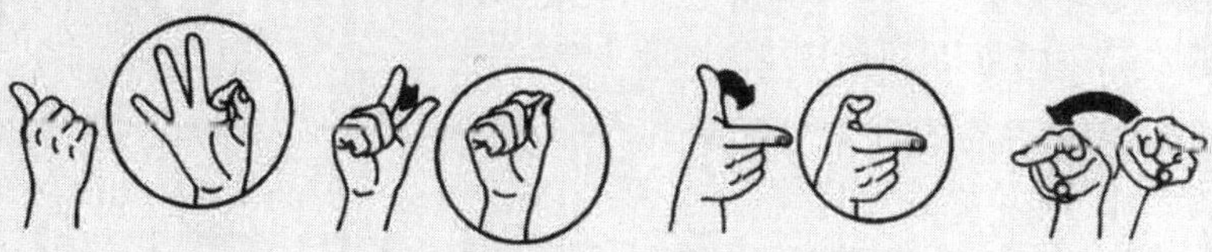

Nineteen, 19 Twenty, 20 Twenty-one, 21 Twenty-two, 22

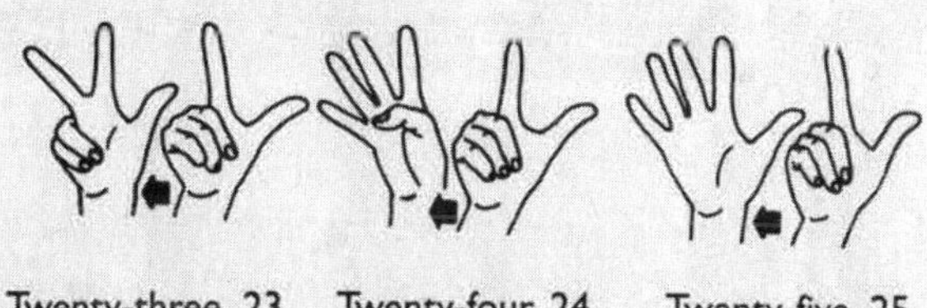

Twenty-three, 23 Twenty-four, 24 Twenty-five, 25

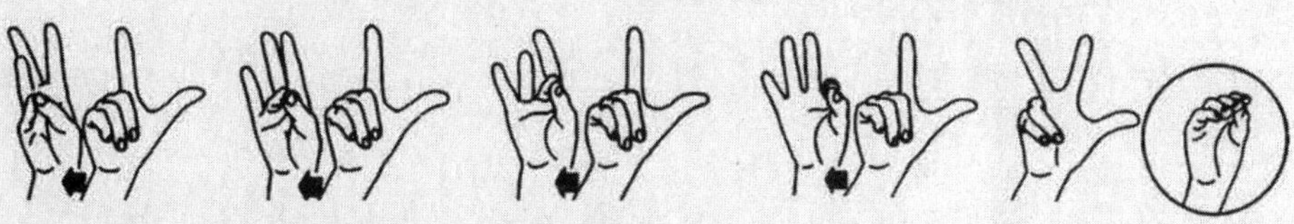

Twenty-six, 26 Twenty-seven, 27 Twenty-eight, 28 Twenty-nine, 29 Thirty, 30